American Politics Today

THIRD ESSENTIALS EDITION

The Presidential Election of 2012

Obama (Democrat)
Romney (Republican)
(7) Number of electoral votes

Pacific Ocean

WASHINGTON
(12)

OREGON
(7)

MONTANA
(3)

NORTH

IDAHO
(4)

SOUTH

WYOMING
(3)

NEVADA
(6)

UTAH
(6)

COLORADO
(9)

NEB

CALIFORNIA
(55)

ARIZONA
(11)

NEW MEXICO
(5)

HAWAII
(4)

0   100 mi
0   100 km

ALASKA
(3)

CANADA

0   400 mi
0   400 km

MEXICO

3e

William T. Bianco
INDIANA UNIVERSITY, BLOOMINGTON

David T. Canon
UNIVERSITY OF WISCONSIN, MADISON

W. W. NORTON & COMPANY · NEW YORK · LONDON

American Politics Today

W. W. Norton & Company has been independent since its founding in 1923, when William Warder Norton and Mary D. Herter Norton first published lectures delivered at the People's Institute, the adult education division of New York City's Cooper Union. The firm soon expanded its program beyond the Institute, publishing books by celebrated academics from America and abroad. By midcentury, the two major pillars of Norton's publishing program—trade books and college texts—were firmly established. In the 1950s, the Norton family transferred control of the company to its employees, and today—with a staff of four hundred and a comparable number of trade, college, and professional titles published each year—W. W. Norton & Company stands as the largest and oldest publishing house owned wholly by its employees.

Editor: Ann Shin

Managing Editor, College: Marian Johnson

Senior Production Manager, College: Ben Reynolds

Project Editors: Jack Borrebach, Diane Cipollone, Lory Frenkel

Electronic Media Editor: Peter Lesser

Ancillaries Editor: Lorraine Klimowich

Marketing Manager, Political Science: Sasha Levitt

Editorial Assistant: Sarah Wolf

Editorial Assistant, Media: Kathryn Young

Photo Editor: Michael Fodera

Photo Researcher: Dena Beglio Betz

Permissions Clearing: Bethany Salminen

Text and Cover Design: Jillian Burr

Composition: Jouve International—Brattleboro, VT

Manufacturing: R. R. Donnelley & Sons—Jefferson City, MO

Library of Congress Cataloging-in-Publication Data has been applied for.

ISBN: 978-0-393- 92106-9

W. W. Norton & Company, Inc., 500 Fifth Avenue, New York, NY 10110–0017

wwnorton.com

W. W. Norton & Company Ltd., Castle House, 75/76 Wells Street, London W1T 3QT

2 3 4 5 6 7 8 9 0

For our families,
Regina, Anna, and Catherine,
Sarah, Neal, Katherine, and Sophia,
who encouraged, empathized, and
helped, with patience,
grace, and love.

ABOUT THE AUTHORS

WILLIAM T. BIANCO

William T. Bianco is professor of political science at Indiana University, Bloomington, and Co-Chair of the Working Group on the Political Economy of Sustainable Democracy at the Workshop in Political Theory and Policy Analysis. He is the author of *Trust: Representatives and Constituents; American Politics: Strategy and Choice*; and numerous articles on American politics. He has received three National Science Foundation grants. He has also served as a consultant to congressional candidates and party campaign committees, as well as to the U.S. Department of Energy, the U.S. Department of Health and Human Services, and other state and local government agencies.

DAVID T. CANON

David T. Canon is professor of political science at the University of Wisconsin, Madison. His teaching and research interests focus on American political institutions, especially Congress, and racial representation. He is the author of *Actors, Athletes, and Astronauts: Political Amateurs in the U.S. Congress; Race, Redistricting, and Representation: The Unintended Consequences of Black Majority Districts* (winner of the Richard F. Fenno Prize); *The Dysfunctional Congress?* (with Kenneth Mayer); and various articles and book chapters. He recently finished a term as the Congress editor of *Legislative Studies Quarterly*. He is an AP consultant and has taught in the University of Wisconsin Summer AP Institute for U.S. Government & Politics since 1997. Professor Canon is the recipient of a University of Wisconsin Chancellor's Distinguished Teaching Award.

CONTENTS IN BRIEF

CONTENTS

PART II: POLITICS

PART III: INSTITUTIONS

PREFACE

This book is based on three simple premises: politics is conflictual, political process matters, and politics is everywhere. It reflects our belief that politics is explainable, that political outcomes can be understood in terms of decisions made by individuals—and that the average college undergraduate can make sense of the political world in these terms. It focuses on contemporary American politics, the events and outcomes that our students have lived through and know something about. The result, we believe, is a book that provides an accessible but rigorous account of the American political system.

American Politics Today is also the product of our dissatisfaction with existing texts. Twenty-five years ago we were assistant professors at the same university, assigned to teach the introductory class in alternate semesters. While our graduate training was quite different, we found that we shared a deep disappointment with available texts. Their wholesale focus on grand normative concepts such as civic responsibility or their use of analytic themes such as collective action left students with little idea of how American politics really works, how events in Washington affect their everyday lives, and how to piece together all the facts about American politics into a coherent explanation of why things happen as they do. These texts did not engender excitement, fascination, or even passing interest. What they did was put students to sleep.

In this Essentials Edition, our themes continue to embody our belief that it is possible to make sense of American politics—that we can move beyond simply describing what happens in political life to predicting and explaining behavior and outcomes, and, moreover, that this task can be accomplished in the introductory class. In part we wish to counter the widespread belief among students that politics is too complicated, too chaotic, or too secretive to make sense of. More than that, we want to empower our students, to demonstrate that everyday American politics is relevant to their lives. This emphasis is also a response to the typical complaint about American Government textbooks—that they are full of facts but devoid of useful information, and that after students finish reading, they are no better able to answer "why" questions than they were before they cracked the book.

In this Essentials Edition, we maintain our central focus on conflict and compromise in American politics—identifying what Americans agree and disagree about and assessing how conflict shapes American politics, from campaign platforms to policy outcomes. While this emphasis seems especially timely given the debt ceiling crisis of 2011, the hotly contested presidential election in 2012, and the intense debates in Congress over health care reform, immigration, and budget deficits, our aim is to go beyond these events to identify a fundamental constant in American politics: the reality that much of politics is driven by disagreements over the scope and form of government policy, and that compromise is an essential component of virtually all significant changes in government policy. Indeed, it is impossible to imagine politics without conflict. Conflict was embedded in the American political system by the Founders, who set up a system of checks and balances to make sure that no single group could dominate. The Constitution's division of power guarantees that enacting and implementing laws will involve conflict and compromise. Accordingly, despite the general dislike people have for conflict, our students must recognize that conflict and compromise lie at the heart of politics.

Throughout the text, we emphasize common sense, showing students that politics inside the Beltway is often strikingly similar to the students' own everyday interactions. For example, what sustains policy compromises made by members of Congress? The fact that the members typically have long careers, that they interact frequently with each other, and that they only deal with colleagues who have kept their word in the past. These strategies are not unique to the political world. Rather, they embody rules of thumb that most people follow (or are at least aware of) in their everyday interactions. In short, we try to help students understand American politics by emphasizing how it is not all that different from the world they know.

We do not frame the text in terms of any one theory or approach. We present the essential facts and concepts, motivated by real-world political phenomena and explained using text or simple diagrams. This approach gives students a set of tools for understanding politics and matches up well with students' common-sense intuitions about everyday life. While we do not ignore American history, our stress is on contemporary politics—on the debates, actions, and outcomes that most college students are aware of. The text is, as one of us put it, "ruthlessly contemporary." Focusing on recent events emphasizes the utility of the concepts and insights that we develop in the text. It also goes a long way toward establishing the relevance of the intro class.

Finally, our book offers an individual-level perspective on America's government. The essential message is that politics—elections, legislative proceedings, regulatory choices, and everything else we see—is a product of the decisions made by real flesh-and-blood people. This approach grounds our discussion of politics in the real world. Many texts focus on abstractions such as "the eternal debate," "the great questions," or "the pulse of democracy." The problem with these constructs is that they don't explain where the debate, the questions, or even democracy come from. Nor do they help students understand what's going on in Washington and elsewhere, as it's not obvious that the participants care much about these sorts of abstractions—quite the opposite, in fact.

We replace these constructs with a focus on real people and actual choices. The primary goal is to make sense of American politics by understanding why politicians, bureaucrats, judges, and citizens act as they do. That is, we are grounding our description of American politics at the most fundamental level— an individual facing a decision. How, for example, does a voter choose among candidates? Stated that way, it is reasonably easy to talk about where the choice came from, how the individual might evaluate different options, and why one choice might look better than the others. Voters' decisions may be understood by examining the different feasible strategies they employ (issue voting, retrospective evaluations, stereotyping, etc.) and by asking ourselves why some voters use one strategy while others use a different one.

By focusing on individuals and choices, we can place students in the shoes of the decision makers, and in so doing, give them insight into why people act as they do. We can discuss, for example, why a House member might favor enacting wasteful pork-barrel spending, even though a proposal full of such projects will make his constituents economically worse off—and why constituents might reward such behavior, even if they suspect the truth. By taking this approach, we are not trying to let legislators off the hook. Rather, we believe that any real understanding of the political process must begin with a sense of the decisions the participants make and why they make them.

Focusing on individuals also segues naturally into a discussion of consequences, allowing us to move from examining decisions to describing and evaluating outcomes. In this way, we can show students how large-scale outcomes in politics, such as inefficient programs, don't happen by accident or because of malfeasance. Rather, they are the predictable results of choices made by individuals (here, politicians and voters).

The policy chapters—on civil rights, domestic policy, and foreign policy—also represent a distinctive feature of this book. The discussion of policy at the end of an intro class often fits awkwardly with the material covered earlier. It is supposed to be a culmination of the semester-long discussion of institutions, politicians, and political behavior, but instead it often becomes an afterthought that gets discarded when time runs out in the last few weeks of class. Our policy chapters explicitly draw on previous chapters' discussions of the actors that shape policy: the president, Congress, the courts, interest groups, and parties. By doing so, these chapters show how all the pieces of the puzzle fit together.

Finally, this book reflects our experience as practicing scholars and teachers, as well as interactions with over fifteen thousand students in introductory classes at several universities. Rather than thinking of the intro class as a service obligation, we believe it offers a unique opportunity for faculty to develop a broader sense of American politics and American political science, while at the same time giving students the tools they need to behave as knowledgeable citizens or enthusiastic political science majors. We hope that it works for you as well as it does for us.

FEATURES OF THE TEXT

THE BOOK'S "THREE KEY IDEAS"—politics is conflictual, political process matters, and politics is everywhere—are fully integrated throughout the text.

► **Politics Is Conflictual** and conflict and compromise are a normal, healthy part of politics. The questions debated in elections and the policy options considered by people in government are generally marked by disagreement at all levels. Making policy typically involves important issues on which people disagree, sometimes strongly; so compromise, bargaining, and tough choices about trade-offs are often necessary.

► **Political Process Matters** because it is the mechanism we have established to resolve conflicts and achieve compromise. Governmental actions result from conscious choices made by voters, elected officials, and bureaucrats. The media often cover political issues in the same way they do sporting events, and while this makes for entertaining news, it also leads citizens to overlook the institutions, rules, and procedures that have a decisive influence on American life. Politics really is not just a game.

► **Politics Is Everywhere** in that the results of the political process affect all aspects of Americans' everyday lives. Politics governs what people can and cannot do, their quality of life, and how they think about events, other people, and situations.

CONFLICT AND COMPROMISE CHAPTER OPENERS reflect our "politics is conflictual" emphasis. Each chapter begins with an example of conflict in American politics, from debates over what the Constitution means to disagreements within the Democratic and Republican parties. In the Third Edition, all of these openers are new. Within each chapter and especially in the chapter conclusions, we return to the examples, showing how disagreements and efforts to mitigate them shape every area of American politics.

A NEW ORGANIZATION AROUND CHAPTER GOALS stresses learning objectives and mastery of core material.

► **Chapter Goals** appear at the beginning of the chapter and then recur at the start of the relevant sections throughout the chapter to create a more active reading experience that emphasizes important learning objectives.

► **NEW: Extensive end-of-chapter review sections organized around the Chapter Goals** include section summaries, practice quiz questions, key terms, and suggested reading lists. Students have everything they need to master the material in each section of the chapter.

BOXED FEATURES reinforce the three key ideas while introducing other important ways to think about American politics.

► **NEW "How It Works" infographics** show how the political process works and how it resolves (or fails to resolve) conflicts. These complement the chapter-opening stories, depicting the processes that underlie the conflicts and compromises we see in American politics. Critical-thinking questions ask students to consider the implications of the process and how it affects the outcome.

ACKNOWLEDGMENTS

This edition of *American Politics Today* is again dedicated to our families. Our wives, Regina and Sarah, have continued to accommodate our deadlines and schedules and have again served as our most accurate critics and sources of insight and inspiration. Our five children, several of whom are now undergraduates themselves, have again been forced to contend with politics and textbook writing as a perennial topic of conversation and have responded with critiques and insights of their own, which appear throughout the text.

Our colleagues at Indiana University and the University of Wisconsin (and before that, Duke University for both of us) provided many opportunities to talk about American politics and teaching this course.

Bill thanks his colleagues at Indiana University and elsewhere, including Christine Barbour, John Brehm, Ted Carmines, Mike Ensley, Russ Hansen, Jeff Hill, Yanna Krupnikov, Lin Ostrom, Regina Smyth, and Gerry Wright, for sharp insights and encouragement at crucial moments. He is also grateful to the legion of teaching assistants who have helped him organize and teach the intro class at three universities. Finally, he thanks the students at the Higher School of Economics in Moscow, Russia, where he taught the introductory class as a Fulbright Scholar in 2012.

David gives special thanks to Ken Mayer, whose daily "reality checks" and consistently thoughtful professional and personal advice are greatly appreciated. John Coleman, Barry Burden, Charles Franklin, Ken Goldstein, Ben Marquez, Don Moynihan, Ryan Owens, Howard Schweber, Byron Shafer, Dave Weimer, Kathy Walsh, Susan Yackee, and all the great people at Wisconsin have provided a wonderful community within which to teach and research American politics. David would also like to thank the students at the University of Debrecen in Hungary, where he taught American politics as a Fulbright Scholar in 2003–04, and the Eberhard Karls University of Tübingen, Germany, where he taught as a Fulbright Scholar in 2011–12. The Hungarian students' unique perspective on democracy, civil liberties, and the role of government required David to think about American politics in a different way. The German students' views on the role of political parties, campaigns, and the social welfare state also provided a strong contrast to the views of his American students.

Both of us are grateful to the political science faculty at Duke University, who, in addition to providing us with our first academic jobs, worked to construct a hospitable and invigorating place to research and to teach. In particular, Rom Coles, Ruth Grant, John Aldrich, Tom Spragens, Taylor Cole, and David Barber were model colleagues and scholars. We both learned to teach by watching them, and we are the better teachers and scholars for it.

The outstanding people at W. W. Norton made this a much better book than we could have produced on our own. Steve Dunn was responsible for getting the process started and providing good commentary and encouragement from beginning to end. Roby Harrington has been a source of constant encouragement and feedback. We are also extraordinarily grateful for Ann Shin's editorial insights, vision, and judgment, which are reflected in improvements made throughout the text. Once again, Pete Lesser's clear vision for the electronic media and for the textbook itself was a major help, and Lorraine Klimowich ensured order and accuracy in the support materials. Marian Johnson and Jack Borrebach were superb project editors, bringing to the project their talent for clarity of words and visuals. Sarah Wolf and Kathryn Young made sure everyone had the right versions of everything. Dena Betz and Michael Fodera put together an excellent photo program. Bethany Salminen cleared reprint permissions for the figures and tables. Ben Reynolds handled production with efficiency and good humor. Jillian Burr created a beautiful design for the book interior and cover. The entire crew at Norton has been incredibly professional and supportive. We feel very fortunate to work with them.

We are also indebted to the many reviewers who have commented on the text.

FIRST EDITION REVIEWERS

Dave Adler, Idaho State University

Rick Almeida, Francis Marion University

Jim Bailey, Arkansas State University, Mountain Home

Todd Belt, University of Hawaii, Hilo

Scott Buchanan, Columbus State University

Randy Burnside, Southern Illinois University, Carbondale

Carolyn Cocca, SUNY College at Old Westbury

Tom Dolan, Columbus State University

Dave Dulio, Oakland University

Matt Eshbaugh-Soha, University of North Texas

Kevin Esterling, University of California, Riverside

Peter Francia, East Carolina University

Scott Frisch, California State University, Channel Islands

Sarah Fulton, Texas A&M University

Keith Gaddie, University of Oklahoma

Joe Giammo, University of Arkansas, Little Rock

Kate Greene, University of Southern Mississippi

Steven Greene, North Carolina State University

Phil Habel, Southern Illinois University, Carbondale

Charles Hartwig, Arkansas State University, Jonesboro

Ted Jelen, University of Nevada, Las Vegas

Jennifer Jensen, Binghamton University (SUNY)

Terri Johnson, University of Wisconsin, Green Bay

Luke Keele, Ohio State University

Linda Keith, University of Texas, Dallas

Chris Kelley, Miami University

Jason Kirksey, Oklahoma State University

Jeffrey Kraus, Wagner College

Chris Kukk, Western Connecticut State University

Mel Kulbicki, York College

Joel Lieske, Cleveland State University

Steve Light, University of North Dakota

Baodong (Paul) Liu, University of Utah

Ken Long, Saint Joseph College, Connecticut

Michael Lynch, University of Kansas

Cherie Maestas, Florida State University

Tom Marshall, University of Texas, Arlington

Scott McClurg, Southern Illinois University, Carbondale

Jonathan Morris, East Carolina University

Jason Mycoff, University of Delaware

Sean Nicholson-Crotty, University of Missouri, Columbia

Timothy Nokken, Texas Tech University

Sandra O'Brien, Florida Gulf Coast University

John Orman, Fairfield University

L. Marvin Overby, University of Missouri, Columbia

Catherine Paden, Simmons College

Dan Ponder, Drury University

Paul Posner, George Mason University

David Redlawsk, University of Iowa

Russell Renka, Southeast Missouri State University

Travis Ridout, Washington State University

Andy Rudalevige, Dickinson College

Denise Scheberle, University of Wisconsin, Green Bay

Tom Schmeling, Rhode Island College

Pat Sellers, Davidson College

Dan Smith, Northwest Missouri State University

Dale Story, University of Texas, Arlington

John Vile, Middle Tennessee State University

Mike Wagner, University of Nebraska

Dave Wigg, St. Louis Community College

Maggie Zetts, Purdue University

SECOND EDITION REVIEWERS

Danny Adkison, Oklahoma State University

Hunter Bacot, Elon College

Tim Barnett, Jacksonville State University

Robert Bruhl, University of Illinois, Chicago

Daniel Butler, Yale University

Jennifer Byrne, James Madison University

Jason Casellas, University of Texas, Austin

Jeffrey Christiansen, Seminole State College

Richard Conley, University of Florida

Michael Crespin, University of Georgia

Brian DiSarro, California State University, Sacramento

Ryan Emenaker, College of the Redwoods

John Evans, California State University, Northridge

John Fliter, Kansas State University

Jimmy Gleason, Purdue University

Dana Glencross, Oklahoma City Community College

Jeannie Grussendorf, Georgia State University

Phil Habel, Southern Illinois University, Carbondale

Lori Han, Chapman University

Katy Harriger, Wake Forest University

Richard Himelfarb, Hofstra University

Doug Imig, University of Memphis

Daniel Klinghard, College of the Holy Cross

Eddie Meaders, University of North Texas

Kristy Michaud, California State University, Northridge

Kris Miler, University of Illinois, Urbana-Champaign

Melinda Mueller, Eastern Illinois University

Michael Mundt, Oakton Community College

Emily Neff-Sharum, University of North Carolina, Pembroke

David Nice, Washington State University
Tim Nokken, Texas Tech University
Stephen Nuño, Northern Arizona University
Richard Powell, University of Maine, Orono
Travis Ridout, Washington State University
Sara Rinfret, University of Wisconsin, Green Bay
Martin Saiz, California State University, Northridge
Gabriel Ramon Sanchez, University of New Mexico
Charles Shipan, University of Michigan
Dan Smith, Northwest Missouri State University
Rachel Sondheimer, United States Military Academy
Chris Soper, Pepperdine University
Walt Stone, University of California, Davis
Greg Streich, University of Central Missouri
Charles Walcott, Virginia Tech
Rick Waterman, University of Kentucky
Edward Weber, Washington State University
Jack Wright, Ohio State University

THIRD EDITION REVIEWERS

Steve Anthony, Georgia State University
Marcos Arandia, North Lake College
Richard Barberio, SUNY College at Oneonta
Jody Baumgartner, East Carolina University
Brian Berry, University of Texas, Dallas
David Birch, Lone Star College, Tomball
Eileen Burgin, University of Vermont
Randolph Burnside, Southern Illinois University, Carbondale
Kim Casey, Northwest Missouri State University
Christopher Chapp, University of Wisconsin, Whitewater
Daniel Coffey, University of Akron
William Corbett, University of Texas at El Paso
Jonathan Day, Western Illinois University
Rebecca Deen, University of Texas, Arlington
Brian DiSarro, California State University, Sacramento
Nelson Dometrius, Texas Tech University
Stan Dupree, College of the Desert
David Edwards, University of Texas, Austin
Ryan Emenaker, College of the Redwoods
John Evans, University of Wisconsin, Eau Claire
Brandon Franke, Blinn College, Bryan
Rodd Freitag, University of Wisconsin, Eau Claire
Donna Godwin, Trinity Valley Community College
Craig Goodman, Texas Tech University
Amy Gossett, Lincoln University
Tobin Grant, Southern Illinois University

Stephanie Hallock, Harford Community College
Alexander Hogan, Lone Star College, CyFair
Marvin King, University of Mississippi
Timothy LaPira, James Madison University
Mary Linder, Grayson University
Christine Lipsmeyer, Texas A&M University
Michael Lyons, Utah State University
Jill Marshall, University of Texas, Arlington
Thomas Masterson, Butte College
Daniel Matisoff, Georgia Institute of Technology
Jason McDaniel, San Francisco State University
Mark McKenzie, Texas Tech University
Leonard McNeil, Contra Costa College
Melissa Merry, University of Louisville
Ann Mezzell, Lincoln University
Eric Miller, Blinn College, Bryan
Jonathan Morris, East Carolina University
Leah Murray, Weber State University
Farzeen Nasri, Ventura College
Brian Newman, Pepperdine University
David Nice, Washington State University
Stephen Nichols, Cal State University, San Marcos
Tim Nokken, Texas Tech University
Barbara Norrander, University of Arizona
Andrew Reeves, Boston University
Michelle Rodriguez, San Diego Mesa College
Dan Smith, Northwest Missouri State University
Christopher Soper, Pepperdine University
Jim Startin, University of Texas, San Antonio
Jeffrey Stonecash, Syracuse University
Linda Trautman, Ohio University
Kevin Unter, University of Louisiana, Monroe
Michelle Wade, Northwest Missouri State University
Michael Wagner, University of Nebraska, Lincoln
Adam Warber, Clemson University
Wayne Wolf, South Suburban College

It is a humbling experience to have so many smart people helping us find our voice and make our arguments. Their reviews were often critical, but always insightful, and we have been fortunate to have them guide our revisions. Again, they have our profound thanks.

William T. Bianco
David T. Canon
October 2012

American Politics Today

THIRD ESSENTIALS EDITION

1

Understanding American Politics

PRESIDENT OBAMA CAME INTO conflict with the Republican majority in the House of Representatives over many issues, including the federal debt. In 2011, Obama and House Speaker John Boehner met on numerous occasions, but reaching a compromise on the debt limit and other issues proved difficult. Why?

IN SUMMER 2011, CONGRESSIONAL REPUBLICANS CAME INTO sharp conflict with President Obama and congressional Democrats over raising the federal government's debt limit. Each side argued that it could not accept the plan proposed by the other side, even if the delay in finding a solution risked harming the economy. The debate arose because the federal government's expenditures currently exceed the revenues it collects through taxes and other sources. So the Treasury Department must issue bonds to fund operations. This essentially involves borrowing money from the bondholders, who must eventually be repaid, with interest. However, the total amount of federal borrowing is limited by law, so when Congress authorizes spending that requires more borrowing, it must also enact legislation to raise the debt limit.

In 2011, after Congress passed a spending budget that would require an increase in the debt limit, congressional Republicans announced they would not support the increase without significant spending reductions. Many opponents of the increase had been elected in 2010 with the support of "Tea Party" groups, who wanted to reduce federal spending. President Obama and congressional Democrats argued that funding the government's current activities and upholding its obligations was necessary, even if that meant borrowing more money. Negotiations spanned several months, as the date approached when the debt limit would be reached and the government would have to either refuse to repay bonds that came due or make drastic spending cuts.

CONFLICT & COMPROMISE
in American Politics

Ultimately, a deal was reached that raised the debt limit, implemented cuts in federal spending, and established a bipartisan committee to recommend additional cuts—a commission that ultimately failed, however. The prolonged negotiations contributed to declines in the stock market and the decision by a key bond ratings agency to lower its ratings on federal bonds.

How did this happen? How did politicians decide to push debate over the debt limit right to the brink, to the point of harming the American economy? The episode seems like a classic example of elected officials creating conflict in order to gain political advantage, ignoring the damage they were doing to the country as a whole.

However, political motivations are only a partial explanation. Debates over budgets and debt limits are not just about money; they are also about determining what government does. How much should the government spend on defense—but also how should America's armed forces be used? How much should be spent on Medicare—but also what are the limits on the government's responsibility to provide health care to senior citizens? How much taxes should people with different incomes pay—but should people get tax breaks for purchasing a home, adopting a child, or certain other actions? Every disagreement over taxing and spending contains a disagreement over policies like these.

Differences among Democrats and Republicans in Congress reflect real divisions among American citizens. If the debate was only about the size of the federal budget, it might be easy to find a compromise. But since the debate is over policy as well as spending, both sides have to make multiple offers and counteroffers before a compromise wins enough support to be enacted.

Two features of the legislative process provide additional insight into the debt limit negotiations. First, the fact that legislation was required to raise the debt limit was not inevitable. However, requiring a separate vote gives members of Congress an opportunity to oppose the limit and thereby gain favor with constituents who worry about excessive government spending—but only if enough of their colleagues forgo these benefits and vote to increase the limit. Thus the debt limit vote illustrates the trade-off members face between maintaining and building political support on the one hand, and doing what is necessary to keep the government in business on the other. Second, the fact that America in 2011 had a divided government (Democrats controlled the Senate and the presidency, and a Republican majority controlled the House of Representatives) meant that a bipartisan compromise was necessary for success: even if one party could get all its members to support a deal, they could not enact it without some support from the other party. Reaching this compromise required intense negotiation.

This example shows how digging below the surface of political events can help to explain why things happen in American politics—and in particular, why raising the debt limit was so difficult. Our goal is to give you a similar understanding of the entire range of American politics. Indeed, the central theme of this book is that *politics is about conflict and compromise.* People often view political compromise as "selling out" or giving up on core values and principles. However, because Americans disagree over what to do about most policy questions, conflict is an essential part of politics and compromise is usually needed to enact changes in government policy.

MAKING SENSE OF AMERICAN GOVERNMENT AND POLITICS

The premise of this book is simple: *American politics makes sense*. What happens in elections, in Congress, in the White House, and everywhere else in the political process has a logical and often simple explanation.

This claim may seem unrealistic and naive. On the surface, American politics is full of bewildering complexities, from the enumerated powers in the Constitution to the unwritten rules that govern how Congress works. Many policy questions— from confronting economic crises to dealing with climate change—seem hopelessly intractable. As our chapter-opening story suggested, politicians often seem more interested in publicizing their disagreements than in solving them. Election outcomes look random or even chaotic.

Many people, we believe, have given up on American politics because they don't understand the political process, feel helpless to influence election outcomes or policy making, and believe that politics is irrelevant to their lives. Since you are taking a class on American politics, we hope you have not given up on politics entirely. It is *not* our goal to turn you into a political junkie or a policy expert. And you need not be completely immersed in politics to make sense of it, but we hope that after finishing this book you will have a basic understanding of the political process.

One goal of this book is to help you take an active role in the political process. A functioning democracy allows citizens to defer complicated policy decisions to their elected leaders, but it also requires citizens to monitor what those politicians do and to hold them accountable at the voting booth. This book will help you accomplish this important duty by providing the analytical skills necessary to make sense of politics. We will answer questions about politics by applying three key ideas: politics is conflictual, political process matters, and politics is everywhere. But first we begin with an even more basic question: Why do we have a government?

DESCRIBE THE BASIC FUNCTIONS OF GOVERNMENT

WHY DO WE HAVE A GOVERNMENT?

government The system for implementing decisions made through the political process.

As we prepare to address this question, let's agree on a definition: **government** is the system for implementing decisions made through the political process. All countries have some form of government, which in general serves two broad purposes: to provide order and to promote the general welfare.

FORMS OF GOVERNMENT

The Greek political philosopher Aristotle, writing in the fourth century B.C., developed a classification scheme for governments that remains useful today. Aristotle distinguished three pure types of government based on the number of rulers versus the number of people ruled: monarchy (rule by one), aristocracy (rule by the few), and polity (rule by the many—such as the general population).

Today Aristotle's third type of government would include constitutional republican governments. Within such structures, additional distinctions can be made according to how the governing systems allocate power among the executive, legislative, and judicial branches. Presidential systems such as ours in the United States tend to follow a separation of power among the three branches, while parliamentary systems such as the United Kingdom's elect the chief executive from the legislature, so there is much closer coordination between those two branches.

We can further refine Aristotle's third type by considering the relationships among different levels of the government. In a *federal system* such as we have in the United States, power is shared among local, state, and national levels of government. In a *unitary system* all power is held at the national level. A *confederation* is a less common form of government in which states retain their sovereignty and autonomy but form a loose association at the national level.

GOVERNMENTS PROVIDE ORDER

At a basic level the answer to "Why do we have a government?" seems obvious: without government there would be chaos. As the seventeenth-century British philosopher Thomas Hobbes said, life in the "state of nature" (that is, without government) would be "solitary, poor, nasty, brutish, and short."[1] Without government there would be no laws—people could do whatever they wanted. Even if people tried to develop informal rules, there would be no way to guarantee enforcement of those rules.

The Founders of the U.S. Constitution noted this crucial role in the document's preamble: two of the central goals of our government are to "provide for the common defence" and to "insure domestic Tranquility." The former refers to military protection (by the Army and Navy at the time of the Founding; it now also includes the Marines, Coast Guard, and Air Force) against foreign invasion and the defense of our nation's common security interests. The latter refers to law enforcement within the nation, which today includes the National Guard, FBI, Department of Homeland Security, state and local police, and courts. So at a minimal level, government is necessary to provide security.

However, the Founders also cited the desire to "establish Justice . . . and secure the Blessings of Liberty to ourselves and our Posterity." Do we need government to do these things? It may be obvious that the police power of the state is required to prevent anarchy, but can't people have justice and liberty without government? In a perfect world, maybe; but the Founders had a more realistic view of human nature. As the Founder James Madison said, "But what is government itself, but the greatest of all reflections on human nature? If men were angels, no government would be necessary. If angels were to govern men, neither external nor internal controls on government would be necessary."[2] Furthermore, Madison continued, people have a variety of interests that have "divided mankind into parties, inflamed them with mutual animosity, and rendered them much more disposed to vex and oppress each other than to co-operate for their common good."[3] That is, without government we would quickly head toward Hobbes's nasty and brutish state of nature.

Madison assumed that people are self-interested: we want what is best for ourselves and for our families, and to satisfy those interests we form groups with like-minded people. Madison saw these groups, which he called **factions**, as being opposed to the public good, and his greatest fear was of tyranny by a faction imposing its will on the rest of the nation. For example, if one group took power and established an official state religion, that faction would be tyrannizing people who practiced a different religion. This type of oppression is exactly what drove many American colonists to flee Europe in the first place.

So government is necessary to avoid the anarchy of the state of nature, and the right kind of government is needed to avoid oppression by whoever controls the policy-making process. As we will discuss in Chapters 2 and 3, America's government seeks to control the effects of factions by dividing governmental power in three main ways. First, the **separation of powers** divides the government into three branches—judicial, executive, and legislative—and assigns distinct duties to each branch. Second, the system of **checks and balances** gives each branch some power over the other two. (For example, the president can veto legislation passed

factions Groups of like-minded people who try to influence the government. American government is set up to avoid domination by any one of these groups.

separation of powers The division of government power across the judicial, executive, and legislative branches.

checks and balances A system in which each branch of government has some power over the others.

TWO IMPORTANT GOVERNMENT FUNCTIONS are to "provide for the common defence" and "insure domestic Tranquility." The military and local police are two of the most commonly used forces the government maintains to fulfill those roles.

federalism The division of power across the local, state, and national levels of government.

by Congress; Congress can impeach the president; and the Supreme Court has the power to interpret laws written by Congress to determine whether they are constitutional.) Third, **federalism** divides power yet again by allotting different responsibilities to local, state, and national governments. With power divided in this fashion, Madison reasoned, no single faction could dominate the government.

GOVERNMENTS PROMOTE THE GENERAL WELFARE

public goods Services or actions (such as protecting the environment) that, once provided to one person, become available to everyone. Government is typically needed to provide public goods because they will be underproduced by the free market.

collective action problems Situations in which the members of a group would benefit by working together to produce some outcome, but each individual is better off refusing to cooperate and reaping benefits from those who do the work.

free rider problem The incentive to benefit from others' work without making a contribution, which leads individuals in a collective action situation to refuse to work together.

The preamble to the Constitution also states that the federal government exists to "promote the general Welfare." This means tackling the hard problems that Americans cannot solve on their own, such as taking care of the poor, the sick, or the aged, and dealing with global issues like climate change, terrorist threats, and poverty in other countries. However, government is not inevitable—people can decide that these problems aren't worth solving. But if people *do* want to address these large problems, government action is necessary because individuals, working by themselves, generally do not provide **public goods** such as these.

Often people find it difficult to achieve shared goals because of **collective action problems**. Collective action problems occur when the members of a group would benefit by working together to produce some outcome, but each individual is better off refusing to cooperate and reaping benefits from those who do the work. Government helps solve collective action problems. It is easy for two people or even a small group to tackle a common problem without the help of government, but a thousand people (or the more than 300 million in the United States today) would have a very difficult time. They would suffer from the **free rider problem**: because it is in everyone's interest to let others pay the costs—in effort and resources—to tackle the problem, and because everyone likely thinks this way, the collective goal would never be achieved. But a government representing 300 million people can provide public goods, such as defending the nation, that all those people acting on their own would be unable to provide, so they elect leaders and pay taxes to ensure the provision of those goods.

Now that we understand *why* we have a government, the next question is, *what* does the government do to "insure domestic Tranquility" and "promote the general Welfare"? Many components of the government promote these goals, from the police and armed services to the Internal Revenue Service, Post Office, Social Security Administration, National Aeronautics and Space Administration, Department of Education, and Food and Drug Administration. More generally, the government does several things:

▶ It creates and enforces laws and protects private property through the criminal justice system.

▶ It establishes a common currency and regulates commerce among the states and trade with other nations.

▶ It provides public goods that would not be produced or would be undersupplied by the free market, including national defense, an interstate highway system, and national parks.

▶ It regulates the market to promote the general good, specifically by addressing market failures in areas such as environmental pollution and product safety.

▶ It protects individual civil liberties, such as the freedom of speech and the free exercise of religion.

All of these government roles are significant, in that they affect the lives of many Americans. They are controversial, in that Americans disagree about what government should do in each area. Government actions in each area are shaped by process, or the rules that determine who gets to select different policies.

WHAT IS POLITICS?

DEFINE *POLITICS* AND IDENTIFY THREE KEY IDEAS THAT HELP EXPLAIN POLITICS

We define **politics** as the process that determines what government does. It includes ways of behaving and making decisions that are common in everyday life. Many aspects of our discussion of politics will probably sound familiar because your life involves politics on a regular basis. This statement will become clear in light of the three key ideas of this book.

politics The process that determines what government does.

First, *politics is conflictual*. As the struggle over the debt limit illustrates, the questions debated in election campaigns and the options considered by policy makers generally involve disagreement at all levels. The federal government does not spend much time resolving issues that everyone agrees should be decided in a particular way. Rather, the making of government policy largely involves issues on which people disagree, sometimes strongly, which makes compromise difficult—and this is a normal, healthy part of politics. Compromise is often necessary to produce an outcome that can be enacted and implemented.

Second, *political process matters*. Governmental actions don't happen by accident—they result from conscious choices made by elected officials and bureaucrats. Politics, as the process that determines what governments do, puts certain individuals into positions of power and makes the rules that structure their choices. Indeed, the political process is the mechanism for resolving conflict. The most obvious example is elections, which democracies use to resolve a fundamental conflict: deciding who should lead the country.

Third, *politics is everywhere*. Decisions about what government should do or who should be in charge are integral to society, and they influence the everyday lives of all Americans. Politics helps to determine what people can and cannot do, their quality of life, and how they think about events, other people, and situations.

In the following sections we take a closer look at each of these three key ideas.

KEY IDEA 1: POLITICS IS CONFLICTUAL

Political scientists have long recognized the central role of conflict in politics. In fact, one prominent theory in the mid-twentieth century saw conflict among interest groups as explaining most outcomes in American politics. The political scientist E. E. Schattschneider argued that the scope of political conflict—that is, how many people are involved in the fight—determines who wins in politics. Others have argued that some conflict is essential for small-group decision making: if nobody challenges a widely shared but flawed view, people may convince themselves that the flaws are not a problem. Bureaucratic politics, congressional politics, elections, and even Supreme Court decision making have all been studied through the lens of political conflict.[4]

Despite the consensus that conflict in politics is essential, most people do not like conflict, either in their personal lives or in politics. Rather than talking about controversial subjects, many people simply avoid them. Indeed, since the 1950s political scientists have found strong evidence that people avoid discussing politics in order to maintain social harmony.[5] Many people apply their disdain for conflict to politicians as well. "Why is there so much partisan bickering?" our students frequently ask. "Why can't they just get along?" Similar comments were voiced during negotiations over the debt limit in 2011 and during many other legislative fights in recent years.

The idea that conflict is nearly always a part of politics should be no surprise. Whereas issues on which there is consensus tend to resolve quickly, conflictual issues remain on the agenda as the winners try to extend their gains and the losers work to roll back the policies that are currently in place. Thus one reason that abortion rights is a perennial issue in campaigns and congressional debates is that there is no national consensus on when to allow abortions, no indication that the issue is becoming less important to citizens or elected officials, and no compromise policy that would attract widespread support.

An important implication of the inevitable conflicts in American politics is that compromise and bargaining are essential to getting things done. Politicians who bargain with opponents are not necessarily abandoning their principles; indeed, striking a deal may be the only way to make some of the policy changes they want. Moreover, agreement sometimes exists even in the midst of controversy. For example, surveys that measure attitudes about abortion—as noted, a highly controversial topic—find widespread support for prohibiting government funding for abortions, requiring parental notification when a minor has an abortion, or requiring doctors who perform the procedure to present their patients with information on alternatives such as adoption.

Another implication of conflict is that it is almost impossible to get exactly what you want from the political process. Even when a significant percentage of the population is united behind common goals—such as supporters of Barack Obama after the 2008 election, who favored expanding the federal government, or Tea Party sympathizers after the 2010 midterm election, who wanted to shrink government and eliminate regulations—these individuals almost always have to accept something short of their ideal in order to attract enough support to implement policy change. The need for compromise does not mean that change is impossible, only that what is achievable often falls short of individuals' initial demands.

CONFLICT IS INHERENT IN AMERICAN politics, a fact that was driven home by the national debate in 2009 and 2010 over health care reform.

Finally, we are not arguing that all conflict is good. For example, obstruction for the sake of obstruction in Congress does not serve the greater public good. Our point here—as it is throughout this book—is simply that conflict and compromise are inherent parts of politics.

KEY IDEA 2: POLITICAL PROCESS MATTERS

The political process is often described like a sporting event, with a focus on strategies and "winning." In fact, a politics news show on CNN has a daily segment titled "The Play of the Day." This focus overlooks an important point: politics is the process that determines what government does, none of which is inevitable. Public policy—everything from defending the nation to spending on Medicare—is up for grabs. And the political process determines these government actions. It is not just a game.

Elections are an excellent example of the importance of the political process. Elections allow voters to give fellow citizens the power to enact laws, write budgets, and appoint senior bureaucrats and federal judges—so it does matter who gets elected. After the 2008 election, when Democrats captured control of Congress and the presidency, they enacted a massive economic stimulus package and new policies for alternative energy, global warming, education, health care, regulation of the mortgage and financial sectors, and the wars in Iraq and Afghanistan. But if the 2008 election had gone the other way (with Republicans controlling Congress and the presidency), policies in these important areas would be significantly different. As it turned out, the Republican takeover of the House in the 2010 midterm election and Republican gains in the Senate ended the Democrats' ability to pass similar proposals—unless they could craft them in a way that gained Republican support. Clearly, elections matter.

Yet politics is more than elections. Many members of the federal bureaucracy have influence over what government does by virtue of their roles in developing and implementing government policies. The same is true for federal judges, who review government actions to see if they are consistent with the Constitution and other federal laws. These individuals' decisions are part of the political process, even though they are not elected to their positions.

Ordinary citizens are also part of politics. They can vote; donate time or money to interest groups, party organizations, or individual candidates; or demand action from these groups or individuals. Such actions can influence government policy, either by determining who holds the power to change policy directly or by signaling which options have public support.

Another important element of politics is the web of rules and procedures that determine who has the power to make choices about government policy. These rules range from the requirement that the president must have been born in the United States, to the structure of debates and voting in the House and the Senate, to the procedures for approving new federal regulations. Seemingly innocuous rules can have an enormous impact on what can or does happen, which means that choices about these rules are actually choices about outcomes.

Consider the cloture rule for ending debate in the Senate. It states that 60 votes out of 100 are needed to enact a new law, not just a simple majority of 51. For the last half of 2009, the Democrats controlled the 60 Senate sets needed to stop a Republican filibuster. (A filibuster is a way to extend debate and thereby prevent a vote on a proposal.) However, the Democrats' filibuster-proof majority was

short-lived as Republican Scott Brown won a special election in early 2010 to fill the late (Democratic) senator Ted Kennedy's seat in Massachusetts, and as Democrats lost additional seats in the 2010 midterm election.

As the cloture example implies, the ability to determine political rules empowers the people who make them. To paraphrase a favorite saying of Representative John Dingell, a long-serving Democrat from Michigan, "If you let me decide procedure and I let you decide substance, I'll beat you every time."

KEY IDEA 3: POLITICS IS EVERYWHERE

Even though most Americans have little interest in politics, most of us encounter it every day. When you read the newspaper, watch TV, surf the web, or listen to the radio, you'll almost surely encounter a political story. When walking down the street you may see billboards, bumper stickers, or T-shirts advertising a candidate, a political party, an interest group, or an issue position. Someone may ask you to sign a petition. You may read about the war in Afghanistan and wonder whether members of Congress and the president were right to pursue their current policy. Politics is also a fundamental part of how Americans think about themselves. Virtually everyone can name their party identification (Democrat, Republican, or independent)[6] and can place their views on a continuum between liberal and conservative.[7]

Politics is everywhere in another important way, too: actions by the enormous federal government touch virtually every aspect of our lives. Figure 1.1 shows a timeline for a typical college student on a typical day and the myriad ways in which federal programs, spending, and regulations influence that student's day. As you will see in later chapters, it's not surprising that the federal government touches everyday life in so many places. The federal government is extraordinarily large in terms of spending (over \$3.5 trillion for fiscal year 2012, ending in October 2012), number of employees (nearly 10 million, including contractors and the postal service), and new regulations (over 80 thousand pages in 2011).[8]

Moreover, the idea that politics is everywhere has a deeper meaning because people's political behavior is similar to their behavior in other contexts. For example, many voters form judgments about candidates based on their ethnic background, gender, or age. Such stereotyping also shapes people's judgments about

THREE KEY IDEAS FOR UNDERSTANDING POLITICS

POLITICS IS CONFLICTUAL

Conflict and compromise are natural parts of politics.

Political conflict over issues like the national debt, abortion, and health care reflect disagreements among the American people and often require compromises within government.

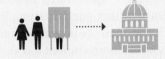

POLITICAL PROCESS MATTERS

How political conflicts are resolved is important.

Elections determine who represents citizens in government. Rules and procedures determine who has power in Congress and other branches of government.

POLITICS IS EVERYWHERE

What happens in government affects our lives in countless ways.

Policies related to jobs and the economy, food safety and nutrition, student loans, and many other areas shape our everyday lives. We see political information in the news and encounter political situations in many areas of our lives.

POP QUIZ!

1 The rule that the president must receive a majority of votes in the electoral college (not just the most votes from citizens) illustrates the idea that

a politics is conflictual.

b political process matters.

c politics is everywhere.

d the government has police powers.

e the government promotes the general welfare.

2 The fact that virtually no one got exactly what they wanted in the recent health care law (the Affordable Care Act) illustrates the idea that

a politics is conflictual.

b political process matters.

c politics is everywhere.

d the government has police powers.

e the government promotes the general welfare.

Answers: 1.b; 2.a

FIGURE » 1.1

GOVERNMENT IN A STUDENT'S DAILY LIFE

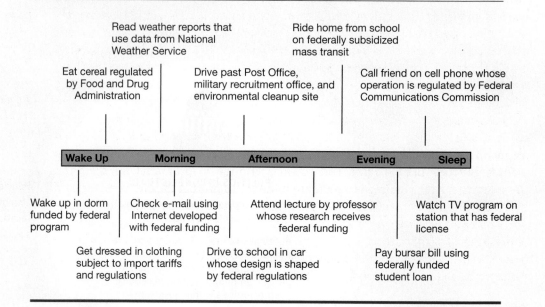

Read weather reports that use data from National Weather Service

Ride home from school on federally subsidized mass transit

Eat cereal regulated by Food and Drug Administration

Drive past Post Office, military recruitment office, and environmental cleanup site

Call friend on cell phone whose operation is regulated by Federal Communications Commission

| Wake Up | Morning | Afternoon | Evening | Sleep |

Wake up in dorm funded by federal program

Check e-mail using Internet developed with federal funding

Attend lecture by professor whose research receives federal funding

Watch TV program on station that has federal license

Get dressed in clothing subject to import tariffs and regulations

Drive to school in car whose design is shaped by federal regulations

Pay bursar bill using federally funded student loan

individuals whom they meet in other areas of life. Also, consider that convincing like-minded individuals to contribute to a group's lobbying efforts is not easy. Each would-be contributor of time or money has the opportunity to be a free rider who doesn't participate yet reaps the benefits of others' participation. Because of these difficulties, some groups of people with common goals remain unorganized. College students are a good example: many want more student aid and lower interest rates on government-subsidized student loans, but they do not organize politically toward those ends. Similar collective action problems occur when you live with roommates and need to keep common areas neat and clean: despite having the same goal, each roommate is inclined to let someone else do the work. In each case individual free riders acting in their own self-interest may undermine the outcome that most people prefer.

This similarity between behavior in political situations and in other contexts is no surprise; everything that happens in politics is the result of individuals' choices. And the connections between politics and daily life mean you already know more about politics than you realize.

IDENTIFY MAJOR SOURCES OF CONFLICT IN AMERICAN POLITICS

SOURCES OF CONFLICT IN AMERICAN POLITICS

Conflict must be addressed in order to find compromise and enact policy. Sometimes, however, disagreements resist resolution because of inherent differences among people and their opinions about government and politics.

ECONOMIC INTERESTS

People's economic interests today vary widely, and they constitute a source of conflict in politics. In contrast, relative economic equality characterized our nation's early history—at least among white men, since small landowners, businessmen, craftsmen, and their families were a majority of the population. Over time our nation became more stratified by class, to the point that the United States now ranks about 91 among the world's 194 countries in terms of income equality.[9] However, a commitment to the **free market** and **economic individualism** remains central to our national identity.

Today there are important differences among American citizens, interest groups, and political parties in terms of their economic interests and favored economic policies. Democratic politicians and activists tend to favor more **redistributive tax policies** and social spending on programs for the poor. Democrats are also inclined to regulate industry to protect the environment and worker and product safety, but they favor fewer restrictions on individual behavior. Republicans prefer lower taxes and less spending on social policies. They are more supportive than Democrats of the free market and less inclined to interfere with business interests, although many Republicans favor regulation of individual behaviors such as abortion rights and gay marriage.

free market An economic system based on competition among businesses without government interference.

economic individualism The autonomy of individuals to manage their own financial decisions without government interference.

redistributive tax policies Policies, generally favored by Democratic politicians, that use taxation to attempt to create greater social equality (i.e., higher taxation of the rich to provide programs for the poor).

CULTURAL VALUES

Another source of conflict is differing cultural values. For example, political analysts often focus attention on the **culture wars** in the United States between "red-state" Americans, who tend to have strong religious beliefs, and "blue-state" Americans, who tend to be more secular. (The color coding of the states comes from the election-night maps on television that show the states carried by Republican candidates in red and those won by Democrats in blue.)

There is no doubt that many Americans disagree on cultural and moral issues. These include the broad category of "family values" (such as whether and how to regulate pornography, gambling, and media obscenity and violence); whether to supplement the teaching of evolution in public schools with the perspectives

culture wars Political conflict in the United States between "red-state" Americans, who tend to have strong religious beliefs, and "blue-state" Americans, who tend to be more secular.

ECONOMIC INEQUALITY HAS LONG been a source of political conflict, but in recent years an increasing gap between rich and poor has heightened disagreements about what—if anything—government should do about it. The Occupy movement drew attention to the issue starting in 2011.

of intelligent design and creationism; gay marriage; abortion; stem cell research; school prayer; the war on drugs; gun control; school vouchers; and religious displays in public places. Interest groups and activists on all sides attempt to keep these hot-button issues at the top of the policy agenda.

RACIAL, GENDER, AND ETHNIC DIFFERENCES

Many political differences arise from racial, ethnic, and gender differences. For example, over the last generation about 90 percent of African Americans have been strong supporters of Democratic candidates. Other racial and ethnic groups have been less cohesive in their voting. Whites tend to vote Republican; Latinos tend to vote Democratic, with the exception of Cuban Americans, who generally vote Republican; Asian Americans tend to vote Democratic but less consistently than Latinos. A gender gap in national politics is also evident, with women being somewhat more likely to vote for Democrats and men for Republicans.[10] Because these tendencies are not fixed, however, the political implications of racial, ethnic, and gender differences can change over time.

One longstanding debate concerns whether ethnic and racial differences should be tied to political interests. For example, differing perspectives on bilingual public education and English as the nation's official language reflect the views of groups such as assimilationists (supporters of the "melting pot" image), racial separatists (such as the Nation of Islam), and multiculturalists (those who see strength in diversity). Though debates will continue about the policies best suited to our nation's diverse population, our multiracial makeup is clear (see Table 1.1). The extent to which this diversity continues to be a source of political conflict depends on the broader role of race and ethnicity in our society. As long as there are racial and ethnic differences in employment, education, health, housing, and crime, and as long as discrimination is present, race and ethnicity will continue to matter for politics. The long-running debate over immigration reform is strong evidence of this.

Many of the same observations apply to gender and politics. The women's movement is usually viewed as beginning in 1848 at the first Women's Rights Convention at Seneca Falls, New York. The fight for women's suffrage and legal rights dominated the movement through the late nineteenth and early twentieth centuries. In the 1960s and 1970s, feminism and the women's liberation movement highlighted workplace issues such as maternity leave, equal pay, and sexual harassment; reproductive rights and abortion; domestic violence; and sexual violence. Despite progress on many fronts, gender remains an important source of political disagreement.

IDEOLOGY

Another source of differences in interests is **ideology**—a set of ideas and beliefs that enables an individual to evaluate the political world. Ideology may seem most obviously related to political interests through political parties, since Republicans tend to be **conservative** and Democrats tend to be **liberal**. Conservatives favor traditional social practices and lower taxes, a free market, and more limited government, whereas liberals support social tolerance, stronger government programs, and more market regulation. Nonetheless, few Americans consider their views ideologically extreme.[11]

CIVIL AND VOTING RIGHTS POLICIES contributed to the realignment of the South in the second half of the twentieth century, as more whites began supporting the Republican Party, and the Democratic Party came to be seen as the champion of minority rights. Here, blacks and whites in Alabama wait in line together to vote at a city hall after enactment of the 1965 Voting Rights Act.

ideology A cohesive set of ideas and beliefs used to organize and evaluate the political world.

conservative One side of the ideological spectrum defined by support for lower taxes, a free market, and a more limited government; generally associated with Republicans.

liberal One side of the ideological spectrum defined by support for stronger government programs and more market regulation; generally associated with Democrats.

TABLE » 1.1

THE RACIAL COMPOSITION OF THE UNITED STATES

These census data show the racial diversity of the United States. Only about 75 percent of Americans describe themselves as white. Moreover, the proportion of Hispanics and Latinos in the population is 16.3 percent and rising, although this category contains many distinct subgroups.

RACE	NUMBER	PERCENT
Total U.S. population	309,349,689	100.0
White	229,397,472	74.2
Hispanic or Latino (any race)	50,477,594	16.3
Mexican	31,798,258	10.3
Puerto Rican	4,623,716	1.5
Cuban	1,785,547	0.6
Dominican	1,414,703	0.5
Other, Hispanic or Latino	9,163,850	2.5
Black or African American	38,874,625	12.6
Asian	14,728,302	4.7
American Indian and Alaska Native	2,553,566	0.8
Native Hawaiian and other Pacific Islander	507,916	0.1
Some other race	14,889,440	4.8
Two or more races	8,398,368	2.7

Source: U.S. Census Bureau, 2010 American Community Survey.

Also, personal ideologies are not always consistent. Someone could be both a fiscal conservative (favoring balanced budgets) and a social liberal (favoring the pro-choice position on abortion and marital rights for gay men and lesbians), or a liberal on foreign policy issues (supporting humanitarian aid and opposing the war in Afghanistan) and a conservative on moral issues (being pro-life on abortion and opposing stem cell research). In Chapter 5, Public Opinion and the Media, we explore whether America is becoming more ideological and polarized, deepening our conflicts and making compromise more difficult.

You may be surprised to find that the American public has fairly centrist views and that there are relatively few systematic differences between residents of blue states and red states on a broad range of policies. For example, red-state and blue-state residents have very similar views on immigration, English as the official language, environmental policy, school vouchers, affirmative action, equal rights for women, and tolerance of others' views.[12] Figure 1.2 illustrates this finding with data from the 2012 presidential election. The map shows the

FIGURE » 1.2

PURPLE AMERICA: THE 2012 PRESIDENTIAL ELECTION

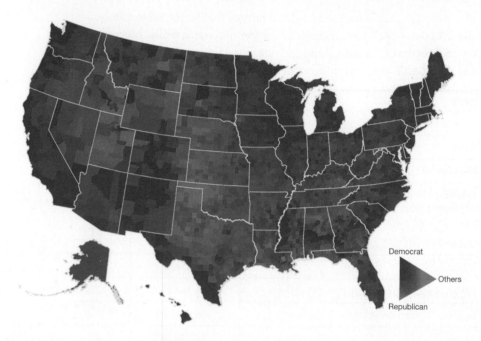

Democrat

Others

Republican

Source: Robert J. Vanderbei, Princeton University, "2012 Presidential Election, Purple America," www.princeton.edu/nrydb/JAVA/election2012 (accessed 11/10/12).

relative strength by state of Mitt Romney and Barack Obama, with the reddest states showing the strongest Republican support and the bluest states showing the Democratic strongholds. As you can see, most of the country is purple, which indicates a geographic intermixing between the parties and their associated ideological beliefs.

CONCLUSION

By understanding that politics is conflictual, that it is rooted in process, and that it is everywhere, you will see that modern American political life makes more sense than you might have thought before you read this chapter. As you proceed through this book, you will learn important "nuts and bolts" of the American political process as well as some political history. In general, though, this book will focus on contemporary questions, debates, and examples to illustrate broader points about our nation's political system. After all, American politics in its current form is the politics that will have the greatest impact on your life. Though you will likely disagree with some aspects of American politics, our goal in this book is to provide you with the tools to understand *why* government operates as it does.

WHY DO WE HAVE A GOVERNMENT?

▶ Describe the basic functions of government. **Pages 6–9**

SUMMARY

Forms of governments can be characterized by the number of people who hold power (many vs. few) and by the number of levels over which power is distributed (national vs. state vs. local). Government exists primarily to provide order, although it must do so while avoiding oppression by the rulers. Government also needs to provide public goods because they will be underprovided by the free market.

KEY TERMS

government (p. 6)

factions (p. 7)

separation of powers (p. 7)

checks and balances (p. 7)

federalism (p. 8)

public goods (p. 8)

collective action problems (p. 8)

free rider problem (p. 8)

PRACTICE QUIZ QUESTIONS

1. What did Aristotle call "a government ruled by the many"?
   a) monarchy
   b) aristocracy
   c) polity
   d) unitary system
   e) democracy

2. Which term describes giving each branch of government power over the other two branches?
   a) separation of powers
   b) checks and balances
   c) federalism
   d) plutocracy
   e) unitary system

3. Which term describes the inability to get individuals to cooperate to achieve a common goal?
   a) positive externality
   b) the Samaritan's dilemma
   c) collective action problem
   d) principal-agent problem
   e) public goods

ⓢ PRACTICE ONLINE

"Big Think" video exercise: *Self-Government for a Modern Age*

WHAT IS POLITICS?

▶ Define *politics* and identify three key ideas that help explain politics. **Pages 9–13**

SUMMARY

Conflict cannot be avoided in politics: the American people disagree on nearly every issue on which politicians make policy decisions. Compromise and bargaining are essential to enacting policy, but this means that it is almost impossible to get exactly what you want from the political process. Policy outcomes are also influenced by the policy process itself—different procedures of making policy can lead to different outcomes. Whether it is on the news or directly influencing most aspects of your life, politics is all around us.

KEY TERM

politics (p. 9)

CRITICAL THINKING AND DISCUSSION

What are some examples from your life that illustrate that "politics is everywhere"? How do government policies affect the things you do every day? Can you think of past decisions or experiences that you may not have seen as political, but that illustrate this idea as well?

PRACTICE QUIZ QUESTIONS

4. What is the main reason politicians have a hard time resolving the issue of abortion?
   a) Politicians don't listen to the people.
   b) The parties are divided on what abortion policy should look like.
   c) Politicians don't know what their constituents' views are.
   d) The country is divided on what abortion policy should look like.
   e) Abortion is a relatively new issue.

5. Which concept describes the idea that actions by the government touch most aspects of your life?
   a) Politics is understandable.
   b) Politics is conflictual.
   c) Political process matters.
   d) Politics is everywhere.
   e) People have different interests.

6. Rules such as those regulating debate in the Senate serve as evidence that _____.
   a) politics is understandable
   b) politics is conflictual
   c) political process matters
   d) politics is everywhere
   e) people have different interests

ⓢ PRACTICE ONLINE

"What Do Political Scientists Do?" video exercise: *William Bianco and David Canon discuss how political scientists develop and apply research methods.*

SOURCES OF CONFLICT IN AMERICAN POLITICS

▶ Identify major sources of conflict in American politics. **Pages 14–18**

SUMMARY

Although Americans generally agree on a free market system, there is considerable conflict over how much the government should support tax policies that redistribute wealth. Conflict also arises on cultural grounds, pitting religious "red-state" Americans against the more secular "blue-state" Americans. There is also disagreement on the extent to which racial, ethnic, and gender diversity should be celebrated or minimized. Last, although Americans are not as polarized as one would think, liberals and conservatives come into conflict on ideological grounds.

KEY TERMS

free market (p. 15)

economic individualism (p. 15)

redistributive tax policies (p. 15)

culture wars (p. 15)

ideology (p. 16)

conservative (p. 16)

liberal (p. 16)

CRITICAL THINKING AND DISCUSSION

What are your views on the role of conflict in politics? What types of issues are most likely to be resolved through political conflict and compromise, and which issues are more resistant to compromise?

PRACTICE QUIZ QUESTIONS

7. Democrats tend to favor _____ tax policies and are _____ inclined to regulate industry.
   a) redistributive; more
   b) conservative; more
   c) redistributive; less
   d) conservative; less
   e) regressive; less

8. Which issue is commonly associated with the culture wars?
a) the national debt
b) environmental regulation
c) affirmative action
d) the tax code
e) gay marriage

 **PRACTICE ONLINE**

"Critical Thinking" exercise: *Polling Report Data on Congressional Job Approval Ratings*

SUGGESTED READING

Dahl, Robert. *On Democracy*. New Haven, CT: Yale University Press, 1998.

Fiorina, Morris P., with Samuel J. Abrams and Jeremy C. Pope. *Culture War? The Myth of a Polarized America,* 2nd ed. New York: Pearson, Longman, 2006.

Gutman, Amy. *Identity in Democracy*. Princeton, NJ: Princeton University Press, 2003.

Schattschneider, E. E. *The Semi-Sovereign People: A Realist's View of Democracy in America*. New York: Holt, Rinehart, and Winston, 1960.

2

The Constitution and the Founding

RECENTLY, THE CONSTITUTION ITSELF HAS BECOME THE focus of political debate and conflict. Starting in the 2010 midterm elections and continuing through the 2012 presidential election, a popular movement known as the Tea Party has supported candidates who endorse a return to the Constitution's founding principles. While the range of views within the Tea Party movement is vast, its supporters generally see the expansion of federal power—which began with Theodore Roosevelt, exploded during the New Deal of the 1930s and Great Society of the 1960s, and continues today with President Obama's health care reform—as constitutional overreach. Many Tea Partiers see Social Security, Medicare, and the Federal Reserve as unconstitutional because they are not expressly permitted by the Constitution. Jim DeMint, a Republican senator from South Carolina and a leading Tea Partier, recently wrote, "If President Obama's motto is 'Yes, we can,' the Constitution's is 'No, you can't.' . . . Although the Constitution does give some defined powers to the federal government, it is overwhelmingly a document of limits, and those limits must be respected."[1]

The Tea Party's efforts to establish constitutional limits on government activity have met resistance from those who challenge the Tea Party's take on the Constitution and the Founding. These critics argue that rather than serving as a document that created a limited national government and protected state power, the Constitution was intended to create a strong national government while limiting state power.[2] Differences of opinion about the Constitution have been part of American politics since the debates between Federalists and

CONFLICT & COMPROMISE
in American Politics

23

Antifederalists over the document's ratification. Unfortunately, the Constitution itself provides few definitive answers because its language was intentionally general so that it would stand the test of time. Consequently, in every major political debate in our nation's history, both sides have claimed to ground their views in the Constitution. Abolitionists and secessionists during the pre–Civil War period, New Deal supporters and opponents, and civil rights activists and segregationists all claimed to have the Constitution on their side. Today's vigorous debate about the proper scope of the national government's powers is only the most recent chapter in this perpetual conflict.

Our Constitution has survived so long because rather than taking up arms, since the earliest years of our republic Americans have relied on elections and representative government to settle disputes. Losers of one round of elections know that they have an opportunity to compete in the next election and that their voices can be heard in another part of the government. The peaceful transitions of power and stability in our political system may be attributed to the hallmark characteristics of U.S. constitutional government: the separation of power across the levels of government (national, state, and local) and within government (legislative, executive, and judicial), as well as the checks and balances of power across the institutions of government.

The separation of powers in government does not mean that the Constitution *resolves* our political conflicts. The Founders recognized that self-interest and conflict are inherent parts of human nature and cannot be eliminated, so they attempted to control conflict by dispersing power across different parts of government. Thus parts of the political system are always competing with one another in pursuit of various interests: for example, Republicans in Congress may want to cut spending to balance the budget, while a Democratic president may want a mix of spending cuts and tax increases. This conflictual process is often criticized as "gridlock" and "partisan bickering." But that is the system our Founders created. Think about it this way: dictatorships do not have political conflict because dissenters are imprisoned or murdered; in contrast, we *do* have political conflict because under our constitutional government there is free and open competition among different interests and ideas.

In addition to guaranteeing that politics is conflictual, the Constitution clearly exemplifies the other two themes of this textbook. The sweeping influence of the Constitution also shows that politics is everywhere. The document shapes every aspect of national politics, which in turn influences many parts of your life. The Constitution establishes the basic rules for our nation's institutions of government, prevents the government from doing certain things to citizens (such as denying them freedom of speech), and guarantees specific individual rights. In other words, the Constitution determines the ground rules for the process that guides politics. We will return to these themes throughout this chapter.

Finally, the Constitution is highly readable. You do not have to be a lawyer or a political philosopher to understand it. It contains only 4,543 words (about the length of a 15-page term paper), and although the writing is somewhat old-fashioned in places, it uses everyday language rather than the legalese that one would confront in a modern document of this type. If you haven't read it recently (or at all), turn to the Appendix and read it now.

THE HISTORICAL CONTEXT OF THE CONSTITUTION

DESCRIBE THE HISTORICAL CIRCUMSTANCES THAT LED TO THE CONSTITUTIONAL CONVENTION OF 1787

The Constitution was created through conflict and compromise, and it is important to understand the historical context within which that process occurred. Key events shaped the Constitutional Convention, including the period of British rule over the American colonies, the Revolutionary War, and problems with the first form of government in the United States—the Articles of Confederation.

The first event that led many American colonists to question the fairness of British rule and shaped their ideas about self-governance was the Stamp Act of 1765, which imposed a tax on many publications and legal documents in the colonies. The British Parliament enacted the tax to help pay for the French and Indian War (1754–1763), claiming the tax was fair because the American colonists were benefiting from the protection of British troops. Many colonists saw this as unfair "taxation without representation" because they had no say in the legislation's passage (because they had no representation in the British Parliament). A series of escalating events, including the Tea Act (1773) and the Boston Tea Party later that year, in which colonists dumped tea from the British Indian Tea Company into the harbor rather than pay new tax, moved the colonies closer to the inevitable break with Great Britain. Attempts at a political solution failed, so the Continental Congress declared independence from Britain on July 4, 1776.[3]

ARTICLES OF CONFEDERATION: THE FIRST ATTEMPT AT GOVERNMENT

Throughout the Revolutionary and early post-Revolutionary era, the future of the American colonies was very much in doubt. While many Americans were eager to sever ties with the oppressive British government and establish a new nation

THE FOUNDERS WANTED TO CREATE a constitution that was general enough to stand the test of time. Their approach succeeded and the U.S. Constitution is the oldest written constitution still in use today. However, by leaving some passages open to interpretation, they also set the stage for conflict over the meaning of the Constitution.

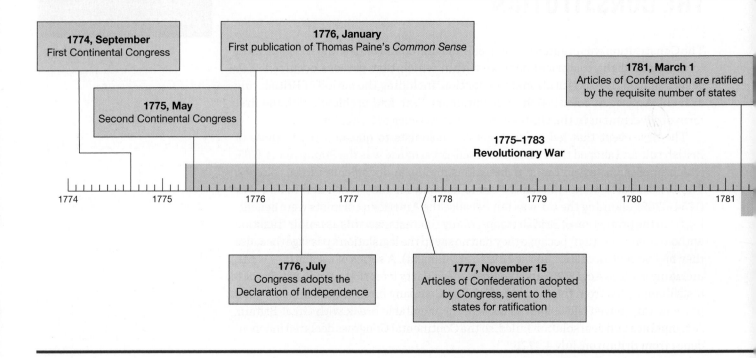

1774, September
First Continental Congress

1776, January
First publication of Thomas Paine's *Common Sense*

1781, March 1
Articles of Confederation are ratified by the requisite number of states

1775, May
Second Continental Congress

1775–1783
Revolutionary War

1774   1775   1776   1777   1778   1779   1780   1781

1776, July
Congress adopts the Declaration of Independence

1777, November 15
Articles of Confederation adopted by Congress, sent to the states for ratification

---

Articles of Confederation
Sent to the states for ratification in 1777, these were the first attempt at a new American government. It was later decided that the Articles restricted national government too much, and they were replaced by the Constitution.

limited government A political system in which the powers of the government are restricted to prevent tyranny by protecting property and individual rights.

that rejected the trappings of royalty, there was still a large contingent of Tories (supporters of the British monarchy) and probably an even larger group of Americans who wished the conflict would just go away. This context of uncertainty and conflict made the Founders' task of creating a lasting republic extremely difficult.

The first attempt to structure an American government, the **Articles of Confederation**, swung too far in the direction of **limited government**. The Articles were written in the summer of 1776 during the Second Continental Congress, which also authorized and approved the Declaration of Independence. The Articles were submitted to all 13 states in 1777 for approval, but they did not take effect until the last state ratified them in 1781. However, in the absence of any alternative, the Articles of Confederation served as the basis for organizing the government during the Revolutionary War. (See Figure 2.1, "Constitutional Timeline.")

In their zeal to reject monarchy, the authors of the Articles did not even include a president or any other executive leader. Instead, they assigned all national power to a Congress in which each state had a single vote. Members of Congress were elected by state legislatures rather than directly by the people. There was no judicial branch; all legal matters were left to the states, with the exception of disputes among the states, which would be resolved by special panels of judges appointed on an as-needed basis by Congress. In their eagerness to limit the power of government, the authors of the Articles gave each state veto power over any changes to the Articles and required approval from 9 of the 13 states on any legislation.

More important, the states maintained autonomy and did not sacrifice any significant power to the national government. Powers granted to the national government, such as making treaties and coining money, were not exclusive powers; that is, they were not denied to the states. Congress also lacked any real authority over

FIGURE » 2.1

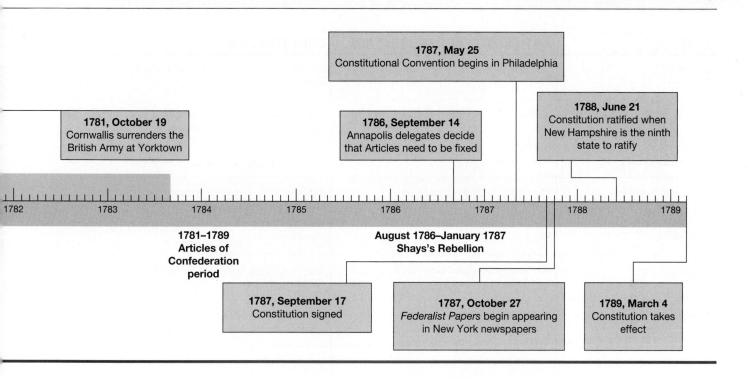

1787, May 25
Constitutional Convention begins in Philadelphia

1781, October 19
Cornwallis surrenders the British Army at Yorktown

1786, September 14
Annapolis delegates decide that Articles need to be fixed

1788, June 21
Constitution ratified when New Hampshire is the ninth state to ratify

1782   1783   1784   1785   1786   1787   1788   1789

1781–1789
Articles of Confederation period

August 1786–January 1787
Shays's Rebellion

1787, September 17
Constitution signed

1787, October 27
Federalist Papers begin appearing in New York newspapers

1789, March 4
Constitution takes effect

the states. For example, Congress could suggest the amount of money each state owed to support the Revolutionary army but could not enforce payment. After the Revolutionary War ended with the British surrender in 1781, the same weaknesses continued to plague Congress. For example, even though the new government owed millions of dollars to foreign governments and domestic creditors, it had no way to make the states pay their share. And if a foreign government negotiated a trade agreement with Congress, any state government could veto or amend the agreement, which meant that the foreign government might have to negotiate separate agreements with Congress and each state legislature. Even trade among states was complicated and inefficient.

In the face of such issues, a small group of leaders decided that something had to be done. A group from Virginia urged state legislatures to send delegates to a convention on interstate commerce in Annapolis, Maryland, in September 1786. Only five sent delegates. However, Alexander Hamilton and James Madison salvaged the effort by getting those delegates to agree to convene again in Philadelphia the following May. They also proposed that the next convention examine the defects of the current government and "devise such further provisions as shall appear to them necessary to render the Constitution of the Federal Government adequate to the exigencies of the Union."[4]

The issues that motivated the Annapolis Convention gained new urgency as subsequent events unfolded. In the years after the war, economic chaos led to a depression, and many farmers lost their land because they could not pay their debts or state taxes. Frustration mounted, and early in 1787 a former captain in the Revolutionary army, Daniel Shays, led a force of 1,000 farmers in an attempt to take over the Massachusetts state government arsenal in Springfield. Their goal was to force the state

COMPARING THE ARTICLES OF CONFEDERATION AND THE CONSTITUTION

ISSUE	ARTICLES OF CONFEDERATION	CONSTITUTION
Legislature	Unicameral Congress	Bicameral Congress divided into the House of Representatives and the Senate
Members of Congress	Between two and seven per state	Two senators per state; representatives apportioned according to population of each state
Voting in Congress	One vote per state	One vote per representative or senator
Selection of members	Appointed by state legislatures	Representatives elected by popular vote; senators appointed by state legislatures
Executive	None	President
National judiciary	Maritime judiciary established, no general federal courts	Supreme Court; Congress authorized to establish national judiciary
Amendments to the document	When approved by all states	When approved by two-thirds of each house of Congress and three-fourths of the states
Power to coin money	Federal government and the states	Federal government only
Taxes	Apportioned by Congress, collected by the states	Apportioned and collected by Congress
Ratification	Unanimous consent required	Consent of nine states required

courts to stop prosecuting debtors and taking their land, but the rebels were repelled by a state militia. Similar protests on a smaller scale happened in Pennsylvania and Virginia. Some state legislatures gave in to the debtors' demands, causing national leaders to fear that Shays's Rebellion had exposed fundamental discontent with the new government. The very future of the fledgling nation was at risk.

POLITICAL THEORIES OF THE FRAMERS

monarchy A form of government in which power is held by a single person, or monarch, who comes to power through inheritance rather than election.

republican democracy A form of government in which the interests of the people are represented through elected leaders.

Although the leaders who gathered in Philadelphia in the summer of 1787 to write the Constitution were chastened by the failure of the Articles of Confederation, they still supported many of the principles that motivated the Revolution. There was broad consensus on: (1) rejection of **monarchy**, (2) popular control of government through a **republican democracy**, and (3) limitations on government power that would protect individual rights and personal property (that is, protect against tyranny).

First among these principles was rejection of monarchy in favor of a form of government based on self-rule. In its broadest sense, **republicanism** is the ideology of any state that is not a monarchy. As understood by the framers, it is a government in which elected leaders represent the views of the people. Thomas Paine, an influential political writer of the Revolutionary era, wrote a pamphlet entitled *Common Sense* in 1776 that was a widely read[5] indictment of monarchy and an endorsement of the principles that fueled the Revolution and underpinned the framers' thinking. Paine wrote that a monarchy was the "most bare-faced falsity ever imposed on mankind" and that the common interests of the community should be served by elected representatives.

The Founders' views of republicanism were combined with liberal principles of liberty and individual rights to create their views of the proper form of government. The Declaration of Independence expresses these core principles:

> *We hold these truths to be self-evident, that all men are created equal, that they are endowed by their Creator with certain unalienable Rights, that among these are Life, Liberty, and the pursuit of Happiness. That to secure these rights, Governments are instituted among Men, deriving their just powers from the consent of the governed. That whenever any Form of Government becomes destructive of these ends, it is the Right of the People to alter or to abolish it, and to institute new Government.*

Three crucial ideas are packed into this passage: equality, self-rule, and natural rights. Equality was not given much attention in the Constitution (in later chapters we discuss how the problem of slavery was handled), but the notion that a government gains its legitimacy from the **"consent of the governed"** and that its central purpose is to uphold the "unalienable" or **natural rights** of the people were central to the framers. The "right of the people to alter or abolish" a government that did not protect these rights served both to justify the revolt against the British and to remind the framers of their continuing obligation to ensure that those needs were met. The leaders who met in Philadelphia thought the Articles of Confederation had become "destructive to those ends" and therefore needed to be altered.

The most comprehensive statement of the framers' political philosophy and democratic theory was a series of essays written by James Madison, Alexander Hamilton, and John Jay entitled the ***Federalist Papers***. These essays explained and justified the framework of government created by the Constitution. They also revealed the framers' view of human nature and its implications for democracy. The framers' view of human nature as basically self-interested led to Madison's assessment that "In framing a government which is to be administered by men over men, the great difficulty lies in this: you must first enable the government to control the governed; and in the next place oblige it to control itself." This analysis (from *Federalist 51*) is often considered the clearest articulation of the need for republican government and a system of separated powers.

In *Federalist 10* Madison described the central problem for government as the need to control factions.

He argued that governments cannot control the causes of factions, because differences of opinion—based on the fallibility of reason; differences in wealth, property, and native abilities; and attachments to different leaders—are part of human nature. The only way to eliminate factions would be to either remove liberty or try to make everyone the same. The first remedy Madison called "worse

republicanism As understood by James Madison and the framers, the belief that a form of government in which the interests of the people are represented through elected leaders is the best form of government.

"consent of the governed" The idea that government gains its legitimacy through regular elections in which the people living under that government participate to elect their leaders.

natural rights Also known as "unalienable rights," the Declaration of Independence defines them as "Life, Liberty, and the pursuit of Happiness." The Founders believed that upholding these rights should be the government's central purpose.

Federalist Papers A series of 85 articles written by Alexander Hamilton, James Madison, and John Jay that sought to sway public opinion toward the Federalists' position.

than the disease," and the second he found "as impracticable as the first would be unwise." Because people are driven by self-interest, which sometimes conflicts with the common good, government must, however, try to control the effects of factions. This was the task facing the framers at the Constitutional Convention.

ECONOMIC INTERESTS

Political ideas were central to the framers' thinking at the Constitutional Convention, but economic interests were equally important. Both the economic status of the framers themselves and the broader economic context of the time played a role. The historian Charles Beard famously argued that the framers wanted to revise the Articles of Confederation and strengthen the national government largely to

THE ECONOMIC CONTEXT OF the American Founding had an important impact on the Constitution. Most Americans worked on small farms or as artisans or business owners, which meant that economic power was broadly distributed. This woodcut shows New York City (in the distance, upper right) around the time the Constitution was written, viewed from upper Manhattan, probably about where Harlem is today.

protect their own property holdings and investments.[6] In fact, some undemocratic features of the Constitution probably do reflect the framers' privileged position; however, Beard's argument has been countered by research showing, among other things, that opponents of the Constitution also came from the upper class.[7] Most constitutional scholars now view the Constitution as the product of both ideas and interests.[8]

The broader economic context of the American Founding was more important than the delegates' individual interests. First, while there were certainly class differences among Americans in the late eighteenth century, they were insignificant compared to those in Europe. America did not have the history of feudalism that had created tremendous inequality in Europe between landowners and propertyless serfs who worked the land. In contrast, most Americans owned small farms or worked as middle-class artisans and craftsmen. Thus, while political equality did not figure prominently in the Constitution, citizens' relative economic equality did indeed influence the context of debates at the Constitutional Convention.

Second, despite Americans' general economic equality, there were significant regional differences. The South was largely agricultural with cotton and tobacco plantations that depended on slave labor. The South favored free trade because of its export-based economy (bolstered by westward expansion) and the slave trade. The middle Atlantic and northern states, however, had smaller farms and a broad economic base of manufacturing, fishing, and trade. These states favored government-managed trade and commercial development.

Federalists Those at the Constitutional Convention who favored a strong national government and a system of separated powers.

Antifederalists Those at the Constitutional Convention who favored strong state governments and feared that a strong national government would be a threat to individual rights.

Despite these differences the diverse population favored a stronger national government and reform of the Articles of Confederation. Creditors wanted a government that could pay off its debts to them, southern farmers wanted free trade that could only be efficiently promoted by a central government, and manufacturers and traders wanted a single national currency and uniform interstate commerce regulations. However, there was a deep division between the supporters of empowering the national government and those who still favored strong state governments. These two groups became known as the **Federalists** and the **Antifederalists**. The stage was set for a productive but contentious convention.

THE POLITICS OF COMPROMISE AT THE CONSTITUTIONAL CONVENTION

ANALYZE THE MAJOR ISSUES DEBATED BY THE FRAMERS OF THE CONSTITUTION

Although the delegates to the Constitutional Convention generally agreed that the Articles of Confederation needed to be changed, there were many tensions over the changes that required political compromise. Among them were the following:

- ► majority rule versus minority rights,
- ► small states versus large states,
- ► legislative power versus executive power (and how to elect the executive),
- ► national power versus state and local power, and
- ► slave states versus nonslave states.

These complex and competing interests meant that the delegates had to focus on pragmatic, achievable solutions rather than on proposals that represented particular groups' ideals but could not gain majority support.

MAJORITY RULE VERSUS MINORITY RIGHTS

A central problem for any representative democracy is protecting minority rights within a system ruled by the majority. The framers did not think of this issue in terms of racial and ethnic minorities (as we might today), but in terms of regional and economic minorities. How could the framers be sure that small landowners and poorer people would not impose onerous taxes on the wealthier minority? How could they guarantee that dominant agricultural interests would not impose punitive tariffs on manufacturing while allowing the free export of farmed commodities? The answers to these questions can be found in Madison's writings on the problem of factions.

Madison defined a faction as a group motivated by selfish interests against the common good. If these interests prevailed, he felt, it could produce the very kind of tyranny that the Americans had fought to escape during the Revolutionary War. Madison's solution to this problem provided justification for the American form of government. To control majority tyranny, he argued, factions must be set against one another to counter one another's ambitions and prevent the tyranny of any single majority faction. This would be accomplished through the "double protection" of the separation of powers within the national government in the form of checks and balances, and also through the further division of power across the levels of state and local governments.

Madison also argued that additional protection against majority tyranny would come from the "size principle." That is, the new nation would be a large and diverse republic in which majority interests would be less likely to organize,

JAMES MADISON ARGUED THAT IT is beneficial to put the interests of one group in competition with the interests of other groups, so that no one group can dominate government. He hoped to achieve this through the separation of powers across different branches of the national government and across the national, state, and local levels.

pluralism The idea that having a variety of parties and interests within a government will strengthen the system, ensuring that no group possesses total control.

and therefore less able to dominate. This insight provides the basis for modern **pluralism**, a political theory that makes the same argument about the cross-cutting interests of groups today.

The precise contours of Madison's solution still had to be hammered out at the Constitutional Convention, but the general principle pleased both the Antifederalists and the Federalists. State governments would maintain some autonomy, but the national government would become stronger than it had been under the Articles. The issue was how to strike an appropriate balance: none of the framers favored a pure populist majoritarian democracy, and few wanted to protect minority rights to the extent that the Articles had.

SMALL STATES VERSUS LARGE STATES

Virginia Plan A plan proposed by the larger states during the Constitutional Convention that based representation in the national legislature on population. The plan also included a variety of other proposals to strengthen the national government.

New Jersey Plan In response to the Virginia Plan, smaller states at the Constitutional Convention proposed that each state should receive equal representation in the national legislature, regardless of size.

Great Compromise A compromise between the large and small states, proposed by Connecticut, in which Congress would have two houses: a Senate with two legislators per state and a House of Representatives in which each state's representation would be based on population (also known as the Connecticut Compromise).

The question of the appropriate balance came to a head in a debate between small states and large states over representation in the national legislature. Under the Articles every state had a single vote, but this did not seem fair to large states. They were pushing for representation based on population. This proposal, along with other proposals to strengthen the national government, constituted the **Virginia Plan**. The small states countered with the **New Jersey Plan**, which proposed maintaining equal representation for every state. Rhode Island, the smallest state, was so concerned about small-state power that it boycotted the convention. Tensions were running high; this issue appeared to have all the elements of a deal breaker, and there seemed to be no way to break the impasse.

Just as it appeared that the convention might grind to a halt, Connecticut proposed what became known as the **Great Compromise**, or the Connecticut Compromise. The plan suggested establishing a Congress with two houses: a Senate with two senators from each state, and a House of Representatives with each state's number of representatives being based on its population. That system is still in place today.

LEGISLATIVE POWER VERSUS EXECUTIVE POWER

An equally difficult challenge was how to divide power at the national level. Here the central issues revolved around the executive—the president. How much power should the president have relative to the legislative branch? (The courts also figured into the discussions, but they were less central.) And how would the president be elected? One of the main problems was that the convention delegates did not have any positive role models for the executive.

LIMITING PRESIDENTIAL POWER

The delegates knew what they did not want: the king of England and his colonial governors were viewed as tramplers of liberty. Many delegates rejected outright the idea of a single executive because they believed it was impossible to have an executive who would not be oppressive. For this reason Edmund Randolph proposed a three-person executive. In contrast, the Virginia Plan envisioned a single executive who would share some legislative power with federal judges in a Council of Revision with the power to veto legislation passed by Congress (however, the veto could be overridden by a simple majority vote in Congress). The delegates finally agreed on the single executive because the president would have the most "energy, dispatch, and responsibility for the office," but they constrained the president's power through the system of checks and balances. One significant power they granted to the executive was the veto. It could be overridden by Congress, but only with the support of two-thirds of both chambers. This requirement gave the president a significant role in the legislative process.

The arguments for a strong executive relied heavily on the work of the English philosopher John Locke. Locke recognized the general superiority of a government of laws created by legislatures, but he also saw the need for an executive with more flexible leadership powers, or what he called "prerogative powers." Legislatures are unable, Locke wrote, "to foresee, and so by laws to provide for all accidents and necessities." They also are, by virtue of their size and unwieldiness, too slow to alter and adapt the law in times of crisis, when the executive could step in to pursue policies in the public's interest.

Although there was support for this view, the Antifederalists were concerned that if such powers were viewed as open-ended, they could give rise to the type of oppressive leader the framers were trying to avoid. Madison attempted to reassure the opponents of executive power, arguing that any prerogative powers would have to be clearly enumerated in the Constitution. In fact, the Constitution explicitly provides only one extraordinary executive power: the right to grant reprieves and pardons, which means that the president can forgive any crimes against the federal government.

SELECTING THE PRESIDENT

The second contentious issue concerning the executive was the method of selecting a president. The way the president was to be elected incorporated the issues of majority rule and minority rights, state versus national power, and the nature of executive power itself. Would the president be elected by the nation as a whole, by the states, or by coalitions within Congress? If the state-level governments played a central role, would this mean that the president could not speak for national interests? If Congress elected the president, could the executive still provide a check on the legislative branch?

Most Americans do not realize how unique our presidential system is and how close we came to having a parliamentary system, which is the form of government that exists in most other established democracies. In a **parliamentary system** the executive branch depends on the support of the legislative branch. The Virginia Plan proposed that Congress elect the president, just as Parliament elects the British prime minister. However, facing lingering concerns that the president would be too beholden to Congress, a committee of framers subsequently made the following recommendations: (1) that the president would be selected by an electoral college, representation in which would be based on the number of representatives and senators each state has in Congress, and (2) that members of each state's legislature would determine the method for choosing their state's electors.[9] The delegates ultimately approved this recommendation.

However, the solution did not work out the way the framers intended. First, if the electoral college was supposed to provide an independent check on the voters, it never played this role because the framers did not anticipate the quick emergence of political parties. Electors soon became agents of the parties (as they remain today) rather than independent actors who would use their own judgment to pick the most qualified candidate for president. Second, the emergence of parties

parliamentary system A system of government in which legislative and executive power are closely joined. The legislature (parliament) selects the chief executive (prime minister) who forms the cabinet from members of the parliament.

created a serious technical error in the Constitution: the provision that gave each elector two votes and elected the candidate with the most votes as president and the second-place finisher as vice president. With electors acting as agents of the parties, they ended up casting one vote each for the presidential and vice presidential candidate of their own party. This created a tie in the 1800 presidential election when Thomas Jefferson and Aaron Burr each received 73 electoral votes. The problem was easily fixed by the Twelfth Amendment, which required that electors cast separate votes for president and vice president.

reserved powers As defined in the Tenth Amendment, powers that are not given to the national government by the Constitution, or not prohibited to the states, are reserved by the states or the people.

national supremacy clause Part of Article VI, Section 2, of the Constitution stating that the Constitution and the laws and treaties of the United States are the "supreme Law of the Land," meaning national laws take precedent over state laws if the two conflict.

NATIONAL POWER VERSUS STATE AND LOCAL POWER

Tensions over the balance of power cut across virtually every debate at the convention: presidential versus legislative power, whether the national government could supersede state laws, apportionment in the legislature, slavery, regulation of commerce and taxation, and the amending process. The overall compromise that addressed these tensions was the system of federalism, which divided power among autonomous levels of government that controlled different areas of policy.

Federalism is such an important topic that we devote the entire next chapter to it, but two brief points about it are important here. First, federalism is an example of how careful compromises can alter the Constitution's meaning by changing a single word. The Tenth Amendment, which was added as part of the Bill of Rights shortly after ratification, was a concession to the Antifederalists who were concerned about the national government gaining too much power in the new political system. The Tenth Amendment says, "The powers not delegated to the United States by the Constitution, nor prohibited by it to the States, are reserved to the States respectively, or to the people." This definition of **reserved powers** was viewed as setting outer limits on the reach of national power.

However, the Antifederalists were not happy with this wording because of the removal of a single word; they wanted the Tenth Amendment to read, "The powers not *expressly* delegated to the United States. . . ." The new wording would have more explicitly restricted national power. With the word *expressly* removed, the amendment became much more ambiguous and less restrictive of national power.

A SLAVE AUCTION IN VIRGINIA. SLAVERY created several problems at the Constitutional Convention: Would there be limits on the importation of slaves? How would runaway slaves be dealt with by nonslave states? And how would slaves be counted for the purposes of congressional representation?

Second, the **national supremacy clause** of the Constitution (Article VI) says that any national law is the supreme law of the land and takes precedence over any state law that conflicts with it. This is especially important in areas where the national and state governments have overlapping responsibilities for policy. (The relationship between the national government and the states is discussed in Chapter 3, Federalism.)

SLAVE STATES VERSUS NONSLAVE STATES

Slavery was another nearly insurmountable issue for the delegates. Southern states would not agree to any provisions limiting slavery. Although the nonslave

MAJOR COMPROMISES AT THE CONSTITUTIONAL CONVENTION

	Position of the Large States	Position of the Small States	Compromise
Apportionment in Congress	By population	State equality	Great Compromise created the Senate and House
Method of election to Congress	By the people	By the states	House elected by the people; Senate elected by the state legislatures
Electing the executive (president)	By Congress	By the states	By the electoral college
Who decides federal–state conflicts?	Some federal authority	State courts	State courts to decide[a]

	Position of the Slave States	Position of the Nonslave States	Compromise
Control over commerce	By the states	By Congress	By Congress, but with 20-year exemption for the importation of slaves
Counting slaves toward apportionment	Counted 1:1 like citizens	Not counted	Three-Fifths Compromise
Protection for individual rights	Secured by state constitutions; national Bill of Rights not needed	National Bill of Rights needed	Bill of Rights passed by the 1st Congress; ratified by all states as of December 1791

[a] This was changed by the Judiciary Act of 1789, which provided for appeals from state to federal courts.

states opposed the practice, they were not willing to scuttle the entire Constitution by taking a principled stand. Even after these basic divisions had been recognized, many unresolved issues remained. Could the importation of slaves be restricted in the future? How would northern states deal with runaway slaves? Most important, how would the slave population be counted for the purpose of slave states' representation in Congress?

In reaching compromises on these questions, the delegates went through similar negotiations over how slaves would be counted for purposes of states' congressional representation. The states had been through this debate once before, when they addressed the issue of taxation under the Articles of Confederation. At that point slave states had argued that slaves should not be counted because they did not receive the same benefits as citizens and were not the same burden to the government. Nonslave states had countered that slaves should be counted in the same way as citizens when determining a state's fair share of the tax burden. They had reached a compromise by agreeing that slaves would count as three-fifths of a person for

UNION AND CONFEDERATE TROOPS clash in close combat in the Battle of Cold Harbor, Virginia, in June 1864. The inability of the framers to resolve the issue of slavery allowed tensions over the issue to grow throughout the early nineteenth century, culminating in the Civil War.

Three-Fifths Compromise
The states' decision during the Constitutional Convention to count each slave as three-fifths of a person in a state's population for the purposes of determining the number of House members and the distribution of taxes.

purposes of taxation. Now the arguments over the issue of representation were even more contentious at the Constitutional Convention. Here the positions were reversed, with slave states arguing that slaves should be counted like everyone else for the purposes of determining the number of House representatives for each state. Ultimately, both sides managed to agree on the **Three-Fifths Compromise**.

The other two issues involved the importation of slaves and how to deal with runaway slaves. In terms of the latter issue, northern states either would be obligated to return runaway slaves to their southern owners or they would not. Because there was no middle ground, the opposing sides looked for other issues on which to trade votes. The nonslave states wanted more national government control over commerce and trade than under the Articles, a change that the slave states opposed. So a vote trade developed as a way to compromise the competing regional interests of slavery and regulation of commerce. Northern states agreed to return runaway slaves, and southern states agreed to allow Congress to regulate commerce and tax imports with a simple majority vote (rather than the supermajority required under the Articles).

The importation of slaves was included as part of this solution. Northern states wanted to allow future Congresses to ban the importation of slaves; southern states wanted to allow the importation of slaves to continue indefinitely, arguing that slavery was essential to produce their labor-intensive crops. After much negotiation the final language of the Article prevented a constitutional amendment from banning the slave trade until 1808.[10]

From a modern perspective it is difficult to understand how the framers could have taken such a purely political approach to the moral issue of slavery. Many of the delegates believed slavery was immoral, yet they were willing to negotiate in order to gain the southern states' support of the Constitution. Some southern delegates were apologetic about slavery, even as they argued for protecting their own interests. Numerous constitutional scholars view the convention's treatment of slavery as its central failure. In fairness to the delegates, it is not clear that they could have done much better if the goal was to create a document that all states would support. However, the delegates' inability to resolve this issue meant that it would simmer below the surface for the next 70 years, finally boiling over into the bloodiest of all American wars, the Civil War.

The convention ended on a relatively harmonious note with Benjamin Franklin moving for adoption. His motion was worded ambiguously to allow those who still had reservations to sign the Constitution anyway: "Done in Convention by the unanimous consent of the States present the 17th of September . . . In Witness whereof we have hereunto subscribed our names." His clever wording meant that the signers were only bearing witness to the approval by the states and therefore could still, in good faith, oppose substantial parts of the document. Franklin's motion passed with ten ayes, no nays, and one delegation divided. All but three of the remaining delegates signed.

//

RATIFICATION

CONTRAST THE ARGUMENTS OF THE FEDERALISTS WITH THOSE OF THE ANTIFEDERALISTS

Article VII of the Constitution, which described the process for ratifying the document, was also designed to maximize its chance of success. Only nine states were needed to ratify, rather than the unanimity rule that had applied to changing the Articles of Confederation. Equally important, ratification votes would be taken in state conventions set up specifically for that purpose, bypassing the state legislatures, which would be more likely to resist some of the Constitution's state–federal power-sharing arrangements.

The near-unanimous approval at the Constitutional Convention's end masked the very strong opposition that remained. Subsequently, the ratifying conventions in each state subjected the Constitution to intense scrutiny, as attendees examined every sentence for possible objections. A national debate raged over the next nine months.

THE ANTIFEDERALISTS' CONCERNS

The Antifederalists were most worried about the role of the president, the transfer of power from the states to the national government, and the lack of specific guarantees of civil liberties. In short, they feared that the national government would become tyrannical. State power and the ability to regulate commerce were also central concerns. States such as New York would lose substantial revenue if they could no longer charge tariffs on goods that came into their ports. Other states were concerned that they would pay a disproportionate share of national taxes.

The Antifederalists' most important objection was the lack of protections for civil liberties in the new political system. During the last week of the convention, Elbridge Gerry and George Mason offered a resolution "to prepare a Bill of Rights." However, the resolution was unanimously defeated by the state delegations. Some believed that the national government posed no threat to liberties such as freedom of the press because it did not have the power to restrict them in the first place. Others thought that because it would be impossible to enumerate all rights, it was better to list none at all. Federalists such as Roger Sherman argued that state constitutions, most of which protected freedom of speech, freedom of the press, right to a trial by jury, and other civil liberties, would be sufficient to protect liberty. However, many Antifederalists still wanted assurances that the *national* government would not trample their rights. Thus they argued against ratification until such assurances were in place.

THE FEDERALISTS' STRATEGIES

The Federalists counterattacked on several fronts. First, they published a series of articles that came to be known as the *Federalist Papers*. Although originally published in New York newspapers, these articles were widely read throughout the nation. The *Federalist Papers* were one-sided arguments aimed at changing public opinion; the authors downplayed potentially unpopular aspects of the new system, such as the power of the president, while emphasizing points they knew would appeal to the opposition. Despite their biased arguments, the *Federalist Papers* are considered the best comprehensive discussion of the political theory underlying the Constitution and the framers' interpretations of many of its key provisions.

Bill of Rights The first 10 amendments to the Constitution; they protect individual rights and liberties.

Second, the Federalists agreed that the new Congress's first order of business would be to add a **Bill of Rights** to the Constitution to protect individual rights and liberties. This promise was essential for securing the support of New York, Massachusetts, and Virginia. The crucial ninth state, New Hampshire, ratified the Constitution on June 21, 1788, but New York and Virginia were still dragging their heels, and their support was viewed as necessary for the legitimacy of the United States, even if it technically was not needed. By the end of the summer both Virginia and New York finally voted for ratification. Rhode Island and North Carolina refused to ratify until Congress made good on its promise of a Bill of Rights. The 1st Congress submitted 12 amendments to the states, and 10 were ratified by all the states as of December 15, 1791. We will take a close look at the Bill of Rights in Chapter 4, Civil Liberties.

OUTLINE THE MAJOR PROVISIONS OF THE CONSTITUTION

THE CONSTITUTION: A FRAMEWORK FOR GOVERNMENT

The Constitution certainly has its flaws (some of which have been corrected through amendments), but the document's longevity is testimony to the framers' foresight in crafting a flexible framework for government. Perhaps its most important feature is the system of separation of powers and checks and balances that prevent majority tyranny while maintaining sufficient flexibility for decisive leadership during times of crisis. The system of checks and balances means that each branch of national government has certain exclusive powers, some shared powers, and the ability to check the other two branches (see "How It Works").

CHECKS AND BALANCES

President can veto congressional legislation.

The Court interprets actions by the executive.

The Senate approves presidential nominations, and Congress can pass laws over the president's veto.

President nominates judges.

IN THE CONSTITUTION

The Senate confirms the president's nominations. Congress can impeach and remove judges from office.

IN THE CONSTITUTION

If one branch tries to assert too much power, the other branches have certain key powers that allow them to fight back and restore the balance. (In addition to the powers noted in the diagram, the Congress also can impeach the president and remove him or her from office.)

The Court interprets the laws passed by Congress.

Congress passed an anti-torture law and held hearings.

The Court ruled that the executive violated the rights of suspected terrorists.

AN EXAMPLE

AN EXAMPLE

During the war on terror, concerns arose that President Bush and the executive branch had assumed too much power—especially the unilateral power to disregard due process rights for suspected terrorists. In response, Congress checked the president by passing an anti-torture law and holding hearings to determine if the Department of Justice had acted illegally. The Supreme Court limited the president's power by ruling that the executive branch violated the rights and liberties of suspected terrorists, but the president and Congress responded to limit the scope of the Court's ruling.

POP QUIZ!

1 How can the president (the executive branch) stop Congress (the legislative branch) from asserting too much power?

  a by declaring laws unconstitutional
  b by impeaching members of Congress
  c by vetoing legislation
  d by holding hearings
  e through nominations

2 How did the Supreme Court "check" the Bush administration in the cases involving the rights of terror suspects?

  a by declaring presidential/executive branch acts unconstitutional
  b by impeaching the president
  c by passing legislation
  d through nominations
  e through ratification

Answers: 1.c; 2.a

EXCLUSIVE POWERS

The framers viewed Congress as the "first branch" of government and granted it significant exclusive powers. Congress was given the power to raise revenue for the federal government through taxes and borrowing, regulate interstate and foreign commerce, coin money, establish post offices and roads, grant patents and copyrights, declare war, "raise and support armies," make rules for the military, and create and maintain a navy. Most important is the so-called power of the purse—control over taxation and spending.

Congress's exclusive powers take on additional significance through the **necessary and proper clause**, also known as the elastic clause. It gives Congress the power to "make all Laws which shall be necessary and proper for carrying into Execution the foregoing Powers, and all other Powers vested by this Constitution in the Government of the United States, or in any Department or Officer thereof." In other words, Congress could pass laws related to any of its exclusive powers. For example, while the Constitution did not explicitly mention Congress's right to compel people to serve in the military, its power to enact a draft was clearly given by the necessary and proper clause, in conjunction with its power to "raise and support armies."

The exclusive powers of Congress are more numerous and specific than the limited powers granted to the president. As commander in chief of the armed forces, the president has the power to receive ambassadors and foreign ministers and to issue pardons. The president's most important powers are contained in the executive powers clause, which says, "The executive power shall be vested in a President of the United States of America," and in the directive to ensure "that the laws are faithfully executed."

The courts did not receive as much attention in the Constitution as either Congress or the president. The most important positive powers that the framers gave the Supreme Court were lifetime tenure for justices in good behavior and relative independence from the other two branches. The critical negative power of judicial review, the ability to strike down the laws and actions of other branches, will be discussed below.

necessary and proper clause
Part of Article I, Section 8, of the Constitution that grants Congress the power to pass all laws related to one of its expressed powers; also known as the elastic clause.

CONGRESS ALONE HAS "THE POWER of the purse" to fund government programs. Although President Bush ordered the invasion of Iraq, the ongoing effort there depended on congressional authorization of funds to pay for the war.

SHARED POWERS

Along with dividing the exclusive powers among the branches of government, checks and balances designate some shared powers. These are areas where no branch has exclusive control. For example, the president has the power to negotiate treaties and make appointments to the federal courts and other government offices, but these executive actions are to be undertaken with the "advice and consent" of the Senate, which means they were intended to be shared powers. In the twentieth century these particular powers became executive-centered, with the Senate providing almost no advice to the president and routinely giving its consent. However, the Senate still can assert its shared power, as shown by the Senate's relatively recent blocking of several of President George W. Bush's and President Obama's lower court nominees.

The war powers, which include decisions about when and how to use military force, were also intended to be shared but have become executive-dominated powers. The framers disagreed about who should control the war powers. The ultimate compromise shows checks and balances at work, with the president serving as commander in chief of the armed forces, while Congress has the power to declare war and to appropriate the funds to conduct a war. Since very early in the nation's history, the president has taken a lead role in the war powers. Presidents have authorized the use of American troops on hundreds of occasions, but Congress has declared war only five times. Of these, Congress debated the merits of entering only one war, the War of 1812. The other "declarations" recognized a state of war that already existed. As the 2003 invasion of Iraq demonstrated, if a president is intent on going to war, Congress must go along or get out of the way.

However, since the Vietnam War, Congress has tried to redress the imbalance in the war powers in other ways. In 1970, during the Vietnam War, Congress passed a resolution that prevented any funds from supporting ground troops in Laos or Cambodia (nations that bordered Vietnam). In the 1980s, Democrats in Congress prevented President Ronald Reagan from using any appropriated funds to support the Contra rebels in their fight against the Sandinista government in Nicaragua.[11] These examples show that while the president continues to dominate the war powers, Congress can assert its power when it has the will—just as it can by advising the president in treaty negotiations or by withholding approval of the president's nominees for appointed positions.

NEGATIVE OR CHECKING POWERS

The last part of the system of checks and balances is the negative power that the branches have over one another. These powers are especially important because they ensure that no single branch dominates the national government.

SONIA SOTOMAYOR IS SWORN in before the Senate Judiciary Committee at her confirmation hearings to become a justice of the Supreme Court. The president and the Senate share the appointment power to the federal courts: the president makes the nominations, and the Senate provides its "advice and consent."

CONGRESSIONAL CHECKS

Congress has two important negative checks on the other two branches: impeachment and the power of the purse. **Impeachment** was based on the British practice of removing unpopular or corrupt ministers of the king through a vote of no confidence, but the framers made one important change. The president, vice president, or other "officers of the United States" (including federal judges) could not be removed for political reasons, but only for abuses of power—specifically, "Treason, Bribery, or other High Crimes or Misdemeanors."

Through the **power of the purse** Congress can punish executive agencies by freezing or cutting their funding or by holding hearings on, investigations of, or audits of their operations to make sure money is being spent properly. Congress can also freeze judges' salaries to show displeasure with court decisions, and it has the power to limit the issues that federal courts can consider. Even today the system of checks and balances is not fixed in stone but evolves according to the changing political climate.

PRESIDENTIAL CHECKS

The framers placed important checks on congressional power as well, and the president's most important check on Congress is the veto. Again there was very little agreement on this topic. The Antifederalists argued that it was "a political error of the greatest magnitude, to allow the executive power a negative, or in fact any kind of control over the proceedings of the legislature." But the Federalists worried that Congress would slowly strip away presidential powers and leave the president too weak. Ultimately, the Federalist view won the day. However, the veto has developed into a major policy-making tool for the president, which is probably broader than the check against "depredations" envisioned by the framers. The Constitution also gives the president a formal check on the courts through the power to appoint judges.

JUDICIAL REVIEW

The Constitution did not provide the Supreme Court with any formal checks on the other two branches. Instead, the practice of **judicial review**—the ability of the Supreme Court to strike down a law or an executive branch action as unconstitutional—was established by the Court much later, in the landmark decision *Marbury v. Madison* in 1803. While judicial review is not explicitly mentioned in the Constitution, supporters of the practice point to the supremacy clause, which states that the "Constitution, and the Laws of the United States which shall be made in Pursuance thereof . . . shall be the supreme Law of the Land."

As Chief Justice John Marshall argued in *Marbury v. Madison*, in order to enforce the Constitution as the supreme law of the land, the Court must determine which laws are "in pursuance thereof." Critics of judicial review argue that the Constitution is supreme because it gains its legitimacy from the people, and therefore elected officials—Congress and the president—should be the primary interpreters of the Constitution rather than the courts. This dispute may never fully be resolved, but Marshall's bold assertion of judicial review made the Supreme Court an equal partner in the system of separate powers and checks and balances.

impeachment A negative or checking power over the other branches that allows Congress to remove the president, vice president, or other "officers of the United States" (including federal judges) for abuses of power.

power of the purse The constitutional power of Congress to raise and spend money. Congress can use this as a negative or checking power over the other branches by freezing or cutting their funding.

judicial review The Supreme Court's power to strike down a law or executive branch action that it finds unconstitutional.

IS THE CONSTITUTION A "LIVING" DOCUMENT?

EXPLORE HOW THE MEANING OF THE CONSTITUTION HAS EVOLVED

How has the Constitution remained relevant after more than 200 years? Why does this framework of government still work? How can the framers' values still be meaningful to us? There are several reasons that the Constitution continues to be a "living" document.

CHANGING THE CONSTITUTION

The most obvious way that the Constitution keeps up with the times is by allowing for changes to its language. The framers broadly supported the idea behind Article V, which lays out the formal process for amending the Constitution: the people must control their own political system, which includes the ability to change it through a regular, nonviolent process.

PROPOSAL AND RATIFICATION

While there was strong consensus on including in the Constitution a set of provisions for amending it, there was no agreement on how this should be done. The Virginia Plan envisioned a relatively easy process of changing the Constitution "whensoever it shall seem necessary" by means of ratification by the people, while the New Jersey Plan proposed a central role for state governments. Madison suggested the plan that was eventually adopted, which accommodated both those who wanted a stronger national government and those who favored the states.

FIGURE » 2.2

AMENDING THE CONSTITUTION

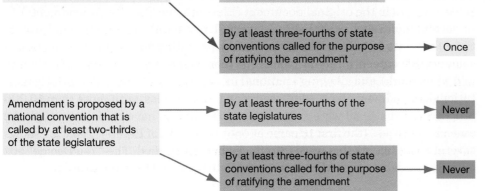

Proposal	Ratification	Frequency of Use
Congress proposes amendment by at least a two-thirds vote	By at least three-fourths of the state legislatures	All but once
	By at least three-fourths of state conventions called for the purpose of ratifying the amendment	Once
Amendment is proposed by a national convention that is called by at least two-thirds of the state legislatures	By at least three-fourths of the state legislatures	Never
	By at least three-fourths of state conventions called for the purpose of ratifying the amendment	Never

Article V describes the two steps necessary to change the Constitution: proposal and ratification. Congress may *propose* an amendment that has the approval of two-thirds of the members in both houses, or an amendment may be proposed by a national convention that has been called by two-thirds of the states' legislatures. In either case the amendment must be *ratified* by three-fourths of the states' legislatures or state conventions (see Figure 2.2). A national convention has never been used to propose an amendment, and every amendment except for the Twenty-First, which repealed Prohibition, has been ratified by state legislatures rather than state conventions.

FLAWS IN THE AMENDING PROCESS

Article V was a brilliant compromise that struck a balance between opposing views and made it neither too difficult nor too easy to amend the Constitution. However, the amending process has its flaws. First, one reason that a new constitutional convention has never been called is fear of a "runaway convention." Some scholars argue that nothing in Article V would constrain the convention to consider only a single issue, so it is possible that the convention could start from scratch, the way the framers did, even proposing a new method of ratification. Others dispute this view, but we have come close to finding out on several occasions. In the 1960s, 35 states—one short of the necessary two-thirds—called for a convention to propose a constitutional amendment that would overturn a Supreme Court decision concerning legislative redistricting. In the late 1970s, 30 states called for a convention to propose an amendment requiring a balanced federal budget.

Second, Article V does not specify voting procedures for a constitutional convention and is silent on the mechanism for choosing delegates to attend the state conventions. Third, Article V does not address the question of time limits on amendments; rather, this issue has been left up to Congress. The Eighteenth Amendment (Prohibition) was the first to have a time limit: it had to be ratified within seven years. All amendments before the Eighteenth and some after have been approved by Congress and sent to the states for ratification without time limits. This led to the odd situation surrounding the Twenty-Seventh Amendment, which required that no legislation granting a congressional pay raise could go into effect until after the following election. This amendment was originally proposed in 1789 as part of the original Bill of Rights, but it took until 1992 for enough states to ratify the amendment and add it to the Constitution, after a lag of more than 202 years!

A RANGE OF AMENDMENTS

Constitutional amendments have ranged from fairly narrow, technical corrections of errors in the original document (Eleventh and Twelfth Amendments), to important topics such as abolishing slavery (Thirteenth), mandating equal protection of the laws for all citizens (Fourteenth), providing for the popular election of senators (Seventeenth), giving blacks and then women the right to vote (Fifteenth and Nineteenth), and allowing a national income tax (Sixteenth). Potential constitutional amendments have addressed many other issues, with more than 10,000 proposed; of those, 33 were sent to the states and 27 have made it through the amending process (the first 10 came at once in the Bill of Rights). Table 2.1 shows several amendments that were introduced but not ratified. The "You Decide" box outlines the debate over when it is appropriate to amend the Constitution.

AMENDING THE CONSTITUTION

In a typical Congress there are between 50 and 100 proposals to amend the Constitution. Some of the proposed amendments reflect efforts to overturn particularly controversial Supreme Court decisions. Recent examples include amendments to prohibit abortion, guarantee the right to obtain an abortion, make flag desecration a crime, and permit prayer in public school. Some amendments are designed to change the government's basic structure and process, such as proposals to replace the electoral college with a direct popular vote, choose presidential electors at the congressional-district level, repeal the Twenty-Second Amendment (which limits presidents to two terms), require a two-thirds congressional vote to raise taxes, impose term limits on representatives and senators, or repeal the Sixteenth Amendment (which permitted a federal income tax). And some proposed amendments would guarantee specific benefits or create new classes of constitutionally guaranteed rights like affordable housing, quality health care, a clean environment, or full employment. The only thing that cannot be changed in the Constitution is the equal apportionment of states' votes in the Senate (two senators per state).[a] Anything short of that is fair game.

One controversial question concerning the amending process is whether it should be used to address specific policy issues such as term limits, balancing the federal budget, burning the flag, the Pledge of Allegiance, or whether a person may be detained for not wearing a seatbelt. The only adopted amendments that fall into this category are Prohibition (which was subsequently repealed with another amendment) and the long-delayed Twenty-Seventh Amendment regarding congressional pay raises. The other amendments address broader policy concerns, expand or protect individual rights and liberties, modify electoral laws and institutions, or address basic concerns about the working of government. Constitutional scholar Kathleen Sullivan is critical of efforts to alter the Constitution. Constitutional principles should not, she concludes, be "up for grabs" or politicized but should be slow to change; amendments should be reserved for setting out the basic structure of government and defining "a few fundamental political ideals."[b] The alternative perspective chides those who "treat the Constitution like an untouchable religious text and the republic's founders as omniscient," and maintains that "meaningful democratic politics requires an aggressive constitutional politics."[c] Many of the recently proposed amendments (see Table 2.1) are clearly policy related, thus many members of Congress view amending the Constitution as a legitimate policy-making tool.

One policy area in the debate over the appropriateness of policy-related constitutional amendments concerns gay marriage. Many states have amended their constitutions to define marriage to exclude same-sex couples. Advocates of this view are pushing for an amendment to the Constitution to define marriage the same way at the national level. Would you support such an amendment? Try to separate your view on the spe-

Some people argue that the Constitution should not be used to make policy, except for broader purposes such as expanding political rights or protecting equality. The Eighteenth Amendment, ratified in 1919, prohibited the consumption of alcohol and is often upheld as an example of a failed policy attempt. In this 1933 photo, a beer distributor readies his first shipment following ratification of the Twenty-First Amendment, which repealed Prohibition.

cific issue, gay marriage, from your position on the question of amending the Constitution. If you oppose gay marriage, is it possible that the better path of action would be through the state legislatures?

Critical Thinking Questions

1. What kinds of policies would you favor addressing through constitutional amendments? Do you agree that amendments should be reserved for a "few fundamental political ideas"—things like the right to vote and the structure of government—or that more frequent amendments are necessary for "meaningful democratic politics"?

2. Do you support any of the amendments proposed in Table 2.1? Choose one and explain why a constitutional amendment is (or is not) the best way to address the issue.

TABLE » 2.1

AMENDMENTS INTRODUCED IN CONGRESS THAT DID NOT PASS

Many proposed constitutional amendments have almost no chance of passing. Indeed, most of those listed here did not even make it to the floor of the House or Senate for a vote. Why do you think a member of Congress would propose an amendment that he or she knew would fail?

112th Congress (2011–12)	Amend the First Amendment to allow limitations on federal campaign contribution and expenditures.
	Protect the right of parents to raise and educate their children without interference from government.
	Require that the federal budget is balanced.
111th Congress (2009–10)	Abolish the electoral college and provide for the direct election of the president and vice president.
	Provide a high-quality education to all citizens of the United States.
	Repeal the Sixteenth Amendment (prohibit an income tax).
110th Congress (2007–08)	Repeal the Twenty-Second Amendment (abolish term limits for the president).
	Provide the right to a clean, safe, and sustainable environment for all persons.
	Permit voluntary school prayer.
	Impose 12-year term limits for the House and Senate.
109th Congress (2005–06)	Make the filibuster in the Senate a part of the Constitution.
	Provide for continuity of government in case of a catastrophic event.
	Prohibit desecration of the U.S. flag.
108th Congress (2003–04)	Include use of the word "God" in the Pledge of Allegiance and the national motto as protected speech.
	Define marriage in all states as a union between a man and a woman.
	Prohibit courts from protecting child pornography.

Source: The U.S. Constitution Online: Some Proposed Amendments, www.usconstitution.net/constamprop.html (accessed 3/22/12); http://thomas.loc.gov (accessed 3/22/12).

FLEXIBILITY AND INTERPRETATION

The Constitution also remains relevant because it allows for some flexibility in how it is interpreted. First, some parts of the Constitution are simply ignored today because they have no meaning in a modern context. For example, Article I, Section 4, says that "Congress shall assemble at least once in every Year," but the modern Congress is in session throughout the year (with various recesses). Nobody pays attention to this passage anymore because it simply does not matter.

AMBIGUITY

A more important characteristic of the Constitution that has kept the document relevant is its ambiguity. Key passages were written in very general language, which has enabled the Constitution to evolve along with changing norms, values, and political

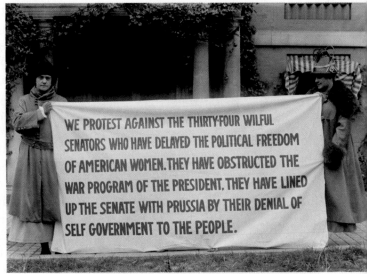

AMENDING THE CONSTITUTION IS difficult and can be controversial. Some amendments that are widely accepted today, like the Nineteenth Amendment, which gives women the right to vote, were intensely debated prior to their ratification.

contexts. This ambiguity was a political necessity: not only were the framers aware that the document would need to survive for generations, but in many instances the language that they chose was simply the only wording that all the framers could agree on. For instance, the necessary and proper clause gives Congress the power to enact laws that are related to its **enumerated powers**, or those that are explicitly granted. But what does "necessary and proper" mean? Congress for the most part gets to answer that question.

enumerated powers Powers explicitly granted to Congress, the president, or the Supreme Court in the first three articles of the Constitution. Examples include Congress's power to "raise and support armies" and the president's power as commander in chief.

IMPLIED POWERS

Furthermore, there have been significant changes in the way that the Constitution structures the policy-making process, even though the pertinent text of the Constitution has not changed.[12] This point is best understood by examining the concept of **implied powers**—that is, powers not explicitly stated in the Constitution but that can be inferred from an enumerated power. The Supreme Court often defines the boundaries of implied powers, but Congress, the president, and the public can also play key roles.

implied powers Powers supported by the Constitution that are not expressly stated in it.

To take a recent example of Congress's interpretation of implied powers, the president's appointment powers have evolved as the Senate has become much more aggressive in providing "advice and consent" on presidential nominations to the federal courts. As we explore in Chapter 12, in the past 20 years the Senate has blocked court appointments at a significantly higher rate than it did in the first half of the twentieth century. The relevant language in the Constitution is the same, yet the Senate's understanding of its role in this important process has changed.

CHANGING SOCIAL NORMS

Public opinion and social norms also influence the prevailing interpretation of the Constitution, as is evident in the evolving meanings of capital punishment (the

THE EIGHTH AMENDMENT'S BAN on "cruel and unusual punishment" is generally viewed as excluding capital punishment, but the execution of juveniles and the mentally retarded has been found unconstitutional. This picture shows the electric chair in the Southern Ohio Correctional Facility in Lucasville, Ohio.

death penalty) and freedom of speech. When the Constitution was written, capital punishment was broadly accepted, even for horse thieves. Therefore, the prohibition in the Eighth Amendment against "cruel and unusual punishment" certainly did not mean to the framers that the death penalty was unconstitutional. However, in 1972 the Supreme Court struck down capital punishment as unconstitutional because it was being applied arbitrarily.[13] Subsequently, after procedural changes were made, the Court once again upheld the practice. However, the Court has since decided that capital punishment for a mentally retarded man and minors constituted cruel and unusual punishment—a decision that reflects modern sensibilities but not the framers' thinking.[14] Similarly, the text of the First Amendment protections for freedom of speech has never changed, but the Supreme Court has been willing to uphold significant limitations on free speech, especially in wartime. When external threats are less severe, the Court has been more tolerant of controversial speech.

The line between a new interpretation of the Constitution and constitutional change is difficult to define. Clearly, not every new direction taken by the Court or new interpretation of the constitutional roles of the president or Congress is comparable to a constitutional amendment. In one respect a constitutional amendment is much more permanent than a new interpretation. For example, the Supreme Court could not unilaterally decide that 18- to 20-year-olds, women, and African Americans no longer have the right to vote. Constitutional amendments expanded the right to vote to include these groups, and only further amendments could either expand or restrict the right to vote. However, gradual changes in constitutional interpretation are probably just as important as the amending process in explaining the Constitution's ability to keep pace with the times.

CONCLUSION

The debate between Tea Party supporters and opponents outlined in this chapter's introduction illustrates many of the chapter's themes: the conflictual nature of politics established by the Constitution, multiple interpreters, and ambiguous language. The separation of powers and the system of checks and balances in our political system divide power to protect against majority tyranny. To Tea Party supporters, we have strayed too far from the limited government roots of the founding. Tea Party opponents claim that the Constitution centralized power in the national government, while moving away from the state-centered Articles of Confederation. Which side is right? The rather unsatisfying answer is: both are correct. The Founders *did* create a system of limited government that was intended to protect individual liberty from government tyranny, but at the same time the Founders wanted a strong and effective government that could overcome the limitations of state-centered government.

Congress, the president, and the Supreme Court all must interpret the Constitution in the normal course of playing their institutional roles. The general and ambiguous language of the Constitution means that both supporters and opponents of the Tea Party can stake a claim to having views that are informed by the Constitution. When a Tea Party advocate claims that the Federal Reserve is unconstitutional because it is not specifically mentioned in the document, the other side can point out that under that logic the Air Force is unconstitutional as well (the Constitution mentions Congress's power to support the Army and Navy, but obviously not the Air Force). Furthermore, Tea Party opponents would say, the commerce clause and the necessary and proper clause give Congress all the power it needs.

The Constitution's flexibility and general language mean that there will never be definitive answers to the conflict over its meaning, but they ensure that these debates will be enduring and meaningful.

THE HISTORICAL CONTEXT OF THE CONSTITUTION

▶ Describe the historical circumstances that led to the Constitutional Convention of 1787. **Pages 25–30**

SUMMARY

The U.S. Constitution was shaped by historical events preceding its creation, particularly the period of British rule over the colonies, the Revolutionary War, and the states' experience under the Articles of Confederation. Under British rule, the colonies were relatively independent of one another, and the framers sought to create a strong nation while still maintaining the autonomy of the states in the system. The framers based the Constitution on three key principles: the rejection of a monarchy, popular control of the government, and a limited government that protected against tyranny.

KEY TERMS

Articles of Confederation (p. 26)

limited government (p. 26)

monarchy (p. 28)

republican democracy (p. 28)

republicanism (p. 29)

"consent of the governed" (p. 29)

natural rights (p. 29)

Federalist Papers (p. 29)

Federalists (p. 30)

Antifederalists (p. 30)

PRACTICE QUIZ QUESTIONS

1. How were members of Congress selected under the Articles of Confederation?
a) by the state governor
b) by the state legislature
c) by the state supreme court
d) by popular election
e) by random lot

2. What power did the president have under the Articles of Confederation?
a) power to raise an army
b) power to veto congressional legislation
c) power to negotiate foreign agreements
d) power to nominate federal judges
e) There was no president under the Articles of Confederation.

3. At the American Founding, what is the best way to describe the economic inequality among classes and the economic inequality among regions?
a) high / high
b) high / low
c) low / high
d) low / low

THE POLITICS OF COMPROMISE AT THE CONSTITUTIONAL CONVENTION

▶ Analyze the major issues debated by the framers of the Constitution. **Pages 31–37**

SUMMARY

While the framers of the Constitution agreed that the Articles of Confederation needed to be changed, there was little consensus otherwise. The Federalists and Antifederalists clashed on several issues, though the most important were (1) balancing majority rule with minority rights, (2) allocating power between large and small states, (3) allocating power between the legislature and executive, (4) allocating power between the national government and the states, and (5) determining how to handle slavery.

KEY TERMS

pluralism (p. 32)

Virginia Plan (p. 32)

New Jersey Plan (p. 32)

Great Compromise (p. 32)

parliamentary system (p. 33)

reserved powers (p. 34)

national supremacy clause (p. 34)

Three-Fifths Compromise (p. 36)

CRITICAL THINKING AND DISCUSSION

If you had been at the Constitutional Convention, which part of the document would you have worked to change? How would you have negotiated a compromise to make that change possible?

PRACTICE QUIZ QUESTIONS

4. Madison argued that the best way to prevent the tyranny of factions was to _____.
   a) outlaw political parties
   b) establish a strong national government
   c) have various groups compete against each other in the government
   d) establish strong local governments
   e) try to ensure that all people were equal

5. The Great Compromise provided solutions to which issue?
   a) balancing majority rule with minority rights
   b) allocating power between big and small states

   c) allocating power between the legislature and executive
   d) allocating power between national and state governments
   e) determining how to handle slavery

6. How are executives chosen in most other established democracies?
   a) by popular election
   b) by the electoral college
   c) through selection by the judiciary
   d) through selection by the legislature
   e) by the United Nations

7. The outcome of the Three-Fifths Compromise was that slaves counted for three-fifths of a person for the purposes of _____ and _____.
   a) voting; taxation
   b) congressional representation; taxation
   c) voting; congressional representation
   d) taxation; congressional appropriations
   e) congressional representation; agricultural subsidies

ⓢ PRACTICE ONLINE

"Big Think" video exercise: *What Is the Legacy of Slavery in America?*

RATIFICATION

▶ Contrast the arguments of the Federalists with those of the Antifederalists. **Pages 37–38**

SUMMARY

After the Constitution was written and approved at the Constitutional Convention, it still needed to be ratified by nine states. The Constitution was primarily criticized by the Antifederalists, which gave way to a lengthy public debate over the merits of the proposed framework. Ultimately, the framers had to include the Bill of Rights, which was tailored to protect the rights of states and individuals from the national government, in order to win over the necessary support in the states.

KEY TERM

Bill of Rights (p. 38)

PRACTICE QUIZ QUESTIONS

8. What group was concerned about the constitution's provisions for the strength of the president and the lack of specific guarantees of civil liberties?
   a) Tories
   b) Unionists
   c) Federalists
   d) Antifederalists
   e) Free Soilers

9. James Madison, Alexander Hamilton, and John Jay wrote a series of arguments in support of the Constitution that outlined the political theory behind it. What are their assembled works called?
    a) *Pickwick Papers*
    b) *Federalist Papers*
    c) *Antifederalist Papers*
    d) *Common Sense*
    e) *The Second Treatise of Government*

Ⓢ **PRACTICE ONLINE**

"Critical Thinking" exercise: *Politics Is Conflictual—The Bill of Rights*

THE CONSTITUTION: A FRAMEWORK FOR GOVERNMENT

▶ Outline the major provisions of the Constitution. **Pages 38–42**

SUMMARY

The defining feature of the Constitution is its separation of powers while still maintaining flexibility for leadership in times of crisis. The system of checks and balances gives each branch of the federal government some explicit powers, some shared powers, and some ability to limit the power of the other two branches of government.

KEY TERMS

necessary and proper clause (p. 40)

impeachment (p. 42)

power of the purse (p. 42)

judicial review (p. 42)

CRITICAL THINKING AND DISCUSSION

The president has clearly dominated the decision to go to war in the past century, despite the founders' view that war powers are a shared power. How would a Tea Partier respond to this change? What other areas of the Constitution as a framework for government have evolved?

PRACTICE QUIZ QUESTIONS

10. The "necessary and proper clause" gives flexibility to which part of government?
    a) the president
    b) the Supreme Court
    c) the bureaucracy
    d) the Congress
    e) interest groups

11. Which branch has the fewest explicit powers?
    a) the president
    b) the Supreme Court
    c) the bureaucracy
    d) the Congress

12. Which of the following negative powers does the president enjoy?
    a) the power to veto legislation
    b) the power to freeze judicial salaries
    c) the power to review the constitutionality of a law
    d) the power to impeach federal justices
    e) the power to dissolve Congress and call new elections

Ⓢ **PRACTICE ONLINE**

"Critical Thinking" exercise: *Political Process Matters—Impeachment*

IS THE CONSTITUTION A "LIVING" DOCUMENT?

▶ Explore how the meaning of the Constitution has evolved. **Pages 43–48**

SUMMARY

The Constitution is more than 200 years old, yet it still provides a blueprint for modern governance. It has maintained its relevance due to its ambiguity on several key passages, its ability to be amended rather than entirely rewritten, and the designation of multiple interpreters of the Constitution.

CRITICAL THINKING AND DISCUSSION

Should the Constitution be a "living document" that evolves with the values and norms of our society, or should interpretation of the Constitution follow more closely the original intentions of the framers?

PRACTICE QUIZ QUESTIONS

13. Which route for *proposing* a constitutional amendment has been used for all successful amendments to date?
a) approval by two-thirds of the members of Congress
b) approval by a national convention
c) approval by two-thirds of the state legislatures
d) approval by the Supreme Court
e) approval by the president

14. After an amendment is successfully proposed, what step must occur in order for it to become part of the Constitution?
a) signature by the president
b) approval by a popular vote
c) ratification by three-fourths of the states
d) nullification by all 50 state legislatures
e) a national referendum vote

15. Which part of government often defines the boundaries of implied powers?
a) the president
b) the Supreme Court
c) the bureaucracy
d) the Congress
e) the people

Ⓢ PRACTICE ONLINE

"Big Think" video exercise: *The Challenge of Constitutional Interpretation*

SUGGESTED READING

Balkin, Jack M., ed. *The Constitution in 2020*. New York: Oxford University Press, 2009.

Currie, David P. *The Constitution of the United States: A Primer for the People*, 2nd ed. Chicago: University of Chicago Press, 2000.

Dahl, Robert A. *How Democratic Is the American Constitution?* New Haven, CT: Yale University Press, 2001.

Davis, Sue. *Corwin and Peltason's Understanding the Constitution*, 17th ed. Boston: Wadsworth Publishing, 2007.

Hamilton, Alexander, James Madison, and John Jay. *The Federalist Papers*. 1788. Reprint, 2nd ed., edited by Roy P. Fairfield. Baltimore, MD: Johns Hopkins University Press, 1981.

Ketcham, Ralph. *The Anti-Federalist Papers and the Constitutional Convention Debates*. New York: Signet Classics, 2003.

Kurland, Philip B., and Ralph Lerner, eds. *The Founders' Constitution*. Chicago: University of Chicago Press, 1987.

Rossiter, Clinton. *1787: The Grand Convention*. New York: Macmillan, 1966.

Sunstein, Cass R. *Designing Democracy: What Constitutions Do*. New York: Oxford University Press, 2001.

Wood, Gordon S. *The Creation of the American Republic*. New York: Norton, 1969.

3

Federalism

FOLLOWING PASSAGE OF THE 2010 AFFORDABLE CARE ACT (ACA),[1] 26 states sued the national government over the new law. Intended to provide health care coverage to more than 30 million uninsured Americans, the law seemed to these states to be an unconstitutional overreach of federal power: "the individual mandate exceeds Congress's enumerated powers, the Medicaid expansions are unconstitutionally coercive, and the employer mandates impermissibly interfere with state sovereignty."[2] This is the federalism trifecta, hitting on all three major themes concerning the balance of power among levels of government: (1) Congress's power to enact broad national legislation under the Constitution's commerce clause, (2) Congress's power to compel states to act through "coercive federalism," and (3) states' sovereign powers under the Tenth and Eleventh Amendments.

Supporters of the law argued that standardizing these provisions across all 50 states was crucial to ensuring health care for all Americans because otherwise millions of Americans would be unable to get health insurance. At present some states do an excellent job of providing access to health care, but others do not.[3] As President Obama explained when signing the legislation, "we have now just enshrined—as soon as I sign this bill—the core principle that everybody should have some basic security when it comes to their health care."[4] Furthermore, the national law eliminates state-based insurance monopolies that drive up health care costs; competition across state lines through the health insurance exchanges mandated by the ACA will help keep health care costs lower.

CONFLICT & COMPROMISE
in American Politics

The Obama administration and other supporters of the law have rebutted each of the challenges to its constitutionality. The strongest legal challenge to the law is whether Congress can force individuals to buy health insurance under the commerce clause of the Constitution. Opponents say that the decision to *not* buy insurance is not economic activity (but rather is "inactivity") and therefore cannot be regulated by Congress. Supporters point out that everyone participates in the health care system at some point: people who do not buy insurance drive up health care costs for those who do have insurance because the uninsured use emergency rooms when they get sick or injured (which is much more expensive than normal care). Therefore, supporters say, the decision not to buy insurance does have an impact on economic activity.

Opponents' objection regarding "coercive federalism" concerns the national government's expanding of Medicaid eligibility while shifting more of the costs of Medicaid onto the states. Supporters of the law say that states could opt out by not accepting the federal money, in which case they would not be forced to do anything. Finally, proponents argue that the Tenth and Eleventh Amendments do not restrain Congress from enacting laws that are "necessary and proper" under their Article I powers. The Supreme Court largely upheld the ACA, but there were two parts of the decision that accepted the critics' view and have important implications for federalism. First, the basis for upholding the controversial individual mandate was Congress's taxing power, rather than the commerce clause. The Court agreed with critics of the law who argued that Congress's power to regulate interstate commerce does not apply to penalizing economic inactivity (that is, failing to buy health insurance). Second, the Court ruled that the expansion of Medicaid, which would provide health care for an additional 17 million low-income Americans, was unconstitutionally coercive in requiring states to expand Medicaid or lose all their federal funding for the existing Medicaid program. States could still choose to accept the federal funding to expand Medicaid, but they would not lose their other Medicaid funding if they opted out of the expansion (as of this writing, ten states have indicated that they may opt out).

The battles over the ACA illustrate our central theme that politics is about conflict and compromise. Our system of federalism is bound to produce conflict as the national and state governments disagree over the best direction for any specific policy. Sometimes disputes are resolved by the national government imposing its views on the states. In that instance, there may appear to be little compromise. However, even in the case of health care reform, the states still have a significant impact on the policy's implementation.

Federalism also illustrates our other two themes. By dividing power across the levels of government, federalism highlights the importance of the political process. While the U.S. Congress wrote the ACA law, the 50 states will be implementing it, which means that the political process of each state will come into play. Federalism also shows that politics is everywhere: decentralizing power across levels of government provides a much broader range of *individual-level* choices than a unitary system does. For example, a retiree trying to decide where to live could choose between low-tax, low-service states such as Texas and high-tax, high-service states such as New York. Business owners often decide where to locate a new facility by considering the "business climate"—the corporate tax structure, environmental laws, regulatory policy, and levels of education and unionization of the workforce. States differ in regard to these factors because our federal system gives them autonomy to choose policies that meet their residents' needs.

WHAT IS FEDERALISM AND WHY DOES IT MATTER?

Federalism can be defined as a form of government that divides sovereign power across at least two political units. Dividing **sovereign power** means that each unit of government (in the U.S. context, the national and state governments) has some degree of authority and autonomy. As discussed in Chapter 2, this division of power across levels of government is central to the system of separated powers in the United States. The concept of dividing power across levels of government seems simple, but as we will see later in this chapter, the political battles over *how* that power is divided have been intense.

In practical terms, federalism is about intergovernmental relations: how the different levels of government interact, and how power is divided. But even that may seem a little abstract. Why does federalism matter? On a broad range of issues, the level of government that dictates policy can make a real difference. The conflict over health care reform is an obvious example, but other recent issues include whether the national government should be able to prevent states from allowing marijuana use for medical purposes or allowing assisted suicides, or be able to compel states to ban guns within or around public schools or set a uniform speed limit on federal highways. These questions involve defining the disputed boundaries between what the states and national government are allowed to do. Much of U.S. history has been rooted in this struggle to define American federalism.

Another important point concerns the *politics* of federalism: while the states' rights perspective of federalism has traditionally been associated with conservative political causes (most prominently, opposition to civil rights and racial integration in the South in the 1950s and 1960s, and more recently opposition to health

federalism The division of power across the local, state, and national governments.

sovereign power The national and state government each have some degree of authority and autonomy.

THE RELATIONSHIP BETWEEN THE national government and the states also involves cooperation. After a series of devastating tornadoes hit the Midwest and the South in 2011, President Obama and federal agencies worked with the states to provide emergency relief funds and services. Here, President Obama visits Joplin, Missouri, with Governor Jay Nixon.

care reform and gun control), on many issues such as environmental policy and gay rights the states have been pushing for more progressive policies than the federal government sets.

Thus federalism influences both the direction of policy outcomes and the politics of the process, but with evolving roles for the national and state governments. Before we consider the changing balance of intergovernmental power in American federalism, however, we will take a closer look in this section at what federalism means.

LEVELS OF GOVERNMENT AND THEIR DEGREES OF AUTONOMY

A distinguishing feature of federalism is that each level of government has some degree of autonomy from the other levels; that is, each level can carry out some policies that the others may not prefer. In the United States, this means that the national and state governments have distinct powers and responsibilities. The national government, for example, is responsible for national defense and foreign policy. State and local governments have primary responsibility for conducting elections and promoting public safety, or **police powers**. In other areas, such as transportation, the different levels of government share responsibilities in the **concurrent powers** (see Nuts and Bolts 3.1). The national government also has additional responsibilities through implied powers that are inferred from the powers explicitly granted in the Constitution (see later discussion in this chapter).

Local governments—cities, towns, school districts, and counties—are not autonomous units of government. State governments create them and control the types of activities they can engage in, by specifying in the state charter either what they *can* do or only what they *cannot* do (that is, they are allowed to do anything not prohibited in the charter). Despite this lack of autonomy, local governments play an important role in providing public education, police and fire departments, and land use policies. They also raise money through property taxes, user fees, and in some cases local sales taxes. But overall, local governments do not directly share power within our federal system with the state and national governments because of their lack of autonomy.

A COMPARATIVE PERSPECTIVE

It is useful to compare U.S. federalism to forms of government in other countries. In some countries, power is centralized within the national government. This system is known as a **unitary government**. Unitary governments are the most common in the modern world (about 80 percent); examples include the United Kingdom, Israel, Italy, France, Japan, and Sweden. In these countries, the states or subunit governments are not autonomous; they cannot carry out policies if the national government opposes them. At the opposite end of the spectrum is a **confederal government**, in which the states have most of the power and often can veto the actions of the central government. This was the first type of government in the United States under the Articles of Confederation. Because there

police powers The power to enforce laws and provide for public safety.

concurrent powers Responsibilities for particular policy areas, such as transportation, that are shared by federal, state, and local governments.

unitary government A system in which the national, centralized government holds ultimate authority. It is the most common form of government in the world.

confederal government A form of government in which states hold power over a limited national government.

NATIONAL AND STATE RESPONSIBILITIES

National Government Powers	State Government Powers	Concurrent Powers
Print money	Issue licenses	Collect taxes
Regulate interstate commerce and international trade	Regulate intrastate (within the state) businesses	Build roads
Make treaties and conduct foreign policy	Conduct elections	Borrow money
Declare war	Establish local governments	Establish courts
Provide an army and navy	Ratify amendments to the Constitution	Make and enforce laws
Establish post offices	Promote public health and safety	Charter banks and corporations
Make laws necessary and proper to carry out these powers	May exert powers the Constitution does not delegate to the national government or does not prohibit the states from using	Spend money for the general welfare; take private property for public purposes, with just compensation

Powers Denied to the National Government	Powers Denied to State Governments
May not violate the Bill of Rights	May not enter into treaties with other countries
May not impose export taxes among states	May not print money
May not use money from the Treasury without an appropriation from Congress	May not tax imports or exports
May not change state boundaries	May not interfere with contracts
	May not suspend a person's rights without due process

Source: GPO Access: Guide to the U.S. Government, http://bensguide.gpo.gov/3-5/government/federalism.html (accessed 12/5/11).

are many problems associated with having such a weak national government (see Chapter 2), few successful modern examples exist. The Commonwealth of Independent States (CIS), which formed in 1991 after the breakup of the Soviet Union, was initially successful as a confederal structure, but rifts among the member states today are making it largely ineffective.[5]

Although true confederations are rare, **intergovernmental organizations** have proliferated in recent decades. More than 1,200 multilateral organizations have been created by member nations seeking to coordinate their policies on, for example, economic activity, security, or environmental protection. The United Nations (UN), the International Monetary Fund (IMF), and the North Atlantic

intergovernmental organizations Organizations that seek to coordinate policy across member nations.

Treaty Organization (NATO) are important examples. The European Union is an intergovernmental organization that began as a loose confederation, but it is becoming more federalist in its decision-making process and structure.

EXPLAIN WHAT THE CONSTITUTION SAYS ABOUT FEDERALISM

BALANCING NATIONAL AND STATE POWER IN THE CONSTITUTION

Although our nation's Founders wanted a national government that was stronger than it had been under the Articles of Confederation, they also wanted to preserve the states' autonomy. These goals are reflected in different parts of the Constitution, which provides ample evidence for advocates of both state-centered and nation-centered federalism. The nation-centered position appears in the document's preamble, which begins, "We the People of the United States," compared to the Articles of Confederation, which began, "We the undersigned delegates of the States." The Constitution's phrasing emphasizes the nation as a whole over the separate states.

A STRONG NATIONAL GOVERNMENT

Other aspects of the Constitution also support the nation-centered perspective. These reflect the Founders' desire for a strong national government to provide national security and a healthy, efficient economy.

In terms of national security, Congress was granted the power to raise and support armies, declare war, and "suppress Insurrections and repel Invasion," while the president, as commander in chief of the armed forces, would oversee the conduct of war. Congress's power to regulate interstate commerce promoted economic efficiency and centralized an important economic power at the national level, and many restrictions on state power had similar effects. States were *prohibited* from entering into "any Treaty, Alliance, or Confederation" or keeping troops or "Ships of War" during peacetime. They also could not coin money or impose duties on imports or exports (see Article I, Section 10). These provisions ensured that states would not interfere with the smooth operation of interstate commerce or create problems for national defense. Imagine, for example, that Oklahoma had the power to tax oil produced in other states or that California decided to create its own army. This would create inefficiencies and potential danger for the rest of the country.

The necessary and proper clause (Article I, Section 8) was another broad grant of power to the national government: it gave Congress the power "To make all Laws which shall be necessary and proper for carrying into Execution the foregoing Powers." Similarly, the national supremacy clause (Article VI) says that the Constitution and all laws and treaties that are made under the Constitution shall be the "supreme Law of the Land" and that "the Judges in every State shall be bound thereby, any Thing in the Constitution or Laws of any State to the Contrary notwithstanding." This is perhaps the clearest statement of the nation-centered focus of the Constitution. If any state law or state constitution conflicts with national law or the Constitution, the national perspective wins. Thus, the laws passed by states to limit implementation of the ACA will have no effect now that the Supreme Court upheld the central parts of the national law.

STATE POWERS AND LIMITS ON NATIONAL POWER

Despite the Founders' nation-centered bias, many parts of the Constitution also address state powers and limits on national power. Article II gives the states the power to choose electors for the electoral college, and Article V grants the states a central role in the process of amending the Constitution. Three-fourths of the states must ratify any constitutional amendment (either through conventions or the state legislatures, as specified by Congress), but the states can also bypass Congress in proposing amendments if two-thirds of the states call for a convention. This route to amending the Constitution has never been used, but the Founders clearly wanted to provide an additional check on national power.

Article I of the Constitution enumerates many powers for Congress, but the list of state powers is much shorter. One could interpret this as more evidence for the nation-centered perspective, but at the time of the Founding the default position was to keep most power at the state level. Therefore, the federal powers that were exceptions to this rule had to be clearly specified, while state governments received authority over all other matters. The Tenth Amendment supports this view, saying, "The powers not delegated to the United States by the Constitution, nor prohibited by it to the states, are reserved to the states respectively, or to the people."

The Eleventh Amendment, the first one passed after the Bill of Rights, was another important affirmation of state sovereignty. Antifederalists were concerned that the part of Article III that gave the Supreme Court authority over cases involving a "State and Citizens of another State" would undermine state sovereignty by giving the Court too much power over state laws. Federalists assured them this would not happen, but the Supreme Court ruled in *Chisholm v. Georgia* (1793) that citizens of one state could sue the government of another state. The majority opinion ridiculed the "haughty notions of state independence, state sovereignty, and state supremacy." The states struck back by adopting the Eleventh Amendment, which made such lawsuits unconstitutional. While the Supreme Court lost this skirmish over state power, it continued to serve as the umpire in disputes between the national and state governments.

CLAUSES THAT FAVOR BOTH PERSPECTIVES

Article IV of the Constitution has elements that favor both the state-centered and the nation-centered perspectives. For example, its **full faith and credit clause** specifies that states must respect one another's laws, granting citizens the "Full Faith and Credit" of their home state's laws if they go to another state. At the same time, though, the article's **privileges and immunities clause** says

full faith and credit clause Part of Article IV of the Constitution requiring that each state's laws be honored by the other states. For example, a legal marriage in one state must be recognized across state lines.

privileges and immunities clause Part of Article IV of the Constitution requiring that states must treat nonstate residents within their borders as they would treat their own residents. This was meant to promote commerce and travel between states.

that citizens of each state are "entitled to all Privileges and Immunities" of citizens in the other states, which means that states must treat visitors from other states the same as their own residents. This part of the Constitution favors a nation-centered perspective because it was intended to promote free travel and economic activity among the states.

There are many examples of the full faith and credit clause at work today. If you have a New York driver's license and are traveling to California, you do not need to stop at every state line to get a new license; each state will honor your New York license. Similarly, a legal marriage in one state must be honored by another state, a provision that has fueled the ongoing controversy over same-sex marriage. In 1996, after Hawaii courts gave homosexual marriages most of the same legal rights as heterosexual marriages, many states passed laws saying they would not have to honor those marriages. Similarly, Congress passed the Defense of Marriage Act, which said that states would not have to recognize same-sex marriages. Hawaii courts have since overturned the decision to recognize same-sex marriages, but as of late 2012 nine states allow gay marriages and five states recognize civil unions between homosexual partners, but not marriage.[6] However, current law holds that the full faith and credit clause does not apply to gay marriage because of the "policy exception."[7]

We can also cite examples of the privileges and immunities clause at work in a modern context. For example, Michigan cannot charge the owner of a lake cabin different property taxes based on whether she lives in Michigan or in another state. Also, states may not deny welfare benefits to new residents or deny police protection to visitors even though they do not pay state taxes.[8] However, states are allowed to make some distinctions between residents and nonresidents. For example, states do not have to permit nonresidents to vote in state elections, and public colleges and universities may charge out-of-state residents higher tuition than in-state residents. Therefore, the privileges and immunities clause cuts both ways on the question of the balance of power: it allows the states to determine and uphold these laws autonomously, but it also emphasizes that national citizenship is more important than state citizenship.

The Constitution sets the boundaries for the battles over federalism. For example, no state can decide to print its own currency, and the U.S. government cannot take over any public school district in the country. But within those broad boundaries, the balance between national and state power at any given point in history is a political decision, the product of choices made by elected leaders and the courts. Decisions by the Supreme Court have figured prominently in this evolution.

SHOULD SAME-SEX MARRIAGES performed in one state be recognized in another state where such marriages are banned? Here, demonstrators protest Proposition 8, which was intended to ban gay marriage in California.

THE EVOLVING CONCEPT OF FEDERALISM

TRACE THE MAJOR SHIFTS IN STATE AND FEDERAL GOVERNMENT POWER OVER TIME

The nature of federalism has changed as the relative positions of the national and state governments have evolved. In the first century of our nation's history, the national government played a relatively limited role and the boundaries among the levels of government were distinct. As the national government took on more power in the twentieth century, intergovernmental relations became more cooperative and the boundaries less distinct. Even within this more cooperative framework, federalism remains a source of conflict within our political system as the levels of government share law-making authority (as the health care example that opened the chapter illustrates).

THE EARLY YEARS

As the United States gained its footing, clashes between the advocates of state-centered and nation-centered federalism evolved into a partisan struggle. The Federalists (the party of George Washington, John Adams, and Alexander Hamilton) controlled the new government for its first twelve years and favored strong national power. Their opponents, the Democratic-Republicans (led by Thomas Jefferson and James Madison), favored state power.

ESTABLISHING NATIONAL SUPREMACY

The first confrontation came when the Federalists established a national bank in 1791, over Jefferson's objections. This controversy did not come to a head until Congress chartered the second national bank in 1816. At that time the state of Maryland, which was controlled by the Democratic-Republicans, tried to tax the National Bank's Baltimore branch out of existence, but the head cashier of the bank refused to pay the tax and the case eventually ended up at the Supreme Court. The Court had to decide whether Congress had the power to create the bank, and if it did, whether Maryland had the right to tax the bank.

In the landmark decision *McCulloch v. Maryland* (1819), the Court ruled in favor of the national government on both counts. In deciding whether Congress could create the bank, the Court held that even though the word *bank* does not appear in the Constitution, Congress's power to create one is implied through its enumerated powers—such as the power to coin money, levy taxes, and borrow money. The Court also ruled that Maryland did not have the right to tax the bank because of the Constitution's national supremacy clause. Both the concept of implied powers and the validation of national supremacy were critical for establishing the centrality of the national government.

A few years later, the Supreme Court decided another case that cemented Congress's power to act based on the commerce clause. In *Gibbons v. Ogden* (1824), the Supreme Court held that Congress has broad power to regulate interstate commerce and struck down a New York law that had granted a monopoly to a private company operating steamboats on the Hudson River between New York and

New Jersey. By granting this monopoly, the ruling stated, New York was interfering with interstate commerce.

PRESSING FOR STATES' RIGHTS

states' rights The idea that states are entitled to a certain amount of self-government, free of federal government intervention. This became a central issue in the period leading up to the Civil War.

Despite such Court rulings in favor of national government, the following decades saw a push for broader **states' rights**, as when the southern states challenged federalism on issues such as tariffs and slavery. John Calhoun, a South Carolina senator, used the term *nullification* to refer to the same principle, urging South Carolina to ignore a tariff law passed by Congress in 1832. The states' rights perspective was at the center of the dispute between southern and northern states over slavery, which ultimately led to the secession of the Confederate states and, subsequently, the Civil War. The stakes were enormous in the battles over federalism: about 528,000 people died in that bloodiest of American wars.[9] As Abraham Lincoln forcefully argued, concepts such as nullification and states' rights, when taken to their logical extremes, were too divisive to be allowed to stand. If states were allowed to ignore national laws, the basis of the United States would fall apart.

DUAL FEDERALISM

The ideas of states' rights and nullification did not produce the Civil War by themselves. They had some help from the Supreme Court's infamous *Dred Scott* decision. In this section we will discuss the significance of that case as well as the broader system of dual federalism, which defined intergovernmental relations for nearly the first 150 years of our nation's history.

For nearly three decades during the mid-1800s, the Supreme Court was able to limit the reach of the national government through Chief Justice Roger Taney's

TABLE » 3.1

EARLY LANDMARK SUPREME COURT DECISIONS ON FEDERALISM

CASE	HOLDING AND SIGNIFICANCE
Chisholm v. Georgia (1793)	Held that citizens of one state could sue another state; led to the Eleventh Amendment, which prohibited such lawsuits.
McCulloch v. Maryland (1819)	Upheld the national government's right to create a bank and reaffirmed the idea of "national supremacy."
Gibbons v. Ogden (1824)	Held that Congress, rather than the states, has broad power to regulate interstate commerce.
Barron v. Baltimore (1833)	Endorsed a notion of "dual federalism" in which the rights of a U.S. citizen under the Bill of Rights did not apply to that same person under state law.
Dred Scott v. Sandford (1857)	Sided with southern states' view that slaves were property and ruled that the Missouri Compromise violated the Fifth Amendment, since making slavery illegal in some states deprived slave owners of property. Contributed to the start of the Civil War.
National Labor Relations Board v. Jones & Laughlin Steel Corporation (1937)	Upheld the National Labor Relations Act of 1935 as consistent with Congress's commerce clause powers, reversing the Court's more narrow interpretation of that clause.

vision of federalism, which is known as dual federalism (see Table 3.1). Under **dual federalism** the national and state governments were viewed as distinct, with little overlap in their activities or the services they provided. In this view the national government's activities are confined to powers strictly enumerated in the Constitution, despite the necessary and proper clause and the implied powers endorsed in *McCulloch v. Maryland*. Within this framework of distinct national and state powers, the Taney Court expanded the power of the states over commerce in ways that would not be accepted today. For example, this Court gave the mayor of New York City the right to control immigration by requiring shipmasters to post bonds for foreign passengers who might later go on welfare,[10] and it allowed the city of Philadelphia to require ships to use local captains when entering the harbor.[11] Today these areas of commerce are regulated by Congress, not by local governments.

dual federalism The form of federalism favored by Chief Justice Roger Taney in which national and state governments are seen as distinct entities providing separate services. This model limits the power of the national government.

DRED SCOTT AND CIVIL WAR

The state-centered views of the Taney Court also produced a tragic decision, *Dred Scott v. Sandford* (1857). Dred Scott was a slave who had lived for many years with his owner in the free Wisconsin Territory but was living in Missouri, a slave state, when his master died. Scott petitioned for his freedom under the Missouri Compromise, which said that slavery was illegal in any free state. The Taney Court's decision held that slaves were not citizens but private property, and that therefore the Missouri Compromise violated the Fifth Amendment because it deprived people (slave owners) of property without the due process of law. This unfortunate decision contributed to the Civil War, which started four

AFTER THE SUPREME COURT STRUCK down the 1875 Civil Rights Act, southern states were free to impose Jim Crow laws. These state and local laws led to complete racial segregation, even for public drinking fountains.

years later, because it indicated that there could not be a political solution to the problem of slavery.

Ultimately the Civil War ended the dispute over slavery, but it did not resolve basic questions about the balance of power between the national and state systems. Right after the Civil War, the Constitution was amended to ensure that the Union's views on states' rights were the law of the land. The Civil War amendments banned slavery (the Thirteenth), prohibited states from denying citizens due process or equal protection of the laws (Fourteenth), and gave newly freed male slaves the right to vote (Fifteenth). The Fourteenth Amendment was the most important in terms of federalism because it served as the constitutional basis for many of the civil rights laws passed by Congress during Reconstruction.

THE SUPREME COURT AND LIMITED NATIONAL GOVERNMENT

However, the Supreme Court soon stepped in again to limit the power of the national government. In 1873 the Court reinforced the notion of dual federalism, ruling that the Fourteenth Amendment did not change the balance of power between the national and state governments despite its clear language aimed at state action. Moreover, the Court ruled that the Fourteenth Amendment right to due process and equal treatment under the law only applied to individuals' rights as citizens of the United States, not to their state citizenship.[12] By extension, freedom of speech, freedom of the press, and the other liberties protected in the Bill of Rights only applied to laws passed by Congress, not to state laws. This distinction between state and national citizenship sounds odd today, partly because the Fourteenth Amendment has long been viewed as the basis for ensuring that states do not violate basic rights.

Ten years later, the Court overturned the 1875 Civil Rights Act, which guaranteed equal treatment in public accommodations. The Court argued that the Fourteenth Amendment did not give Congress the power to regulate private conduct, such as whether a white restaurant owner had to serve a black customer, but only the conduct of state governments.[13] This narrow view of the Fourteenth Amendment left the national government powerless to prevent southern states from implementing state and local laws that led to complete segregation of blacks and whites in the South (called Jim Crow laws) and the denial of many basic rights to blacks after northern troops left the South at the end of Reconstruction.

The other area in which the Supreme Court limited the reach of the national government concerned Congress's power to regulate the economy through its **commerce clause powers**. In several cases in the late nineteenth and early twentieth centuries, the Supreme Court endorsed a view of laissez-faire capitalism—French for "leave alone"—aimed at protecting business from regulation by the national government. To this end, the Court defined clear boundaries between *inter*state and *intra*state commerce, ruling that Congress could not regulate any economic activity that occurred *within* a state (intrastate).

On similar grounds the Court also struck down attempts by Congress to regulate child labor.[14] In some instances, the Court's laissez-faire perspective even led the justices to strike down state laws, as in one case that ruled unconstitutional a New York law limiting the working hours of bakers to no more than 60 hours a week or 10 hours a day.[15] Therefore, the limits that the Court placed on Congress during this antiregulation phase did not necessarily tip the balance to the state governments. Rather, big business was the clear winner over both national and state government.

commerce clause powers The powers of Congress to regulate the economy granted in Article I, Section 8, of the Constitution.

COOPERATIVE FEDERALISM

The Progressive Era policies of the early twentieth century and the New Deal policies of the 1930s ushered in a new period of American federalism. Now the national government became much more involved in activities that were formerly reserved for the states, such as education, transportation, civil rights, agriculture, social welfare, and management–labor relations. Starting in 1937 with the landmark ruling *National Labor Relations Board v. Jones and Lauglin Steel Corporation,* the Supreme Court gave Congress far more latitude in shaping economic and social policy for the nation.[16]

SHIFTING NATIONAL-STATE RELATIONS

The type of federalism that emerged in the Progressive Era and blossomed in the late 1930s is called **cooperative federalism**, or "marble cake" federalism, as opposed to the "layer cake" model of dual federalism.[17] As the image of a marble cake suggests, the boundaries of state and national responsibilities are not as well defined under cooperative federalism as under dual federalism. With the increasing industrialization and urbanization of the late 1930s and the 1940s, more complex problems arose that could not be solved at one level of government. Cooperative federalism adopted a more practical focus on intergovernmental relations and how to efficiently provide services. State and local governments maintained some influence as the implementers of national programs, but the national government played an enhanced role as the initiator of key policies.

cooperative federalism A form of federalism in which national and state governments work together to provide services efficiently. This form emerged in the late 1930s, representing a profound shift toward less concrete boundaries of responsibility in national–state relations.

THIS IS ONE RABBIT THAT NEVER FAILED ME!

SPENDING

OLD RELIABLE!

FRANKLIN DELANO ROOSEVELT'S NEW Deal shifted power to the federal government. Through major programs to address the Great Depression, the government expanded its reach, though it spent greatly to pay for the programs.

DESCRIBE THE MAJOR TRENDS AND DEBATES IN FEDERALISM TODAY

picket fence federalism A more refined and realistic form of cooperative federalism in which policy makers within a particular policy area work together across the levels of government.

fiscal federalism A form of federalism in which federal funds are allocated to the lower levels of government through transfer payments or grants.

Cooperative federalism accurately describes this important shift in national–state relations in the first half of the twentieth century, but it does not capture the complexity of modern federalism. The marble cake metaphor falls short in one important way: the lines of authority and patterns of cooperation are not as messy as implied by the swirly flow of chocolate through white cake. Instead, the 1960s metaphor of **picket fence federalism** is a better description of cooperative federalism in action. As the "How It Works" box shows, each picket of the fence represents a different policy area, and the horizontal boards that hold the pickets together represent the different levels of government. This is a much more orderly image than the marble cake, and it has important implications about how policy is made across levels of government.

The most important point is that activity within the cooperative federal system occurs *within* pickets of the fence—that is, within policy areas. Policy makers within a given policy area will have more in common with others in that area at different levels of government than with people at the same level of government who work on different issues. For example, someone working in a state's education department will have more contact with people working in local school districts and in the national Department of Education than with people who also work at the state level but who focus on, say, transportation policy. Overall, this version of federalism provides good opportunities for coordination and the sharing of expertise within policy areas.

FEDERALISM TODAY

Federalism today is a complex mix of all the elements our nation's political system has experienced in the past. Our current system is predominantly characterized by cooperative federalism, but it has retained strong elements of national supremacy, dual federalism, and states' rights. Therefore, rather than categorizing types of federalism into neat time periods, the following discussion characterizes the dominant tendency within each period, keeping in mind that competing versions of federalism have always been just below the surface (see Nuts and Bolts 3.2). In the past twenty years, the competing versions are so evident that this period could be considered the "era of balanced federalism."[18]

COOPERATIVE FEDERALISM LIVES ON: FISCAL FEDERALISM

The cooperative relationship between the national and state governments is rooted in the system of transfer payments, or grants from the national government to lower levels of government. This is called **fiscal federalism**. However, just because money flows from Washington does not mean that cooperation by the recipients follows. Depending on how the money is transferred, the national government can either help the local and state governments to achieve their own goals or use its centralized fiscal power to impose its will.

VERSIONS OF FEDERALISM

LAYER CAKE FEDERALISM

No interactions between the levels of government.

NATIONAL
STATE
LOCAL

MARBLE CAKE FEDERALISM

Interactions between the levels of government are common.

NATIONAL
STATE
LOCAL

PICKET FENCE FEDERALISM

Horizontal boards represent levels of government that connect the different policy areas (pickets).

NATIONAL
STATE
LOCAL

AGRICULTURE
EDUCATION
HIGHWAYS
HOUSING
ENVIRONMENT
MEDICAL CARE
TAX POLICY

COERCIVE FEDERALISM

National government uses regulations, mandates, and conditions to pressure states to fall into line with national policy goals.

POP QUIZ!

1 Which of the following best describes the system in the United States in the 1800s?

a layer cake federalism
b marble cake federalism
c picket fence federalism
d coercive federalism
e none of the above

2 Requiring all states to comply with the Motor Voter Act is an example of which version of federalism?

a layer cake federalism
b marble cake federalism
c picket fence federalism
d coercive federalism
e none of the above

THE EVOLUTION OF FEDERALISM

Type of Federalism	Period	Characteristics
Dual federalism (layer cake)	1789–1937	The national and state governments were viewed as very distinct with little overlap in their activities or the services they provided. Within this period, federalism could have been state-centered or nation-centered, but relations between levels of government were limited.
Cooperative federalism (marble cake)	1937–present	This indicates greater cooperation and collaboration between the levels of government.
Picket fence federalism	1961–present	This version of cooperative federalism emphasizes that policy makers within a given policy area have more in common with others in their area at different levels of government than with people at the same level of government who work on different issues.
Fiscal federalism	1937–present	This system of transfer payments or grants from the national government to lower-level governments involves varying degrees of national control over how the money is spent: categorical grants give the national government a great deal of control while block grants involve less national control.
New federalism	1969–present	New federalism attempts to shift power to the states by consolidating categorical grants into block grants and giving the states authority over programs such as welfare.
Coercive federalism	1970s–present	This involves federal preemptions of state and local authority and unfunded mandates on state and local governments to force the states to change their policies to match national goals or policies established by Congress.

categorical grants Federal aid to state or local governments that is provided for a specific purpose, such as a mass transit program within the transportation budget or a school lunch program within the education budget.

block grants Federal aid provided to a state government to be spent within a certain policy area, but the state can decide how to spend the money within that area.

GRANTS IN AID

Today most federal aid to the states comes in one of two forms. **Categorical grants** are for specific purposes—they have strings attached, and therefore we discuss them in the section on coercive federalism below. **Block grants** are financial aid to states for use within a specific policy area, but within that area the states have discretion on how to spend the money. For example, Community Development Block Grants were started in 1974 to help state and local governments revitalize their communities; such grants may support ongoing programs or help with large capital expenditures, such as building a waste treatment plant or a highway. Since the 1970s, grants to the states as a proportion of the size of the national economy (gross domestic product, or GDP) has been relatively constant, while the rate of state and local spending has inched up (see Figure 3.1).

NEW FEDERALISM

New Federalism, which shifted some important powers back to the states, was introduced in a limited form by Richard Nixon in the early 1970s and was revived

FIGURE » 3.1

FEDERAL AND STATE/LOCAL GOVERNMENT SPENDING (INCLUDING GRANTS), 1946–2011

Since the early 1950s, federal spending as a percentage of the overall size of the economy has been flat, while the share of state and local spending has nearly tripled. What does this say about the debates between nation-centered and state-centered federalism?

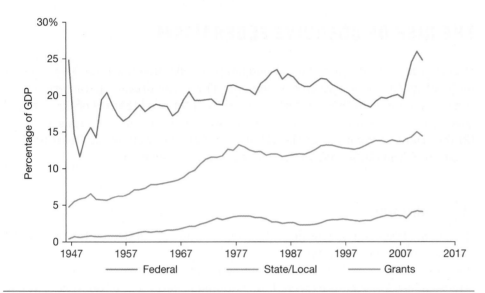

Source: 2012 Statistical Abstract of the United States, Table 4.31, and the Bureau of Economic Analysis, Table 3.2 and Table 3.3 (accessed 8/16/12).

during Ronald Reagan's presidency in the 1980s. In his inaugural address, Reagan emphasized, "All of us need to be reminded that the federal government did not create the states. The states created the federal government." This classic statement of the states' rights position is similar to the Antifederalists' position at the Constitutional Convention.

Reagan's goal of returning more power to the states involved consolidating seventy-seven categorical grants into nine general block grants that gave local politicians more control over how money was spent. This change reflected the belief that because state and local politicians were closer to the people, they would know better how to spend the money. However, the increase in state control came with a 25 percent cut in the amount of federal money granted to the states.

The next phase of New Federalism came when Republicans won control of Congress in 1994. Working with President Clinton, a moderate Democrat, Republicans passed several pieces of significant legislation that shifted power toward the states. For example, in 1996 the Personal Responsibility and Work Opportunity Act reformed welfare by creating a block grant to the states, Temporary Assistance to Needy Families (TANF), to replace the largest nationally administered welfare program. Another piece of legislation, the Unfunded Mandate

unfunded mandates Federal laws that require the states to do certain things but do not provide state governments with funding to implement these policies.

Reform Act of 1995, made it more difficult for Congress to impose **unfunded mandates** on the states.

The shift from categorical grants to block grants has not substantially affected the balance of power between the national and state governments. In fact, the amount of money going to the states through block grants has been surpassed by categorical grants since 1982. We will explore the reason for this below: Congress prefers categorical grants because they allow more control over how the money is spent.

THE RISE OF COERCIVE FEDERALISM

Despite the overall shift toward cooperative federalism, strong overtones of national government supremacy remain. Three important characteristics of American politics in the past forty years have reinforced the role of the national government: (1) reliance on the national government in times of crisis and war, (2) the "rights revolution" of the 1950s and 1960s, as well as the Great Society programs of the 1960s, and (3) the rise of coercive federalism.

CRISIS AND WAR

Even in the 1800s, during the period of dual federalism and strong state power, the national government's decisive actions were needed during the Civil War to hold the nation together. More recently, following the September 11, 2001, terrorist attacks, most Americans expected the national government to improve national security and retaliate for the attacks. Even Republicans, who normally oppose increasing the size of government, largely supported President Bush's proposal to create a cabinet-level Department of Homeland Security and the USA PATRIOT Act. Other major crises that occurred during the twentieth century (the Great Depression's New Deal policies, the massive mobilization for World War II, and the response to the banking meltdown of 2008–09) also dramatically shifted the balance of power toward Washington.

THE "RIGHTS REVOLUTION" AND GREAT SOCIETY PROGRAMS

During the mid-twentieth century, the "rights revolution" created by the Supreme Court, as well as Lyndon Johnson's Great Society programs, contributed to more national control over state policies. Landmark Court decisions thrust the national government into policy areas that had typically been reserved to the states. In the school desegregation and busing cases of the 1950s and 1960s, for example, the Court upheld the national goal of promoting racial equality and fighting discrimination over the earlier norm of local control of school districts.[19] The rights revolution also applied to police powers, another area of traditional state control, including protection against self-incrimination and preventing illegally obtained evidence from being used in a criminal trial.[20]

These Court actions were paralleled by a burst of legislation that tackled civil rights, education, the environment, medical care for the poor, and housing. These so-called Great Society policies gave the national government much more leverage over policy areas previously controlled by state and local governments.

For example, under the 1965 Voting Rights Act federal marshals were sent to the South to ensure that African Americans were allowed to vote. Another part of this act required local governments to submit changes in their electoral practices, including the boundaries of voting districts, to the Justice Department to make sure they did not have a discriminatory impact.

During this period, the national government also expanded its reach through an explosion in categorical grants, which the states sorely needed even though the monies came with strings attached. For example, the 1964 Civil Rights Act required nondiscrimination as a condition for receiving any kind of federal grants.

OTHER SHIFTS TOWARD NATIONAL SUPREMACY

Categorical grants aimed at a broad national goal have also reinforced national supremacy in recent decades—for example, requiring a state drinking age of twenty-one before granting federal highway funds. This policy direction from Washington is part of a trend known as **coercive federalism**. The practice involves the use of federal regulations, mandates, or conditions to force or entice the states to change their policies to match national goals or policies established by Congress. The Clean Air and Water Acts, the Americans with Disabilities Act (which promotes handicapped access to public buildings and commercial facilities), and the "Motor Voter Act" (which requires states to provide voter registration services at motor vehicle departments) are all laws that forced states to change their policies. The laws most objectionable to the states are unfunded mandates, which require states to do certain things but force them to come up with the money on their own.

Along with these mandates, federal preemption is another method of coercive federalism. Derived from the Constitution's national supremacy clause, **federal preemptions** involve the imposition of national priorities on the states. Many preemptions also include unfunded mandates, making the state and local governments pick up the tab for policies that the national government wants them to implement. The presidency of George W. Bush provided strong evidence of this shift toward national power. Beyond the apparent centralization of power associated with fighting terrorism, Bush pushed the national government into more areas that previously had been dominated by the states—including significant mandates and preemptions in education testing, sales tax collection, emergency management, infrastructure, and election administration.[21]

President Obama continued the shift toward national power with one of the most active domestic policy agendas since the New Deal of the 1930s. A $787 billion economic stimulus package of tax cuts and spending designed to address the financial collapse of 2008–09, a $938 billion health care reform law, cap-and-trade legislation, efforts to prop up and stimulate the battered housing industry, strengthened regulations of finance and banking, and an expanded jobs program all were on the agenda in Obama's first term. Health care reform was especially controversial with state governments, many of which saw the law as an unwarranted expansion of federal power (recall this chapter's opening discussion). This view was supported by the Supreme Court's ruling that states could not be coerced by the federal government into expanding their Medicaid coverage. This Court decision means that there are limits on the scope of coercive federalism. While the overall impact of national health care reform is to centralize more power at the national level, states remain very important in this period of "balanced federalism," as the next section demonstrates.

coercive federalism A form of federalism in which the federal government pressures the states to change their policies by using regulations, mandates, and conditions (often involving threats to withdraw federal funding).

federal preemptions Impositions of national priorities on the states through national legislation that is based on the Constitution's supremacy clause.

WITH THE NO CHILD LEFT BEHIND Act, the George W. Bush administration increased the national government's power over education. States are required to test students and meet goals determined by the federal government in order to receive federal funding.

THE STATES FIGHT BACK

Most Americans support the national policies that have been imposed on the states: racial equality, clean air and water, a fair legal process, safer highways, and equal access to the voting booth. At the same time, there has always been strong support for state and local governments. In most national surveys, Americans typically say that they trust state and local government more than the national government. Indeed, the shift in public opinion toward favoring national power after the terrorist attacks of September 11 was temporary, and it appears that state and local governments quickly reasserted their position as the more trusted level of government.

States appear to be reversing their traditional role of resisting change and protecting the status quo. Lately, for example, they have taken the lead on environmental policy. Many policies to address climate change—including the development of renewable energy sources, carbon emissions limits, and carbon cap-and-trade programs—have been advocated at the state level.[22] States have also taken a lead role on health care policy, immigration, gay marriage, and stem cell research. However, this willingness to fight back in recent years has not always been for progressive causes. Indeed, with the Republican gains in the 2010 midterm elections and the influence of the Tea Party movement, many states have been attempting to curb national power and protect their more conservative policies in a broad range of areas, including land use, gun control, immigration, and health care. For example, Alabama, Tennessee, and Washington are considering legislation that would assert local police powers over federal authority, even on federal lands. "There's a tsunami of interest in states' rights and resistance to an overbearing federal government; that's what all these measures indicate," said Gary Marbut, a states' rights activist from Montana.[23]

To complicate the ideological picture even more, one of the recent moves by states to resist national power cuts in the liberal direction: Vermont, Rhode Island, and Wisconsin have introduced legislation to require their governors to recall or take control of National Guard troops, arguing that the use of the National Guard by the federal government is unconstitutional (because Article I of the Constitution says that the "militia"—today's National Guard—should only be used for defensive purposes). Many of the state laws mentioned in this discussion will not stand up in federal court, but they are clearly a reflection of state frustration with assertions of federal power.

States have one important advantage over the national government when it comes to experimenting with new policies: their numbers. The fact that there are 50 states potentially trying a mix of different policies is another argument cited by advocates of state-centered federalism. In this view, such a mix of policies produces **competitive federalism**—competition among states to provide the best policies to attract businesses, create jobs, and maintain a healthy social fabric.[24]

But competitive federalism can also create a "race to the bottom" as states compete in a negative way. For example, when states compete for businesses and jobs, they may do so by eliminating more environmental or occupational regulations than would be desirable. Likewise, a priority to keep taxes low may lead to cuts in benefits to those who can least afford it, such as welfare or Medicaid recipients.[25] Thus while competitive federalism provides citizens with a broad range of choices about the type of government they prefer, it also can be a source of political conflict over the national direction of policy.

competitive federalism A form of federalism in which states compete to attract businesses and jobs through the policies they adopt.

FIGHTING FOR STATES' RIGHTS: THE ROLE OF THE MODERN SUPREME COURT

Just as the Supreme Court played a central role in defining the boundaries of dual federalism in the nineteenth and early twentieth centuries and in introducing a more nation-centered cooperative federalism in the late 1930s, today's Court is once again reshaping federalism. But this time the move is decidedly in the direction of state power.

THE TENTH AMENDMENT

The Tenth Amendment ensures that all powers not delegated to the national government are reserved to the states or to the people. Interestingly, the amendment has had little significance except during the early 1930s and in the recent era.

Thirty-five years ago, a leading text on the Constitution said that the Tenth Amendment "does not alter the distribution of power between the national and state governments. It adds nothing to the Constitution."[26] To understand why, consider the following example. State and local governments have always controlled their own public schools. Thus public education is a power reserved to the states under the Tenth Amendment. However, a state law concerning public education is void if it conflicts with the Constitution or with a national law based on an enumerated power. For example, a state could not compel an 18-year-old to attend school if the student had been drafted to serve in the army. Under the Tenth Amendment, the constitutionally enumerated national power to "raise and support armies" would trump the reserved state power to support public education. This view supporting the primacy of national government power was validated as recently as 1985 when the Supreme Court ruled that Congress had the power to impose a national minimum wage law on state governments, even if this was an area of traditional state power.[27]

But times change. With the appointment of three conservative justices in the 1980s who favored a stronger role for the states, the Court started to limit

Congress's reach. One technique has been to require that Congress provide an unambiguous statement of its intent to overrule state authority when issuing legislation that does so. Moreover, a potentially far-reaching decision in 2011 said that individuals, as well as states, have the right to challenge the constitutionality of a federal law under the Tenth Amendment. The case involved a woman who was trying to hurt her husband's lover with dangerous chemicals and was prosecuted under a federal law aimed at attempting to limit the spread of chemical weapons.[28] This ruling, which supported the woman's right to sue the federal government, opens a new path of potential challenges to congressional limitations on state power.

THE FOURTEENTH AMENDMENT

The Fourteenth Amendment was intended to give the national government control over the potentially discriminatory laws of southern states after the Civil War. Section 1 guarantees that no state shall make or enforce any law depriving any person of "life, liberty, or property, without due process of law," or denying any person the "equal protection of the laws." Section 5 empowers Congress "to enforce" those guarantees by "appropriate legislation."

The Supreme Court narrowly interpreted the Fourteenth Amendment in the late nineteenth century, severely limiting Congress's ability to affect state policy. However, throughout most of the twentieth century the Court interpreted Section 5 to give Congress broad discretion to pass legislation to remedy bad state laws. For example, discriminatory application of literacy tests prevented millions of African Americans from voting in the South before Congress passed the Voting Rights Act in 1965. As part of the federalism revolution of the 1990s, the Court started to chip away at Congress's Fourteenth Amendment powers.

An important case in 1997 established a new standard to justify **remedial legislation**—national legislation that fixes discriminatory state law—under Section 5, saying, "There must be a congruence and proportionality between the injury to be prevented or remedied and the means adopted to that end."[29] In one application of the new standard, the Court struck down the portion of the Americans with Disabilities Act (ADA) that applied to the states. Passed in 1990, the ADA required employers, including state agencies, to make "reasonable accommodations" for a "qualified individual with a disability." However, the majority opinion said that states could refuse to hire people in wheelchairs, or deaf or blind people, as "States are not required . . . to make special accommodations for the disabled."[30] Three years later the Court made a narrow exception to this ruling, saying that states did need to provide access for the disabled to courthouses.[31]

In another exception to the federalism revolution, the Court upheld Congress's power to apply the 1993 Family Leave Act to state employees as "appropriate legislation" under Section 5 of the Fourteenth Amendment.[32] The key difference between this case and the disability case is that in passing the Family Leave Act, Congress recognized the gender inequality of family care: when a family member gets sick, the mother or wife typically bears the burden. Constitutional protections for discrimination based on disability are much weaker than those for discrimination based on gender. (For a summary of recent important Court decisions on federalism, see Table 3.2.)

remedial legislation National laws that address discriminatory state laws. Authority for such legislation comes from Section 5 of the Fourteenth Amendment.

THE AMERICANS WITH DISABILITIES Act of 1990 requires that public accommodations and commercial facilities be handicapped accessible, and recent Supreme Court rulings have held that the law applies to state and local government buildings. Disabled activists are shown in front of the White House lobbying for stronger legislation.

TABLE » 3.2

RECENT IMPORTANT SUPREME COURT DECISIONS ON FEDERALISM

CASE	HOLDING AND SIGNIFICANCE
Gregory v. Ashcroft (1991)	The Missouri constitution's requirement that state judges retire by age 70 did not violate the Age Discrimination in Employment Act.
United States v. Lopez (1995)	Carrying a gun in a school did not fall within "interstate commerce," thus Congress could not prohibit the possession of guns on school property.
Seminole Tribe v. Florida (1996)	The Court used the Eleventh Amendment to strengthen states' sovereign immunity, ruling that Congress could not compel a state to negotiate with Indian tribes about gaming and casinos.
Printz v. United States (1997)	The Court struck down part of the Brady Handgun Violence Prevention Act, saying that Congress cannot require local law enforcement officers to perform background checks on prospective handgun purchasers.
City of Boerne v. Flores (1997)	The Court struck down the Religious Freedom Restoration Act as an overly broad attempt to curtail the state-sponsored harassment of religion, saying that national legislation aimed at remedying states' discrimination must be "congruent and proportional" to the harm.
Alden v. Maine (1999)	State employees could not sue the state of Maine for violating the overtime pay provisions of the federal Fair Labor Standards Act.
United States v. Morrison (2000)	The Court struck down part of the Violence against Women Act, saying that Congress did not have the power under the commerce clause to provide a national remedy for gender-based crimes.
Kimel et al. v. Florida Board of Regents (2000)	The Age Discrimination in Employment Act of 1967 could not be applied to state employees because it was not considered "appropriate legislation" under Section 5 of the Fourteenth Amendment.
Alabama v. Garrett (2001)	The Court struck down the portion of the Americans with Disabilities Act that applied to the states, saying that state governments are not required to make special accommodations for the disabled.
Nevada Department of Human Resources v. Hibbs (2003)	The Court upheld Congress's power to apply the 1993 Family Leave Act to state employees as "appropriate legislation" under Section 5 of the Fourteenth Amendment.
United States v. Bond (2011)	The Court upheld individuals' right to challenge the constitutionality of a federal law under the Tenth Amendment.
National Federation of Independent Business v. Sebelius (2012)	The Court upheld most provisions of the Affordable Care Act, but struck down the expansion of Medicaid as an unconstitutional use of coercive federalism (states could voluntarily take the additional funding to cover the expansion, but they would not lose existing funds if they opted out).

THE COMMERCE CLAUSE

Another category of cases leading to more state power concerns the commerce clause of the Constitution. A significant recent Court case that limited Congress's commerce powers involved the Gun-Free School Zones Act of 1990, which made it a federal offense to have a gun within 1,000 feet of a school. Congress assumed that it had the power to pass this legislation, given the Court's previously expansive interpretation of the commerce clause, even though it concerned a traditional area of state power. Although it was a stretch to claim that carrying a gun in or around a school was related to interstate commerce,

Congress could have demonstrated the point by showing that (1) most guns are made in one state and sold in another (thus commercially crossing state lines), (2) crime affects the economy and commerce, and (3) the quality of education, which is also crucial to the economy, is harmed if students and teachers are worrying about guns in their schools. However, members of Congress did not present this evidence because they did not think it was necessary.

Alfonso Lopez, a high school senior, was arrested for carrying a concealed handgun with five bullets in it. Lopez moved to dismiss the charges, arguing that the law was unconstitutional because carrying a gun in a school could not be regulated as "interstate commerce." The Court agreed in *United States v. Lopez*.[33] If Congress wanted to encroach on the states' turf in the future, the Court indicated, Congress would have to demonstrate that the law in question was a legitimate exercise of the commerce clause powers.

As a result, the next time Congress passed legislation that affected law enforcement at the state level, it documented the impact on interstate commerce. The Violence Against Women Act was passed in 1994 after weeks of testimony and evidence showing the links between violence against women and commerce. Nevertheless, the Supreme Court subsequently ruled that Congress did not have the power under the commerce clause to make a national law that gave victims of gender-motivated violence the right to sue their attackers in federal court. (However, the Court only struck down that part of the law; the program funding remained unaffected.)[34]

The significance of such rulings is enormous. Not only has the Court set new limits on Congress's ability to address national problems (the "congruence and proportionality" test), but it has also clearly stated that the Court alone will determine which rights warrant protection by Congress. However, the Court does not consistently rule against Congress; it often rules against the states because of broader constitutional principles or general public consensus behind a specific issue. For example, the Court struck down Arkansas's three-term limit for members of Congress, ruling that states could not impose any additional limits on the qualifications for being a member of Congress beyond those in the Constitution.[35] The Court has also struck down state laws limiting gay rights as a violation of the equal protection clause of the Fourteenth Amendment[36] and has upheld Congress's power to regulate marijuana over states that had attempted to allow its medical use,[37] and while the Court rejected the commerce clause as the constitutional justification for national health care reform, it did uphold the ACA based on Congress's taxing power.[38]

Based on these and other cases, some would argue that the shift in power toward the states has been relatively marginal. Furthermore, the national government still has the upper hand in the balance of power and can readily blunt the impact of a Court decision: First, Congress can pass new laws to clarify its legislative intent and can overturn any cases that involve statutory interpretation. Second, Congress can use its financial power to impose its will on the states. So, for example, Congress could pass a law stating that before a state could receive money from the federal government related to the relevant law, it would have to agree to abide by the Americans with Disabilities Act or the Age Discrimination in Employment Act. Thus while the Supreme Court has

THE *LOPEZ* DECISION STRUCK DOWN the 1990 Gun-Free School Zones Act, ruling that Congress did not have the power to forbid people to carry guns near schools. After the shooting of 12 students and one teacher at Columbine High School in Jefferson County, Colorado, on April 20, 1999, there were renewed calls nationwide for strengthening gun control laws.

limited Congress's power under the commerce clause, Congress still may induce states to act according to its policy goals. However, as noted above, there are new limits on budgetary coercion. In the health care reform case, the Court ruled that the threat to withhold Medicaid funds was a "gun to the head" of states,[39] meaning states did not have a real choice. This was the first time the Court limited Congress's coercive budgetary power over the states, and the boundaries of the new limits will have to be decided in future cases.

ASSESSING FEDERALISM TODAY

From protecting individual liberty to allowing states to be "laboratories of democracy" in policy innovation, there is much to recommend federalism as a cornerstone of our political system. However, there are disadvantages as well, such as inefficiency in the policy process and inequality in policy outcomes. How does federalism in the United States fare from a twenty-first-century perspective?

IDEOLOGICAL COMPLEXITIES

Historically, issues concerning federalism have seemed to break down along traditional liberal and conservative lines. Liberals generally favor strong national power to fight discrimination, and they push for progressive national policies on issues such as protecting the environment, providing national health care, and supporting the poor. Conservatives, in contrast, tend to favor limited intrusion from the national government and allowing the states to decide their own mix of social welfare and regulatory policies.

However, in recent years the tables have turned, and in many cases liberals today are arguing for states' rights while conservatives are advocating the virtues of uniform national laws. On a broad range of new issues, such as medical uses of marijuana, gay marriage, cloning, and assisted suicide, state governments are passing socially liberal legislation.[40] And the Court's earlier, state-centered rulings give it little precedent for striking down these laws. The Court's current conservative majority will either have to continue applying its state-centered federalism and uphold these liberal state laws, or strike them down on ideological grounds, which would undermine the Court's credibility.

ADVANTAGES OF A STRONG ROLE FOR THE STATES

The advantages of a strong role for the states can be summarized in four main points: states can be laboratories of democracy, state and local government is closer to the people, states provide more access to the political system, and states provide an important check on national power.

The first point refers to the role that states play as the source of policy diversity and innovation. If many states are trying to solve problems creatively, they can complement the efforts of the national government. Likewise, successful policies first adopted at the state level often percolate up to the national level. Welfare reform, health care, and environmental policy are key areas in which states have innovated.

IN THE DEBATE OVER HEALTH CARE reform and the Affordable Care Act, supporters of nationalized health care argued that the federal government could do a better job than the patchwork of state policies to ensure that all Americans received sufficient care.

FIGURE » 3.2

TYPES OF SPENDING PER CAPITA BY STATE

Spending varies dramatically by state. What are some of the advantages and disadvantages of living in a low-spending state or in a high-spending state? Which type of state would you rather live in?

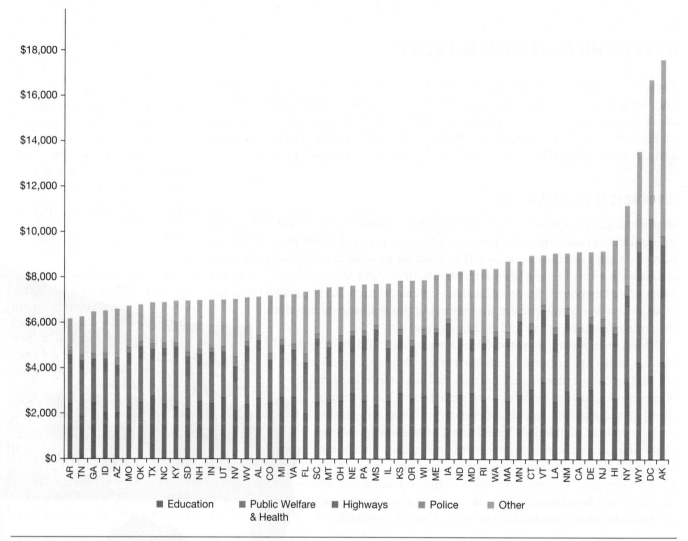

Legend: ■ Education ■ Public Welfare & Health ■ Highways ■ Police ■ Other

Source: State and Local Government Finance Data Query System, www.taxpolicycenter.org/slf-dqs/pages.cfm (accessed 8/16/12).

Second, government that is closer to the people encourages participation in the political process. Local politicians know better what their constituents want than farther-removed national politicians do. On the one hand, if voters want higher taxes to pay for more public benefits, such as public parks and better schools, they can enact these changes at the state and local levels. On the other hand, if they prefer lower taxes and fewer services, local politicians can be responsive to those desires. Also, local government provides a broad range of opportunities for direct involvement in politics, from working on local political campaigns to attending school board or city council meetings. When citizens are able to directly affect policies, they are more likely to get involved in the political process.

MEDICAL MARIJUANA AND ASSISTED SUICIDE

The debate over devolving power from the national government to the states has grown increasingly complicated in the past several years. The partisan nature of the debate has shifted, the courts have played a larger but inconsistent role, and issues of states' rights increasingly cut across normal ideological and partisan divisions. In the 1990s, Republicans continued to favor greater state control, and Democratic president Bill Clinton also supported devolution to the states in several areas, including welfare policy. Since the mid-1990s, the Supreme Court has played a central role in the shift of power to the states, but two recent cases involving medical marijuana (*Gonzales v. Raich*, 2005) and assisted suicide (*Gonzales v. Oregon*, 2006) show how the typical debate between national and state power can shift when a moral dimension is introduced.

In both cases, state voters supported liberal policies. In 1996, California voters passed the Compassionate Use Act, by a margin of 56 to 44 percent. This law allowed seriously ill Californians, typically AIDS and cancer patients, to use marijuana as part of their medical treatment with the permission of a doctor. Oregon voters approved the Death with Dignity Act in 1994 by a margin of 51 to 49 percent. This law allows physicians to prescribe a lethal drug dosage for terminally ill patients who wish to end their lives. A court order delayed implementation of the law until 1997, the same year that the matter was put before the voters again, but they rejected repealing the law by a margin of 60 to 40 percent. Both of these states' laws were challenged in federal court in classic confrontations between the states' rights and national power perspectives. Surprisingly, the Supreme Court ruled against medical marijuana and in favor of assisted suicide (this oversimplifies the legal arguments, but these were the bottom-line outcomes).

Should Congress be able to tell a state that it cannot allow the use of medical marijuana? Can the attorney general interpret a congressional law as a prohibition of assisted suicide? Unlike many of the cases discussed in this chapter, the states' rights position in these cases represented the liberal perspective, rather than the conservative position typically associated with state-centered federalism. Social liberals tended to support both the medical marijuana law and the assisted suicide law, while social conservatives tended to oppose them both. However, if you examine these cases in terms of the question of federal versus state power, a central ideological divide in this nation since the Constitutional Convention, the traditional liberal and conservative perspectives both look more complex. That is, a national-power liberal and a social conservative would agree that the national government should regulate medical marijuana and assisted suicide. Likewise, states' rights conservatives and social liberals would share the view that the states should decide these issues on their own.

Federal drug enforcement agents raid a medical marijuana club.

Somewhat surprisingly, there was almost no consistency among the eight justices who voted on both cases (Chief Justice William Rehnquist was replaced by John Roberts between the two cases). Only Justice Sandra Day O'Connor supported the states' rights position in both cases while Justice Antonin Scalia voted as a moral conservative against both laws—and counter to his previously articulated views on national power and federalism. The other six justices mixed their views, voting to uphold one of the laws and to strike down the other. The resulting rulings were inconsistent on the question of federalism as well. In the medical marijuana case, the Court upheld Congress's power to regulate the medical use of marijuana under the Controlled Substances Act. But in the assisted suicide case, the Court said that under that same congressional law, the U.S. attorney general did not have the power to limit the drugs that doctors in Oregon could prescribe for use in an assisted suicide.

Critical Thinking Questions

1. As a matter of policy, should doctors be able to prescribe marijuana to alleviate pain? Should they be able to prescribe lethal drugs to terminally ill patients?

2. Do you tend to support a state-centered or nation-centered perspective on federalism? Now revisit your answers to the first two questions. Are your positions more consistent with your views on federalism or with your policy concerns?

FIGURE » 3.3A

POVERTY RATES BY STATE, 2010

There are huge differences between the wealthiest states and the poorest states in terms of their income levels and poverty rates. What do these disparities imply about the role of the national government in terms of supporting a "social safety net"? How do recent developments in federalism support or undermine the notion of a social safety net?

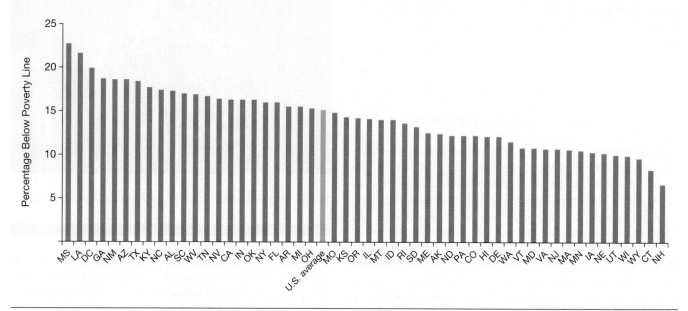

Source: Current Population Survey, 2011 Annual Social and Economic Supplement, www.census.gov/hhes/www/cpstables/032011/pov/new46_100125_01 .htm (accessed 8/17/12).

Third, our federalist system provides more potential paths to address problems. For example, the court system allows citizens to pursue complaints under either state or federal law. Likewise, cooperative federalism can draw on the strengths of different levels of government to solve problems.

Finally, federalism provides a check on national tyranny. Competitive federalism ensures that Americans have a broad range of social policies, levels of taxation and regulation, and public services to choose from (see Figure 3.2). When people "vote with their feet" by deciding whether to move and where to live, they encourage healthy competition among states that would be impossible under a unitary government.

DISADVANTAGES OF TOO MUCH STATE POWER

A balanced assessment must acknowledge that there are problems with a federalist system that gives too much power to the states. The disadvantages include unequal distribution of resources across the states, unequal protection for civil rights, and competitive federalism that produces a "race to the bottom."

One problem of giving too much responsibility to the states is the huge variation in the distribution of resources. Without federal funding, poor states simply cannot provide an adequate level of benefits because they have the greatest needs (see Figure 3.3a) but the lowest incomes (see Figure 3.3b)—a situation that leads to significant disparities in important areas such as public education. The resource problem becomes more acute in dealing with national-level problems

FIGURE » 3.3B

PER CAPITA INCOME BY STATE, 2010

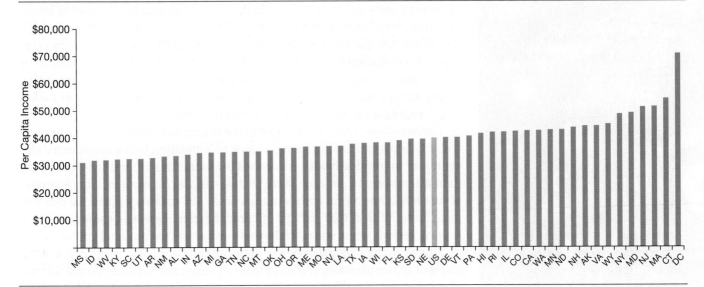

Source: U.S. Department of Commerce, Bureau of Economic Analysis, State Annual Personal Income, August 17, 2012, www.bea.gov/iTable/iTable.cfm?reg10=99/step=1 (accessed 8/17/12).

that are intractable at the local or state level. For example, pollution spills across state lines, and the deteriorating public infrastructure, like the highway system, crosses state boundaries. Solving such problems individually would vastly outstrip the resources of state and local governments.[41]

The second problem, unequal civil rights protection, is evident in various federalism cases that have passed before the Supreme Court. These clearly show that states are not uniformly willing to protect the civil liberties and civil rights of their citizens. Without national laws, there will continue to be large differences in the levels of protection against discrimination based on age, disability, and sexual orientation.

Finally, competitive federalism can create a "race to the bottom" as states attempt to lure businesses by keeping taxes and social spending low. This can place an unfair burden on states that take a more generous position toward the poor.

Thus, overall, there is no clear "winner" in determining the appropriate balance of national and state power in our nation today. The advantages and disadvantages of our federal system insure that federalism will always remain a central source of conflict in the policy-making process as the various levels of government fight it out.

CONCLUSION

Alexis de Tocqueville, a French observer of American politics in the early nineteenth century, noted the tendency of democratic governments to centralize. This is especially true during wartime or times of crisis, as in the aftermath of the September 11 attacks, but it is also true during normal political times.

ONE OF THE STRENGTHS OF FEDERALISM is that it allows regional diversity to flourish. Green Bay Packers fans proudly wear their cheesehead hats at Lambeau Field, showing that what passes for normal behavior in one part of the country would be viewed differently in other areas.

Powerful interest groups have an incentive to claim national importance for their causes to increase their likelihood of success. As the political scientist Michael Greve explains, "Interest groups and parties thrive on redistribution, which is best accomplished at a highly centralized level of government—because it spreads the costs over a larger number of losers and eliminates exit options for them."[42] That is, when interest groups get a national law passed that benefits their group (for example, dairy price support legislation for dairy farmers, which increases the price of milk by 26 percent for the average consumer), the entire country pays the costs. These groups win by expanding the conflict to the entire nation rather than keeping it contained within a specific state.

The health care reform example at the beginning of the chapter also illustrates this point. Passing a single piece of legislation was a much more efficient way to provide health insurance for more than 30 million Americans than attempting to get each state to pass similar legislation. This scenario occurs again and again across many issues and creates a powerful centralizing force. Within that pattern of centralization, however, there have been lengthy periods when states' rights held sway over the national government.

This evolving balance of power between the national government and the states obscures a broader reality of federalism: we are citizens of several levels of government simultaneously. One leading scholar of American federalism says that the basic question of federalism involves choices about how many communities we will be.[43] If you asked most people in our nation about their primary geopolitical community, they would probably not say "I am a Montanan" or "I am an Arizonan"; most would likely say "I am an American." Yet we have strong attachments to our local communities and state identities. Most Texans would not be caught dead wearing a styrofoam cheesehead, but thousands of football fans in Green Bay, Wisconsin, regularly don the funny-looking things to watch their beloved Packers. We are members of multiple communities, a fact that has had an indelible impact on our political system. The beauty of our federal system is that despite its complex and evolving nature, it makes a lot of sense.

WHAT IS FEDERALISM AND WHY DOES IT MATTER?

▶ Define federalism and explain its significance. **Pages 57–60**

SUMMARY

A federal system simultaneously allocates power to both the state and federal governments, while a confederal system only gives power to the states, and a unitary government only gives power to the federal government.

KEY TERMS

federalism (p. 57)

sovereign power (p. 57)

police powers (p. 58)

concurrent powers (p. 58)

unitary government (p. 58)

confederal government (p. 58)

intergovernmental organizations (p. 59)

PRACTICE QUIZ QUESTIONS

1. What system of government did the Articles of Confederation establish?
   a) unitary
   b) federal
   c) confederal
   d) monarchy
   e) dictatorship

2. Which is an example of a concurrent power?
   a) print money
   b) build roads
   c) conduct elections
   d) declare war
   e) establish post offices

BALANCING NATIONAL AND STATE POWER IN THE CONSTITUTION

▶ Explain what the Constitution says about federalism. **Pages 60–62**

SUMMARY

The framers of the Constitution wanted a federal government that was stronger than under the Articles of Confederation, but they also wanted to preserve the autonomy of the states. While the state governments have considerable power in our system, the Founders ultimately favored the federal government in the Constitution, so that the federal government's powers superseded those of the states in the event of a conflict.

KEY TERMS

full faith and credit clause (p. 61)

privileges and immunities clause (p. 61)

PRACTICE QUIZ QUESTIONS

3. States' rights are protected in the reserve clause, which is found in _____.
   a) the Ninth Amendment
   b) the Tenth Amendment
   c) Article I of the Constitution
   d) Article III of the Constitution
   e) the First Amendment

4. Contemporary conflict over same-sex marriage falls under which constitutional provision?
   a) privileges and immunities clause
   b) exclusionary clause
   c) national supremacy clause
   d) full faith and credit clause
   e) establishment clause

THE EVOLVING CONCEPT OF FEDERALISM

▶ Trace the major shifts in state and federal government power over time. **Pages 63–68**

SUMMARY

The relationship between the state and federal governments has changed dramatically over time. Whereas the federal and state governments traditionally operated with little interaction under the era of dual federalism, the trend over the past 80 years has been one of increasing federal interaction with state governments to address particular policy areas.

KEY TERMS

states' rights (p. 64)

dual federalism (p. 65)

commerce clause powers (p. 67)

cooperative federalism (p. 67)

picket fence federalism (p. 68)

PRACTICE QUIZ QUESTIONS

5. Which analogy best describes the federalism arrangement today?
   a) layer cake federalism
   b) marble cake federalism
   c) picket fence federalism
   d) gumbo federalism
   e) dual federalism

6. Which case bolstered the federal government's power over the states?
   a) *United States v. Lopez*
   b) *McCulloch v. Maryland*
   c) *Dred Scott v. Sanford*
   d) *Mapp v. Ohio*
   e) *U.S. v. Lopez*

7. When did the federal government begin cooperating with the states on policy goals?
   a) 1890s
   b) 1930s
   c) 1950s
   d) 1970s
   e) 1990s

---

⑤ PRACTICE ONLINE

"Critical Thinking" exercise: *Process Matters—Federal and State Relationships*

FEDERALISM TODAY

▶ Describe the major trends and debates in federalism today. **Pages 68–83**

SUMMARY

Today's federal structure offers a complex mix of all previous components of federalism: some elements of national supremacy combine with states' rights for a varied federal landscape. While the federal and state governments still exercise cooperative federalism to achieve joint policy goals, the federal government has utilized coercive federalism to impose federal priorities on the states without offering compensation. However, in several recent cases the Supreme Court has ruled in favor of the states, limiting federal power.

KEY TERMS

fiscal federalism (p. 68)

categorical grants (p. 70)

block grants (p. 70)

unfunded mandates (p. 72)

coercive federalism (p. 73)

federal preemptions (p. 73)

competitive federalism (p. 75)

remedial legislation (p. 76)

CRITICAL THINKING AND DISCUSSION

On which issues is the national government particularly well suited to serve the people's interests? Which issues are the states better suited to handle? Explain the reasons for your choices.

PRACTICE QUIZ QUESTIONS

8. This form of revenue sharing is given to the states by the federal government with explicit conditions on how it is to be allocated.
   a) block grant
   b) categorical grant
   c) general revenue sharing

d) federal mandate

e) tax refund

9. Ronald Reagan's efforts to increase states' rights led to an increase in _____.

a) block grants

b) categorical grants

c) general revenue sharing

d) federal mandates

e) state taxes

10. The imposition of national priorities on the states through congressional legislation and the imposition of the national supremacy clause is called

_____.

a) cooperative federalism

b) dual federalism

c) competitive federalism

d) federal preemption

e) remedial legislation

11. A state would usually challenge the constitutionality of a federal law under which amendment(s)?

a) Eighth Amendment

b) Tenth and Eleventh Amendments

c) Thirteenth Amendment

d) Fourteenth Amendment

e) First Amendment

12. The Eleventh Amendment's protections of state sovereign immunity guarantee that _____.

a) residents of one state cannot sue the government of another state

b) state governments cannot commit a legal wrong

c) ambassadors from foreign countries cannot be detained by state governments

d) state governments can sue the federal government

e) state governments cannot be sued by anybody

13. The Court has recently overturned a number of congressional laws rooted in the _____.

a) national supremacy clause

b) reserve clause

c) establishment clause

d) commerce clause

e) free exercise clause

ⓢ PRACTICE ONLINE

"Big Think" video exercise: *Improving Government Controls*

SUGGESTED READING

Beer, Samuel. *To Make a Nation: The Rediscovery of American Federalism.* Cambridge, MA: Harvard University Press, 1993.

Conlan, Timothy. *From New Federalism to Devolution: Twenty-Five Years of Intergovernmental Reform.* Washington, DC: Brookings Institution, 1998.

Derthick, Martha. *Keeping the Compound Republic: Essays on American Federalism.* Washington, DC: Brookings Institution, 2001.

Elkins, Stanley, and Eric McKitrick. *The Age of Federalism: The Early American Republic, 1788–1800.* New York: Oxford University Press, 1993.

Grodzins, Martin. *The American System: A New View of Government in the United States.* Chicago: Rand McNally, 1966.

LaCroix, Alison L. *The Ideological Origins of American Federalism.* Cambridge, MA: Harvard University Press, 2010.

Manna, Paul. *School's In: Federalism and the National Education Agenda.* Washington, DC: Georgetown University Press, 2006.

McDonald, Forrest. *States' Rights and the Union: Imperium in Imperia, 1776–1876.* Lawrence: University Press of Kansas, 2000.

Nagel, Robert F. *The Implosion of American Federalism.* New York: Oxford University Press, 2001.

Peterson, Paul E. *The Price of Federalism.* Washington, DC: Brookings Institution, 1995.

Posner, Paul L. *The Politics of Unfunded Mandates: Whither Federalism?* Washington, DC: Georgetown University Press, 1998.

Scheberle, Denise. *Federalism and Environmental Policy: Trust and the Politics of Implementation,* 2nd ed. Washington, DC: Georgetown University Press, 2004.

4

Civil Liberties

SHOULD FREE SPEECH be protected even when the ideas are offensive? The Supreme Court ruled that the Westboro Baptist Church had a right to protest at military funerals, even though many Americans found their arguments and approach deeply offensive.

SINCE 2005, MEMBERS OF THE WESTBORO BAPTIST CHURCH (WBC) have protested at more than 400 funerals of members of the armed services who were killed in Iraq and Afghanistan. However, these were not typical antiwar protests. Instead, the protesters claimed that the troops' deaths were God's punishment for "the homosexual lifestyle of soul-damning, nation-destroying filth."[1]

The church has drawn strong reactions and counterprotests for its members' confrontational approach at military funerals, including the protesters' use of signs that say "God Hates Fags," "Thank God for Dead Soldiers," "God Killed Your Sons," and "God Hates America." Critics, including many veterans groups and states' attorneys general, argue that the protests should not be considered protected speech under the First Amendment. While recognizing that the First Amendment protects offensive speech, these critics argue that it does not allow "personal attacks targeted at private individuals during a time of mourning."[2] A group of veterans called the Patriot Guard Riders have gathered at the funerals to serve as a buffer for the grieving families by riding motorcycles along the funeral routes and singing patriotic songs or revving their engines to drown out the hateful speech.

State legislatures and Congress have also attempted to limit the disruption caused by the WBC protests. Forty-three states have passed laws limiting protests at military funerals to a certain distance from the actual services. In 2006 Congress passed the Respect for Fallen American Heroes Act, which prohibits protests within 300 feet of a federal cemetery for one hour before or after a funeral.

CONFLICT & COMPROMISE

in American Politics

When the WBC protested at the funeral of Marine Lance Corporal Matthew Snyder, his father, Albert Synder, sued the church for defamation, intentional infliction of emotional distress, and invasion of privacy. The district federal court ruled in Snyder's favor, awarding $5 million in damages. But the appeals court reversed the ruling, setting up an appeal to the Supreme Court. The case drew extensive attention with 48 states, 42 U.S. senators, and many veterans groups—including the American Legion and Veterans of Foreign Wars—filing briefs on behalf of Snyder, while more than 20 national news organizations filed briefs arguing that the WBC's protests should be protected by the First Amendment. In its 2011 decision, the Supreme Court ruled 8–1 that the WBC's protests were protected speech: "Speech is powerful. It can stir people to action, move them to tears of both joy and sorrow, and—as it did here—inflict great pain. On the facts before us, we cannot react to that pain by punishing the speaker. As a nation we have chosen a different course—to protect even hurtful speech on public issues to ensure that we do not stifle public debate."[3] The justices said that the speech was not defamation because most of the WBC's signs were related to political issues, such as American involvement in wars and the service of homosexuals in the military. They also argued that the Snyder family's privacy rights were not violated because the protesters were 1,000 feet from the funeral. Justice Samuel Alito, the only dissenter, disagreed: "Our profound national commitment to free and open debate is not a license for the vicious verbal assault that occurred in this case. . . . In order to have a society in which public issues can be openly and vigorously debated, it is not necessary to allow the brutalization of innocent victims."[4]

The Court's strong reaffirmation of the First Amendment's protection of hurtful and unpopular speech is an excellent illustration of our central theme that politics is conflictual. It is difficult to imagine speech that is more conflictual than the WBC's protests. Indeed, the entire purpose of the protesters' speech is to generate conflict. But the case also shows that compromise is possible. The "time, manner, and place" restrictions that limit the protests to areas away from the funeral maintain the privacy rights of the grieving families, at least to some extent, while protecting the First Amendment rights of the protesters. While the plaintiffs and their supporters were not happy with this compromise, it represents the outcome of the legislative and judicial process.

The case also illustrates our other two themes. The evolution of the meaning of civil liberties, as largely defined by the courts, is a great example that the political process matters. Despite the WBC members' overwhelmingly unpopular views, they may continue picketing because the legal process has endorsed their interpretation of the Constitution. Civil liberties also are an excellent example that politics is everywhere. Freedom of speech, religion, and assembly; privacy rights; and the rights of criminal defendants generate great public interest because they are so central to our political system and our daily lives.

DEFINING CIVIL LIBERTIES

DEFINE "CIVIL LIBERTIES," AND EXPLAIN HOW THE BILL OF RIGHTS CAME TO APPLY TO THE STATES

The terms *civil rights* and *civil liberties* are often used interchangeably, but there are some important differences (see Nuts & Bolts 4.1). To oversimplify a bit, civil liberties are about freedom and civil rights are about equality. (For more on this distinction, see Chapter 13.)

Civil liberties are deeply rooted in our key idea that politics is conflictual and that it involves trade-offs. When the Supreme Court rules on civil liberties cases, it must balance an individual's freedom with the government's interests and the public good. For example, in the war on terrorism the government has had to balance civil liberties with national security. Many Americans have been concerned that government surveillance invades people's privacy and that the treatment of suspected terrorists violates due process rights;[5] at the same time, most Americans would probably agree that in some instances these measures might be warranted. For example, if a nuclear device were set to detonate in Manhattan in three hours, few would insist on protecting the civil liberties of someone who knew where the bomb was hidden. Once we recognize that our freedoms are not absolute, it becomes a question of how they are balanced against other interests, such as national security, public safety, and public health.

Along with balancing competing interests, court rulings must also draw the lines to define the limits of permissible conduct by the government or by an individual in the context of a specific civil liberty. For example, despite the First Amendment's protection of freedom of speech, it is obvious that some speech absolutely cannot be permitted; the classic example is falsely yelling "fire!" in a crowded theater. Therefore, the courts must interpret the law to draw the line between protected speech and impermissible speech. The same challenge applies to other civil liberties such as the establishment of religion, freedom of the press, freedom from illegal searches, or other due process rights.

4.1 NUTS & bolts

DISTINGUISHING CIVIL LIBERTIES FROM CIVIL RIGHTS

Civil Liberties	Civil Rights
Basic freedoms and liberties	Protection from discrimination
Rooted in the Bill of Rights and the "due process" protection of the Fourteenth Amendment	Rooted in laws and the "equal protection" clause of the Fourteenth Amendment
Primarily restrict what the government can do to you ("*Congress* shall make no law . . . abridging the freedom of speech")	Protect you from discrimination both by the government and by individuals

HOW CAN CONFLICTS BE RESOLVED between civil liberties and other legitimate interests, such as public safety and public health? Sometimes freedom is forced to give way. Courts have upheld bans on the religious practice of snake handling and laws requiring the Amish to display reflective triangles when driving slow-moving buggies on public roads, despite religious objections to doing so.

Courts define the boundaries of civil liberties, but the other branches of government and the public often get involved as well. The earliest debates during the American Founding illustrate the broad public involvement concerning the basic questions of how our civil liberties would be defined: Should government be limited by an explicit statement of individual liberties? Would these limitations apply to the state governments or just the national government? How should these freedoms evolve as our society changes? As we will see in this section, interpretations of these constitutional protections have changed over time.

ORIGINS OF THE BILL OF RIGHTS

Originally, the Constitution provided very limited protection of civil liberties: (1) a guarantee of habeas corpus rights (a protection against illegal incarceration), and (2) a prohibition of bills of attainder (legislation punishing someone for a crime without the benefit of a trial) and ex post facto laws (laws that retroactively change the legal consequences of some behavior). There were a few attempts to include a broader statement of civil liberties, including one proposed by George Mason and Elbridge Gerry five days before the Constitutional Convention adjourned, but their motion to appoint a committee to draft a bill of rights was rejected. Charles Pinckney and Gerry also tried to add a provision protecting the freedom of the press, but that too was rejected.[6]

Mason and Gerry opposed ratification of the Constitution partly because it did not include a bill of rights, and many Antifederalists echoed this view. Some states ratified the Constitution but urged Congress to draft specific protections for individuals' and states' rights from federal action. (They believed that protection

DRAWING LINES AND THE FOURTH AMENDMENT

The Supreme Court has ruled that police do not need a search warrant to have drug-sniffing dogs search luggage at an airport or a car that has been stopped for a traffic violation unrelated to drugs. Lower courts have also ruled that sniffs are not considered searches in a hotel hallway, school locker, outside a passenger train's sleeper compartments, or outside an apartment door. However, lower courts have been split on whether drug-sniffing dogs may be used outside a home without a warrant, due, in part, to a Supreme Court precedent giving homes stronger Fourth Amendment protection than cars, lockers, or other areas. For example, in 2001 the Court ruled that police needed a warrant to use a thermal imaging device outside a home in an attempt to detect marijuana growing under heat lamps inside.

Another case provided an opportunity for the Court to sort out the lower court conflict by determining which precedent from its own decisions was most relevant (the thermal imaging case involving homes or the dog-sniffing cases about airports and cars). The case involved a Houston man, David Smith, who was arrested when a trained dog smelled methamphetamine in his garage. Based on the dog's positive indication, the police obtained a search warrant and found the meth and other evidence of criminal activity. Smith was sentenced to 37 years in prison but has appealed the conviction on the grounds that the evidence against him was illegally obtained. His lawyers argued to the Supreme Court that the thermal imaging case was the relevant precedent and that the charges should be thrown out, saying, "No distinction exists between a thermal imaging device and drug sniffing dog in that they are both sense-enhancing and permit information regarding the interior of a home to be gathered which could not otherwise be obtained without a physical intrusion into a constitutionally protected area." The district attorney, urging the Court to reject the appeal, said the thermal imaging case was not relevant because the Court's ruling in that case was focused on protecting the original meaning of the Fourth Amendment from erosion by new technology. He said that in contrast to thermal imaging devices, "The use of a drug detection dog does not constitute the use of any technology, let alone advanced technology."[a] The Supreme Court declined to hear the case. While this means the conviction stands, it does not imply Court agreement or disagreement with the conviction. Interestingly, in the very same term in which the Court declined to hear this case, they decided the case noted above ruling that using a drug-sniffing dog during a routine traffic stop did not violate the Fourth Amendment.[b]

At the opposite end of the technological spectrum from a drug-sniffing dog are all the new surveillance technologies that are available to law enforcement officials. Video surveillance in public places, cell phones with tracking chips, collection of Wi-Fi data, "E-ZPass" highway toll collection systems, roadside assistance devices, and web traffic data kept by online merchants and social networking sites are some of the more obvious technologies that could be used by law enforcement

Federal agents use a drug-sniffing dog to inspect a car.

officials. Others that are becoming more common or will be used soon include RFIDs (radio frequency identifications), which are the size of a grain of rice and transmit information wirelessly through radio waves; facial recognition software and iris scanners; "smart dust devices"—tiny wireless micromechanical sensors—that can detect light and movement; and drones, which have primarily been used for military purposes but also have vast potential for tracking suspects in any context.

In the context of rapidly changing technology, what is the public's "reasonable expectation" for privacy? Justice Alito raised this question in oral arguments in a Supreme Court case involving a GPS tracking device (we discuss the case later in the chapter). He said, "Technology is changing people's expectations of privacy. . . . Maybe 10 years from now 90 percent of the population will be using social networking sites and they will have on average 500 friends and they will have allowed their friends to monitor their location 24 hours a day, 365 days a year, through the use of their cell phones. Then—what would the expectation of privacy be then?"[c]

Critical Thinking Questions

1. If you had to decide the case of the drug-sniffing dog, how would you have ruled? Do you think that homes should have stronger privacy expectations than cars? Even when it concerns illegal drugs?

2. How would you answer Justice Alito's question about the expectation of privacy in an era of rapidly changing technology? When should law enforcement officials have to get a warrant to monitor our behavior?

of civil liberties from state actions should reside in state constitutions.) In other states, the Antifederalists who lost the ratification battle continued making their case to the public and Congress.

When the first Congress took up this contentious issue, state conventions submitted 124 amendments for consideration. That list was whittled down to 17 by the House and then to 12 by the Senate. This even dozen was approved by the House and sent to the states, which in 1791 ratified the 10 amendments that became the Bill of Rights.[7] Despite the document's profound significance, however, one point limited its reach: it applied only to the national government, not to the states. This decision proved consequential because the national government was quite weak for the first half of our nation's history. Given that the states exercised at least as much power over people's lives as the national government, it would have been more important for the Bill of Rights to limit the states rather than the federal government, but this did not occur.

Interestingly, because the Bill of Rights only applied to the national government, it played a relatively small role for more than a century. The Supreme Court used it only once before 1866 to invalidate a federal action—in the infamous *Dred Scott* case that contributed to the Civil War (see Chapter 3).

4.2 NUTS & bolts

THE BILL OF RIGHTS: A STATEMENT OF OUR CIVIL LIBERTIES

First Amendment	Freedom of religion, speech, press, and assembly; the separation of church and state; and the right to petition the government.
Second Amendment	Right to bear arms.
Third Amendment	Protection against the forced quartering of troops in one's home.
Fourth Amendment	Protection from unreasonable searches and seizures; requirement of "probable cause" for search warrants.
Fifth Amendment	Protection from forced self-incrimination or double jeopardy (being tried twice for the same crime); no person can be deprived of life, liberty, or property without due process of law; private property cannot be taken for public use without just compensation; and no person can be tried for a serious crime without the indictment of a grand jury.
Sixth Amendment	Right of the accused to a speedy and public trial by an impartial jury, to an attorney, to confront witnesses, to a compulsory process for obtaining witnesses in his or her favor, and to counsel in all felony cases.
Seventh Amendment	Right to a trial by jury in civil cases involving common law.
Eighth Amendment	Protection from excessive bail, excessive fines, and cruel and unusual punishment.
Ninth Amendment	The enumeration of specific rights in the Constitution shall not be construed to deny other rights retained by the people. This has been interpreted to include a general right to privacy and other fundamental rights.
Tenth Amendment	Powers not delegated by the Constitution to the national government, nor prohibited by it to the states, are reserved to the states or to the people.

SELECTIVE INCORPORATION AND THE FOURTEENTH AMENDMENT

The significance of the Bill of Rights increased somewhat with ratification of the Fourteenth Amendment in 1868. It was one of the three **Civil War Amendments** that attempted to guarantee the newly freed slaves equal rights as citizens of the United States. (The other two Civil War Amendments were the Thirteenth, which abolished slavery, and the Fifteenth, which gave male former slaves the right to vote.) Northern politicians were concerned that southerners would deny basic rights to the former slaves, so the sweeping language of the Fourteenth Amendment was adopted.

Section 1 of the Fourteenth Amendment says:

> *All persons born or naturalized in the United States, and subject to the jurisdiction thereof, are citizens of the United States and of the State wherein they reside. No State shall make or enforce any law which shall abridge the privileges or immunities of citizens of the United States; nor shall any State deprive any person of life, liberty, or property, without due process of law; nor deny to any person within its jurisdiction the equal protection of the laws.*

This language sought to ensure that states would not deny newly freed slaves the full protection of the law.[8] The **due process clause**, which forbids any state from denying "life, liberty, or property, without due process of law," led to an especially important expansion of civil liberties because the Supreme Court had previously interpreted a similar clause in the Fifth Amendment to apply only to the federal government.

However, in 1873, in its first opportunity to interpret the Fourteenth Amendment, the Court continued to rule in favor of protection from national government actions only. Despite the amendment's clear language that "No State shall make or enforce any law" limiting citizens' legal "privileges or immunities," the Court ruled that the Fourteenth Amendment protected U.S. citizens against actions of the national government only, not the state governments. The Court also rejected the plaintiffs' claim that the state was denying them "the equal protection of the laws" on the grounds that the Fourteenth Amendment was intended to strike down laws that discriminated against blacks.[9] This particular case involved a slaughterhouse monopoly in Louisiana in which all parties on both sides of the issue were white.

Over the next 50 years a few justices tried mightily to interpret the Fourteenth Amendment to protect civil liberties against state government action, culminating in the 1925 case *Gitlow v. New York*.[10] Here the Court said for the first time that the Fourteenth Amendment incorporated one of the amendments in the Bill of Rights and applied it to the states. The case involved Benjamin Gitlow, a radical Socialist convicted under New York's Criminal Anarchy Act of 1902 for advocating the overthrow of the government. The Court upheld his conviction, arguing that

Civil War Amendments The Thirteenth, Fourteenth, and Fifteenth Amendments to the Constitution, which abolished slavery and granted civil liberties and voting rights to freed slaves after the Civil War.

due process clause Part of the Fourteenth Amendment that forbids states from denying "life, liberty, or property" to any person without due process of law. (A nearly identical clause in the Fifth Amendment applies only to the national government.)

CAN THE POLICE SEARCH YOUR HOME without a warrant? After Dollree Mapp was arrested for possession of pornographic material, the case made its way to the Supreme Court and the search was ruled unconstitutional. This case established the "exclusionary rule" for evidence that is obtained without a warrant.

TABLE » 4.1

SELECTIVE INCORPORATION

AMENDMENT	ISSUE	CASE
First Amendment	Freedom of speech	*Gitlow v. New York* (1925)
	Freedom of the press	*Near v. Minnesota* (1931)
	Freedom of assembly	*DeJonge v. Oregon* (1937)
	Right to petition the government	*Hague v. CIO* (1939)
	Free exercise of religion	*Hamilton v. Regents of the University of California* (1934), *Cantwell v. Connecticut* (1940)
	Separation of church and state	*Everson v. Board of Education of Ewing Township* (1947)
Second Amendment	Right to bear arms	*McDonald v. Chicago* (2010)
Fourth Amendment	Protection from unreasonable search and seizure	*Wolf v. Colorado (1949), Mapp v. Ohio* (1961)[a]
Fifth Amendment	Protection from forced self-incrimination	*Malloy v. Hogan* (1964)
	Protection from double jeopardy	*Benton v. Maryland* (1969)
Sixth Amendment	Right to a public trial	*In re Oliver 333 U.S. 257* (1948)
	Right to a fair trial and an attorney in death-penalty cases	*Powell v. Alabama* (1932)
	Right to an attorney in all felony cases	*Gideon v. Wainwright* (1963)
	Right to an attorney in cases involving jail time	*Argersinger v. Hamlin* (1972)
	Right to a jury trial in a criminal case	*Duncan v. Louisiana* (1968)
	Right to cross-examine a witness	*Pointer v. Texas* (1965)
	Right to compel witnesses to testify who are vital for the defendant's case	*Washington v. Texas* (1967)
Eighth Amendment	Protection from cruel and unusual punishment	*Robinson v. California* (1962)[b]
	Protection from excessive bail	*Schilb v. Kuebel* (1971)[c]
Ninth Amendment	Right to privacy and other nonenumerated, fundamental rights	*Griswold v. Connecticut* (1965)[d]

NOT INCORPORATED		
Third Amendment	Prohibition against the quartering of troops in private homes	
Fifth Amendment	Right to indictment by a grand jury	
Seventh Amendment	Right to a jury trial in a civil case	
Eighth Amendment	Prohibition against excessive fines	

[a]*Wolf v. Colorado* applied the Fourth Amendment to the states (which meant that states could not engage in unreasonable searches and seizures); *Mapp v. Ohio* applied the exclusionary rule to the states (which excludes the use in a trial of illegally obtained evidence).

[b]Some sources list *Louisiana ex rel. Francis v. Resweber* (1947) as the first case that incorporated the Eighth Amendment. While the decision mentioned the Fifth and Eighth Amendments in the context of the due process clause of the Fourteenth Amendment, this argument was not included in the majority opinion that upheld as constitutional the bizarre double-electrocution of Willie Francis (the electric chair malfunctioned on the first attempt but was successful on the second attempt; see Abraham and Perry, *Freedom and the Court*, pp. 71–72).

[c]Justice Blackmun "assumed" in this case that "the 8th Amendment's proscription of excessive bail [applies] to the states through the 14th Amendment," but later decisions did not seem to share this view. However, Justices Stevens and O'Connor agreed with Blackmun's view in *Browning-Ferris v. Kelco Disposal* (1989). Some sources argue that the excessive bail clause of the Eighth Amendment is unincorporated.

[d]Justice Goldberg argued for explicit incorporation of the Ninth Amendment in a concurring opinion joined by Justices Warren and Brennan. The opinion of the Court referred more generally to a privacy right rooted in five amendments, including the Ninth, but did not explicitly argue for incorporation.

his writings were the "language of direct incitement," but it also warned state governments that there were limits on such suppression of speech.

Over the ensuing decades most civil liberties covered in the Bill of Rights were applied to the states on a case-by-case basis through the Fourteenth Amendment (see Table 4.1). However, this process of **selective incorporation** was not smooth and incremental; rather, it progressed in surges. The first flurry of activity came in the 1930s when most of the First Amendment was incorporated, requiring the states to allow a free press, the right to assemble, free exercise of religion, and the right to petition. The next flurry came in the 1960s with a series of cases on criminal defendants' rights and due process.

Following another decades-long gap, in 2010 the incorporation of the Second Amendment's right to bear arms meant that all the significant amendments now apply to state and local governments. As a result, we can now say that the Bill of Rights has evolved from the nineteenth century's limitations that affected only national government action to a robust set of widespread protections for freedom and liberty today.

selective incorporation The process through which the civil liberties granted in the Bill of Rights were applied to the states on a case-by-case basis through the Fourteenth Amendment.

FREEDOM OF SPEECH, ASSEMBLY, AND THE PRESS

DESCRIBE THE MAJOR FIRST AMENDMENT RIGHTS RELATED TO FREEDOM OF SPEECH

The First Amendment's ringing words are the most famous statement of personal freedoms in the Constitution: "Congress shall make no law respecting an establishment of religion, or prohibiting the free exercise thereof; or abridging the freedom of speech, or of the press; or the right of the people peaceably to assemble, and to petition the Government for a redress of grievances." (The "How It Works" diagram on page 107 illustrates how much is packed into this one amendment.) As noted earlier, defining the scope of our civil liberties depends on balancing interests and drawing lines. This is especially true of First Amendment freedoms, which can best be envisioned on a continuum from most to least protected based on the Supreme Court cases that have tested their limits.

GENERALLY PROTECTED EXPRESSION

Anytime you attend a religious service or a political rally, write an article for your student paper, or express a political idea, you are being protected by the First Amendment. However, the nature of this protection is continually evolving due to political forces and shifting constitutional interpretations. Only recently have the courts developed a complex continuum ranging from strongly protected political speech to less protected speech.

STANDARDS FOR PROTECTION

The basis for the continuum of protected speech lies in the content of the speech. Typically, the Court does not allow content-based regulation of speech (unless it falls into one of the categories of exceptions we discuss below). For example, in 1972 the Court struck down a local ordinance that banned picketing outside of schools except for labor picketing.[11] This ordinance was deemed to be content-based regulation because it favored one form of speech (from labor unions) over others. Such regulation is subject to the **strict scrutiny** standard of judicial review, which means the regulation must be narrowly tailored (that is, the least restrictive means) to serve a compelling state interest. In most cases this means that the speech will be protected and the regulation struck down. If a regulation is "content neutral" and does not favor any given viewpoint, then it is subject to the less demanding **intermediate scrutiny** standard. This means that the government must only demonstrate a substantial interest, that the interest must be unrelated to the content of the speech, and that there are alternative opportunities for communication.[12]

POLITICAL SPEECH

Freedom of speech got off to a rocky start when Congress passed the Alien and Sedition Acts in 1798. The controversial Sedition Act made it a crime to "write, print, utter or publish . . . any false, scandalous and malicious writing or writings against the government of the United States." Supporters of the acts claimed they were necessary to strengthen the national government in response to the French Revolution, but in reality they were an attempt by the governing Federalist Party to neutralize the opposition Democratic-Republican Party. The outcry against the laws helped propel Thomas Jefferson to the presidency in 1800. Jefferson pardoned those who had been convicted under the law (mostly newspaper editors), Congress repealed one of the acts in 1802, and the others were allowed to expire before the Supreme Court had a chance to rule them unconstitutional.

The next big challenge to freedom of speech came from the states. During the battles over slavery early in the nineteenth century, northern states outlawed positive statements about slavery, while southern states prohibited criticism of slavery. By the end of the nineteenth century such sedition laws prohibiting behavior considered subversive were quite common at the state level, and hundreds of people had been jailed for criticizing the government and its policies (recall that the First Amendment did not apply to the states in the nineteenth century).

In the twentieth century World War I prompted the harshest crackdowns on free speech since the Sedition Act of 1798. The most important case from this period involved the general secretary of the Socialist Party, Charles Schenk, who opposed U.S. involvement in the war. He had printed a leaflet urging young men to resist the draft. Schenk was arrested and appealed all the way to the Supreme Court, arguing that the First Amendment permitted him to protest the war and urge others to resist the draft. But the Court sustained his conviction, noting that free speech is not an absolute right:

> *The most stringent protection of free speech would not protect a man in falsely shouting fire in a theatre and causing a panic. . . . The question in every case is whether the words used are used in such circumstances and are of such a nature as to create a clear and present danger that they will bring about the substantive evils that Congress has a right to prevent.*[13]

strict scrutiny The highest level of scrutiny the courts use when determining whether a law is constitutional. To pass this test, the law or policy must be shown to serve a "compelling state interest" or goal, it must be narrowly tailored to achieve that goal, and it must be the least restrictive means of achieving the goal.

intermediate scrutiny The middle level of scrutiny the courts use when determining whether a law is constitutional. To pass this test, the law or policy must further an important government interest in a way that is "substantially related" to that interest. That is, the law must use means that are a close fit to the government's goal and not substantially broader than necessary to accomplish that goal.

This **clear and present danger test** meant that the government could suppress any speech it thought was dangerous—in this instance, preventing the government from fighting the war. However, critics of the decision argue that Schenk's actions were not dangerous for the country.[14]

Over the next several decades the Court struggled to draw the line between dangerous speech and words that were simply unpopular. Then, in 1969, the Court established a strong protection for free speech that still holds today. This case involved a Ku Klux Klan leader who made a threatening speech at a cross-burning rally that was subsequently shown on television. Twelve hooded figures were shown, many with weapons. The speech said that "revengence" [sic] might be taken if "our president, our Congress, our Supreme Court continues to suppress the white, Caucasian race." He continued, "We are marching on Congress July the Fourth, four hundred thousand strong." The Klan leader was convicted under an Ohio law banning "sabotage, violence, or unlawful methods of terrorism as a means of accomplishing industrial or political reform," but the Court unanimously reversed his conviction, arguing that threatening speech could not be suppressed just because it sounded dangerous. Specifically, the **direct incitement test** holds that speech is protected "except where such advocacy is directed to inciting or producing imminent lawless action and is likely to incite or produce such action."[15] Under this new standard *Schenk* and many other previous sedition convictions would have been overturned.

SYMBOLIC SPEECH

The use of signs, symbols, or other unspoken acts or methods to communicate in a political manner—**symbolic speech**—enjoys many of the same protections as regular speech. For example, during the Vietnam War the Court protected the First Amendment right of a protester to wear an American flag patch sewn on the seat of his pants,[16] a high school student's right to wear an armband to protest the war,[17] and an individual's right to tape a peace symbol on the flag and fly it upside-down outside an apartment window.[18]

A 1989 case provided the strongest protection for symbolic speech yet, overturning a flag desecration law in Texas on the grounds that symbolic political speech is protected by the First Amendment.[19] In response to this unpopular decision, Congress passed the Flag Protection Act of 1989, which the Court also struck down as an unconstitutional infringement on political expression.[20] Congress then attempted six times to pass a constitutional amendment to overturn the Court decision, but each time the measure failed in the Senate.

Spending money in political campaigns may also be protected by the First Amendment since it provides the means for more conventional types of political speech. Here the question is whether the government can control campaign contributions and spending for a broader public purpose such as controlling corruption, or whether such laws violate the First Amendment rights of candidates or their supporters. You probably have heard the old saying "Money talks," which implies that money is speech. Given the importance

clear and present danger test Established in *Schenk v. United States*, this test allows the government to restrict certain types of speech deemed dangerous.

direct incitement test Established in *Brandenberg v. Ohio*, this test protects threatening speech under the First Amendment unless that speech aims to and is likely to cause imminent "lawless action."

THE AMERICAN FLAG IS A POPULAR target for protesters: it has been spat upon, shredded, turned into underwear, and burned, as it was during this 2004 demonstration at the Democratic National Convention in Boston. Despite multiple efforts in Congress to ban flag desecration, these activities remain constitutionally protected symbolic speech.

symbolic speech Nonverbal expression, such as the use of signs or symbols. It benefits from many of the same constitutional protections as verbal speech.

of advertising in modern campaigns, limitations on raising and spending money could limit the ability of candidates and groups to reach voters with their message. The Court has walked a tightrope on this one, balancing the public interest in honest and ethical elections and the First Amendment rights of candidates and their advocates. The Court has upheld individual candidates' right to spend their own money in federal elections, but presidential candidates give up that right if they accept federal campaign funds (taxpayers' money) in a presidential election. Also, candidates in federal elections are subject to limits on the types and size of contributions they can receive, and they must report all contributions and spending to the Federal Election Commission.[21]

The Bipartisan Campaign Reform Act, which went into effect for the 2004 elections, included a "Millionaires' Amendment" that lifted restrictions on campaign contributions for candidates whose opponent spent more than $350,000 of his or her own money in the election. This attempt to level the campaign finance playing field was struck down by the Supreme Court in 2008 as a violation of wealthy candidates' First Amendment rights.[22] In the 2010 case *Citizens United,* the Court also extended First Amendment rights to corporations and labor unions that want to spend money on campaign ads.[23] (For more on these cases, see Chapter 8.) However, the Court upheld a ban on unlimited "soft money" contributions because they have the most potential for corruption.[24]

HATE SPEECH

hate speech Expression that is offensive or abusive, particularly in terms of race, gender, or sexual orientation. It is currently protected under the First Amendment.

Free speech has been a hot topic on many college campuses in the context of **hate speech**. Do people have a right to say things that are offensive or abusive, especially in terms of race, gender, and sexual orientation? By the mid-1990s more than 350 public colleges and universities said no by regulating some forms of hate speech.[25] One example was a speech code adopted at the University of Michigan that prohibited "any behavior, verbal or physical, that stigmatizes or victimizes an individual on the basis of race, ethnicity, religion, sex, sexual orientation, creed, national origin, ancestry, age, marital status, handicap, or Vietnam veteran status" and "creates an intimidating, hostile, or demeaning environment for educational pursuits, employment or participation in University-sponsored extra-curricular activities."[26] The Supreme Court has yet to rule on this issue, but lower courts have struck down the University of Michigan's speech code as well as similar rules at several other universities. If the Supreme Court were to take up any of these cases, the justices would likely strike down the speech codes because they are not "content neutral" regulations and they do not meet the direct incitement test of targeting only expressions that would spur imminent violence.

ARE LAWS BANNING HATE SPEECH constitutional? Sometimes yes, but the threshold is relatively high. These Ku Klux Klan members are free to hold rallies, preach racism and xenophobia, and burn crosses, as long as they do not directly incite violence or display an "intent to intimidate."

Another significant issue combines the topics of symbolic speech and hate speech. For example, can a person who burned a cross on a black family's lawn be convicted under a city ordinance that prohibits conduct "arous[ing] anger, alarm, or resentment in others on the basis of race, color, creed, religion, or gender"? Or is the ordinance an unconstitutional limit on First Amendment rights? In this case the Court said the cross burner could be punished for arson, terrorism, trespassing, or other violations of the law, but he could not be convicted under the city ordinance because it was overly broad and vague.[27] However, the Court has since upheld more carefully worded bans of cross burning.[28]

FREEDOM OF ASSEMBLY

The Supreme Court has consistently protected the right to assemble peaceably. Perhaps the most famous assembly case involved a neo-Nazi group that wanted to march in a suburb of Chicago whose population of 70,000 was nearly 60 percent Jewish. (And of those, many were Holocaust survivors.) The village passed ordinances that banned the group from marching, arguing that residents would be so upset by the Nazi marchers that they might become violent. But the lower courts did not accept this argument, ruling that if "the audience is so offended by the ideas being expressed that it becomes disorderly and attempts to silence the speaker, it is the duty of the police to attempt to protect the speaker, not to silence his speech."[29] Otherwise, the right to assemble would be restricted by a "heckler's veto." The Court elaborated on this responsibility to protect expressions of unpopular views by striking down another town's ordinance that allowed it to charge a higher permit fee to groups whose march would likely require more police protection.[30]

While broad protection is provided for peaceable assemblies, governments may regulate the time, manner, and place of expression as long as the regulation does not favor certain groups or messages over others. For example, antiabortion protesters were not allowed to picket a doctor's home in Brookfield, Wisconsin. The Court ruled that the ordinance banning all residential picketing was content neutral and that there was a government interest in preserving the "sanctity of the home, the one retreat to which men and women can repair to escape from the tribulations of their daily pursuits."[31] "Time, manner, and place" restrictions also may be invoked for practical reasons. For example, if the Ku Klux Klan planned to hold a march around a football stadium on the day of a game, the local city council could deny them a permit and suggest they choose another day that would be more convenient. The legal standard for these regulations is that they are "reasonable." While vague, this standard allows the courts to balance the right to assemble against other practical considerations.

FREEDOM OF THE PRESS

The task of balancing interests is central to many First Amendment cases involving the freedom of the press. The general issue here is **prior restraint**, the government's right to prevent the media from publishing (or later, broadcasting) something of social or political significance. Prior restraint has never been clearly defined by the Supreme Court, but several landmark cases have set a very high bar for applying it.

prior restraint A limit on freedom of the press that allows the government to prohibit the media from publishing certain materials.

The first case, brought in the 1930s, involved a Minnesota law that banned "obscene, lewd and lascivious" publications or "malicious, scandalous and defamatory" content. Under this law the state shut down a racist, bigoted publication that railed against many groups of people. The Court subsequently struck down the law in *Near v. Minnesota*, saying, "The fact that the liberty of the press may be abused by miscreant purveyors of scandal does not make any less necessary the immunity of the press from previous restraint."[32] However, the Court did not specify when prior restraint would be acceptable. Another suit, brought in 1971 and known as the Pentagon Papers case, involved disclosure of parts of a top-secret

THE PUBLICATION OF THOUSANDS of government documents, including some sensitive reports and communications, raised new questions about press freedom and national security. Here, WikiLeaks founder Julian Assange discusses the leaked documents.

report on internal planning for the Vietnam War. Ultimately, the Court decided that the government could not prevent publication of the Pentagon Papers, but at least five justices supported the view that under some circumstances the government could use prior restraint—though they could not agree on the standard.[33]

Recently, prior restraint has gained new significance in the war on terrorism. The media, especially the *New York Times*, skirmished with the Bush administration over publishing stories on classified programs, including extraordinary rendition of suspected terrorists, domestic surveillance, and the Terrorist Finance Tracking Program, which monitors all large financial transactions in the international banking system. The sensational leaking of more than 91,000 reports concerning the war in Afghanistan by WikiLeaks ratcheted up the stakes. Some members of Congress labeled the leaks "treason" and called for prosecution. However, supporters of an unrestrained press point to the Pentagon Papers case as precedent for the role of journalists in holding the government accountable. They argue that the conduct of war and programs such as warrantless wiretapping of U.S. citizens may violate international or domestic law and that the public has the right to know about them. None of these issues has yet to appear in a suit before the Supreme Court.

The forms of expression discussed in this section—speech, assembly, and press—all have strong protection from the First Amendment. The strongest protections are for content-based expression. However, there are exceptions, such as speech that directly incites an imminent danger. If the regulation is content neutral and does not favor one viewpoint over another, then it is easier to uphold. But even then, the government must have a substantial reason for limiting expression.

LESS PROTECTED SPEECH AND PUBLICATIONS

Some forms of speech do not warrant the same level of protection as political speech because they do not contribute to public debate or express ideas that have important social value. Governments may more easily regulate four categories of such speech: fighting words, slander and libel, commercial speech, and obscenity.

FIGHTING WORDS

fighting words Forms of expression that "by their very utterance" can incite violence. These can be regulated by the government but are often difficult to define.

Governments may regulate **fighting words**, "which by their very utterance inflict injury or tend to incite an immediate breach of the peace."[34] Such laws must be narrowly written; it is not acceptable to ban all foul language, and the prohibited speech must target a single person rather than a group. Moreover, the question of whether certain words provoke a backlash depends on the reaction of the targeted person. Inflammatory words directed at a pacifist would not be fighting words because he or she would turn the other cheek, whereas the same words yelled at a hothead *would* be fighting words because that individual would likely respond with violence. The Court has further clarified the test, based on "what persons of common intelligence would understand to be words likely to cause an average addressee to fight."[35]

SLANDER AND LIBEL

A more extensive line of cases prohibiting speech concerns **slander**, spoken false statements that damage someone's reputation, and **libel**, written statements that do the same thing. However, it is difficult to draw the line between permissible speech and slander or libel. The current legal standard distinguishes between speech about a public figure, such as a politician or celebrity, and speech about a regular person. It is much more difficult for public figures to prove libel because they must demonstrate that the defamatory statement was made with "actual malice" and "with knowledge that it was false or with reckless disregard of whether it was false or not."[36]

One of the most famous libel cases occurred when Reverend Jerry Falwell, a well-known televangelist and political activist, sued *Hustler* magazine for libel and emotional distress after the magazine published a parody of a liquor advertisement depicting him in a "drunken incestuous rendezvous with his mother in an outhouse" (this quote is from the Supreme Court case).[37] The Court ruled against Falwell, saying that public figures and public officials have to put up with such things and compared the parody to outrageous political cartoons, which have always been protected by the First Amendment.

COMMERCIAL SPEECH

Commercial speech, which mostly refers to advertising, has evolved from having almost no protection under the First Amendment to enjoying quite strong protection by the 1970s. In a 1976 case the Court struck down a law against advertising prescription drug prices and one prohibiting placing newspaper racks on city streets to distribute commercial publications such as real estate guides.[38] Another key decision in 1980 established a test that is still central today. The Court ruled that the government may regulate commercial speech if it concerns an illegal activity, if the advertisement is misleading, or if regulating speech directly advances a substantial government interest and the regulation is not excessive. In practice, this test means that commercial speech can be regulated but that the government has to have a very good reason to do it.[39] Even public health concerns have not been allowed to override commercial speech rights. For example, the Court struck down a Massachusetts regulation that limited the content of advertisements aimed at children (the ban on R. J. Reynolds's Joe Camel character is the classic example) in a manner that was more restrictive than federal law.[40]

OBSCENITY

One area in which the press has never experienced complete freedom involves the publication of pornography and material considered obscene. The difficulty arises in deciding where to draw the line. Nearly everyone would agree that child pornography should not be published[41] and that pornography should not be available to minors. However, beyond these points there is little consensus. For example, some people are offended by nude paintings in art museums, while others enjoy watching hardcore X-rated movies.

Defining obscenity has proven difficult for the courts. In an often-quoted moment of frustration, Justice Potter Stewart wrote that he could not define obscenity, but "I know it when I see it."[42] The Supreme Court took a stab at it in 1973 in a case

slander and **libel** Spoken false statements (slander) and written false statements (libel) that damage a person's reputation. Both can be regulated by the government but are often difficult to distinguish from permissible speech.

commercial speech Public expression with the aim of making a profit. It has received greater protection under the First Amendment in recent years but remains less protected than political speech.

JOE CAMEL PEDDLES HIS WARES on a New York City billboard. Commercial speech, as a general category, is not as strongly protected by the First Amendment as political speech, but advertising can be limited by the government only in specific circumstances.

Miller test Established in *Miller v. California*, the Supreme Court uses this three-part test to determine whether speech meets the criteria for obscenity. If so, it can be restricted by the government.

that gave rise to the **Miller test**, which is still applied today.[43] The test has three standards that must all be met in order for material to be banned as obscene: if it appeals to prurient interests, if it is "patently offensive," and if the work as a whole lacks serious literary, artistic, political, or scientific value. The Court also clarified that *local* community standards are to apply rather than a single national standard.

Congress and the president also get in on the act of controlling obscenity. Recent efforts have focused on the Internet as a pornography medium. Congress passed the Communications Decency Act in 1996, which criminalized the use of any computer network to display "indecent" material, unless the provider could offer an effective way of screening out potential users under age 18. The Court struck down the law in 1997 because it was vague and because it is technically impossible to limit access to websites based on age. This ruling gives the Internet the same free speech protection as print.[44] But in 1998 Congress enacted the Child Online Protection Act, which prohibited commercial websites from distributing material that is "harmful to minors," using the *Miller* test to specify what this means. The law bounced around in federal courts for six years before the Supreme Court ultimately struck it down.[45]

///

DESCRIBE THE FIRST AMENDMENT RIGHTS RELATED TO FREEDOM OF RELIGION

FREEDOM OF RELIGION

establishment clause Part of the First Amendment that states "Congress shall make no law respecting an establishment of religion," which has been interpreted to mean that Congress cannot sponsor or favor any religion.

The First Amendment has two parts that deal with religion: the **establishment clause**, which says that Congress cannot sponsor or endorse any particular religion, and the **free exercise clause**, which states that Congress cannot interfere in the practice of religion. Essentially, the former says that Congress should not *help* religion and the latter that it should not *hurt* religion. The establishment clause is primarily concerned with drawing lines; for example, does a prayer at a public high school fooball game or a nativity scene on government property constitute state sponsorship of religion? The free exercise clause has more to do with balancing interests, such as balancing public safety concerns against snake handling in religious services and the use of Amish buggies on public highways.

free exercise clause Part of the First Amendment that states Congress cannot prohibit or interfere with the practice of religion.

The combination of the establishment and free exercise clauses results in a general policy of noninterference and government neutrality toward religion. As Thomas Jefferson said in 1802, the First Amendment provides a "wall of eternal separation between church and state." This language continues to be cited in Court cases[46] in which religion and politics intersect. Since both areas carry great moral weight and emotional charge, the boundaries of religious expression remain difficult to draw.

THE ESTABLISHMENT CLAUSE AND SEPARATION OF CHURCH AND STATE

Determining the boundaries between church and state—the central issue of the establishment clause—is very difficult. We know that the Founders did not want an official state religion or for the government to favor one religion over another, but beyond that it's hard to say. Jefferson's "eternal wall of separation" has been cited in Court decisions that prohibit state aid for religious activities, but lately the Court has been displaying a more "accommodationist" perspective that sometimes allows religious activity in public institutions.

SCHOOL PRAYER

The issue of prohibition of prayer in public schools exploded onto the political scene in 1962 when the Court ruled in *Engle v. Vitale* that a prayer written by the New York Board of State Regents and read every day in the state's public schools violated the separation of church and state.[47] Banning the prayer caused a public outcry protesting the perceived attack on religion.

Over the next 50 years Congress repeatedly tried, unsuccessfully, to amend the Constitution to allow school prayer. Meanwhile, the Court continued to take a hard line on school-sponsored prayer. In 1985 the Court struck down the practice of observing a one-minute moment of silence for "meditation or voluntary prayer" in the Alabama public schools.[48] More recently, the Court said that benedictions or prayers at public school graduations and a school policy that allowed an elected student representative to lead a prayer at a high school football game also violated the establishment clause.[49] Yet the Court has upheld the practice of opening every session of Congress with a prayer and has let stand without comment a lower court ruling that allowed a prayer that was planned and led by students (rather than being school policy) at a high school graduation.[50]

AID TO RELIGIOUS ORGANIZATIONS

The Court has had an even more difficult time determining principles to govern aid to religious organizations, either directly, through tax dollars, or indirectly, through the use of public space. One early attempt was known as the **Lemon test**, after one of the parties in a 1971 case involving government support for religious schools (*Lemon v. Kurtzman*). Here the justices ruled that a practice violated the establishment clause if it (1) did not have a "secular legislative purpose," (2) either

Lemon test The Supreme Court uses this test, established in *Lemon v. Kurtzman*, to determine whether a practice violates the First Amendment's establishment clause.

CAN A CROSS BE DISPLAYED ON federal land? The Supreme Court has ruled that religious displays on government property must be part of larger, secular displays. This cross on federal land in the Mojave Desert was covered up after it became controversial.

advanced or inhibited religion, or (3) fostered "an excessive government entanglement with religion."[51] The third part of the test was later found open to interpretation by lower courts and therefore led to conflicting rulings.

The Court started to move away from the *Lemon* test in a 1984 case involving a city-owned creche that was displayed in a park owned by a nonprofit corporation. The Court allowed the nativity display, saying, "The Constitution does not require complete separation of church and state; it affirmatively mandates accommodation, not merely tolerance, of all religions, and forbids hostility toward any."[52] This "endorsement test" simply says that government action is unconstitutional if a "reasonable observer" would think that the action either endorses or disapproves of religion. Later rulings upheld similar religious displays, especially if they conformed to what observers have labeled the "three plastic animals rule"—if the baby Jesus is surrounded by Rudolph the red-nosed reindeer and other secular symbols, the overall display is considered sufficiently nonreligious to pass constitutional muster.[53] This picture became more muddled in 2005 when the Court said that the Ten Commandments could not be posted in two Kentucky courthouses but could be displayed on a monument outside the capitol in Austin, Texas. Justice Breyer noted that Austin's monument was one of 40 on the capitol grounds, so the display served a "mixed but primarily non-religious purpose," whereas the Kentucky courthouses' displays were clearly religious.[54]

The Court has also applied the accommodationist perspective to funding for religious schools by looking more favorably on providing tax dollars to students' families to subsidize tuition costs rather than funding the parochial schools directly. In 2011 the Court expanded taxpayer support for religious education when it upheld an Arizona law that provides state tax credits for contributions to organizations that provide tuition for religious schools.[55]

Another case involved a clash between the First Amendment's free speech and establishment clauses. The University of Virginia declined to support a Christian newspaper because of its religious content (despite funding 118 other student organizations with a range of views), and the editor of the paper sued the university for violating his freedom of speech. The Court ruled that free speech concerns trumped possible establishment issues, so that refusing to fund the Christian paper while funding so many others amounted to "viewpoint discrimination."[56]

THE FREE EXERCISE CLAUSE

While the freedom of belief is absolute, freedom of religious conduct cannot be unrestricted. That is, you can believe whatever you want without government interference, but if you *act* on those beliefs, the government may regulate your behavior. And while the government has restricted religious conduct in dozens of cases, the freedom of religion has been among the most consistently protected civil liberties.

Hundreds of cases have come before the Court in the area of the free exercise of religion. Here are some examples of the questions they addressed:[57] May Amish parents be forced to send their children to schools beyond the eighth grade? (no); Is animal sacrifice as part of a religious ceremony protected by the First Amendment? (generally yes); May Mormons have multiple wives? (no); May the Amish be compelled to follow traffic laws and put license plates on their buggies? (yes);

How It Works

THE FIRST AMENDMENT

Political speech and symbolic speech

Less protected forms of speech

FREEDOM OF THE PRESS

FREE EXERCISE
The government cannot prevent people from practicing their religion.

FREEDOM OF SPEECH

FREEDOM TO PETITION THE GOVERNMENT

ESTABLISHMENT
The government cannot establish an official state religion or favor one religion over others.

FREEDOM OF ASSEMBLY

FREEDOM OF RELIGION

FREEDOM OF EXPRESSION

1ST AMENDMENT

Congress shall make no law respecting an establishment of religion, or prohibiting the free exercise thereof; or abridging the freedom of speech, or of the press; or the right of the people peaceably to assemble, and to petition the Government for a redress of grievances.

POP QUIZ!

1 Which type of speech is strongly protected under the First Amendment?

- **a** political speech
- **b** commercial speech
- **c** obscenity
- **d** libel
- **e** fighting words

2 The First Amendment's "establishment clause" says that the government cannot

- **a** establish categories of speech.
- **b** prevent people from practicing their religion.
- **c** ban offensive speech.
- **d** create an official state religion.
- **e** prevent people from peaceably assembling.

Answers: 1.a; 2.d

May people be forced to work on Friday night and Saturday if those are their days of worship? (no); May religious dress be regulated? (generally no, but in some contexts, such as the military, yes). Keep in mind that this list is not exhaustive.

One case in 1990 addressed whether the state may deny unemployment benefits to someone who is fired for taking illegal drugs as part of a religious ceremony. The Court ruled that the state of Oregon had not violated the free exercise clause in denying unemployment benefits to the plaintiffs because they were fired from their jobs in a drug rehabilitation clinic for using peyote. The broader significance of the ruling came with the Court's announcement of a new interpretation of the free exercise clause: the government does not need a "compelling interest" in regulating a particular behavior to justify a law that limits a religious practice.[58] In other words, after this decision it would be easier for the government to limit the exercise of religion because the Court would no longer require a "compelling" reason for the restrictions, just a good one.

Although Congress responded by passing the Religious Freedom Restoration Act in 1993, reinstating the need to demonstrate a "compelling state interest" before limiting religious freedoms, in 1997 the Court ruled that Congress could not usurp its power to define the constitutional protections for religion and that the 1993 law did not apply to the states.[59] Then in 2000 Congress passed a more narrowly written law that only concerned zoning and the religious rights of people in prisons and government-run mental institutions. Under its power to regulate commerce and control spending, Congress told states that if they accepted federal tax dollars, they would have to reinstate the "compelling interest" standard when restricting religious practices in these two areas.

The Supreme Court gave partial support to this law in deciding a case involving the religious freedoms of prison inmates in Ohio.[60] The Court also upheld the law in allowing members of a small religion in New Mexico to use a hallucinogenic tea in their services even though the tea is a federally controlled substance. The Court ruled that the government had not demonstrated a compelling interest in barring

LAWYERS FOR TOM GREEN ARGUED that laws against bigamy and polygamy infringed on his religious freedom. Green belonged to a fundamentalist sect of Mormonism that teaches plural marriage. When this photo was taken in 2000, he had five wives and at least 29 children.

the sacramental use of the tea, indicating a shift back toward the stricter standard for justifying limits on religious practices.[61]

The struggle between Congress and the Court in defining civil liberties illustrates the importance of the political process. When Congress decides to tackle an important civil liberty such as religious freedom, it can influence outcomes in an area that is usually dominated by the courts.

THE RIGHT TO BEAR ARMS

EXPLORE WHY THE SECOND AMENDMENT'S MEANING ON GUN RIGHTS IS OFTEN DEBATED

Between 1791 and 2007 the Court issued only four rulings directly pertaining to the Second Amendment and the right to bear arms. The federal courts had always interpreted the Second Amendment's awkward phrasing—"A well regulated Militia, being necessary to the security of a free State, the right of the people to keep and bear Arms, shall not be infringed"—as a right to bear arms within the context of serving in a militia, rather than an individual right to own a gun.

Interest groups such as the National Rifle Association have long asserted that the Second Amendment guarantees an individual the right to bear arms. Critics of this view emphasize the first clause of the amendment and point to the frequent mentions of state militias in congressional debates at the time the Bill of Rights was adopted. They argue that the Second Amendment was adopted to reassure Antifederalist advocates of states' rights that state militias, not a national standing army, would provide national security. In this view the national armed forces and the National Guard have made the Second Amendment obsolete.

Before the Court's recent entry into this debate, Congress and state and local lawmakers had largely defined gun ownership and carrying rights, creating significant variation among the states. (Wyoming and Montana have virtually no restrictions on gun ownership, for example, whereas California and Connecticut have many.) However, following an assassination attempt on President Reagan in 1981, a push for stronger gun control laws intensified. In 1993 Congress passed the Brady bill, which mandates a background check and a five-day waiting period for any handgun purchase.

AFTER A MENTALLY ILL STUDENT shot and killed 32 people at Virginia Tech in 2007, many people called for stricter gun laws.

In 2008 a landmark ruling recognized for the first time an individual right to bear arms for self-defense and hunting.[62] The decision struck down the District of Columbia's ban on handguns, while noting that state and local governments could enforce ownership restrictions, such as preventing felons or the mentally impaired from buying guns. The Court did not apply the Second Amendment to the states in this decision but did so two years later in striking down a gun control ordinance in Chicago, while reaffirming the ownership restrictions noted in the Washington, D.C., case.[63]

Given the strong public support for gun ownership (there are about 200 million privately owned guns in the United States) and the Supreme Court's endorsement of an individual right to bear arms, stronger gun control at the national level is highly unlikely. However, extensive litigation will be necessary to define the acceptable boundaries of gun control and to identify which state and local restrictions will be allowed to stand.

DESCRIBE THE PROTECTIONS PROVIDED FOR PEOPLE ACCUSED OF A CRIME

LAW, ORDER, AND THE RIGHTS OF CRIMINAL DEFENDANTS

due process rights The idea that laws and legal proceedings must be fair. The Constitution guarantees that the government cannot take away a person's "life, liberty, or property, without due process of law." Other specific due process rights are found in the Fourth, Fifth, Sixth, and Eighth Amendments, such as protection from self-incrimination and freedom from illegal searches.

Every advanced democracy protects the rights of people who have been accused of a crime. In the United States the **due process rights** of the Fourth, Fifth, Sixth, and Eighth Amendments include the right to a fair trial, the right to consult a lawyer, freedom from self-incrimination, knowing what crime you are accused of, the right to confront the accuser in court, and freedom from unreasonable police searches. Difficulties in applying these abstract principles to concrete situations indicate how hard it is to define due process, especially in a way that protects civil liberties without jeopardizing order.

The difference between abstract principles of due process and their specific application also raises difficult political questions. Most people endorse the principle of "due process of law" and general ideas such as requiring that police legally obtain any evidence used in court. However, when the Court applies these principles to protect the rights of criminal defendants, there is a public outcry that too many suspects are going free on "legal technicalities" (such as having to inform a suspect of his or her right to talk to an attorney before being questioned by the police).

THE FOURTH AMENDMENT: UNREASONABLE SEARCHES AND SEIZURES

The Fourth Amendment says, "The right of the people to be secure in their persons, houses, papers, and effects, against unreasonable searches and seizures, shall not be violated." Over the years the Court provided strong protections against searches within a person's physical space, typically defined as his or her home. With the introduction of new technology—telephones and wiretapping, then more sophisticated listening and searching devices—the Court had to confront a broad array of complicated questions. It has attempted to achieve a balance between security and privacy by requiring court approval for search warrants, while carving out limited exceptions to this general rule.

SEARCHES AND WARRANTS

Under most circumstances a law enforcement official seeking a search warrant must provide the court with "personal knowledge" of a "probable cause" of specific criminal activity and outline the evidence that is the target of the search. Broad "fishing expeditions" for evidence are not allowed.

Police searches inherently involve a clash between public safety and the private freedom from government intrusions. These issues came to the fore with passage of the USA PATRIOT Act of 2001 after the terrorist attacks of September 11. Several of the most controversial parts of the act strengthen police surveillance powers; make it easier to conduct "sneak and peek" searches (the police enter a home with a warrant, look for evidence, and do not tell the suspect of their search until months later); broaden Internet surveillance; increase the government's access to library, banking, and medical records; and permit roving wiretaps for suspected terrorists.

The most common reason for police searches without warrants is consent of the suspect (the officers are not required to tell the suspect that he or she may say "no" or request a warrant). Other cases in which the Court allows a warrantless search include: conducting a search that happens at the time of a legal arrest and "is confined to the immediate vicinity of the arrest"; collecting evidence that was not included in the search warrant but is out in plain view; searching the passenger area and passengers of a car if the driver has been stopped for a traffic offense; and searching school lockers with probable cause.[64] The Supreme Court recently upheld strip searches after an arrest and before the suspect is put in jail even when there was no suspicion of illegal substances. Dissenting justices argued that "the humiliation of a visual strip-search" after being "arrested for driving with a noisy muffler, failing to use a turn signal and riding a bicycle without an audible bell" should not be allowed under the Fourth Amendment.[65]

The Court has generally made it easier for law enforcement officials to conduct searches without warrants, but one important decision in the other direction was a 2012 case that required a warrant to place a GPS tracking device on a vehicle. The FBI suspected Antoine Jones of selling cocaine, so they placed a tracking device on his vehicle without a warrant, monitored his movements for four weeks, and then used the evidence to convict him. Jones was sentenced to life in prison. While the Court required a warrant in this specific case, the basis for the majority's decision was fairly narrow: the placement of the device was a "physical trespass," and the lengthy monitoring of his movement constituted an illegal search.[66] Remote tracking without physical trespass or shorter term monitoring with a GPS device without a warrant may be acceptable to the Court. Additional cases will be required to sort this out.

If the police illegally obtain evidence, the need to balance security and privacy becomes concrete. Either the evidence is excluded from a criminal trial to protect privacy rights, or it is allowed in order to support conviction of the suspect.

THE EXCLUSIONARY RULE

In 1961 the Fourth Amendment was incorporated (applied to the states through the Fourteenth Amendment) in a case that established the **exclusionary rule** for all courts.[67] Previously, the rule had applied only at the national level. The rule

exclusionary rule The principle that illegally or unconstitutionally acquired evidence cannot be used in a criminal trial.

states that illegally obtained evidence cannot be used in a criminal trial. The landmark case involved police breaking into a woman's residence without a warrant looking for a suspect thought to be hiding there. The officers did not find him, but they did find illegal pornographic material. Although the woman was convicted of possessing it, the Court ultimately threw out the conviction.

Subsequent Courts started weakening the exclusionary rule. The public was concerned that too many criminals were being set free because of the limits on obtaining and using evidence, and most justices agreed. In 1974 the Court allowed the use of illegally obtained evidence in grand jury testimony.[68] Several years later it relaxed the general rule to allow the use of evidence if the "totality of circumstances" suggests that a police officer's action was justified.[69] The following year the Court established a "good faith exception" to the exclusionary rule, allowing evidence to be used as long as the officer believed that he or she had conducted a legal search. In the specific case the officer had a warrant that turned out to have errors on it, such as the wrong address.[70] The bottom line is that the exclusionary rule remains in effect, but lately it has become easier for prosecutors to use evidence obtained under questionable circumstances.

DRUG TESTING

Another area of Fourth Amendment law concerns drug testing. The clause granting people the right "to be secure in their persons" certainly seems to cover drug testing. However, the courts have long recognized the right of private companies to test their employees for illegal drugs, and testing for performance-enhancing drugs is increasingly common in professional sports.

What about drug testing by the state? The Court has upheld random drug testing for high school athletes and mandatory drug testing for any junior high or high school students involved in extracurricular activities.[71] Federal employees became subject to drug testing in 1986, with all employees required to refrain from using illegal drugs as a condition of federal employment, and with each agency required to implement drug testing for sensitive positions. Two years later the Drug-Free Workplace Act applied the same rule to all executive agencies, the uniformed services, and any service providers under contract with the federal government. Despite these prohibitions, drug testing of federal employees is actually limited to people who hold security clearances, carry firearms, or work in public safety or national security. Some employees receive random tests; others are tested only when they apply for a job, are involved in a workplace accident, or show signs of drug use.

The Court has upheld drug testing of public employees, with one exception. It struck down a Georgia law that would have required all candidates for state office to pass a drug test within 30 days of announcing a run for office because candidates are not public employees.[72] Rather than appealing to the courts, former senator Ernest Hollings of South Carolina had a different approach to avoid drug testing. When his opponent, Representative Tommy Hartnett, challenged him to take a drug test, the senator shot back, "I'll take a drug test if you take an I.Q. test."

DOMESTIC SURVEILLANCE POST-SEPTEMBER 11

The debate over the trade-off between civil liberties and security intensified in 2005 when a White House–approved domestic surveillance program was revealed. Since the September 11, 2001, attacks, the National Security Agency (NSA) had been monitoring the phone calls of many U.S. citizens who have had contact with suspected terrorists overseas. These calls were intercepted without the approval of the Foreign Intelligence Surveillance Court (FISA), which Congress created in 1978 for approving the interception of calls. A few months later in 2005, another NSA program aimed at creating a database of every phone call made within the borders of the United States was revealed. Phone companies AT&T, Verizon, and BellSouth reportedly had turned over records of millions of customers' phone calls to the government.[73] Critics warn that phone surveillance may be just the tip of the domestic surveillance iceberg because the government might be monitoring travel, credit card, and banking records more widely than we think.[74]

As you can imagine, the debate over domestic surveillance has generated intense disagreement. The idea that politics is everywhere may seem threatening if you are concerned about protecting your civil liberties, or it may seem reassuring if you are more concerned about national security. Either way, this issue will remain significant in your daily life for the foreseeable future.

THE FIFTH AMENDMENT: SELF-INCRIMINATION

The familiar phrase "I plead the Fifth" has been part of our criminal justice system since the Bill of Rights was ratified, ensuring that a suspect cannot be compelled to provide court testimony that would cause him or her to be prosecuted for a crime. However, what about outside a court of law? If a police officer coerces a confession out of a suspect, is that self-incrimination?

Such police interrogations were allowed until a landmark case in 1966. Ernesto Miranda had been convicted in an Arizona court of kidnapping and rape, on the basis of a confession extracted after two hours of questioning in which he was not read his rights. The Court overturned the conviction, saying that police interrogation "is inherently intimidating" and in these circumstances "no statement obtained from the defendant can truly be the product of his free choice."[75]

DEFENDANT	LOCATION

SPECIFIC WARNING REGARDING INTERROGATIONS

1. YOU HAVE THE RIGHT TO REMAIN SILENT.

2. ANYTHING YOU SAY CAN AND WILL BE USED AGAINST YOU IN A COURT OF LAW.

3. YOU HAVE THE RIGHT TO TALK TO A LAWYER AND HAVE HIM PRESENT WITH YOU WHILE YOU ARE BEING QUESTIONED.

4. IF YOU CANNOT AFFORD TO HIRE A LAWYER ONE WILL BE APPOINTED TO REPRESENT YOU BEFORE ANY QUESTIONING, IF YOU WISH ONE.

SIGNATURE OF DEFENDANT	DATE
WITNESS	TIME

☐ REFUSED SIGNATURE   SAN FRANCISCO POLICE DEPARTMENT   PR.9.1.4

THIS IS A TYPICAL EXAMPLE OF THE Miranda Warning card that police officers carry with them and read to a suspect after an arrest.

Miranda rights The list of civil
liberties described in the Fifth
Amendment that must be read to a
suspect before anything the suspect
says can be used in a trial.

To ensure a confession is truly a free choice, the Court established **Miranda
rights**. If police do not read a suspect these rights, nothing the suspect says can
be used in court.

Over time the Court has carved out exceptions to the *Miranda* rights requirement because the public has viewed the practice as "coddling criminals" and letting too many people go free on legal technicalities. However, in 2000 the Court
rejected Congress's attempt to overturn *Miranda* by designating all voluntary con-
fessions as legally admissible evidence. The Court ruled that it, not Congress, has
the power to determine constitutional protections for criminal defendants. The
justices also affirmed their intent to protect the *Miranda* rule, saying, "*Miranda*
has become embedded in routine police practice to the point where the warnings
have become part of our national culture."[76]

double jeopardy Being tried
twice for the same crime. This is
prevented by the Fifth Amendment.

Another Fifth Amendment right for defendants is protection against being
tried more than once for a particular crime. This **double jeopardy** prohibition
was extended to the states in 1969.[77] However, prosecutors can exploit two loopholes in this civil liberty: (1) a suspect may be tried in federal court and state court
for the same crime, and (2) if a suspect is found innocent of one set of *criminal*
charges brought by the state, he or she may still be found guilty of the same or similar offenses based on *civil* charges brought by a private individual.

The final part of the Fifth Amendment is at the heart of a legal debate over
property rights; the clause says, "nor shall private property be taken for public use,
without just compensation." For most of American history this civil liberty has
been noncontroversial. When the government needs private property for a public use such as a highway or a park, it may enforce "physical takings" by making a
property owner sell at a fair market value. But lately a controversial interpretation
of the "takings" clause has attempted to expand just compensation for "regulatory
takings" as well. For example, if the Endangered Species Act protects an animal
whose habitat is on your land, you would not be able to develop that property and
thus its market value would probably drop. Therefore, the argument goes, because
of this law the government has "taken" some of your land's value by protecting the
species, so the government should compensate you.

One key case ruled that if a regulation "deprives a property owner of all beneficial use of his property," the owner must receive compensation.[78] The issue
became especially controversial around a case involving a development project
in New London, Connecticut. A working-class neighborhood was sold to a private
developer to build a waterfront hotel, office space, and higher-end housing, but a
homeowner sued the city to stop the development. The Court supported the local
government, saying that "promoting economic development is a traditional and
long accepted function of government," so a "plausible public use" is satisfied.[79]
Ironically, after the homes had been moved or bulldozed, the developer failed to
get the necessary financing. As of this writing, the waterfront property remains
an empty lot.

THE SIXTH AMENDMENT: THE RIGHT TO LEGAL COUNSEL AND A JURY TRIAL

The right to an attorney is a key civil liberty, because the legal system is too complicated for a layperson to navigate. However, at one time poor people accused of
a felony had to defend themselves in court because they could not afford a lawyer

(except in death penalty cases, for which the state would provide a lawyer).[80] This changed in 1963 with *Gideon v. Wainwright*, when the Court overturned the conviction of a man who had been accused of breaking into a pool hall to steal beer, wine, and money. Unable to afford an attorney, Clarence Gideon defended himself—quite well, in fact, but the (false) testimony of the actual guilty party brought Gideon a conviction. Ultimately, the Court overturned it, saying, "In our adversary system of criminal justice, any person hauled into court who is too poor to hire a lawyer cannot be assured a fair trial unless counsel is provided for him."[81]

The right to an attorney has been strengthened over time, through both legislation and subsequent Court rulings. One year after *Gideon*, Congress passed the Criminal Justice Act, which provided better legal representation for criminal defendants in federal court; soon 23 states had taken similar action. The Court has defined a general right to *effective* counsel (although the bar is set low in defining *effective*) and recently mandated that defense attorneys must conduct any reasonable investigation into possible lines of defense when presenting evidence that could help the defendant.[82]

The Sixth Amendment also protects the right to a speedy and public trial by an impartial jury in criminal cases. The Court affirmed the right to a speedy trial in 1967,[83] and today under the Federal Speedy Trial Act a trial must begin within 70 days of the defendant's arrest or first appearance in court. In addition, a defendant may not waive the right to a speedy trial.[84] The most important disputes over the "impartial jury" issue concern jury selection and peremptory challenges, in which lawyers may eliminate certain people from the jury pool without providing any reason. Race and gender may not be the basis for a peremptory challenge.[85] The Court has also ruled that the right to a jury trial limits the way that judges can use sentencing guidelines.[86]

THE FIGHT AGAINST TERRORISM HAS raised controversial questions about due process rights. After the United States killed Anwar al-Awlaki—an Al Qaeda leader living in Yemen, and a U.S. citizen—critics argued that his due process rights, such as the right to a fair trial, had been violated.

THE EIGHTH AMENDMENT: CRUEL AND UNUSUAL PUNISHMENT

The Founders would be surprised by the intense debates over whether the Eighth Amendment prohibition against "cruel and unusual punishment" applies to the death penalty. Clearly, the death penalty was accepted in their time (even stealing a horse was a capital offense!), and the language of the Constitution reflects that. Both the Fifth and Fourteenth Amendments say that a person may not be deprived of "life, liberty, or property, without due process of law," which implies that someone *could* be deprived of life as long as the state follows due process. In the United States, 33 states still allow capital punishment. However, five states have abolished the death penalty since 2007, and dozens of other countries have done the same in recent years.

After being silent on this issue for nearly two centuries, in 1972 the Supreme Court ruled that the death penalty was unconstitutional because the process of applying it was inconsistent. Thereafter, Congress and 35 states rushed to make their laws compliant with the Court decision. The typical fix was to make explicit which crimes were punishable by death and to make capital sentencing a two-step process: first the determination of guilt or innocence, and then a sentencing phase after a guilty finding. Four years later the Court allowed states to bring back the death penalty.[87]

While never again challenging the death penalty, the Court has been chipping away at its edges for two decades. The Court has struck down state laws mandating the death penalty in murder cases and another law requiring it for rape. It has also prohibited the execution of insane prisoners and abolished the death penalty for the mildly retarded (2002), for juveniles (2005), and for child rapists (2008).[88]

One unsettled area of Eighth Amendment law concerns "proportionality"—the idea that some punishments may be so disproportionate to the crime that they constitute "cruel and unusual punishment." Recently, the Court has applied proportionality (disallowed these punishments) in the following situations: taking away citizenship as punishment for a crime,[89] incarceration for drug addiction,[90] beating of prison inmates,[91] and issuing a disproportionate prison sentence.[92] In the latter case the Court ruled that a life sentence without the possibility of parole for a seventh nonviolent felony (cashing a $100 check on a closed account) was unconstitutional.

In 1991, however, the Court began to limit application of the principle to cases with a "gross disproportionality," saying that "the Eighth Amendment contains no proportionality guarantee."[93] More recently, the Court ruled in two cases that California's "three strikes and you're out" law (which mandates very harsh sentences for third felony convictions) did not violate the Eighth Amendment. In the first case Gary Ewing stole three golf clubs, each valued at $399, and received 25 years to life. In the other case Leandro Andrade stole nine videotapes valued at $150 from two different K-Marts and received two consecutive terms of 25 years to life (because there were two crimes).[94] In each case the defendants' previous felony convictions were for nonviolent crimes.

PRIVACY RIGHTS

EXPLAIN WHY THE RIGHTS ASSOCIATED WITH PRIVACY ARE OFTEN CONTROVERSIAL

privacy rights Liberties protected by several amendments in the Bill of Rights that shield certain personal aspects of citizens' lives from governmental interference, such as the Fourth Amendment's protection against unreasonable searches and seizures.

You may be surprised to learn that the word *privacy* does not actually appear in the Constitution. **Privacy rights** were developed in a 1965 case that questioned the constitutionality of an 1879 Connecticut law against using birth control. Estelle Griswold, the director of Planned Parenthood in Connecticut, was arrested after opening a clinic that dispensed contraceptives. She was fined $100 and appealed her conviction all the way to the Supreme Court, which overturned it.

In a fractured decision the Court agreed that the law was outdated, but the justices agreed on little else. Even those who based their opinions on an implied constitutional right to privacy cited various constitutional roots: the First Amendment right of association, the Third's protection against the quartering of troops, the Fourth's prohibition against unreasonable searches and seizures, the Fifth's protection against self-incrimination, and the Ninth's statement, "The enumeration in the Constitution, of certain rights, shall not be construed to deny or disparage others retained by the people."[95] *Griswold* was significant for establishing the constitutional basis for a right to privacy, but the dissenters worried where this right would lead. Justice Black warned that privacy "is a broad, abstract and ambiguous concept" that could be shrunken or expanded in subsequent decisions as judges determine what is constitutional on the basis of their own appraisal of what laws are unwise or unnecessary.[96]

ABORTION RIGHTS

Eight years after *Griswold* the landmark ruling in *Roe v. Wade* struck down laws in 46 states that limited abortion. Twelve of those states allowed abortions for pregnancies due to rape or incest, to protect the life of the mother, and in cases of severe fetal handicap. The much-criticized trimester analysis in the *Roe* ruling said that states could not limit abortions in the first trimester; in the second trimester, states could regulate abortions in the interests of the health of the mother; and in the third trimester, states could forbid all abortions except those necessary to protect the health or life of the mother.[97]

Subsequent decisions have upheld *Roe* but endorsed various state restrictions on abortion, such as requiring parental consent, a waiting period, or counseling sessions aimed at convincing the woman not to have an abortion. Most significant, the trimester analysis of *Roe* has been replaced by a focus on fetal viability. When the fetus would be viable (generally at 22 or 23 weeks), states can ban abortions "except where it is necessary, in appropriate medical judgment, for the preservation of the life or health of the mother."[98]

Since *Roe*, most political action concerning abortion has taken place in the courts, but that could all change if the Supreme Court overturns this decision. Overturning *Roe* would shift the politics of abortion back to state legislatures and make it an even more highly contested political issue. One effort to force a challenge to *Roe* was a "personhood amendment" to the Mississippi constitution that defined life beginning at conception. However, the amendment was soundly defeated in a statewide vote in 2011.[99]

THE RIGHT TO DIE

Privacy rights have become central in debates over the right to die, in which two types of political issues arise. The first involves the right of a person who is brain dead or in a persistent vegetative state to refuse medical treatment so he or she may die. The second is more complicated: May states allow assisted suicide for people with terminal illnesses, even if that practice conflicts with federal law?

In terms of the first issue, courts have approved living wills in which a person documents specific wishes in advance about end-of-life medical care. The problem arises when a person who can no longer communicate has not left instructions on how much medical intervention to receive. Every month thousands of families have to make these decisions during the last few weeks of a patient's life, in consultation with their doctors. Most decisions are extremely difficult but without legal conflict. The high-profile case of Terri Schiavo illustrated how complicated the situation can get. After a heart failure that resulted in severe brain damage, Schiavo remained in a vegetative state from 1990 though 2005. Her husband said she would not have wanted to be kept alive in that condition, but Schiavo's parents wanted to keep her alive. After the Supreme Court refused to intervene, she was taken off life support at her husband's request. Given this precedent, the courts seem unlikely to get involved in matters traditionally resolved between a family and their doctor.

The assisted suicide issue applied to a case involving Oregon's Death with Dignity Act. This law allows a terminally ill patient to get a doctor's prescription to end his or her life. In the law's first 14 years, 596 people ended their lives through this procedure.[100] Only three states have such a law, and it has been highly controversial; Attorney General John Ashcroft attempted to revoke the medical licenses of doctors who prescribed the drugs. According to Ashcroft's interpretation of the federal Controlled Substances Act, use of prescription drugs in doctor-assisted suicide is not a "legitimate medical purpose" of the drugs and therefore is not allowed under the law. However, the Supreme Court upheld the Oregon law in 2006.[101]

GAY RIGHTS

Gay rights have typically been seen more as a civil right (that is, freedom from discrimination) than a civil liberty. However, a recent Court ruling established very broad privacy rights for sexual behavior. The case involved two Houston men who were prosecuted for same-sex sodomy after police entered one of the men's apartments—upon receiving a false tip about an armed man in an apartment complex—and found the two having sex. Under Texas law, sodomy was illegal for homosexuals but not for heterosexuals. In a landmark ruling the Court said that the liberty guaranteed by the Fourteenth Amendment's due process clause allows homosexuals to have sexual relations. "Freedom presumes an autonomy of self that includes freedom of thought, belief, expression, and certain intimate conduct."[102]

substantive due process doctrine One interpretation of the due process clause of the Fourteenth Amendment; in this view the Supreme Court has the power to overturn laws that infringe on individual liberties.

The reasoning in this case is rooted in the **substantive due process doctrine** that underlies the constitutional protections for birth control, abortion, and decisions about how to raise one's children. Five members of the majority signed on to the broad "due process" reasoning of the decision, while Justice O'Connor wrote a concurring opinion in which she agreed that the Texas law was unconstitutional but on narrower grounds. With the broader due process logic, 13 state laws that banned sodomy were struck down.

OPPONENTS OF THE MILITARY'S "DON'T ask, don't tell" policy argued that it infringed on the rights and liberties of gay and lesbian service members, in part because they could be dismissed based on their private sexual behavior. The policy was repealed in 2011.

While privacy rights may not be as firmly grounded in the Constitution as the freedom of speech or religion, this evolving area of the law has provided important protections for millions of Americans. These civil liberties also remain among the most controversial political issues in our nation, contributing to our observation that politics is conflictual.

///

CONCLUSION

Every day you are likely affected by your civil liberties, whether when speaking in a public place, attending church, being searched at an airport, participating in a political demonstration, writing or reading an article in your school newspaper, or being free from illegal police searches in your home. Because civil liberties are defined as those things the government *cannot* do to us, defining our civil liberties is a political process. Often this process is confined to the courts; but on many issues—including free speech, freedom of the press, pornography, criminal rights, abortion, and gun control—these debates take place in the broader political world where the process involves balancing competing interests and drawing lines by interpreting and applying the law. For example, debates over how to balance national security and civil liberties—whether newspapers should publish stories about classified programs that may threaten civil liberties; whether government surveillance powers should be strengthened to fight terrorism—will rage for years to come. Other cases, such as this chapter's opening story of homophobic protests at military funerals, illustrate how difficult and politically unpopular it can be to protect our freedoms and liberty. As with all political questions, the evolving nature of our civil liberties is sure to generate more political conflict. But that process affirms the essence of our political system.

STUDY *guide*

DEFINING CIVIL LIBERTIES

▶ Define "civil liberties," and explain how the Bill of Rights came to apply to the states. **Pages 91–97**

SUMMARY

The Bill of Rights—the first ten amendments to the Constitution—lists individual protections from the federal government. For the majority of the nineteenth century these individual freedoms were only guaranteed from the *federal* government and did not extend to protections from *state* governments. With the ratification of the Fourteenth Amendment and the process of selective incorporation, federal freedoms have been gradually extended to the state level.

KEY TERMS

Civil War Amendments (p. 95)

due process clause (p. 95)

selective incorporation (p. 97)

PRACTICE QUIZ QUESTIONS

1. The Bill of Rights originally protected individuals from which level of government?
   a) all levels of American government
   b) state governments
   c) local governments
   d) federal government
   e) the bureaucracy

2. Which amendment has been used as the basis for selective incorporation?
   a) Eighth Amendment
   b) Fourteenth Amendment
   c) Tenth Amendment
   d) Nineteenth Amendment
   e) Fifth Amendment

FREEDOM OF SPEECH, ASSEMBLY, AND THE PRESS

▶ Describe the major First Amendment rights related to freedom of speech. **Pages 97–104**

SUMMARY

The Court's attempt to balance individual freedoms and the public good is evident in the scope of protections guaranteed by the First Amendment. The Court generally prioritizes protecting individual rights to political speech, hate speech, symbolic speech, the freedom to assemble, and the freedom of the press unless under extreme circumstances (such as speech that poses a direct incitement to violence). By contrast, the Court regularly places a lower priority on, and affords far less protection to, fighting words, slander, libel, and commercial speech.

KEY TERMS

strict scrutiny (p. 98)

intermediate scrutiny (p. 98)

clear and present danger test (p. 99)

direct incitement test (p. 99)

symbolic speech (p. 100)

hate speech (p. 100)

prior restraint (p. 101)

fighting words (p. 102)

slander (p. 103)

libel (p. 103)

commercial speech (p. 103)

Miller **test** (p. 104)

CRITICAL THINKING AND DISCUSSION:

Do you support complete freedom of speech for the most despicable group you can think of? When should speech be limited, if at all?

PRACTICE QUIZ QUESTIONS

3. Which test does the Court use to determine if speech is considered dangerous and should not be legally protected?
   a) *Lemon* test
   b) clear and present danger test
   c) *Miller* test
   d) direct incitement test
   e) balancing test

4. Flag burning is an example of _____ that is currently _____ under the First Amendment.
   a) symbolic speech; protected
   b) symbolic speech; not protected
   c) hate speech; protected
   d) hate speech; not protected
   e) offensive slander; not protected

5. Prior restraint involves limits on what form of expression?
   a) freedom of assembly
   b) freedom of association
   c) freedom of speech
   d) freedom of the press
   e) freedom of religion

Ⓢ **PRACTICE ONLINE**

"Critical Thinking" exercise: *Politics Is Conflictual—Free Speech and Flag Burning*

FREEDOM OF RELIGION

▶ Describe the First Amendment rights related to freedom of religion. **Pages 104–09**

SUMMARY

Religious freedoms are defined by two clauses in the First Amendment: the establishment clause and the free association clause. Together, they do not allow the government to do anything to benefit any particular religion, nor is it allowed to do anything to hinder religious practice. As is often the case, the Court has struggled to precisely define exactly what constitutes "excessive government entanglement" in religion.

KEY TERMS

establishment clause (p. 104)

free exercise clause (p. 104)

Lemon **test** (p. 105)

CRITICAL THINKING AND DISCUSSION:

Has the Supreme Court balanced protection for the free exercise of religion without allowing the state establishment of religion, or has the Court swung too far in one direction? Which rulings support your conclusion?

PRACTICE QUIZ QUESTIONS

6. The establishment clause is invoked under which of the following circumstances?
   a) allowing "conscientious objectors" to avoid the military draft
   b) outlawing polygamy
   c) prayer in public schools
   d) allowing the Amish to keep children home from school after eighth grade
   e) banning the handling of snakes in church services

7. Which test does the Supreme Court use to establish whether there has been "excessive government entanglement with religion?"
   a) *Lemon* test
   b) *Kreutz* test
   c) *Miller* test
   d) *Meyer* test
   e) *Brandenburg* test

THE RIGHT TO BEAR ARMS

▶ Explore why the Second Amendment's meaning on gun rights is often debated. **Pages 109–10**

SUMMARY

The Supreme Court has done little to define exactly what freedoms are established in the Second Amendment, largely preferring to allow the national, state, and local governments the autonomy to make their own laws. The majority of public sentiment appears in favor of continued gun ownership, and limitations on Second Amendment rights appear unlikely.

PRACTICE QUIZ QUESTIONS

8. Until 2008, the Supreme Court had been _____ in defining Second Amendment laws, and its decisions generally _____ gun rights.
    a) passive; limited
    b) passive; supported
    c) active; limited
    d) active; supported

LAW, ORDER, AND THE RIGHTS OF CRIMINAL DEFENDANTS

▶ Describe the protections provided for people accused of a crime. **Pages 110–16**

SUMMARY

The Fourth, Fifth, Sixth, and Eighth Amendments provide protections to individuals accused of a crime, known as due process rights. These rights protect us from unreasonable searches and seizures, permit us to avoid testifying against ourselves in court, give us the right to a lawyer and jury trial, and protect us from suffering cruel and unusual punishment if convicted of a crime. Interpreting these general due process rights in specific cases is difficult, however, because specific standards of fairness and justice are very hard to define.

KEY TERMS

due process rights (p. 110)

exclusionary rule (p. 111)

Miranda **rights** (p. 114)

double jeopardy (p. 114)

CRITICAL THINKING AND DISCUSSION:

Do you support due process rights for defendants in criminal cases, even if it means that some potentially guilty people go free? If so, why? If not, are you concerned about convicting innocent people?

PRACTICE QUIZ QUESTIONS

9. Protections from unreasonable searches and seizures are guaranteed by which constitutional amendment?
    a) Third Amendment
    b) Fourth Amendment
    c) Fifth Amendment
    d) Seventh Amendment
    e) Eighth Amendment

10. The *Miranda* rights are protections that fall under which constitutional amendment?
    a) Third Amendment
    b) Fourth Amendment
    c) Fifth Amendment
    d) Seventh Amendment
    e) Eighth Amendment

11. In 1972 the Supreme Court banned the death penalty for what reason?
    a) It deprived individuals of their rights to "life, liberty or property."

b) It was cruel and unusual.

c) It was being inconsistently applied.

d) It was racially biased.

e) It was inconsistent with international law.

⑤ PRACTICE ONLINE

"Big Think" video exercise: *Problems with the War on Terror*

PRIVACY RIGHTS

▶ Explain why the rights associated with privacy are often controversial. **Pages 116–19**

SUMMARY

The term *privacy rights* is not found in the Constitution—rather, it was established in a 1965 Supreme Court case—but it may be implied in several amendments to the Bill of Rights. The right to privacy is controversial because of the lack of explicit language in the Constitution and the lack of consensus on exactly what the right to privacy means. It has remained a hot-button issue because recognition of the right to privacy is an important facet of the contemporary debate on abortion.

KEY TERMS

privacy rights (p. 116)

substantive due process doctrine (p. 118)

PRACTICE QUIZ QUESTIONS

12. Which of the following freedoms guaranteed in the Bill of Rights is thought to imply a right to privacy?

a) right to bear arms

b) protection against unreasonable searches

c) right to secure legal counsel

d) right to request a jury trial

e) freedom of speech

13. In what case did the Supreme Court establish the right to privacy?

a) *Roe v. Wade*

b) *Lawrence v. Texas*

c) *Griswold v. Connecticut*

d) *Gonzalez v. Oregon*

e) *Lemon v. Kurtzman*

⑤ PRACTICE ONLINE

"Critical Thinking" exercise: *Political Process Matters—Civil Liberties and Privacy*

SUGGESTED READING

Abraham, Henry J., and Barbara A. Perry. *Freedom and the Court: Civil Rights and Liberties in the United States*, 8th ed. Lawrence: University Press of Kansas, 2003.

Amar, Akhil Reed. *The Bill of Rights*. New Haven, CT: Yale University Press, 1998.

Bondenhamer, David J., and James W. Ely, eds. *The Bill of Rights in Modern America*. Bloomington: Indiana University Press, 2008.

Lewis, Anthony. *Gideon's Trumpet*. New York: Random House, 1964.

Moynihan, Daniel Patrick. *Secrecy: The American Experience*. New Haven, CT: Yale University Press, 1998.

Posner, Richard A. *Not a Suicide Pact: The Constitution in a Time of National Emergency*. New York: Oxford University Press, 2006.

Pritchett, C. Herman. *Constitutional Civil Liberties*. Englewood Cliffs, NJ: Prentice Hall, 1984.

Schweber, Howard. *Speech, Conduct, and the First Amendment*. New York: Peter Lang Publishing, 2003.

5

Public Opinion and the Media

SHOULD SAME-SEX COUPLES BE allowed to marry? Americans are almost evenly split on this question, making it difficult to find a compromise. However, public opinion also changes over time, so an issue that is sharply divisive today may become easier to resolve as opinions shift.

AMERICANS ARE SHARPLY DIVIDED ON THE QUESTION OF WHETHER TO allow gay and lesbian couples to marry: a 2012 Pew Trust poll found that 48 percent of Americans support same-sex marriage, while 44 percent are opposed.[1] Moreover, there is a sharp partisan split in opinions, as 65 percent of Democrats are supportive of same-sex marriage rights, while only 24 percent of Republicans feel the same way. Similar divisions can be found in many other areas, from opinions about specific policies such as President Obama's health care reforms to broader questions such as whether America is divided into "haves" and "have nots."[2]

Such polling date gives rise to two questions. First, can common ground be found given the apparently profound disagreements? Some people look at opinion data on issues such as same-sex marriage and see a "culture war" in which Americans are divided into opposing camps across a range of issues, with secular Democrats facing off against religious Republicans.[3] We have said throughout this book that politics is conflictual and that compromise is often necessary to get anything done in Washington, D.C. But if most Americans hold extreme positions on many policy questions and are unwilling to compromise, it is hard to see how politicians can get anything done, unless they are willing to offend large segments of the population—and risk losing their positions in the next election. Moreover, when Americans are divided, as in the case of single-sex marriage, it may be impossible to find a policy option that satisfies even a majority of the population, so no matter what politicians do, majority dissatisfaction is virtually guaranteed.

CONFLICT & COMPROMISE
in American Politics

A second question concerns the quality of public opinion in America. Candidates, political parties, journalists, and political scientists take thousands of polls to determine who is likely to vote; what sorts of arguments, slogans, and platforms would appeal to these voters; and which policies are in demand by the electorate. Yet some scholars have argued that most Americans make up their responses to survey questions on the spot, have no firm opinions about government policy, and are easily swayed by candidates, advocacy groups, or the media.[4] In other words, what do people mean when they say they support marriage rights for gays and lesbians? What does it mean when people say they are opposed?

This chapter shows that Americans hold measurable opinions on a wide range of topics and that these opinions shape their political behavior. The fact that most people can express a wide range of opinions about politics and public policy is one of the strongest pieces of evidence for the idea that politics is everywhere. We examine the sources of public opinion, from everyday events to what politicians say and do, to biological explanations as well as group characteristics such as race, gender, and ethnicity. We consider how politicians take account of public opinion—how their campaign strategies, as well as their actions in office (in particular, their willingness to compromise policy differences), are shaped by information about what the public wants or might want in the future.

The case of gay marriage also illustrates one way that these conflicts are resolved, which is by "generational replacement." Many polis have found a gradual shift in American public opinion over the last generation toward support for single-sex marriage. In the main, this shift is the result of the replacement of older Americans, who tend to oppose gay marriage, by younger Americans, who are much more likely to support this policy. If this trend continues, citizen support for single-sex marriage will gradually increase, leading additional states to adopt legislation or referenda to allow single-sex marriage. These shifts in opinion also make it much less likely that Congress will enact legislation or a constitutional amendment to ban such marriages.

As you will see, process matters in the way individual opinions are formed and the methods used to measure public opinion. These processes shape what people demand from government and how politicians respond to those demands. While most Americans are not policy experts, they tend to think about politics in the same way that they think about most things in their lives. Aside from a few broad principles, such as party identification, that typically form early in life, opinions take form only when they are needed, such as when people vote on Election Day or answer a survey question. In other words, relatively few Americans form concrete opinions about issues such as same-sex marriage until they are asked about the policy in a survey. This process of opinion formation has important consequences for how we should interpret survey results.

Finally, examining American public opinion allows us to identify issues where Americans disagree on policy questions and to better understand the political conflicts they raise. We will also see that although Americans disagree about many important issues, *profound* polarization (such as in current polls on same-sex marriage) is relatively rare, meaning that compromise is sometimes easier to reach than you might think. When polls are designed to tap consensus, they reveal that on a wide range of policy questions, most Americans hold opinions that are squarely in the middle of the political spectrum. Thus, there is little evidence of a "culture war" in American politics. Although much of this chapter details how Americans disagree, and the generational and demographic sources of these splits, it is important to remember that disagreement does not always exist, and when it does, acceptable compromises often can be found.

ARE AMERICANS POORLY INFORMED about politics? One survey found that more Americans could identify characters on *The Simpsons* than could list which liberties the Bill of Rights guarantees, and another found most respondents unable to name any Supreme Court justices.

WHAT IS PUBLIC OPINION?

DEFINE *PUBLIC OPINION*, AND EXPLAIN WHY IT MATTERS IN AMERICAN POLITICS

Public opinion describes what the population thinks about politics and government—what government should be doing, evaluations of what government *is* doing, and judgments about elected officials and others who participate in the political process—as well as the wider set of beliefs that shape these opinions.

Public opinion matters for three reasons.

First, citizens' political actions—including voting, contributing to campaigns, writing letters to senators, and undertaking other kinds of activism—are driven by their opinions.[5] Therefore, if we want to explain either an individual's behavior or broader political outcomes, such as who wins an election or the fate of a legislative proposal, we need good data on public opinion.

Second, examining public opinion helps explain the behavior of candidates, political parties, and other political actors. Politicians look to public opinion to determine what citizens want them to do and how happy citizens are with their behavior in office.

Third, because public opinion is a key to understanding what motivates citizens and political officials, it can shed light on the reasons for specific policy outcomes. For example, changes in the policy mood—the public's demand for new policies— are linked to changes in government spending.[6] When people want government to do more, spending increases more rapidly; when people want less from government, spending goes down (or increases more slowly). Thus, to explain what government does and why, we need to measure and understand public opinion.

public opinion Citizens' views on politics and government actions.

DESCRIBING PUBLIC OPINION

Modern theories of public opinion distinguish between two types of opinions. The first are broad expressions such as how a person thinks about politics, what he or she wants from government, or principles that apply across a range of issues. These kinds of beliefs typically form early in life and remain stable over

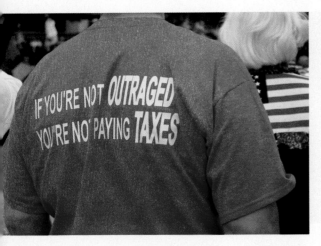

A PERSON'S IDEOLOGICAL PERSPECTIVE is relatively stable over time. People who have a conservative ideology generally oppose increasing government spending and taxes.

time. Some of these beliefs are obviously political, such as party identification, ideology (liberal or conservative), and judgments about whether elected officials lose touch with citizens. The second, more specific type of opinion, such as beliefs about homosexuality or religion, may seem irrelevant to politics, but in fact a wide range of seemingly nonpolitical beliefs directly shape Americans' political opinions.

As noted, broad beliefs that people form early in life are relatively stable. Consider liberal–conservative ideology: the best way to predict an American's ideology at age 40 is to assume it will match his or her ideology at age 20. The same is true for party identification. However, even fundamental opinions like these sometimes change in response to events. For example, although party identification often persists throughout an individual's life, it can change as new issues arise or when candidates' positions contradict a citizen's notion of the differences between parties.[7] In a later section we look more closely at how such opinions form and why they change.

MANY OPINIONS ARE LATENT

One important thing to understand about public opinion is that although ideology and party identification are largely consistent over time, they are exceptions to the rule.[8] The average person does not maintain a set of fully formed opinions on all political topics. Instead, most Americans' political judgments are **latent opinions**: they are constructed only as needed, such as when answering a survey question or deciding just before Election Day how to vote. For example, when an individual is first asked about his opinions on global warming, he will probably not have a specific response in mind because he has not thought much about the question. His opinions on global warming become more concrete only when he has to describe them.

latent opinion An opinion formed on the spot, when it is needed (as distinct from a deeply held opinion that is stable over time).

People who follow politics closely have more preformed opinions than the average American, whose interest in politics is relatively low. But very few people are so well informed that they have ready opinions on a wide range of political questions. Moreover, even when people do form opinions in advance, they may not remember every factor that influenced their opinions. Thus an individual may identify as a liberal or a conservative, or as a supporter of a particular party, but may be unable to explain the reasons behind these ideological leanings.[9]

HOW PEOPLE FORM OPINIONS

considerations The many pieces of information a person uses to form an opinion.

When people form opinions on the spot, they are based on **considerations**, which are the pieces of relevant information—such as ideology, party identification, religious beliefs, and personal circumstances—that come to mind when the opinion is requested.[10] The process of forming an opinion usually is not thorough or systematic, since most people don't take into account everything they know about an issue.[11] Rather, they only use considerations that come to mind immediately.[12] Highly informed people who follow politics use this process, as do those with low levels of political interest and knowledge.[13]

Many studies of public opinion support the idea that most people form opinions on the spot using a wide range of considerations. Consider the following research findings: Attitudes about immigration are shaped by evaluations of the state of the economy.[14] People judge government spending proposals differently depending on whether a Republican or a Democrat made the proposal, using their own party identification as a consideration.[15] Evaluations of affirmative action programs vary depending on whether the survey question reminds respondents that such programs might hurt their own economic well-being.[16] Voters' party identification and ideology influence their evaluations of candidates.[17] Individuals' willingness to allow protests and other expressions of opinions they disagree with depends on their belief in tolerance.[18] And if people feel obligated to help others in need, they are more likely to support government programs that benefit the poor.[19] As all these examples show, diverse considerations play a significant role in influencing citizens' political opinions.

IMAGES OF CONFRONTATION BETWEEN pro-choice and pro-life protesters may conceal the more nuanced considerations that underlie most Americans' opinions about abortion. Most Americans believe that the decision to have an abortion should be left up to the woman but are uncomfortable allowing unrestricted access to the procedure.

Sometimes, competing or contradictory considerations influence the opinion-formation process. In the case of abortion laws, many people believe in protecting human life but also in allowing women to make their own medical decisions.[20] When a survey asks someone with both beliefs for her opinion about abortion laws, her response will depend on which consideration comes to mind and seems most relevant as she is answering the question. Opinions about other morally complex issues such as right-to-die legislation, or about race-related issues such as affirmative action, also often involve competing considerations.[21]

Even events can become considerations. For example, following the September 11 attacks, researchers began surveying Americans about their fears of another terrorist attack. For example, every time a terrorist attack occurred in the next few years, regardless of its location, the percentage of Americans answering that they were "very worried" about a future attack rose significantly. What other events can you think of that have galvanized American public opinion?

SOURCES OF OPINIONS

EXPLAIN HOW PEOPLE FORM POLITICAL ATTITUDES AND OPINIONS

There are numerous sources of public opinion. Some arise from early life experiences, such as exposure to the beliefs of parents, relatives, or teachers; others result from later life events. Politicians and other political actors also play a critical role in the opinion-formation process.

SOCIALIZATION: FAMILIES AND COMMUNITIES

Theories of **political socialization** show that many people's political opinions start with what they learned from their parents, including liberal–conservative ideology, level of trust in others, class identity, and ethnic identity.[22] Although people

political socialization The process by which an individual's political opinions are shaped by other people and the surrounding culture.

CHILDREN TEND TO ADOPT THEIR parents' ideology and party affiliation. Senator Rand Paul (right) and his father, the presidential candidate and House member Ron Paul, are both Republicans and share a libertarian ideology.

sometimes respond to events by modifying their opinions, for many individuals the ideas learned during childhood shape their political opinions throughout their lives.[23]

Beyond the influence of parents and family, research finds broader aspects of socialization that shape political opinions. Consider the following five examples: People are socialized by their communities—by the people they interact with while growing up, such as neighbors, teachers, clergy, and others.[24] Support for democracy as a system of government and for American political institutions is higher for individuals who take a civics class in high school.[25] Growing up in a homogenous community, where many people share the same cultural, ethnic, or political beliefs, increases an adult's sense of civic duty—his belief that voting or other forms of political participation are important social obligations.[26] Volunteering in community organizations as a child shapes political beliefs and participation in later life.[27] Engaging in political activity as a teenager, such as volunteering in a presidential campaign, generates higher levels of political interest as an adult; it also strengthens the belief that people should care about politics and participate in political activities.[28] As indicated by the range of activities and interactions summarized here, many aspects of socialization can influence one's political outlook.

EVENTS

Although socialization often influences individuals' fairly stable core beliefs, public opinion is not fixed. All kinds of events—from everyday interactions to traumatic, life-changing disasters—can capture a person's attention and cause her to revise her understanding of politics and the role of government. For example, though an individual's initial partisan affiliation likely reflects her parents' leanings, it may change in response to subsequent events such as who runs for office, what platforms they campaign on, and their performance in office—especially if those factors affect the individual directly.[29]

Some events that shape beliefs are specific, individual experiences. For example, someone who believes that he managed to get a college degree only because of government grants and guaranteed student loans might favor a large, activist government that provides numerous benefits to its citizens. Other events affect large numbers of people. Political realignments are a good example. A realignment is a nationwide shift in which many people move from identifying with one political party to identifying with another (see Chapter 6). Beginning in the early 1960s, large numbers of white southerners shifted their party identification from Democratic to Republican. This gradual change was driven by national events, including support of civil rights and voting rights legislation by many Democratic officials in Washington, D.C.[30]

Recent events also shape beliefs. After the September 11 terrorist attacks, many citizens became more willing to restrict civil liberties to reduce the chances of future attacks.[31] Support for restrictions remained elevated 10 years later, suggesting a long-term change in public opinion.[32] Less specific events such as changes in the economy hold a similar sway over opinions, such as presidential approval. Presidents are more likely to have high approval ratings when economic growth is high and inflation and unemployment are low, whereas their ratings fall when growth is sluggish or negative and unemployment and inflation are high. Many of these factors also shape attachments to political parties.[33]

Finally, the reaction to events depends on how political information is disseminated. A study of public opinion on the death penalty found that opposition increased as media coverage of death penalty cases began to deemphasize moral arguments and focused instead on the possibility that innocent people were being mistakenly executed.[34] We discuss this phenomenon, known as framing, later in the chapter.

GROUP IDENTITY

Other influences on an individual's opinions are social categories or groups, such as gender, race, and education level. These characteristics might shape opinions in three ways. The first two ways relate to the fact that individuals learn about politics from the people around them. Therefore, those who live in the same region or who were born in the same era might have similar beliefs because (1) they experienced the same historical events at similar points in their lives or (2) they learned political viewpoints from one another. In the United States, opinions on many issues are highly correlated with the state or region where a person grew up.[35]

Third, individuals may rely on others who "look like" them as a source of opinions. Some political scientists, for example, argue that group identities shape partisanship: when a person decides between being a Republican or a Democrat, she thinks about which demographic groups are associated with each party and picks the party that has more members from the groups she feels she is a part of.[36]

One reason for looking at group variations in public opinion is that candidates and political consultants often formulate their campaign strategies in terms of groups. For example, analyses of the 2008 election argued that Barack Obama's presidential win and the Democratic gains in t-he House and Senate were driven by high levels of support from young Americans, African Americans, and people with advanced degrees. Similarly, Democratic losses in 2009 and 2010 special elections were the result of lower turnout among the same groups and strong

support for Republican candidates by people who live in suburbs and those with strong religious beliefs.[37]

Table 5.1 reports data on the variation in opinions across different groups of Americans. These data reveal two important facts about group affiliations and public opinion. First, there are sharp differences among groups on some questions. For example, people of different education levels tended to respond very differently to the question about interpreting the Bible literally. Second, in some respects the data show considerable consensus. There is little variation between men and women on the role of women in politics, although relatively sharp regional and educational differences are apparent. Moreover, no one group holds strong views on all three issues. For example, opinions on the Bible vary with respondents' education level, but this characteristic shows only a weak correlation with respondents' opinions about income redistribution.

These data indicate that group characteristics can be important predictors of some of an individual's opinions, but they are not the whole story.[38] Americans' opinions are a product of their socialization and life experiences as well as their group characteristics.

POLITICIANS AND OTHER POLITICAL ACTORS

Opinions and changes in opinion are also subject to influence by politicians and other political actors (such as political parties and party leaders, interest groups, and leaders of religious, civic, and other large organizations). In part, this link exists because Americans look to these individuals for information due to their presumed expertise. For example, if you do not know what to think about health care reform, you might seek out someone who knows more about the issues than you do; if her opinions seem reasonable, you might adopt them as your own.[39] Of course, most people only take account of an expert's opinions when they generally agree with the expert—perhaps because they hold matching conservative or liberal views, or because they have some other basis for thinking their preferences match the expert's.

Politicians and other political actors also work to shape public opinion. Some political scientists argue that politicians describe proposals through arguments and images designed to tap the public's strong opinions, with the goal of winning support for these proposals.[40] While President Obama and his staff expended much effort to promote health care reform, giving dozens of speeches, holding rallies, and briefing legislators, opponents managed to shape many Americans' opinions by making dire pronouncements of the proposal's potentially negative outcomes.[41] Even though health care reform was eventually enacted, these opposition efforts turned initial majority public support into a dead heat and very nearly defeated the proposal.

In sum, public opinion at the individual level is driven by many factors—so many that it is often difficult to explain why an individual holds one belief rather than another. This difficulty partly explains why, when interpreting pubic opinion data, political scientists often focus on average opinions for groups or for the entire nation.

POLITICIANS ON BOTH SIDES OF THE debate tried to influence public opinion about health care reform. While Obama and the Democrats sought to convince Americans that the new plan was necessary, opponents played up the possible disadvantages, with references to "death panels" and other dangers.

RESPONDING TO PUBLIC OPINION ON GAYS AND LESBIANS IN THE MILITARY

As we discuss in Chapter 9, elected officials in America work hard to cast votes and take other actions that their constituents will like. At first glance, this behavior seems easy. All a politician needs to do is take a poll, measure public opinion in her state or district, and comply with the demands expressed in the survey responses.

Actually, it is not easy for a representative to find out what her constituents want, because public opinion is hard to measure. Everything you have learned in this chapter suggests that taking a poll doesn't necessarily tell the whole story. Poll results need interpretation and may not provide clear guidance to elected officials.

Consider public opinion on allowing gays and lesbians to serve in the military. Suppose a member of the House represents a district where public opinion on this issue is the same as the national data in Table 5.2 (p. 137). Also assume that this representative wants to mirror district opinion to gain political support and stay in office. What sort of guide does the survey data provide to the representative?

The first problem is that the survey provides different guidance depending on which question the representative looks at. As we discuss in this chapter, small differences in question wording can produce large changes in responses. Our representative could find data showing support for several different interpretations—that her district is sharply divided or that it is in favor of changing the policy.

These data reveal two problems with reading public opinion for guidance. In many cases, opinions are sensitive to question wording, so a representative cannot be sure that survey results are indicative of actual feelings or are an artifact of how the questions were asked. Moreover, since opinions are typically formed on the spot, based on relatively little information, even if the survey questions were not changed, opinions might look very different if a survey was taken a day, a month, or a year later, as people take account of new or different information. The problem is not that the people who conduct surveys try to bias their results—rather, the difficulty in measuring public opinion stems from how Americans think about politics and respond to survey questions.

For these reasons, voting in line with polls may not be politically advantageous. A representative who did so might find later find that the poll's results were shaped by question wording, and that her constituents actually preferred a different policy and a different vote—or that opinions shifted between the time she voted and the next election because people changed how they formed their opinions on the issue. And, as we discussed earlier, when opinions are changing, as they are in the case of gay marriage, a poll taken at one point in time may not be a good guide to public opinion a short time afterward.

Polls on the military's "Don't Ask, Don't Tell" policy reported very different findings, making it difficult to know what the public really thought. The policy was eventually repealed, enabling gay men and lesbians to serve openly.

These findings create a quandary for elected officials: even if they want to vote in accordance with constituent opinion, these opinions are hard to measure and may change over time for a variety of reasons. But representatives must vote, even when they are not sure what their constituents want. How should they vote? You decide.

Critical **Thinking Questions**

1. Looking though this chapter, do you see cases where you think opinion surveys provide an accurate picture of public opinion?

2. What advice would you give representatives on the limits of polling and how to read survey findings?

TABLE » 5.1

THE IMPORTANCE OF GROUPS

		"THE BIBLE IS THE ACTUAL WORD OF GOD AND IS TO BE TAKEN LITERALLY, WORD FOR WORD." (PERCENTAGE WHO AGREE)	"MEN ARE BETTER SUITED [THAN WOMEN] FOR POLITICS." (PERCENTAGE WHO AGREE)	"GOVERNMENT SHOULD REDUCE THE INCOME DIFFERENCES BETWEEN THE RICH AND THE POOR." (PERCENTAGE WHO STRONGLY AGREE)
Gender	Male	28%	32%	17%
	Female	39	31	22
Age	18–30	31%	27%	18%
	31–40	35	26	18
	41–55	34	39	19
	Over 55	36	42	21
Education	High school	38%	30%	18%
	Bachelor's degree	17	23	9
	Advanced degree	11	17	11
Race	White	30%	31%	16%
	African American	56	31	33
	Other	36	31	26
Family income	Less than $15,000	43%	35%	39%
	$15,000–$20,000	37	33	24
	$20,000–$25,000	31	29	49
	More than $25,000	17	25	18
Region	New England	17%	23%	16%
	Middle Atlantic	31	29	21
	Midwest	32	31	20
	South	52	43	19
	Mountain	29	25	15
	Pacific	23	27	17

Source: Data from 2010 General Social Survey, http://sda.berkeley.edu/archive.htm (accessed 9/15/12).

DESCRIBE BASIC SURVEY METHODS AND POTENTIAL ISSUES AFFECTING ACCURACY

MEASURING PUBLIC OPINION

For the most part, information about public opinion comes from **mass surveys**—that is, face-to-face or telephone interviews with hundreds or thousands of voters. A mass survey seeks to measure the attitudes of a particular

population, or group of people, such as the residents of a specific congressional district, evangelicals, senior citizens, or even the nation's entire adult population. For large groups such as these, it would be impossible to survey everyone. So surveys typically involve **samples** of between a few hundred and several thousand individuals.

MASS SURVEYS

One of the principal attractions of mass surveys is that they can in theory provide very accurate estimates of public opinion for a large population by using relatively small samples (see Nuts and Bolts 5.1). For example, while polls taken very early in a presidential campaign (such as a year in advance of the general election) are poor predictors of the ultimate outcome, polls taken after the campaign has gotten started, when both party's nominees are known, provide very good predictions of who will win the election and how many votes that candidate will receive.[42]

Large-scale surveys such as the American National Election Study (NES), conducted every election year, use various types of questions to measure citizens' opinions. In presidential election years, participants in the NES are first asked whether they voted for president. If they say yes, they are asked which candidate they voted for: a major party candidate (Barack Obama or Mitt Romney in 2012), an independent candidate, or some other candidate.

Another kind of survey question uses an issue scale. For example, respondents might be asked about the government's role in protecting morality or their own liberal–conservative ideology. Two opposing statements are given for each topic, and respondents are asked to agree with the one that comes closest to their views, including options in the middle of the two extremes.

A typical survey includes a hundred or so questions asking respondents to evaluate issues and candidates, along with questions about the respondents' age, education, and marital status. Some surveys conducted by candidates or political parties are shorter, focusing on voter evaluations of specific candidates and the reasons for these evaluations. In the main, the length of a survey reflects the fact that interviewing people is expensive, so there is a trade-off between learning more about each respondent's opinions and maximizing the number of respondents. The fewer questions asked, the more people can be interviewed.

PROBLEMS IN MEASURING PUBLIC OPINION

While measuring public opinion seems an easy task—just find some people and ask them questions—it is actually very complicated. The problems begin with gathering an appropriate sample and are compounded with issues such as question wording and the nature of public opinion itself. As a result, survey results must be read carefully, taking into account who the respondents are, what opinions they are being asked to give, when they are being surveyed, and what mechanism is used to ask the survey questions.

mass survey A way to measure public opinion by interviewing a large sample of the population.

population The group of people that a researcher or pollster wants to study, such as evangelicals, senior citizens, or Americans.

sample Within a population, the group of people surveyed in order to gauge the whole population's opinion. Researchers use samples because it would be impossible to interview the entire population.

SAMPLING ERROR IN MASS SURVEYS

The **sampling error** in a survey (the predicted difference between the average opinion expressed by survey respondents and the average opinion in the population, sometimes called the margin of error) using a random sample depends on the sample size. Sampling error is large for small samples of around 100 or less, but it decreases rapidly as sample size increases.

The graph shows how the sampling error for a random sample decreases as sample size increases. For example, in surveys with 1,000 respondents the sampling error is 2 percent, meaning that 95 percent of the time, the results of a 1,000-person survey will fall within the range of 2 percentage points above or below the actual percentage in the population that holds a particular opinion surveyed. If the sample size was increased to 5,000 people, the sampling error would decline to 0.5 percent.

Sampling errors need to be taken into account in interpreting what a poll says about public opinion. Suppose a 1,000-person survey finds that 60 percent of the sample favor candidate Smith, while 40 percent support candidate Jones. Since the difference in support for the two candidates (20 points) exceeds the sampling error (4 points), it is reasonable to conclude that Smith has more supporters in the population than Jones and should be considered the favorite to win the election.

In contrast, suppose the poll found a narrow 51 to 49 percent split slightly favoring Smith over Jones. Since the difference in support is smaller than the sampling error, it would be a mistake to conclude that Smith is the likely winner. Even though Smith is ahead among the sample, Jones may have more supporters in the population. Put another way, given the sampling error, the survey results tell us that there is a 95 percent chance that Smith's support in the population is between 49 and 53 percent, and Jones is between 47 and 51 percent. In other words, when a poll shows a difference in support smaller than the sampling error, the only thing that poll tells us is that neither candidate is the clear favorite.

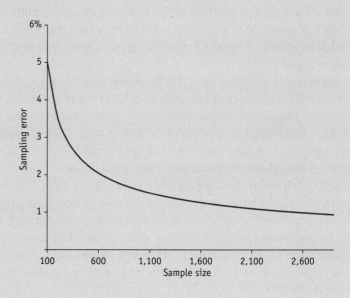

ISSUES WITH SURVEY METHODS

sampling error A calculation that describes what percentage of the people surveyed may not accurately represent the population being studied. Increasing the number of respondents lowers the sampling error.

Building a random sample of respondents is not easy. One standard strategy is to choose households at random from census data and send interviewers out for face-to-face meetings. Another strategy involves contacting people by telephone using random digit dialing, which allows surveyors to find people who have unlisted phone numbers or who just use a cell phone. While each technique in theory produces a random sample, in practice they both may deviate from this ideal. For example, face-to-face interviewing risks losing households in which both adults work away from the home during the day.

To keep costs down, many organizations use other strategies. These may include Internet polling, in which volunteer respondents log on to a website to participate in a survey, or robo-polls, in which a computer program phones people and interviews them. While these techniques are less expensive, there are serious doubts about the randomness of the samples they produce.[43]

Question wording can also influence survey results. Table 5.2 shows four different questions asked during late 2010 to measure opinions about the change in

TABLE » 5.2

QUESTION WORDING AND OPINIONS ABOUT GAYS IN THE MILITARY

POLL	QUESTION	RESPONSES
ABC News/Wash. Post Poll, Dec. 9-12, 2010	"Do you think gays and lesbians who do NOT publicly disclose their sexual orientation should be allowed to serve in the military or not?"	Allowed: 83% Not allowed: 14% Unsure: 4%
	"Do you think gays and lesbians who DO publicly disclose their sexual orientation should be allowed to serve in the military or not?"	Allowed: 77% Not allowed: 21% Unsure: 4%
Quinnipiac University Poll, Nov. 8-15, 2010	"Federal law currently prohibits openly gay men and women from serving in the military. Do you think this law should be repealed or not?"	Should be: 58% Should not be: 34% Unsure: 8%
McClatchy-Marist Poll, Nov. 15-18, 2010	"Do you think the current Democratic Congress should repeal the 'Don't Ask, Don't Tell' policy and allow gay men and women to serve openly in the military or do you think they should not repeal it so they continue to serve but not openly?"	Should repeal: 47% Should not repeal: 48% Unsure: 5%

For additional details on these polls, see www.pollingreport.com/civil.htm (accessed 9/15/12).

government policy to allow gay men and lesbians to serve openly (that is, disclose their sexual orientation) in the U.S. military. As you can see, respondents' support for this change depended on whether a question (1) mentioned serving openly versus keeping one's sexual orientation private, (2) described the policy change in terms of repealing a law, or (3) tied the repeal to action by the then-Democratic Congress. Depending on how the question is worded, support for repeal can be almost cut in half, from 83 percent to 47 percent.

UNRELIABLE RESPONSES

People are sometimes reluctant to reveal their opinions. Rather than speaking truthfully, they often give socially acceptable answers or the ones that they think the interviewers want to hear. In the case of voter turnout in elections, up to one-fourth of respondents who say they voted when surveyed actually did not vote at all.[44] Political scientists refer to this behavior as the social desirability bias, meaning that people are less willing to admit actions or express opinions (such as racial prejudice) that they think their neighbors or society at large will disapprove of.[45] Pollsters use various techniques to address this problem, such as framing a question in terms of the entire country rather than the respondent's own beliefs.

Opinion researchers also have to contend with the opinion-formation process discussed earlier. Since many people develop their opinions on the basis of considerations that come to mind at the moment they are asked, their answer may change a day, a week, or a month later. This problem often arises in polls taken early in a presidential campaign; results vary from week to week not necessarily because of what the candidates have done but because the respondents' opinions are based on relatively little information and can shift according to very small changes in what they know.[46]

THE ACCURACY OF PUBLIC OPINION

Early theories of public opinion held that the average American's opinions about politics were incomplete at best and wildly inaccurate at worst. Modern theories have revised these conclusions. It is true that many Americans have significant gaps in factual information, such as which party controls the House or the Senate,[47] and routinely overestimate the amount of federal money spent on government programs such as foreign aid. However, rather than reflecting ignorance, these misperceptions often result from poor survey design or the respondents' misinterpretation of survey questions.

Claims about health care reform are a good example. In a 2009 survey, 86 percent of respondents said they had heard that reform legislation would create so-called death panels. (The question asked about "government organizations that will make decisions about who will and will not receive health services when they are critically ill.")[48] Moreover, 30 percent of these respondents believed these claims about death panels, even though no such provision was included in any of the health care reform proposals. How can we explain these findings?

We can offer four explanations. (1) Many respondents likely had not thought about the questions beforehand. When asked for an opinion as part of a survey, there was no time to do research or think things through, so the respondents probably guessed, and a significant percentage said (guessed) that death panels were part of the bill. (2) Incomplete or inaccurate responses to survey questions may reflect respondents' unwillingness to admit they don't know about something: survey participants sometimes make up responses to avoid appearing ill informed.[49] Thus, when asked about death panels and health care reform, respondents might have affirmed that a link existed even if they knew little about the actual proposals. (3) Because opinions are subject to influence by politicians and others, survey respondents might have mentioned death panels because they formed their opinions after hearing certain public figures denounce the health care reform plan in terms of possible death panels. (4) Many supposed facts are "contested truths," meaning that it is reasonable for individuals to hold a range of views.[50] So respondents might have known that the proposals did not contain a provision for death panels but answered in the affirmative because they thought that the health care reforms might lead to such panels in the future.

Such problems do not arise in all areas of public opinion. Respondents' ability to express specific opinions, as well as the accuracy of their opinions, rises if the survey questions relate to their everyday life.[51] Thus the average American would be more likely to have an accurate sense of the state of the economy or his own personal economic condition than of the situation in Afghanistan. Everyday life gives us information about the economy; in contrast, we learn about Afghanistan only if we take the time to gather information.

CHARACTERISTICS OF AMERICAN PUBLIC OPINION

PRESENT FINDINGS ON WHAT AMERICANS THINK ABOUT MAJOR POLITICAL ISSUES

American public opinion encompasses what people think of the federal government, their ideological beliefs, and their positions on key public policy questions. These opinions drive public demands for government action, from spending to regulation and other types of policy. So, to understand what America's national government does and why, we have to determine what Americans ask of it. We also need to understand differences of opinion that divide Americans, from specific questions of policy to general statements of belief.

IDEOLOGICAL POLARIZATION

We begin by examining liberal–conservative ideology and party identification to see if historical data show evidence of polarization. Are there fewer moderates and more strong liberals and conservatives today compared to a generation ago? Figure 5.1 shows data on Americans' ideological opinions from the 1970s to 2010, aggregated (grouped) by decade. The plots show no evidence of **ideological polarization**—a culture war that expresses itself in Americans' ideology. Over the last several decades a strong majority of Americans have continued to say they

ideological polarization The effect on public opinion when many citizens move away from moderate positions and toward either end of the political spectrum, identifying themselves as either liberals or conservatives.

FIGURE » 5.1

LIBERAL–CONSERVATIVE IDEOLOGY IN AMERICA

Many commentators describe politics in America as highly conflictual, with most Americans holding either liberal or conservative points of view and very few people in between. Do opinion data confirm or disprove this description?

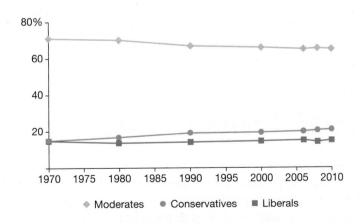

Source: Data from 2008 General Social Survey, http://sda.berkeley.edu/archive.htm (accessed 9/5/12).

FIGURE » 5.2

PARTY IDENTIFICATION IN AMERICA, 1970–2010

Party identification is another place to look for evidence of an increasingly polarized America. Do these data show evidence of polarization?

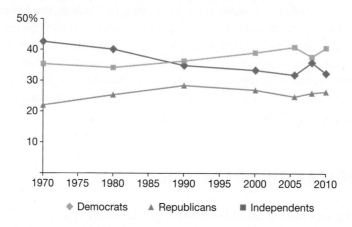

Source: Data from General Social Survey, http://sda.berkeley.edu/archive.htm (accessed 9/5/12).

are moderates, with fewer than 40 percent saying they are liberal or conservative. There is also no evidence that ideological polarization has increased; in fact, the percentage of liberals and of conservatives has remained relatively constant.[52]

Figure 5.2 shows decade-by-decade data about how citizens describe their party identification. Here again, there is little evidence of polarization. Since 1970 the percentage of Republicans has increased slightly, while the percentage of Democrats has declined significantly, with some increase in 2008. The number of independents (people who have no strong attachment to either party) has also increased. The long-term trend for party identification is toward moderation and no strong attachments to parties.

Finally, survey responses that reveal conflict over broad principles do not indicate whether these differences translate into conflicts over specific policy questions. As we have seen, opinions have many sources, some of which may lead to consensus rather than conflict. One such example is the reaction to well-publicized events, as we saw earlier in widespread public approval of restricted civil liberties following the September 11 terrorist attacks.

EVALUATIONS OF GOVERNMENT AND OFFICEHOLDERS

Another set of opinions addresses how people view the government: how well or poorly they think it is doing, whether they trust it, and their evaluations of individual politicians, notably their own representatives in Congress. These opinions matter for several reasons. First, a citizen's judgments about the government's overall performance may shape his evaluations of specific policies, especially if he does not know much about them.[53] Also, evaluations of specific policies may be shaped by how much a citizen trusts the government; more trust brings higher evaluations.[54] Finally, trust in government and overall evaluations of it might influence a citizen's willingness to vote for incumbent congressional representatives or a president seeking reelection.[55]

Table 5.3 reveals that the average American is fairly disenchanted with the government. A majority believes that elected officials lose touch with the people and don't care what average people think, and that corporations have too much power. A near-majority believes that government is almost always wasteful and inefficient. Many surveys over the last two generations show similar responses.[56]

This impression of a disenchanted and disapproving public is amplified by Figure 5.3, which shows declining levels of trust in government since the 1960s. Many scholars have argued that low levels of trust make it harder for elected officials to enact new policies, especially those involving large expenditures.[57] Some scholars even argue that low levels of trust raise questions about the future of democracy in America.[58] How can we say that American democracy is a good or popular form of government when so many people are unhappy with the performance of elected officials and bureaucrats?

One important insight is that although Americans don't like their government in general, they tend to be happier with their own representatives in Washington (see Chapter 9). For example, when a survey question asks about "the government" it may cause respondents to picture a roomful of bureaucrats pushing paperwork, whereas asking about "your representative" may lead respondents to think of someone working on their behalf. Also, as we discuss in Chapter 9 (Congress), members of Congress work hard to convince their constituents that they are doing everything possible to satisfy constituents' demands. Sometimes, members blame the institution

TABLE » 5.3

MEASURING AMERICAN PUBLIC OPINION: BELIEFS ABOUT GOVERNMENT

Surveys show that Americans generally like their elected representatives in Congress. Presidents are sometimes extremely popular. Do Americans have positive feelings about government itself?

	STRONGLY AGREE	AGREE	NEITHER, DON'T KNOW	AGREE	STRONGLY AGREE	
Government is almost always wasteful and inefficient.	46%	9%	6%	12%	27%	Government often does a better job than people give it credit for.
Too much power is concentrated in the hands of a few large companies.	66	12	6	7	9	The largest companies do not have too much power.
Elected officials in Washington lose touch with the people pretty quickly.	60	12	5	8	14	Elected officials in Washington try hard to stay in touch with voters back home.
Most elected officials care about what people like me think.	15	11	5	60	10	Most elected officials don't care about what people like me think.

Source: Pew Research Center, "Beyond Red and Blue: the Political Topology," May 4, 2010, www.people-press.org/2011/05/04/beyond-red-vs-blue-the-political-typology/ (accessed 9/15/12).

FIGURE » 5.3

TRUST IN GOVERNMENT

In America, trust in government varies widely over time. What factors drive these changes?

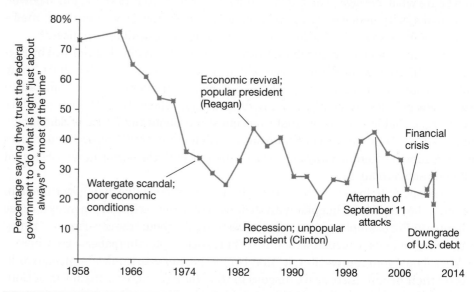

Source: Pew Research Center, "Obama Leadership Image Takes a Hit, GOP Ratings Decline," Pew Research Center, August 25, 2011, www.people-press.org/files/legacy-pdf/8-25-11%20Political%20Release.pdf (accessed 9/5/12).

of Congress and the government bureaucracy for shortcomings, portraying themselves as standing between their constituents and an inefficient government.

POLICY PREFERENCES

policy mood The level of public support for expanding the government's role in society; whether the public wants government action on a specific issue.

In a diverse country of more than 300 million, people care about a wide range of policies. One useful measure of Americans' policy preferences is the **policy mood**, which captures the public's collective demands for government action on domestic policies.[59] Policy mood measures are constructed from surveys that address a wide range of policy questions.[60]

Fluctuations in the policy mood in America have led to changes in defense spending, environmental policy, and race-related policies, among others—and have influenced elections.[61] Figure 5.4 shows that when the policy mood leans in a liberal direction, such as in the early 1960s, conditions are ripe for an expansion of the federal government involving more spending and new programs. But when the policy mood becomes more conservative, such as in the late 1970s and early 1980s, officials generally enact smaller increases in government spending and fewer new programs.

Turning to specific issues, surveys show that most Americans focus on the same issues: the wars in Iraq and Afghanistan, economic conditions, energy policy, health care, immigration, global warming, abortion, and gay rights.[62] The

FIGURE » 5.4

POLICY MOOD

As the labels in the figure indicate, sharp changes in the policy mood often precede changes in the composition of Congress or the party that holds the presidency. Could you have used the recent policy mood data to predict the outcomes of the 2012 presidential and congressional elections?

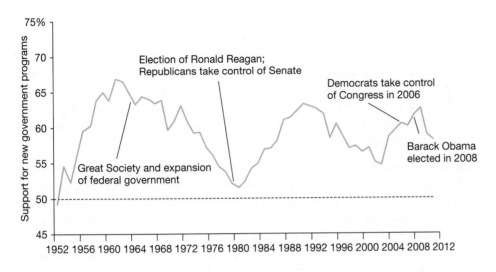

Source: James Stimson, University of North Carolina, Chapel Hill, www.unc.edu/~jstimson (accessed 11/13/12).

list below summarizes opinion data on some of these issues. Certain issues carry significant levels of conflict; others involve much less.

▶ *Iraq and Afghanistan:* Public opinion on both conflicts has changed profoundly since U.S. troops invaded those countries in 2003 and 2001, respectively. There has been a move from strong support initially to less support by 2008.

▶ *Economic conditions:* Throughout 2006 and 2007 the economy ranked a distant second to the wars in Iraq and Afghanistan. However, by 2008 a collapse in housing prices and the near meltdown of the global financial system led many Americans to revise their opinions about the most important economic problems facing the country.

▶ *Health care:* In surveys from 2008 and 2009, many Americans worried about losing health coverage and complained about its high cost. But there was no strong support for reforms to America's health care system. Respondents might have thought that the reform proposals included other provisions, such as "death panels," or would cause other problems, such as increased health care costs.

▶ *Immigration:* There is broad consensus for specific reforms. In a recent survey most respondents favored allowing illegal immigrants to become citizens after several years. The government's failure to reform immigration laws may have more to do with conflict within Congress, pressures from a small number of intensely opinionated voters, or the fact that economic concerns have overshadowed immigration issues.

▶ *Gay rights:* A majority of Americans favor allowing gay couples to form civil unions (partnershsips that confer the same legal standing as a marriage), but only about one-third support allowing gay couples to marry. A majority of Republicans oppose gay marriage, and a majority of Democrats favor civil unions or marriage rights. Support for gay marriage and civil unions is higher among younger voters than among older voters.

▶ *Climate change:* Democrats are more likely to believe that global warming is real and is caused by humans; Republicans are more likely to think that it isn't happening or that it is a natural phenomenon that humans have no decisive role in influencing. Given this split, members of Congress and the president have been unable to agree on policies to combat climate change.

As these examples and the data behind them illustrate, it is hard to find an issue on which nearly everyone agrees about what should be done. In a country as large and diverse as the United States, this is no surprise. What is surprising is the potential for compromise, which argues against describing American politics in terms of a culture war. Survey questions that ask about ideology or party identification find that most Americans are moderates. While Americans in 2010 and 2011 disagreed on the source of economic hard times, they agreed that the economy is the most important problem. And questions on immigration and gay rights find strong majority support for certain policy changes. Thus, while disagreement is a fact of life in American politics, it may not be so profound as to eliminate the possibility for compromise.

DOES PUBLIC OPINION INFLUENCE GOVERNMENT?

There is considerable evidence that government policy reflects public opinion. Congressional actions on a wide range of issues, from votes on defense policy to the confirmation of Supreme Court nominees, are shaped by constituent opinion.[63] Moreover, this linkage does not occur because politicians shape public opinion in line with what they themselves prefer; rather, politicians behave in line with constituents' opinions because to do otherwise would place them in jeopardy of losing the next election.[64]

Of course, all politicians, particularly those with a national audience such as the president, work to shape public opinion. However, these efforts mainly serve to publicize opinions that people already hold, as a way of influencing other elected officials rather than changing what citizens believe.[65]

Recent events also speak to the influence of public opinion. Regarding the war in Iraq, as long as public support remained high, members of Congress barely criticized military strategy or reconstruction efforts. However, as public support waned, more members of Congress from both parties expressed reservations, disagreed with President Bush's claims that conditions were improving, and suggested that Congress revise the war policy.[66] These comments likely reinforced declining public support for the war and may have influenced the pro-Democratic shift in the 2006 and 2008 elections (see Chapter 7). The ebbing of combat opera-

POLITICIANS READ PUBLIC OPINION polls closely to gauge whether their behavior will anger or please constituents. Few politicians always follow survey results—but virtually none would agree with Calvin's father that polls should be ignored entirely.

tions in late 2009 and the continued reductions in troop levels in 2010 and 2011 were also consistent with public opinion during this period.

In fact, it is hard to find a major policy change that did not have majority support at the time it was made. Consider 2011: efforts ranging from the U.S. intervention in Libya to budget reduction agreements and establishment of a debt supercommittee all reflected the demands of a majority of Americans. This is exactly what we should expect if public opinion is relevant to what happens in politics.

THE NEWS MEDIA

> DESCRIBE THE MAJOR TYPES OF NEWS SOURCES AND THE ROLE THEY PLAY IN AMERICAN POLITICS

Closely related to our discussion of public opinion is the role of the news media, for it is generally through the media that Americans receive political information. This section describes the **mass media**, the many sources of political information available to Americans. It also identifies dramatic changes in new forms of media and the way these changes affect not only the amount of political information available and how it is delivered, but also how people use it. Finally, we consider how the media may influence public opinion and politics.

mass media Sources that provide information to the average citizen, such as newspapers, television networks, radio stations, and websites.

MEDIA SOURCES

There are many sources of political information—from **mainstream media** such as newspapers, TV and radio stations, books, and magazines, to countless Internet-based sources. As you will see, media sources are not interchangeable: what you learn about politics depends on where you look. Here we consider each major type of media before discussing how the Internet is changing the way Americans experience politics.

mainstream media Media sources that predate the Internet, such as newspapers, magazines, television, and radio.

PRINT MEDIA

National newspapers, such as the *New York Times, Washington Post, Los Angeles Times*, and *Wall Street Journal*, cover American politics using a large, worldwide staff. Of the many magazines that cover politics, national weeklies such as *Time* and *Newsweek* often feature political events as front-page news. Smaller regional and local papers serve medium- to large-size cities and smaller towns. Recent years have seen significant declines in newspaper readership. Companies that once owned newspapers in Chicago, Philadelphia, and Minneapolis have gone bankrupt, and one major U.S. city, Seattle, now has no hometown daily newspaper. Moreover, decreases in circulation and advertising revenues are forcing many newspapers to cut foreign bureaus, some local reporters, and the amount of news in every edition.[67] Nonetheless, many books with political content continue to be published each year.

BROADCAST MEDIA

The four major national TV networks (ABC, CBS, Fox, and NBC) and many cable channels, such as CNN, offer nightly news as well as **prime-time** news programs. Some cable stations offer news coverage throughout the day and night, creating the 24-hour **news cycle**. Local TV stations also cover local political events in addition to running the national networks' programming. News coverage varies from the "talking head" format of a person behind a desk reading copy to the camera, to investigative reporting that involves reporters and camera crews gathering information in the field, to talk shows that air interviews with political figures.

The major radio networks, such as ABC, CBS, and Clear Channel Communications, offer brief news programs throughout the day; but most political content on the radio consists of talk radio programs featuring a host discussing politics with listeners who phone in. The major nationwide talk radio shows, such as *The Rush Limbaugh Show*, generally offer a politically conservative viewpoint—and openly advertise this orientation.[68] Liberal talk radio programs have a very small audience compared to the conservative programs' audience. Other political programs air on National Public Radio, an organization funded by the government and private donations. Overall, there are more than 13,000 radio stations in America. As with other media sources, only a fraction of these stations focus on news or political coverage.

THE INTERNET

The Internet has quickly become a major source of information about American politics (Table 5.4). Some Internet sources are electronic versions of sources that originate in other kinds of media; for example, you can read the *New York Times* on its website or listen to Rush Limbaugh's radio program online. Other sources exist only in cyberspace; these include Politico.com as well as blogs authored by political scientists, political consultants, elected officials, and others. Video sites such as YouTube offer coverage of congressional proceedings, campaign events, major political speeches, and many other political topics.

Social media sites are another new information source on the Internet; these include Facebook, Twitter, and countless sites that offer forums, chat rooms, and other venues for interaction. Virtually every political organization in America uses such tools for keeping in touch with supporters and offering its own viewpoint on issues. For example, during Occupy Wall Street protests, organizers have used Facebook and Twitter to inform supporters about upcoming protests and to post pictures of protests and police response in different cities. These tools have also enabled Occupy supporters to exchange ideas about the movement's goals, to report on local activities that other media may have missed, and to compare notes about successful protest tactics. Because the Internet has become such a significant source of political information, we explore its role in more detail below.

TABLE » 5.4

KNOWLEDGE LEVELS BY NEWS SOURCE

One of the most important questions about media usage is whether people who know a lot about politics get their information from different sources than those used by people who don't know as much. Does this table show differences between high-information and low-information?

	PERCENTAGE WHO COULD . . .			
	HIGH-KNOWLEDGE GROUP	IDENTIFY SUNNIS	IDENTIFY LIBBY	IDENTIFY PUTIN	APPROXIMATE U.S. DEATHS IN IRAQ
Nationwide	35%	32%	29%	36%	55%
THE AUDIENCE OF . . .					
The Daily Show/The Colbert Report	54%	50%	44%	52%	59%
Major newspaper websites	54	52	42	58	64
NewsHour	53	46	45	54	67
The O'Reilly Factor	51	43	44	53	64
National Public Radio	51	49	43	51	66
The Rush Limbaugh Show	50	40	42	52	70
Local daily newspaper	43	36	35	43	60
News from Google, Yahoo, etc.	41	44	33	44	60
CNN	41	38	36	41	60
Network evening news	38	31	33	37	61
Online news discussion blogs	37	35	32	36	57
Fox News Channel	35	32	29	38	58
Local TV news	35	30	30	35	57
Network morning shows	34	30	30	35	57

Entries show the percentage of regular viewers, readers, or listeners of each outlet who fall in the high-knowledge group (correctly answered at least 15 of 23 questions about politics and world affairs) and the percentage who correctly answered some of the individual questions on the test.

Source: Pew Research Center, "What Americans Know: 1989–2007," April 15, 2007, http://people-press.org/reports/pdf/319.pdf (accessed 8/30/12).

WHAT DIFFERENCE DOES THE INTERNET MAKE?

The Internet has made new kinds of political information available to the average citizen. Many sites offer the full text of government reports and analyses: for example, the president's annual budget request, new regulations published in the *Federal Register*, or evaluations of government programs released by the Government Accountability Office.[69] Twenty years ago such documents were available only at major libraries.

The Internet also provides access to a wealth of analytic information. During the 2011 debate over reducing the federal deficit, many websites—including that of the Congressional Budget Office—offered detailed analyses of how people would be affected by different budget-cutting plans. Prior to the Internet, analyses like these circulated only among a few scholars and policy makers. Similarly, the proliferation of videos on the Internet allows average Americans to see politics at first hand, ranging from online videos of Occupy Wall Street protests to just about any other political event of significance.

A RANGE OF ONLINE SOURCES

Most American newspapers, television networks, radio stations, and cable stations offer free access to most or all of their daily news via Internet sites. Most also provide some web-only information and post blogs written by their reporters. One highly influential conservative weekly magazine, *National Review*, has a web version, National Review Online, where many of the magazine's reporters publish web-exclusive stories.[70] Also, most major newspapers use Twitter feeds to announce new articles or photos, especially about time-critical events.

Other Internet-only news providers, such as Politico's Playbook, offer links to daily political coverage throughout the nation or a preview of upcoming political events in Washington.[71] SCOTUSblog (Supreme Court of the United States blog) analyzes Supreme Court decisions, judicial nominations, and other legal questions.[72] And many blogs such as The Monkey Cage discuss political science research to explain contemporary American politics.[73] Finally, a wealth of professional and amateur video coverage of politics is available on YouTube and many other websites. Various political organizations and candidates use Facebook, Twitter, and other social networking sites to recruit and organize supporters.

THE RISE OF DIGITAL MEDIA HAS transformed the media industry, as an increasing number of Americans get news and other information online. How does this change affect the media's role in politics?

LOWERED BARRIERS TO PUBLICATION

The Internet has lowered the barriers to publication. A generation ago it was all but impossible for average citizens to report on what they knew or to present their analyses to the general public.[74] Today the Internet provides more opportunities for home-grown media, enabling a would-be political reporter to easily set up a website or Facebook page. For example, thousands of active-duty and retired military personnel have used blogs to chronicle their service in Iraq and Afghanistan, a phenomenon known as milblogging.[75] In addition, many interest groups use Facebook to keep supporters informed about issues and events. One of the major Tea Party organizations, Tea Party Patriots, had nearly a million "likes" on its Facebook page as of late 2012.

Similarly, YouTube posts videos of campaign events and campaign ads, many prepared by people with no official connections to the candidates. These videos have the potential to change elections. For example, in the 2006 Virginia Senate race a volunteer for challenger James Webb recorded incumbent George Allen using a Tunisian racial slur, *macaca,* to refer to the volunteer, who was of Indian descent.[76] The episode, which mainstream media later picked up, dogged Allen for the entire campaign. After initially seeming a shoo-in for reelection, Allen lost by more than 9,000 votes.

The Internet also creates new opportunities for two-way interaction among citizens, reporters, and government officials. Many reporters respond to comments posted by readers or host live chat sessions, allowing people to ask follow-up questions about published stories.[77] Politicians do the same: in April 2011, President Obama used Facebook for "town hall meetings" where he responded to questions posted online.[78]

Finally, the Internet enables ordinary citizens to report on events as they happen. For example, when New York City police arrested Occupy Wall Street protesters on the Brooklyn Bridge in October 2011, the first reports and videos of the event appeared as Twitter posts. Politicians must now assume that anything they say or do (good or bad) will be instantly publicized via the same technology.

A BETTER-INFORMED CITIZENRY?

How much difference does all this Internet information make? Some pundits argue that the Internet will transform American politics, leading to a better-informed, more politically active citizenry.[79] And it may—someday. Some studies do show that Internet usage is associated with higher levels of political participation, but others show no such association.[80] Moreover, there is no clear evidence that surfing the web makes people more politically informed.[81]

Why hasn't the Internet created a better-informed citizenry? First, although the percentage of people who routinely use the Internet is very high, access is only the first step in becoming informed. Finding information on the Internet still requires doing your own research, and despite the availability of search engines it is not always obvious where to look for political information.

Second, some of the vast quantity of information on the Internet is of questionable reliability. For example, it is easy to find fake photographs of the U.S. president, other prominent figures and celebrities, or international terrorist leaders. Some websites identify these pictures as fabrications, but others do not. When citizens do not take the time to investigate what they see or read, it is easy to accept false information as true.

Third, most people do not consult a wide range of media sources. Instead, they focus on sites whose take on political events is compatible with their own. Thus Democrats look for sites that favor Democratic policies, conservatives look for sites run by conservative individuals or organizations, and so on.[82] The use of information supplied by political blogs shows the same pattern.[83]

In short, despite the Internet's wealth of information, there is no guarantee that people will sit down, search for what they want or need to know, distinguish truth from falsehood, and assemble their findings into coherent conclusions. In fact, people may prefer to focus on events that capture their attention, such as a new celebrity scandal or viral video, and thus avoid current events in politics.[84]

REGULATING THE MEDIA

Federal Communications Commission (FCC) A government agency created in 1934 to regulate American radio stations and later expanded to regulate television, wireless communications technologies, and other broadcast media.

broadcast media Communications technologies, such as television and radio, that transmit information over airwaves.

The Communications Act of 1934 authorized the **Federal Communications Commission (FCC)** to regulate **broadcast media**, which at the time meant radio stations and subsequently included television stations, cable TV, and other communications technologies. FCC regulations considered the airways to be public property, so no one had an inherent right to operate a radio or TV station. Rather, station owners were expected to serve the public interest, as defined by the FCC.

LIMITS ON OWNERSHIP AND CONTENT

A central concern in the 1930s was that one company or organization might buy enough stations to dominate the airwaves in an area, so that only one set of programs or point of view would be available. Over the next two generations the FCC developed regulations to limit the number of radio and TV stations a company could own in a community and the total nationwide audience that a company's TV stations could reach.[85]

The 1940s saw the rise of TV as Americans' primary news source. Television made it possible to report on stories using instantly accessible visual footage rather than printed words—a crucial distinction, given many citizens' lack of interest in political events and issues. In fact, decades later a frequent argument about public opinion during the Vietnam War was that declining public support for the war arose from the fact that stories depicting the war's horror firsthand were a staple on nightly news broadcasts.[86] Although previous wars led to graphic photos in magazines and newsreels, such images became much more commonplace with the advent of television.

fairness doctrine An FCC regulation requiring broadcast media to present several points of view to ensure balanced coverage. It was created in the late 1940s and eliminated in 1987.

equal time provision An FCC regulation requiring broadcast media to provide equal airtime on any non-news programming to all candidates running for an office.

In the late 1940s the FCC also developed the **fairness doctrine,** which required TV and radio stations to broadcast a variety of political views.[87] As a result, stations offered debates and presentations supporting different political positions as part of their news programs, as well as talk shows and interviews featuring diverse political figures. The FCC also created the **equal time provision**, which states that if a radio or television station gives air time to a candidate outside its news coverage—such as during an entertainment show—it has to give equal time to other candidates running for the same office.

DEREGULATION

The FCC's limits on ownership and content assumed that radio and TV stations were public trustees with a responsibility to provide full and unbiased coverage of political events. This assumption changed with the development of cable TV, satellite TV, and the Internet. After all, with so many sources of information, if one broadcaster ignored a candidate, issue, or viewpoint, citizens could still find what they wanted from another source. Pressure for deregulation also came from the owners of media companies, who wanted to buy more TV, radio, and cable stations, as well as from book and magazine publishers, Internet service providers, and newspapers, in order to increase efficiencies and profits.[88] Ultimately, the Telecommunications Act of 1996 gave the FCC the power to revise all ownership and content restrictions enacted over the last two generations; since then, the FCC has abolished most ownership restrictions. (The equal time provision is still in place, but the fairness doctrine was eliminated in 1987.)[89]

These regulatory changes accelerated two trends in American news media. The first is **concentration**, which involves one company owning more than one media source in a town or community. For example, Clear Channel Communications owns multiple AM and FM radio stations in more than 30 cities. The

concentration The trend toward single-company ownership of several media sources in one area.

5.2 NUTS & bolts

HOLDINGS OF NEWS CORPORATION

News Corporation is an example of a media conglomerate, a company that controls a variety of different media outlets throughout the world. It owns cable television networks, TV and radio stations, newspapers, movie production companies, magazines, and even sports teams. This structure allows the company to operate more efficiently, as it can rebroadcast or reprint stories in different outlets, but opponents are concerned that conglomerates might expand to control most or even all of the sources that are available to the average citizen, making it impossible to access alternate points of view.

Fox Television Stations	Film Companies	Books and Magazines
27 U.S. stations	20th Century Fox	*The Weekly Standard*
	Fox Searchlight Pictures	*TV Guide* (partial)
	Fox Television Studios	3 other magazines
	Blue Sky Studios	45 book publishers worldwide
	11 other film companies	

Satellite and Cable Holdings	Newspapers	Other Holdings
DirecTV	*New York Post*	Los Angeles Kings (40 percent ownership)
Fox News Channel	*Wall Street Journal*	Los Angeles Lakers (10 percent ownership)
46 other cable channels worldwide	4 UK newspapers	Hulu.com (32 percent ownership)
		18 news and entertainment websites
	20 Australian newspapers	15 other businesses
	24 local U.S. newspapers	

cross-ownership The trend toward single-company ownership of several kinds of media outlets.

media conglomerates Companies that control a large number of media sources across several types of media outlets.

second trend is **cross-ownership**, which involves one company owning several different kinds of media outlets, often in the same community. For example, the Tribune Company in Chicago owns the WGN radio station, the WGN TV station, and the *Chicago Tribune* daily newspaper. These trends have given rise to **media conglomerates**, companies that control a wide range of news sources.[90] Today all four major television networks (ABC, NBC, CBS, and Fox) are part of larger companies that own many other broadcast and cable stations, movie production and distribution companies, radio stations, newspapers, and other media outlets. Nuts and Bolts 5.2 shows the diverse holdings of one such company, News Corporation.

Deregulation has been controversial. Some FCC commissioners have argued in particular that concentration limits citizens' choices and forces programming to become increasingly homogenized. Despite this and other concerns, at the moment there is no sign that the increased number of sources is leading to a better-informed population—or that media concentration in some markets is having the opposite effect.

MEDIA EFFECTS ON CITIZENS AND GOVERNMENT

media effects The influence of media coverage on average citizens' opinions and actions.

The study of **media effects** explores whether exposure to media coverage of politics changes what people think or do. There is considerable evidence that media coverage influences its audience. However, much of the impact stems from what such stories leave out, how they present certain information, or even whether a story is reported at all. Political scientists label these mechanisms as priming, filtering (also called agenda-setting), slant, and framing.[91]

Modern theories of media influence distinguish various ways in which coverage can affect media consumers' beliefs. Most obvious is the use of the media as a forum for persuasion, overtly seeking to persuade people to change their minds about a candidate or an issue. However, people are not always conscious of this

AS THESE STARK IMAGES from Vietnam and Iraq illustrate, photos and televised images of war have the potential to capture attention and shape public opinion.

phenomenon. Theorists describe four media effects that work largely without consumers' awareness.

▶ **Filtering** reflects journalists' and editors' decisions about which news stories to report.

▶ **Slant** in a story gives favorable coverage to one candidate or policy without providing "balanced" favorable coverage of other sides.

▶ **Priming** occurs when media coverage of a story affects the importance people place on the issues or events mentioned in the coverage.

▶ **Framing** refers to the way in which the presentation of a story, including details, explanations, and context, changes people's reaction to the information.

The existence of these media effects does not imply that reporters or editors try to mislead the public or sway public opinion to conform to their own ideas. If you read an article about a particular issue and decide to change your position, this doesn't suggest that the story was inaccurate or biased. Your decision may be justified by the facts of the situation. Similarly, when slanted campaign coverage praises one candidate and dismisses another as unqualified, you might conclude that the author agrees with the first candidate's positions and wrote the story to help that candidate get elected. But what if the first candidate is actually the most qualified? If so, then slanted coverage of the campaign might be objective.

The same is true for other media effects. Space limitations mean that some filtering is inevitable as reporters and editors decide which stories to cover. Similar decisions about what to report and how to present the information lead to priming and framing effects. Even if everyone in the political media adhered to the highest standards of accuracy, these influences would still exist. And it would be impossible to escape their effects. In fact, diverse research studies have confirmed that the details of media coverage do indeed affect what citizens know about politics and government policy, how they evaluate officeholders and government programs, their vote decisions, and the demands they put on elected officials. For example, regular readers of a paper that endorsed a particular candidate were more likely to hold a positive opinion of that candidate and more likely to vote for him.[92] And a study of priming found that exposure to press coverage of the Persian Gulf War in 1990 and 1991 moved citizens to evaluate then-president George H. W. Bush on the basis of his effectiveness in managing the war rather than on other factors such as the state of the economy.[93]

filtering The influence on public opinion that results from journalists' and editors' decisions about which of many potential news stories to report.

slant The imbalance in a story that covers one candidate or policy favorably without providing similar coverage of the other side.

priming The influence on the public's general impressions caused by positive or negative coverage of a candidate or issue.

framing The influence on public opinion caused by the way a story is presented or covered, including the details, explanations, and context offered in the report.

CONCLUSION

Public opinion and the media matter in American politics. Our nation's citizens have ideas about what they want government to do, and they use these ideas to guide their political choices. Most of the time these beliefs are formed only when needed, so they are sensitive to recent events. In a country as large and diverse as the United States, disagreements over government policy are inevitable. However, even though public opinion data shows disagreement in many areas, it also shows areas where compromise is possible.

News media are Americans' primary source of public information about politics and policy. The news media landscape today is undergoing a massive transition, as the Internet supports an ever-growing variety of new information sources and fewer people rely on newspapers or television for news. Even so, these traditional sources remain the most popular for political information. Although journalists can shape public opinion, media coverage is also substantially influenced by the need to attract an audience. There is little evidence, however, to support claims of an ideological bias in media coverage.

The average American is not an expert on government policies and knows relatively little about possible alternatives. But even a small amount of information is enough to inform his or her beliefs about what policies should be enacted. Politicians, moreover, generally take care to behave in accordance with the public's demands. Changes in the last few years in government policy, politicians' statements, and election outcomes all reflect changes in the policy mood.

WHAT IS PUBLIC OPINION?

▶ Define *public opinion*, and explain why it matters in American politics. **Pages 127–29**

SUMMARY

What the population thinks about politics and government matters for three reasons: people's political actions are driven by their opinions; there is a strong linkage between people's opinions and political actors' behavior; and public opinion helps us understand how specific policy outcomes are achieved.

KEY TERMS

public opinion (p. 127)

latent opinion (p. 128)

considerations (p. 128)

CRITICAL THINKING AND DISCUSSION:

Given that many Americans cannot answer basic political questions, and given that many of the opinions they express vary from day to day without anything changing in the political world, how can we say that public opinion exists?

PRACTICE QUIZ QUESTIONS

1. What does it mean that most political judgments are latent opinions?
    a) Most Americans have preformed opinions.
    b) Most Americans have well-thought-out reasons for preferring a policy.
    c) Most Americans do not have any meaningful political attitudes.
    d) Most Americans form their opinions only as needed.
    e) Most opinions are not accurate.

2. Which of the following is *not* true regarding considerations?
    a) Well-informed and poorly informed people use them in forming opinions.
    b) Opinions on morally complex issues do not involve considerations.
    c) Political events can become considerations.
    d) They may be contradictory.
    e) Party identification is often used in considerations.

SOURCES OF OPINIONS

▶ Explain how people form political attitudes and opinions. **Pages 129–34**

SUMMARY

Political opinions are influenced by a wide range of factors. The belief systems of our parents and relatives influence our opinions early on, and our social groups influence our perspectives later in life. Personal events such as attending college or moving to a new city may influence how we think about politics, as do national events such as the September 11 attacks or the government's decision to go to war. Even political debates by political elites and party leaders shape our political attitudes.

KEY TERMS

political socialization (p. 129)

PRACTICE QUIZ QUESTIONS

3. Theories of political socialization say that people's opinions are influenced most by _____.
    a) what they learned from their parents
    b) the way political parties change over time
    c) their genetic and biological factors

d) their personality traits

e) politicians

4. The idea that individuals will rely on others who "look like" them for opinions relates to _____.

a) political socialization

b) group identity

c) political events

d) generational effects

e) generational effects

5. Which phrase best completes the following statement regarding the sources of public opinion? "Politicians and other political actors work to _____ public opinion."

a) respond to

b) ignore

c) disregard

d) stabilize

e) shape

ⓢ **PRACTICE ONLINE**

"Critical Thinking" exercise: *Politics Is Everywhere—State Opinions and the Election*

MEASURING PUBLIC OPINION

▶ Describe basic survey methods and potential issues affecting accuracy. **Pages 134–38**

SUMMARY

Most information on public opinion comes from mass surveys involving hundreds or thousands of respondents. The accuracy of surveys is influenced by several factors, including the size of the sample and whether the people in the sample are randomly selected. Using a randomly selected sample, researchers can draw conclusions about public opinion across the American population.

KEY TERMS

mass survey (p. 135)

population (p. 135)

sample (p. 135)

sampling error (p. 136)

CRITICAL THINKING AND DISCUSSION

In light of the many problems with measuring public opinion, how should you read survey results?

PRACTICE QUIZ QUESTIONS

6. Why are random samples helpful in understanding public opinion?

a) They provide deep insights into why people hold the views that they do.

b) They eliminate people with strong ideological biases.

c) They enable researchers to use a small number of respondents to draw conclusions about the entire country.

d) It's impossible to understand public opinion any other way.

e) They restrict respondents to a few answer choices.

7. Which of the following is *not* a problem with survey data?

a) It's impossible to get a random sample.

b) People often give the socially desirable answer to a question.

c) Even a well constructed survey may have a sampling error that makes it difficult to say who is ahead in a close election.

d) Question wording can influence survey responses.

e) People may invent responses to avoid appearing uninformed.

ⓢ **PRACTICE ONLINE**

"Big Think" video exercise: *Why Does Polling Matter?*

CHARACTERISTICS OF AMERICAN PUBLIC OPINION

▶ Present findings on what Americans think about major political issues. **Pages 139–45**

SUMMARY

As a whole, the American electorate is ideologically moderate, with relatively little ideological polarization. Moreover, there is considerable agreement on the most important problems in the country, and the potential exists for compromise on most policy areas. Paradoxically, while trust in the government has declined steadily since the 1960s, people are still generally rather happy with their own representatives in Washington, DC.

KEY TERMS

ideological polarization (p. 139)

policy mood (p. 142)

CRITICAL THINKING AND DISCUSSION

How much conflict is there in American public opinion?

PRACTICE QUIZ QUESTIONS

8. In the 1970s the majority of people identified themselves as ideologically _____; in the 2000s most people identified as _____.
   a) moderate; conservative
   b) moderate; moderate
   c) moderate; liberal
   d) conservative; moderate
   e) conservative; conservative

9. Americans generally _____ of the government; Americans generally _____ of their own representatives.

   a) approve; approve
   b) approve; disapprove
   c) disapprove; approve
   d) disapprove; disapprove

10. What is policy mood?
   a) public support for Congress
   b) presidential approval rating
   c) public demand for government action on domestic policies
   d) public demand for government action on international policies
   e) public demand for government action on international policies

11. Which policy area is always near the top of Americans' concerns?
   a) economic conditions
   b) health care
   c) gay rights
   d) immigration
   e) the environment

Ⓢ PRACTICE ONLINE

"Critical Thinking" exercise: *Politics Is Conflictual—Public Opinion and Health Care*

THE NEWS MEDIA

▶ Describe the major types of news sources and the role they play in American politics. **Pages 145–53**

SUMMARY

While the term *media* traditionally only referred to print sources, technological advances allowed political information to be spread through radio, TV, and now the Internet. Nearly all modern research finds that the media has significant effects on public opinion. By determining which stories to cover, how a story is written, or how many stories to write on a given topic, media sources influence the way that citizens think about politics.

KEY TERMS

mass media (p. 145)

mainstream media (p. 145)

prime time (p. 146)

news cycle (p. 146)

Federal Communications Commission (FCC) (p. 150)

broadcast media (p. 150)

fairness doctrine (p. 150)

equal time provision (p. 150)

concentration (p. 151)

cross-ownership (p. 152)

media conglomerates (p. 152)

media effects (p. 152)

filtering (p. 153)

slant (p. 153)

priming (p. 153)

framing (p. 153)

CRITICAL THINKING AND DISCUSSION:

One argument against deregulating the media is that consolidation and the formation of media conglomerates would reduce the number of independent sources of information that are available to the average American. Based on the media sources that you and your friends use, do you agree or disagree with this argument? Why?

PRACTICE QUIZ QUESTIONS

12. What is one result of the decreased barriers to publication on the Internet?
   a) Few opportunities exist for citizens to interact with reporters or government officials.
   b) People with no official connection to candidates can have significant influence on elections.
   c) The accuracy of political information has improved.
   d) Few average citizens report on events as they happen.
   e) Like-minded political supporters have difficulty organizing and staying informed on issues.

13. Why hasn't the Internet increased citizens' political knowledge?
   a) It can be hard to find political news on the Internet.
   b) Most people do not have access to the Internet.
   c) Most people read content from a wide range of balanced media sources.
   d) Most people only focus on sites that reinforce their own views.
   e) Search engines don't include political topics.

14. What is the fairness doctrine?
   a) TV and radio stations must offer a variety of political views in programs.

   b) TV and radio stations must give equal time to candidates running advertisements.
   c) News anchors cannot slander political candidates.
   d) Radio station owners cannot also own TV and print media outlets.
   e) Journalists must investigate challengers as well as incumbents.

15. The deregulation of the media has resulted in _____.
   a) increasing enforcement of the equal time provision
   b) increasing enforcement of the fairness doctrine
   c) increasing use of the Internet
   d) increasing scrutiny of media concentration
   e) increasing frequency of cross-ownership

16. What is priming?
   a) a journalist's decision about which story to report on and which story to skip
   b) a journalist giving favorable coverage to one candidate without providing balanced coverage on the opponent
   c) the phenomenon of a journalist's story affecting the importance people place on the issue covered in the story
   d) the particular way that a journalist decides to present and describe a story
   e) the decision to prioritize one story over another

17. Space limitations mean that some _____ is inevitable.
   a) filtering
   b) slant
   c) priming
   d) framing
   e) soft news

ⓢ PRACTICE ONLINE

"What Do Political Scientists Do?" video exercise: *Issue Framing*

SUGGESTED READING

Campbell, David. *Why We Vote: How Schools and Communities Shape Our Civic Life*. Princeton, NJ: Princeton University Press, 2006.

Cappella, J. N., and K. H. Jamieson. *Spiral of Cynicism: The Press and the Public Good*. New York: Oxford University Press, 1997.

Carmines, Edward G., and James A. Stimson. *Issue Evolution: Race and the Transformation of American Politics*. Princeton, NJ: Princeton University Press, 1990.

Converse, Phillip E. "The Nature of Belief Systems in Mass Publics." In *Ideology and Discontent*, edited by David E. Apter, 206–61. Glencoe, IL: The Free Press of Glencoe, 1964.

Davenport, Christian. *Media Bias, Perspective, and State Repression: The Black Panther Party*. New York: Cambridge University Press, 2010.

Delli Carpini, Michael X., and Scott Keeter. *What Americans Know about Politics and Why It Matters*. New Haven, CT: Yale University Press, 1997.

Green, Donald P., Bradley Palmquist, and Eric Schickler. *Partisan Hearts and Minds*. New Haven, CT: Yale University Press, 2002.

Hibbing, John R., and Elizabeth Theiss-Morse. *Congress as Public Enemy: Public Attitudes toward American Political Institutions*. New York: Cambridge University Press, 1995.

Iyengar, Shanto. *Is Anyone Responsible? How Television Frames Political Issues*. Chicago: University of Chicago Press, 1991.

Jacobs, Lawrence R., and Robert Y. Shapiro. *Politicians Don't Pander: Political Manipulation and the Loss of Democratic Responsiveness*. Chicago: University of Chicago Press, 2000.

Lippman, Walter. *Public Opinion*. 1922. Reprint, New York: Free Press, 1997.

Lupia, Arthur, and Mathew D. McCubbins. *The Democratic Dilemma*. New York: Cambridge University Press, 1998.

Marcus, George E., John L. Sullivan, Elizabeth Theiss-Morse, and Sandra L. Wood. *With Malice toward Some: How People Make Civil Liberties Judgments*. New York: Cambridge University Press, 1995.

Patterson, Thomas. *Out of Order*. New York: Knopf, 1993.

Peffley, Mark, and Jon Hurwitz. *Justice in America: The Separate Realities of Blacks and Whites*. New York: Cambridge University Press, 2010.

Prior, Markus. *Post-Broadcast Democracy: How Media Choice Increases Inequality in Political Involvement and Polarizes Elections*. New York: Cambridge University Press, 2007.

Zaller, John. *The Nature and Origins of Mass Opinion*. New York: Cambridge University Press, 1992.

6

Political Parties

BEGINNING IN 2009, GROUPS AFFILIATED WITH THE Tea Party movement began encouraging candidates sympathetic to their goals to run for office in 2010. The Tea Party movement encompasses numerous loosely affiliated groups that organized in opposition to a broad range of developments in 2009 and 2010, including the following: federal economic stimulus spending; bailouts of banks, auto companies, and other businesses; health care reform; immigration reform; and affirmative action. These groups, ranging from the Tea Party Patriots to the Tea Party in Space, have attracted a wide range of citizens to their rallies, used face-to-face meetings and social networks to discuss issues, and recruited candidates.

Their recruitment efforts bore fruit in the 2010 midterm elections, when nearly 150 candidates ran for the House and Senate with the endorsement of one or more Tea Party groups. About a third were elected. These candidates ran as Republicans or independents. Some won the Republican nomination with little or no opposition, but others defeated candidates who were supported by the state or local Republican Party organization. One Tea Party candidate in Utah even defeated an incumbent Republican senator for the nomination; another in Delaware won the Republican Senate nomination by defeating a well-known Republican House member who had the support of most state and local party officials.

As we will see repeatedly throughout this textbook, political parties are often at the center of conflicts in American politics. The two main American political

CONFLICT & COMPROMISE
in American Politics

parties, the Republicans and the Democrats, come into conflict over what government should do and how to do it. But even within parties, groups of party members (both in Washington and throughout the nation) often squabble over what the party stands for. In this way conflict in American politics occurs within as well as between the Democratic and Republican parties—both in Congress and throughout the nation. For example, the rise of the Tea Party movement as a force within the Republican Party caused the party to confront conflicting points of view and forge compromises among its members.

During the 110th Congress (2011–12), candidates who won with support from Tea Party groups formed a Tea Party Caucus, comprising over 70 Republican House and Senate members. These legislators were among the most vocal in demanding cuts in federal spending; they were also the focus of intense lobbying efforts by Republican Party leaders during negotiations over enacting the annual federal budget, raising the federal debt limit, and crafting a deficit-reduction package. Many of the details of these packages were added in order to reach a compromise between Tea Party members and other Republicans, and thereby win enough Tea Party votes to enact the proposals.

The rise of the Tea Party movement and its impact in the 2010 and 2012 elections highlights the enduring conflict in American politics over the proper role of government in society. While Tea Party groups differ on the specifics, in the main they are unified around the goal of reducing the size of the federal government and its regulation of individuals, groups, and corporations. (Members do, however, disagree somewhat on other issues.) As we will see in this chapter, the Tea Party movement is not generally considered a political party, but it has played an important role in influencing the priorities of the Republican Party.

In a broader perspective, American political parties have been at the center of debates over the role of government ever since the Founding. By competing for control of the presidency, House, and Senate, as well as state and local offices, and by offering different visions of what government should do, parties and their candidates embody some of the most fundamental conflicts that underlie American politics. Parties help shape the way Americans think about candidates, policies, and vote decisions. Parties also impact elections by recruiting candidates, paying for campaign ads, and mobilizing supporters. After elections, the winning party's candidates implement their vision, while the losers try to derail these efforts and develop an alternative vision that will attract support in the next election. In so doing, parties unify and mobilize disparate groups, simplify the choices that voters face, and bring efficiency and coherence to government policy making. The Tea Party organizations, for all their impact on American politics, have fulfilled some—but not all—of this job description.

Why do parties play these roles in American politics? The rise of the Tea Party organizations, along with periodic conflicts within the Democratic and Republican parties, illustrates that the question "Why parties?"[1] does not have an obvious answer. Although American political parties often have an impact on elections and policy, the same organizations can seem inept and irrelevant in other situations. A good answer to "Why parties?" must explain this variation. Why are American political parties sometimes powerful and sometimes powerless? The answer developed in this chapter rests on the notion that the political process matters: understanding what parties do (and cannot do) requires an appreciation of how they are organized, as well as the rules and regulations that shape the behavior of party leaders, politicians, and citizens.

PARTIES AND PARTY SYSTEMS

SHOW HOW AMERICAN POLITICAL PARTIES AND PARTY SYSTEMS HAVE EVOLVED OVER TIME

Political parties are organizations that run candidates for political office and coordinate the actions of officials elected under the party banner. Looking around the world, we find many different kinds of parties. In numerous western European countries, the major political parties have millions of dues-paying members, and party leaders control what their elected officials do. In contrast, in many new democracies, candidates run as representatives of a party, but party leaders have no control over what candidates say during the campaign or how they act once they win office. America's major political parties, the Republicans and the Democrats, lie somewhere between these extremes. Many Americans have a deep, enduring connection to one of these parties, and these organizations' actions affect both election returns and policy outcomes.

However, rather than being unified organizations with party leaders at the top, candidates and party workers in the middle, and citizen-members at the bottom, American political parties are decentralized: they constitute a loose network of organizations, groups, and individuals who share a party label but are under no obligation to work together.[2] For example, the Speaker of the House of Representatives, John Boehner, is the leader of House members from his party, the Republicans, but he works independently of the party's national organization, the Republican National Committee (RNC); neither one is in charge of the other. Boehner is also not in charge of other Republican groups in Congress, such as the Tea Party Caucus; while Caucus members may listen to Boehner's arguments, they are under no obligation to do what he asks. Similarly, the RNC cannot command state and local Republican Party organizations to take some actions and not others. Moreover, while many Americans think of themselves as members of a political party, neither the Republicans nor the Democrats have formal membership. Someone

AMERICAN POLITICAL PARTIES have three largely separate components: the party organization, represented here by Debbie Wasserman Schultz, chair of the Democratic National Committee; the party in government, represented by House minority leader Nancy Pelosi and her leadership team; and the party in the electorate, exemplied by the crowd at a rally for Barack Obama.

party organization A specific political party's leaders and workers at the national, state, and local levels.

party in government The group of officeholders who belong to a specific political party and were elected as candidates of that party.

party in the electorate The group of citizens who identify with a specific political party.

party system A period in which the names of the major political parties, their supporters, and the issues dividing them remain relatively stable.

who identifies with the Republican Party does not have to work for the party, give money to the party, or vote for its candidates.

In light of this defining characteristic of American political parties, scholars describe these organizations as comprising three separate and largely independent pieces.[3] The **party organization** involves the structure of national, state, and local parties, including party leaders and workers. The **party in government** is made up of the politicians who were elected as candidates of the party. And the **party in the electorate** includes all the citizens who identify with the party. As you will see, organization matters: the fact that American political parties are split into three parts has important implications for what they do and for their impact on the nation's politics.

Political scientists use the term **party system** to describe periods in which the major parties' names, their groups of supporters, and the issues dividing them have all been constant. As Table 6.1 shows, there have been six party systems in America.[4] For each party system the table gives the names of the two major parties, indicates which party dominated (that is, won the most presidential elections or controlled Congress), and describes the principal issues dividing the parties.

THE FIRST FIVE PARTY SYSTEMS

THE FIRST PARTY SYSTEM, 1789–1828

Political parties formed soon after the Founding of the United States. While many of the Founders expressed their dislike of political parties, most affiliated with a party soon after the first elections. The first American parties, the Federalists and the Democratic-Republicans, were primarily parties in government. Federalists wanted a strong central government and a national bank, and they favored assumption of state war debts by the national government; Democratic-Republicans took

TABLE » 6.1

AMERICAN PARTY SYSTEMS

PARTY SYSTEM	MAJOR PARTIES (dominant party in boldface)	KEY ISSUES
First (1789–1828)	**Federalists**, Democratic-Republicans	Location of the capital, financial issues (e.g., national bank)
Second (1829–56)	**Democrats**, Whigs	Tariffs (farmers vs. merchants), slavery
Third (1857–96)	Democrats, **Republicans**	Slavery (pre–Civil War), Reconstruction (post–Civil War), industrialization
Fourth (1897–1932)	Democrats, **Republicans**	Industrialization, immigration
Fifth (1933–68)	**Democrats**, Republicans	Size and scope of the federal government
Sixth (1969–present)	Democrats, Republicans (neither party is dominant)	Size and scope of the federal government, civil rights, social issues, foreign policy

the opposite positions based on their preference for concentrating power at the state level. These political parties were quite different from their modern counterparts. In particular, there were no national party organizations, few citizens thought of themselves as party members, and candidates for office did not campaign as representatives of a political party.

THE SECOND PARTY SYSTEM, 1829-56

The second American party system began with the disintegration of the Federalist Party. Many Federalist legislators had opposed the War of 1812 and supported a politically unpopular pay raise for members of Congress.[5] Ultimately, Federalist politicians were either defeated for reelection or switched their party affiliation, thereby eliminating the Federalist Party as a political force in American politics.

The demise of the Federalists gave way to the so-called Era of Good Feelings, a period when there was only one political party, the Democratic-Republicans. Following the election of President Andrew Jackson in 1828, the organization that elected Jackson was transformed by him and by then-senator (later president) Martin Van Buren into the Democratic Party, the ancestor of the modern-day organization. At the same time another new party, the Whigs, was formed, and the Democratic-Republican Party dissolved, with most of its politicians becoming Democrats.

The new Democratic Party embodied two important innovations. First, it cultivated electoral support as a way of strengthening the party's hold on power in Washington. The party built organizations at the state and local levels to mobilize citizens to support its candidates. These efforts helped to bind citizens to the party, encouraging them to think of themselves as party members and creating the first American party in the electorate. The Democrats' second innovation was what Van Buren called the **party principle**, the idea that a party is not just

party principle The idea that a political party exists as an organization distinct from its elected officials or party leaders.

FOLLOWING HIS ELECTION IN 1828, President Andrew Jackson strengthened the Democratic Party by encouraging party organizations at the state and local level and by creating the spoils system to reward loyal party members. Here, Jackson makes a speech while on his way to Washington to take office.

spoils system The practice of rewarding party supporters with benefits like federal government positions.

a group of elected officials but an organization that exists apart from its candidates.[6] Jackson and Van Buren also created the **spoils system**, whereby individuals who worked for the party were rewarded with benefits such as jobs in the federal government.

THE THIRD PARTY SYSTEM, 1857-96

The issue of slavery split the second party system, leading to a third party system. Most Democratic politicians and party officials either supported slavery outright or wanted to avoid debating the issue.[7] The Whig Party was split between (1) politicians who agreed with the Democrats and (2) abolitionists who wanted to end slavery. Ultimately, antislavery Whigs left the party and formed a new organization, the Republican Party, which also attracted antislavery Democrats. As the remaining Whig candidates began to have difficulty winning office against both Republican and Democratic opponents, Whig officeholders left the party and joined one of these two more powerful parties. This move divided the country into a largely Republican Northeast, a largely Democratic South, and politically split midwestern and border states.[8]

political machine An unofficial patronage system within a political party that seeks to gain political power and government contracts, jobs, and other benefits for party leaders, workers, and supporters.

Although the Civil War settled the issue of slavery, it did not change the identity of the major American parties. In the postwar era, the Republicans and the Democrats remained the two prominent, national parties, and the same regional split persisted between these organizations. Slavery was no longer an issue, but the parties were divided on related concerns such as the withdrawal of the Union Army from southern states. At about the same time, the rapid growth of American cities and increased immigration raised new debate over the size and scope of the federal government: should it help farmers and rural residents, or the inhabitants of rapidly expanding cities, or neither group? A related concern was whether the federal government should regulate America's rapidly growing industrial base.

THE TAMMANY HALL POLITICAL machine, depicted here as a rotund version of one of its leaders, William "Boss" Tweed, controlled New York City politics for most of the nineteenth and early twentieth centuries. Its strategy was "honest graft," rewarding party workers, contributors, and voters for their efforts to keep the machine's candidates in office.

THE FOURTH PARTY SYSTEM, 1897-1932

The political parties took opposing positions on the issues identified above, leading to a fourth party system. Democrats, led by three-time presidential candidate William Jennings Bryan, attempted to build a coalition of rural and urban voters by proposing a larger, more active federal government and other policies that would help these groups. Although Bryan was never elected president, the issues he stood for divided the major parties and defined the debate in Washington for more than a generation.

During this period, especially in the late 1800s, political machines were common in cities and towns. A **political machine** is a party organization built around the goal of gaining political power to enrich party leaders, party workers, and citizen supporters.[9] Political machines give government services to citizens, government jobs to party workers, and government contracts to higher-level party officials and contributors. In return, the recipients of these benefits are expected to help by campaigning and voting for the machine's candidates, as well as by contributing to the party. One classic example of a political machine was Tammany Hall, an organization of Democratic Party politicians in New York City who were especially powerful during the late 1800s and early 1900s.[10]

However, civil service legislation in the 1890s and other reforms brought about a decline in party machines.

The move from the third to the fourth party system shows how American political parties reflect the basic divisions in society over what government should do. In the third party system, the parties were divided over slavery and, after the Civil War, the pace of Reconstruction. Once these issues were settled, politicians and party leaders found new issues to campaign on—partly because they cared about these issues and partly because taking these positions helped to attract votes and other support to themselves and to their party.

THE FIFTH PARTY SYSTEM, 1933–68

The fifth party system was born out of the Great Depression, a worldwide economic collapse. Many Republican politicians, especially Republican president Herbert Hoover, argued that conditions would improve over time and that government intervention would be costly and do little good to relieve declining prices, massive unemployment, and long lines of Americans seeking food assistance. However, Democratic challenger Franklin Roosevelt proposed new government programs that would help people in need and spur economic growth. Roosevelt won the 1932 presidential election, and many other Democrats won seats in Congress. Together, the president and Congress enacted the New Deal, a series of federal programs designed to stimulate the national economy, help needy people, and impose a variety of new regulations.

Debate over the New Deal brought together the **New Deal Coalition** of African Americans, Catholics, Jewish people, union members, and white southerners, who became strong supporters of Democratic candidates over the next generation.[11] This transformation also established the basic division between the Republican

New Deal Coalition The assemblage of groups who aligned with and supported the Democratic Party in support of New Deal policies during the fifth party system, including African Americans, Catholics, Jewish people, union members, and white southerners.

DEBATE OVER ROOSEVELT'S NEW DEAL programs established the basic divide between Democrats and Republicans that continues to this day: Democrats favor a strong federal government that takes an active role in the economy; Republicans prefer a smaller federal government and fewer programs and regulations.

and Democratic parties that persists to the present day: Democrats generally favor a large federal government that takes an active role in managing the economy and regulating individual and corporate behavior, while Republicans believe that many such programs should either be provided by state and local governments or be kept entirely separate from government.

THE SIXTH PARTY SYSTEM, 1969–PRESENT

A sixth party system emerged as new political questions and debates divided the parties.[12] Beginning in the late 1940s, and continuing more decisively during the 1960s, many Democratic candidates and party leaders, particularly outside the South, came out against the "separate but equal" system of racial discrimination in southern states and in favor of programs designed to ensure equal opportunity for minority citizens throughout the nation.

At the same time, Democratic politicians, particularly President Lyndon Johnson, argued for expanding the federal government into health care funding (in the form of the Medicare and Medicaid programs), antipoverty programs, education, and public works. Johnson called his plan the Great Society. Although some Republican politicians supported portions of the Great Society, particularly the civil rights reforms, there was considerable Republican opposition to expanding the role of government in society.

This division on civil rights—along with differences on other issues such as foreign policy, abortion rights, and the size and scope of government—produced a gradual but significant shift in the groups that identified with each party. White southerners and some Catholics gradually moved to the Republican Party, and minorities, particularly African Americans, started identifying more strongly as Democrats. Candidates (particularly those entering politics) either chose or changed their party affiliations to reflect the new party coalitions. By the late 1980s all three elements of the Republican and Democratic parties (organization, government, and electorate) were much more like-minded than they had been a generation earlier.

The sixth party system also brought changes in the party organizations. Both the Republican and the Democratic parties became parties in service, increasing their involvement in recruiting, training, conducting fund-raising, and campaigning for their party's congressional and presidential candidates.[13] Just as in the first party system, the parties in government became more involved in campaigns as a way of electing like-minded colleagues who would vote with them to enact their preferred policies. At the same time, the parties in government began to play a larger role in building policy compromises within and across the parties and in working to shape legislative proceedings to enact these compromises into law.

realignment A change in the size or composition of the party coalitions or in the nature of the issues that divide the parties. Realignments typically occur within an election cycle or two, but they can also occur gradually over the course of a decade or longer.

REALIGNMENTS

Each party system is separated from the next by a **realignment**—a change in one or more of the factors that define a party system. These factors include the issues that divide supporters and candidates from each party, the nature and function of the party organizations, the composition of the party coalitions, and the specifics of government policy.

In some cases a realignment begins with the emergence of a new question or issue debate that captures the attention of large numbers of ordinary citizens, activists, and politicians.[14] For example, in the case of the second party system (1829–56), the new issue was slavery.[15] Although most Democratic Party leaders and elected officials supported keeping slavery legal, the Whig Party was split between proslavery and abolitionist members. The result was the formation of a new political party, the Republicans, by antislavery Whigs and some Democrats. Likewise, as noted, the fifth party system (1933–68) was born during the Great Depression, when the parties were primarily divided by their positions on the appropriate size of the federal government and how much it should control the behavior of individuals and corporations.

While issues appear to be the driving force behind realignments and the move from one party system to another, other factors also contribute to the separation between party systems. For example, one important factor that separated the fifth from the sixth party system was the introduction of new technologies such as television and the ability to measure public opinion by using mass surveys, which enabled candidates to win political office without the help of a party organization. Moreover, the changes between the fifth and sixth party systems were to some extent the result of changes in the party coalitions, as white southerners moved to the Republican Party.

MODERN AMERICAN POLITICAL PARTIES

DESCRIBE THE MAIN CHARACTERISTICS OF AMERICAN PARTIES AS ORGANIZATIONS, IN THE GOVERNMENT, AND IN THE ELECTORATE

In this section we examine the contemporary Democratic and Republican parties in terms of their party organization, party in government, and party in the electorate. We show how these distinct parts work, and we consider some implications of the parties' three-part structure.

THE PARTY ORGANIZATION

The principal body in each party organization is the **national committee**, which consists of representatives from state party organizations, usually one man and one woman per state. The state party organizations in turn are made up of professional staff plus thousands of party organizations at the county, city, and town levels. The job of these organizations is to run the party's day-to-day operations, recruit candidates and supporters, raise money for future campaigns, and work to build a consensus on major issues.

Both major parties also include a number of constituency groups (the Democrats' term) or teams (the Republicans' term). These organizations within the party work to attract the support of demographic groups considered likely to share the party's issue concerns—such as specific racial or ethnic groups, people with strong religious beliefs, senior citizens, women, and many others—and assist in fund-raising.[16]

national committee An American political party's principal organization, comprising party representatives from each state.

Each party organization also includes groups designed to build support for or coordinate the efforts of particular individuals or politicians. These include the Democratic and the Republican Governors' Associations, the Young Democrats, the Young Republicans, and more specialized groups such as the Republican Lawyers' Organization or the Democratic Leadership Council (DLC), an organization of moderate Democratic politicians.[17]

Many other groups, such as **political action committees (PACs)** or **527 organizations**, labor unions, and other interest groups and organizations, are loosely affiliated with one of the major parties. For example, the organization MoveOn.org typically supports Democratic candidates. Similar organizations on the Republican side include the Club for Growth and many evangelical groups. Though these groups often favor one party over the other, they are not part of the party organization and do not always agree with the party's positions or support its candidates; in fact, many have to operate independently of the parties and their candidates in order to preserve their tax-exempt status. (For more details on campaign finance see Chapters 7, Elections, and 8, Interest Groups.) While the Tea Party organizations discussed at the beginning of this chapter share the label of "party" with the Republican and Democratic parties, in function and appearance they more closely resemble these other loosely affiliated organizations. For example, they do not run candidates on their own; rather, they support candidates—almost always Republicans—who are running for a major-party nomination.

As this description suggests, the party organization has a fluid structure rather than a rigid hierarchy.[18] Individuals and groups work with a party's leaders and candidates when they share the same goals, but unless they are paid party employees, they are under no obligation to do so (even paid party workers can quit rather than work for a candidate or a cause they oppose).

PARTY ORGANIZATIONS AT THE LOCAL level coordinate support for the party's candidates, but they don't necessarily have to follow the lead of the national party organization.

political action committee (PAC) An interest group or a division of an interest group that can raise money to contribute to campaigns or to spend on ads in support of candidates. The amount a PAC can receive from each of its donors and the amount it can spend on federal electioneering are strictly limited.

527 organization A tax-exempt group formed primarily to influence elections through voter mobilization efforts and issue ads that do not directly endorse or oppose a candidate. Unlike political action committees, they are not subject to contribution limits and spending caps.

PARTY BRAND NAMES

The Republican and Democratic Party organizations have well-established **brand names**. Because the parties stand for different things, both in terms of their preferred government policies and in terms of their ideological leanings, the party names themselves become a shorthand way of providing information to voters about the parties' candidates.[19] Hearing the term *Democrat* or *Republican* calls to mind ideas about what kinds of positions the members of each party support, what kinds of candidates each party runs, and how these candidates are likely to behave in office. Citizens can use these brand names as a cue to decide whom to vote for in an election. (See Chapter 7 for more information on voting cues.)

brand names The use of party names to evoke certain positions or issues. For instance, "Adidas" might immediately call to mind athletics in the same way that "Democrat" might remind you of environmental policies or universal health care.

THE LIMITS OF THE PARTY ORGANIZATION

One critical thing to understand about the Democratic and Republican party organizations is that they are not hierarchies. No one person or group in charge determines what either organization does. Within the Republican National Committee (RNC) and Democratic National Committee (DNC), the party organization's issue positions are set not by the committee chair but by DNC or RNC members from all 50 states. If the committee chair and the committee disagree, the chair cannot force the committee members to do what he or she wants. In many cases, from civil rights proposals in the 1950s to health care reform in 2009, the Democratic Party has been internally divided, but party leaders have been unable to force a consensus. The Republican Party is likewise subject to the same limitations.

The national party organization is also unable to force state and local parties to share its positions on issues or comply with other requests. State and local parties make their own decisions about state- and local-level candidates and issue positions. The National Committee can ask nicely, cajole, or even threaten to withhold funds (although such threats are rare), but if a state party organization, an independent group, or even an individual candidate disagrees with the National Committee, there's little the National Committee can do to force compliance.

THE PARTY IN GOVERNMENT

The party in government consists of elected officials holding national, state, and local offices who have taken office as candidates of a particular party. They are the public face of the party, somewhat like the players on a sports team. Though players are only one part of a sports franchise—along with owners, coaches, trainers, and support staff—their identities are what most people call to mind when they think of the team. Because the party in government is made up of officeholders, it has a direct impact on government policy. Members of the party organization can recruit candidates, write platforms, and pay for campaign ads, but only those who win elections—that is, the party in government—get to serve as members of Congress or as executive officials and actually propose, debate, vote on, and sign the legislation that determines what government does.

The party in government is largely independent of the party organization. Some elected officials or former elected officials serve as members of their party's national committee or hold a position in a state or local organization, but most American politicians go through their entire political careers without holding a position in their party organization.

CAUCUSES AND CONFERENCES

The Democratic and Republican parties in government in the House and Senate are organized around working groups—Democrats call theirs a **caucus**, and Republicans have a **conference**. The party caucus or conference serves as a forum for debate, compromise, and strategizing among a party's elected officials. For example, throughout 2009 members of the House Democratic Caucus held numerous meetings to decide their group's position on health care reform.[20] The Democrats' strategy for addressing these proposals reflected the consensus reached in the caucus.

Each party's caucus or conference also meets to decide legislative committee assignments, leadership positions on committees, and leadership positions within the caucus or conference.[21] Caucus or conference leaders serve as spokespeople for their respective parties, particularly when the president is from the other party. The party in government also contains groups that recruit and support candidates for political office, the Democratic Congressional Campaign Committee (DCCC),

caucus (congressional) The organization of Democrats within the House and Senate that meets to discuss and debate the party's positions on various issues in order to reach a consensus and to assign leadership positions.

conference The organization of Republicans within the House and Senate that meets to discuss and debate the party's positions on various issues in order to reach a consensus and to assign leadership positions.

the Democratic Senatorial Campaign Committee (DSCC), the National Republican Senatorial Committee (NRSC), and the National Republican Congressional Committee (NRCC).

POLICY POSITIONS

The modern Congress is polarized: in both the House and the Senate, Republicans and Democrats hold different views on government policy. Figure 6.1 compares legislators on the basis of their ideology, or their general feelings about government policy, as measured by a liberal–conservative scale. The data reflect two House sessions: the contemporary 112th House (served 2011–12) and the 83rd House of almost 60 years ago (served 1953–55).

These graphs tell us two things. First, over the last 60 years the magnitude of ideological differences between the parties in Congress has increased. In the 83rd House there was some overlap between the positions of Democrats and Republicans, but it had disappeared by the time of the 112th House.[22]

The second fact that Figure 6.1 reveals is that both parties in government include a mixture of ideologies, not a uniform consensus opinion. In the 83rd House plot, for example, Democrats vary from the relatively liberal left end of the scale to

---

FIGURE » 6.1

IDEOLOGY OF THE PARTIES IN GOVERNMENT: HOUSE OF REPRESENTATIVES, 1952 AND 2010

Over the last several decades, ideological differences between Democrats and Republicans in Congress have increased significantly. However, even in the 112th House, both parties still included a wide range of views. In light of these data, would you expect more or less partisan conflict in the modern Congress than there was in the early 1950s? According to these data, would you expect House members in each party to agree on what policies to pursue?

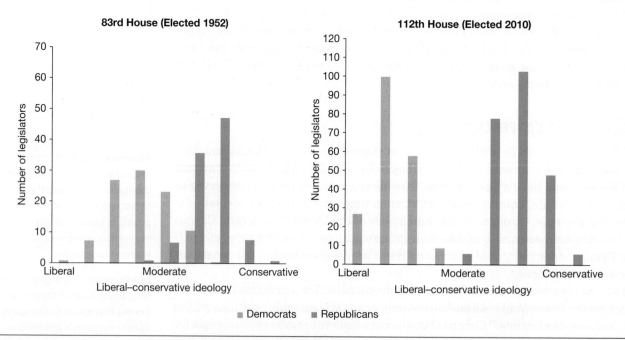

Source: Calculated from Royce Carroll, Jeff Lewis, James Lo, Nolan McCarty, Keith Poole, and Howard Rosenthal, "DW-NOMINATE Scores with Bootstrapped Standard Errors," January 23, 2009, www.voteview.com/dwnomin.htm (accessed 8/31/12).

the moderate (middle) and even somewhat conservative right side. Democrats in the 112th House were, on average, more liberal than their colleagues in the 83rd, but a wide range of ideologies were still represented in the Democratic caucus. The same is true for Republicans, who leaned in the conservative direction in both the 112th and the 83rd Houses.

The range of positions among members of the party in government can create situations in which a caucus or conference is divided on a policy question. Compromise within a party's working group is not inevitable—even though legislators share a party label, they may not be able to find common ground. On the Republican side, divisions arose in 2011 over the need for tax increases in deficit-reduction packages, with one group (including Tea Party members and some Democrats) opposing any tax increases, while other Republicans were willing to accept some modest increases.[23]

THE PARTY IN THE ELECTORATE

The party in the electorate consists of citizens who identify with a particular political party. Most Americans say they are either Democrats or Republicans, although the percentage has declined over the last two generations. **Party identification (party ID)** is a critical variable in understanding votes and other forms of political participation.

party identification (party ID) A citizen's loyalty to a specific political party.

PARTY IDENTIFICATION

Party identification is different from formal membership in a political party. Although the Republicans and the Democrats have websites where people can sign up to receive e-mail alerts and to contribute to party causes, joining a party does not give a citizen any direct influence over what the party does. It is the party leaders and the candidates themselves who make the day-to-day decisions. These individuals often heed citizens' demands, but there is no requirement that they do so. Real participation in party operations is open to citizens who become activists by working for a party organization or one of its candidates. Activists' contributions vary from stuffing envelopes to helping out with a phone bank, being a delegate to a party convention, attending campaign rallies, or campaigning door-to-door. Relatively few Americans are activists, only a small percentage of the population.

Figure 6.2 gives data on party identification in America over the last 60 years. The first plot shows that the Democratic Party had a considerable advantage in terms of the number of citizens identifying with the party from the 1930s until the late 1980s. During the 1970s nearly half of adults identified with the Democratic Party, and only about 20 percent identified with the Republicans. During the 1990s the percentage of Democratic identifiers decreased significantly and the percentage of Republican identifiers increased slightly, to the point that in 2002 the parties had roughly the same percentage of identifiers.[24] However, beginning in 2003 the Democrats again opened up a significant advantage in terms of identifiers, although the difference has largely disappeared in recent years. The two lines in Figure 6.2 do not add up

ACTIVIST VOLUNTEERS UNDERTAKE most of the one-on-one efforts to mobilize support for a party and its candidates.

FIGURE » 6.2

PARTY IDENTIFICATION TRENDS AMONG AMERICAN VOTERS

In terms of party identification, the parties have moved from rough parity in the 1930s and 1940s, to a period of Democratic advantage that lasted from the 1950s to the 1980s. Beginning in 2003, Democrats appeared to be opening up another advantage, although this change has eroded in recent years. What events might have caused these changes in party identification?

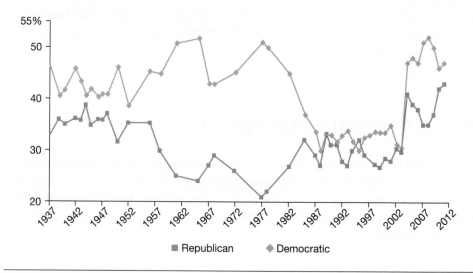

Source: Pew Research Center, "GOP Makes Big Gains among White Voters," July 22, 2011, www.people-press .org/2011/07/22/gop-makes-big-gains-among-white-voters/ (accessed 9/17/12).

to 100 percent, and the difference represents the percentage of independent voters who do not identify with either party. Just like the percentages of Republican and Democratic identifiers, the percentage of independents fluctuates over time.

Looking more closely at vote decisions, Figure 6.3 shows how Democrats, Republicans, and independents voted in the 2012 presidential election. Almost all Democrats voted for Barack Obama, the Democratic nominee; and almost all Republicans voted for Mitt Romney, the Republican nominee. Independent voters slightly favored Romney, but Obama won because Democrats are the largest group in the electorate. Simply put, if you are trying to predict how someone will vote, the most important thing to know is his or her party identification.[25] Party ID also influences other kinds of political behavior; for example, people whose identification is strong are more likely to work for the party or to make a contribution compared to people with weak party identification.[26]

PARTY COALITIONS

party coalitions The groups that identify with a political party, usually described in demographic terms such as African American Democrats or evangelical Republicans.

Data on party ID enable scholars to identify the **party coalitions**, or groups of citizens who identify with each party. Table 6.2 shows the contemporary Democratic and Republican party coalitions. As you can see, some groups are disproportionately likely to identify as Democrats (African Americans), some are disproportionately likely to be Republicans (white evangelicals), and other groups have no clear favorite party (people with some college education).

FIGURE » 6.3

THE IMPACT OF PARTY IDENTIFICATION ON VOTE DECISIONS IN THE 2012 PRESIDENTIAL ELECTION

Americans are much more likely to vote for candidates who share their party affiliation. What does this relationship tell us about the impact of campaign events (including speeches, debates, and gaffes) on vote decisions?

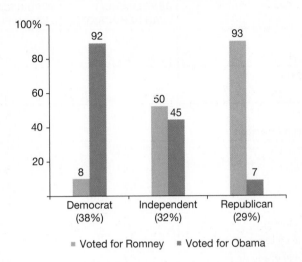

■ Voted for Romney   ■ Voted for Obama

Source: CNN Exit Poll, www.cnn.com/election/2012/results/race/president#exit-polls (accessed 11/7/12).

The Republican and Democratic party coalitions differ systematically in terms of their policy preferences—what they want government to do—as shown in Table 6.3 The second and third columns give the percentages of Republican and Democratic identifiers who considered each item a priority. The fourth column shows the differences between the Republican and Democratic party coalitions, which disagree about the relative importance of issues such as providing health insurance to the uninsured, addressing global warming, and strengthening the military. These data demonstrate that party labels are meaningful: if you know someone is a Republican (or a Democrat), this information tells you something about what that person probably wants government to do, and how he or she will likely vote in the next election.

THE ROLE OF POLITICAL PARTIES IN AMERICAN POLITICS

EXPLAIN THE IMPORTANT FUNCTIONS THAT PARTIES PERFORM IN THE POLITICAL SYSTEM

Political parties play an important dual role in American politics, based on contesting elections yet also building consensus across branches of government. However, these activities are not necessarily coordinated. Candidates and groups at different levels of a party organization may work together, refuse to cooperate, or even actively oppose one another's efforts.

TABLE » 6.2

THE PARTY COALITIONS

Many groups, such as African Americans and white evangelicals, are much more likely to affiliate with one party than the other. What are the implications of these differences for the positions taken by each party's candidates?

		DEMOCRATIC/ LEAN DEMOCRATIC	REPUBLICAN/ LEAN REPUBLICAN
Gender	Male	43%	47%
	Female	52	42
Age	18–29	52%	39%
	30+	45	47
Race	White	39%	52%
	African American	86	8
Region	Northeast	45%	41%
	Midwest	38	50
	South	35	57
	West	41	50
Education	No college	48%	44%
	Some college	46	45
	College graduate	59	41
Religion	White evangelical	32%	60%
	White mainline Protestant	40	49
	White Catholic	40	50

Source: Pew Research Center, "GOP Makes Big Gains among White Voters," July 22, 2011, http://www .people-press.org/2011/07/22/gop-makes-big-gains-among-white-voters/ (accessed 9/17/12).

CONTESTING ELECTIONS

In modern American politics virtually everyone elected to a state or national political office is either a Republican or a Democrat. In the 111th Congress, elected in 2012, there were only two independent senators and no independent House members. In fall 2012, a total of 49 of 50 states' governors were either Democrats or Republicans; and of more than 7,300 state legislators, very few were independents or minor-party candidates, including those elected with Tea Party support.

RECRUITING AND NOMINATING CANDIDATES

Actions taken inside party organizations shape citizens' choices on Election Day. Historically, the recruitment of candidates was left up to local party organizations. But the process has become much more systematic, with national party leaders playing a central role in finding and recruiting candidates—and often promising those candidates help in assembling a staff, organizing a campaign, and raising money.[27]

For all of these efforts, though, parties do not control who runs in House or Senate races. In most states, candidates for these offices are selected in a **primary**

primary A ballot vote in which citizens select a party's nominee for the general election.

TABLE » 6.3

ISSUE DIFFERENCES BETWEEN THE REPUBLICAN AND DEMOCRATIC PARTIES IN THE ELECTORATE

PERCENTAGE CONSIDERING EACH AS A "TOP PRIORITY"	REPUBLICANS	DEMOCRATS	REPUBLICAN–DEMOCRATIC DIFFERENCE
Providing health insurance to uninsured	26%	75%	–49
Dealing with global warming	11	43	–32
Dealing with problems of poor	40	67	–27
Protecting the environment	34	60	–26
Reducing health care costs	48	71	–23
Improving educational system	54	75	–21
Securing Medicare	54	72	–18
Dealing with U.S. energy problem	43	56	–13
Improving job situation	80	90	–10
Reducing crime	46	55	–9
Securing Social Security	62	68	–6
Strengthening nation's economy	81	87	–6
Dealing with global trade	32	37	–5
Reducing middle-class taxes	45	45	0
Reducing budget deficit	61	60	+1
Dealing with moral breakdown	52	45	+7
Defending U.S. against terrorism	89	80	+9
Reducing influence of lobbyists	45	27	+18
Dealing with illegal immigration	49	30	+19
Strengthening the military	64	44	+20

Source: Pew Research Center, "Energy Concerns Fall, Deficit Concerns Rise," January 25, 2010, www.people-press.org/files/legacy-pdf/584.pdf (accessed 9/17/12).

election or a **caucus**, in which they compete for a particular party's spot on the ballot. (Most states use primaries; a few state parties use conventions to select candidates.) Nuts and Bolts 6.1 further explains these different ways that the parties select candidates.

Running as a party's nominee is almost always the easiest way to get on the general election ballot. Some states give the Republican and Democratic nominees an automatic spot on the ballot; even in states that don't automatically allocate ballot slots this way, the requirements for the major parties to get a candidate on the

caucus (electoral) A local meeting in which party members select a party's nominee for the general election.

TYPES OF PRIMARIES AND CAUCUSES

PRIMARY ELECTION	An election in which voters choose the major party nominees for political office, who subsequently compete in a general election.
Closed primary	A primary election system in which only registered party members can vote in their party's primary.
Nonpartisan primary	A primary election system in which candidates from both parties are listed on the same primary ballot. Following a nonpartisan primary, the two candidates who receive the most votes in the primary compete in the general election, even if they are from the same party.
Open ("crossover") primary	A primary election system in which any registered voter can participate in either party's primary, regardless of the voter's party affiliation.
Semi-closed primary	A primary election system where voters registered as party members must vote in their party's primary, but registered independents can vote in either party's primary.
CAUCUS ELECTION	A series of local meetings at which registered voters select a particular candidate's supporters as delegates who will vote for the candidate in a later, state-level convention. (In national elections, the state-convention delegates select delegates to the national convention.) Caucuses are used in some states to select delegates to the major parties' presidential nominating conventions. Some states' caucuses are open to members of any party, while others are closed.

ballot are much less onerous than those for minor parties and independents. In California, for example, a party and its candidates automatically qualify for a position on the ballot if any of the party's candidates for statewide office received more than 2 percent of the vote in the previous election. In contrast, independent candidates need to file petitions with more than 150,000 signatures to get on the ballot without a major-party label—an expensive, time-consuming task.[28] These advantages help explain why virtually all prominent candidates for Congress and the presidency run as Democrats or Republicans—including many congressional candidates who ran with Tea Party support in 2010 and 2012.

National parties also manage the nomination process for presidential candidates. This process involves a series of primaries and caucuses held over a six-month period beginning in January of a presidential election year. The type of election (primary or caucus; about two-thirds of states use primaries) and its date are determined by state legislatures, although national party committees can limit the allowable dates, using their control over seating delegates at the party conventions to motivate compliance. Voters in these primaries and caucuses don't directly select the parties' nominees. Instead, citizens' votes are used to determine how many of each candidate's supporters become delegates to the party's national **nominating convention**, where delegates vote to choose the party's presidential and vice-presidential nominees. The national party organizations determine how many delegates each state sends to the convention based on factors such as state population, the number of votes the party's candidate received in each state in the last presidential election, and the number of House members and senators from the party that each state elected.

nominating convention A meeting held by each party every four years at which states' delegates select the party's presidential and vice-presidential nominees and approve the party platform.

How It Works

NOMINATING PRESIDENTIAL CANDIDATES

OPEN PRIMARIES
Open to voters from any political party and independents

CLOSED PRIMARIES
Only voters registered with party vote

CAUCUSES
Party members meet in groups to select delegates

SELECT DELEGATES TO NATIONAL CONVENTION

Republican Party
States can divide delegates or give all to the winning candidate.

Democratic Party
The state's delegates are divided up proportionately.

NATIONAL NOMINATING CONVENTIONS

Delegates from all states attend the national convention, where they vote for the party's presidential and vice presidential nominees, based on the primary and caucus results. Superdelegates—important party leaders—also vote at the convention.

POP QUIZ!

1 In an open primary
a only voters from that party vote.
b members of any party and independents may vote.
c party members meet in groups.
d voters select more than one candidate for each office.
e delegates are not selected.

2 Primary elections and caucuses select
a delegates, who support a specific candidate at the national convention.
b superdelegates, who support a specific candidate at the national convention.
c state party leaders.
d the president and vice president.
e members of the electoral college.

ONE OF THE MOST IMPORTANT WAYS parties help candidates is by raising money to fund campaigns. In 2012, the DNC raised nearly a billion dollars to help re-elect Obama and to support other Democratic candidates. The RNC raised a similar amount.

CAMPAIGN ASSISTANCE

One of the most visible ways that the political parties support candidates is by contributing to and spending money on campaign activities. By and large, federal law mandates that these funds be spent by the organization that raised them; the national party, for example, is limited in the amount of money it can contribute to congressional and presidential candidates or to state party organizations. As we discuss in Chapter 7, however, party organizations that raise campaign funds can use them to help candidates get elected through independent expenditures—by running their own ads in a candidate's district or state.

Figure 6.4 shows the amount of money raised by the top groups within the Republican and Democratic parties for the 2012 election (through November 2). The final figures show that the parties and their various committees raised nearly a billion dollars each. The Democratic and Republican national committees (DNC and RNC) raised the most money, but the congressional campaign committees also raised significant sums. Congressional Democratic committees outraised their Republican counterparts. State and local party committees also raised large sums in the 2012 election.

Along with supplying campaign funds, party organizations give candidates other assistance, ranging from offering campaign advice (on which issues to emphasize, how to deal with the press, and the like) to conducting polls. Party organizations at all levels also undertake get-out-the-vote activities, encouraging supporters to get to the polls.

PARTY PLATFORMS

party platform A set of objectives outlining the party's issue positions and priorities. Candidates are not required to support their party's platform.

The **party platform** is a set of promises about what candidates from the party will do if they are elected. The most visible party platform is the one approved at each party's presidential nominating convention, but the party organizations in the House and Senate also release platforms, as do other groups in the major parties. Party platforms generally reflect the brand-name differences between the parties discussed earlier. For example, in the case of abortion rights the 2012 Republican presidential platform favored a total ban on abortions, while the Democratic presidential platform in 2012 expressed support for a woman's right to choose, meaning that abortion would be legal under a wider range of conditions.

FIGURE » 6.4

DEMOCRATIC AND REPUBLICAN FUND-RAISING IN THE 2011–12 ELECTION CYCLE

In the 2011–12 election cycle, party committees raised more than $1.7 billion in campaign funds. Although most of this money was raised by the national committees, the state, local, and candidate committees also raised significant sums. To what extent might these funds allow the national committees to force candidates to run on the party platform?

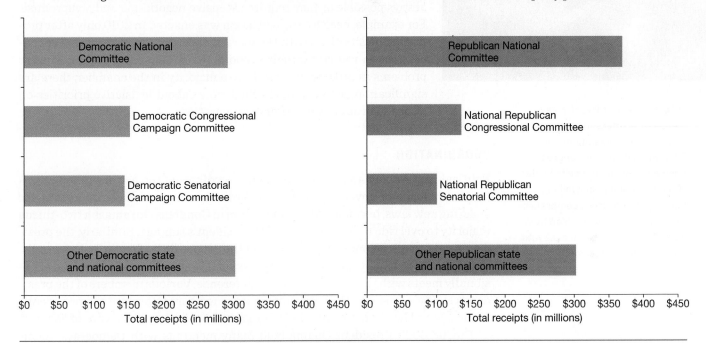

Note: Figures are based on Federal Election Commission data released on November 2, 2012.

Source: Federal Election Commission data provided by the Center for Responsive Politics, www.opensecrets.org/parties/index.php (accessed 11/2/12).

In theory, party platforms describe differences between the major parties, capture each party's diagnosis of the problems facing the country, and present the party's plan for solving those problems. In this way, party platforms give citizens an easy way to evaluate candidates. However, candidates are not obligated to support their party's platform, and many take divergent stances on some issues. For example, notwithstanding the consistently strong prochoice position on abortion in the Democratic Party's presidential platforms over the last generation, some Democratic congressional candidates, such as Pennsylvania senator Robert Casey, have promised to vote to restrict abortions if elected—a position closer to the Republican platform.[30] For some of these candidates, this position has reflected personal or religious beliefs; for others, it has been driven by the desire to reflect the opinion of voters in their district or state.

COOPERATION IN GOVERNMENT

Parties also play an important role in enabling like-minded politicians to cooperate on policy plans and strategies for enacting these proposals. Parties in government develop agendas, coordinate the actions of members across branches of government, and provide accountability to voters.

FOCUSING ON PARTIES CAN MAKE it easier for voters to issue rewards and punishments. In 2011, Republicans in Congress (including Senate minority leader Mitch McConnell, shown here) held numerous press conferences to contrast their position on the budget and the national debt with the Democrats' position.

AGENDA SETTING

Throughout the year the parties in government meet to devise strategies for legislative action—that is, to set agendas. What proposals should they offer, and in what order should they be considered? Should they try to make a deal with the president or with legislators from the other party?

However, the party in government can act collectively this way only when its members can agree on what they want. Such agreement is not always possible or may require extensive negotiation and compromise. For example, health care legislation was enacted in 2010 only after protracted negotiations with Democratic senators and the granting of concessions in return for their support. House Republicans faced similar problems in 2011: while they have a majority in the chamber, there are significant disagreements in their ranks about legislative priorities on issues such as budget cuts and immigration.

COORDINATION

Political parties play an important role in coordinating the actions taken in different branches of government. Such coordination is extremely important for enacting new laws, because unless supporters in Congress can amass a two-thirds majority to override a veto, they need the president's support. Similarly, the president needs congressional support to enact the proposals he favors. To these ends, the president routinely meets with congressional leaders from his party and occasionally meets with the entire caucus or conference. Various members of the president's staff also meet with House and Senate members to present the president's proposals and hear what members of Congress from both parties want to enact.

During 2009 President Obama held many meetings with Democratic members of Congress to lobby them to support his proposals for health care reform. Although many congressional Democrats supported Obama's proposals, enactment was nearly derailed by several Democratic representatives and senators who demanded amendments to restrict government payment for abortions. Obama opposed these efforts but was powerless to stop them. In fact, getting the last few votes needed for enactment required Obama to promise to issue an executive order that had essentially the same effect as the proposed amendments.

Coordination can also occur between caucuses or conferences in the House and Senate. At the same time that President Obama and Democrats in Congress were negotiating over health care reform, congressional Republicans were devising strategies for delaying and defeating these proposals. Although their efforts did not prevent the enactment of reform legislation, their strong opposition required the president and congressional leaders to accept many changes favored by moderate and conservative Democrats in order to enact the legislation without Republican support. Such coordination efforts require real work and compromise, as party leaders in the House and the Senate do not have authority over each other or over the elected members of their party. Nor can the president order a House member or senator to do anything, even if the legislator is from the president's own party.

ACCOUNTABILITY

One of the most important roles of political parties in a democracy is giving citizens identifiable groups to reward or punish for government actions, thereby providing a means for voters to focus their desire for accountability. By rewarding and punishing elected officials, often based on their party affiliation and other party members' behavior in office, voters use the party system to hold officials accountable for outcomes such as the state of the economy or America's relations with other nations.

During periods of **unified government**, when one party holds majorities in both the House and the Senate *and* controls the presidency, that party is the **party in power**. It has enough votes to enact policies in Congress and a good chance of having them signed into law by the president. During times of **divided government**, when one party controls Congress but not the presidency, or when different parties control the House and Senate, the president's party is considered the party in power. Focusing on parties makes it easy for a citizen to issue rewards and punishments. Is the economy doing well? Then that citizen is likely to vote for the candidates from the party in power. But if the economy is doing poorly, or if the citizen feels that government is wasting tax money or enacting bad policies, she or he can vote for candidates from the party that is currently out of power. When citizens behave this way, they strengthen the incentive for elected officials from the party in power to work together to develop policies that address voters' concerns— on the premise that if they do, voters will reward them with another term in office.

Consider the 2010 midterm election, when many Americans voted against Democratic candidates because of poor economic conditions. While Democrats lost seats in both the House and the Senate, most Democratic incumbents were returned to office. Why? Some were elected from states or districts dominated by Democratic identifiers. But many others were reelected because they campaigned on a platform of changing policy or because of their efforts to help local businesses, saying in effect, "Instead of punishing me for my party affiliation, reward me for working on your behalf."

In sum, while parties in government can do all of these things, there is no guarantee that individuals elected under a party's banner will agree to do so. For example, candidates may refuse to endorse their party's platform because it conflicts with their own policy goals, or because it would be unpopular with their constituents. Accordingly, one of the biggest problems for party leaders is to forge compromise among their candidates and elected members—to ensure that the party can act as a unified, disciplined organization.

unified government A situation in which one party holds a majority of seats in the House and Senate and the president is a member of that same party.

party in power Under unified government, the party that controls the House, Senate, and the presidency. Under divided government, the president's party.

divided government A situation in which the House, Senate, and presidency are not controlled by the same party, such as if Democrats hold the majority of House and Senate seats, and the president is a Republican.

MINOR PARTIES

CONSIDER THE ROLE OF MINOR PARTIES IN A SYSTEM DOMINATED BY TWO MAJOR PARTIES

So far, this chapter has focused on the major American political parties—the Republicans and the Democrats—and paid less attention to other party organizations. The reason is that minor political parties in America are *so* minor that they are generally not significant players on the political stage. Many such parties exist, but few run candidates in more than a handful of races, and very few minor-party candidates win political office. Few Americans identify with minor parties, and most exist for only a relatively short period.

MINOR-PARTY PRESIDENTIAL CANDIDATES

Even so, you may think we're giving minor parties too little attention. Consider Ralph Nader, who ran as the Green Party nominee for president in 2000, winning almost 5 percent of the vote. In some states the number of votes Nader received exceeded the margin separating Democrat Al Gore from Republican George Bush. In particular, in Florida, where Bush won by only a few hundred votes after

SHOULD PARTIES CHOOSE THEIR CANDIDATES?

One of the facts of life for the leaders of the Democratic and Republican parties is that they cannot determine who runs as their party's candidate for political office. They can encourage some candidates to run and attempt to discourage others by endorsing their favorites and funneling money, staff support, and other forms of assistance to the candidates they prefer. But in the end, congressional candidates get on the ballot by winning a primary or a vote at a state party convention; presidential candidates compete in a series of primaries and caucuses.

Political parties don't always get the nominees that their leaders want. In the 2010 election cycle, for example, insurgent (and Tea Party–backed) candidates Christine O'Donnell in Delaware and Joe Miller in Alaska captured their party's nominations for U.S. Senate seats. In Alaska, Miller defeated incumbent Lisa Murkowski; in Delaware, O'Donnell won an open seat contest against a veteran House member, Mike Castle. After their primary victories, both candidates struggled to justify extreme positions they had taken in the past. These problems came as no surprise to Delaware and Alaska Republican state party leaders, virtually all of whom had favored the losing candidates, based on the calculation that they were more likely to win in the general election. The expectations of the state party leaders proved correct, as Miller lost in the general election to a write-in campaign by Murkowski and O'Donnell was defeated by a little-known Democratic opponent. However, because both state parties chose their nominees in primaries, state party leaders had to accept whoever won the primary, even if they preferred another candidate.

Party leaders cannot force candidates out of a race. In spring 2008, many Democratic Party leaders wanted Hillary Clinton to end her presidential candidacy as it became increasingly clear that Barack Obama would win the nomination. Clinton stayed in the race until the primaries ended, forcing Obama to campaign aggressively, spend additional campaign funds, and respond to attacks from the Clinton campaign.

Why not let party leaders pick their candidates? Many scholars have argued that doing so would increase the chances of getting experienced, talented candidates on the ballot.[a] After all, party leaders probably know more than the average primary voter about who would make a good candidate or elected official. Plus, party leaders have a strong incentive to find good candidates and convince them to run—their party's influence over government policy increases with the number of people they can elect to political office.

Why, then, do voters in America get to pick party nominees in primaries? Direct primaries were introduced in American politics during the late 1800s and early 1900s.[b] The goal was explicit: reform-minded party activists wanted to take the choice of nominees out of the hands of party leaders and give it to the electorate, with the assumption that voters should be

In 2012, some Republicans worried that the fierce fight in the primary elections turned off voters, divided the party, and depleted campaign funds that would be better spent campaigning against Obama in the general election.

able to influence the choice of candidates for the general election. Moreover, reformers believed that this goal outweighed the expertise held by party leaders.

Here is the trade-off: if party leaders selected nominees, they would likely choose electable candidates who share the policy goals held by party leaders. If voters choose nominees, they can pick whoever they want, using whatever criteria they like—but there is no guarantee that these candidates will be skilled general-election campaigners or effective in office.

Of course, our system of primary elections is unlikely to go away. However, it would be possible to increase the influence that party leaders have over the process. One option would be to change campaign finance laws to increase the importance of the parties as a source of campaign funds. Another is to create a mechanism such as a state or district-level convention where party leaders could select candidates for a primary—and making it harder for candidates to get on the ballot without the leaders' endorsement.

Critical **Thinking** Questions

1. Would a system that gave additional power to party leaders in selecting nominees generally help incumbents more than challengers or the reverse?

2. What kind of nomination procedure would be favored by insurgent groups such as the various Tea Party organizations?

a disputed recount, Nader received almost 100,000 votes—enough to swing the state, and the election, to Gore.

However, the outcome of Nader's 2000 presidential campaign doesn't so much highlight the importance of minor parties as it illustrates the closeness of the 2000 presidential election. If Nader had not run, Gore might have received enough additional support to win. But given that Bush's margin of victory in Florida was so small, any number of seemingly minor events (a polling station closing early, or rain in some areas and sunshine in others) could have changed the outcome.

EFFECTS ON ELECTION OUTCOMES

Minor parties did not play a decisive role in the 2008 presidential election, but in several swing states they received more votes than the margin of difference between Obama and McCain. The most successful were the Independent Party (661,000 votes) and the Libertarian Party (491,000), while others like the Boston Tea Party and the U.S. Pacifist Party received far fewer votes (2,305 and 97, respectively). Minor parties won about 1.5 million votes in the 2008 presidential race, whereas the two major parties received 121 million votes.

Even in terms of lower offices, minor-party candidates typically attract only meager support. The Libertarian Party claimed to have more than 154 officeholders as of 2011. However, many of these officials held unelected positions such as seats on county planning boards or ran unopposed for relatively minor offices such as justice of the peace.[31]

Looking back in history, some minor-party candidates for president have attracted a substantial percentage of citizens' votes. George Wallace (governor of Alabama at the time) ran as the candidate of the American Independent Party in 1968, receiving about 13 percent of the popular vote nationwide. Texas millionaire Ross Perot, the Reform Party candidate for president in 1996, won 8.4 percent of the popular vote. Perot also ran as an independent in 1992, winning 18.2 percent of the popular vote. And as noted above, consumer advocate Ralph Nader ran as the Green Party nominee for president in 2000, winning almost 5 percent of the vote.

MINOR PARTY PRESIDENTIAL candidates, such as Ralph Nader in 2000, sometimes attract considerable press attention because of their distinctive, often extreme policy preferences—but they rarely affect election outcomes. Nader ran again, as an independent, in 2004 and 2008.

STRUCTURAL AND ISSUE DIFFERENCES

The differences between major and minor political parties in contemporary American politics grow even more substantial when considered in terms other than election outcomes. For most minor parties the party in government does not exist, as few of their candidates win office. Many minor parties have virtually no organization beyond a small party headquarters and a website. Some minor parties, such as the Green Party, the Libertarian Party, and the Reform Party, have local chapters that meet on a regular basis. But these modest efforts pale in comparison to the nationwide network of offices, thousands of workers, and millions of dollars deployed by Republican and Democratic Party organizations. Nonetheless, research shows that some people vote for minor-party candidates in order to show their support of these candidates' positions and to express their belief that neither major party can govern effectively.[32]

The issues and issue positions taken by minor parties and their candidates are almost always very different from

those espoused by the major parties. The Constitution Party, for example, advocates an end to government civil service regulations; a ban on compulsory school attendance laws; withdrawal of the United States from the United Nations and all international trade agreements; abolishing foreign aid, the income tax, the Internal Revenue Service, and all federal welfare programs; and repealing all campaign finance legislation, the Endangered Species Act, and federal firearms regulations.[33] These positions are extreme, not in the sense of being silly or dangerous, but in the sense that relatively few Americans feel the same way.

VOTERS MAY PUNISH THE PARTY IN power if they are unhappy with its policies. In 2010, frustration with many of President Obama's policies worked against Democrats and helped Republicans. Senator Marco Rubio of Florida was one of the new Republican members elected to Congress that year.

CONCLUSION

American political parties help organize elections, unify disparate social groups, simplify the choices facing voters, and build compromises around party members' shared policy concerns. A close look at how parties operate demonstrates that groups such as the various Tea Party organizations, for all their activities and press attention, fall far short of what it takes to make a political party.

However, in all their activities the success of political parties depends on whether individual party members—candidates, citizens, and party leaders—are willing to take the actions necessary to achieve these goals. Sometimes they are, but at other times they decide that their own interests, or those of their constituents, are best served by ignoring or working against party priorities. And when party members refuse to cooperate, political parties may be unable to do the things that help American democracy to work well.

The case of the Democratic Party from 2006 to 2012 illustrates these limits. It was an easy choice for Democratic candidates to emphasize their party affiliation in the 2006 and 2008 elections, but the brand name was valuable during these contests only because of the unpopularity of then-president Bush and the Republicans in the House and Senate. Those individuals were seen as being responsible for the poor state of the economy and the unpopular wars in Iraq and Afghanistan.

After the 2008 election, however, divisions within the Democratic Party in government soon became apparent. Though Democrats were able to unite to enact an economic stimulus package, building consensus around health care reform legislation took considerable time and required jettisoning provisions that many Democratic legislators supported. Despite having strong majorities in both houses of Congress, Democratic leaders had to worry as much about keeping their own members in line as they did about thwarting Republican opposition.

And in the 2010 midterm and 2012 presidential elections, with Democrats now seen as the party responsible for poor economic conditions, many Democratic candidates tried to disassociate themselves from the party and campaigned on their personal accomplishments.

Of course, these difficulties do not reflect a problem with Democrats per se. Republicans did little better when they controlled the House, Senate, and presidency, and they may have similar problems given the additional seats their candidates won in 2010. Rather, the difficulties show that the individuals who make up American political parties often do not have an incentive to behave in the interests of their party or as theories of democracy suggest they should.

PARTIES AND PARTY SYSTEMS

▶ Show how American political parties and party systems have evolved over time. **Pages 163–69**

SUMMARY

Political parties are a central feature of American politics, though they look and act very differently today than they have over time. Political scientists use the term *party system* to refer to a period of party stability; in all, there have been six different party systems in the country's history. Party systems have been separated by realignments, which occur when some of the defining factors of the party system are changed or specified, and when rifts in the group develop because of these changes.

KEY TERMS

party organization (p. 164)

party in government (p. 164)

party in the electorate (p. 164)

party system (p. 164)

party principle (p. 165)

spoils system (p. 166)

political machine (p. 166)

New Deal Coalition (p. 167)

realignment (p. 168)

CRITICAL THINKING AND DISCUSSION

Is the spoils system a good idea or a bad idea? Why?

PRACTICE QUIZ QUESTIONS

1. Which were the first well-known parties in the United States?
   a) Federalists and Democratic-Republicans
   b) Democrats and Republicans
   c) Whigs and Federalists
   d) Democratics and Whigs
   e) Whigs and Republicans

2. The idea that a party is not just a group, but an organization that exists apart from its candidate, is called the
   _____.
   a) party system
   b) spoils system
   c) conditional party government
   d) party identification
   e) party principle

3. The third party system (1857–96) was broken up by which issue?
   a) the creation of a national bank
   b) the size and regulatory power of government
   c) the admission of California to the Union
   d) the adoption of the greenback
   e) the New Deal

CRITICAL THINKING AND DISCUSSION

How would we know when a realignment takes place in American politics?

MODERN AMERICAN POLITICAL PARTIES

▶ Describe the main characteristics of American parties as organizations, in the government, and in the electorate. **Pages 169–75**

SUMMARY

The modern party comprises three parts. The party organization is a loosely defined group of individuals and organizations focused on supporting political candidates who share the same policy goals. The party in government consists of elected officials who are members of a particular party. The party in the electorate consists of citizens who identify with a particular party.

KEY TERMS

national committee (p. 169)

political action committee (PAC) (p. 170)

527 organization (p. 170)

brand names (p. 170)

caucus (congressional) (p. 171)

conference (p. 171)

party identification (party ID) (p. 173)

party coalitions (p. 174)

PRACTICE QUIZ QUESTIONS

4. The Democratic and Republican party organizations _____ hierarchical; they are _____ to force state and local parties to share their positions on issues.
   a) are not; able
   b) are not; unable

c) are; able
d) are; unable
e) are; sometimes able

5. A group of elected officials of the same party who organize to debate and strategize is called a _____.
   a) cabal
   b) conditional party government
   c) primary
   d) political action committee
   e) caucus or conference

6. The modern Congress is _____; the distance between the parties has _____ over the past 60 years.
   a) polarized; increased
   b) polarized; stayed the same
   c) not polarized; decreased
   d) not polarized; stayed the same
   e) not polarized; increased

ⓢ PRACTICE ONLINE

"Critical Thinking" exercise: *Politics Is Everywhere— Party Identification*

THE ROLE OF POLITICAL PARTIES IN AMERICAN POLITICS

▶ Explain the important functions that parties perform in the political system. **Pages 175–83**

SUMMARY

Political parties serve two major roles in the political system. First, they contest elections by recruiting and nominating candidates and supporting candidate campaigns. Second, they facilitate cooperation in government by providing a framework for agenda setting, coordination, and accountability among members of the same party.

KEY TERMS

primary (p. 176)

caucus (electoral) (p. 177)

nominating convention (p. 178)

party platform (p. 180)

unified government (p. 183)

party in power (p. 183)

divided government (p. 183)

CRITICAL THINKING AND DISCUSSION

Suppose you are the leader of your party's caucus or conference in the House of Representatives. In what situations would you want to convince your party's elected officials to support the party's position on an issue? In what situations might you want to let them vote as they think best?

7. Which is *not* one of the ways that political party organizations support candidates?
a) by controlling who runs in House and Senate races
b) by contributing money to campaign activities
c) by offering advice on how to deal with the press
d) by organizing get-out-the-vote activities
e) by offering advice on which issues to emphasize

8. Why do most candidates support their party platforms?
a) because candidates are required to support the platforms
b) because all candidates vote on the platforms that are written
c) because candidates get kicked out of the party for not doing so
d) because both major parties' platforms are essentially the same
e) because most candidates and their constituents generally agree with the platform

9. When the president, House, and Senate are controlled by the same party, this is called _____. .
a) party in government
b) responsible party government
c) unified government
d) divided government
e) conditional party government

MINOR PARTIES

▶ Consider the role of minor parties in a system dominated by two major parties. **Pages 183-86**

SUMMARY

There are many minor political parties, and while they rarely make a significant impact on the political stage, they do occasionally influence election outcomes. The two big issues facing minor parties are (1) their platforms do not appeal to a large portion of Americans, and (2) the electoral system makes it hard for minor parties to win elections.

PRACTICE QUIZ QUESTIONS

10. In American politics, minor parties _____.
a) are very prominent at the state and local levels
b) are only prominent in congressional elections
c) win few offices at any level of government
d) win a significant number of offices at all levels
e) are more influential today than in the past

11. The issue positions of minor parties are usually _____.
a) very different from those of the major parties and most Americans
b) very similar to those of the major parties and most Americans
c) developed with input from a national network
d) based on the preferences of the party's members in government
e) not the reason people vote for minor party candidates

Ⓢ **PRACTICE ONLINE**

"Big Think" video exercise: *Are Two Parties Enough?*

SUGGESTED READING

Aldrich, John. *Why Parties?* Chicago: University of Chicago Press, 1995.

Carmines, Edward G., and James A. Stimson. *Issue Evolution: Race and the Transformation of American Politics*. Princeton, NJ: Princeton University Press, 1989.

Cohen, Marty, David Karol, Hans Noel, and John Zaller. *The Party Decides: Presidential Nominations Before and After Reform*. Chicago: University of Chicago Press, 2008.

Cox, Gary, and Mathew McCubbins. *Setting the Agenda: Party Government in the U.S. House of Representatives*. New York: Cambridge University Press, 2005.

Fiorina, Morris. *Retrospective Voting in American National Elections*. New Haven, CT: Yale University Press, 1981.

Green, Donald, Bradley Palmquist, and Eric Schickler. *Partisan Hearts and Minds*. New Haven, CT: Yale University Press, 2004.

Key, V. O. *Politics, Parties, and Pressure Groups*. New York: Crowell, 1956.

Polsby, Nelson. *Consequences of Party Reform*. New York: Oxford University Press, 1983.

Rohde, David. *Parties and Leaders in the Post-Reform House*. Chicago: University of Chicago Press, 1991.

Schattschneider, E. E. *Party Government*. New York: McGraw-Hill, 1942.

Schlesinger, Joseph. *Political Parties and the Winning of Office*. Ann Arbor: University of Michigan Press, 1994.

Sundquist, James L. *Dynamics of the Party System*. Rev. ed. Washington, DC: Brookings Institution, 1983.

7

Elections

IN THE 2012 ELECTION, BARACK Obama and Mitt Romney offered Americans a choice between two distinct visions of government. Throughout the campaigns, and especially during their three debates, the candidates competed to appeal to voters.

CONFLICT & COMPROMISE
in American Politics

AMERICAN NATIONAL ELECTIONS ARE ABOUT CONFLICT—THEY ARE contests in which candidates compete for political office, offering voters a choice between different backgrounds, records, and promises. In the 2012 presidential elections, Democrat Barack Obama and Republican Mitt Romney gave the electorate two distinct, competing visions of what the federal government should do, from what the tax code should look like to how this money should be spent and what regulations should be imposed on individuals and corporations. One of the central themes of this chapter is that elections matter; what government does depends on who wins these political contests. Some policies remain the same no matter who wins—but there is no doubt that a President Romney would make many different choices if he was in office, from defense spending to Medicare, alternative energy, corporate regulations, and Supreme Court nominees.

The same is true in House and Senate elections. As we have seen over the last two years, the policies emerging from a Republican-led House of Representatives look very different that those enacted when the Democrats were in the majority. And if the Senate had switched from a Democratic to a Republican majority in 2012, the policies emerging from that chamber would be very different as well. Even at the level of individual House and Senate seats, elections determine who represents a given state or district—which policies they fight for, whose demands they consider when deciding what to do, and which party agenda they will support in Congress.

191

The presence of conflict in American elections is no surprise: as we discussed in Chapter 5 on public opinion, Americans often disagree about what government should do. These differences are reflected among the candidates for the House, Senate, and presidency—both in the promises they make during campaigns and in the actions they take in office. Even when candidates largely agree on policy questions, which occasionally happens in House and Senate races, elections are still conflictual, as debate centers on which one is better-qualified to make the choices he or she will face if elected.

Elections are also about compromise. Some of the voters who supported Mitt Romney during the Republican nomination process did so not because he was their most-preferred candidate, but because he was good enough in their view, and they believed that he had the best chance of beating Barack Obama. Similarly, as Romney's rivals, including Herman Cain, Newt Gingrich, and Rick Santorum, dropped out of the race, they endorsed Romney and campaigned for him. While each would have preferred to be the nominee rather than Romney, their endorsement reflected the fact that they would rather see Romney win than have four more years of Obama in office.

On the Democratic side, after Obama won the presidency in 2008, he named his principal rival for the Democratic nomination, Hillary Clinton, as his secretary of state. Obama's vice president, Joe Biden, had also competed for the Democratic nomination. While Clinton's and Biden's policy views differed from Obama's in some areas, their interest in Obama succeeding in office was enough to overcome their disagreements. And, while there was some conflict within the Democratic Party over some decisions Obama made in his first term in office, most dissenters supported Obama because they believed he was the best candidate the party could put forth. As these examples illustrate, compromise is often an essential ingredient in a winning electoral strategy, both for voters and for candidates.

Elections also demonstrate that political process matters. Candidates in American elections compete for a wide variety of offices. They are elected for different periods of time to represent districts, states, or the entire nation—places that vary tremendously in terms of what constituents want from government. A variety of rules determine who can run, who can vote, and how candidates can campaign. Even ballot layouts and how votes are cast and counted vary across states. Elections also differ in the amount of media coverage they receive, the level of involvement of political parties and other organizations, and the amount of attention citizens pay to the contests. All these aspects of the election process— who runs, how they campaign, and how voters respond—shape outcomes.

Elections, as prominent, public forums that give Americans the opportunity to debate policy preferences, provide further evidence that politics is everywhere. During election season, campaign coverage and ads for candidates become almost impossible to avoid. Even so, one of the most important tasks all campaigns face is getting citizens' attention and convincing them to listen.

Our goal in this chapter is to explain how American elections work. By making the election process more comprehensible and by focusing on the promises candidates make in campaigns, we aim to demonstrate how and why elections matter. We show that there are real differences between candidates in races for national office and that these differences have profound implications for public policy. We show that the actions candidates take during campaigns shape citizens' perceptions and their vote decisions. And we show that despite Americans' general detachment from politics, their votes reflect both their policy preferences and considerable insight into candidates' promises and performance.

HOW DO AMERICAN ELECTIONS WORK?

The American political system is a representative democracy: Americans do not make policy choices themselves, but they vote for individuals who make these choices on their behalf. Thus we begin by describing the rules and procedures that define American national elections. These rules and actions are tied directly to what elections do: select representatives, enable citizens to influence the direction of government policy, and give citizens the opportunity to reward and punish officeholders seeking re-election.

The most visible function of American national elections is the selection of officeholders: members of the House and Senate, and the president and vice president. Candidates can be **incumbents** or challengers. America has a representative democracy, which means that by voting in elections Americans have an indirect effect on government policy. Although citizens do not make policy choices themselves, they determine which individuals get to make these choices. In this way elections connect citizen preferences and government actions.

incumbent A politician running for re-election to the office he or she currently holds.

The fundamental choice in an election is between two or more candidates running for some political office—in national elections this means a seat in the House or the Senate, or the presidency. In part, voters choose between candidates, deciding which individual they would prefer to see in office. But elections also involve a choice between candidates' policy platforms, the set of policies and programs they promise to carry out if elected. By investigating candidates' platforms, citizens learn about the range of options for government policy. Moreover, their vote decisions, which lead to the election of some candidates and the defeat of others, determine who gets to make choices about future government policy and thereby shape policy itself.

The election process also creates a way to hold incumbents accountable. When citizens choose between voting for an incumbent or a challenger, they can consider the incumbent's performance, asking, "Has she done a good job on the issues I care about?"[1] Citizens who answer yes typically vote for the incumbent, and those who say no typically vote for the challenger. These evaluations are significant because they make incumbents responsive to their constituents' demands.[2] If an elected official anticipates that some constituents will consider his performance when making their decision, he will try to take actions that these constituents will like. Otherwise, voters can opt to remove him from office because they disapprove of his performance and believe the country will fare better if a different candidate wins.

AMERICAN CANDIDATES, such as California House member Tom McClintock, shown here, compete for different offices under a complex set of regulations. At the national level, their large campaign organizations often spend millions. Even so, elections are best understood in individual terms: one candidate trying to win one citizen's vote.

TWO STAGES OF ELECTIONS

House and Senate candidates face a two-step procedure. First, if the prospective candidate wants to run on behalf of a political party, she must win the party's nomination in a primary election. If the would-be candidate wants to run as an independent, she needs to gather signatures on a petition to secure a spot on the ballot. Different states hold either

open primary A primary election in which any registered voter can participate in the contest, regardless of party affiliation.

closed primary A primary election in which only registered members of a particular political party can vote.

general election The election in which voters cast ballots for House members, senators, and (every four years) a president and vice president.

open primaries or **closed primaries**, and state law sets the timing of these elections. A few states hold single primaries, in which there is one election involving candidates from both parties, with the top two finalists (regardless of party) receiving nominations to the general election.

The second step in the election process, the **general election**, is held throughout the nation on the first Tuesday after the first Monday in November, which federal law designates as Election Day. General elections determine who wins elected positions in government. The offices at stake vary depending on the year. Presidential elections occur every four years (2008, 2012, . . .). In a presidential election year Americans elect the entire House of Representatives, one-third of the Senate, and a president and vice president. During midterm elections (2006, 2010, . . .) there is no presidential contest, but the entire House and another one-third of the Senate are up for election.

The Constitution limits voting rights to American citizens who are at least 18 years old. There are also restrictions on voter eligibility; these vary across states, including residency requirements (usually 30 days) and whether people convicted of a major crime can vote. A new development in American elections is an increase in the practice of early voting, or casting a general election vote prior to Election Day.[3] This has always been an option for voters who cannot get to the polls on Election Day because of travel, illness, religious obligations, or similar reasons. These voters may cast an absentee ballot, typically by mailing it to a designated location. Recently, many states have established no-excuse-required absentee ballots or simply have allowed voters to vote early by mail or at polling stations.

CONSTITUENCIES: WHO CHOOSES REPRESENTATIVES?

In American elections, officeholders are elected in single-member districts in which only the winner of the most votes takes office. (Although each state's senators both represent the whole state, they are elected separately; they are not the first- and second-place election winners.) Senate candidates compete at the state level; House candidates compete in congressional districts. In most states the congressional district lines are drawn by state legislatures. In a few states nonpartisan commissions or committees of judges perform this function. (For details on redistricting, see Chapter 9.)

Because members of the House and Senate are elected from specific geographic areas, they often represent very different kinds of people. These constituents differ in terms of age, race, income level, occupation, and political leaning, including party affiliation and ideology. Therefore, legislators from different areas of the country face highly diverse demands from their constituents—leading them to pursue very dissimilar kinds of policies. For example, Democratic senator John Kerry, elected from Massachusetts, represents a fairly liberal state where gay marriage is legal, while Republican senator Orrin Hatch is from the conservative state of Utah. Suppose the Senate votes on a measure to ban gay marriage nationwide. Kerry knows that most of his constituents would probably want him to vote against the proposal, and Hatch knows that most of his constituents would probably want him to vote for it. Thus, in general, congressional conflicts over policy often reflect differences in constituents' demands.

DETERMINING WHO WINS

Most House and Senate contests involve **plurality voting**: the candidate who gets the most votes wins. However, some states use **majority voting,** meaning that a candidate needs more than 50 percent of the vote to win. In these states if no candidate has a majority, a **runoff election** takes place between the top two finishers.

The two-step process of primary and general elections can have a similar effect on the election's outcome. Sometimes the winner of a primary is not a party's best candidate for the general election. For example, in the 2010 Alaska Senate Republican primary, politically inexperienced challenger Joe Miller defeated incumbent Lisa Murkowski. However, Murkowski won the general election as a write-in candidate.[4]

Americans vote by using a range of machines and ballots.[5] Some counties use paper keypunch ballots, on which voters use a stylus to punch out holes in a ballot card next to the names of their preferred candidates. These ballots are then scanned, although they can also be hand-counted. Other counties use mechanical voting machines that require voters to pull a lever next to the name of their preferred candidates. Touch-screen voting machines are becoming increasingly popular, but this type of voting is controversial because of its cost, the potential for delays on Election Day (voters often take longer to cast their votes when using this technology), and concerns that the machines could be manipulated to change election outcomes.[6] However, the widespread use of touch screens in recent elections has occurred without major problems.

Different voting methods show different rates of undervotes. These can happen when a voter casts an unmarked ballot, votes in some races on the ballot but not others, or casts a ballot that cannot be counted for some reason. And ballot counting itself adds more complexities. Most states have laws that allow vote recounts if a race is sufficiently close (within 1 percent or less). Even when a recount occurs, it may be impossible to definitively determine who won a particular election, as the statutes that determine which ballots are valid are often open to interpretation.

plurality voting A voting system in which the candidate who receives the most votes within a geographic area wins the election, regardless of whether that candidate wins a majority (more than half) of the votes.

majority voting A voting system in which a candidate must win more than 50 percent of votes to win the election. If no candidate wins enough votes to take office, a runoff election is held between the top two vote-getters.

runoff election Under a majority voting system, a second election held only if no candidate wins a majority of the votes in the first general election. Only the top two vote-getters in the first election compete in the runoff.

primary A ballot vote in which citizens select a party's nominee for the general election.

caucus A local meeting in which party members select a party's nominee for the general election.

proportional allocation During the presidential primaries, the practice of determining the number of convention delegates allotted to each candidate based on the percentage of the popular vote cast for each candidate. All Democratic primaries and caucuses use this system, as do some states' Republican primaries and caucuses.

winner-take-all During the presidential primaries, the practice of assigning all of a given state's delegates to the candidate who receives the most popular votes. Some states' Republican primaries and caucuses use this system.

What *is* clear is that election rules can affect results. Particularly in close races, small changes in the rules governing elections can easily change outcomes. In a close 2008 Minnesota Senate race, for example, press reports suggested that some voters were turned away because of a shortage of voting supplies. If polling stations had been required to stock extra supplies, the election outcome might have been different.

PRESIDENTIAL ELECTIONS

Many of the rules governing elections, such as who is eligible to vote, are the same for both presidential and congressional elections. However, presidential contests have several unique rules regarding how nominees are determined and how votes are counted.

THE NOMINATION: PRIMARIES AND CAUCUSES

Presidential nominees from the Democratic and Republican parties are determined by state-level **primaries** and **caucuses** over a five-month period beginning in January of an election year.[7] These elections select delegates to attend the nominating conventions that take place during the summer. There the delegates cast the votes that determine their party's presidential and vice-presidential nominees. The format of these elections, including their timing and the number of delegates selected per state, is determined on a state-by-state basis by the state and national party organizations.[8] A candidate's principal goal is to win as many delegates as possible.

The details of translating primary and caucus votes into convention delegates vary from state to state, but some general rules apply. All Democratic primaries and caucuses use **proportional allocation** to divide each state's delegate seats between the candidates; thus if a candidate receives 40 percent of the votes in a state's primary, the candidate gets roughly 40 percent of the convention delegates from that state. Some Republican contests use proportional allocation, but others are **winner-take-all**. In these, the candidate who receives the most votes gets all of the state's convention delegates. While these rules were not significant in 2012, they had a significant effect on the 2008 Republican presidential nomination. John McCain's early victories in winner-take-all primaries helped him build a large lead in delegates that caused some other candidates to drop out. Overall, McCain won only 47 percent of the primary and caucus vote but claimed 72 percent of the delegates. In contrast, in 2012, with fewer states using winner-take-all, candidates' delegate totals more closely matched the total votes they received. However, states are free to move back to using winner-take-all, which might advantage certain candidates in a future contest.

The ordering of state primaries and caucuses is another important factor, because many candidacies do not survive beyond the early contests.[9] Most presidential candidates pour everything they have into the first few contests. Candidates who do well

THE DESIGN OF THE INFAMOUS Palm Beach County, Florida, butterfly ballot, used in the 2000 presidential election, inadvertently led some people who intended to vote for Democrat Al Gore to select Reform Party candidate Patrick Buchanan.

Office	Minimum Age	Residency Requirement	Term of Office
President	35	Born in the United States	Four years
Senator	30	Resident of state; U.S. citizen for at least 9 years	Six years
Representative	25	Resident of state; U.S. citizen for at least 7 years	Two years

early on attract contributions, campaign workers, endorsements, and additional media coverage, all of which enable them to move on to subsequent primaries or caucuses. For many years Iowa and New Hampshire have held the first presidential nomination contests in January, with the Iowa caucus taking place a week before the New Hampshire primary. These states' position at the beginning of the process is largely a historical accident, but party officials from other states often complain about the disproportionate influence of these states. For example, in 2012, Rick Santorum's emergence as an early challenger to Mitt Romney was the product of Santorum's surprisingly strong showing in the Iowa caucuses, which was due to strong support from evangelical voters in Iowa. In contrast, Santorum did far worse a week later in the New Hampshire primary, where there are far fewer evangelical voters. Without his early Iowa success Santorum would likely have dropped out of the race in January and would never have emerged as Romney's principal opponent.

The parties' national committees can issue rules and requirements about the timing of state presidential primaries, but state law sets the election dates, meaning that a national committee's directives may not be followed. As a result, the 2012 nomination process was roughly the same as in previous years, with Iowa and New Hampshire holding the initial contests, in early January 2012, followed by primaries in South Carolina and Florida later in the month, and the remaining contests beginning in February and continuing to June.

THE NATIONAL CONVENTION

Presidential nominating conventions happen late in the summer of an election year. Their main task is to select the party's presidential nominee, although the vote at the convention is largely a formality, as in all recent contests one candidate has emerged from the nomination process with a clear majority of delegates and wins the nomination on the first ballot.[10] To get the nomination, a candidate needs the support of a majority of the delegates. If no candidate receives a majority after the first round of voting at the convention, the voting continues until someone does. When a sitting president runs for re-election, as Barack Obama did in 2012, he typically faces little opposition for the party's general-election nomination.

After the delegates nominate a presidential candidate, they select a vice-presidential nominee. The presidential nominee chooses this running mate, and the delegates almost always ratify this choice without much debate. Convention delegates also vote on the party platform, which describes what kinds of policies its candidates will supposedly seek to enact if they are elected.

The final purpose of a convention is to attract public attention to the party and its nominees. Public figures give speeches during the evening sessions when all major television networks have live coverage. At some recent conventions both parties have drawn press attention by recruiting speakers who support their political goals despite being associated with the opposing party.

Once presidential candidates are nominated, the general election campaign officially begins—though it often unofficially starts much earlier, as soon as the presumptive nominees are known. We say more about presidential campaigns in a later section.

ONE OF THE PRIMARY PURPOSES of presidential nominating conventions is to showcase a party's nominee before a national audience. Here, Barack Obama and Joe Biden appear after being officially nominated at the 2012 Democratic National Convention.

electoral college The body that votes to select America's president and vice president based on the popular vote in each state. Each candidate nominates a slate of electors who are selected to attend the meeting of the college if their candidate wins the most votes in a state or district.

COUNTING PRESIDENTIAL VOTES

Let's assume for a moment that the campaigning is over and that Election Day has arrived. Even though in the voting booth you choose between the candidates by name, you actually don't vote directly for a presidential candidate. Rather, when you select your preferred candidate's name, you are choosing that person's slate of pledged supporters from your state to serve as electors, who will then vote to elect the president. The number of electors for each state equals the state's number of House members (which varies by state population) plus the number of senators (two per state). Altogether, the electors chosen by the citizens of each state constitute the **electoral college**, the body that formally selects the president.

In most states the electoral votes are allocated on a winner-take-all basis: the candidate who receives the most votes from a given state's citizens gets all of that state's electoral votes. Two states, Maine and Nebraska, allocate most of their electoral votes at the congressional district level: in those states the candidate who wins the most votes in each congressional district wins that district's single electoral vote. Then the remaining two electoral votes go to the candidate who gets the most votes statewide.[11]

The winner-take-all method of allocating most states' electoral votes makes candidates focus their attention on two kinds of states: high-population states with lots of electoral votes to be gained, and, more important, swing states where the contest is relatively close. It's better for a candidate to spend a day campaigning in California, with its 55 electoral votes, than in Montana, where only 3 electoral votes are at stake. However, if one candidate is sure to win a particular state, both candidates will direct their efforts elsewhere. This is why both campaigns in 2012 spent so much time and campaign funds on states such as Virginia, Ohio, and Florida (swing states with many electoral votes)—and why they largely ignored the District of Columbia and other states in the small-state, one-party-dominant category.

While most Americans believe that the winner of the presidential election is decided on Election Day, this outcome is actually just the first step in a process that determines the winner. After citizens' votes are counted in each state, the slates of electors meet in December in the state capitals. At their meetings the electors

ELECTORAL VOTES AND SWING STATES

As discussed in the text, presidential campaigns focus on states with high electoral votes and swing states, those where each candidate has a good chance of winning. In this box, we group states based on these two variables, dividing them into three categories based on their number of electoral votes, and on whether one party always won the state in the 2000, 2004, and 2008 presidential elections.

		One Party Dominates in Recent Elections	
		Yes	No
Electoral Votes (2012 Election)	3–5	D.C., Delaware, Alaska, Montana, North Dakota, South Dakota, Vermont, Wyoming, Hawaii, Maine, Rhode Island, Idaho, Nebraska, West Virginia	New Hampshire, New Mexico
	6–10	Arkansas, Kansas, Utah, Connecticut, Oregon, Oklahoma, Kentucky, Louisiana, Alabama, South Carolina, Wisconsin, Maryland, Missouri, Mississippi	Iowa, Nevada, Colorado, Minnesota
	More than 10	Massachusetts, Arizona, Tennessee, Washington, New Jersey, Michigan, Georgia, Illinois, Pennsylvania, New York, Texas, California	Indiana, Virginia, North Carolina, Ohio, Florida

almost always vote for the presidential candidate they have pledged to support. After the votes are certified by a joint session of Congress, the candidate who wins a majority of the nation's electoral votes (at least 270) is the new president. If no candidate receives a majority of the electoral college votes, the members of the House of Representatives choose the winner. They follow a procedure in which the members from each state decide which candidate to support and then cast one collective vote per state, with the winner needing a majority of these state-level votes to win. This procedure has not been used since 1824, although it might be required if a third-party candidate wins a significant number of electoral votes or if a state's electors refuse to cast their votes.[12]

A presidential candidate can win the electoral college vote, and thus the election, without receiving a majority of the votes cast by citizens. When a third-party candidate for president receives a substantial number of votes, the winner can easily end up receiving more votes than any other candidate without winning a majority of the popular vote. Bill Clinton won a substantial electoral college majority in 1992, while receiving only 43 percent of the popular vote. This was due to the fact that Ross Perot, a third-party candidate, received almost 19 percent of the national popular vote but not enough support in any one state to win electoral votes. In 2012, Barack Obama won about 50 percent of the popular vote, but nearly 62 percent of the electoral votes. It is also possible for a candidate who loses the popular vote to receive the majority of electoral votes and win the election. George W. Bush, the winner of the 2000 election, received about 540,000 fewer popular votes than his main rival, Al Gore.

FIGURE » 7.1

POPULAR VOTE vs. ELECTORAL VOTE, 2000–2012

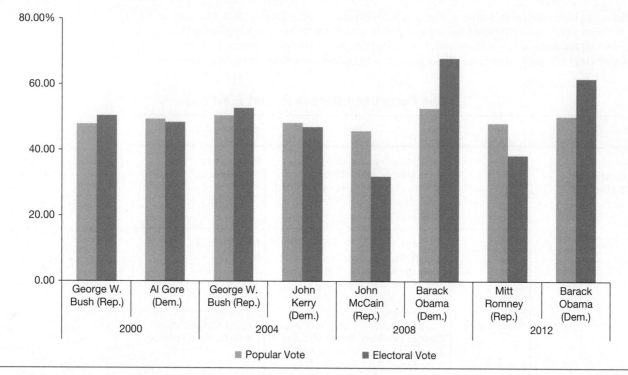

Source: U.S. National Archives and Records Administration, www.archives.gov/federal-register/electoral-college/historical.html (accessed 11/12/12).

DESCRIBE THE FEATURES AND STRATEGIES OF CAMPAIGNS FOR FEDERAL OFFICE

election cycle The two-year period between general elections.

ELECTORAL CAMPAIGNS

Now that we have reviewed the main steps of how American elections work, we will focus in this section on the campaign process and what candidates do to convince people to vote for them on Election Day. Our emphasis is on things that candidates do regardless of the office they are running for, across the entire **election cycle**, the two-year period between general elections.

SETTING THE STAGE

On the day after any election, candidates, party officials, and interest groups all start thinking about the next election cycle. They consider who won and who lost, which incumbents look like safe bets for re-election and which ones might be vulnerable, who might retire soon or run for another office in the next election, and whether the election returns reveal new information about the kinds of campaigns or issues that might increase voter turnout or support the next time.

How It Works

THE ELECTORAL COLLEGE

ELECTORAL VOTES PER STATE

The number of electors from each state equals the state's number of House members (which varies based on state population) plus the number of senators (two per state). Each elector has one vote in the electoral college.

WHO ARE THE ELECTORS?

Candidates to be electors are nominated by their political parties. They pledge to support a certain candidate if they are elected to the electoral college. When you cast your vote for a presidential candidate, you are in fact voting for the slate of potential electors who support that candidate.

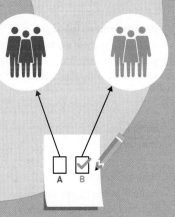

100% OF ELECTORAL VOTES GO TO WINNER

37%

61%

WINNING A STATE

Most states give all of their electoral college votes to the candidate who wins the most votes from citizens in the state. So, even if a candidate only gets 51% of the vote in the state, his or her entire slate of electors is elected, and he or she gets all of the state's votes in the electoral college.

POP QUIZ!

1 The number of electors that each state has in the electoral college is based on

  a voter turnout in the previous election.

  b an equal number for all states.

  c the number of parties in the state.

  d the date the state joined the Union.

  e population.

2 When you cast your vote in a presidential general election, you are actually voting for

  a a political party.

  b delegates who pledge to support a specific candidate at the party's national convention.

  c electors who pledge to support a specific candidate in the electoral college.

  d whoever gets the most votes in the state.

  e a slate of presidential candidates.

open seat An elected position for which there is no incumbent.

Party committees and candidates have particular interest in the likelihood that incumbents might retire, thereby creating an **open seat**. Open seats are of special interest because incumbents generally hold an election advantage.[13] So, when a seat opens, candidates from the party that does not control the seat know that they might have a better chance to win because they will not have to run against an incumbent.

Presidential campaigns work the same way. Virtually all first-term presidents run for re-election. So potential challengers in the opposing party study the results of the last election to see how many votes the president received and how this support was distributed across the states, in order to determine their own chances of winning against the president. Candidates in the president's party make the same calculations, although no sitting president in the twentieth century was denied renomination. Some presidents (Harry Truman in 1952, Lyndon Johnson in 1968) retired because their chances of being renominated were not good, while others (Gerald Ford in 1976, Jimmy Carter in 1980) faced tough primary contests.[14]

BEFORE THE CAMPAIGN

permanent campaign The actions officeholders take throughout the election cycle to build support for their re-election.

MOST OFFICE HOLDERS ARE ALWAYS campaigning—traveling around their states or districts, talking with constituents, and explaining their actions in office—all in the hope of winning and keeping support for the next election. Here, Republican representative Sam Graves greets constituents during a 2008 parade in Kearney, Missouri.

Most incumbent House members, senators, and presidents work throughout the election cycle to secure their re-election. Political scientists label this activity the **permanent campaign**:[15] it involves keeping the constituents happy and raising money for the campaign. As we see in Chapter 9, congressional incumbents try to keep their constituents happy by taking actions that ensure the voters can identify something good that the incumbent has done.[16] Incumbent presidents make the same calculations. During Barack Obama's first months in office, many of his advisers argued that he had to offer an economic stimulus plan in light of polls showing that the economy was an overriding concern to most Americans. Obama did so—a decision driven by political as well as policy concerns. Of course, many presidential actions are taken in response to events rather than initiated to gain voter support. Particularly in the case of wars and other conflicts, it is far-fetched to say that presidents initiate hostilities for political gain. Even so, presidents, just like other politicians, are keenly aware of the political consequences of their actions and the need to build a record they can run on in the next election.

Candidates for all offices, incumbents and challengers alike, also devote considerable time before the campaign to raising campaign funds. Fund-raising helps an incumbent in two ways.[17] First, it ensures that if the incumbent faces a strong opponent, she or he will have enough money to run an aggressive campaign. Second, successful fund-raising deters opposition. Potential challengers are less likely to run against an incumbent if that individual is well funded with a sizable campaign war chest.[18]

Another thing candidates do before the campaign is build their campaign organization.[19] The success or failure of these efforts is another signal of a candidate's prospects. If experienced, well-respected people work in a candidate's campaign, observers conclude that the candidate's prospects for being elected are probably good. Indeed, skilled campaign consultants are highly desirable. They plan strategies, run public opinion polls, assemble ads and buy television time, and talk with members of the media on the candidate's behalf, among

other things. While only the most well-funded campaigns can afford top consultants, almost all campaigns have paid and volunteer staff, ranging from the dozen or so people who work for a typical House candidate to the thousands that run a major-party candidate's presidential campaign.

THE GENERAL ELECTION CAMPAIGN

General election campaigns begin in early September. By this point several important steps have occurred: candidates have announced their intent to run and have built their campaign organizations, primary campaigns and elections have taken place, and both parties have chosen their presidential nominees and their congressional candidates. Interest groups, candidates, and party committees have raised most of the funds they will use or donate in the campaign. The race is on.

BASIC CAMPAIGN STRATEGIES

One fundamental campaign strategy, particularly in congressional campaigns, is to build name recognition. Since many citizens know fairly little about congressional candidates, efforts to increase a candidate's name recognition can deliver a few extra percentage points of support—enough to turn a close defeat into a victory. (Practically all voters can identify the major party presidential candidates, so name recognition efforts are not as central to these elections.)

A second basic strategy is mobilization. Turnout is not automatic: candidates have to make sure that their supporters actually go to the polls and vote. Campaign professionals refer to voter mobilization efforts as **GOTV ("get out the vote")** or the **ground game**.[20] Most campaigns for Congress or the presidency use extensive door-to-door canvassing, as well as phone banks and e-mail. Both Republican and

GOTV ("get out the vote") or the **ground game** A campaign's efforts to "get out the vote" or make sure their supporters vote on Election Day.

AMERICAN PRESIDENTIAL CAMPAIGNS depend on thousands of paid and volunteer staff. Here, workers for Republican candidate Mitt Romney contact potential supporters.

Democratic campaigns use sophisticated databases, combining voter registration data with demographic information and even purchasing data to determine who their potential supporters are and how best to reach them.[21]

Today the Internet and social media sites play important roles in campaigns. In part, these technologies help candidates to do things that they always have done, such as recruiting supporters and informing them about a candidate's appearances and issue positions. Whereas previously this information might have been disseminated using a phone bank, flyers, or volunteers going door-to-door, now candidates use e-mail, Twitter, Facebook updates, or similar tools. Social media sites are especially useful for organizing large numbers of volunteers—in 2008, for example, Barack Obama's campaign ran extensive GOTV operations during the nomination process and the general election using the Internet as the primary point of contact between the campaign and the volunteers.

The Internet also enables candidates to do things that were impossible a generation ago. For example, many candidates prepare Internet-only campaign ads, counting on media attention to spread the word about the ads' content. Twitter and other social media help candidates and their staff to instantly comment on their opponent's campaign or respond to similar attacks, or post campaign videos. While most of these efforts have little long-term consequences—just as most campaign advertising is ignored by most voters—there are examples of Internet-based campaigning having a real effect on election outcomes. For example, during the 2012 Republican primaries Texas governor Rick Perry's gaffe during a debate, in which he claimed that if elected he would abolish three Cabinet departments but could only name two, became a popular video clip.[22] While Perry's campaign was in trouble before his performance spread across the Internet, the popularity of the video contributed to his poor performance in Republican primaries and caucuses.

PROMISES AND PLATFORMS

Issues matter in American elections. A candidate's issue positions help to mobilize supporters and attract volunteers, activists, interest-group endorsements, and contributions. Issue positions also define what government will seek to do differently depending on who gets elected. Thus another important set of campaign decisions involves the candidate's campaign platform, which presents his or her stances on issues and promises about how the candidate will act in office.

In writing their platform, candidates may be constrained by positions they have taken in the past or by their party affiliation. Chapter 6 showed that the parties have strong brand identities that lead many citizens to associate Democrats with liberal policies and Republicans with conservative ones; as a result, candidates often find it difficult to make campaign promises that contradict these perceptions. Also influencing a candidate's positions are demands from potential supporters. For example, in a state or district with many conservative or Republican voters, opposition to health care reform legislation or to amnesty for illegal immigrants might be a winning electoral strategy—just as support for these proposals would generally be helpful for candidates running in states or districts where most voters are moderate to liberal or Democrats.

DURING CAMPAIGNS, CANDIDATES often seek to strengthen the perception that they share (or at least are sympathetic to) average Americans' beliefs and interests. Here, Democratic candidate Hillary Clinton enjoys a beverage with patrons in an Indiana bar during the 2008 presidential primaries.

The two-step electoral process in American elections also influences candidate positions. To win office, candidates have to campaign twice, first in a primary and then in a general election. Voters in primary elections generally hold more extreme views than the average voters in a general election. As a result, in the typical congressional district Republican candidates win primaries by taking conservative positions, while Democratic candidates win primaries by upholding liberal views. However, a position or promise that attracts votes in a primary election might not work so well in the general election, or vice versa. For example, during debates before the 2012 Iowa caucuses, some Republican presidential candidates cited their religious beliefs as an influence on their personal lives and political stands—a useful strategy given the large number of religious conservatives expected to attend the Iowa caucuses, but a less useful strategy in the general election given the lower proportion of such voters across the entire nation.

CONFRONTING OTHER CANDIDATES

Candidates often contrast their own records or positions with those of opposing candidates or make claims designed to lower voters' opinions of their opponents. Sometimes these interactions occur during a formal debate. Most congressional campaigns involve debates in front of an audience of likely voters, a group of reporters, or the editorial board of a local newspaper. Typically candidates take questions from reporters, although sometimes candidates question each other or answer questions from the audience.

Presidential campaigns involve multiple debates during the primary and caucus season. Throughout the months before the first primaries and caucuses, each party's candidates gather for many single-party debates using a variety of formats. During the general election the Republican and Democratic nominees meet for several debates. (The number and format are negotiated between the campaigns and the Commission on Presidential Debates, the organization that hosts the debates.)[23] The 2012 presidential campaign featured three debates between the presidential nominees and one between the vice presidential nominees. The debates offer valuable free exposure: given a relatively uninterested electorate, candidates must present themselves in a way that captures voters' attention and gains their support.

Candidates attempt to win support by emphasizing their understanding of citizens' concerns and their willingness to address those concerns. They also try to raise doubts about their opponents by citing politically damaging statements or unpopular past behavior. In conducting opposition research, candidates and interest groups dig into an opponent's past for embarrassing incidents or personal indiscretions, either by the candidate or a by member of the candidate's family or staff. Campaigns may then leak this information to the media or release it on their own. Candidates, parties, and interest groups also routinely use trackers, staff who attend their opponents' events with video cameras in the hopes of recording embarrassing behavior or statements. The resulting videos may be posted on the Internet, given to the press, or used in a campaign ad.

Another way that candidates may confront one another involves the use of **attack ads**, which are campaign ads that criticize the opponent. Many such ads stretch the truth (or break it outright), trying to get voters to stop and think—or to get the opposing candidate to spend time and money denying the ads' claims. In the 2010 campaign various candidates were accused of "wanting to gas house pets, inject young girls with dangerous drugs, let men beat their wives, and assist child molesters, whether by buying them Viagra or protecting their privacy."[24] Candidates who are behind in the polls sometimes resort to this type of ad.

attack ads Campaign advertising that criticizes a candidate's opponent—typically by making potentially damaging claims about the opponent's background or record—rather than focusing on positive reasons to vote for the candidate.

CAMPAIGN ADVERTISING: GETTING THE WORD OUT

One of the realities of modern American electoral campaigns is that they are conducted largely through campaign advertising. Candidates, party committees, and interest groups spend more than several billion dollars during each election cycle for federal office. Most of that money goes to campaign advertising, usually as 30-second television spots. Such advertising is critical because candidates cannot assume that citizens will take the time to learn from other sources about the candidates, their qualifications, and their issue positions.

Campaign advertising has evolved considerably over the last generation.[25] During the early years of television, many campaign ads consisted of speeches by candidates or endorsements from supporters, and they ran several minutes in length. Today, in contrast, campaign ads are short, feature arresting images, and often use photo montages and bold text to engage a distracted citizenry. Content varies depending on who is running the ads. Yet despite all the money and effort poured into campaign advertising, these messages must deliver a message that all viewers can understand without too much interpretation.

One critical question about campaign advertising is whether the ads work: whether they shape what people know or influence their vote decisions or other forms of participation. Some observers have complained that campaign ads—especially attack ads and negative campaigning—depress voter turnout and reinforce citizens' negative perceptions of government.[26] During the 2010 campaign one candidate's ad showed the opponent as an evil blimp hovering over Washington; another used video of a kindergarten class while talking about the need to reduce conflict in Congress.[27] These ads seek to capture voters' attention, to get them to focus on a race long enough to consider the candidates and their real messages. With regard to negative campaigning, early evidence suggested that attack ads depress voter turnout, but later studies have shown that they do not have much effect.[28]

IN THE 2012 PRESIDENTIAL RACE, many of the ads aired by the Romney campaign and Republican groups criticized President Obama, blaming him for the nation's ongoing economic problems.

Other evidence suggests that campaign advertising has several beneficial effects. Scholars have found that people who are exposed to campaign ads tend to be more interested in the campaign and know more about the candidates.[29] Moreover, many campaign ads highlight real differences between the candidates and the parties.[30] Even so, average citizens know that they cannot believe everything they see on television, so campaign advertising typically captures their attention without necessarily changing their minds.[31]

CAMPAIGN FINANCE

Campaign finance refers to money collected for and spent on campaigns and elections by candidates, political parties, and other organizations and individuals. The **Federal Election Commission** is in charge of administering election laws, including the complex regulations pertaining to how campaigns can spend money. The most recent changes in campaign finance rules, which were passed as the Bipartisan Campaign Reform Act (BCRA), took effect after the 2002 elections and have been modified by subsequent Supreme Court decisions. (In particular, the 2010 decision in *Citizens United v. Federal Election Commission* removed all restrictions on campaign funding by corporations and labor unions.)

Federal Election Commission The government agency that enforces and regulates election laws; made up of six presidential appointees, of whom no more than three can be members of the same party.

TYPES OF FUNDING ORGANIZATIONS

The limits on campaign contributions in the BCRA—also known as the McCain–Feingold Act—vary depending on whether contributions are made by an individual or a group, and by the type of group, as Table 7.1 shows. During the 2012 elections, for example, individuals could contribute up to $2,500 to a candidate per election (donations to the primary and general elections count separately), $28,500 to a political party, $10,000 to a state party, and $5,000 to a political action committee (PAC), with an overall limit of about $100,000. Individuals and corporations can also (1) make unlimited contributions to 527 organizations (see below), which can use the money for voter mobilization efforts or issue advocacy as long as they do not directly support or oppose a particular candidate, and (2) spend unlimited amounts on expenditures that are not connected to a particular candidate, party, or committee.

PACs are groups that aim to elect or defeat particular candidates or political parties. A company or organization can form a PAC and solicit contributions from employees or group members. As Table 7.1 shows, the amount PACs can give to each candidate in an election is limited, but these limits only pertain to **hard money**—the funds given directly to a candidate. PACs can also form what are known as 527 organizations (named after the Internal Revenue Code provision that allows them), which can then accept unlimited amounts of **soft money**. Ads by 527s cannot advocate the election or defeat of a particular candidate or political party.[32] Another type of organization, again described using the IRS code, is a 501(c)(4). The principal difference between 527s and 501(c)(4)s is that the latter type of organization does not have to disclose the names of its contributors. (See Chapter 8 for more on PACs, 527s, and 501(c)(4)s.)

As discussed in Chapter 6, political party committees are entities within the Republican and Democratic parties. Both major parties have a national committee and a campaign committee in each house of Congress. Party committees are

hard money Donations that are used to help elect or defeat a specific candidate.

soft money Contributions that can be used for voter mobilization or to promote a policy proposal or point of view as long as these efforts are not tied to supporting or opposing a particular candidate.

TABLE » 7.1

CONTRIBUTION LIMITS IN THE 2012 ELECTIONS

	INDIVIDUAL CANDIDATES	NATIONAL PARTY COMMITTEE	STATE PARTY	POLITICAL ACTION COMMITTEE	LIMIT ON TOTAL CONTRIBUTIONS
Individuals	$2,500	$30,800	—	—	$46,200 to candidates, $70,800 to organizations
Political action committees	$5,000	$15,000	$5,000	$5,000	—
National party committee	$5,000	—	Unlimited transfers	$5,000	—
State and local party committees	$5,000	Unlimited transfers	Unlimited transfers	$5,000	—

Source: Federal Election Commission "Contribution Limits for 2011–2012," www.fec.gov/info/contriblimits1112 .pdf (accessed 11/10/12).

limited in the amount of hard money they can give to a candidate's campaign and in the amount they can spend on behalf of the candidate as a coordinated expenditure. However, a party committee (and, after *Citizens United*, corporations and labor unions) can spend an unlimited amount in independent expenditures to elect a candidate or candidates. To be considered independent, expenditures must not be controlled, directed, or approved by any candidate's campaign. Independent expenditures can pay for campaign advertising, but the candidate or candidates cannot be consulted on the content.

FUNDING FOR PRESIDENTIAL CAMPAIGNS

Presidential campaigns have different financing rules. During the primary process, the federal government provides matching funds to candidates who raise $5,000 in each of at least 20 states in contributions of $250 or less. Once a candidate passes this threshold, the government matches the first $250 of each subsequent contribution. In order to receive these funds, candidates must agree to an overall cap on the amount they will spend during the nomination process ($42.05 million in 2008) and to spending caps for each primary or caucus of 67 cents per voting-age person in the state. If candidates forgo the federal matching funds in the primaries, they can ignore these spending caps—a strategy followed by all of the major presidential candidates in 2008 and 2012.

During the general election, presidential candidates can receive federal funding for their campaigns. Candidates do not have to accept this funding, although every major party nominee did so between 1976, when the law took effect, and 2008, when Democrat Barack Obama became the first candidate to opt out. He continued to do so in 2012, as did his opponent, Mitt Romney. Funds are also given to minor political parties if their candidate received more than 5 percent of the vote in the previous election.

These federal funds are generated, in part, by money that taxpayers voluntarily allocate out of their federal taxes by checking off a box on their tax return form. The amount an individual taxpayer can choose to allocate is $3. (This donation does not reduce the refund or increase the taxes.) When this voluntary check-off procedure has not allocated sufficient funds to pay for candidates' public funding, the rest comes out of general government revenues.

These complex campaign finance regulations reflect two simple truths. First, any limits on campaign activities involve balancing (1) the right to free speech about candidates and issues with (2) the idea that rich people or well-funded organizations should not be allowed to dominate what voters hear during the campaign. Second, an enormous amount of money is spent on American elections (see Table 7.2).

INTERPRETING CAMPAIGN FINANCE DATA

The raw data on campaign finance do not always tell the whole story. For example, the huge amounts make more sense when you consider what is at stake during

TABLE » 7.2

CANDIDATE, PARTY, AND INTEREST GROUP ELECTION FUND-RAISING, 2006–12

Candidates and political parties raise and spend a great deal of money in their campaigns. Do these numbers help to explain the high re-election rates for members of Congress?

	2006	2008	2010	2012
PRESIDENTIAL CANDIDATES*				
Republican		(McCain)		(Romney)
	—	$360,000,000	—	$989,652,023
Democrat		(Obama)		(Obama)
	—	$639,000,000	—	$928,497,835
CONGRESSIONAL CANDIDATES				
House incumbents	$198,137,808	$539,879,135	$481,226,815	$631,553,983
House challengers	$27,680,023	$193,381,140	$256,639,703	$198,720,761
House open seat candidates	$16,453,309	$150,938,532	$141,773,031	$163,615,546
Senate incumbents	$190,492,258	$361,183,002	$186,563,786	$282,484,082
Senate challengers	$44,307,619	$100,188,001	$129,210,379	$162,483,481
Senate open seat candidates	$18,382,257	$59,328,470	$320,664,118	$265,825,062
POLITICAL PARTIES				
Republicans	$598,127,532	$1,228,025,068	$497,570,243	$906,957,839
Democrats	$493,311,599	$1,210,831,060	$559,585,362	$859,745,655
INDEPENDENT EXPENDITURES	$59,861,371	$286,459,718	$294,379,276	$977,495,372
TOTALS	$1,881,827,402	$5,268,316,289	$2,867,612,713	$6,367,026,932

*Presidential spending includes federal matching funds for the general election.
Source: Data compiled from the Center for Responsive Politics, November 2, 2012, www.opensecrets.org (accessed 11/2/12).

each election cycle: control of the federal government, with a budget of about $3 trillion a year and the power to start wars and regulate many aspects of citizens' lives. Also, the total amount spent on electioneering represents all funding for the 435 House contests, 33 or 34 Senate races, and a presidential election. Moreover, in terms of television advertising alone, a 30-second ad on a major network can cost tens or hundreds of thousands of dollars.[33] Given that even House campaigns may run hundreds of ads, and presidential campaigns run tens of thousands, it is easy to see why campaign costs pile up so quickly.

The principal concern about all this campaign cash is that the amount of money spent on a candidate's campaign might matter more than the candidate's qualifications or issue positions. That is, a candidate—in particular, a wealthy one who can self-fund his campaign—could get elected regardless of how good a job he would do, simply because he has more money than competing candidates to pay for ads, polls, a large staff, and mobilization efforts. Another concern is that individuals and organizations or corporations that can afford to make large contributions (or to fund their own electioneering efforts) might be able to dictate election outcomes or, by funding certain candidates' campaigns, garner disproportionate influence over the subsequent behavior of elected officials.

However, there is little evidence that campaign contributions alter legislators' behavior or that contributors are rewarded with votes supporting their causes or favorable policies.[34] Contributions may help contributors gain access, getting an appointment to present arguments to a politician or her staff. But people and organizations who contribute are already friendly with the politicians they support, and the politicians would likely hear their arguments in any case.

In sum, although money helps to shape elections, claims about the power of large contributors and big spenders are typically overstated. Much of the campaign spending in American elections is funded by average Americans making small donations. Moreover, no candidate, political organization, or corporation has the ability to dominate the airwaves and crowd out other voices. In the end, citizens are exposed to campaign advertising from a variety of sources, and they must decide which arguments to take seriously.

EXPLAIN THE KEY FACTORS THAT INFLUENCE VOTERS' CHOICES

HOW DO VOTERS DECIDE?

All the electoral activities we have considered so far are directed at citizens: making sure they are registered to vote, influencing their vote decisions, and getting them to the polls. Now we examine how citizens respond to these influences. The first things to understand are that only a minority of citizens report high levels of interest in campaigns, many people know little about the candidates or the issues, and many people do not vote.[35]

THE DECISION TO VOTE

Politics is everywhere, but getting involved is your choice; voting and other forms of political participation are optional. Even a strong preference between two candidates may not drive a citizen to the polls because each person's vote is just one of many.[36] The only time a vote "counts," in the sense that it changes the outcome,

CAMPAIGN FINANCE REGULATIONS

Campaign finance regulations place restrictions on what Americans can do to influence election outcomes. Suppose you are a wealthy person or the head of a corporation with deep pockets. Under current law, you and your corporation can only donate about $15,000 to a candidate's campaign; corporations have to form a political action committee to do so and cannot pay for the contribution with business revenues. You can also form an organization called a 527 that can run campaign ads designed to help elect your preferred candidates or donate to an existing 527. You can also spend unlimited amounts on independent expenditures, efforts that help a particular candidate, as long as the candidate or campaign has no control over these expenditures. But if your goal is to help your favorite candidate directly, whether by a cash contribution or an ad linked to the campaign, you face serious limits.

These limits on campaign spending arguably conflict with fundamental tenets of American democracy. The Bill of Rights states that Congress cannot abridge "freedom of speech, or of the press; or the right of the people peaceably to assemble, and to petition the Government for a redress of grievances." One interpretation of the First Amendment is that people should be free to spend whatever they want on contesting elections—excluding bribes, threats, and other illegal actions, of course. Thus, ending limits on campaign contributions would support free speech rights, although in practice it would affect only a small number of individuals, those who had large sums of money to spend.

The principal argument for restricting campaign contributions is that money conveys political power. That is, if we let rich people spend as much as they want on electioneering, they could control election outcomes by giving their favored candidates enough money to win regardless of who ran against them. This argument implies that removing contribution restrictions would result in election outcomes driven purely by campaign spending rather than by voters' preferences. (Of course, the lack of limits on independent expenditures works against this logic.)

However, even with unlimited funds, it is hard to get voters' attention—and harder still to change their minds. There are many examples of candidates who lost despite outspending their opponents. And there is no evidence in the corporate world that a company that spends enough on advertising can dominate its market and put its competitors out of business.

Even so, because money for ads is a necessary component of a political campaign, the possibility remains that a rich donor could change election outcomes by giving large sums to challengers in congressional elections. Many challengers never find out how voters would respond to their platforms because they lack the funds to run a full-blown campaign, including paying for an extensive ad campaign. Though most poorly funded challengers would stand no chance of beating their incumbent opponents even with an unlimited advertising budget, some

In a 2010 decision, the Supreme Court ruled that the Citizens United group (whose leader, David Bossie, is shown here) should have been allowed to release the film Hillary: The Movie *during the 2008 presidential campaigns. This decision opened the door to more campaign spending by groups and corporations.*

might. And in close races, giving a candidate extra funds to increase his or her get-out-the-vote efforts or to run additional campaign ads might be enough to change the outcome.

Critical Thinking Questions

1. Limits on individual campaign contributions guard against allowing wealthy people to dominate elections. What are some of the possible drawbacks of such regulations?

2. Since the *Citizens United* decision in 2010, corporations and unions (not just individuals) are allowed unlimited political expenditures as long as they are independent of a candidate's campaign organization. Why do you think independent expenditures are less regulated than direct contributions to campaigns?

paradox of voting The question of why citizens vote even though their individual votes stand little chance of changing the election outcome.

is when the other votes are split evenly so that one vote breaks the tie. Moreover, voting involves costs. Even if you don't learn about the candidates but vote anyway, you still have to get to the polls on Election Day. Thus the **paradox of voting** is this: Why does anyone vote, given that voting involves costs and the chances of affecting the outcome are small?

Figure 7.2 shows that among Americans the percentage of registered voters who actually voted has been, in recent presidential elections, around 60 percent, although the turnout has been close to 50 percent. (Voter turnout is calculated on the whole voting age population, including people who didn't vote because they opted not to register or were ineligible to register because of a felony conviction or other factors.)[37] As the figure shows, turnout is significantly higher in presidential elections than in midterm elections. Turnout is even lower in primaries and caucuses.

In the main, turnout is higher for whites than nonwhites, and among older Americans compared to younger cohorts, and for college graduates relative to people with a high school education or less. Men and women, however, say they vote at roughly the same rate. Many factors explain variation in turnout. People who vote regularly are more likely to see it as an obligation of citizenship, to feel guilty when they do not vote, and to think that the election matters. In contrast, turnout is much lower among those who are angry with the government, think that government actions do not affect them, or think that voting will have no impact on government policy.[38]

FIGURE » 7.2

TURNOUT IN PRESIDENTIAL AND MIDTERM ELECTIONS, 1992–2012

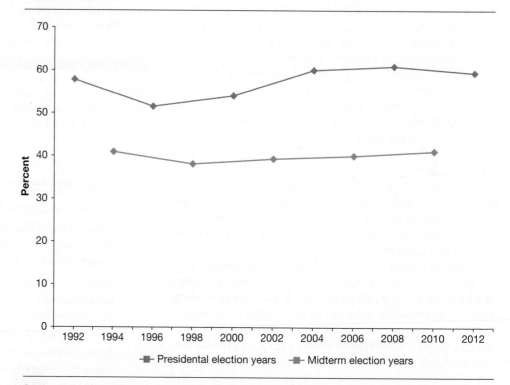

Source: United States Election Project, http://elections.gmu.edu/voter_turnout.htm (accessed 9/20/12).

These findings demonstrate the importance of mobilization in elections. As discussed earlier, many candidates for political office spend at least as much time trying to convince their supporters to vote as they do attempting to persuade others to become supporters in the first place. Because many Americans either do not vote or vote only sporadically, mobilization is vital for winning elections.

HOW DO PEOPLE VOTE?

Although candidates, parties, and other organizations release a blizzard of endorsements, reports, and press releases throughout the campaign, much of this information may be difficult to interpret. It is a daunting task, even for the rare, highly motivated voter. The combination of a lack of interest and a relatively complex task leads most Americans to base their vote decisions on easily interpretable pieces of information, or **voting cues**.[39] Voters in American national elections use many kinds of cues, including:

▶ *Incumbency*: Vote for the incumbent candidate.[40]

▶ *Partisanship*: Vote for the candidate whose party affiliation matches your own.[41]

▶ *Personal vote*: Vote for the incumbent if he or she has helped you to get assistance from a government agency or has helped your community to benefit from desirable government projects.[42]

▶ *Personal characteristics*: Vote for the candidate whose personal characteristics (age, race, gender, ethnicity, or religious beliefs) match your own or suggest that you have common values, ideologies, or policy preferences.[43]

▶ *Retrospective evaluations*: Focus on a small set of votes the incumbent has cast while in office or other duties of the office that you care about, and vote for the incumbent if he or she has behaved the way you want in these circumstances.[44]

▶ *For (or against) the party in power*: Vote for a candidate based on a comparison of that candidate's party with an assessment of the party in power (the party that controls the presidency and has majorities in the House and Senate).[45]

voting cues Pieces of information about a candidate that are readily available, easy to interpret, and lead a citizen to decide to vote for a particular candidate.

IN ORDER TO VOTE, CITIZENS MUST BE registered. Until recently, people who had either moved or turned 18 just before an election often could not register in time to vote, but the 1993 Motor Voter Act lowered barriers to registration. The act required states to give citizens the opportunity to register to vote when applying for or renewing a driver's license.

Cues give people a low-effort way to cast a vote that, more likely than not, is consistent with the voter's true preference among candidates.[46] Studies have found that citizens who use cues and are politically well informed are more likely to cast a reasonable vote (one that's consistent with their underlying policy preferences relative to candidates' positions), compared to those who use cues but are otherwise relatively politically ignorant. In essence, information helps people to select the right cue.[47]

Consider the partisanship cue. Because Republican and Democratic candidates usually hold different positions on many important issues, a candidate's party affiliation tells a voter something about how the candidate is likely to behave if elected. But the signal is not foolproof: in 2004 a Republican voter who was pro-gay rights might have used a partisan cue to vote for George Bush because he was the Republican nominee, even though more investigation would have revealed that Bush's position on gay rights was the opposite of her own. Even so, because partisan cues are so easy to employ, they are a favorite voting strategy in American elections.

All the strategies identified above for making vote decisions are used to some extent in every election. However, in **normal elections**, when congressional re-election rates are high and the seat shift between the parties is small, voters generally use cues that focus on the candidates themselves—such as incumbency, partisanship, a personal connection to a candidate, or the candidate's personal characteristics or past performance. This behavior is consistent with the saying that "all politics is local": congressional elections are independent, local contests in which a candidate's chances of winning depend on what voters think of the candidate in particular—not the president, Congress, or national issues. It also explains why electoral **coattails** are typically very weak in American elections and why so many Americans cast **split tickets** rather than **straight tickets**. In the main, vote decisions in presidential and congressional elections are made independently of each other.

VOTING IN NATIONALIZED ELECTIONS

Nationalized elections are atypical congressional elections in which the re-election rate is relatively low for one party's House and Senate incumbents and national-level issues exert more influence than usual on the House and Senate races. Such elections generally occur when a large number of voters switch to using the anti-party-in-power cue, which leads them to vote against candidates from the president's party. Typically, this shift happens when voters become highly concerned about a national issue such as the state of the economy or an international conflict. In 2006 many voters disapproved of how the war in Iraq was being conducted.[48] And in 2010 many voters disapproved of economic conditions in general as well as corporate bailouts, economic stimulus legislation, and health care reform.

National-level concerns such as these cause citizens to lower their evaluations of the president and of Congress, so they use different cues to guide their voting decisions.[49] Many voters look for someone to blame, focusing on members of Congress from the party in power. They then vote against these members, either as a protest vote or because they want to put different individuals in charge in the hopes that conditions will improve.

In nationalized elections, re-election rates for members of Congress (the percentage of incumbents who successfully ran for re-election) are generally high, as

normal election A typical congressional election in which the reelection rate is high and the influences on House and Senate contests are largely local.

coattails The idea that a popular president can generate additional support for candidates affiliated with his party. Coattails are weak or nonexistent in most American elections.

split ticket A ballot on which a voter selects candidates from more than one political party.

straight ticket A ballot on which a voter selects candidates from only one political party.

FIGURE » 7.3

INCUMBENTS RE-ELECTED

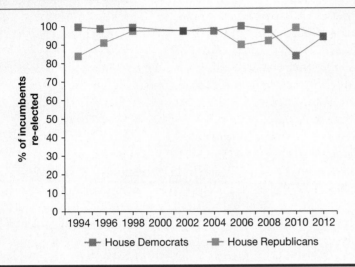

Figure 7.3 shows for the House of Representatives over the last generation. During that period neither party had a House re-election rate of less than 80 percent—even in 2006, when 100 percent of Democratic House incumbents running for re-election were re-elected, the re-election rate for House Republican incumbents was almost 90 percent.

Re-election rates for members of Congress are so high because senators and representatives work to insulate themselves from electoral challenges through tactics discussed in this chapter and in Chapter 9. Even so, congressional incumbents are not necessarily safe from electoral defeat. Rather, their high re-election rates result from the actions they take every day, which are calculated to win favor with their constituents. In normal elections these strategies are generally enough to ensure re-election. In nationalized elections, however, they are not enough to protect some legislators from protest votes against the disadvantaged party, as the Democrats learned in 2010.

UNDERSTANDING THE 2012 ELECTIONS

ANALYZE THE ISSUES AND OUTCOMES IN THE 2012 ELECTIONS

In contrast to the previous three elections, the 2012 elections might have seemed much less dramatic: Democrats held on to their majority in the Senate, Republicans continued to control the House, and President Obama was re-elected, albeit by a narrow margin. There appeared to be no major changes in the balance of power in the national government.

Despite this stability, the 2012 elections confirmed that politics is conflictual. The two presidential candidates, Democrat Barack Obama and Republican Mitt Romney, along with the congressional candidates from each party, offered very different ideas about the size and scope of the federal government in areas ranging

ALTHOUGH THE 2012 ELECTIONS confirmed the status quo, with President Obama re-elected and control of the House and Senate remaining the same, Americans and the major parties were sharply divided on many issues. In his 2012 acceptance speech, Obama alluded to these conflicts and the need for compromise in the coming months and years.

from deficit reduction to social issues. The 2012 elections also illustrate the idea that process matters. For example, one reason that Republican losses in the House were small was that Republican legislators in many states drew voting districts that favored their Republican colleagues in the House of Representatives. Finally, the 2012 returns also confirm our argument that focusing on the general election campaign ignores many important factors outside this narrow window of time. Accordingly, we begin our discussion of the 2012 elections by reviewing what happened in the 2008 and 2010 elections.

THE PATH TO 2012: THE 2008 AND 2010 ELECTIONS

The 2008 and 2010 elections were very different contests. In 2008, Barack Obama defeated John McCain with 365 electoral votes and nearly 53 percent of the popular vote. Democrats gained 8 seats in the Senate and 21 in the House. In contrast, Republicans dominated the 2010 midterms, gaining 63 House seats and control of the chamber, and they narrowed the Democrats' advantage in the Senate. In the end, the two elections illustrate the findings that Americans are sharply divided on many issues and that short-term factors such as the state of the economy or international conflicts can produce large changes from election to election.

THE 2008 ELECTION

Some characteristics of the 2008 contest distinguished it from all previous American elections. For the first time, an African American was elected president. The election also included the first female candidate to have a significant chance of winning a major party's nomination, Democrat Hillary Clinton, and only the second female vice-presidential nominee, Alaska governor Sarah Palin. For the first time since 2001, the wars in Iraq and Afghanistan were not central issues. And the American economy was faltering due to high energy prices, the failure of several large financial firms, the collapse of house prices, and banks' unwillingness to lend money, even to well-established, secure firms.

In the general election, Obama's get-out-the-vote operation was far more elaborate than McCain's, which helped Obama win key swing states. The Obama campaign did all the usual things, from knocking on doors to organizing shuttle vans to drive voters to the polls, but their operation was one of the largest and most effective ever seen in a presidential race. Similar efforts were crucial to Obama's success in the 2012 contest.

There were real differences in 2008 between Republican and Democratic candidates on issues such as how to address economic problems, how to reform health care, and what to do in Iraq and Afghanistan. Exit poll data showed that a clear majority of voters cited the economy as the most important issue and that Obama was the favorite among people who wanted the government to address the economy.

THE 2010 MIDTERM ELECTION

In the two years following the 2008 election, Democrats managed to enact significant portions of the party's policy agenda. However, debate over these policies exposed deep divisions within the House and Senate Democratic caucuses, as well as strong differences of opinion among voters who had elected Democrats to Congress and put Obama in the White House. More important, Republicans regained the initiative, offering proposals for sharp changes in government policy, while most Democratic candidates seemed to avoid talking about their party's policy accomplishments. Many who supported Democratic candidates in 2008 switched to become equally strong supporters of Republican candidates in 2010.

While some explanations of the 2010 contest focus on Obama's declining popularity, the flood of independent spending, or the rise of the Tea Party, perhaps a better explanation is found in the procedural advantages on the Republican side. For example, Democratic gains in the 2006 and 2008 House elections meant that as many as 50 to 60 incumbent Democrats were running in pro-Republican districts. These seats were winnable for Democrats as long as Republicans were tagged with an extremely unpopular war (as in 2006) or an economy in freefall (as in 2008). But in 2010, Republican candidates in these districts were free of these burdens for the first time in six years, giving them a decided advantage.

THE STATE OF THE COUNTRY IN 2012

As in 2008 and 2010, the economy was the central issue in the 2012 campaign. At first glance, the economic data appeared to pose a serious threat to President Obama's re-election chances—historically, a poor economy dooms a president's chance of re-election. In Obama's case, though, many Americans seemed to hold him only partially responsible for the economy, believing that he inherited many of the problems from previous administrations. The result was that at the national level, Obama's economic policies, including the economic stimulus legislation, did not hinder his chances of re-election, although they did not help much either.

Many Republican candidates ran on platforms emphasizing the need to reduce government spending and regulations, generally citing the repeal of President Obama's health care reforms as a central priority. Debates about the federal budget deficit were also significant. However, while virtually all candidates argued that something needed to be done about the deficit, very few were willing to commit to the painful policy changes that would be needed to deal with the problem. Social issues such as gay marriage were not often mentioned during the campaign—perhaps due to poll results that show a solid majority of Americans are not opposed to changes that would give gay and lesbian couples some form of marriage rights.

One difference between 2012 and the previous few elections was that international conflicts, including the wars in Afghanistan and Iraq, were not central issues in the campaign, both because of the withdrawal of American ground forces from Iraq and the gradual drawdown of forces from Afghanistan and because of the Obama administration's successes in the war on terror and the NATO operation in Libya.

In sum, while many issues arose during the 2012 campaign, none of them gave Republican or Democratic candidates a solid advantage. Instead, victory or defeat hinged on candidates' personal characteristics, their campaign promises, and, for incumbents, their record in office. For example, President Obama's approval rating hovered near 50 percent throughout the campaign—showing that he was neither a sure winner nor certain of defeat.

THE PRESIDENTIAL NOMINATION PROCESS AND CONVENTIONS

The Republican and Democratic presidential nomination campaigns were very different. On the Republican side, Mitt Romney was the front-runner from the beginning of the race to the end, although he faced serious opposition for most of the primary season from several candidates, including former senator Rick Santorum, former House Speaker Newt Gingrich, and businessman Herman Cain.

Thus, Romney's winning the nomination was not a surprise. He was experienced, having run for president in 2008 and served as governor of Massachusetts. His record as a businessman appealed to voters who thought that government should be run more efficiently. He was conservative but had not taken many controversial stands, such as calling for a total ban on abortion, although he did say that he would sign such a measure if Congress enacted it. He also opposed gay marriage. So, while Romney was not a perfect candidate—some voters disliked him because of his Mormon faith and his personal fortune, which together suggested to some that he was unfamiliar with the conditions facing average Americans—he was well-positioned to win the Republican nomination. Doubts about whether he was sufficiently conservative were muted after he selected conservative representative Paul Ryan of Wisconsin as his vice presidential candidate.

In contrast to Romney and the Republicans, President Obama won renomination with no significant opposition, as is usual for incumbent presidents. Both parties officially announced their nominees for president and vice president at their national conventions in late summer. The message at the Republican convention, articulated by Romney, Ryan, and others, was that President Obama should be blamed for poor economic conditions and pay the price for his support of programs such as health care reform that expanded the role of government in society. Democrats, in turn, emphasized how bad the economy was when Obama came into office and noted the many policy successes of Obama's first term.

THE GENERAL ELECTION: OBAMA VS. ROMNEY

Early in the general election campaign, Obama appeared to be opening up a significant lead over Romney, after a Democratic convention that was perceived to have made an effective case for his re-election. With most states squarely in one candidate's camp or the other, attention focused on nine swing states where neither candidate was significantly ahead: North Carolina, Ohio, Virginia, Florida, New Hampshire, Nevada, Wisconsin, Colorado, and Iowa.

THE DEBATES

The presidential debates in 2012 were an exception to the rule that debates have little influence on voter preferences: Obama's poor performance in the first debate, coupled with a strong performance by Romney, shifted the electorate two or three points toward Romney, which made the race effectively tied at the national level and extremely close in the swing states. Obama recovered in the second and third debates, responding effectively to Romney's criticisms and winning back a significant portion of the ground he lost in the first debate. After the debates, the polls settled back close to where they were before the convention, with the candidates roughly tied in national polls, but Obama was favored to win enough swing states to gain the electoral votes needed for another term.

CAMPAIGN STRATEGY

While both candidates refused federal funding and spent over a billion dollars each on the campaign (along with an equal amount spent by outside groups), as

FIGURE » 7.4

THE 2012 PRESIDENTIAL ELECTION: STATE BY STATE

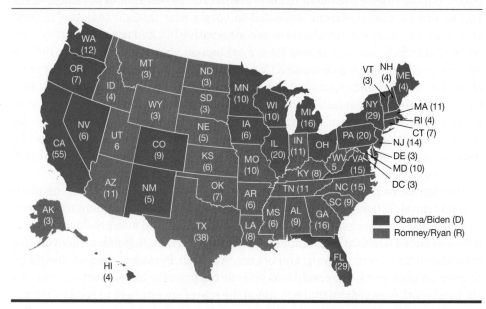

we have seen in other campaigns, there is little evidence that spending had much impact on the outcome. Part of the problem, as we discussed in earlier chapters, is that many Americans pay relatively little attention to politics, so even a large amount of campaign advertising may not get the message heard. Moreover, in the presidential race, polls showed that most Americans had largely made up their minds fairly early in the campaign, and few were open to persuasion.

Under these conditions, voter mobilization played a crucial role—and Obama's campaign was much better organized to get people to the polls, both for early voting and on Election Day. Many Democrats also went to court to contest laws that required voters to show picture ID at the polls, believing that this requirement would lower turnout by their supporters.

OBAMA'S VICTORY

In the end, Obama's record and campaign organization were just enough: he defeated Romney by a slight margin in the popular vote and a somewhat larger margin in the electoral college. Figure 7.4 displays the state-by-state results, showing Obama's strength in the Northeast, Midwest, and West Coast states, and Romney's dominance of western and southern states. Obama's victory was due to his strength in high-population states that had large electoral vote counts (such as California, New York, and Illinois) and his dominance of the so-called swing states.

CONGRESSIONAL RACES

At the beginning of the 2012 campaigns, many political scientists believed that the Democrats would lose seats in both the House and the Senate regardless of the outcome of the presidential election. In the House, the expectation was that

Republican-controlled state legislatures would use redistricting to put Democratic incumbents in vulnerable districts. Moreover, Democrats controlled 23 (including 2 independents who caucus with Democrats) of the 33 seats that were contested in the campaign and had several vulnerable incumbents.

Surprisingly, Democrats won one additional Senate seat (counting 2 independents expected to caucus with Democrats) and gained 8 House seats. Their success was due to two factors. First, Republicans' control of redistricting was limited by the fact that in some states, redistricting is determined by nonpartisan commissions, while in others, Democratic governors had to approve districting schemes. Republican prospects were also constrained by their large gains in the 2010 election. There were not that many vulnerable Democratic incumbents in 2012 because many such candidates had been defeated or had retired in 2010. Conversely, Republicans faced the problem of securing their gains from that election, helping a large class of freshmen House members get re-elected. Moreover, while there were vulnerable Democratic senators in 2012, some Republican senators were vulnerable as well, most notably Scott Brown of Massachusetts, who won a special election in 2009 in a state that typically sends Democrats to Congress. Brown was defeated by Democrat Elizabeth Warren in 2012.

Democrats also benefited from campaign gaffes by Republican candidates. For example, Representative Todd Akin's prospects in running for senator in Missouri were severely harmed by his claim during an interview that it was nearly impossible for a woman to become pregnant from a rape. After this remark produced a nationwide firestorm of protest, many organizations, including the Republican National Committee and Senate Campaign Committee, refused to support his candidacy. His opponent, Claire McCaskill, who was regarded as one of the most vulnerable Democratic incumbents, ultimately won re-election.

SENATOR CLAIRE MCCASKILL OF Missouri—shown here canvassing for votes in the state—was one of several Democratic incumbents considered vulnerable in 2012. However, McCaskill prevailed after her opponent Todd Akin's remarks about rape drew wide criticism.

ANALYZING THE 2012 ELECTIONS

It is always easy to attribute an election outcome to a single event or factor. We might say that Mitt Romney lost the presidential election because he was a Mormon or because of his remarks at a campaign event that 47 percent of Americans want to be dependent on government. If Obama had lost, we could attribute it to a poor performance in the first debate, dissatisfaction with his health care or economic stimulus proposals, or the September 11, 2012, attack on the U.S. Consulate in Bengazi, Libya, which killed the American ambassador and three others.

Sometimes campaigns do turn on a single event or decision. Todd Akin probably lost his Senate race in Missouri because of his comments about rape and pregnancy—polls showed that Claire McCaskill gained considerable support after the remarks and never lost it.

More commonly, however, elections are decided by broadly held perceptions that develop over time and are hard to change. Obama's appeal was based on his economic stimulus programs, health care reform, ending of the wars in Iraq and Afghanistan, promises of immigration reform, and positions on social issues such as gay marriage and abortion rights. Romney's campaign emphasized opposition to the stimulus and health care reforms and promised to roll back regulations, promote a more aggressive foreign policy, and champion more conservative stands on social policy. These differences are reflected in the kinds of voters that supported each candidate, as shown in Table 7.3.

Table 7.3 shows that Obama's coalition was younger, more female, more diverse, and had lower incomes than those supporting Romney. These differences make sense given the issue positions and records of the two candidates and the opinions and preferences held by these groups, as discussed in Chapter 5.

Why, then, was the presidential contest so close—even at the end? For one thing, presidents who win overwhelming victories either have a strong economy to talk about or an opponent who can be criticized for a weak performance or empty promises. Obama had neither of these things; nor did Romney. Moreover, the country is divided almost evenly on several major issues, from health care to social policy. Even on deficit reduction, where most people favor quick action, there is no consensus about what policies are best. Under these conditions, it is extraordinarily hard for any candidate to take issue positions that generate a large supporting coalition—positions that attract some votes will drive others away. As long as these conflicts persist, it is likely that we will continue to see close presidential elections.

TABLE » 7.3

GROUPS AND VOTES IN THE 2012 PRESIDENTIAL ELECTION

		PERCENT VOTE FOR	
		OBAMA	ROMNEY
Gender	Male	48%	53%
	Female	55	45
Age	18–29	60	40
	30–44	52	48
	45–64	51	49
	65 and over	44	56
Race/Ethnicity	White	41	59
	Black	93	7
	Hispanic	71	29
	Asian	73	27
Income	Under 30K	63	37
	30–49K	57	43
	50–100K	53	47
	100K or more	46	54

Source: Exit poll data at http://elections.nytimes.com/2012/results/president/exit-polls (accessed 11/7/12).

CONCLUSION

Candidates in American national elections compete for different offices using a variety of rules that determine who can run for office, who can vote, and how ballots are counted and winners determined. Election outcomes are shaped by who runs for office and how they campaign, who decides to vote, and how they decide whom to support, but also by the rules that govern electoral competition.

It is easy to complain about American elections. Citizens are not experts about public policy. They often know little about the candidates running for office. Candidates sensationalize, attack, and dissemble, rather than giving constructive details about who they are and what they would do if elected. Even so, there are clear, systematic differences between Democratic and Republican candidates that translate into different government policies depending on who holds office. In addition, the criteria that average Americans use to make vote decisions reflect these differences. People don't know everything about politics or about elections, but their votes are, by and large, reasonable.

Moreover, many examples of seemingly strange behavior in American elections make more sense once you examine them. It makes sense that so few Americans are issue voters and that many abstain. It also makes sense that candidates seeking the attention of distracted voters tend to emphasize sensationalism over sober discussion of policies. The outcome of the election is the result of all these individual-level choices added together. In that sense, election outcomes reflect the preferences of the American people.

American elections are not perfect, but it is impossible to say that they are irrelevant. By determining who holds political office, elections determine what government does. The 2010 and 2012 elections illustrate this point. After Republicans gained control of the House and won additional Senate seats in 2010 and 2012, congressional Democrats and President Obama had to scale back plans for new policy initiatives, as they now required substantial Republican support to enact legislation. The last two years have also seen extended deadlock over deficit reduction and government spending, reflecting the divided control of government. The 2012 elections, which preserved this outcome, are likely to produce deadlock on many issues as well. However, if Mitt Romney had won the presidency and Republicans gained control of the Senate, the result would have been significant changes in policies throughout the federal government.

STUDY*guide*

HOW DO AMERICAN ELECTIONS WORK?

▶ Present the major rules and procedures of American elections. **Pages 193–200**

SUMMARY

Elections in America generally have two steps. Primary elections select each party's nominees, and general elections determine who wins the office. Some of the rules for presidential elections differ from those for other elections; notably, the electoral college system determines the winner of the general election.

KEY TERMS

incumbent (p. 193)

open primary (p. 194)

closed primary (p. 194)

general election (p. 194)

plurality voting (p. 195)

majority voting (p. 195)

runoff election (p. 195)

primary (p. 196)

caucus (p. 196)

proportional allocation (p. 196)

winner-take-all (p. 196)

electoral college (p. 198)

PRACTICE QUIZ QUESTIONS

1. Runoff elections only occur in states that use
_____.

a) majority voting
b) primary elections
c) plurality voting
d) absentee ballots
e) proportional allocation

2. The winner-take-all method of allocating most states' electoral votes results in candidates focusing on
_____ states and _____ states.

a) low-population; safe
b) high-population; safe
c) low-population; swing
d) high-population; swing
e) safe; swing

(S) PRACTICE ONLINE

"Big Think" video exercise: *Abolish the Electoral College?*

ELECTORAL CAMPAIGNS

▶ Describe the features and strategies of campaigns for federal office. **Pages 200–210**

SUMMARY

Party organizations and candidates begin preparing for the next election the day after the last election ends. They focus on fund-raising and determining which races are likely to be competitive. Incumbents work throughout the election cycle to maintain their good standing among the voters and to secure their re-election bids. During a campaign, candidates work hard, particularly through the use of advertise-

ments, to increase their name recognition and mobilize their supporters.

KEY TERMS

election cycle (p. 200)

open seat (p. 202)

permanent campaign (p. 202)

GOTV ("get out the vote") (p. 203)

ground game (p. 203)

attack ads (p. 206)

Federal Election Commission (p. 207)

hard money (p. 207)

soft money (p. 207)

CRITICAL THINKING AND DISCUSSION

What kinds of candidates are helped by limits on campaign contributions by individuals and organizations such as PACs? What kinds of candidates do these restrictions hurt? Why do such limits affect these types of candidates differently?

PRACTICE QUIZ QUESTIONS

3. An open seat election is one in which _____.
   a) there is no challenger in the race
   b) there is no incumbent in the race
   c) an incumbent loses his/her seat due to redistricting
   d) an incumbent faces a challenger in his/her own primary
   e) an incumbent faces a challenger in the general election

4. What effect does fundraising have for incumbents?
   a) It ensures the potential for an aggressive campaign, but it has no effect on opposition.
   b) It ensures the potential for an aggressive campaign, and it deters opposition.
   c) It ensures the potential for an aggressive campaign, and it encourages opposition.
   d) It has no effect on the potential for an aggressive campaign, but it does deter opposition.
   e) It has no effect on the potential for an aggressive campaign, nor does it deter opposition.

5. GOTV and "ground game" refer to a candidate's attempts to _____.
   a) boost name recognition
   b) mobilize supporters
   c) increase fund-raising
   d) deter opposition
   e) win endorsements

6. What is soft money?
   a) money that can be given directly to a candidate
   b) money that is given by members of the opposing party
   c) money that can be spent to mobilize voters for a specific candidate
   d) money that candidates spend to boost the party's reputation
   e) money that is not tied to a specific candidate

7. Research shows that modern campaign ads are likely to _____.
   a) change voters' minds
   b) feature speeches by the candidate
   c) have beneficial effects, such as informing voters
   d) run several minutes in length
   e) increase turnout

Ⓢ PRACTICE ONLINE

"Critical Thinking" exercise: *Politics Is Conflictual— Campaign Ads*

HOW DO VOTERS DECIDE?

▶ Explain the key factors that influence voters' choices. **Pages 210–15**

SUMMARY

Despite the fact that politics is everywhere, ordinary voters don't pay much attention to politics. Turnout rates are modest, and people know relatively little about the candidates and their positions. While some voters are highly interested in politics and vote after collecting all the information they can about the candidates, most voters rely on voting cues for their vote choice.

KEY TERMS

paradox of voting (p. 212)

voting cues (p. 213)

normal election (p. 214)

coattails (p. 214)

split ticket (p. 214)

straight ticket (p. 214)

CRITICAL THINKING AND DISCUSSION

Using cues to make vote decisions lowers the cost of voting, in terms of the time and effort involved in a voter's decision. Under what conditions will cues help a voter to make the right choice in an election? ("The right choice" may be defined as the same choice that would result from having complete information about the candidates.) Under what conditions will cues lead a voter to make the wrong choice?

PRACTICE QUIZ QUESTIONS

8. The paradox of voting is this: Why does anyone vote, given that _____?
   a) voting is costly, and the chances of affecting the outcome are small
   b) voting is costly and approval for government is high.
   c) voting is easy, and the chances of affecting the outcome are large
   d) voting is easy, but informing yourself about the candidates takes time
   e) approval for government is low, but turnout rates are high

9. Voters who rely on voting cues to determine their vote choice are _____.
   a) likely to cast a reasonable vote, regardless of their information level
   b) unlikely to cast a reasonable vote, regardless of their information level
   c) likely to cast a reasonable vote, and more so if they are informed
   d) unlikely to cast a reasonable vote, and less so if they are informed
   e) neither more nor less likely to cast a reasonable vote than voters who ignore cues

10. Weak coattails and split tickets serve as indicators that _____.
    a) most voters don't know anything about the candidates
    b) most elections are determined by local issues
    c) most elections are determined by national issues
    d) most voters use political parties as their dominant voting cue
    e) most voters use incumbency as their dominant voting cue

Ⓢ PRACTICE ONLINE

"What Do Political Scientists Do?" video exercise: *Party Identification and Independent Voters*

UNDERSTANDING THE 2012 ELECTIONS

▶ Analyze the issues and outcomes in the 2012 elections. **Pages 215–22**

SUMMARY

The 2012 elections preserved the status quo, with a Republican House, a Democratic Senate, and the re-election of President Obama. With the nation divided on many questions and a lackluster national economy, the presidential campaigns focused on a small number of swing states, including Ohio, Florida, and Virginia. President Obama's victory owed much to his campaign's extensive mobilization efforts and its success at portraying Republican Mitt Romney as out of touch with the concerns of average Americans.

PRACTICE QUIZ QUESTIONS

11. What is the most accurate statement about the role of economic conditions in the 2012 election?
    a) Looking across the entire nation, economic conditions did not strongly favor either candidate.
    b) The Obama campaign's mobilization efforts offset the loss of support from a weak economy.
    c) Mitt Romney's campaign avoided talking about the economy.
    d) Economic conditions did not matter because most Americans based their vote on other issues.
    e) The Obama campaign convinced voters that Republican Senate leaders were to blame for the poor economy.

12. What role did the question of expanding marriage rights to gays and lesbians play in the 2012 election?
    a) Surveys showed that President Obama gained many votes because of his continued opposition to allowing gays to marry.
    b) Neither campaign emphasized this issue.
    c) Mitt Romney did not talk about this issue because of his Mormon religious beliefs.
    d) In contrast to 2010, more voters saw the issue as important.
    e) Both candidates supported a constitutional amendment to allow gays and lesbians to marry.

13. Why was congressional turnover so low in 2012?
    a) Incumbents used the redistricting process to build safe districts.
    b) Spending on campaign ads by outside groups favored House and Senate incumbents.
    c) Neither party could find enough qualified challengers to run in House and Senate races.
    d) Too many House members and senators lost primary elections.
    e) Most vulnerable House members and senators had already lost in 2008 and 2010.

....

SUGGESTED READING

Abramson, Paul, John Aldrich, and David Rohde. *Change and Continuity in the 2004 and 2006 Elections*. Washington, DC: CQ Press, 1995.

Bartels, Larry *Presidential Primaries and the Dynamics of Public Choice*. Princeton, NJ: Prrinceton University Press, 1998.

Cramer, Richard Ben. *The Way to the White House*. New York: Vintage, 1993.

Donovan, Todd, and Shaun Bowler. *Reforming the Republic: Democratic Institutions for the New America*. New York: Pearson, 2007.

Florina, Morris P. *Retrospective Voting in American National Elections*. New Heaven, CT: Yale University Press, 1981.

Hellemann, John, and Mark Halpren. *Game Change: Obama and the Clintons, McCain and Palin, and the Race of a Lifetime*. New York: Random House, 2009.

Jacobson, Gary. *The Politics of Congressional Electronics*, 6th ed. New York: Pearson Longman, 2004.

Key, V.O. *The Responsible Electorate*. New York: Vintage, 1966.

Museum of the Moving Image, "The Living Room Candidate: exhibit at http://livingroomcandidate.movingimage.us.

Niemi, Richard G, and Herbert F. Weisberg. *Controversies in Voting Behavior*, 4th ed. Washington, DC: CQ Press, 2001.

Popkin, Samuel. *The Reasoning Voter*. Chicago: University of Chicago Press, 1991.

8

Interest Groups

THE GROUPS INVOLVED IN THE Occupy Wall Street movement argued that the government showered benefits on wealthy corporations and individuals, while ordinary Americans ("the 99%") struggled. They claimed that lobbying efforts by corporations influenced government policy.

DESPITE DISAGREEING ABOUT ASPECTS OF AMERICAN politics and public policy, one thing that the groups involved in the Occupy Wall Street movement generally opposed was the federal government's bailout in 2008 and 2009 of major banks and financial institutions. The federal bailouts, they argue, rewarded the same firms whose actions had caused widespread economic distress in the first place—distress that made the bailouts crucial to the firms' survival. These disgruntled groups also agree on why the bailout occurred: it was the result of intense lobbying efforts by the corporations that stood to gain from a bailout. In the protesting groups' view, lobbying enabled these firms to achieve a change in government policy that made them vastly better off—in some cases, saved them from going bankrupt—at the expense of most of the American public, many of whom lost their jobs or saw their home values plummet but received no bailouts.

There seems to be evidence to support these claims. An analysis conducted by the Center for Responsive Politics (CRP) argued that a firm's success in getting funds from the government's principal bailout program, the Troubled Assets Relief Program (TARP), hinged on the firm's lobbying efforts. Twenty-five firms spent a total of $114 million on lobbying in 2008 and received a total of $295 billion from TARP. Many of the firms that spent a lot on lobbying, such as AIG, Citigroup, and Bank of America, received some of the higher TARP allocations. As the head of the CRP put it, "Even in the best economic times, you won't find an investment with a greater payoff than what these companies

CONFLICT & COMPROMISE
in American Politics

229

have been getting. Some of the companies and industries that have received payments may now consider their contributions and lobbying to be the smartest investments they've made in years."[1] Looking at the same evidence, one member of Congress claimed that "Wall Street owns Washington."[2]

With examples like these, it is not surprising that Americans are suspicious of interest groups and worry about their ability to dominate the political process. What do these companies get from lobbying? How can average Americans change government policy when they are fighting against organizations that have millions of dollars and extensive connections on their side? Even if individuals try to form new groups to advance certain policy goals, their battle against well-entrenched groups does not seem like a fair fight. Moreover, despite the proliferation of interest groups and lobbyists in America, some large groups of like-minded Americans have no interest group fighting for their policy concerns. Where, for example, are groups that lobby for what college students want? And how can debates over policy be considered a fair fight when some groups are unrepresented?

This chapter surveys the wide range of interest groups in American politics, from large, powerful groups such as the National Rifle Association (NRA) to small organizations that lobby on issues that concern only a few Americans. In part, our discussion will confirm that conflicts over government policy are the driving force behind interest group activities. For example, the NRA fights to maintain and extend Americans' ability to own and carry firearms, while other groups, such as Handgun Control, work to impose restrictions on these rights. Government policy reflects, at least in part, the actions taken by these different groups.

However, interest groups are not only the tools of the rich and powerful. Virtually all Americans belong to interest groups or have groups that lobby on their behalf. And many of the clubs, groups, and organizations to which Americans belong have little-known yet extensive lobbying arms. Moreover, policy victories do not always go to the organization that spends the most money or hires the most expensive talent. Groups can succeed by mobilizing their members, forming alliances with other groups, becoming sources of political or policy expertise, or using the courts to fight policy battles. Thus, although people are correct to understand interest groups in terms of conflict, they are wrong in thinking that these groups invariably work against the interests of average Americans. Moreover, interest groups often serve as a source of compromise in the policy process, either in the proposals they offer or in their efforts to work together with other groups.

This chapter also shows that evidence does not support many of the claims about the vast influence of interest groups. In the case of TARP, for example, some firms received relatively little in bailout funds even though they lobbied a lot—General Motors (GM), for example, spent the most of any firm on lobbying but received far less than the top TARP recipients. One bank, Wells Fargo, spent only a tenth of what GM did on lobbying but received more than twice the TARP allocation. Other firms, such as E*Trade, spent considerable amounts on lobbying but were denied TARP funding.

In the end, the TARP example does not reveal that interest groups are all-powerful in American politics. Rather, it shows how America's political institutions provide many opportunities for groups to influence policy making. Thus, while it is surely wrong to say that interest groups are irrelevant—in many cases, their efforts have an important impact on public policy—it is equally wrong to say that they are the dominant force in the policy process.

THE INTEREST GROUP UNIVERSE

DEFINE INTEREST GROUPS AND DESCRIBE THE CHARACTERISTICS OF DIFFERENT TYPES OF GROUPS

Interest groups are organizations that seek to influence government policy by helping to elect candidates who support the organizations' policy goals and by **lobbying** elected officials and bureaucrats. Lobbying involves persuasion—using reports, protests, informal meetings, or other techniques to convince an elected official or bureaucrat to help enact a law, craft a regulation, or do something else that a group wants. The members of an interest group can be individual citizens, local governments, businesses, foundations or nonprofit organizations, churches, or virtually any other entity. An interest group's employees or members may lobby on the group's behalf, or a group may hire a lobbyist or lobbying firm to do the work for it. Nuts and Bolts 8.1 gives some examples of the types of interest groups found in contemporary American politics.

Interest groups and political parties both hope to change what government does, but there are three critical differences between these types of organizations. First, political parties focus on running candidates for office and coordinating the activities of elected officials. Some interest groups do these things, but they do not have an official position on electoral ballots to offer their candidates. Moreover, many interest groups do not get involved in elections at all. Second, the major political parties hold certain legal advantages over even the largest interest groups when it comes to influencing policy (one such advantage is having guaranteed positions on electoral ballots). Third, the elected members of political parties have a direct influence over government activity: they propose, debate, and vote on policies. In contrast, interest groups have an indirect influence: they must either persuade elected officials to support their point of view or help elect candidates who already share their goals.

Sometimes interest groups are primarily political organizations. One such group is Public Citizen, which conducts research projects, lobbies legislators and bureaucrats, and tries to rally public opinion on a range of environmental, health, and energy issues. Usually, though, lobbying is only one part of what an organization does. The NRA, for example, endorses candidates, contributes to campaigns, and lobbies elected officials; but it also runs gun safety classes, holds competitions, and sells hardware to its members. In other cases, interest group activity is almost hidden within an organization. For example, most drivers know the Automobile Association of America (AAA) as a provider of emergency roadside service and maps, but AAA is also an interest group that lobbies for increased funding for highways and less funding for mass transit.

As these descriptions suggest, interest groups and lobbying are ubiquitous in American politics. Many organizations have lobbying operations or hire lobbyists to work on their behalf. You may think that you don't belong to a group that lobbies the federal government, but the odds are that you do.

ORGANIZATIONAL STRUCTURES

Interest groups differ in how they are organized—whether the group is one unitary body, or made up of many smaller, local groups. How a group is organized makes a difference for the kinds of lobbying tactics it can use, as well as how decisions are made about what to lobby for.

interest group An organization of people who share common political interests and aim to influence public policy by electioneering and lobbying.

lobbying Efforts to influence public policy through contact with public officials on behalf of an interest group.

MORE THAN 4 MILLION INDIVIDUALS belong to the National Rifle Association, one of the most powerful interest groups in America. At their national convention, shown here, members have the opportunity to visit a gun show.

TYPES OF INTEREST GROUPS

Scholars often divide interest groups into categories based on who their members are or the number or kinds of things they lobby for. While it's important not to take these categories too literally—very few groups, for example, lobby on only one issue—the categories explain what kinds of interest groups exist and what they lobby for.

▶ *Economic groups* include corporations, trade associations, labor groups, and professional organizations. Economic interest groups aim to influence policy in ways that will bring their members economic—that is, monetary—benefits. Many corporations such as Microsoft, Exxon, or Boeing have lobbying operations that petition government for contracts or favorable regulations of their firm or industry.

▶ *Labor organizations* are another kind of economic group. The American Federation of Labor and Congress of Industrial Organizations (AFL-CIO) lobbies for regulations that make it easy for workers to form labor unions, and a range of other policies. Professional organizations, a third type of economic group, lobby

for government policies that financially benefit their members.

▶ The second interest group category is *citizen groups*, or public interest groups. This category captures a range of organizations, from those with mass membership (such as the Sierra Club) to those that have no members but claim to speak for large segments of the population. One such group is the Family Research Council, which describes itself as "promoting the Judeo-Christian worldview as the basis for a just, free, and stable society." This group lobbies for a range of policies, from legislation that defines marriage as between a man and a woman to legislation that would eliminate estate taxes.

▶ The third category of interest group is the *single-issue groups*. These groups focus on a narrow range of topics or a single government program or piece of legislation. Examples include the National Right to Life Committee, which lobbies for restrictions on abortion rights, and NumbersUSA, which lobbies against guest worker programs for noncitizens.

CENTRALIZED GROUPS OR CONFEDERATIONS

centralized groups Interest groups that have a headquarters, usually in Washington, D.C., as well as members and field offices throughout the country. In general, these groups' lobbying decisions are made at headquarters by the group leaders.

confederations Interest groups made up of several independent, local organizations that provide much of their funding and hold most of the power.

There are two main models of interest group structure. Most large, well-known organizations are **centralized groups**; two examples are the NRA and the American Association of Retired Persons (AARP). National organizations like these typically have headquarters in Washington, D.C., operate field offices in large state capitals, and have members nationwide. Each organization's leadership is located in its headquarters, and these leaders determine the group's lobbying goals and tactics. The other structural model is a **confederation**, which comprises largely independent, local organizations. For example, the National Independent Automobile Dealers Association (NADA) encompasses fifty state-level organizations that provide most of the membership benefits to car dealers who join and that also raise much of the money that NADA contributes to political candidates (several million dollars in recent elections).

Both organizational structures have advantages and disadvantages. A centralized organization controls all the group's resources and can deploy them efficiently, but it can be challenging for these groups to find out what their members want. In contrast, because confederations maintain independent chapters at the state and local levels, their national headquarters can easily learn what the members want simply by contacting the local groups. But this strength is related to a weakness: because state and local chapters mostly function independently of the national headquarters, confederated groups often experience conflict as different local chapters disagree over what to lobby for and which candidates to support.

MASS ASSOCIATIONS OR PEAK ASSOCIATIONS

Interest groups can also be distinguished according to the size of their membership and the members' role in the group's activities. Some are **mass associations** with many dues-paying members. One example is the Sierra Club, which has more than 750,000 members who pay annual dues of about $30 each. Besides keeping its members informed about the making of environmental policy in Washington, D.C., the Sierra Club endorses judicial nominees and candidates for elected positions and works with members of Congress to develop legislative proposals. The group's members elect the organization's board of directors.

However, not all mass associations give members a say in selecting a group's leaders or determining its mission. For example, AARP claims to lobby for policies its members favor, but members actually have no control over which legislative causes the group chooses. Moreover, AARP does not poll members to determine its issue positions, nor do members pick AARP leadership.

Peak associations have a different type of membership,[3] exemplified by the Business-Industry Political Action Committee (BIPAC). This association of several hundred businesses and trade associations aims to elect "pro-business individuals" to Congress.[4] Individuals cannot join peak associations—they may work for member companies or organizations, but they cannot become dues-paying members on their own.

mass associations Interest groups that have a large number of dues-paying individuals as members.

peak associations Interest groups whose members are businesses or other organizations rather than individuals.

MEMBERSHIP: BENEFITS AND INCENTIVES

Attracting members is important for an interest group's success. Society is full of groups of like-minded people (such as college students) who do not organize to lobby or who choose to enjoy the benefits of organizations without participating. Therefore, most organizations develop mechanisms to promote participation. These mechanisms fall into three categories: benefits from participation, coercion, and selective incentives.

CENTRALIZED INTEREST GROUPS in America often have an office in Washington, D.C., which helps them to stay in touch with members of Congress, bureaucrats, and the president and his staff. It also provides a venue for attracting press coverage of the group's concerns. This 2009 town hall meeting on health care held at the Washington headquarters of AARP was attended by President Obama.

solidary benefits Satisfaction derived from the experience of working with like-minded people, even if the group's efforts do not achieve the desired impact.

purposive benefits Satisfaction derived from the experience of working toward a desired policy goal, even if the goal is not achieved.

coercion A method of eliminating nonparticipation or free riding by potential group members by requiring participation, as in many labor unions.

selective incentives Benefits that can motivate participation in a group effort because they are available only to those who participate, such as member services offered by interest groups.

Studies of political parties and interest groups find that some individuals volunteer out of a sense of duty or because they enjoy working together toward a common goal. These benefits of participation are called either **solidary benefits**, which come from working with like-minded people, or **purposive benefits**, which come from working to achieve a desired policy goal.[5] When these benefits are not enough to prompt participation, groups try other measures to promote active membership.

A second mechanism is **coercion**, or required participation. Consider labor unions. They provide public goods to workers by negotiating with management on behalf of worker-members over pay issues and work requirements. In many cases, worker-members have to join the union: union shop laws require them to pay union dues as a condition of their employment.

Finally, **selective incentives** (also called material incentives) are benefits given only to the members of a given interest group. Thus, for example, AAA members can call AAA at any time for emergency service when they have car trouble. AAA also provides its members with annotated maps and travel guides, discounts at hotels and restaurants, and other benefits. These services mask the interest group role of AAA. For example, its Foundation for Traffic Safety delivers research reports to legislators on topics ranging from lowering the blood alcohol level threshold that legally defines drunk driving to increasing the restrictions on driving by senior citizens.[6] It's unlikely that many AAA members—who join for the selective incentives— are aware of the organization's lobbying efforts. The inducements drive membership, which funds the organization's lobbying operation.

RESOURCES

The resources that interest groups use to support their lobbying efforts are people (the members), money, and expertise. Although we examine interest group strategies in a later section, here we emphasize that a group's resources influence its

INTEREST GROUPS USE A VARIETY of tactics to draw attention to their concerns, including events designed to generate media coverage. Jon Davids, a Public Interest Research Group staffer, traveled nearly 20,000 miles across America with an eighteen-foot inflatable largemouth bass named Freddie to events that publicized the dangers of mercury pollution in lakes and streams.

available lobbying strategies. Some groups have sufficient funding and staff to pursue a wide range of strategies, while smaller groups with fewer resources have only a few lobbying options.

A crucial resource for most interest groups is the membership. Group members can write to or meet with elected officials, travel to Washington for demonstrations, and even offer expertise or advice to the group's leaders. When the "members" of a group are corporations, as is the case with trade associations, CEOs and other corporate staff can help with the group's lobbying efforts.

Money is another important resource. Virtually everything interest groups do, from meeting with elected officials to fighting for what they want in court, can be purchased as services. Money can also go toward campaign contributions or developing and running campaign ads. And, of course, money is necessary to fund interest groups' everyday operations. Well-funded interest groups have a considerable advantage in the lobbying process. If they need an expert, a lobbyist, or a lawyer, they can hire one. Also, they can pay for campaign ads and make campaign contributions, while groups with less cash cannot use these strategies.

Expertise is a third type of group resource. It takes many forms. Some interest group leaders know a lot about their members' preferences or about what people in a community, congressional district, or state want,[7] and they can relay this information to elected officials and bureaucrats. Other groups offer information that ranges from reports on policy questions to concrete legislative proposals. Group leaders can use this information to negotiate with officials or bureaucrats as part of a trade to get what the group wants. Expertise can also involve knowledge of political factors, such as what kinds of policies certain party caucuses or individual legislators support, or information about the constitutionality of proposed laws. Lobbying firms that employ former members of Congress and bureaucrats are a good source of such information.

AAA (FORMERLY THE AUTOMOBILE Association of America) is a well-known provider of emergency road service, yet few people are aware of its role as an interest group that lobbies for a wide range of policy changes.

STAFF

Interest group staff falls into two categories: experts on the group's main policy areas, and people with useful government connections and knowledge of procedures. The first group includes scientists, engineers, and others with advanced degrees; the second primarily comprises people who have worked inside government as elected officials, bureaucrats, or legislative staff.[8] Sometimes these former members of government are also policy experts, but their unique contribution is their knowledge of how government works and their already-existing relationships with officeholders and other former coworkers in government.

The practice of transitioning from government positions to working for interest groups or lobbying firms, or transitioning from lobbyist to officeholder, is often called the **revolving door**.[9] A 2005 study found that from 1998 to 2005, more than 40 percent of members leaving the House or Senate joined a lobbying firm after their departure.[10] A separate study in 2006 found that more than two-thirds of the Department of Homeland Security's original senior staff left their positions to work for corporations or lobbying firms.[11] Examples such as these highlight the dilemma of the revolving door.

revolving door The movement of individuals from government positions to jobs with interest groups or lobbying firms, and vice versa.

RESTRICTIONS ON INTEREST GROUP LOBBYING

In 2005, a major lobbyist, Jack Abramoff, was accused of using "golf junkets, meals at his restaurant, seats at sporting events, and, in some cases, old-fashioned cash" to lobby members of Congress.[a] Abramoff was convicted in 2006 of conspiracy, fraud, and tax evasion. Representative Bob Ney (R-Ohio) and several aides and high-ranking bureaucrats were also convicted of accepting Abramoff's bribes or making false statements about their relationship with him.[b] The case suggests that some interest groups and lobbying firms are not playing by the rules. Rather than just making their case to officials, they are offering money and other inducements in return for policy change.

It seems that to solve this problem, interest groups and lobbying firms should be regulated to ensure that they cannot unfairly dominate the policy process by buying support from members of Congress and bureaucrats. This proposal raises two questions. First, would new regulations prevent abuses of power? Second, are such abuses of power commonplace enough to justify a new regulation?

Consider the six-point lobbying reform proposal offered after the Abramoff scandal by a coalition of six public interest groups.[c]

1. Place low limits on interest groups' contributions to candidates.

2. Ban interest groups from providing subsidized travel to people in government.

3. Ban gifts from interest groups and their staff to members of Congress and congressional staff.

4. Establish an independent ethics review board to oversee interactions between lobbyists and both Congress and the bureaucracy, and increase penalties for ethics violations.

5. Ban former members of Congress, legislative staff, and bureaucrats from lobbying for two years after leaving office.

6. Require electronic filing of lobbying registration forms and congresspersons' financial disclosure forms.

Most of these proposals seem unobjectionable. Even so, there are three fundamental problems with these restrictions. First, some of them violate freedoms that many Americans value. The campaign finance restrictions in point one would make it harder for people to organize to influence elections. For example, the amount that groups such as the NRA or AARP contribute to political campaigns would be severely limited compared to the current rules. A second problem is that it is difficult to tell whether these regulations would work as intended. As discussed in this chapter, interest groups are already highly regulated in terms of who can lobby, how they can lobby, and what kinds of gifts and assistance they can offer to government officials. Giving legisla-

This cartoon summarizes public assumptions about lobbying and its impact on members of Congress. In reality, Jack Abramoff's conduct is the exception rather than the rule among lobbyists.

tors, staffers, or bureaucrats gifts in return for policy changes is already against the law, and if those laws aren't working, it is hard to see how new, similar laws will solve the problem.

Finally, this chapter shows that these reforms are, to some extent, based on a misunderstanding of how interest groups operate. The case of Jack Abramoff is interesting precisely *because* it is a glaring exception. Most interest groups are small and have such limited resources that they couldn't offer gifts or threaten to withhold large campaign donations even if they wanted to. Moreover, interest groups tend to focus on offering advice and information to people in government who already support their goals. None of the reforms described here would change anything about those practices, except to add some additional reporting requirements and further limit their (already restricted) ability to hire people who used to work in government. (Moreover, additional restrictions on electioneering might not be possible given the *Citizens United* decision discussed in Chapter 7.)

Critical **Thinking Questions**

1. To what extent do you think these laws will curb illegal behavior by interest groups—especially in light of the fact that existing laws do not?

2. Are these laws aimed at exceptional cases or at average interest groups?

What is this dilemma? On one hand, people who have worked in industry or as lobbyists already know a particular field and the relevant laws, making them well qualified to work in this area for the executive branch. Similarly, former officeholders, congressional staff, and bureaucrats are attractive to lobbying firms, as they have first-hand knowledge of how policies are made and they enjoy established relationships with people in government. On the other hand, the problem with the revolving door is that people in government may try to help particular firms and interest groups in return for a well-paid position after they leave government service. Or, when the influence works in the opposite direction, lobbyists-turned-lawmakers may favor the firms and organizations that once employed them. It is very hard to craft restrictions that avoid these problems. At the least, most executive or legislative branch employees who take lobbying jobs are legally required to refrain from lobbying people in their former office or agency for one year; elected officials who become lobbyists must wait two years.

THE BUSINESS OF LOBBYING

Interest group lobbying is heavily regulated.[12] Such firms must file annual reports identifying their clients and specifying how much each client paid. Similarly, interest groups and corporations must file reports that list staff members who spent more than 20 percent of their time lobbying Congress and that detail expenditures to lobbying firms. Data from these sources and others offer insight into the extent of lobbying in American politics.

Today, lobbying involves billions of dollars a year. Figure 8.1 presents annual lobbying expenditures for 2000 through 2011. As the figure shows, a total of $3.27 billion was spent on lobbying in 2011. Figure 8.2 indicates that a multitude of groups and organizations lobby the federal government. The amount spent as well as the number of groups lobbying government has increased significantly over the last decade.

Why are there so many interest groups and registered lobbyists, and why are their numbers increasing? Figure 8.2 suggests that this proliferation is related to the large size and widespread influence of the federal government. People lobby because they have a stake in what the government does: they want their company to get a government contract, they want a new regulation to favor their business sector, or they want the government to either limit what citizens can do or relax restrictions on citizens' behavior. Simply put, the federal government does so many things and spends so much money that many individuals, organizations, and corporations have strong incentives for lobbying.[13] Moreover, as groups form on one side of a policy question and start to lobby, people who oppose them may form their own interest groups and start lobbying as well, either separately or together.[14]

The expenditures shown in Figure 8.1 pay for many things. For example, beginning in 2003, lobbyists for the Boeing Corporation were working to secure a government contract with the U.S. military for Boeing to build tanker aircraft (planes that can refuel other planes in midair). Along with meetings between Boeing employees and Department of Defense staff to negotiate the contract, Boeing's lobbyists and employees met with members of Congress, congressional staff, senior members of President Bush's staff, and the leaders of labor unions whose members worked for Boeing.[15] Boeing also ran ads in Washington newspapers promoting its tanker proposal. Thus, in pursuing the contract, Boeing paid the salaries of its employees who planned and executed the lobbying effort, paid for outside lobbyists and their

WHEN THE SCANDALS SURROUNDING Jack Abramoff came to light in 2005, many Americans considered him a typical lobbyist who used gifts, bribes, and favors to get advantageous policy decisions from elected officials and bureaucrats. Abramoff's actions were illegal, but the question remains: Are his tactics common in Washington, or was he a rare exception?

FIGURE » 8.1

TOTAL SPENDING ON LOBBYING, 2000–2011

These data show that in recent years, interest groups have spent several billion dollars lobbying the federal government. Does this amount seem surprisingly large or surprisingly small, given what lobbyists do?

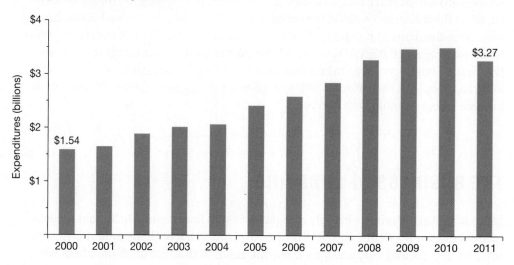

Source: Center for Responsive Politics, "Total Lobbying Spending," www.opensecrets.org/lobby/index.php; "Lobbying Database," www.opensecrets.org/lobby/index.php (accessed 1/30/12).

meetings on Capitol Hill, and spent additional money on broader publicity efforts. Ultimately, Boeing won the contract.

The disclosure data in Table 8.1 reveal the big spenders. Dominating the list are corporations like General Electric and business groups such as the U.S. Chamber of Commerce. Of General Electric's $11.4 million spent on lobbying in 2006, more than $8 million was spent on GE employees, and the remaining $3 million paid for the services of fourteen lobbying firms.[16] Most interest groups or corporations spend much less on lobbying efforts. The Sierra Club, for example, spent less than $100,000 on lobbying in 2006.[17] Many other groups barely scrape together enough cash to send someone to plead their case in Washington.

trade association An interest group composed of companies in the same business or industry (the same "trade") that lobbies for policies that benefit members of the group.

Other companies lobby through their membership in **trade associations**. Consider the National Beer Wholesalers Association (NBWA), a nationwide group of local businesses that buy beer from brewers and resell it to stores and restaurants. The NBWA's principal lobbying goal is to ensure that laws remain in place requiring middlemen between beer producers and the stores, bars, and restaurants that sell beer to consumers. If the rules change to allow beer producers to deal with the end-sellers directly, then the NBWA's members are out of a job.

Although the amount of money spent on lobbying by interest groups may seem like a lot, it is small compared to how much is at stake.[18] The federal government now spends more than $3 trillion every year. In recent years, spending by interest groups and by the lobbying arms of organizations and corporations has totaled $3 billion every year. That's a lot of money, but it's still only about 0.1 percent of

FIGURE » 8.2

GROWTH IN FEDERAL SPENDING AND IN LOBBYING

In general, as the federal government has grown, so has the number of lobbyists. One explanation is that lobbyists get the government to spend money that it otherwise would not. Can you think of a different explanation that is consistent with the data?

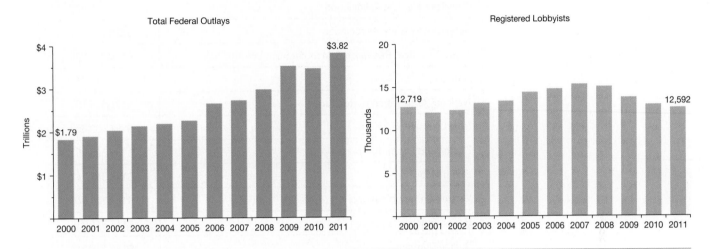

Source: "Lobbying Database," www.opensecrets.org/lobby/index.php (accessed 1/30/12); GPO Access, Budget of the United States Government, Historical Table 1.1 (FY 2012), available at www.gpo.gov/fdsys/pkg/BUDGET-2012-TAB/pdf (accessed 10/31/12).

total federal spending. This difference raises a critical question: If interest groups could control policy choices by spending money on lobbying, why aren't they spending more? We will address this question throughout the remainder of this chapter, focusing on how groups lobby and the limits of their influence over government policy.

INTEREST GROUP STRATEGIES

EXPLORE THE WAYS INTEREST GROUPS TRY TO INFLUENCE GOVERNMENT POLICIES

Once a group has organized and determined its goals, the next step is to decide how to lobby. There are two types of possible tactics: **inside strategies**, which are actions taken in Washington, and **outside strategies**, which are actions taken outside of Washington.[19]

INSIDE STRATEGIES

Inside strategies involve contact with elected officials or bureaucrats. Thus, inside strategies require a group to establish an office in Washington or hire a lobbying firm to act on its behalf.

inside strategies The tactics employed within Washington, D.C., by interest groups seeking to achieve their policy goals.

outside strategies The tactics employed outside Washington, D.C., by interest groups seeking to achieve their policy goals.

TABLE » 8.1

TOP 20 SPENDERS ON LOBBYING, 1998–2012

U.S. Chamber of Commerce	$885,975,680
General Electric	$274,100,000
American Medical Association	$274,017,500
American Hospital Association	$225,269,136
Pharmaceutical Research & Manufacturers of America	$224,263,920
AARP	$217,612,064
National Association of Realtors	$194,515,133
Blue Cross/Blue Shield	$191,452,052
Northrop Grumman	$180,565,253
Exxon Mobil	$176,362,742
Verizon Communications	$167,546,543
Edison Electric Institute	$165,566,789
Boeing Company	$164,139,310
Business Roundtable	$162,910,000
Lockheed Martin	$158,350,688
AT&T, Inc.	$145,529,336
Southern Company	$138,680,694
National Cable & Telecommunications Association	$132,340,000
General Motors	$131,704,170
Pfizer, Inc.	$126,227,268

Source: "Top Spenders," www.opensecrets.org/lobby/top.php?indexType=s (accessed 9/11/12).

DIRECT LOBBYING

direct lobbying Attempts by interest group staff to influence policy by speaking with elected officials or bureaucrats.

When interest group staff meet with officeholders or bureaucrats, they plead their case through **direct lobbying**, asking government officials to change policy in line with the group's goals.[20] Direct lobbying is generally aimed at officials and bureaucrats who are sympathetic to the group's goals.[21] In these efforts, interest groups and their representatives help like-minded legislators to secure policy changes that they both want. The interest groups' help can range from sharing information about the proposed changes, to providing lists of legislators who might be persuaded to support the group's goals, to drafting legislative proposals or regulations.

Interest groups also contact legislators who disagree with their goals, as well as fence sitters (legislators who are not supporters or opponents), with the goal of converting them into supporters. These efforts are less extensive than the lobbying of supporters, because opponents are unlikely to change their minds unless a group can provide new information that causes them to rethink their position.

As these descriptions indicate, interest groups place a high priority on maintaining access to their lobbying targets, on being able to present their arguments, regardless of whether they expect to get what they want. Of course, groups want to achieve their policy goals, but access is the first step that makes persuasion possible. Therefore, many interest groups try to keep their efforts low-key, providing information to friends and opponents alike, avoiding threats or harsh words, in the hope that they will leave a favorable impression and be able to gain access the next time they want to lobby. After all, people who oppose a group's current priorities one day may agree with them on some future issue.

In their efforts at direct lobbying, interest groups contact elected officials, members of the president's staff, and bureaucrats in the executive branch. They seek this wide range of contacts because different officials play distinct roles in the policy-making process and thus have various types of influence. Members of Congress shape legislation and budgets; members of the president's staff influence the formation of new policies and obtain presidential consent for new laws; and executive branch bureaucrats change the ways regulations are written and policies are implemented.

DRAFTING LEGISLATION AND REGULATIONS

Interest groups sometimes draft legislative proposals and regulations, which they deliver to legislators and bureaucrats as part of their lobbying efforts.[22] Interest groups don't give proposals to just anyone. As with direct lobbying, they seek out legislators who already support their cause and who have significant influence within Congress. For example, a lobbying effort aimed at cutting interest rates on student loans would target supporters of this change who are also members of the congressional committee with jurisdiction over student loan programs—preferably someone who chairs the committee or one of its subcommittees.[23] Interest groups also lobby bureaucrats to influence the details of new regulations.[24] If the type of regulations involved can go into effect without congressional approval, then lobbying can give groups what they want directly. If new regulations require approval by Congress or White House staff, then interest groups can increase their chances of success by getting involved in the initial drafting.

RESEARCH

Interest groups often prepare research reports on topics of interest to the group. For example, Public Citizen recently featured on its website a series of research reports on topics such as medical malpractice, the house building industry, toy safety, and international trade.[25] Such reports may sway public opinion or help persuade elected officials or bureaucrats. They also help interest group staff claim expertise on some aspect of public policy. Members of Congress are more likely to accept a group's legislative proposal if they think that the group's staff have solid research to back up their claims. Journalists are also more likely to respond to an interest group's requests for publicity if they think that the group's staff has viable evidence supporting their claims.

HEARINGS

Interest group staff often testify before congressional committees. In part, this activity seeks to inform members of Congress about issues that matter to the group. For example, the NRA's website

THE AMERICAN CIVIL LIBERTIES Union is an interest group that often uses litigation strategies in its efforts to change government policy. Here, an ACLU attorney describes the group's efforts to limit the Department of Homeland Security's use of "no fly lists" to screen airline passengers.

shows that its staff have testified in favor of "right to carry" laws as well as laws that would grant immunity to gun manufacturers for harm committed with weapons they produced.[26]

LITIGATION

Another inside strategy involves taking the government to court. In bringing their case, groups can argue that the government's actions are not consistent with the Constitution or that the government has misinterpreted the existing law.[27] Groups can also become involved in an existing case by filing *amicus curiae* ("friend of the court") briefs; these are documents that offer the group's rationale for how the judges should decide the case. The drawback of litigation is that it is costly and time-consuming; cases can take years to work through the federal courts system. In fact, most groups that use the litigation strategy combine it with direct lobbying or other strategies.

WORKING TOGETHER

To increase their chances for success, interest groups can work together in their lobbying efforts, formulating a common strategy and future plans. Legislators are more likely to respond, or at least provide access, when many groups with large or diverse memberships are all asking for the same thing.[28] Generally these are short-term efforts focused on achieving a specific outcome, like supporting or opposing the confirmation of judicial and cabinet nominees.[29]

The problem with working together is that groups may agree on general goals but disagree on specifics. If differences cannot be bridged, groups may undertake separate and possibly conflicting lobbying efforts or decide against lobbying entirely. For example, during the 2009 debate over climate change legislation, many environmental interest groups sat on the sidelines despite having pressed for such legislation for more than a decade. The problem? The groups disagreed on which policies should be implemented, who should pay for them, and whether the government should aid companies that would be forced to purchase new antipollution equipment.[30] Here, again, we see how conflict and compromise infuse another aspect of the American political process.

OUTSIDE STRATEGIES

Outside strategies involve actions that interest groups undertake across the country rather than in Washington. Again, these activities can be orchestrated by the group or be organized by a firm that the group hires.

GRASSROOTS LOBBYING

grassroots lobbying A lobbying strategy that relies on participation by group members, such as a protest or a letter-writing campaign.

Directly involving interest group members in lobbying efforts is called **grassroots lobbying**. Members may send letters, make telephone calls, participate in a protest, or express their demands in other ways. Mass protests, another form of grassroots lobbying, seek to capture the attention of government officials and also to draw media coverage, with the idea of publicizing the group's goals and perhaps gaining new members or financial support.

Grassroots strategies are useful because elected officials do not like to act against a large group of citizens who care enough about an issue to express their position.[31] Officials may not agree with the group's goals, but they will likely arrange a meeting with its staff so that they appear willing to learn about their constituents' demands.[32] However, these member-based strategies work only for interest groups with a large number of members, because legislators pay attention to a letter-writing campaign only when they receive several thousand pieces of mail. In addition, the letters or other efforts have to come from a member's own constituents. For example, a representative who opposes increases in student aid will not worry about a letter-writing campaign if most of the letters come from people outside his or her district.

The effectiveness of grassroots lobbying also depends on perceptions of how much a group has done to motivate participation. Suppose a representative gets 10,000 e-mails demanding an increase in student aid, but virtually all the messages contain the same appeal because they were generated and sent from a group's website. People in Washington refer to these efforts as **astroturf lobbying**.[33] Given the letters' similarity, the representative may discount the effort, believing that it says more about the group's ability to make campaign participation accessible than it does about the number of district residents who strongly support an increase in student aid. Even so, the fact that so many people participated, even with facilitation by an interest group, means that their demands should at least be considered.

The Internet has important implications for grassroots lobbying. Technological developments such as blogs and e-mail lower the costs of encouraging an interest group's members and would-be members to get involved by writing a letter, sending an e-mail, making a phone call, or showing up for a protest. However, if Internet-driven grassroots lobbying looks like astroturf lobbying, it may be less likely to achieve its goal of influencing elected officials and bureaucrats.

> **astroturf lobbying** Any lobbying method initiated by an interest group that is designed to look like the spontaneous, independent participation of many individuals.

MOBILIZING PUBLIC OPINION

One strategy related to grassroots lobbying involves trying to change what the public thinks about an issue. The goal is not to get citizens to do anything, but simply to influence public opinion in the hope that elected officials will notice this change and respond by enacting (or opposing) new laws or regulations in order to keep their constituents happy. Virtually all interest groups try to influence opinion. Most maintain a web page that presents their message and write press releases to get media coverage. Any contact with citizens, whether to encourage them to join the group, contribute money, or engage in grassroots lobbying, also involves elements of persuasion—trying to transform citizens into supporters, and supporters into true believers. A focused mobilization effort involves contacting large numbers of potential supporters through e-mail, phone calls, direct mail, television advertising, print media, and websites. In order to get legislators to respond, a group has to persuade large numbers of people to become involved.

> **MASS PROTESTS, SUCH AS THIS** April 4, 2009, Tea Party rally in California, attract media attention and demonstrate the depth of public support for a group's goals.

ELECTIONEERING

Interest groups get involved in elections by making contributions to candidates, urging people to help in a campaign, endorsing candidates, funding campaign ads, or mobilizing a candidate's or party's supporters. All these efforts seek to influence who gets elected, with the expectation that changing who gets elected will affect what government does.

501(c)(3) organization A tax code classification that applies to most interest groups; this designation makes donations to the group tax-deductible but limits the group's political activities.

political action committee (PAC) An interest group or a division of an interest group that can raise money to contribute to campaigns or to spend on ads in support of candidates. The amount a PAC can receive from each of its donors and the amount it can spend on federal campaigning are strictly limited.

527 organization A tax-exempt group formed primarily to influence elections through voter mobilization efforts and issue ads that do not directly endorse or oppose a candidate. Unlike political action committees, 527s are not subject to contribution limits and spending caps.

Federal laws limit groups' electioneering and lobbying efforts. Nuts and Bolts 8.2 provides information on what different types of organizations can and cannot do. For example, most private organizations and associations in America are organized as **501(c)(3) organizations**, a designation based on their Internal Revenue Service classification, which means that donations to the group are tax-deductible. However, 501(c)(3)s must not engage in any political activities or lobbying (other than certain voter education programs or voter registration drives that are conducted in a nonpartisan manner). Groups that want to engage in lobbying or electioneering can incorporate under other IRS designations and operate as a **political action committee (PAC)**, a **527 organization**, or a 501(c)(4). While contributions to these organizations are not tax-deductible, they have fewer restrictions on the size of contributions or how money can be spent: 527 organizations, for example, have no contribution or spending limits.

In 2012, federally focused 527 organizations spent more than $300 million on electioneering, and PACs spent nearly $375 million.[34] Table 8.2 reports campaign spending for the top ten 527 organizations. In the 2012 election, the 576 active 527 organizations that participated in the campaign spent an average of about $486,000 each.

Data on the top ten PACs in 2012 show that the largest PAC contributed just under $3 million to candidates in the 2012 election, and the tenth largest slightly less than $2 million. These organizations donating millions of dollars are the exception: in the 2008 election, the average PAC gave only $100,000 in contributions. Part of the reason for this lower spending is that PACs' direct contributions

8.2 **NUTS** *& bolts*

INTEREST GROUPS AND ELECTIONEERING: TYPES OF ORGANIZATIONS

The ability of an interest group to engage in electioneering depends on how it is organized—what section of the IRS code applies to the organization. The following table gives details on four common organizations: 501(c) organizations, 527 organizations, political action committees (PACs), and so-called Super PACs.

Therefore, many choose to contribute money to nonprofits organized as 501(c)(4) groups, which can lobby and engage in electioneering as long as their "primary activity" (at least half of their overall activity) is not political.

Type of Organization	Advantages	Disadvantages
501(c)(3)	Contributions tax-deducible	Cannot engage in political activities or lobbying, only voter education and mobilization
527	Can spend unlimited amounts on issue advocacy and voter mobilization	Cannot make contributions to candidates or coordinate efforts with candidates or parties
501(c)(4)	Can spend unlimited amounts on electioneering, do not have to disclose contributors	At least half of their activities must be nonpolitical, cannot coordinate efforts with candidates or parties
PACs	Can contribute directly to candidates and parties	Strict limits on direct contributions
Super PACs	Can spend unlimited amounts on electioneering, support or oppose specific candidates	Cannot make contributions to candidates or coordinate efforts with candidates or parties

to candidates are capped at $5,000 per candidate, and their contributions to party committees are also strictly limited.

Two new options for electioneering for interest groups emerged in the 2010 election: "Super PACs" and 501(c)(4) organizations. The former was a consequence of the *Citizens United* Supreme Court decision that authorized unlimited independent spending by corporations and labor unions in federal elections. Many groups set up new political action committees to take advantage of these new rules—the "super" label reflects the fact that these groups take in and spend much more money than the typical PAC. However, many businesses prefer that their contributions remain secret because they are afraid of angering shareholders and customers who might disagree with their political spending; thus, they donate through 501(c)(4) groups, which do not have to disclose their donors.

The data highlight a sharp difference in electioneering strategies between the very few large, well-funded interest groups and everyone else. A few 527s, Super PACs, 501(c)(4)s, and PACs have the money to deploy massive advertising and mobilizing efforts for a candidate or issue they like or against one they don't. There are also some mass associations that can persuade large numbers of members to work and vote for candidates the group supports or against candidates the group wants to defeat. But these strategies are not available to the vast majority of interest groups, which simply don't have the resources. They give modest help to candidates who are sympathetic to the group's goals in the hope that once elected, the officeholder will remember their contribution when the group asks for a meeting.

TABLE » 8.2

BIG SPENDERS IN THE 2012 ELECTION: 527 ORGANIZATIONS

This table shows the amount of money spent on electioneering by the top ten 527 organizations. Does this information support claims of interest groups having a disproportionate influence over election outcomes, especially in light of the high costs of campaigning described in Chapter 7?

ORGANIZATION	GENERALLY SUPPORTS	TOTAL EXPENDITURES
ActBlue	Democrats	$11,648,124
College Republican National Committee	Republicans	$9,172,430
Citizens United	Republicans	$8,120,525
EMILY's List	Democrats	$7,716,027
Service Employees International Union	Democrats	$6,191,200
Plumbers/Pipefitters Union	Democrats	$4,700,542
Gay & Lesbian Victory Fund	Democrats	$3,792,865
GOPAC	Republicans	$3,303,261
New Conservative Coalition	Republicans	$3,030,479
International Brotherhood of Electrical Workers	Democrats	$2,858,540

Source: Center for Responsive Politics, "527 Committees: Top Fifty Federally Focused Organizations," available at www.opensecrets.org/527s/527cmtes.php. Based on data released by the Federal Election Commission on November 2, 2012 (accessed 11/2/12).

Some groups do no electioneering at all because they lack sufficient funds, want to avoid making enemies (because of whom they do or do not support), or choose to pursue other strategies. Many groups opt for quiet lobbying efforts that utilize their expertise or undertake grassroots efforts to build public support for their policy goals. Massive electioneering operations by interest groups are relatively rare.

CULTIVATING MEDIA CONTACTS

Media coverage helps a group publicize its concerns without spending any money. Such attention may mobilize public opinion indirectly by getting people to join the group, contribute money, or demand that elected officials support the group's agenda. Favorable media coverage also helps a group's leaders assure members that they are actively working on members' concerns.

Journalists listen when interest groups call if they feel that a group's story will catch their readers' attention or address their concerns. Smart interest group leaders make it easy for journalists to cover their cause, holding events that produce intriguing news stories. These stories may not change anyone's mind, but the media coverage provides free publicity for the groups' policy agendas.

EVALUATE INTEREST GROUP INFLUENCE

SUPER PACS, SUCH AS THE American Conservative Union Foundation, have been influential in recent elections. Here, Senator Jim DeMint of South Carolina addresses the group's Conservative Political Action Conference in 2012.

HOW MUCH POWER DO INTEREST GROUPS HAVE?

Many observers worry that interest groups have too much power over government, influencing which issues the government takes up, the nature of legislation that Congress passes, and even the outcomes of elections. Interest groups are also thought to have enormous influence over the actions of unelected bureaucrats, whose policy goals may be displaced by the aims of the individuals and corporations they are supposed to regulate. When this happens, bureaucrats become more interested in catering to interest groups than in implementing policies that are good for the general population.[35] (See also Chapter 11.)

However, the evidence on interest group influence does not support these claims.[36] Research has shown that some interest groups get what they want from government some of the time, but success can prove elusive even for groups with many members and large budgets.[37] More important, there is no correlation between the amount of money spent on lobbying and a group's success at achieving its policy goals.[38]

WHAT DETERMINES WHEN INTEREST GROUPS SUCCEED?

Rather than asking why interest groups are so powerful, it makes more sense to ask when they are powerful—that is, when they succeed.[39]

LOBBYING THE FEDERAL GOVERNMENT: INSIDE AND OUTSIDE STRATEGIES

INSIDE STRATEGIES

Groups lobby government officials directly in Washington, D.C.

Examples: meeting with lawmakers, drafting legislation, providing research and testimony, taking the government to court.

OUTSIDE STRATEGIES

Groups use public pressure, elections, and the media to influence government.

Examples: grassroots email, letter, or phone campaigns; contributing to election campaigns; getting media coverage of their cause.

POP QUIZ!

1 Which of the following is an example of outside lobbying?

  a providing research to lawmakers

  b suing the government

  c working with bureaucrats

  d making campaign contributions

  e meeting with lawmakers

2 When officials in Washington, D.C., work with lobbyists, it is typically because

  a officials are afraid of being sued.

  b officials are hoping to benefit personally.

  c lobbyists are good at "converting" politicians to their cause.

  d lobbyists provide valuable information.

  e lobbyists threaten them with negative publicity.

WHILE MANY OBSERVERS CREDIT lobbying by the pharmaceutical industry for policies such as the Medicare Prescription Drug Benefit (and its ban on importing medicines), favorable public opinion, the efforts of AARP, and bureaucrats' independent judgments probably had greater influence on passing the Drug Benefit.

AMOUNT OF PUBLIC ATTENTION

Interest groups are more likely to succeed when their request attracts little public attention.[40] When the average voter does not know or care about a group's request, legislators and bureaucrats do not have to worry about the political consequences of giving the group what it wants. The only question is whether the officials themselves favor the request or can be convinced that the group's desired change is worthwhile. In contrast, when the issue attracts a lot of public attention, a legislator's response to lobbying will hinge on her judgment of constituent opinion: Do voters favor what the group wants? After all, the average legislator has a strong interest in re-election and is unlikely to act against her constituents' wishes. As a result, lobbying may count for nothing in the face of public opposition or be superfluous when the group's position already has public support.[41]

The idea of interest group lobbying probably brings to mind titanic struggles on controversial issues (such as gun control, abortion rights, or judicial nominations) over which groups try to capture public attention as a way of pressuring the government. But not all interest group lobbying is so high profile. Consider the National Turkey Federation, an association of turkey farmers and processors. The Federation sponsors the annual ritual of presenting the president with a live Thanksgiving turkey, which is officially "pardoned" and sent to a local petting zoo. In 2002, the Federation persuaded federal bureaucrats to change federally funded school lunch program regulations in a way that increased the allowable amount of turkey in various entrees. The policy change resulting from the Federation's lobbying efforts attracted no publicity, which is precisely the point. When few people know or care about a policy change, interest groups are able to dominate the policy-making process.

LEVEL OF CONFLICT

Conflict can also make it difficult for interest groups to get what they want. Lobbying is subject to two kinds of conflict. One involves disagreements between interest groups: some prefer spending more on a given program, some less. The other involves differences between what a particular interest group wants and the preferences of the general public. Both kinds of conflict can work against the success of a lobbying effort.[42]

In the case of the National Turkey Federation, no one in the general public knew about its proposal, and no interest group lobbied against it. In essence, bureaucrats heard one group asking for something and, hearing no opposition, decided the policy change was worth making. The situation might have been different if another group—perhaps the American Pork Producers or the American Cattlemen—had lobbied against the Turkey Federation. If so, satisfying one group would have required displeasing at least one other group. Faced with this no-win situation, bureaucrats or legislators would be less likely to give the group what it wanted.

The picture gets more complicated on highly conflictual issues—those over which public opinion is split and groups are active on all sides of the question. Consider health care reform. The 2009–10 debate over health care reform attracted many well-funded interest groups and coalitions, but there was no consensus among members of Congress, interest groups, or the American public about which policy changes were needed. Under these conditions, access doesn't count for much; legislators have a keen sense of the political costs of accommodating a group's demands. Moreover, policy changes are likely to reflect a complex process of bargaining and compromise, with no groups getting exactly what they want—which is what happened with health care reform.

Health care reform also illustrates that being large or well funded does not always help an interest group convince government officials to comply with its requests. Although many people worry that well-funded interest groups will use their financial resources to dominate the policy-making process, even if public opinion is against them, these fears are largely unfounded. The conditions that are ripe for well-funded interest groups to become involved in a policy debate typically ensure that there will be well-funded groups on all sides of a question. Then no group is likely to get everything it wants, and no group's lobbying efforts are likely to be decisive. Some groups may not get anything.

HOW GROUPS SUCCEED

Even when issues attract much attention and involve heated conflict, interest groups can still be influential. Research and testimony may help members of Congress develop legislative proposals and give them arguments to use in the bargaining process. Grassroots and media efforts may mobilize public opinion, pressuring members of Congress to vote for options that their constituents favor. If a particular group decided against doing these things and no other group took its place, then groups on the other side of the debate might carry the day. But interest group leaders are aware of the potentially dire consequences of not getting involved and are unlikely to be inactive on questions that matter to them and their group—even if a full-fledged lobbying effort is unlikely to produce many identifiable benefits, given the opposition by other groups.

Lobbying efforts may produce identifiable benefits when they target relatively small details of a policy change. However, groups are successful in these efforts precisely because they seek modest policy changes, which are nonetheless important to their members but generate minimal opposition. Particularly when policy questions are complex, interest groups may focus on achieving seemingly minor policy changes that have large benefits for their members.

Another measure of the limits of lobbying on conflictual questions is evident in groups' decisions about which issues to avoid lobbying on. Think about one of the most powerful interest groups, the NRA, and its advocacy of concealed carry laws. There is little doubt the NRA's leaders and most of its members favor the passage of such laws, but its efforts are unlikely to be successful given public opinion and well-funded opposition. As a result, the NRA chooses to lobby on other matters—policy questions where it might succeed or where its efforts are necessary to prevent other groups from succeeding in changing policies in ways that the NRA opposes.

Thus, success depends on what the group is asking for and whether there is significant opposition from opposing groups or public opinion. It would be a considerable overstatement to say that interest groups have no power and lobbying makes no difference, because, if nothing else, groups may lobby to prevent the policy changes that would occur if they stayed inactive. And interest groups often succeed in efforts to change policies that are less important to the public or in the small details of proposals. But when large, powerful groups seek controversial changes, their resources are matched by the difficulty of the task. Fears of large groups dominating the policy-making process to the exclusion of public opinion are largely unfounded.

///

CONCLUSION

The number of interest groups in America and the amount those groups spend on lobbying have increased in recent years, bringing a larger variety of organizations and lobbying tactics. Contrary to the image of interest groups as powerful manipulators, one of their biggest challenges involves galvanizing members to participate in their efforts. Interest groups are more likely to get what they want when their demands attract little public attention and no opposition from other groups. When a group asks for a large or controversial policy change, it stands little chance of success even if the group has many members, a large lobbying budget, or an influential leader directing its operation. Moreover, because interest groups are more likely to succeed when they work together, and because many of their strategies help to inform members of Congress and bureaucrats about the details of public policy and the shape of public opinion, interest group lobbying can be a force for compromise in American politics as well as a source of conflict.

In sum, while individual lobbying efforts often reflect the efforts of small groups to achieve favored policy outcomes at the expense of the majority of the population, looking across the entire range of interest group activities, a different picture emerges. In the main, interest groups reflect the conflictual nature of American politics and the resulting drive of individuals, groups, and corporations to shape American public policy in line with their diverse policy goals.

THE INTEREST GROUP UNIVERSE

▶ Define interest groups and describe the characteristics of different types of groups. **Pages 231–39**

SUMMARY

Interest groups are organizations that seek to influence government policy by helping elect candidates who support their policy goals, and by lobbying elected officials and bureaucrats. Though they are generally viewed with disdain, interest groups are ubiquitous—most organizations have lobbyists working on their behalf—and under the theory of pluralism, are regarded as fundamental actors in American politics.

KEY TERMS

interest group (p. 231)

lobbying (p. 231)

centralized groups (p. 232)

confederations (p. 232)

mass associations (p. 233)

peak associations (p. 233)

solidary benefits (p. 234)

purposive benefits (p. 234)

coercion (p. 234)

selective incentives (p. 234)

revolving door (p. 235)

trade association (p. 238)

PRACTICE QUIZ QUESTIONS

1. In contrast to political parties, interest groups can _____.
    a) run candidates for office and coordinate activities
    b) coordinate the activities of elected officials
    c) guarantee positions on electoral ballots
    d) directly influence government activity
    e) indirectly influence government activity

2. Why is the number of lobbyists increasing?
    a) The federal government is growing in size and influence.
    b) Lobbying is not closely regulated.
    c) Citizens are now more supportive of special interests.
    d) Politicians can concurrently serve their terms and work as lobbyists.
    e) Interest groups have more money to spend.

3. In contrast to a confederation, a centralized interest group _____.
    a) maintains a number of independent chapters
    b) often has local chapters competing over resources
    c) deploys the group's resources more efficiently
    d) is able to find out what their members want
    e) has no weaknesses

4. The practice of moving from government positions to working for interest groups is called _____.
    a) interest group capture
    b) the revolving door
    c) an iron triangle
    d) escalator politics
    e) the spoils system

5. Purposive benefits come from _____; solidary benefits come from _____.
    a) working with like-minded people; working to achieve a desired policy goal
    b) receiving material goods; working with like-minded people
    c) receiving material goods; working to achieve a desired policy goal

d) working to achieve a desired policy goal; receiving material goods

e) working to achieve a desired policy goal; working with like-minded people

ⓢ **PRACTICE ONLINE**

"Critical Thinking" exercise: *Politics Is Everywhere– Whom Do 527 Organizations Represent?*

INTEREST GROUP STRATEGIES

▶ Explore the ways interest groups try to influence government policies. **Pages 239–46**

SUMMARY

Interest groups have two types of tactics for lobbying elected officials. They can either attempt to influence politics by taking action in Washington, or they can take action elsewhere. The decision to pursue an inside or outside strategy comes down to the interest group's resources, and which strategy they think will be most effective.

KEY TERMS

inside strategies (p. 239)

outside strategies (p. 239)

direct lobbying (p. 240)

grassroots lobbying (p. 242)

astroturf lobbying (p. 243)

501(c)(3) organization (p. 244)

political action committee (PAC) (p. 244)

527 organization (p. 244)

CRITICAL THINKING AND DISCUSSION

The chapter describes the last few decades' significant increases in the number of interest groups and lobbyists and in the amount spent on lobbying. What factors could cause this increase to level off or even reverse?

PRACTICE QUIZ QUESTIONS

6. Asking government officials to change policy in line with the group's goals is _____.
a) revolving door lobbying
b) astroturf lobbying
c) direct lobbying
d) indirect lobbying
e) outside lobbying

7. Interest groups generally _____ draft legislation; they generally _____ provide testimony before committees.
a) do; do
b) do not; do
c) do; do not
d) do not; do not

8. Directly involving interest group members in lobbying efforts is called _____.
a) astroturf lobbying
b) grassroots lobbying
c) democratic lobbying
d) lobbying through referendum
e) inside lobbying

9. For indirect lobbying to be effective _____.
a) only a few pieces of mail are necessary
b) mail is necessary from all over the country
c) all messages have to have exactly the same appeal
d) letters have to come from constituents
e) letters have to come from prominent officials

ⓢ **PRACTICE ONLINE**

"Big Think" video exercise: *How Do You Lobby?*

HOW MUCH POWER DO INTEREST GROUPS HAVE?

▶ Evaluate interest group influence. **Pages 246–50**

SUMMARY

It is common to argue that elected officials are letting interest groups define their agenda. However, the evidence does not support these claims: there is no correlation between the amount of money spent on lobbying and a group's success, nor is there conclusive evidence that group lobbying influences policy. Groups are generally most influential when the issues attract little public attention, and when the issue does not have organized opposition.

CRITICAL THINKING AND DISCUSSION

A friend complains to you about the enormous power of organized interests in American politics, citing a group's recent victory in getting members of Congress to approve its policy proposal. Present three other possible explanations for this victory that are not related to the political power of the interest group.

PRACTICE QUIZ QUESTIONS

10. Interest groups generally lobby _____ in government.
   a) their opponents
   b) their friends
   c) the undecided
   d) the newly elected
   e) the less informed

11. Interest groups are more likely to succeed when their request has _____ salience; and when it has _____ conflict.
   a) low; little
   b) high; little
   c) low; high
   d) high; high
   e) high; zero

> Ⓢ **PRACTICE ONLINE**
>
> "Big Think" video exercise: *How Do Lobbies Affect the Way We Eat?*

....

SUGGESTED READING

Ainsworth, Scott. *Analyzing Interest Groups: Group Influence on People and Policies*. New York: Norton, 2002.

Baumgartner, Jeffrey, M. Berry, Marie Hojnacki, David C. Kimball, and Beth L. Leech. *Lobbying and Policy Change: Who Wins, Who Loses, and Why*. Chicago: University of Chicago Press, 2009.

Carpenter, Daniel. *The Forging of Bureaucratic Autonomy: Reputations, Networks, and Policy Innovation in Executive Agencies, 1862–1928*. Princeton, NJ: Princeton University Press, 2002.

Kollman, Kenneth. *Outside Lobbying: Public Opinion and Interest Group Strategies*. Princeton, NJ: Princeton University Press, 1998.

Lowi, Theodore. *The End of Liberalism: The Second Republic of the United States*. New York: Norton, 1979.

Olson, Mancur. *The Logic of Collective Action*, 2nd ed. Cambridge, MA: Harvard University Press, 1971.

Schattschneider, E. E. *The Semi-Sovereign People*. New York: Harper and Row, 1959.

Schlozman, Kay Lehman, and John Tierney. *Organized Interests and American Democracy*. New York: HarperCollins, 1986.

Stigerwalt, Amy. *The Battle over the Bench: Senators, Interest Groups, and Lower Court Confirmations*. Charlottesville: University of Virginia Press, 2010.

Verba, Sidney, Kay Lehman Schlozman, and Henry Brady. *Voice and Equality: Civic Participation in America*. Cambridge, MA: Harvard University Press, 1995.

Walker, Jack. *Mobilizing Interest Groups in America*. Ann Arbor: University of Michigan Press, 1991.

9

Congress

DEMOCRATS GIVE A STANDING ovation while Republicans sit silently during a speech by President Obama to a joint session of Congress. Is Congress hopelessly divided, or is compromise still possible?

AS THE DUST SETTLED FROM THE 2012 ELECTIONS, Congress and the nation faced a problem that came to be known as the "fiscal cliff." This term referred to the $100 billion in spending cuts and the $500 billion in tax increases scheduled to occur in 2013 because the "Supercommittee" formed in 2011 to decide how to reduce the deficit failed to reach an agreement (see Chapter 1). Half the cuts triggered by the Supercommittee's failure would come from military spending and half from domestic spending, and taxes would increase as the Bush-era income tax cuts expired. If Congress did not act, it was feared that the spending cuts and tax increases would send the economy back into a recession in 2013.

Democrats and Republicans in Congress had very different ideas on how to proceed. Nobody wanted deep cuts in defense spending or tax increases on 98 percent of Americans. However, Republicans wanted to extend tax cuts to everyone, while Democrats wanted to raise taxes on the wealthiest 2 percent of Americans back to the levels they were at in the 1990s. Democrats offered to accept 2.5 dollars in spending cuts for every dollar in tax increases, but Republicans wanted much deeper cuts in spending. Another point of contention was that Republicans only wanted to raise revenue by limiting deductions and closing loopholes, while Democrats wanted to raise the top tax rate on the wealthy. Many observers worried that if a compromise wasn't reached the nation would end up hurtling off the fiscal cliff. As of late 2012, both sides were playing tough, but it seemed likely the Congress would agree on a "bridge" solution that would postpone the changes until after the new Congress took over in January, allowing legislators more time to work out a compromise.

CONFLICT & COMPROMISE
in American Politics

The essential nature of conflict and compromise in the legislative process is not very well understood by the general public. Americans often view the wheeling and dealing that is necessary to reach compromises as improper and wonder why there is so much conflict; a typical sentiment is, "Why does there have to be so much partisan bickering? Can't they just implement the best solutions to our problems?" Many Americans don't even attempt to understand the legislative process and the nature of conflict and compromise because it seems hopelessly complex. Anyone who has watched congressional debates on C-SPAN knows that legislative maneuvers and discussions can make your head spin. Certainly, the legislative details of the bill to address the fiscal cliff would be too complicated for more than a few experts to comprehend.

In this chapter we show that the basic characteristics of Congress are straightforward and that the motivations that guide members' behavior and the way that Congress works are transparent. This chapter argues that members' behavior is driven by their desire to respond to constituent interests (and the related goal of re-election) and is constrained by the institutional structures within which they operate (such as the committee system, parties, and leadership). At the same time, members try to be responsible for the broader national interests, which are often at odds with constituent interests and the goal of re-election.

This tension between being responsible and responsive is a source of conflict, and it requires members of Congress to make tough decisions that often involve political trade-offs and compromises. Should a House member vote for dairy price supports for her local farmers even if it means higher milk prices for families around the nation? Should a senator vote to subsidize the production of tobacco, the biggest cash crop in his state, despite the tremendous health costs it imposes on millions of Americans? Should a member vote to close a military base, as requested by the Pentagon, even if doing so means the loss of thousands of jobs back home? These are difficult questions. On a complex issue such as the fiscal cliff, there is no obvious "responsible" solution: Republicans favor spending cuts with no changes in tax rates, while Democrats want both tax increases on the wealthy and spending cuts to reduce the deficit.

The tension between responsibility and responsiveness illustrates the other two themes of this book as well. Members of Congress regularly make decisions that affect our everyday lives. Indeed, they spend much of their time trying to respond to our desires, which means that many laws are relevant for our interests, such as government support for education, transportation, tax laws, and energy policy. The idea that political process matters is probably more evident in this chapter than any other. By controlling the legislative agenda, determining which amendments will be allowed on a given bill, or stacking an important committee with sympathetic partisans, the legislative process affects political outcomes.

CONGRESS'S PLACE IN OUR CONSTITUTIONAL SYSTEM

DESCRIBE HOW THE FOUNDERS ENVISIONED CONGRESS'S ROLE

Congress was the "first branch" early in our nation's history. The Constitution gave Congress the lead role in a vast array of enumerated powers, including regulating commerce, coining money, raising and supporting armies, creating the courts, establishing post offices and roads, declaring war, and levying taxes (see Article I, Section 8, of the Constitution in the Appendix). The president, in contrast, was given few explicit powers and played a much less prominent role early in our history. Many of Congress's extensive powers come from its implicit powers rooted in the elastic clause of Article I, which gives Congress the power "to make all Laws which shall be necessary and proper for carrying into Execution the foregoing Powers."

The compromises that gave rise to Congress's initial structure reflected an attempt to reconcile the competing interests of the day (large vs. small states, northern vs. southern interests, and proponents of strong national power vs. state power). These compromises included establishing a **bicameral** (two-chambered) institution made up of a popularly elected House and a Senate chosen by state legislatures. Other compromises involved allowing slaves to count as three-fifths of a person for purposes of apportionment for the House, and setting longer terms for senators (six years) than for House members (two years).

But these compromises also laid the foundation for the split loyalties that members of Congress have between their local constituencies and the nation's interests. Although the Founders hoped that Congress would pass legislation emphasizing the national good over local interests, they also recognized the importance of local constituencies. Thus the two-year House term was intended to tie legislators to public sentiment. In general, the Founders viewed the Senate as the more likely institution to speak for the national interests; it was intended to check the more responsive and passionate House. Because senators were indirectly elected and served longer terms than House members, the Senate was more insulated from the people. A famous (though maybe fictional) story that points out the differences between the House and Senate involves an argument between George Washington and Thomas Jefferson. Jefferson did not think the Senate was necessary, while Washington supported having two chambers. During the argument Jefferson poured some coffee he was drinking into his saucer. Washington asked him why he had done so. "To cool it," replied Jefferson. "Even so," said Washington, "we pour legislation into the senatorial saucer to cool it."

This idea of a more responsible Senate survived well into the twentieth century, even after the Seventeenth Amendment in 1913 allowed the direct, popular election of senators. Today the Senate is still more insulated than the House. Because of the six-year term, only one-third of the 100 Senate seats are contested in each election, while all 435 House members are elected every two years. However, differences between the House and Senate's representational roles

bicameralism The system of having two chambers within one legislative body, like the House and Senate in the U.S. Congress.

THE FOUNDERS VIEWED THE HOUSE AS more passionate than the Senate, or as the "hot coffee" that needed to be cooled in the "saucer" of the Senate. This perception probably did not include coming to blows over differences in policy as Congressmen Albert G. Brown and John A. Wilcox did in 1851 about whether Mississippi should secede from the Union.

have become muted as senators seem to campaign for re-election 365 days a year, every year, just like House members.[1] This "permanent campaign" means that senators are less insulated from electoral forces than previously.

The relationship between the president and Congress has also evolved significantly. Congress's roots in geographic constituencies made it well suited for the politics of the nineteenth century. Early in U.S. history several great presidents left their mark on national politics (George Washington, Andrew Jackson, and Abraham Lincoln, among others), but Congress dominated much of the day-to-day politics, which revolved around issues such as the tariff (taxes on imported or exported goods), slavery, and internal improvements such as building roads and canals. Given the tendency to address these issues with patronage and the **pork barrel** (that is, jobs and policies targeted to benefit specific constituents), Congress was better suited for the task than the president was.

Beginning around the turn of the twentieth century and accelerating with the New Deal of the 1930s (which established modern social welfare and regulatory policies), the scope of national policy expanded and politics became more centered in Washington. With this nationalization of politics and the increasing importance of national security issues, the president has assumed a more central policy-making role. However, the tensions between representing local versus national interests remain key in understanding the legislative process and the relationship between members of Congress and their constituents.

pork barrel Legislative appropriations that benefit specific constituents, created with the aim of helping local representatives win re-election.

EXPLAIN HOW MEMBERS OF CONGRESS REPRESENT THEIR CONSTITUENTS AND HOW ELECTIONS HOLD MEMBERS ACCOUNTABLE

CONGRESS AND THE PEOPLE

Americans have a love–hate relationship with Congress; that is, we generally love our own member of Congress, but we hate the Congress as a whole. Well, *hate* is a strong word, but as we show later in this section, individual members of Congress routinely have approval ratings 30 to 40 points higher than the institution's. Before explaining that puzzling pattern, we'll explore the nature of representation in Congress.

REPRESENTATION AND THE CONSTITUENCY

It may seem obvious why members of Congress are called "representatives," but that role is more complex than you might imagine. Factors that influence this complexity include the different ways in which the members can represent the citizens who elected them to office, and the different characteristics, desires, and needs of the district populations that each member represents.

TYPES OF REPRESENTATION

First let's examine the two basic components of the relationship between a constituency and its member of Congress: descriptive representation and substantive representation. The former is rooted in the politician's side of the relationship: Does the member of Congress "look like" his or her constituents in demographic terms—for example, African American, Latino, or white; male or female; Catho-

lic, Protestant, or some other religion? Many people believe that such **descriptive representation** is a distinct value in itself. Having positive role models for various demographic groups helps create greater trust in the system, and there are benefits from being represented by someone who shares something as basic as skin color with constituents.

Descriptive representation is also related to the perceived responsiveness of a member of Congress. In general, constituents report higher levels of satisfaction with representatives who are of the same racial or ethnic background as the constituents themselves.[2] If you doubt that descriptive representation makes a difference, ask yourself whether it would be fair if all 435 House members and 100 senators were white, male Protestants. Although the demographics of Congress are considerably more diverse than this, the legislature does not come close to "looking like us" on a nationwide scale (see Figures 9.1 A and B).

More important than a member's race, gender, or religion, many people argue, is the *substance* of what that person does. **Substantive representation** moves beyond appearances to specify how the member serves his or her constituents' interests. Two longstanding models are: (1) the **trustee**, who represents the constituents' interests from a distance, weighing numerous national, collective, local, and moral concerns, and (2) the **delegate**, who carries out the direct desires of the voters. In a sense, trustees are more concerned with being responsible, and delegates are more interested in being responsive.

A trustee, by definition, will do what she thinks is in the best long-term interests of her constituents and the nation, even though it may mean voting against her constituents' immediate wishes and risking defeat in the next election. A delegate, in contrast, does not have to worry about angering voters because he simply does what they want. Truth be told, the trustee/delegate distinction is mostly important as a theoretical point of departure for talking about representation roles. Nearly all members of Congress act like trustees in some circumstances and like delegates in

descriptive representation
When a member of Congress shares the characteristics (such as gender, race, religion, or ethnicity) of his or her constituents.

substantive representation
When a member of Congress represents constituents' interests and policy concerns.

trustee A member of Congress who represents constituents' interests while also taking into account national, collective, and moral concerns that sometimes cause the member to vote against the preference of a majority of constituents.

delegate A member of Congress who loyally represents constituents' direct interests.

others. A third model of representation is the **politico**, who is more likely to act as a delegate on issues that are especially important to the constituency (such as immigration reform) but is more likely to be a trustee on issues that constituents don't feel strongly about or on very complex issues (such as some foreign policies). Therefore, the crucial component of representation is the nature of the constituency and how the member of Congress attempts to balance and represent constituents' conflicting needs and desires.

THE ROLE OF THE CONSTITUENCY

Our characterization of the representative–constituency relationship raises numerous questions. For example: How much do voters monitor their representatives' behavior? Can representation work if voters are not paying attention? Although most constituents do not follow congressional politics, representational links remain strong through indirect mechanisms. Members of Congress behave as if voters were paying attention, even when constituents are inattentive. Incumbents know that at election time the challengers may raise issues that become important after the public thinks about them, so they try to deter challengers by anticipating what the constituents would want *if they were fully informed.*[3] For example, the public didn't know much about the "fiscal cliff" that the nation could fall from in January 2013, until it became a big issue in the 2012 elections. Savvy incumbents would have tried to preempt their vulnerability on that issue *before*

FIGURE » 9.1A

WOMEN IN CONGRESS, 1933–2013

While Congress still does not have gender parity, there have been substantial gains in recent years (with the exception of 2011, when the number of women in the House dropped for the first time in thirty years). What difference does it make for policy to have more women in Congress?

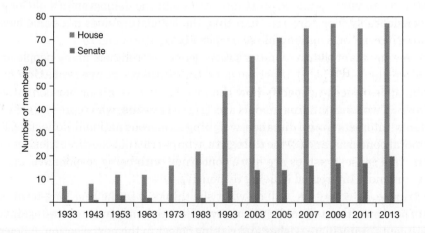

Source: Jennifer E. Manning and Colleen J. Shogan, "Women in the United States Congress: 1917–2009," Congressional Research Service Report RL30261, December 23, 2009, www.senate.gov/CRSReports/crs-publish.cfm?pid=%270E%2C*PLS%3D%22%40%20%20%0A (accessed 1/4/10). Source for 2009–13: Roll Call, www.rollcall.com (accessed 11/9/12).

FIGURE » 9.1B

MINORITIES IN THE HOUSE, 1933–2013

Hispanics now comprise the largest ethnic minority in the United States, yet they still lag behind African Americans in terms of representation in the House. What do you think explains this difference? How might it affect policy?

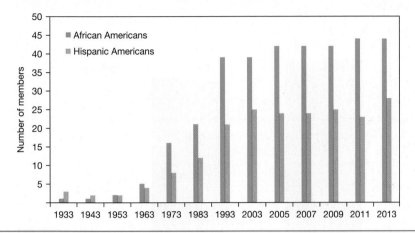

Source: Compiled from Mildred L. Amer, "Black Members of the United States Congress: 1870–2005," Congressional Research Service Report RL30378, August 4, 2005; Government Printing Office, Hispanic Americans in Congress, 1822–1995. 1995, www.loc.gov/rr/hispanic/congress/ (accessed 1/4/10). Source for 2009–13: Roll Call, www.rollcall.com (accessed 11/9/12).

a strong challenger raised the issue in a campaign—the incumbents would have staked out a position consistent with what their constituents would want once they knew more about the issue.

Another way to examine the representative–constituency relationship is to look at differences across districts. How do districts vary? First, they differ in size: Senate "districts" (that is, states) vary in terms of both area and population. House districts all have about 700,000 people, but they vary tremendously in geographic size. Districts also differ in terms of who lives there and what they want from government.

Because districts are so multifaceted, the legislators they elect differ from one another as well. Regardless of the office, most voters want to elect someone whose policy positions are close to theirs. As a result, legislators tend to reflect the central tendencies of their districts. At one level, electing a legislature that "thinks like America" sounds good: if legislators act and think like their districts, then the legislature will contain a good mixture of the interests representing the country or state. But finding an acceptable compromise is not easy. We elect legislators to get things done, but they may be unable to agree on anything because their disagreements are too fundamental to bridge. For example, the country is sharply divided on abortion rights, as are the House, the Senate, and most state legislatures. The fact that legislators have not come to a decision on this issue is no surprise: just as citizens disagree, so do their elected representatives.

Despite the vast differences among congressional constituencies, voters nationwide want many of the same things: a healthy economy, a safe country (in terms of national defense and local crime), good schools, and effective and

FIGURE » 9.2

THE JOB OF A MEMBER OF CONGRESS

Congress is often criticized for passing pork-barrel policies that benefit specific districts. Yet this survey clearly shows that people want their "fair share" and are less concerned with whether their representative works on "national bills." Why do you think that is?

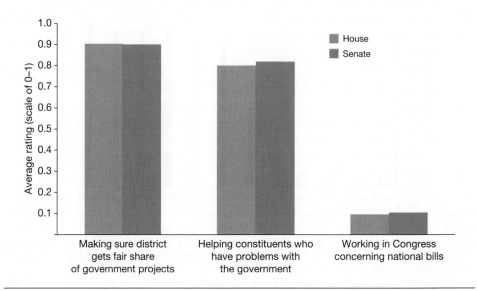

Source: Adapted from Paul Gronke, The Electorate, the Campaign, and the Office: A Unified Approach to Senate and House Elections *(Ann Arbor: University of Michigan Press, 2001), Table 6.5.*

casework Assistance provided by members of Congress to their constituents in solving problems with the federal bureaucracy or addressing other specific concerns.

affordable health care. As Figure 9.2 shows, citizens clearly want their elected officials to get them a fair share of the federal pie and to do **casework** for the district. But survey respondents show little interest in having their representatives "work in Congress concerning national bills." Thus responsibilities for national interests may be more difficult for members of Congress to explain to their constituents.

THE ELECTORAL CONNECTION

Members' relationship to their constituents also must be understood within the context of their desire to be re-elected. Political scientist David Mayhew argues that re-election must come first.[4] Members of Congress certainly hold multiple goals, including making good policy; but if they cannot maintain their seats, then they cannot attain other goals while in office.

After assuming that re-election is central, Mayhew asks this question: "Members of Congress may be electorally motivated, but are they in a position to do anything about it?"[5] Although individual members of Congress cannot do much to alter national economic or political forces, they can control their own activities in the House or Senate. The importance of the **electoral connection** in explaining members' behavior seems especially clear for marginal incumbents who are

electoral connection The idea that congressional behavior is centrally motivated by members' desire for re-election.

constantly trying to shore up their electoral base, but even incumbents in "safe" districts realize that their job security is not guaranteed.

Mayhew outlines three ways that members of Congress promote their chances for re-election: through advertising, credit claiming, and position taking. Each approach shapes the way members relate to their constituents. *Advertising* in this context refers to appeals or appearances without issue content that get the member's name before the public in a favorable way. Advertising includes "working the district," such as by attending town meetings, appearing in a parade, or sending letters of congratulation for graduations, birthdays, or anniversaries. Members of Congress also spend a fair amount of time meeting with constituents in Washington.

The second activity, *credit claiming,* involves the member of Congress taking credit for something of value to the voter—most commonly, pork-barrel policies targeted to specific constituents or the district. Another source of credit claiming is casework for individual constituents who request help with tasks such as tracking down a lost Social Security check or expediting the processing of a passport. This activity, like advertising, has both district-based and Washington-based components.

SOME DEMOCRATS WHO WERE successful in the 2010 elections had to distance themselves from the national party. One example is Joe Manchin, who won a Senate seat by emphasizing that he would fight for the people of West Virginia, even when it meant going against his party.

Position taking refers to any public statement—such as a roll call vote, speech, editorial, or position paper—about a topic of interest to constituents or interest groups. This may be the toughest aspect of a member's job, because on many issues the member is likely to alienate a certain segment of the population no matter what position she takes. Members try to appeal to specific audiences within their district. For example, while speaking to the Veterans of Foreign Wars, a member might emphasize his support for a particular new weapons program, but in a meeting with college students, he might highlight his opposition to the war in Afghanistan.

The focus on re-election has some costs, two of which reflect widespread public opinion. First, the perception that Congress has granted itself too many special privileges aimed at securing re-election (such as funding for large staffs and the privilege of sending mail at no cost) leads to harsh criticism. Second, there is concern that members' time spent actively campaigning takes time away from the responsibilities of enacting laws and overseeing their implementation. Another cost is the possibility of passing contradictory policies in an effort to satisfy diverse interest groups.

REDISTRICTING

To understand legislative constituencies, we must consider their physical boundaries. District boundaries determine who is eligible to vote in any given congressional race, and these boundaries are redrawn every 10 years, after each national census. **Redistricting** is the task of state legislatures. Its official purpose is to ensure that districts are roughly equal in population, which in turn ensures that every vote counts equally in determining the composition of the legislature.

District populations vary over time as people move from state to state or from one part of a state to another. At the national level, states gain or lose legislative seats after each census through a process called **apportionment** as the fixed number of House seats (435) is divided among the states. (States growing the

redistricting Redrawing the geographic boundaries of legislative districts. This happens every ten years to ensure that districts remain roughly equal in population.

apportionment The process of assigning the 435 seats in the House to the states based on increases or decreases in state population.

fastest gain seats, and those that are not growing as fast lose seats.) The one legislature in America that is not redistricted is the U.S. Senate, which contains two legislators per state, thus giving voters in small states more influence than those in large states.

CRITERIA FOR REDISTRICTING

In theory, redistricting proceeds from a set of principles that define what districts should look like. One criterion is that districts should be roughly equal in population. They should also capture "communities of interest" by grouping like-minded voters in the same district. There are also technical criteria, including compactness (districts should not have extremely bizarre shapes) and contiguity (one part of a district cannot be completely separated from the rest of the district). Mapmakers also try to respect traditional natural boundaries, avoid splitting municipalities, preserve existing districts, and avoid diluting the voting power of racial minorities.

PARTISAN REDISTRICTING

Although the principles listed above are important, they are not the driving force in the redistricting process. In most states the state legislature draws district boundaries, and the majority party tries to draw districts that will give the greatest advantage to candidates from their party. Suppose a Democrat holds a state assembly seat from an urban district populated mainly by citizens with strong Democratic Party ties. After a census the Republican-dominated state legislature develops a new plan that extends the representative's district into the suburbs, claiming that the change counteracts population declines within the city by adding suburban voters. However, these suburban voters will likely be Republicans, thus increasing the chance that the Democrat will face strong opposition in future elections and maybe lose her seat. Such changes have an important impact on voters as well. Voters who are "moved" to a new district by a change in boundaries may be unable to vote for the incumbent they have supported for years, instead getting a representative who doesn't share their views.

In congressional redistricting, a reduction in the number of seats allocated to a state can lead to districting plans that put two incumbents in the same district, forcing them to run against each other. Incumbents from one party use these opportunities to defeat incumbents from the other party. Both parties use this technique and other tools of creative cartography to gain partisan advantage. In the 2012 redistricting cycle Illinois drew the most egregious map in favor of Democrats, including one district in Chicago that looks like a pair of earmuffs, while Pennsylvania drew a "group of Rorschach-inkblot districts" that turned a state with a normally Democratic leaning into one where 12 of 18 districts lean Republican.[6]

The most dramatic recent example of redistricting for partisan purposes was in Texas. Deviating from the standard practice of redrawing district lines only once every decade, Republicans decided to change the district boundaries that had only been in effect for one election. Democratic legislators were outraged by the partisan power grab and fled the state (they hid out in Oklahoma) to prevent the special session of the legislature from convening. Eventually, Republicans were able to implement their plan and gain five House seats in the 2004 elections. The Supreme Court upheld the Texas plan, saying that even when partisan advantage is the only motivation for redistricting, this does not make the resulting plan unconstitutional.[7]

TYPES OF GERRYMANDERS

Partisan gerrymanders: Elected officials from one party draw district lines that benefit candidates from their party and hurt candidates from other parties. This usually occurs when one party has majorities in both houses of the state legislature and occupies the governorship, and can therefore enact redistricting legislation without votes from the minority party.

Incumbent gerrymanders: Lines are drawn to benefit the current group of incumbents. This usually occurs when control of state government is divided between parties and support from both parties is required to enact a districting plan, or when plans must be approved by judges or bipartisan panels.

Racial gerrymanders: Redistricting is used to help or hurt the chances of minority legislative candidates. The Voting Rights Act (VRA) of 1965 mandated that districting plans for many parts of the South be approved by the U.S. Department of Justice or a Washington, D.C., district court. Subsequent interpretation of the 1982 VRA amendments and Supreme Court decisions led to the creation of districts in which racial minorities are in the majority. The original aim of these majority-minority districts was to raise the percentage of African American and Latino elected officials. However, Republicans in some southern states have used this requirement to enact plans that elect minorities (who tend to be Democrats) in some districts but favor Republicans in adjoining districts.

Candidate gerrymanders: District plans that favor certain individuals, particularly state legislators planning to run for the U.S. House. For example, a Republican state legislator would want to construct a congressional district with a high percentage of Republican voters and as many of his current constituents as possible.

Such attempts to use the redistricting process for political advantage are called **gerrymandering**. The term is named after Elbridge Gerry, an early Massachusetts House member and governor, vice president under James Madison, and author of one of the original partisan redistricting plans (including a district with a thin, winding shape resembling a salamander). In addition to the partisan gerrymanders discussed above, Nuts and Bolts 9.1 describes several other types.

gerrymandering Attempting to use the process of redrawing district boundaries to benefit a political party, protect incumbents, or change the proportion of minority voters in a district.

RACIAL REDISTRICTING

Redistricting may yield boundaries that look highly unusual, especially when such efforts address population groups based on race. During the 1992 redistricting in North Carolina, the Justice Department told state legislators that they needed to create two districts with majority populations of minority voters (called majority-minority districts). Figure 9.3 shows the plan they enacted, in which the district boundaries look like a pattern of spider webs and ink blots. Moreover, one of the districts had parts that ended up being only as wide as Interstate I-85, following the highway off an exit ramp, over a bridge, and down the entrance ramp on the other side. This move prevented the I-85 district from bisecting the district it was traveling through, which would have violated the state law requiring contiguous districts.

The North Carolina example shows how convoluted redistricting plans can become. Part of the complexity is due to the availability of census databases that enable line-drawers to divide voters as closely as they want, moving neighborhood by neighborhood, even house by house. Why bother with this level of detail? Because redistricting influences who gets elected; it is active politicking in its most fundamental form. The North Carolina plan was ultimately declared unconstitutional by the Supreme Court—a ruling that opened the door for dozens

FIGURE » 9.3

NORTH CAROLINA REDISTRICTING, 1992

This set of House districts was the subject of the landmark Supreme Court ruling *Shaw v. Reno* (1993), in which the Court said that "appearances matter" when drawing district lines. Do you agree? Should other factors such as race, party, and competitiveness play a greater role than district shape?

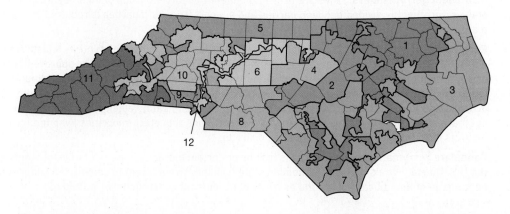

Source: North Carolina General Assembly, 1992 Congressional Base Plan No. 10, www.ncga.state.nc.us/ Redistricting/Archives/Defuncan10/92BP10_Map_ Detail.pdf, http://ncga.state.nc.us/GIS/Download/Reference Docs/2011/NC%20 Congressional%20Districts%20–%20Historical%20Plans%20–%201941–1992.pdf (accessed 10/26/12).

• of lawsuits about racial redistricting. The current legal standard is that race cannot be the *predominant* factor in drawing congressional district lines, but it may still be a factor.

CONGRESS'S IMAGE PROBLEM

Despite members' strong links to their constituents, efforts to secure re-election, and districts that are designed in their favor, public approval of Congress is generally very low. Its approval rate rarely tops 50 percent (a recent exception was following the terrorist attacks of September 11, 2001). Through most of 2012, approval for Congress hovered in the low teens and was only 16 percent before Election Day in November. And the public's cynical view of Congress runs deep. Well over half of all Americans agree with polling statements such as "The government is pretty much run by a few big interests looking out for themselves." Another poll found that members of Congress landed fifth from the bottom in a ranking of 26 professions in terms of perceived honesty and ethical standards.[8]

Why does Congress have such an image problem? Some of it is self-inflicted. Although political corruption for personal gain is rare in Congress (only four members have been indicted on bribery charges since 1981), there are periodic scandals. The two most serious recent cases involved bribery. In one, Rep. William Jefferson (D-La.) was found guilty of soliciting bribes, money laundering, and using his office as a racketeering enterprise. In addition, Mark Foley (R-Fla.)

brought shame on the House when his steamy e-mails to 16-year-old House pages were revealed. Foley quickly resigned when his inappropriate behavior was exposed. Other sex scandals involved Senator Larry Craig (R-Ida.), who pled guilty to a "disorderly conduct" charge for an apparent attempt to solicit sex in a men's bathroom in the Minneapolis airport, and Rep. Anthony Weiner (D-N.Y.), who resigned after sending lewd pictures of himself on Twitter. Yet, despite such scandals, most members of Congress are dedicated public servants who work hard for their constituents.

MEDIA INFLUENCES

Politicians traditionally blame the media for their poor standing in the polls, and there is some basis for the complaints. One study examined stories on Congress in various national newspapers and magazines during 10 political periods between 1946 and 1992 and concluded that "press coverage of Congress focuses on scandal, partisan rivalry, and interbranch conflict rather than the more complex subjects such as policy, process, and institutional concerns."[9] From this perspective the professional context of journalism, with its short news cycle and the need to produce a salable product, creates pressure for superficial coverage that perpetuates Congress's image problem. However, a recent study using more than 8,000 newspaper stories on members of Congress over a two-year period found that 70 percent of news stories were neutral; and of the 30 percent that had some spin, positive stories outnumbered negative stories five to one.[10]

THE RESPONSIBILITY-RESPONSIVENESS DILEMMA

Congress's image problem isn't simply a matter of negative media coverage or a cynical public. It is rooted in the basic representational conflicts that arise from Congress's dual roles: responsibility for national policy making and responsiveness to local constituencies.[11] Part of the national frustration with Congress arises because we want our representatives to be both responsible *and* responsive; we want them to be great national leaders *and* take care of our local and, at times, personal concerns.

But often it is impossible to satisfy both of these demands at the same time. Rather than understanding these issues as inherent in the legislative process, we often accuse members of **gridlock** and partisan bickering when our conflicting demands are not met. For example, public opinion polls routinely show that the public wants lower taxes; more spending in education, the environment, and health care; and balanced budgets—but those three things cannot happen simultaneously. We often expect the impossible from Congress and then are frustrated when it doesn't happen.

The responsibility–responsiveness dilemma brings us back to the puzzle we posed at the beginning of this section: Why is there a persistent 30 to 40 percent gap between approval ratings for individual members and for the institution? The answer may simply be that members of Congress tend to respond more to their constituents' demands than take on the responsibility of solving national problems. And when Congress becomes embroiled in debates about constituencies' conflicting demands, the institution may appear ineffectual. But as long as members keep the "folks back home" happy, their individual popularity will remain high. In the next section we describe how members use this and other techniques to cultivate an incumbency advantage.

UNFORTUNATELY, MEMBERS OF Congress do include some of the "criminal class" noted by Mark Twain. Former representatives Randy "Duke" Cunningham (R-Calif.), shown with his wife Nancy (top), and William Jefferson (D-La.) are both serving time in federal prison.

gridlock An inability to enact legislation because of partisan conflict within Congress or between Congress and the president.

THE INCUMBENCY ADVANTAGE AND ITS SOURCES

The desire to be re-elected influences House members' and senators' behavior both in the district and in Congress. As we have mentioned, incumbents look for opportunities to shore up support for the next election, and their success at pleasing constituents produces large election rewards. As Figures 9.4 A and B show, few members are defeated in re-election races. This is known as the **incumbency advantage**. In the past two decades incumbent re-election rates have been near record-high levels, with 95 to 98 percent of House incumbents winning.[12] For example, in 2008, in an election that many called "transformational," 95 percent of House incumbents were re-elected. Although the Democrats picked up some seats in the Senate, re-election was the norm there as well. Even in the "tsunami" election of 2010, in which Republicans made the largest gains in the House since 1948, picking up at least 60 seats, 86 percent of incumbents were elected. Why are incumbents so successful?

incumbency advantage The relative infrequency with which members of Congress are defeated in their attempts for re-election.

IN THE DISTRICT: HOME STYLE

One explanation for the increasing incumbency advantage is rooted in the diversity of congressional districts and states. Members of Congress typically respond to the diversity in their districts by developing an appropriate home style—a way of relating to the district.[13] A home style shapes the way members allocate resources, the way incumbents present themselves to others, and the way they explain their policy positions.

Given the variation among districts, members' home styles vary as well. In some rural districts it is important for representatives to have local roots, and voters expect extensive contact with members. Urban districts expect a different kind of style. Because they have a more mobile population, voters there expect less direct contact and place more emphasis on how their elected members of Congress explain their policy positions.

Incumbency advantage may be explained in part by the skill with which members have cultivated their individual home styles in the last two decades. Members spend more time at home and less time in Washington than was true a generation ago. This familiarity with voters has helped them remain in office.

MEMBERS OF CONGRESS TRY TO KEEP the "folks back home" happy with projects like this groundbreaking ceremony in St. Louis for a $670 million Mississippi River bridge connecting Illinois and Missouri.

FIGURE » 9.4A

HOUSE INCUMBENCY RE-ELECTION RATES, 1948–2012

The rate of defeat for incumbent House members is very low, typically in the 5 percent to 10 percent range, while total turnover is quite a bit higher. Which data are more central for debates about the importance of term limits? Which data are more central to discussions of electoral accountability?

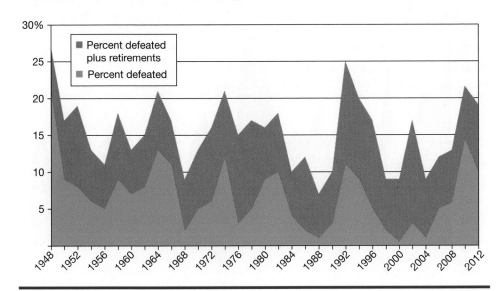

CAMPAIGN FUND-RAISING

Raising money is also key to staying in office. Incumbents need money to pay for campaign staff, travel, and advertising. It takes at least $1 million to make a credible challenge to an incumbent in most districts, and in many areas with expensive media markets the minimum price tag is $2 million or more. Few challengers can raise that much money. The gap between incumbent and challenger spending has grown dramatically in the past decade, with incumbents now spending about three times as much as challengers. Incumbents have far greater potential to raise vast sums of money, in part because political action committees (PACs) are unwilling to risk alienating an incumbent by donating to challengers. (For more on campaign finance, see Chapter 7 and Chapter 8.)

Money also functions as a deterrent to potential challengers. A sizeable re-election fund signals that an incumbent knows how to raise money and will run a strong campaign. The aim is to convince would-be challengers that they have a slim chance of beating the incumbent—and to convince contributors and party organizations that there's no point in trying to support a challenger. This point is crucial in explaining incumbency advantage because it is nearly impossible for a weak challenger to beat an incumbent. Consider that only 10 to 15 percent of challengers in a typical election year have any previous elective experience; when such a high proportion of challengers are amateurs, it is not surprising that so many incumbents win.

FIGURE » 9.4B

SENATE INCUMBENCY RE-ELECTION RATES, 1948–2012*

Incumbency re-election rates are noticeably more volatile in the Senate than in the House. What implications does this have for the Founders' belief that the Senate should be more insulated from popular control than the House? Does the Senate's six-year term help provide that insulation?

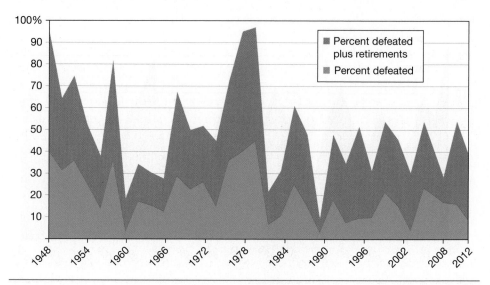

*Percentage for the Senate is of those up for re-election.

Source: Compiled from Center for Responsive Politics, Reelection Rates over the Years, www.opensecrets.org/bigpicture/reelect.php; and Norman J. Ornstein, Thomas E. Mann, and Michael J. Malbin, Vital Statistics on Congress: 1999–2000 *(Washington, DC: CQ Press, 2000), pp. 60–63; 2010 and 2012 percentages calculated from election results, http://elections.nytimes.com (accessed 11/10/12).*

CONSTITUENCY SERVICE

Another thing incumbents do to get re-elected is "work their districts," taking every opportunity to meet with constituents, listen to their concerns, and perform casework (helping constituents interact with government programs or agencies). High levels of constituency service may help explain why some incumbents have become electorally secure.

Members of Congress love doing constituency service because it is an easy way to make voters happy. If a member can help a constituent solve a problem, that person will be more likely to support the member in the future.[14] Many voters might give the incumbent some credit simply for being willing to listen. Therefore, most members devote a significant portion of their staff to constituency service, publish newsletters that tout their good deeds on behalf of constituents, and solicit citizens' requests for help through their newsletters and websites.

This combination of factors gives incumbents substantial advantages over candidates who might run against them. By virtue of their position they can help constituents who have problems with an agency or program. They attract media attention because of their actions in office. And they use their official position as a platform for raising campaign cash. Finally, most incumbents represent states or districts whose partisan balance (the number of likely supporters of their party versus the number likely to prefer the other party) is skewed in their favor—if it wasn't, they probably wouldn't have won the seat in the first place.

THE STRUCTURE OF CONGRESS

EXAMINE HOW PARTIES, THE COMMITTEE SYSTEM, AND STAFFERS ENABLE CONGRESS TO FUNCTION

Much of the structure of Congress is set up to meet the electoral needs of its members. Several elements facilitate their re-election, including informal structures (norms) and formal structures (staff, the committee system, parties, and the leadership). However, the goal of being re-elected cannot explain everything about members' behavior and the congressional structure. Other explanations include the policy motivations of members, the partisan basis for congressional institutions, and the informational advantages of the committee system.

INFORMAL STRUCTURES

Various norms provide an informal structure for the way that Congress works. Universalism is a norm stating that when benefits are divided up, as many districts and states as possible should benefit. Thus, for example, when it comes to handing out federal highway dollars or expenditures for the Pentagon's weapons programs, the benefits are broadly distributed across the entire country. (This means, however, that votes on such bills tend to be lopsided, as some areas of the country need the federal funds more urgently than others.)

Another norm, reciprocity, reinforces universalism with the idea that "if you scratch my back, I'll scratch yours." This norm (also called logrolling) leads members of Congress to support bills that they otherwise might oppose in exchange for another member's vote on a bill that is very important to them. For example, a House member from a dairy state might vote for tobacco price supports even if there are no tobacco farmers in his state, and in return he would expect a member from the tobacco state to vote for the dairy price support bill. This norm can produce wasteful pork-barrel spending. In 2011 a $1.1 trillion omnibus appropriations bill contained more than 6,488 **earmarks** worth $8.3 billion, so nearly everyone gained something by passing it. The 2012 omnibus appropriations bill did not include any traditional earmarks, following congressional efforts to limit the practice; however, there was still $3.5 billion in unauthorized spending on defense alone.[15] The "You Decide" box describes some of the fierce debates in Congress and among political commentators about the merit of this type of spending.[16]

earmarks Federally funded local projects attached to bills passed through Congress.

The norm of specialization is also important, both for the efficient operation of Congress and for members' re-election. By specializing and becoming expert on a given issue, members provide valuable information to the institution as a whole and also create a basis for credit claiming. This norm is stronger in the House, where members often develop a few areas of expertise, whereas senators tend to be policy generalists.

The **seniority** norm also serves individual and institutional purposes. This norm holds that the member with the longest service on a committee will chair the committee. Although there have been numerous violations of the norm, whereby the most senior member is passed over for someone whom the party leaders favor instead, the norm benefits the institution by ensuring orderly succession in committee leadership.[17] The norm also benefits members by providing a tangible reason why voters should return them to Congress year after year.

FORMAL STRUCTURES

Formal structures also shape members' behavior in Congress. Political parties, party leadership, the committee system, and staff provide the context within which members of Congress make policy and represent their constituents.

PARTIES AND PARTY LEADERS

Political parties are important for allocating power in Congress. Party leaders are always elected on straight party-line votes, and committee leadership, the division of seats on committees, and the allocation of committee resources are all determined by the majority party. Without parties, the legislative process would be much more fractured because members would be autonomous agents in battle with one another. Parties provide a team framework that allows members to work together for broadly beneficial goals. Just think how difficult it would be for a member of Congress to get a bill passed if she had to build a coalition from scratch every time. Instead, parties provide a solid base from which coalition building may begin. As discussed in Chapter 6, political parties provide the collective good of brand name recognition for members.

The top party leader in the House—and the only House leader mentioned in the Constitution—is the **Speaker of the House**. This individual is the head of the majority party, and he or she influences the legislative agenda, committee assignments, scheduling, and overall party strategy. The Speaker is aided by the **majority leader**, the majority whip, and the caucus chair (in addition to many other lower-level party positions). The majority leader not only is a key national spokesperson for the party but also helps with the day-to-day operation of the legislative process.

PARTY LEADERSHIP IS CENTRAL IN THE legislative process. Following the overwhelming victory in the 2010 midterm elections that swept their party to power, Republicans Eric Cantor (R-Va.) and John Boehner (R-Ohio) met to talk about strategy for the upcoming Congress. Boehner became the Speaker and Cantor the House majority leader in January 2011.

THE POLITICS OF PORK

The infamous "bridge to nowhere," a $435 million project to connect Ketchikan, Alaska, with a barely inhabited island, is one of the most famous examples of wasteful pork-barrel spending, but it is unusual only in its scale rather than its kind. It is also unusual because the outcry over the bridge prompted Alaska to pull the plug on the project, whereas most pork-barrel spending survives. Pork typically takes the form of earmarked funding for a specific project that is not subjected to standard, neutral spending formulas or a competitive process.

One tactic legislators often use to win approval for pork is to insert it into emergency spending bills that are expected to pass, such as disaster relief for flood and hurricane victims, spending for national security after the September 11 attacks, or funding for the wars in Iraq and Afghanistan. For example, the $636.3 billion 2010 defense appropriations bill included $128.3 billion for the wars in Iraq and Afghanistan and was stuffed with 1,719 earmarks worth $7.6 billion.[a] One controversial earmark was $2.5 billion for ten C-17 transport planes that had not been requested by the Pentagon. Senator John McCain (R-Ariz.) opposed the earmark, saying that the bill would "fund the purchase of new aircraft that we neither need nor can afford. . . . That would have a significant impact on our ability to provide the day-to-day operational funding that our servicemen and women and their families deserve." Other earmarks in that bill included $23 million for the Hawaii Healthcare Network, $18.9 million for the Edward M. Kennedy Institute for the Senate, and $20 million for the National World War II museum in New Orleans.

Some broader definitions of pork include any benefit targeted to a particular political constituency (typically an important business in a member's district or a generous campaign contributor), even if the benefit is part of a stand-alone bill. Examples of this type of targeted federal largesse include the bill that provided federal support to the airlines after the September 11 attacks, which sailed through Congress without much debate, and the lucrative contracts to rebuild Iraq that were awarded to politically well-connected businesses.

Pork has plenty of critics. Citizens against Government Waste, one of the most outspoken groups to tackle pork-barrel spending, compiles each year's federal pork-barrel projects into their annual *Pig Book* to draw attention to pork. Representative Dave Obey (D-Wis.) and Senator John McCain (R-Ariz.), among others, have been trying to get Congress to cut back on earmarks. The ban on earmarks imposed by House Republicans in 2011 has helped a great deal, but committee and informal earmarks are still pervasive. The arguments against pork are especially urgent during a time of massive budget deficits. According to this view, the national interest in a balanced budget should take priority over localized projects.

However, some argue that pork is the "glue of legislating," because these small side payments secure the passage of larger bills. If it takes a little pork for the home district or state

Surrounded by members of Congress, President Obama signs the National Defense Authorization Act for 2010. The law included 1,719 earmarks worth $7.6 billion.

in order to get important legislation through Congress, so be it. The motives of budget reform groups that call for greater fiscal discipline in Congress may also be questioned, since many of these groups oppose government spending in general—not just on pork. In some cases, policies they identify as pork have significant national implications: military readiness, road improvements to support economic infrastructure, or the development of new agricultural and food products. National interests can be served, in other words, by allowing local interests to take a dip into the pork barrel. Put another way, "pork is in the eye of the beholder," or one person's pork is another person's essential spending. Finally, defenders of pork point out that even according to the critics' own definition, pork spending constitutes about one-half of 1 percent of the total federal budget. If you were a member of Congress, would you work hard to deliver pork to your district or work to eliminate as much pork as you could from the budget?

Critical Thinking Questions

1. If you were a member of Congress, would you work hard to deliver pork to your district or work to eliminate as much pork as you could from the budget?

2. Why is it so difficult to ban earmarks even in the face of massive budget deficits?

whip system An organization of House leaders who work to disseminate information and promote party unity in voting on legislation.

minority leader The elected head of the party holding the minority of seats in the House or Senate.

president pro tempore A largely symbolic position usually held by the most senior member of the majority party in the Senate.

roll call vote A recorded vote on legislation; members may vote yes, no, abstain, or present.

party vote A vote in which the majority of one party opposes the position of the majority of the other party.

party unity The extent to which members of Congress in the same party vote together on party votes.

The majority whip oversees the extensive **whip system**, which has three functions: information gathering, information dissemination, and coalition building. The whips meet regularly to discuss legislative strategy and scheduling. The whips then pass along this information to colleagues in their respective parties and indicate the party's position on a given bill. Whips also take a headcount of party members in the House on specific votes and communicate this information to the party leaders. If a vote looks close, whips try to persuade members to support the party's position. The conference chair (or caucus chair for the Democrats) runs the party meetings to elect floor leaders, make committee assignments, and set legislative agendas. The minority party in the House has a parallel structure: its leader is the **minority leader**, and the second in command is the minority whip. (*Whip* comes from English fox hunting, referring to the person who keeps the hounds from wandering too far from the pack—the *whipper-in*.)

The Senate leadership does not have as much power as that of the House, mostly because individual senators have more power than House members on account of the Senate's rule of unlimited debate. The majority leader and minority leader are the leaders of their respective parties; second in command are the assistant majority and minority leaders. The Senate also has a whip system, but it is not as extensive as the House system. Republicans have a separate position for the conference chair, while the Democratic leader serves also as conference chair. The country's vice president is officially the president of the Senate, but he only appears in the chamber when needed to cast a tie-breaking vote. The Constitution also mentions the **president pro tempore** of the Senate, whose formal duties involve presiding over the Senate when the vice president is not present. This is typically the most senior member of the majority party, although the position does not have any real power. (In fact, the actual president pro tempore rarely presides over the Senate, and the task is typically given to a more junior senator.)

THE ROLE OF PARTIES

Political parties in Congress reflect the individualism of the institution. In the U.S. Congress, the parties do not impose a party line or penalize members who vote against the party. Indeed, they have virtually no ability to impose electoral restrictions (such as denying the party's nomination) on renegade members. Thus from the perspective of a member seeking re-election, parties are more useful for what they are not—they do not force members to vote with the party—than for what they are. Though there are significant party differences on many issues, on about half of all **roll call votes** majorities of both parties are on the same side.

Parties in Congress have greatly strengthened since the 1960s (see Figures 9.5 A and B). Partisanship—evident when party members stick together in opposition to the other party—reached its highest levels of the post–World War II era in the mid-1990s. About 70 percent of all roll call votes were **party votes**, in which a majority of one party opposed a majority of the other party. The proportion of party votes has since fallen but remains between 50 and 60 percent; however, in 2009 the Senate hit a high of 72 percent as contention over Barack Obama's policy agenda was running high. **Party unity**, the percentage of party members voting together on party votes, soared during this period as well, especially in the House.

This greater cohesiveness within parties and separation across parties means that strong party leadership is possible in Congress, but only with the consent of party members.[18] That consent is more likely if there are strong differences between the parties and homogeneity within the parties. Leaders' primary respon-

FIGURE » 9.5A

PARTY VOTES IN CONGRESS, 1962–2011

These graphs make two important points. First, partisanship has increased in the last two decades, both in terms of the proportion of party votes and the level of party unity. Second, despite these increased levels of partisanship, only about half of all votes in the House and Senate divide the two parties. Given these potentially conflicting observations, how would you assess the argument that partisanship in Congress is far too intense?

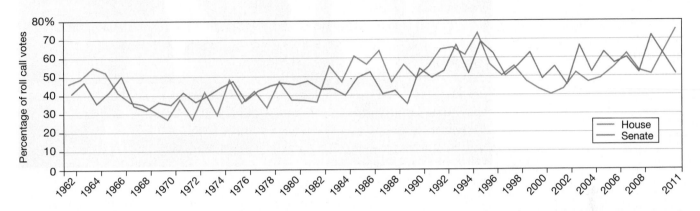

FIGURE » 9.5B

PARTY UNITY IN CONGRESS, 1962–2011

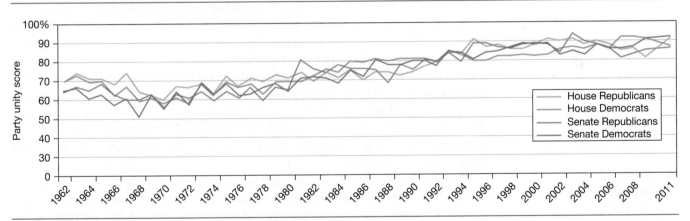

Sources for 10.6A and 10.6B: Data from Norman J. Ornstein, Thomas E. Mann, and Michael J. Malbin, Vital Statistics on Congress: 1999–2000 *(Washington, DC: CQ Press, 2000), pp. 201–3, and more recent editions of* Congressional Quarterly Almanac.

sibility is to get their party's legislative agenda through Congress; their positive powers in this regard are agenda control and persuasion. Leaders' success largely depends on their personal skills, communicative abilities, and trustworthiness. Some of the most successful leaders, such as Lyndon Johnson (D-Tex.), majority leader of the Senate from 1955 to 1961, and Sam Rayburn (D-Tex.), Speaker of the House for more than 17 years, kept in touch with key members on a daily basis.

PRESIDENT BARACK OBAMA WORKED tirelessly as his party's chief fund-raiser and campaigner in the 2010 midterm elections. He is shown here at a campaign rally in Nevada for Senator Harry Reid.

Leaders also must have the ability to bargain and compromise. One observer noted, "To Senator Johnson, public policy evidently was an inexhaustibly bargainable product."[19] Such leaders find solutions where none appear possible. Leaders also do favors for members to engender a feeling of personal obligation to the leadership when it needs a key vote. Such favors include making campaign appearances, helping with fund-raising, contributing to campaigns, helping members get desired committee assignments, or guiding pet projects through the legislative process.

The party's most powerful positive incentives are in the area of campaign finance. In recent years the congressional campaign committees of both parties and the national party organizations have been supplying candidates with money and other resources in an attempt to gain more influence in the electoral process. Party leaders may also help arrange a campaign stop or a fund-raiser for a candidate with party leaders or the president. For example, President Obama held dozens of fund-raisers for Democrats in 2010, earning him the label "Fundraiser-in-Chief" from CBS News.[20] Such events typically raise $500,000 to more than $1 million.

Despite these positive reinforcements, members' desire for re-election always comes before party concerns, and leadership rarely tries to force a member to vote against his or her constituents' interests. For example, Democrats from rural areas, where most constituents support gun ownership and many are hunters, would not be expected to vote the party line favoring a gun-control bill. To be disciplined by the party, a member of Congress must do something much more extreme than not supporting the party on roll call votes; extreme moves would include supporting the opposing party's candidate for Speaker or passing strategic information to the opposition. In such cases disciplinary measures might involve stripping the member of all committee assignments or even expelling the member from his or her seat. Despite occasional strong-arm tactics, party leaders have moved toward a service-oriented leadership, recognizing that their power is only as strong as the leeway granted by the rank-and-file membership.

THE COMMITTEE SYSTEM

The committee system in the House and Senate is another crucial part of the legislative structure. There are four types of committees: standing, select, joint, and conference. **Standing committees**, which have ongoing membership and jurisdictions, are where most of the work of Congress gets done. These committees draft legislation and oversee the implementation of the laws they pass. For example, the Agriculture Committees in the House and Senate have jurisdiction over farm programs such as commodity price supports, crop insurance, and soil conservation. But they also create and oversee policy for rural electrification and development, the food stamp and nutrition programs, and the inspection of livestock, poultry, seafood, and meat products. Many committees share jurisdiction on policy: for example, the House Natural Resources Committee oversees the National Forest Service and forests on federally owned lands, and the Agriculture Committee oversees policy for forests on privately owned lands.

    Select committees typically address a specific topic for one or two terms, such as the Select Committee on Energy Independence and Global Warming that operated from 2007 to 2010. These committees do not have the same legislative authority as standing committees; they mostly collect information, provide policy options, and draw attention to a given issue. **Joint committees** comprise members of the House and Senate, and they rarely have legislative authority. The Joint Committee on Taxation, for example, does not have authority to send legislation concerning tax policy to the floor of the House or Senate. Instead, it gathers information and provides estimates of the consequences of proposed tax legislation. Joint committees may also be temporary, such as the "Supercommittee" (officially, the Joint Select Committee on Deficit Reduction) discussed in the chapter opener. **Conference committees** are formed to resolve differences between the House and Senate versions of legislation that passes each chamber. These committees mostly comprise standing committee members from each chamber who worked on the bill. Table 9.2 shows the policy areas covered by each type of committee.

    The committee system creates a division of labor that helps re-election by supporting members' specialization and credit claiming. For example, a chair of the Agriculture Committee or of a key agricultural subcommittee may reasonably take credit for passing an important bill for the farmers back home, such as the Cottonseed Payment Program that provides assistance to cottonseed farmers who have lost crops due to hurricanes. The number of members who could make these credible claims expanded dramatically in the 1970s with the proliferation of subcommittees (there are 108 in the House and 73 in the Senate). One observer of Congress suggested, with some exaggeration, that if you ever forget a member's name, you can simply refer to him or her as "Mr. or Ms. Chairman" and you will be right about half the time.

    This view of congressional committees is based on the *distributive theory*, which is rooted in the norm of reciprocity and the incentive to provide benefits for the district. The theory holds that members will seek committee assignments to best serve their district's interests, the leadership will accommodate those requests, and the floor will respect the views of the committees (that is, committee members will support one another's legislation). This means that members tend to have an interest in and support the policies produced by the committees they serve on. For example, members from farm states will want to serve on the Agriculture Committee, and members with a lot of military bases

standing committees Committees that are a permanent part of the House or Senate structure, holding more importance and authority than other committees.

select committees Committees in the House or Senate created to address a specific issue for one or two terms.

joint committees Committees that contain members of both the House and Senate but have limited authority.

conference committees Temporary committees created to negotiate differences between the House and Senate versions of a piece of legislation that has passed through both chambers.

TABLE » 9.2

CONGRESSIONAL COMMITTEES

Equivalent or similar committees in both chambers are listed across from each other.

HOUSE COMMITTEES	SENATE COMMITTEES	JOINT COMMITTEES
Agriculture	Agriculture, Nutrition, and Forestry	Joint Economic Committee
Appropriations	Appropriations	Joint Committee on the Library
Armed Services	Armed Services	Joint Committee on Printing
Budget	Budget	Joint Committee on Taxation
Education and Workforce	Health, Education, Labor, and Pensions	
Energy and Commerce	Commerce, Science, and Transportation	
Ethics	Select Committee on Ethics	
Financial Services	Banking, Housing, and Urban Affairs	
Foreign Affairs	Foreign Relations	
Homeland Security	Homeland Security and Governmental Affairs	
House Administration	Rules and Administration	
Select Committee on Intelligence	Select Committee on Intelligence	
Judiciary	Judiciary	
Natural Resources	Energy and Natural Resources	
Small Business	Small Business and Entrepreneurship	
Transportation and Infrastructure	Environment and Public Works	
Veterans' Affairs	Veterans' Affairs	
Ways and Means	Finance	
The committees below are specific to one chamber.	*Specific to one chamber*	
Oversight and Government Reform	Special Committee on Aging	
Rules	Indian Affairs	
Science, Space, and Technology		

or defense contractors in their districts will want to be on the Armed Services Committee.

However, the committee system does not exist simply to further members' electoral goals. The structure of committees creates more expertise than if the policy process were more ad hoc.[21] This expertise provides collective benefits to the rest of the members because it helps reduce uncertainty about policy outcomes. By deferring to expert committees, members are able to achieve beneficial outcomes while using their own time more efficiently.

Committees also serve the policy needs of the majority party, largely because it controls a majority of seats on every committee. The party ratios on each committee generally reflect the partisan distribution in the overall chamber, but the majority party gives itself somewhat larger majorities on the important committees such as Ways and Means (which controls tax policy), Appropriations, and Rules. The Rules Committee is important to the majority party because it structures the nature of debate in the House by setting the length of debate and the type

FIGURE » 9.6

IDEOLOGICAL DISTRIBUTION OF MEMBERS

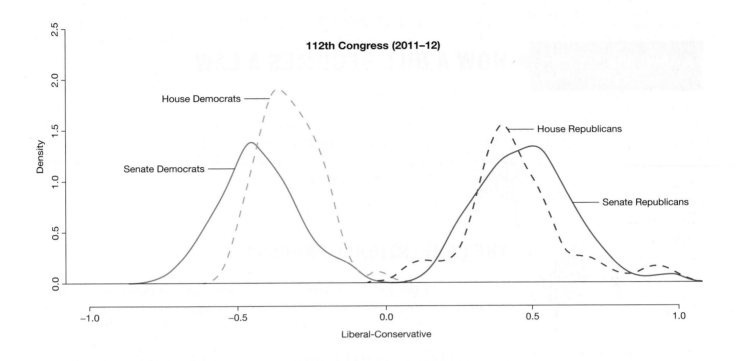

Source: "Forecasting Polarization in the 113th Senate," September 10, 2012, voteview, http://voteview.com/blog/?p=567 (accessed 9/19/12).

and number of amendments to a bill that will be allowed. These decisions must be approved by a majority of the House floor. The Rules Committee has become an arm of the majority party leadership, and in many instances it provides rules that support the party's policy agenda or protect its members from having to take controversial positions. For example, the Rules Committee prevented many amendments on the 2010 health care reform bill that would have divided the Democratic Party if they had come to a vote. Majority members are expected to support their party on votes concerning rules, even if they end up voting against the related legislation.

CONGRESSIONAL STAFF

The final component of the formal structure of Congress is congressional staff. The size of personal and committee staff exploded in the 1970s and 1980s and has since leveled off. Today the total number of congressional staff is more than four times as large as it was 50 years ago. Part of the motivation for this growth was to reduce the gap between the policy-making capability of Congress and the president, especially with regard to fiscal policy. The larger committee staffs gave members of Congress independent sources of information and expertise with which to challenge the president. The other primary motivation was electoral: by increasing the size of their personal staff, members were able to open multiple district offices and expand the opportunities for casework.

TRACE THE STEPS IN THE LEGISLATIVE PROCESS ▶

HOW A BILL BECOMES A LAW

Every introductory textbook on American politics presents a diagram that describes how a bill becomes a law. This book is no exception. However, we provide an important truth-in-advertising disclosure: many important laws do not follow this orderly path.[22] After presenting the standard view, we describe the most important deviations from that path.

THE CONVENTIONAL PROCESS

The details of the legislative process can be incredibly complex, but its basic aspects are fairly simple. The most important thing to understand about the process is that before a piece of legislation can become a law it must be passed *in identical form* by both the House and the Senate and signed by the president. If the president vetoes the bill, it can still be passed with a two-thirds vote in each chamber. The basic steps of the process are:

1. A member of Congress introduces the bill.
2. A subcommittee and committee craft the bill.
3. Floor action on the bill takes place in the first chamber (House or Senate).
4. Committee and floor action takes place in the second chamber.
5. The conference committee works out any differences between the House and Senate versions of the bill. (If the two chambers pass the same version, steps 5 and 6 are not necessary.)
6. The floor of each chamber passes the final conference committee version.
7. The president either signs or vetoes the final version.
8. If the bill is vetoed, both chambers can attempt to override the veto.

EARLY STEPS

The first part of the process, unchanged from the earliest Congresses, is the introduction of the bill. Only members of Congress can introduce a bill, either by dropping it into the "hopper," a wooden box at the front of the chamber in the House, or by presenting it to one of the clerks at the presiding officer's desk in the Senate. Even the president would need to have a House member or senator introduce his bill. Each bill has one or more sponsors and often many co-sponsors. (See Nuts and Bolts 9.2 for a description of the different types of bills.)

The next step is to send the bill to the relevant committee. House and Senate rules specify committee jurisdictions (there are more than 200 categories), and the

TYPES OF LEGISLATION

Bill: A legislative proposal that becomes law if it is passed by both the House and the Senate in identical form and approved by the president. Each is assigned a bill number, with "HR" indicating bills that originated in the House and "S" denoting bills that originated in the Senate. Private bills are concerned with a specific individual or organization and often address immigration or naturalization issues. Public bills affect the general public if enacted into law.

Simple resolution: Legislation used to express the sense of the House or Senate, designated by "H.Res." or "S.Res." Simple resolutions only affect the chamber passing the resolution, are not signed by the president, and cannot become public law. Resolutions are often used for symbolic legislation, such as congratulating sports teams.

Concurrent resolution: Legislation used to express the position of both chambers on a nonlegislative matter to set the annual budget, or to fix adjournment dates, designated by "H.Con.Res" or "S.Con.Res." Concurrent resolutions are not signed by the president and therefore do not carry the weight of law.

Joint resolution: Legislation that has few practical differences from a bill unless it proposes a constitutional amendment. In that case, a two-thirds majority of those present and voting in both the House and the Senate, and ratification by three-fourths of the states, are required for the amendment to be adopted.

bill is matched with the committee that best fits its subject matter. In the House, major legislation may be sent to more than one committee in a practice known as multiple referral, but only one of them is designated the primary committee, and the bill is reviewed by different committees sequentially or in parts. The practice is less common in the Senate, partly because senators have more opportunities to amend legislation on the floor.

Once the bill goes to a committee, the chair refers it to the relevant subcommittee where much of the legislative work occurs. The subcommittee holds hearings, calls witnesses, and gathers the information necessary to rewrite, amend, and edit the bill. The final language of the bill is determined in a collaborative process known as the **markup**. During this meeting members debate aspects of the issue and offer amendments to change the language or content of the bill. After all amendments have been considered, a final vote is taken on whether to send the bill to the full committee. The full committee then considers whether to pass it along to the floor. They, too, have the option of amending the bill, passing it as-is, or tabling it (which kills the bill). Every bill sent to the floor by a committee is accompanied by a report and full documentation of all the hearings. These documents constitute the bill's legislative history, which the courts, executive departments, and the public use to determine the purpose and meaning of the law.

markup One of the steps through which a bill becomes a law, in which the final wording of the bill is determined.

DEBATING THE BILL

When the bill makes it to the floor, it is placed on one of the various legislative calendars. Bills are removed from the calendar to be considered by the floor under a broad range of possible rules. When the bill reaches the floor, the majority party and minority party each designate a bill manager who is responsible for guiding the debate on the floor. Debate in the House proceeds according to tight time limits and rules governing the nature of amendments. Senate debate is much more open and unlimited in most circumstances (unless all the senators agree to a limit).

IN 2010 SENATOR BERNARD SANDERS of Vermont spoke on the Senate floor for 8 hours and 37 minutes to draw attention to his concerns about a proposed tax plan. However, Sanders's long speech wasn't technically a filibuster because it didn't prevent Senate business from proceeding (none was scheduled for that day).

Unless restricted by a unanimous consent agreement, senators can speak as long as they want and offer any amendment to a bill, even if it isn't germane (that is, directly related to the underlying bill). Debate may be cut off only if a supermajority of 60 senators agrees in a process known as invoking **cloture**. Therefore, one senator can stop any bill by threatening to talk the bill to death if 40 of his or her colleagues agree. This practice, which is known as a **filibuster**, strengthens the hand of the minority party in the Senate, giving it veto power over legislation unless the majority party has 60 senators who unanimously support a bill.

When debate is completed and all amendments have been considered, the presiding officer calls for a voice vote, with those in favor saying "aye" and those opposed "no." If it is unclear which side has won, any member may call for a "division vote," which requires members on each side to stand and be counted. At that point any member may call for a recorded vote (there is no way of recording members' positions on voice votes and division votes). If at least 25 members agree that a recorded vote is desired, buzzers go off in the office buildings and committee rooms, calling members to the floor for the vote. Once they reach the floor, members vote by an electronic system in which they insert ATM-like cards into slots and each vote is recorded on a big board at the front of the chamber.

RESOLVING DISCREPANCIES

cloture A procedure through which the Senate can limit the amount of time spent debating a bill (cutting off a filibuster), if a supermajority of sixty senators agree.

filibuster A tactic used by senators to block a bill by continuing to hold the floor and speak—under the Senate rule of unlimited debate—until the bill's supporters back down.

If the bill passes the House and the Senate in different forms, the discrepancies have to be resolved. On many minor bills, one chamber may simply accept the other chamber's version to solve the problem. On other minor bills and some major bills, differences are resolved through a process known as amendments between the chambers. In this case one chamber modifies a bill passed by the other chamber and sends it back. These modifications can go back and forth several times before both chambers agree on an identical bill. A complicated version of this approach was used to pass health care reform in 2010.

The most common way to resolve differences on major legislation is through a conference committee comprising key players in the House and the Senate. About three-fourths of major bills go to a conference committee, but only 12 percent of all bills follow this route.[23] Sometimes the conferees split the difference between the House and Senate versions, but at other times the House and Senate approaches are so different that one must be chosen—an especially tricky prospect when different parties control the two chambers. Sometimes the conference committee cannot resolve differences, and the bill dies. If the committee can agree on changes, each chamber must pass the final version—the conference report—by a majority vote, and neither chamber is allowed to amend it.

One final point on how a bill becomes a law is important: any bill that appropriates money must pass through the two-step process of authorization and appropriation. In the authorization process, members debate the merits of the bill, determine its language, and limit the amount that can be spent on the bill. The appropriations process involves both the Budget Committees in the House and the Senate, which set the overall guidelines for the national budget, and the Appropriations Committees in the two chambers, which determine the actual amounts of money that will be spent (see "How It Works" in Chapter 14). In recent years Congress has been unable to pass appropriations bills in time for the start of the new fiscal year, so it ends up passing "continuing resolutions" that spend money at the previous year's levels in order to keep the government open. Congress passed four continuing resolutions for the 2012 fiscal year. That may sound like a lot, but the record is 21 for the 2001 fiscal year.[24]

PRESIDENTIAL APPROVAL OR VETO

The bill is then sent to the president. If he approves and signs the measure within 10 days (not counting Sundays), it becomes law. If the president objects to the bill, he may veto it within 10 days by sending it back to the chamber where it originated, along with a statement of objections. Unless both the House and the Senate vote to override the veto by a two-thirds majority, the bill dies. If the president does not act within 10 days and Congress is in session, the bill becomes law without the president's approval. If Congress is not in session, the measure dies through a **pocket veto**.

pocket veto The automatic death of a bill passed by the House and Senate when the president fails to sign the bill in the last ten days of a legislative session.

DEVIATIONS FROM THE CONVENTIONAL PROCESS

There are many ways in which legislation may not follow the typical path. First, in some congresses up to 20 percent of *major* bills bypass the committee system. This may be done by a discharge petition, in which a majority of the members force a bill out of its assigned committee, or by a special rule in the House. In some cases a bill may go to the relevant committee, but then party leadership may impose its version of the bill later in the process. Consider the USA PATRIOT Act, which Congress passed in the wake of the terrorist attacks of 9/11 to give the government stronger surveillance powers. It was unanimously reported by the Judiciary Committee after five days of hard bipartisan work; but a few days later, according to committee member Rep. Jerrold Nadler (D-N.Y.), "Then the bill just disappeared. And we had a new several hundred page bill revealed from the Rules Committee" that had to be voted on the next day. Most members of Congress did not have a chance to read it.[25] The Affordable Care Act passed in 2010 also deviated from the standard path (see "How It Works").

Second, about one-third of major bills are adjusted post-committee and before the legislation reaches the floor by supporters of the bill to increase the chances of passage. Sometimes the bill goes back to the committee after these changes, and sometimes it does not. Thus although most of the legislative work is accomplished in committees, a significant amount of legislation bypasses committee review.

Third, summit meetings between the president and congressional leaders may bypass or jump-start the normal legislative process. For example, rather than going through the Budget Committees to set budgetary targets, the president may meet with top leaders from both parties and hammer out a compromise that is presented to Congress as a done deal.

Fourth, **omnibus legislation**—massive bills that run hundreds of pages long and cover many different subjects and programs—often requires creative approaches by the leadership to guide the bill through the legislative maze. Leadership task forces may be used in the place of committees, and alternatives to the conference committee may be devised to resolve differences between the two chambers. In addition, the massive legislation often carries riders—extraneous legislation attached to the "must pass" bill to secure approval for pet projects that would otherwise fail. This form of pork-barrel legislation is another mechanism used in the quest for re-election.

omnibus legislation Large bills that often cover several topics and may contain extraneous, or pork-barrel, projects.

KEY DIFFERENCES BETWEEN HOUSE AND SENATE PROCESSES

There are three central differences between the legislative processes of the House and the Senate: the continuity of the membership and the impact that has on the rules; the way in which bills get to the floor; and the structure of the floor process, including debate and amendments. First, because the Senate is a continuing body, with two-thirds of its members returning every session without facing re-election, there has been greater stability in the rules of the Senate than the House. However, Senate rules can be changed at the start of a session if necessary to accommodate new members' needs.

Second, the process by which a bill gets to the floor is much more complicated in the House than in the Senate. Although new bills generally get placed at the bottom of the legislative calendar in the House, the leadership can move a bill to the top of the agenda in several ways. One way is to have the bill considered under what is called suspension of the rules; another is to have the Rules Committee make a special rule that gives the bill top priority if a majority of the House members approve. The entire procedure is much easier in the Senate, where the leadership can give bills privileged status simply by putting them at the top of the agenda via a motion or unanimous consent.

Finally, the floor process itself is simpler in the Senate than in the House. This is partly due to the relative size of the two chambers: the House with 435 members needs more rules than the 100-person Senate. Moreover, the Senate has unlimited debate and a very open amendment process. As mentioned earlier, unless restricted by a unanimous consent agreement, senators can speak as long as they want and offer any type of amendment to a bill. In contrast, the House is a more complex institution. The Rules Committee governs the nature of debate on a bill there: closed rules do not allow any amendments, open rules allow related amendments, and modified rules allow some amendments but not others. Floor managers control general debate under a five-minute rule, although that restriction is frequently circumvented through an elaborate process that allows more time.

Ironically, although the Senate is formally committed to unlimited debate, senators often voluntarily place limits on themselves, which makes them operate more like the House. Similarly, although the House has strict rules concerning debate and amendments, there are ways of bending those rules to make that chamber operate more like the potentially free-wheeling Senate.

DESCRIBE HOW CONGRESS ENSURES THAT THE BUREAUCRACY IMPLEMENTS POLICIES CORRECTLY

OVERSIGHT

Once a bill becomes a law, Congress plays another crucial role by overseeing the implementation of the law to make sure the bureaucracy interprets it as Congress intended. Other motivations driving the oversight process are the desire to gain publicity that may help in the re-election quest or to embarrass the presi-

How It Works

PASSING LEGISLATION: THE CONVENTIONAL METHOD

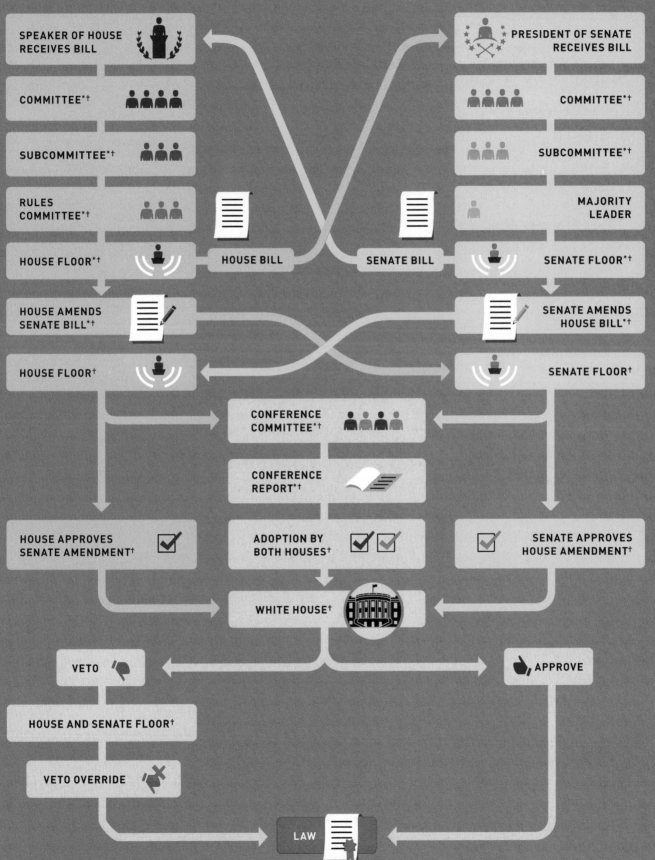

SPEAKER OF HOUSE RECEIVES BILL

COMMITTEE*†

SUBCOMMITTEE*†

RULES COMMITTEE*†

HOUSE FLOOR*†

HOUSE BILL

PRESIDENT OF SENATE RECEIVES BILL

COMMITTEE*†

SUBCOMMITTEE*†

MAJORITY LEADER

SENATE BILL

SENATE FLOOR*†

HOUSE AMENDS SENATE BILL*†

HOUSE FLOOR†

SENATE AMENDS HOUSE BILL*†

SENATE FLOOR†

CONFERENCE COMMITTEE*†

CONFERENCE REPORT*†

HOUSE APPROVES SENATE AMENDMENT†

ADOPTION BY BOTH HOUSES†

SENATE APPROVES HOUSE AMENDMENT†

WHITE HOUSE†

VETO

APPROVE

HOUSE AND SENATE FLOOR†

VETO OVERRIDE

LAW

*Points at which a bill can be amended.
†Points at which a bill can die.

How It Works

DEVIATIONS FROM THE CONVENTIONAL METHOD: AN EXAMPLE

CONVENTIONAL STEPS after a bill is introduced. (See the preceding page.)

THE 2010 AFFORDABLE CARE ACT (ACA) provides an example of how passing legislation often deviates from the conventional method.

A committee and a subcommittee revise the bill

In the House, **3 committees** crafted the bill.

5 committees worked on the Senate version.

Speaker Nancy Pelosi assumed a central role in shaping the final bill, adding things that weren't in the committee version.

After a deadlock between two committees, Majority Leader Harry Reid pushed through a merged version of the bill, adding things that weren't in the committee version.

President Obama was intensely involved. The White House held daily meetings with the committees.

Floor action

Floor action

Floor action

Conference committee reconciles House and Senate versions.

No conference committee. Instead, committee leaders, White House staff, and party leadership negotiated the details of the bill.

Adoption of final bill by both House and Senate

The Senate version of the bill was passed by the House, but then the House also passed a separate reconciliation bill that included many amendments to the Senate version.

That reconciliation bill was then passed by the Senate.

President signs bill into law.

President Obama signed the ACA into law.

POP QUIZ!

1 A conference committee's job is to

  a draft an original bill.

  b determine whether a bill should be considered by Congress.

  c determine whether a bill is constitutional.

  d reconcile differences between House and Senate versions of a bill.

  e convince the president to sign the bill.

2 One way the passage of the ACA differed from the conventional process is that

  a committees were not involved.

  b President Obama and party leaders were directly involved in shaping the bill.

  c no floor action took place.

  d only one house voted on the bill.

  e the president signed it into law.

dent if he is of the opposite party. For example, in President Bush's last two years, Democrats investigated fraud and cost overruns in Defense Department contracts to rebuild Iraq that went to corporations with close Republican Party ties. In 2011, Republicans used their oversight powers to highlight policy failures in the Obama administration such as "Operation Fast and Furious" (a Justice Department program to sell guns to drug dealers that could then be tracked to Mexican drug lords; the program went horribly awry when hundreds of the guns went missing and two were found where a Border Patrol agent was killed).[26] However, the basic motivation for oversight is to ensure that laws are implemented properly.

Congress may use several mechanisms to accomplish this goal; we examine these in Chapter 11 but briefly describe them here. First, the bluntest instrument is the power of the purse. If members of Congress think an agency is not properly implementing their programs, they can simply cut off the funds. However, this approach is rarely used because budget cuts often end up cutting good aspects of the agency along with the bad.

Second, Congress may hold hearings and investigations. By summoning administration officials and agency heads to a public hearing, Congress can use the media spotlight to focus attention on problems within the bureaucracy or on issues that have been overlooked. For example, the economic meltdown of 2008–09 produced dozens of hearings on topics ranging from the bailout of the auto industry to the use of TARP (Troubled Assets Relief Program, another government bailout program) money by financial institutions, executive pay in the financial sector, the housing market and subprime mortgage crises, and accountability of the Federal Reserve. This type of oversight is known as fire alarm oversight—that is, members wait until there is a crisis before they spring to action.[27] It is in contrast to so-called police patrol oversight, which involves constant vigilance in overseeing the bureaucracy. Of the two, fire alarm oversight is more common because Congress does not have the resources to constantly monitor the entire bureaucracy.

Third, Congress may use **legislative vetoes**. In writing laws Congress often gives the bureaucracy broad discretion over how to implement policies, because it is impossible for Congress to foresee every scenario that might arise. However, Congress is reluctant to give full control to the implementing agencies. Legislative vetoes resolve this dilemma by allowing Congress to overturn bureaucratic decisions. In 1983 the Supreme Court ruled that many forms of legislative vetoes are unconstitutional.[28] Despite this ruling, Congress has enacted more than 400 new legislative vetoes since 1983.[29]

Finally, the Senate exercises specific control over other executive functions through its constitutional responsibilities to provide "advice and consent" on presidential appointments and approval of treaties. The Senate typically defers to the president on these matters, but it may assert its power, especially when constituent interests are involved. Current examples include the Senate's increasing skepticism about free trade agreements negotiated by the president's trade representatives and its holds on presidential nominations.

The ultimate in congressional oversight is the process of removing the president, vice president, other civil officers, or federal judges through impeachment. The House and Senate share this power. The House issues articles of impeachment, which outline the charges against the official, and the Senate conducts the trial of

THE CEOS OF GENERAL MOTORS, FORD, and Chrysler testify before the Senate Banking, Housing, and Urban Affairs Committee about a proposed $34 billion federal bailout for the auto industry. When members of Congress took this extraordinary step in 2009, they wanted to make sure that taxpayers' money would be wisely spent.

legislative veto A form of oversight in which Congress overturns bureaucratic decisions.

the impeached officials. Two presidents have been impeached: Andrew Johnson in the controversy over Reconstruction after the Civil War, and Bill Clinton over the scandal involving White House intern Monica Lewinsky. However, neither president was convicted and removed by the Senate.

CONCLUSION

Though the details of the legislative process and the institutions of Congress can be complicated, the basic explanations for member behavior are straightforward when viewed in terms of the trade-off between responsiveness and responsibility. Members of Congress want to be re-elected, so they are generally quite responsive to constituents' interests. They spend considerable time on casework, meeting with people in the district and delivering benefits for the district. At the same time, members are motivated to be responsible—to rise above local interests and attend to the nation's best interests.

The conflict between these two impulses can create contradictory policies that contribute to Congress's image problem. For example, we subsidize tobacco farming at the same time that we spend billions of dollars to treat the health problems that tobacco use creates. We have laws on water rights that encourage farmers to irrigate the desert at the same time that we pay farmers to leave parts of their land unplanted in areas of the country that are well suited for agriculture. These policies, and others, reflect both the desire to serve local interests and the norms of reciprocity and universalism.

Considering members' motivations is crucial to understanding how Congress functions, but their behavior is also constrained by the institutions in which they operate. The committee system is an important source of expertise and information, and it provides a platform from which members can take positions and claim credit. Parties in Congress provide coherence to the legislative agenda and help structure voting patterns on bills. Rules and norms constrain the nature of debate and the legislative process. Although these institutions shape members' behavior, members can also change those rules and institutions. Therefore, Congress has the ability to evolve with changing national conditions and demands from voters, groups, and the president.

In this context, much of what Congress does can be understood in terms of the conflicts inherent in politics. How can members act responsibly without sacrificing responsiveness? Can Congress be structured in a way that allows members to be responsive (and therefore have a better chance of getting re-elected) without losing the ability to make unpopular decisions when needed? The example discussed in the chapter introduction concerning the "fiscal cliff" shows that partisan conflict in Congress makes it difficult to resolve basic disputes over taxes and spending. But ultimately, both sides have to give up something and compromise if we are going to solve the nation's budget problems. Congress does not always live up to the expectations of being the "first branch" of government, but it often does an admirable job of balancing the conflicting pressures it faces.

STUDY *guide*

CONGRESS'S PLACE IN OUR CONSTITUTIONAL SYSTEM

▶ Describe how the Founders envisioned Congress's role. **Pages 257–58**

SUMMARY

The Constitution gave Congress vast enumerated powers, making it the "first branch" of government. The bicameral structure represented a number of compromises between competing interests among the Founders—notably, the compromises included differences in constituency size, election mechanisms, and length of terms. While Congress has long dominated day-to-day politics, the president has become considerably more powerful over time.

KEY TERMS

bicameralism (p. 257)

pork barrel (p. 258)

PRACTICE QUIZ QUESTIONS

1. What did the Seventeenth Amendment do?
   a) repealed prohibition
   b) granted women's suffrage
   c) gave senators six-year terms
   d) allowed for direct election of senators
   e) lowered the voting age to 18

2. Why do senators have longer terms than members of the House of Representatives?
   a) to reduce the number of candidates in each election
   b) to make sure senators are tied to public sentiment
   c) to provide opportunities for pork barrel legislation
   d) to make elections easier to administer
   e) to make sure that senators are somewhat insulated from the people

CONGRESS AND THE PEOPLE

▶ Explain how members of Congress represent their constituents and how elections hold members accountable. **Pages 258–71**

SUMMARY

Despite low approval ratings for Congress, most voters like their members of Congress. Members work hard to strike a balance between responding to constituents and acting in the nation's best interest. In the balance, they prioritize district interests over national policy. Incumbents are re-elected at high rates because they can relate to their constituents well, generally succeed in raising money for their political campaigns, and perform lots of constituency service.

KEY TERMS

descriptive representation (p. 259)

substantive representation (p. 259)

trustee (p. 259)

delegate (p. 259)

politico (p. 260)

casework (p. 262)

electoral connection (p. 262)

redistricting (p. 263)

apportionment (p. 263)

gerrymandering (p. 265)

gridlock (p. 267)

incumbency advantage (p. 268)

PRACTICE QUIZ QUESTIONS

3. How would most members of Congress classify their representation style?
   a) trustee
   b) politico
   c) delegate
   d) consulate
   e) advisor

Members of Congress generally hold multiple goals. Which goal comes first?

    a) getting re-elected

    b) passing good policy

    c) serving their political party

    d) blocking the opposing party

    e) serving special interests

5. What is apportionment?

    a) determining presidential primary winners

    b) determining whether the state legislature or courts will re-draw district lines

    c) determining which states gain/lose seats in the Senate

    d) determining which states gain/lose seats in the House

    e) determining how many seats a party has in Congress

6. On average, incumbents spend _____ times as much as challengers on campaigning.

    a) one and one-half

    b) three

    c) five

    d) ten

    e) twenty

ⓢ PRACTICE ONLINE

"Critical Thinking" exercise: *Politics Is Conflictual— Congressional and Presidential Fund-Raising*

THE STRUCTURE OF CONGRESS

▶ Examine how parties, the committee system, and staffers enable Congress to function. **Pages 271–80**

SUMMARY

Many aspects of Congress meet the electoral needs of its members. The norms of universalism and reciprocity still dominate, meaning that members of Congress share resources more broadly than partisan politics would dictate.

KEY TERMS

earmarks (p. 271)

seniority (p. 272)

Speaker of the House (p. 272)

majority leader (p. 272)

whip system (p. 274)

minority leader (p. 274)

president pro tempore (p. 274)

roll call vote (p. 274)

party vote (p. 274)

party unity (p. 274)

standing committees (p. 277)

select committees (p. 277)

joint committees (p. 277)

conference committees (p. 277)

CRITICAL THINKING AND DISCUSSION

If you were in charge of the Commission on Congressional Reform, what proposals would you make to change how Congress operates? Would your proposals have a chance of being implemented? Why or why not?

PRACTICE QUIZ QUESTIONS

7. Under the norm of _____, federal highway dollars are likely to be divided up so that many districts benefit.

    a) reciprocity

    b) seniority

    c) party unity

    d) universalism

    e) specialization

8. The Senate leadership is _____ the House leadership.

    a) more powerful than

    b) as powerful as

    c) less powerful than

9. Party leaders have the power to _____.

    a) force members of Congress to vote a particular way

    b) keep a member of Congress off the ballot in the next election

    c) force their members to share campaign money

    d) exclude a member from a roll call vote

    e) help their members get favorable committee assignments

10. Committee leadership, division of seats on committees, and allocation of committee resources are determined by _____.

    a) majority party

    b) size of election margin

c) unanimous consent
d) seniority
e) the president pro tempore

ⓢ **PRACTICE ONLINE**

"Critical Thinking" exercise: *Politics Is Everywhere—Earmarks*

HOW A BILL BECOMES A LAW

▶ Trace the steps in the legislative process. **Pages 280–84**

SUMMARY

Most bills become law in a conventional manner, but major legislation generally deviates considerably from this path. The process differs for the House and Senate, sometimes making it difficult to reconcile differences between bills.

KEY TERMS

markup (p. 281)

cloture (p. 282)

filibuster (p. 282)

pocket veto (p. 283)

omnibus legislation (p. 283)

PRACTICE QUIZ QUESTION

11. Compared to the Senate, the floor process in the House is very _____ and _____.
   a) unstructured; majoritarian
   b) structured; majoritarian
   c) unstructured; individualistic
   d) structured; individualistic
   e) individualistic; majoritarian

OVERSIGHT

▶ Describe how Congress ensures that the bureaucracy implements policies correctly. **Pages 284–88**

SUMMARY

After passing bills into law, Congress oversees the bureaucracy in its implementation of every law to ensure that it fits Congress's intentions. Although controlling funding is the most powerful mechanism for this, Congress has other mechanisms for achieving bureaucratic fidelity. Generally, Congress does not constantly monitor the bureaucracy, but waits to act until a crisis occurs.

KEY TERM

legislative veto (p. 287)

CRITICAL THINKING AND DISCUSSION

If you had to choose between having a responsive or responsible member of Congress, which would you choose and why?

PRACTICE QUIZ QUESTION

12. Waiting for a crisis to emerge before taking action is called _____.
   a) police patrol oversight
   b) fire alarm oversight
   c) emergency room oversight
   d) reactionary oversight
   e) bureaucratic oversight

SUGGESTED READING

Bianco, William T. *Trust: Representatives and Constituents*. Ann Arbor: University of Michigan Press, 1994.

Canon, David T. Race, *Redistricting and Representation: The Unintended Consequences of Black Majority Districts*. Chicago: University of Chicago Press, 1999.

Fenno, Richard F. *Congressmen in Committees*. Boston: Little, Brown, 1973.

Hall, Richard L. *Participation in Congress*. New Haven, CT: Yale University Press, 1996.

Jacobson, Gary C. *The Politics of Congressional Elections*, 5th ed. New York: Addison-Wesley, 2001.

Mayhew, David R. *Congress: The Electoral Connection*. New Haven, CT: Yale University Press, 1974.

Theriault, Sean. *Party Polarization in Congress*. New York: Cambridge University Press, 2008.

10

The Presidency

PRESIDENTIAL DECISIONS, SUCH as President Obama's choice to use drones for attacks on enemy targets in Afghanistan and elsewhere, are often controversial. Here, Obama discusses military and defense strategy in 2012.

ONE OF THE CORE ELEMENTS OF PRESIDENT BARACK OBAMA'S strategy to fight terrorist groups has been the increased use of drones—small, unmanned aircraft that fly into foreign airspace, monitor the activities of terror suspects on the ground, and, once the identities of suspects have been verified and the president's approval received, launch missles to attack these suspects and their facilities. Over the last four years, drone attacks in countries such as Afghanistan, Yemen, and Pakistan have decimated the leadership and infrastructure of terrorist groups and inflicted significant casualties on lower-level fighters. Drones also played a key role in identifying the safe house in Pakistan where Al Qaeda leader Osama bin Laden was located, making possible the helicopter attack by U.S. Special Forces that resulted in bin Laden's death in 2011.

Decisions involving military force provide an example of presidential power and how it may be controversial. In the case of using drones, virtually all Americans support the idea of fighting back against terror groups such as Al Qaeda. The controversy arises because some Americans favor a more aggressive approach that would involve sending ground forces to fight terrorist strongholds rather than attacking from the air. Others are uncomfortable with the use of drones because of the difficulty of being absolutely sure that the people being attacked are all terrorists. Finally, some observers have criticized the Obama administration drone strategy on the grounds that it is motivated by politics rather than a judgment about the most effective approach. They worry that Obama and his advisers favor unmanned attacks in order to minimize American casualties, which would be politically unpopular even if they were part of a more effective strategy.

CONFLICT & COMPROMISE
in American Politics

These dissenting opinions reflect the fact that the reliance on unmanned drones is actually a compromise among different strategies for fighting the war on terror—between aggressive strategies that rely on ground forces and more defensive approches that focus on preventing attacks against Americans. Drone attacks are an intermediate option, allowing attacks on terrorist groups without putting U.S. troops in harm's way. This compromise helps the president obtain the support of Congress and the American public. While such support is not necessary to order individual attacks, in the long run presidents generally need congressional and public support in order to carry out their decisions.

The president's power to order American forces into combat is only one example of presidential power. As we discuss in this chapter, America's presidents have considerable power over foreign and domestic policy and have used this power to make real, significant changes in government policy that have had real consequences for the lives of ordinary Americans. For example, Barack Obama's first term in office was marked by the enactment of landmark health care legislation, new financial regulations, economic stimulus, and the appointment of two Supreme Court justices. Accomplishments such as these are often cited as evidence that presidential power has gotten out of control—that presidents are virtual dictators, able to do almost whatever they want without congressional consent or judicial review.

This chapter offers a different interpretation of presidential power. U.S. presidents face decisions that are highly conflictual, with many people holding strong opinions on both sides of the question. Although some Americans approved of Obama's accomplishments, many others were opposed. Success for presidents is not automatic; they face the problem of reaching their own policy goals while at the same time trying to satisfy the demands of their supporters in Congress and among the American people—and seeking to avoid alienating people who disagree with presidential decisions.

To put it another way, while presidents are powerful, they are not dictators: in most cases, their actions either require congressional consent to take effect or can be undone by subsequent congressional action. Presidents must also cultivate public opinion in order to get re-elected or to elect members of Congress from their party, and must monitor the bureaucracy to make sure that their decisions are faithfully implemented. And sometimes, as with health care reform for Obama or George W. Bush's failed 2005 Social Security reform initiative, presidents must decide whether to scale back their proposals in an effort to get them enacted or risk completely failing to accomplish their goals.

Accordingly, one of the fundamental questions we ask in this chapter is, what are the limits of presidential power? When are presidents able to prevail in the face of conflict in the country, in Congress, or in the bureaucracy? Has presidential power grown over time? How does conflict affect the decisions that presidents make and the ways they try to implement their policy goals?

The second fundamental question we ask is, what are the sources of presidential power? The answer lies in the idea that political process matters. In some situations, the powers allocated in the Constitution enable the president to change government policy unilaterally. However, there are limits on this power. Congress and the Supreme Court can and at times do overturn presidential actions. Moreover, many policy changes require explicit congressional approval. This chapter shows that all presidents face opportunities and constraints, and their success in office depends on the particular challenges that arise, their personal policy goals, and their skill at using the power of the presidency.

AMERICA'S PRESIDENTS

TRACE THE EVOLUTION OF PRESIDENTIAL POWER OVER TIME

As we consider the histories of America's 44 presidents, three facts stand out. First, presidents get their power from a variety of sources, from provisions of the Constitution to their administration of the executive branch of government. Second, presidential power has increased over time, not because of changes in the Constitution but because of America's growth as a nation, its emergence as a dominant actor in international politics, the expansion of the federal government, and acts of legislation that gave new authority to the president. Third, there are sharp limits to presidential power. Presidents are often forced to compromise in the face of public, congressional, or foreign opposition.

EARLY YEARS THROUGH WORLD WAR I

Since the early years of the Republic, presidents' actions have had profound consequences for the nation. Presidents George Washington, John Adams, and Thomas Jefferson forged compromises on issues such as choosing a permanent location for the nation's capital, establishing the federal courts, and devising a system for financing the government.[1] Presidents Andrew Jackson and Martin Van Buren were instrumental in forming the Democratic Party and its local party organizations.

Early presidents also made important foreign policy decisions. For example, the Monroe Doctrine, issued by President James Monroe in 1823, stated that America would remain neutral in wars involving European nations and that these nations must cease attempts to colonize or occupy areas in North and South America.[2] Presidents John Tyler and James Polk oversaw the admission of the huge territory of Texas into the Union following the Mexican-American War. Polk also negotiated the Oregon Treaty with Britain, which led to acquisition of land that later became Oregon, Washington, Idaho, and parts of Montana and Wyoming.[3]

Several presidents sought compromise on slavery prior to the Civil War and during the war itself. President Millard Fillmore's support helped to enact the Compromise of 1850, which limited slavery in California, and Franklin Pierce supported the Kansas-Nebraska Act, which regulated slavery in these territories. Abraham Lincoln, who helped form the Republican Party in the 1850s, played a transformative role in setting policy as president during the Civil War. His orders raised the huge Union Army, and as commander in chief he directed the conduct of the bloody war that kept the southern states from seceding permanently. Lincoln issued the Emancipation Proclamation, which freed the slaves in the South, and temporarily suspended the writ of habeas corpus, which allowed the government to imprison people without filing charges against them.[4]

During the late 1800s and early 1900s, presidents were instrumental in federal responses to the nation's rapid expansion and industrialization.[5] The country's growing size and economy generated conflict over which services the federal government should provide to citizens and how much the government should regulate individual and corporate behavior.[6] Various acts of legislation created new federal agencies and, in doing so, also created new presidential powers and responsibilities. For example, Republican president Theodore Roosevelt used the Sherman Antitrust Act to break up the Northern Securities Company, a mammoth nationwide railroad trust. He increased the power of the Interstate Commerce Commission to regulate businesses and expanded federal conservation programs. Democrat Woodrow

GEORGE WASHINGTON REMAINS, FOR many Americans, the presidential ideal—a leader whose crucial domestic and foreign policy decisions shaped the growth of America's democracy.

Wilson further increased the government's role in managing the economy through his support of the Clayton Antitrust Act, the Federal Reserve Act, the first federal income tax, and legislation banning child labor.[7]

As these examples illustrate, presidential power has grown over time as the president and members of the executive branch have obtained new regulatory powers over corporations and individual Americans, and as presidents have responded to shifts in public opinion by proposing new policies. Essentially, because the president is the head of the bureaucracy, as the number of agencies and bureaucrats grows, so does presidential power.

At the same time, Wilson's foreign policy activities illustrate the limits of presidential power. While he campaigned in the 1916 election on a promise to keep America out of World War I, he ultimately ordered American troops to fight on the side of the Allies. After the war, Wilson offered a peace plan that proposed (1) reshaping the borders of European countries in order to prevent future conflicts; (2) creating an international organization, the League of Nations, to prevent future conflicts; and (3) taking other measures to encourage free trade and democracy.[8] However, America's allies rejected most of Wilson's proposals, and the Senate refused to allow American participation in the League of Nations.

THE GREAT DEPRESSION THROUGH THE PRESENT

Presidential actions defined the government's response to the Great Depression, a worldwide economic collapse in the late 1920s and 1930s marked by high unemployment, huge stock market declines, and bank failures. Republican president Herbert Hoover favored only modest government actions in response, arguing that more substantial efforts would be of little use.[9] After Hoover lost the 1932 election, Democrat Franklin Roosevelt and his staff began reshaping American government. Roosevelt's New Deal reforms created numerous federal agencies that helped individual Americans and imposed many new corporate regulations.[10] This expansion continued under Roosevelt's successors. Even Republican Dwight Eisenhower, whose party had initially opposed many New Deal reforms, presided over the creation of new agencies and the building of the interstate highway system.[11]

Presidents were instrumental in the civil rights reforms and expansion of the federal government in the 1960s. Democrat John Kennedy established the Peace Corps and began bargaining with members of Congress over legislation that would guarantee voting rights and civil rights for African Americans. Democrat Lyndon Johnson, who assumed the presidency after Kennedy's assassination, campaigned for re-election on his proposals for the Great Society and a War on Poverty. Johnson's administration created a wide range of domestic programs, such as the Department of Housing and Urban Development, Medicare, Medicaid, and federal funding for schools; his administration also finished the job of enacting voting rights and civil rights legislation. Again, this expansion of the federal government through legislation added to presidential power.

Both Johnson and his successor, Richard Nixon, directed America's involvement in the Vietnam War, with the goal of forcing the North Vietnamese to abandon their plans to unify North and South Vietnam. Here again, presidential efforts did not meet with success: despite enormous deployments of American forces and more than 58,000 American soldiers killed, Nixon eventually signed an agreement that allowed American troops to leave but did not end the conflict, which concluded only after a North Vietnamese victory in 1975.

The two presidents after Nixon, Republican Gerald Ford and Democrat Jimmy Carter, faced the worst economic conditions since the Great Depression, largely due to increased energy prices. Both presidents offered plans to reduce unemployment and inflation, restore economic growth, and enhance domestic energy sources. However, their efforts were largely unsuccessful, and their inability to move the economy became a critical factor in their failed re-election bids.

In the last generation, the political and policy importance of presidential actions has increased. Republican Ronald Reagan's popular campaign platform of tax cuts, fewer regulations, smaller government, and a tougher stand against the Soviet Union helped Republicans gain majority control of the Senate in 1980 and attract many new voters to the party. Reagan and his staff negotiated important arms control agreements with the Soviet Union, efforts that accelerated under Reagan's successor, George H. W. Bush. Bush led American and international participation in the Persian Gulf War during 1990 and 1991, which succeeded in removing Iraqi forces from Kuwait with minimal American casualties.

Democrat Bill Clinton's presidency was marked by passage of the North American Free Trade Agreement, welfare reform, arms control agreements, successful peacekeeping efforts by U.S. troops in Haiti and the Balkans, one of the longest periods of economic growth in U.S. history, and the first balanced budgets since the 1960s. However, despite efforts to cultivate public support for health care reform, congressional and public opposition doomed Clinton's proposals. The same factors delayed peacekeeping efforts in Bosnia and Kosovo and deterred American efforts to stop the genocide from civil war in Rwanda. President George W. Bush's two terms were marked by substantial achievements in domestic policy, such as the No Child Left Behind education reforms, but his presidency will be remembered mostly for his response to the 9/11 attacks, including the Patriot Act's restrictions on civil liberties and the wars in Iraq and Afghanistan. President Obama has secured several notable changes in foreign and domestic policy, such as the enactment of health insurance reform and the end of active military operations in Iraq. However, he had to compromise on many of these questions, and in other cases, such as his efforts to enact comprehensive immigration reform, he was completely unsuccessful in his first term. In this chapter, we examine these and other presidential successes and failures in order to understand the limits of presidential power.

PRESIDENT FRANKLIN DELANO Roosevelt called on the public to support his New Deal programs and other policies. Here, he delivers one of his "fireside chat" radio broadcasts, designed to communicate his arguments to the American people and win their support.

constitutional authority (presidential) Powers derived from the provisions of the Constitution that outline the president's role in government.

statutory authority (presidential) Powers derived from laws enacted by Congress that add to the powers given to the president in the Constitution.

THE PRESIDENT'S JOB DESCRIPTION

DESCRIBE THE CONSTITUTIONAL AND STATUTORY POWERS OF THE PRESIDENT TODAY

This section describes both the president's **constitutional authority**, which derives from the provisions of the Constitution that identify the president's governmental role, and his **statutory authority**, which comes from laws that give the president additional responsibilities. These powers are summarized in Nuts and Bolts 10.1. As the box indicates, some presidential powers arise from one source, such as the Constitution, while others derive from a combination of constitutional and statutory authority. Our aim is to show how these provisions operate in modern-day American politics: what kinds of opportunities and constraints they create for the current president and future holders of the office.

HEAD OF THE EXECUTIVE BRANCH

vesting clause Article II, Section 1, of the Constitution, which states that "executive Power shall be vested in a President of the United States of America," making the president both the head of government and the head of state.

head of government One role of the president, through which he or she has authority over the executive branch.

head of state One role of the president, through which he or she represents the country symbolically and politically.

The president's job description begins with the list of constitutional responsibilities of the office. The Constitution's **vesting clause**, "The executive Power shall be vested in a President of the United States of America," makes the president the **head of government**, granting him authority over the executive branch, as well as the **head of state**, serving as the symbolic and political representative of the country. The Constitution also places the president in charge of the implementation of laws, saying, "he shall take Care that the Laws be faithfully executed."

Sometimes the implementation of a law is nearly automatic, and all the president needs to do is ensure that bureaucrats use proper, lawful procedures to accomplish the implementation. More commonly, the president's authority to implement the law requires using judgment to translate legislative goals into programs, budgets, and regulations. For example, the bank bailout legislation enacted in late 2008 gave bureaucrats in the Bush (and later the Obama) administration funds to be used to help banks and other companies in financial distress but let the bureaucrats decide who would receive the money, how much, and under what terms.[12] Similarly, the Military Commissions Act of 2006 established the goal of using military tribunals to review evidence against terror suspects but allowed President Bush and his appointees to determine these tribunals' procedures—such as whether defendants could see classified information that was part of the evidence against them and whether evidence obtained through coercive interrogation could be used in the trials.[13] Presidents and their staff can also delay implementation of a law, either to avoid putting in place new policies they disapprove of or to give them time to lobby Congress to reverse the decision.

Finally, the president's control of the executive branch enables him to issue orders to government agencies that make significant policy changes. For example, in April 2010 President Obama directed the Department of Health and Human Services to prohibit discrimination against gay and lesbian couples in hospital visitation rules.[14] While this order could be overturned by Congress, the president's ability to act unilaterally in this way conveys significant power: unless opponents in Congress can organize, write appropriate legislation, shepherd it through the House and Senate, and override a presidential veto, the president's decision will prevail.

APPOINTMENTS

The president appoints ambassadors, senior bureaucrats, and members of the federal judiciary, including Supreme Court justices.[15] As head of the executive branch, the president controls about 8,000 positions, ranging from high-profile jobs such as secretary of state to routine administrative and secretarial positions. About 1,200 of these appointments—generally high-level positions such as cabinet secretaries—require Senate confirmation. In the main, the Senate approves the majority of the president's nominees without much debate or controversy, with exceptions concentrated in defense, intelligence, and justice positions.

In addition, presidents make nominations to the federal courts; Presidents Bill Clinton and George W. Bush each appointed more than 400 judges. Because federal judgeships are lifetime appointments, they enable the president to put people into positions of power who will remain after he leaves office. For example, President George W. Bush appointed two conservative justices to the Supreme Court whose impact was immediately apparent in a series of Court decisions released in 2007 on issues such as abortion rights, gun control, and affirmative action.[16]

THE PRESIDENT AS HEAD OF THE EXECUTIVE BRANCH

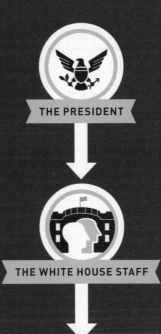

THE PRESIDENT

THE WHITE HOUSE STAFF

White House Office
Office of Management & Budget
Council of Economic Advisers
National Security Council
Office of National Drug Control Policy
Office of the U.S. Trade Representative

Council on Environmental Quality
Office of Science & Tech. Policy
Office of Policy Development
Office of Administration
Vice President

EXECUTIVE OFFICE OF THE PRESIDENT

Examples:
Federal Election Commission
Federal Trade Commission
Social Security Administration
National Transportation Safety Board

INDEPENDENT AGENCIES & GOV. CORPORATIONS

THE CABINET

Dept. of Housing & Urban Development
Dept. of the Interior
Dept. of Commerce
Dept. of Labor
Dept. of Education
Dept. of Transportation
Dept. of Energy
Dept. of Veterans Affairs
Dept. of Justice
Dept. of Defense
Dept. of State
Dept. of Homeland Security
Dept. of Health & Human Services
Dept. of the Treasury
Dept. of Agriculture

POP QUIZ!

1 The president has direct control over the cabinet departments, but his control of _____ is more limited.

  a the White House staff

  b the Executive Office of the President

  c the Cabinet

  d the independent agencies

  e the vice president

2 Officials who serve on the National Security Council and the Council of Economic Advisers are part of the

  a White House staff.

  b Executive Office of the President.

  c Cabinet.

  d independent agencies.

  e government corporations.

Answers: 1.d; 2.b

PRESIDENTIAL POWERS

Constitutional Authority	Statutory Authority	Other
Head of government, head of state (vesting clause)		Executive privilege
Implementation of laws ("faithful execution")	Implementation of laws (as directed in statutes)	Recommend annual federal budget and other legislative initiatives
Executive orders and similar directives (rare)	Executive orders and similar directives	
Administer executive branch		
Nominations and appointments to executive branch and judiciary	Nominations and appointments to executive branch and judiciary	
Commander in chief of armed forces		
Negotiation of treaties and executive agreements	Negotiation of treaties and executive agreements	
Veto of congressional actions		
Presidential pardons		
Other ceremonial powers		

The Senate approves the vast majority of the president's nominees without much controversy, but the need for Senate confirmation of his appointments fundamentally limits this presidential power. Rather than demanding that the Senate vote on every nomination, presidents have often compromised by withdrawing the most controversial names and proposing other candidates who are more satisfactory to the Senate. For example, President Obama's nominee for secretary of health and human services, former senator Tom Daschle, withdrew his name from consideration after it was revealed that he had to pay more than $100,000 in back taxes for the use of a car and driver while he was a lobbyist.[17]

One way the president can temporarily dodge the need for Senate approval is to make a **recess appointment** during a period when Congress is not in session. These appointments, however, are temporary, lasting only for the rest of the legislative term. By making recess appointments, the president can fill vacant ambassadorships or designate heads of cabinet departments without waiting for a Senate vote. This provision was included in the Constitution because it was expected that Congress would not be in session for much of the year; but in the modern era, when Congress is in session almost continuously, recess appointments are sometimes used to bypass the confirmation process for controversial nominees.

EXECUTIVE ORDERS

Presidents have the power to issue **executive orders**, proclamations that unilaterally change government policy without subsequent congressional consent.[18] (Presidents can also issue other kinds of orders that change policy, such as National Security Presidential Directives and Presidential Findings.) One executive order issued by President Obama on December 29, 2009, changed the guidelines for

recess appointment Selection by the president of a person to be an ambassador or the head of a department while the Senate is not in session, thereby bypassing Senate approval. Unless approved by a subsequent Senate vote, recess appointees serve only to the end of the congressional term.

executive orders Proclamations made by the president that change government policy without congressional approval.

classified information, declaring that if there is significant doubt about the need to classify information, it should not be classified. Another executive order, issued on January 17, 2010, mobilized some reserve military personnel to participate in relief operations after the earthquake in Haiti.

It has been estimated that more than 1,000 executive orders issued between 1949 and 1999 were the subject of press coverage, congressional hearings, litigation, scholarly articles, or presidential public statements.[19] Most adressed relatively minor matters. However, some executive orders, such as the one about classifying information, make significant policy changes.

Executive orders may appear to give the president authority to do whatever he wants, even when facing strong opposition from Congress. However, a president's power to issue executive orders is limited. In many cases, Congress enacts a law giving presidents the authority to issue an executive order on a particular question. Moreover, regardless of the authority used to issue an order, if members object to the policy changes, they can work to pass a law overturning any executive orders or deny funding to implement them—although they would need support from two-thirds of both houses to override the expected presidential veto. The threat of congressional response often influences the specifics of executive orders, so that they reflect a compromise between what the president wants and what the members of Congress are willing to tolerate.

COMMANDER IN CHIEF

The Constitution makes the president the commander in chief of America's military forces but gives Congress the power to declare war. These provisions are potentially contradictory, and the Constitution leaves open the broader question of who controls the military.[20] In practice, however, the president controls day-to-day military operations through the Department of Defense and has the power to order troops into action without explicit congressional approval. This happened in 2002 when President George W. Bush deployed more than 100,000 troops, hundreds of aircraft, and dozens of warships in anticipation of action against Iraq. Although Congress eventually passed a resolution authorizing combat operations against Iraq, this happened after the deployments had occurred. (Subsequent deployments of troops to Iraq and Afghanistan also occurred without further congressional approval.)

Congress has the power to declare war, but this power by itself does not constrain the president. In fact, even though the United States has been involved in hundreds of military conflicts since the Founding, there have been only five declarations of war: the War of 1812, the Mexican-American War (1846), the Spanish-American War (1898), World War I (1917), and World War II (1941). However, especially in recent years, members of Congress have used other methods to try to constrain presidential war-making powers.

In particular, Congress enacted the War Powers Resolution in 1973 (see Nuts and Bolts 10.2). However, between 1975 and 2003, despite dozens of U.S. military actions—ranging from embassy evacuations to large-scale operations, including the 1991 Persian Gulf War and the invasions of Iraq and Afghanistan—the War Powers Resolution has been invoked only once.[21] Moreover, despite being in effect for nearly 40 years, it has never faced Supreme Court review. Some scholars have argued that the resolution actually expands presidential power because it gives the president essentially unlimited control for the first 90 days of a military operation.[22]

Despite its limitations, the War Powers Resolution has forced presidents to gain congressional approval, in the form of congressional resolutions, for large-scale military actions such as the invasion of Iraq, as well as for lesser operations such as the deployments of peacekeeping forces in Bosnia during the 1990s. Members of Congress can also curb a president's war-making powers through budget restrictions, legislative prohibitions, and, ultimately, impeachment (we discuss impeachment later in this chapter).[23]

TREATY MAKING AND FOREIGN POLICY

Treaty-making power is shared between Congress and the president: presidents and their staff negotiate treaties; these are then sent to the Senate for approval, which requires the support of a two-thirds majority. Congress considers trea-

10.2 NUTS & bolts

THE WAR POWERS RESOLUTION OF 1973

1. The president is required to report to Congress any introduction of U.S. forces into hostilities or imminent hostilities.

2. The use of force must be terminated within 60 days unless Congress approves of the deployment. The time limit can be extended to 90 days if the president certifies that additional time is needed to safely withdraw American forces.

3. The president is required whenever possible to consult with Congress before introducing American forces into hostilities or imminent hostilities.

4. Any congressional resolution authorizing the continued deployment of American forces will be considered under expedited procedures.

Source: Richard F. Grimmett, "The War Powers Resolution: After Thirty Years," Congressional Research Service Report RL32267, March 11, 2004.

ties only after negotiations have ended; there is no way for members of Congress to force the president to negotiate a treaty. However, the need for congressional approval often leads presidents to consider senators' preferences when negotiating treaties, leading again to significant compromise between the two branches.

Presidents have two strategies for avoiding a congressional treaty vote. One is to announce that the United States will voluntarily abide by a treaty without ratifying it. President Clinton used this tactic to implement the 1997 Kyoto Protocol, an agreement that set limits on carbon emissions by industrialized nations.[24] It is also possible to structure a deal as an **executive agreement** between the executive branch and a foreign government, which does not require Senate approval. Relative to a ratified treaty, which remains in force after the president who negotiated it leaves office, both voluntary compliance and executive agreements have the disadvantage that a subsequent president can simply undo the action. For example, President George W. Bush did this in the case of compliance with the Kyoto Protocol.

The president also serves as the principal representative of the United States in foreign affairs other than treaty negotiations. These duties include communicating with foreign leaders, nongovernmental organizations, and even ordinary citizens to persuade them to act in what the president believes is in the United States' interest. For example, in June 2009, President Obama gave a speech in Cairo, Egypt, aimed at "convincing people throughout the Middle East of America's sympathy to their concerns, such as the creation of a Palestinian state."[25]

The amount of time the president devotes to foreign policy is subject to world events and therefore is not entirely under his control. George W. Bush campaigned on the priorities of tax cuts and education reform[26] and against nation-building abroad. Nonetheless, in response to the September 11 attacks, he initiated efforts to build stable democracies in Afghanistan and Iraq.[27] Similarly, Barack Obama campaigned on a largely domestic agenda but spent considerable time reformulating American policy in Iraq and Afganistan, as well as on trips and speeches such as the one concerning the Middle East mentioned earlier.

executive agreement An agreement between the executive branch and a foreign government, which acts as a treaty but does not require Senate approval.

AS HEAD OF STATE, THE PRESIDENT often negotiates agreements with other countries. In 2009, President Obama visited China and met with Chinese president Hu Jintao and other officials to discuss a number of issues, including exchange rates, human rights, and cooperation on sanctions against Iran.

LEGISLATIVE POWER

The Constitution establishes lawmaking as a shared power between the president and Congress, meaning that compromise is fundamental to this activity.[28] The president can recommend policies to Congress, notably in the annual **State of the Union** address. The president and his staff also work with members of Congress to develop legislative proposals, and although the president cannot formally introduce legislation, it is typically easy to find a member of Congress willing to sponsor a presidential proposal.[29] Presidents and their legislative staff also spend time lobbying members of Congress to support their proposals and negotiating with legislative leaders over policy details.

The president's legislative power also stems from the ability to veto legislation (see Chapter 9). Once both chambers of Congress have passed a bill by simple majority, the president must decide within two weeks whether to sign it or issue a veto. Signed bills become law, but vetoed bills return to the House and Senate for a vote to override the veto. If both chambers enact the bill again with at least two-thirds majorities, the bill becomes law; otherwise it is defeated. If Congress adjourns before the president has made his decision, the president can pocket veto the proposal by not responding to it. Pocket vetoes cannot be overridden, but congressional leaders can avoid them by keeping Congress in session for two weeks after a bill is enacted, thereby forcing the president either to sign the bill or to veto it.

Studies show that vetoes are most likely to occur under divided government, when a president from one party faces a House and Senate controlled by the other party.[30] Under these conditions, the veto allows the president to block proposals supported by legislators from the other party, producing gridlock.[31] Vetoes are much less likely under unified government, when one party controls Congress and the presidency, because the chances are much higher that the president and legislators from his party hold similar policy priorities. By vetoing legislation, presidents gain raw power over the legislative process and can stop a proposal dead in its tracks unless it has strong support in both houses of Congress.

Democratic president Bill Clinton faced divided government, working with a Republican-controlled Congress for all but the first two of his eight years in office. Republican president George W. Bush, in contrast, had divided government with Democratic control of the Senate during most of his first two years, unified government for the middle four years, and divided government once again when the Democrats took control of Congress in the 2006 midterms. Clinton issued almost 40 vetoes in his eight years in office, whereas Bush vetoed only 11 pieces of legislation in the same time. Bush's low number of vetoes was a consequence of the more unified government he enjoyed while in office. As of late 2012, President Obama has vetoed only two pieces of legislation, reflecting unified government during his first two years in office, and little legislation of consequence passed during the second half of his term.

A president's threats to veto legislation provide an additional source of power: they allow the president to specify what kinds of proposals he is willing or unwilling to accept from Congress. Legislators then know that they need to write a proposal that attracts two-thirds support in both houses or else accede to the president's demands. For example, during the 2007 debate over funding for the war in Iraq, then-president Bush said he would veto any legislation that included a timetable for troop withdrawal. Whether Bush was willing to follow through with his threat is unclear, but the threat worked. The funding bill that ultimately passed Congress did not include any sort of timetable. In this sense, the veto power can facilitate

State of the Union An annual speech in which the president addresses Congress to report on the condition of the country and recommend policies.

compromise between presidents and members of Congress—compromises that favor the president's point of view.

While the veto is useful to block legislation or issue a threat that encourages legislators to negotiate before casting their votes, it cannot force members of Congress to enact a proposal they oppose.[32] The president and his staff bargain with legislators, trying to craft proposals that a majority will support and sometimes offering inducements to individual lawmakers, such as presidential support for other favored policies. House members and senators from the president's party may feel obligated to help him, but it is very hard for a president to win over opponents in Congress, especially if helping the president will anger a legislator's constituents. Under these conditions, compromises are likely to favor congressional preferences.

For example, one of President Obama's greatest domestic priorities in 2009 was enactment of health care legislation. Obama made speeches on the subject, held meetings with the public, attended bargaining sessions with legislators from both parties, and dispatched aides to lobby members of Congress in favor of proposals that would reduce the number of uninsured individuals, end the ability of insurance companies to deny coverage for preexisting conditions, and, in theory, reduce the rate of increase in health care costs. However, although Obama's goals were popular, his proposals were not. As public opposition increased, congressional support even among Democrats began to waver, and Republicans were unified in their opposition. Although Obama ultimately prevailed and health care legislation was enacted in 2010, the president had to make significant compromises to win support from reluctant Democrats—and he was unable to bridge the conflict with congressional Republicans. So although enactment of health care reform is rightly cited as an example of presidential power, it also illustrates the limits of this power.

In sum, by using a combination of their proposal power, lobbying, issuing vetoes and veto threats, and the other powers discussed in this section, presidents have considerable—but not unlimited—influence over legislative outcomes.

OTHER DUTIES AND POWERS

The Constitution gives the president several additional powers, including the authority to pardon people convicted of federal crimes or commute their sentences. The only limit on this power is that a president cannot pardon anyone who has been impeached and convicted by Congress. (Thus, if a president is removed from office via impeachment, he can neither pardon himself nor be pardoned when his vice president assumes the presidency.)

Although most presidential pardons attract little attention, some have been extremely controversial. Presidents have pardoned their own appointees for crimes committed while serving in their administrations, as well as campaign contributors and personal friends. In July 2007, President Bush commuted a thirty-month jail term given to Lewis "Scooter" Libby, Vice President Dick Cheney's former aide. Libby had been convicted of lying to a grand jury about his role in leaking the name of a covert CIA agent to several journalists.

The Constitution also gives the president a number of largely ceremonial powers, such as the power to convene Congress or to adjourn it if legislators cannot agree on an adjournment date. This provision gave the president real power during the early days of the Republic, when Congress was in session for only a few months every year. Now that Congress is in session for most of the year and party leaders set dates for the beginning and end of legislative sessions well in advance, this power is irrelevant. Similarly, the Constitution gives the president the responsibility for receiving ambassadors from other nations by officially recognizing that they speak on behalf of their countries' rulers. The president also signs commissions to formally appoint military officers.

EXECUTIVE PRIVILEGE

executive privilege The right of the president to keep executive branch conversations and correspondence confidential from the legislative and judicial branches.

Finally, although this power is not formally set out in the Constitution or a statute, all presidents have claimed to hold the power of **executive privilege**. This refers to the ability to shield themselves and their subordinates from revealing White House discussions, decisions, or documents (including e-mails) to members of the legislative or judicial branches of government.[33] The nature of executive privilege—exactly what it protects versus what Congress can force the president to release—is an unsettled question. Some constitutional scholars even argue that in legal terms, executive privilege doesn't exist.[34]

Although claims of executive privilege have been made since the ratification of the Constitution in 1789, it is still not clear exactly what falls under the privilege and what does not. In the 1974 case *United States v. Nixon*, a special prosecutor appointed by the Justice Department to investigate the Watergate scandal challenged President Nixon's claims of executive privilege to force him to hand over tapes of potentially incriminating Oval Office conversations involving Nixon and his senior aides. The Supreme Court ruled unanimously that executive privilege does exist, but that the privilege is not absolute. The Court's decision required Nixon to release the tapes, which proved his involvement with attempts to cover up the scandal; but the ruling did not clearly state the conditions under which a future president could withhold such information.[35]

Claims of executive privilege present a dilemma. On the one hand, members of Congress need to know what is happening in the executive branch. In the case of President Nixon and the Watergate scandal, claims of executive privilege allowed the Watergate cover-up to continue for more than a year and would have kept this information secret permanently if the Court had ruled in Nixon's favor.[36] Claims of executive privilege can also weaken accountability to the public, as restricting information may leave the average voter unaware of what an administration

THE PRESIDENT IS THE UNOFFICIAL head of his party and works with fellow party members in government. In 2011, President Obama and the Democrats met with congressional Republicans to try to resolve the conflict between the two parties over the deficit and the national debt.

THE LIMITS OF EXECUTIVE PRIVILEGE

Deciding which information a president can be compelled to release to the public or to other branches of government and what he can keep confidential requires confronting fundamentally political questions. There are no right answers, and the limits of executive privilege remain unclear. On the one hand, members of Congress need facts, predictions, and estimates from the executive branch to make good public policy. More important, members need to be able to weigh the pros and cons of a range of policy alternatives.

Consider the controversy over the Obama administration's grant of federal loan guarantees to the Solyndra Corporation.[a] These loan guarantees were supposed to allow Solyndra to bring cheaper, more efficient solar power panels to market. However, the company's efforts were unsuccessful and it declared bankruptcy in August 2011, at a cost to taxpayers exceeding $500 million. Republican critics in Congress charged that a high-level Obama appointee in the Department of Energy whose wife did legal work for Solyndra had pushed for the loans and that the Obama administration had ignored warnings because they wanted to claim credit for a "green energy" program. There were several congressional investigations during 2011 and 2012, and numerous congressional subpoenas for documents—some of which were challenged by the Obama administration on grounds of executive privilege.

The Solyndra case may seem like a situation in which executive privilege does not apply. Shouldn't the American people know the reasons the loan guarantees were made? If the Energy Department staff did nothing wrong, why wouldn't the Obama administration comply with congressional subpoenas and make their staff available for congressional hearings?

The problem is that testifying before Congress, or even releasing documents in response to a congressional request, is enormously time-consuming and can be surprisingly expensive. Presidential appointees who have testified before Congress have faced personal legal bills of $100,000 or more. If members of Congress could require information and testimony of executive branch employees whenever they wanted, it would be hard for the executive bureaucracy to get anything done—and hard to convince anyone to work there.

Of course, there are two sides to this story. Republicans opposed the loan guarantees on policy grounds, believing that the free market rather than the government should decide which new companies get funded. And of course, the investigations did help to publicize the fact that the Obama administration's decision to lend money to Solyndra was, at least in retrospect, a mistake. But even leaving these concerns aside, it is not surprising that the administration invoked executive privilege, as the costs of complying with the subpoenas in terms of time, effort, and a loss of confidentiality were substantial.

In sum, although being able to get information from a president can help members of Congress make better policy

The Obama administration refused to have some energy department staffers testify before Congress about loans to the Solyndra Corporation, claiming executive privilege.

choices, there are situations in which confidentiality helps the president and his staff make good choices as well. However, executive privilege can also be used to hide crimes or questionable political tactics, or to prevent members of Congress from embarrassing the president by publicizing his mistakes or private comments. Should presidents have an executive privilege? What limits should apply to congressional requests for information and testimony? You decide.

Critical **Thinking Questions**

1. Decisions about executive privilege involve a tradeoff between informing the public and members of Congress about executive branch deliberations, and facilitating the free exchange of information between a president and his or her aides. What criteria or decision rules should determine whether claims of executive privilege are upheld or dismissed?

2. In the case of the Solyndra program, would you allow President Obama to claim executive privilege or force him to release all of the information requested by members of Congress? Would your answer be different if Obama were a Republican?

is doing. On the other hand, the president and his staff need to be able to communicate freely, discussing alternative strategies and hypothetical situations or national security secrets without fearing that they will be forced to reveal conversations that could become politically embarrassing or costly. (Suppose the discussions included political strategies for the next election or a sarcastic remark about jailing their opponents.) Moreover, allowing aides to testify before Congress is enormously time-consuming and can be costly for the aides if they hire lawyers.

Even when executive privilege does not apply (if Congress has not issued a subpoena), presidents can and do refuse to provide information to the media, Congress, or the general public. For example, despite President Obama's promises to increase the transparency of government, his administration did not disclose the specifics of White House negotiations over health care reform, announcing details of the deal only after it was carried out. However, this reluctance is not surprising given the conflict over heath care reform. Disclosure of what participants said in meetings and what they were willing to trade away would be politically embarrassing. In this sense, some confidentiality may be necessary for a president to arrive at the compromises needed to change government policy.

THE PRESIDENT AS POLITICIAN

As head of the executive branch, the president has considerable influence over policy. However, much of what presidents do (or want to do) requires support from legislators, bureaucrats, and ordinary citizens. As a result, the presidency is an inherently political office. The president has to take into account the political consequences of his decisions—both for his own re-election prospects and for the re-election of legislators from his party. He must also contend with the fact that achieving his policy goals often requires bargaining and compromising with others, both inside and outside government.

Presidents try to deliver on their campaign promises not only because they believe in them but also because fulfilling them is politically advantageous. For example, one of President Obama's central campaign promises was to work to restore economic growth, a promise partly fulfilled by the enactment of economic stimulus legislation in 2010. While these measures did not restore robust economic growth by the 2012 elections, Obama gained support from voters who believed that the measures had prevented a more extreme economic downturn. Obama also benefited from the positive impact of the stimulus in swing states such as Ohio.

presidential approval rating The percentage of Americans who feel that the president is doing a good job in office.

The president also typically keeps a close eye on the **presidential approval rating**, a survey-based measurement of the percentage of the public who thinks he is doing a good job in office. Particularly during his first term, one of the president's primary concerns is to build a record that will get him re-elected, and keeping approval levels as high as possible is a crucial part of this strategy. Figure 10.1, which shows approval ratings for the last six presidents who ran for re-election, reveals that first-term presidents with less than 50 percent approval are in real trouble. No recent president has been re-elected with less than a 50 percent approval rating.

THE PRESIDENT AS PARTY LEADER

The president is the unofficial head of his political party and generally picks the day-to-day leadership of the party, or at least has considerable influence over the

FIGURE » 10.1

PRESIDENTIAL POPULARITY AND RE-ELECTION

This figure shows the pre-election year average approval ratings for recent presidents who ran for re-election. It shows that a president's chances of winning re-election are related to his popularity. At what level of approval would you say that an incumbent president is likely to be re-elected?

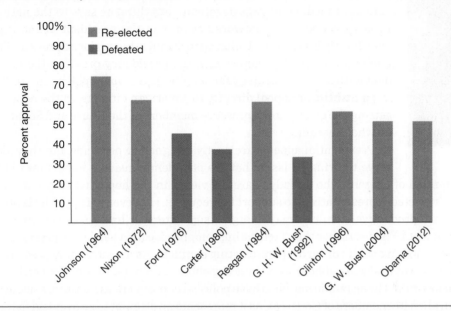

Source: Approval data from the Roper Center for Public Opinion Research, University of Connecticut, "Data Access: Presidential Approval," http://webapps.ropercenter.uconn.edu/CFIDE/roper/presidential/webroot/presidential_rating.cfm (accessed 10/26/12).

selection. This process begins when a presidential candidate captures the party's nomination. For example, soon after Barack Obama became the presumptive Democratic Party nominee by amassing a majority of convention delegates, some of his senior aides and advisers took on leadership positions in the Democratic Party organization.[37]

The president's connection to the party reflects their intertwined interests. The president needs support from his party members in Congress to enact legislation, and the party and its candidates need the president to compile a record of policy achievements that reflect well on the party and to help raise the funds needed for the next election. Therefore, party leaders generally defer to a presidential candidate's (or a president's) staffing requests, and most presidents and presidential candidates take time to meet with national party leaders and the congressional leadership from their party to plan legislative strategies, make joint campaign appearances, and raise funds for the party's candidates.

When presidential approval ratings drop to low levels, most members of Congress see no political advantage in campaigning with the president or supporting his proposals, and they may become increasingly reluctant to comply with his requests. In the 2010 elections, for example, Democratic incumbents in many districts believed that campaigning with President Obama would reduce their chances of re-election,

as it would remind voters of unpopular proposals championed by Obama, such as health care reform and the economic stimulus legislation, both enacted in 2009.

GOING PUBLIC

The president would appear to be in an excellent position to communicate with the American people because of his prominent role and the extensive media coverage devoted to anything he says to the nation. Broadcast and cable networks even give the president prime time slots for his State of the Union speech and other major addresses. The media attention that comes with the presidency provides the president with a unique strategy for shaping government policy: the ability to **go public**, or appeal directly to American citizens, in the hopes of getting the electorate to pressure members of the House and Senate to do what he wants.[38]

Presidential appeals are partly designed to persuade, but they also serve to bring an issue that the president considers important to the attention of citizens who already share his views, in the hope that they will urge their elected representatives to support his requests. However, going public is often counterproductive—while it may energize supporters, it has a similar effect on opponents.[39] Thus, rather than facilitating compromise (or a wholesale presidential victory), going public often deepens existing conflicts. As a result, while presidents might want to shape public opinion by going public, in general they find it hard to be successful.[40] Going public may also have political consequences for the president. It can alienate members of Congress, as it represents an attempt to go over legislators' heads to reach the American people directly, thereby forcing Congress to agree with the president without the benefit of the usual bargaining and negotiations.[41]

President Obama's experiences illustrate the limits and possibilities of going public. During the campaign, his organization made excellent use of social networking sites and e-mail to stay in contact with millions of supporters.[42] This crucial mobilization network helped Obama win the nomination by dominating caucus elections where turnout is low and candidates need to get supporters to the polls. The network proved less useful as a way to lobby Congress in favor of Obama's proposals, such as health care.

PRESIDENTIAL SUCCESSION

Under the Constitution, presidents are limited to two full terms in office. A vice president who becomes president in between elections can, if re-elected, serve two more full terms if he or she takes over during the second half of his predecessor's term; otherwise they can serve only one additional term. Under the Twenty-Fifth Amendment, a vice president can also temporarily take over as president, a procedure used in 2007 when President George W. Bush had a medical procedure requiring anesthesia.[43]

If both the president and the vice president were to die or become incapacitated, the Speaker of the House of Representatives would become president. Next in line is the president pro tempore of the Senate, and then certain cabinet secretaries. Whenever the entire cabinet and Congress gather in one place, such as at the

THE CONSTITUTION MAKES THE president commander in chief but limits that power by giving Congress the power to raise and support armies. When President Obama ordered a "surge" in the number of American troops in Afghanistan in 2009, he needed Congress to approve the $30 billion it was estimated to cost. The day after announcing the decision, Obama made the case for the "surge" in a speech at West Point.

go public A president's use of speeches and other public communications to appeal directly to citizens about issues the president would like the House and Senate to act on.

annual State of the Union address, at least one member of the cabinet is assigned to be somewhere else, so that in the event of a catastrophe someone in the line of succession would survive to assume the presidency.

In the event that the vice president must be replaced due to resignation, impeachment, or incapacity, the Twenty-Fifth Amendment allows the president to nominate a new vice president, who must be confirmed by majority votes in the House and the Senate.

THE EXECUTIVE BRANCH

EXPLAIN HOW THE EXECUTIVE OFFICE OF THE PRESIDENT (EOP), THE VICE PRESIDENT, AND THE CABINET HELP THE PRESIDENT

As head of the executive branch, the president runs a huge, complex organization with hundreds of thousands of employees. This section describes the organizations and staff who help the president exercise his vast responsibilities, from managing disaster-response efforts to implementing policy changes.[44] Among these employees are appointees who hold senior positions in the government. These individuals serve as the president's eyes and ears in the bureaucracy, making sure that bureaucrats are following presidential directives.

Many other executive branch employees work within the Executive Office of the President, which has employed about 1,800 people in recent administrations. About one-third of these employees are concentrated in two offices, the Office of Management and Budget, which develops the president's budget proposals and monitors spending by government agencies, and the Office of the United States Trade Representative, which negotiates trade agreements with other nations.[45]

THE EXECUTIVE OFFICE OF THE PRESIDENT

Nuts and Bolts 10.3 lists the organizations that make up the **Executive Office of the President (EOP)** and one of its main components, the White House Office. Both include offices that have clear policy-related or political missions.

One of the most important duties of EOP staff is helping the president and candidates from his party achieve their policy goals and get re-elected. Consider the Office of National Drug Control Policy (ONDCP). During 2006, representatives from the office traveled throughout the country to hold joint press conferences with Republican and Democratic members of Congress to announce federal grants for drug abuse prevention programs. However, three months before that year's midterm elections, with Republicans in danger of losing majority control of the House and Senate, ONDCP officials began holding press conferences exclusively with Republican legislators.[46] An e-mail from the head of the office revealed that this strategy was an attempt to help vulnerable Republican candidates. In other words, people in the ONDCP did not abandon their official duties, but they also did everything they could to help Republicans in the 2006 election.

The most influential EOP staff occupy the offices in the West Wing of the White House. The West Wing contains the president's office, known as the Oval Office,

Executive Office of the President (EOP) The group of policy-related offices that serves as support staff to the president.

THE EXECUTIVE OFFICE OF THE PRESIDENT

Council of Economic Advisers

Council on Environmental Quality

National Security Council

Office of Administration

Office of Management and Budget

Office of National Drug Control Policy

Office of Science and Technology Policy

Office of United States Trade Representative

President's Foreign Intelligence Advisory Board

White House Office

White House Office

Domestic Policy Council

Homeland Security Council

National Economic Council

Office of Faith-Based and Community Initiatives

Office of the First Lady

Office of National AIDS Policy

Privacy and Civil Liberties Oversight Board

USA Freedom Corps

White House Fellows Office

White House Military Office

and space for the president's chief aide and personal secretary, as well as senior aides such as the vice president, the president's press secretary, and the chief of staff, who coordinates White House operations. Many recent chiefs of staff have been central in the development of policy proposals and negotiations with members of Congress. However, the chief of staff serves as the agent of the president—what matters is what the president wants, not a chief of staff's policy preferences.

Most EOP staff members are presidential appointees who retain their positions only as long as the president who appointed them remains in office, though some EOP offices—such as the Office of Management and Budget, the Office of the United States Trade Representative, and the National Security Council—also have a significant number of permanent staff analysts and experts.[47] When the president appoints people to EOP positions, his primary expectation of them is loyalty rather than a concern for the general public or policy expertise.[48] The president needs staff who understand what he wants the government to do and who will dedicate themselves to implementing his vision.[49] However, the emphasis on loyalty in presidential appointments also has an obvious drawback: appointees may not know much about the jobs they are given and may not be very effective at managing the agencies they are supposed to control. As we discuss in Chapter 11, The Bureaucracy, many observers believe that delays in the provision of federal disaster relief after Hurricane Katrina occurred partly because quite a few senior positions in the Federal Emergency Management Agency were held by political appointees who knew little about such operations.[50]

THE VICE PRESIDENT

As set out in the Constitution, the vice president's job is to preside over Senate proceedings. This largely ceremonial job is usually delegated to the president pro tempore of the Senate, who in turn typically gives the duty to a more junior member. The vice president also has the power to cast tie-breaking votes in the Senate. As mentioned earlier, the vice president's other formal responsibility is to become president if the current president dies, becomes incapacitated, resigns, or is impeached. Of the 44 people who have become president, nine were vice presidents who became president in midterm.

These rather limited official duties of the vice president pale in comparison to the influential role played by recent vice presidents. Vice President Dick Cheney, who served with President George W. Bush, exerted a significant influence over many policy decisions, including the rights of terror suspects, tax and spending policy, environmental decisions, and the writing of new government regulations.[51] Many critics claimed that Cheney had too much power, and some even described him as a co-president.[52]

Although Cheney's level of influence was unique, other recent vice presidents have also had real power. For example, Vice President Al Gore was an important adviser to President Bill Clinton. And Barack Obama's vice president, Joe Biden, appears to play an important role, attending all significant meetings and serving as the last person the president consults before making a decision.

The vice president's role as a senior adviser and trusted confidante is a recent development. Before this change, vice presidents were often chosen to provide political or regional balance to a presidential candidate's electoral appeal. For example, in 1952 Dwight Eisenhower chose then-senator Richard Nixon as his vice president in order to appeal to conservative groups in the Republican Party (but then Eisenhower excluded Nixon from many meetings once in office). The expansion of the federal government beginning in the 1960s appears to have led recent presidents to look beyond political or regional factors when choosing a vice president to find a like-minded individual who can help them manage the bureaucracy and achieve their policy goals. Barack Obama's choice of Joe Biden reflected these priorities, as Biden's foreign policy expertise was expected to offset Obama's relative inexperience in this area.

TODAY, VICE PRESIDENTS ARE MORE influential than they were in the past. President Obama drew on Vice President Joe Biden's foreign policy expertise and entrusted him with numerous important initiatives.

THE PRESIDENT'S CABINET

The president's **Cabinet** is composed of the heads of the 15 executive departments in the federal government, along with other appointees given cabinet rank by the president. Nuts and Bolts 10.4 lists the cabinet positions. The cabinet members' principal job is to be the frontline implementers of the president's agenda in their executive departments. As we discuss in more detail in Chapter 11, they monitor the actions of the lower-level bureaucrats who retain their jobs regardless of who is president and who are not necessarily sympathetic to the president's priorities.

Like other presidential appointees, cabinet members are chosen for a combination of loyalty to the president and expertise. Barack Obama's secretary of transportation, Ray LaHood, a former moderate Republican congressman, had been on the Transportation and Infrastructure Committee while serving in the House of Representatives, so he had a good working knowledge of federal transportation programs. And Secretary of Energy Steven Chu was a Nobel Prize–winning physicist who had directed a major energy research laboratory.

Cabinet The group of 15 executive department heads who implement the president's agenda in their respective positions.

CABINET POSITIONS

The president's Cabinet is composed of the heads of the 15 executive departments along with other appointees given cabinet rank by the president.

Secretary of Agriculture

Secretary of Commerce

Secretary of Defense

Secretary of Education

Secretary of Energy

Secretary of Health and Human Services

Secretary of Homeland Security

Secretary of Housing and Urban Development

Secretary of the Interior

Secretary of Labor

Secretary of State

Secretary of the Treasury

Secretary of Transportation

Secretary of Veterans Affairs

Vice President

White House Chief of Staff

Attorney General

Head of the Environmental Protection Agency

Head of the Office of Management and Budget

Head of the Office of National Drug Control Policy

United States Trade Representative

EXPLAIN HOW AMERICANS EVALUATE PRESIDENTS

THE AMERICAN PUBLIC AND THE PRESIDENT

As we have described, presidents need to cultivate public support to get re-elected and to enact their policy proposals. Thus, to understand the kinds of policy goals presidents set and how they seek to come across to the public, it is important to consider what Americans want from their presidents and which characteristics they associate with a successful president.

Table 10.1 shows survey results about the qualities Americans want in a president. Large majorities want the president to have good judgment and to be ethical and compassionate; smaller majorities want a president who says what he believes, holds consistent positions, and is forceful and decisive. A third or fewer want the president to be willing to compromise, to have political experience and savvy, to have Washington experience, or to be loyal to his party. Relatively few Americans consider military experience an important presidential asset.

Various factors shape presidential popularity. In general, any issue that is at the top of the public's list of most important problems is likely to be reflected in presidential popularity. For example, the slow decline in public support for the war in Iraq, and the increase in the number of people who saw the war as the most important problem, was reflected in a systematic decline in then-president Bush's popularity in 2006 and 2007. By the time the war dropped from the top of the most important problem list, it was replaced by the economy, which did not help Bush's approval ratings because most people were dissatisfied with economic conditions and blamed it on Bush's administration. The slow recovery from poor economic

TABLE » 10.1

CITIZEN DEMANDS ON THE PRESIDENT

These data show that many Americans want the president to stick to his principles, say what he believes, and be forceful and decisive. Fewer consider political experience and willingness to compromise essential presidential qualities. How might the political necessity for bargaining and compromise affect a president's ability to satisfy citizens' expectations?

ESSENTIAL QUALITIES	1995	1999	2003
Sound judgment	76%	78%	76%
High ethical standards	67	63	67
Compassion	64	63	63
Saying what one believes	59	57	56
Consistent positions	51	50	52
Forcefulness and decisiveness	50	46	49
Willingness to compromise	34	33	38
Experience in public office	30	38	37
Political savvy	31	–	36
Experience in Washington	21	27	32
Party loyalty	25	33	30
Military experience	–	–	16

Source: Pew Research Center, "Bush Reelect Margin Narrows to 45%–43%," news release, September 25, 2003, www.people-press.org/reports/pdf/194.pdf (accessed 9/20/12).

conditions also contributed to President Obama's relatively low approval ratings during his first term in office.

As this example indicates, presidential approval is mostly about outcomes, not a president's policies or actions. Approval doesn't arise from voters learning about a president's programs and voicing their support or opposition. Rather, most people look at the world around them, decide whether they like what they see, and express approval or disapproval accordingly. In this sense, presidential approval is to some extent out of a president's control. Bill Clinton enjoyed relatively high approval ratings during most of his eight years in office due to a strong domestic economy, but this economic strength probably had less to do with Clinton's policies than it did with factors that were well beyond Clinton's control. In contrast, Presidents Carter and Ford had the misfortune to be in office at a time when economic conditions were relatively weak and largely out of their control. In this sense, presidential popularity is to some extent a matter of luck.

All presidents have staff and consultants who regularly poll the public to discern its feelings about the president and find out what

PRESIDENTIAL APPROVAL IS influenced by international events that concern Americans, such as the taking of American hostages by militant Iranian students in 1979. President Jimmy Carter initially saw his approval ratings increase, but they declined steadily as the crisis continued into 1980.

actions might increase approval. Political considerations matter somewhat less to a second-term president (since running for re-election is not an option), but politics still matters in the second term. Members of Congress are more likely to support policy initiatives proposed by a popular president, believing that this popularity reflects public support for the president's goals. Conversely, an unpopular president finds it much harder to build support for new programs.[53]

Presidential popularity is more than just a measure of opinion—it is a resource that presidents can draw on to advance their policy agendas. However, high popularity doesn't allow presidents to do whatever they want, nor does low popularity make it impossible to do anything. Moreover, presidential popularity is shaped by factors such as the state of the economy that are only partly under a president's control.

//

ANALYZE WHY PRESIDENTS HAVE BECOME MUCH MORE POWERFUL SINCE THE FOUNDING

ASSESSING PRESIDENTIAL POWER

Throughout American history, presidents have realized major achievements. They have expanded the United States, fought wars, and enacted large government programs. Yet the Constitution grants the president only rather limited powers. Assessing presidential power requires examining this contradiction. Saying that the presidents gained power because of the expansion of the United States or the increased size of the federal budget or bureaucracy tells only part of the story. Why did this power go to the presidents rather than to Congress or to bureaucrats?

Debates over the source and extent of presidential powers have a long history. In the 1790s, Alexander Hamilton and James Madison, writing anonymously as Helvidius and Pacificus, argued about whether George Washington needed congressional approval to declare the United States neutral in the war between Britain and France.[54] Even after more than two centuries, many of the limits to presidential powers—including which executive actions require congressional approval and which ones can be reversed by Congress—are not well defined.

Presidents also derive power from the very fact that they are Head of State and Head of Government. One classic work in presidential studies argues that this influence comes from a president's power to persuade legislators to accept his point of view. Presidents can offer small inducements like visits to the Oval Office and campaign assistance, and they can draw on the natural respect that most people (including members of Congress) feel for the presidency regardless of who holds the office, thereby achieving compromises that enable the president to reach his policy goals.[55] Most presidents have considerable success in their persuasion efforts.

The very ambiguity of the Constitution also creates opportunities for the exercise of presidential power. Consider the president's war-making powers: the Constitution makes the president military commander in chief but gives Congress the power to declare war and to raise and support armies, without specifying which branch of government is in charge of the military. Thus, at least part of presidential authority must be derived or assumed from what the Constitution *does not say*—that is, the ways in which it fails to define or delineate presidential power or grants inherent power to the president.[56]

unilateral action (presidential) Any policy decision made and acted upon by the president and his staff without the explicit approval or consent of Congress.

UNILATERAL ACTIONS AND SIGNING STATEMENTS

Constitutional ambiguities about presidential power have enabled presidents to take **unilateral action**—that is, changing policy on their own without consulting

Congress or anyone else. The 2007 debate over funding the war in Iraq provides a good example. During the debate, many members of Congress wanted to cut off war funding to force the withdrawal of American forces from Iraq; but supporters of the Bush administration maintained that the Constitution's description of the president as commander in chief meant that even if Congress refused to appropriate funds for the war, the president could (1) order American forces to stay in Iraq and (2) order the Treasury Department to spend any funds necessary to continue operations. Ultimately, members of Congress approved a funding resolution.

Even when a president takes a unilateral action, it may not lead to policy change. Presidents and their staffs still have to monitor subsequent actions by bureaucrats to make sure they are implementing the president's decision. Most presidents have tried to control the interpretation and implementation of laws by issuing a **signing statement** when signing a bill into law. These documents, which explain the president's interpretation of the new law, are issued most often when the president disagrees with the interpretation of members of Congress who supported the legislation but still wishes to approve the bill. Presidents issue signing statements so that if the courts have to resolve uncertainties about the bill's intent, judges can take into account not only the views expressed during congressional debates about the bill, but also the president's interpretation of it.[57]

signing statement A document issued by the president when signing a bill into law explaining his interpretation of the law, which often differs from the interpretation of Congress, in an attempt to influence how the law will be implemented.

CONGRESSIONAL RESPONSES TO UNILATERAL ACTION

In theory, members of Congress can undo a president's unilateral action by enacting a law to overturn it, but this is harder than it may sound.[58] Some members of Congress may approve of what the president has done or be indifferent to it, or may give a higher priority to other policies. Still, reversals do happen: after Obama announced plans to close the Guantánamo Bay detention center for terrorist suspects, the House and Senate added an amendment to a spending bill stating that the prison could not be closed until the administration released plans explaining where the prisoners would be sent.

Members of Congress can also write laws in a way that limits the president's authority over their implementation.[59] The problem with this approach is that members of Congress delegate authority to the president or the executive branch bureaucracy for good reasons—either because it is difficult for legislators to predict how a policy should be implemented, or because they cannot agree among themselves on an implementation plan.[60] Members of Congress from the president's party may also want him to have the authority because they hold similar policy goals and would therefore benefit from the exercise of unilateral power.

In sum, ambiguities in the Constitution create opportunities for unilateral presidential action. These actions are subject to reversal through legislation, court decisions, and impeachment, but members of Congress face significant costs if they undertake any of these options. As long as the president is careful to limit the exercise of unilateral power to actions that do not generate intense opposition in Congress, he can implement a wide range of policy goals without official congressional consent—provided that bureaucrats go along with the president's wishes (see Chapter 11). Thus, presidential power has important consequences for government policy—but it is not unlimited.

CONCLUSION

A president's power over government policy is derived from constitutional authority, statutory authority, and ambiguities within these official grants of power that give the president a substantial ability to act unilaterally. Even so, presidential power is limited. The president shares many powers with Congress, including lawmaking, treaty-making, and war-making powers. Moreover, presidents are politicians who need public support, both to win re-election and to persuade members of Congress to approve their policy initiatives. The public evaluates the president based on how he handles issues that are a priority for many Americans, such as the economy, health care, and national security.

These factors suggest a very different explanation for the seemingly expansive power of President Barack Obama, which we discussed at the beginning of this chapter. For one thing, Obama's successes, from fighting terrorist groups to the enactment of health care reform, are not unusual. Many presidents have similar records of accomplishment. Moreover, although Obama enjoyed notable successes, he was forced to compromise in many areas in order to win congressional support. Also, many of Obama's (and other presidents') successful unilateral actions concerned policy areas in which members of Congress and the public either favored their proposals or had no strong feelings about them. Thus, the president remains an important figure in American politics but is clearly not solely responsible for setting government policy.

AMERICA'S PRESIDENTS

▶ Trace the evolution of presidential power over time. **Pages 295–97**

SUMMARY

Presidents get their powers from a variety of sources: some are from the Constitution; others have more informal origins. Although the president's constitutional powers have not changed, presidential power has grown substantially over time. Nonetheless, even presidents' power is still limited in a number of contexts.

PRACTICE QUIZ QUESTION

1. The government's response to the Great Depression was defined by _____.
   a) presidential actions
   b) presidential inaction
   c) congressional action
   d) popular protest
   e) international pressure

THE PRESIDENT'S JOB DESCRIPTION

▶ Describe the constitutional and statutory powers of the president today. **Pages 297–311**

SUMMARY

The president's formal powers arise from a combination of constitutional provisions and laws that give him additional responsibilities. The president has many duties but his primary responsibilities are to oversee the executive branch and implement the laws passed by Congress. While presidents have the authority to focus on domestic policy and foreign policy, most tend to focus on only one aspect.

KEY TERMS

constitutional authority (presidential) (p. 297)

statutory authority (presidential) (p. 297)

vesting clause (p. 298)

head of government (p. 298)

head of state (p. 298)

recess appointment (p. 300)

executive orders (p. 300)

executive agreement (p. 303)

State of the Union (p. 304)

executive privilege (p. 306)

presidential approval rating (p. 308)

go public (p. 310)

PRACTICE QUIZ QUESTIONS

2. Presidents use recess appointments when they are trying to _____.
   a) fill a judicial vacancy outside the scheduled period
   b) fill a vacant seat in Congress
   c) temporarily dodge the need for Senate approval
   d) temporarily dodge the need for House approval
   e) fill vacancies with a permanent replacement

3. A presidential proclamation that unilaterally changes government policy without congressional consent is called _____.
   a) executive privilege
   b) fast track authority
   c) an executive agreement
   d) an executive order
   e) statutory authority

4. The War Powers Resolution was intended to constrain the power of _____.
   a) the president
   b) Congress
   c) the Supreme Court
   d) the Department of Defense
   e) the State Department

5. For most presidents, the problem with going public is that _____.
   a) the public is more focused on Congress
   b) they are not very persuasive
   c) they energize their opponents
   d) they generally address unimportant issues
   e) they do not reach their target audience

⑤ **PRACTICE ONLINE**

"What Do Political Scientists Do?" video exercise: *Ken Mayer on presidential power and executive orders*

THE EXECUTIVE BRANCH

▶ Explain how the Executive Office of the President (EOP), the vice president, and the Cabinet help the president. **Pages 311–14**

SUMMARY

The executive branch is a huge, complex organization that helps the president exercise vast responsibilities. Presidential appointments to the branch serve as eyes and ears on the bureaucracy. Most positions turn over with new administrations.

KEY TERMS

Executive Office of the President (EOP) (p. 311)

Cabinet (p. 313)

CRITICAL THINKING AND DISCUSSION

Why might bureaucrats who are not presidential appointees be more responsive to congressional mandates and demands than to the president's orders, even though the president heads the executive branch?

PRACTICE QUIZ QUESTIONS

6. In most presidential appointments to EOP positions, presidents generally emphasize _____.
   a) experience
   b) expertise
   c) effectiveness
   d) public opinion
   e) loyalty

7. Recent vice presidents have had _____ official duties and/but _____ been influential in their role.
   a) no; have not
   b) limited; have
   c) limited; have not
   d) extensive; have
   e) extensive; have not

THE AMERICAN PUBLIC AND THE PRESIDENT

▶ Explain how Americans evaluate presidents. **Pages 314–16**

SUMMARY

Presidential popularity is critical for presidents to get re-elected and enact their policy proposals. Nonetheless, presidential popularity itself is affected by factors that may not actually be influenced by the president himself.

CRITICAL THINKING AND DISCUSSION

Why do you think Americans often hold the president more accountable than Congress for the state of the economy?

PRACTICE QUIZ QUESTIONS

8. Most Americans want a president who is _____; while few Americans want a president who is _____.
   a) consistent; decisive
   b) consistent; politically savvy
   c) politically savvy; decisive
   d) politically savvy; consistent
   e) decisive; consistent

9. Presidential approval is generally based on _____.
   a) policy outcomes
   b) policy positions
   c) presidential actions
   d) presidential appointments
   e) an absence of scandals

10. Presidents in their second term worry about public opinion _____ than/as presidents in their first term.
    a) much more
    b) somewhat more
    c) somewhat less
    d) far less
    e) to the same degree

Ⓢ PRACTICE ONLINE

"Critical Thinking" exercise: *Politics Is Conflictual–Presidential Approval Ratings*

ASSESSING PRESIDENTIAL POWER

▶ Analyze why presidents have become much more powerful since the Founding. **Pages 316–18**

SUMMARY

While presidents have gained much power over time, the Constitution grants the president rather limited powers. The growth of presidential power is closely related to the reality that most of the limits are not well defined, and presidents have been successful at taking advantage of these constitutional ambiguities.

KEY TERMS

unilateral action (presidential) (p. 316)
signing statement (p. 317)

CRITICAL THINKING AND DISCUSSION

What can members of Congress do to stop a president from changing policy unilaterally? Which of these methods seems most effective, and why?

PRACTICE QUIZ QUESTIONS

11. Most presidents use a(n) _____ to control the interpretation and implementation of laws.
    a) line item veto
    b) recess appointment
    c) executive order
    d) signing statement
    e) pocket veto

12. Congressional challenges to presidential authority are _____ used, and are generally _____ at constraining presidential power.
    a) rarely; successful
    b) rarely; unsuccessful
    c) commonly; successful
    d) commonly; unsuccessful

Ⓢ PRACTICE ONLINE

"Big Think" video exercise: *What Is the Case for a Strong Executive?*

SUGGESTED READING

Alter, Jonathan. *The Promise: President Obama, Year One.* New York: Simon and Schuster, 2010.

Canes-Wrone, Brandice. *Who Leads Whom? Presidents, Policy, and the Public.* Chicago: University of Chicago Press, 2006.

Howell, William G. *Power without Persuasion: The Politics of Direct Presidential Action.* Princeton, NJ: Princeton University Press, 2003.

Krehbiel, Keith. *Pivotal Politics: A Theory of U.S. Lawmaking.* Chicago: University of Chicago Press, 1998.

Lewis, David E. *Presidents and the Politics of Agency Design.* Palo Alto, CA: Stanford University Press, 2003.

Mayer, Kenneth. *With the Stroke of a Pen: Executive Orders and Presidential Power.* Princeton, NJ: Princeton University Press, 2001.

Neustadt, Richard E. *Presidential Power and the Modern Presidents: The Politics of Leadership from Roosevelt to Reagan.* New York: Free Press, 1990.

Rudalevige, Andrew. *Managing the President's Program: Presidential Leadership and Legislative Policy Formation.* Princeton, NJ: Princeton University Press, 2002.

Skowronek, Stephen. *The Politics Presidents Make: Leadership from John Adams to Bill Clinton.* Cambridge, MA: Harvard University Press, 1997.

11

The Bureaucracy

THE FEDERAL HOUSING FINANCE Agency (FHFA) supervises corporations responsible for the mortgages on millions of American homes. In 2011, the FHFA came into conflict with the Obama administration over a plan to help homeowners who were unable to make their mortgage payments and risked losing their homes to the bank.

MILLIONS OF AMERICANS WORK IN THE FEDERAL bureaucracy. Most of the time, their workdays involve routine actions that attract little attention from elected officials or the general public. However, even professional bureaucrats who were hired for their technical expertise—rather than their connections to a politician or party—can find themselves at the center of political conflict. Consider the case of Edward DeMarco, acting director of the Federal Housing Finance Agency (FHFA) in 2011.[1]

One of the primary roles of DeMarco's agency is to supervise two federally sponsored corporations, the Federal National Mortgage Association and the Federal Home Loan Mortgage Corporation (also known as Fannie Mae and Freddie Mac), that own trillions of dollars of home mortgages. If you or your parents own a home with a mortgage, your monthly payment may well go to one of these agencies. After the sharp declines of housing prices in 2007–08, Fannie Mae and Freddie Mac required federal bailouts totaling over $170 billion, and their futures are now uncertain.

The conflict DeMarco faced involved the Obama administration's attempts in 2010 and 2011 to help homeowners whose mortgages were "under water"— meaning their homes were worth less than they owed on their mortgages. Obama proposed new regulations that would encourage mortgage-holding corporations to reduce the amount owed, thereby shrinking homeowners' monthly payments and enabling them to continue paying their mortgages rather than abandoning their homes to foreclosure.

CONFLICT &
COMPROMISE
in American Politics

323

These programs could be implemented only if DeMarco certified that they would be "loss minimizing" for Fannie Mae and Freddie Mac—that the two corporations would be better off because reduced mortgages were more likely to be repaid. Based on his assessment of the programs, DeMarco refused. His decision did not appear to reflect political considerations or opposition to the Obama administration's initiatives. Rather, DeMarco was following the legal mandate of the FHFA as he interpreted it and trying to do what was best for the agency. This is not to say that the Obama administration didn't want what was best for Fannie Mae and Freddie Mac; rather, the situation was one in which reasonable people could disagree about the consequences of the proposed policy.

The Obama administration attempted to sidestep DeMarco by finding a new permanent head of the FHFA or by removing DeMarco in favor of a different acting director who presumably would be more sympathetic to their initiatives. However, these efforts were blocked by congressional disapproval and by regulations that make it hard to remove bureaucrats from their positions. Ultimately, the Obama plan was rewritten to eliminate the aspects that DeMarco objected to, and as of summer 2012, DeMarco remained in his position at the FHFA.

This case highlights just one instance of conflict and compromise within the federal bureaucracy. It also illustrates the impact of bureaucratic agencies on life in America. The bureaucracy, it seems, is everywhere. Americans encounter the work of government employees every day: when they sort through mail delivered by the Postal Service, drive on highways funded by the Department of Transportation, or purchase food inspected by the Food and Drug Administration. The prices Americans pay to surf the Web, watch television, or use a cell phone are influenced by regulations issued by the Federal Communications Commission. When Americans go on vacation, their bags are inspected by the Transportation Security Administration; the aircraft and pilots are scrutinized by the Federal Aviation Administration, and the beaches may be maintained by the Army Corps of Engineers.

While many federal bureaucrats work diligently to serve the American public, examination of what they do and how they do it reveals a paradox: the same organization that accomplishes so many huge tasks also does things that are inefficient, wasteful, and downright dumb. Do these shortcomings result from inevitable accidents, or are they the consequences of deliberate actions? And if so, why are agencies designed to fail or to do things that look a lot like failure?

In this chapter, we show that it's possible to explain many bureaucratic failures in terms of the bureaucracy's complex decision-making procedures and the political conflicts that ensue when elected officials and interest groups attempt to control bureaucrats' actions. These conflicts underlie many seemingly inexplicable bureaucratic actions and outcomes. For example, the need to monitor bureaucrats to ensure that they carry out congressional mandates often leads to rigid procedures that make it impossible for bureaucrats to shift policies in light of changing circumstances. In many cases, these structures reflect compromises among lawmakers holding different ideas of what bureaucrats should do. In this sense, the bureaucracy is just like Congress, multinational corporations, or other large enterprises that have many employees and undertake complex tasks.

This chapter also shows that the public's disdain for bureaucrats is not uniform. Most Americans award higher ratings to government agencies and offices with which they have personal experience. Similarly, most bureaucrats believe deeply in their agency's mission and work hard to achieve its goals.

WHAT IS THE FEDERAL BUREAUCRACY?

> **DEFINE BUREAUCRACY AND EXPLAIN ITS MAJOR FUNCTIONS**

The federal **bureaucracy** that makes up the government's executive branch comprises millions of **civil servants**, who work for the government in permanent positions, and thousands of **political appointees** holding short-term, usually senior positions, who are appointed by the president. Another name for the bureaucracy is the administrative state, or the state.

bureaucracy The system of civil servants and political appointees who implement congressional or presidential decisions; also known as the administrative state.

civil servants Employees of bureaucratic agencies within the government.

political appointees People selected by an elected leader, such as the president, to hold a government position.

WHAT DO BUREAUCRATS DO?

The task of the bureaucracy is to implement policies established by congressional acts or presidential decisions. These tasks are summarized in Nuts and Bolts 11.1. Sometimes the tasks are very specific. For example, in the appropriations bill for fiscal year 2010, Congress mandated a 3.4 percent pay increase for military personnel and funds for certain new military equipment.[2] These provisions required no discretion on the part of the bureaucrats who implement them. Their tasks were limited to making the administrative changes necessary to raise military pay and following through with the purchase of specified equipment.

More commonly, however, legislation determines only the general guidelines for meeting governmental goals, allowing bureaucrats to develop specific policies and programs. In these cases, bureaucrats' actions constitute the essence of government action, determining "who gets what, when, and how."[3] For example, the 1938 Federal Food, Drug, and Cosmetic Act gave the Food and Drug Administration

(FDA) the job of determining which drugs are safe and effective, but it allowed FDA bureaucrats to develop their own procedures for making these determinations.[4]

In general, the job of the federal bureaucracy includes a wide range of activities, from regulating the behavior of individuals and corporations to buying everything from pencils to jet fighters. These activities are inherently political and often conflictual: ordinary citizens, elected officials, and bureaucrats themselves often disagree about aspects of these activities, and they work to influence bureaucratic actions to suit their own goals.

REGULATIONS

regulation A rule that allows the government to exercise control over individuals and corporations by restricting certain behaviors.

A **regulation** is a government rule that affects the choices that individuals or corporations make. It does so by either allowing or prohibiting behavior, setting out the conditions under which certain behaviors can occur, or assessing costs or granting benefits based on behavior. Consider deepwater offshore drilling, which became an issue in 2010 after an explosion at a BP oil well in the Gulf of Mexico created a massive oil spill. That crisis focused attention on a government agency known as the Minerals Management Service, which regulates every aspect of the drilling process—from how many lifeboats should be on a rig to what kinds of hardware should be used to drill and maintain the well site on the ocean floor. Bureaucrats gain the authority to write regulations by the statute that establishes their agency or by a subsequent act of Congress.

notice and comment procedure A step in the rule-making process in which proposed rules are published in the Federal Register and made available for debate by the general public.

Regulations are developed according to the **notice and comment procedure**.[5] Before a new regulation can take effect, it must be published in the *Federal Register*, an official publication that includes rules, proposed rules, and other types of government documents. Individuals and companies that will be affected by the regulation can then respond to the agency that proposed it, either supporting or opposing it, and offering different versions for consideration. Those potentially affected can also appeal to members of Congress or to the president's staff for help in getting the proposed rule revised. The agency then issues a final regulation, incorporating changes based on the comments. This final regulation is also published in the *Federal Register* and then put into effect.

The process of devising or modifying regulations is often political. Members of Congress and the president usually have strong opinions about how new reg-

11.1 **NUTS** *& bolts*

WHAT DO BUREAUCRATS DO?

The fundamental job of the bureaucracy is to implement executive orders and legislation enacted by Congress. To this end, bureaucrats take a variety of actions each day, such as

▶ Develop and enforce regulations that shape choices made by individuals and corporations

▶ Purchase goods and services for the federal government, from office space to pencils and fighter aircraft

▶ Deliver services to Americans, such as mail delivery and student loans

▶ Do research and development on health care and other scientific questions

▶ Manage contractors who provide services to the government and to individuals

ulations should look—and even when they don't, they may still get involved on behalf of a constituent or interest group. Bureaucrats take account of these pressures for two reasons. First, the bureaucrats' policy-making power may derive from a statute that members of Congress could overturn if they disapprove of bureaucrats' actions. Second, bureaucrats need congressional support to get larger budgets and more important tasks for their agency, and to prevent budget cuts. Thus, despite bureaucrats' power to implement policies, their agencies' budgets, appointed leaders, and overall missions are subject to elected officials' oversight.

Federal regulations affect every aspect of everyday life. They influence the gas mileage of cars sold in the United States, the materials used to build roads, and the price of gasoline. They determine the amounts that doctors can charge senior citizens for medical procedures; the hours that medical residents can work; and the criteria used to determine who gets a heart, lung, or kidney transplant. Regulations set the eligibility criteria for student loans, limit how the military can recruit on college campuses, determine who can get a home mortgage and what their interest rate will be, and describe what constitutes equal funding for men's and women's college sports teams. Regulations also shape contribution limits and spending decisions in political campaigns.

Regulations are often controversial because they involve trade-offs between incompatible goals as well as decisions made under uncertain circumstances. For example, the FDA drug approval process prioritizes the goal of preventing harmful drugs from coming to market.[6] As a result, patients sometimes cannot get access to experimental treatments because FDA approval has not been granted, even when those treatments are the patients' only remaining option.[7] Advocates for patients have argued that people with dire prognoses should be allowed to use an experimental treatment as a potentially life-saving last resort.[8] However, FDA regulations prevent them from doing so except under very special circumstances, arguing that unapproved treatments may do more harm than good and that allowing wider access to these drugs may tempt manufacturers to market new drugs without adequate testing.

PROCUREMENT

Bureaucrats also handle government purchases, buying everything from pencils to aircraft carriers. The General Services Administration (GSA) manages 8,600 buildings owned or leased by the government and a fleet of 208,000 vehicles, and provides government agencies with most of their supplies.[9]

Procurement seems a straightforward task: agencies determine what they need, find out who can supply it, and choose the lowest-cost provider. However, procurement for the federal government can be surprisingly complicated. Consider the purchase of a new model of fighter plane or an attack submarine. Bureaucrats must devise criteria for choosing among designs with very different strengths and weaknesses. Procurement decisions are also shaped by congressional and executive mandates. For example, when the GSA searches for suppliers of a particular product, it often has to give preference to small businesses or firms owned by minorities or veterans. These guidelines are the result of the political process, as elected officials try to shape government actions to suit their own policy goals.

PROVIDING SERVICES

Street-level bureaucrats provide services to help ordinary Americans.[10] These services include certain job-training programs and disaster assistance. In addition, federal employees manage tourist attractions from the National Zoo to the Statue of Liberty to Mount Rushmore. They inspect passenger baggage at airports, monitor aircraft maintenance, and direct aircraft in flight.

RESEARCH AND DEVELOPMENT

Government scientists work in areas from medicine to astronomy to agriculture. Sometimes they do basic research, such as working for the National Institutes of Health to discover mechanisms that govern cell reproduction and death. Government scientists also do applied research, from developing new cancer drugs to improving crop management techniques. Federal funds support research in many universities and corporations that examine similar issues.

MANAGING AND DIRECTING

Some bureaucrats supervise actions taken by people outside government. For example, the Department of Defense uses civilian contractors to provide support services in Afghanistan, from doing laundry to performing maintenance work on planes, trucks, and ships. Many workers at government facilities and public works projects are employees of private corporations working on government contracts.

AFTER NEWS OF AN $800,000 GSA conference at a Las Vegas resort came to light in 2012, Congress held hearings on the agency's practices. Here, Representative John Mica criticizes the apparent misuse of taxpayer money.

BUREAUCRATIC EXPERTISE AND ITS CONSEQUENCES

Bureaucrats are experts. Even compared to most members of Congress or presidential appointees, the average bureaucrat is a specialist in a certain policy area, with a better grasp of his or her agency's mission. For example, people who hold scientific or management positions in the FDA usually know more about the benefits and risks of new drugs than people outside the agency do. A bureaucracy of experts is an important part of **state capacity**—the knowledge, personnel, and institutions needed to implement policies that benefit society.[11]

RED TAPE AND STANDARD OPERATING PROCEDURES

Despite bureaucrats' policy expertise, their decisions often appear to take too much time, rely on arbitrary judgments of what is important, and have unintended consequences—to the point that actions designed to solve one problem may create worse ones. Many critics cite the abundance of **red tape**, which refers to unnecessarily complex procedures, or **standard operating procedures**, which are the rules that lower-level bureaucrats must follow when implementing policies regardless of whether those rules are applicable. The performance of the Federal Emergency Management Agency (FEMA) after Hurricane Katrina in 2008 is a classic example: while many observers criticized FEMA for taking several days to fully implement disaster relief, FEMA employees were in fact following long-established plans that had been approved by FEMA managers and members of Congress.

There have been many attempts to make the bureaucracy operate more effectively by mandating that bureaucrats make decisions using specific procedures or criteria. Though each of these efforts can claim modest success, none have fundamentally changed the way the government does business. Thus, cases of bureaucratic ineptitude and failed reform efforts raise a critical question: How can an organization full of experts develop such dysfunctional ways of doing business? Bureaucrats are neither clueless nor malevolent. What, then, explains red tape and counterproductive standard operating procedures? The answer is the very strength of the American bureaucracy: its expertise.

Because bureaucrats know things that elected officials do not and because bureaucrats have their own policy goals, it is hard for elected officials to evaluate what bureaucrats are doing. For example, FEMA was criticized for using a cruise ship to house relief workers after Hurricane Katrina, which cost more than it would have to send these employees on a Caribbean cruise. While the contract was expensive, the FEMA staffer who signed the contract may have found that all other options were more expensive or simply not feasible. Without looking deeper into these issues, it is impossible to be sure.

Of course, sometimes bureaucrats simply make mistakes. For example, the FDA has delayed helpful drugs from reaching the market or has approved drugs that were later found to have harmful side effects. However, these decisions may have been justified based on the information available to bureaucrats at the time. Here again, it is hard to say whether bureaucrats are at fault for such decisions.

state capacity The knowledge, personnel, and institutions that the government requires to effectively implement policies.

red tape Excessive or unnecessarily complex regulations imposed by the bureaucracy.

standard operating procedures Rules that lower-level bureaucrats must follow when implementing policies.

DESPITE THEIR POLICY EXPERTISE, bureaucrats still make mistakes. When the Medicare program implemented the Prescription Drug Benefit in 2006, information about the new coverage was available on an easy-to-read website, but the agency soon learned that many seniors who needed the information did not know how to use a web browser.

THE PROBLEM OF CONTROL

problem of control A difficulty faced by elected officials in ensuring that when bureaucrats implement policies, they follow these officials' intentions but still have enough discretion to use their expertise.

principal–agent game The interaction between a principal (such as the president or Congress), who needs something done, and an agent (such as a bureaucrat), who is responsible for carrying out the principal's orders.

The difficulty that elected officials and their staff face when trying to interpret or influence bureaucratic actions is the **problem of control**.[12] A classic example is the **principal–agent game**, which describes an interaction that involves an individual or group (an "agent") acting on behalf of another (the "principal"). In the federal government, for example, the president and Congress are principals, and bureaucrats are agents. An agent may prefer outcomes that the principal does not like. Moreover, because the agent is an expert at the task he has been given, he has private information inaccessible to the principal. The problem for the principal, then, is this: giving the agent very specific orders prevents the agent from acting based on his expertise; but if the principal gives the agent the freedom to make decisions based on expertise, the principal has less control over the agent's actions.

Suppose Congress and the president direct the FDA to shorten its drug approval process. FDA officials might have mandated a lengthy process based on their expert assessment of the best way to screen out harmful drugs. By giving orders that supersede the FDA officials' screening process, elected officials would be sacrificing the valuable bureaucratic expertise behind the policy and risking the hasty approval of unsafe drugs. But if Congress and the president allow FDA bureaucrats to devise their own procedures and regulations, the FDA might use this freedom to pursue goals that have nothing to do with drug safety. For example,

FIGURE » 11.1

HOW AMERICANS VIEW THE FEDERAL BUREAUCRACY

Many Americans believe the bureaucracy is wasteful and inefficient. Note, however, that the magnitude of negative feelings varies over time. Consider the time frame represented on the graph. What happened during these years that might explain the changes in citizens' opinions about the government?

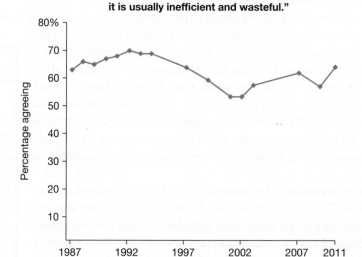

"When something is run by the government, it is usually inefficient and wasteful."

Source: Pew Research Center, "The Generation Gap and the 2012 Elections," Pew Research Center, November 1, 2011, www.people-press.org/files/legacy-pdf/11-3-11%20Generations%20Release.pdf (accessed 9/22/12).

critics of the FDA's procedures have asserted that a drawn-out approval process favors large companies that already have drugs on the market over smaller companies trying to get approval for drugs that would compete with existing products.

The principal–agent game can also be framed in terms of citizens. Figure 11.1 shows that a majority of survey respondents agreed that the federal government is typically inefficient and wasteful—although the percentage agreeing with this assessment declined from its peak in 1992 until recent years, where it again increased. These opinions give citizens a strong motivation to demand that elected officials control the bureaucracy—to reduce the waste and inefficiency that many see as commonplace.

The problem of control has existed throughout the history of the federal government. It affects both the kinds of policies that bureaucrats implement and the structure of the federal bureaucracy, including the number of agencies and their missions, staff, and tasks. Moreover, elected officials use a variety of methods to solve the problem of control, including making it easier for people outside government to learn about agency actions before they take effect. However, all these tactics are at best partial solutions to the problem of control. The trade-off between expertise and control remains.

HISTORY OF THE AMERICAN BUREAUCRACY

> TRACE THE EXPANSION OF THE FEDERAL BUREAUCRACY OVER TIME

The evolution of America's federal bureaucracy was not steady or smooth. Most of its important developments occurred during three short periods: the late 1890s and early 1900s, the 1930s, and the 1960s.[13] In all three periods, the driving force was a combination of demands from citizens for enhanced government services and the desire of people in government to either respond to these demands or increase the size and scope of the federal government in line with their own policy goals.

THE BEGINNING OF AMERICA'S BUREAUCRACY

From the beginning of the United States until the election of Andrew Jackson in 1828, the staff of the entire federal bureaucracy numbered at most in the low thousands. There were only three executive departments (State, Treasury, and War), along with a Postmaster General.[14] The early federal government also performed a narrow range of tasks. It collected taxes on imports and exports and delivered the mail. The national army consisted of a small Corps of Engineers and a few frontier patrols. The attorney general was a private attorney who had the federal government as one of his clients. Members of Congress outnumbered civil servants in Washington; the president had very little staff at all.[15] The small size of the federal government during those years reflected Americans' deep suspicion of government, especially unelected officials.[16]

The election of Andrew Jackson brought the first large-scale use of the spoils system, in which people who had worked in Jackson's campaign were rewarded with new positions in the federal government (usually as local postmasters).[17] The spoils system was extremely useful to party organizations, as it gave them a

THIS CARTOON OF A MONUMENT TO President Andrew Jackson riding a pig decries his involvement in the spoils system, which allowed politicians to dole out government service jobs in return for political support.

federal civil service A system created by the 1883 Pendleton Civil Service Act in which bureaucrats are hired on the basis of merit rather than political connections.

powerful incentive with which to convince people to work for the party—a particularly important tool for Jackson, as his campaign organization was at that time the largest ever organized.

The challenge facing the spoils system was ensuring that these government employees, who often lacked experience in their new fields, could actually carry out their jobs. The solution was to develop procedures so that these employees knew exactly what to do even if they had no experience or training.[18] These instructions became one of the earliest uses of standard operating procedures. They ensured that the government could function even if many employees had been hired in reward for political work rather than because of their qualifications.[19]

As America expanded, so did the federal government, which saw an almost eightfold increase in the bureaucracy between 1816 and the beginning of the Civil War in 1861. This growth did not reflect a fundamental change in what the government did; in fact, much of the increase came in areas such as the Post Office, which needed to serve a geographically larger nation—and, of course, to provide "spoils" for party workers in the form of government jobs.[20] Even by the end of the Civil War, the federal government still had very little involvement in the lives of ordinary Americans. State and local governments provided services such as education, public works, and welfare benefits, if they were provided at all. The federal government's role in daily life was limited to mail delivery, collecting import and export taxes, and a few other areas.

BUILDING A NEW AMERICAN STATE: THE PROGRESSIVE ERA

Changes in the second half of the nineteenth century transformed America's bureaucracy.[21] This transformation began after the Civil War, but the most significant changes occurred during the Progressive Era, 1890–1920. Many laws and executive actions increased the government's regulatory power during this period, including the Sherman Antitrust Act of 1890, the Pure Food and Drug Act of 1906, the Meat Inspection Act, expansion of the Interstate Commerce Commission, and various conservation measures.[22] Now the federal government had an indirect impact on several aspects of everyday life: when Americans bought food or other products, went to work, or traveled, the choices available to them were shaped by the actions of federal bureaucrats.

These developments were matched by a fundamental change in the federal bureaucracy following passage of the 1883 Pendleton Civil Service Act. This measure created the **federal civil service**, in which the merit system (qualifications, not political connections) became the basis for hiring and promoting bureaucrats.[23] In other words, when a new president took office, he could not replace members of the civil service with his own campaign workers. Initially, only about 13,000 federal jobs acquired civil service protections, but subsequently many additional positions were incorporated into the civil service, to the point that today virtually all full-time, permanent government employees have civil service protection. These reforms created a bureaucracy in which people could build a career in government without having to fear being fired when a new president or Congress took office.[24]

When civil service reforms were adopted, their impact on party organizations was well understood. As one New York City machine politician, George Washington Plunkitt, put it, "This civil service law is the biggest fraud of the age. It is the curse of the nation. . . . How are you going to interest our young men in their country if you have no offices to give them when they work for their party?"[25] Plunkitt meant that without the spoils system, organizations like his would be in serious danger of losing their hold on government, as they would be unable to use the promise of a government job to motivate people to help elect the machine's candidates.

THE NEW DEAL, THE GREAT SOCIETY, AND THE REAGAN REVOLUTION

Dramatic expansion of the federal bureaucracy occurred during the New Deal period in the 1930s and during the mid-1960s Great Society era. In both cases, the changes were driven by a combination of citizen demands and the preferences of elected officials who favored an increased role of government in society. This expansion was only marginally curtailed during the Reagan Revolution of the 1980s.

THE NEW DEAL

The New Deal comprised government programs implemented during Franklin Roosevelt's first term as president in the 1930s. These programs were partly a response to the Great Depression and the inability of local governments and private charities to respond to this economic crisis. Many advocates of the New Deal also favored an expanded role for government in American society, regardless of the immediate need for intervention.[26] Roosevelt's programs included reforms to the financial industry as well as efforts to help people directly and to stimulate employment, economic growth, and the formation of labor unions. The Social Security Act, the first federally funded pension program for all Americans, was also passed as part of the New Deal.[27]

These reforms represented a vast increase in the size and responsibilities of the bureaucracy, as well as a large transfer of power to bureaucrats and to the president.[28] Before the New Deal, the federal government influenced citizens' choices through activities such as regulating industries and workplace conditions. Afterward, it took on the role of delivering a wide range of benefits and services directly to individuals, from jobs to electricity, as well as increased regulation of many industries, including the banking and financial industries.

Expansion of the federal government and the subsequent delegation of power to bureaucrats and to the president were controversial changes.[29] Many Republicans opposed New Deal reforms because they believed that the federal government could not deliver services efficiently and that an expanded federal bureaucracy would create a modern spoils system. Many southerners worried that the federal government's increased involvement in everyday life would endanger the system of racial segregation in southern states.[30] Even so, Democratic supporters of the New Deal, aided by public support, carried the day.

THE GREAT SOCIETY

The Great Society was a further expansion in the size and activities of the bureaucracy that occurred during Lyndon Johnson's presidency (1963–69). Johnson proposed and Congress enacted programs that funded bilingual education, loans and

grants for college students, special education, preschools, construction of elementary and secondary schools, mass transit programs in many cities, health care for seniors and poor people, job training and urban renewal, enhanced voting rights and civil rights for minorities, environmental protection, and funding for the arts and cultural activities.[31]

The Great Society programs had mixed success. Voting rights and civil rights reforms ended the "separate but equal" system of social order in southern states and dramatically increased political participation by African Americans.[32] At the same time, many antipoverty programs were dismal failures. Poverty rates among most groups remained relatively constant, and other indicators, such as the rate of teen pregnancies, actually increased.[33] In retrospect, the people who designed and implemented these programs did not realize the complexities of the problems they were trying to address.[34] Despite these shortcomings, the expansion of the federal government during the New Deal and Great Society has remained in place over the last generation.

THE REAGAN REVOLUTION

The election of Ronald Reagan to the presidency in 1980, along with a Republican takeover of the Senate and significant Republican gains in the House of Representatives, created an opportunity for conservatives to roll back the size and scope of the federal government. However, after eight years of Reagan in office followed by four years of George H. W. Bush, and Republican control of Congress during most of Democrat Bill Clinton's presidency as well as during most of the presidency of Republican George W. Bush, the growth of the federal government did not slow. Few programs were eliminated, and the federal budget steadily increased.[35]

Conservative presidents and members of Congress have enacted programs and regulations that increased the impact of government on society. For example, George W. Bush's administration added the No Child Left Behind education reforms, which imposed many new requirements on local schools; the Medicare Prescription Drug Benefit, which was the biggest new health care program since the 1960s; the Sarbanes–Oxley Act, which increased financial reporting requirements for corporations; and a host of other regulations, from specifications on backyard play sets to inspections of baggage on commercial aircraft.[36] The trend toward increased federal regulation continued in the Obama administration, especially with health care and financial industry reforms enacted in Obama's first term.

DESCRIBE THE SIZE AND STRUCTURE OF THE EXECUTIVE BRANCH TODAY

THE MODERN FEDERAL BUREAUCRACY

The size and scope of the modern federal bureaucracy reflect the expansion of the federal government over the last half-century and its increased role in citizens' lives. The bureaucracy's structure also reflects ongoing attempts by presidents, members of Congress, and others to control bureaucratic actions in line with their policy goals.

THE STRUCTURE OF THE FEDERAL GOVERNMENT

Figure 11.2 shows the structure of the executive branch of the federal government. As discussed in Chapter 10, the Executive Office of the President (EOP) contains organizations that support the president and implement presidential policy initiatives; individuals working in these organizations are part of the administrative presidency that seeks to ensure that bureaucrats implement the president's policy priorities, bringing the actions of bureaucrats (agents) in line with the president's (principal's) preferences.[37] Among its many offices, the EOP contains the **Office of Management and Budget**, which prepares the president's annual budget proposal and monitors government spending as well as the development of new regulations. Below the EOP are the 15 executive departments, from the Department of Agriculture to the Department of Veterans Affairs. The heads of these 15 organizations make up the president's cabinet.

Each executive department contains many smaller organizations. Figure 11.3 shows the organizational chart for the Department of Agriculture.

Below the executive departments, but not subordinate to them, are agencies, commissions, and government corporations that are called **independent agencies**, or independent establishments, to highlight that they are not part of an executive department. Most of these carry out specialized functions, such as the Federal Reserve (which manages the money supply, banking system, and interest rates) and the Federal Deposit Insurance Corporation (which regulates the banking industry). The figure only includes some noteworthy agencies; there are many more.

Office of Management and Budget An office within the Executive Office of the President that is responsible for creating the president's annual budget proposal to Congress, reviewing proposed rules, and other budget-related tasks.

independent agencies Government offices or organizations that provide government services and are not part of an executive department.

FIGURE » 11.2

THE EXECUTIVE BRANCH OF THE FEDERAL GOVERNMENT

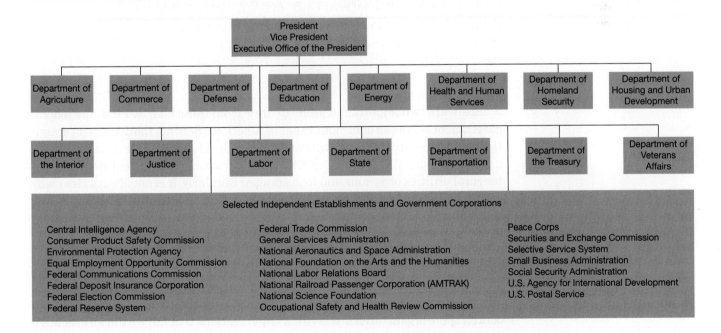

Source: Based on GPO Access: Guide to the U.S. Government, http://bensguide.gpo.gov/files/gov_chart.pdf (accessed 9/22/12).

FIGURE » 11.3

THE STRUCTURE OF THE DEPARTMENT OF AGRICULTURE

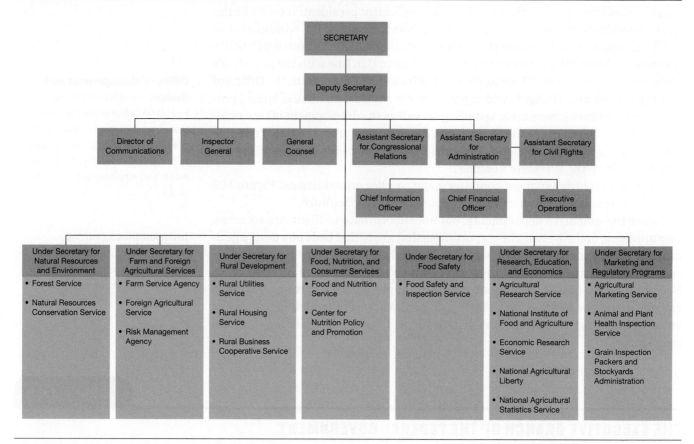

Source: U.S. Department of Agriculture, USDA Organization Chart, www.usda.gov/documents/AgencyWorkflow.pdf (accessed 4/23/10).

There are two important lessons to draw from these charts. First, the federal government serves an enormous range of functions. Second, the division of activities among executive departments and independent agencies does not always have an obvious logic. Why, for example, does the Department of Agriculture administer rural utilities programs and food stamps? Similarly, it is not always clear why certain tasks are handled by an independent agency while others fall within the scope of an executive department.[38] Why is the Federal Reserve an independent agency rather than part of the Department of the Treasury?

Organizational decisions like these often reflect elected officials' attempts to shape agency behavior—and the extent to which political process matters.

Part of the difference between independent agencies and the organizations contained within executive departments has to do with the president's ability to control these organizations' activities. Organizations that fall within an executive department, such as the Internal Revenue Service, can be subject to presidential control (to some extent) through his appointees.[39] In contrast, independent agencies have more freedom from oversight and control by the president and Congress. For example, the president nominates governors of the Federal Reserve, who (if the Senate confirms them) serve for 14 years. Outside the nomination and confirmation process, the president and Congress have very little control over the Federal Reserve's policies; the organization is self-financing, and its governors can be removed from office only if Congress impeaches them. These kinds of details about the hiring and firing of bureaucrats and the location of agencies in the structure of the federal government matter because they determine the amount of political control that other parts of the government can exercise over an agency, as well as who gets to exercise this power.[40]

THE SIZE OF THE FEDERAL GOVERNMENT

The federal government employs millions of people. Table 11.1 reports the number of employees in each executive department and selected independent agencies. Millions of additional people work for the government as members of the armed forces, as employees of the Postal Service, for civilian companies that contract with the government, or as recipients of federal grant money.

Figure 11.4 shows the size of the federal budget since 1968. Clearly, the budget has steadily increased, to the point that recent annual spending tops $3 trillion per year. The best explanation for the size of the federal government is the size of America itself—more than 300 million people spread out over an area more than twice the size of the European Union—coupled with America's position as the most powerful nation in the world.

However, some observers argue that the real explanation has to do with bureaucrats themselves. This view suggests that the government is so large because bureaucrats never pass up a chance to increase their own funding, regardless of whether the new spending is worthwhile.[41] This argument misses some important points. First, the increase in total federal spending masks the fact that many agencies see their budgets shrink.[42] Particularly in recent administrations, one of the principal missions of presidential appointees, both in agencies and in the Executive Office of the President, has been to scrutinize budget requests with an eye to cutting spending as much as possible.[43] And every year, some government agencies are eliminated.[44]

Moreover, public opinion data demonstrate the American public's demand for services.[45] Despite complaints about the federal bureaucracy, polls find little evidence of demands for less government. When the Harris Poll asked people in 2007 to decide which two programs should have their spending cut as a way of reducing the budget deficit, a majority favored cutting relatively small programs: 52 percent picked the space program and 79 percent picked foreign economic aid. Far fewer people favored cuts in the programs that account for most federal spending: defense (42%), health care (22%), and Social Security (12%).[46] In other words, while in the abstract Americans might want a smaller government that is less involved in everyday life, they do not support the large-scale budget cuts that would be necessary to achieve this goal. The public's desire for more government services is often encouraged by elected officials, who create new government programs (and expand existing ones) as a way of building support and improving their chances of re-election.

TABLE » 11.1

EMPLOYMENT IN SELECTED FEDERAL ORGANIZATIONS

Some federal agencies, such as the Department of Defense, have many employees, but many others are quite small. The Department of Education, for example, has only 4,000 employees. Does this variation in size make sense given the differences in the missions of these organizations?

ORGANIZATION	TOTAL EMPLOYEES
CABINET DEPARTMENTS	
Defense (civilian only)	652,000
Veterans Affairs	280,000
Homeland Security	171,000
Justice	108,000
Treasury	88,000
Agriculture	82,000
Interior	67,000
Health and Human Services	64,000
Transportation	55,000
Commerce	39,000
Labor	16,000
Energy	15,000
State	15,000
Housing and Urban Development	9,000
Education	4,000
INDEPENDENT AGENCIES	
Social Security Administration	64,000
National Aeronautics and Space Administration	18,000
Environmental Protection Agency	18,000
General Services Administration	12,000
Federal Deposit Insurance Corporation	5,000
Smithsonian Institution	4,000

Source: U.S. Bureau of Labor Statistics, Career Guide to Industries, "Federal Government, Excluding the Postal Service," Table 1, March 2012, www.bls.gov/oco/cg/cgs041.htm (accessed 9/22/12).

FIGURE » 11.4

THE SIZE OF THE FEDERAL BUDGET

The graph on the left shows that federal spending has increased sharply since the 1960s. However, the one on the right shows that as a percentage of gross domestic product (GDP), which measures the size of the American economy, the increase is much smaller, except for the financial bailout and economic stimulus programs enacted in 2008 and 2009. What might these figures suggest about the increase in government spending?

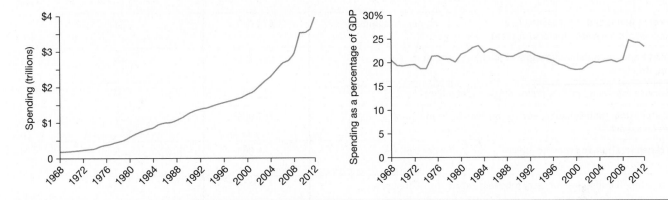

Source: Congressional Budget Office, Historical Budget Data, "Revenues, Outlays, Deficits, Surpluses, and Debt Held by the Public," www.cbo.gov/budget/data/historical.shtml; "CBO's 2011 Long-Term Budget Outlook," http://cbo.gov/publication/41486 (accessed 3/21/12).

THE HUMAN FACE OF THE BUREAUCRACY

> DESCRIBE WHO BUREAUCRATS ARE AND THE REGULATIONS THAT GOVERN THEIR EMPLOYMENT

The term "bureaucrat" applies to an array of people with different qualifications and job descriptions (see Nuts and Bolts 11.2). There are a lot of managers (680,000 people) and administrative support staff (273,000), but there are also 670,000 professionals such as scientists and 8,000 people whose positions involve farming, fishing, and forestry. The federal government includes so many different kinds of jobs because of the vast array of services it provides. While complaints about federal bureaucrats' efficiency or motivations are common, survey data show that many have a strong interest in public service.[47] This section describes who these people are and the terms of their government employment.

CIVIL SERVICE REGULATIONS

Most jobs in the federal bureaucracy are subject to the civil service regulations mentioned earlier.[48] The current civil service system sets out job descriptions and pay ranges for all federal jobs.[49] People with less than a college degree are generally eligible for clerical and low-level technical jobs. As in the private sector, a college degree or an advanced degree and work experience qualify an individual for higher-level positions. Federal salaries are supposed to be comparable to what

TYPES OF FEDERAL WORKERS

Occupation	Employees	Percentage of Federal Work Force
Management, business, and financial jobs (e.g., purchasing agents, accountants, tax collectors)	680,000	34%
Professional and related jobs (e.g., scientists, engineers, computer specialists, lawyers, doctors, nurses)	670,000	33
Office and administrative support jobs (e.g., secretaries, record clerks)	273,000	14
Service jobs (e.g., jailers, police officers, detectives)	161,000	8
Installation, maintenance, and repair jobs (e.g., mechanics, electricians)	101,000	5
Transportation and moving jobs (e.g., air traffic controllers, transportation inspectors)	61,000	3
Farming, fishing, and forestry jobs (e.g., agricultural inspectors, farmworkers, loggers)	8,000	0.4

Source: Based on the U.S. Bureau of Labor Statistics, "Career Guide to Industries, 2010–2011 Edition," Table 3, available at www.bls.gov/oco/cg/cgs041.htm (accessed 2/4/10).

people earn in similar, private sector positions, and salaries are increased somewhat for federal employees who work in areas with a high cost of living.

The civil service system also establishes tests that determine who is hired for low-level clerical and secretarial positions. The people who receive the highest scores are hired as vacancies arise. A similar system applies for Postal Service employees and for federal air traffic controllers. Hiring for higher-level jobs involves comparing the qualifications and experience of candidates who meet the educational requirements for the position. Seniority, or the amount of time a person has worked for the government or at a particular type of position, also determines which employees receive promotions.

Civil service regulations provide job security. After three years of satisfactory performance, employees cannot be fired except "for cause," meaning that the firing agency must cite a reason. Civil service regulations set out a multistep procedure for firing someone, beginning with low performance evaluations, then warning letters given to the employee, followed by a lengthy appeals process before a firing takes place. In simple terms, it is very hard to fire someone from the federal bureaucracy as long as he or she shows up for work.[50] A subpar performer may be assigned other duties, transferred to another office, or even given nothing to do in the hope that the person will leave voluntarily out of boredom.

Despite the difficulties associated with firing an individual underperforming bureaucrat, it is possible to reduce the size of the federal workforce through reductions in force (RIF), which occasionally occur when an entire office or program is terminated. Employees who have been laid off due to an RIF can apply for civil service positions in other parts of government. Another strategy for reducing the federal workforce is simply not to replace employees who decide to leave government service, or to hire contractors, who lack civil service protections and can be terminated at will.

Civil service regulations are extraordinarily cumbersome.[51] The hiring criteria remove a manager's discretion to hire someone who would do an excellent job but lacks the education or work experience that the regulations specify as necessary for the position. The firing requirements make it difficult to remove poor performers. The salary and promotion restrictions create problems with rewarding excellent performance or promoting the best employees rather than those with the most seniority.

Why do civil service requirements exist? Recall that the aim of these regulations was to separate politics from policy. The mechanism for achieving this goal was a set of rules that made it hard for elected officials to control the hiring and firing of government employees to further their own political goals. In effect, even though civil service regulations have drawbacks, they also provide this very important benefit. Although loyalty to the president is a widely accepted criterion for hiring agency heads and other presidential appointees, professionals with permanent civil service positions are supposed to be hired on the basis of their qualifications, not their political beliefs.

POLITICAL APPOINTEES AND THE SENIOR EXECUTIVE SERVICE

Not every federal employee is a member of the civil service. The president appoints over 7,000 individuals to senior positions in the executive branch who are not subject to civil service regulations, such as the leaders of executive departments and independent agencies, as well as members of the Executive Office of the President. (In some cases, the Senate must confirm these nominees.)

The majority of a president's appointees act as his eyes, ears, and hands throughout the executive branch. They hold positions of power within government agencies, serving as secretaries of executive departments, agency heads, or senior deputies. Their jobs involve finding out what the president wants from their agency and ordering or persuading their subordinates to implement presidential directives.

In many agencies, people in the top positions are members of the Senior Executive Service (SES), who are also exempt from civil service restrictions.[52] As of 2012, there were a few thousand SES members—mostly career government employees who held relatively high-level agency positions before moving to the SES. This change of employment status costs them their civil service protections but allows them to apply for senior leadership positions in the bureaucracy. Some political appointees are also given SES positions, although most do not have the experience or expertise held by career bureaucrats who typically move to the SES.

The president's ability to appoint bureaucrats in many different agencies helps him control the bureaucracy. By selecting people who are loyal or like-minded, he can attempt to control the actions of lower-level bureaucrats and implement his policy agenda. The SES also gives civil servants an incentive to do their jobs well, as good performance in an agency position can help build a career that might allow them to transfer to the SES.

THE PRESIDENT APPOINTS OVER 7,000 top officials in the executive branch, including his closest advisors. Political appointees are usually selected based on their loyalty to the president and his policy goals. Here, some of President Obama's advisors work to plan his visit to Baghdad in 2009.

FEDERAL LAW PROHIBITS THE USE OF government money, facilities, or services for political activities. Here, former Republican representative Tom DeLay (left), whose Texas district included NASA's Johnson Space Center, attends an awards ceremony with NASA administrator Michael Griffin. Although Griffin flew to Houston on a government plane primarily to present awards to NASA employees, his trip was cited as an illegal use of funds because his speech praised DeLay, who was running for re-election.

LIMITS ON POLITICAL ACTIVITY

Federal employees are limited in their political activities. The Hatch Act, enacted in 1939 and amended in 1940, prohibited federal employees from engaging in organized political activities:[53] employees could vote and contribute to candidates but could not work for candidates or for political parties. These restrictions were modified under the 1993 Federal Employees Political Activities Act, allowing federal employees to undertake a wider range of political activities, including fund-raising and serving as an officer of a political party. Senior members of the president's White House staff and political appointees are exempt from most of these restrictions, though they cannot use government resources for political activities.

These regulations make life difficult for presidential appointees whose job duties often mix government service with politics, such as helping the president they work for get reelected. Moreover, it is not completely clear which activities these laws allow or prohibit. For example, in spring 2007, congressional Democrats complained that Karl Rove, deputy White House chief of staff and a close political adviser to President George W. Bush, had given briefings to senior political appointees on Republican losses in the 2006 midterm elections and plans for the 2008 campaign. Although these meetings had been approved as legal by the White House counsel, their political content is obvious. During one briefing, the head of the General Services Administration asked how her agency could help elect Republican candidates in 2008.[54] As a senior member of the White House staff, Rove was exempt from the Hatch Act's prohibitions, but the more junior White House staff involved in the briefings probably were not. While ultimately no action was taken against Rove or his aides, this example illustrates the ambiguities inherent in separating the political and policy role of federal bureaucrats, especially those who work in the White House.

CONTROLLING THE BUREAUCRACY

EXPLAIN HOW CONGRESS AND THE PRESIDENT OVERSEE THE EXECUTIVE BRANCH

As the expert implementers of legislation and presidential directives, bureaucrats hold significant power to influence government policy. This situation creates the problem of political control illustrated by the principal–agent game: elected officials must figure out how to reap the benefits of bureaucratic expertise without simply giving bureaucrats free rein to do whatever they want.

One strategy is to take away discretion and give bureaucrats simple, direct orders. For example, after NASA scientist James Hansen gave a speech in 2006 calling for policies to combat global warming that did not reflect the Bush administration's preferences, he was told to submit all future papers, lectures, and interview requests to NASA political appointees for review.[55] In this case, NASA reversed the order after it received press attention, and the agency's head released a statement supporting scientific openness.[56] Soon after this episode, however, NASA's official mission statement was modified to exclude studies of Earth, thereby choking off its studies of climate change entirely.[57]

Such attempts to control the bureaucracy are common. The problem with eliminating bureaucrats' discretion is that it limits the positive influence of their expertise. Particularly when new policies are being developed, taking away bureaucratic discretion is costly for legislators or presidential appointees, as it forces them to work out the policy details themselves—and it may produce less effective policies than those constructed by bureaucrats with specialized knowledge.[58] Moreover, preventing bureaucrats from using their judgment makes it impossible for them to craft policies that take into account new developments or unforeseen circumstances.[59] Directives may also make it impossible for bureaucrats to develop and implement policies incrementally (over time) as opposed to all at once.[60] Incrementalism is a good strategy when policies are complex and no one is sure what the impact of new regulations will be, but directives from elected officials to develop and implement regulations as fast as possible can make this strategy impossible.

For all these reasons, elected officials must find ways to reduce or eliminate **bureaucratic drift** (that is, bureaucrats pursuing their own goals rather than their assignments from officeholders or appointees) while still reaping the benefits of bureaucratic expertise. This section describes two common strategies: changing the way agencies are organized and staffed, and using standardized procedures for monitoring agency actions.

bureaucratic drift Bureaucrats' tendency to implement policies in a way that favors their own political objectives rather than following the original intentions of the legislation.

AGENCY ORGANIZATION

Political scientists have shown how agencies can be organized to minimize bureaucratic drift.[61] Specifically, when an agency is set up or given new responsibilities, the officials who initiated the change don't simply tell the agency what to do. To ensure that they get the policies they want, they also determine where the agency is located within the federal government structure and who runs it. These efforts may occur solely within Congress, or involve both Congress and the president, or be arranged by presidential actions.[62]

For example, when legislation was written to form the Department of Homeland Security in 2002, the Bush administration pushed to have the Coast Guard transferred out of the Department of Transportation and into the new department. This move sought to change the Coast Guard's priorities from search and rescue operations and routine patrol to a focus on port security, without increasing its budget. The shift worked: subsequently the amount of effort expended by Coast Guard personnel on port security increased from a small percentage of total effort to nearly 50 percent, with a corresponding decrease in other activities.[63]

Another strategy is to impose limits on who is allowed to run the agency. In the case of the Federal Communications Commission, elected officials were concerned that the organization would adopt regulations on political advertising that favored one political party over the other. To prevent this, the legislation that created the agency mandates that it will be run by five commissioners, all of whom are nominated by the president and confirmed by the Senate.[64] However, no more than three of the commissioners can be from the same political party. As a result, if a partisan majority on the commission tries to enact laws that favor one party, opponents only need to convince one supporter to switch positions in order to block the measure. The same rule applies when selecting commissioners for other agencies. In many cases, commissioners are also prohibited from having a business relationship (as a consultant, stockholder, or otherwise) with any company that is subject to their agency's rulings.

Delegation of rule-making power to an agency can also allow federal courts to review agency action.[65] One study of rule making by the Federal Communications Commission, which regulates television, radio, and other broadcasting firms, found that relying on the courts reduced the uncertainties faced by members of Congress, because they have more faith in the impartiality of federal judges than of bureaucrats or other members of Congress.

MONITORING

oversight Congressional efforts to make sure that laws are implemented correctly by the bureaucracy after they have been passed.

One of the most important ways elected officials prevent bureaucratic drift is to know what bureaucrats are doing or planning to do. Information gathering by members of Congress about bureaucratic actions is termed **oversight**. Congressional committees often hold hearings to question agency heads, secretaries of executive departments, or senior agency staff. Similarly, one responsibility of presidential appointees is to monitor how bureaucrats are responding to presidential directives. However, presidential appointees may be unable to fulfill this role. Because they are chosen for their loyalty to the president, they may lack the experience needed to fully understand what bureaucrats in their agency are doing. Moreover, given that appointees typically hold their position for only a year or two, they have little time to learn the details of agency operations.

ADVANCE WARNING

Members of Congress, the president, and his staff gain advance knowledge of bureaucratic actions through the notice and comment procedure described earlier, which requires bureaucrats to disclose proposed changes before they take effect.[66] This delay gives opponents the opportunity to register complaints with their congressional representatives, and it allows these legislators time either to pressure the agency to revise the regulation or even to enact another law undoing or modifying the agency action.

IS POLITICAL CONTROL OF THE BUREAUCRACY BENEFICIAL?

When working with bureaucrats, elected officials face the problem of political control: Should they allow bureaucrats to exercise judgment when implementing policies or give them specific, narrow directives? Letting bureaucrats set policy allows them to base decisions on their expertise or private information, but it also gives them the freedom to ignore elected officials' policy goals and preferences in favor of their own. While this exercise of expertise sounds like a good idea—shouldn't we let government policy be formulated by the most-knowledgeable people—in practice it remains a difficult decision.

Consider the case of America's involvement in the Libyan Civil War in 2011. The United States, along with its allies in NATO, provided the Libyan rebels with weapons and other supplies, and conducted manned and drone airstrikes on the government's military bases and infrastructure. After some initial strikes, the U.S. involvement was limited to drone missions, refueling of NATO aircraft, and logistics support. However, by the provisions of the War Powers Act (see Chapter 10), after sixty days the president was obligated to determine whether U.S. involvement constituted "hostilities," and, if it did, to inform members of Congress, who could vote on whether to continue the mission or end it.

While the final decision about whether an operation constitutes hostilities rests with the president, typically presidents have relied on the judgment of lawyers in the State Department to make this determination. In the case of Libya, these lawyers argued that the Libyan mission constituted hostilities. However, the president ignored this advice and relied on the judgment of his advisers in the Executive Office of the President, who came to the opposite conclusion, meaning that there was no need to ask Congress to pass judgment on the operation.

Many observers criticized the president's decision to overrule the judgment of his legal experts. As Speaker of the House Republican John Boehner put in, "The White House says there are no hostilities taking place. Yet we've got drone attacks under way. We're spending $10 million a day. We're part of an effort to drop bombs on Qaddafi's compounds. It just doesn't pass the straight-face test, in my view, that we're not in the midst of hostilities." Even leaving politics aside—the Libya operation was opposed by many Republicans, including Boehner—the episode raises an important question: If bureaucrats are experts, why shouldn't they make policy decisions, rather than leaving them up to politicians, who may know far less about the decisions they face?

The problem with bureaucratic discretion is that it cuts both ways. Allowing bureaucrats to act as they think best means that they can disregard the stated goals of legislation or the preferences of elected officials and simply implement the policies they favor. Even bureaucrats' public statements can have policy consequences—they may influence public opinion and in turn shape government policy. If experts in the bureaucracy sound the alarm, people outside government may listen and even take action in the form of protests, legal action, or other organized

While legal experts in the State Department said that U.S. involvement in Libya in 2011 constituted "hostilities" and was therefore subject to a possible vote in Congress, the Obama administration chose to ignore the experts and follow their own plan.

attempts to overturn the decision inside government. Even if their efforts are unsuccessful, the president and the people working for him or her may spend considerable time responding to public pressure.

Another down side that comes with bureaucratic discretion is that bureaucrats are unelected and most are very difficult to fire because of their civil service protections. Moreover, if bureaucrats are given a great deal of leeway to use their judgment in policy making, it becomes very difficult to determine the criteria for judging whether their removal is warranted or not. How much discretion should elected officials allow bureaucrats to use? You decide.

Critical Thinking Questions

1. It's easy to see why opponents of the president's policies would like to reduce political control of the bureaucracy. However, there are situations where even a president might want to reduce his or her control over bureaucratic actions. Why?

2. The benefits and costs of political control vary across the different agencies and departments that make up the bureaucracy. Where do you think the benefits are high, and where do you think they are low? What about costs?

INVESTIGATIONS: POLICE PATROLS AND FIRE ALARMS

Investigations involve Congress, legislative staff, or presidential appointees scrutinizing some government program or office, its expenditures, and its activities. The two types of oversight, police patrols and fire alarms, are described in "How It Works." Ideally, every agency would be investigated as often as possible, with agencies that have large budgets or carry out important functions being investigated more frequently. These investigations may involve fact-finding trips to local offices, interviews with senior personnel, audits of agency accounts, and calls to the agency to see how it responds to citizens' requests. This method of investigation is called **police patrol oversight**.[67] Think of a police officer walking her beat, rattling doors to see if they are locked, checking out broken windows, and looking down alleys for suspicious behavior.

The disadvantage of police patrol oversight is that it is costly in terms of money and staff time. Moreover, these investigations often find that agencies are doing what they should. Because of these drawbacks, Congress and the president also look outside government for information on what bureaucrats are doing. Rather than initiating investigations, they wait until they receive a complaint about bureaucratic actions and then focus investigative efforts on those cases, a practice labeled **fire alarm oversight**.[68]

The so-called fire alarm can take many different forms. Representatives and their staff meet frequently with constituents, who may let them know of a problem with the bureaucracy. Similarly, lobbyists, corporate executives, and ordinary citizens often contact the president and his staff with complaints about bureaucratic actions. Newspaper reporters and Internet bloggers, too, provide information on what bureaucrats are doing. Some agencies have advisory committees that not only help make agency decisions but also keep Congress and the president informed about them.[69] Such fire alarm communications tell Congress and the president where to focus their efforts to monitor the bureaucracy, rather than trying to oversee the entire government at once.

CORRECTING VIOLATIONS

When members of Congress or the president find a case of bureaucratic drift, they can choose from many tactics to bring a wayward agency into line. Legislation or an executive order can send a clear directive to an agency or remove its discretion, tasks and programs can be moved to an agency more closely aligned with elected officials' goals, political appointees at an agency can be replaced, and agencies can be reorganized. In extreme situations, members of Congress can even fail to renew an agency's statutory authority, in effect putting the agency out of business.

A significant difficulty in dealing with bureaucratic drift is disagreement between members of Congress and the president about whether an agency is doing the right thing—regardless of whether it is following its original orders. Most of the tactics listed require joint action by the president and congressional majorities. Without presidential support, members of Congress need a two-thirds majority to impose corrections. Without congressional support, the president can only threaten to cut an agency's proposed budget, change its home within the federal bureaucracy, or establish a new agency to do what the errant agency refuses to do; actually carrying out these threats requires congressional approval. As a result,

police patrol oversight
A method of oversight in which members of Congress constantly monitor the bureaucracy to make sure that laws are implemented correctly.

fire alarm oversight A method of oversight in which members of Congress respond to complaints about the bureaucracy or problems of implementation only as they arise rather than exercising constant vigilance.

How It Works

OVERSEEING THE BUREAUCRACY

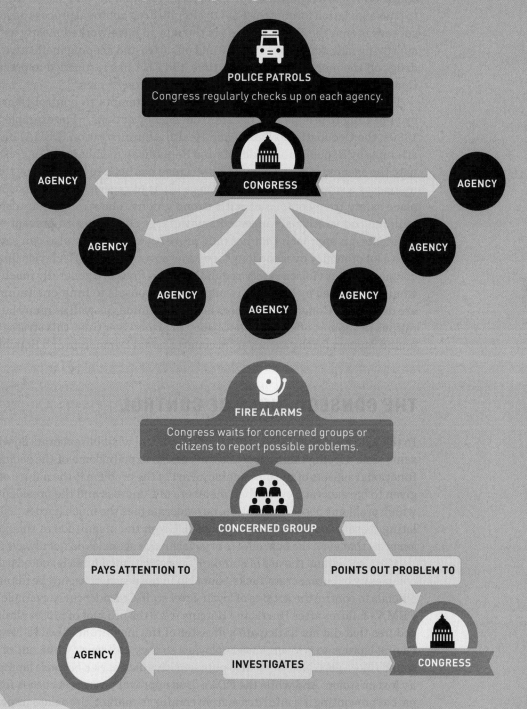

POLICE PATROLS
Congress regularly checks up on each agency.

AGENCY — CONGRESS — AGENCY

AGENCY · AGENCY · AGENCY · AGENCY · AGENCY

FIRE ALARMS
Congress waits for concerned groups or citizens to report possible problems.

CONCERNED GROUP

PAYS ATTENTION TO · POINTS OUT PROBLEM TO

AGENCY ← INVESTIGATES ← CONGRESS

POP QUIZ!

1 Which method of oversight relies on groups or citizens to alert Congress when a bureaucratic agency gets out of line?

  a police patrol

  b fire alarm

  c investigative

  d all of the above

  e none of the above

2 The main reason police patrol oversight is difficult is that

  a members of Congress don't care what the bureaucracy does.

  b most bureaucrats are corrupt.

  c citizens don't care what the bureaucracy does.

  d Congress can't hold hearings when a problem is found.

  e the bureaucracy is huge and complex.

disagreements between the president and Congress can give an agency significant freedom, as long as it retains the support of at least one branch of government.

An agency may also be able to fend off elected officials' attempts to take political control if it has a reputation for expertise. For example, one reason that attempts to pass legislation forcing the FDA to alter its drug approval process have had little success is that the FDA's process is thought to have worked mostly as intended, approving new drugs that are safe and effective and keeping ineffective or unsafe drugs off the market. At the same time, the FDA has responded to pressure from Congress and the president to revise some rules on its own.[70]

Finally, agencies can sometimes combat attempts to control their behavior by appealing to groups that benefit from agency actions.[71] For example, since the 1980s, the Occupational Safety and Health Administration (OSHA) has resisted attempts by Republican presidents and Republican members of Congress to eliminate the agency.[72] One element of its strategy has been to build strong ties to labor unions; as a result, OSHA is much more likely to receive complaints about workplace safety from companies with strong unions. The strategy has also involved building cooperative arrangements with large companies to prevent workplace accidents, an approach that not only protects workers but also can save companies a lot of money over the long term. Moreover, when OSHA levies fines against companies that violate safety regulations, the fines are generally much less than would be allowed by law. As a result, when proposals to limit or eliminate OSHA are debated in Congress, members hear from unions as well as many large corporations in support of keeping the agency in place. Over time, this strategy has generated support for the agency from congressional Democrats and Republicans.

THE CONSEQUENCES OF CONTROL

In the following discussion of attempts to control what bureaucrats do while at the same time tapping their expertise, we seek to explain some of the seemingly dysfunctional aspects of the bureaucracy. Part of the problem is the nature of the tasks given to bureaucrats: even when members of Congress and the president agree on which problems deserve attention, bureaucrats face the much harder task of translating these goals into concrete policies. Given the magnitude of this job, it is no surprise that even the best efforts of government agencies do not always succeed.

Most important, the use of standard operating procedures is rooted partly in the complexity of bureaucrats' tasks—but also in the desire of agency heads and elected officials to control the actions of lower-level staff. Consider three examples. Some of FEMA's failures after Hurricane Katrina were the product of preset plans and procedures that did not anticipate a disaster of the magnitude faced in New Orleans. Giving laptops to government employees so they can work while out of the office sounds like a good idea, but it also puts sensitive data at risk because laptops are easily lost or stolen. And while the FDA's drug approval process succeeds for the most part at preventing harmful drugs from coming to market, the delays imposed by the process do prevent some patients from receiving life-saving treatments. However, in all these cases the decisions do not reflect incompetence or malice. Rules and procedures are needed in any organization to ensure that decisions are fair and reflect the goals of the organization. Yet it is impossible to find procedures that will work well in all cases, particularly for the kinds of policy decisions bureaucrats must make.

It is also important to remember that many government regulations, even those that are the product of standard operating procedures, work as intended and do provide socially beneficial results. For example, regulations restricting pollution have led to dramatic increases in air and water quality throughout the United States.

Dysfunctional bureaucratic behavior can also arise from the problem of political control. Overly specific directives may prevent bureaucrats from pursuing what they consider the most effective course of action, but the president and his appointees are genuinely worried about being undercut by unelected bureaucrats who may disagree with their plans. Similarly, government reorganizations such as those that occurred during the formation of the Department of Homeland Security may be intentionally designed to bring about some bureaucratic "failures" as priorities shift and agencies' goals are redefined. For example, no one expects the Coast Guard to take on new responsibilities without shifting resources away from the jobs it is already doing. In a sense, the Guard has fallen short in its routine patrol mission since it became part of Homeland Security. But the reason for moving the Guard into the new department was to refocus its efforts on port security. From the viewpoint of political control, the reorganization worked exactly as planned.

In sum, when government agencies do things that seem counterproductive, it would be wrong to conclude that the agencies are inept or willfully shirking their responsibilities. Rather, they may be doing the best they can to achieve formidable goals, carrying out procedures that are often—but not always—productive, or responding to directives from elected officials.

MANY GOVERNMENT REGULATIONS work as intended. An increase in regulatory attention to environmental protection and cleanup of polluted sites has dramatically improved water quality nationwide, including that of the Hudson River in New York, shown here.

CONCLUSION

Bureaucrats implement government policy—often in situations where the problems and potential solutions are vast and poorly understood, and in the face of sharp disagreements about what government should do. On the government's behalf, bureaucrats spend money on everything from paper clips to aircraft carriers. They formulate regulations that determine what can be created, produced, transported, bought, sold, consumed, and disposed of in America. Elected officials want to control what bureaucrats do while also tapping into their expertise on policy matters. In this way, conflict over public policy often translates into conflicting ideas about what bureaucrats should do, resulting in complex, often contradictory mandates and directions imposed on those workers.

These characteristics of the bureaucracy and the fundamentally political nature of bureaucrats' jobs explain many cases of ineptitude and red tape. Sometimes bureaucrats simply make mistakes, choosing the wrong policy because they lack full information about the tasks they were given. Bureaucrats may drag their feet when they oppose their tasks on policy grounds. Policies may reflect direct orders given by elected officials or political appointees. Attempts at political control also shape the structure of the bureaucracy, from influencing which agencies function independently and which ones fall within executive departments, to determining the qualifications for commissioners and agency heads and the rules they must follow when making decisions.

WHAT IS THE FEDERAL BUREAUCRACY?

▶ Define bureaucracy and explain its major functions. **Pages 325–31**

SUMMARY

The bureaucracy is composed of both civil servants and political appointees and is in charge of interpreting and implementing a wide range of government policies. While bureaucrats are policy experts, most members of Congress are not. Nonetheless, Congress still tries to control how the bureaucracy operates, which can result in inefficiencies.

KEY TERMS

bureaucracy (p. 325)

civil servants (p. 325)

political appointees (p. 325)

regulation (p. 326)

notice and comment procedure (p. 326)

state capacity (p. 329)

red tape (p. 329)

standard operating procedures (p. 329)

problem of control (p. 330)

principal-agent game (p. 330)

PRACTICE QUIZ QUESTIONS

1. A government rule that affects the choices that individuals or corporations make is called _____.
   a) an initiative
   b) a referendum
   c) a regulation
   d) a procurement
   e) an appropriation

2. One of the reasons bureaucrats take account of pressure from elected officials is because _____.
   a) they need congressional support to get larger budgets
   b) elected officials have more expertise
   c) they are all appointed by members of Congress
   d) their offices are housed in the Congress
   e) they are required by law to do so

3. In the problem of control, the _____ is the principal and the _____ is the agent.
   a) bureaucracy; president
   b) bureaucracy; Congress
   c) president; Congress
   d) president; bureaucracy
   e) Congress; president

ⓢ PRACTICE ONLINE

"Critical Thinking" exercise: *Politics Is Conflictual—Popular Perceptions of Bureaucracy*

HISTORY OF THE AMERICAN BUREAUCRACY

▶ Trace the expansion of the federal bureaucracy over time. **Pages 331–34**

SUMMARY

The bureaucracy has grown substantially since the turn of the twentieth century, largely in response to citizen demands that the government do more for the people. Though the federal government had a very limited role in daily life for much of the nineteenth century, it expanded during the Progressive Era, when regulatory activity increased and the spoils system was replaced by the federal civil service. The bureaucracy expanded again with the New Deal and Great Society programs, which increased the number of services the government provided.

KEY TERM

federal civil service (p. 332)

PRACTICE QUIZ QUESTIONS

4. How did the bureaucracy change during the Progressive Era?
   a) It expanded the delivery of government services directly to individuals.
   b) The spoils system was established.
   c) It created a number of antipoverty and educational programs.
   d) It reduced the government's regulatory activity.
   e) It increased the government's regulatory activity.

5. The civil service reforms of the Progressive Era _____ the spoils system and _____ the power of party organizations.
   a) ended; increased
   b) ended; decreased
   c) instituted; increased
   d) instituted; decreased
   e) expanded; increased

6. What effect did the Reagan Revolution have on bureaucracy?
   a) The government stopped passing regulatory policies.
   b) The size of the federal government shrunk.
   c) The size of the federal government expanded.
   d) The civil service reforms were weakened.
   e) The civil service reforms were strengthened.

THE MODERN FEDERAL BUREAUCRACY

▶ Describe the size and structure of the executive branch today. **Pages 334–39**

SUMMARY

The modern bureaucracy serves a wide range of functions, but the division of labor within the bureaucracy does not always have an obvious logic. Overlapping or confusing jurisdictions can be the result of elected officials attempting to shape the agency's behavior by assigning a task to an executive department rather than an independent agency. The overall size of the bureaucracy reflects the demands of constituents but also fits the needs of elected officials who can improve their chances of re-election.

KEY TERMS

Office of Management and Budget (p. 335)

independent agencies (p. 335)

CRITICAL THINKING AND DISCUSSION

Suppose you are a member of Congress who must decide whether to give bureaucrats in a particular agency direct orders that allow them little or no input, or to allow them to exercise their own discretion. What factors should you consider when making this decision?

7. What is the job of the Office of Management and Budget?
   a) preparing the annual budget proposal for the Congress
   b) preparing the annual budget proposal for the president
   c) preparing annual budget proposals for the states
   d) monitoring government spending for the Supreme Court
   e) monitoring government spending for the Congress

8. Independent agencies have _____ freedom from oversight than executive departments; and _____ be controlled by the president through his appointees.
   a) more; cannot
   b) more; can
   c) less; cannot
   d) less; can

9. The federal budget continues to grow because _____.
   a) bureaucrats are budget maximizers
   b) politicians do not scrutinize budget requests
   c) government agencies are never eliminated
   d) the public does not support large-scale budget cuts
   e) a growing percentage of Americans are going into civil service

Ⓢ PRACTICE ONLINE

"Critical Thinking" exercise: *Process Matters—Executive Agencies and Bureaucratic Organization*

THE HUMAN FACE OF THE BUREAUCRACY

▶ Describe who bureaucrats are and the regulations that govern their employment. **Pages 339–42**

SUMMARY

The regulations within the civil service system were established to separate politics from policy—rather than getting and retaining a job for political considerations, individuals are hired based on merit and are quite difficult to fire. On the other hand, the president makes senior level appointments that are not protected by civil service regulations and are more political in nature. These appointments are instrumental in helping the president control the bureaucracy.

CRITICAL THINKING AND DISCUSSION

What are the advantages and disadvantages of the fact that bureaucrats often have their own preferences about how to implement the policies they administer?

PRACTICE QUIZ QUESTIONS

10. Which job category is most common in the bureaucracy?
    a) clerks and secretaries
    b) management, business, and financial jobs
    c) farming, fishing, and forestry jobs
    d) scientists and engineers
    e) maintenance jobs

11. The civil service regulations _____ the flexibility that managers have in their hiring decisions and _____ the influence of elected officials.
    a) decrease; decrease
    b) increase; increase
    c) increase; decrease
    d) decrease; increase
    e) increase; have no effect on

Ⓢ PRACTICE ONLINE

"Big Think" video exercise: *What Happens Inside the Department of Defense?*

CONTROLLING THE BUREAUCRACY

▶ Explain how Congress and the president oversee the executive branch. **Pages 343–49**

SUMMARY

With their expertise, bureaucrats have the power to significantly influence government policy. This creates a dilemma for elected officials, who want to enjoy the benefits of the expertise while retaining control of the bureaucracy. Lawmakers can generally organize agencies and monitor their behavior to reduce, but not eliminate, bureaucratic drift.

KEY TERMS

bureaucratic drift (p. 343)

oversight (p. 344)

police patrol oversight (p. 346)

fire alarm oversight (p. 346)

CRITICAL THINKING AND DISCUSSION

Why might bureaucrats pay more attention to orders and directives from members of Congress than those from the president or his political appointees?

PRACTICE QUIZ QUESTIONS

12. When bureaucrats pursue their own goals rather than assignments from officeholders, this is called _____.
   a) an iron triangle
   b) regulatory capture
   c) the problem of control
   d) turkey farming
   e) bureaucratic drift

13. Giving direct orders to bureaucrats _____ the influence of their policy expertise and _____ the potential for incrementalism.
   a) limits; reduces
   b) increases; reduces
   c) limits; increases
   d) increases; increases
   e) limits; has no effect on

14. While police patrol oversight has the advantage of being _____, it has the drawback of being _____.
   a) affordable; unresponsive
   b) responsive; costly
   c) affordable; generally unnecessary
   d) responsive; unpopular
   e) affordable; ineffective

---

⑤ PRACTICE ONLINE

"Big Think" video exercise: *Sen. George Mitchell on Congress and Bureaucracy*

SUGGESTED READING

Aaron, Henry J. *Politics and the Professors: The Great Society in Perspective.* Washington, DC: Brookings Institution Press, 1978.

Brehm, John, and Scott Gates. *Working, Shirking and Sabotage.* Ann Arbor: University of Michigan Press, 1998.

Carpenter, Daniel P. *The Forging of Bureaucratic Autonomy: Reputations, Networks, and Policy Innovation in Executive Agencies, 1862–1928.* Princeton, NJ: Princeton University Press, 2001.

Epstein, David, and Sharyn O'Halloran. *Delegating Powers: A Transaction Cost Politics Approach to Policy Making under Separate Powers.* New York: Cambridge University Press, 1999.

Huber, John D., and Charles R. Shipan. *Deliberate Discretion? The Institutional Foundations of Bureaucratic Autonomy.* New York: Cambridge University Press, 2002.

Lewis, David E. *The Politics of Presidential Appointments: Political Control and Bureaucratic Performance.* Princeton, NJ: Princeton University Press, 2010.

Light, Paul. *A Government Well-Executed: Public Service and Public Performance.* Washington, DC: Brookings Institution Press, 2003.

McCubbins, Mathew D., Roger G. Noll, and Barry R. Weingast. "Structure and Process as Solutions to the Politician's Principal–Agency Problem," *Virginia Law Review* 74 (1989): 431–82.

Miller, Gary. *Managerial Dilemmas: The Political Economy of Hierarchy.* New York: Cambridge University Press, 1987.

Moe, Terry M. "Political Control and the Power of the Agent." *Journal of Law, Economics, and Organization* 22 (2006): 1–21.

Nelson, Michael. "A Short, Ironic History of American National Bureaucracy." *Journal of Politics* 44 (1982): 747–78.

Skowronek, Stephen. *Building a New American State: The Expansion of National Administrative Capacities, 1877–1920.* New York: Cambridge University Press, 1982.

Wilson, James Q. *Bureaucracy: What Government Agencies Do and Why They Do It.* 2nd ed. New York: Basic Books, 2000.

12

The Courts

IN 2012, THE SUPREME COURT RULED on a controversial immigration law passed by the state of Arizona. Conflict surrounded the issue, but the Court's decision also reflected a compromise between national power and states' rights.

I N JUNE 2012, THE SUPREME COURT THRUST itself into the middle of election-year politics by deciding two cases—one concerning health care reform (see Chapters 3 and 14) and one on immigration policy—that had important political implications. In the 2012–13 term, the Court was slated to hear cases on politically controversial issues, including affirmative action in higher education, same-sex marriage, and the Voting Rights Act. Scholars of the Court had to reach back to 1936 and the battles between the Court and President Franklin Roosevelt to find a comparable period in which the Court was so involved with the central political debates of the day.

In the 2012 health care and immigration cases, the Supreme Court largely ruled in favor of national power, disappointing conservatives who had hoped that the Court would strike down the laws that were involved. The Court's decision about which path to take in a given case is often very political, involving conflict, tradeoffs, and compromise, much like decision-making in Congress. That the Supreme Court is a policy-making and political institution may seem inappropriate. After all, the guiding principles of the "rule of law" in the American political system—embodied in the words carved above the entrance to the Supreme Court ("equal justice under the law") and the statue of Justice represented as a blindfolded woman holding a set of scales—seem to contradict the view of a political Supreme Court. We normally think of the court as objectively applying the law and interpreting the Constitution for each case. But the immigration and health care cases clearly represented

CONFLICT & COMPROMISE
in American Politics

355

compromises. The health care case upheld the most important part of the Affordable Care Act—the so-called individual mandate, requiring people to obtain insurance—but did so on narrower constitutional grounds than liberals wanted, while striking down the expansion of Medicaid as an unfair example of coercive federalism, which made conservatives happy. The immigration case struck down three part of Arizona's immigration law while upholding the most controversial "show your papers" part of the law, allowing both liberals and conservatives to claim victory in the case.

Although we certainly expect them to be fair and objective, judges have their own political views and opinions, and these often shape their views of cases, in part *because* there are usually multiple legal justifications for any case. For example, there is no simple or clear-cut way to determine objectively the relative legal merits of Justice Scalia's dissenting view in the immigration case that "the federal executive's refusal to enforce the nation's immigration laws" opens the door for states to enforce the law or the majority's view that Congress has the power to dictate immigration policy because of the supremacy clause of the Constitution. To a large extent, this depends on the justices' views of whether the supremacy clause applies in this context.

For those who resist the view that the courts are a policy-making institution, at least in the same way that Congress is, the theme "political process matters" may not seem to apply in this chapter. However, the courts often *do* make policy, and the manner in which they make decisions has an impact on outcomes. To see how political process matters for the courts, it is important to answer the following questions: What are the different roles of the courts? What is the structure of the judicial system? How do court decisions shape policy? In a nutshell, what is the nature of judicial decision making?

The role of the Supreme Court as a policy-making and political institution also illustrates the third theme of this book. On the one hand, the courts seem to resist our characterization that politics is everywhere. There is an aura of mystery and prestige to the courts that seems to isolate them from the rest of the political process. However, most Americans will come into contact with the court system at some point in their lives, whether it is to contest a traffic ticket, fight a local zoning change, or serve on a jury (we assume that you will not be on the "wrong side" of the law). The relevance of the courts in national politics is similarly self-evident. Dramatic moments, such as the *Bush v. Gore* decision that determined the 2000 presidential election and the health care reform case, are the most obvious examples of the relevance (and political nature!) of the courts. Less visible decisions that are handed down every day in the federal courts affects the lives of millions of Americans across a broad range of areas, including environmental policy, employment law, tax policy, civil rights, and civil liberties. In fact, some critics of the courts complain about and "imperial judiciary" that has become *too* powerful in the political system. This chapter examines the issues centered on the proper place of the courts within our political system. How much power should unelected judges have? Are they a necessary check on the other branches of government or a source of unaccountable power that contradicts core principles of democracy? How do the courts interact with the other branches? Before addressing these questions, we discuss how the Founders viewed the judicial system.

THE DEVELOPMENT OF AN INDEPENDENT AND POWERFUL FEDERAL JUDICIARY

EXPLAIN HOW THE POWER OF JUDICIAL REVIEW WAS ESTABLISHED

The role of the courts in American politics and the Supreme Court's authority as the ultimate interpreter of the Constitution were not definitively established in the Constitution. The powers of the Supreme Court evolved over time, and debates about its proper role continue to this day.

THE FOUNDERS' VIEWS OF THE COURTS: THE WEAKEST BRANCH?

The Federalists and Antifederalists did not see eye-to-eye on much, and the judiciary was no exception. Alexander Hamilton, writing in *Federalist 78*, said that the Supreme Court would be "beyond comparison the weakest of the three departments of power." In contrast, the author of the *Antifederalist Papers* wrote, "The supreme court under this constitution would be exalted above all other power in the government and subjected to no control."[1] Hmmm, which is it, weakest or strongest? While the framers could not agree on the likely relative power of the Court, there was surprisingly little debate at the Constitutional Convention about the judiciary. Article III of the Constitution created one Supreme Court and gave the courts independence by providing federal judges with lifetime terms (assuming "good behavior"). However, the Federalists and Antifederalists did not see eye-to-eye on much, and the judiciary was no exception.

The main disagreements about the judiciary had to do with how independent the courts should be vis-à-vis the other branches of government and how much power to give the courts. Some of the framers feared a tyrannical Congress and wanted to create judicial and executive branches that could check this power. Others argued for making the executive and judicial branches more closely related so they would be better able to balance Congress. A central debate was whether to give the judiciary some "revisionary power" over Congress, similar to the president's veto power. This idea of judicial review would have given the Supreme Court the power to strike down laws passed by Congress that violated the Constitution. The framers could not agree on judicial review, so the Constitution remained silent on the matter. As the power of judicial review has evolved, it has become a central part of the system of checks and balances (see Chapter 2).

Many details about the Supreme Court were left up to Congress, including its size, the time and place it would meet, and its internal organization. These details, as well as the system of lower federal courts, were outlined in the **Judiciary Act of 1789**. This law set the number of justices at six (one chief justice and five associates). The number of justices gradually increased to 10 by the end of the Civil War and was then restricted to seven under Reconstruction policies. The number was set at nine in 1869, where it has remained since.[2]

The 1789 Act also created a system of federal courts, which included thirteen **district courts** and three circuit courts—the intermediate-level courts that heard appeals from the district courts. The district courts each had one judge; the circuits comprised two Supreme Court justices and one district judge. Today, separate judges are appointed to fill the circuit courts (what we call "appeals courts"). Furthermore, the act refined the jurisdiction of the federal courts—the limits within which they could exercise their authority. One controversial provision was Section 25, which expanded the Court's **appellate jurisdiction** (cases heard on appeal from lower courts) to include state supreme court cases involving conflicts between state law and federal law or treaties or the U.S. Constitution.

The Supreme Court had a rough start. Indeed, it seemed determined to prove Alexander Hamilton right that it was the weakest branch. Of the six original justices appointed by George Washington, one declined to serve and another never showed up for a formal session. The Court's first sessions lasted only a few days because it did not have much business. In fact, the Court did not decide a single case in 1791 or 1792. When Justice Rutledge resigned in 1791 to take a state court position, two potential appointees turned down the job in order to keep their positions in their state legislatures! Such career decisions would be unimaginable today, when serving on the Supreme Court is considered the pinnacle of a legal career.[3]

JUDICIAL REVIEW AND *MARBURY V. MADISON*

The Court started to gain more power when John Marshall was appointed chief justice in 1801. Marshall single-handedly transformed the Court into an equal partner in the system of checks and balances. The most important step was the decision *Marbury v. Madison* (1803), which gave the Supreme Court the power of **judicial review**. As noted, the framers were split on the wisdom of giving the Court the power to strike down laws passed by Congress; therefore the Constitution does not explicitly address the issue. However, historians have established that a majority of the framers, including the most influential ones, favored judicial

Judiciary Act of 1789 The law in which Congress laid out the organization of the federal judiciary. The law refined and clarified federal court jurisdiction and set the original number of justices at six. It also created the Office of the Attorney General and established the lower federal courts.

district courts Lower-level trial courts of the federal judicial system that handle most U.S. federal cases.

appellate jurisdiction The authority of a court to hear appeals from lower courts and change or uphold the decision.

judicial review The Supreme Court's power to strike down a law or executive branch action that it finds unconstitutional.

review. Given the silence of the Constitution, Marshall simply asserted that the Supreme Court had the power to determine when a law was unconstitutional.

Although the idea was not original to Marshall (the framers debated the issue and Hamilton endorsed it in some detail in *Federalist 78*), the Court had never exercised its authority to rule on the constitutionality of a federal law. The facts of the *Marbury* case involved a partisan dispute over last-minute appointments to a lower court by the outgoing Adams administration. The new Jefferson administration did not honor those appointments and one of the people who didn't get his position, Mr. Marbury, brought the case to the Supreme Court. Marshall said that Marbury was due his commission, but the Court did not have the power to give him his job because the part of the Judiciary Act of 1789 that gave it that power was unconstitutional! The core issue was Section 13 of the act, which gave the Court the power to issue orders (writs of mandamus) to anyone holding federal office. This section expanded the **original jurisdiction** of the Supreme Court, and that was where Congress overstepped its bounds, according to Marshall. The original jurisdiction of the Court is clearly specified in the Constitution, so any attempt by Congress to change that jurisdiction through legislation would be unconstitutional; the only way to change original jurisdiction would be through a constitutional amendment.[4] Marshall writes, "It is emphatically the province and duty of the judicial department to say what the law is. . . . If two laws conflict with each other, the courts must decide on the operation of each. So if a law be in opposition to the Constitution . . . the courts must determine which of these conflicting rules governs the case. This is of the very essence of judicial duty."[5]

By asserting its power to review the constitutionality of laws passed by Congress, the Court became an equal partner in the institutional balance of power. Although more than 50 years would pass before the Court would use judicial review again to strike down a law passed by Congress (in the unfortunate 1857 *Dred Scott* case concerning slavery that basically led to the Civil War), the reasoning behind *Marbury* has never been challenged by subsequent presidents or Congresses.[6]

Interpreting federal laws may seem a logical responsibility for the Supreme Court, but what about state laws? Should the Supreme Court have final say over them as well? The Constitution does not answer this question. However, the supremacy clause requires that the Constitution and national laws take precedence over state constitutions and state laws when they conflict. And the Judiciary Act of 1789 made it clear that the Supreme Court would rule on these matters.

It didn't take long for the Court to assert its power in this area. In 1796 the Court heard a case concerning a British creditor who was trying to collect a debt from the state of Virginia. The state had passed a law canceling all debts owed by Virginians (or the state) to British subjects. However, the Treaty of Paris, which ended the Revolutionary War and recognized American independence, ensured the collection of such debts. This conflict was resolved when the Court struck down the state law and upheld Americans' commitments under the treaty.[7] Advocates of states' rights were not happy with this development, but it was crucial for the national government that the Constitution be applied uniformly rather than be subject to different interpretations by every state.

original jurisdiction The authority of a court to handle a case first, as in the Supreme Court's authority to initially hear disputes between two states. However, original jurisdiction for the Supreme Court is not exclusive; it may assign such a case to a lower court.

CHIEF JUSTICE JOHN MARSHALL favored the idea of judicial review and claimed this power for the Court in the *Marbury v. Madison* decision.

JURISDICTION OF THE FEDERAL COURTS AS DEFINED IN ARTICLE III OF THE CONSTITUTION

JURISDICTION OF LOWER FEDERAL COURTS

▶ Cases involving the U.S. Constitution, federal laws, and treaties.

▶ Controversies between two or more states. (Congress passed a law giving the Supreme Court exclusive jurisdiction over these cases.)

▶ Controversies between citizens of different states.

▶ Controversies between a state and citizens of another state. (The Eleventh Amendment removed federal jurisdiction in these cases.)

▶ Controversies between a state or its citizens and any foreign states, citizens, or subjects.

▶ Cases affecting ambassadors, public ministers, and consuls.

▶ Cases of admiralty and maritime jurisdictions.

▶ Controversies between citizens of the same state claiming lands under grants of different states.

JURISDICTION OF THE SUPREME COURT

Original Jurisdiction[a]

▶ Cases involving ambassadors, public ministers, and consuls.

▶ Cases to which a state is a party.

Appellate Jurisdiction

▶ Cases falling under the jurisdiction of the lower federal courts, "with such exceptions, and under such Regulations as the Congress shall make."

[a]This does not imply exclusive jurisdiction. For example, the Supreme Court may refer to a district court a case involving an ambassador (the more likely outcome).

Source: Lee Epstein and Thomas G. Walker, Constitutional Law for a Changing America: Institutional Powers and Constraints, *5th ed. (Washington, DC: CQ Press, 2004), p. 65.*

JUDICIAL REVIEW IN PRACTICE

The contours of the relationship between the national government and the states were largely defined by how active the Supreme Court was in asserting judicial review and how willing it was to intervene in matters of state law. For much of the nineteenth century the Court embraced dual federalism, in which the national government and the states operated on two separate levels (see Chapter 3). Later the Court involved itself more in state law as it moved toward an increasingly active role for the national government in regulating interstate commerce and using the Fourteenth Amendment to selectively incorporate the amendments that constitute the Bill of Rights (see Chapter 4).

All in all, the Court has struck down more than 170 acts of Congress and about 1,400 state laws. This sounds like a lot, but Congress passed more than 60,000 laws in its first 220 years, so only about one-quarter of 1 percent have been struck down by the Court. The number of state laws passed throughout U.S. history is more difficult to measure, but the percentage of state laws that have been struck down is also quite small. Over time the Court has ruled on state laws in many important areas, including civil liberties, desegregation and civil rights, abortion, privacy, redistricting, labor laws, employment and discrimination, and business and environmental regulation.

When the Supreme Court strikes down a congressional or state law, it engages in **constitutional interpretation**—that is, it determines that the law is unconstitutional. But the Supreme Court also engages in **statutory interpretation**—that is, it applies national and state laws to particular cases (statutes are laws that are passed by legislatures). Often the language of a statute may be unclear, and the Court must interpret how to apply the law. For example, should the protection of endangered species prevent economic development that destroys the species' habitat? How does one determine whether an employer is responsible for sexual harassment in the workplace? How should the voting rights of minorities be protected? In cases such as these, the Court must interpret the relevant statutes to determine what Congress or the state legislatures really meant when issuing them.

Although politicians and other political actors accept judicial review as a central part of the political system, critics are concerned about its antidemocratic nature. Why, for example, do we give nine unelected justices such awesome power over our elected representatives? Debates about the proper role for the Court will continue as long as it is involved in controversial decisions. We take up this question later in the chapter when we address the concepts of judicial activism and judicial restraint.

constitutional interpretation The process of determining whether a piece of legislation or governmental action is supported by the Constitution.

statutory interpretation The various methods and tests used by the courts for determining the meaning of a law and applying it to specific situations. Congress may overturn the courts' interpretation by writing a new law; thus it also engages in statutory interpretation.

///

THE AMERICAN LEGAL AND JUDICIAL SYSTEM

OUTLINE THE STRUCTURE OF THE COURT SYSTEM

Two sets of considerations shed light on the overall nature of our judicial system: the fundamentals of the legal system that apply to all courts in the United States, and the structure of the court system within our system of federalism.

COURT FUNDAMENTALS

The general characteristics of the court system begin with the people who are in the courtroom. The **plaintiff** brings the case, and the **defendant** is the party who is being sued or charged with a crime. If the case is appealed, the petitioner is the person bringing the appeal, and the respondent is the party on the other side of the case. In a civil case, the plaintiff sues to determine who is right or wrong and to gain something of value, such as monetary damages, the right to vote, or admission to a university. In a criminal case, the plaintiff is the government, and the prosecutor attempts to prove the guilt of the defendant (the person accused of the crime).

plaintiff The person or party who brings a case to court.

defendant The person or party against whom a case is brought.

O. J. SIMPSON DONS A PAIR OF GLOVES during testimony in his double-murder trial in Los Angeles in June 1995. The jury was not convinced of his guilt "beyond all reasonable doubt" and thus acquitted Simpson in this criminal trial. However, a subsequent civil trial found that a "preponderance of evidence" was against him.

plea bargain An agreement between a plaintiff and defendant to settle a case before it goes to trial or the verdict is decided. In a civil case this usually involves an admission of guilt and an agreement on monetary damages; in a criminal case it often involves an admission of guilt in return for a reduced charge or sentence.

class-action lawsuit A case brought by a group of individuals on behalf of themselves and others in the general public who are in similar circumstances.

common law Law based on the precedent of previous court rulings rather than on legislation. It is used in all federal courts and forty-nine of the fifty state courts.

precedent A legal norm established in court cases that is then applied to future cases dealing with the same legal questions.

Many, but not all, civil and criminal cases are heard before a jury that decides the outcome in the case, which is called the verdict. Often cases get settled before they go to trial (or even in the middle of the trial) in a process known as **plea bargaining**. In a civil case, this would mean that the plaintiff and defendant agree on a monetary settlement and admission of guilt (or not; in some cases the defendant may agree to pay a fine or damages but not to admit guilt). In a criminal case, the defendant may agree to plead guilty in exchange for being charged with a lesser crime or for receiving a shorter sentence than might be imposed in a jury trial. Plea bargaining is an excellent example of how legal conflict between two parties can be resolved through a compromise that is satisfactory to both sides.

One type of civil suit is the **class-action lawsuit**, a case brought by a group of individuals on behalf of themselves and others in similar circumstances. The target may be a corporation that produced hazardous or defective products, or that engaged in illegal behavior that harmed a particular group. For example, in 1999, 1.5 million current and former female Walmart employees sued the retailing giant for sex discrimination, claiming that the store has paid women less than men for the same work and has promoted fewer women than men.[8] Class-action suits are often filed on behalf of shareholders of companies that have lost value because of fraud committed by corporate leaders. Cases like these are a very important mechanism for providing accountability and justice in our economic system.

COMMON LAW AND PRECEDENT

Forty-nine of the 50 states and the federal courts operate under a system of **common law**, which means that legal decisions build from precedent established in previous cases and apply commonly throughout the jurisdiction of the court. The alternative, which is practiced only in Louisiana, is the civil law tradition that is based on a detailed codification of the law that is applied to each specific case.

The notion of **precedent** (or stare decisis—"let the decision stand") deserves special attention. Precedent is a previously decided case or set of decisions that serves as a guide for future cases on the same topic. Lower courts are bound by Supreme Court decisions when there is a clear precedent that is relevant for a given case. In many cases, following precedent is not clear-cut because several precedents may seem relevant. The lower courts have considerable discretion in sorting out which precedents are the most important. The Supreme Court tries to follow its own precedents, but in the past 50 years justices have been willing to deviate from earlier decisions when they think that the precedent is flawed. As Table 12.1 shows, precedent is not a rule the Court must follow but a norm that constrains its behavior.

STANDING

Another factor must be considered before a case is filed: the person bringing the case must have **standing** to sue in a civil case, which means that there is a legitimate basis for bringing the case. This usually means that the individual has suffered some direct and personal harm from the action addressed in the court case. Standing is easy to establish for private parties—for example, if your neighbor destroys your fence, you have been harmed. However, it gets more interesting when

TABLE » 12.1

SUPREME COURT CASES OVERRULING PRECEDENT AND ACTS OF CONGRESS, 1789–2011

The Supreme Court has overruled precedent in a far higher proportion of cases in the past 60 years than it did during the first 160 years of U.S. history. More acts of Congress have also been struck down in recent years—but even in some earlier periods, the Court has played an activist role. What do these data say about the role of the Supreme Court within our constitutional system?

COURT (CHIEF JUSTICE)	YEARS	CASES OVERRULING PRECEDENT	PRECEDENTS OVERRULED	CASES OVERRULING ACTS OF CONGRESS	ACTS OVERRULED PER YEAR
Jay Court	1789–1795	0	0	0	0
Rutledge Court	1795	0	0	0	0
Ellsworth Court	1796–1800	0	0	0	0
Marshall Court	1801–1836	1	1	1	0.03
Taney Court	1836–1864	2	3	1	0.03
Chase Court	1864–1874	1	1	8	0.8
Waite Court	1874–1888	9	11	7	0.5
Fuller Court	1888–1910	3	4	13	0.52
White Court	1910–1921	4	4	10	1.1
Taft Court	1921–1930	5	6	13	1.44
Hughes Court	1930–1941	15	22	15	1.36
Stone Court	1941–1946	8	11	1	0.20
Vinson Court	1946–1953	6	11	2	0.28
Warren Court	1953–1969	37	53	23	1.44
Burger Court	1969–1986	46	62	31	1.82
Rehnquist Court	1986–2005	38	44	35	1.84
Roberts Court	2005–present	8	n.a.	8	1.3

Note: This table includes only cases in which the reversal of precedent is clearly stated in the Court decision. A single case can overrule more than one precedent.

Source: For 1789–2003, David G. Savage, Guide to the Supreme Court, *4th ed. (Washington, DC: CQ Press, 2004), pp. 320, 1192–1204. For 2004–11, The Supreme Court Database, Washington University, http://scdb.wustl.edu (accessed 10/2/12).*

the government is a party. For example, when an environmental group challenged the Interior Department's interpretation of the Endangered Species Act, the Court ruled that it did not have standing because it did not demonstrate that the government's policy would cause "imminent" injury to the group.[9] As we discuss below in the section on how cases get to the Supreme Court, federal judges have some leeway in defining standing.

standing Legitimate justification for bringing a civil case to court.

JURISDICTION

jurisdiction The sphere of a court's legal authority to hear and decide cases.

The final general characteristic of the legal system is the **jurisdiction** of the court: when bringing a case before the court, you must choose a court that actually has the power to hear your case. For example, if you want to contest a speeding ticket, you would not file your case in the state supreme court or the federal district court, but in your local traffic court. What if you believed you were the victim of discrimination in the workplace? Would you sue in state or federal court? You probably could do either, but the decision would be based on which set of laws would provide you more protection from discrimination. This varies by state, so the proper jurisdiction for a given case is often a judgment call based on specific legal questions.

STRUCTURE OF THE COURT AND FEDERALISM

The structure of the court system is just like that of the rest of the political system: it is divided within and across levels of government. Across the levels of government, the court system operates on two parallel tracks within the state and local courts and the national courts. Within each level of government, both tracks include courts of original jurisdiction, appeals courts, and courts of special jurisdiction. As the "How It Works" diagram shows, the state courts are entirely separate from the federal courts, with the exception of the small proportion of cases that are appealed from a state supreme court to the U.S. Supreme Court. There is much variation in the structure of state courts in terms of their names and the number of levels of courts. However, they all follow the same general pattern of trial courts with limited and general original jurisdiction and appeals courts (either one or two levels, depending on the state).

appeals courts The intermediate level of federal courts that hear appeals from district courts. More generally, an appeals court is any court with appellate jurisdiction.

PRESIDENTS CAN INFLUENCE THE direction of the federal courts by selecting judges who share their views. In his first term, President Obama had the opporutunity to nominate two justices to the Supreme Court: Sonia Sotomayor and Elena Kagan (shown here).

DISTRICT COURTS

The Judiciary Act of 1789 created the lower federal courts. Workhorses of the federal system, the district courts handle more than a quarter of a million filings a year. There are 89 districts in the 50 states, with at least one district court for each state. There are also district courts in Puerto Rico, the Virgin Islands, the District of Columbia, Guam, and the Northern Mariana Islands; this brings the total to 94 districts with 678 judges.[10] There are two limited jurisdiction district courts: the Court of International Trade, which addresses cases involving international trade and customs issues, and the U.S. Court of Federal Claims, which handles most claims for money damages against the United States, disputes over federal contracts, unlawful "takings" of private property by the federal government, and other claims against the United States.

APPEALS COURTS

The **appeals courts** (called "circuit courts" until 1948) are the intermediate courts of appeals, but in practice they are the final court for most federal cases that are appealed from the lower courts. The losing side in a federal case can appeal to the Supreme Court, but the highest court in the land hears so few cases that the appeals courts usually get the final word. Appeals courts did not always have this much power; in fact, through much of the nineteenth century they had very limited appellate jurisdiction and did not hear many significant cases.

The number of appeals courts slowly expanded as the workload grew, to the current 12 regional courts (the 11 numbered districts shown in Figure 12.1, plus the appeals court for the District of Columbia) and the Court of Appeals for the Federal Circuit, which handles specialized cases from all over the country. Today the only appeals of district court cases that go directly to the Supreme Court and bypass the appeals court are cases that concern legislative reapportionment and redistricting, voting rights, and some issues related to the 1964 Civil Rights Act.

THE SUPREME COURT

The Supreme Court sits at the top of the federal court system. The rest of this chapter outlines many important aspects of the Court, including how cases get to the Court, nominations, and judicial decision making. The immediate discussion concerns the Court's place within the judicial system and its relationship to the other courts.

The Supreme Court is the "court of last resort" for cases coming from both the state and the federal courts. One important function of the Court is to resolve conflicts between lower courts, or between a state law and federal law, or between the states, to ensure that the application and interpretation of the Constitution is consistent nationwide. For example, before the Court took up the issue of affirmative action in higher education, there were several conflicting lower court decisions,

FIGURE » 12.1

MAP OF THE FEDERAL APPEALS COURTS

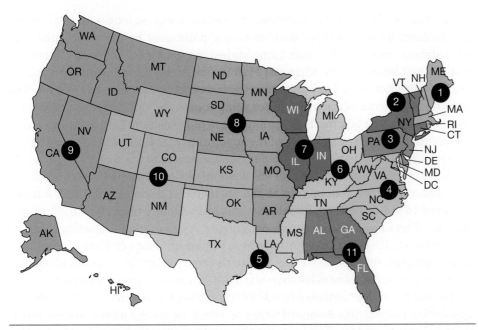

Source: U.S. Courts, Circuit Map, www.uscourts.gov/courtlinks (accessed 10/5/12).

which meant that affirmative action was legal in certain parts of the country and unconstitutional in other parts. A district court or appeals court ruling is applicable only for the specific region of that court, whereas Supreme Court rulings apply to the entire country.

Although the Supreme Court is the most important interpreter of the Constitution, the president and Congress also interpret the Constitution on a regular basis. This means that the Supreme Court does not always have the final say. For example, if the Court strikes down a federal law for being overly vague, Congress can rewrite the law to clarify the offending passage. When this happens, Congress may have the final word. For example, Congress overturned *Ledbetter v. Goodyear Tire and Rubber* (2007) when it passed the Lilly Ledbetter Fair Pay Act in 2009. The law said that the Supreme Court had misinterpreted the 1964 Civil Rights Act when it ruled in 2007 that Ledbetter would have had to file her pay discrimination suit within 180 days of being hired.[11]

Even on matters of constitutional interpretation rather than statutory interpretation, Congress can fight back by passing a constitutional amendment. However, this is a difficult and time-consuming process; hundreds of amendments are proposed every year, but very few even get a hearing or come to a vote in Congress, and even fewer are passed and submitted to the states for ratification (see Chapter 2). Nevertheless, that option is available as a way of overturning an unpopular Court decision.

HOW JUDGES ARE SELECTED

There are many mechanisms for placing judges in courts. At the national level, the president makes the appointments with the advice and consent of the Senate. At the state level, various methods are in use.

STATE-LEVEL JUDGES

At the state level there are five different means for selecting judges for trial courts: appointment by the governor (two states), appointment by the state legislature (two states), partisan elections (nine states), nonpartisan elections (17 states), and the system called the Missouri Plan in which the governor makes appointments from a list compiled by a nonpartisan screening committee (17 states; four more states use the Missouri Plan for some courts and another means for other courts).[12] With this last method, the appointed judge usually has to run in a retention election within several years of the appointment, making this system a hybrid of the political nomination and popular election routes to the court.

There is some controversy over the wisdom of electing judges. Such elections may undermine the courts' role as the protector of unpopular minority rights and even in states where judicial elections are officially nonpartisan, it is clear who the liberal and conservative candidates are, so judicial elections can be very partisan. Electing judges also raises the potential for conflicts of interest if campaign contributors have cases before the court.[13] On the other hand, elected judges will be more responsive to public opinion, especially on salient issues such as the death penalty[14] and abortion.[15] Furthermore, the alternative to elections—appointing judges—has been criticized as elitist by giving power over nominations to lawyers and for claiming that the process is "merit-based" without much evidence.[16]

How It Works

THE COURT SYSTEM

If federal question

State Supreme Courts
About 85,000 cases in 50 courts.

FINAL APPEALS COURTS

United States Supreme Court
Received 7,857 filings for the 2010–11 term; 86 cases argued; 83 disposed of in 75 signed opinions.*

Courts of Appeals
300,000 cases in the 38 states with courts of appeals.

INTERMEDIATE APPEALS COURTS

U.S. Courts of Appeals
12 regional courts and the U.S. Court of Appeals for the Federal Circuit; decided 55,126 cases in 2010–11.

TRIAL COURTS OF LIMITED AND SPECIAL JURISDICTION

Examples: Juvenile Court, Traffic Court, Small Claims Court, Justice of the Peace, Family Court.

TRIAL COURTS OF GENERAL AND ORIGINAL JURISDICTION

District Courts, County Courts, Municipal Courts
About 90 million filing in state and local courts of original jurisdiction.

TRIAL COURTS

TRIAL COURTS OF GENERAL AND ORIGINAL JURISDICTION

94 District Courts
Decided 289,252 civil cases and 78,440 criminal cases in 2010–11.

TRIAL COURTS OF LIMITED AND SPECIAL JURISDICTION

Examples: Federal Claims Court, Tax Court, Court of International Trade, Court of Veterans Appeals.

STATE AND LOCAL COURTS

FEDERAL COURTS

*Data on federal courts are from the U.S. Supreme Court, "2011 Year-End Report on the Federal Judiciary," www.supremecourt.gov/publicinfo/year-end/2011year-endreport.pdf (accessed 9/5/12).

POP QUIZ!

1 If you are convicted in a U.S. district court and want to appeal the ruling, with which court would you file an appeal?

a the state supreme court

b the state court of appeals

c the U.S. court of appeals for your region

d the U.S. Supreme Court

e none of the above

2 If your case is heard by your state supreme court and you want to appeal the decision, with which court would you file an appeal?

a the trial court of original jurisdiction

b the state court of appeals

c the U.S. court of appeals for your region

d the U.S. Supreme Court (if the case involves a federal question)

e none of the above

Answers: 1.c; 2.d

FEDERAL JUDGES

The Constitution does not specify requirements for serving on the federal courts, unlike the detailed stipulations for members of Congress and the president. Federal judges don't even have to have a law degree! (This is probably due to the limited number of law schools at the time of the Founding; someone who wanted to be a lawyer usually would have served as an apprentice to learn the trade.) The president appoints federal judges with the "advice and consent" of the Senate (the Senate must approve the nominees with a majority vote).

Nomination battles for federal judges can be intense because the stakes are high. As the discussion of judicial review made clear, the Supreme Court plays a central role in the policy process, and because a justice has life tenure, a justice's impact can outlive the president and Senate who put him or her on the Court. Judges often serve for decades, much longer than the people who appoint them.

THE ROLE OF THE PRESIDENT

Given the Constitution's silence on the qualification of federal judges, presidents have broad discretion over whom to nominate. Presidents have always tried to influence the direction of the federal courts and especially the Supreme Court by picking people who share their views. Because the Senate often has different ideas about the proper direction for the court, nomination disputes end up being a combination of debates over the merit of a nominee and of partisan battles about the ideological composition of the courts.

Although presidents would *like* to influence the direction of the courts, it is not always possible to predict how judges will behave once they are on the federal bench. However, the president can make a good guess about how a justice is likely to vote based on the nominee's party affiliation and the nature of his or her legal writings and decisions (if the nominee has prior judicial experience). Not surprisingly, 98 of 108 justices who have served on the Supreme Court have shared the president's party. Overall, more than 90 percent of the lower court judges appointed by presidents in the twentieth century also belonged to the same party as the president.

The most partisan move to influence the Court was President Franklin Delano Roosevelt's infamous plan to pack the Court. FDR was frustrated because the Court had struck down several pieces of important New Deal legislation, so to get a more sympathetic Court he proposed nominating a new justice for every justice who was more than 70 years old. Six justices were over 70, so this would have increased the size of the Court to 15. The plan to pack the Court ran into opposition, but in the "switch in time that saved nine," as it was called, the Court started ruling in favor of the New Deal legislation, so the plan was dropped.

In addition to ideological considerations about whom to nominate, the president also considers the individual's reputation as a legal scholar and his personal relationship to the candidate, as well as the candidate's ethical standards, gender, and race. See Table 12.2 for data on the latter two points.

THE ROLE OF THE SENATE

The other half of the equation to determine the composition of the federal courts is the Senate. It has shifted from having a very active role in providing "advice and consent" on court appointments to playing a passive role and then back to an active role. One constant is that the Senate rarely rejects nominees because of their qualifications, but rather for political reasons. Of 28 nominees rejected by the Senate in the history of the United States, only two were turned down because they were

TABLE » 12.2

THE DEMOGRAPHICS OF THE FEDERAL BENCH

All presidents try to appoint qualified candidates to the federal courts; however, there is variation in the types of people they nominate. Identify some characteristics common to most judges and some that vary across presidents. Which traits vary by the president's party?

	OBAMA[a]		W. BUSH		CLINTON		BUSH		REAGAN	
Experience[b]										
Judicial	61%	(36)	52%	(136)	52%	(159)	47%	(69)	46%	(134)
Prosecutorial	54	(32)	47	(123)	41	(126)	39	(58)	44	(128)
Neither	24	(14)	25	(65)	29	(88)	32	(47)	29	(83)
Average age at nomination	51		49.1		49.5		48.2		48.6	
Law school education										
Public	39%	(23)	49%	(128)	40%	(121)	53%	(78)	45%	(130)
Private	37	(22)	39	(102)	41	(124)	33	(49)	43	(126)
Ivy League	24	(14)	12	(31)	20	(60)	14	(21)	12	(34)
Gender										
Male	51%	(30)	79%	(207)	72%	(218)	80%	(119)	92%	(226)
Female	49	(29)	21	(54)	29	(87)	20	(29)	8	(24)
Ethnicity/race										
White	56%	(33)	82%	(213)	75%	(229)	89%	(132)	92%	(268)
African American	27	(16)	7	(18)	17	(53)	7	(10)	2	(6)
Hispanic	7	(4)	10	(26)	6	(18)	4	(6)	5	(14)
Asian	10	(6)	1	4	1.3	(4)	–	–	0.7	(2)
Native American	–		–	–	0.3	(1)	–	–	–	–
Percentage white male	30	(18)	67	(176)	52	(160)	73	(108)	85	(246)
Political identification										
Democrat	90%	(53)	8%	(21)	88%	(267)	6%	(9)	5%	(14)
Republican	–		83	(217)	6	(19)	89	(131)	92	(266)
Other	–		–	–	0.3	(1)	–	–	–	–
None	10%	(6)	9	(23)	6	(18)	5	(8)	3	(10)
Net worth										
Under $200,000	3%	(2)	5%	(13)	13%	(41)	10%	(15)	18%	(52)
$200–499,999	7	(6)	18	(47)	22	(66)	31	(46)	38	(109)
$500–999,999	20	(12)	22	(57)	27	(82)	26	(39)	22	(63)
$1+ million	66	(39)	55	(144)	38	(116)	32	(48)	23	(66)
Total number of appointees		59		261		305		148		290

[a]Through 2010.

[b]Percentages sum to more than 100 because some appointees have both judicial and prosecutorial experience.

Source: Sheldon Goldman, Sara Schiavoni, and Elliot Slotnick, "Obama's Judiciary at Midterm," Judicature 94:6 (May–June 2011): 296–97.

SENATE HEARINGS ON SUPREME
Court nominations have been more conflictual since the 1960s. Although Sonia Sotomayor was confirmed by a 68–31 vote in 2009, Senate Republicans challenged her to explain and defend her views on several issues.

senatorial courtesy A norm in the nomination of district court judges in which the president consults with his party's senators from the relevant state in choosing the nominee.

seen as unqualified. The other 26 nominees were rejected for political reasons. Most commonly, when a "lame duck" president makes a nomination and the Senate is controlled by the opposing party, the Senate will kill the nomination, hoping that its party will win the presidency and nominate a justice more to its liking.

However, not all recent Supreme Court nominations have been controversial. President Bill Clinton's two Supreme Court picks were judicial moderates who were overwhelmingly confirmed—Ruth Bader Ginsburg by a 96-to-3 vote and Stephen Breyer by an 87-to-9 margin. George W. Bush's nominees, John Roberts and Samuel Alito, were confirmed by comfortable margins; the former by a 78-to-22 vote, with half of the Democrats supporting him, and the latter by a 58-to-42 margin. President Obama appointed the first Hispanic to serve on the Supreme Court, Sonia Sotomayor, who was confirmed by a 68-to-31 vote. Elena Kagan's confirmation by a 63-to-37 vote in 2010 meant that three women are serving on the Court for the first time.

Contentious battles do occur, though, between the president and the Senate over nominees to the federal bench and the Supreme Court, and these have recently expanded to include nominees to the district and appeals courts. For much of the nation's history, the president did not play a very active role in the nomination process for district courts; instead, he deferred to the home-state senator of his own party to suggest candidates—a norm called **senatorial courtesy**. If there was no senator of the president's party from the relevant state, the president would consult House members and other high-ranking party members from the state. The president typically has shown more interest in appeals court nominations. The Justice Department plays a key role in screening candidates, but the local senators of the president's party remain active.

Lately, the process has become much more contentious. The confirmation rate for federal judges has gone from between about 80 and 100 percent to less than

FIGURE » 12.2

CONFIRMATION DELAY FOR FEDERAL JUDGES, 1981–2012

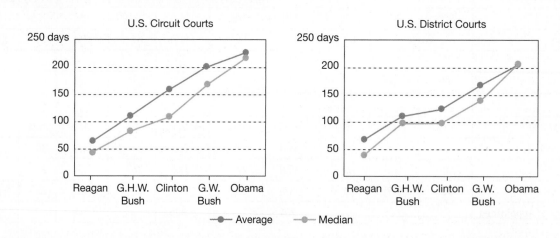

Source: "Length of Time from Nomination to Confirmation for 'Uncontroversial' U.S. Circuit and District Court Nominees: Detailed Analysis," Barry J. McMillion, Congressional Research Service, September 18, 2012, www.fas.org/sgp/crs/misc/R42732.pdf (accessed 10/2/12).

ADVICE AND CONSENT: PRINCIPLED OPPOSITION OR OBSTRUCTIONISM?

The use of the filibuster to stop presidential nominations to the federal courts has been the source of intense partisan battles in the past fifteen years (recall that forty-one senators can stop action on any bill or nomination through a filibuster). However, the positions in those battles are determined by which party controls the Senate and the presidency. Democrats who railed against Republican obstruction when Clinton was president used the same tactics when they were in the minority party and Bush was president. Now the tables are turned again and some of the strongest Republican critics of Democratic filibusters, such as Jeff Sessions, led the first filibuster against an Obama appeals court nominee (which failed).

The partisan struggles have led to serious discussion about limiting the use of the filibuster for court nominations. In Bush's first term, Senate Democrats stopped lower court nominees through the filibuster. After winning reelection in 2004, President Bush resubmitted seven nominees who had been rejected in the previous Senate (and thirteen more who were nominated in the previous term but did not come up for a vote). After Democrats indicated that they were not going to abandon the filibusters, the Republican leadership in the Senate considered implementing the "nuclear option," which would have prevented filibusters on judicial nominations (this plan gets its name because Democrats threatened to essentially shut down the Senate if they lost the filibuster). This crisis was defused when the "Gang of 14"—seven moderate Republicans and seven moderate Democrats—agreed to a compromise that preserved the Democrats' right to filibuster but only in the most extreme cases. The compromise was not put to a critical test (both of Bush's Supreme Court nominees were confirmed without filibusters), and Republicans have pursued an approach of delaying nominations through holds in the Judiciary Committee and on the floor.

Let's do a thought experiment to try to strip partisanship from this issue and figure out if you support the principle of filibustering judicial nominations. Put yourself in the place of a Democratic senator on the Judiciary Committee during the Bush years. President Bush has nominated a candidate for an appeals court position whom you believe is unqualified. Should you support a filibuster to stop the nomination even if it means that the Republican leadership might take away the filibuster? Now put yourself in the place of a Republican senator. You strongly favor President Bush's right to nominate whom he wants to the federal courts, and you support his policy positions, especially on abortion and the regulation of the free market. However, the Democrats are opposed and threatening to filibuster. You have to decide whether to support the "nuclear

When they are the minority party in the Senate, both Democrats and Republicans have been willing to use the filibuster to block judicial nominees.

option" to take away the Democrats' right to filibuster the nomination. There are at least fifty-six votes in favor of the nominee but not the sixty needed to cut off the filibuster. On the one hand, you don't think it is fair that Democrats are obstructing the vote. On the other hand, you were in the Senate back when the Republicans were in the minority, and you remember how important the filibuster was to protect the views of the minority party. You are worried that supporting the "nuclear option" would seriously damage the institution that you value and respect as the world's greatest deliberative body. What is the best option? You decide. What do you do?

Critical **Thinking** Questions

1. What would you do in the situation just described? Why?

2. Now to complete the thought experiment, flip the positions of the senators for an Obama nominee to the appeals court. Is your position still the same?

50 percent in recent years. When Republicans took control of the Senate in 1995, they stopped more than 60 of President Clinton's nominees to the lower federal courts. The average length of delay from nomination to confirmation has increased as well (see Figure 12.2). The situation has intensified since then (see "You Decide"). Democrats blocked 39 of President Bush's nominees between 2001 and 2009,[17] and Republicans have been returning the favor since then, blocking 20 of President Obama's nominees.[18]

///

DESCRIBE HOW CASES REACH THE SUPREME COURT

ACCESS TO THE SUPREME COURT

It is extremely difficult to have a case heard by the Supreme Court. Currently the Court hears about 1 percent of the cases submitted (roughly 85 of about 8,000 cases per year). This section explains how the Court decides which cases to hear. When a case is submitted, the clerk of the Court assigns it a number and places it on the docket, which is the schedule of cases.

THE COURT'S WORKLOAD

Statistics on the Supreme Court's workload initially suggest that the size of the docket has increased dramatically since the 1970s (see Figure 12.3). However, a majority of cases are frivolous and are dismissed after limited review.

Though the increase in workload is not as significant as it appears due to the high number of frivolous cases, another change is more important: the number of opinions issued by the Court has fallen by more than half in the past 20 years. The Court heard about 150 cases each year through the 1980s, but this number has fallen to only 75 to 85 in recent years (see again Figure 12.3).[19] There is no good explanation for why the Court issues half as many opinions as it used to, other than that the chief justices have decided that the Court shouldn't issue so many opinions.[20]

RULES OF ACCESS

With the smaller number of cases being heard, it is even more important to understand how the Court decides which ones to hear. There are four paths that a case may take to get to the Supreme Court.

First, Article III of the Constitution specifies that the Court has original jurisdiction in cases involving foreign ambassadors or foreign countries, or cases in which a state is a party. As a practical matter, the Court shares jurisdiction with the lower courts on these issues. In recent years, the Court has invoked original jurisdiction only in cases involving disputes between two or more states over territorial or natural resource issues. For example, New Jersey and New York disagreed over which state should control about 25 acres of filled land that the federal government had added around Ellis Island, and Kansas and Colorado disagreed over which state should have access to water from the Arkansas River (recent disputes

FIGURE » 12.3

THE COURT SEES MORE OPPORTUNITIES . . . BUT HEARS FEWER CASES

The Supreme Court's workload appears to be headed in two directions: the Court is receiving more cases but hearing fewer of them. What are the implications of having the Supreme Court hear fewer cases? Should something be done to try to get the Court to hear more cases?

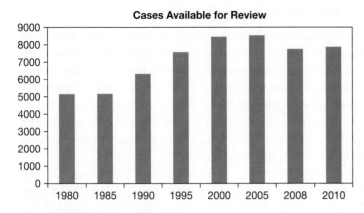

Cases Available for Review

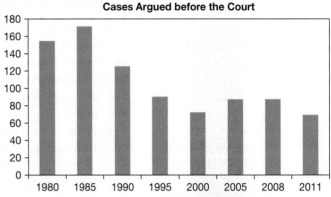

Cases Argued before the Court

Sources: Data compiled from "Chief Justice's Year-End Reports on the Federal Judiciary," www.supremecourtus.gov/publicinfo/year-end/2011year-endreport.html, and Kedar Bhatia, "Final Term 2011 Stat Pack and Summary Memo," SCOTUSblog, June 30, 2012, www.scotus.blog.com/2012/06/final-October-term-2011-stat-pack-and-summary-memo (accessed 10/2/12).

often concern water rights).[21] In the history of our nation, only about 175 cases have made it to the Court through this path, and typically these cases do not have any broader significance beyond the interest of the parties involved.[22]

The other three routes to the Court are all on appeal: as a matter of right (usually called "on appeal"), through certification, or through the writ of certiorari. Cases "on appeal" are those that Congress has determined to be so important that the Supreme Court must hear them. Lately Congress has given the Court much more discretion on these cases; the only ones that the Court is still compelled to take on appeal are some voting rights and redistricting cases.

A writ of certification occurs when an appeals court asks the Court to clarify a new point of federal law in a specific case. The Court can agree to hear the case, but given that appeals court judges and state supreme court judges are the only people who can make these requests, this path to the Court is very rare. (In fact, since 1982 the Court has not taken up a certified question from one of the appeals courts and has certified only five cases from state supreme courts.)[23]

The third path is the most common: at least 95 percent of the cases in most sessions arrive through a **writ of certiorari** (from the Latin "to be informed"). In these cases, a litigant who lost in lower court can file a petition to the Supreme Court explaining why it should hear the case. If four justices agree, the case will get a full hearing (this is called the "Rule of Four"). This process may sound simple, but sifting through the 8,000 or so cases that the Court receives every year and deciding which 85 of them will be heard is daunting. In fact, former justice William O. Douglas said that this winnowing process is "in many respects the most important and interesting of all our functions."[24]

writ of certiorari The most common way for a case to reach the Supreme Court, in which at least four of the nine justices agree to hear a case that has reached them via an appeal from the losing party in a lower court's ruling.

THE COURT'S CRITERIA

How does the Court decide which cases to hear? Several factors come into play, including the specific characteristics of the case and the broader politics surrounding it. Although several criteria generally must be met before the Court will hear the case, justices still have leeway in defining the boundaries of these conditions.

COLLUSION, STANDING, MOOTNESS, AND RIPENESS

First, there are the constitutional guidelines, which are sparse. The Constitution limits the Court to hearing actual "cases and controversies," which has been interpreted to mean that the Court cannot offer advisory opinions about hypothetical situations but must deal with actual cases. The term "actual controversy" also includes several other concepts that limit whether a case will be heard: collusion, standing, mootness, and ripeness. Collusion simply means that the litigants in the case cannot want the same outcome and cannot be testing the law without an actual dispute occurring between the two parties.[25]

Standing is the most general criterion; as noted above, it means that the party bringing the case must have a personal stake in the outcome. The Court has discretion in defining standing: it may hear cases that the justices think are important even when the plaintiff may not have standing, as traditionally understood, or it may duck cases that may be politically sensitive on the grounds that there is no standing. For example, the Court has decided several important racial redistricting cases even when the white plaintiffs had not suffered any personal harm by being in the black-majority districts.[26] On the other hand, in a politically sensitive case involving the pledge of allegiance and the First Amendment, the Court decided not to hear the case, saying the father of the student who brought the case did not have standing because he did not have sufficient custody over his daughter (he was divorced and the mother had primary custody).[27] Clearly the Court was more eager to voice its views on redistricting than on the pledge of allegiance because it could have just as easily ducked the former case by saying the plaintiffs did not have standing and ruled on the merits of the latter case.

Mootness means that the controversy must still be relevant when the Court hears the case. For example, a student sued a law school for reverse discrimination, saying that he had not been admitted because of the university's affirmative action policy. A lower court agreed and ordered that the student be admitted. The appeals court reversed the decision, but the student was allowed to remain enrolled while the case was appealed to the Supreme Court. By the time the Supreme Court received the case, the student was in his last semester of law school and the university said that he would graduate no matter the outcome of the case. Therefore, the Court refused to hear the case because it was moot.[28] However, there have to be exceptions to this principle because some types of cases would always be moot by the time they reach the Supreme Court. For example, exceptions have been made for abortion cases because a pregnancy lasts only nine months and the time that it takes to get a case from district court, to the appeals court, to the Supreme Court always takes longer than that.

Ripeness can be considered the opposite of mootness. With mootness the controversy is already over; with ripeness the controversy has not started yet. Just as you wouldn't want to eat a piece of fruit before it is ripe, the Court doesn't want to hear a case until it is ripe. Sometimes ripeness can affect standing. One exam-

mootness The irrelevance of a case by the time it is received by a federal court, causing the court to decline to hear the case.

ripeness A criterion that federal courts use to decide whether a case is ready to be heard. A case's ripeness is based on whether its central issue or controversy has actually taken place.

ple is the line item veto, which Congress gave to President Clinton at the start of his second term. Almost immediately some members of Congress challenged the constitutionality of the law because they believed that the president should not be able to veto part of a bill. The case was ultimately appealed to the Supreme Court, but the justices refused to hear it: because the issue was not ripe, the members of Congress did not have standing. That is, President Clinton had not yet used the line item veto, so there was no controversy and the members had not been harmed. Two months later Clinton used the veto, another case was filed, and the Court eventually struck down the law.[29]

Thousands of cases every year meet the basic criteria. One very simple guideline eliminates the largest number of cases: if a case does not involve a "substantial federal question," it will not be heard. This essentially means that the Court does not have to hear a case if the justices do not think the case is important enough. Of course, the "federal" part of this standard is also important: if a case is governed by state law rather than by federal law, the Court would decline to hear the case.

INTERNAL POLITICS

Since the late 1970s most justices have used a **cert pool**, whereby their law clerks take a first cut at the cases. (Law clerks to the justices are top graduates of elite law schools who help the justices with background research at several stages of the process.) Clerks write joint memos about groups of cases, providing their recommendations about which cases should be heard. The ultimate decisions are up to the justices, but clerks have significant power to help shape the agenda.

The chief justice has an important agenda-setting power: he decides the "discuss list" for a given day. Any justice can add a case to the list, but there is no systematic evidence on how often this happens. Only 20 to 30 percent of the cases are discussed in conference, which means that about three-quarters of the cases that are submitted to the Supreme Court are never even discussed by the Court. In most cases this is justified because of the high proportion of frivolous suits submitted to the Court.[30]

Many factors outside the legal requirements or internal processes of the Court influence access to the Court and which cases will be heard. Cases that have generated a lot of activity from interest groups or other governmental parties, such as the solicitor general, are more likely to be heard. The **solicitor general** is a presidential appointee who works in the Justice Department and supervises the litigation of the executive branch. In cases in which the federal government is a party, the solicitor general or someone else from that office will represent the government in court. The Court accepts about 70 to 80 percent of cases in which the U.S. government is a party, compared to about 1 percent overall.[31]

Even with these influences, the Court has a great deal of discretion on which cases it hears. Well-established practices such as standing, ripeness, and mootness may be ignored (or modified) if the Court wants to hear a specific case. However, one final point is important: although the justices may pick and choose their cases, they cannot set their own agenda. They can only select from the cases that come to them.

cert pool A system initiated in the Supreme Court in the 1970s in which law clerks screen cases that come to the Supreme Court and recommend to the justices which cases should be heard.

solicitor general A presidential appointee in the Department of Justice who conducts all litigation on behalf of the federal government before the Supreme Court and supervises litigation in the federal appellate courts.

IF HE OR SHE IS IN THE MAJORITY, THE chief justice decides who will write the majority opinion. Otherwise, the most senior justice in the majority makes the assignment. Since being named chief justice in 2005, John Roberts has spread opinion writing duties fairly evenly among the justices.

HEARING CASES BEFORE THE SUPREME COURT

A surprisingly small proportion of the Court's time is actually spent hearing cases—only 40 days in the 2012–13 term. The Court is in session from the first Monday in October through the end of June or early July. It hears cases on Mondays through Wednesdays in alternating two-week cycles in which it is in session from 10 A.M. to 3 P.M. with a one-hour break for lunch. In the other two weeks of the cycle when it is not in session, justices review briefs, write opinions, and sift through the next batch of petitions. On most Fridays when the Court is in session the justices meet in conference to discuss cases that have been argued and decide which cases they will hear. Opinions are released throughout the term, but the bulk of them come in May and June.[32]

The Court is in recess from July through September. The justices may take some vacation, but they mostly use the time for studying, reading, writing, and preparing for the next term. During the summer the Court also considers emergency petitions (such as stays of execution) and occasionally hears exceptionally important cases—as it did in 1974, for example, during the Watergate scandal when deciding whether President Nixon had to turn over tapes of conversations that had secretly been recorded in the White House.

BRIEFS

During the regular sessions, the Court follows rigidly set routines. The justices prepare for a case by reading the briefs that both parties submit. Because the Supreme Court hears only appeals, it does not call witnesses or gather new evidence. Instead, in structured briefs of no more than 50 pages, the parties present their arguments about why they either support the lower court decision or believe the case was improperly decided. Interest groups often submit **amicus curiae** ("friend of the court") briefs that convey their opinions to the Court; in fact, 85 percent of cases before the Supreme Court have at least one amicus brief.[33] The federal government also files amici curiae on important issues such as school busing, school prayer, abortion, reapportionment of legislative districts, job discrimination against women, and affirmative action in higher education.

It is difficult to determine the impact of amici curiae on the outcome of a case, but those that are filed early in the process increase the chances that the case will be heard. Interestingly, even amici curiae that are filed *against* a case increase the chances that the case will be heard.[34] Given the limited information that the justices have about any given case, interest group involvement can be a strong signal about the importance of a case.

ORAL ARGUMENT

Once the briefs are filed and have been reviewed by the justices, cases are scheduled for **oral arguments**. Except in unusual circumstances, each case gets one hour, which is divided evenly between the two parties. In especially

amicus curiae Latin for "friend of the court," referring to an interested group or person who shares relevant information about a case to help the Court reach a decision.

oral arguments Spoken presentations made in person by the lawyers of each party to a judge or appellate court outlining the legal reasons their side should prevail.

CAMERAS ARE NOT ALLOWED IN the Supreme Court, so artists' sketches are the only images of oral arguments. This sketch shows solicitor general Donald Verrilli arguing for the Affordable Care Act in 2012, as justices Antonin Scalia and John Roberts listen.

important cases, extra time may be granted. Usually there is only one lawyer for each side who presents the case, but parties that have filed amicus briefs may participate if their arguments "would provide assistance to the Court not otherwise available." Given the tight time pressures, the Court generally does not extend the allotted time to allow "friends of the court" to testify; their participation is usually limited to written briefs rather than oral arguments.

Some lawyers may not use all of their time because their train of thought is interrupted by aggressive questioning. Transcripts reveal that justices jump in with questions almost immediately, and some attorneys never regain their footing. The frequency and pointedness of the questions vary by justice, with Justices Scalia, Breyer, Kagan, and Sotomayor being the most aggressive on the current Court, while Justice Thomas has gone more than six years without asking a single question.[35] Cameras are not allowed in the courtroom, so most Americans have never seen the Court in action—though a small live audience is admitted every morning the Court is in session. If you are curious about oral arguments, audio recordings of every case since 1995 are available at www.oyez.org.

CONFERENCE

After oral arguments, the justices meet in conference to discuss and then vote on the cases. As with the initial conferences, these meetings are conducted in secret. We know, based on notes in the personal papers of retired justices, that the conferences are orderly and structured but can become quite heated. The justices take turns discussing the cases and outlining the reasons for their positions. This is the kind of internal debate that the justices have argued should remain confidential. They have expressed concern that premature disclosure of their private debates and doubts may undermine the Court's credibility and inhibit their exchange of ideas.

OPINION WRITING

After the justices indicate how they are likely to vote on a case, if the chief justice is in the majority (which is most of the time), he decides who will write the majority opinion. Otherwise, the most senior justice in the majority assigns the opinion. Many considerations determine how a case will be assigned. First, the chief justice will try to ensure the smooth operation of the Court, including considerations such as which justices may be able to take on the work of writing a given opinion. A second factor is the justices' individual areas of expertise. For example, Justice O'Connor developed expertise in racial redistricting cases and authored most of those decisions in the 1990s.

The final set of factors is more strategic: it includes the Court's external relations, internal relations, and the personal policy goals of the opinion assigner. The Court must be sensitive to how others might respond to its decisions because it must rely on the other branches of government to enforce its decisions. One famous example of this consideration in an opinion assignment came in a case from the 1940s that struck down a practice that had prevented African Americans from voting in Democratic primaries.[36] Originally, the opinion was assigned to Justice Felix Frankfurter, but Justice Robert Jackson wrote a memo suggesting that it might be unwise to have a liberal, politically independent Jew from the Northeast write an opinion that was sure to be controversial in the South. Chief Justice Harlan Fiske Stone agreed and reassigned the opinion to Justice Stanley Reed,

TYPES OF SUPREME COURT DECISIONS

Majority opinion: The core decision of the Court that must be agreed upon by at least five justices. The majority opinion presents the legal reasoning for the Court's decision.

Concurring opinion: Written by a justice who agrees with the outcome of the case but not with the legal reasoning. Concurring opinions may be joined by other justices. A justice may sign on to the majority opinion and write a separate concurring opinion.

Plurality opinion: Occurs when a majority cannot agree on the legal reasoning in a case. The plurality opinion is the one that has the most agreement (usually three or four justices). Because of the fractured nature of these opinions, they typically are not viewed as having as much clout as majority opinions.

Dissent: Submitted by a justice who disagrees with the outcome of the case. Other justices can sign on to a dissent or write their own, so there can be as many as four dissents. Justices can also sign on to part of a dissent but not the entire opinion.

Per curiam opinion: (Latin for "by the court") An unsigned opinion of the Court or a decision written by the entire Court. However, this is not the same as a unanimous decision that is signed by the entire Court. Per curiam opinions are usually very short opinions on noncontroversial issues, but not always. For example, *Bush v. Gore*, which decided the outcome of the 2000 presidential election, was a per curiam opinion. Per curiam decisions may also have dissents.

a Protestant and Democrat from Kentucky.[37] It may not seem that the Court is sensitive to public opinion, but these kinds of considerations happen fairly frequently in important cases. Internal considerations occasionally cause a justice to vote strategically— that is, different from his or her sincere preference—in order to be in the majority so the justice can assign the opinion (often to himself or herself).

After the opinions are assigned, the justices work on writing a draft opinion. Law clerks typically help with this process. The drafts are circulated to the other justices for comment and reactions. Some bargaining may occur, in which a justice says he or she will withdraw support unless a provision is changed. Justices may join the majority opinion, may write a separate concurring opinion, or may dissent (see Nuts and Bolts 12.2 for details on the types of opinions).

Two final points about the process of writing and issuing opinions are important. First, until the 1940s a premium was placed on unanimous decisions. This changed dramatically in the 1940s, when most cases had at least one dissent. Lately, about two-thirds of cases have a dissent. Second, dissents serve an important purpose: not only do they allow the minority view to be expressed but they also often provide the basis for subsequently reversing a poorly reasoned case. Moreover, when justices strongly oppose the majority decision, they may take the unusual step of reading a portion of their dissent from the bench.

ANALYZE THE FACTORS THAT INFLUENCE SUPREME COURT DECISIONS

SUPREME COURT DECISION MAKING

There are many different influences on judicial decision making. The two main categories are legal and political. Legal factors include the precedent of earlier cases and norms that justices must follow the language of the Constitution. Political influences include the justices' preferences or ideologies, their stances on whether the Court should take a restrained or activist role with respect to the elected branches, and external factors such as public opinion and interest group involvement.

LEGAL FACTORS

The most basic legal factor is stare decisis, or precedent, which we discussed earlier. Precedent does not determine the outcome of any given case, because every case has a range of precedent that can serve to justify a justice's decision. The "easy" cases, in which settled law makes the outcome obvious, are less likely to be heard by the Court because of the justices' desire to focus on the more controversial areas of unsettled law. However, in some areas of the law—such as free speech, the death penalty, and search and seizure—precedent is an important explanation for how the justices decide a case.

The various perspectives that emphasize the language of the Constitution all fall under the heading of **strict construction**. The most basic of these is the literalist view of the Constitution. Literalists argue that justices need to look no farther than the actual words of the Constitution. However, critics of strict construction point out that the Constitution is silent on many important points (such as a right to privacy) and could not have anticipated the changes in technology in the twentieth and twenty-first centuries that have many legal implications, such as eavesdropping devices, cloning, and the Internet. Also, though the language of the First Amendment is relatively clear when it comes to political speech, other equally important words of the Constitution such as "necessary and proper," "executive power," "equal protection," and "due process" are open-ended and vague.

Critics of the strict constructionist view are often described as supporting a **living Constitution** perspective on the document (see Chapter 2). They argue that strict construction can "make a nation the prisoner of its past, and reject any constitutional development save constitutional amendment."[38] If the justices are bound to follow the literal words of the Constitution, *with the meaning they had when the document was written,* we certainly could be legally frozen in time. Amending the Constitution is a long and difficult process, so that option is not always a viable way for the Constitution to reflect changing norms and values.

strict construction A way of interpreting the Constitution based on its language alone.

living Constitution A way of interpreting the Constitution that takes into account evolving national attitudes and circumstances rather than the text alone.

POLITICAL FACTORS

The living Constitution perspective points to the second set of influences on Supreme Court decision making: political factors. Indeed, many people are uncomfortable thinking about the Court in political terms and prefer to think of the image of "blind justice," in which constitutional principles are fairly applied. However, political influences are clearly evident in the Court—maybe less than in Congress or the presidency, but they are certainly present. This means that the courts respond to and shape politics in ways that often involve compromise, both within the courts themselves and in the broader political system.

POLITICAL IDEOLOGY AND ATTITUDES

The most important political factor is the justice's ideology or attitudes about various issues. Liberal judges are strong defenders of individual civil liberties (including defendants' rights), tend to be prochoice on abortion, support regulatory

policy to protect the environment and workers, support national intervention in the states, and favor race-conscious policies such as affirmative action. Conservative judges favor state regulation of private conduct (especially on moral issues), support prosecutors over defendants, tend to be pro-life on abortion, and support the free market and property rights over the environment and workers, states' rights over national intervention, and a color-blind policy on race. These are, of course, just general tendencies. However, they do provide a strong basis for explaining patterns of decisions, especially on some types of cases.

THE STRATEGIC MODEL

A strategic approach to understanding Supreme Court decision making focuses on justices' calculations about the preferences of the other justices, the president, and Congress, the choices that other justices are likely to make, and the institutional context within which they operate. After all, justices do not operate alone: at a minimum they need the votes of four of their colleagues if they want their position to prevail. Therefore, it makes sense to focus on the strategic interactions that take place to build coalitions.

The median voter on the Court—the one in the middle when the justices are arrayed from the most liberal to the most conservative—has an especially influential role in the strategic model. For many years the median justice was Sandra Day O'Connor; when Samuel Alito replaced her, Anthony Kennedy became the new median (see Figure 12.4). The four conservatives to his right and the four liberals to his left all wanted to attract his vote. When Justice Sotomayor replaced Justice Souter and when Justice Kagan replaced Justice Stevens, Kennedy remained the median voter on the Court. Research shows that at least one justice switches his or her vote at some stage in the process (from the initial conference to oral arguments to the final vote) on at least half of the cases, so strategic bargaining appears to be fairly common.[39] Our earlier discussion of opinion assignment and writing opinions to attract the support of a specific justice is more evidence in support of the strategic model.

SEPARATION OF POWERS

Another political influence on justices' decision making is their view of the place of the Court with respect to the democratically elected institutions (Congress and the president). Specifically, do they favor an activist or a restrained role for the Court? Advocates of **judicial restraint** argue that judges should defer to the elected branches and not strike down their laws or other actions. In contrast, advocates of **judicial activism** argue that the Court must play an active role in interpreting the Constitution to protect minority rights even if it means overturning the actions of the elected branches. Yet another approach says that these normative arguments about how restraint or activism ought to work don't really matter because the Court usually follows public opinion and rarely plays a lead role in promoting policy change.

Often, assessments of the Court's role vary with the views of a specific line of cases. A political conservative may favor "activist" decisions striking down environmental laws or workplace regulations but oppose activist decisions that defend

CHAPTER 5 CITED A SURVEY in which most respondents were unable to name any Supreme Court justices. Just so you are not in danger of falling into that category, as of fall 2012 the justices are (front row, left to right) Clarence Thomas, Antonin Scalia, John G. Roberts Jr. (chief justice), Anthony M. Kennedy, Ruth Bader Ginsburg, (standing, left to right) Sonia Sotomayor, Stephen Breyer, Samuel Alito Jr., and Elena Kagan.

judicial restraint The idea that the Supreme Court should defer to the democratically elected executive and legislative branches of government rather than contradicting existing laws.

judicial activism The idea that the Supreme Court should assert its interpretation of the law even if it overrules the elected executive and legislative branches of government.

flag burning or defendants' rights. Political liberals may be the opposite—calling for judicial restraint on the first set of cases but activism in protecting civil liberties. Sometimes, the popular media mistakenly assert that liberal justices are more activist than conservative justices. In fact, though, that is not always the case. The current Court is quite conservative, but it is also activist.[40]

The separation of powers continues to play a role after the justices have issued their rulings. In some instances the Court can force its view on the other branches; in other cases it needs their support to enforce its decisions. Some decisions are nearly self-enforcing because of their visibility and narrow application. For example, in 1974 Richard Nixon had to go along with the Court ruling forcing him to give up his secret tapes in the Watergate investigation or else face impeachment. Yet the Court's lack of enforcement power is especially evident when a ruling applies broadly to millions of people who care deeply about the issues. Consider school prayer, which still exists in hundreds of public schools despite having been ruled unconstitutional over forty years ago. It is impossible to enforce the ban unless someone in a school complains and brings a lawsuit.

The president and Congress often fight back when they think the Court is exerting too much influence, which can limit the Court's power as a policy-making institution. For example, the president can fail to enforce a decision vigorously, and Congress can block appointments it disagrees with, limit the jurisdiction of the federal courts, change the size of the Court, or even impeach a judge. The latter three options are rarely used. The most common way for Congress to respond to a Court decision that it disagrees with is to pass legislation that overturns the decision (if the case concerns the interpretation of a law). In general, the Court avoids stepping on the toes of the other branches unless it is absolutely necessary. The Court often exercises self-imposed restraint and refuses to act on "political questions"—issues that are outside the judicial domain and should be decided by elected officials.

OUTSIDE INFLUENCES: INTEREST GROUPS AND PUBLIC OPINION

Finally, there are external influences on the Court, such as public opinion and interest groups. We have already talked about the role of interest groups in filing amicus briefs. When it comes to the Court, this is the only avenue of influence open to interest groups; other tactics such as lobbying or fund-raising are either inappropriate or irrelevant (because justices are not elected). The role of public opinion is more complex. Obviously, justices do not consult public opinion polls the way elected officials do. However, there are several indirect ways that the Court expresses the public's preferences.

The first indirect way involves the fact that the public elects the president and the Senate, who appoint and confirm the justices. Therefore, sooner or later, the Court should reflect the views of the public. Work by political scientists has

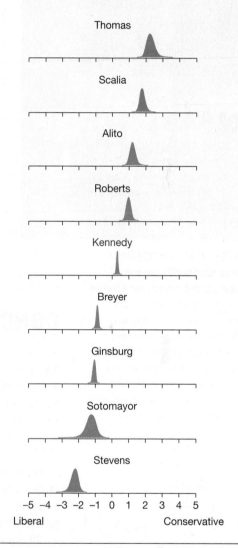

FIGURE » 12.4

IDEOLOGY OF SUPREME COURT JUSTICES, 2010

Notice that the estimates of the justices' ideology vary in their precision. What might explain the relatively tight distribution for Breyer or Kennedy, compared to the broad distribution for Sotomayor?

Source: Alexander Tahk and Stephen Jessee, Supreme Court Ideology Project, http://sct.tahk.us/current.html (accessed 10/2/12).

confirmed this to be largely the case,[41] especially in recent years when Supreme Court nominations have become more political and more important to the public.[42]

The second mechanism through which public opinion may influence the Court is somewhat more direct: when the public has a clear position on an issue that is before the Court, the Court tends to agree with the public.[43] Several high-profile examples support the idea that the Court is sensitive to public opinion: the Court's switch during the New Deal in the 1930s to support Roosevelt's policy agenda after standing in the way for four years, giving in to wartime opinion to support the internment of Japanese Americans during World War II, limiting an accused child molester's right to confront his accuser in a courtroom, and declaring that laws limiting sex between consenting gay adults were unconstitutional. In each of these cases the justices reflected the current public opinion of the nation rather than a strict reading of the Constitution or the Founders' intent.

Another way that the Court may consider the public mood is to shift the timing of a decision. The best example here is the landmark school desegregation case, *Brown v. Board of Education* (1954), that the Court sat on for more than two years—until after the 1952 presidential election—because it didn't think the public was ready for its bombshell ruling.[44] Others have argued that the Court rarely *changes* its views to reflect public opinion, but at a minimum the evidence supports the notion that the Court is usually in step with the public.

HIGH SCHOOL STUDENTS IN MAIZE, Kansas, join hands around a flagpole at the annual nationwide event calling Christian youth to preclass schoolyard prayer at the start of the new school year. Enforcing the prohibition of school prayer and drawing the line between permissible and impermissible prayer have both been difficult for the Court.

CONCLUSION

The judicial branch as a whole contains a paradox: it may simultaneously be seen as the least democratic and the most democratic branch of government.[45] The least democratic aspect is obvious: federal judges and many state and local judges are unelected and are not accountable to voters (except indirectly through the leaders who appoint them). But the courts can also be seen as the most democratic branch. Cases that are brought to the courts come from the people, and as long as the legal criteria for bringing a case are met, the courts must hear those cases. Although only a small fraction of the cases brought to the Supreme Court are heard, the court system as a whole may be seen as providing an important outlet for participation in our political system.

The courts also demonstrate that politics is conflictual. Although plenty of unanimous Supreme Court decisions do not involve much conflict among the justices, many landmark cases deeply divide the Court on constitutional interpretation and how to balance those competing interpretations against other values and interests. These conflicts in the Court often reveal deeper fault lines in the broader political system.

It shouldn't be surprising that political process matters in the courts. The rules of courtroom procedures, including how evidence is gathered and presented, can have an important impact on outcomes. If lawyers do not follow these procedural rules, a case that otherwise could have been won, might be thrown out by

a judge. Political process is also important for selecting judges and determining which cases the Supreme Court hears.

Politics is indeed everywhere, even in the courts, where you would least expect to see it. Despite the idealized image of Justice as a blindfolded woman holding a set of scales, politics affects everything from the selection of judges to the decisions they make. Some characteristics of the federal courts (most important being judges' lifetime tenure) insulate the system from politics. However, courts are subject to influence by judges' ideologies, interest groups, and the president and Senate, who try to shape their composition through the nomination process.

Returning to the example that opened this chapter demonstrates the important role that the courts play in the political system. The Supreme Court endorsed the national government's dominant role in shaping immigration policy, but also recognized the states' right to enforce the federal law. The federal courts may serve as a referee between the other branches, and between the national and state government, defining the boundaries of permissible conduct.

THE DEVELOPMENT OF AN INDEPENDENT AND POWERFUL FEDERAL JUDICIARY

▶ Explain how the power of judicial review was established. **Pages 357–61**

SUMMARY

In contrast to other branches of government, the Constitution offers few specifics on the organization of the judiciary. In fact, most of the details on the arrangement of the judiciary do not come from the Constitution at all, but from congressional action. In addition, the Supreme Court's strongest power—judicial review—is not even mentioned in the Constitution but was established in the *Marbury v. Madison* decision.

KEY TERMS

Judiciary Act of 1789 (p. 358)

district courts (p. 358)

appellate jurisdiction (p. 358)

judicial review (p. 358)

original jurisdiction (p. 359)

constitutional interpretation (p. 361)

statutory interpretation (p. 361)

CRITICAL THINKING AND DISCUSSION

What do recent decisions on immigration and health care reform reveal about the role of the Supreme Court in our political system? Did the Founders approve of the practice of judicial review?

PRACTICE QUIZ QUESTIONS

1. Most of the details about the Supreme Court were established in _____.
    a) the Judiciary Act of 1789
    b) Article I of the Constitution
    c) Article II of the Constitution
    d) the *Federalist Papers*
    e) *Marbury v. Madison*

2. *Marbury v. Madison* is significant because it _____.
    a) established the Supreme Court
    b) introduced the process of selective incorporation
    c) changed the manner of judicial selection
    d) established judicial review
    e) gave Supreme Court justices lifetime appointments

3. Judicial review enables the Supreme Court to _____.
    a) submit legislation to Congress
    b) strike down laws passed by Congress
    c) revise laws passed by Congress
    d) oversee presidential appointments to the bureaucracy
    e) approve judicial appointments to lower courts

THE AMERICAN LEGAL AND JUDICIAL SYSTEM

▶ Outline the structure of the court system. **Pages 361–72**

SUMMARY

All courts within the United States have a similar set of fundamental attributes, such as the distinction between civil and criminal cases and the reliance on legal precedent. The judicial system is divided between state and federal courts, and within each level of government, there are courts of original jurisdiction and appeals courts.

KEY TERMS

plaintiff (p. 361)

defendant (p. 361)

plea bargain (p. 362)

class-action lawsuit (p. 362)

common law (p. 362)

precedent (p. 362)

standing (p. 363)

jurisdiction (p. 364)

appeals courts (p. 364)

senatorial courtesy (p. 370)

CRITICAL THINKING AND DISCUSSION

What is the proper role for the Senate in providing "advice and consent" on the selection of federal judges? Should the Senate play the role of an equal partner to the president or simply approve most of the president's choices?

PRACTICE QUIZ QUESTIONS

4. A system of _____ relies on legal decisions that built from precedent established in previous cases.
   a) common law
   b) civil law
   c) statutory law
   d) stare decisis
   e) plea bargaining

5. When one has suffered direct and personal harm from the action addressed in a case, it is called

   _____.
   a) precedent
   b) appellant
   c) plea bargaining
   d) jurisdiction
   e) standing

6. The president appoints federal judges with the "advice and consent" of the _____.
   a) House of Representatives
   b) Senate
   c) Supreme Court
   d) Attorney General
   e) vice president

ⓢ PRACTICE ONLINE

"Critical Thinking" exercise: *Political Process Matters— Senatorial Approval and the Nomination Process*

ACCESS TO THE SUPREME COURT

▶ Describe how cases reach the Supreme Court. **Pages 372–75**

SUMMARY

The Supreme Court hears only about 1 percent of the cases that are brought to it. To help decide which cases to hear, the Court generally uses four factors: collusion, standing, mootness, ripeness. Ultimately, the justices have a great deal of discretion in deciding to hear a case, but they can only hear cases that come to them.

KEY TERMS

writ of certiorari (p. 373)

mootness (p. 374)

ripeness (p. 374)

cert pool (p. 375)

solicitor general (p. 375)

7. When a litigant who lost in a lower court files a petition, the case reaches the Supreme Court _____.
   a) as a matter of right
   b) through a writ of certification
   c) through a writ of certiorari
   d) as a matter of original jurisdiction
   e) through senatorial courtesy

8. _____ means that the controversy is not relevant when the Court hears the case.
   a) Mootness
   b) Ripeness
   c) Collusion
   d) Standing
   e) Precedent

9. Most justices _____ in initially deciding which cases should be heard.
   a) personally review all cases
   b) personally review a random sample of cases
   c) follow the recommendations of the chief justice
   d) use a random selection process
   e) use a cert pool

HEARING CASES BEFORE THE SUPREME COURT

▶ Describe the Supreme Court's procedures for hearing a case. **Pages 376–78**

SUMMARY

When hearing a case, the justices prepare by reading briefs before they hear the oral arguments. After oral arguments, the justices meet in conference to discuss and vote on the cases. The majority opinion explains the rationale for how a decision is reached, though justices can also write dissenting and concurring opinions if they agree with the outcome of the case, but not the legal reasoning.

KEY TERMS

amicus curiae (p. 376)

oral arguments (p. 376)

PRACTICE QUIZ QUESTIONS

10. Oral arguments generally last _____, and justices _____ wait until the end of the arguments to ask questions.
   a) one hour; do
   b) one hour; do not
   c) one day; will
   d) one week; do
   e) one week; do not

11. Generally, the chief justice or the _____ justice decides who writes the majority opinion; justices' individual areas of expertise _____ a factor in making this assignment.
   a) most junior; are not
   b) most junior; are
   c) most senior; are not
   d) most senior; are
   e) dissenting; are not

> ⑤ **PRACTICE ONLINE**
>
> "Critical Thinking" exercise: *Politics Is Conflictual— Sandra Day O'Connor on* The Daily Show

SUPREME COURT DECISION MAKING

▶ Analyze the factors that influence Supreme Court decisions. **Pages 378–82**

SUMMARY

The Court makes decisions based on legal factors, such as legal precedent and informal legal norms, and political factors, such as the justices' own ideologies and position on the role that the Court plays in government. Though the Court does not consult public opinion the way elected officials do, most of its decisions generally stay in step with the views of the public.

KEY TERMS

strict construction (p. 379)

living Constitution (p. 379)

judicial restraint (p. 380)

judicial activism (p. 380)

CRITICAL THINKING AND DISCUSSION

Should unelected judges have the ability to overturn laws passed by the elected branches? If so, should there be any mechanism for *political* accountability?

PRACTICE QUIZ QUESTIONS

12. The perspective that when the Constitution is not clear, the justices should be guided by what the Founders wanted is called _____.
   a) judicial activism
   b) strict construction
   c) original intent
   d) attitudinalist approach
   e) interpretive statute

13. Advocates of _____ argue that the Court must defer to the elected branches and not strike down their laws.
   a) judicial restraint
   b) judicial activism
   c) judicial limitation
   d) legal maximization
   e) the strategic model

14. In general, the Court _____ challenges with the elected branches and often _____ to act on "political questions."
   a) avoids; agrees
   b) avoids; refuses
   c) pursues; agrees
   d) pursues; refuses

ⓢ PRACTICE ONLINE

"Big Think" video exercise: *The Challenge of Constitutional Interpretation*

SUGGESTED READING

Baum, Lawrence. *Judges and Their Audiences: A Perspective on Judicial Behavior*. Princeton, NJ: Princeton University Press, 2006.

Cornell University Law School, Supreme Court Collection, http://supct/law.cornell.edu/supct.

Eisgruber, Christopher L. *Constitutional Self-Government*. Cambridge, MA: Harvard University Press, 2001.

Hansford, Thomas G., and James F. Spriggs II. *The Politics of Precedent on the U.S. Supreme Court*. Princeton, NJ: Princeton University Press, 2006.

Northwestern University, Oyez: Supreme Court Multimedia, www.oyez.org.

O'Brien, David M. *Storm Center: The Supreme Court in American Politics*. 9th ed. New York: Norton, 2011.

Rosen, Jeffrey. *The Most Democratic Branch: How the Courts Serve America*. New York: Oxford University Press, 2006.

Sunstein, Cass R., David Schkade, Lisa M. Ellman, and Andres Sawicki. *Are Judges Political? An Empirical Analysis of the Federal Judiciary*. Washington, DC: Brookings Institution Press, 2006.

Tushnet, Mark. *A Court Divided: The Rehnquist Court and the Future of Constitutional Law*. New York: Norton, 2006.

U.S. Supreme Court website, www.supremecourt.gov.

13

Civil Rights

ve your papers ready—
acial profiling just ahead.

uéntame   paid for by Brave New Foundation

CRITICS OF A 2010 IMMIGRATION law in Arizona worried that it would subject Latinos to racial profiling. One group opposing the law sponsored this billboard in Phoenix to draw attention to their concerns. Supporters of the law, such as Phoenix sheriff Joe Arpaio, argued that strong measures were necessary to discourage illegal immigration.

JOE ARPAIO OF PHOENIX, ARIZONA, IS THE self-described "toughest sheriff in America." He was also the target of a U.S. Justice Department investigation of discriminatory practices in the enforcement of immigration laws. He is either a hero or villain, depending on one's views concerning illegal immigration. Supporters see him as a courageous fighter who enforces the law that the federal government seems unable or unwilling to do. Critics see him as a bigoted publicity hound who abuses the civil rights of nonwhites living in Maricopa County, Arizona.

A Justice Department report issued in 2011 concluded that Arpaio's county sheriff office has "a pervasive culture of discriminatory bias against Latinos . . . that violates the Constitution and federal law."[1] In an example of "egregious racial profiling," Latino drivers were four to nine times more likely to be stopped than non-Latino drivers.[2] Sheriffs used minor traffic violations, such as failure to signal a lane change, to pull over Latinos and ask for their documents. One incident that drew international attention was a sweep of a town of about 6,000 Yaqui Indians and Latinos outside of Phoenix. Over two days, more than 100 deputies conducted hundreds of searches, netting nine undocumented immigrants. Subsequently one report said, "The community was so scarred by the event that families are still terrified to leave their homes when they see the Sheriff's patrol cars."[3]

Sheriff Arpaio defended his office, saying, "We are proud of the work we have done to fight illegal immigration."[4] One of the most popular politicians in Arizona, Arpaio has been re-elected four times since taking office in 1993. All the

CONFLICT & COMPROMISE
in American Politics

Republican presidential candidates heavily courted him in 2011, demonstrating his political clout within the party. While the federal abuse of power investigation was closed without criminal charges being brought against Arpaio, a class action civil suit is still in the courts as of early 2013.

Enforcing immigration law is extremely conflictual. Hardliners want to secure our nation's borders while deporting all illegal immigrants; the alternative is to control illegal immigration while protecting the civil rights of citizens and legal residents and providing a path to citizenship for illegal residents who are productive and law abiding. The issue seems to defy compromise: President Bush tried and failed to enact comprehensive immigration reform, and President Obama has not fared any better in his first term. However, nearly everyone agrees that the current immigration system is broken. Obama is determined to enact reforms in his second term. Any reform that secures our borders while protecting the civil rights of law-abiding people will involve compromise.

Civil rights policy encompasses much more than immigration policy. It demonstrates that politics is everywhere: policies concerning discrimination in the workplace, in housing, and against women, minorities, gay men and lesbians, and the disabled affect millions of Americans every day. To see how civil rights policy may affect you, consider the following scenarios:

▶ You are driving home with friends after a party. You have not had anything to drink and are following all traffic laws. Suddenly red flashing lights signal you to pull over. As the police officer approaches, you wonder if this happened because you and your friends are African Americans driving in an all-white neighborhood. Have your civil rights been violated? Now imagine a car full of white teenagers with all the other facts the same. Can an officer pull you over just because he thinks that teenagers are more likely to be engaging in criminal activity than older people?

▶ Scenario two: you are a 21-year-old Asian American woman applying for your first job out of college. After being turned down for the job at an engineering firm, you suspect that you didn't get the job because you are a woman and would not fit in with the "good ol' boy" atmosphere of the firm. Have your civil rights been violated?

▶ You and your gay partner are told that "your kind" are not welcome in the apartment complex where you would like to live. Should you call a lawyer?

▶ You are a white male graduating from high school. After you receive a rejection letter from the college that was your first choice, a friend tells you that one of your classmates got into the same school even though he had the same grades as you and his SAT scores were slightly lower. Your friend says that it is probably because of the school's affirmative action policy— the classmate who was accepted is Latino. Are you a victim of "reverse discrimination"? Have your civil rights been violated?

All these scenarios seem to be civil rights violations. However, some are, some are not, and some depend on additional considerations (we will return to these examples in the Conclusion). Applying civil rights law can be very complex, but a central goal of this chapter is to clarify the origins of specific civil rights by examining the policy-making process. This chapter will also focus on the theme that political process matters by highlighting how civil rights enforcement has varied over time and across institutions. That is, sometimes the Supreme Court is a strong defender of civil rights and Congress is not. At other times, the reverse has been true.

A GROUP OF TEENAGERS IS DETAINED and questioned by police. When is a police stop legitimate? How do we know if it might be a violation of civil rights?

THE CONTEXT OF CIVIL RIGHTS

DESCRIBE THE HISTORICAL STRUGGLES GROUPS HAVE FACED IN WINNING CIVIL RIGHTS

We begin by examining the context of civil rights: we define civil rights and then provide a historical overview of the struggle for civil rights.

In general, **civil rights** involve the right to be free from discrimination. The terms *civil rights* and *civil liberties* are often used interchangeably, but there are important differences. Civil liberties are the freedoms guaranteed in the Bill of Rights, such as freedom of speech, religious expression, and the press, as well as the "due process" protection of the Fourteenth Amendment. In contrast, civil rights protect all persons from discrimination and are rooted in laws and the equal protection clause of the Fourteenth Amendment. Moreover, civil liberties primarily limit what the government can do to you ("*Congress* shall make no law . . . abridging the freedom of speech"), whereas civil rights protect you from discrimination both by the government and by individuals. To oversimplify, civil liberties are about freedom, and civil rights are about equality.

Neither civil liberties nor civil rights figured prominently at the Constitutional Convention. Equality is not even mentioned in the Constitution or the Bill of Rights. The Bill of Rights is centrally concerned with freedom, but it was not added to the Constitution until the Antifederalists made it a condition for ratification, as discussed in Chapter 2. However, equality was very much on the Founders' minds, as is evident in this ringing passage from the Declaration of Independence: "We hold these truths to be self evident, that all men are created equal, that they are endowed by the Creator with certain unalienable rights, that among these are life, liberty, and the pursuit of happiness." Despite the broad language, this was a limited conception of equality because women had no political or economic rights at that time. Similarly, equality did not apply to slaves or to Native Americans. Even propertyless white men did not have full political rights until several decades after

civil rights Rights that guarantee individuals freedom from discrimination. These rights are generally grounded in the equal protection clause of the Fourteenth Amendment and more specifically laid out in laws passed by Congress, such as the 1964 Civil Rights Act.

the Constitution was ratified. Indeed, equality and civil rights in the United States have been a continually evolving work in progress.

AFRICAN AMERICANS

From the early nineteenth century, with the abolitionists' efforts, until the mid-twentieth century and the civil rights movement, the central focus of civil rights was on African Americans. Other groups received attention more gradually. For example, starting in the mid-nineteenth century women began their fight for equal rights, and over the next century the civil rights movement expanded to include groups such as Native Americans, Latinos, and Asian Americans. Most recently, attention has turned to the elderly, the disabled, and the LGBT community (lesbian, gay, bisexual, and transgender people). The most divisive civil rights issue with the greatest long-term impact, however, has been slavery and its legacy.

SLAVERY AND ITS IMPACT

Slavery was part of the American economy from nearly the beginning of the nation's history. Dutch traders brought 20 slaves to Jamestown, Virginia, in 1619, a year before the Puritans came to Plymouth Rock. Between 1619 and 1808, when the importation of slaves was banned, about 600,000 to 650,000 slaves were forcibly brought from Africa to the United States (and about 75,000 to 100,000 more were brought from Africa but died in transit).[5]

It is impossible to overstate the importance of slaves to the southern economy. The 1860 census shows that there were 2.3 million slaves in the Deep South, constituting 47 percent of its population, and nearly 4 million slaves overall. Most slaves worked on plantations, but others labored as shipyard workers, carpenters, bakers, stone masons, millers, spinners, weavers, and domestic servants. In the states that later seceded from the Union, 30.8 percent of households owned slaves. The economic benefits of slavery for the owners were clear. By 1860, the per capita income for whites in the South was $3,978; in the North it was $2,040. The South had only 30 percent of the nation's free population, but it had 60 percent of the wealthiest men.[6]

Abolitionists worked to rid the nation of slavery as its importance to the South grew, setting the nation on a collision course that would not be resolved until the Civil War. The Founders largely ducked the issue (see Chapter 2), and subsequent legislatures and courts did not fare much better. The **Missouri Compromise** of 1820, which limited the expansion of slavery and kept the overall balance between slave states and free states, eased tensions for a while, but the issue persisted. Slave owners became increasingly frustrated with the success of the Underground Railroad, which helped some slaves escape to the North. The debate over admitting California as a free state or a slave state (or making it half free and half slave) threatened to split the nation once again. Southern states agreed to admit California as a free state, but only if Congress passed the Fugitive Slave Act, which required northern states to treat escaped slaves as property and return them to their owners. Soon after, Congress enacted the Compromise of 1850, which overturned the Missouri Compromise and allowed each new state to decide for itself whether to be a slave state or a free state.

All possibility of further compromise ended when the misguided *Dred Scott v. Sandford* decision of 1857 ruled that states could not be prevented from allow-

Missouri Compromise An agreement between pro- and antislavery groups passed by Congress in 1820 in an attempt to ease tensions by limiting the expansion of slavery while also maintaining a balance between slave states and free states.

ing slavery. It also held that slaves were property rather than citizens and had no legal rights. With Abraham Lincoln's victory in the 1860 presidential election, the southern states believed that slavery was in jeopardy, so they seceded from the Union and formed the Confederacy.

The outcome of the Civil War restored national unity and ended slavery, but the price was very high. About 528,000 Americans died in the war, with an astonishingly high casualty rate of 25 percent among combatants.[7] Republicans moved quickly to ensure that the changes accomplished by the war could not be easily undone: they promptly adopted the Civil War Amendments to the Constitution. The Thirteenth Amendment banned slavery, the Fourteenth guaranteed that states could not deny newly freed slaves the equal protection of the laws and provided citizenship to anyone born in the United States, and the Fifteenth gave African American men the right to vote. These amendments were ratified within five years, although southern states resisted giving freed slaves "equal protection of the laws" over the next 100 years.

SLAVERY WAS PART OF THE AMERICAN economy from the 1600s until the Civil War in 1861. The system of slavery in the South created a highly unequal society in which African Americans were denied virtually all rights.

SLOW PROGRESS AFTER RECONSTRUCTION

During Reconstruction (1866–77), blacks in the South gained political power through institutions such as the Freedmen's Bureau and the Union League. With the protection of the occupying northern army, blacks were able to vote and even hold public office. However, when federal troops withdrew and the Republican Party abandoned the South, blacks were almost completely **disenfranchised** through the imposition of residency requirements, poll taxes, literacy tests, the **grandfather clause**, physical intimidation, and other forms of disqualification. Later the practice known as the "white primary" allowed only whites to vote in Democratic primary elections; given that the Republican Party did not exist in most southern states, blacks were effectively disenfranchised. Although most of these provisions claimed to be race neutral, their impact fell disproportionately on black voters and virtually eliminated black voting. Despite the constitutional guarantees of the Fourteenth and Fifteenth Amendments, blacks had little access to the political system in the South, and they had little success in winning office at any level in the rest of the nation.[8]

The social and economic position of blacks in the South followed a path similar to their political fortunes. When Reconstruction ended in 1877 the southern states enacted "black codes," or **Jim Crow laws,** that led to complete segregation of the races. Jim Crow laws forbade interracial marriage and mandated the separation of the races in neighborhoods, hotels, apartments, hospitals, schools, restrooms, drinking fountains, restaurants, elevators, and even cemetery plots. In cases where it would have been inconvenient to completely separate the races, as in public transportation, blacks had to sit in the back of the bus or in separate cars on the train and give up their seats to whites if asked. The Supreme Court validated these practices in *Plessy v. Ferguson* (1896) in establishing the **"separate but equal"** doctrine, officially permitting segregation as long as blacks had equal facilities.

Initially after Reconstruction, the rest of the nation mostly ignored the status of blacks because 90 percent of all African Americans lived in the South. But as blacks' northward migration gradually transformed the nation's demographic

disenfranchised To have been denied the ability to exercise a right, such as the right to vote.

grandfather clause A type of law enacted in several southern states to allow those who were permitted to vote before the Civil War, and their descendants, to bypass literacy tests and other obstacles to voting, thereby exempting whites from these tests while continuing to disenfranchise African Americans and other people of color.

Jim Crow laws State and local laws that mandated racial segregation in all public facilities in the South, many border states, and some northern communities between 1876 and 1964.

"separate but equal" The idea that racial segregation was acceptable as long as the separate facilities were of equal quality; supported by *Plessy v. Ferguson* and struck down by *Brown v. Board of Education.*

profile and its racial politics, America's "race problem" was no longer a southern problem. Although conditions for blacks were generally better outside the South, they still faced discrimination and lived largely segregated lives throughout the nation. In World Wars I and II, black soldiers fought and died for their country in segregated units. Professional sports teams were segregated, and black musicians and artists could not perform in many of the nation's leading theaters. Blacks largely were hired for the lowest-paying, menial jobs.

Real progress began in the 1940s. The Supreme Court struck down the white primary in 1944, Jackie Robinson broke the color line in major league baseball in 1947, and President Harry Truman issued an executive order integrating the U.S. armed services in 1948. Then came the landmark decision *Brown v. Board of Education* (1954), which rejected the "separate but equal" doctrine, followed by *Brown II* (1955), which ordered that public schools be desegregated "with all deliberate speed." These events set the stage for the growing success of the civil rights movement, discussed later in this chapter.

NATIVE AMERICANS, ASIANS, AND LATINOS

The legacy of slavery and racial segregation has been the dominant focus of U.S. civil rights policies, but many other groups as well have fought for equal rights. Understanding the history of these struggles is also necessary to understand today's civil rights policies.

Native Americans were the first group to confront the European immigrants. Though most initial relations were good, the settlers' appetite for more land and their insensitivity to Native American culture fostered continual conflict. The Native Americans were systematically pushed from their land and placed on reservations. The most infamous example was the removal of 46,000 members of the "Five Civilized Tribes" from the southeastern United States under the Indian Removal Act of 1830. Thousands of Native Americans died on the "trail of tears" on their way to reservations in Oklahoma.[9] Native Americans had no political rights; they were considered "savages" to be eliminated. They did not gain the right to vote until 1924, just after women and well after black men. Although the U.S. government signed treaties with them that regarded their tribes as sovereign nations (not foreign nations but "domestic dependent nations"),[10] in practice the government ignored most of the agreements. Only recently has it started to uphold its obligations, although compliance remains spotty. Native Americans have struggled to maintain their cultural history and autonomy in the face of widespread poverty and unemployment.

Latinos also have struggled for political and economic equality. The early history is rooted in the Mexican-American War (1846–48) and the conquest by the United States of much of the territory that today makes up most of the southwestern states. One of their first major political successes was Cesar Chavez's effort to organize farm workers in the 1960s and 1970s. He established the United Farm Workers union and forced growers to bargain with 50,000 mostly Mexican American field-workers in California and Florida. While many Mexican Americans have roots that go back hundreds of years, most Latinos have been in the United States for less than two generations and have become a political force only recently, despite now constituting the nation's largest minority.

Latinos' relative lack of political clout when compared to African Americans derives from two factors. First, Latinos vote at a much lower rate than African

Americans because of language barriers and because about one-third of Latinos are not U.S. citizens (a requirement for voting in national elections). Second, unlike African Americans, Latinos are a relatively diverse group politically. They include Mexican Americans, Cuban Americans, Puerto Ricans, Dominicans, and people from many other Latin American nations. Most Latino voters are loyal to the Democratic Party, but a majority of Cuban Americans are strong Republicans. Although this diversity means that Latino voters do not speak with one voice, it brings opportunity for increased political clout in the future because both parties are eager to attract them as new voters.

Asian Americans have experienced discrimination since their arrival in the United States in the nineteenth century. The first wave of Chinese immigrants came with the 1848 California gold rush and staked out their claims along with Americans. However, by 1850, when the easy-to-find gold was gone, Americans tried to drive out the Chinese through violence and the Foreign Miners Tax. Subsequently, Chinese immigrants worked on building the intercontinental railroad between 1865 and 1869; but since they were given the more dangerous jobs, many lost their lives. After the railroad was completed, Chinese workers returned to the West Coast, where they experienced increasing discrimination and violence. When Congress passed the Chinese Exclusion Act of 1882, Chinese already in the United States were prevented from becoming U.S. citizens. (The Supreme Court later granted their American-born children automatic citizenship under the Fourteenth Amendment.)[11] The Chinese Exclusion Act also barred virtually all immigration from China—the first time in U.S. history that a specific ethnic group was singled out in this way. Later, during World War II, Japanese Americans were singled out and placed in internment camps for fear that they were enemy supporters. In recent decades a diverse range of Asians have emigrated to the United States, including Koreans, Filipinos, Hmong, Vietnamese, and Asian Indians; their diversity in culture means that they display equally diverse political views and voting patterns.

WOMEN AND CIVIL RIGHTS

When John Adams attended the Constitutional Convention in 1787, his wife, Abigail, advised him not to "put such unlimited power in the hands of the husbands. Remember, all men would be tyrants if they could. . . . If particular care and attention is not paid to the ladies, we . . . will not hold ourselves bound by any laws in which we have no voice or representation."[12] John Adams did not listen to his wife. The Constitution did not give women the right to vote, and they were not guaranteed that civil right until the Nineteenth Amendment was ratified in 1920. Until the early twentieth century, women in most parts of the country could not hold office, serve on juries, bring lawsuits in their own name, own property, or serve as legal guardians for their children. A woman's identity was so closely tied to her husband that if she married a noncitizen she automatically gave up her citizenship. The rationale for these policies was called **protectionism**: women were considered too frail to compete in the business world and were seen as needing to be protected by men.

protectionism The idea under which some people have tried to rationalize discriminatory policies by claiming that some groups, like women or African Americans, should be denied certain rights for their own safety or well-being.

While protectionist sentiment waned by the mid-twentieth century, as recently as 1961 a court upheld a Florida law that automatically exempted women, but not men, from compulsory jury duty. Later in this chapter we describe how the Supreme Court has moved away from this discriminatory position and rejected protectionist thinking toward women.

GAY MEN AND LESBIANS

The most recent group in the struggle for civil rights is the LGBT community. For most of American history, gay men and lesbians lived secret lives and faced abuse and discrimination if they came out. The critical moment that spurred the gay rights movement occurred in 1969, during a police raid on the Stonewall Inn in New York City. (Police often raided gay bars to harass patrons and selectively enforce liquor laws.)[13] Rather than submitting to the arrests, the customers fought back, throwing stones and beer bottles, breaking windows, and starting small fires. Several hundred people gathered, and the fighting raged for three nights. The Stonewall Rebellion was a galvanizing event for the gay community by demonstrating the power of collective action.

Since Stonewall, the gay rights movement has made progress through political mobilization and protest, legislative action, and legal action. Public support for gay rights has increased dramatically in recent years. In fact, a CBS News poll showed that 63 percent of Americans believe that same-sex couples should be entitled to the same benefits as heterosexual couples, whereas only 32 percent think they should not.[14] In May 2012, President Obama endorsed same-sex marriage for the first time, completing his gradual evolution on the issue. Thus, public support for equal rights based on sexual orientation is growing.

> ANALYZE INEQUALITY AMONG RACIAL, ETHNIC, AND SOCIAL GROUPS TODAY

THE RACIAL DIVIDE TODAY

Why does the history of civil rights matter for politics today? First, the effects of slavery and Jim Crow laws are still evident: legal racial segregation ended less than 50 years ago, and its legacy—especially in the relative quality of education available to most whites and blacks—remains. As noted, other racial and ethnic minorities have also faced exclusion and discrimination. Second, active discrimination based on race, gender, and sexual orientation is still evident in our society. In addition to unequal treatment, a gulf remains between the quality of life of minorities and that of whites, as well as between each group's political views. Although substantial progress has been made in bridging that gulf, inequalities in political, social, and economic conditions remain.

DIFFERENCES IN VOTING ACCESS

The political divide is mostly evident in lower levels of voter turnout among racial minorities relative to whites. Different rates of voter turnout can mostly be accounted for by education and income—especially between blacks and whites—but there are many examples of practices and institutions that depress minority turnout. And many of these are intentional. They include moving and reducing the number of polling places in minority-majority areas, changing from district-based to at-large elections, redistricting to dilute minority voting power, withholding information about registration and voting procedures from blacks, and "causing or taking advantage of election day irregularities."[15]

Consider the 2008 elections, in which numerous practices likely led to voter suppression and intimidation. Some were based on race. Three states removed voters from the voting rolls if there wasn't an identical match between the name the voter used when registering to vote and the name as it appeared in another state database (often, driver's license information). States also used voter purges (seven states), challenges targeting minority voters (five states), technical barriers to voter registration and voting (six states), student voting barriers (seven states), voter registration access (a number of states did not comply with the law that requires voter registration services at social services offices), voter intimidation and deceptive practices (fourteen states), and poor ballot design (three states).[16]

DESPITE THE REMOVAL OF MOST formal barriers to voting, Latinos are less likely to vote and participate in politics than whites, blacks, and Asian Americans. Groups like Voto Latino (represented here by Rosario Dawson and John Leguizamo) have tried to mobilize Latino voters in recent elections.

SOCIOECONOMIC INDICATORS

The racial divide is also evident in social and economic terms, as an overview of demographic data reveals. Nearly three times as many black families are below the poverty line as white families, and the poverty rate of 25.3 percent for Hispanic families in 2009 was similar to that of black families.[17] Furthermore, black median household income in 2011 was only 58.2 percent of median white family income, and the average white household had more than six times the assets of the typical nonwhite family. In 2010 the median household net worth was $130,600 for whites and $20,400 for nonwhites. Figures for Hispanics are somewhat better, but the gaps are still large. Hispanic household income was 69.7 percent of white income, $38,626 compared to $55,412.[18] Poverty is concentrated in areas of the country where the minority population is highest (see Figures 13.1A and 13.1B).

FIGURE » 13.1A

PERCENTAGE OF PEOPLE IN POVERTY, 2010

Together, these maps show that the poverty rate in the United States is closely related to the minority population. How do you think these patterns might affect the politics of civil rights policies that are aimed at reducing discrimination in the workplace or housing?

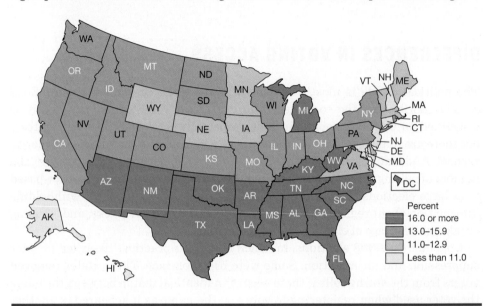

Percent
- 16.0 or more
- 13.0–15.9
- 11.0–12.9
- Less than 11.0

FIGURE » 13.1B

PERCENTAGE OF THE POPULATION THAT IS WHITE, 2010

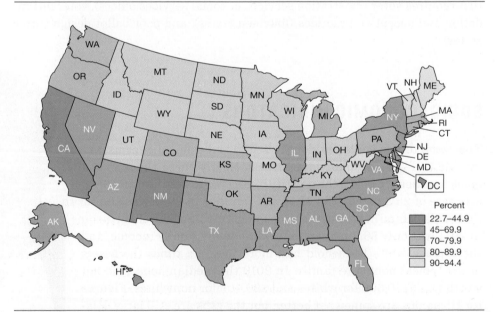

Percent
- 22.7–44.9
- 45–69.9
- 70–79.9
- 80–89.9
- 90–94.4

Source: Poverty data from U.S. Census Bureau, "Poverty: 2010 and 2011 American Community Surveys," September 2010, www.census.gov/acs; race data from U.S. Census Bureau, 2012 Statistical Abstract, Population Table 18, "Resident Population by Hispanic Origin and State; 2010," www.census.gov/compendia/statab/2012/tables/12s0018.pdf (accessed 11/3/12).

Other indicators show similar patterns. For example, the rate of black, adult male unemployment has been about twice as high as that of white adult males for the past 45 years. On every measure of health—life expectancy, infectious diseases, infant mortality, cancer rates, heart disease, and strokes—the gaps between whites and blacks are large and, in many cases, increasing.[19]

CRIMINAL JUSTICE AND HATE CRIMES

The greatest disparity between racial minorities and whites may be in the criminal justice system. Racial profiling subjects many innocent blacks to intrusive searches. In addition, blacks are not only more likely than whites to be convicted for the same crimes but also likely to serve longer sentences.[20] And African Americans and other minorities are subjected to hate crimes much more frequently than whites. According to the FBI, of the 6,624 hate crimes committed in 2010, 47.3 percent were race related. Of these, nearly 70 percent were "anti-black" and only 18 percent were "anti-white," which means that the rate of anti-black hate crimes is more than five times what would be expected based on the percentage of African Americans in the United States, while the rate of anti-white hate crimes is about one-fourth as high as would be expected.[21]

This backdrop of racial inequality, discrimination, and violence drives civil rights activists to push their agenda in the three branches of government: legislative, executive, and judicial. In some instances, activists work in several arenas simultaneously; in others, they seek redress in one arena after exhausting alternatives. The civil rights movement, which was crucial in the early policy successes, also continues to mobilize the grass roots.

JAMES BYRD JR. WAS MURDERED In Jasper, Texas, by three white supremacists who chained him to a pickup truck and dragged him down a road until he was decapitated. According to FBI statistics, in 2008 nearly three-quarters of race-related hate crimes in the United States were "anti-black."

THE POLICY-MAKING PROCESS AND CIVIL RIGHTS

> EXPLAIN THE APPROACHES USED TO BRING ABOUT CHANGE IN CIVIL RIGHTS POLICY

Our nation's system of separated and shared powers almost ensures that each branch has some say in making policy. Each has played a central role at different points in history. For example, in the 1940s and 1950s the courts were considered the most sympathetic branch for advancing the civil rights agenda because segregationist southern Democrats controlled key congressional committees and none of the presidents of this era made civil rights a top priority. Then, in the mid-1960s, Congress took the lead role by passing landmark legislation.

The policy-making process in the area of civil rights also provides insight into the importance of federalism. To promote African Americans' civil rights, the national government required the southern states to desegregate schools, allow blacks to vote, and generally dismantle the system of segregation, thus demonstrating the importance of nation-centered federalism. However, in terms of gay rights, state and local governments have taken the lead role. Congress, in contrast, has taken steps to restrict gay rights, especially gay marriage (although with a few important exceptions, such as the service of gay men and lesbians in the military).

In terms of women's rights, both the national and state governments have taken important actions.

SOCIAL MOVEMENTS

It is important not to overlook the importance of social movements. From the early women's rights movement and abolitionists of the nineteenth century to the gay rights and civil rights movements of the mid-twentieth century, activists have pressured the political system to change civil rights policies. Through collective action, these social movements have made sure that such controversial issues remained on the policy agenda.

Women started to push for the right to vote at a convention in 1848 at Seneca Falls, New York. Subsequently, a constitutional amendment to give women the right to vote was regularly introduced in Congress between 1878 and 1913 but never was passed, despite the efforts of women such as Susan B. Anthony and Elizabeth Cady Stanton. After a parallel movement at the state level had some success, the constitutional amendment finally passed in 1919 and was ratified in 1920.

The civil rights movement of the 1950s and 1960s, aimed at ending segregation and gaining equal political and social rights for blacks, is the most famous example of a successful social movement (see Figure 13.2). Although the *Brown v. Board of Education* decision, which struck down segregation in public schools, gave the movement a boost, most southern blacks saw little change in their daily lives after

CIVIL RIGHTS TIMELINE

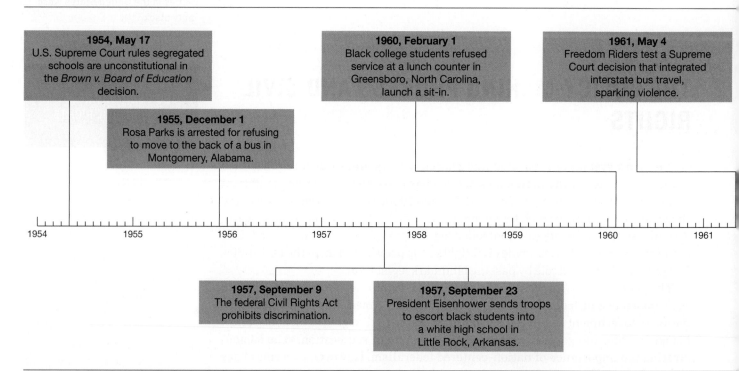

1954, May 17
U.S. Supreme Court rules segregated schools are unconstitutional in the *Brown v. Board of Education* decision.

1955, December 1
Rosa Parks is arrested for refusing to move to the back of a bus in Montgomery, Alabama.

1960, February 1
Black college students refused service at a lunch counter in Greensboro, North Carolina, launch a sit-in.

1961, May 4
Freedom Riders test a Supreme Court decision that integrated interstate bus travel, sparking violence.

1957, September 9
The federal Civil Rights Act prohibits discrimination.

1957, September 23
President Eisenhower sends troops to escort black students into a white high school in Little Rock, Arkansas.

Source: Adapted from "Key Moments in Civil Rights History," Ann Arbor News, *January 11, 2004, www.mlive.com/news/aanews/index.ssf?/base/features-0/1073819921106320.xml.*

the ruling. As white school boards and local governments resisted integration, black leaders became convinced that the only way to change the laws was to get the public, both black and white, to demand change.

The spark came in 1955 in Montgomery, Alabama, when Rosa Parks refused to give up her seat on a bus to a white person, as she was required to do by law. When she was arrested, local civil rights leaders organized a boycott of the bus company. Whites in Montgomery tried to stop the boycott, including arresting and fining blacks who arranged a car pooling system to get to work: people waiting for a ride were arrested for loitering, and car pool drivers were arrested for lacking appropriate insurance or having too many people in their car. Martin Luther King Jr., the group's elected leader, was subjected to harassment and violence—his house was firebombed, and he was arrested several times. Finally a federal district court ruled that the segregation policy was unconstitutional, and the Supreme Court upheld the ruling.

NONVIOLENT PROTEST

In 1960, four black students in Greensboro, North Carolina, went to a segregated lunch counter at a local Woolworth's and asked to be served. They waited for an hour without being served and had to leave when the store closed. When 20 students returned the next day, national wire services picked up the story. Within two weeks the sit-ins spread to 11 cities. In some cases the students encountered violence; in others they were simply arrested. However, they continued to respond with passive resistance, and succeeding waves of protesters replaced those who were arrested. The Student Nonviolent Coordinating Committee (SNCC) was

FIGURE » 13.2

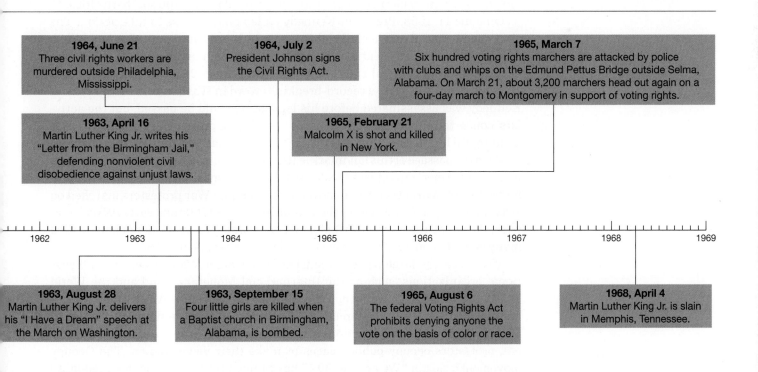

1964, June 21
Three civil rights workers are murdered outside Philadelphia, Mississippi.

1964, July 2
President Johnson signs the Civil Rights Act.

1965, March 7
Six hundred voting rights marchers are attacked by police with clubs and whips on the Edmund Pettus Bridge outside Selma, Alabama. On March 21, about 3,200 marchers head out again on a four-day march to Montgomery in support of voting rights.

1963, April 16
Martin Luther King Jr. writes his "Letter from the Birmingham Jail," defending nonviolent civil disobedience against unjust laws.

1965, February 21
Malcolm X is shot and killed in New York.

1962   1963   1964   1965   1966   1967   1968   1969

1963, August 28
Martin Luther King Jr. delivers his "I Have a Dream" speech at the March on Washington.

1963, September 15
Four little girls are killed when a Baptist church in Birmingham, Alabama, is bombed.

1965, August 6
The federal Voting Rights Act prohibits denying anyone the vote on the basis of color or race.

1968, April 4
Martin Luther King Jr. is slain in Memphis, Tennessee.

CIVIL RIGHTS LEADER MARTIN LUTHER KING JR. waves to supporters from the steps of the Lincoln Memorial on August 28, 1963, in Washington, DC. The March on Washington drew an estimated 250,000 people who heard King deliver his famous "I Have a Dream" speech.

created to coordinate the protests. The Greensboro Woolworth's was integrated on July 26, 1961, but the protests continued in other cities. By August 1961, the sit-ins had 70,000 participants and 3,000 arrests.[22] The sit-ins marked an important shift in the tactics of the civil rights movement away from the court-based approach and toward the nonviolent civil disobedience that had been successful in Montgomery.

The next significant events occurred in Birmingham, Alabama, which experienced 18 unsolved bombings of black churches and homes in a six-year period. During a peaceful protest in 1963, Martin Luther King Jr. and many others were arrested. While in solitary confinement, King wrote his "Letter from the Birmingham Jail," an eloquent statement of the principles of nonviolent civil disobedience. Responding to white religious leaders who said that King's actions were "unwise and untimely" and that "when rights are consistently denied, a cause should be pressed in the courts and in negotiations among local leaders, and not in the streets," King wrote a justification for civil disobedience, asserting that everyone had an obligation to follow just laws but an equal obligation to break unjust laws.

PUBLIC OPINION AND LEGISLATIVE ACTION

Following King's release from jail, the situation escalated. The protest leaders decided to use children in the next round of demonstrations. After more than 1,000 children were arrested and the jails were overflowing, the police turned fire hoses and police dogs on children trying to continue their march. Media coverage turned public opinion in favor of the marchers as the country expressed outrage over the violence in Birmingham. Similar protests occurred in over 100 southern cities.

On June 11, 1963, President Kennedy called on Congress to take action. The next day Medgar Evers, a civil rights leader in Mississippi, was shot and killed. A week later Kennedy sent a civil rights bill to Congress that would guarantee equal social and political rights to blacks. On August 28, King delivered his "I Have a Dream" speech to a record-breaking crowd in Washington, D.C. President Kennedy was assassinated before his legislation could be passed, but the activists' concerted efforts over two decades were key in pressuring Congress to pass meaningful legislation. (For details, see "The Legislative Arena" in this chapter.)

With the passage of this landmark legislation, large-scale activity for civil rights for African Americans started to decline. However, mass protest became the preferred tool of many other social movements. Vietnam War protesters marched on Washington by the hundreds of thousands in the late 1960s and early 1970s. Likewise, the women's rights, gay rights, and environmental movements have staged many mass demonstrations in Washington and other major cities.

Most recently, large-scale demonstrations against Wall Street and international organizations, such as the International Monetary Fund and the World Trade Organization have swept the nation. The "Occupy Wall Street" movement, which started in September 2011, has spread to more than 1,500 cities in 82 nations. Modeling their actions after the nonviolent protests of the civil rights era, protestors occupy public spaces to make their views known. The Occupy movement's slogan "We are the 99%" has drawn attention to income inequality and helped set the tone for the 2012 presidential election. Conservative activists, such as those in the pro-life movement, have also used nonviolent protest, sit-ins, and mass demonstrations. Protests against President Obama's policies early in

2009 evolved into the "Tea Party" movement (evoking the Boston Tea Party of the American Revolution). Rooted in an opposition to high taxes and activist government, the Tea Party movement organized protests on Tax Day (April 15) that drew more than 300,000 people in 346 cities.[23] Clearly, the legacy of the civil rights movement has been not only to help change unjust laws but also to provide a new tool for political action across a broad range of policy areas.

THE JUDICIAL ARENA

Early in the civil rights movement in the 1930s and 1940s, the Supreme Court provided most of the successes, especially in voting rights and desegregation. Later the Court's attention turned to discrimination cases in employment (in addition to cases in voting rights), and here its record was more mixed from the perspective of civil rights supporters.

CHALLENGING "SEPARATE BUT EQUAL" IN EDUCATION

In the 1930s the National Association for the Advancement of Colored People (NAACP), which fights for equal rights for blacks, started a concerted effort to nibble away at the "separate but equal" doctrine. Rather than tackle segregation head-on, the NAACP challenged an aspect of segregation that would be familiar to the Supreme Court justices: the ways in which states kept blacks out of all-white law schools.

The Court's first ruling in this area came in 1938, in a case from Missouri. Here, the state paid black students' tuition to attend an out-of-state school, while white students attended the in-state school tuition-free. The state defended the practice under the separate but equal doctrine, but the Court rejected these arguments. The bottom line was that white students could attend law school in the state and similarly qualified black students could not, which violated the Fourteenth Amendment's equal protection of the laws.[24]

Another case chipped away at the principle itself. In 1950 Texas had a separate law school for black students, but this school had only four part-time faculty, no librarian in the law library, and a library with few of the promised books. The situation started to improve after the case was under way, but the Court ruled that *this*

BUSING STUDENTS FROM ONE school district to another in the interest of desegregation has been controversial since the 1960s. In 2007, the Supreme Court invalidated voluntary desegregations plan in the Louisville and Seattle school districts.

was not good enough. There were intangible aspects of the quality of law school, such as the school's reputation, the "position and influence of the alumni," and "traditions and prestige." This ruling came very close to saying that "separate but equal" was a contradiction in terms, but the Court stopped just short of reaching that conclusion.[25]

After these victories, the signals increasingly indicated that the Supreme Court was ready to strike down the separate but equal doctrine. As background, in addition to the law school cases, in 1948 the Court had ruled that "restrictive covenants"—clauses in real estate contracts that prevented a property owner from selling to an African American—could not be enforced by state or local courts because of the Fourteenth Amendment's prohibition against a state denying blacks the "equal protection of the laws." This application of the Fourteenth Amendment was expanded in the landmark ruling *Brown v. Board of Education.*

The *Brown* case arrived on the Court's docket in 1951, was postponed for argument until after the 1952 elections, and was re-argued in December 1953. The postponement was intentional because the Court knew that a firestorm would ensue. In its unanimous decision the Court ruled, "In the field of public education, the doctrine of separate but equal has no place. Separate educational facilities are inherently unequal, depriving the plaintiffs of the equal protection of the laws."[26] The case was significant not only because it required all public schools to desegregate but also because it used the equal protection clause of the Fourteenth Amendment in a way that had potentially far-reaching consequences. Also, even though the decision did not rule segregation unconstitutional in all contexts, *Brown* provided an important boost to the civil rights movement.

THE PUSH TO DESEGREGATE SCHOOLS

In 1955, *Brown v. Board of Education II* addressed the implementation of desegregation and required the states to "desegregate with all deliberate speed."[27] The odd choice of words, "all deliberate speed" was read as a signal by southerners that they could take their time with desegregation. The phrase does seem to be contradictory: being deliberate does not usually involve being speedy. Southern states engaged in "massive resistance" to the desegregation order. In some cases they even closed public schools rather than integrate them—and then reopened the schools as "private," segregated schools for which the white students received government vouchers. However, Maryland, Kentucky, Tennessee, Missouri, and the District of Columbia desegregated their schools within two years.

Eight years after *Brown I,* little had changed in the Deep South: fewer than 1 percent of black children attended school with white children.[28] The Supreme Court became frustrated with the lack of progress in desegregating the schools, saying there was "too much deliberation and not enough speed."[29] Through the 1960s the courts had to battle against the continued resistance. In 1971 the Court shifted its focus from **de jure** segregation (segregation mandated by law) to **de facto** segregation (segregation that existed because of segregated housing patterns) and approved school busing as a tool to integrate schools.[30] This approach was extremely controversial. The Court almost immediately limited the application of busing by ruling in a Detroit case that busing could not go beyond the boundaries of a city's school district: students did not have to be bused from suburbs to cities unless it could be shown that the school district's lines were drawn

de jure Relating to actions or circumstances that occur "by law," such as the legally enforced segregation of schools in the American South before the 1960s.

de facto Relating to actions or circumstances that occur outside the law or "by fact," such as the segregation of schools that resulted from housing patterns and other factors rather than from laws.

in an intentionally discriminatory way.[31] This rule encouraged "white flight" from the cities to the suburbs in response to court-ordered busing.

The Supreme Court retreated further from enforcing desegregation in 1991 when it ruled that a school district could be released from a court-ordered desegregation plan if the district had taken "all practicable steps" to desegregate. Furthermore, districts do not have to address segregation in public schools that is caused by segregated housing.[32] The Court ruled in 1995 that low minority achievement scores are not evidence of a district's failure to desegregate, and it said that school districts cannot be forced by the courts to spend money to establish magnet schools with special programs that could attract white students from the suburbs.[33] In a significant recent decision, in 2007 the Court invalidated voluntary desegregation plans implemented by public school districts in Seattle and Louisville. Both districts set goals for racial diversity and denied assignment requests if they tipped the racial balance above or below certain thresholds. In these cases, the discrimination was against white students who wanted to be in schools with few minority students rather than black students who wanted to be in integrated schools.[34]

A FIFTEEN-YEAR-OLD CIVIL RIGHTS demonstrator, defying an anti-parade ordinance, is attacked by a police dog in Birmingham, Alabama, on May 3, 1963. The next day, during a meeting at the White House, President Kennedy discussed this photo, which had appeared on the front page of the *New York Times*. Reaction against this police brutality helped spur Congress and the president to enact civil rights legislation.

EXPANDING CIVIL RIGHTS

Other significant rulings struck down state laws that forbid interracial marriages (16 states had such laws), upheld all significant parts of the Civil Rights Act, and expanded the scope of the Voting Rights Act. The central cases ruled that Congress had the power to eliminate segregation in public places, such as restaurants and hotels, under the commerce clause of the Constitution.

One important area of cases was in employment law. In 1971 the Court ruled that employment tests, such as written exams or general aptitude tests, that are not related to job performance and that discriminate against blacks violate the 1964 Civil Rights Act.[35] The burden of proof was on the employer to show that the test was a "reasonable measure of job performance" and not simply an excuse to exclude African Americans from certain jobs. Under this standard, the *intent* of the company or person who is discriminating does not matter; whether the practice has an adverse *effect* on a racial group is the key point. This decision had a tremendous impact on integrating the workplace. In 1989, however, the Supreme Court reversed itself and placed the burden of proof on the employee to show that the discriminatory practice did not result from a business necessity.[36] This ruling made it much more difficult to prove workplace discrimination, and Congress subsequently overruled the Court on the issue, as discussed later in the chapter. (See also Nuts and Bolts 13.1.)

THE COLOR-BLIND COURT AND JUDICIAL ACTIVISM

Over the past two decades the Court has been gradually imposing a "color-blind jurisprudence" over numerous issues. One significant area was the 1992 racial redistricting in which 15 new U.S. House districts were drawn to help elect African Americans and 10 districts were drawn to help elect Latino members. The resulting dramatic change in the number of minorities in Congress (more than 50 percent) was rooted in the 1982 amendments to the Voting Rights Act. Instead of mandating a fair *process*, this law and subsequent interpretation by the Supreme Court mandated that minorities be able to "elect representatives of their choice" when their

RACE-RELATED DISCRIMINATION AS DEFINED BY THE EQUAL EMPLOYMENT OPPORTUNITY COMMISSION

Excerpts from the U.S. Equal Employment Opportunity Commission's publication defining race/color discrimination:

RACE/COLOR DISCRIMINATION

Race discrimination involves treating someone (an applicant or employee) unfavorably because he/she is of a certain race or because of personal characteristics associated with race (such as hair texture, skin color, or certain facial features). Color discrimination involves treating someone unfavorably because of skin color complexion. . . . Discrimination can occur when the victim and the person who inflicted the discrimination are the same race or color.

RACE/COLOR DISCRIMINATION AND WORK SITUATIONS

The law forbids discrimination when it comes to any aspect of employment, including hiring, firing, pay, job assignments, promotions, layoff, training, fringe benefits, and any other term or condition of employment.

RACE/COLOR DISCRIMINATION AND HARASSMENT

It is unlawful to harass a person because of that person's race or color. Harassment can include, for example, racial slurs, offensive or derogatory remarks about a person's race or color, or the display of racially-offensive symbols. Although the law doesn't prohibit simple teasing, offhand comments, or isolated incidents that are not very serious, harassment is illegal when it is so frequent or severe that it creates a hostile or offensive work environment or when it results in an adverse employment decision (such as the victim being fired or demoted). The harasser can be the victim's supervisor, a supervisor in another area, a co-worker, or someone who is not an employee of the employer, such as a client or customer.

RACE/COLOR DISCRIMINATION AND EMPLOYMENT POLICIES/PRACTICES

An employment policy or practice that applies to everyone, regardless of race or color, can be illegal if it has a negative impact on the employment of people of a particular race or color and is not job-related and necessary to the operation of the business.

Source: U.S. Equal Employment Opportunity Commission, "Race/Color Discrimination," www.eeoc.gov/laws/types/race_color.cfm (accessed 5/25/10).

numbers and configuration permit. As a result, the legislative redistricting process now had to avoid discriminatory *results* rather than being concerned only with discriminatory *intent*.

However, in several decisions starting with the 1993 case *Shaw v. Reno*, the Supreme Court's adherence to a color-blind jurisprudence has thrown the constitutionality of black-majority districts into doubt. The Court has ruled that black-majority districts are legal as long as they are "done right,"[37] but it has consistently held that if race is the predominant factor in drawing district lines, the districts are unconstitutional because they violate the equal protection clause of the Fourteenth Amendment. This line of cases struck down black-majority districts in North Carolina, Georgia, Louisiana, Virginia, Texas, and Florida. The most recent case, in 2001, upheld the redrawn 12th District in North Carolina, which no longer was black majority, arguing that when race and partisanship are so intertwined—as they are when 90 percent of African Americans vote for the Democratic candidate—plaintiffs cannot assume that African Americans were placed together for racial reasons. This ruling opens the door for a greater consideration of race than had been allowed in the previous cases. However, racial redistricting is an unsettled area of the law, and many other countries have used more aggressive policies such as quotas to ensure more equal representation for minorities and women.[38]

The racial redistricting cases illustrate that the Supreme Court is increasingly activist in civil rights. It is generally unwilling to defer to any other branch of government that disagrees with its view of discrimination and equal protection (see Chapter 12 for a discussion of judicial activism). In some periods, judicial activism may serve to further civil rights, as in the 1950s and 1960s, or to limit them, as in the recent period.

WOMEN'S RIGHTS

The Supreme Court has also been central in determining women's civil rights. Until relatively recently the Court did not apply the Constitution to women, despite the Fourteenth Amendment's language that states may not deny any *person* the equal protection of the laws. Apparently, women were not regarded as people when it came to political and economic rights in the nineteenth and early twentieth centuries. These protectionist notions were finally rejected in three cases between 1971 and 1976, when the Court made it much more difficult for states to treat men and women differently.

The first case involved an Idaho state law that gave a man priority over a woman when they were otherwise equally entitled to execute a person's estate. This law was justified on the "reasonable" grounds that it reduced the state courts' workload by having an automatic rule that would limit challenges. However, the Court ruled that the law was arbitrary, did not meet the "reasonableness" test, and therefore violated the woman's equal protection rights under the Fourteenth Amendment.[39] The second case involved a female Air Force officer who wanted to count her husband as a dependent for purposes of health and housing benefits. Under the current law a military man could automatically count his wife as a dependent, but a woman could claim her husband only if she brought in more than half the family income. The Court struck down this practice, saying that protectionist laws "in practical effect, put women not on a pedestal, but in a cage."[40]

These two cases still relied on the **rational basis test** for discrimination between men and women. It wasn't until 1976 that the Court established the **intermediate scrutiny test** in a case involving the drinking age. In the early 1970s some states had a lower drinking age for women than for men on the "reasonable (or rational) basis" that 18- to 20-year-old women are more mature than men of that age (and thus less likely to abuse alcohol). The new intermediate scrutiny standard meant that the government's policy must be "substantially related" to an "important government objective" to justify the unequal treatment of men and women, so the law was struck down.[41] (See Nuts and Bolts 13.2.)

Before this case, only two standards served to apply the Fourteenth Amendment to different categories of people: the reasonable basis test and the strict scrutiny test. Racial minorities received the strongest protection as the "suspect classification" where the **strict scrutiny test** is applied. Under this test there must be a "compelling state interest" to discriminate among people if race is involved. The only other test before the new intermediate one said that it was acceptable to discriminate against a group of people as long as there was a "reasonable basis" for that state law. Today, for example, states can pass a 21-year-old drinking law on the grounds that traffic fatalities will be lower with that drinking age rather than with a law that allows 18-year-olds to drink. The intermediate scrutiny test gives women stronger protections than the rational basis test, but it is not as strong as strict scrutiny.

The more aggressive application of the Fourteenth Amendment for women helped in providing them the equal protection of the laws, as shown in a Court decision that struck down the Virginia Military Institute's male-only admission

rational basis test The use of evidence to suggest that differences in the behavior of two groups can rationalize unequal treatment of these groups.

intermediate scrutiny test The middle level of scrutiny the courts use when determining whether a law is constitutional. To pass this test, the law or policy must further an important government interest in a way that is "substantially related" to that interest. This means that the law uses means that are a close fit to the government's objective and not substantially broader than necessary to accomplish that important objective.

strict scrutiny test The highest level of scrutiny the courts use when determining whether a law is constitutional. To pass this test, the law or policy must be shown to serve a "compelling state interest" or goal, it must be narrowly tailored to achieve that goal, and it must be the least restrictive means of achieving the goal.

LEVELS OF SCRUTINY IN DISCRIMINATION LAW SUITS

When deciding a lawsuit, federal judges use different levels of scrutiny to determine whether discrimination is allowed, based on the status of the plaintiff.

rational basis test The use of evidence to suggest that differences in the behavior of two groups can rationalize unequal treatment of these groups, such as charging 16- to 21-year-olds higher prices for auto insurance than people over 21 because younger people have higher accident rates.

intermediate scrutiny test The middle level of scrutiny the courts use when determining whether unequal treatment is justified by the effect of a law; this is the standard used for gender-based discrimination cases and for many cases based on sexual orientation.

strict scrutiny test The highest level of scrutiny the courts use when determining whether unequal treatment is justified by the effect of a law. It is applied in all cases involving race. Laws rarely pass the strict scrutiny standard; a law that discriminates based on race must be shown to serve some "compelling state interest" in order to be upheld.

policy. The ruling stated that VMI violated the Fourteenth Amendment's equal protection clause because it failed to show an "exceedingly persuasive justification" for its sex-biased admissions policy.[42]

Two other areas where the Court helped advance women's rights were affirmative action and protection against sexual harassment. In 1987 the Court approved affirmative action in a case involving a woman who was promoted over a man despite the fact that he scored slightly higher than she did on a test. The Court ruled that this was acceptable to make up for past discrimination.[43] The Court made it easier to sue employers for sexual harassment in 1993, saying that a woman did not have to reach the point of a nervous breakdown before claiming that she was harassed; it was enough to demonstrate a pattern of "repeated and unwanted" behavior that created a "hostile workplace environment."[44] Later rulings stated that if a single act is flagrant, the conduct did not have to be repeated to create a hostile environment.

The Court has also restricted the rights of women in some instances. In 1984 it ruled that Title IX of the Education Amendments of 1972, which prohibits sex discrimination in "any education program or activity receiving Federal financial assistance," applied to private colleges and universities in which students received federal financial aid. However, in a blow to equal treatment for women, the Court said that only the program receiving federal funds could not discriminate, rather than the institution as a whole. This ruling released many athletic programs from their obligation to provide equal opportunity for women athletes.[45] Congress overturned the ruling with the Civil Rights Restoration Act in 1988.

More recently, Lilly Ledbetter sued Goodyear Tire and Rubber Company for receiving lower pay than men for the same work over a 20-year period, which she claimed was gender discrimination. However, the Court rejected her claim, saying that she did not meet the time limit required by the law, as the discrimination must have occurred within 180 days of the claim. Dissenters pointed out that pay discrimination usually occurs in increments over long periods, so it would be impossible to recognize the discrimination within 180 days. The long-standing policy of the Equal Employment Opportunity Commission (EEOC) was that each new paycheck restarted the 180-day clock as a new act of discrimination, but the Court overturned that policy, making it almost impossible to sue for discriminatory pay

How It Works

DETERMINING IF DISCRIMINATION IS LEGAL

CASES INVOLVING "SUSPECT CLASSIFICATION" (race, ethnicity, creed, or national origin)

STRICT SCRUTINY TEST

1. Is unequal treatment justified by a "compelling state interest"?
2. Is unequal treatment the "least restrictive" option?

YES If yes to both, discrimination is legal. However, very few cases meet this standard.

NO If not, discrimination is illegal.

CASES INVOLVING SEX OR GENDER EQUALITY

INTERMEDIATE SCRUTINY TEST

1. Is the discriminatory policy "substantially related" to an "important government objective"?
2. Is the discrimination "no greater than necessary" to achieve this objective?

YES If yes to both, discrimination is legal. Some discrimination based on gender is permitted, but this test is harder to pass than the rational basis test applied to gender cases in the past.

NO If not, discrimination is illegal.

CASES INVOLVING AGE, ECONOMIC STATUS, OR OTHER CRITERIA

RATIONAL BASIS TEST

1. Is the law rationally related to furthering a legitimate government interest?
2. Does the policy avoid "arbitrary, capricious, or deliberate" discrimination?

YES If yes to both, discrimination is legal. This is the easiest hurdle for a law or policy to pass.

NO If not, discrimination is illegal.

POP QUIZ!

1 Unequal treatment based on race is typically subject to

a strict scrutiny by the courts.
b intermediate scrutiny by the courts.
c rational basis test by the courts.
d First Amendment protections.
e majority preferences.

2 An example of unequal treatment that would pass the rational basis test is

a affirmative action programs.
b hiring whites only.
c banning Jews from certain government positions.
d systematically paying men more than women.
e banning people under a certain age from driving.

Answers: 1.a; 2.e

based on gender or race under the Civil Rights Act.[46] Congress overturned this decision and restored the old standard in January 2009 by passing the Lilly Ledbetter Fair Pay Act. As Figure 13.3 shows, significant pay disparities between men and women remain throughout much of the United States.

Recent verdicts won by the EEOC include a $19 million settlement that Outback Steakhouse agreed to pay in a sex discrimination and "glass ceiling" lawsuit. Thousands of female employees at hundreds of restaurants alleged they were denied equal opportunities for advancement. The EEOC has also won large settlements for sexual harassment and pay discrimination in recent years against FedEx, Jack in the Box, Dunkin' Donuts, Ruby Tuesday, IHOP, and dozens of other corporations.[47]

GAY RIGHTS

The Supreme Court has a similarly mixed record on gay rights. Early cases were not supportive of gay rights. One of the first concerned Georgia's law banning sodomy. The Supreme Court ruled in *Bowers v. Hardwick* (1986) that homosexual behavior was not protected by the Constitution and that state laws banning it could be justified under the most lenient "reasonable basis" test.[48] In other cases the Court sidestepped the controversial issue of gay rights, choosing alternative constitutional grounds to reach its decisions.[49]

FIGURE » 13.3

WOMEN'S EARNINGS AS A PERCENTAGE OF MEN'S EARNINGS, 2007

There is a substantial difference between women's and men's earnings in the United States. What could account for this variation? How much do you think it has to do with levels of discrimination and how much with differences in the nature of the jobs that men and women hold?

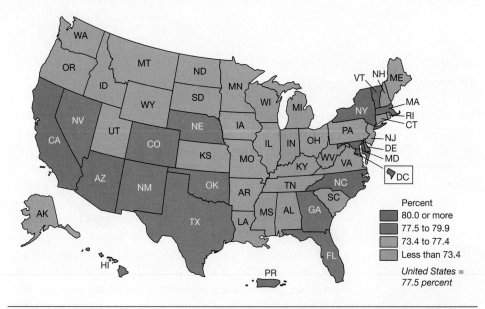

Source: Alemayehu Bishaw and Jessica Semega, "Income, Earnings, and Poverty Data from the 2007 American Community Survey," U.S. Census Bureau, August 2008, www.census.gov/prod/2008pubs/acs-09.pdf (accessed 11/3/12).

In the first endorsement of civil rights for gay men and lesbians, the Court struck down an amendment to the Colorado state constitution that prevented them from suing for discrimination in employment or housing. The Court said that the amendment violated homosexuals' equal protection rights because it "withdrew from homosexuals, but no others, specific legal protection from the injuries caused by discrimination."[50] A more important ruling came seven years later in a case involving two Houston men who were prosecuted for same-sex sodomy after police entered an apartment—upon receiving a false tip about an armed man in the complex—and found the two having sex. Under Texas law, sodomy was illegal for homosexuals but not for heterosexuals. In its ruling, the Court said that the liberty guaranteed by the Fourteenth Amendment's due process clause allows homosexuals to have sexual relations. "Freedom presumes an autonomy of self that includes freedom of thought, belief, expression, and certain intimate conduct."[51]

The Court has yet to rule on gay marriage, but California may provide the test case. In 2008, California voters narrowly passed Proposition 8, striking down the state's gay marriage law. In 2010, a federal district court struck down Proposition 8, and then the state said that it would not defend the proposition in court. After the state supreme court ruled that proponents of the proposition had standing to defend the case, the appeal went forward.[52] Gay marriage in California is still on hold until appeals are decided.

This summary of cases demonstrates that the courts can be both a strong advocate of and an impediment to civil rights. In general, however, the courts have a limited *independent* impact on policy. Indeed, the Supreme Court must rely on the other branches of government to carry out its policy decisions.

THE LEGISLATIVE ARENA

Congress has provided the basis for protection of civil rights through laws enacted starting in the 1960s. Applying to racial and ethnic minorities and women, these laws attempted to ensure a "level playing field" of equal opportunity.

INITIAL LEGISLATION OF THE 1960S

The bedrock of equal protection that exists today stems from the 1964 Civil Rights Act, the 1965 Voting Rights Act, and the 1968 Fair Housing Act. President Lyndon Johnson, a former segregationist, helped push through the Civil Rights Act when he became president. The act barred discrimination in employment based on race, sex, religion, or national origin; banned segregation in public places; and established the EEOC as the enforcement agency for the legislation.

The Voting Rights Act of 1965 (VRA) eliminated direct obstacles to minority voting in the South, such as discriminatory literacy tests and other voter registration tests and provided the means to enforce the law: federal marshals were charged with overseeing elections in the South. The VRA, often cited as one of the most significant pieces of civil rights legislation,[53] precipitated an explosion in black political participation in the South. The most dramatic gains came in Mississippi, where black registration increased from 6.7 percent before the VRA to 59.8 percent in 1967.

The Fair Housing Act of 1968 barred discrimination in the rental or sale of a home based on race, sex, religion, and national origin. Important amendments to the law enacted in 1988 added disability and familial status (having children under age 18), provided new administrative enforcement mechanisms, and expanded Justice Department jurisdiction to bring suit on behalf of victims in federal district courts.[54]

Among other amendments to civil rights laws, most important were the 1975 amendments to the VRA that extended coverage of many of the law's provisions to language minorities; the 1982 VRA amendments, which extended important provisions of the law for 25 years and made it easier to bring a lawsuit under the act; the 1991 Civil Rights Act; and the 2006 extension of the VRA for another 25 years. The 1991 law overruled or altered parts of 12 Supreme Court decisions that had eroded the intent of Congress when it passed the civil rights legislation. It expanded earlier legislation and increased the costs to employers for intentional, illegal discrimination.

PROTECTIONS FOR WOMEN

Women have also received extensive protection through legislation. In 1966 the National Organization for Women (NOW) was formed to push for enforcement of Title VII of the Civil Rights Act, which barred discrimination based on gender. NOW's members convinced President Johnson to sign an executive order that eliminated sex discrimination in federal agencies and among federal contractors, but it was difficult to enforce. Finally in 1970 the EEOC started enforcing the law. Before long, one-third of civil rights cases involved sex discrimination, and those numbers remain high (see Figure 13.4).

In 1972 Congress passed Title IX of the Higher Education Act, which prohibits sex discrimination in institutions that receive federal funds. The law has had the greatest impact in women's sports. In the 1960s and 1970s, opportunities for women to play sports in college or high school were limited owing to few scholarships and small budgets for women's sports. Though it took nearly 30 years to reach parity between men and women, most universities are now in compliance with Title IX. Nonetheless, many men's sports, such as baseball, tennis, wrestling, and gymnastics, were cut at universities that had to bring the number of student athletes into rough parity, and critics argued that such cuts were unfair, especially as the interest in women's sports was not as high as for men's sports. Defenders of the law argue that the gap in interest in women's and men's sports will not change until there is equal opportunity. There is some evidence to support that claim, as interest is increasing in women's soccer and professional basketball with the WNBA, as well as in well-established women's professional sports such as golf and tennis.

Another significant effort was the failed Equal Rights Amendment. It was passed in 1972 with simple wording: "Equality of rights under the law shall not be denied or abridged by the United States or any state on the account of sex." Many states passed it within months, but it fell three states short of the required 38 states after the required seven years. The amendment received a three-year extension from Congress but still did not get passage by the additional three states.

In 1994 Congress passed the Violence against Women Act, which allowed women who were the victims of physical abuse and violence to sue in federal court. Part of this law was overturned by the Supreme Court, which ruled that Congress had exceeded its powers under the commerce clause.[55]

PROTECTIONS FOR THE DISABLED AND FOR GAY RIGHTS

Other important civil rights legislation included the 1990 Americans with Disabilities Act, which provided federal protections for disabled Americans in terms of workplace discrimination and access to public facilities. This law produced the curb-cuts in sidewalks, access for wheelchairs to public buses and trains, special seating in sports

BETTY DUKES, A PLAINTIFF IN A SEXUAL discrimination lawsuit—the largest in the nation's history—filed against Wal-Mart, leaves a San Francisco courthouse with her attorney. Wal-Mart lost its appeal to remove the class-action status for plaintiffs and will face billions of dollars in damages if it loses the case.

FIGURE » 13.4

DISCRIMINATION CASES IN THE EQUAL EMPLOYMENT OPPORTUNITY COMMISSION, 2009

Discrimination based on race and on sex are the types that are most frequently reported, but there is a significant amount of discrimination based on age and disability as well. What types of discrimination do you think would be most likely to go unreported?

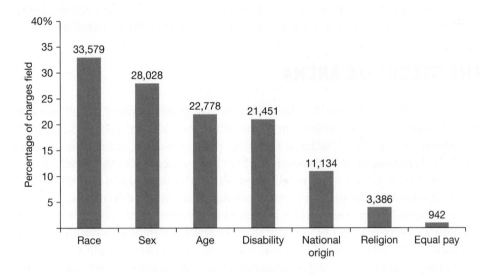

Note: Percentages do not sum to 100 because complaints may be filed in more than one category.

Source: U.S. Equal Employment Opportunity Commission, Charge Statistics, www.eeoc.gov/eeoc/statistics/ enforcement/charges.cfm (accessed 11/3/12).

stadiums, and many other changes that provide the disabled an equal opportunity to participate more fully in society. The Supreme Court narrowed the law's scope in 2001 when it ruled that the law did not apply to state employees.[56]

Congress's track record in protecting gay rights is not as strong. In fact, most of the steps taken by Congress have been to restrict gay rights. In 1996 Congress reacted to the possibility that some liberal states would allow same-sex marriage by passing the Defense of Marriage Act. Its concern was rooted in the "full faith and credit clause" of the Constitution, which says that all states have to respect the laws of other states. Thus, if same-sex marriages were allowed in one state, all other states would have to recognize that marriage as legal if the couple were to move to another state.

More recently, Congress has proposed an amendment that would ban same-sex marriage. President George W. Bush endorsed the amendment, and Democrats have criticized it as a divisive gimmick to appeal to the conservative base of the Republican Party. President Obama opposes the amendment, and while the Democrats are in control of the Senate, any action on the amendment is unlikely.

In a possible change of course, in 2009 Congress passed the Matthew Shepard and James Byrd Jr. Hate Crimes Prevention Act. This legislation expanded the hate crime laws based on race, color, religion, or national origin to include attacks based on sexual orientation, gender identity, or mental or physical disability. The law also lifted a requirement that a victim had to be attacked while engaged in a federally protected activity, such as attending school, for it to be a federal hate crime. In signing the bill, President Obama said, "After more than a decade of opposition and delay, we've passed inclusive hate crimes legislation to help protect our citizens from violence based on what they look like, who they love, how they pray or who they are."[57] The law commemorates the murders of James Byrd Jr., an African American man who was dragged behind a pickup truck by three men believed to be white supremacists (mentioned earlier), and Matthew Shepard, a gay teenager who in 1998 was beaten by two men, tied to a fence, and left to die. Also, the Employment Non-Discrimination Act, which would prohibit discrimination in employment based on sexual orientation, has been proposed in nearly every Congress since 1994. A version of the bill passed the House in 2007 but died in the Senate. President Obama supports it, but it is unlikely to pass the Republican-controlled House.

THE EXECUTIVE ARENA

The civil rights movement has benefited greatly from presidential action, such as President Truman's integration of the armed services in 1948 and President Eisenhower's use of the National Guard to enforce a court order to integrate a school in Arkansas in 1957. Executive orders by presidents Kennedy and Johnson in 1961 and 1965, respectively, established affirmative action; and in 1969 Richard Nixon expanded the "goals and numerical ranges" for hiring minorities.

The most significant action by a president in the area of civil rights for gay men and lesbians was President Clinton's effort to end the ban on homosexuals in the military. Under his policy of "don't ask, don't tell," the military would stop actively searching for and discharging homosexuals from the military ranks, and recruits would not need to reveal their sexual orientation. However, if without an investigation the military found out a person was gay, he or she still could be disciplined or discharged. Subsequently President Obama promised to repeal "don't ask, don't tell," and under his administration Congress passed the "Don't Ask, Don't Tell Repeal Act of 2010." The repeal went into effect on September 20, 2011. Minutes afterward, Navy Lt. Gary Ross and his long-term partner were married in Vermont to become the first openly gay married person in the military.[58]

The low priority that recent presidential candidates have given to civil rights policy more generally means that it is less likely that significant and dramatic change will come from unilateral action by the president. Instead, attention to civil rights concerns in the executive branch has primarily been in two areas since 1993: racial diversity in presidential appointments and use of the bully pulpit to promote racial concerns and interests.

President Clinton was active on both dimensions. His cabinet, subcabinet, and judicial appointments achieved the greatest gender and racial balance in history. Fourteen percent of Clinton's first-year presidential appointments were African American (compared to 12 percent of the population in 1992), 6 percent were Hispanic (compared to 9.5 percent of the population), and the percentages of Asian American and Native American appointees were identical to their proportions in the population. (The proportion of women appointees—27 percent—was well short of their proportion in the population, but it still was a record high.) Clinton also used the bully pulpit to advocate a civil rights agenda focusing on problems faced by minorities.

President George W. Bush did not achieve the same level of diversity in his appointments as Clinton, but his administration was more diverse than that of other Republican presidents. Moreover, Bush

IN 2011, THE U.S. MILITARY REPEALED its controversial "don't ask, don't tell" policy, which prevented gay men and lesbians from serving openly in the armed forces. At midnight on September 20, 2011, as the repeal formally took effect, Navy Lieutenant Gary Ross (right) married his longtime partner, Dan Swezy.

made serious overtures to minorities, especially Latinos, in his effort to expand the Republican Party base. In terms of Barack Obama's presidency, the historical significance of his successful campaign as a minority candidate is clear. And like his predecessors, Obama nominated a diverse cabinet—with 14 men, seven women, and seven racial minorities. Eric Holder is the first African American to serve as attorney general and Sonia Sotomayor is the first Latina on the Supreme Court. Obama also nominated Elena Kagan to the Supreme Court, putting three women on the Court for the first time.

Race also played a role in the 2012 presidential election. In the Republican primary, Newt Gingrich caused a stir when he called Obama "the greatest food stamp president." When asked whether this label was demeaning to African Americans and to the president, he defended the remark, saying that record numbers of Americans are on food stamps. A brief stir was also caused when Mitt Romney referred to the "birthers" claim that President Obama was not born in the United States by joking that "No one's ever asked to see my birth certificate. They know that this is the place that we were born and raised." However, race did not play a very prominent role in the general election as both candidates focused on the economy.[59]

CONTINUING AND FUTURE CIVIL RIGHTS ISSUES

EXAMINE AFFIRMATIVE ACTION AND OTHER ONGOING CIVIL RIGHTS ISSUES

There is vigorous debate over the likely direction of the civil rights movement in the twenty-first century. These debates play out over a broad range of issues, three of which are outlined in this section.

AFFIRMATIVE ACTION

Even though the Civil Rights Act of 1964 ensured that all Americans would enjoy equality of opportunity, blacks continued to lag behind whites in socioeconomic status. In 1965, President Johnson required all federal agencies and government contractors to submit written proposals to provide an equal opportunity for employment of blacks, women, Asian Americans, and Native Americans within various job categories and to outline programs to achieve those goals. The policy was expanded under President Nixon, and throughout the 1970s and 1980s affirmative action programs grew in the private sector, higher education, and government contracting. Through such programs, employers and universities gave special opportunities to minorities and women.

Affirmative action takes many forms. The most passive type involves recruiting women and minorities for employment or college admission by placing ads in newspapers and magazines, visiting inner-city schools, or sending out targeted mailings. A more active form involves including race or gender as a "plus factor" in the admissions or hiring decision. That is, from a pool of qualified candidates, a minority applicant may receive an advantage over white applicants. (Women generally do not receive special consideration in admissions decisions, but gender may be a "plus factor" in some employment decisions.) The strongest form of affirmative action is the use of quotas—strict numerical targets to hire or admit a specific number of applicants from underrepresented groups.

Affirmative action has been a controversial policy. Many whites view it as "preferential treatment" and "reverse discrimination." Polls indicate that minorities are much more supportive of the practice than whites. A majority of whites support more passive forms of affirmative action, such as "education programs to assist minorities in competing for college admissions" but draw the line at preferences, even when they are intended to make up for past discrimination.[60]

The Supreme Court has helped define the boundaries of this policy debate. The earliest cases concerning affirmative action in employment upheld preferential treatment and rigid quotas when the policies were necessary to make up for past discrimination.[61] In each instance there had been a previous pattern of discrimination and exclusion. Then in 1989 the Court started moving in a "color-blind" direction concerning "set-aside" programs in government contracting. In 1983 Richmond, Virginia, began requiring contractors who had won city construction contracts to subcontract at least 30 percent of the work to minority-owned businesses. After a white business owner sued, the Court ruled that set-asides were unconstitutional without evidence of discrimination against minorities and that any such programs had to be "narrowly tailored to meet a compelling state interest."[62] The same reasoning was applied to federal contracting set-aside programs in 1995.[63]

The Court applied a similar line of analysis to an important reverse-discrimination employment case in 2009. In that case, 17 white firefighters and one Hispanic firefighter sued the city of New Haven, Connecticut, for throwing out the results of a test that would have been used to promote them. The city tried to ignore the test results because no African American firefighters would have qualified for promotion and the city feared a "disparate impact" lawsuit. However, the Court ruled that the exam did appear to be "job related and consistent with business necessity" (as required by Section VII of the Civil Rights Act) and that unless the city could provide a "strong basis in evidence" that it would have been sued, it had to consider the results of the exam.[64]

The landmark decision for affirmative action in higher education is *University of California Regents v. Bakke* (1978).[65] Allan Bakke, a white student, sued when he was denied admission to medical school at the University of California, Davis, in successive years. Bakke's test scores and GPA were significantly higher than those of some minority students who were admitted under the school's affirmative action program. The Supreme Court agreed with Bakke that rigid racial quotas were unconstitutional but allowed race to be used in admissions decisions as a "plus factor" to promote diversity in the student body.

In two 2003 cases from the University of Michigan, the Court's rulings were consistent with *Bakke*, saying that the law school's "holistic approach" that considered race as one of the factors in the admission decision was acceptable but that the University of Michigan's more rigid approach, which automatically gave minority students 20 of the 100 points needed to guarantee admission, was unacceptable.[66] Though these two decisions affirmed *Bakke*, it was the first time that a majority of the Court clearly stated that "student body diversity is a compelling state interest that can justify the use of race in university admissions."[67]

MULTICULTURAL ISSUES

Issues involving the multicultural, multiracial nature of American society will become more important as whites cease to be the majority of the population by mid-century. Two key issues are English as the official language and immigration.

AFFIRMATIVE ACTION AT THE UNIVERSITY OF MICHIGAN

If you were serving on the Supreme Court, how would you have decided the University of Michigan affirmative action cases? In the undergraduate case, Jennifer Gratz had a high school GPA of 3.76 and an ACT score of 25 (eighty-third percentile), and Patrick Hamacher had a GPA of 3.37 and an ACT of 28 (eighty-ninth percentile), but they were denied admission to Michigan. The student in the law school case, Barbara Grutter, was a forty-three-year-old returning student who had an undergraduate GPA of 3.81 at Michigan State University and a 161 on the LSAT. All three students showed that they had higher scores than some of the minority students who were admitted under the university's affirmative action program. The legal question that the Court had to decide was whether the university's affirmative action program violated the equal protection clause of the Fourteenth Amendment and civil rights laws barring discrimination on the basis of race, or if the program could be justified as serving a "compelling state interest" under the strict scrutiny standard.

The crucial point of contention in the debate over the use of race in college admissions decisions is "viewpoint diversity"; the claimed advantage of affirmative action is the diversity that it brings to classroom discussions. Advocates of affirmative action argue that viewpoint diversity is essential to learning and that having racial diversity in the student body is likely to produce more viewpoint diversity than having an all-white student body. Furthermore, proponents argue, the courts are not the proper place to decide these issues. Instead, as with the complex and highly charged topic of racial redistricting, the political branches of government are where these decisions should be made. Advocates also make a very pragmatic argument that getting rid of affirmative action would almost certainly lead to a system that is *less* rooted in merit-based admissions than the current system. This is because states that get rid of race as a factor in admissions often adopt a "10 percent solution," which says that the top 10 percent of any graduating high school class can be admitted to the state university. This means that a student who may be in the top 20 percent of an excellent school might not be admitted even if she had better test scores and grades than a student who was in the top 10 percent of a high school that was not as good.

Opponents reply that supporters of affirmative action have not provided convincing evidence that racial diversity in colleges has any beneficial effects. They also argue that "viewpoint diversity" arguments assume that members of all racial minorities think alike, drawing a comparison to racial profiling in law enforcement. It is just as offensive, they say, that an admissions committee thinks that one black student has the

In 2003, when the University of Michigan affirmative action cases were heard by the Supreme Court, some students demonstrated to show their support for the university's admissions process. Others protested that it was unfair to white students.

same views as another black student as it is that a police officer may pull over a black teenage male just because he fits a certain criminal profile. Opponents also argue that affirmative action amounts to "reverse discrimination" and that any racial classification is harmful.

The Supreme Court has agreed to hear an affirmative action case from Texas in the 2012–13 term. Many are predicting that the Court will endorse a more color-blind approach to college admissions than is allowed by the Michigan precedent.

Critical **Thinking Questions**

1. To what extent should race be used as a "plus factor" to promote racial diversity and viewpoint diversity, if at all?

2. Think of your own experiences in high school and college. Has racial diversity contributed to viewpoint diversity?

Decisions to establish English as the official language in many states have had wide-reaching consequences. For example, the Supreme Court upheld an Alabama state law requiring that the state driver's license test be conducted only in English. A Mexican immigrant sued under Title VI of the 1964 Civil Rights Act, claiming that the Alabama law had a disparate impact on non-English-speaking residents. However, the Court held in *Alexander v. Sandoval* (2001) that individuals may not sue federally funded state agencies over policies that have a discriminatory effect on minorities under Title VI.[68] This decision has far-reaching consequences for the use of the Civil Rights Act to fight patterns of discrimination, especially in education policy (for example, civil rights advocates have challenged the use of standardized testing because of its disparate impact on minorities) and environmental policy (lawsuits brought under Title VI have alleged "environmental racism" in decisions to site hazardous waste dumps in predominantly minority areas).

Immigration regained center stage after the September 11 terrorist attacks, when some people saw immigration as a threat that must be curtailed. The government asserted that it would not engage in racial profiling of Arab Americans—for example, subjecting them to stricter screening at airports—but many commentators argued that such profiling would be justified, and there was at least anecdotal evidence of increased discrimination against people of Middle Eastern descent.

Recently, immigration has been central in many political debates. Some are nominally about social welfare benefits, but deeper racial issues often are just below the surface. For example, in 1994 voters in California adopted Proposition 187, which denied most public benefits to illegal immigrants but seemed to critics to discriminate against Mexican Americans. Debates over immigration have important political implications. Republicans supported Proposition 187, while Democrats opposed it. When the courts struck down the measure and Democrats won the 1998 gubernatorial race in California with the support of the growing Hispanic population, Republicans softened their position. President George W. Bush cultivated the Hispanic vote, often presenting part of his speeches in Spanish, and won a record (for Republican presidential candidates) 44 percent of the Latino vote in 2004. Bush pushed for comprehensive immigration reform in 2006. However, anti-immigration Republicans in Congress passed a measure aimed at enforcing existing immigration laws and building a barrier along the border with Mexico. Strong Latino turnout in 2006 is credited, in part, with a return of control of Congress to the Democrats, and Obama won 67 percent of the Latino vote in 2008.

The immigration debate intensified in 2010 when Arizona enacted an anti-immigration law that requires local law enforcement officials to check the immigration status of a person in a "lawful stop, detention, or arrest" if there is a "reasonable suspicion" that the person is an illegal alien. The law also requires immigrants to always carry papers and bans people without proper documents from seeking work in public places. Opponents of the law argue that it requires illegal racial profiling and that the federal government has the sole responsibility for deciding immigration law. As noted earlier, the Supreme Court struck down three of the four main provisions of the law, citing the supremacy clause of the Constitution. This meant that Congress, not the states, decides immigration law when the two laws conflict. The Court upheld the controversial "show me your papers" part of the law, saying that the state was simply enforcing the federal law. However, the Court indicated that the law must be applied in a race-neutral way and could be struck down if there was clear evidence of racial profiling.[69] Several months later a federal district court judge cleared the way for implementation of the "show me your papers"

BORDER PATROL AGENTS DETAIN undocumented immigrants apprehended near the Mexican border outside McAllen, Texas. Illegal immigration continues to be a "hot-button" issue in national electoral and legislative politics.

law, saying that the Supreme Court wanted to see actual evidence of discrimination rather than speculation that the law could have a discriminatory effect.[70]

As noted in the introduction, the immigration system is widely viewed as broken and in need of reform. However, both Bush and Obama were unable to get their proposals approved by Congress that would have provided a "path to citizenship" for illegal aliens.

The debates over affirmative action, English as a second language, and immigration reform clearly illustrate the conflictual nature of civil rights policy. However, history has shown that when public opinion strongly supports a given application of civil rights, as with African Americans in the South in the 1960s and more recently the service of homosexuals in the military, public policy soon reflects those views. While it is impossible to say how soon same-sex marriage will be nationally recognized or comprehensive immigration reform will become law, given the trends in public opinion, policy appears to be headed in that direction.

CONCLUSION

Enforcing civil rights means providing equal protection of the law to individuals and groups that are discriminated against, which may include noncitizens and illegal immigrants. But figuring out exactly when an individual's' civil rights have been violated can be tricky. When does a routine traffic stop by a police officer turn into racial profiling? To help figure that out, we now can answer the questions about possible civil rights violations that introduced this chapter.

▶ The African American teenagers who were pulled over by the police may or may not have had their civil rights violated, depending on the laws in their state. In Massachusetts, for example, it is prohibited to consider the "race, gender, national or ethnic origin of members of the public in deciding to detain a person or stop a motor vehicle" except in "suspect specific incidents."[71] Pulling over the white teenagers would have been acceptable as long as there was "probable cause" to justify the stop.

▶ The Asian American woman who did not get the job could certainly talk to a lawyer about filing a "disparate impact" discrimination suit. Under the 1991 Civil Rights Act, the employer would have the burden of proof to show that she was not a victim of the "good ol' boy" network.

▶ The gay couple who could not rent the apartment because of their sexual orientation may have a basis for a civil rights lawsuit based on the Fourteenth Amendment; however, this would depend on where they live, given that there is no federal protection against discrimination against gay men and lesbians (and the Supreme Court has not applied the Fourteenth Amendment in this context).

▶ Court decisions concerning affirmative action in Michigan show that the white student who was not admitted to the university of his choice would have to take his lumps, as long as the affirmative action program considered race as a general "plus factor" rather than assigning more or fewer points for it.

This review of civil rights policy has highlighted only some of the most important issues, but a significant agenda remains. The civil rights movement will continue to use the multiple avenues of the legislative, executive, and judicial branches to secure equal rights for all Americans.

THE CONTEXT OF CIVIL RIGHTS

▶ Describe the historical struggles groups have faced in winning civil rights. **Pages 391–96**

SUMMARY

Civil rights are protections from discrimination by both the government and individuals, and are rooted in laws and the equal protection clause of the Fourteenth Amendment. The concept of equality has evolved over time, with protections now for women, African Americans, Native Americans, Asians, and Latinos. Despite our attempts to live in a color-blind society, awareness of race still influences many people's opinions and behavior.

KEY TERMS

civil rights (p. 391)

Missouri Compromise (p. 392)

disenfranchised (p. 393)

grandfather clause (p. 393)

Jim Crow laws (p. 393)

"separate but equal" (p. 393)

protectionism (p. 396)

PRACTICE QUIZ QUESTIONS

1. The distinction between civil rights and civil liberties is that civil rights _____ while civil liberties _____.

   a) protect against discrimination; are guaranteed in the Bill of Rights

   b) are guaranteed in the Bill of Rights; protect against discrimination

   c) are guaranteed in the Bill of Rights; limit what the government can do to you

   d) limit what the government can do to you; protect against discrimination

   e) limit what the government can do to you; are guaranteed in the Bill of Rights

2. The Missouri Compromise _____.

   a) ruled that people held as slaves are not protected by the Constitution

   b) ruled that three-fifths of the slaves could count in a state's population

   c) limited the expansion of slavery while maintaining the balance of slave states

   d) gave slaves the right to vote

   e) ended slavery in the South

3. *Plessy v. Ferguson* established _____.

   a) the legitimacy of poll taxes

   b) the "separate but equal" doctrine

   c) that Jim Crow laws were illegal

   d) the process of desegregation in the South

   e) the legality of slavery

4. The principle of _____ was used in many court cases to deny women equal rights.

   a) matriarchy

   b) "separate but equal"

   c) sectionalism

   d) misandry

   e) protectionism

ⓢ PRACTICE ONLINE

"Big Think" video exercise: *C. Raj Kumar on the Origin of Human Rights*

THE RACIAL DIVIDE TODAY

▶ Analyze inequality among racial, ethnic, and social groups today. **Pages 396–99**

SUMMARY

Beyond the unequal treatment of racial minorities, women, and gays and lesbians, inequalities on political, social, and economic conditions also persist. More whites are able than minorities to politically participate at a higher rate, enjoy a better standard of living, and avoid prejudice in the criminal justice system.

PRACTICE QUIZ QUESTIONS

5. *Most* of the differences in voter turnout among whites relative to racial minorities can be accounted for by _____.

    a) contemporary Jim Crow laws

    b) voter purge lists

    c) voter ID laws

    d) poll taxes

    e) education and income

6. The gaps between whites and blacks on health measures are _____ and in many cases, _____.

    a) large; decreasing

    b) large; increasing

    c) small; decreasing

    d) small; increasing

    e) small; staying the same

CRITICAL THINKING AND DISCUSSION

Have you ever faced discrimination based on your race, gender, or sexual orientation? If so, what did you learn in this chapter about whether your civil rights were violated?

Ⓢ PRACTICE ONLINE

"Critical Thinking" exercise: *Politics Is Everywhere— Census Scope*

THE POLICY-MAKING PROCESS AND CIVIL RIGHTS

▶ Explain the approaches used to bring about change in civil rights policies. **Pages 399–415**

SUMMARY

Depending on the political context, each branch of government has played a role in the expansion of civil rights. Moreover, federalism has played a role in this process: while state governments often lagged behind the federal government in African Americans' civil rights, they have been on the forefront on protecting the rights of gays and lesbians.

KEY TERMS

de jure (p. 404)

de facto (p. 404)

rational basis test (p. 407)

intermediate scrutiny test (p. 407)

strict scrutiny test (p. 408)

PRACTICE QUIZ QUESTIONS

7. The most successful social movement has been the _____.

    a) women's rights movement

    b) gay and lesbian civil rights movement

    c) African Americans' civil rights movement

    d) United Farm Workers' movement

    e) Native American rights movement

8. Early in the civil rights movement, which branch provided most of the successes?

    a) state governments

    b) Congress

    c) presidency

    d) bureaucracy

    e) Supreme Court

9. The difference between de facto segregation and de jure segregation is that de facto _____; while de jure segregation _____.
   a) is the result of circumstances; is mandated by law
   b) is mandated by law; is the result of circumstances
   c) applies to racial minorities; applies to women
   d) applies to women; applies to racial minorities
   e) applies to all groups; applies to racial minorities

10. The strongest protection as the "suspect classification" applies which test?
   a) reasonable basis
   b) strict scrutiny
   c) intermediate scrutiny
   d) privileged interest
   e) disparate impact

11. The Voting Rights Act of 1965 _____.
   a) established "majority-minority" districts
   b) established compulsory voter registration for African Americans
   c) eliminated direct obstacles to minority voting in the South

   d) barred discrimination in the rental or sale of a home
   e) reduced participation by African Americans in the South

12. Relative to the protection of individuals with disabilities, Congress's track record in protecting gay rights is _____.
   a) stronger
   b) about the same
   c) weaker
   d) nonexistent
   e) more focused on job discrimination

CRITICAL THINKING AND DISCUSSION

Which policy-making institution has historically played the most important role in protecting the civil rights of Americans? Does that institution still play that role today?

Ⓢ PRACTICE ONLINE

"Critical Thinking" exercise: *Process Matters—Little Rock and Desegregation*

CONTINUING AND FUTURE CIVIL RIGHTS ISSUES

▶ Examine affirmative action and other ongoing civil rights issues. **Pages 416–19**

SUMMARY

The public is divided on the appropriateness of civil rights policies, with different groups preferring a "color-blind" or color-specific approach. Moreover, the debates over issues such as affirmative action, immigration reform, and English as a second language indicate the level of conflict over civil rights policy. Nonetheless, when public opinion does strongly support the application of civil rights in a particular arena, policy makers generally respond to these views.

PRACTICE QUIZ QUESTIONS

13. The Supreme Court's implementation of "color-blind jurisprudence" fits the agenda of those who argue that _____.
   a) the gap between blacks and whites has narrowed
   b) the civil rights movement needs to continue to fight for equal opportunity

   c) African Americans need to be separate and fully self-sufficient
   d) that equality of outcomes is important
   e) that the gap between blacks and whites has widened

14. What did the case *University of California Regents v. Bakke* establish?
   a) that race could play no role in the college admissions process
   b) that gender could play no role in the college admissions process
   c) that strict racial quotas in the admissions process were legal
   d) that race could be used as a "plus factor" in the admissions process
   e) that gender could be used as a "plus factor" in the admissions process

CRITICAL THINKING AND DISCUSSION

Should government attempt to provide a level playing field by making sure that there is no discrimination, or should it go beyond providing equality of opportunity to also be concerned with the equality of outcomes?

Ⓢ **PRACTICE ONLINE**

"Big Think" video exercise: *Laurène Tribe and the Shifting Supreme Court*

SUGGESTED READING

Canon, David T. *Race, Redistricting, and Representation: The Unintended Consequences of Black-Majority Districts.* Chicago: University of Chicago Press, 1999.

Dawson, Michael C. *Behind the Mule: Race and Class in African-American Politics.* Princeton, NJ: Princeton University Press, 1994.

Gross, Ariela J. *What Blood Won't Tell: A History of Race on Trial in America.* Cambridge, MA: Harvard University Press, 2008.

Hochschild, Jennifer L. *Facing Up to the American Dream: Race, Class, and the Soul of the Nation.* Princeton, NJ: Princeton University Press, 1995.

Katznelson, Ira. *When Affirmative Action Was White: An Untold History of Racial Inequality in Twentieth-Century America.* New York: Norton, 2005.

Kluger, Richard. *Simple Justice: The History of* Brown v. Board of Education *and Black America's Struggle for Equality.* New York: Vintage, 2004.

Kousser, J. Morgan. *Colorblind Injustice: Minority Voting Rights and the Undoing of the Second Reconstruction.* Chapel Hill: University of North Carolina Press, 1999.

Lublin, David. *The Paradox of Representation: Racial Gerrymandering and Minority Interests in Congress.* Princeton, NJ: Princeton University Press, 1997.

Tate, Katherine. *Black Faces in the Mirror: African Americans and Their Representatives in Congress.* Princeton, NJ: Princeton University Press, 2003.

Thernstrom, Stephan, and Abigail Thernstrom. *America in Black and White: One Nation, Indivisible: Race in Modern America.* New York: Simon and Schuster, 1997.

14

Economic and Social Policy

Government Spending (As Percentage of GDP)

President's Budget

ECONOMIC POLICIES HAVE GENERATED intense conflicts in recent years. Republicans, like Representative Paul Ryan, have argued that the government must cut spending and focus on reducing the national debt and deficit. Both parties have claimed that they have a better plan for helping spur economic growth.

PRESIDENT OBAMA SIGNALED EARLY IN THE 2012 presidential campaign that tax policy and income inequality would be important themes in the election. He argued, "Today, the wealthiest Americans are paying the lowest taxes in over half a century. . . . Today, thanks to loopholes and shelters, a quarter of all millionaires now pay lower tax rates than millions of you, millions of middle-class families. Some billionaires have a tax rate as low as one percent. One percent. That is the height of unfairness. It is wrong."[1] This argument soon gained political relevance when the leading Republican candidate for president, Mitt Romney, revealed that he paid only 13.9 percent in federal taxes on the $21.7 million income he earned in 2010. Many people with high incomes pay 25 to 30 percent in federal taxes (for example, President Obama paid 26 percent on $1.8 million in 2010).[2]

How is it possible that Romney's tax rate was only 13.9 percent? His taxes were so low because most of his income came from dividends and capital gains, which are taxed at 15 percent, rather than at the top marginal rate of 35 percent (in 2012 the 35 percent rate was paid on all earned income above $388,350, after deductions and exemptions; single tax payers pay 33 percent on income between $178,650 and $388,350, 28 percent on income between $85, 650 and $178,650, all the way down to 10% on the first $8,700). Middle-income people who have a marginal rate of 25 percent (on income between $35,350 and $85,650) and pay 7.65 percent of their income in payroll taxes can easily have a total tax burden higher than 13.9 percent. To address this inequity in the tax code, Obama called

CONFLICT & COMPROMISE
in American Politics

425

for a "millionaire's tax" that would set a minimum rate of 30 percent for incomes that reach that level.

Republicans rejected Obama's call for a millionaire's tax, arguing that the problem is not low taxes on the rich, but excessive government spending. They argue that low taxes stimulate job creation and that lower taxes on capital gains and dividends encourage investment. Furthermore, taxes on dividends represent double taxation because corporations pay both a corporate income tax that is among the highest in the world and then pay taxes on payouts to shareholders.[3]

Tax policies are inherently conflictual due to their redistributive nature: when the government takes money from one group and gives it to another, there will be conflict over those decisions. For example, if tax policy is used to help the poor, the wealthy will pay a larger share of their income in taxes than the poor. But even taxes that do not seem obviously redistributive hit some people harder than others. A 5 percent sales tax is more of a burden for the poor than the nonpoor because poor people spend a higher proportion of their income on basic living costs.

Social policies that redistribute wealth, such as food stamps and welfare, are even more controversial. Many of America's political debates concern economic and social policy: Should we run deficits or have balanced budgets? Should we have a largely unregulated free market, or regulations for things like pollution and health care? What should the government do to help the poor, the uneducated, and others who are at a disadvantage? Democrats generally favor an activist government that supports a range of redistributive programs and regulates the economy to ensure numerous public goods, such as rebuilding the infrastructure. Republicans generally favor limited government that promotes lower taxes and less regulation and allows the free market to determine more social and economic decisions, such as allowing greater development of domestic energy sources.

The conflict over economic and social policy is clear, but how about compromise? The policy responses to the economic meltdown of 2008–09 were very conflictual, as the public questioned the use of taxpayers' money to support Wall Street and the auto industry. But ultimately, bipartisan majorities agreed on a plan to shore up the banking system and get the economy on sounder footing. The stimulus bill of 2009 was also a compromise package comprising roughly equal parts of tax cuts, federal spending, and support for the states. President Obama has vowed to increase taxes on the wealthy to help reduce the deficits, but House Republicans prefer tax simplification through reducing loopholes and deductions (both sides agree that spending should be cut, but Republicans want more cuts with less tax revenue).

Economic and social policy also illustrate the other themes of this book. The idea that political process matters is evident in the ways Congress, the president, and the bureaucracy all have a hand in attempting to achieve economic and social policy goals. The politics of social and economic policy is also everywhere: these policies directly affect all Americans.

This chapter has three main parts. First we discuss the policy-making process and the main players in domestic policy making. Next we examine economic policies, and then social policies. Although we can only scratch the surface of the many important policies that each of these categories encompasses, this chapter will provide a basic understanding of how the political process shapes these policies.

FIGURE » 14.1

TOP MARGINAL TAX RATES, 1913–2012

The top marginal tax rate, which is the tax rate paid by the richest Americans on their income above some threshold ($388,350 in 2012), has plummeted in the past 50 years from more than 90 percent to 35 percent. What are the arguments for and against increasing the top marginal tax rate?

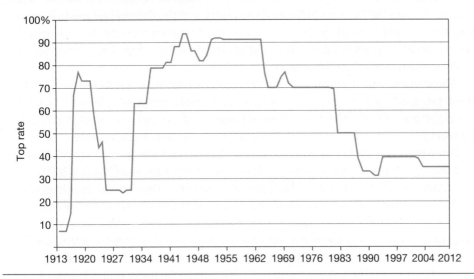

Source: Data from the Internal Revenue Service, "Internal Revenue Bulletin: 2007–45," November 5, 2007, Rev. Proc. 2007-66, www.irs.gov/irb/2007-45_IRB/ar19.html (accessed 5/12/12; 2008–2012 rates from www.irs.gov (accessed 11/5/12).

MAKING PUBLIC POLICY

Public policy is a course of action pursued by government to address a specific problem. For example, various social policies, such as Medicare or Social Security, are aimed at addressing the medical and economic needs of retired American citizens. In this section we outline the policy-making process and discuss the key players in shaping economic and social policy.

THE POLICY-MAKING PROCESS

How are policies shaped and implemented? All policies go through similar stages in this process. The "How It Works" diagram shows the various stages for Social Security, but the steps are the same for most policies. The first stage involves defining a problem as an issue that requires the federal government's attention. Of the thousands of possible issues, Congress only acts on a relatively small number. Consider food stamps: poor and hungry people have been part of American society since the arrival of the first settlers, but this was not seen as a problem requiring government

> **TRACE THE STEPS THROUGH WHICH PROBLEMS ARE ADDRESSED BY GOVERNMENT POLICIES**

public policy A law, rule, statute, or edict that expresses the government's goals and provides for rewards and punishments to promote their attainment.

intervention until the twentieth century. What causes a society to change its assumptions about whether and how government should address social problems?

Sometimes there is a triggering event: the assassination of President John F. Kennedy led to the passage of gun control legislation, the energy crisis of the early 1970s led to the first comprehensive discussions of energy policy, and Hurricane Katrina in 2005 led to a reexamination of our readiness for emergencies and our social safety net. Sometimes redefining an issue can move the policy to the next step of the process. For example, the estate tax has been part of our tax system since 1917, but when Republican leaders in Congress redefined it as the "death tax" in the late 1990s, it transformed the politics of the debate and made it a problem that needed a solution. After all, who could support a tax on dead people? (Of course, dead people don't pay taxes—the estate's heirs do—but that nuance was lost in the redefinition of the problem.)

Recognizing and defining a problem is just the first step; it still needs to come to the attention of political leaders and get on the **policy agenda**. When conditions are right, with the appropriate national political mood and participation from key interest groups and government actors, an issue can reach the agenda.

Once the issue is on the active agenda, alternatives are proposed and debated, and the final version of the policy is formulated in Congress (if it is a bill) or the executive branch (if it is an administrative action). Enactment involves either (1) a roll call vote in the House and the Senate and then a signature by the president, (2) a regulatory decision or administrative action by the bureaucracy, or (3) unilateral action by the president (such as an executive order or agreement).

Many factors determine whether the policy is implemented successfully. First, the problem has to be solvable and the policy must be clear and consistent in its objectives. It wouldn't make sense for Congress to pass a law telling the Department of Health and Human Services to "eliminate poverty," because such a law could not indicate how to accomplish that broad goal. Second, the policy must be funded adequately and administered by competent bureaucrats who have the required expertise. Finally, external support from the public and relevant interest groups may be critical to the policy's success. For example, AARP's support is absolutely essential for the success of any social policy that affects older Americans. Its support helped pass the prescription drug benefit that was added to Medicare in 2003 and comprehensive health care reform in 2010, and its opposition to the Catastrophic Coverage Act forced Congress to repeal the program one year after it was passed.[4]

Implementation of a policy is an ongoing process. To ensure that the desires of Congress and the president are being followed, policy evaluation is a critical stage of the process. (See Chapter 11 for a discussion of Congress's and the president's attempts to control the bureaucracy.) Although policy evaluation has become increasingly visible since passage of the Government Performance and Results Act of 1993, which requires agencies to publish strategic plans and performance measures, it is incredibly difficult to assess whether a government program is achieving its aims.

Political scientist James Q. Wilson explains the difference in measuring success in the private sector and the public sector—specifically, he compares McDonald's to the Department of Motor Vehicles (DMV).[5] It is relatively easy to know whether McDonald's is doing a good job: simply compare the profits being generated to those of the previous period. If profits are going up at a reasonable pace, the burger flippers and fry cooks are doing their jobs. The DMV's performance is much more difficult to assess because there is no simple measure, such as profit, to assess. Maybe you could review the number of people served per hour or the average time that people have to wait to get their driver's license. But that would ignore many other considerations,

policy agenda The set of desired policies that political leaders view as their top priorities.

How It Works

THE BUDGET PROCESS

1ST MONDAY IN FEB. — The president submits budget to Congress.

FEB. 15TH — CBO issues budget and economic outlook report.

WITHIN SIX WEEKS OF PRESIDENT'S SUBMISSION — Other committees with budgetary responsibilities submit "views and estimates" to budget committees.

EARLY APRIL — House Budget Committee creates its budget resolution and the House votes on it.

Senate Budget committee creates its budget resolution and the Senate votes on it.

Budget Conference Committee reconciles House and Senate versions of the budget resolution.

BY APRIL 15TH — House votes on conference version.

Senate votes on conference version.

APPROPRIATIONS

After both houses approve the budget resolution, appropriations committees draft legislation authorizing expenditures to the relevant agencies. Each appropriations bill must be passed by both houses and signed into law by the president. If this process is not completed by October 1st, and no temporary measure (a "continuing resolution") is in place, the government will shut down.

OCT 1ST — Start of the fiscal year.

POP QUIZ!

1 When does each house of Congress vote on its own version of a budget resolution?

- **a** the first Monday in February
- **b** February 15th
- **c** within 6 weeks of receiving the president's budget proposal
- **d** early April
- **e** October 1st

2 If the budget process is not completed by October 1st and no temporary measure is in place

- **a** the president withdraws his proposal.
- **b** both houses of Congress vote on the conference version.
- **c** the government shuts down.
- **d** the start of the fiscal year is postponed until January.
- **e** the appropriations committees draft legislation.

Answers: 1.d; 2.c

such as how well the DMV serves disadvantaged populations or people for whom English is a second language. In a DMV office where 50 percent of the applicants don't speak English, we wouldn't expect the workers to be as efficient as in one where all applicants speak English.

Evaluating a public agency such as the State Department is even more difficult. How do we know if diplomacy is being conducted in a manner consistent with congressional and presidential preferences? Would success be defined as staying out of war? Increasing economic activity or cultural exchanges between countries? Strengthening democratic institutions in emerging democracies? Getting cooperation in the war on terrorism? Measuring the achievement of objectives like these is very difficult even if those goals can be clearly defined.

Despite these limitations, extensive efforts to evaluate policy do provide decision makers with some basis for deciding whether to modify, expand, or terminate a policy. Programs are notoriously difficult to cut or eliminate.

HEALTH CARE REFORM HAS BEEN ONE of the most controversial social policies. When the Supreme Court heard arguments for and against the Affordable Care Act in 2012, groups on both sides of the issue demonstrated outside the Court.

THE KEY PLAYERS IN ECONOMIC AND SOCIAL POLICY MAKING

Congress, the president, and the bureaucracy all play important roles in making economic and social policy. Congress, through the "power of the purse," has the constitutional authority to determine the nation's fiscal policy, but the president also can shape taxing and spending policy for the nation. The Federal Reserve and the Treasury implement the nation's monetary policy, while other bureaucratic agencies implement social policy. Additional significant players include the courts, state governments, and interest groups.

CONGRESS

The Constitution places Congress at the center of economic policy making by giving legislators the "power of the purse"—that is, power over the nation's fiscal policy of taxing and spending. In a way, everything Congress does has an impact on the economy, whether it is providing money for an interstate highway or a student loan, regulating the level of air pollutants, or funding the Social Security system. Some committees are more directly related to economic policy: budget, appropriations, and tax committees direct Congress's **fiscal policy**—taxing and spending—whereas the banking committees have a hand in overseeing aspects of the nation's **monetary policy**—controlling the money supply and interest rates. (However, as we discuss later in the chapter, monetary policy is primarily the domain of the Federal Reserve System, or the Fed.) The commerce committees, especially in the House, also influence a range of economic policies. The budget process is the most important of Congress's economic policy-making responsibilities.

Budget making in Congress was decentralized through much of the nation's history, with various committees and subcommittees serving as the centers of

fiscal policy Government decisions about how to influence the economy by taxing and spending.

monetary policy Government decisions about how to influence the economy using control of the money supply and interest rates.

budget making The processes carried out in Congress to determine how government money will be spent and revenue will be raised.

the legislative process and no real way to coordinate activity among them. The appropriations committees tried to be the "guardians of the Treasury," but it was difficult to keep the spending requests from other committees in line with overall budgetary expectations because of Congress's two-step process to approve spending: the authorizing committee writes the law that authorizes the spending, and then the appropriations committee approves the level of spending.[6] As a result, budgetary power shifted from Congress to the president, starting with the Budget and Accounting Act of 1921. Since then presidents have played a central role in the budget process by submitting their budgets to Congress. The president's budget often serves as the starting point for the congressional budget (see "How It Works").

Today, as evidence that politics is conflictual, increased partisan polarization is occurring in Congress over budget making. Differences between Democrats' and Republicans' views of taxing and spending policy make it difficult to pass a budget on time. Recently, Congress has relied on "continuing resolutions," which keep spending at the level of the previous year's budget, when they cannot agree on a new budget. Even traditionally noncontroversial aspects of fiscal policy, such as increasing the debt ceiling to authorize government borrowing, have become opportunities for partisan politics.

Congress also plays a central role in shaping social policy. Many important social policies such as Social Security, Medicare, Medicaid, and food stamps, started out as presidential initiatives. But Congress writes the laws and then reforms and expands them over the years.

THE PRESIDENT

Presidents know that the public expects them to promote a healthy economy. Indeed, the state of the economy influences the public's assessment of presidential performance and also influences election outcomes. President Obama focused on the economy in his first months in office, pushing through a massive stimulus bill; later, facing high levels of unemployment, Obama also signed legislation aimed at creating more jobs.

As mentioned in Chapter 10, on the economic front the president cannot accomplish much single-handedly: Congress, the Fed, and broader domestic and international economic forces all have an impact on the health of the economy. However, the president has a large advising structure to help formulate economic policy. The Office of Management and Budget (OMB), the Council of Economic Advisers (CEA), the Office of the **United States Trade Representative (USTR)**, and the **National Economic Council (NEC)** all provide important economic advice to the president.

The OMB, formerly the Bureau of the Budget, solicits spending requests from all federal agencies, suggests additional cuts, and then coordinates these requests with presidential priorities. It ultimately puts together the president's budget, which is then submitted to Congress. The OMB also oversees government reorganization plans and recommends improvements in departmental operations.

The CEA primarily provides the president with objective data on the state of the economy and expert advice on economic policy. The CEA is responsible for creating the *Annual Economic Report of the President*, which has a wealth of data on the economy and an overview of the president's policies. Although presidents have varied in how closely they work with the CEA or other parts of their economic team, some prominent CEA members have significantly influenced the administration's tax policy and jobs program.

United States Trade Representative (USTR) An agency founded in 1962 to negotiate with foreign governments to create trade agreements, resolve disputes, and participate in global trade policy organizations. Treaties negotiated by the USTR must be ratified by the Senate.

National Economic Council (NEC) A group of economic advisers created in 1993 to work with the president to coordinate economic policy.

Interactions between Congress and the president are central to understanding economic and social policy. If the president's party controls Congress, then the president's budget becomes the starting point for congressional negotiations over the budget. If the opposing party controls Congress, then the president's budget is usually considered "dead on arrival" and Congress creates its own document. Of course, the president can use the veto threat to try to move Congress closer to his position; but when the budget is contained in one large package that must be signed or vetoed in its entirety, it is difficult to carry out such threats.[7]

Similarly, in some instances the president may take the lead in formulating social policy, as Franklin D. Roosevelt did with the New Deal and Lyndon Johnson with the Great Society. In other instances Congress plays a central role, as with health care reform in 2009–10. In all cases the president and Congress must find some common ground.

THE BUREAUCRACY

You might assume that the bureaucracy makes little difference in social policy and simply implements the policies determined by Congress and the president. For some policies, that is somewhat true—such as Social Security, whose benefit levels are determined by law. Implementing this policy largely involves determining that the proper amount of money is going to the right people and distributing the payments. However, as discussed in Chapter 11, with many social policies the "on-the-ground" public employees have a great deal of discretion. One study found that welfare agencies that distributed AFDC benefits had a more "hostile and punitive" attitude toward their clients than those that administered the disability program under Social Security. Welfare offices in general tend not to be very welcoming places. People often have to wait for hours, and office workers are sometimes rude. Some potential welfare recipients are so alienated by the process that they give up.[8] (This is not true of all welfare offices, but there are general differences in how recipients are treated in different types of social welfare programs.)

Bureaucratic discretion may also serve more positive ends, though. In fact, many bureaucratic agencies in the late nineteenth and early twentieth centuries developed political autonomy and strong reputations that enabled them to analyze and solve problems, create new programs, and plan and administer programs efficiently.[9] Many of the same insights apply to agencies that deliver social policies today, such as the Social Security Administration, which has a very strong base of popular and political support.

In terms of economic policy, two bureaucratic agencies are key in creating monetary policy: the **Federal Reserve System** (the Fed), an independent agency; and the **Treasury Department**, a cabinet-level department. (For a discussion of the Fed, see pages 440–44.) The Treasury Department's mission "is to promote the conditions for prosperity and stability in the United States and encourage prosperity and stability in the rest of the world."[10] Some of these responsibilities overlap with the Fed's, especially supervising banks and managing the public debt. In most instances the responsibilities are complementary rather than competing, such as the management of currency and coins: the Treasury produces currency and coins, and the Fed distributes them to member banks.[11] Financing federal debt is another matter. The Treasury prefers lower interest rates to keep down the cost of financing the debt and to promote economic growth, while the Fed is also concerned about keeping rates high enough to avoid inflation. Therefore, the Fed and the Treasury must coordinate their policies to avoid working at cross-purposes.

Federal Reserve System An independent agency that serves as the central bank of the United States to bring stability to the nation's banking system.

Treasury Department A cabinet-level agency that is responsible for managing the federal government's revenue. It prints currency, collects taxes, and sells government bonds.

OTHER IMPORTANT PLAYERS

By providing a necessary legal foundation, *the courts* ensure fair application of economic and social policy laws and regulations. For example, contract law, patent law, banking and finance law, and property rights are all elements of a legal system that provides the foundation for economic development. Courts issue rulings on the regulation of telecommunications, banking, and energy industries and decisions on environmental law and eminent domain that affect property rights. All these policies have an impact on economic policy. Courts are also important in helping to shape economic and social policy by deciding when laws passed by Congress may be unconstitutional.

State governments have a central role in areas such as education and welfare. Welfare has always been administered at the state and local level, with varying degrees of national control. Medicaid is administered at the state level (with federal assistance), and education is almost completely controlled by local and state governments. One sticking point with health care reform in 2009–10 was the extent to which policy would be centered in the states or have a stronger national component. (The stronger national approach failed, but the new law signaled a definite shift to a more national role in health care.)

Education policy, too, is seeing more involvement by the national government. But even with the national accountability mechanisms and testing requirements established by President Bush's No Child Left Behind Act, and the incentives provided by President Obama's "Race to the Top" program, education policy remains largely a state and local affair.

In contrast, economic policy making is more of a national responsibility. States are severely constrained in making fiscal policy because they must have balanced budgets every year (unlike the national government, which may run deficits to stimulate the economy). Monetary policy is entirely the domain of the national government.

Interest groups constitute another important player in shaping policy, although those advocating for social policy are not as influential as groups focusing on business, labor, the environment, or gun ownership. A major exception is AARP, a highly powerful lobby that addresses policy issues affecting the elderly (see

Chapter 8). AARP has had an especially strong voice on behalf of Social Security and Medicare. Many other interest groups and think tanks work on behalf of the poor, homeless, and other disadvantaged people, but Washington is generally less responsive to their concerns because these groups are not politically powerful.

Lately, interest groups and social movements have gotten involved in economic policy. The Tea Party advocates less government spending and more focus on the debt, while the Occupy movement directs attention to income inequality and the need for more regulation of Wall Street. More long-standing groups, such as the Concord Coalition, have organized to influence fiscal policy in Washington.

EXPLAIN THE MAIN PURPOSE OF GOVERNMENT INVOLVEMENT IN THE ECONOMY AND HOW FISCAL, MONETARY, REGULATORY, AND TRADE POLICIES INFLUENCE THE ECONOMY

ECONOMIC POLICY

Here we take a closer look at the goals and theories that influence specific economic policies passed by the government. We also examine the trade-offs among various goals.

GOALS OF ECONOMIC POLICY

Policy makers have specific goals in mind when they try to influence the economy. Many seem obvious, such as full employment (it's better to have more people working than not working), but others may be less clear. Also, it is difficult to pursue all the goals simultaneously because there are trade-offs among some of them.

FULL EMPLOYMENT

Employment seems like a good starting point for a healthy economy. If people have jobs, they pay taxes and do not depend on the government for support. Despite this, **full employment** was not an explicit goal of economic policy until 1946, when Congress passed the Employment Act. Leaders were concerned that with millions of returning World War II veterans and the wartime economy gearing down, the nation might slide back into the **economic depression** that had created so much hardship in the 1930s. Although the act was largely symbolic (there was no guaranteed right to employment), it did create the **Council of Economic Advisers**, which provides the president with economic information and advice. A more concrete effort to ensure that returning veterans could find jobs was the Servicemen's Readjustment Act (the GI Bill). Enacted in 1944, it provided higher education assistance and low-interest home mortgages for millions of veterans. Today the government seeks to support the creation of as many jobs as possible through a strong economy.

STABLE PRICES

The importance of price stability is not as obvious as the need for jobs. Why are rising prices—**inflation**—a problem? This is a common question during periods of low inflation. Especially for workers who have automatic raises (cost of living adjustments, or COLAs) as part of their basic pay package, moderate inflation isn't much of a problem. For example, if your rent goes up by 4 percent, the price of gro-

full employment The theoretical point at which all citizens who want to be employed have a job.

economic depression A deep, widespread downturn in the economy, like the Great Depression of the 1930s.

Council of Economic Advisers A group of economic advisers, created by the Employment Act of 1946, which provides objective data on the state of the economy and makes economic policy recommendations to the president.

inflation The increase in the price of consumer goods over time.

FIGURE » 14.2

INFLATION AND UNEMPLOYMENT, 1960–2012

The Misery Index is the sum of the unemployment rate and the inflation rate. Which periods have had the highest misery rate since 1960? Were there any external explanations for the high misery rate? How did the government respond to the high levels of unemployment and inflation?

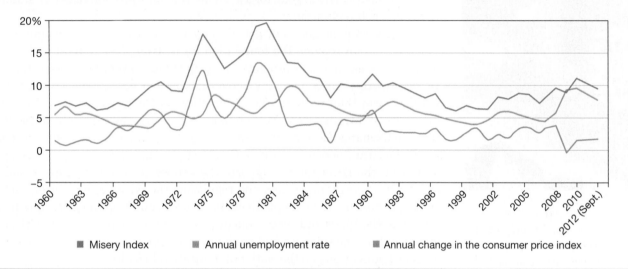

■ Misery Index   ■ Annual unemployment rate   ■ Annual change in the consumer price index

Source: Data from the U.S. Department of Labor, Bureau of Labor Statistics. Inflation data from "Consumer Price Index," www.bls.gov/CPI, and unemployment data from "Labor Force Statistics from the Current Population Survey," www.bls.gov/cps (accessed 9/24/12).

ceries goes up by 3 percent, and you get a 4 percent raise, you will probably manage to be at least as well off as you were in the previous year (see Figure 14.2).

However, high inflation can have serious effects on the economy. First, some people see an erosion of their purchasing power. So if your rent goes up by 10 percent and groceries are up by 15 percent, but your pay goes up by only 4 percent, you will be substantially worse off. Second, high inflation penalizes savers and rewards debtors as savings interest rates may be outstripped by inflation (so savings are worth less over time), but people who go into debt can repay those debts with cheaper dollars in the future. Finally, long-term economic planning by businesses becomes more difficult when inflation is high, because investors demand high interest rates to compensate for the added risk of future inflation.

Typically, unemployment and inflation are not high at the same time, so there can be a trade-off in focusing on one or the other in economic policy. There tend to be basic partisan differences on the goals of full employment and stable prices, with Democrats being more concerned about employment and Republicans more concerned about inflation. This is no surprise, given the Democratic Party's base of support within labor unions and blue-collar workers and the Republican Party's stronger support on Wall Street and with investors whose income is likely to be eroded by high inflation.

PROMOTING THE FREE MARKET AND GROWTH

The American economy is a capitalist system, which means that most economic decisions are voluntarily made between individuals and firms for their mutual benefit. The government generally stays out of most economic activity, except to regulate the market when it produces too much of something that is not in the public's interest, such as pollution or unsafe products. Economists tout the advantage of the free market as promoting the most efficient use of resources. Economic growth is also a central goal, for a growing economy provides a better standard of living for each generation.

The government does not get directly involved in most economic transactions, but it can provide the foundation for a strong free market and economic growth. The government protects property rights so that businesses that invest in the growth of their company know that another firm or the government cannot take away their property. The foundation for the free market is also provided by secure and transparent capital markets through the oversight of the Securities and Exchange Commission, and through a secure banking system as ensured by the Federal Deposit Insurance Corporation and the Federal Reserve System. Moreover, the government supports the economic infrastructure by subsidizing the transportation system and regulating the telecommunication system. It accomplishes this through public works such as building the interstate highway system in the 1950s and 1960s, and by promoting economic growth with support of research in the sciences and medicine through agencies such as the National Science Foundation and the National Institutes of Health.

As we will see later in the chapter, the economic meltdown of 2008–09 raised basic questions about the efficiency of economic markets and the need for more regulation of the financial sector.

BALANCED BUDGETS

Maintaining a **balanced budget** has been a central economic goal since the 1980s, when **budget deficits** skyrocketed (see Figure 14.3A and Nuts and Bolts 14.1). Large deficits are a concern for several reasons. First, they take a big bite out of current spending. About $258 billion, or 7.3 percent, of the 2012 fiscal year budget went to financing the federal debt. These dollars went to people who own federal bonds and securities; the monies did not buy a single uniform for a soldier, highway exit ramp, or student loan. Second, the total federal debt is a burden on future generations. Each man, woman, and child in the United States in effect carries more than $51,386 of federal debt. (Total debt has grown steadily; see Figure 14.3B.)

TRADE-OFFS AMONG ECONOMIC POLICY GOALS

One challenge facing economic policy makers is that it is difficult to "have it all." The period of economic growth, low unemployment, and low inflation with falling budget deficits that the United States enjoyed through much of the 1990s was relatively unusual. Typically, at least part of the economy is not performing well and some goals are not being met, so policy makers must tread carefully when addressing economic problems to ensure that they do not make some other problem worse.

ONE IMPORTANT WAY THAT THE government supports the free market and economic growth is by promoting the stability of the banking system. The Federal Deposit Insurance Corporation (FDIC) bolsters confidence in banks by insuring each account holder's deposits in its member banks up to $250,000.

balanced budget A spending plan in which the government's expenditures are equal to its revenue.

budget deficits The amount by which a government's spending in a given fiscal year exceeds its revenue.

DEFICITS AND DEBT

Budget deficits and the federal debt are related concepts that are easily confused.

▶ A *budget deficit* occurs when tax revenue is not sufficient to cover government spending in a given year. If tax revenue is higher than spending, then there is a budget surplus.

▶ The *federal debt* is the total accumulation of all outstanding borrowing by the government.

▶ The concepts of deficit and debt are related because when the government runs a deficit, it must borrow money to cover the gap. This borrowing then builds up the federal debt.

You can think of this in terms of your own spending habits. Any time you spend more money in a given month than you earn, you are running a deficit. You must borrow money to make up that deficit from a bank, from your parents, or by running up the balance on your credit card. The accumulated sum of your monthly deficits is the total debt that you owe.

TOOLS AND THEORIES OF ECONOMIC POLICY

Here we explore the various tools that policy makers use to achieve the goals outlined in the previous section. We do not want to give the impression that policy makers can pull levers and push buttons to achieve desired outcomes, or that they are immune from external forces that can sink the economy despite their best efforts. However, leaders can do certain things to move the massive U.S. economy in the right direction.

FISCAL POLICY

Fiscal policy is the use of the government's taxing and spending power to influence the direction of the economy. In the 1930s the economist John Maynard Keynes developed the idea of fine-tuning the economy through "countercyclical" taxing and spending policy, usually called **Keynesian economics**. Keynes argued that policy makers can soften the effects of a recession by stimulating the economy when overall demand is low—during a recession, when people aren't spending much—through tax cuts or increased government spending. Tax cuts put more money in people's pockets, enabling them to spend more than they otherwise would, while government spending stimulates the economy through the purchase of various goods, such as highways or military equipment, or direct payments to individuals, such as Social Security checks. From this perspective it is acceptable to run budget deficits in order to increase employment and national income to give a short-term boost to the economy. Keynes also pointed out that if overall demand is too high, which might result in inflation, policy makers should cool off the economy by cutting spending or raising taxes.[12]

A more recent version of fiscal policy was the basis for Ronald Reagan's tax cuts in 1981 and has been the centerpiece of economic policy for many Republicans since

Keynesian economics The theory that governments should use economic policy, like taxing and spending, to maintain stability in the economy.

FIGURE » 14.3A

FEDERAL BUDGET DEFICITS AND SURPLUSES

The federal deficit is the amount by which the government's spending exceeds its revenue in a given year; the federal debt is the accumulation of these annual deficits. Why do the federal deficits and debt matter? Does the answer depend on the state of the economy?

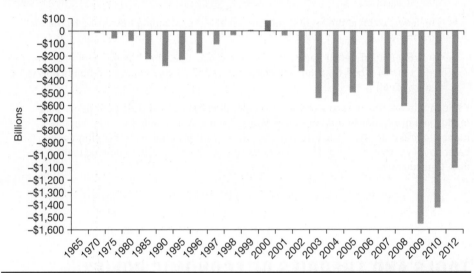

FIGURE » 14.3B

FEDERAL DEBT

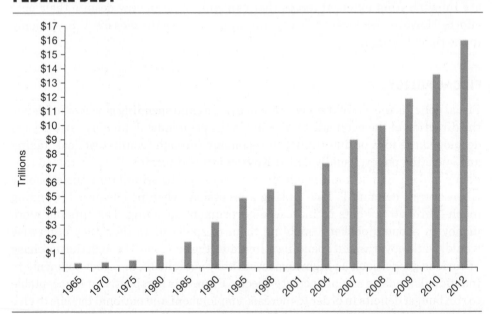

Note: Totals in Figure 14.2A exclude the Social Security Trust Fund and reflect total public debt, including intragovernmental holdings.

Source: Data on budget deficits from the Congressional Budget Office, Historical Budget Data, www.cbo.gov/publication/42911. Data on federal debt from the U.S. Department of the Treasury, TreasuryDirect, www.treasurydirect.gov/govt/reports/pd/histdebt/histdebt.htm (accessed 11/4/12).

then. **Supply-side economics** focuses on the ways that tax policy and regulations affect the labor supply rather than on these policies' impact on overall demand. The primary focus is on the way tax rates affect how much people work rather than how they spend. The idea is that if tax rates are too high, people will work less because a large percentage of their income goes to the government.

However, when taxes were cut under Reagan, with the top marginal rate (the income tax rate paid on the top slice of earned income) going from 70 to 50 percent, revenue fell and the budget deficits exploded. Supporters of the supply-side theory argue that the problem was on the spending side of the equation rather than on tax revenue. While overall government spending did increase during the 1982–83 recession, spending from the beginning of Reagan's term to the end dropped slightly from 22.2 percent to 21.2 percent of **gross domestic product** (GDP), and tax revenue fell from 19.6 percent of GDP in 1981, the last year before the tax cuts went into effect, to 18.1 percent of GDP in 1988, the last year of the Reagan presidency.[13] This observation suggests that lower taxes, not higher spending, were not the source of the budget deficits in the 1980s.

Economists continue to debate the extent to which fiscal policy can influence the economy. Two factors have limited the effectiveness of fiscal policy. First, fiscal policies often cannot be implemented quickly enough to have the intended impact on the **business cycle**—the normal expansion and contraction of the economy. This is especially true when one party controls Congress and the other controls the presidency, but it happens even during unified government. The $787 billion American Recovery and Reinvestment Act of 2009, designed to stimulate the economy and create jobs, encountered problems along these lines. Although the legislation had some immediate impact on the economy, it is impossible to spend that much money (or implement tax cuts) without some time lag. Republicans criticized Democrats for spending too much money and not enacting policies that would have had a more immediate effect (such as payroll tax cuts), and other critics argued that the stimulus wasn't big enough.

Second, on the other side of the Keynesian coin, increasing taxes or cutting spending during good economic times is much more difficult to implement than the more politically popular tax cuts or spending increases. After all, politicians do not like to raise taxes or cut spending. Furthermore, even if politicians *wanted* to cut spending, this aspect of fiscal policy is becoming increasingly difficult to use because a growing portion of the federal budget is devoted to **mandatory spending**—that is, entitlements such as Social Security, which must be spent by law, and interest on the federal debt, which must be paid (if the United States defaulted on its debt, there would be an international economic meltdown). So reducing the federal deficit by cutting spending is increasingly difficult. With the 2013 deficit running close to $900 billion, Congress would have to eliminate nearly all **discretionary spending**—spending that can be cut from the budget without changing the underlying law—including defense spending and everything else the government does, to balance the budget.[14] (See Figure 14.4.)

Fiscal policy may have a relatively modest impact on the economy, but it determines how the tax burden is distributed and which parts of the economy and policy areas benefit from federal spending. In other words, fiscal policy has *redistributive* implications. There are two ways of thinking about the characteristics of federal taxes: (1) the different types of taxes and (2) their redistributive nature—that is, whether a specific tax is regressive, neutral, or progressive (defined later in the chapter). There are four major types of federal taxes: personal income taxes, corporate taxes, payroll taxes (for Social Security and Medicare), and excise taxes (such as taxes on cigarettes, alcohol, gasoline, air travel,

supply-side economics The theory that lower tax rates will stimulate the economy by encouraging people to save, invest, and produce more goods and services.

gross domestic product The value of a country's economic output taken as a whole.

business cycle The normal pattern of expansion and contraction of the economy.

mandatory spending Expenditures that are required by law, such as the funding for Social Security.

discretionary spending Expenditures that can be cut from the budget without changing the underlying law.

FIGURE » 14.4

MANDATORY AND DISCRETIONARY SPENDING, 1962-2013

The percentage of the budget allocated for discretionary spending has been shrinking since the 1960s. What implications does this have for members of Congress and the president as they try to reduce the federal deficits?

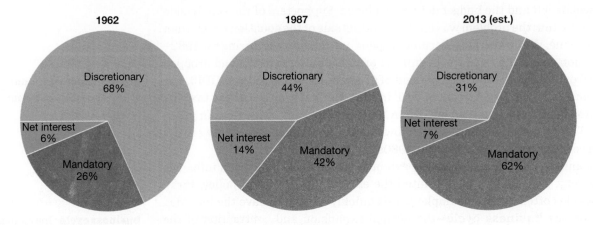

1962
Discretionary 68%
Net interest 6%
Mandatory 26%

1987
Discretionary 44%
Net interest 14%
Mandatory 42%

2013 (est.)
Discretionary 31%
Net interest 7%
Mandatory 62%

Source: The President's Budget for Fiscal Year 2013, Office of Management and Budget, www.whitehouse.gov/omb/budget (accessed 10/7/12).

and telephone lines). Figure 14.5 shows how the distribution of tax revenue changed between 1962 and 2013. The proportion of personal income taxes held fairly steady, but excise taxes and corporate taxes fell, and payroll taxes more than doubled.

The increasing share of revenue that comes from payroll taxes has important implications for the redistributive nature of taxes. Payroll taxes are **regressive** because everyone pays the same rate of 6.2 percent (with a temporary rate of 4.2 percent in 2011 and 2012) up to a certain income level ($110,100 in 2012; everyone also pays an additional 1.45 percent on all income to support Medicare). Thus someone who earns $110,100 pays the same *amount* of Social Security tax ($6,826) as a wealthy individual such as Bill Gates, but it is a much larger share of that person's income than it is for a person like Gates. Income taxes, in contrast, are **progressive**: upper-income people pay a larger share of their income in taxes than low-income people do (however, as the example of Mitt Romney's taxes illustrated, wealthy people may pay a smaller proportion of their total income in taxes than middle-class people if most of their income comes from capital gains and dividends).

regressive Taxes that take a larger share of poor people's income than wealthy people's income, such as sales taxes and payroll taxes.

progressive Taxes that require upper-income people to pay a higher tax rate than lower-income people, such as income taxes.

MONETARY POLICY AND THE FEDERAL RESERVE SYSTEM

Monetary policy includes influencing interest rates and the money supply and regulating the lending activity of banks. The Federal Reserve Act of 1913 established the Federal Reserve System to bring stability and continuity to the nation's banking system. The chair and six other governors serve on the board of governors of the Federal Reserve System. The board is responsible for establishing monetary policy for the nation. There are 12 regional Federal Reserve banks and more than 2,900 member banks out of the approximately 7,800 banks in the nation.[15] The Fed moni-

FIGURE » 14.5

FEDERAL REVENUES AND SPENDING, 1962 AND 2013

A much larger share of tax revenue comes from payroll taxes than was true in the 1960s. What implications does this have for the redistributive nature of federal taxes? What have been the biggest changes since the 1960s in the way the federal tax dollar is spent? Are these trends likely to reverse or continue in the next 30 years?

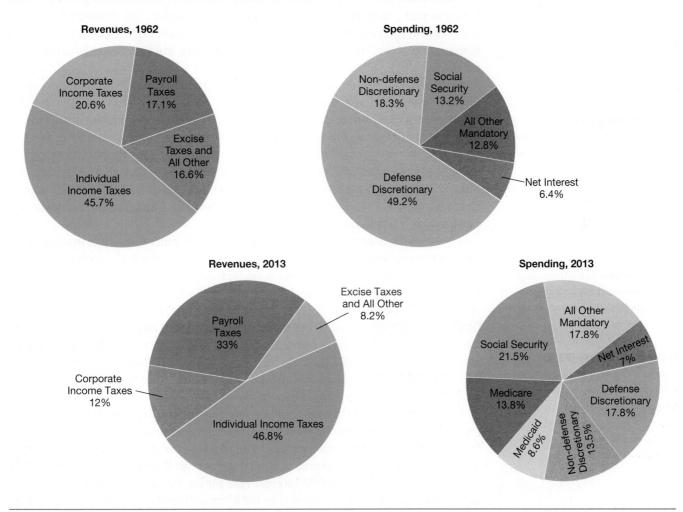

Source: The President's Budget for Fiscal Year 2013, Office of Management and Budget, www.whitehouse.gov/omb/budget (accessed 10/7/12).

tors levels of bank lending, the money supply, and interest rates. Bank lending is important for economic growth because businesses borrow money to expand, and as they grow, they add jobs. If credit is tight and businesses cannot borrow money, economic growth will suffer, as became painfully evident in late 2008 and 2009.

The second target of monetary policy, the money supply, is also central to economic growth and directly related to levels of lending activity. The Fed can influence the amount of money in the system by making it easier or harder for banks to lend money. According to the **monetarist theory**, the amount of money in circulation is the most important determinant of economic activity and inflation. If too much money is chasing too few goods, there could be inflationary pressure on

monetarist theory The idea that the amount of money in circulation (the money supply) is the primary influence on economic activity and inflation.

the economy and prices might rise too quickly.[16] In contrast, if enough money isn't available, a recession could occur.

Perhaps the most obvious targets of monetary policy are interest rates. Changing interest rates affect the economy by making borrowing money either less or more expensive. Businesses and consumers are more likely to borrow if the interest rate is 6 percent than 12 percent. Consumer purchases of big-ticket items, things that are financed by borrowing rather than purchased with cash, also increase when interest rates are low and dry up when interest rates are high. That is why so many appliance stores and car dealers advertise, "Zero dollars down, and zero percent interest until next January!" Entire sectors of the economy, such as housing, construction, consumer durables, and cars, are very sensitive to interest rates.

What can the Fed do to meet its targets on credit availability, the money supply, and interest rates? There are three central tools of monetary policy. First, the **reserve requirement** is the most potentially powerful tool for affecting the availability of credit: banks are required to have a certain amount of money in reserve to ensure they have cash on hand to cover withdrawals. By simply changing the amount of money that banks are required to hold for every deposit, the Fed can significantly influence the amount of money that banks can lend. However, because changing the reserve requirement has such a powerful impact on the economy, the Fed has rarely used this tool.[17]

The second monetary policy tool, interest rates, is more difficult to manage than the reserve requirement. With the reserve requirement, the Fed simply announces the change in the rate. With interest rates, there is only one rate—the **discount rate**—that the Fed directly sets. It is the rate the Fed charges to member banks for short-term loans. However, it is far less important as a policy tool than the **federal funds rate (FFR)**, the rate that member banks charge one another on overnight loans (these are short-term loans that banks use to meet their reserve requirements). Beginning in 1995 the FFR has been the central interest rate target for the Fed.[18] The FFR is set by the demand for overnight loans that are necessary to settle accounts, but the Fed greatly affects those rates.

Despite the Fed's ability to influence short-term interest rates, it has only indirect impact on long-term interest rates, including consumer rates such as those for mortgages and home equity loans. The market sets these rates. If an investor thinks that inflation will increase from 3 percent to 6 percent over the next five years, he will demand a higher interest rate for lending his money to the government or a corporation than if he thinks inflation will hold steady at about 3 percent.

The last tool the Fed uses to meet its monetary targets is **open market operations**—the buying and selling of securities. This is the most important tool because it influences the FFR and the level of bank reserves—and thus the money supply. If the Fed wants to increase the money supply and put downward pressure on the FFR, it will purchase securities such as government bonds from a bank. The bank gives the Fed its bond, and the Fed deposits the appropriate amount of money into the bank's account at the Fed. The bank can use this money to support new loans. Open market operations may also serve to contract the money supply or raise interest rates; if this is the desired outcome, the Fed will sell government securities. The member bank will give the Fed money to cover the cost of the bond and therefore take money out of circulation.

Fed chair Ben Bernanke used these tools to help stop the "credit crunch" that emerged with the meltdown of the subprime mortgage market and related problems in the bond markets in 2008. The Fed increased its balance sheet (its state-

reserve requirement The minimum amount of money that a bank is required to have on hand to back up its assets.

discount rate The interest rate that a bank must pay on a short-term loan from the Federal Reserve Bank.

federal funds rate (FFR) The interest rate that a bank must pay on an overnight loan from another bank.

open market operations The process by which the Federal Reserve System buys and sells securities to influence the money supply.

ment of assets and liabilities) from $927 billion on September 10, 2008, to an eye-popping $2.26 trillion by November 11, 2008. About $1.6 trillion of the money injected into the economy came through efforts to stabilize short-term lending, money market funds, and the bailout of AIG (among other things). By October 2012 those loans had been almost entirely repaid as credit markets stabilized. However, overall Fed assets remained at $2.26 trillion, as the securities held by the Fed climbed from $514 billion to $2 trillion from February 2009 to September 2010 (including $1.1 trillion in mortgage-backed securities that the Fed purchased from stressed financial institutions).[19] In the next two years, the Fed continued to expand its injection of money into the economy by purchasing an additional $600 billion in securities. This unprecedented intervention in the financial sector prevented a serious crisis, but critics argue that the Fed has become too powerful and unaccountable a player in economic policy making.

One crucial characteristic of the Fed is its political independence: its decisions are not subject to presidential or congressional review. A strong indication of the Fed's independence is that presidents typically reappoint chairs who were initially appointed by presidents of the other party: Alan Greenspan's tenure spanned the presidencies of Reagan, Bush, Clinton, and the second Bush.[20] Ben Bernanke was nominated by Bush and renominated by Obama. But the Fed is not immune to political influence. In fact, one line of research argues that the Fed tries to help presidents during re-election years by encouraging a pro-growth economy.[21] Evidence on this point is mixed, but at a minimum, presidents do have the ability to make it clear when they disagree with the Fed's policies. Presidents also have the opportunity to appoint the chair and vice chair of the Fed, but presidents rarely fire them because they do not want to upset the financial markets. Other research has shown that the Fed is at least somewhat sensitive to the preferences of the president and Congress.[22]

The Fed's ultimate accountability is to Congress, because if things really get out of hand—for example, if the Fed were to increase interest rates to 20 percent

FEDERAL RESERVE CHAIRMAN BEN Bernanke (left) presents his semiannual report to Congress in February 2010. Although the Fed makes regular reports to Congress and the president, it is an independent agency and its decisions are not subject to presidential and congressional review.

without good reason—Congress could amend the Federal Reserve Act and remove the Fed's responsibility or autonomy in specific areas. The Fed must report to Congress annually on its activities and to the banking committees of Congress twice a year on its plans for monetary policy. The Fed's annual report is subject to an outside audit. Fed officials also frequently testify before Congress on a range of issues. And Congress may publicly criticize the Fed when it disagrees with the Fed's policies.

REGULATORY POLICY

Government regulation has a huge impact on the economy. For example, the federal government regulates the quality of food and water, the safety of workplaces and airspaces, and the integrity of the banking and finance system. In general, regulations address market failures such as monopolies and imperfect information (discussed later). There are two main types of regulation: economic and social. Economic regulation sets prices or conditions on entry of firms into an industry, whereas social regulation addresses issues of quality and safety.[23] Both types influence the economy.

A common type of economic regulation involves price regulation of monopolies. A monopoly occurs when a single firm controls the entire market for a product so it is not subject to competition. When this happens, the monopoly could charge extremely high prices if the government did not regulate it. Concern about this type of behavior led to the Interstate Commerce Act (1887), which created the Interstate Commerce Commission to regulate railroad rates, and the Sherman Antitrust Act (1890), which served to break up Standard Oil in 1910, among other monopolies. More common than a true monopoly are firms that control most of a market rather than all of it and start acting like a monopoly. For example, Microsoft was sued by the Justice Department and 19 states in 1998 for trying to quash its competition in the rapidly growing area of Internet browsers.

The most common market failures that lead to social regulation occur in situations when the costs of a firm's behavior are not entirely borne by the firm but are passed on to other people. The classic example is pollution. In a free market, the owners of a coal-fired power plant do not bear the cost of the pollution spewing out of its smokestacks; instead, the people who live downwind from the plant bear the cost. Therefore, the power plant owners have little incentive to curb pollution unless the government regulates it. Other examples of agencies that set social regulations are those that promote safety, such as the National Highway Traffic Safety Administration, the Consumer Product Safety Commission, and the Occupational Safety and Health Administration.

Social regulation has generally received strong political support since the 1960s and 1970s, but Congress has pared back economic regulation in the past 30 years. (One exception is in the financial sector, for which regulations were strengthened in 2010.) Regulatory policy also involves interbranch politics between Congress and the bureaucracy. Even when members of Congress agree on a general policy goal—for example, limiting air pollution—they often cannot agree on the precise mechanisms for achieving that goal, so they delegate authority to a regulatory agency. As discussed in Chapter 11, this produces a "principal-agent problem" in which Congress (the principal) cannot be sure that the bureaucracy (the agent) will implement policy according to its goals. Another area in which regulatory policy has generated political heat concerns the debate about the trade-off between regulation and economic growth. Regulations impose costs on the free market, which may limit job growth. However, in recent years new approaches in environmental regulation have attempted to address that concern. Environmentalists have learned that using market principles can work to their advantage, as the example of grazing rights in the West shows (see "You Decide)".

Thus while political debates over regulatory policy can still be intense, common ground may be found in pursuing market solutions to regulatory problems. In general, the public interest is often served by regulations that protect the environment, ensure the safety of the food supply, and regulate the dumping of hazardous chemicals, whether it is through traditional economic regulations or more recent market approaches. In each instance, *politics* defines how the public interest is served through regulation.

CASE STUDY: THE 2008-09 ECONOMIC CRISIS

The economic meltdown of 2008–09 is an excellent example of how policy makers respond to a crisis and how they can influence the direction of the economy.

BACKGROUND

Problems in the subprime, or high-risk, mortgage market, the collapse of housing prices, and the tightening of credit markets had been putting pressure on the economy through the spring and summer of 2008. The first sign of serious trouble came in March when the New York Federal Reserve loaned $30 billion to JP Morgan Chase to facilitate the buyout of Bear Stearns, the investment bank that was going bankrupt because of its exposure to mortgage-backed securities. Concerns deepened in September, when the federal government took over the Federal National Mortgage Association and the Federal Home Mortgage Corporation because they were about to go under. These two government-sponsored enterprises, nicknamed "Fannie Mae" and "Freddie Mac," fund most of the home loans in the nation. This federal acquisition, involving a commitment of $200 billion to back up Fannie and Freddie's assets, was "one of the most sweeping government interventions in private financial markets in decades."[24] The takeover calmed the credit markets for a few days, until it became evident that two Wall Street giants, the investment banks Lehman Brothers and Merrill Lynch, were also going under. Lehman Brothers went bankrupt, Merrill Lynch was bought by Bank of America, and the markets panicked.

The next day brought more bad news: the world's largest insurance company, AIG, was also deep in the subprime mess and teetering on the edge of bankruptcy, so the Fed stepped in with an $85 billion loan to save it. Despite these dramatic moves, credit markets seized up, and investors started pulling money out of anything remotely related to the financial crisis. A few days later, Washington Mutual, the nation's sixth-largest bank, failed.

CRAFTING A FINANCIAL RESCUE

Throughout the crisis, which was the worst since the Great Depression, Fed Chair Ben Bernanke, Treasury Secretary Henry Paulson, and congressional leaders worked together to restore confidence in financial institutions.[25] After a couple of false starts, Congress passed a $700 billion Troubled Asset Relief Program

GRAZING RIGHTS AND FREE MARKET ENVIRONMENTALISM

Imagine you are a Republican U.S. House member who represents a western state. You are a firm believer in the free market, capitalism, and limited government. In other words, whenever possible you would like people to make choices in the free market without government interference or regulation. By the way, this conveniently is a view that is held by a large majority of your constituents. You also are a strong supporter of grazing rights for ranchers in your state. You have often done battle with environmentalists who want to reserve more public lands for recreational uses and conservation than for grazing cattle. On this issue, your constituents are more divided: there is strong support for ranchers, but an increasing proportion of the residents in your district are dependent on tourism.

The scenario that you have to consider here is an actual case that was first publicized in a *New York Times* op-ed piece.[a] The case involves a fifth-generation rancher in southern Utah named Dell LeFevre. He is no friend of environmentalism, saying, "We've got Easterners who don't know the land telling us what to do with it. I am a bitter old cowboy." His bitterness was deepened back in 1991 when he found two dozen of his cows shot to death. He thinks the deed was done by an environmentalist who was trying to get ranchers to leave a scenic part of the Escalante River canyon. So he seems to be a very unlikely candidate to have sat down with an environmentalist named Bill Hedden to accomplish that very goal of ending ranching in the area. Hedden works for a group called the Grand Canyon Trust (GCT) that, as the *Times* article explained, "doesn't use lobbyists or lawsuits (or guns) to drive out ranchers. These environmentalists get land the old-fashioned way. They buy it." Hedden spent about $100,000 to buy and retire the grazing rights from LeFevre for this scenic canyon area. The environmentalists are happy because the vegetation is coming back, and LeFevre is happy because he doesn't have to battle the environmentalists anymore and was able to buy grazing rights in a different area that is better for his cattle. Supporters of "free market environmentalism" say this is a perfect example of allowing the market to determine the best use of the land. If an environmentalist is willing to buy a rancher's grazing rights, this means that the market has determined that hiking and conservation have a greater value than grazing for that piece of land.

If the story ended here, there would be no controversy for you to consider. But as you probably guessed, the story does not end here. Local groups, such as the Canyon Country Rural Alliance, which opposed all limitations on ranchers' grazing rights, lobbied Congress and the Interior Department to disallow such arrangements that remove grazing rights from some public lands. Bowing to pressure, the Interior Department decided that "only Congress may permanently exclude lands from grazing use," so GCT had no guarantee that the Bureau of Land Management wouldn't change its mind and allow grazing. The process of resolving this conflict bounced around the Interior Department and the federal courts for nearly 10 years.

Using free-market forces is an increasingly common way to address a variety of environmental issues, from grazing and water rights to air pollution and global warming.

In the meantime, GCT went to Plan B from the "if you can't lick 'em, join 'em" school of thought: they decided to become ranchers. If the Interior Department wouldn't grant permanent conservation use permits on land designated for grazing, they would buy some cattle. GCT is now one of the largest ranchers in the Colorado Plateau with 1,000 acres of private land and grazing permits that cover 860,000 acres of federal and state lands, including a large part of the Kaibab National Forest adjacent to the North Rim of the Grand Canyon. They are managing the land in an eco-friendly manner with only 800 head of cattle. Though it may seem odd that an environmental group had to take up ranching to get the policy outcome they wanted, it was a compromise that made all sides of the dispute relatively happy. As one opponent of GCT put it, "We turned them from environmentalists into cowboys. I guess what they can do is get their cows and start losing money like the rest of us."[b]

If you were the member of Congress representing this district, what would you decide to do?

Critical **Thinking Questions**

1. Would you support the limitations on permanently removing grazing rights because they are consistent with the desires of many of your constituents? If so, how would you reconcile this with your free market views, and how would you justify the decision to your constituents who support free market environmentalism?

2. Does the compromise position of GCT taking up ranching strike you as a reasonable middle ground? Why or why not?

(TARP) and increased the amount of savings insured by the federal government from $100,000 to $250,000 per account to help restore confidence in regular savings accounts. President Bush signed the Emergency Economic Stabilization Act into law on October 3, 2008.

Despite this significant rescue plan, the crisis spiraled out of control in the following weeks. Stock markets plunged worldwide, with the U.S. stock market shedding 35 percent of its value in the two months after the crisis began. Credit markets remained frozen, and it became clear that an alternative approach was needed. The government's purchase of "toxic debt" posed many technical obstacles, and financial markets had no confidence that the plan would work. The Treasury decided to abandon its plan to buy toxic debt and use all the funds to directly invest in banks. By mid-November, the economic panic had eased, but the situation remained fragile.

When President Obama took office in 2009, things were still very grim. Stocks finally bottomed in March 2009 (down 56 percent from their October 2007 high), shortly after Treasury Secretary Timothy Geithner announced the administration's Financial Stability Plan. The plan focused on four problems: frozen credit markets, weakened bank capital, a backlog of troubled mortgage assets on bank balance sheets, and falling home prices. Working with the Fed to stabilize the financial markets, the Treasury had largely resolved three of those four problems one year later. Credit markets were operating, and banks were in much better shape, having raised more than $140 billion in capital and $60 billion in unsecured debt. Banks used these funds to repay the Treasury, which as of October 2012 had recovered 89 percent of its investments in banks. The Treasury expects to eventually recover all of the TARP expenditures. The housing market, though not fully recovered, has also stabilized, with sales up and prices steady in most markets. Troubled mortgage assets remained on the balance sheets of many banks, but with their stronger base of capital and the strengthened housing market, they were in much better shape.[26]

Despite the broad success of the financial rescue, it remained a political liability. The rescue was widely perceived as a bailout of Wall Street. Many citizens were outraged over corporate salaries and bonuses, the bailout of the auto industry, and the perception that not enough was being done to help average Americans. The economy lost 8.4 million jobs in 2008–09, millions of Americans were losing their homes, and unemployment remained stuck around 8 percent through 2012. Discontent with the bailout contributed to the crushing defeat for Democrats in the 2010 midterm elections, despite the fact that it was a bipartisan plan passed at the end of the Bush administration.[37] While the financial rescue remains unpopular, it is clear that things would have been much worse without the swift action by Congress, the Treasury, and the Fed. Still, the financial rescue and the regulation of Wall Street remained issues in the 2012 election.

SOCIAL POLICY

EXPLAIN WHAT WE MEAN BY SOCIAL POLICY, DISCUSS HOW THE NATIONAL GOVERNMENT'S ROLE IN SOCIAL POLICY HAS EVOLVED, AND ANALYZE THE CURRENT MAJOR AREAS OF SOCIAL POLICY

Social policy is generally defined in terms of the "social safety net," or **welfare**, which the *American Heritage Dictionary* defines as "receiving regular assistance from the government or a private agency because of need." A broader conception includes government programs aimed at achieving a general social goal, such as support for public education, the income tax deduction for interest paid on home mortgages (to encourage home ownership), or job creation and growth. This section addresses both conceptions of social policies and also discusses how some traditional social welfare programs such as Social Security are not based on need.

social policy An area of public policy related to maintaining or enhancing the well-being of individuals.

welfare Financial or other assistance provided to individuals by the government, usually based on need.

HISTORY AND CONTEXT OF SOCIAL POLICY

This section outlines the evolution of social policy in the United States and describes the various types of social policy. It is also important to understand the need for social policy by examining the nature of poverty in the United States.

HISTORICAL OVERVIEW

Early in our nation's history, the federal government took little responsibility for social welfare. Private charities, churches, and families largely took responsibility for the poor and disadvantaged. The first significant social policy appeared in the nineteenth century in the form of federal financial support for Civil War veterans and their families. Between 1880 and 1910 the national government spent more than a quarter of its budget on Civil War pensions and support for veterans' widows.[27] During the recession of the mid-1890s, populist and progressive reformers sought a national system of unemployment compensation, but the desire for such extensive policies was several decades ahead of its time (see Nuts and Bolts 14.2).

Not until the 1930s and Franklin Delano Roosevelt's presidency did the government undertake broad-scale social policies. The stock market crash in 1929

TYPES OF SOCIAL POLICY

There are two main types of social policy:

▶ *contributory* (or social insurance) programs include Social Security, Medicare, disability insurance, and unemployment compensation.

– similar to insurance programs in that people pay a specified amount of money to cover some future benefit (either expected, as with the programs related to retirement, or unexpected, as with disability and unemployment)

– not means-tested; that is, all people may participate in the program regardless of their income

▶ *noncontributory* (or public assistance) programs include Medicaid, food stamps, housing assistance, welfare, and school lunches.

– recipients are not expected to pay for the programs, which are means-tested, meaning that they are aimed at helping poor people

▶ The new health care law has elements of both a contributory and noncontributory program. People who are required to buy health insurance are "contributing" to their own insurance. However, those who cannot afford to pay for their insurance receive government subsidies (and thus are participating in a noncontributory program).

and the ensuing Great Depression created a desperate economic situation for millions of Americans. An immediate concern was to alleviate the suffering caused by unemployment, but FDR also wanted to implement a broader "preventative social policy."[28] Thus his **New Deal** policies, enacted between 1933 and 1935, included

▶ the Agricultural Adjustment Administration, which provided farmers with much-needed assistance;

▶ the National Recovery Administration and Public Works Administration, which reinvigorated the business sector;

▶ the Federal Emergency Relief Administration, which provided $500 million in emergency aid for the poor (about $7 billion in today's dollars);

▶ jobs programs such as the Civil Works Administration and Civilian Conservation Corps, which put more than 2 million people to work, and later the Works Progress Administration, a broader program that employed at least one-third of the nation's unemployed;

▶ Social Security, which included the familiar retirement policy and supported the states for spending on unemployment compensation, disability programs, and support for dependent children of single mothers—the precursor of the central welfare program;

▶ the National Labor Relations Act, which guaranteed the right to organize a union and set regulations for collective bargaining between management and labor.[29]

With these policies, the role of the federal government in social policy was forever changed. Although some aspects of the New Deal, such as the jobs programs, were never repeated on a similarly broad

New Deal The set of policies proposed by President Franklin Roosevelt and enacted by Congress between 1933 and 1935 to promote economic recovery and social welfare during the Great Depression.

BEFORE THE NEW DEAL PROGRAMS in the 1930s, poverty relief was provided mainly by private charities. Here future first lady Eleanor Roosevelt serves meals to unemployed women and their children in a New York restaurant.

PRESIDENT GEORGE W. BUSH emphasized the idea of an "ownership society," in which people would take more responsibility for their own social welfare. For example, Bush proposed privatizing Social Security to allow people to invest the money themselves.

Great Society The wide-ranging social agenda promoted by President Lyndon Johnson in the mid-1960s that aimed to improve Americans' quality of life through governmental social programs.

ownership society The term used to describe the social policy vision of President George W. Bush, in which citizens take responsibility for their own social welfare and the free market plays a greater role in social policy.

scale, most of its other programs became the cornerstone of social policy for subsequent generations.

The next major expansion of social policy occurred during the **Great Society** of President Lyndon Johnson in the mid-1960s. We discussed part of this social agenda in Chapter 13: the civil rights movement, which culminated with the passage of the Civil Rights Act in 1964 and the Voting Rights Act in 1965. The other important aspect of Johnson's Great Society included the War on Poverty and programs concerning health, education, and housing. Perhaps most significant was the creation of Medicare, the national program that funds medical care for the elderly, and Medicaid, which funds health care for the poor.[30] By the late 1960s the mounting costs of the Vietnam War created a trade-off: it wasn't possible to continue funding ambitious social programs and the war without causing inflation. Over the following decades conservative backlash against the "welfare state" especially during the Reagan years (1981–89), led to cuts in spending on social programs.

President George W. Bush continued this general direction for social policy, maintaining most programs with some cuts and one major expansion—the addition of a prescription benefit to Medicare. Bush attempted to place his stamp on social policy as a "compassionate conservative" with his idea of an **ownership society**, in which people take more responsibility for their own social welfare. He proposed privatizing part of Social Security and creating private savings accounts to cover more out-of-pocket medical expenses, in combination with more free market forces and a bigger role for private charity. President Obama has favored an approach that emphasizes the market and community, while preserving an important role for government. Obama's social policies in his first term focused on enacting comprehensive health care reform, while maintaining and expanding the social safety net for those devastated by the recent recession.

POVERTY AND INCOME INEQUALITY TODAY

The persistence of poverty remains the primary motivator for most social policy today. In 2012 the poverty line for a family of four was an annual income of $23,050; for a single person it was $11,170. In 2009 fully 43.6 million Americans lived in poverty—14.3 percent of the population. In 2011, 46.2 million Americans were in poverty—15 percent of the population. Even the social programs that do not directly help the poor and disadvantaged, such as Social Security and Medicare, have an impact on poverty. As Figure 14.6 shows, the percentage of the elderly population living in poverty plummeted from more than 35 percent in 1959 to 8.7 percent in 2011.[31]

Another source of concern is the growing income and wealth inequality in the United States. Since 1980, 80 percent of the net income gains have gone to the top 1 percent of the income distribution.[32] From 1979 to 2009 the average income of the top 1 percent grew by $700,000 to $1,220,100 (a 133 percent gain), compared to a $2,600 gain to $18,900 (16 percent) for the bottom fifth of the income levels.[33] The wealth gap is even greater: the median (half are above this level and half are below) net worth of U.S. households in 2007 was $120,300, but the median wealth for the top 10 percent was $1.89 million, and this group held 73 percent of the nation's wealth.

FIGURE » 14.6

POVERTY RATES BY AGE

Children today are in poverty at nearly twice the rate of the elderly, whereas 40 years ago the poverty rate among the elderly was twice that of children. What changes in social policies in the past 75 years could help explain this change?

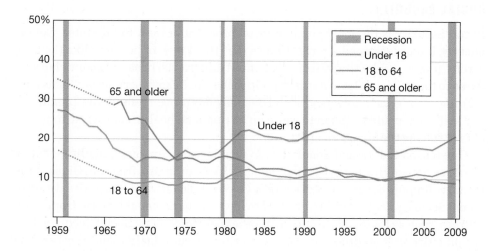

Note: The data points are placed at the midpoints of the respective years. Data for people age 18 and older are not available from 1960 to 1965.

Source: U.S. Census Bureau, Current Population Survey, 1960 to 2010 Annual Social and Economic Supplements, available at www.census.gov/hhes/www/poverty/publications/pubs-cps.html (accessed 6/12/12).

Despite these patterns of inequality, people who earn more than $100,000 receive more benefits from the federal government ($5,690 on average) than people who earn less than $10,000 ($5,560). How can that be? Consider, for example, that 68 percent of the tax savings from deducting mortgage interest goes to people in the top fifth of the income ladder.[34] Other government policies that help the wealthy include patent and copyright law, bankruptcy law, bailouts of the financial sector, immigration policy, enforcement of tax law, and monetary policy.[35] Government programs that help the wealthy also benefit corporations. These policies, often called "corporate welfare," include programs such as crop subsidies to large corporate farmers and tax deductions for oil companies to encourage exploration and drilling.[36] Clearly, there is much more to welfare policies than programs for the poor.

Politicians' differing reactions to the types of statistics presented here remind us that politics is conflictual. Republicans argue that the best way to address poverty is to create jobs and have a healthy economy through supply-side tax cuts that promote the creation of capital, investment, and jobs. Democrats argue that making the wealthy pay a larger share of their income in taxes could fund programs to help the poor directly rather than waiting for the trickle-down effect of tax cuts for the wealthy. From this perspective a trade-off exists between inequality and reducing poverty, and progressive taxes are needed to help the poor.

SOCIAL POLICY TODAY

In the 2013 fiscal year Social Security, Medicare, and Medicaid constitute nearly half of all federal spending. With an aging population and health care costs that are rising as a percentage of the economy, these policies will continue to take an even greater share of the budget. Here we explain the nature of these important programs and discuss recent efforts to reform them.

SOCIAL SECURITY

Social Security is the most popular social program in the United States. Consequently, it has developed a reputation as the "third rail" of politics (like the dangerous, power-conducting rail on electrified train tracks) because a politician who dares to touch Social Security risks political death. Despite serious problems concerning its long-term solvency, Social Security has proven remarkably immune to any steps that could be taken to shore up its financial health, such as cutting benefits or raising the Social Security tax.

One reason that Social Security is so popular is its universal quality—that is, nearly every working American participates in the program, from Bill Gates to the teenager flipping burgers at McDonald's. Once people retire, they are all entitled to Social Security checks without regard to how much income they have from other sources, such as dividends, interest, or other pensions. Thus Social Security does not pit citizens from different classes or ethnic groups against one another. The program is also popular because it works. Fewer than 10 percent of the nation's elderly are in poverty today. Census data show that nearly half of the elderly (46.2 percent) would be in poverty today without their Social Security payments.[37] (See Nuts and Bolts 14.3.)

However, Social Security faces long-term problems. The source of the problem is changes in the nation's demographic profile. The **Baby Boom generation**, born between 1946 and 1964, is just starting to retire, and between 2000 and 2030 the

Baby Boom generation Americans born between 1946 and 1964, who will be retiring in large numbers over the next 20 years.

14.3 NUTS & bolts

SOCIAL SECURITY

Number of recipients for old-age, survivors, and disability insurance:

▶ Old-age insurance (the basic retirement program)   37,123,000

▶ Survivors insurance (retirement program for widows, widowers, and the children of deceased primary wage earners)   6,325,000

▶ Disability insurance (payments for people and their families who cannot work because of a disability and are not yet retired)   9,942,000

Monthly Retirement Benefits:

▶ Individual: Average = $1,171, maximum = $2,346

▶ Couple: Average = $1,902, maximum = $3,539 (if one spouse does not work and the other earns the maximum)

Source: All figures are from the U.S. Social Security Administration Office of Policy, "Monthly Statistical Snapshot, July 2012," available at www.ssa.gov/policy/docs/ quickfacts/stat_snapshot/ (accessed 9/24/12).

FIGURE » 14.7

THE SOCIAL SECURITY TRUST FUND

As of 2011, the cost of the Social Security program exceeds Social Security payroll taxes, so taxes will need to be raised to cover the trust fund's obligations and the program's ongoing expenses. What do you think are the best solutions to address the long-term future of Social Security? What are the politically viable solutions?

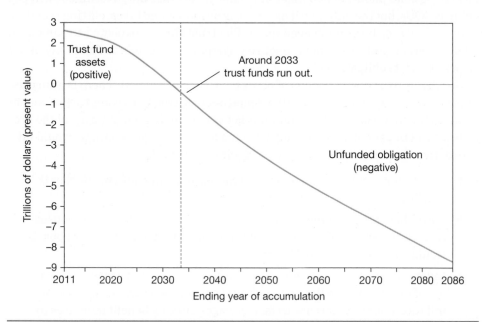

Source: Social Security Administration, 2012 OASDI Trustees Report, Figure II D5, available at www.ssa.gov/OACT/TR/2012/tr2012.pdf (accessed 9/24/12).

number of Americans over age 65 will more than double, while the number under 65 will grow by only 18 percent.[38] When this happens there will be fewer workers to support the retirees.[39] See Figure 14.7 for evidence of the aging population. "Wait a minute," you may be saying. "Why does it matter how many workers there are for each retiree? I thought that Social Security was a pension program that you pay into while you're working and then get the benefits when you retire." Not exactly. Social Security is a "pay-as-you-go" system under which today's workers support today's retirees. Therefore, the huge increase in the number of retirees will strain the system because each worker will have to pay higher taxes to maintain the same level of Social Security benefits for retirees.

Social Security faced its first real crisis in the early 1980s, well before the Boomers started retiring. Benefits had increased faster than payroll taxes throughout the 1970s, and the Social Security Administration estimated that it would not be able to meet its obligations as early as 1983. New laws passed in 1983 provided for a gradual increase in the retirement age from 65 to 67 and increases in the payroll tax that generated surpluses for a trust fund to cover the Boomers' retirement. The first change was relatively straightforward: people born in 1937 or earlier could retire in 2002 at age 65 and receive full benefits. Between 2003 and 2027 the retirement age increases gradually to 67 for a person to qualify for full benefits.

Early retirement at 62 is an option if the retiree is willing to accept a permanently reduced benefit level.

A second change, concerning the trust fund, is the source of great confusion and controversy. The idea behind the trust fund was sound: build up a surplus while the Boomers are working, and use that money to pay for their retirement. The problem is that the money wasn't really saved but went for general government spending (for example, the war in Afghanistan, food stamps, school loans, and funding the FBI), and in turn the government gave the Social Security trust fund an IOU in the form of "special public-debt obligation." This means that the government will pay off these IOUs, but the only way it can do so is by increasing taxes, cutting spending in other areas, or borrowing even more. The trust fund is expected to run out in 2033, at which point the Social Security system will be able to fund only about 75 percent of its obligations.[40]

So what is to be done? Dozens of plans have been suggested. There is a surprising amount of agreement that saving Social Security requires a mixture of benefit cuts and tax increases. The calculations get very complicated in terms of the projected fiscal impact of various reforms, but a mixture of these options would take care of the long-term fiscal problems of Social Security:[41]

▶ Raise payroll taxes by 1 percent and increase the income ceiling that is taxable.

▶ Lower benefits for nonworking spouses. Currently nonworking spouses receive 50 percent of the benefit of their working spouse. Some proposals would cut that benefit to 33 percent.

▶ Index current and future benefits to inflation instead of wages. Currently, benefit increases are linked to national average wage increases. Because inflation does not increase as fast as wages, linking benefit increases to inflation would generate significant savings.

▶ Gradually raise the retirement age to 70 (by 2030). Changing the retirement age to 70 would save $620 billion by 2040.

More controversial proposals include these:

▶ Lower benefits for wealthier recipients. The strongest argument in favor of this approach is that wealthy people don't need the measly couple of thousand dollars they will receive each month from Social Security. The main argument against this proposal is that it would end the universal nature of Social Security and possibly turn it into another welfare program.

▶ Partial or full **privatization** of Social Security. This is the main issue that divides Democrats and Republicans: Democrats favor maintaining the basic structure of Social Security's public social insurance system, and Republicans favor moving part or all of the "pay-as-you-go" system to private accounts. The central argument in favor of private accounts is that over the long term, investing in the stock market has historically provided higher returns than the expected returns from Social Security. Advocates argue that if everyone were able to take their 6.2 percent payroll tax and put that in a retirement account, they would have a modest nest egg by the time they retired that would almost certainly provide a stream of benefits larger than the Social Security check they would receive under the current system. Democrats point out the problems with this approach—most important, the transition costs. Because the current system is "pay-as-you-go," if we stopped taking payroll taxes and allowed people to put the money into private accounts, there wouldn't be any money to pay for today's retirees. These transition costs—having to cover the retirement of all current retirees and everyone else who has paid into the system for a substantial number of years—are estimated to be $7 to 8 *trillion*! A second criticism of these plans is that investing in the stock market is fine as a supplement to Social Security, but everyone needs that dependable check, and investing in the stock market is too risky (as the collapse of the stock market in 2008–09 reminded us).

These issues are not likely to be resolved anytime soon, which illustrates that politics is conflictual. Social Security reform can pit one generation against another or wealthy people against poor people. The stakes in Social Security are extremely high because it is the most popular and visible social program, which makes it all the more difficult to handle.

HEALTH CARE

Health care policy has seemed as difficult to reform as Social Security. Every president since Theodore Roosevelt who attempted comprehensive reform failed until President Obama's success in 2010. In order to understand the current issues we have to understand how health care is provided in the United States and what factors it addresses: the nation's aging population, health care costs that are rising faster than inflation, and the more than 46 million Americans who have no health insurance.[42] Americans spend more on health care than citizens of any other nation in the world—more than $2.6 trillion, or 17.9 percent of GDP, compared to 9.5 percent on average for citizens of other developed countries.

The current system combines government spending (Medicare and Medicaid), private insurance, charity (donated care), and out-of-pocket payments. **Medicare**, the federal health care program for retired people, covers most health care costs and about 75 percent of the cost of prescription drugs.

The other government health care program is **Medicaid**, which serves poor people who otherwise would have no health care. Medicaid is administered through the states with substantial funding from the federal government. Although Medicaid is an **entitlement**, states have considerable discretion over the program. Each state (1) establishes its own eligibility standards; (2) determines the type, amount, duration, and scope of services; (3) sets the rate of payment for services; and (4) administers its own program.[43] (See Nuts and Bolts 14.4.)

The variation in state Medicaid coverage means that some states cover virtually all poor people and others cover as few as one-third of those in need. Overall, nearly 40 million Americans receive health care through Medicaid at a projected cost of $395 billion in 2013 ($276 by the national government and $119 billion by the states).[44] The federal government reimburses the states for about 60 percent of the costs, but this percentage varies by the relative total personal income in the states (that is poorer states get more of their costs reimbursed than wealthier states).[45] Like Medicare, Medicaid faces growing budgetary pressures in the coming years. An increasing share of Medicaid's costs goes toward long-term nursing home care for the indigent elderly, which continues to grow as the population ages.

The long-term fiscal problems of Medicare and Medicaid are severe. In fact, they dwarf Social Security's problems. The 2010 Medicare Trustees report estimates that Social Security's unfunded liabilities through 2085, or the amount of additional money (beyond the current payroll tax) required to fund all the

Medicare The federal health care plan created in 1965 that provides coverage for retired Americans for hospital care (Part A), medical care (Part B), and prescription drugs (Part D).

Medicaid An entitlement program funded by the federal and state governments that provides health care coverage for low-income Americans who would otherwise be unable to afford health care.

entitlement Any federal government program that provides benefits to Americans who meet requirements specified by law.

14.4 **NUTS** *& bolts*

MEDICARE COVERAGE

Medicare Premiums for 2010

Part A (hospital insurance): Most people do not pay Part A premiums because they or a spouse has 40 or more quarters of Medicare-covered employment.

Part B (medical insurance): $110.50 per month.

Part D (prescription drugs): $32.34 per month.

Medicare Deductible and Co-Insurance Amounts for 2010

Part A: Medicare pays all covered costs except a deductible of $1,156 during the first 60 days and co-insurance amounts of $289 per day for days 61 through 90 of a hospital stay and $578 per day for up to 60 "lifetime reserve days" that can be used at any time during one's lifetime. No costs beyond 150 days are covered.

Part B: $140 per year and then a 20 percent co-pay after meeting the $140 deductible.

Part D: $320 per year and then a 25 percent co-pay for the first $2,840 of drugs. The beneficiary then pays 50 percent of the next $2,840 of drug costs. After a $4,550 out-of-pocket annual limit is reached, Medicare pays 95 percent of the costs of drugs.

Note: Part C, known as Medicare Advantage, is not included here because it is not used nearly as widely as Part A or Part B and its provisions get quite complicated.

Source: Health and Human Services, "Strengthening Health and Opportunity for All Americans: Fiscal Year 2013 Budget in Brief," pp. 56–57, available at www.hhs.gov/budget/budget-brief-fy2013.pdf (accessed 9/24/12).

program's commitments, are $8.6 trillion, while Medicare has unfunded liabilities of $20 trillion (plus another $2.7 trillion to pay for trust fund redemptions).[46] Even though such projections depend on assumptions about future economic performance, demographic trends, and other uncertain variables, the *relative* difference between the two programs is significant. Medicare's troubles are more than two and a half times as serious as those of Social Security!

Another study estimates that by 2080 federal health care spending will reach about 19 percent of GDP. That is, if the size of the federal government stays around its historic average of 20 percent of GDP, health care spending will constitute nearly all of federal spending that is not interest on the debt by 2080. The choices are clear: either everything else must be cut from the budget (defense, education, transportation), health care costs must be reined in, or the size of government will grow. Clearly, the current trends are not sustainable.

Although comprehensive health care reform had been shot down repeatedly before 2010, several incremental reforms added up to substantial change. In 1996 Congress passed the Health Insurance Portability and Accountability Act, which guaranteed that people could not be denied health care coverage when they switch jobs. Medicaid was expanded in 1997 to provide health care for children in families that make too much to qualify for Medicaid but not enough to buy private insurance for their children (incomes that are no more than double the poverty level). By 2011 more than 7.7 million children were enrolled in the program.[47] Under the Bush administration Congress passed limited tax-free health savings accounts that may be used for paying routine out-of-pocket health care expenses or saving

FIGURE » 14.8

PROJECTED NATIONAL SPENDING ON HEALTH CARE

If current spending patterns hold, an increasing percentage of federal spending will be devoted to health care, crowding out other programs. Clearly such trends are not sustainable. What changes do you support to reduce health care spending in the long run?

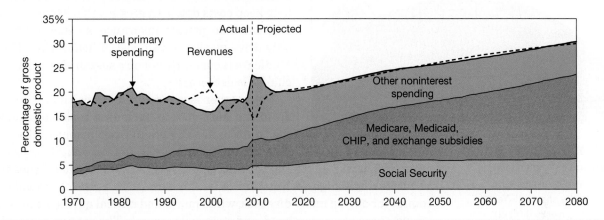

Source: Congressional Budget Office, "The Long-Term Budget Outlook," June 2010 (revised August 2010), Figure A-1, p.68, available at www.cbo.gov/ftpdocs/115xx/doc11579/06-30-LTBO.pdf (accessed 9/24/12).

for more substantial, unexpected health care costs. Also, Medicare's prescription drug plan went into effect in 2006. Despite these reforms, though, discontent with the system continued.

President Obama's primary focus when he took office in 2009 was to get the economy going; however, he also campaigned on reforming our health care system—controlling costs, providing as close to universal coverage as possible, and paying for the program without adding to the deficit. His goal of comprehensive coverage was essential. If insurance companies were forced to cover people with preexisting conditions without a mandate that everyone have insurance, people would wait until they were seriously ill to get coverage. Healthy people had to be pooled with sick people to spread the costs of expensive care. This was achieved by requiring businesses with more than 50 employees to provide coverage, and individuals not covered by employers to purchase insurance through state-regulated private health insurance exchanges (to be in place by 2014). Businesses and individuals who do not comply with the mandate will face fines. However, individuals who cannot afford insurance will receive federal subsidies on a sliding scale (a formula that provides the biggest subsidies to the poorest people and some support all the way up to four times the federal poverty rate). Other features of the law include incentives to computerize medical records, which would improve the quality of care, reduce the number of mistakes, and facilitate evaluating quality of care.

Another goal was that health care had to pay for itself. With a price tag of just under $1 trillion over the first 10 years, paying for the bill was a challenge. However, a combination of higher Medicare taxes, a new investment tax on the wealthy, an excise tax on insurers for expensive health care plans, new fees for drug companies and health insurers, and cuts in Medicare reimbursement meant

WE'D BETTER DO SOMETHING, THIS COULD EXPLODE...

SOCIAL SECURITY

CONGRESS

MEDICARE

THE UNFUNDED LIABILITIES FOR Medicare are estimated to be about 6 times as large as the Social Security shortfall. Yet Congress has a very difficult time acting, because any solution involves the politically unpopular combination of tax increases and benefit cuts.

income support Government programs that provide support to low-income Americans, such as welfare, food stamps, unemployment compensation, and the Earned Income Tax Credit.

that the law would actually reduce the federal deficit by $143 billion over the first decade.[48]

Yet the battle over health care reform was not over when Obama signed the bill into law. Opponents promised to repeal the law and featured this pledge in their campaign strategy during the 2010 midterm elections. Republicans have argued for market-based reforms that would introduce more competition into the system to help keep costs down. Critics say that Medicare is more efficient than private insurance, so such reforms will only drive up the overall cost of health care. However, Medicare is currently not on a sustainable path, so some change is necessary.

Many other issues related to health care will come up in the next decade, including assisted suicide and the "right to die." Voters in Oregon approved a law that went into effect in 1997 allowing the terminally ill to take a fatal dose of medication, which was upheld by the Supreme Court in 2006.[49] Other issues involve the increasingly high-tech nature of health care: DNA research provides great promise for curing many diseases, while moral and ethical questions arise about cloning, surrogate parenthood, and stem cell research. The coming years will be a challenging period for health care policy.

INCOME SUPPORT AND WELFARE

Welfare is usually thought of as cash support for people who cannot support themselves. However, **income support** can take many forms, including food stamps, unemployment insurance, Supplemental Security Income, and the Earned Income Tax Credit. Moreover, a significant reform of welfare occurred in 1996.

The Supplemental Nutrition Assistance Program provides food stamps, which today are government-issued debit cards that may be used as cash to buy groceries. Anyone whose income is less than 130 percent of the poverty level and whose resources do not exceed specific levels may qualify for food stamps. In 2012 the maximum monthly gross income for a family of four to qualify for food stamps was $2,422. As the effects of the recent economic crisis lingered through 2011, the number of people using food stamps hit a record of nearly 44.7 million, with an average monthly benefit of $133.85 per person.[50]

The Federal-State Unemployment Compensation Program was established in 1935 as part of the Social Security Act. The U.S. Department of Labor oversees the program, but it is administered by the states. The program provides temporary and partial wage replacement for people who have been laid off and to help stabilize the economy during recessions. States set a broad range in benefit levels, minimum amount of income earned, and hours worked during the period leading up to unemployment. Also, laid-off workers have to make themselves "available for work." About 97 percent of all workers are covered by unemployment insurance, but only about half of the eligible unemployed make use of the benefit. The regular state programs provide up to 26 weeks of income support, and the Federal-State Extended Benefits Program temporarily provides up to 20 additional weeks in states with relatively high unemployment rates. In January 2012 the average weekly benefit check was $296, which replaced 32.8 percent of the average worker's previous salary.[51]

The Earned Income Tax Credit (EITC) is one of the most successful programs for providing income support for the working poor. Established in 1975, the program aims to help poor people move from welfare to work: it provides tax credits to those who do not earn enough to pay income taxes and are relatively poor. It is intended to offset the burden of Social Security taxes, which all workers pay as part of payroll taxes. In 2011 an individual could qualify for an EITC if she or he had two children and earned less than $40,964, one child and earned less than $36,052, or no children and earned less than $13,660; the figures are slightly higher if the individuals are married and filing jointly.[52] The federal government provided $59.5 billion in EITCs in 2010 to 26.8 million recipients, with an average monthly benefit of $185 per recipient.[53]

Welfare is straight cash assistance for people who are not working and do not qualify for unemployment compensation. The primary welfare program for the latter half of the twentieth century was **Aid to Families with Dependent Children (AFDC)**. This program became increasingly unpopular through the 1980s, and in 1992 Bill Clinton was the first Democratic presidential nominee to campaign against welfare, promising to "end welfare as we know it."[54] President Clinton did not make this the top priority of his first year in office and instead focused on health care reform and balancing the budget. Clinton began addressing welfare reform in 1993 by appointing a task force on the issue. When the Republicans took over Congress in 1994, the momentum for reform grew. Clinton and Congress haggled over the specifics for two years but then agreed on a major reform called **Temporary Assistance for Needy Families (TANF)**.

The new law set a five-year lifetime limit on welfare benefits, required single mothers with children above age five to find work after two years of receiving benefits, required unmarried mothers who were under age 18 to live with an adult and attend school to get full benefits, denied benefits to drug users who were convicted of a felony, and limited people who were not raising children and were between the ages of 18 and 50 to three months of food stamps in any three-year period in which they were not working. Perhaps most important, welfare lost its status as an entitlement and would be administered by the states with the assistance of federal block grants. In February 2006, Congress reauthorized TANF and required that half the recipients in a state's caseload participate in work activities for at least 30 hours per week.

Welfare reform significantly reduced the number of people on welfare, as Figure 14.9 shows, but it has been criticized for being too hard on the people who need government assistance the most. Critics also point out that TANF block grants have not been adjusted for inflation since they were first created in 1996.[55]

EDUCATION POLICY

Education policy is largely the domain of state and local governments. For the first century of our nation's history, the national government played virtually no role in education. One important exception was the Morrill Act in 1862, also known as the Land Grant College Act, which gave land to eligible states to establish colleges focusing on practical professions such as agriculture and mechanical arts. More than 75 colleges and universities today are land grant institutions. The next major forays by the federal government into education policy came with the GI Bill of Rights in 1944, which provided access to higher education for returning World War II veterans, and the Elementary and Secondary Education Act of 1965, which was part of President Johnson's War on Poverty. The Department of Education

Aid to Families with Dependent Children (AFDC) The federal welfare program in place from 1935 until 1995, when it was replaced by Temporary Assistance for Needy Families (TANF) under President Clinton.

Temporary Assistance for Needy Families (TANF) The welfare program that replaced Aid to Families with Dependent Children (AFDC) in 1996, eliminating the entitlement status of welfare, shifting implementation of the policy to the states, and introducing several new restrictions on receiving aid. These changes led to a significant decrease in the number of welfare recipients.

FIGURE » 14.9

PARTICIPATION IN MEANS-TESTED PROGRAMS

The social policy "safety net" is supposed to protect poor Americans during periods of economic recession. A deep recession happened in the early 1980s, and the other recession during the time frame depicted here was in the early 1990s. To what extent did the safety net play its intended role?

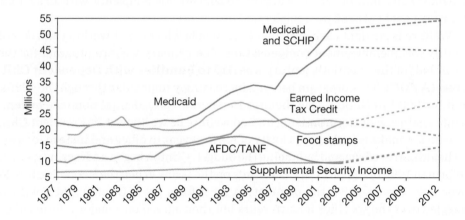

Source: Congressional Budget Office, Economic and Budget Issue Brief, "Changes in Participation in Means-Tested Programs," April 20, 2005, p. 3, available at www.cbo.gov/ftpdocs/63xx/ doc6302/04-20-Means-Tested .pdf, for data through 2003 (accessed 9/24/12). Various sources for 2012 (2012 is reported in 2003 dollars to allow comparison with the previous study).

was created in 1980, signaling the government's interest in playing an important role in education policy.

A recent debate concerning the national government's role in education policy has focused on standards-based education reform: Should the national government establish standards and impose accountability as a way to improve public schools? The No Child Left Behind Act of 2001 requires yearly statewide standardized testing in math and reading. If the test results show that a school is not meeting annual academic benchmarks, it loses some federal funding and its students may transfer to another public school. Critics argue that standardized test results are a poor measurement of progress, as schools "teach to the test" and manipulate other aspects of the evaluation system.

President Obama's "Race to the Top" program dedicated $4 billion to competitive grants in 2010 and a proposed $1.35 billion in 2011 to encourage schools to adopt more challenging standards and better tools of assessment, promote better leadership and methods for assessing and rewarding excellent teaching, create better data systems for tracking students' progress, and obtain stronger commitments for improving the worst-performing schools. These grants were aimed at strengthening the quality of public education while improving accountability.[56] Early in 2012 the Obama administration proposed the RESPECT project (Recognizing Educational Success, Professional Excellence and Collaborative Teaching), which is another set of incentive grants aimed at improving education.[57]

Even with these efforts at imposing a national approach, there can be variations in state and local implementation of the national law. States and local school districts are also experimenting with policies aimed at introducing more competition for public schools, including public school choice and publicly funded vouchers for attending private schools.

CONCLUSION

The experiences with social policy reform illustrate the themes of this book. First, health care reform illustrates the conflictual nature of politics.

Similarly, conflict is natural in many economic policy decisions, and politics is a part of this process. Any economic policy has winners and losers and elected leaders must be involved in this process if representative democracy is to have any meaning. This is especially true of the budget process because the redistributive implications of taxing and spending are so clear, but even monetary policy is not insulated from politics. This role for politics is guaranteed by our system of checks and balances: Congress, the president, and to some extent the courts all have a hand in shaping economic policy.

It shouldn't be surprising when politics enters the economic policy debate. Elected leaders should be responsive to what their constituents think about the central questions concerning the direction of the economy. The struggles over economic and social policies—especially in Congress—demonstrate that political process matters. Politicians' decisions have a key impact on policy outcomes, and the timing and politics of the policy-making process drive the results. Finally, politics is everywhere: social and economic policies touch every American.

MAKING PUBLIC POLICY

▶ Trace the steps through which problems are addressed by government policies. **Pages 427–34**

SUMMARY

Once an issue is recognized and defined as a problem, and when the conditions are right, the issue reaches the congressional agenda. Once a policy is in place, its effectiveness and implementation are evaluated in an ongoing process, though very few programs are ultimately terminated.

KEY TERMS

public policy (p. 427)

policy agenda (p. 428)

fiscal policy (p. 430)

monetary policy (p. 430)

budget making (p. 430)

United States Trade Representative (USTR) (p. 431)

National Economic Council (NEC) (p. 431)

Federal Reserve System (p. 432)

Treasury Department (p. 432)

CRITICAL THINKING AND DISCUSSION

What differences may be expected in the shaping of social policy with Barack Obama having been re-elected president in 2012? Does it matter which party controls Congress?

PRACTICE QUIZ QUESTIONS

1. What is the policy agenda?
   a) the set of policies political leaders view as priorities
   b) the set of issues political leaders view as priorities
   c) the set of issues that issue groups view as priorities
   d) the set of policies that issue groups view as priorities
   e) the set of policies that issue groups and political leaders view as priorities

2. Relative to the private sector, public sector programs are _____ to evaluate
   a) easier
   b) equally easy
   c) harder
   d) equally as hard
   e) not important

3. States influence policies on _____, but not _____.
   a) Social Security; education
   b) education; Medicaid
   c) Medicaid; education
   d) Medicaid; Social Security
   e) Medicare, Medicaid

4. The difference between fiscal policy and monetary policy is that fiscal policy is concerned with _____, while monetary policy is concerned with _____.
   a) taxing and spending; controlling the money supply and interest rates
   b) controlling the money supply and interest rates; taxing and spending
   c) controlling the money supply and spending; taxing and interest rates
   d) taxing and controlling the money supply; spending and interest rates
   e) taxing and interest rates; spending and controlling the money supply

5. The Treasury generally prefers _____ interest rates; the Federal Reserve board generally prefers _____.

   a) higher; lower
   b) higher; higher
   c) lower; lower
   d) lower; higher
   e) stable; lower

ⓢ PRACTICE ONLINE

"Critical Thinking" exercise: *Politics Is Conflictual— Social Security Reform and Party Platforms?*

ECONOMIC POLICY

▶ Explain the main purposes of government involvement in the economy and how fiscal, monetary, regulatory, and trade policies influence the economy. **Pages 434–48**

SUMMARY

Policy makers' pursuit of economic goals—such as full employment, stable prices, or growth—is a complex process. Policy makers have a variety of tools at their disposal to help push the economy in their desired direction. The government utilizes fiscal policy, monetary policy, and regulation to influence the country's economic performance, but the pursuit of one goal often comes at the expense of other economic goals.

KEY TERMS

full employment (p. 434)

economic depression (p. 434)

Council of Economic Advisers (p. 434)

inflation (p. 434)

balanced budget (p. 436)

budget deficits (p. 436)

Keynesian economics (p. 437)

supply-side economics (p. 439)

gross domestic product (p. 439)

business cycle (p. 439)

mandatory spending (p. 439)

discretionary spending (p. 439)

regressive (p. 440)

progressive (p. 440)

monetarist theory (p. 441)

reserve requirement (p. 442)

discount rate (p. 442)

federal funds rate (FFR) (p. 442)

open market operations (p. 442)

CRITICAL THINKING AND DISCUSSION

Do you support an active role for the government in regulating the economy, or would you prefer the free market to be largely unregulated?

PRACTICE QUIZ QUESTIONS

6. The Council of Economic Advisors was established _____.

   a) by the Employment Act
   b) by the Balanced Budget Amendment
   c) in Article I of the Constitution
   d) in Article III of the Constitution
   e) by the Federal Reserve Board

7. When the government attempts to reduce inflation, it typically results in _____.
   a) businesses growing
   b) higher interest rates
   c) lower unemployment
   d) an increase in GDP
   e) lower interest rates

8. Keynesian economics argues that the effects of an economic recession can be reduced by _____.
   a) decreasing government spending
   b) increasing government spending
   c) increasing income taxes
   d) reducing the budget deficit
   e) discouraging consumer spending

9. Reducing the federal deficit by cutting spending is difficult because _____.
   a) the interest rates are too high
   b) the majority of the budget is mandatory spending

c) the majority of the budget is discretionary spending

d) members of Congress put too much pork in budgetary bills

e) large deficits benefit the economy in the long run

10. Regressive taxes, like the payroll tax, means that compared to the wealthy, poor people spend _____ of their income on taxes.

a) slightly less

b) an equal amount

c) more

d) considerably less

e) none

11. The "reserve requirement" refers to _____.

a) the interest rates the Fed charges to member banks

b) the rate member banks charge one another on overnight loans

c) the minimum activity level of the Fed's open market operations

d) the lowest price for government bonds

e) the minimum level of money banks must always have on hand

---

⑤ PRACTICE ONLINE

"Big Think" video exercise: *The Free Market and Politics*

SOCIAL POLICY

▶ Explain what we mean by social policy, discuss how the national government's role in social policy has evolved, and analyze the current major areas of social policy. **Pages 448–61**

SUMMARY

Social policy is the catch-all term for government programs that are designed to achieve a general social goal. While the early federal government took little responsibility for social welfare, it currently plays a significant role in ensuring the welfare of its people. The most important social programs currently center on the issues of poverty, an aging population, and health care. Unfortunately, the political realities of the system make reforms difficult.

KEY TERMS

social policy (p. 448)

welfare (p. 448)

New Deal (p. 449)

Great Society (p. 449)

ownership society (p. 450)

Baby Boom generation (p. 452)

privatization (p. 454)

Medicare (p. 455)

Medicaid (p. 455)

entitlement (p. 455)

income support (p. 458)

Aid to Families with Dependent Children (AFDC) (p. 459)

Temporary Assistance for Needy Families (TANF) (p. 459)

CRITICAL THINKING AND DISCUSSION

What do you think should be the government's responsibilities in the area of social policy? Do you favor more of an "ownership society" or more of a direct role for the government?

PRACTICE QUIZ QUESTIONS

12. Social Security was established under the _____ program; Medicare was established under the _____ program.

a) New Deal; Great Society

b) New Deal; New Deal

c) Great Society; Great Society

d) Great Society; New Deal

13. The principle of the "ownership society" is that _____.

a) the government has responsibility for the people's social welfare

b) the government has responsibility for the poor's social welfare

c) the government has responsibility for health care but not education

d) the rich have responsibility for the poor's social welfare

e) people have responsibility for their own welfare

14. The primary motivator for social policy is _____.

a) economic dislocation

b) poverty

c) the deficit

d) care for the elderly

e) gender inequality

15. The primary reason Social Security will be financially strained in the coming years is because _____.

a) it is a pay-as-you-go program

b) its stipends are indexed to inflation

c) it is transitioning to privately held accounts

d) compensation to nonworking spouses is equal to benefits for the working spouse

e) most Americans don't approve of Social Security

16. In President Obama's health care plan, why was it essential to guarantee comprehensive coverage?

a) to make sure enough people were paying into the system

b) to pool risk between sick and healthy people

c) to reduce the risks of fraud

d) to prevent individuals from only having one price to pay

e) to win broad political support

Ⓢ PRACTICE ONLINE

"Big Think" video exercise: *Paul Krugman on the Retirement Age*

SUGGESTED READING

Altman, Nancy J. *The Battle for Social Security: From FDR's Vision to Bush's Gamble*. New York: Wiley, 2005.

Bartels, Larry M. *Unequal Democracy: The Political Economy of the New Gilded Age*. Princeton, NJ: Princeton University Press, 2008.

Friedman, Milton. *Capitalism and Freedom*, 40th Anniversary ed. Chicago: University of Chicago Press, 2002.

Friedman, Thomas L. *The World Is Flat: A Brief History of the Twenty-First Century*. New York: Farrar, Straus and Giroux, 2005.

Keynes, John Maynard. *General Theory of Employment, Interest and Money*. New York: Macmillan, 2007, originally published in 1936.

King, Ronald F. *Budgeting Entitlements: The Politics of Food Stamps*. Washington, DC: Georgetown University Press, 2000.

Krugman, Paul. *The Great Unraveling: Losing Our Way in the New Century*. New York: Norton, 2003.

Lewis, Michael. *The Big Short: Inside the Doomsday Machine*. New York: Norton, 2010.

Oberlander, Jonathan. *The Political Life of Medicare*. Chicago: University of Chicago Press, 2003.

Phillips, Kevin. *Bad Money: Reckless Finance, Failed Politics, and the Global Crisis of American Capitalism*. New York: Viking, 2008.

Skocpol, Theda. *Social Policy in the United States: Future Possibilities in Historical Perspective*. Princeton, NJ: Princeton University Press, 1995.

Soros, George. *The New Paradigm for Financial Markets: The Credit Crash of 2008 and What It Means*. New York: PublicAffairs Books, 2008.

Soss, Joe. *Unwanted Claims: The Politics of Participation in the U.S. Welfare System*. Ann Arbor: University of Michigan Press, 2000.

Stiglitz, Joseph E. *Globalization and Its Discontents*. New York: Norton, 2003.

Weaver, R. Kent. *Ending Welfare as We Know It*. Washington, DC: Brookings Institution Press, 2000.

15

Foreign Policy

GENERAL STANLEY MCCHRYSTAL was removed from his position as commander of U.S. forces in Afghanistan after he was quoted making critical comments about the Obama administration's handling of the situation. Members of the military are expected to carry out the civil leaders' policies and to support those policies, at least in public.

MANY AMERICANS EXPECT FOREIGN POLICY TO BE an area of consensus—that we all hold similar ideas of what our country should be doing outside our borders. As a result many Americans agree with Senator Arthur Vandenberg, who in 1945 argued that "Politics stops at the water's edge," and tend to see disagreement over foreign policy as somehow unpatriotic and motivated by political factors.

One recent example of these beliefs in action occurred in 2010 when General Stanley McChrystal, then commander of U.S. forces in Afghanistan, was quoted in a *Rolling Stone* article making critical comments about various members of the Obama administration, questioning their knowledge of the situation in Afghanistan and their beliefs about how military action should proceed.[1] McChrystal was soon removed from his position by President Obama. Some responses to the removal echoed Vandenberg's comments—shouldn't Americans defer to the judgments of military leaders, who presumably are in the best position to plan and execute military operations in Afghanistan and elsewhere?

One of the central goals of this chapter is to demonstrate that simple answers are rare in foreign policy. The situation in Afghanistan is a good example. After more than a decade of military action and efforts to build a stable democracy and a growing economy, Afghanistan remains a dangerous, unstable place. Should the United States be responsible for creating a stable, prosperous Afghan nation? What will happen if the United States withdraws

CONFLICT & COMPROMISE
in American Politics

467

its ground forces? Can the Afghan government control its own borders and aid its own citizens? Would terrorist organizations such as Al Qaeda, the group that organized the September 11 attacks on the United States, return to using Afghanistan as an organizational haven? These questions are difficult to answer with certainty. Even if we could, reasonable people might reach different conclusions. For example, suppose Afghanistan were to develop into a stable, vibrant society if the United States kept ground forces there for another decade. One person might conclude that staying the course would be the best option, but another might decide that this outcome would not be worth the monetary and human costs.

This example illustrates that we should expect disagreement over America's foreign policy, both in Afghanistan and elsewhere. And we should not be surprised when these disagreements occur in government, even between civilians and military personnel. As we discuss in Chapters 10 and 11, the very fact that bureaucrats are experts, who know a great deal about the policies they administer, means that they will often disagree about the best course of action in any given situation. McChrystal was removed not because he disagreed with the Obama administration's policy but because that disagreement became public.

This chapter will show how other areas of foreign policy are beset with conflict—and how making and executing policy often requires actors to compromise on their differences. Our discussion will also highlight how America's foreign and domestic policies are increasingly intertwined. Consider the state of America's economy. Over the last generation American politicians have approved numerous treaties that reduced tariffs on imports and exports, thereby generating enormous profits for some American companies. American aircraft manufacturers, for example, prospered under trade liberalization, selling passenger and cargo jets to airlines worldwide. However, trade liberalization has hurt companies that could not respond to increased foreign competition, such as the financially troubled American auto producers that have required substantial federal aid just to stay in business. Many of their workers have been laid off or have taken buyouts to quit their jobs or retire early rather than face an uncertain future of layoffs and wage cuts.

Examples of national unity in foreign policy are actually quite rare. Even after the September 11 attacks, the initial surge of unity and common purpose dissolved into debate over the specifics of America's response—from the initial decisions to invade Afghanistan and Iraq, to contemporary debates over how best to fight the ongoing threat of terrorist attacks. Again, this conflict is nothing new. Throughout American history there have been many disagreements over foreign policy issues, from whether and how to use military force or to form alliances, to questions about foreign trade agreements and human rights policies. Although these debates often have political consequences, with positions sometimes taken for political gain, in the main they reflect sincere differences of opinion; in this sense foreign policy closely resembles domestic policy.

Finally, political process matters in foreign policy. The president's central role in the making of foreign policy stems in part from constitutional allocations of executive power, such as the president's leadership of the executive branch and his role as commander in chief of the U.S. armed forces. The president also benefits from his ability to act unilaterally, as we saw in Chapter 10. Even so, presidents do not have complete authority to determine America's foreign policy. Factors such as congressional control over federal spending, as well as judicial review exercised by federal judges, impose significant limits on presidential power in this area.

WHAT IS FOREIGN POLICY?

DESCRIBE THE MAJOR APPROACHES TO UNDERSTANDING FOREIGN POLICY AND TRACE HOW AMERICA'S ROLE IN THE WORLD HAS EVOLVED

Foreign policy encompasses government actions involving countries, groups, individuals, and corporations that lie outside America's borders. Foreign policy includes military operations, economic interactions, human rights policies, environmental agreements, foreign aid, democracy assistance, interventions in civil wars and other conflicts, and international efforts to limit weapons of mass destruction, including nuclear weapons.

The goals behind many foreign policy actions are complex. For example, some observers have argued that America's invasion of Iraq in 2003 was aimed at securing inexpensive oil for American businesses and consumers. Although this goal may have motivated some politicians to support the war, others might have believed that Iraq possessed weapons of mass destruction or was supporting terrorist groups. Alternatively, they might have thought that establishing a democratic government in Iraq would serve as a model for other Middle Eastern countries, or they might have wanted to end human rights abuses by the Iraqi government. As this example illustrates, foreign policy questions are not only complex but also often highly conflictual.

Because foreign policy is so complex, debates over what the United States should do in a particular situation tend to be framed in terms of general principles. These principles summarize the arguments on each side of a foreign policy question or, in some cases, show how foreign policy issues that seem different are actually quite similar. The discussion in this section outlines an important distinction: unilateral versus multilateral action; it also delineates two pairs of important concepts: isolationism versus internationalism, and idealism versus realism. An additional concept, constructivism, addresses how the leaders of a state interpret all of these terms. Nuts and Bolts 15.1 summarizes these terms. The concepts are more than theoretical guides for decision making; many international relations scholars see them as descriptions of how states actually act.

Unilateral action occurs when one country does something on its own, without coordinating with other countries. For example, some U.S. antiterror operations under both President Bush and President Obama, particularly in Pakistan,

foreign policy Government actions that affect countries, corporations, groups, or individuals outside America's borders.

unilateral action Independent acts of foreign policy undertaken by a nation without the assistance or coordination of other nations.

15.1 **NUTS** *& bolts*

THE LANGUAGE OF FOREIGN POLICY

Realism	Foreign policy is driven by a state's national interest, as defined by its leaders.
Idealism	Foreign policy reflects the ideals held by a state's leaders, such as protection of human rights.
Isolationism	States should, whenever possible, pursue their foreign policy goals by working together with other nations.
Internationalism	States should, whenever possible, work alone to define and implement their foreign policy, working with other nations only when absolutely necessary.
Constructivism	Foreign policy is not determined by objective factors such as national interest, by ideologies such as idealism, or by admonitions about working alone or with other nations but by how a state's leaders define these factors.

multilateral action Foreign policy carried out by a nation in coordination with other nations or international organizations.

isolationism The idea that a country should refrain from involvement in international affairs.

internationalism The idea that a country should be involved in the affairs of other nations, out of both self-interest and moral obligation.

realism The idea that a country's foreign policy decisions are motivated by self-interest and the goal of gaining more power.

idealism The idea that a country's foreign policy decisions are based on factors beyond self-interest, including upholding important principles or values.

have been undertaken without any consultation with or notice to U.S. allies—not even the Pakistanis.[2] However, American foreign policy more commonly involves **multilateral action** by the United States alongside other countries or international organizations such as the United Nations. For example, since early 2008 more than 20 nations, including the United States, have conducted naval patrols in the Gulf of Aden in an attempt to deter pirate attacks against civilian shipping in that area of the Indian Ocean. As another example, after civil strife broke out in Syria in 2011, the United States, in cooperation with the United Nations and several other nations, has sought to force the Syrian government to negotiate with rebel forces and end the civil war there peacefully.

A second important distinction in foreign policy is between **isolationism** and **internationalism**. Isolationists believe that the United States should avoid making alliances and agreements with other nations, concentrate on defending our own borders, and let the people in other countries work out their problems for themselves. In the case of Syria, an isolationist might argue that U.S. intervention would be futile or potentially counterproductive, too costly, or simply inappropriate.[3] An internationalist, however, would likely argue that the United States should establish many agreements with other nations and intervene in international crises whenever it may be able to help, both because of possible economic and security gains and because intervening in civil wars and helping to solve humanitarian crises is morally right. In the case of Syria, internationalists would support U.S. efforts to help and protect the local population, either in concert with other nations or alone if other nations are unwilling to intervene.[4]

The third major distinction in foreign policy making is between **realism** and **idealism**.[5] Realists believe that countries pursue their own interests, seeking to increase their economic and military power and their international influence. In approaching a policy decision, a realist would choose the policy that maximizes U.S. military and economic power relative to that of other states. Idealists, in contrast, believe that states' concerns extend beyond increasing their power, including the promotion of principles such as freedom, liberty, or democracy. For an idealist, upholding these principles should be a primary goal of U.S. foreign policy. **Constructivists** offer an alternative to both positions, arguing that state actions are shaped by past events rather than by ideological beliefs.

These terms are used often in foreign policy debates because they offer convenient ways to summarize the motivations behind policy decisions. That is how we use the terms in this chapter, but in reality none of them provides a fully accurate definition of what motivates nations or individuals. No one is a realist or an idealist all the time. Consider President Obama and his foreign policy actions. While he was a candidate for president, his campaign promise to meet with hostile foreign leaders suggested an idealist perspective; but now that he is president his increased use of drone aircraft against Al Qaeda in Pakistan and other countries, as well as his decision to assist in NATO operations in Libya's civil strife but to avoid getting involved with the civil war in Syria, is more consistent with realism. For any leader, the realist and idealist labels summarize the motivations behind individual policy decisions and may not necessarily suggest what kinds of policies that leader might prefer in the future.

constructivism The idea that foreign policy is shaped by how a state's leaders define the national interest, ideology, and other factors.

HISTORY OF AMERICAN FOREIGN POLICY

In this section we review the evolution of American foreign policy. Our aim is to illustrate what foreign policy encompasses, including the types of choices American politicians face, how these policy options have changed over time, and the lack of agreement among American politicians about how to resolve these issues.

THE FOUNDING TO WORLD WAR I

Until America's entry into World War I in 1917, American foreign policy was primarily but not completely isolationist. Isolationism made sense during this period for several reasons: America's distance from Europe reduced the potential for international economic interactions, lowered the level of military threat, and gave early America room to expand without conflicting with European nations.[6] The **Monroe Doctrine**, established by President James Monroe in 1823, stated that America would remain neutral in wars involving European nations and that the United States expected these nations to stop trying to colonize or occupy areas in North and South America.[7] During this time America expanded by purchasing land from other countries (it added much of the Midwest through the Louisiana Purchase) and by annexing land after military conflicts (it acquired a large section of the Southwest from Mexico following the Mexican-American War).

America's foreign policy was never completely isolationist, however, even in the early years. The navy was deployed on many occasions to protect U.S. ships and citizens, and America had colonies far beyond its borders. America also built the Panama Canal, leasing land from Panama in the process, and sent troops into conflicts in Nicaragua and other Central American countries. Moreover, America maintained significant trading relationships with nations in Europe and elsewhere.

Still, America's involvement in World War I (1914–18) marked a sharp departure in foreign policy, both in the nation's participation in an international alliance and

Monroe Doctrine The American policy initiated under President James Monroe in 1823 stating that the United States would remain neutral in conflicts between European nations, and that these nations should stop colonizing or occupying areas of North and South America.

in the president's willingness to continue these activities after the conflict.[8] With the war almost over, President Woodrow Wilson offered a peace plan, the Fourteen Points, which proposed (1) reshaping the borders of European countries in order to mitigate future conflict, (2) taking measures to encourage free trade and democracy, and (3) establishing an international organization that would prevent future conflicts.[9] American diplomats participated in the negotiations that culminated in the Treaty of Versailles, which officially ended the war.[10] The treaty created the League of Nations, an organization similar to the modern United Nations; but the U.S. Senate rejected the treaty, with the result that the United States never joined the League of Nations.[11] (Again, this example illustrates the conflicts that have marked American foreign policy over the last 200 years.)

THE RISE OF INTERNATIONALISM

A great transition in American foreign policy occurred during World War II (1939–45). The United States did not become directly involved in the conflict until December 8, 1941, declaring war on Japan the day after Japanese air attacks on Pearl Harbor in Hawaii and American bases in the Philippines. Germany subsequently declared war on the United States on December 11. However, prior to the United States' official involvement, the U.S. military had been supplying Great Britain and its allies with arms, ships, and other supplies in return for payments and long-term leases on British military bases throughout the world. (All these actions had narrowly escaped a congressional veto—yet another illustration that making foreign policy is conflictual.)

During World War II, the Allied Powers—the United States, Great Britain, the Soviet Union, and other countries—fought as a formal alliance, forming joint plans and sharing military hardware and intelligence. After World War II, though, American politicians and scholars felt that the United States should be a central actor in world affairs. This new policy was justified on the basis of realist arguments, such as the need to deter future conflicts and the desire for economic benefits through trade with other nations.[12] Yet idealists argued for the same policies on the grounds that America had a moral obligation to preserve world peace.[13] However, the nation's shift toward internationalism only increased the amount of conflict in American foreign policy, as actors disagreed on where the United States should get involved; what the goals should be; whether intervention should involve military force, foreign aid, diplomacy, or some other policy tool; and whether the United States should act alone or in concert with other nations.

THE COLD WAR

Cold War The period of tension and arms competition between the United States and the Soviet Union that lasted from 1945 until 1991.

containment An important feature of American Cold War policy in which the United States used diplomatic, economic, and military strategies in an effort to prevent the Soviet Union from expanding its influence.

Soon after World War II ended, the **Cold War** (1945–91) began as the victorious Allies disagreed over the reconstruction of Germany and the reformation of Eastern European countries that Germany had occupied during the war. In a 1946 speech, former British prime minister Winston Churchill referred to an "iron curtain" that had split Eastern and Western Europe, leaving the East under Soviet domination with few political freedoms.[14] The American diplomat George Kennan argued for **containment**, the idea that America should use diplomatic, economic, and military means to prevent the Soviet Union from expanding the set of countries that it controlled or was allied with.[15] This policy constituted the Truman Doctrine, which served as a guiding principle for American foreign policy over the next generation.[16]

During this period the United States implemented several measures to build and strengthen alliances against the Soviet threat. The first was the Marshall Plan, a series of aid and development programs enacted in the late 1940s to restore the economies of Western European countries that had been devastated during World War II.[17] In addition, the United States was instrumental in the formation of the World Bank and the International Monetary Fund, as well as other international trade agreements. (See later discussion.)

The United States also formed alliances with other countries, including the North Atlantic Treaty Organization (NATO) in 1949. The goal of these alliances and organizations was collective security, based on the principle that "an attack against one is an attack against all."[18] The aim was to deter Soviet attacks throughout the world by formalizing America's commitment to defend its allies. Of course, the Soviets formed their own alliances, most notably the Warsaw Pact with nations in Eastern Europe.[19]

On another front the United States was behind the 1945 creation of the United Nations (UN), an international organization with the goal of preventing wars by facilitating negotiations between combatants and, if necessary, by sending military forces from member states to stop conflicts. Other aspects of the UN's role have included administering relief efforts for refugees, undertaking development efforts, codifying international law, and publicizing and condemning human rights violations.

Clearly, the goal of containment influenced every aspect of American foreign policy after World War II.[20] America maintained large military forces, beginning its first peacetime draft in the 1950s and building up a large store of nuclear weapons. These weapons were intended to deter war with the Soviet Union through the threat of **mutually assured destruction**—the idea that even if the Soviet Union unleashed an all-out nuclear assault on the United States, enough American weapons would remain intact to deliver a similarly devastating counterattack. As part of this effort, throughout much of the mid-twentieth century the United States stationed hundreds of thousands of troops in Western Europe and elsewhere to deter the Soviet threat. Yet in 1962 war nearly broke out during the Cuban Missile Crisis, when the Soviets attempted to station nuclear missiles in Cuba—within striking range of the United States. However, the issue was defused by a Soviet withdrawal in the face of an American naval blockade of Cuba and a secret American promise to withdraw similar missiles from Turkey in return.

In the early 1960s America also became involved in the conflict in Vietnam, believing that North Vietnam's drive to take over South Vietnam was part of the Soviet Union's plan for world domination.[21] A popular theory at the time held that if the United States did not prevent the fall of South Vietnam, the next step would be a Soviet-backed conflict in the Philippines, in Australia, or in the territory of some other American ally. However, the initial conflict between North and South Vietnam was a civil war rather than an international event.[22] Though the North Vietnamese accepted Soviet support, they did not take orders from the Soviets.

Beginning in the early 1970s President Richard Nixon and his national security adviser, Henry Kissinger, began a process of **détente** with the Soviet Union. This involved a series of negotiations and cultural exchanges designed to reduce tensions and promote cooperation.[23] These efforts culminated in the 1972 Strategic Arms Limitation Treaty (SALT I), which limited the growth of U.S. and Soviet missile forces.[24]

At the same time, the Arab nations' embargo prohibiting oil shipments to Western nations after the 1973 Arab–Israeli war was a reminder that containment of the Soviet Union could not be America's only foreign policy priority. Tensions over

mutually assured destruction The idea that two nations that possess large stores of nuclear weapons—like the United States and the Soviet Union during the Cold War—would both be annihilated in any nuclear exchange, thus making it unlikely that either country would launch a first attack.

détente An approach to foreign policy in which cultural exchanges and negotiations are used to reduce tensions between rival nations, such as between the United States and the Soviet Union during the 1970s.

oil increased again when the Organization of the Petroleum Exporting Countries (OPEC) raised prices in 1979. Both events contributed to a recession in America and the electoral defeats of two incumbent presidents, Gerald Ford in 1976 and Jimmy Carter in 1980.

AFTER THE COLD WAR: HUMAN RIGHTS, TRADE, TERRORISM, AND OTHER CONCERNS

In 1991 the Soviet Union splintered into 15 countries, effectively ending the Cold War. The end of this conflict, along with the growing number of democracies worldwide and the development of democratic peace theories (which argue that democracies will not fight other democracies), suggested to some observers that military conflicts would become much rarer, so that other concerns would more strongly influence America's foreign policy.[25] Events early in the post–Cold War era seemed to support this thesis. For example, human rights became a more important foreign policy topic,[26] and the United States became involved in humanitarian relief and nation-building efforts in Somalia, Bosnia, and Kosovo. Moreover, a series of agreements, including the North American Free Trade Agreement (NAFTA) in 1994 and the formation of the World Trade Organization (WTO) in 1995, lowered tariffs throughout the world.

However, new security threats emerged in the form of terrorist groups, most notably Al Qaeda, led by Osama bin Laden. Al Qaeda organized several attacks on Americans, including the bombing of U.S. embassies in Tanzania and Kenya in 1998 and an attack on an American warship in 2000. Then came the attacks of September 11, 2001. Some analysts and politicians, including President George W. Bush, described these attacks as part of a worldwide "clash of civilizations" or a global war on terrorism, pitting the secular, open West against radical Islam.[27] After the attacks President George W. Bush announced a new U.S. policy, the **Bush Doctrine**, or the doctrine of preemption, whereby the United States would not wait until after an attack to respond but, rather, would use military force to eliminate potential threats before they could be put in motion. This policy was behind the decision to invade Iraq in 2003 and the ongoing operations against Al Qaeda, including the attack in May 2011 that resulted in bin Laden's death.

In several important respects Barack Obama's presidency represents a sharp reversal of many Bush-era policies. The emphasis now is on improving foreign perceptions of America and Americans, and avoiding unilateral action in favor of multilateral coalitions. Obama's 2009 speech in Cairo, in which he acknowledged past American mistakes and called for cooperation around shared interests, is typical of this new approach. However, as we describe throughout this chapter, many of Obama's policies in regard to the war on terrorism and other areas are quite similar to those established by the Bush administration.

Finally, the Arab Spring of 2012, during which citizen protests toppled governments in Middle Eastern countries from Tunisia to Yemen, creates new challenges for American foreign policy. While the establishment of democratically elected governments in these countries would seem to be consistent with American interests, the concern is that citizens there might demand policies that are contrary to stated American goals, including support for Israel. In fall 2012 these countries held their first free elections, and it is not clear what policies will ultimately emerge. Clearly, though, the changes initiated by the Arab Spring raise new concerns for American policy makers.

Bush Doctrine The foreign policy of President George W. Bush, under which the United States would use military force preemptively against threats to its national security.

THE AL QAEDA TERRORIST organization headed by Osama bin Laden was the driving force behind many terrorist attacks on Americans, including the October 2000 bombing of the USS *Cole* and the 2001 attacks on the World Trade Center and the Pentagon.

FOREIGN POLICY MAKERS

This section focuses on the makers of American foreign policy. We begin with the president and the executive branch, and then we consider Congress, the courts, and finally, other groups and individuals outside the government. Nuts and Bolts 15.2 summarizes the foreign policy powers of the two most important actors, the president and Congress.

THE PRESIDENT AND THE EXECUTIVE BRANCH

The president is the dominant actor in American foreign policy.[28] He and his staff can negotiate treaties or executive agreements with other nations, change policy through executive orders or findings, mobilize public opinion to prompt action by Congress, and shape foreign policy by appointing people to agencies and departments that administer these policies (see Chapter 10). The president also serves as commander in chief of America's armed forces.

Within the Executive Office of the President (EOP), the principal foreign policy agency is the **National Security Council (NSC)**, which develops foreign policy options and presents them to the president. The EOP also includes the Office of the U.S. Trade Representative, which focuses on tariffs and trade disputes; the president's Foreign Intelligence Advisory Board, a group of academics, politicians, and former government officials who advise the president; the Homeland Security Council, which coordinates antiterrorism policies; and the Office of Management and Budget, which prepares the president's annual budget proposals for federal agencies and departments, including those with foreign policy responsibilities.

National Security Council (NSC) Within the Executive Office of the President, a committee that advises the president on matters of foreign policy.

15.2 NUTS & bolts

FOREIGN POLICY POWERS OF THE PRESIDENT AND CONGRESS

President	Congress
Commander in chief of armed forces	Can declare war
Nominates and appoints senior officials in Department of Defense	Senate must approve defense nominees
Negotiates treaties and executive agreements with other nations	Treaties take effect only if approved by senate
Changes policy with executive orders and findings	Can overturn orders and findings with legislation
Attempts to mobilize public opinion behind foreign policy goals	Makes policy using "Power of the Purse" (annual budget)

AS OBAMA'S FIRST SECRETARY of state, Hillary Clinton was instrumental in getting Myanmar—widely viewed as having one of the world's most oppressive governments—to introduce economic and political reforms. The United States rewarded Myanmar by lifting sanctions and increasing aid.

civilian control The idea that military leaders do not formulate military policy, but rather implement directives from civilian leaders.

THE DEPARTMENT OF STATE

The principal foreign policy department in the executive branch is the Department of State. Its head, the secretary of state, acts as the official spokesperson for the United States in foreign relations and is an important adviser to the president. Aside from senior staff like the secretary of state, who is nominated by the president and confirmed by the Senate, State Department personnel are generally career civil servants who remain in their positions even after a new president takes office.

State Department officials operate U.S. embassies abroad and interact extensively with the leaders of other countries; they also offer expertise on the politics, economics, and cultures of other nations. There are many different offices and working groups in the State Department, from people who deal with treaties to coordinators of international aid, arms control, or assistance for refugees. This wide variation highlights the broad range of issues that are considered foreign policy.

THE DEPARTMENT OF DEFENSE

The Department of Defense carries out military actions as ordered by civilian authorities, ranging from full-scale wars such as those in Iraq and Afghanistan, to smaller operations such as the ongoing drone attacks against Al Qaeda forces throughout the Middle East.

The military's role in foreign policy is not limited to uses of force. Military personnel also deliver humanitarian aid and help American citizens evacuate from areas of conflict. For example, U.S. Navy ships and helicopters delivered relief aid to Haiti after the 2010 earthquake, and wounded Haitians were airlifted to military ships and facilities in the United States for medical treatment. Moreover, the American military advises and trains armed forces in other countries, and senior military personnel sometimes serve as consultants during foreign policy debates.

The overriding principle of America's military is the concept of **civilian control**—the idea that military personnel do not formulate policy but, rather, implement directives from their civilian leaders in the executive branch (the president and senior leaders in the Defense Department) and Congress. In general, the norm is that disagreements between the civilians and the military are accepted as long as (1) they are kept private and (2) military leaders carry out without hesitation the orders they are ultimately given. However, as in the case of General McChrystal discussed in this chapter's introduction, when disagreements become public and when military leaders express a lack of confidence in their civilian leaders, the usual response is to replace these leaders immediately. Such a move reflects the bedrock principle of civilian control.

THE DEPARTMENT OF HOMELAND SECURITY

The Department of Homeland Security was formed after the September 11 attacks by combining the Coast Guard, the Transportation Security Administration, the Border Patrol, and several other agencies. Its responsibilities are to secure America's borders, prevent future terrorist attacks, and coordinate intelligence gathering. Although there has not been a major terrorist attack on American soil since September 11, 2001, the Department of Homeland Security still works toward its goal of successfully facilitating information-sharing and cooperation among various intelligence agencies in government.

INTELLIGENCE AGENCIES

Agencies such as the Central Intelligence Agency (CIA) and National Security Agency (NSA) are primarily responsible for government intelligence gathering. Most of their work consists of gathering information from public or semipublic sources, such as data on industrial outputs. However, these agencies also undertake covert operations to acquire intelligence, use satellites and other technology to monitor communications, or even attack individuals, other nations, or organizations. The director of national intelligence in the EOP leads and coordinates the activities of the various intelligence agencies.

CONGRESS

Although the president dominates foreign policy, several groups within Congress participate in making foreign policy, and Congress can reverse or thwart any presidential initiatives. The Committee on Foreign Affairs in the House, and the Foreign Relations Committee in the Senate, are responsible for writing legislation that deals with foreign policy, including setting the annual budget for agencies that carry out those policies. These committees also hold hearings in which they pose questions to foreign policy experts from inside and outside the government.

There is an Intelligence Committee in both the House and the Senate; these committees oversee covert operations and the actions of the CIA, NSA, and similar agencies. Current law requires the president to give Congress "timely notification" of covert intelligence operations.[29] The intent is to ensure that someone outside the executive branch knows about secret operations and can organize congressional opposition if these actions are deemed illegal, immoral, or unwise.

Congress holds three types of influence over foreign policy, all of which force presidents to compromise with members of Congress when their policy goals are in conflict. The first is the power of the purse. Since members of Congress write annual budgets for every government department and agency, one way for members to shape foreign policy is to forbid expenditures on activities that members want to prevent.

Second, the Senate has the power to approve treaties and confirm the appointments of senior members of the president's foreign policy team—including the secretaries of state and defense, the director of national intelligence, and America's ambassador to the UN. Although it is rare for senators to reject a treaty or a nominee, sometimes they issue preemptive warnings about what kinds of treaties they will accept or, more commonly, never put to a vote any treaties that might be voted down.

Third, the Constitution grants Congress the power to declare war on other nations. However, as we saw in Chapter 10, the Constitution does not say that this declaration must occur before hostilities can begin or whether the declaration is necessary at all. In an attempt to codify war-making powers, in 1973 Congress adopted the War Powers Resolution, although as we discussed in Chapter 10, the question of which branch of the government ultimately controls America's armed forces remains controversial.

Of course, members of Congress always have the power to block a president's foreign policy initiatives, but doing so requires enacting a law with enough votes to override a presidential veto (often an impossible task). In the debate over funding for the Iraq War, in 2007 the House and Senate passed a funding resolution that included a withdrawal timeline for U.S. troops, but it was approved by a margin of only a few votes in each chamber. After President Bush vetoed the resolution, the two Houses passed a new funding resolution that dropped these restrictions. The "How It Works" diagram illustrates the basic powers of Congress and the president when it comes to military conflict.

THE FEDERAL COURTS

The federal courts, including the Supreme Court, weigh in on foreign policy questions through judicial review. This involves determining whether laws, regulations, and presidential actions are consistent with the Constitution. For example, a series of lower court and Supreme Court decisions forced the Bush administration to revise its policies of holding terror suspects indefinitely without charges; the rulings required that the suspects be charged with crimes and tried on those charges.[30] Although the courts can reverse presidential actions, it is worth noting that these trials occurred only after several cases spent years proceeding through the judicial system. During that time the administration's policy remained in place.[31]

GROUPS OUTSIDE THE FEDERAL GOVERNMENT

Foreign policy choices are also influenced by a variety of individuals and groups outside government. These actors range from corporate, citizen, and single-interest groups to the media, public opinion, and international and nongovernmental organizations. Here we explore how these groups participate in the making of foreign policy.

INTEREST GROUPS

Interest groups are organizations that work to convince elected officials and bureaucrats to implement policy changes in line with the group's goals. A diverse set of groups and organizations lobby government over foreign policy, including some foreign corporations.[32] Lobbying efforts can even involve foreign governments. In these cases, lobbying efforts center on economic and military aid, trade deals, and more general efforts to improve a country's image among members of Congress and the bureaucracy.

Sometimes interest group lobbying pits business interests against moral concerns. For example, during the debate over granting China more favorable trade terms with U.S. companies in 2007, some groups argued that the legislation should be shelved until the Chinese government guaranteed religious freedoms to its citizens.[33] Other groups favored imposing tariffs on Chinese goods as retaliation for the Chinese government's refusal to revalue its currency—a move that would make Chinese goods more expensive and help U.S. manufacturers. Ultimately, members of Congress sympathetic to both groups blocked the trade proposals, although the U.S. government did implement some trade agreements with China that did not require congressional approval.[34]

WAR POWERS: WHO CONTROLS THE ARMED FORCES?

As commander in chief, has the power to deploy troops.

THE PRESIDENT

Under the War Powers Resolution, has to notify Congress, and the use of force must be terminated within 60 days if Congress does not approve. However, Congress has never voted to terminate military action, and most presidents have argued that the act is unconstitutional.

Has the power to declare war (but has not used this power since World War II).

ARMED FORCES

CONGRESS

Has the power of the purse: can provide or withhold funding for military action.

POP QUIZ!

1 The Constitution gives _____ the power to declare war.

a the president

b Congress

c the Pentagon

d the State Department

e the ambassador to the target country

2 However, in the past century, almost all military action has been initiated by

a the president.

b Congress.

c the Pentagon.

d the State Department.

e the ambassador to the target country.

IN 2010, PRESIDENT OBAMA HELD
bilateral talks with President
Hu Jintao of China in an effort
to increase nuclear security. In
addition to being the United States'
chief diplomat, the president
also tends to dominate decisions
related to war and security.

One of the most prominent foreign policy interest groups is the American Israel Public Affairs Committee (AIPAC). This group has lobbied for increased military aid to Israel and American sanctions against Iran, among other matters, and the group contributes to the campaigns of congressional candidates who share its goals.[35] Other groups focus on publicizing international events in the hope of prompting citizens to demand government action. For example, the Stop Kony organization created a video to increase global awareness of Joseph Kony, leader of the Lords Resistance Army based in Uganda, and the alleged use of child soldiers in his fight against the governments of Congo, the Central African Republic, and South Sudan.

As mentioned in Chapter 8, the impact of lobbying efforts like these is hard to determine. For example, although AIPAC is a powerful interest group, it is likely that America's foreign policy would largely favor Israel regardless of AIPAC's actions.[36] Similarly, as of spring 2012 the Kony video had been viewed over 100 million times on various websites and attracted considerable press attention, but it has not prompted any new international action against Kony. Interest groups' influence over foreign policy depends mainly on the same two factors as their influence over domestic policy: groups hold the most sway when few citizens care about the matter and when the issue is noncontroversial.

THE MEDIA

Television, radio, print media, and the Internet all inform the public about events in America and elsewhere. However, it is not clear that evaluations of America's foreign policy are driven solely by the news media's decisions about what to cover and how to report it. In the case of Afghanistan there is no doubt that media coverage during 2011 and 2012 was generally negative and that public opinion on the war declined during this period. However, both trends reflected the facts on the ground during that time: a persistent insurgency, limited reconstruction, political stalemate, and steadily rising American casualties.

PUBLIC OPINION

Foreign policy decisions are also sensitive to public opinion. For example, congressional attempts in 2007 to make funding for the Iraq conflict conditional on setting troop withdrawal deadlines were driven in part by the shift in public opinion against the war—and by the influence of that shift on the 2006 midterm elections, in which many Republicans who had supported the war were defeated or came close to defeat.[37] More recently, declines in public support for the war in Afghanistan have probably stimulated congressional calls to accelerate the withdrawal of American ground forces.

Though elected officials generally consider public opinion when making foreign policy decisions, their judgments must take into account the problems of measuring opinions (see Chapter 5). After all, public opinion is sensitive to context, including both how and when survey questions are asked. For example, fears of another terrorist attack on the United States increase sharply every time there is an attack elsewhere in the world.

The fact that public opinion is sensitive to context means that Americans may sometimes ignore foreign policy questions (or their representative's positions on these issues) in favor of other concerns. For example, as we discussed in Chapter 5, as economic conditions in the United States worsened in 2008 and 2009, mentions in mass surveys of the economy as the most important issue facing the country rose sharply, while mentions of Iraq, Afghanistan, fears of a terrorist attack, and other foreign policy issues declined. Politicians must also consider that many Americans know little about other countries.

When citizens are relatively less interested in foreign policy and uninformed about it, elected officials can place a low priority on responding to public opinion and can instead pursue their own foreign policy goals. For example, in March 2012 President Obama decided to join in NATO's operations in favor of Libyan rebel forces despite public opposition.[38]

INTERGOVERNMENTAL ORGANIZATIONS, NONGOVERNMENTAL ORGANIZATIONS, AND INTERNATIONAL ORGANIZATIONS

America's relationship with the rest of the world is not just about government action; it also reflects actions on the part of several types of organizations. For example, members of **intergovernmental organizations (IGOs)** and **nongovernmental organizations (NGOs)** provide information and humanitarian assistance, and carry out other activities that the U.S. government is unable or unwilling to undertake. IGOs are associations of sovereign states, while NGOs are private organizations. Thousands of IGOs and NGOs operate throughout the world.[39]

A primary goal of NGOs is to promote global economic development and growth. Thus one of the largest IGOs, the **World Bank**, funds economic development projects worldwide. Another IGO, the **International Monetary Fund (IMF)**, helps countries manage budget deficits and control the value of their currencies. Many NGOs, such as the Asia Foundation, focus on development in a particular region or on certain activities.

A second goal of NGOs is to provide humanitarian relief. In the wake of a disaster such as an earthquake or a flood, or during a famine or a war, organizations such as Oxfam International supply populations in crisis with basic necessities. Other groups such as Doctors without Borders provide medical care to populations threatened by violence, epidemics, or natural disasters. Some NGOs also promote human rights. For example, Amnesty International spotlights international cases of people jailed for their political beliefs or held without trial, or the use of cruel punishments such as stoning. Amnesty's campaigns, as well as those of other NGOs, are not always supportive of U.S. policy. For example, Amnesty decries the rendition of terror suspects by the United States.[40]

Finally, NGOs help build democracies. The Open Society Institute funds efforts to increase mass political participation, strengthen political organizations, and verify the fairness of elections in new democracies throughout the world. The National Democratic Institute and the International Republican Institute conduct similar activities. Both organizations, for example, sent groups in 2011 and 2012 to new democracies in the Middle East to assist with building party organizations and developing election rules in the wake of the Arab Spring.[41]

The United States is also a member of many international organizations. Best known is the **United Nations (UN)**, an assembly of ambassadors representing almost all of the world's nations that addresses issues of worldwide concern. The UN is involved in economic development, environmental protection, humanitarian relief, and peacekeeping efforts. Inside the UN, the Security Council—a group of 15 nations (permanent members Britain, China, France, Russia, and the United

intergovernmental organizations (IGOs) Associations of sovereign states that work to protect human rights, increase living standards, and achieve policy goals throughout the world.

nongovernmental organizations (NGOs) Groups operated by private institutions (rather than governments) to promote growth, economic development, and other agendas throughout the world.

World Bank A nongovernmental organization established in 1944 that provides financial support for economic development projects in developing nations.

International Monetary Fund (IMF) A nongovernmental organization established in 1944 to help stabilize the international monetary system, improve economic growth, and aid developing nations.

United Nations (UN) An international organization made up of representatives from nearly every nation, with a mission to promote peace and cooperation, uphold international law, and provide humanitarian aid.

SHOULD AMERICA JOIN THE INTERNATIONAL CRIMINAL COURT?

Foreign policy presents Americans with a fundamental choice: Should America act alone or cooperate with other nations? Unilateral action means that American policy makers can act to further America's self-interest—as these individuals define it, of course. The advantage of multilateral action is that working with other nations may allow the United States to achieve goals that would be unattainable by acting alone. However, multilateral action may sometimes produce policies that are not ideal, or even acceptable, to the United States.

As an example, consider the International Criminal Court (ICC), an agency within the United Nations that was set up in 2002 to prosecute cases of genocide, war crimes, and crimes against humanity.[a] Before the ICC was established, new courts had to be created every time someone was tried for such crimes, such as the International Criminal Tribunal for the Former Yugoslavia, which prosecuted more than 100 political leaders, military leaders, and soldiers. The ICC was created as a permanent international body that would adjudicate these high-profile, international cases.

As of July 2012, over 120 nations have ratified the ICC treaty, which essentially gives the ICC jurisdiction over their citizens.[b] These nations include U.S. allies Great Britain, France, and Germany. However, the United States has not ratified the treaty, nor have allies Israel and Japan. Others who have not ratified include China and Russia.

The United States signed the ICC treaty during President Clinton's administration, but the treaty was never sent to the Senate for a ratification vote. (Clinton expressed doubts about the treaty and faced a Senate in which support for the treaty was weak.) Clinton's successor, George W. Bush, nullified the signature and declared that the United States would not allow its citizens to be prosecuted by the ICC. Bush administration officials even threatened to withhold U.S. forces from UN peacekeeping missions unless they were granted full immunity from ICC prosecution.[c] As of late 2012, this policy remains in place under President Obama, although the United States has sent observers to monitor ICC proceedings.[d]

U.S. criticism of the ICC centers on whether defendants are given full due process rights as they are in American courts, such as the right to see the evidence against them and protection against self-incrimination.[e] However, an analysis by the group Human Rights Watch, which supports the ICC, argued that ICC procedures are similar to those in U.S. courts.[f]

These debates miss a deeper concern. By joining the ICC, the United States would lose the ability to protect its citizens from prosecution by this court. In theory, the ICC could prosecute American forces and military leaders for such actions as the invasion and occupation of Iraq or the interrogation techniques used against terror suspects in the detention facility

The International Criminal Court, shown here during a meeting, was set up to allow the prosecution of terrorists and international war criminals, such as individuals involved in genocide. The United States, whose empty seat at the Court is shown here, has refused to join the organization, partly due to concerns that American troops might be tried for their actions during armed conflicts.

at Guantánamo Bay. These concerns are not merely abstract. British soldiers have been prosecuted and convicted by the ICC for abuse of prisoners in Iraq.[g] And American military lawyers expressed concerns that interrogation methods that were commonly used by American forces would put these individuals at risk of ICC prosecution.[h]

The stakes are high on both sides of the question. If the United States joins the ICC, it will pressure other holdout nations to do so, thus increasing the Court's value as a potential deterrent to future cases of genocide, crimes against humanity, and war crimes. But joining the ICC would also put American soldiers and statesmen at risk of prosecution. What would you decide?

Critical Thinking Questions

1. The discussion gives several reasons why U.S. leaders might be reluctant to join the ICC. Besides the argument about encouraging holdouts, what are the advantages of joining this organization?

2. When might civilian and military leaders disagree about the decision to join the ICC? Why might military leaders favor joining the organization?

States, plus 10 rotating nations)—makes the most important decisions, particularly those involving UN military missions. The UN General Assembly, in which each nation has one vote, debates and votes on other concerns.

THE TOOLS OF FOREIGN POLICY

EXAMINE THE WAYS AMERICAN FOREIGN POLICY IS IMPLEMENTED

The tools or methods used to implement American foreign policy include, most obviously, the use of military force but also changes in trade policy or the provision of foreign or military aid. Although these strategies differ in terms of cost, and although some, such as military force, seem morally questionable to many Americans, all nations use these strategies in the pursuit of desired policy outcomes.

MILITARY FORCE

Military force is a fundamental tool of foreign policy. America's military forces serve throughout the world as a deterrent to conflict, and military exercises by U.S. troops, aircraft, and ships serve to remind potential adversaries of America's military power. For example, in early 2012 Iran threatened to close the Strait of Hormuz, a narrow passage connecting the Persian Gulf and the Gulf of Oman that tankers carrying Middle Eastern oil exports must transit; the United States responded by sending a carrier battle group to the strait to conduct flight operations—and to demonstrate that America was ready to keep the passage open by using force if necessary.[42]

The United States has also fought wars and lesser conflicts to further its foreign policy goals. Some are all-out military operations, such as the invasion of Iraq. More commonly, these deployments are short-lived operations ranging from the evacuation of American civilians from areas of unrest to the delivery of humanitarian

AS AMERICAN OPERATIONS IN IRAQ began to wind down in 2009 and 2010, additional forces were sent to Afghanistan in the hopes that the "surge" tactic used to good effect in Iraq would be similarly successful in Afghanistan. Here, a group of U.S. Marines participating in the surge listens to a briefing at Camp Dwyer in Helmand Province, Afghanistan.

assistance or the use of ship-launched cruise missiles to attack terrorist camps and similar targets.[43]

The size and power of America's military provide numerous options for policy makers. For example, after the September 11 attacks, in an attempt to prevent future terror attacks by Al Qaeda, U.S. forces invaded Afghanistan, which had been used as a base of operations for the organization.[44] It is highly unlikely that any other country could carry out such a large-scale operation so far from home. Nonetheless, military force is not all-powerful. At the end of 2012 American troops were still fighting in Afghanistan, with their mission by no means successfully accomplished.

TRADE AND ECONOMIC POLICIES

Foreign policy is also aimed at sustaining economic growth in the United States and elsewhere, as well as creating foreign markets for the goods produced by America's domestic industries. Figure 15.1 shows total American trade (imports and exports) with other countries over the last 40 years, expressed as a percentage of U.S. gross domestic product (GDP, a measure of the size of the U.S. economy). In recent years imports and exports have constituted more than 40 percent of GDP.

FIGURE » 15.1

U.S. IMPORTS AND EXPORTS AS A PERCENTAGE OF GROSS DOMESTIC PRODUCT (GDP)

This figure illustrates the importance of trade to the U.S. economy. In recent years, imports and exports have made up more than 40 percent of U.S. economic activity, and the percentage is steadily increasing. Based on these data, what arguments would you make for lowering or increasing barriers to trade?

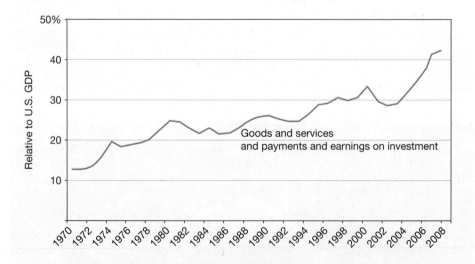

Source: Office of the U.S. Trade Representative, "2010 Trade Policy Agenda and 2009 Annual Report," February 2010, www.ustr.gov/2010-trade-policy-agenda (accessed 9/25/12).

The main tools of trade policy are tariffs and trade agreements. A **tariff** is a tax collected by the government for the import or export of certain commodities, and a trade agreement sets tariff levels or limits the quantities of particular items that can be imported or exported. The United States International Trade Commission maintains a list of all tariffs in effect.[45] By adjusting tariff rates the government can help or hurt domestic industries: high tariffs on imports help American producers charge lower prices than foreign competitors can, and low tariffs on exports help American producers sell to overseas markets.

Over the last two generations the United States and most other nations have been lowering tariffs and establishing free trade zones, which reflect agreements to eliminate tariffs on all imports and exports among specific nations. Examples include the North American Free Trade Agreement (NAFTA), involving the United States, Canada, and Mexico; and the Central America Free Trade Agreement (CAFTA) among the United States, five Central American nations, and the Dominican Republic. Other organizations, such as the **World Trade Organization (WTO),** facilitate negotiations over tariffs and provide a mechanism for adjudicating cases in which one nation believes that another is using tariffs unfairly. Finally, the United States has granted many other countries **most-favored-nation status**: tariffs on imports to the United States from these nations are set at the lowest rate placed on any other nation.

Clearly, trade is an important part of foreign policy. The United States can use free trade agreements and tariffs to bargain with countries for concessions in other areas. For example, in the 1990s the Clinton administration used tariffs, most-favored-nation status, and other inducements to force China to moderate its human rights policies and crack down on illegal copying of software and videos.[46]

Economic policies, which may involve the United States acting alone or with other nations, are also used to threaten or sanction countries as a way of inducing them to change their behavior. For example, in 2007 the UN Security Council authorized sanctions against Iran aimed at forcing the nation to stop enriching uranium, a first step in the production of nuclear weapons.[47] These sanctions included freezing bank accounts held by members of Iran's nuclear team and banning arms sales to the country. Additional sanctions imposed in 2012 cut off Iranian banks from international funds transfer networks, making it difficult for Iranian citizens and corporations to do business outside their nation's borders. If Iran agreed to stop its program, it would receive incentives such as civilian nuclear reactor technology and direct talks with the United States over various issues. At the same time, the United States also discouraged Israel from attacking Iranian nuclear facilities. This combination of carrots and sticks led to ongoing negotiations between the Iranians and a group of nations, including the United States and the European Union. However, as of the end of 2012, no deal had been reached.

DIPLOMACY

The process of diplomacy involves using personal contact and negotiations with national leaders and representatives to work out international agreements or persuade other nations to change their behavior. Sometimes these efforts involve the threat of military action or economic sanctions, or incentives such as economic assistance or other forms of aid. The United States may participate directly in such efforts or mediate between parties in a dispute.

ONE OF THE MOST CONFLICTUAL issues involving international trade is the enforcement of copyrights on movies, music, and computer software. The Chinese government's refusal to enforce American copyrights has been a source of tension between the two nations.

tariff A tax levied on imported and exported goods.

World Trade Organization (WTO) An international organization created in 1995 to oversee trade agreements between nations by facilitating negotiations and handling disputes.

most-favored-nation status A standing awarded to countries with which the United States has good trade relations, providing the lowest possible tariff rate. World Trade Organization members must give one another this preferred status.

Diplomacy has often been a useful but limited foreign policy tool. For example, American and Mexican diplomats signed an agreement in 2010 to deter the transportation of illegal drugs across the U.S.–Mexican border. And American diplomats are involved in many behind-the-scenes efforts to help resolve international disputes, such as the ongoing disagreement between Argentina and Great Britain over ownership of the Falkland Islands.

FOREIGN AID

IRAN'S NUCLEAR PROGRAM IS A CAUSE of concern for U.S. officials and IAEA inspectors. Although Iran claims its program is focused on energy, not weapons, this claim is widely doubted. Here, Iranian president Mahmoud Ahmadinejad tours a nuclear enrichment facility.

Foreign aid comprises money, products, or services given to other countries or the citizens of these countries. Sometimes foreign aid reflects the desire to provide basic assistance to satisfy fundamental human needs. For example, the American military is often tasked to deliver food and medical supplies to the victims of earthquakes and other natural disasters. Foreign aid also serves to stimulate economic growth in other nations and to facilitate international agreements. For example, the peace treaty between Egypt and Israel in 1979 was facili-

FIGURE » 15.2

U.S. FOREIGN AID IN COMPARATIVE PERSPECTIVE

This figure shows foreign aid contributions expressed as a percentage of gross national income. Do these data imply that America is less generous than other nations in its willingness to donate aid?

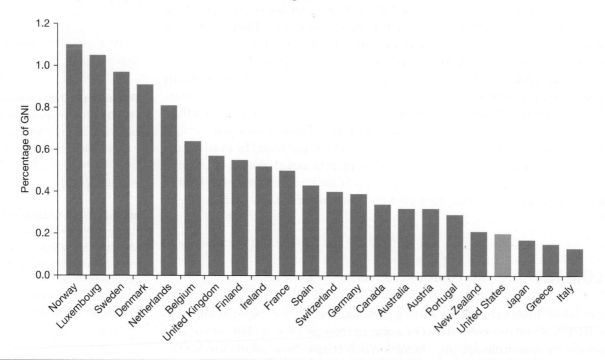

Source: Organization for Economic Co-operation and Development, "Development Co-operation Report 2010," April 23, 2010, www.oecd.org/dac/dcr (accessed 9/25/12).

tated by America's agreement to provide substantial military and economic assistance to both countries.[48]

Figure 15.2 shows the level of American nonmilitary foreign aid in 2010, measured as a percentage of gross national income (GNI) compared to that of other members of the Organization for Economic Cooperation and Development. (GNI includes GDP as well as investment income from other countries.) Considering the amount of U.S. foreign aid as a percentage of GNI suggests that the United States gives relatively little to other countries. Part of the reason for this perception lies in the size of the U.S. economy: America's foreign aid contributions are the largest of any country when measured in total dollars, but it also has the largest GNI of any country.

ALLIANCES AND TREATIES

A treaty is an agreement between nations to work together on economic or security issues. An alliance is an agreement that commits nations to security guarantees, which are assurances that one country will help another if it is attacked. America is a member of many international alliances, most notably the **North Atlantic Treaty Organization (NATO)**. It was formed by the North Atlantic Treaty after World War II to provide collective security against the Soviet Union and Warsaw Pact countries, but after the Cold War the organization's mission shifted to coordinating military force toward common goals. NATO's operations in Libya in 2011 were the first instance of operations outside Europe.[49]

The United States is a party to many treaties: bilateral agreements between the United States and one other country, and multilateral agreements involving the United States and several countries.[50] Treaties and alliances enable the United States to commit itself to a course of action or signal its intentions to other nations.[51] By joining NATO and stationing troops in Europe, for example, the United States guaranteed that if Warsaw Pact troops invaded the West, U.S. forces would be part of the resistance. Moreover, if the United States should fail to honor its treaty obligations, it would be difficult for it to convince other nations to enter into future agreements.

North Atlantic Treaty Organization (NATO) An international alliance among the United States, Canada, and several European nations, originally created to provide security against the Soviet Union during the Cold War.

THE POLITICS OF FOREIGN POLICY

ANALYZE SEVERAL MAJOR AREAS OF FOREIGN POLICY AND WHY THEY ARE OFTEN CONTROVERSIAL

The making of foreign policy, like everything else in the federal government, is a political act—a contest involving elected officials, bureaucrats, interest groups, and other actors, all with their own goals. In this sense there are always conflicts over what American's foreign policy should look like, and compromise will always be fundamental to the making of foreign policy. Moreover, as with domestic issues, the amount of attention paid to foreign policy matters varies over time.

Conflict over foreign policy has several sources, including Americans' different ideas of what such policy should look like. One source of disagreement is the realist–idealist distinction discussed earlier. Self-interest is another powerful factor. For example, several studies have found that as National Guard units were mobilized for service in Iraq, support for the war declined in the communities where these units were based.[52]

Disagreements over foreign policy may also reflect citizens' exposure to different information or their disparate ways of understanding the world. Indeed, there are sharp disagreements among citizens over the existence of climate change and its cause—natural phenomena or human activity (see Chapter 5).[53] The same study that documented those disagreements found that an individual's support for policies to combat climate change depends on his or her diagnosis of the problem. Most people who see human activity as the cause favor policies that would alleviate the problem, and most who believe climate change is a natural phenomenon favor the status quo.

Disagreements may also originate in differing expectations about whether policies will work as intended, as well as the basic facts of a situation. For example, during the debate over whether the United States and its allies should support rebel groups in the Syrian civil war that began in 2011, some members of Congress and Obama administration officials argued that Syria's central geographic and political position in the Middle East made intervention essential—while others cited the same factors to argue against getting involved.[54] Both sides in the debate were unsure of the size and capabilities of the various rebel groups, whether the groups were willing to work together, whether arming these groups would prolong the conflict or end it, and what kind of political system would result if the rebel groups succeeded in winning control of the country.

In sum, disagreements about foreign policy are unavoidable, both in government and among the general public. These conflicts will surely continue. For a variety of reasons, citizens and elected officials will disagree on what America's foreign policy should look like, and they will work in elections and in the government to influence those choices.

IN 1989 THE FALL OF THE BERLIN WALL, which separated West Berlin from communist East Berlin, provided a powerful symbol of the end of the Cold War. With just one superpower—the United States—left, many predicted that democracy would spread and peace would prevail. However, new foreign policy challenges quickly emerged.

CONCLUSION

Foreign policy definitely matters. Consider the following four statements: (1) National security is a top priority for many Americans. (2) The state of the American economy, from home prices to the unemployment rate, is affected by economic conditions elsewhere. (3) Trade agreements with other nations determine how much American companies are allowed to export and what taxes and fees they must pay to import raw materials and other goods. (4) Solutions to pressing environmental problems such as climate change are inherently international. As these statements show, it is hard to find a domestic issue that does not have a foreign policy component.

Foreign policy is also conflictual. Disagreements among elected officials over what to do in Afghanistan, or over trade agreements or any other question of foreign policy, are not just attempts to attract political support or gain media attention. These differences of opinion reflect real dilemmas over what government should do.

In all these respects, events such as the September 11 attacks, the invasions of Iraq and Afghanistan, and the worldwide economic crisis of 2008–09 are not exceptions to the rule. Rather, these events epitomize just how close to home foreign policy is. Foreign policy is not something that happens "out there," in isolation from the American public; from the state of the economy to public safety, ordinary Americans are finding their lives increasingly affected by actions taken by individuals, organizations, and countries outside America's borders.

STUDY *guide*

WHAT IS FOREIGN POLICY?

▶ Describe the major approaches to understanding foreign policy and trace how America's role in the world has evolved.
Pages 469–74

SUMMARY

Foreign policy is any government action with a group outside of America's borders. Foreign policy goals are complex, and debates on what America's goals should be are traditionally framed in terms of general principles. American foreign policy has changed its goals over time and has become increasingly internationalist.

KEY TERMS

foreign policy (p. 469)

unilateral action (p. 469)

multilateral action (p. 470)

isolationism (p. 470)

internationalism (p. 470)

realism (p. 470)

idealism (p. 470)

constructivism (p. 471)

Monroe Doctrine (p. 471)

Cold War (p. 472)

containment (p. 472)

mutually assured destruction (p. 473)

détente (p. 473)

Bush Doctrine (p. 474)

PRACTICE QUIZ QUESTIONS

1. When one country does something on its own without coordinating with other countries, it is
    _____.
    a) isolationist
    b) internationalist
    c) acting unilaterally
    d) acting multilaterally
    e) nation building

2. _____ believe that countries pursue their own interests.
    a) Realists
    b) Idealists
    c) Constructivists
    d) Internationalists
    e) Isolationists

3. The Monroe Doctrine stated that in European wars, America would _____.
    a) support Britain
    b) support the attacking country
    c) support the attacked country
    d) provide arms but not troops
    e) remain neutral

4. American foreign policy became increasingly internationalist following _____.
    a) the Civil War
    b) World War I
    c) World War II
    d) the Vietnam War
    e) the Cold War

5. The goal of containment influenced the _____ and _____.
    a) war in Iraq; war in Afghanistan
    b) Korean war; war in Iraq
    c) Vietnam war; war in Iraq
    d) Vietnam war; Cuban Missile Crisis
    e) Vietnam war; World War II

CRITICAL THINKING AND DISCUSSION

Pick one of the foreign policy problems described in this chapter. What policy choices would a realist make? What choices would an idealist make?

⑤ PRACTICE ONLINE

"Critical Thinking" exercise: *Politics Is Conflictual— The League of Nations*

FOREIGN POLICY MAKERS

▶ Explain how the various branches of government shape foreign policy. **Pages 475–83**

SUMMARY

The major actors in foreign policy are the president and Congress, though the Supreme Court, interest groups, and public opinion all influence foreign policy decisions to a degree. The president's advantage over Congress lies in the ambiguity in the Constitution and the unilateral presidential power.

KEY TERMS

National Security Council (NSC) (p. 475)

civilian control (p. 476)

intergovernmental organizations (IGOs) (p. 481)

nongovernmental organizations (NGOs) (p. 481)

World Bank (p. 481)

International Monetary Fund (IMF) (p. 481)

United Nations (UN) (p. 481)

PRACTICE QUIZ QUESTIONS

6. The principal foreign policy department in the executive branch is _____.
   a) the Department of Defense
   b) the Council on Foreign Relations
   c) the Department of International Relations
   d) the Department of State
   e) the Foreign Intelligence Advisory Board

7. The idea that military personnel do not formulate policy, but rather implement directives from civilians is _____.
   a) military deference
   b) civilian control
   c) the Geneva system

   d) civilian-military alliance
   e) the Bush Doctrine

8. Congress holds _____ and _____, which both influence foreign policy.
   a) the power to deploy troops; the power of the purse
   b) the power to approve treaties; the power to deploy troops
   c) the power to declare war; the power of the purse
   d) the power to deploy troops; the power to declare war
   e) the power to approve appointments; the power to deploy troops

9. The War Powers Resolution was designed to _____.
   a) limit the president's war-making powers
   b) limit the Congress's war-making powers
   c) limit the Department of Defense's war-making powers
   d) limit the Pentagon's war-making powers
   e) limit the State Department's war-making powers

CRITICAL THINKING AND DISCUSSION

The American president has much more influence over foreign policy than members of Congress do. What are the pros and cons of this allocation of power?

⑤ PRACTICE ONLINE

"Critical Thinking" exercise: *Political Process Matters—The War Powers Resolution*

THE TOOLS OF FOREIGN POLICY

▶ Examine the ways American foreign policy is implemented. **Pages 483–87**

SUMMARY

American foreign policy is implemented using a variety of tools—beyond the use of military force, other tools include the provision of foreign aid or changes to trade policy. Though all tools can be used in pursuit of desired policy outcomes, the specific tool will be selected based on careful consideration of context.

KEY TERMS

tariff (p. 485)

World Trade Organization (WTO) (p. 485)

most-favored-nation status (p. 485)

North Atlantic Treaty Organization (NATO) (p. 487)

PRACTICE QUIZ QUESTIONS

10. When a country is given "most-favored-nation" status, it means that the United States _____ to any other nation.
    a) gave the country higher levels of foreign aid than
    b) gave the country higher levels of military aid than
    c) set tariffs on imports to the United States to the lowest rate given
    d) set tariffs on exports from the United States to the lowest rate given
    e) sends more troops to that country than

11. The process of _____ involves using personal contact and negotiations with leaders to work out international agreements.
    a) nation building
    b) diplomacy
    c) unilateralism
    d) the Bush Doctrine
    e) the use of force

12. The North American Free Trade Agreement (NAFTA) is an example of _____.
    a) a bilateral agreement
    b) an alliance
    c) a trade compact
    d) a multilateral agreement
    e) a sanction

ⓢ PRACTICE ONLINE

"Critical Thinking" exercise: *Politics Is Everywhere— U.S. Military Presence Worldwide*

SUGGESTED READING

Bueno de Mesquita, Bruce. *Principles of International Politics.* Washington, DC: CQ Press, 2005.

Fisher, Louis. *Presidential War Power.* Lawrence: University Press of Kansas, 2004.

Friedman, Thomas L. *The World Is Flat 3.0: A Brief History of the Twenty-first Century.* New York: Farrar, Straus and Giroux, 2007.

Huntington, Samuel P. *The Clash of Civilizations and the Remaking of World Order.* New York: Free Press, 2002.

Keohane, Robert O. *After Hegemony: Cooperation and Discord in the International System.* Princeton, NJ: Princeton University Press, 2005 (originally published 1984).

Mearsheimer, John J. *The Tragedy of Great Power Politics.* New York: Norton, 2001.

National Commission on Terrorist Attacks upon the United States. *The 9/11 Commission Report: Final Report of the*

National Commission on Terrorist Attacks upon the United States. New York: Norton, 2004. Full text also available from the U.S. Government Printing Office at www.gpoaccess .gov/911/index.html.

Ricks, Thomas. *The Gamble: General David Petraeus and the American Military Adventure in Iraq, 2006–2008.* New York: Penguin Press, 2009.

Roach, Stephen. *The Next Asia: Opportunities and Challenges for a New Globalization.* New York: Wiley, 2009.

Sen, Amartya. *Identity and Violence: The Illusion of Destiny.* New York: Norton, 2007.

Simmons, Beth, Frank Dobbin, and Geoffrey Garrett. *The Global Diffusion of Markets and Democracy.* New York: Cambridge University Press, 2008.

Stiglitz, Joseph E. *Making Globalization Work.* New York: Norton, 2007.

APPENDIX

The Declaration of Independence

In Congress, July 4, 1776

The unanimous Declaration of the thirteen united States of America,

When in the Course of human events, it becomes necessary for one people to dissolve the political bands which have connected them with another, and to assume among the powers of the earth, the separate and equal station to which the Laws of Nature and of Nature's God entitle them, a decent respect to the opinions of mankind requires that they should declare the causes which impel them to the separation.

We hold these truths to be self-evident, that all men are created equal, that they are endowed by their Creator with certain unalienable Rights, that among these are Life, Liberty and the pursuit of Happiness.—That to secure these rights, Governments are instituted among Men, deriving their just powers from the consent of the governed. —That whenever any Form of Government becomes destructive of these ends, it is the Right of the People to alter or to abolish it, and to institute new Government, laying its foundation on such principles and organizing its powers in such form, as to them shall seem most likely to effect their Safety and Happiness. Prudence, indeed, will dictate that Governments long established should not be changed for light and transient causes; and accordingly all experience hath shewn, that mankind are more disposed to suffer, while evils are sufferable, than to right themselves by abolishing the forms to which they are accustomed. But when a long train of abuses and usurpations, pursuing invariably the same Object evinces a design to reduce them under absolute Despotism, it is their right, it is their duty, to throw off such Government, and to provide new Guards for their future security.—Such has been the patient sufferance of these Colonies; and such is now the necessity which constrains them to alter their former Systems of Government. The history of the present King of Great Britain is a history of repeated injuries and usurpations, all having in direct object the establishment of an absolute Tyranny over these States. To prove this, let Facts be submitted to a candid world.

He has refused his Assent to Laws, the most wholesome and necessary for the public good.

He has forbidden his Governors to pass Laws of immediate and pressing importance, unless suspended in their operation till his Assent should be obtained; and when so suspended, he has utterly neglected to attend to them.

He has refused to pass other Laws for the accommodation of large districts of people, unless those people would relinquish the right of Representation in the Legislature, a right inestimable to them and formidable to tyrants only.

He has called together legislative bodies at places unusual, uncomfortable, and distant from the depository of their public Records, for the sole purpose of fatiguing them into compliance with his measures.

He has dissolved Representative Houses repeatedly, for opposing with manly firmness his invasions on the rights of the people.

He has refused for a long time, after such dissolutions, to cause others to be elected; whereby the Legislative powers, incapable of Annihilation, have returned to the People at large for their exercise; the State remaining in the mean time exposed to all the dangers of invasion from without, and convulsions within.

He has endeavoured to prevent the population of these States; for that purpose obstructing the Laws for Naturalization of Foreigners; refusing to pass others to encourage their migrations hither, and raising the conditions of new Appropriations of Lands.

He has obstructed the Administration of Justice, by refusing his Assent to Laws for establishing Judiciary powers.

He has made Judges dependent on his Will alone, for the tenure of their offices, and the amount and payment of their salaries.

He has erected a multitude of New Offices, and sent hither swarms of Officers to harrass our people, and eat out their substance.

He has kept among us, in times of peace, Standing Armies without the Consent of our legislatures.

He has affected to render the Military independent of and superior to the Civil power.

He has combined with others to subject us to a jurisdiction foreign to our constitution, and unacknowledged by our laws; giving his Assent to their Acts of pretended Legislation:

For Quartering large bodies of armed troops among us:

For protecting them, by a mock Trial, from punishment for any Murders which they should commit on the Inhabitants of these States:

For cutting off our Trade with all parts of the world:

For imposing Taxes on us without our Consent:

For depriving us in many cases, of the benefits of Trial by Jury:

For transporting us beyond Seas to be tried for pretended offences:

For abolishing the free System of English Laws in a neighboring Province, establishing therein an Arbitrary government, and enlarging its Boundaries so as to render it at once an example and fit instrument for introducing the same absolute rule into these Colonies:

For taking away our Charters, abolishing our most valuable Laws, and altering fundamentally the Forms of our Governments:

For suspending our own Legislatures, and declaring themselves invested with power to legislate for us in all cases whatsoever.

He has abdicated Government here, by declaring us out of his Protection and waging War against us.

He has plundered our seas, ravaged our Coasts, burnt our towns, and destroyed the lives of our people.

He is at this time transporting large Armies of foreign Mercenaries to compleat the works of death, desolation and tyranny, already begun with circumstances of Cruelty & perfidy scarcely parelleled in the most barbarous ages, and totally unworthy the Head of a civilized nation.

He has constrained our fellow Citizens taken Captive on the high Seas to bear Arms against their Country, to become the executioners of their friends and Brethren, or to fall themselves by their Hands.

He has excited domestic insurrections amongst us, and has endeavoured to bring on the inhabitants of our frontiers, the merciless Indian Savages, whose known rule of warfare, is an undistinguished destruction of all ages, sexes and conditions.

In every stage of these Oppressions We have Petitioned for Redress in the most humble terms: Our repeated Petitions have been answered only by repeated injury. A Prince whose character is thus marked by every act which may define a Tyrant, is unfit to be the ruler of a free people.

Nor have We been wanting in attentions to our Brittish brethren. We have warned them from time to time of attempts by their legislature to extend an unwarrantable jurisdiction over us. We have reminded them of the circumstances of our emigration and settlement here. We have appealed to their native justice and magnanimity, and we have conjured them by the ties of our common kindred to disavow these usurpations, which, would inevitably interrupt our connections and correspondence. They too have been deaf to the voice of justice and of consanguinity. We must, therefore, acquiesce in the necessity, which denounces our Separation, and hold them, as we hold the rest of mankind, Enemies in War, in Peace Friends.

We, Therefore, the Representatives of the United States of America, in General Congress, Assembled, appealing to the Supreme Judge of the world for the rectitude of our intentions, do, in the Name, and by Authority of the good People of these Colonies, solemnly publish and declare, That these United Colonies are, and of Right ought to be Free and Independent States; that they are Absolved from all Allegiance to the British Crown, and that all political connection between them and the State of Great Britain, is and ought to be totally dissolved; and that as Free and Independent States, they have full Power to levy War, conclude Peace, contract Alliances, establish Commerce, and to do all other Acts and Things which Independent States may of right do. And for the support of this Declaration, with a firm reliance on the protection of divine Providence, we mutually pledge to each other our Lives, our Fortunes and our sacred Honor.

The foregoing Declaration was, by order of Congress, engrossed, and signed by the following members:

John Hancock

NEW HAMPSHIRE
Josiah Bartlett
William Whipple
Matthew Thornton

MASSACHUSETTS BAY
Samuel Adams
John Adams
Robert Treat Paine
Elbridge Gerry

RHODE ISLAND
Stephen Hopkins
William Ellery

CONNECTICUT
Roger Sherman
Samuel Huntington
William Williams
Oliver Wolcott

NEW YORK
William Floyd
Philip Livingston
Francis Lewis
Lewis Morris

NEW JERSEY
Richard Stockton
John Witherspoon
Francis Hopkinson
John Hart
Abraham Clark

PENNSYLVANIA
Robert Morris
Benjamin Rush
Benjamin Franklin
John Morton
George Clymer
James Smith
George Taylor
James Wilson
George Ross

DELAWARE
Caesar Rodney
George Read
Thomas M'Kean

MARYLAND
Samuel Chase
William Paca
Thomas Stone
Charles Carroll,
  of Carrollton

VIRGINIA
George Wythe
Richard Henry Lee
Thomas Jefferson
Benjamin Harrison
Thomas Nelson, Jr.
Francis Lightfoot Lee
Carter Braxton

NORTH CAROLINA
William Hooper
Joseph Hewes
John Penn

SOUTH CAROLINA
Edward Rutledge
Thomas Heyward, Jr.
Thomas Lynch, Jr.
Arthur Middleton

GEORGIA
Button Gwinnett
Lyman Hall
George Walton

Resolved, That copies of the Declaration be sent to the several assemblies, conventions, and committees, or councils of safety, and to the several commanding officers of the continental troops; that it be proclaimed in each of the United States, at the head of the army.

The Articles of Confederation

Agreed to by Congress November 15, 1777;
ratified and in force March 1, 1781

To all whom these Presents shall come, we the undersigned Delegates of the States affixed to our Names, send greeting. Whereas the Delegates of the United States of America, in Congress assembled, did, on the fifteenth day of November, in the Year of Our Lord One thousand Seven Hundred and Seventy seven, and in the Second Year of the Independence of America, agree to certain articles of Confederation and perpetual Union between the States of Newhampshire, Massachusetts-bay, Rhodeisland and Providence Plantations, Connecticut, New-York, New-Jersey, Pennsylvania, Delaware, Maryland, Virginia, North-Carolina, South-Carolina and Georgia in the words following, viz. "Articles of Confederation and perpetual Union between the states of Newhampshire, Massachusettsbay, Rhodeisland and Providence Plantations, Connecticut, New-York, New-Jersey, Pennsylvania, Delaware, Maryland, Virginia, North-Carolina, South-Carolina and Georgia.

Art. I. The Stile of this confederacy shall be "The United States of America."

Art. II. Each state retains its sovereignty, freedom and independence, and every Power, Jurisdiction and right, which is not by this confederation expressly delegated to the United States, in Congress assembled.

Art. III. The said states hereby severally enter into a firm league of friendship with each other, for their common defence, the security of their Liberties, and their mutual and general welfare, binding themselves to assist each other, against all force offered to, or attacks made upon them, or any of them, on account of religion, sovereignty, trade, or any other pretence whatever.

Art. IV. The better to secure and perpetuate mutual friendship and intercourse among the people of the different states in this union, the free inhabitants of each of these states, paupers, vagabonds and fugitives from Justice excepted, shall be entitled to all privileges and immunities of free citizens in the several states; and the people of each state shall have free ingress and regress to and from any other state, and shall enjoy therein all the privileges of trade and commerce, subject to the same duties, impositions and restrictions as the inhabitants thereof respectively, provided that such restriction shall not extend so far as to prevent the removal of property imported into any state, to any other state, of which the Owner is an inhabitant; provided also that no imposition, duties or restriction shall be laid by any state, on the property of the united states, or either of them.

If any Person guilty of, or charged with treason, felony, or other high misdemeanor in any state, shall flee from Justice, and be found in any of the united states, he shall, upon demand of the Governor or executive power, of the state from which he fled, be delivered up and removed to the state having jurisdiction of his offence.

Full faith and credit shall be given in each of these states to the records, acts and judicial proceedings of the courts and magistrates of every other state.

Art. V. For the more convenient management of the general interests of the united states, delegates shall be annually appointed in such manner as the legislature of each state shall direct, to meet in Congress on the first Monday in November, in every year, with a power reserved to each state, to recall its delegates, or any of them, at any time within the year, and to send others in their stead, for the remainder of the Year.

No state shall be represented in Congress by less than two, nor by more than seven Members; and no person shall be capable of being a delegate for more than three years in any term of six years; nor shall any person, being a delegate, be capable of holding any office under the united states, for which he, or another for his benefit receives any salary, fees or emolument of any kind.

Each state shall maintain its own delegates in a meeting of the states, and while they act as members of the committee of the states.

In determining questions in the united states, in Congress assembled, each state shall have one vote.

Freedom of speech and debate in Congress shall not be impeached or questioned in any Court, or place out of Congress, and the members of congress shall be protected in their persons from arrests and imprisonments, during the time of their going to and from, and attendance on congress, except for treason, felony, or breach of the peace.

Art. VI. No state without the Consent of the united states in congress assembled, shall send any embassy to, or receive any embassy from, or enter into any conference, agreement, or alliance or treaty with any King, prince or state; nor shall any person holding any office of profit or trust under the united states, or any of them, accept of any present, emolument, office or title of any kind whatever from any king, prince or foreign state; nor shall the united states in congress assembled, or any of them, grant any title of nobility.

No two or more states shall enter into any treaty, confederation or alliance whatever between them, without the consent of the united states in congress assembled, specifying accurately the purposes for which the same is to be entered into, and how long it shall continue.

No state shall lay any imposts or duties, which may interfere with any stipulations in treaties, entered into by the united states in congress assembled, with any king, prince or state, in pursuance of any treaties already proposed by congress, to the courts of France and Spain.

No vessels of war shall be kept up in time of peace by any state, except such number only, as shall be deemed necessary by the united states in congress assembled, for the defence of such state, or its trade; nor shall any body of forces be kept up by any state, in time of peace, except such number only, as in the judgment of the united states, in congress assembled, shall be deemed requisite to garrison the forts necessary for the defence of such state; but every state shall always keep up a well regulated and disciplined militia, sufficiently armed and accoutred, and shall provide and constantly have ready for use, in public stores, a due number of field pieces and tents, and a proper quantity of arms, ammunition and camp equipage.

No state shall engage in any war without the consent of the united states in congress assembled, unless such state be actually invaded by enemies, or shall have received certain advice of a resolution being formed by some nation of Indians to invade such state, and the danger is so imminent as not to admit of a delay, till the united states in congress asssembled can be consulted; nor shall any state grant commissions to any ships or vessels of war, nor letters of marque or reprisal, except it be after a declaration of war by the united states in congress assembled, and then only against the kingdom or state and the subjects thereof, against which war has been so declared, and under such regulations as shall be established by the united states in congress assembled, unless such state be infested by pirates; in which case vessels of war may be fitted out for that occasion, and kept so long as the danger shall continue, or until the united states in congress assembled shall determine otherwise.

Art. VII. When land-forces are raised by any state for the common defence, all officers of or under the rank of colonel, shall be appointed by the legislature of each state respectively, by whom such forces shall be raised, or in such manner as such state shall direct, and all vacancies shall be filled up by the state which first made the appointment.

Art. VIII. All charges of war, and all other expences that shall be incurred for the common defence or general welfare, and allowed by the united states in congress assembled, shall be defrayed out of a common treasury, which shall be supplied by the several states in proportion to the value of all land within each state, granted to or surveyed for any Person, as such land and the buildings and improvements thereon shall be estimated according to such mode as the united states in congress assembled, shall from time to time direct and appoint.

The taxes for paying that proportion shall be laid and levied by the authority and direction of the legislatures of the several states within the time agreed upon by the united states in congress assembled.

Art. IX. The united states in congress assembled, shall have the sole and exclusive right and power of determining on peace and war, except in the cases mentioned in the sixth article—of sending and receiving ambassadors—entering into treaties and alliances, provided that no treaty of commerce shall be made whereby the legislative power of the respective states shall be restrained from imposing such imposts and duties on foreigners, as their own people are subjected to, or from prohibiting the exportation of any species of goods or commodities whatsoever—of establishing rules for deciding in all cases, what captures on land or water shall be legal, and in what manner prizes taken by land or naval forces in the service of the united states shall be divided or appropriated—of granting letters of marque and reprisal in times of peace—appointing courts for the trial of piracies and felonies committed on the high seas and establishing courts for receiving and determining finally appeals in all cases of captures, provided that no member of congress shall be appointed a judge of any of the said courts.

The united states in congress assembled shall also be the last resort on appeal in all disputes and differences now subsisting or that hereafter may arise between two or more states concerning boundary, jurisdiction or any other cause whatever; which authority shall always be exercised in the manner following. Whenever the legislative or executive authority or lawful agent of any state in controversy with another shall present a petition to congress stating the matter in question and praying for a hearing, notice thereof shall be given by order of congress to the legislative or executive authority of the other state in controversy, and a day assigned for the appearance of the parties by their lawful agents, who shall then be directed to appoint by joint consent, commissioners or judges to constitute a court for hearing and determining the matter in question: but if they cannot agree, congress shall name three persons out of each of the united states, and from the list of such persons each party shall alternately strike out one, the petitioners beginning, until the number shall be reduced to thirteen; and from that number not less than seven, nor more than nine names as congress shall direct, shall in the presence of congress be drawn out by lot, and the persons whose names shall be so drawn or any five of them, shall be commissioners or judges, to hear and finally determine the controversy, so always as a major part of the judges who shall hear the cause shall agree in the determination: and if either party shall neglect to attend at the day appointed, without shewing reasons, which congress shall judge sufficient, or being present shall refuse to strike, the congress shall proceed to nominate three persons out of each state, and the secretary of congress shall strike in behalf of such party absent or refusing; and the judgment and sentence of the court to be appointed, in the manner before prescribed, shall be final and conclusive; and if any of the parties shall refuse to submit to the authority of such court, or to appear to defend their claim or cause, the court shall nevertheless proceed to pronounce sentence, or judgment, which shall in like manner be final and decisive, the judgment or sentence and other proceedings being in either case transmitted to congress, and lodged among the acts of congress for the security of the parties concerned: provided that every commissioner, before he sits in judgment, shall take an oath to be administered by one of the judges of the supreme or superior court of the state, where the cause shall be tried, "well and truly to hear and determine the matter in question, according to the best of his judgment, without favour, affection or hope of reward:" provided also, that no state shall be deprived of territory for the benefit of the united states.

All controversies concerning the private right of soil claimed under different grants of two or more states, whose jurisdictions as they may respect such lands, and the states which passed such grants are adjusted, the said grants or either of them being at the same time claimed to have originated antecedent to such settlement of jurisdiction, shall on the petition of either party to the congress of the united states, be finally determined as near as may be in the same manner as is before prescribed for deciding disputes respecting territorial jurisdiction between different states.

The united states in congress assembled shall also have the sole and exclusive right and power of regulating the alloy and value of coin struck by their own authority, or by that of the respective states—fixing the standard of weights and measures throughout the united states—regulating the trade and managing all affairs with the Indians, not members of any of the states, provided that the legislative right of any state within its own limits be not infringed or violated—establishing and regulating post-offices from one state to another, throughout all the united states, and exacting such postage on the papers passing thro' the same as may be requisite to defray the expences of the said office—appointing all officers of the land forces, in the service of the united states, excepting regimental officers—appointing all the officers of the naval forces, and commissioning all officers whatever in the service of the united states—making rules for the government and regulation of the said land and naval forces, and directing their operations.

The united states in congress assembled shall have authority to appoint a committee, to sit in the recess of congress, to be denominated "A Committee of the States," and to consist of one delegate from each state; and to appoint such other committees and civil officers as may be necessary for managing the general affairs of the united states under their direction—to appoint one of their number to preside, provided that no person be allowed to serve in the office of president more than one year in any term of three years; to ascertain the necessary sums of Money to be raised for the service of the united states, and to appropriate and apply the same for defraying the public expenses—to borrow money, or emit bills on the credit of the united states, transmitting every half year to the respective states an account of the sums of money so borrowed or emitted,—to build and equip a navy—to agree upon the number of land forces, and to make requisitions from each state for its quota, in proportion to the number of white inhabitants in such state; which requisition shall be binding, and thereupon the legislature of each state shall appoint the regimental officers, raise the men and cloath, arm and equip them in a soldier like manner, at the expense of the united states; and the officers and men so cloathed, armed and equipped shall march to the place appointed, and within the time agreed on by the united states in congress assembled: But if the united states in congress assembled shall, on consideration of circumstances judge proper that any state should not raise men, or should raise a smaller number than its quota, and that any other state should raise a greater number of men than the quota thereof, such extra number shall be raised, officered, cloathed, armed and equipped in the same manner as the quota of such state, unless the legislature of such state shall judge that such extra number cannot be safely spared out of the same, in which case they shall raise officer, cloath, arm and equip as many of such extra number as they judge can be safely spared. And the officers and men so cloathed, armed and equipped, shall march to the place appointed, and within the time agreed on by the united states in congress assembled.

The united states in congress assembled shall never engage in a war, nor grant letters of marque and reprisal in time of peace, nor enter into any treaties or alliances, nor coin money, nor regulate the value thereof, nor ascertain the sums and expenses necessary for the defence and welfare of the united states, or any of them, nor emit bills, nor borrow money on the credit of the united states, nor appropriate money, nor agree upon the number of vessels of war, to be built or purchased, or the number of land or sea forces to be raised, nor appoint a commander in chief of the army or navy, unless nine states assent to the same: nor shall a question on any other point, except for adjourning from day to day be determined, unless by the votes of a majority of the united states in congress assembled.

The congress of the united states shall have power to adjourn to any time within the year, and to any place within the united states, so that no period of adjournment be for a longer duration than the space of six Months, and shall publish the Journal of their proceedings monthly, except such parts thereof relating to treaties, alliances or military operations, as in their judgment require secrecy; and the yeas and nays of the delegates of each state on any question shall be entered on the Journal, when it is desired by any delegate; and the delegates of a state, or any of them, at his or their request shall be furnished with a transcript of the said Journal, except such parts as are above excepted, to lay before the legislatures of the several states.

Art. X. The committee of the states, or any nine of them, shall be authorised to execute, in the recess of congress, such of the powers of congress as the united states in congress assembled, by the consent of nine states, shall from time to time think expedient to vest them with; provided that no power be delegated to the said committee, for the exercise of which, by the articles of confederation, the voice of nine states in the congress of the united states assembled is requisite.

Art. XI. Canada acceding to this confederation, and joining in the measures of the united states, shall be admitted into, and entitled to all the advantages of this union: but no other colony shall be admitted into the same, unless such admission be agreed to by nine states.

Art. XII. All bills of credit emitted, monies borrowed and debts contracted by, or under the authority of congress, before the assembling of the united states, in pursuance of the present confederation, shall be deemed and considered as a charge against the united states, for payment and satisfaction whereof the said united states and the public faith are hereby solemnly pledged.

Art. XIII. Every state shall abide by the determinations of the united states in congress assembled, on all questions which by this confederation are submitted to them. And the Articles of this confederation shall be inviolably observed by every state, and the union shall be perpetual; nor shall any alteration at any time hereafter be made in any of them; unless such alteration be agreed to in a congress of the united states, and be afterwards confirmed by the legislatures of every state.

And Whereas it hath pleased the Great Governor of the World to incline the hearts of the legislatures we respectively represent in congress, to approve of, and to authorize us to ratify the said articles of confederation and perpetual union. Know Ye that we the undersigned delegates, by virtue of the power and authority to us given for that purpose, do by these presents, in the name and in behalf of our respective constituents, fully and entirely ratify and confirm each and every of the said articles of confederation and perpetual union, and all and singular the matters and things therein contained: And we do further solemnly plight and engage the faith of our respective constituents, that they shall abide by the determinations of the united states in congress assembled, on all questions, which by the said confederation are submitted to them. And that the articles thereof shall be inviolably observed by the states we respectively represent, and that the union shall be perpetual. In Witness whereof we have hereunto set our hands in Congress. Done at Philadelphia in the state of Pennsylvania the ninth day of July, in the Year of our Lord one Thousand seven Hundred and Seventy-eight, and in the third year of the independence of America.

The Constitution of the United States of America

[PREAMBLE]

We the People of the United States, in Order to form a more perfect Union, establish Justice, insure domestic Tranquility, provide for the common defence, promote the general Welfare, and secure the Blessings of Liberty to ourselves and our Posterity, do ordain and establish this Constitution for the United States of America.

Article I

SECTION 1

[LEGISLATIVE POWERS]

All legislative Powers herein granted shall be vested in a Congress of the United States, which shall consist of a Senate and House of Representatives.

SECTION 2

[HOUSE OF REPRESENTATIVES, HOW CONSTITUTED, POWER OF IMPEACHMENT]

The House of Representatives shall be composed of Members chosen every second Year by the People of the several States, and the Electors in each State shall have the Qualifications requisite for Electors of the most numerous Branch of the State Legislature.

No Person shall be a Representative who shall not have attained to the Age of twenty five Years, and been seven Years a Citizen of the United States, and who shall not, when elected, be an Inhabitant of that State in which he shall be chosen.

Representatives and *direct Taxes*[1] shall be apportioned among the several States which may be included within this Union, according to their respective Numbers, *which shall be determined by adding to the whole Number of free Persons, including those bound to Service for a Term of Years, and excluding Indians not taxed, three fifths of all other Persons.*[2] The actual Enumeration shall be made within three Years after the first Meeting of the Congress of the United States, and within every subsequent Term of ten Years, in such Manner as they shall by Law direct. The Number of Representatives shall not exceed one for every thirty Thousand, but each State shall have at Least one Representative; *and until such enumeration shall be made, the State of New Hampshire shall be entitled to chuse three, Massachusetts eight, Rhode-Island and Providence Plantations one, Connecticut five, New-York six, New Jersey four, Pennsylvania eight, Delaware one, Maryland six, Virginia ten, North Carolina five, South Carolina five, and Georgia three.*[3]

When vacancies happen in the Representation from any State, the Executive Authority thereof shall issue Writs of Election to fill such Vacancies.

The House of Representatives shall chuse their Speaker and other Officers; and shall have the sole Power of Impeachment.

SECTION 3

[THE SENATE, HOW CONSTITUTED, IMPEACHMENT TRIALS]

The Senate of the United States shall be composed of two Senators from each State, *chosen by the Legislature thereof,*[4] for six Years; and each Senator shall have one Vote.

Immediately after they shall be assembled in Consequence of the first Election, they shall be divided as equally as may be into three Classes. The Seats of the Senators of the first Class shall be vacated at the Expiration of the second Year, of the second Class at the Expiration of the fourth Year, and of the third Class at the Expiration of the sixth Year, so that one third may be chosen every second Year; *and if Vacancies happen by Resignation, or otherwise, during the Recess of the Legislature of any State, the Executive thereof may make temporary Appointments until the next Meeting of the Legislature, which shall then fill such Vacancies.*[5]

No Person shall be a Senator who shall not have attained to the Age of thirty Years, and been nine Years a Citizen of the United States, and who shall not, when elected, be an Inhabitant of that State for which he shall be chosen.

The Vice President of the United States shall be President of the Senate, but shall have no Vote, unless they be equally divided.

The Senate shall chuse their other Officers, and also a President pro tempore, in the Absence of the Vice President, or when he shall exercise the Office of President of the United States.

The Senate shall have the sole Power to try all Impeachments. When sitting for that Purpose, they shall be on Oath or Affirmation. When the President of the United States is tried, the Chief Justice shall preside: And no Person shall be convicted without the Concurrence of two thirds of the Members present.

Judgment in Cases of Impeachment shall not extend further than to removal from Office, and disqualification to hold and enjoy any Office of honor, Trust or Profit under the United States: but the Party convicted shall nevertheless be liable and subject to Indictment, Trial, Judgment and Punishment, according to Law.

SECTION 4

[ELECTION OF SENATORS AND REPRESENTATIVES]

The Times, Places and Manner of holding Elections for Senators and Representatives, shall be prescribed in each State by the Legislature thereof; but the Congress may at any time by Law make or alter such Regulations, except as to the Places of chusing Senators.

The Congress shall assemble at least once in every Year, and such Meeting shall be on the first Monday in December, unless they shall by Law appoint a different Day.[6]

SECTION 5

[QUORUM, JOURNALS, MEETINGS, ADJOURNMENTS]

Each House shall be the Judge of the Elections, Returns and Qualifications of its own Members, and a Majority of each shall constitute a Quorum to do Business; but a smaller Number may adjourn from day to day, and may be authorized to compel the Attendance of absent Members, in such Manner, and under such Penalties as each House may provide.

Each House may determine the Rules of its Proceedings, punish its Members for disorderly Behaviour, and, with the Concurrence of two thirds, expel a Member.

Each House shall keep a Journal of its Proceedings, and from time to time publish the same, excepting such Parts as may in their Judgment require Secrecy; and the Yeas and Nays of the Members of either House on any questions shall, at the Desire of one fifth of those Present, be entered on the Journal.

Neither House, during the Session of Congress, shall, without the Consent of the other, adjourn for more than three days, nor to any other Place than that in which the two Houses shall be sitting.

---

[1]Modified by Sixteenth Amendment.
[2]Modified by Fourteenth Amendment.
[3]Temporary provision.
[4]Modified by Seventeenth Amendment.
[5]Modified by Seventeenth Amendment.
[6]Modified by Twentieth Amendment.

SECTION 6
[COMPENSATION, PRIVILEGES, DISABILITIES]

The Senators and Representatives shall receive a Compensation for their Services, to be ascertained by Law, and paid out of the Treasury of the United States. They shall in all Cases, except Treason, Felony and Breach of the Peace, be privileged from Arrest during their Attendance at the Session of their respective Houses, and in going to and returning from the same; and for any Speech or Debate in either House, they shall not be questioned in any other Place.

No Senator or Representative shall, during the Time for which he was elected, be appointed to any civil Office under the Authority of the United States, which shall have been created, or the Emoluments whereof shall have been encreased during such time; and no Person holding any Office under the United States, shall be a Member of either House during his Continuance in Office.

SECTION 7
[PROCEDURE IN PASSING BILLS AND RESOLUTIONS]

All Bills for raising Revenue shall originate in the House of Representatives; but the Senate may propose or concur with Amendments as on other Bills.

Every Bill which shall have passed the House of Representatives and the Senate, shall, before it become a Law, be presented to the President of the United States: If he approve he shall sign it, but if not he shall return it, with his Objections to that House in which it shall have originated, who shall enter the Objections at large on their Journal, and proceed to reconsider it. If after such Reconsideration two thirds of that House shall agree to pass the Bill, it shall be sent, together with the Objections, to the other House, by which it shall likewise be reconsidered, and if approved by two thirds of that House, it shall become a Law. But in all such Cases the Votes of both Houses shall be determined by yeas and Nays, and the Names of the Persons voting for and against the Bill shall be entered on the Journal of each House respectively. If any Bill shall not be returned by the President within ten Days (Sundays excepted) after it shall have been presented to him, the Same shall be a Law, in like Manner as if he had signed it, unless the Congress by their Adjournment prevent its Return, in which Case it shall not be a Law.

Every Order, Resolution, or Vote to which the Concurrence of the Senate and House of Representatives may be necessary (except on a question of Adjournment) shall be presented to the President of the United States; and before the Same shall take Effect, shall be approved by him, or being disapproved by him, shall be repassed by two thirds of the Senate and House of Representatives, according to the Rules and Limitations prescribed in the Case of a Bill.

SECTION 8
[POWERS OF CONGRESS]

The Congress shall have Power

To lay and collect Taxes, Duties, Imposts and Excises, to pay the Debts and provide for the common Defence and general Welfare of the United States; but all Duties, Imposts and Excises shall be uniform throughout the United States;

To borrow Money on the credit of the United States;

To regulate Commerce with foreign Nations, and among the several States, and with the Indian Tribes;

To establish an uniform Rule of Naturalization, and uniform Laws on the subject of Bankruptcies throughout the United States;

To coin Money, regulate the Value thereof, and of foreign Coin, and fix the Standard of Weights and Measures;

To provide for the Punishment of counterfeiting the Securities and current Coin of the United States;

To establish Post Offices and post Roads;

To promote the Progress of Science and useful Arts, by securing for limited Times to Authors and Inventors the exclusive Right to their respective Writings and Discoveries;

To constitute Tribunals inferior to the supreme Court;

To define and punish Piracies and Felonies committed on the high Seas, and Offences against the Law of Nations;

To declare War, grant Letters of Marque and Reprisal, and make Rules concerning Captures on Land and Water;

To raise and support Armies, but no Appropriation of Money to that Use shall be for a longer Term than two Years;

To provide and maintain a Navy;

To make Rules for the Government and Regulation of the land and naval Forces;

To provide for calling forth the Militia to execute the Laws of the Union, suppress Insurrections and repel Invasions;

To provide for organizing, arming, and disciplining, the Militia, and for governing such Part of them as may be employed in the Service of the United States, reserving to the States respectively, the Appointment of the Officers, and the Authority of training the Militia according to the discipline prescribed by Congress;

To exercise exclusive Legislation in all Cases whatsoever, over such District (not exceeding ten Miles square) as may, by Cession of particular States, and the Acceptance of Congress, become the Seat of the Government of the United States, and to exercise like Authority over all Places purchased by the Consent of the Legislature of the State in which the Same shall be, for the Erection of Forts, Magazines, Arsenals, dock-Yards, and other needful Buildings;—And

To make all Laws which shall be necessary and proper for carrying into Execution the foregoing Powers, and all other Powers vested by this Constitution in the Government of the United States, or in any Department or Officer thereof.

SECTION 9
[SOME RESTRICTIONS ON FEDERAL POWER]

The Migration or Importation of such Persons as any of the States now existing shall think proper to admit, shall not be prohibited by the Congress prior to the Year one thousand eight hundred and eight, but a Tax or duty may be imposed on such Importation, not exceeding ten dollars for each Person.[7]

The Privilege of the Writ of Habeas Corpus shall not be suspended, unless when in Cases of Rebellion or Invasion the public Safety may require it.

No Bill of Attainder or ex post facto Law shall be passed.

No Capitation, or other direct, Tax shall be laid, unless in Proportion to the Census or Enumeration herein before directed to be taken.[8]

No Tax or Duty shall be laid on Articles exported from any State.

No Preference shall be given by any Regulation of Commerce or Revenue to the Ports of one State over those of another; nor shall Vessels bound to, or from, one State, be obliged to enter, clear, or pay Duties in another.

No Money shall be drawn from the Treasury, but in Consequence of Appropriations made by Law; and a regular Statement and Account of the Receipts and Expenditures of all public Money shall be published from time to time.

No Title of Nobility shall be granted by the United States: And no Person holding any Office of Profit or Trust under them, shall, without the Consent of the Congress, accept of any present, Emolument, Office, or Title, of any kind whatever, from any King, Prince, or foreign State.

---

[7]Temporary provision.
[8]Modified by Sixteenth Amendment.

SECTION 10

[RESTRICTIONS UPON POWERS OF STATES]

No State shall enter into any Treaty, Alliance, or Confederation; grant Letters of Marque and Reprisal; coin Money; emit Bills of Credit; make any Thing but gold and silver Coin a Tender in Payment of Debts; pass any Bill of Attainder, ex post facto Law, or Law impairing the Obligation of Contracts, or grant any Title of Nobility.

No State shall, without the Consent of the Congress, lay any Imposts or Duties on Imports or Exports, except what may be absolutely necessary for executing its inspection Laws: and the net Produce of all Duties and Imposts, laid by any State on Imports or Exports, shall be for the Use of the Treasury of the United States; and all such Laws shall be subject to the Revision and Control of the Congress.

No State shall, without the Consent of Congress, lay any Duty of Tonnage, keep Troops, or Ships of War in time of Peace, enter into any Agreement or Compact with another State, or with a foreign Power, or engage in War, unless actually invaded, or in such imminent Danger as will not admit of delay.

Article II

SECTION 1

[EXECUTIVE POWER, ELECTION, QUALIFICATIONS OF THE PRESIDENT]

The executive Power shall be vested in a President of the United States of America. *He shall hold his Office during the Term of four Years, and, together with the Vice President, chosen for the same Term, be elected, as follows*[9]

Each State shall appoint, in such Manner as the Legislature thereof may direct, a Number of Electors, equal to the whole Number of Senators and Representatives to which the State may be entitled in the Congress: but no Senator or Representative, or Person holding an Office of Trust or Profit under the United States, shall be appointed an Elector.

The electors shall meet in their respective States, and vote by ballot for two Persons, of whom one at least shall not be an Inhabitant of the same State with themselves. And they shall make a List of all the Persons voted for, and of the Number of Votes for each; which List they shall sign and certify, and transmit sealed to the Seat of the Government of the United States, directed to the President of the Senate. The President of the Senate shall, in the Presence of the Senate and House of Representatives, open all the Certificates, and the Votes shall then be counted. The Person having the greatest Number of Votes shall be the President, if such Number be a Majority of the whole Number of Electors appointed; and if there be more than one who have such Majority, and have an equal Number of Votes, then the House of Representatives shall immediately chuse by Ballot one of them for President; and if no Person have a Majority, then from the five highest on the List the said House shall in like Manner chuse the President. But in chusing the President, the Votes shall be taken by States, the Representation from each State having one Vote; A quorum for this Purpose shall consist of a Member or Members from two thirds of the States, and a Majority of all the States shall be necessary to a Choice. In every Case, after the Choice of the President, the person having the greatest Number of Votes of the Electors shall be the Vice President. But if there should remain two or more who have equal Votes, the Senate shall chuse from them by Ballot the Vice President.[10]

The Congress may determine the Time of chusing the Electors, and the Day on which they shall give their Votes; which Day shall be the same throughout the United States.

---

[9]Number of terms limited to two by Twenty-second Amendment.
[10]Modified by the Twelfth and Twentieth Amendments.

No Person except a natural born Citizen, or a Citizen of the United States, at the time of the Adoption of this Constitution, shall be eligible to the Office of President; neither shall any Person be eligible to that Office who shall not have attained to the Age of thirty five Years, and been fourteen Years a Resident within the United States.

In Case of the Removal of the President from Office, or his Death, Resignation, or Inability to discharge the Powers and Duties of the said Office, the Same shall devolve on the Vice President, and the Congress may by Law provide for the Case of Removal, Death, Resignation or Inability, both of the President and Vice President, declaring what Officer shall then act as President, and such Officer shall act accordingly, until the Disability be removed, or a President shall be elected.

The President shall, at stated Times, receive for his Services, a Compensation, which shall neither be increased nor diminished during the Period for which he shall have been elected, and he shall not receive within that Period any other Emolument from the United States, or any of them.

Before he enter on the Execution of his Office, he shall take the following Oath or Affirmation:—"I do solemnly swear (or affirm) that I will faithfully execute the Office of President of the United States, and will to the best of my Ability, preserve, protect and defend the Constitution of the United States."

SECTION 2

[POWERS OF THE PRESIDENT]

The President shall be Commander in Chief of the Army and Navy of the United States, and of the Militia of the several States, when called into the actual Service of the United States; he may require the Opinion, in writing, of the principal Officer in each of the executive Departments, upon any Subject relating to the Duties of their respective Offices, and he shall have Power to grant Reprieves and Pardons for Offences against the United States, except in Cases of Impeachment.

He shall have Power, by and with the Advice and Consent of the Senate, to make Treaties, provided two thirds of the Senators present concur; and he shall nominate, and by and with the Advice and Consent of the Senate, shall appoint Ambassadors, other public Ministers and Consuls, Judges of the supreme Court, and all other Officers of the United States, whose Appointments are not herein otherwise provided for, and which shall be established by Law: but the Congress may by Law vest the Appointment of such inferior Officers, as they think proper, in the President alone, in the Courts of Law, or in the Heads of Departments.

The President shall have Power to fill up all Vacancies that may happen during the Recess of the Senate, by granting Commissions which shall expire at the End of their next Session.

SECTION 3

[POWERS AND DUTIES OF THE PRESIDENT]

He shall from time to time give to the Congress Information of the State of the Union, and recommend to their Consideration such Measures as he shall judge necessary and expedient; he may, on extraordinary Occasions, convene both Houses, or either of them, and in Case of Disagreement between them, with Respect to the Time of Adjournment, he may adjourn them to such Time as he shall think proper; he shall receive Ambassadors and other public Ministers; he shall take Care that the Laws be faithfully executed, and shall Commission all the Officers of the United States.

SECTION 4

[IMPEACHMENT]

The President, Vice President and all civil Officers of the United States, shall be removed from Office on Impeachment for, and Conviction of, Treason, Bribery, or other high Crimes and Misdemeanors.

Article III

SECTION 1
[JUDICIAL POWER, TENURE OF OFFICE]

The judicial Power of the United States, shall be vested in one supreme Court, and in such inferior Courts as the Congress may from time to time ordain and establish. The Judges, both of the supreme and inferior Courts, shall hold their Offices during good Behaviour, and shall, at stated Times, receive for their Services, a Compensation, which shall not be diminished during their Continuance in Office.

SECTION 2
[JURISDICTION]

The judicial Power shall extend to all Cases, in Law and Equity, arising under this Constitution, the Laws of the United States, and Treaties made, or which shall be made, under their Authority;—to all Cases affecting Ambassadors, other public Ministers and Consuls;—to all Cases of admiralty and maritime Jurisdiction;—to Controversies to which the United States shall be a Party;—to Controversies between two or more States;—*between a State and Citizens of another State;*—between Citizens of different States,—between Citizens of the same State claiming Lands under Grants of different States, *and between a State,* or the Citizens thereof, *and foreign States, Citizens or Subjects.*[11]

In all Cases affecting Ambassadors, other public Ministers and Consuls, and those in which a State shall be Party, the supreme Court shall have original Jurisdiction. In all the other Cases before mentioned, the supreme Court shall have appellate Jurisdiction, both as to Law and Fact, with such Exceptions, and under such Regulations as the Congress shall make.

The Trial of all Crimes, except in Cases of Impeachment, shall be by Jury; and such Trial shall be held in the State where the said Crimes shall have been committed; but when not committed within any State, the Trial shall be at such Place or Places as the Congress may by Law have directed.

SECTION 3
[TREASON, PROOF, AND PUNISHMENT]

Treason against the United States, shall consist only in levying War against them, or in adhering to their Enemies, giving them Aid and Comfort. No Person shall be convicted of Treason unless on the Testimony of two Witnesses to the same overt Act, or on Confession in open Court.

The Congress shall have Power to declare the Punishment of Treason, but no Attainder of Treason shall work Corruption of Blood, or Forfeiture except during the Life of the Person attainted.

Article IV

SECTION 1
[FAITH AND CREDIT AMONG STATES]

Full Faith and Credit shall be given in each State to the public Acts, Records, and judicial Proceedings of every other State. And the Congress may by general Laws prescribe the Manner in which such Acts, Records and Proceedings shall be proved, and the Effect thereof.

SECTION 2
[PRIVILEGES AND IMMUNITIES, FUGITIVES]

The Citizens of each State shall be entitled to all Privileges and Immunities of Citizens in the several States.

A Person charged in any State with Treason, Felony or other Crime, who shall flee from Justice, and be found in another State, shall on Demand of the executive Authority of the State from which he fled, be delivered up, to be removed to the State having Jurisdiction of the Crime.

No person held to Service or Labour in one State, under the Laws thereof, escaping into another, shall, in Consequence of any Law or Regulation therein, be discharged from such Service or Labour, but shall be delivered up on Claim of the Party to whom such Service or Labour may be due.[12]

SECTION 3
[ADMISSION OF NEW STATES]

New States may be admitted by the Congress into this Union; but no new State shall be formed or erected within the Jurisdiction of any other State; nor any State be formed by the Junction of two or more States, or Parts of States, without the Consent of the Legislatures of the States concerned as well as of the Congress.

The Congress shall have Power to dispose of and make all needful Rules and Regulations respecting the Territory or other Property belonging to the United States; and nothing in this Constitution shall be so construed as to Prejudice any Claims of the United States, or of any particular State.

SECTION 4
[GUARANTEE OF REPUBLICAN GOVERNMENT]

The United States shall guarantee to every State in this Union a Republican Form of Government, and shall protect each of them against Invasion; and on Application of the Legislature, or of the Executive (when the Legislature cannot be convened), against domestic Violence.

Article V
[AMENDMENT OF THE CONSTITUTION]

The Congress, whenever two thirds of both Houses shall deem it necessary, shall propose Amendments to this Constitution, or, on the Application of the Legislatures of two thirds of the several States, shall call a Convention for proposing Amendments, which, in either Case, shall be valid to all Intents and Purposes, as Part of this Constitution, when ratified by the Legislatures of three fourths of the several States, or by Conventions in three fourths thereof, as the one or the other Mode of Ratification may be proposed by the Congress; *Provided that no Amendment which may be made prior to the Year One thousand eight hundred and eight shall in any Manner affect the first and fourth Clauses in the Ninth Section of the first Article;* and that no State, without its Consent, shall be deprived of its equal Suffrage in the Senate.

Article VI
[DEBTS, SUPREMACY, OATH]

All Debts contracted and Engagements entered into, before the Adoption of this Constitution, shall be as valid against the United States under this Constitution, as under the Confederation.

---

[11]Modified by the Eleventh Amendment.

[12]Repealed by the Thirteenth Amendment.

This Constitution, and the Laws of the United States which shall be made in Pursuance thereof; and all Treaties made, or which shall be made, under the Authority of the United States, shall be the supreme Law of the Land; and the Judges in every State shall be bound thereby, any Thing in the Constitution or Laws of any State to the Contrary notwithstanding.

The Senators and Representatives before mentioned, and the Members of the several State Legislatures, and all executive and judicial Officers, both of the United States and of the several States, shall be bound by Oath or Affirmation, to support this Constitution; but no religious Test shall be required as a Qualification to any Office or public Trust under the United States.

Article VII

[RATIFICATION AND ESTABLISHMENT]

The Ratification of the Conventions of nine States, shall be sufficient for the Establishment of this Constitution between the States so ratifying the Same.

Done in Convention by the Unanimous Consent of the States present the Seventeenth Day of September in the Year of our Lord one thousand seven hundred and Eighty seven and of the Independence of the United States of America the Twelfth. *In Witness* whereof We have hereunto subscribed our Names,

G:⁰ WASHINGTON—
Presidt. and deputy from Virginia

NEW HAMPSHIRE
John Langdon
Nicholas Gilman

MASSACHUSETTS
Nathaniel Gorham
Rufus King

CONNECTICUT
Wm. Saml. Johnson
Roger Sherman

NEW YORK
Alexander Hamilton

NEW JERSEY
Wil: Livingston
David Brearley
Wm. Paterson
Jona: Dayton

PENNSYLVANIA
B Franklin
Thomas Mifflin
Robt. Morris
Geo. Clymer
Thos. FitzSimons
Jared Ingersoll
James Wilson
Gouv Morris

DELAWARE
Geo: Read
Gunning Bedford jun
John Dickinson
Richard Bassett
Jaco: Broom

MARYLAND
James McHenry
Dan of St Thos. Jenifer
Danl. Carroll

VIRGINIA
John Blair—
James Madison Jr.

NORTH CAROLINA
Wm. Blount
Richd. Dobbs Spaight
Hu Williamson

SOUTH CAROLINA
J. Rutledge
Charles Cotesworth Pinckney
Charles Pinckney
Pierce Butler

GEORGIA
William Few
Abr Baldwin

Amendments to the Constitution

Proposed by Congress and Ratified by the Legislatures of the
Several States, Pursuant to Article V of the Original Constitution.

Amendments I–X, known as the Bill of Rights, were proposed by Congress on September 25, 1789, and ratified on December 15, 1791.

Amendment I
[FREEDOM OF RELIGION, OF SPEECH, AND OF THE PRESS]

Congress shall make no law respecting an establishment of religion, or prohibiting the free exercise thereof; or abridging the freedom of speech, or of the press; or the right of the people peaceably to assemble, and to petition the Government for a redress of grievances.

Amendment II
[RIGHT TO KEEP AND BEAR ARMS]

A well regulated Militia, being necessary to the security of a free State, the right of the people to keep and bear Arms, shall not be infringed.

Amendment III
[QUARTERING OF SOLDIERS]

No Soldier shall, in time of peace be quartered in any house, without the consent of the Owner, nor in time of war, but in a manner to be prescribed by law.

Amendment IV
[SECURITY FROM UNWARRANTABLE SEARCH AND SEIZURE]

The right of the people to be secure in their persons, houses, papers, and effects, against unreasonable searches and seizures, shall not be violated, and no Warrants shall issue, but upon probable cause, supported by Oath or affirmation, and particularly describing the place to be searched, and the persons or things to be seized.

Amendment V
[RIGHTS OF ACCUSED PERSONS IN CRIMINAL PROCEEDINGS]

No person shall be held to answer for a capital, or otherwise infamous crime, unless on a presentment or indictment of a Grand Jury, except in cases arising in the land or naval forces, or in the Militia, when in actual service in time of War or in public danger; nor shall any person be subject for the same offence to be twice put in jeopardy of life or limb; nor shall be compelled in any criminal case to be a witness against himself, nor be deprived of life, liberty, or property, without due process of law; nor shall private property be taken for public use, without just compensation.

Amendment VI
[RIGHT TO SPEEDY TRIAL, WITNESSES, ETC.]

In all criminal prosecutions, the accused shall enjoy the right to a speedy and public trial, by an impartial jury of the State and district wherein the crime shall have been committed, which district shall have been previously ascertained by law, and to be informed of the nature and cause of the accusation; to be confronted with the witnesses against him; to have compulsory process for obtaining witnesses in his favor, and to have the Assistance of Counsel for his defence.

Amendment VII
[TRIAL BY JURY IN CIVIL CASES]

In suits at common law, where the value in controversy shall exceed twenty dollars, the right of trial by jury shall be preserved, and no fact tried by a jury, shall be otherwise reexamined in any Court of the United States, than according to the rules of the common law.

Amendment VIII
[BAILS, FINES, PUNISHMENTS]

Excessive bail shall not be required, nor excessive fines imposed, nor cruel and unusual punishments inflicted.

Amendment IX
[RESERVATION OF RIGHTS OF PEOPLE]

The enumeration in the Constitution, of certain rights, shall not be construed to deny or disparage others retained by the people.

Amendment X
[POWERS RESERVED TO STATES OR PEOPLE]

The powers not delegated to the United States by the Constitution, nor prohibited by it to the States, are reserved to the States respectively, or to the people.

Amendment XI
[*Proposed by Congress on March 4, 1794;
declared ratified on January 8, 1798.*]
[RESTRICTION OF JUDICIAL POWER]

The Judicial power of the United States shall not be construed to extend to any suit in law or equity, commenced or prosecuted against one of the United States by Citizens of another State, or by Citizens or Subjects of any Foreign State.

Amendment XII
[*Proposed by Congress on December 9, 1803;
declared ratified on September 25, 1804.*]
[ELECTION OF PRESIDENT AND VICE PRESIDENT]

The Electors shall meet in their respective states and vote by ballot for President and Vice-President, one of whom, at least, shall not be an inhabitant of the same state with themselves; they shall name in their ballots the person voted for as President, and in distinct ballots the person voted for as Vice-President, and they shall make distinct lists of all persons voted for as President, and of all persons voted for as Vice-President, and of the number of votes for each, which lists they shall sign and certify, and transmit sealed to the seat of the government of the United States, directed to the President of the Senate;—the President of the Senate shall, in presence of the Senate and House of Representatives, open all the certificates and the votes shall then be counted;—The person having the greatest number of votes for President, shall be the President, if such number be a majority of the whole number of Electors appointed; and if no person have such majority, then from the persons having the highest numbers not exceeding three on the list of those voted for as

President, the House of Representatives shall choose immediately, by ballot, the President. But in choosing the President, the votes shall be taken by states, the representation from each state having one vote; a quorum for this purpose shall consist of a member or members from two-thirds of the states, and a majority of all the states shall be necessary to a choice. And if the House of Representatives shall not choose a President whenever the right of choice shall devolve upon them, before the fourth day of March next following, then the Vice-President shall act as President, as in the case of the death or other constitutional disability of the President.—The person having the greatest number of votes as Vice-President, shall be the Vice-President, if such number be a majority of the whole number of Electors appointed, and if no person have a majority, then from the two highest numbers on the list, the Senate shall choose the Vice-President; a quorum for the purpose shall consist of two-thirds of the whole number of Senators, and a majority of the whole number shall be necessary to a choice. But no person constitutionally ineligible to the office of President shall be eligible to that of Vice-President of the United States.

Amendment XIII

[*Proposed by Congress on January 31, 1865;*
declared ratified on December 18, 1865.]

SECTION 1
[ABOLITION OF SLAVERY]

Neither slavery nor involuntary servitude, except as a punishment for crime whereof the party shall have been duly convicted, shall exist within the United States, or any place subject to their jurisdiction.

SECTION 2
[POWER TO ENFORCE THIS ARTICLE]

Congress shall have power to enforce this article by appropriate legislation.

Amendment XIV

[*Proposed by Congress on June 13, 1866;*
declared ratified on July 28, 1868.]

SECTION 1
[CITIZENSHIP RIGHTS NOT TO BE ABRIDGED BY STATES]

All persons born or naturalized in the United States, and subject to the jurisdiction thereof, are citizens of the United States and of the State wherein they reside. No State shall make or enforce any law which shall abridge the privileges or immunities of citizens of the United States; nor shall any State deprive any person of life, liberty, or property, without due process of law; nor deny to any person within its jurisdiction the equal protection of the laws.

SECTION 2
[APPORTIONMENT OF REPRESENTATIVES IN CONGRESS]

Representatives shall be apportioned among the several States according to their respective numbers, counting the whole number of persons in each State, excluding Indians not taxed. But when the right to vote at any election for the choice of electors for President and Vice-President of the United States, Representatives in Congress, the Executive and Judicial officers of a State, or the members of the Legislature thereof, is denied to any of the male inhabitants of such State, being twenty-one years of age, and citizens of the United States, or in any way abridged, except for participation in rebellion, or other crime, the basis of representation therein shall be reduced in the proportion which the number

of such male citizens shall bear to the whole number of male citizens twenty-one years of age in such State.

SECTION 3
[PERSONS DISQUALIFIED FROM HOLDING OFFICE]

No person shall be a Senator or Representative in Congress, or elector of President and Vice-President, or hold any office, civil or military, under the United States, or under any State, who, having previously taken an oath, as a member of Congress, or as an officer of the United States, or as a member of any State legislature, or as an executive or judicial officer of any State, to support the Constitution of the United States, shall have engaged in insurrection or rebellion against the same, or given aid or comfort to the enemies thereof. But Congress may by a vote of two-thirds of each House, remove such disability.

SECTION 4
[WHAT PUBLIC DEBTS ARE VALID]

The validity of the public debt of the United States, authorized by law, including debts incurred for payment of pensions and bounties for services in suppressing insurrection or rebellion, shall not be questioned. But neither the United States nor any State shall assume or pay any debt or obligation incurred in aid of insurrection or rebellion against the United States, or any claim for the loss or emancipation of any slave; but all such debts, obligations and claims shall be held illegal and void.

SECTION 5
[POWER TO ENFORCE THIS ARTICLE]

The Congress shall have power to enforce, by appropriate legislation, the provisions of this article.

Amendment XV

[*Proposed by Congress on February 26, 1869;*
declared ratified on March 30, 1870.]

SECTION 1
[NEGRO SUFFRAGE]

The right of citizens of the United States to vote shall not be denied or abridged by the United States or by any State on account of race, color, or previous condition of servitude.

SECTION 2
[POWER TO ENFORCE THIS ARTICLE]

The Congress shall have power to enforce this article by appropriate legislation.

Amendment XVI

[*Proposed by Congress on July 2, 1909; declared*
ratified on February 25, 1913.]
[AUTHORIZING INCOME TAXES]

The Congress shall have power to lay and collect taxes on incomes, from whatever source derived, without apportionment among the several States, and without regard to any census or enumeration.

Amendment XVII

[*Proposed by Congress on May 13, 1912; declared ratified on May 31, 1913.*]
[POPULAR ELECTION OF SENATORS]

The Senate of the United States shall be composed of two Senators from each State, elected by the people thereof, for six years; and each Senator shall have one vote. The electors in each State shall have the qualifications requisite for electors of the most numerous branch of the State legislatures.

When vacancies happen in the representation of any State in the Senate, the executive authority of such State shall issue writs of election to fill such vacancies: *Provided,* That the legislature of any State may empower the executive thereof to make temporary appointments until the people fill the vacancies by election as the legislature may direct.

This amendment shall not be so construed as to affect the election or term of any Senator chosen before it becomes valid as part of the Constitution.

Amendment XVIII

[*Proposed by Congress December 18, 1917; declared ratified on January 29, 1919.*]

SECTION 1

[NATIONAL LIQUOR PROHIBITION]

After one year from the ratification of this article the manufacture, sale, or transportation of intoxicating liquors within, the importation thereof into, or the exportation thereof from the United States and all territory subject to the jurisdiction thereof for beverage purposes is hereby prohibited.

SECTION 2

[POWER TO ENFORCE THIS ARTICLE]

The Congress and the several States shall have concurrent power to enforce this article by appropriate legislation.

SECTION 3

[RATIFICATION WITHIN SEVEN YEARS]

This article shall be inoperative unless it shall have been ratified as an amendment to the Constitution by the legislatures of the several States, as provided in the Constitution, within seven years from the date of the submission hereof to the States by the Congress.[1]

Amendment XIX

[*Proposed by Congress on June 4, 1919; declared ratified on August 26, 1920.*]

[WOMAN SUFFRAGE]

The right of citizens of the United States to vote shall not be denied or abridged by the United States or by any State on account of sex.

Congress shall have power to enforce this article by appropriate legislation.

Amendment XX

[*Proposed by Congress on March 2, 1932; declared ratified on February 6, 1933.*]

SECTION 1

[TERMS OF OFFICE]

The terms of the President and Vice President shall end at noon on the 20th day of January, and the terms of Senators and Representatives at noon on the 3d day of January, of the years in which such terms would have ended if this article had not been ratified; and the terms of their successors shall then begin.

---

[1]Repealed by the Twenty-first Amendment.

SECTION 2

[TIME OF CONVENING CONGRESS]

The Congress shall assemble at least once in every year, and such meeting shall begin at noon on the 3d day of January, unless they shall by law appoint a different day.

SECTION 3

[DEATH OF PRESIDENT-ELECT]

If, at the time fixed for the beginning of the term of the President, the President elect shall have died, the Vice President elect shall become President. If a President shall not have been chosen before the time fixed for the beginning of his term, or if the President elect shall have failed to qualify, then the Vice President elect shall act as President until a President shall have qualified; and the Congress may by law provide for the case wherein neither a President elect nor a Vice President elect shall have qualified, declaring who shall then act as President, or the manner in which one who is to act shall be selected, and such person shall act accordingly until a President or Vice President shall have qualified.

SECTION 4

[ELECTION OF THE PRESIDENT]

The Congress may by law provide for the case of the death of any of the persons from whom the House of Representatives may choose a President whenever the right of choice shall have devolved upon them, and for the case of the death of any of the persons from whom the Senate may choose a Vice President whenever the right of choice shall have devolved upon them.

SECTION 5

[AMENDMENT TAKES EFFECT]

Sections 1 and 2 shall take effect on the 15th day of October following the ratification of this article.

SECTION 6

[RATIFICATION WITHIN SEVEN YEARS]

This article shall be inoperative unless it shall have been ratified as an amendment to the Constitution by the legislatures of three-fourths of the several States within seven years from the date of its submission.

Amendment XXI

[*Proposed by Congress on February 20, 1933; declared ratified on December 5, 1933.*]

SECTION 1

[NATIONAL LIQUOR PROHIBITION REPEALED]

The eighteenth article of amendment to the Constitution of the United States is hereby repealed.

SECTION 2

[TRANSPORTATION OF LIQUOR INTO "DRY" STATES]

The transportation or importation into any State, Territory, or Possession of the United States for delivery or use therein of intoxicating liquors, in violation of the laws thereof, is hereby prohibited.

SECTION 3

[RATIFICATION WITHIN SEVEN YEARS]

This article shall be inoperative unless it shall have been ratified as an amendment to the Constitution by conventions in the several States, as provided in the Constitution, within seven years from the date of the submission hereof to the States by the Congress.

Amendment XXII

[*Proposed by Congress on March 21, 1947;
declared ratified on February 27, 1951.*]

SECTION 1

[TENURE OF PRESIDENT LIMITED]

No person shall be elected to the office of President more than twice, and no person who has held the office of President or acted as President, for more than two years of a term to which some other person was elected President shall be elected to the office of the President more than once. But this Article shall not apply to any person holding the office of President when this Article was proposed by the Congress, and shall not prevent any person who may be holding the office of President, or acting as President, during the term within which this Article becomes operative from holding the office of President or acting as President during the remainder of such term.

SECTION 2

[RATIFICATION WITHIN SEVEN YEARS]

This article shall be inoperative unless it shall have been ratified as an amendment to the Constitution by the legislatures of three-fourths of the several States within seven years from the date of its submission to the States by the Congress.

Amendment XXIII

[*Proposed by Congress on June 16, 1960; declared
ratified on March 29, 1961.*]

SECTION 1

[ELECTORAL COLLEGE VOTES FOR THE DISTRICT OF COLUMBIA]

The District constituting the seat of Government of the United States shall appoint in such manner as the Congress may direct:

A number of electors of President and Vice President equal to the whole number of Senators and Representatives in Congress to which the District would be entitled if it were a State, but in no event more than the least populous State; they shall be in addition to those appointed by the States, but they shall be considered, for the purposes of the election of President and Vice President, to be electors appointed by a State; and they shall meet in the District and perform such duties as provided by the twelfth article of amendment.

SECTION 2

[POWER TO ENFORCE THIS ARTICLE]

The Congress shall have power to enforce this article by appropriate legislation.

Amendment XXIV

[*Proposed by Congress on August 27, 1962;
declared ratified on January 23, 1964.*]

SECTION 1

[ANTI-POLL TAX]

The right of citizens of the United States to vote in any primary or other election for President or Vice President, for electors for President or Vice President, or for Senator or Representative of Congress, shall not be denied or abridged by the United States or any State by reason of failure to pay any poll tax or other tax.

SECTION 2

[POWER TO ENFORCE THIS ARTICLE]

The Congress shall have power to enforce this article by appropriate legislation.

Amendment XXV

[*Proposed by Congress on July 6, 1965; declared
ratified on February 10, 1967.*]

SECTION 1

[VICE PRESIDENT TO BECOME PRESIDENT]

In case of the removal of the President from office or his death or resignation, the Vice President shall become President.

SECTION 2

[CHOICE OF A NEW VICE PRESIDENT]

Whenever there is a vacancy in the office of the Vice President, the President shall nominate a Vice President who shall take the office upon confirmation by a majority vote of both houses of Congress.

SECTION 3

[PRESIDENT MAY DECLARE OWN DISABILITY]

Whenever the President transmits to the President pro tempore of the Senate and the Speaker of the House of Representatives his written declaration that he is unable to discharge the powers and duties of his office, and until he transmits to them a written declaration to the contrary, such powers and duties shall be discharged by the Vice President as Acting President.

SECTION 4

[ALTERNATE PROCEDURES TO DECLARE AND TO END
PRESIDENTIAL DISABILITY]

Whenever the Vice President and a majority of either the principal officers of the executive departments, or of such other body as Congress may by law provide, transmit to the President pro tempore of the Senate and the Speaker of the House of Representatives their written declaration that the President is unable to discharge the powers and duties of his office, the Vice President shall immediately assume the powers and duties of the office as Acting President.

Thereafter, when the President transmits to the President pro tempore of the Senate and the Speaker of the House of Representatives his written declaration that no inability exists, he shall resume the powers and duties of his office unless the Vice President and a majority of either the principal officers of the executive department, or of such other body as Congress may by law provide, transmit within four days to the President pro tempore of the Senate and the Speaker of the House of Representatives their written declaration that the President is unable to discharge the powers and duties of his office. Thereupon Congress shall decide the issue, assembling within forty eight hours for that purpose if not in session. If the Congress, within twenty one days after receipt of the latter written declaration, or, if Congress is not in session, within twenty one days after Congress is required to assemble, determines by two-thirds vote of both Houses that the President is unable to discharge the powers and duties of his office, the Vice President shall continue to discharge the same as Acting President; otherwise, the President shall resume the powers and duties of his office.

Amendment XXVI

[*Proposed by Congress on March 23, 1971; declared ratified on July 1, 1971.*]

SECTION 1
[EIGHTEEN-YEAR-OLD VOTE]

The right of citizens of the United States, who are eighteen years of age or older, to vote shall not be denied or abridged by the United States or by any State on account of age.

SECTION 2
[POWER TO ENFORCE THIS ARTICLE]

The Congress shall have power to enforce this article by appropriate legislation.

Amendment XXVII

[*Proposed by Congress on September 25, 1789; declared ratified on May 8, 1992.*]

[CONGRESS CANNOT RAISE ITS OWN PAY]

No law varying the compensation for the services of the Senators and Representatives, shall take effect, until an election of representatives shall have intervened.

The Federalist Papers

No. 10: Madison

Among the numerous advantages promised by a well constructed Union, none deserves to be more accurately developed than its tendency to break and control the violence of faction. The friend of popular governments never finds himself so much alarmed for their character and fate, as when he contemplates their propensity to this dangerous vice. He will not fail therefore to set a due value on any plan which, without violating the principles to which he is attached, provides a proper cure for it. The instability, injustice, and confusion introduced into the public councils have, in truth, been the mortal diseases under which popular governments have everywhere perished, as they continue to be the favorite and fruitful topics from which the adversaries to liberty derive their most specious declamations. The valuable improvements made by the American constitutions on the popular models, both ancient and modern, cannot certainly be too much admired; but it would be an unwarrantable partiality to contend that they have as effectually obviated the danger on this side, as was wished and expected. Complaints are everywhere heard from our most considerate and virtuous citizens, equally the friends of public and private faith and of public and personal liberty, that our governments are too unstable, that the public good is disregarded in the conflicts of rival parties, and that measures are too often decided, not according to the rules of justice and the rights of the minor party, but by the superior force of an interested and overbearing majority. However anxiously we may wish that these complaints had no foundation, the evidence of known facts will not permit us to deny that they are in some degree true. It will be found, indeed, on a candid review of our situation, that some of the distresses under which we labor have been erroneously charged on the operation of our governments; but it will be found, at the same time, that other causes will not alone account for many of our heaviest misfortunes; and, particularly, for that prevailing and increasing distrust of public engagements and alarm for private rights which are echoed from one end of the continent to the other. These must be chiefly, if not wholly, effects of the unsteadiness and injustice with which a factious spirit has tainted our public administration.

By a faction I understand a number of citizens, whether amounting to a majority or minority of the whole, who are united and actuated by some common impulse of passion, or of interest, adverse to the rights of other citizens, or to the permanent and aggregate interests of the community.

There are two methods of curing the mischiefs of faction: the one, by removing its causes; the other, by controlling its effects.

There are again two methods of removing the causes of faction: the one, by destroying the liberty which is essential to its existence; the other, by giving to every citizen the same opinions, the same passions, and the same interests.

It could never be more truly said than of the first remedy, that it is worse than the disease. Liberty is to faction what air is to fire, an aliment without which it instantly expires. But it could not be a less folly to abolish liberty, which is essential to political life, because it nourishes faction, than it would be to wish the annihilation of air, which is essential to animal life, because it imparts to fire its destructive agency.

The second expedient is as impracticable, as the first would be unwise. As long as the reason of man continues fallible, and he is at liberty to exercise it, different opinions will be formed. As long as the connection subsists between his reason and his self-love, his opinions and his passions will have a reciprocal influence on each other; and the former will be objects to which the latter will attach themselves.

The diversity in the faculties of men, from which the rights of property originate, is not less an insuperable obstacle to a uniformity of interests. The protection of these faculties is the first object of Government. From the protection of different and unequal faculties of acquiring property, the possession of different degrees and kinds of property immediately results; and from the influence of these on the sentiments and views of the respective proprietors, ensues a division of the society into different interests and parties.

The latent causes of faction are thus sown in the nature of man; and we see them everywhere brought into different degrees of activity, according to the different circumstances of civil society. A zeal for different opinions concerning religion, concerning Government, and many other points, as well of speculation as of practice; an attachment to different leaders ambitiously contending for pre-eminence and power; or to persons of other descriptions whose fortunes have been interesting to the human passions, have in turn divided mankind into parties, inflamed them with mutual animosity, and rendered them much more disposed to vex and oppress each other, than to co-operate for their common good. So strong is this propensity of mankind to fall into mutual animosities, that where no substantial occasion presents itself, the most frivolous and fanciful distinctions have been sufficient to kindle their unfriendly passions, and excite their most violent conflicts. But the most common and durable source of factions has been the various and unequal distribution of property. Those who hold and those who are without property have ever formed distinct interests in society. Those who are creditors, and those who are debtors, fall under a like discrimination. A landed interest, a manufacturing interest, a mercantile interest, a moneyed interest, with many lesser interests, grow up of necessity in civilized nations, and divide them into different classes, actuated by different sentiments and views. The regulation of these various and interfering interests forms the principal task of modern Legislation, and involves the spirit of party and faction in the necessary and ordinary operations of Government.

No man is allowed to be judge in his own cause, because his interest would certainly bias his judgment and, not improbably, corrupt his integrity. With equal, nay with greater reason, a body of men are unfit to be both judges and parties at the same time; yet what are many of the most important acts of legislation but so many judicial determinations, not indeed concerning the rights of single persons, but concerning the rights of large bodies of citizens; and what are the different classes of legislators but advocates and parties to the causes which they determine? Is a law proposed concerning private debts? It is a question to which the creditors are parties on one side and the debtors on the other. Justice ought to hold the balance between them. Yet the parties are, and must be, themselves the judges; and the most numerous party, or in other words, the most powerful faction must be expected to prevail. Shall domestic manufacturers be encouraged, and in what degree, by restrictions on foreign manufacturers? are questions which would be differently decided by the landed and the manufacturing classes, and probably by neither with a sole regard to justice and the public good. The apportionment of taxes on the various descriptions of property is an act which seems to require the most exact impartiality; yet there is, perhaps, no legislative act in which greater opportunity and temptation are given to a predominant party to trample on the rules of justice. Every shilling with which they overburden the inferior number is a shilling saved to their own pockets.

It is in vain to say that enlightened statesmen will be able to adjust these clashing interests and render them all subservient to the public good. Enlightened statesmen will not always be at the helm. Nor, in many cases, can such an adjustment be made at all without taking into view indirect and remote considerations, which will rarely prevail over the immediate interest which one party may find in disregarding the rights of another or the good of the whole.

The inference to which we are brought is that the *causes* of faction cannot be removed and that relief is only to be sought in the means of controlling its *effects*.

If a faction consists of less than a majority, relief is supplied by the republican principle, which enables the majority to defeat its sinister views by regular vote. It may clog the administration, it may convulse the society; but it will be unable to execute and mask its violence under the forms of the Constitution. When a majority is included in a faction, the form of popular government, on the other hand, enables it to sacrifice to its ruling passion or interest both the public good and the rights of other citizens. To secure the public good and private rights against the danger of such a faction, and at the same time to preserve the spirit and the form of popular government, is then the great object to which our enquiries are directed. Let me add that it is the great desideratum by which alone this form of government can be rescued from the opprobrium under which it has so long labored and be recommended to the esteem and adoption of mankind.

By what means is this object attainable? Evidently by one of two only. Either the existence of the same passion or interest in a majority at the same time must be prevented, or the majority, having such co-existent passion or interest, must be rendered, by their number and local situation, unable to concert and carry into effect schemes of oppression. If the impulse and the opportunity be suffered to coincide, we well know that neither moral nor religious motives can be relied on as an adequate control. They are not found to be such on the injustice and violence of individuals, and lose their efficacy in proportion to the number combined together, that is, in proportion as their efficacy becomes needful.

From this view of the subject it may be concluded that a pure Democracy, by which I mean a Society consisting of a small number of citizens, who assemble and administer the Government in person, can admit of no cure for the mischiefs of faction. A common passion or interest will, in almost every case, be felt by a majority of the whole; a communication and concert results from the form of Government itself; and there is nothing to check the inducements to sacrifice the weaker party or an obnoxious individual. Hence it is that such Democracies have ever been spectacles of turbulence and contention; have ever been found incompatible with personal security or the rights of property; and have in general been as short in their lives as they have been violent in their deaths. Theoretic politicians, who have patronized this species of Government, have erroneously supposed that by reducing mankind to a perfect equality in their political rights, they would at the same time be perfectly equalized and assimilated in their possessions, their opinions, and their passions.

A Republic, by which I mean a Government in which the scheme of representation takes place, opens a different prospect and promises the cure for which we are seeking. Let us examine the points in which it varies from pure Democracy, and we shall comprehend both the nature of the cure and the efficacy which it must derive from the Union.

The two great points of difference between a Democracy and a Republic are: first, the delegation of the Government, in the latter, to a small number of citizens elected by the rest; secondly, the greater number of citizens and greater sphere of country over which the latter may be extended.

The effect of the first difference is, on the one hand, to refine and enlarge the public views by passing them through the medium of a chosen body of citizens, whose wisdom may best discern the true interest of their country and whose patriotism and love of justice will be least likely to sacrifice it to temporary or partial considerations. Under such a regulation it may well happen that the public voice, pronounced by the representatives of the people, will be more consonant to the public good than if pronounced by the people themselves, convened for the purpose. On the other hand, the effect may be inverted. Men of factious tempers, of local prejudices, or of sinister designs, may, by intrigue, by corruption, or by other means, first obtain the suffrages, and then betray the interests of the people. The question resulting is, whether small or extensive Republics are most favorable to the election of proper guardians of the public weal; and it is clearly decided in favor of the latter by two obvious considerations.

In the first place it is to be remarked that however small the Republic may be, the Representatives must be raised to a certain number in order to guard against the cabals of a few; and that however large it may be they must be limited to a certain number in order to guard against the confusion of a multitude. Hence, the number of Representatives in the two cases not being in proportion to that of the Constituents, and being proportionally greatest in the small Republic, it follows that if the proportion of fit characters be not less in the large than in the small Republic, the former will present a greater option, and consequently a greater probability of a fit choice.

In the next place, as each Representative will be chosen by a greater number of citizens in the large than in the small Republic, it will be more difficult for unworthy candidates to practise with success the vicious arts by which elections are too often carried; and the suffrages of the people being more free, will be more likely to centre on men who possess the most attractive merit and the most diffusive and established characters.

It must be confessed that in this, as in most other cases, there is a mean, on both sides of which inconveniencies will be found to lie. By enlarging too much the number of electors, you render the representative too little acquainted with all their local circumstances and lesser interests; as by reducing it too much, you render him unduly attached to these, and too little fit to comprehend and pursue great and national objects. The Federal Constitution forms a happy combination in this respect; the great and aggregate interests being referred to the national, the local and particular to the State legislatures.

The other point of difference is the greater number of citizens and extent of territory which may be brought within the compass of Republican than of Democratic Government; and it is this circumstance principally which renders factious combinations less to be dreaded in the former than in the latter. The smaller the society, the fewer probably will be the distinct parties and interests composing it; the fewer the distinct parties and interests, the more frequently will a majority be found of the same party; and the smaller the number of individuals composing a majority, and the smaller the compass within which they are placed, the more easily will they concert and execute their plans of oppression. Extend the sphere and you take in a greater variety of parties and interests; you make it less probable that a majority of the whole will have a common motive to invade the rights of other citizens; or if such a common motive exists, it will be more difficult for all who feel it to discover their own strength and to act in unison with each other. Besides other impediments, it may be remarked, that where there is a consciousness of unjust or dishonorable purposes, communication is always checked by distrust in proportion to the number whose concurrence is necessary.

Hence, it clearly appears that the same advantage which a Republic has over a Democracy in controlling the effects of faction is enjoyed by a large over a small republic—is enjoyed by the Union over the States composing it. Does this advantage consist in the substitution of representatives whose enlightened views and virtuous sentiments render them superior to local prejudices and to schemes of injustice? It will not be denied that the representation of the Union will be most likely to possess these requisite endowments. Does it consist in the greater security afforded by a greater variety of parties, against the event of any one party being able to outnumber and oppress the rest? In an equal degree does the increased variety of parties comprised within the Union increase this security? Does it, in fine, consist in the greater obstacles opposed to the concert and accomplishment of the secret wishes of an unjust and interested majority? Here again the extent of the Union gives it the most palpable advantage.

The influence of factious leaders may kindle a flame within their particular States but will be unable to spread a general conflagration through the other States: a religious sect may degenerate into a political faction in a part of the Confederacy; but the variety of sects dispersed over the entire face of it must secure the national Councils against any danger from that source: a rage for paper money, for an abolition of debts, for an equal division of property, or for any other improper or wicked project, will be less apt to pervade the whole body of the Union than a particular member of it; in the same proportion as such a malady is more likely to taint a particular county or district than an entire State.

In the extent and proper structure of the Union, therefore, we behold a republican remedy for the diseases most incident to Republican Government. And according to the degree of pleasure and pride we feel in being republicans ought to be our zeal in cherishing the spirit and supporting the character of federalist.

PUBLIUS

No. 51: Madison

To what expedient, then, shall we finally resort, for maintaining in practice the necessary partition of power among the several departments as laid down in the constitution? The only answer that can be given is that as all these exterior provisions are found to be inadequate the defect must be supplied, by so contriving the interior structure of the government as that its several constituent parts may, by their mutual relations, be the means of keeping each other in their proper places. Without presuming to undertake a full development of this important idea I will hazard a few general observations which may perhaps place it in a clearer light, and enable us to form a more correct judgment of the principles and structure of the government planned by the convention.

In order to lay a due foundation for that separate and distinct exercise of the different powers of government, which to a certain extent is admitted on all hands to be essential to the preservation of liberty, it is evident that each department should have a will of its own; and consequently should be so constituted that the members of each should have as little agency as possible in the appointment of the members of the others. Were this principle rigorously adhered to, it would require that all the appointments for the supreme executive, legislative, and judiciary magistracies should be drawn from the same fountain of authority, the people, through channels having no communication whatever with one another. Perhaps such a plan of constructing the several departments would be less difficult in practice than it may in contemplation appear. Some difficulties, however, and some additional expense would attend the execution of it. Some deviations, therefore, from the principle must be admitted. In the constitution of the judiciary department in particular, it might be inexpedient to insist rigorously on the principle: first, because peculiar qualifications being essential in the members, the primary consideration ought to be to select that mode of choice which best secures these qualifications; second, because the permanent tenure by which the appointments are held in that department must soon destroy all sense of dependence on the authority conferring them.

It is equally evident that the members of each department should be as little dependent as possible on those of the others for the emoluments annexed to their offices. Were the executive magistrate, or the judges, not independent of the legislature in this particular, their independence in every other would be merely nominal.

But the great security against a gradual concentration of the several powers in the same department consists in giving to those who administer each department the necessary constitutional means and personal motives to resist encroachments of the others. The provision for defence must in this, as in all other cases, be made commensurate to the danger of attack. Ambition must be made to counteract ambition. The interest of the man must be connected with the constitutional rights of the place. It may be a reflection on human nature that such devices should be necessary to control the abuses of government. But what is government itself but the greatest of all reflections on human nature? If men were angels, no government would be necessary. If angels were to govern men, neither external nor internal controls on government would be necessary. In framing a government which is to be administered by men over men, the great difficulty lies in this: You must first enable the government to control the governed; and in the next place oblige it to control itself. A dependence on the people is, no doubt, the primary control on the government; but experience has taught mankind the necessity of auxiliary precautions.

This policy of supplying, by opposite and rival interests, the defect of better motives, might be traced through the whole system of human affairs, private as well as public. We see it particularly displayed in all the subordinate distributions of power, where the constant aim is to divide and arrange the several offices in such a manner as that each may be a check on the other; that the private interest of every individual may be a sentinel over the public rights. These inventions of prudence cannot be less requisite in the distribution of the supreme powers of the State.

But it is not possible to give to each department an equal power of self-defense. In republican government, the legislative authority necessarily predominates. The remedy for this inconveniency is to divide the legislature into different branches; and to render them, by different modes of election and different principles of action, as little connected with each other as the nature of their common functions and their common dependence on the society will admit. It may even be necessary to guard against dangerous encroachments by still further precautions. As the weight of the legislative authority requires that it should be thus divided, the weakness of the executive may require, on the other hand, that it should be fortified. An absolute negative on the legislature appears, at first view, to be the natural defense with which the executive magistrate should be armed. But perhaps it would be neither altogether safe nor alone sufficient. On ordinary occasions it might not be exerted with the requisite firmness, and on extraordinary occasions it might be perfidiously abused. May not this defect of an absolute negative be supplied by some qualified connection between this weaker branch of the stronger department, by which the latter may be led to support the constitutional rights of the former, without being too much detached from the rights of its own department?

If the principles on which these observations are founded be just, as I persuade myself they are, and they be applied as a criterion to the several State constitutions, and to the federal Constitution, it will be found that if the latter does not perfectly correspond with them, the former are infinitely less able to bear such a test.

There are, moreover, two considerations particularly applicable to the federal system of America, which place that system in a very interesting point of view.

First. In a single republic, all the power surrendered by the people is submitted to the administration of a single government; and usurpations are guarded against by a division of the government into distinct and separate departments. In the compound republic of America, the power surrendered by the people is first divided between two distinct governments, and then the portion allotted to each subdivided among distinct and separate departments. Hence a double security arises to the rights of the people. The different governments will control each other, at the same time that each will be controlled by itself.

Second. It is of great importance in a republic not only to guard the society against the oppression of its rulers, but to guard one part of the society against the injustice of the other part. Different interests necessarily exist in different classes of citizens. If a majority be united by a common interest, the rights of the minority will be insecure. There are but two methods of providing against this evil: The one by creating a will in the community independent of the majority—that is, of the society itself; the other, by comprehending in the society so many separate descriptions of citizens as will render an unjust combination of a majority of the whole very improbable, if not impracticable. The first method prevails in all governments possessing an hereditary or self-appointed authority. This, at best, is but a precarious security; because a power independent of the society may as well espouse the unjust views of the major as the rightful interests of the minor party, and may possibly be turned against both parties. The second method will be exemplified in the federal republic of the United States. Whilst all authority in it will be derived from and dependent on the society, the society itself will be broken into so many parts, interests and classes of citizens, that the rights of individuals, or of the minority, will be in little danger from interested combinations of the majority. In a free government the security for civil rights must be the same as that for religious rights. It consists in the one case in the multiplicity of interests, and in the other in the multiplicity of sects. The degree of security in both cases will depend on the number of interests and sects; and this may be presumed to depend on the extent of country and number of people comprehended under the same government. This view of the subject must particularly recommend a proper federal system to all the sincere and considerate friends of republican government: Since it shows that in exact proportion as the territory of the Union may be formed into more circumscribed Confederacies, or States, oppressive combinations of a majority will be facilitated; the best security, under the republican form, for the rights of every class of citizens, will be diminished; and consequently the stability and independence of some member of the government, the only other security, must be proportionally increased. Justice is the end of government. It is the end of civil society. It ever has been and ever will be pursued until it be obtained, or until liberty be lost in the pursuit. In a society under the forms of which the stronger faction can readily unite and oppress the weaker, anarchy may as truly be said to reign as in a state of nature, where the weaker individual is not secured against the violence of the stronger: And as, in the latter state, even the stronger individuals are prompted, by the uncertainty of their condition, to submit to a government which may protect the weak as well as themselves: So, in the former state, will the more powerful factions or parties be gradually induced, by a like motive, to wish for a government which will protect all parties, the weaker as well as the more powerful. It can be little doubted that if the State of Rhode Island was separated from the Confederacy and left to itself, the insecurity of rights under the popular form of government within such narrow limits would be displayed by such reiterated oppressions of factious majorities that some power altogether independent of the people would soon be called for by the voice of the very factions whose misrule had proved the necessity of it. In the extended republic of the United States, and among the great variety of interests, parties, and sects which it embraces, a coalition of a majority of the whole society could seldom take place on any other principles than those of justice and the general good; and there being thus less danger to a minor from the will of the major party, there must be less pretext, also, to provide for the security of the former, by introducing into the government a will not dependent on the latter, or, in other words, a will independent of the society itself. It is no less certain than it is important, notwithstanding the contrary opinions which have been entertained, that the larger the society, provided it lie within a practicable sphere, the more duly capable it will be of self-government. And happily for the *republican cause,* practicable

sphere may be carried to a very great extent by a judicious modification and mixture of the *federal principle.*

PUBLIUS

No. 78: Hamilton

To the People of the State of New York:

WE PROCEED now to an examination of the judiciary department of the proposed government.

In unfolding the defects of the existing Confederation, the utility and necessity of a federal judicature have been clearly pointed out. It is the less necessary to recapitulate the considerations there urged, as the propriety of the institution in the abstract is not disputed; the only questions which have been raised being relative to the manner of constituting it, and to its extent. To these points, therefore, our observations shall be confined.

The manner of constituting it seems to embrace these several objects: 1st. The mode of appointing the judges. 2d. The tenure by which they are to hold their places. 3d. The partition of the judiciary authority between different courts, and their relations to each other.

First. As to the mode of appointing the judges; this is the same with that of appointing the officers of the Union in general, and has been so fully discussed in the two last numbers, that nothing can be said here which would not be useless repetition.

Second. As to the tenure by which the judges are to hold their places; this chiefly concerns their duration in office; the provisions for their support; the precautions for their responsibility.

According to the plan of the convention, all judges who may be appointed by the United States are to hold their offices DURING GOOD BEHAVIOR; which is conformable to the most approved of the State constitutions and among the rest, to that of this State. Its propriety having been drawn into question by the adversaries of that plan, is no light symptom of the rage for objection, which disorders their imaginations and judgments. The standard of good behavior for the continuance in office of the judicial magistracy, is certainly one of the most valuable of the modern improvements in the practice of government. In a monarchy it is an excellent barrier to the despotism of the prince; in a republic it is a no less excellent barrier to the encroachments and oppressions of the representative body. And it is the best expedient which can be devised in any government, to secure a steady, upright, and impartial administration of the laws.

Whoever attentively considers the different departments of power must perceive, that, in a government in which they are separated from each other, the judiciary, from the nature of its functions, will always be the least dangerous to the political rights of the Constitution; because it will be least in a capacity to annoy or injure them. The Executive not only dispenses the honors, but holds the sword of the community. The legislature not only commands the purse, but prescribes the rules by which the duties and rights of every citizen are to be regulated. The judiciary, on the contrary, has no influence over either the sword or the purse; no direction either of the strength or of the wealth of the society; and can take no active resolution whatever. It may truly be said to have neither FORCE nor WILL, but merely judgment; and must ultimately depend upon the aid of the executive arm even for the efficacy of its judgments.

This simple view of the matter suggests several important consequences. It proves incontestably, that the judiciary is beyond comparison the weakest of the three departments of power; that it can never attack with success either of the other two; and that all possible care is requisite to enable it to defend itself against their attacks. It equally proves, that though individual oppression may now and then proceed from the courts of justice, the general liberty of the people can never be endangered from that quarter; I mean so long as the judiciary remains truly distinct from both the legislature and the Executive. For I agree, that "there is no liberty, if the power of judging be not separated from the legislative and executive powers." And it proves, in the last place, that as liberty can have nothing to fear from the judiciary alone, but would have every thing to fear from its union with either of the other departments; that as all the effects of such a union must ensue from a dependence of the former on the latter, notwithstanding a nominal and apparent separation; that as, from the natural feebleness of the judiciary, it is in continual jeopardy of being overpowered, awed, or influenced by its co-ordinate branches; and that as nothing can contribute so much to its firmness and independence as permanency in office, this quality may therefore be justly regarded as an indispensable ingredient in its constitution, and, in a great measure, as the citadel of the public justice and the public security.

The complete independence of the courts of justice is peculiarly essential in a limited Constitution. By a limited Constitution, I understand one which contains certain specified exceptions to the legislative authority; such, for instance, as that it shall pass no bills of attainder, no ex-post-facto laws, and the like. Limitations of this kind can be preserved in practice no other way than through the medium of courts of justice, whose duty it must be to declare all acts contrary to the manifest tenor of the Constitution void. Without this, all the reservations of particular rights or privileges would amount to nothing.

Some perplexity respecting the rights of the courts to pronounce legislative acts void, because contrary to the Constitution, has arisen from an imagination that the doctrine would imply a superiority of the judiciary to the legislative power. It is urged that the authority which can declare the acts of another void, must necessarily be superior to the one whose acts may be declared void. As this doctrine is of great importance in all the American constitutions, a brief discussion of the ground on which it rests cannot be unacceptable.

There is no position which depends on clearer principles, than that every act of a delegated authority, contrary to the tenor of the commission under which it is exercised, is void. No legislative act, therefore, contrary to the Constitution, can be valid. To deny this, would be to affirm, that the deputy is greater than his principal; that the servant is above his master; that the representatives of the people are superior to the people themselves; that men acting by virtue of powers, may do not only what their powers do not authorize, but what they forbid.

If it be said that the legislative body are themselves the constitutional judges of their own powers, and that the construction they put upon them is conclusive upon the other departments, it may be answered, that this cannot be the natural presumption, where it is not to be collected from any particular provisions in the Constitution. It is not otherwise to be supposed, that the Constitution could intend to enable the representatives of the people to substitute their WILL to that of their constituents. It is far more rational to suppose, that the courts were designed to be an intermediate body between the people and the legislature, in order, among other things, to keep the latter within the limits assigned to their authority. The interpretation of the laws is the proper and peculiar province of the courts. A constitution is, in fact, and must be regarded by the judges, as a fundamental law. It therefore belongs to them to ascertain its meaning, as well as the meaning of any particular act proceeding from the legislative body. If there should happen to be an irreconcilable variance between the two, that which has the superior obligation and validity ought, of course, to be preferred; or, in other words, the Constitution ought to be preferred to the statute, the intention of the people to the intention of their agents.

Nor does this conclusion by any means suppose a superiority of the judicial to the legislative power. It only supposes that the power of the people is superior to both; and that where the will of the legislature, declared in its statutes, stands in opposition to that of the people, declared in the Constitution, the judges ought to be governed by the latter rather than the former. They ought to regulate their decisions by the fundamental laws, rather than by those which are not fundamental.

This exercise of judicial discretion, in determining between two contradictory laws, is exemplified in a familiar instance. It not uncommonly happens, that there are two statutes existing at one time, clashing in whole or in part with each other, and neither of them containing any repealing clause or expression. In such a case, it is the province of the courts to liquidate and fix their meaning and operation. So far as they can, by any fair construction, be reconciled to each other, reason and law conspire to dictate that this should be done; where this is impracticable, it becomes a matter of necessity to give effect to one, in exclusion of the other. The rule which has obtained in the courts for determining their relative validity is, that the last in order of time shall be preferred to the first. But this is a mere rule of construction, not derived from any positive law, but from the nature and reason of the thing. It is a rule not enjoined upon the courts by legislative provision, but adopted by themselves, as consonant to truth and propriety, for the direction of their conduct as interpreters of the law. They thought it reasonable, that between the interfering acts of an EQUAL authority, that which was the last indication of its will should have the preference.

But in regard to the interfering acts of a superior and subordinate authority, of an original and derivative power, the nature and reason of the thing indicate the converse of that rule as proper to be followed. They teach us that the prior act of a superior ought to be preferred to the subsequent act of an inferior and subordinate authority; and that accordingly, whenever a particular statute contravenes the Constitution, it will be the duty of the judicial tribunals to adhere to the latter and disregard the former.

It can be of no weight to say that the courts, on the pretense of a repugnancy, may substitute their own pleasure to the constitutional intentions of the legislature. This might as well happen in the case of two contradictory statutes; or it might as well happen in every adjudication upon any single statute. The courts must declare the sense of the law; and if they should be disposed to exercise WILL instead of JUDGMENT, the consequence would equally be the substitution of their pleasure to that of the legislative body. The observation, if it prove any thing, would prove that there ought to be no judges distinct from that body.

If, then, the courts of justice are to be considered as the bulwarks of a limited Constitution against legislative encroachments, this consideration will afford a strong argument for the permanent tenure of judicial offices, since nothing will contribute so much as this to that independent spirit in the judges which must be essential to the faithful performance of so arduous a duty.

This independence of the judges is equally requisite to guard the Constitution and the rights of individuals from the effects of those ill humors, which the arts of designing men, or the influence of particular conjunctures, sometimes disseminate among the people themselves, and which, though they speedily give place to better information, and more deliberate reflection, have a tendency, in the meantime, to occasion dangerous innovations in the government, and serious oppressions of the minor party in the community. Though I trust the friends of the proposed Constitution will never concur with its enemies, in questioning that fundamental principle of republican government, which admits the right of the people to alter or abolish the established Constitution, whenever they find it inconsistent with their happiness, yet it is not to be inferred from this principle, that the representatives of the people, whenever a momentary inclination happens to lay hold of a majority of their constituents, incompatible with the provisions in the existing Constitution, would, on that account, be justifiable in a violation of those provisions; or that the courts would be under a greater obligation to connive at infractions in this shape, than when they had proceeded wholly from the cabals of the representative body. Until the people have, by some solemn and authoritative act, annulled or changed the established form, it is binding upon themselves collectively, as well as individually; and no presumption, or even knowledge, of their sentiments, can warrant their representatives in a departure from it, prior to such an act. But it is easy to see, that it would require an uncommon portion of fortitude in the judges to do their duty as faithful guardians of the Constitution, where legislative invasions of it had been instigated by the major voice of the community.

But it is not with a view to infractions of the Constitution only, that the independence of the judges may be an essential safeguard against the effects of occasional ill humors in the society. These sometimes extend no farther than to the injury of the private rights of particular classes of citizens, by unjust and partial laws. Here also the firmness of the judicial magistracy is of vast importance in mitigating the severity and confining the operation of such laws. It not only serves to moderate the immediate mischiefs of those which may have been passed, but it operates as a check upon the legislative body in passing them; who, perceiving that obstacles to the success of iniquitous intention are to be expected from the scruples of the courts, are in a manner compelled, by the very motives of the injustice they meditate, to qualify their attempts. This is a circumstance calculated to have more influence upon the character of our governments, than but few may be aware of. The benefits of the integrity and moderation of the judiciary have already been felt in more States than one; and though they may have displeased those whose sinister expectations they may have disappointed, they must have commanded the esteem and applause of all the virtuous and disinterested. Considerate men, of every description, ought to prize whatever will tend to beget or fortify that temper in the courts: as no man can be sure that he may not be to-morrow the victim of a spirit of injustice, by which he may be a gainer to-day. And every man must now feel, that the inevitable tendency of such a spirit is to sap the foundations of public and private confidence, and to introduce in its stead universal distrust and distress.

That inflexible and uniform adherence to the rights of the Constitution, and of individuals, which we perceive to be indispensable in the courts of justice, can certainly not be expected from judges who hold their offices by a temporary commission. Periodical appointments, however regulated, or by whomsoever made, would, in some way or other, be fatal to their necessary independence. If the power of making them was committed either to the Executive or legislature, there would be danger of an improper complaisance to the branch which possessed it; if to both, there would be an unwillingness to hazard the displeasure of either; if to the people, or to persons chosen by them for the special purpose, there would be too great a disposition to consult popularity, to justify a reliance that nothing would be consulted but the Constitution and the laws.

There is yet a further and a weightier reason for the permanency of the judicial offices, which is deducible from the nature of the qualifications they require. It has been frequently remarked, with great propriety, that a voluminous code of laws is one of the inconveniences necessarily connected with the advantages of a free government. To avoid an arbitrary discretion in the courts, it is indispensable that they should be bound down by strict rules and precedents, which serve to define and point out their duty in every particular case that comes before them; and it will readily be conceived from the variety of controversies which grow out of the folly and wickedness of mankind, that the records of those precedents must unavoidably swell to a very considerable bulk, and must demand long and laborious study to acquire a competent knowledge of them. Hence it is, that there can be but few men in the society who will have sufficient skill in the laws to qualify them for the stations of judges. And making the proper deductions for the ordinary depravity of human nature, the number must be still smaller of those who unite the requisite integrity with the requisite knowledge. These considerations apprise us, that the government can have no great option between fit character; and that a temporary duration in office, which would naturally discourage such characters from quitting a lucrative line of practice to accept a seat on the bench, would have a tendency to throw the administration of justice into hands less able, and less well qualified, to conduct it with utility and dignity. In the present circumstances of this country, and in those in which it is likely to be for a long time to come, the disadvantages on this score would be greater than they may at first sight appear; but it must be confessed, that they are far inferior to those which present themselves under the other aspects of the subject.

Upon the whole, there can be no room to doubt that the convention acted wisely in copying from the models of those constitutions which have established GOOD BEHAVIOR as the tenure of their judicial offices, in point of duration; and that so far from being blamable on this account, their plan would have been inexcusably defective, if it had wanted this important feature of good government. The experience of Great Britain affords an illustrious comment on the excellence of the institution.

PUBLIUS

GLOSSARY

activists People who dedicate their time, effort, and money to supporting a political party or particular candidates.

Aid to Families with Dependent Children (AFDC) The federal welfare program in place from 1935 until 1995, when it was replaced by Temporary Assistance for Needy Families (TANF) under President Clinton.

amicus curiae Latin for "friend of the court," referring to an interested group or person who shares relevant information about a case to help the Court reach a decision.

Antifederalists Those at the Constitutional Convention who favored strong state governments and feared that a strong national government would be a threat to individual rights.

appeals courts The intermediate level of federal courts that hear appeals from district courts. More generally, an appeals court is any court with appellate jurisdiction.

appellate jurisdiction The authority of a court to hear appeals from lower courts and change or uphold the decision.

apportionment The process of assigning the 435 seats in the House to the states based on increases or decreases in state population.

Articles of Confederation Sent to the states for ratification in 1777, these were the first attempt at a new American government. It was later decided that the Articles restricted national government too much, and they were replaced by the Constitution.

astroturf lobbying Any lobbying method initiated by an interest group that is designed to look like the spontaneous, independent participation of many individuals.

attack ads Campaign advertising that criticizes a candidate's opponent— typically by making potentially damaging claims about the opponent's background or record—rather than focusing on positive reasons to vote for the candidate.

Baby Boom generation Americans born between 1946 and 1964, who will be retiring in large numbers over the next 20 years.

balanced budget A spending plan in which the government's expenditures are equal to its revenue.

bicameralism The system of having two chambers within one legislative body, like the House and Senate in the U.S. Congress.

Bill of Rights The first 10 amendments to the Constitution; they protect individual rights and liberties.

block grants Federal aid provided to a state government to be spent within a certain policy area, but the state can decide how to spend the money within that area.

brand names The use of party names to evoke certain positions or issues. For instance, "Adidas" might immediately call to mind athletics in the same way that "Democrat" might remind you of environmental policies or universal health care.

broadcast media Communications technologies, such as television and radio, that transmit information over airwaves.

budget deficits The amount by which a government's spending in a given fiscal year exceeds its revenue.

budget making The processes carried out in Congress to determine how government money will be spent and revenue will be raised.

bureaucracy The system of civil servants and political appointees who implement congressional or presidential decisions; also known as the administrative state.

bureaucratic drift Bureaucrats' tendency to implement policies in a way that favors their own political objectives rather than following the original intentions of the legislation.

Bush Doctrine The foreign policy of President George W. Bush, under which the United States would use military force preemptively against threats to its national security.

business cycle The normal pattern of expansion and contraction of the economy.

Cabinet The group of 15 executive department heads who implement the president's agenda in their respective positions.

casework Assistance provided by members of Congress to their constituents in solving problems with the federal bureaucracy or addressing other specific concerns.

categorical grants Federal aid to state or local governments that is provided for a specific purpose, such as a mass transit program within the transportation budget or a school lunch program within the education budget.

caucus A local meeting in which party members select a party's nominee for the general election.

caucus (congressional) The organization of Democrats within the House and Senate that meets to discuss and debate the party's positions on various issues in order to reach a consensus and to assign leadership positions.

caucus (electoral) A local meeting in which party members select a party's nominee for the general election.

centralized groups Interest groups that have a headquarters, usually in Washington, D.C., as well as members and field offices throughout the country. In general, these groups' lobbying decisions are made at headquarters by the group leaders.

cert pool A system initiated in the Supreme Court in the 1970s in which law clerks screen cases that come to the Supreme Court and recommend to the justices which cases should be heard.

checks and balances A system in which each branch of government has some power over the others.

civilian control The idea that military leaders do not formulate military policy, but rather implement directives from civilian leaders.

civil rights Rights that guarantee individuals freedom from discrimination. These rights are generally grounded in the equal protection clause of the Fourteenth Amendment and more specifically laid out in laws passed by Congress, such as the 1964 Civil Rights Act.

civil servants Employees of bureaucratic agencies within the government.

Civil War Amendments The Thirteenth, Fourteenth, and Fifteenth Amendments to the Constitution, which abolished slavery and granted civil liberties and voting rights to freed slaves after the Civil War.

class-action lawsuit A case brought by a group of individuals on behalf of themselves and others in the general public who are in similar circumstances.

clear and present danger test Established in *Schenk v. United States*, this test allows the government to restrict certain types of speech deemed dangerous.

closed primary A primary election in which only registered members of a particular political party can vote.

cloture A procedure through which the Senate can limit the amount of time spent debating a bill (cutting off a filibuster), if a supermajority of sixty senators agree.

coattails The idea that a popular president can generate additional support for candidates affiliated with his party. Coattails are weak or nonexistent in most American elections.

coercion A method of eliminating nonparticipation or free riding by potential group members by requiring participation, as in many labor unions.

coercive federalism A form of federalism in which the federal government pressures the states to change their policies by using regulations, mandates, and conditions (often involving threats to withdraw federal funding).

Cold War The period of tension and arms competition between the United States and the Soviet Union that lasted from 1945 until 1991.

collective action problems Situations in which the members of a group would benefit by working together to produce some outcome, but each individual is better off refusing to cooperate and reaping benefits from those who do the work.

commerce clause powers The powers of Congress to regulate the economy granted in Article I, Section 8, of the Constitution.

commercial speech Public expression with the aim of making a profit. It has received greater protection under the First Amendment in recent years but remains less protected than political speech.

common law Law based on the precedent of previous court rulings rather than on legislation. It is used in all federal courts and forty-nine of the fifty state courts.

competitive federalism A form of federalism in which states compete to attract businesses and jobs through the policies they adopt.

concentration The trend toward single-company ownership of several media sources in one area.

concurrent powers Responsibilities for particular policy areas, such as transportation, that are shared by federal, state, and local governments.

confederal government A form of government in which states hold power over a limited national government.

confederations Interest groups made up of several independent, local organizations that provide much of their funding and hold most of the power.

conference The organization of Republicans within the House and Senate that meets to discuss and debate the party's positions on various issues in order to reach a consensus and to assign leadership positions.

conference committees Temporary committees created to negotiate differences between the House and Senate versions of a piece of legislation that has passed through both chambers.

"consent of the governed" The idea that government gains its legitimacy through regular elections in which the people living under that government participate to elect their leaders.

conservative One side of the ideological spectrum defined by support for lower taxes, a free market, and a more limited government; generally associated with Republicans.

considerations The many pieces of information a person uses to form an opinion.

constitutional authority (presidential) Powers derived from the provisions of the Constitution that outline the president's role in government.

constitutional interpretation The process of determining whether a piece of legislation or governmental action is supported by the Constitution.

constructivism The idea that foreign policy is shaped by how a state's leaders define the national interest, ideology, and other factors.

containment An important feature of American Cold War policy in which the United States used diplomatic, economic, and military strategies in an effort to prevent the Soviet Union from expanding its influence.

cooperative federalism A form of federalism in which national and state governments work together to provide services efficiently. This form emerged in the late 1930s, representing a profound shift toward less concrete boundaries of responsibility in national–state relations.

Council of Economic Advisers A group of economic advisers, created by the Employment Act of 1946, which provides objective data on the state of the economy and makes economic policy recommendations to the president.

cross-ownership The trend toward single-company ownership of several kinds of media outlets.

culture wars Political conflict in the United States between "red-state" Americans, who tend to have strong religious beliefs, and "blue-state" Americans, who tend to be more secular.

de facto Relating to actions or circumstances that occur outside the law or "by fact," such as the segregation of schools that resulted from housing patterns and other factors rather than from laws.

defendant The person or party against whom a case is brought.

de jure Relating to actions or circumstances that occur "by law," such as the legally enforced segregation of schools in the American South before the 1960s.

delegate A member of Congress who loyally represents constituents' direct interests.

descriptive representation When a member of Congress shares the characteristics (such as gender, race, religion, or ethnicity) of his or her constituents.

détente An approach to foreign policy in which cultural exchanges and negotiations are used to reduce tensions between rival nations, such as between the United States and the Soviet Union during the 1970s.

direct incitement test Established in *Brandenberg v. Ohio*, this test protects threatening speech under the First Amendment unless that speech aims to and is likely to cause imminent "lawless action."

direct lobbying Attempts by interest group staff to influence policy by speaking with elected officials or bureaucrats.

discount rate The interest rate that a bank must pay on a short-term loan from the Federal Reserve Bank.

discretionary spending Expenditures that can be cut from the budget without changing the underlaying law.

disenfranchised To have been denied the ability to exercise a right, such as the right to vote.

district courts Lower-level trial courts of the federal judicial system that handle most U.S. federal cases.

divided government A situation in which the House, Senate, and presidency are not controlled by the same party, such as if Democrats hold the majority of House and Senate seats, and the president is a Republican.

double jeopardy Being tried twice for the same crime. This is prevented by the Fifth Amendment.

dual federalism The form of federalism favored by Chief Justice Roger Taney in which national and state governments are seen as distinct entities providing separate services. This model limits the power of the national government.

due process clause Part of the Fourteenth Amendment that forbids states from denying "life, liberty, or property" to any person without due process of law. (A nearly identical clause in the Fifth Amendment applies only to the national government.)

due process rights The idea that laws and legal proceedings must be fair. The Constitution guarantees that the government cannot take away a person's "life, liberty, or property, without due process of law." Other specific due process rights are found in the Fourth, Fifth, Sixth, and Eighth Amendments, such as protection from self-incrimination and freedom from illegal searches.

earmarks Federally funded local projects attached to bills passed through Congress.

economic depression A deep, widespread downturn in the economy, like the Great Depression of the 1930s.

economic individualism The autonomy of individuals to manage their own financial decisions without government interference.

election cycle The two-year period between general elections.

electoral college The body that votes to select America's president and vice president based on the popular vote in each state. Each candidate nominates a slate of electors who are selected to attend the meeting of the college if their candidate wins the most votes in a state or district.

electoral connection The idea that congressional behavior is centrally motivated by members' desire for re-election.

entitlement Any federal government program that provides benefits to Americans who meet requirements specified by law.

enumerated powers Powers explicitly granted to Congress, the president, or the Supreme Court in the first three articles of the Constitution. Examples include Congress's power to "raise and support armies" and the president's power as commander in chief.

equal time provision An FCC regulation requiring broadcast media to provide equal airtime on any non-news programming to all candidates running for an office.

establishment clause Part of the First Amendment that states "Congress shall make no law respecting an establishment of religion," which has been interpreted to mean that Congress cannot sponsor or favor any religion.

exclusionary rule The principle that illegally or unconstitutionally acquired evidence cannot be used in a criminal trial.

executive agreement An agreement between the executive branch and a foreign government, which acts as a treaty but does not require Senate approval.

Executive Office of the President (EOP) The group of policy-related offices that serves as support staff to the president.

executive orders Proclamations made by the president that change government policy without congressional approval.

executive privilege The right of the president to keep executive branch conversations and correspondence confidential from the legislative and judicial branches.

factions Groups of like-minded people who try to influence the government. American government is set up to avoid domination by any one of these groups.

fairness doctrine An FCC regulation requiring broadcast media to present

several points of view to ensure balanced coverage. It was created in the late 1940s and eliminated in 1987.

federal civil service A system created by the 1883 Pendleton Civil Service Act in which bureaucrats are hired on the basis of merit rather than political connections.

Federal Communications Commission (FCC) A government agency created in 1934 to regulate American radio stations and later expanded to regulate television, wireless communications technologies, and other broadcast media.

Federal Election Commission The government agency that enforces and regulates election laws; made up of six presidential appointees, of whom no more than three can be members of the same party.

federal funds rate (FFR) The interest rate that a bank must pay on an overnight loan from another bank.

federalism The division of power across the local, state, and national levels of government.

Federalist Papers A series of 85 articles written by Alexander Hamilton, James Madison, and John Jay that sought to sway public opinion toward the Federalists' position.

Federalists Those at the Constitutional Convention who favored a strong national government and a system of separated powers.

federal preemptions Impositions of national priorities on the states through national legislation that is based on the Constitution's supremacy clause.

federal reserve system An independent agency that serves as the central bank of the United States to bring stability to the nation's banking system.

fighting words Forms of expression that "by their very utterance" can incite violence. These can be regulated by the government but are often difficult to define.

filibuster A tactic used by senators to block a bill by continuing to hold the floor and speak—under the Senate rule of unlimited debate—until the bill's supporters back down.

filtering The influence on public opinion that results from journalists' and editors' decisions about which of many potential news stories to report.

fire alarm oversight A method of oversight in which members of Congress respond to complaints about the bureaucracy or problems of implementation only as they arise rather than exercising constant vigilance.

fiscal federalism A form of federalism in which federal funds are allocated to the lower levels of government through transfer payments or grants.

fiscal policy Government decisions about how to influence the economy by taxing and spending.

501(c)(3) organization A tax code classification that applies to most interest groups; this designation makes donations to the group tax-deductible but limits the group's political activities.

527 organization A tax-exempt group formed primarily to influence elections through voter mobilization efforts and issue ads that do not directly endorse or oppose a candidate. Unlike political action committees, they are not subject to contribution limits and spending caps.

foreign policy Government actions that affect countries, corporations, groups, or individuals outside America's borders.

framing The influence on public opinion caused by the way a story is presented or covered, including the details, explanations, and context offered in the report.

free exercise clause Part of the First Amendment that states Congress cannot prohibit or interfere with the practice of religion.

free market An economic system based on competition among businesses without government interference.

free rider problem The incentive to benefit from others' work without making a contribution, which leads individuals in a collective action situation to refuse to work together.

full employment The theoretical point at which all citizens who want to be employed have a job.

full faith and credit clause Part of Article IV of the Constitution requiring that each state's laws be honored by the other states. For example, a legal marriage in one state must be recognized across state lines.

general election The election in which voters cast ballots for House members, senators, and (every four years) a president and vice president.

gerrymandering Attempting to use the process of redrawing district boundaries to benefit a political party, protect incumbents, or change the proportion of minority voters in a district.

go public A president's use of speeches and other public communications to appeal directly to citizens about issues the president would like the House and Senate to act on.

GOTV ("get out the vote") or the **ground game** A campaign's efforts to "get out the vote" or make sure their supporters vote on Election Day.

government The system for implementing decisions made through the political process.

grandfather clause A type of law enacted in several southern states to allow those who were permitted to vote before the Civil War, and their descendants, to bypass literacy tests and other obstacles to voting, thereby exempting whites from these tests while continuing to disenfranchise African Americans and other people of color.

grassroots lobbying A lobbying strategy that relies on participation by group members, such as a protest or a letter-writing campaign.

Great Compromise A compromise between the large and small states, proposed by Connecticut, in which Congress would have two houses: a Senate with two legislators per state and a House of Representatives in which each state's representation would be based on population (also known as the Connecticut Compromise).

Great Society The wide-ranging social agenda promoted by President Lyndon Johnson in the mid-1960s that aimed to improve Americans' quality of life through governmental social programs.

gridlock An inability to enact legislation because of partisan conflict within Congress or between Congress and the president.

gross domestic product The value of a country's economic output taken as a whole.

hard money Donations that are used to help elect or defeat a specific candidate.

hate speech Expression that is offensive or abusive, particularly in terms of race, gender, or sexual orientation. It is currently protected under the First Amendment.

head of government One role of the president, through which he or she has authority over the executive branch.

head of state One role of the president, through which he or she represents the country symbolically and politically.

idealism The idea that a country's foreign policy decisions are based on factors beyond self-interest, including upholding important principles or values.

ideological polarization The effect on public opinion when many citizens move away from moderate positions and toward either end of the political spectrum, identifying themselves as either liberals or conservatives.

ideology A cohesive set of ideas and beliefs used to organize and evaluate the political world.

impeachment A negative or checking power over the other branches that allows Congress to remove the president, vice president, or other "officers of the United States" (including federal judges) for abuses of power.

implied powers Powers supported by the Constitution that are not expressly stated in it.

income support Government programs that provide support to low-income Americans, such as welfare, food stamps, unemployment compensation, and the Earned Income Tax Credit.

incumbency advantage The relative infrequency with which members of Congress are defeated in their attempts for re-election.

incumbent A politician running for re-election to the office he or she currently holds.

independent agencies Government offices or organizations that provide government services and are not part of an executive department.

inflation The increase in the price of consumer goods over time.

inside strategies The tactics employed within Washington, D.C., by interest groups seeking to achieve their policy goals.

interest group An organization of people who share common political interests and aim to influence public policy by electioneering and lobbying.

intergovernmental organizations (IGOs) Associations of sovereign states that work to protect human rights, increase living standards, and achieve policy goals throughout the world.

intermediate scrutiny The middle level of scrutiny the courts use when determining whether a law is constitutional. To pass this test, the law or policy must further an important government interest in a way that is "substantially related" to that interest. That is, the law must use means that are a close fit to the government's goal and not substantially broader than necessary to accomplish that goal.

intermediate scrutiny test The middle level of scrutiny the courts use when determining whether unequal treatment is justified by the effect of a law.

internationalism The idea that a country should be involved in the affairs of other nations, out of both self-interest and moral obligation.

International Monetary Fund (IMF) A nongovernmental organization established in 1944 to help stabilize the international monetary system, improve economic growth, and aid developing nations.

isolationism The idea that a country should refrain from involvement in international affairs.

Jim Crow laws State and local laws that mandated racial segregation in all public facilities in the South, many border states, and some northern communities between 1876 and 1964.

joint committees Committees that contain members of both the House and Senate but have limited authority.

judicial activism The idea that the Supreme Court should assert its interpretation of the law even if it overrules the elected executive and legislative branches of government.

judicial restraint The idea that the Supreme Court should defer to the democratically elected executive and legislative branches of government rather than contradicting existing laws.

judicial review The Supreme Court's power to strike down a law or executive branch action that it finds unconstitutional.

Judiciary Act of 1789 The law in which Congress laid out the organization of the federal judiciary. The law refined and clarified federal court jurisdiction and set the original number of justices at six. It also created the Office of the Attorney General and established the lower federal courts.

jurisdiction The sphere of a court's legal authority to hear and decide cases.

Keynesian economics The theory that governments should use economic policy, like taxing and spending, to maintain stability in the economy.

latent opinion An opinion formed on the spot, when it is needed (as distinct from a deeply held opinion that is stable over time).

legislative veto A form of oversight in which Congress overturns bureaucratic decisions.

***Lemon* test** The Supreme Court uses this test, established in *Lemon v. Kurtzman*, to determine whether a practice violates the First Amendment's establishment clause.

liberal One side of the ideological spectrum defined by support for stronger government programs and more market regulation; generally associated with Democrats.

limited government A political system in which the powers of the government are restricted to prevent tyranny by protecting property and individual rights.

living Constitution A way of interpreting the Constitution that takes into account evolving national attitudes and circumstances rather than the text alone.

lobbying Efforts to influence public policy through contact with public officials on behalf of an interest group.

mainstream media Media sources that predate the Internet, such as newspapers, magazines, television, and radio.

majority leader The elected head of the party holding the majority of seats in the House or Senate.

majority voting A voting system in which a candidate must win more than 50 percent of votes to win the election. If no candidate wins enough votes to take office, a runoff election is held between the top two vote-getters.

mandatory spending Expenditures that are required by law, such as the funding for Social Security.

markup One of the steps through which a bill becomes a law, in which the final wording of the bill is determined.

mass associations Interest groups that have a large number of dues-paying individuals as members.

mass media Sources that provide information to the average citizen, such as newspapers, television networks, radio stations, and websites.

mass survey A way to measure public opinion by interviewing a large sample of the population.

media conglomerates Companies that control a large number of media sources across several types of media outlets.

media effects The influence of media coverage on average citizens' opinions and actions.

Medicaid An entitlement program funded by the federal and state governments that provides health care coverage for low-income Americans who would otherwise be unable to afford health care.

Medicare The federal health care plan created in 1965 that provides coverage for retired Americans for hospital care (Part A), medical care (Part B), and prescription drugs (Part D).

***Miller* test** Established in *Miller v. California*, the Supreme Court uses this three-part test to determine whether speech meets the criteria for obscenity. If so, it can be restricted by the government.

minority leader The elected head of the party holding the minority of seats in the House or Senate.

***Miranda* rights** The list of civil liberties described in the Fifth Amendment that must be read to a suspect before anything the suspect says can be used in a trial.

Missouri Compromise An agreement between pro- and antislavery groups passed by Congress in 1820 in an attempt to ease tensions by limiting the expansion of slavery while also maintaining a balance between slave states and free states.

monarchy A form of government in which power is held by a single person, or monarch, who comes to power through inheritance rather than election.

monetarist theory The idea that the amount of money in circulation (the money supply) is the primary influence on economic activity and inflation.

monetary policy Government decisions about how to influence the economy using control of the money supply and interest rates.

Monroe Doctrine The American policy initiated under President James Monroe in 1823 stating that the United States would remain neutral in conflicts between European nations, and that these nations should stop colonizing or occupying areas of North and South America.

mootness The irrelevance of a case by the time it is received by a federal court, causing the court to decline to hear the case.

most-favored-nation status A standing awarded to countries with which the United States has good trade relations, providing the lowest possible tariff rate. World Trade Organization members must give one another this preferred status.

multilateral action Foreign policy carried out by a nation in coordination with other nations or international organizations.

mutually assured destruction The idea that two nations that possess large stores of nuclear weapons—like the United States and the Soviet Union during the Cold War—would both be annihilated in any nuclear exchange, thus making it unlikely that either country would launch a first attack.

national committee An American political party's principal organization, comprising party representatives from each state.

National Economic Council (NEC) A group of economic advisers created in 1993 to work with the president to coordinate economic policy.

National Security Council (NSC) Within the Executive Office of the President, a committee that advises the president on matters of foreign policy.

national supremacy clause Part of Article VI, Section 2, of the Constitution stating that the Constitution and the laws and treaties of the United States are the "supreme Law of the Land," meaning national laws take precedent over state laws if the two conflict.

natural rights Also known as "unalienable rights," the Declaration of Independence defines them as "Life, Liberty, and the pursuit of Happiness." The Founders believed that upholding these rights should be the government's central purpose.

necessary and proper clause Part of Article I, Section 8, of the Constitution that grants Congress the power to pass all laws related to one of its expressed powers; also known as the elastic clause.

New Deal The set of policies proposed by President Franklin Roosevelt and enacted by Congress between 1933 and 1935 to promote economic recovery and social welfare during the Great Depression.

New Deal Coalition The assemblage of groups who aligned with and supported the Democratic Party in support of New Deal policies during the fifth party system, including African Americans, Catholics, Jewish people, union members, and white southerners.

New Jersey Plan In response to the Virginia Plan, smaller states at the Constitutional Convention proposed that each state should receive equal representation in the national legislature, regardless of size.

news cycle The time between the release of information and its publication, like the twenty-four hours between issues of a daily newspaper.

nominating convention A meeting held by each party every four years at which states' delegates select the party's presidential and vice-presidential nominees and approve the party platform.

nongovernmental organizations (NGOs) Groups operated by private institutions (rather than governments) to promote growth, economic development, and other agendas throughout the world.

normal election A typical congressional election in which the reelection rate is high and the influences on House and Senate contests are largely local.

North Atlantic Treaty Organization (NATO) An international alliance among the United States, Canada, and several European nations, originally created to provide security against the Soviet Union during the Cold War.

notice and comment procedure A step in the rule-making process in which proposed rules are published in the Federal Register and made available for debate by the general public.

Office of Management and Budget An office within the Executive Office of the President that is responsible for creating the president's annual budget proposal to Congress, reviewing proposed rules, and other budget-related tasks.

omnibus legislation Large bills that often cover several topics and may contain extraneous, or pork-barrel, projects.

open market operations The process by which the Federal Reserve System buys and sells securities to influence the money supply.

open primary A primary election in which any registered voter can participate in the contest, regardless of party affiliation.

open seat An elected position for which there is no incumbent.

oral arguments Spoken presentations made in person by the lawyers of each party to a judge or appellate court outlining the legal reasons their side should prevail.

original jurisdiction The authority of a court to handle a case first, as in the Supreme Court's authority to initially hear disputes between two states. However, original jurisdiction for the Supreme Court is not exclusive; it may assign such a case to a lower court.

outside strategies The tactics employed outside Washington, D.C., by interest groups seeking to achieve their policy goals.

oversight Congressional efforts to make sure that laws are implemented correctly by the bureaucracy after they have been passed.

ownership society The term used to describe the social policy vision of President George W. Bush, in which citizens take responsibility for their own social welfare and the free market plays a greater role in social policy.

paradox of voting The question of why citizens vote even though their individual votes stand little chance of changing the election outcome.

parliamentary system A system of government in which legislative and executive power are closely joined. The legislature (parliament) selects the chief executive (prime minister) who forms the cabinet from members of the parliament.

parties in service The role of the parties in recruiting, training, fund-raising, and campaigning for congressional and presidential candidates. This aspect of party organization grew more prominent during the sixth party system.

party coalitions The groups that identify with a political party, usually described in demographic terms such as African American Democrats or evangelical Republicans.

party identification (party ID) A citizen's loyalty to a specific political party.

party in government The group of officeholders who belong to a specific political party and were elected as candidates of that party.

party in power Under unified government, the party that controls the House, Senate, and the presidency. Under divided government, the president's party.

party in the electorate The group of citizens who identify with a specific political party.

party organization A specific political party's leaders and workers at the national, state, and local levels.

party platform A set of objectives outlining the party's issue positions and priorities. Candidates are not required to support their party's platform.

party principle The idea that a political party exists as an organization distinct from its elected officials or party leaders.

party system A period in which the names of the major political parties, their supporters, and the issues dividing them remain relatively stable.

party unity The extent to which members of Congress in the same party vote together on party votes.

party vote A vote in which the majority of one party opposes the position of the majority of the other party.

peak associations Interest groups whose members are businesses or other organizations rather than individuals.

permanent campaign The actions officeholders take throughout the election cycle to build support for their re-election.

picket fence federalism A more refined and realistic form of cooperative federalism in which policy makers within a particular policy area work together across the levels of government.

plaintiff The person or party who brings a case to court.

plea bargain An agreement between a plaintiff and defendant to settle a case before it goes to trial or the verdict is decided. In a civil case this usually involves an admission of guilt and an agreement on monetary damages; in a criminal case it often involves an admission of guilt in return for a reduced charge or sentence.

pluralism The idea that having a variety of parties and interests within a government will strengthen the system, ensuring that no group possesses total control.

plurality voting A voting system in which the candidate who receives the most votes within a geographic area wins the election, regardless of whether that candidate wins a majority (more than half) of the votes.

pocket veto The automatic death of a bill passed by the House and Senate when the president fails to sign the bill in the last ten days of a legislative session.

police patrol oversight A method of oversight in which members of Congress constantly monitor the bureaucracy to make sure that laws are implemented correctly.

policy agenda The set of desired policies that political leaders view as their top priorities.

policy mood The level of public support for expanding the government's role in society; whether the public wants government action on a specific issue.

political action committee (PAC) An interest group or a division of an interest group that can raise money to contribute to campaigns or to spend on ads in support of candidates. The amount a PAC can receive from each of its donors and the amount it can spend on federal electioneering are strictly limited.

political appointees People selected by an elected leader, such as the president, to hold a government position.

political machine An unofficial patronage system within a political party that seeks to gain political power and government contracts, jobs, and other benefits for party leaders, workers, and supporters.

political socialization The process by which an individual's political opinions are shaped by other people and the surrounding culture.

politico A member of Congress who acts as a delegate on issues that constituents care about (such as immigration reform) and as a trustee on more complex or less salient issues (some foreign policy or regulatory matters).

politics The process that determines what government does.

population The group of people that a researcher or pollster wants to study, such as evangelicals, senior citizens, or Americans.

pork barrel Legislative appropriations that benefit specific constituents, created with the aim of helping local representatives win re-election.

power of the purse The constitutional power of Congress to raise and spend money. Congress can use this as a negative or checking power over the other branches by freezing or cutting their funding.

precedent A legal norm established in court cases that is then applied to future cases dealing with the same legal questions.

presidential approval rating The percentage of Americans who feel that the president is doing a good job in office.

president pro tempore A largely symbolic position usually held by the most senior member of the majority party in the Senate.

primary A ballot vote in which citizens select a party's nominee for the general election.

prime time Evening hours when television viewership is at its highest and networks often schedule news programs.

priming The influence on the public's general impressions caused by positive or negative coverage of a candidate or issue.

principal–agent game The interaction between a principal (such as the president or Congress), who needs something done, and an agent (such as a bureaucrat), who is responsible for carrying out the principal's orders.

prior restraint A limit on freedom of the press that allows the government to prohibit the media from publishing certain materials.

privacy rights Liberties protected by several amendments in the Bill of Rights that shield certain personal aspects of citizens' lives from governmental interference, such as the Fourth Amendment's protection against unreasonable searches and seizures.

privatization The process of transferring the management of a government program (like Social Security) from the public sector to the private sector.

privileges and immunities clause Part of Article IV of the Constitution requiring that states must treat nonstate residents within their borders as they would treat their own residents. This was meant to promote commerce and travel between states.

problem of control A difficulty faced by elected officials in ensuring that when bureaucrats implement policies, they follow these officials' intentions but still have enough discretion to use their expertise.

progressive Taxes that require upper-income people to pay a higher tax rate than lower-income people, such as income taxes.

proportional allocation During the presidential primaries, the practice of determining the number of convention delegates allotted to each candidate based on the percentage of the popular vote cast for each candidate. All Democratic primaries and caucuses use this system, as do some states' Republican primaries and caucuses.

protectionism The idea under which some people have tried to rationalize discriminatory policies by claiming that some groups, like women or African Americans, should be denied certain rights for their own safety or well-being.

public goods Services or actions (such as protecting the environment) that, once provided to one person, become available to everyone. Government is typically needed to provide public goods because they will be underproduced by the free market.

public opinion Citizens' views on politics and government actions.

public policy A law, rule, statute, or edict that expresses the government's goals and provides for rewards and punishments to promote their attainment.

purposive benefits Satisfaction derived from the experience of working toward a desired policy goal, even if the goal is not achieved.

rational basis test The use of evidence to suggest that differences in the behavior of two groups can rationalize unequal treatment of these groups.

realignment A change in the size or composition of the party coalitions or in the nature of the issues that divide the parties. Realignments typically occur within an election cycle or two, but they can also occur gradually over the course of a decade or longer.

realism The idea that a country's foreign policy decisions are motivated by self-interest and the goal of gaining more power.

recess appointment Selection by the president of a person to be an ambassador or the head of a department while the Senate is not in session, thereby bypassing Senate approval. Unless approved by a subsequent Senate vote, recess appointees serve only to the end of the congressional term.

redistributive tax policies Policies, generally favored by Democratic politicians, that use taxation to attempt to create greater social equality (i.e., higher taxation of the rich to provide programs for the poor).

redistricting Redrawing the geographic boundaries of legislative districts. This happens every ten years to ensure that districts remain roughly equal in population.

red tape Excessive or unnecessarily complex regulations imposed by the bureaucracy.

regressive Taxes that take a larger share of poor people's income than wealthy people's income, such as sales taxes and payroll taxes.

regulation A rule that allows the government to exercise control over individuals and corporations by restricting certain behaviors.

remedial legislation National laws that address discriminatory state laws. Authority for such -legislation comes from Section 5 of the Fourteenth Amendment.

republican democracy A form of government in which the interests of the people are represented through elected leaders.

republicanism As understood by James Madison and the framers, the belief that a form of government in which the interests of the people are represented through elected leaders is the best form of government.

reserved powers As defined in the Tenth Amendment, powers that are not given to the national government by the Constitution, or not prohibited to the states, are reserved by the states or the people.

reserve requirement The minimum amount of money that a bank is required to have on hand to back up its assets.

revolving door The movement of individuals from government positions to jobs with interest groups or lobbying firms, and vice versa.

ripeness A criterion that federal courts use to decide whether a case is ready to be heard. A case's ripeness is based on whether its central issue or controversy has actually taken place.

roll call vote A recorded vote on legislation; members may vote yes, no, abstain, or present.

runoff election Under a majority voting system, a second election held only if no candidate wins a majority of the votes in the first general election. Only the top two vote-getters in the first election compete in the runoff.

sample Within a population, the group of people surveyed in order to gauge the whole population's opinion. Researchers use samples because it would be impossible to interview the entire population.

sampling error A calculation that describes what percentage of the people surveyed may not accurately represent the population being studied. Increasing the number of respondents lowers the sampling error.

select committees Committees in the House or Senate created to address a specific issue for one or two terms.

selective incentives Benefits that can motivate participation in a group effort because they are available only to those who participate, such as member services offered by interest groups.

selective incorporation The process through which the civil liberties granted in the Bill of Rights were applied to the states on a case-by-case basis through the Fourteenth Amendment.

senatorial courtesy A norm in the nomination of district court judges in which the president consults with his party's senators from the relevant state in choosing the nominee.

seniority The informal congressional norm of choosing the member who has served the longest on a particular committee to be the committee chair.

"separate but equal" The idea that racial segregation was acceptable as long as the separate facilities were of equal quality; supported by *Plessy v. Ferguson* and struck down by *Brown v. Board of Education*.

separation of powers The division of government power across the judicial, executive, and legislative branches.

signing statement A document issued by the president when signing a bill into law explaining his interpretation of the law, which often differs from the interpretation of Congress, in an attempt to influence how the law will be implemented.

slander and **libel** Spoken false statements (slander) and written false statements (libel) that damage a person's reputation. Both can be regulated by the government but are often difficult to distinguish from permissible speech.

slant The imbalance in a story that covers one candidate or policy favorably without providing similar coverage of the other side.

social policy An area of public policy related to maintaining or enhancing the well-being of individuals.

soft money Contributions that can be used for voter mobilization or to promote a policy proposal or point of view as long as these efforts are not tied to supporting or opposing a particular candidate.

solicitor general A presidential appointee in the Department of Justice who conducts all litigation on behalf of the federal government before the Supreme Court and supervises litigation in the federal appellate courts.

solidary benefits Satisfaction derived from the experience of working with like-minded people, even if the group's efforts do not achieve the desired impact.

sovereign power The national and state government each have some degree of authority and autonomy.

Speaker of the House The elected leader of the House of Representatives.

split ticket A ballot on which a voter selects candidates from more than one political party.

spoils system The practice of rewarding party supporters with benefits like federal government positions.

standard operating procedures Rules that lower-level bureaucrats must follow when implementing policies.

standing Legitimate justification for bringing a civil case to court.

standing committees Committees that are a permanent part of the House or Senate structure, holding more importance and authority than other committees.

state capacity The knowledge, personnel, and institutions that the government requires to effectively implement policies.

State of the Union An annual speech in which the president addresses Congress to report on the condition of the country and recommend policies.

states' rights The idea that states are entitled to a certain amount of self-government, free of federal government intervention. This became a central issue in the period leading up to the Civil War.

statutory authority (presidential) Powers derived from laws enacted by Congress that add to the powers given to the president in the Constitution.

statutory interpretation The various methods and tests used by the courts for determining the meaning of a law and applying it to specific situations. Congress may overturn the courts' interpretation by writing a new law; thus it also engages in statutory interpretation.

straight ticket A ballot on which a voter selects candidates from only one political party.

strict construction A way of interpreting the Constitution based on its language alone.

strict scrutiny The highest level of scrutiny the courts use when determining whether a law is constitutional. To pass this test, the law or policy must be shown to serve a "compelling state interest" or goal, it must be narrowly tailored to achieve that goal, and it must be the least restrictive means of achieving the goal.

strict scrutiny test The highest level of scrutiny the courts use when determining whether unequal treatment is justified by a "compelling state in hereof."

substantive due process doctrine One interpretation of the due process clause of the Fourteenth Amendment; in this view the Supreme Court has the power to overturn laws that infringe on individual liberties.

substantive representation When a member of Congress represents constituents' interests and policy concerns.

supply-side economics The theory that lower tax rates will stimulate the economy by encouraging people to save, invest, and produce more goods and services.

symbolic speech Nonverbal expression, such as the use of signs or symbols. It benefits from many of the same constitutional protections as verbal speech.

tariff A tax levied on imported and exported goods.

Temporary Assistance for Needy Families (TANF) The welfare program that replaced Aid to Families with Dependent Children (AFDC) in 1996, eliminating the entitlement status of welfare, shifting implementation of the policy to the states, and introducing several new restrictions on receiving aid. These changes led to a significant decrease in the number of welfare recipients.

Three-Fifths Compromise The states' decision during the Constitutional Convention to count each slave as three-fifths of a person in a state's population for the purposes of determining the number of House members and the distribution of taxes.

trade association An interest group composed of companies in the same business or industry (the same "trade") that lobbies for policies that benefit members of the group.

Treasury Department A cabinet-level agency that is responsible for managing the federal government's revenue. It prints currency, collects taxes, and sells government bonds.

trustee A member of Congress who represents constituents' interests while also taking into account national, collective, and moral concerns that sometimes cause the member to vote against the preference of a majority of constituents.

unfunded mandates Federal laws that require the states to do certain things but do not provide state governments with funding to implement these policies.

unified government A situation in which one party holds a majority of seats in the House and Senate and the president is a member of that same party.

unilateral action Independent acts of foreign policy undertaken by a nation without the assistance or coordination of other nations.

unilateral action (presidential) Any policy decision made and acted upon by the president and his staff without the explicit approval or consent of Congress.

unitary government A system in which the national, centralized government holds ultimate authority. It is the most common form of government in the world.

United Nations (UN) An international organization made up of representatives from nearly every nation, with a mission to promote peace and cooperation, uphold international law, and provide humanitarian aid.

United States Trade Representative (USTR) An agency founded in 1962 to negotiate with foreign governments to create trade agreements, resolve disputes, and participate in global trade policy organizations. Treaties negotiated by the USTR must be ratified by the Senate.

vesting clause Article II, Section 1, of the Constitution, which states that "executive Power shall be vested in a President of the United States of America," making the president both the head of government and the head of state.

Virginia Plan A plan proposed by the larger states during the Constitutional Convention that based representation in the national legislature on population. The plan also included a variety of other proposals to strengthen the national government.

voting cues Pieces of information about a candidate that are readily available, easy to interpret, and lead a citizen to decide to vote for a particular candidate.

welfare Financial or other assistance provided to individuals by the government, usually based on need.

whip system An organization of House leaders who work to disseminate information and promote party unity in voting on legislation.

winner-take-all During the presidential primaries, the practice of assigning all of a given state's delegates to the candidate who receives the most popular votes. Some states' Republican primaries and caucuses use this system.

World Bank A nongovernmental organization established in 1944 that provides financial support for economic development projects in developing nations.

World Trade Organization (WTO) An international organization created in 1995 to oversee trade agreements between nations by facilitating negotiations and handling disputes.

writ of certiorari The most common way for a case to reach the Supreme Court, in which at least four of the nine justices agree to hear a case that has reached them via an appeal from the losing party in a lower court's ruling.

ENDNOTES

CHAPTER 1

1. Thomas Hobbes, *Leviathan* (1651; repr. Indianapolis, IN: Bobbs, Merrill, 1958).
2. Alexander Hamilton, James Madison, and John Jay, *The Federalist Papers,* ed. Roy P. Fairfield, 2nd ed. (1788; repr. Baltimore, MD: Johns Hopkins University Press, 1981), p. 160.
3. Hamilton, Madison, and Jay, *Federalist Papers,* p. 18.
4. Examples include E. E. Schattschneider, *The Semi-Sovereign People: A Realist's View of Democracy in America* (New York: Holt, Rinehart, and Winston, 1960); Larry Bartels, *Unequal Democracy: The Politics of the New Gilded Age* (Princeton: Princeton University Press, 2008); Jeffrey A. Segal and Howard Spaeth, *The Supreme Court and the Attitudinal Model Revisited* (New York: Cambridge University Press, 2002).
5. Morris Rosenberg, "Some Determinants of Political Apathy," *Public Opinion Quarterly* 18 (Winter 1954–55): 349–66; Jane Mansbridge, *Beyond Adversary Democracy* (New York: Basic Books, 1980); Nina Eliasoph, *Avoiding Politics: How Americans Produce Apathy in Everyday Life* (New York: Cambridge University Press, 1998); Melanie C. Green, Penny S. Visser, and Philip E. Tetlock, "Coping with Accountability Cross-Pressures: Low-Effort Evasive Tactics and High-Effort Quests for Complex Compromises," *Personality and Social Psychology Bulletin* 26, no. 11 (2000): 1380–91.
6. Donald Green, Bradley Palmquist, and Eric Schickler, *Partisan Hearts and Minds* (New Haven, CT: Yale University Press, 2004); Christopher Achen, "Political Socialization and Rational Party Identification," *Political Behavior* 24, no. 2 (2002): 151–70.
7. Robert S. Erikson, Michael B. Mackuen, and James A. Stimson, *The Macro Polity* (New York: Cambridge University Press, 2002).
8. Congressional Budget Office, "Current Budget Projections," available at www.cbo.gov/ftpdocs/108xx/doc10871/budget-projections .pdf; The President's Budget for Fiscal Year 2011, "Total Executive Branch Civilian Full-Time Equivalent (FTE) Employees, 1981–2011," Table 17.1, available at www.white house.gov/ omb/budget/Historicals/; Department of Defense, "Military Personnel Active and Reserve Forces," available at www.whitehouse.gov/omb/budget/fy2011/assets/mil.pdf; Paul Light, "Fact Sheet on the New True Size of Government," Brookings Institution, September 5, 2003, available at www.brookings.edu/articles/2003/0905politics_light.aspx; *The Federal Register,* www.gpoaccess.gov/fr/. (All accessed 7/15/12.)
9. This ranking varies somewhat from year to year and source to source. See, for example, The CIA World Factbook, Country Comparison: Distribution of Family Income - Gini Index, www.cia.gov/library/publications/the-world-factbook/rankorder/2172rank.html (accessed 10/19/12).
10. For details, see Paul R. Abramson, John H. Aldrich, and David W. Rohde, *Change and Continuity in the 2008 and 2010 Elections* (Washington, DC: Congressional Quarterly Press, 2011).
11. Morris P. Fiorina, with Samuel J. Abrams and Jeremy C. Pope, *Culture War?: The Myth of a Polarized America,* 2nd ed. (New York: Pearson, Longman, 2006), pp. 46–47.
12. Fiorina, *Culture War?*

CHAPTER 2

1. Jim DeMint, "Constitution of No," *National Review Online,* June 8, 2010, www.nationalreview.com/articles/229909/constitution-no/jim-demint?pg=2 (accessed 10/16/11).
2. Mark Trumbull, "On Constitution Day, Tea Party and Foes Duel over Our Founding Document," *Christian Science Monitor,* September 17, 2011, www.csmonitor.com/USA/Politics/2011/0917/On-Constitution-Day-tea-party-and-foes-duel-over-our-founding-document (accessed 10/16/11).
3. For a good overview of the political thought of the American Revolution, see Gordon S. Wood, *The Radicalism of the American Revolution* (New York: Vintage Books, 1993). For an excellent summary of the history, see Wood's *The American Revolution: A History* (New York: Modern Library, 2003).
4. J. W. Peltason, *Corwin and Peltason's Understanding the Constitution,* 7th ed. (Hinsdale, IL: Dryden Press, 1976), p. 12.
5. The pamphlet sold 120,000 copies within a few months of publication, a figure that would leave today's Harry Potter books in the dust in terms of the proportion of the literate public that purchased the pamphlet.

6. Charles A. Beard, *An Economic Interpretation of the Constitution of the United States* (New York: Macmillan, 1913).

7. Forrest McDonald, *We the People: The Economic Origins of the Constitution* (Chicago: University of Chicago Press, 1958); Robert E. Brown, *Charles Beard and the Constitution* (New York: Norton, 1956).

8. David Brian Robertson, *The Constitution and America's Destiny* (New York: Cambridge University Press, 2005), p. 4.

9. Many delegates probably assumed that the electors would reflect the wishes of the voters in their states, but there is no clear indication of this in Madison's notes. (Hamilton makes this argument in the *Federalist Papers*.) Until the 1820s many electors were directly chosen by state legislatures rather than by the people. In the first presidential election George Washington won the unanimous support of the electors, but in only five states were the electors chosen by the people.

10. The actual language of the section avoids the term *slavery*. Instead, it says, "The Migration or Importation of such Persons as any of the States now existing shall think proper to admit, shall not be prohibited by Congress prior to the Year one thousand eight hundred and eight." The ban on the importation of slaves was implemented on the earliest possible date, January 1, 1808.

11. This ban prompted the White House to seek covert channels through which to support the Contras, which led to the ill-conceived secret arms deal with Iran (a nation that was under a complete U.S. trade embargo at the time) in which the money from the arms sales was funneled to the Contras.

12. Cass R. Sunstein, "Making Amends," *The New Republic*, March 3, 1997, p. 42.

13. *Furman v. Georgia*, 408 U.S. 238 (1972).

14. The case concerning minors was *Roper v. Simmons*, 543 U.S. 551 (2005), and the case concerning the mentally retarded was *Atkins v. Virginia*, 536 U.S. 304 (2002).

You Decide

a. Douglas Linder, "What in the Constitution Cannot Be Amended?" Arizona Law Review 23 (1981): 717–33.

b. Kathleen M. Sullivan, "What's Wrong with Constitutional Amendments?" in New Federalist Papers, ed. Alan Brinkley, Nelson W. Polsby, and Kathleen M. Sullivan (New York: Norton, 1997), p. 63.

c. Jamin B. Raskin, "A Right to Vote," The American Prospect, August 27, 2001, pp. 10–12.

CHAPTER 3

1. The full title of the law is the Patient Protection and Affordable Care Act (PPACA).

2. *State of Florida, et al. v. U.S. Department of Health and Human Services, et al.*, Petition for Writ of Certiorari to the United States Court of Appeals for the Eleventh Circuit, September 27, 2011, www.azgovernor.gov/dms/upload/PR_092811_Petition.pdf (accessed 10/19/12).

3. State Health Facts.org, Health Care and Coverage, www.statehealthfacts.org/comparecat.jsp?cat=3 (accessed 11/12/11).

4. "Obama's Remarks at the Health Care Bill Signing," *New York Times*, March 23, 2010, www.nytimes.com/2010/03/24/us/politics/24health-text.html?pagewanted=3 (accessed 11/10/11).

5. See www.cisstat.com/eng/cis.htm for more information on the Commonwealth of Independent States.

6. Pam Belluck, "Massachusetts Gay Marriage to Remain Legal," *New York Times*, June 14, 2007, www.nytimes.com/2007/06/15/us/15gay.html (accessed 10/18/07). The state supreme court decision that required the state legislature to recognize gay marriage was *Goodridge v. Dept. of Public Health*, 798 N.E.2d 941 (Mass. 2003).

7. *Nancy Wilson and Paula Schoenwether v. Richard Lake and John Ashcroft* (2005) No. 8:04-cv-1680-T-30TBM.

8. "The Supreme Court; Excerpts from Court's Welfare Ruling and Rehnquist's Dissent," *New York Times*, May 18, 1999, p. A20.

9. John W. Wright, ed., *New York Times 2000 Almanac* (New York: Penguin Reference, 1999), p. 165. Estimates from various online sources are quite a bit higher, averaging about 620,000 deaths.

10. *Mayor of City of New York v. Miln*, 36 U.S. (11 Pet.) 102 (1837).

11. *Cooley v. Board of Wardens of the Port of Philadelphia*, 53 U.S. 229 (1851).

12. Slaughterhouse Cases, 83 U.S. 36 (1873). See Ronald M. Labbe and Jonathan Lurie, *The Slaughterhouse Cases: Regulation, Reconstruction, and the Fourteenth Amendment* (Lawrence: University Press of Kansas, 2003).

13. Civil Rights Cases, 109 U.S. 3 (1883).

14. *Hammer v. Dagenhart*, 247 U.S. 251 (1918).

15. *Lochner v. New York*, 198 U.S. 45 (1905).

16. Four key cases are *West Coast Hotel Company v. Parrish* (1937), *Wright v. Vinton Branch* (1937), *Virginia Railway Company v. System Federation* (1937), and *National Labor Relations Board v. Jones & Laughlin Steel Corporation* (1937).

17. Martin Grodzins, *The American System* (New York: Rand McNally, 1966).

18. John Shannon, "Middle Class Votes Bring a New Balance to Federalism," February 1, 1997, policy paper 10 from the Urban Institute series The Future of the Public Sector, www.urban.org/url.cfm?ID=307051 (accessed 1/3/08).

19. *Brown v. Board of Education*, 347 U.S. 483 (1954); *Swann v. Charlotte-Mecklenburg Board of Education*, 402 U.S. 1 (1971).

20. *Miranda v. Arizona*, 384 U.S. 436 (1966); *Mapp v. Ohio*, 367 U.S. 643 (1961).

21. Paul Posner, "The Politics of Coercive Federalism in the Bush Era," *Publius* 37, no. 3 (May 2007): 390–412.

22. Barry Rabe, "Environmental Policy and the Bush Era: The Collision between the Administrative Presidency and State Experimentation," *Publius* 37, no. 3 (May 2007): 413–31.

23. Quoted in Kirk Johnson, "States' Rights Is Rallying Cry for Lawmakers," *New York Times*, March 17, 2010, p. A1. The Supreme Court endorsed this reassertion of state power in an important case concerning immigration policy. In *Chamber*

of Commerce v. Whiting, 131 S.Ct. 1968 (2011), the Court held that federal immigration law did not preempt an Arizona law that required implementation of federal law in a manner that may have been more aggressive than Congress intended.

24. From a review of Michael S. Greve, *Real Federalism: Why It Matters, How It Could Happen* (Washington, DC: American Enterprise Institute Press, 1999), www.federalismproject.org/publications/books (accessed 10/10/07).

25. Cass Sunstein, *Designing Democracy: What Constitutions Do* (New York: Oxford University Press, 2001), p. 107.

26. J. W. Peltason, *Corwin and Peltason's Understanding the Constitution*, 7th ed. (Hinsdale, IL: Dryden Press, 1976), p. 177.

27. *Garcia v. San Antonio Metropolitan Transit Authority*, 469 U.S. 528 (1985).

28. *Bond. v. United States*, S.C. 09-1227 (2011).

29. *City of Boerne v. Flores*, 521 U.S. 507 (1997), 520.

30. *Alabama v. Garrett*, 531 U.S. 356 (2001).

31. *Tennessee v. Lane*, 541 U.S. 509 (2004).

32. *Nevada Department of Human Resources v. Hibbs*, 538 U.S. 721 (2003).

33. *United States v. Lopez*, 514 U.S. 549 (1995).

34. *United States v. Morrison*, 529 U.S. 598 (2000).

35. *U.S. Term Limits, Inc. v. Thornton*, 514 U.S. 779 (1995).

36. *Romer v. Evans*, 517 U.S. 620 (1996).

37. *Gonzales v. Raich*, 545 U.S. 1 (2005).

38. *National Federation of Independent Business et al. v. Sebelius*, 567 U.S. _____ (2012).

39. Ibid., p. 51.

40. Jonathan Turley, "It's Not the Cannabis, It's the Constitution," *Los Angeles Times*, August 5, 2002, Metro section, part 2, p. 11.

41. American Society of Civil Engineers, "Report Card for America's Infrastructure: 2009," www.infrastructurereportcard.org/ (accessed 11/14/11).

42. From a review of Greve, *Real Federalism*.

43. Martha Derthick, *Keeping the Compound Republic: Essays in American Federalism* (Washington, DC: Brookings Institution, 2001), pp. 9–32.

CHAPTER 4

1. For information about the Westboro Baptist Church, see www.godhatesfags.com/wbcinfo/aboutwbc.html (accessed 12/2/11). The WBC is unaffiliated with the mainstream Baptist church and only has about 40 members, who are mostly relatives of the founder, Fred Phelps. According to the church's website, since 1991 the WBC has held more than 47,000 antigay demonstrations.

2. Timothy J. Nieman, Dean H. Dusinberre, and Lawrence M. Maher, "Brief for the Veterans of Foreign Wars as *Amicus Curiae* in Support of Petitioner," U.S. Supreme Court, *Snyder v. Phelps*, May 28, 2010, p.4.

3. *Snyder v. Phelps*, U.S. Supreme Court slip. op. 09-751 (2011).

4. *Snyder v. Phelps*, Alito dissent.

5. *Arar v. Ashcroft et al.*, 2006 WL 346439 (E.D.N.Y.). The case was also dismissed because Arar, a Canadian citizen, did not have standing to sue the U.S. government. Supporters of this decision (and the practice more generally) say that it is an essential part of the war on terrorism and that the enemy combatants who are arrested have no legal rights. Opponents say that the practice violates international law and our own standards of decency; furthermore, torture almost never produces useful information because people will say anything to get the torture to stop.

6. Max Farrand, ed., *The Records of the Federal Convention of 1787*, rev. ed. (New Haven, CT: Yale University Press, 1937), pp. 587–88, 617–18.

7. The two that were not ratified by the states were a complicated amendment on congressional apportionment and a pay raise amendment.

8. There is an intense scholarly debate on whether the authors of the Fourteenth Amendment intended for it to apply the Bill of Rights to the states. The strongest argument against this position is Raoul Berger, *The Fourteenth Amendment and the Bill of Rights* (Norman: University of Oklahoma Press, 1989), and a good book in support is Akhil Reed Amar, *The Bill of Rights* (New Haven, CT: Yale University Press, 1998).

9. The Slaughterhouse Cases, 83 U.S. 36 (1873). The plaintiffs also made a Thirteenth Amendment claim (that the monopoly forced them to work in "involuntary servitude") and a "due process" claim, but the Court rejected both of those as well. The Court focused on the "privileges and immunities" argument and the idea of dual citizenship.

10. *Gitlow v. New York*, 268 U.S. 652 (1925).

11. *Police Department of Chicago v. Mosley*, 408 U.S. 92 (1972).

12. *United States v. O'Brien*, 391 U.S. 367 (1968); *Ladue v. Gilleo*, 512 U.S. 43 (1994).

13. *Schenk v. United States*, 249 U.S. 47 (1919), 52.

14. Alan Dershowitz, *Shouting Fire: Civil Liberties in a Turbulent Age* (New York: Little, Brown, 2002).

15. *Brandenburg v. Ohio*, 395 U.S. 444 (1969).

16. *Smith v. Goguen*, 415 U.S. 566 (1974).

17. *Tinker v. Des Moines School District*, 393 U.S. 503 (1969).

18. *Spence v. Washington*, 418 U.S. 405 (1974).

19. *Texas v. Johnson*, 491 U.S. 397 (1989).

20. *United States v. Eichman*, 496 U.S. 310 (1990).

21. *Buckley v. Valeo*, 424 U.S. 1 (1976).

22. *Davis v. Federal Election Commission*, 128 S. Ct. 2749 (2008).

23. *Citizens United v. Federal Election Commission*, 558 U.S. 08-205 (2010).

24. *McConnell v. Federal Election Commission*, 540 U.S. 93 (2003).

25. Kermit L. Hall, "Free Speech on Public College Campuses: Overview," www.firstamendmentcenter.org/speech/pubcollege/overview.aspx (accessed 2/10/08).

26. Carolyn J. Palmer, Sophie W. Penney, Donald D. Gehring, and Jan A. Neiger, "Hate Speech and Hate Crimes: Campus Conduct Codes and Supreme Court Rulings," *National Association of Student Personnel Administrators Journal* 34, no. 2 (1997), http://publications.naspa.org/naspajournal/vol34/iss2/art4 (accessed 12/18/07).

27. *City of St. Paul v. RAV*, 505 U.S. 377 (1992).

28. *Virginia v. Black*, 538 U.S. 343 (2003).

29. The Supreme Court declined to review the case in *Smith v. Collin*, 439 U.S. 916 (1978), which meant that the lower court rulings stood: 447 F.Supp. 676 (1978), 578 F 2d 1197 (1978). See Donald A. Downs, *Nazis in Skokie: Freedom, Community and the First Amendment* (Notre Dame, IN: University of Notre Dame Press, 1985), for an excellent analysis of this important case.

30. *Forsyth County v. Nationalist Movement*, 505 U.S. 123 (1992).

31. *Frisby et al. v. Schultz et al.*, 487 U.S. 474 (1988).

32. *Near v. Minnesota*, 283 U.S. 697 (1931), 719–20.

33. *New York Times Co. v. United States*, 403 U.S. 713 (1971).

34. *Chaplinsky v. State of New Hampshire*, 315 U.S. 568 (1942).

35. *Chaplinsky v. State of New Hampshire*.

36. *New York Times v. Sullivan*, 376 U.S. 254 (1964), cited in Henry J. Abraham and Barbara A. Perry, *Freedom and the Court: Civil Rights and Liberties in the United States*, 8th ed. (Lawrence: University Press of Kansas, 2003), p. 193.

37. *Hustler v. Falwell*, 485 U.S. 46 (1988).

38. *Virginia State Board of Pharmacy v. Virginia Citizens Consumer Council, Inc.*, 425 U.S. 748 (1976); *City of Cincinnati v. Discovery Network, Inc., et al.*, 507 U.S. 410 (1993).

39. *Central Hudson Gas & Electric v. Public Service Commission*, 447 U.S. 557 (1980).

40. *Lorillard Tobacco v. Reilly*, 533 U.S. 525 (2001).

41. In 1996 Congress passed the Child Pornography Prevention Act. This law makes the possession, production, or distribution of child pornography a criminal offense punishable with up to 15 years in jail and a fine. However, two parts of the law were struck down by the Court for being "overbroad and unconstitutional." *Ashcroft v. Free Speech Coalition*, 353 U.S. 234 (2002).

42. *Jacobellis v. Ohio*, 378 U.S. 184, 197 (1964).

43. *Miller v. California*, 413 U.S. 15 (1973).

44. *Reno et al. v. American Civil Liberties Union et al.*, 521 U.S. 844 (1997).

45. *Ashcroft v. American Civil Liberties Union*, 535 U.S. 564 (2004).

46. James Hudson, "'A Wall of Separation,'" *Library of Congress Information Bulletin* 57, no.6 (June 1998), www.loc.gov/loc/lcib/9806/danbury.html (accessed 3/3/08).

47. *Engle v. Vitale*, 370 U.S. 421 (1962).

48. *Wallace v. Jaffree*, 482 U.S. 38 (1985).

49. *Lee v. Weisman*, 505 U.S. 577 (1992); *Sante Fe Independent School District v. Doe*, 530 U.S. 290 (2000).

50. *Marsh v. Chambers*, 463 U.S. 783 (1983); *Jones v. Clear Creek Independent School*, 61 LW 3819 (1993).

51. *Lemon v. Kurtzman*, 403 U.S. 602 (1971).

52. *Lynch v. Donnelly*, 465 U.S. 668 (1984), 672–73.

53. Jeffrey Rosen, "Big Ten," *The New Republic*, March 14, 2004, p. 11.

54. *Van Orden v. Perry*, 03-1500 (2005); *McCreary County et al. v. American Civil Liberties Union of Kentucky*, 03-1693 (2005).

55. *Arizona Christian School Tuition Organization v. Winn*, U.S. Supreme Court slip. op. 09-987 and 09-991 (2011).

56. *Rosenberger v. University of Virginia*, 515 U.S. 819 (1995).

57. We will not cite all of the cases here. See Abraham and Perry, *Freedom and the Court*, Chap. 6, for a summary of cases on this topic, especially Tables 6.1 and 6.2.

58. *Employment Division, Department of Human Resources of Oregon v. Smith*, 494 U.S. 872 (1990), 878–80. This case is often erroneously reported as having banned the religious use of peyote. In fact, the Court said, "Although it is constitutionally permissible to exempt sacramental peyote use from the operation of drug laws, it is not constitutionally required."

59. *City of Boerne v. Flores*, 521 U.S. 527 (1997).

60. The court case was *Cutter v. Wilkinson*, No. 03-9877 (2005). See Linda Greenhouse, "Supreme Court Rules in Ohio Prison Case," *New York Times*, June 1, 2005, for a discussion of the broader debate.

61. *Gonzales v. O Centro Espirita Beneficiente Uniao Do Vegetal (UDV) et al.*, 546 U.S. 418 (2006).

62. *District of Columbia v. Heller*, 554 U.S. 290 (2008).

63. *McDonald v. Chicago*, 08-1521 (2010).

64. See Abraham and Perry, *Freedom and the Court*, Chap. 4, for a discussion of these cases.

65. *Florence v. County of Burlington*, U.S. 10-945 (2012),

66. *United States v. Jones*, 565 U.S.   (2012).

67. *Mapp v. Ohio*, 367 U.S. 643 (1961).

68. *United States v. Calandra*, 414 U.S. 338 (1974).

69. *Illinois v. Gates*, 462 U.S. 213 (1983).

70. *Herring v. United States*, 555 U.S.—(2009).

71. *Vernonia School District v. Acton*, 515 U.S. 646 (1995); *Board of Education of Pottawatomie County v. Earls*, 536 U.S. 832 (2002).

72. *Chandler v. Miller*, 520 U.S. 305 (1997).

73. Leslie Cauley, "NSA Has Massive Database of Americans' Phone Calls," *USA Today*, May 11, 2006, p. 1.

74. Lorraine Woellert and Dawn Kopecki, "The Snooping Goes Beyond Phone Calls," *Business Week*, May 29, 2006, p. 38; "Data Mining: Federal Efforts Cover a Wide Range of Uses," GAO Report 04-548, May 2004, www.gao.gov/new.items/d04548.pdf.

75. *Miranda v. Arizona*, 384 U.S. 436 (1966).

76. *Dickerson v. United States*, 530 U.S. 428 (2000).

77. *Benton v. Maryland*, 395 U.S. 784 (1969).

78. *Lucas v. South Carolina Coastal Council*, 505 U.S. 1003 (1992).

79. *Kelo v. City of New London*, 505 U.S. 469 (2005).

80. *Powell v. Alabama*, 287 U.S. 45 (1932).

81. *Gideon v. Wainright*, 372 U.S. 335 (1963).

82. *Evitts v. Lucy*, 469 U.S. 387 (1985); *Wiggins v. Smith*, 539 U.S. 510 (2003). See Elizabeth Gable and Tyler Green, "*Wiggins v. Smith*: The Ineffective Assistance of Counsel Standard Applied Twenty Years after *Strickland*," *Georgetown Journal of Legal Ethics* (Summer 2004), for a discussion of many of these issues.

83. *Klopfer v. North Carolina*, 386 U.S. 213 (1967).

84. The law is 18 U.S.C. § 3161(c)(1) and the ruling is *Zedner v. United States*, 05-5992 (2006).

85. The case concerning African Americans is *Batson v. Kentucky*, 106 S. Ct. 1712 (1986); the case about Latinos is *Hernandez v. New York*, 500 U.S. 352 (1991); and the gender case is *J.E.B. v. Alabama ex rel. T.B.*, 511 U.S. 127 (1994). Two recent cases affirming that peremptory challenges could not be used in a racially discriminatory fashion were *Miller-El v. Dretke*, 545 U.S. 231 (2005), and *Snyder v. Louisiana*, 552 U.S. 472 (2008).

86. *Apprendi v. New Jersey*, 530 U.S. 466 (2000); *United States v. Booker*, 543 U.S. 220 (2005); *Blakely v. Washington*, 542 U.S. 296 (2004). For a discussion of these and other relevant cases see Stephanos Bibas and Susan Klein, "The Sixth Amendment and Criminal Sentencing," *Cardozo Law Review* 30, no.3 (2008): 775–805.

87. *Furman v. Georgia*, 408 U.S. 238 (1972); *Gregg v. Georgia*, 428 U.S. 513 (1976).

88. See Abraham and Perry, *Freedom and the Court*, pp. 72–73, for a discussion of the earlier cases, and Charles Lane, "5–4 Supreme Court Abolishes Juvenile Executions," *Washington Post*, March 2, 2005, p. A1, for a discussion of the 2002 and 2005 cases. The 2008 case was *Kennedy v. Louisiana*, 554 U.S.—(2008).

89. *Trop v. Dulles*, 356 U.S. 86 (1958).

90. *Robinson v. California*, 370 U.S. 660 (1962).

91. *Hudson v. McMillian*, 503 U.S. 1 (1992); *Helling v. McKinney*, 509 U.S. 25 (1993).

92. *Solem v. Helm*, 463 U.S. 277 (1983).

93. *Harmelin v. Michigan*, 501 U.S. 957 (1991).

94. *Ewing v. California*, 538 U.S. 11 (2003); *Lockyer v. Andrade*, 538 U.S. 63 (2003). For a general discussion of these issues, see Editors' Note, "The Eighth Amendment, Proportionality, and the Changing Meaning of 'Punishments,'" *Harvard Law Review* 122, no.3 (January 2009): 960–81.

95. *Griswold v. Connecticut*, 381 U.S. 479 (1965), 482–86.

96. *Griswold v. Connecticut*, 512–13.

97. *Roe v. Wade*, 410 U.S. 113 (1973), 129.

98. *Planned Parenthood of Southeastern Pennsylvania v. Casey*, 505 U.S. 833 (1992).

99. Katharine Q. Seeyle, "Mississippi Voters Reject Anti-Abortion Measure," *New York Times*, November 8, 2011, www.nytimes.com/2011/11/09/us/politics/votes-across-the-nation-could-serve-as-a-political-barometer.html (accessed 12/5/11).

100. Department of Human Services, Office of Disease Prevention and Epidemiology, "Annual Report on Oregon's Death with Dignity Act," March 10, 2012, www.publichealth.oregon.gov/ProviderPartnerResources/EvaluationResearch/DeathWithDignityAct/Documents/year14.pdf (accessed 8/21/12).

101. *Gonzales v. Oregon*, 546 U.S. 23 (2006).

102. *Lawrence v. Texas*, 539 U.S. 558 (2003).

You Decide

a. Linda Greenhouse, "Justices Decline to Rule on Limits for Drug-Sniffing Dogs," New York Times, April 5, 2005, p. A19.

b. Illinois v. Caballes, 543 U.S. 405 (2005).

c. Oral arguments in U.S. v. Jones (2012), November 8, 2011, *www.supremecourt.gov/oral_arguments/argument_transcripts/10-1259.pdf*, p. 44 (accessed 8/20/12).

CHAPTER 5

1. "Two-Thirds of Democrats Now Support Gay Marriage," Pew Research Center, July 31, 2012, www.pewforum.org/Politics-and-Elections/2012-opinions-on-for-gay-marriage-unchanged-after-obamas-announcement.aspx (accessed 9/5/12).

2. "No Consensus about Whether Nation Is Divided into Haves and Have Nots," Pew Research Center, September 29, 2011, www.people-press.org/2011/09/29/no-consensus-about-whether-nation-is-divided-into-haves-and-have-nots (accessed 9/5/17).

3. For a description of this argument and a dissenting view, see Morris P. Fiorina, Samuel J. Adams, and Jeremy C. Pope, *Culture Wars: The Myth of a Polarized America* (New York: Longman, 2010).

4. TK.

5. For a review, see Arthur Lupia and Mathew D. McCubbins, *The Democratic Dilemma* (New York: Cambridge University Press, 1998).

6. Robert S. Erikson, Michael B. Mackuen, and James A. Stimson, *The Macro Polity* (New York: Cambridge University Press, 2002).

7. Donald Green, Bradley Palmquist, and Eric Schickler, "Macropartisanship: A Replication and Critique," *American Political Science Review* 92 (1998): 883–99; Robert S. Erikson, Michael B. Mackuen, and James A. Stimson, "What Moves Macropartisanship? A Response to Green, Palmquist, and Schickler," *American Political Science Review* 92 (1998): 901–12.

8. John Zaller, "Coming to Grips with V. O. Key's Concept of Latent Opinion" (unpublished paper, University of California, Los Angeles, 1998).

9. Morris Fiorina, *Retrospective Voting in American National Elections* (Cambridge, MA: Harvard University Press, 1981).

10. John Zaller, *The Nature and Origins of Mass Opinion* (New York: Cambridge University Press, 1992).

11. R. Michael Alvarez and John Brehm, *Hard Choices, Easy Answers* (Princeton, NJ: Princeton University Press, 2002).

12. John Zaller and Stanley Feldman, "A Theory of the Survey Response: Revealing Preferences versus Answering Questions," *American Journal of Political Science* 36 (1992): 579–616.

13. Janet M. Box-Steffensmeier and Susan DeBoef, "Macropartisanship and Macroideology in the Sophisticated Electorate," *Journal of Politics* 63:1 (2001): 232–48.

14. Jack Citrin, Donald P. Green, Christopher Muste, and Cara Wong, "Public Opinion toward Immigration Reform: The Role of Economic Motivations," *American Journal of Political Science* 59:3 (1997): 858–82.

15. William G. Jacoby, "Issue Framing and Public Opinion on Government Spending," *American Journal of Political Science*

44:4 (2000): 750–67; L. M. Bartels, "Beyond the Running Tally: Partisan Bias in Political Perceptions," *Political Behavior* 24:2 (2002): 117–50.

16. Donald R. Kinder, "Exploring the Racial Divide: Blacks, Whites, and Opinion on National Policy," *American Journal of Political Science* 45:2 (2001): 439–49; Paul M. Sniderman and Thomas Piazza, *The Scar of Race* (Cambridge, MA: Harvard University Press, 1993).

17. Robert Huckfeldt, Jeffery Levine, William Morgan, and John Sprague, "Accessibility and the Political Utility of Partisan and Ideological Orientations," *American Journal of Political Science* 43:3 (July 1999): 888–911.

18. George E. Marcus, John L. Sullivan, Elizabeth Theiss-Morse, and Sandra L. Wood, *With Malice toward Some: How People Make Civil Liberties Judgments* (New York: Cambridge University Press, 1995).

19. Stanley Feldman and Marco R. Steenbergen, "The Humanitarian Foundation of Public Support for Social Welfare," *American Journal of Political Science* 45:3 (2001): 658–77.

20. R. Michael Alvarez and John Brehm, "American Ambivalence towards Abortion Policy: Development of a Heteroskedastic Probit Model of Competing Values," *American Journal of Political Science* 39:4 (1995): 1055–82.

21. R. Michael Alvarez and John Brehm, "Are Americans Ambivalent towards Racial Policies?" *American Journal of Political Science* 41 (1997): 345–74.

22. Virginia Sapiro, "Not Your Parents' Political Socialization: Introduction for a New Generation," *Annual Review of Political Science* 7 (2004): 1–23.

23. M. Kent Jennings and Richard G. Niemi, *Generations and Politics: A Panel Study of Young Adults and Their Parents* (Princeton, NJ: Princeton University Press, 1981).

24. Robert Putnam, *Bowling Alone: The Collapse and Revival of American Community* (New York: Simon and Schuster, 2000).

25. Richard G. Niemi and Mary Hepburn, "The Rebirth of Political Socialization," *Perspectives on Politics* 24 (1995): 7–16.

26. David Campbell, *Why We Vote: How Schools and Communities Shape Our Civic Life* (Princeton, NJ: Princeton University Press, 2006).

27. Sidney Verba, Kay Schlozman, and Henry Brady, *Voice and Equality: Civic Volunteerism in American Politics* (Cambridge, MA: Harvard University Press, 1995).

28. Paul Allen Beck and M. Kent Jennings, "Pathways to Participation," *American Political Science Review* 76 (1982): 94–108.

29. Fiorina, *Retrospective Voting*.

30. Edward G. Carmines and James A. Stimson, *Issue Evolution: Race and the Transformation of American Politics* (Princeton, NJ: Princeton University Press, 1990).

31. Darren W. Davis and Brian D. Silver, "Civil Liberties vs. Security: Public Opinion in the Context of the Terrorist Attacks in America," *American Journal of Political Science* 48:1 (2004): 28–46; Leonie Huddy, Nadia Khatib, and Theresa Capelos, "The Polls: Trends," *Public Opinion Quarterly* 66 (2002): 418–50.

32. Pew Research Center, "Public More Optimistic about the Economy, but Still Reluctant to Spend," June 19, 2009, www .people-press.org/report/523/economy-spending (accessed 11/4/09).

33. Robert S. Erikson, Michael B. Mackuen, and James A. Stimson, "Macro-partisanship," *American Political Science Review* 83 (1989): 1125–42.

34. Frank Baumgartner, Suzanna DeBoef, and Amber Bodston, *The Decline of the Death Penalty and the Discovery of Innocence* (New York: Cambridge University Press, 2008).

35. Richard Nadwau et al., "Class, Party and South-Nonsouth Differences," *American Politics Research* 32 (2004): 52–67.

36. Donald P. Green, Bradley Palmquist, and Eric Schickler, *Partisan Hearts and Minds* (New Haven, CT: Yale University Press, 2002).

37. Don Balz, "Contests Serve as Warning to Democrats: It's Not 2008 Anymore," *Washington Post*, November 4, 2009, p. A1.

38. For elaboration on this point, see William T. Bianco, Richard G. Niemi, and Harold W. Stanley, "Partisanship and Group Support over Time: A Multivariate Analysis," *American Political Science Review* 80 (September 1986): 969–76.

39. Arthur Lupia and Mathew D. McCubbins, *The Democratic Dilemma* (New York: Cambridge University Press, 1998).

40. Lawrence R. Jacobs and Robert Y. Shapiro, *Politicians Don't Pander: Political Manipulation and the Loss of Democratic Responsiveness* (Chicago: University of Chicago Press, 2000).

41. Robert Y. Shapiro and Lawrence Jacobs, "Simulating Representation: Elite Mobilization and Political Power in Health Care Reform," *The Forum* 8:1 (2010), article 4.

42. Christopher Wlezien and Robert S. Erikson, "The Horse Race: What Polls Reveal as the Election Campaign Unfolds," *International Journal of Public Opinion Research* 19:1 (2007): 74–88

43. Pollster.com, "IVR and Internet: How Reliable?" September 28, 2006, www.pollster.com/mystery_pollster/ivr_internet_ how_reliable.php (accessed 2/21/08).

44. For data on reported and actual turnout, see Chapter 7.

45. Anton J. Nederhof, "Methods of Coping with Social Desirability Bias: A Review," *European Journal of Social Psychology* 15:3 (2006): 263–80.

46. Gary Langer, "Two Years from Election, Looking at Early Polls," *ABC News*, January 18, 2007, http://abcnews.go.com/ Politics/story?id=2802742&page=1 (accessed 2/21/08).

47. James H. Kuklinski et al., "Misinformation and the Currency of Democratic Citizenship," *Journal of Politics* 62:3 (2000): 790–816.

48. Pew Research Center, "Health Care Reform Closely Followed, Much Discussed," August 20, 2009, www.people-press.org/ reports/pdf/537.pdf (accessed 11/5/09).

49. George H. Bishop, *The Illusion of Public Opinion: Fact and Artifact in Public Opinion Polls* (Washington, DC: Roman & Littlefield, 2004).

50. Michael X. Delli Carpini and Scott Keeter, *What Americans Know about Politics and Why It Matters* (New Haven, CT: Yale University Press, 1997).

51. Delli Carpini and Keeter, *What Americans Know about Politics*.

52. Morris P. Fiorina, Samuel J. Abrams, and Jeremy C. Pope, *Culture War? The Myth of a Polarized America* (New York: Longman, 2002).

53. For a review of the literature on trust in government, see Karen Cook, Russell Hardin, and Margaret Levi, *Cooperation without Trust* (New York: Russell Sage Foundation, 2005); Marc J. Hetherington, *Why Trust Matters: Declining Political Trust and the Demise of American Liberalism* (Princeton, NJ: Princeton University Press, 2004).

54. William T. Bianco, *Trust: Representatives and Constituents* (Ann Arbor: University of Michigan Press, 1994).

55. Sean M. Theriault, *The Power of the People: Congressional Competition, Public Attention, and Voter Retribution* (Columbus: Ohio State University Press, 2005).

56. John R. Hibbing and Elizabeth Theiss-Morse, *Congress as Public Enemy: Public Attitudes toward American Political Institutions* (New York: Cambridge University Press, 1995).

57. Thomas Rudolph and Jillian Evans, "Political Trust, Ideology, and Public Support for Government Spending," *American Journal of Political Science* 49 (2005): 660–71.

58. Patricia Moy and Michael Pfau, *With Malice toward All? The Media and Public Confidence in Democratic Institutions* (Boulder, CO: Praeger, 2000).

59. Robert S. Erikson, Michael B. Mackuen, and James A. Stimson, *The Macro Polity* (New York: Cambridge University Press, 2002).

60. James A. Stimson, *Public Opinion in America: Moods, Swings, and Cycles* (Boulder, CO: Westview Press, 1999).

61. Robert S. Erikson, Michael B. Mackuen, and James A. Stimson, "American Politics: The Model" (unpublished manuscript, Columbia University, 2000).

62. See, for example, Pew Research Center, "Iraq Looms Large in Nationalized Election," October 5, 2006, www.people-press.org/reports/display.php3?ReportID=290 (accessed 6/1/12), as well as data at www.pollingreport.com.

63. Larry Bartels, "Constituency Opinion and Congressional Policy Making: The Reagan Defense Buildup, *American Political Science Review* 85 (June 1991): 457–74; Jonathan Kastellec, Jeffrey R. Lax, and Justin H. Phillips, "Public Opinion and Senate Confirmation of Supreme Court Nominees," *Journal of Politics* 72 (2010): 767–84.

64. Lawrence R. Jacobs and Robert Y. Shapiro, *Politicians Don't Pander: Political Manipulation and the Loss of Democratic Responsiveness* (Chicago: University of Chicago Press, 2000).

65. Brandice Canes-Wrone, *Who Leads Whom: Presidents, Policy, and the Public* (Chicago: University of Chicago Press, 2005).

66. Thom Shanker and David S. Cloud, "The Reach of War: Bush's Plan for Iraq Runs into Opposition in Congress," *New York Times*, January 12, 2007, p. A1.

67. See, for example, James J. Cramer, "Newspapers Still Stumble Online," RealMoney.com, May 2, 2005, www.thestreet.com/p/_rms/rmoney/jamesjcramer/10221101.html (accessed 2/26/08).

68. Paul Starr, "Reclaiming the Air," *The American Prospect*, March 2004, pp. 57–61.

69. The president's current budget is available at www.whitehouse.gov/omb/budget; the *Federal Register* can be found at www.gpoaccess.gov/fr; and Government Accountability Office reports are available at www.gao.gov.

70. See www.nationalreview.com.

71. See www.politico.com/playbook/.

72. See www.scotusblog.com/movabletype.

73. See www.themonkeycage.org.

74. A. J. Liebling, "Do You Belong in Journalism?" *The New Yorker*, May 14, 1960, p. 105.

75. See www.milblogging.com/.

76. The video *Allen's Listening Tour* is available at http://youtube.com/watch?v=9G7gq7GQ71c (accessed 2/26/08).

77. The *Washington Post* has an archive of previous online discussions at "Post Politics Hour," September 30, 2009, www.washingtonpost.com/wp-dyn/content/linkset/2005/09/30/LI2005093000746.html (accessed 6/1/12).

78. Geoffrey A. Fowler and Carol Lee. 2011. "At Facebook Town Hall, Obama Goes on Offensive." http://online.wsj.com/article/SB10001424052748703838004576275580143706192.html, April 20, 2011 (accessed 6/1/12).

79. For a skeptical introduction to this argument, see the proceedings of "MeetUp, Craigslist, eBay: Has the Web Changed Politics?," a conference at the Harvard School of Law, December 9–11, 2004, http://cyber.law.harvard.edu/is2k4/home (accessed 6/1/12).

80. Bruce Bimber, "Information and Political Engagement in America: The Search for Effects of Information Technology at the Individual Level," *Political Research Quarterly* 54 (2001): 53–67; Caroline J. Tolbert and Ramona S. McNeal, "Unraveling the Effects of the Internet on Political Participation," *Political Research Quarterly* 56 (2003): 175–85.

81. Pew Research Center, "Public Knowledge of Current Affairs Little Changed by News and Information Revolutions," April 15, 2007, www.people-press.org/reports/display.php3?ReportID = 319 (accessed 2/28/08).

82. Shanto Iyengar and Kyu S. Hahn, "Red Media, Blue Media: Evidence of Ideological Selectivity in Media Use," *Journal of Communication* 59 (2009): 19–39.

83. Eric Lawrence, John Sides, and Henry Farrell, "Self-Segregation or Deliberation? Blog Readership, Participation, and Polarization in American Politics," *Perspectives on Politics* 8 (2010): 141–57.

84. Markus Prior, *Post-Broadcast Democracy: How Media Choice Increases Inequality in Political Involvement and Polarizes Elections* (New York: Cambridge University Press, 2007).

85. This discussion draws on the summary "Merging Media: How Relaxing FCC Ownership Rules Has Affected the Media Business," www.pbs.org/newshour/media/conglomeration/fcc2.html (accessed 2/26/08).

86. Peter Braestrup, *Big Story: How the American Press and Television Reported and Interpreted the Crisis of Tet 1968 in Vietnam* (New Haven, CT: Yale University Press, 1983).

87. For an extended discussion of the fairness doctrine and related issues, see "Fairness Doctrine: U.S. Broadcasting Policy,"

www.museum.tv/eotvsection.php?entrycode-fairnessdoct (accessed 10/17/12).

88. The Project for Excellence in Journalism, "The State of the News Media, 2007: Ownership," 2007, www.stateofthenews media.org/2007/narrative_overview_ownership.asp?cat=5 &media=1 (accessed 2/26/08).

89. The FCC website has details of current regulations as well as the agency's strategic goals. See www.fcc.gov/ (accessed 10/17/12).

90. *Columbia Journalism Review* maintains a list of holdings for major media companies at Who Owns What, www.cjr.org/ tools/owners.

91. For a discussion of these concepts, see Paul M. Sniderman and Sean M. Theriault, "The Structure of Political Argument and the Logic of Issue Framing," in *Studies in Public Opinion*, ed. William E. Saris and Paul M. Sniderman (Princeton, NJ: Princeton University Press, 2004); Shanto Iyengar and Donald Kinder, *News That Matters* (Chicago: University of Chicago Press, 1987). See also Maxwell McCombs and Donald L. Shaw, "The Agenda-Setting Functions of Mass Media," *Public Opinion Quarterly* 36 (1972): 176–87; Amos Tversky and Daniel Kahnemann, "The Framing of Decisions and the Psychology of Choice," *Science* 211 (1981): 453–58.

92. James N. Druckman and Michael Parkin, "The Impact of Media Bias: How Editorial Slant Affects Voters," *Journal of Politics* 67 (2005): 4, 1030–49; for similar results, see Kim Fridkin Kahn and Patrick J. Kenney, "The Slant of the News," *American Political Science Review* 96 (2002): 381–94.

93. Jon A. Krosnick and Laura Brannon, "The Impact of the Gulf War on the Ingredients of Presidential Evaluations: Multidimensional Effects of Political Involvement," *American Political Science Review* 87 (1993): 963–75.

CHAPTER 6

1. John Aldrich, *Why Parties?* (Chicago: University of Chicago Press, 2005).

2. Joseph Schlesinger, *Political Parties and the Winning of Office* (Ann Arbor: University of Michigan Press, 1994).

3. The three-part description first appeared in V. O. Key, *Politics, Parties, and Pressure Groups* (New York: Crowell, 1956). For a more recent description, see Paul Allen Beck and Marjorie Hershey, *Party Politics in America* (New York: Longman, 2004).

4. William Nesbit Chambers and Walter Dean Burnham, *The American Party Systems: Stages of Political Development* (Oxford, UK: Oxford University Press, 1966).

5. Donald H. Hickey, "Federalist Party Unity and the War of 1812," *Journal of American Studies* 12 (April 1978): 23–39; William T. Bianco, David B. Spence, and John D. Wilkerson, "The Electoral Connection in the Early Congress: The Case of the Compensation Act of 1816," *American Journal of Political Science* 40 (February 1996): 145–71.

6. Aldrich, *Why Parties?*

7. James MacPherson, *Battle Cry of Freedom: The Civil War Era* (New York: Oxford University Press, 1988).

8. Michael F. Holt, *The Rise and Fall of the Whig Party: Jacksonian Politics and the Onset of the Civil War* (New York: Oxford University Press, 1999).

9. Raymond Wolfinger, "Why Political Machines Have Not Withered Away and Other Revisionist Thoughts," *Journal of Politics* 34:2 (1972): 365–98.

10. For details on Tammany Hall, see William L. Riordon, *Plunkitt of Tammany Hall* (1905; repr., New York: Dutton, 1963), also available at www.marxists.org/reference/archive/ plunkett-george/tammany-hall.

11. Harold W. Stanley, William T. Bianco, and Richard G. Niemi, "Partisanship and Group Support over Time: A Multivariate Analysis," *American Political Science Review* 80 (1986): 969–76.

12. Frank Baumgartner and Bryan D. Jones, *Agendas and Instability in American Politics* (Chicago: University of Chicago Press, 2009).

13. Aldrich, *Why Parties?*

14. James L. Sundquist, *Dynamics of the Party System*, rev. ed. (Washington, DC: Brookings Institution, 1983).

15. Aldrich, *Why Parties?*

16. The full list of Democratic constituency groups is available at www.democrats.org/people. A list of Republican coalition groups is available at www.gop.com/coalition-support (accessed 10/18/12).

17. Jon F. Hale, "The Making of the New Democrats," *Political Science Quarterly* 110:2 (1995): 207–32.

18. James Monroe, *The Political Party Matrix* (Albany, NY: SUNY Press, 2001).

19. Gary Cox and Mathew McCubbins, *Legislative Leviathan* (Berkeley: University of California Press, 1993); James M. Snyder and Michael M. Ting, "An Informational Rationale for Political Parties," *American Journal of Political Science* 46 (2002): 90–110.

20. David Kirkpatrick, "Pelosi Faces Competing Pressures on Health Care," *New York Times*, November 9, 2009, p. A1.

21. Jason Roberts and Steven Smith, "Procedural Contexts, Party Strategy, and Conditional Party Government," *American Journal of Political Science* 47:2 (2003): 205–317.

22. David Rohde, *Parties and Leaders in the Post-Reform House* (Chicago: University of Chicago Press, 1991).

23. Catherine Rampell, "Tax Pledge May Scuttle a Deal on Deficit," *New York Times*, November 18, 2011, p. B1.

24. Michael Meffert, Helmut Norpoth, and Anirudh V. S. Ruhil, "Realignment and Macropartisanship," *American Political Science Review* 95:4 (2001): 953–62.

25. Larry M. Bartels, "Partisanship and Voting Behavior, 1952–1996," *American Journal of Political Science* 44:1 (2000): 35–50.

26. Martin P. Wattenberg, *Where Have All the Voters Gone?* (Cambridge, MA: Harvard University Press, 2002).

27. Jill Lawrence, "Party Recruiters Lead Charge for '06 Vote; Choice of Candidates to Run in Fall May Decide Who Controls the House," *USA Today*, May 25, 2006, p. A5.

28. Compiled from information available at www.ballot-access .org (accessed 12/17/09).

29. Data compiled from Center for Responsive Politics, "Political Parties Overview: Election Cycle 2012," www.opensecrets .org/parties/index.php (accessed 11/2/12).

30. Patricia Zapor, "Pro-life Democrats Describe Lonely Role, but See Improvements," *Catholic News Service*, July 28, 2004, www.catholicnews.com/data/stories/cns/0404122.htm (accessed 3/27/08).

31. See www.lp.org/our-history (accessed 6/5/12).

32. Pew Research & American Life Project surveys 2000-2009," available at www.pewinternet.org/static-pages/trend-data/ online-activities-20002009.aspx (accessed 12/1/09).

33. See www.constitutionparty.com/party_platform.php (accessed 6/5/12).

You Decide

a. Nelson Polsby, *Consequences of Party Reform* (New York: Oxford University Press, 1983).

b. Daniel A. Smith and Caroline J. Tolbert, *Educated by Initiative: The Effects of Direct Democracy on Citizens and Political Organizations in the American States* (Ann Arbor: University of Michigan Press, 2004).

CHAPTER 7

1. Morris P. Fiorina, *Retrospective Voting in American National Elections* (New Haven, CT: Yale University Press, 1981); V. O. Key, *The Responsible Electorate* (New York: Vintage, 1966).

2. David Mayhew, *Congress: The Electoral Connection* (New Haven, CT: Yale University Press, 1973).

3. For details on early voting, see the Early Voting Information Center site, http://earlyvoting.net/ (accessed 10/19/12).

4. See www.cnn.com/ELECTIONS (accessed 10/19/12).

5. For details, see the Caltech/MIT Voting Technology Project site, www.vote.caltech.edu (accessed 10/19/12).

6. Randall Stross, "The Big Gamble on Electronic Voting," *New York Times*, September 24, 2006. p. 3.

7. Minor party candidates are typically selected during party conventions.

8. Barbara Norrander, "Presidential Nomination Politics in the Post-Reform Era," *Political Research Quarterly* 49 (1996): 875–90.

9. Larry Bartels, *Presidential Primaries and the Dynamics of Public Choice* (Princeton, NJ: Princeton University Press, 1988).

10. For a discussion of the 2004 conventions, see Kennedy School of Government, *Campaigning for President: The Managers Look at 2004* (New York: Rowman & Littlefield, 2005).

11. FairVote, "Maine and Nebraska," www.fairvote.org/e_college/ me_ne.htm (accessed 10/19/12).

12. James Q. Wilson, "Is the Electoral College Worth Saving?" *Slate*, November 3, 2000, www.slate.com/id/92663 (accessed 10/19/12).

13. Steven Ansolabehere and Allan Gerber, "Incumbency Advantage and the Persistence of Legislative Majorities," *Legislative Studies Quarterly* 22 (1997): 161–80.

14. For a discussion of Johnson's decision, see Robert A. Caro, *The Path to Power* (New York: Knopf, 1983).

15. Thomas Mann and Norman Ornstein, *The Permanent Campaign and Its Future* (Washington, DC: American Enterprise Institute, 2000).

16. David Mayhew, *Congress: The Electoral Connection* (New Haven, CT: Yale University Press, 1973).

17. Jonathan Krasno and Donald P. Green, "The Dynamics of Campaign Fundraising in House Elections," *Journal of Politics* 56 (1991): 459–74.

18. Michael J. Goff, *The Money Primary: The New Politics of the Early Presidential Nomination Process* (New York: Rowman & Littlefield, 2007).

19. Chris Cillizza, "Consulting Firms Face Conflict in 2008," *Roll Call*, June 20, 2005. p. 1.

20. Matt Bai, "Turnout Wins Elections," *New York Times Magazine*, December 14, 2003, p. 100.

21. Christopher Drew, "New Telemarketing Ploy Steers Voters on Republican Path," *New York Times*, November 6, 2006.

22. Michael Shear and Richard A. Oppel, "For Perry, a Cringe-Worthy Gaffe," *New York Times*, http://thecaucus.blogs .nytimes.com/2011/11/09/for-perry-a-cringe-worthy-gaffe/, November 9, 2011 (accessed 10/19/12).

23. For a history of presidential debates, see the Commission on Presidential Debates site, www.debates.org (accessed 10/19/12).

24. Molly Ball, "This Year's Attack Ads Cut Deeper," *Politico*, October 17, 2010, www.politico.com/news/stories/1010/43698 .html (accessed 10/19/12).

25. For a video library of presidential campaign ads, see Museum of the Moving Image, "The Living Room Candidate: Presidential Campaign Commercials 1952–2012," http://livingroom-candidate.org (accessed 10/19/12).

26. For examples of this argument, see Thomas Patterson, *The Vanishing Voter* (New York: Knopf, 2002); Jules Witcover, *No Way to Pick a President: How Money and Hired Guns Have Debased American Politics* (London: Routledge, 2001).

27. For examples of these and other campaign ads, see "Most Intriguing Campaign Ads of 2010," ABC News, http:// abcnews.go.com/politics/slideshow/intriguing-political -ads-2010-10887147 (accessed 10/19/12).

28. Steven Ansolabehere and Shanto Iyengar, *Going Negative: How Political Advertisements Shrink and Polarize the Electorate* (New York: Free Press, 1997); Richard Lau, Lee Sigelman, Caroline Heldman, and Paul Babbitt, "The Effects of Negative Political Advertisements: A Meta-Analytic Analysis," *American Political Science Review* 93 (1999): 851–70.

29. Paul Freeman, Michael Franz, and Kenneth Goldstein, "Campaign Advertising and Democratic Citizenship," *American Journal of Political Science* 48 (2004): 723–41.

30. Constantine J. Spilotes and Lynn Vavreck, "Campaign Advertising: Partisan Convergence or Divergence," *Journal of Politics* 64 (2002): 249–61.

31. Kathleen Hall Jameson, *Packaging the Presidency: A History and Criticism of Presidential Campaign Advertising* (New York: Oxford University Press, 1996).

32. Jonathan Krasno and Frank J. Sorauf, "For the Defense," *Political Science and Politics* 37 (2004): 777–80.

33. Brian Stelter, "The Price of 30 Seconds," *New York Times*, October 1, 2007, http://mediadecoder.blogs.nytimes.com/2007/10/01/the-price-of-30-seconds (accessed 10/19/12).

34. For a review of this literature, see Michael Malbin, *The Election after Reform: Money, Politics, and the Bipartisan Campaign Reform Act* (Washington, DC: Roman & Littlefield, 2006).

35. For a discussion, see Patterson, *The Vanishing Voter*, especially Chapter 1, "The Incredible Shrinking Electorate," pp. 3–22.

36. William H. Riker and Peter Ordeshook, "A Theory of the Calculus of Voting," *American Political Science Review* 62 (1968): 25–39.

37. Michael McDonald, "The United States Elections Project," http://elections.gmu.edu (accessed 10/19/12).

38. Pew Research Center, "Regular Voters, Intermittent Voters, and Those Who Don't," October 18, 2006, www.people-press.org/reports/pdf/292.pdf.

39. Richard P. Lau and David P. Reslawsk, *How Voters Decide: Information Processing during Electoral Campaigns* (New York: Cambridge University Press, 2006).

40. Gary Cox and Jonathan Katz, "Why Did the Incumbency Advantage in U.S. House Elections Grow?" *American Journal of Political Science* 40 (1996): 478–96.

41. Charles Franklin, "Eschewing Obfuscation: Campaigns and the Perceptions of U.S. Senate Incumbents," *American Political Science Review* 85 (December, 1991): 1193–214; Wendy M. Rahn, "The Role of Partisan Stereotypes in Information Processing about Political Candidates," *American Journal of Political Science* 37 (May 1993): 472–96.

42. Bruce Cain, John Ferejohn, and Morris Fiorina, *The Personal Vote* (Cambridge, MA: Harvard University Press, 1985).

43. Jeffrey Koch, "Gender Stereotypes and Citizens' Impressions of House Candidates' Ideological Orientations," *American Journal of Political Science* 46 (2002): 453–62; Monica McDermott, "Candidate Occupations and Voter Information," *Journal of Politics* 67 (2005): 201–18; Carol Sigelman, Lee Sigelman, Barbara Walkosz, and Michael Nitz, "Black Candidates, White Voters: Understanding Racial Bias in Political Perceptions," *American Journal of Political Science* 39 (February 1995): 243–65.

44. Fiorina, *Retrospective Voting in American National Elections*; Key, *The Responsible Electorate*.

45. Alfred J. Tuchfarber, Stephen E. Bennett, Andrew E. Smith, and Eric W. Rademacher, "The Republican Tidal Wave of 1994: Testing Hypotheses about Realignment, Restructuring, and Rebellion," *Political Science and Politics* 28 (1995): 689–93.

46. Samuel Popkin, *The Reasoning Voter* (Chicago: University of Chicago Press, 1991).

47. Richard R. Lau and David P. Redlawsk, "Advantages and Disadvantages of Cognitive Heuristics in Political Decision Making," *American Journal of Political Science* 45 (2001): 951–71.

48. For 2006 exit poll data, see Pew Research Center, "Public Cheers Democratic Victory," November 16, 2006, http://people-press.org/reports/display.php3?ReportID=296 (accessed 10/19/12).

49. For data on presidential approval and evaluations of Congress in normal and nationalized elections, see Pew Research Center, "Democrats Hold Double-Digit Lead in Competitive Districts," October 6, 2006, http://people-press.org/reports/display.php3?ReportID=293 (accessed 10/19/12).

50. Pew Research Center, "Midterm Snapshot: Enthusiasm for Obama Reelection Bid Greater Than for Reagan in 1982," October 25, 2010, http://pewresearch.org/pubs/1778/public-split-on-obama-run-in-2012-but-better-than-reagan-outlook-in-1982?src=prc-latest&proj=forum (accessed 10/19/12).

51. Amanda Terkel, "The One-Person Funded Super-PAC: How Wealthy Donors Can Skirt Campaign Finance Restrictions," *Huffington Post*, October 22, 2010, www.huffingtonpost.com/2010/10/21/super-pac-taxpayers-earmarks-concerned-citizens-campaign-finance_n_772214.html (accessed 10/19/12).

52. Amy Gardner, "Gauging the Scope of the Tea Party Movement in America," *Washington Post*, October 24, 2010, p. A1.

CHAPTER 8

1. Capital Eye Blog, "TARP Recipients Paid Out $114 Million for Politicking Last Year," February 4, 2009, www.opensecrets.org/news/2009/02/tarp-recipients-paid-out-114-m.html (accessed 9/18/12).

2. see also Joe Weisenthal, "Congressmen: Yep, Wall Street Owns Washington," June 4, 2009, www.businessinsider.com/congressman-yep-wall-street-owns-washington-2009-6 (accessed 8/28/09).

3. Robert H. Salisbury, John P. Heinz, Edward O. Laumann, and Robert L. Nelson, "Who Works with Whom? Interest Group Alliances and Opposition," *American Political Science Review* 81 (1987): 1217–34.

4. Business-Industry Political Action Committee, "About BIPAC," www.bipac.org/about/about.asp (accessed 4/8/08).

5. James Q. Wilson, *Political Organizations* (New York: Basic Books, 1974).

6. American Automobile Association, Foundation for Traffic Safety, www.aaafoundation.org/home (accessed 4/8/08).

7. Scott Ainsworth, "Regulating Lobbyists and Interest Group Influence," *Journal of Politics* 55 (1993): 41–55.

8. Scott Ainsworth, *Analyzing Interest Groups: Group Influence on People and Policies* (New York: Norton, 2002)

9. Timothy Egan, "For Thirsty Farmers, Old Friends at Interior," *New York Times*, March 3, 2006, p. A1.

10. Public Citizen Congress Watch, "Congressional Revolving Doors: The Journey from Congress to K Street," July 2005, www.lobbyinginfo.org/documents/RevolveDoor.pdf (accessed 4/9/08).

11. Eric Lipton, "Former Antiterror Officials Find Industry Pays Better," *New York Times*, June 18, 2006, p. A1.

12. Lobbying regulations are often changed; the discussion here is just a general guide. Regular reports on past, current, and

proposed lobbying regulations can be found on the website of the Congressional Research Service at www.opencrs.com (accessed 9/19/12).

13. Frank Baumgartner and Beth Leech, *Basic Interests: The Importance of Interest Groups in Politics and in Political Science* (Princeton, NJ: Princeton University Press, 1999), p. 109.

14. Timothy M. LaPira, and Nicholas A. Semanko. 2005. "Drawing Lobbyists to Washington: Government Activity and the Demand for Advocacy," Political Research Quarterly 58, 1 (March): 19–30

15. Leslie Wayne, "Documents Show Extent of Lobbying by Boeing," *New York Times*, September 3, 2003.

16. Center for Responsive Politics, Lobbying Spending Database, "General Electric Summary, 2006," www.opensecrets .org/lobbyists/clientsum.asp?txtname=General+Electric& year=2006 (accessed 4/7/08).

17. Center for Responsive Politics, Lobbying Spending Database, "Sierra Club Summary, 2006," www.opensecrets.org/ lobbyists/clientsum.asp?txtname=Sierra+Club&year=2006 (accessed 4/7/08).

18. For more on this argument, see Tim Harford, "There's Not Enough Money in Politics," *Slate*, April 1, 2006, www.slate .com/id/2138874 (accessed 4/8/08); and Stephen Ansolabehere, John M. de Figueiredo, and James M. Snyder, "Why Is There So Little Money in American Politics?" *Journal of Economic Perspectives* 17 (2003): 105–30.

19. Ken Kollman, *Outside Lobbying* (Princeton, NJ: Princeton University Press, 1998).

20. Jack Walker, *Mobilizing Interest Groups in America* (Ann Arbor: University of Michigan Press, 1991).

21. John P. Heinz, Edward O. Laumann, and Robert Salisbury, *The Hollow Core: Private Interests in National Policymaking* (Cambridge, MA: Harvard University Press, 1993).

22. Kay Lehman Schlozman and John Tierney, *Organized Interests and American Democracy* (New York: HarperCollins, 1986).

23. Christine A. DeGregorio, *Networks of Champions: Leadership, Access, and Advocacy in the U.S. House of Representatives* (Ann Arbor: University of Michigan Press, 1992).

24. Daniel Carpenter, *The Forging of Bureaucratic Autonomy: Reputations, Networks, and Policy Innovation in Executive Agencies, 1862–1928* (Princeton, NJ: Princeton University Press, 2002).

25. Public Citizen Publications, www.citizen.org/publications (accessed 7/25/09).

26. Derived from a search of the NRA Institute for Legislative Action site, www.nraila.org (accessed 9/19/12).

27. Kim Scheppele and Jack L. Walker, "The Litigation Strategies of Interest Groups," in *Mobilizing Interest Groups in America*, ed. Jack Walker (Ann Arbor: University of Michigan Press, 1991).

28. Kevin W. Hula, *Lobbying Together: Interest Group Coalitions in Legislative Politics* (Washington, DC: Georgetown University Press, 1999).

29. Lauren Cohen Bell, *Warring Factions: Interest Groups, Money, and the New Politics of Senate Confirmation* (Columbus: Ohio State University Press, 2002).

30. Jeanne Cummings, "Word Games Could Threaten Climate Bill," June 9, 2009, www.politico.com/news/stories/0609/ 24059.html (accessed 9/19/12).

31. Richard Fenno, *Home Style: U.S. House Members in Their Districts* (Boston: Little, Brown, 1978). See also Brandice Caines-Wrone, David W. Brady, and John F. Cogan, "Out of Step, Out of Office: Electoral Accountability and House Members' Voting," *American Political Science Review* 96 (2002): 127–40.

32. Emily Yoffe, "Am I the Next Jack Abramoff?" April 1, 2006, www.slate.com/id/2137886/ (accessed 8/28/09).

33. Kollman, *Outside Lobbying.*

34. For these and other campaign finance data, see the Federal Election Commission website at www.fec.gov, or the Center for Responsive Politics site at www.opensecrets.org (accessed 9/19/12).

35. For a review, see Carpenter, *The Forging of Bureaucratic Autonomy.*

36. Baumgartner and Leech, *Basic Interests,* Chapter 7, especially Table 7.1 and Table 7.2, pp. 130 and 132.

37. Baumgartner and Leech, *Basic Interests,* p. 133.

38. Frank Baumgartner, Jeffrey M. Berry, Marie Hojnacki, David C. Kimball, and Beth L. Leech, *Lobbying and Policy Change: Who Wins, Who Loses, and Why* (Chicago: University of Chicago Press, 2009).

39. Baumgartner and Leech, *Basic Interests,* Chapter 7, pp. 120–46.

40. John M. Berry, *The Interest Group Society* (New York: Harper Collins, 1997); Raymond A. Bauer, Ithiel de Sola Pool, and Lewis Dexter, *American Business and Public Policy* (New York: Atherton Press, 1963).

41. Kollman, *Outside Lobbying.*

42. Austen-Smith and Wright, "Counteractive Lobbying"; Frank R. Baumgartner and Beth L. Leech, "The Multiple Ambiguities of 'Counteractive Lobbying,'" *American Journal of Political Science* 40 (1996): 521–42.

You Decide

a Jacob Weisberg, "Three Cities, Three Scandals: What Jack Abramoff, Anthony Pellicano, and Jared Paul Stern Have in Common," *Slate*, April 9, 2006, www.slate.com/id/2140238 (accessed 10/25/12).

b Associated Press, "Others Caught up in Abramoff Scandal," *New York Times*, March 23, 2007, www.nytimes.com/aponline/ us/AP-Griles-Abramoff-Glance.htm (accessed 4/5/07). Associated Press, "Former Deputy Interior Secretary to Plead Guilty in Lobbyist Case," *New York Times*, March 23, 2007, www .nytimes.com/aponline/washington/AP-Griles-Abramoff .html (accessed 4/5/07).

c For the full text of this proposal, see League of Women Voters et al., "Ethics and Lobbying Reform: Six Benchmarks for Lobbying Reform," January 23, 2006, www.lwv.org (accessed 9/11/12).

CHAPTER 9

1. See Paul Gronke, *The Electorate, the Campaign, and the Office: A Unified Approach to Senate and House Elections* (Ann Arbor: University of Michigan Press, 2000), for research showing that House and Senate elections have many similar characteristics. See Richard F. Fenno, *Senators on the Campaign Trail: The Politics of Representation* (Norman: University of Oklahoma Press, 1996), for a good general discussion of Senate elections.

2. Claudine Gay, "Spirals of Trust? The Effect of Descriptive Representation on the Relationship between Citizens and Their Government," *American Journal of Political Science* 46, no. 4 (October 2002): 717–32; Katherine Tate, *Black Faces in the Mirror: African Americans and Their Representatives in the U.S. Congress* (Princeton, NJ: Princeton University Press, 2003), Chap. 7. However, Tate shows that African Americans who are represented by African Americans in Congress are not any more likely to vote, be involved in politics, or have higher overall approval rates of Congress than African Americans who are not descriptively represented.

3. R. Douglas Arnold, *The Logic of Congressional Action* (New Haven, CT: Yale University Press, 1990), pp. 60–71.

4. David R. Mayhew, *Congress: The Electoral Connection* (New Haven, CT: Yale University Press, 1974).

5. Mayhew, *Congress*, p. 17.

6. Sean Trende, "In Pennsylvania, the Gerrymander of the Decade?" RealClearPolitics, December 14, 2011, www.realclearpolitics.com/articles/2011/12/14/in_pennsylvania_the_gerrymander_of_the_decade_112404.html (accessed 12/20/11); Dennis Byrne, "GOP Can't Catch a Break on Fairness," *Chicago Tribune*, December 20, 2011, www.chicagotribune.com/news/opinion/ct-oped-1220-byrne-20111220,0,7120320.column (accessed 12/20/11).

7. Dan Eggen, "Justice Staff Saw Texas Districting as Illegal: Voting Rights Finding on Map Pushed by DeLay Was Overruled," *Washington Post*, December 2, 2005, p. A1. The court case is *League of United Latin American Citizens v. Perry*, 547 U.S. (2006).

8. All poll data are from PollingReport.com (www.pollingreport.com).

9. Mark J. Rozell, "Press Coverage of Congress, 1946–1992," in *Congress, the Press, and the Public*, ed. Thomas E. Mann and Norman J. Ornstein (Washington, DC: Brookings Institution Press, 1994), p. 110.

10. R. Douglas Arnold, *Congress, the Press, and Political Accountability* (Princeton, NJ: Princeton University Press, 2004), p. 80.

11. See Kenneth R. Mayer and David T. Canon, *The Dysfunctional Congress: The Individual Roots of an Institutional Dilemma*, 2nd ed. (New York: Columbia University Press, 2011), for an extended discussion of this argument.

12. Gary C. Jacobson, *The Politics of Congressional Elections*, 5th ed. (New York: Longman, 2001), pp. 24–30.

13. Richard F. Fenno, *Home Style: House Members in Their Districts* (Boston: Little, Brown, 1978).

14. Morris Fiorina, *Congress: Keystone of the Washington Establishment*, rev. ed. (New Haven: Yale University Press, 1989).

15. John McCain, "Remarks by Senator John McCain on the Conference Report of the FY2012 Omnibus Appropriations Bill," December 16, 2011, http://mccain.senate.gov/public/index.cfm?FuseAction=PressOffice.PressReleases&ContentRecord_id=48f0c068-a39a-0237-fb09-7faf7546fb90 (accessed 12/19/12).

16. Jonathan Weisman and Jim VandeHei, "Road Bill Reflects the Power of Pork: White House Drops Effort to Rein in Hill," *Washington Post*, August 11, 2005, p. A1.

17. Republicans imposed an important qualification to the norm in 1995 when they set a six-year term limit for committee and subcommittee chairs.

18. David Rohde and John Aldrich, "The Transition to Republican Rule in the House: Implications for Theories of Congressional Politics," *Political Science Quarterly* 112, no. 4 (Winter 1997–98): 541–67.

19. Nelson W. Polsby, *Congress and the Presidency*, 4th ed. (Englewood Cliffs, NJ: Prentice Hall, 1986), p. 111.

20. CBS News, "Obama: Fundraiser-in-Chief," August 5, 2010, www.cbsnews.com/video/watch/?id-6747632n (accessed 8/18/10).

21. David E. Price, "Congressional Committees in the Policy Process," in *Congress Reconsidered*, 3rd ed., ed. Lawrence C. Dodd and Bruce I. Oppenheimer (Washington, DC: CQ Press, 1985), pp. 161–88.

22. Barbara Sinclair, *Unorthodox Lawmaking* (Washington, DC: CQ Press, 2000), p. xiv.

23. Sinclair, *Unorthodox Lawmaking*, p. 59.

24. Kenneth Chamberlain, "Government Shutdown Scares through the Years," *National Journal*, December 14, 2011, www.nationaljournal.com/congress/government-shutdown-scares-through-the-years-20111214 (accessed 12/19/11).

25. Dafne Eviatar, "Patriot Act Renewal Kicks Off over Party Lines," *Washington Independent*, September 23, 2009, http://washingtonindependent.com/60575/debate-over-patriot-act-renewal-kicks-off-over-party-lines (accessed 12/19/11).

26. CNN Wire Staff, "Holder to Critics: Have You No Shame?" December 8, 2011, http://articles.cnn.com/2011-12-08/politics/politics_congress-fast-and-furious_1_operation-fast-and-furious-darrell-issa-gop-critics?_s=PM:POLITICS (accessed 12/19/11).

27. Mathew McCubbins and Thomas Schwartz, "Congressional Oversight Overlooked: Police Patrol versus Fire Alarm," *American Journal of Political Science* 28, no. 1 (February 1984): 165–77.

28. *Immigration and Naturalization Service v. Chadha*, 462 U.S. 919 (1983).

29. Louis Fisher, "Legislative Vetoes after *Chadha*," Congressional Research Service Report RS22132, Washington, D.C., May 2, 2005, www.loufisher.org/docs/lv/4116.pdf (accessed 12/20/11).

You Decide

a. This figure comes from a report by the Citizens against Government Waste, "Pork Alert: Defense Conference Report Loaded with Earmarks,"www.cagw.org/newroom/releases/2009/pork -alert-defense.html (accessed 1/6/10). A lower figure of $4 billion in earmarks was reported in John D. McKinnon and Brody Mullins, "Defense Bill Earmarks Total $4 Billion," Wall Street Journal, December 23, 2009, p. A1.

CHAPTER 10

1. John Aldrich, *Why Parties?* (Chicago: University of Chicago Press, 1995).
2. Ernest R. May, *The Making of the Monroe Doctrine* (Cambridge, MA: Harvard University Press, 1975).
3. Arthur M. Schlesinger Jr., *The Age of Jackson* (Boston: Little, Brown, 1945).
4. David Greenberg, "Lincoln's Crackdown," *Slate*, November 30, 2001, www.slate.com/id/2059132 (accessed 4/29/08).
5. Steven Skowronek, *Building a New American State: The Expansion of National Administrative Capacities* (New York: Cambridge University Press, 1982).
6. Theda Skocpol, *Protecting Soldiers and Mothers: The Political Origins of Social Policy in the United States* (Cambridge, MA: Harvard University Press, 1995).
7. Kendrick Clements, *The Presidency of Woodrow Wilson* (Lawrence: University Press of Kansas, 1992).
8. Thomas J. Knock, *To End All Wars: Woodrow Wilson and the Quest for a New World Order* (New York: Oxford University Press, 1992).
9. Arthur M. Schlesinger Jr., *The Crisis of the Old Order, 1919–1933* (Boston: Houghton Mifflin, 1957).
10. William E. Leuchtenburg, *FDR Years: On Roosevelt and His Legacy* (New York: Columbia University Press, 1995).
11. Chester Pach and Elmo Richardson, *The Presidency of Dwight D. Eisenhower* (Lawrence: University Press of Kansas, 1991).
12. Jackie Calmes, "Audit Finds TARP Program Effective," *New York Times*, December 9, 2009, p. D1.
13. Executive Order no. 13425, "Trial of Alien Unlawful Enemy Combatants by Military Commission," February 14, 2007, www .fas.org/irp/offdocs/eo/eo-13425.htm (accessed 4/29/08).
14. Michael D. Shear, "Obama Extends Hospital Visitation Rights to Same-Sex Partners of Gays," *Washington Post*, April 16, 2010, p. A1.
15. Thomas J. Weko, *The Politicizing Presidency: The White House Personnel Office, 1948–1994* (Lawrence: University Press of Kansas, 1995).
16. Walter Dellinger and Dahlia Lithwick, "A Supreme Court Conversation," *Slate*, June 22, 2007, www.slate.com/id/2168856/ entry/2168959 (accessed 4/29/08).
17. Jeff Zeleny, "Daschle Ends Bid for Post; Obama Concedes Mistake," *New York Times*, February 3, 2009, p. A1.
18. Kenneth Mayer, *With the Stroke of a Pen: Executive Orders and Presidential Power* (Princeton, NJ: Princeton University Press, 2001).
19. Kenneth Mayer and Kevin Price, "Unilateral Presidential Powers: Significant Executive Orders, 1949–1999," *Presidential Studies Quarterly* 32 (2002): 367–85.
20. David G. Adler, "The Constitution and Presidential Warmaking: An Enduring Debate," *Political Science Quarterly* 103 (1988): 1–36.
21. Richard F. Grimmett, "The War Powers Resolution: After Thirty Years," Congressional Research Service Report RL32267, March 11, 2004.
22. Lewis Fisher and David G. Adler, "The War Powers Resolution: Time to Say Goodbye," *Political Science Quarterly* 113:1 (1998): 1–20.
23. William G. Howell and Jon C. Pevehouse, *While Dangers Gather: Congressional Checks on Presidential War Powers* (Princeton, NJ: Princeton University Press, 2007).
24. John M. Broder, "The Climate Accord: The Overview; Clinton Adamant on Third World Role in Climate Accord," *New York Times*, December 12, 1997, pp. A1, A16.
25. Jeff Zeleny and Alan Cowell, "Addressing Muslims, Obama Pushes Mideast Peace," *New York Times*, June 4, 2009, p. A1.
26. Richard M. Stevenson, "The Nation; the High-Stakes Politics of Spending the Surplus," *New York Times*, January 7, 2001.
27. Ivo H. Daalder and James M. Lindsay, *America Unbound: The Bush Revolution in American Foreign Policy* (Washington, DC: Brookings Institution Press, 2003).
28. Mark A. Peterson, *Legislating Together: The White House and Capitol Hill from Eisenhower to Reagan* (Cambridge, MA: Harvard University Press, 1990).
29. Andrew Rudalevige, *Managing the President's Program: Presidential Leadership and Legislative Policy Formation* (Princeton, NJ: Princeton University Press, 2002).
30. Charles Cameron and Nolan M. McCarty, "Models of Vetoes and Veto Bargaining," *Annual Review of Political Science* 7 (2004): 409–35.
31. Keith Krehbiel, *Pivotal Politics: A Theory of U.S. Lawmaking* (Chicago: University of Chicago Press, 1998).
32. Charles Jones, *The Presidency in a Separated System* (Washington, DC: Brookings Institution Press, 1994).
33. Mark J. Rozell, "The Law: Executive Privilege: Definition and Standards of Application," *Presidential Studies Quarterly* 29:4 (1999): 918–30.
34. Raoul Berger, *Executive Privilege: A Constitutional Myth* (Cambridge, MA: Harvard University Press, 1974). For commentary, see Saikrisha Prakash, "A Comment on the Constitutionality of Executive Privilege," *Minnesota Law Review* 83:5 (May 1999): 1143–89.
35. See Oyez, *United States v. Nixon*, 418 U.S. 683 (1974), www .oyez.org/cases/1970-1979/1974/1974_73_1766 for a summary of the case (accessed 11/1/12).
36. Mark J. Rozell, *Executive Privilege: The Dilemma of Secrecy and Democratic Accountability* (Baltimore, MD: Johns Hopkins University Press, 1994).
37. Ben Smith and David Paul Kuhn, "Obama Moves Quickly to Reshape DNC," *Politico*, June 13, 2008, www.politico.com/ news/stories/ 0608/11045.html (accessed 7/2/08).
38. George C. Edwards III, *The Public Presidency* (New York: St Martin's Press, 1983); George C. Edwards III, *On Deaf Ears* (New Haven, CT: Yale University Press, 2003).

39. For evidence, see Edwards, *On Deaf Ears.*

40. Edwards, *On Deaf Ears.*

41. Samuel Kernell, *Going Public: New Strategies of Presidential Leadership,* 2nd ed. (Washington, DC: Congressional Quarterly Press, 1993).

42. David Carr, "Obama's Social Networking Was the Real Revolution," *New York Times,* November 9, 2008, www.nytimes.com/2008/11/09/technology/09iht-carr.1.17652000.html (accessed 11/2/10).

43. Associated Press, "Bush Regains Power after Colonoscopy," *New York Times,* July 21, 2007, www.nytimes.com/aponline/us/AP-Bush-Colonoscopy.html?hp (accessed 4/29/08).

44. John Hart, *The Presidential Branch: From Washington to Clinton,* 2nd ed. (Chatham, NY: Chatham House, 1995).

45. John Hart, "President Clinton and the Politics of Symbolism: Cutting the White House Staff," *Political Science Quarterly* 110 (1995): 385–403.

46. Michael Fletcher, "White House Had Drug Officials Appear with GOP Candidates," *Washington Post,* July 18, 2007, p. A8.

47. David E. Lewis, "Staffing Alone: Unilateral Action and the Politicization of the Executive Office of the President, 1988–2004," *Presidential Studies Quarterly* 35 (2005): 496–514.

48. Charles E. Walcott and Karen M. Hult, "White House Staff Size: Explanations and Implications," *Presidential Studies Quarterly* 29 (1999): 638–56.

49. Karen M. Hult and Charles E. Walcott, *Empowering the White House: Governance under Nixon, Ford, and Carter* (Lawrence, KS: University Press of Kansas, 2004).

50. David E. Lewis, *The Politics of Presidential Appointments: Political Control and Bureaucratic Performance* (Princeton, NJ: Princeton University Press, 2008).

51. For a series of articles detailing Cheney's role, see "Angler: The Cheney Vice Presidency," *Washington Post,* June 24–27, 2007, www.washingtonpost.com/cheney (accessed 4/29/08).

52. For example, see David Talbot, "Creepier Than Nixon," *Salon,* March 31, 2004, http://dir.salon.com/story/news/feature/2004/03/31/dean/index.html (accessed 4/29/08).

53. David Kirkpatrick, "Question of Timing on Bush's Push on Earmarks," *New York Times,* January 29, 2008.

54. Alexander Hamilton and James Madison, *The Pacificus-Helvidius Debates of 1793–1794: Toward the Completion of the American Founding,* ed. Martin J. Frisch (1793; repr. Indianapolis, IN: Liberty Fund, 2007).

55. Richard E. Neustart, *Presidential Power and the Modern Presidents* (New York: Simon and Schuster, 1991).

56. Terry M. Moe and William G. Howell, "The Presidential Power of Unilateral Action," *Journal of Law, Economics, and Organization* 15 (1999): 132–46.

57. Louis Fisher, *Presidential War Power,* 2nd ed. (Lawrence: University Press of Kansas, 2004); James M. Lindsay, "Deference and Defiance: The Shifting Rhythms of Executive–Legislative Relations in Foreign Policy," *Presidential Studies Quarterly* 33:3 (2003): 530–46; Lawrence Margolis, *Executive Agreements and Presidential Power in Foreign Policy* (New York: Praeger, 1985), 209–32.

59. David E. Lewis, *Presidents and the Politics of Agency Design: Political Insulation in the United States Government Bureaucracy, 1946–1997* (Palo Alto, CA: Stanford University Press, 2003).

60. David Epstein and Sharyn O'Halloran, *Delegating Powers* (Cambridge, UK: Cambridge University Press, 1999).

You Decide

a. For details on this example, see http://topics.nytimes.com/top/news/business/companies/solyndra/index.html (accessed 4/11/12).

CHAPTER 11

1. Brad Plumer and Ezra Klein, "Analysis: Little-Known Bureaucrat Is Most Powerful Man in Housing Policy," *Washington Post,* August 31, 2011, p. A1.

2. Perry Bacon Jr., "House Passes Defense Spending Bill," *Washington Post,* December 16, 2009, http://voices.washingtonpost.com/44/2009/12/house-passes-defense-spending.html (accessed 2/8/10).

3. The original quote is from Robert Dahl and was used in this context in David E. Lewis, *Presidents and the Politics of Agency Design: Political Insulation in the United States Government* (Palo Alto, CA: Stanford University Press, 2003).

4. For a history of the Food and Drug Administration, see John P. Swann, FDA History Office, "History of the FDA," www.fda.gov/oc/history/historyoffda/section2.html (accessed 7/15/08).

5. For details, see Cornelius Kerwin, *Rulemaking: How Government Agencies Write Law and Make Policy* (Washington, DC: CQ Press, 1999).

6. Andrew Pollack, "New Sense of Caution at FDA," *New York Times,* September 29, 2006.

7. There are two exceptions. A patient can enroll in a clinical trial for a new drug during the approval process, but there is a good chance that he or she will get a placebo or a previously approved treatment rather than the drug being tested. The FDA does allow companies to provide some experimental drugs to patients who cannot participate in a trial but only those drugs that have passed early screening trials.

8. Susan Okie, "Access before Approval—A Right to Take Experimental Drugs?" *New England Journal of Medicine* 355 (2004): 437–40.

9. For details, see the U.S. General Services Administration site at www.gsa.gov.

10. Michael Lipsky, *Street Level Bureaucracy* (New York: Russell Sage Foundation, 1983).

11. Stephen Skowronek, *Building a New American State: The Expansion of National Administrative Capacities, 1877–1920* (New York: Cambridge University Press, 1982).

12. Terry Moe, "An Assessment of the Positive Theory of Congressional Dominance," *Legislative Studies Quarterly* 4 (1987): 475–98.

13. Karen Orren and Steven Skorownek, "Regimes and Regime Building in American Government: A Review of the Literature on the 1940s," *Political Science Quarterly* 113 (1998): 689–702.

14. Michael Nelson, "A Short, Ironic History of American National Bureaucracy," *Journal of Politics* 44 (1982): 747–78.

15. Nelson, "A Short, Ironic History of American National Bureaucracy."

16. Nelson, "A Short, Ironic History of American National Bureaucracy."

17. John Aldrich, *Why Parties?* (Chicago: University of Chicago Press, 1995).

18. Nelson, "A Short, Ironic History of American National Bureaucracy."

19. Matthew A. Crenson, *The Federal Machine: Beginnings of Bureaucracy in Jacksonian America* (Baltimore, MD: Johns Hopkins University Press, 1975).

20. James Q. Wilson, "The Rise of the Bureaucratic State," in *The American Commonwealth*, ed. Nathan Glazer and Irving Kristol (New York: Basic Books, 1976).

21. Skowronek, *Building a New American State*.

22. Robert Harrison, *Congress, Progressive Reform, and the New American State* (New York: Cambridge University Press, 2004).

23. The U.S. State Department has an excellent summary of the Pendleton Act at http://usinfo.state.gov/usa/infousa/facts/democrac/28.htm.

24. Lawrence C. Dodd and Richard L. Schott, *Congress and the Administrative State* (New York: John Wiley, 1979).

25. William Riordan, *Plunkitt of Tammany Hall: A Series of Very Plain Talks on Very Practical Politics* (1924; repr. New York: Signet Classics, 1995).

26. Ira Katznelson and Bruce Pietrykowski, "Rebuilding the American State: Evidence from the 1940s," *Studies in American Political Development* 5:2 (1991): 301–39.

27. David Plotke, *Building a Democratic Political Order: Reshaping American Liberalism in the 1930s and 1940s* (New York: Cambridge University Press, 1996).

28. Theda Skocpol and Kenneth Finegold, "State Capacity and Economic Intervention in the Early New Deal," *Political Science Quarterly* 97 (1999): 255–70.

29. Michael Brown, "State Capacity and Political Choice: Interpreting the Failure of the Third New Deal," *Studies in American Political Development* 9 (1995): 187–212.

30. Ira Katznelson, Kim Geiger, and Daniel Kryder, "Limiting Liberalism: The Southern Veto in Congress, 1933–1950," *Political Science Quarterly* 108 (1993): 283–306.

31. Joseph Califano, "What Was Really Great about the Great Society," *Washington Monthly*, October 1999, www.washingtonmonthly.com/features/1999/9910.califano.html (accessed 7/16/08).

32. David T. Canon, *Race, Redistricting, and Representation: The Unintended Consequences of Black Majority Districts* (Chicago: University of Chicago Press, 1999).

33. Charles Murray, *Losing Ground: American Social Policy, 1950–1980* (New York: Basic Books, 1984)

34. Henry J. Aaron, *Politics and the Professors: The Great Society in Perspective* (Washington, DC: Brookings Institution Press, 1978).

35. Stephen Moore, "How the Budget Revolution Was Lost," Cato Policy Analysis no. 281, September 2, 1997, Cato Institute, www.cato.org/pubs/pas/pa-281.html (accessed 7/21/08).

36. Clyde Wayne Crews Jr., "Ten Thousand Commandments," An Annual Snapshot of the Federal Regulatory State," 2003 ed. (Washington, DC: Cato Institute, 2003), www.cato.org/tech/pubs/10kc_2003.pdf (accessed 7/15/08).

37. Richard P. Nathan, *The Administrative Presidency* (New York: Wiley, 1983).

38. Andrew Rudalevige, "The Structure of Leadership: Presidents, Hierarchies, and Information Flow," *Presidential Studies Quarterly* 35 (2005): 333–60.

39. David E. Lewis, *Presidents and the Policy of Agency Design* (Palo Alto, CA: Stanford University Press, 2003).

40. Terry Moe, "An Assessment of the Positive Theory of Congressional Dominance," *Legislative Studies Quarterly* 4 (1987): 475–98.

41. William A. Niskanen, *Bureaucracy and Public Economics* (Washington, DC: Edward Elgar, 1976); Robert Waples and Jac C. Heckelman, "Public Choice Economics: Where Is There Consensus?" *American Economist* 49 (2005): 66–79.

42. Alan Schick and Felix LoStracco, *The Federal Budget: Politics, Process, Policy* (Washington, DC: Brookings Institution Press, 2000).

43. Joel D. Aberbach, "The Political Significance of the George W. Bush Administration," *Social Policy and Administration* 39:2 (2005): 130–49.

44. David E. Lewis, "The Politics of Agency Termination: Confronting the Myth of Agency Immortality," *Journal of Politics* 64 (2002): 89–107.

45. Ronald A. Wirtz, "Put It on My . . . Er, His Tab: Opinion Polls Show a Big Gap between the Public's Desire for Services and Its Willingness to Pay for These Services," *Fedgazette*, January 2004, www.minneapolisfed.org/pubs/fedgaz/04-01/tab.cfm (accessed 7/16/08).

46. Harris Poll, "Cutting Government Spending May Be Popular But Majorities of the Public Oppose Cuts in Many Big Ticket Items in the Budget," March 1, 2012, www.harrisinteractive.com (accessed 7/19/12).

47. Paul Light, "Measuring the Health of the Public Service," in *Workways of Governance*, ed. Roger Davidson (Washington, DC: Brookings Institution Press, 2003).

48. Paul Light, *A Government Well-Executed: Public Service and Public Performance* (Washington, DC: Brookings Institution Press, 2003).

49. This discussion of the details of the civil service system is based on Bureau of Labor Statistics, "Career Guide to Industries," March 12, 2008, www.bls.gov/oco/cg/cgs041.htm (accessed 7/16/08).

50. Dennis Cauchon, "Some Federal Workers More Likely to Die Than Lose Jobs," *USA Today*, July 19, 2011, p. A1.

51. Ronald N. Johnson and Gary D. Liebcap, *The Federal Civil Service System and the Problem of Bureaucracy* (Chicago: University of Chicago Press, 1993).

52. For details on the Senior Executive Service, see the Office of Personnel Management site at www.opm.gov/ses.

53. For the details of the Hatch Act, see Daniel Engber, "Can Karl Rove Plot Campaign Strategy on the Government's Dime?" *Slate*, April 21, 2006, www.slate.com/id/2140418 (accessed 7/16/08).

54. Stephen Labaton and Edmund Andrews, "White House Calls Political Briefings Legal," *New York Times*, April 27, 2007.

55. Andrew C. Revkin, "Climate Expert Says NASA Tried to Silence Him," *New York Times*, January 29, 2006.

56. Andrew C. Revkin, "A Young Bush Appointee Resigns His Post at NASA," *New York Times*, February 8, 2006.

57. Andrew C. Revkin, "NASA's Goals Delete Mention of Home Planet," *New York Times*, July 22, 2006.

58. John D. Huber and Charles R. Shipan, *Deliberate Discretion? The Institutional Foundations of Bureaucratic Autonomy* (New York: Cambridge University Press, 2002).

59. David Epstein and Sharyn O'Halloran, *Delegating Powers: A Transaction Cost Politics Approach to Policy Making under Separate Powers* (New York: Cambridge University Press, 1999).

60. Charles E. Lindbloom, "The Science of 'Muddling Through,'" *Public Administration Review*, 19 (1959): 79–88.

61. Barry R. Weingast, "Caught in the Middle: The President, Congress, and the Political-Bureaucratic System," in *Institutions of American Democracy: The Executive Branch*, ed. Joel D. Aberbach and Mark A. Peterson (New York: Oxford University Press, 2006).

62. Keith Whittington and Daniel P. Carpenter, "Executive Power in American Institutional Development," *Perspectives on Politics* 1 (2003): 495–513.

63. Dara Cohen, Mariano-Florentino Cuéllar, and Barry R. Weingast, "Crisis Bureaucracy: Homeland Security and the Political Design of Legal Mandates," *Stanford Law Review* 59:3 (2006): 673–760.

64. Federal Communications Commission, "FCC Commissioners," April 1, 2008, www.fcc.gov/commissioners (accessed 7/17/08).

65. Charles Shipan, *Designing Judicial Review: Interest Groups, Congress, and Communication Policy* (Ann Arbor: University of Michigan Press, 2000).

66. Roger Noll, Mathew McCubbins, and Barry Weingast, "Administrative Procedures as Instruments of Political Control," *Journal of Law, Economics and Organization* 3 (1987): 243–77.

67. Mathew McCubbins and Thomas Schwartz, "Congressional Oversight Overlooked: Fire Alarms vs. Police Patrols," *American Journal of Political Science* 28 (1984): 165–79.

68. McCubbins and Schwartz, "Congressional Oversight Overlooked."

69. Steven J. Balla and John R. Wright, "Interest Groups, Advisory Committees, and Congressional Control of the Bureaucracy," *American Journal of Political Science* 45 (2001): 799–812.

70. Daniel P. Carpenter, "The Gatekeeper: Organizational Reputation and Pharmaceutical Regulation at the FDA," unpublished paper, Harvard University, 2006.

71. Terry M. Moe, "Political Control and the Power of the Agent," *Journal of Law, Economics, and Organization* 22 (2006): 1–29.

72. See David Weil, "OSHA: Beyond the Politics," *Frontline*, January 9, 2003, www.pbs.org/wgbh/pages/frontline/shows/workplace/osha/weil.html (accessed 7/17/08).

CHAPTER 12

1. Ralph Ketcham, *The Antifederalist Papers and the Constitutional Convention Debates* (New York: Penguin Putnam, 2003), p. 304.

2. Lester S. Jayson, ed., *The Constitution of the United States of America: Analysis and Interpretation* (Washington, DC: U.S. Government Printing Office, 1973), p. 585.

3. David G. Savage, *Guide to the Supreme Court,* 4th ed. (Washington, DC: CQ Press, 2004), pp. 5–7.

4. Winfield H. Rose, "*Marbury v. Madison*: How John Marshall Changed History by Misquoting the Constitution," *Political Science and Politics* 36:2 (April 2003): 209–14. Rose argues that in a key quotation in the case, Marshall intentionally left out a clause of the Constitution that suggests that Congress *did* have the power to expand the original jurisdiction of the Court. Other constitutional scholars reject this argument.

5. *Marbury v. Madison*, 1 CR. (5 U.S.) 137 (1803).

6. Revisionist historians, legal scholars, and political scientists have challenged the landmark status of *Marbury v. Madison*. For example, Michael Stokes Paulsen's *Michigan Law Review* article points out that *Marbury* was not cited in subsequent Supreme Court cases as a precedent for judicial review until the late nineteenth century. Legal scholars in the early twentieth century were the first to promote the idea that *Marbury* was a landmark decision. Paulsen also notes that when the opinion was delivered in 1803, it was not controversial. Even the Jeffersonian Democrats, who were at odds with Marshall's Federalists, thought that it was a reasonable decision and not the institutional power-grab that modern accounts describe. Finally, Marshall made a very narrow case for judicial review, arguing that the Supreme Court could declare legislation that was contrary to the Court's interpretation of the Constitution null and void only if it concerned judicial powers. Revisionists argue that what appear to be broad claims of judicial power in *Marbury* (e.g., the Court has the power "to say what the law is") are taken out of the context of a much more narrow claim of power. Michael Stokes Paulsen, "Judging Judicial Review: Marbury in the Modern Era: The Irrepressible Myth of *Marbury*," *Michigan Law Review* 101 (August 2003): 2706–43.

7. *Ware v. Hylton*, 3 U.S. 199 (1796).

8. However, in 2011 the Court struck down any class-action claim unless there was "convincing proof of a companywide discriminatory pay and promotion policy"—statistical evidence of pay disparities would not suffice (David Savage,

"Supreme Court Blocks Huge Class-Action Suit against Wal-Mart," Los Angeles Times, June 21, 2011).

9. *Lujan v. Defenders of Wildlife*, 504 U.S. 555 (1992).

10. U.S. Courts, Federal Court Management Statistics, 2007: District Courts, www.uscourts.gov/cgi-bin/cmsd2007.pl (accessed 3/18/08).

11. *Ledbetter v. Goodyear Tire & Rubber Co.*, 550 U.S. 618 (2007).

12. American Judicature Society, "Judicial Selection in the States: Appellate and General Jurisdiction Courts," 2004, www.ajs.org/js/JudicialSelectionCharts_old.pdf (accessed 9/14/06).

13. The Court ruled that the losing party's due process rights under the Fourteenth Amendment had been violated when the justice who benefited from the campaign spending did not recuse himself from the case. Given the disproportionate and significant spending by Massey and the timing of the spending, the majority ruled, "On these extreme facts the probability of actual bias rises to an unconstitutional level." *Caperton v. A.T. Massey Coal Co.*, 556 U.S. 868 (2009).

14. Paul Brace and Brent D. Boyea, "State Public Opinion, the Death Penalty, and the Practice of Electing Judges," *American Journal of Political Science* 52:2 (April 2008): 360-72.

15. Richard P. Caldarone, Brandice Canes-Wrone, and Tom S. Clark, "Partisan Labels and Democratic Accountability: An Analysis of State Supreme Court Abortion Decisions," *Journal of Politics* 71 (2009): 560–73

16. Stephen Ware, "The Missouri Plan in National Perspective," *Missouri Law Review* 74 (2009): 751–75.

17. "President Bush Discusses Judicial Accomplishments and Philosophy," Cincinnati, Ohio, October 6, 2008, georgewbush-whitehouse.archives.gov/news/releases/2008/10/20081006-5.html (accessed 12/14/11).

18. Felicia Sonmez, "Senate Republicans Block Obama Appeals Court Nominee," *Washington Post*, December 6, 2011, p. A1. See http://judicialnominations.org for a comprehensive list of pending nominations and vacancies for federal courts.

19. John Roberts, U.S. Supreme Court, "2007 Year-End Report on the Federal Judiciary," January 1, 2008, www.supremecourtus.gov/publicinfo/year-end/2007year-endreport.pdf (accessed 3/17/08).

20. For a critical account of the Supreme Court's reduced case load, which dates back to the Rehnquist Court, see Philip Allen Lacovara, "The Incredible Shrinking Court," *American Lawyer*, December 1, 2003, www.judicialaccountability.org/download/shrinkinusgcourt.htm (accessed 7/18/08).

21. *New Jersey v. New York*, No. 120 Orig., 118 S. Ct. 1726 (1998), and *Kansas v. Colorado*, No. 105 Orig., 125 S. Ct. 526 (2004).

22. Abraham, *The Judiciary*, p. 25, says that original jurisdiction has been invoked "about 150 times." A Lexis search revealed an additional 27 original jurisdiction cases between 1987 and December 2004. See U.S. Department of Justice, Help/Glossary, www.usdoj.gov/osg/briefs/help.html for a basic discussion of the Supreme Court's original jurisdiction.

23. Amanda L. Tyler, "Setting the Supreme Court's Agenda: Is There a Place for Certification?" *George Washington Law Review Arguendo* 78 (May 2010): 101–18.

24. Savage, *Guide to the U.S. Supreme Court*, p. 848.

25. See Thomas G. Walker and Lee Epstein, *The Supreme Court of the United States: An Introduction* (New York: St. Martin's Press, 1993), pp. 80–85, for a more detailed discussion of these concepts and citations to the relevant court cases.

26. *Shaw v. Reno* (1993) 509 U.S. 630.

27. *Elk Grove Unified School District v. Newdow* (2004) 542 U.S. 1.

28. *DeFunis v. Odegaard*, 416 U.S. 312 (1974).

29. The appeals court case is *Byrd v. Raines*, and the case that was finally heard by the Court was *Clinton v. City of New York*, 524 U.S. 417 (1998).

30. Gregory A. Caldeira and John R. Wright, "The Discuss List: Agenda Building in the Supreme Court," *Law and Society Review* 24 (1990): 813.

31. Walker and Epstein, *Supreme Court*, p. 89.

32. U.S. Supreme Court, "The Court and Its Procedures," www.supremecourtus.gov/about/procedures.pdf (accessed 3/17/08).

33. Lee Epstein, Jeffrey A. Segal, Harold J. Spaeth, and Thomas G. Walker, *The Supreme Court Compendium: Data, Decisions, and Developments*, 3rd ed. (Washington, DC: CQ Press, 2003), Table 7-25.

34. Gregory A. Caldeira and John R. Wright, "Amicus Curiae before the Supreme Court: Who Participates, When, and How Much?" *Journal of Politics* 52 (August 1990): 803.

35. Adam Liptak, "No Argument: Thomas Keeps Five Year Silence," *New York Times*, February 12, 2011, www.nytimes.com/2011/02/13/us/13thomas.html (accessed 1/18/12).

36. *Smith v. Allwright*, 321 U.S. 649 (1944).

37. Walker and Epstein, *Supreme Court*, p. 110.

38. Epstein and Walker, *Constitutional Law for a Changing America*, p. 31.

39. Forrest Maltzman and Paul J. Wahlbeck, "Strategic Considerations and Vote Fluidity on the Burger Court," *American Journal of Political Science* 90 (1996): 581–92; Maltzman, Spriggs, and Wahlbeck, *Crafting Law*.

40. Thomas M. Keck, *The Most Activist Supreme Court in History: The Road to Modern Judicial Conservatism* (Chicago: University of Chicago Press, 2004).

41. Robert Dahl, "Decision-Making in a Democracy: The Supreme Court as a National Policy-Maker," *Journal of Public Law* 6 (1957): 279–95, is the classic work on this topic. More recent work challenged Dahl's methods but largely supports that idea that the Court follows the will of the majority.

42. Jeffrey A. Segal, Richard J. Timpone, and Robert M. Howard, "Buyer Beware? Presidential Success through Supreme Court Appointments," *Political Research Quarterly* 53:3 (September 2000): 557–73; Gregory A. Caldeira and Charles E. Smith Jr., "Campaigning for the Supreme Court: The Dynamics of Public Opinion on the Thomas Nomination," *Political Research Quarterly* 58:3 (August 1996): 655–81.

43. William Mishler and Reginald S. Sheehan, "The Supreme Court as a Countermajoritarian Institution? The Impact of Public Opinion on Supreme Court Decisions," *American Political Science Review* 87:1 (March 1993): 87–101.

44. David O'Brien, *Storm Center: The Supreme Court in American Politics*, 4th ed. (New York: Norton, 1996).

45. We thank Dan Smith for raising this point.

CHAPTER 13

1. "United States' Investigation of the Maricopa County Sheriffs Office," U.S. Department of Justice, Civil Rights Division, December 15, 2011, www.justice.gov/crt/about/spl/documents/mcso_findletter_12-15-11.pdf, accessed January 30, 2012.

2. Mark Lacey, "U.S. Finds Pervasive Bias Against Latinos by Arizona Sheriff," *New York Times*, December 16, 2011, www.nytimes.com/2011/12/16/us/arizona-sheriffs-office-unfairly-targeted-latinos-justice-department-says.html?ref=josephmarpaio (accessed 1/31/12).

3. "The Persistence of Racial and Ethnic Profiling in the United States," American Civil Liberties Union and the Rights Working Group, New York, August 2009, p. 42, www.aclu.org/files/pdfs/humanrights/cerd_finalreport.pdf (accessed 1/31/12).

4. Lacey, "U.S. Finds Pervasive Bias."

5. The number of slaves who died in transit is hotly contested. The most common estimate is that one-sixth of slaves died in transit on the "Middle Passage" to the American colonies. Much higher mortality rates occurred in the slave trade to the Middle East and South America. See "Learning about the Transatlantic Slave Trade," www.antislavery.org/breakingthesilence (accessed 1/26/12).

6. Howard Dodson, "How Slavery Helped Build a World Economy," February 3, 2003, in *Jubilee: The Emergence of African-American Culture* (New York: Schomburg Center for Research in Black Culture, New York City Public Library).

7. John W. Wright, ed., *New York Times 2000 Almanac* (New York: Penguin Reference, 1999), p. 165. Estimates from various online sources are quite a bit higher, averaging about 620,000 deaths.

8. Chandler Davidson, "The Voting Rights Act: A Brief History," in *Controversies in Minority Voting: The Voting Rights Act in Perspective*, ed. Bernard Grofman and Chandler Davidson (Washington, DC: Brookings Institution, 1992), p. 21.

9. "Indian Removal: 1814–1848," Public Broadcasting System," www.pbs.org/wgbh/aia/part4/4p2959.html (accessed 1/26/12).

10. *Cherokee Nation v. Georgia*, 30 U.S. (1831).

11. *United States v. Wong Kim Ark*, 169 U.S. 649 (1898).

12. Institute for Advanced Technology in the Humanities, University of Virginia, Abigail Adams to John Adams, March 31, 1776, www.iath.virginia.edu/seminar/unit1/text/adams.htm (accessed 7/30/08).

13. Lucian K. Truscott IV, "The Real Mob at Stonewall," *New York Times*, June 25, 2009, A19.

14. See a variety of polls at Pollingreport.com, www.pollingreport.com/civil.htm (accessed 1/26/12).

15. Davidson, "The Voting Rights Act," p. 22. See U.S. Department of Justice, Civil Rights Division, "About Section 5 of the Voting Rights Act," www.justice.gov/crt/vot/sec_5/obj_activ.php?, for a complete list of cases in which the Justice Department has denied "preclearance" of a change in an electoral practice under Section 5 of the Voting Rights Act.

16. Wendy Weiser and Margaret Chen, "Voter Suppression Incidents, 2008 Analysis," November 3, 2008, www.brennancenter.org/content/resource/voter_suppression_incidents (accessed 1/19/10).

17. U.S. Census Bureau, "Income, Poverty, and Health Insurance Coverage in the United States: 2008," September 2009, www.census.gov/prod/2009pubs/p60-236.pdf, pp. 7, 14 (accessed 9/8/10).

18. For data on African American and Hispanic income figures, U.S. Census Bureau, "Income, Poverty, and Health Insurance Coverage in the United States: 2008," p. 6: wealth data are from Federal Reserve System, "Changes in U.S. Family Finances from 2007 to 2010: Evidence From the Survey of Consumer Finances," *Federal Reserve Bulletin* 98:2 (June 2012).

19. Life expectancy and infant mortality rates are from the Centers for Disease Control, www.cdc.gov/NCHS/data/nvsr/nvsr58/nvsr58_19.pdf; maternity mortality rates are from the National Center for Health Statistics, http://mchb.hrsa.gov/mchirc/chusa_04/pages/0409mm.htm (both accessed 3/21/08). Other health data are available from the Department of Health and Human Services, www.hhs.gov (accessed 9/20/12).

20. Hundreds of studies have examined these patterns, and, not surprisingly, there are divergent findings. However, most have found differences in sentencing based on race. A meta-analysis of 85 studies by Ojmarrh Mitchell and Doris L. MacKenzie funded by the U.S. Department of Justice found, "after taking into account defendant criminal history and current offense seriousness, African-Americans and Latinos were generally sentenced more harshly than whites." See Mitchell and MacKenzie, "The Relationship between Race, Ethnicity, and Sentencing Outcomes: A Meta-Analysis of Sentencing Research," December 2004, www.ncjrs.gov/pdffiles1/nij/grants/208129.pdf. For government studies of racial profiling, see the Justice Department's "A Resource Guide on Racial Profiling Data Collection Systems," November 2000, www.ncjrs.gov/pdffiles1/bja/184768.pdf. For President Bush's statement on racial profiling, see Department of Justice, "Fact Sheet: Racial Profiling," June 17, 2003, www.usdoj.gov/opa/pr/2003/June/racial_profiling_fact_sheet.pdf. For a GAO study, see "Racial Profiling: Limited Data on Motorist Stops," March 2000, www.gao.gov/new.items/gg00041.pdf. Government statistics on crime may be found on the Federal Bureau of Investigation site at www.fbi.gov. (All documents accessed 3/21/08.)

21. Criminal Justice Information Services Division, Federal Bureau of Investigation, 2006 Hate Crime Statistics, www.fbi.gov/ucr/hc2006/table1.html (accessed 3/21/08).

22. Clayborne Carson, David J. Garrow, Gerald Gill, Vincent Harding, and Darlene Clark Hine, eds., *The Eyes on the Prize Civil Rights Reader* (New York: Penguin Books, 1997).

23. Nate Silver, "Tea Party Nonpartisan Attendance Estimates: Now 300,000," April 16, 2009, www.fivethirtyeight

.com/2009/04/tea-party-nonpartisan-attendance.html (accessed 1/19/10).

24. *Missouri ex rel. Gaines v. Canada*, 305 U.S. 377 (1938).

25. *Sweatt v. Painter*, 339 U.S. 629 (1950).

26. *Brown v. Board of Education*, 347 U.S. 483 (1954).

27. *Brown v. Board of Education (II)*, 349 U.S. 294 (1955).

28. Paul Brest and Sanford Levinson, *Process of Constitutional Decision Making: Cases and Material* (Boston: Little, Brown, 1982), pp. 471–80.

29. *Griffin et al. v. County School Board of Prince Edward County*, 377 U.S. 218 (1964).

30. *Swann v. Charlotte-Mecklenburg Board of Education*, 402 U.S. 1 (1971).

31. *Milliken v. Bradley*, 418 U.S. 717 (1974).

32. *Board of Education of Oklahoma City v. Dowell*, 498 U.S. 237 (1991).

33. *Missouri v. Jenkins*, 515 U.S. 70 (1995).

34. *Parents Involved in Community Schools Inc. v. Seattle School District*, 05-98 (2007); *Meredith v. Jefferson County (Ky.) Board of Education*, 551 U.S. (2007).

35. *Griggs v. Duke Power*, 401 U.S. 424 (1971).

36. *Wards Cove Packing Co. v. Atonio*, 490 U.S. 642 (1989).

37. *Easley v. Cromartie*, 532 U.S. 234 (2001), rehearing denied, 532 U.S. 1076 (2001).

38. *Easley v. Cromartie,* 532 U.S. 1076 (2001).

39. *Reed v. Reed*, 404 U.S. 71 (1971).

40. *Frontiero v. Richardson*, 411 U.S. 677 (1973).

41. *Craig v. Boren*, 429 U.S. 190 (1976).

42. *United States v. Virginia*, 518 U.S. 515 (1996).

43. *Johnson v. Transportation Agency of Santa Clara*, 480 U.S. 616 (1987).

44. *Harris v. Forklift Systems*, 510 U.S. 17 (1993).

45. *Grove City College v. Bell*, 465 U.S. 555 (1984).

46. *Ledbetter v. Goodyear Tire & Rubber Co.*, 550 U.S. (2007).

47. Equal Employment Opportunity Commission, "Outback Steakhouse to Pay $19 Million for Sex Bias against Women in 'Glass Ceiling' Suit by EEOC," press release, December 29, 2009, www.eeoc.gov/eeoc/newsroom/release/12-29-09a.cfm (accessed 1/20/10).

48. *Bowers v. Hardwick*, 478 U.S. 186 (1986), rehearing denied, 478 U.S. 1039 (1986).

49. *Hurley v. Irish-American Gay, Lesbian, and Bisexual Group of Boston*, 515 U.S. 557 (1995) and *Boy Scouts of America v. Dale*, 530 U.S. 640 (2000).

50. *Romer v. Evans*, 517 U.S. 620 (1996).

51. *Lawrence v. Texas*, 539 U.S. 558 (2003). Because the basis for the decision was the due process clause of the Fourteenth Amendment and not the equal protection clause, this ruling upheld a civil liberty rather than a civil right. As such, it applied to all laws regarding sodomy, not just those that applied to gays. However, the decision has been widely regarded as a landmark civil rights case because it provided equal rights for gays.

52. Jerry Markon, "California Supreme Court Clears Way for Same-Sex Marriage Case," *Washington Post,* November 17, 2011, p. A1.

53. Drew S. Days III, "Section 5 Enforcement and the Justice Department," in *Controversies in Minority Voting: The Voting Rights Act in Perspective*, ed. Bernard Grofman and Chandler Davidson (Washington, DC: Brookings Institution Press, 1992), p. 52; Frank R. Parker, *Black Votes Count* (Chapel Hill: University of North Carolina Press, 1990), p. 1.

54. "Fair Housing: It's Your Right." U.S. Department of Housing and Urban Development, http://portal.hud.gov/hudportal/HUD?src=/program_offices/fair_housing_equal_opp/FHLaws/yourrights (accessed 2/2/12).

55. *United States v. Morrison*, 529 U.S. 598 (2000).

56. *Board of Trustees of the University of Alabama v. Garrett*, 531 U.S. 356 (2001). However, in *State of Tennessee v. George Lane and Beverly Jones*, 541 U.S. 509 (2004), the Court ruled that the disabled must have access to courthouses.

57. The White House, "Remarks by the Reception Commemorating the Enactment of the Matthew Shepard and James Byrd Jr. Hate Crimes Prevention Act," October 28, 2009, www.whitehouse.gov/the-press-office/remarks-president-reception-commemorating-enactment-matthew-shephard-and-James-Byrd (accessed 1/21/10).

58. Tim Mak, "Post 'Don't Ask,' Gay Navy Lt. Marries," Politco, September 20, 2011, www.politico.com/news/stories/0911/63909.html (accessed 1/12/12).

59. Sarah Huisenga and Rebecca Kaplan, CBS News, August 24, 2012, "Romney's Birth Certificate Remark Sets off Firestorm," www.cbsnews.com/8301-503544_162-57500031-503544/romney-birth-certificate-remark-sets-off-firestorm/ (accessed 10/5/12).

60. *New York Times*/CBS poll, December 6–9, 1997. Fifty-nine percent of whites and 82 percent of blacks favored the education programs, while 57 percent of whites but only 23 percent of blacks opposed preferences in hiring and promotion "to make up for past discrimination."

61. A training program case was *United Steel Workers of America v. Weber*, 443 U.S. 193 (1979); a labor union case was *Sheet Metal Workers v. EEOC*, 478 U.S. 421 (1986); and a case involving Alabama state police was *U.S. v. Paradise*, 480 U.S. 149 (1987).

62. *Richmond v. J. A. Croson Co.*, 488 U.S. 469 (1989).

63. *Adarand Constructors, Inc. v. Pena*, 515 U.S. 200 (1995).

64. *Ricci v. DeStefano*, 557 U.S. 2009.

65. *Regents of Univ. of California v. Bakke*, 438 U.S. 265 (1978).

66. *Grutter v. Bollinger*, 123 S. Ct. 2325 (2003), was the law school case and *Gratz v. Bollinger*, 123 S. Ct. 2411 (2003), was the undergraduate admissions case.

67. In *Bakke*, Justice Lewis Powell was the only member of the Court who held this position, even if it became the basis for all affirmative action programs over the next 25 years. Four justices in the *Bakke* decision wanted to get rid of race as a factor in admissions, and another four thought that the "strict scrutiny" standard should not even be applied in this instance.

68. *Alexander v. Sandoval*, 532 U.S. 275 (2001).

69. *Arizona v. United States*, 567 U.S. _____ (2012).

70. Fernanda Santos, "Arizona Immigration Law Survives Ruling," *New York Times*, September 6, 2012, www.nytimes.com/2012/09/07/us/key-element-of-arizona-immigration-law-survives-ruling.html?_r=0 (accessed 10/5/12).

71. "An Act Providing for the Collection of Data Relative to Traffic Stops," Massachusetts state law, Chapter 228 of the Acts of 2000, www.mass.gov/legis/laws/seslaw00/sl000228.htm (accessed 7/22/08).

CHAPTER 14

1. "Remarks by the President on the Economy in Osawatomie, Kansas," Osawatomie High School, Osawatomie, Kansas, December 6, 2011, www.whitehouse.gov/the-press-office/2011/12/06/remarks-president-economy-osawatomie-kansas (accessed 2/10/12).

2. "Tales of the 1040s," *Washington Post*, January 23, 2012, www.washingtonpost.com/politics/tales-of-the-1040s/2012/01/23/gIQA83IRMQ_graphic.html (accessed 2/13/12).

3. John Berlau and Trey Kovacs, "Romney and the Burden of Double Taxation," *Wall Street Journal*, January 24, 2012, online.wsj.com/article/SB10001424052970203718504577178831519223426.html (accessed 2/14/12).

4. See William T. Bianco, *Trust: Representatives and Constituents* (Ann Arbor: University of Michigan Press, 1994), Chapter 6, for a discussion of the repeal of the Catastrophic Coverage Act.

5. James Q. Wilson, *Bureaucracy: What Government Agencies Do and Why They Do It* (New York: Basic Books, 1989).

6. The classic work on the appropriations process in the prereform era is Richard Fenno's *The Power of the Purse: Appropriation Politics in Congress* (Boston: Little, Brown, 1966). D. Roderick Kiewiet and Mathew D. McCubbins reexamine the appropriations process in the postreform era and find that the appropriations committees have maintained much of their power; see *The Logic of Delegation: Congressional Parties and the Appropriations Process* (Chicago: University of Chicago Press, 1991).

7. See Charles M. Cameron, *Veto Bargaining: Presidents and the Politics of Negative Power* (New York: Cambridge University Press, 2000), for a general discussion of the strategic elements of issuing veto threats.

8. Joe Soss, *Unwanted Claims: The Politics of Participation in the U.S. Welfare System* (Ann Arbor: University of Michigan Press, 2000).

9. Daniel P. Carpenter, *The Forging of Bureaucratic Autonomy: Reputations, Networks, and Policy Innovation in Executive Agencies, 1862–1928* (Princeton, N.J.: Princeton University Press, 2001).

10. U.S. Department of the Treasury, "Duties and Functions," www.treasury.gov/education/duties (accessed 8/5/08).

11. U.S. Department of the Treasury, "FAQs: Currency: Production and Circulation," www.treasury.gov/education/faq/currency/production.shtml; United States Mint, "Coin Production Figures," www.usmint.gov/about_the_mint/coin_produciton/index.cfm?action=production_figures (accessed 8/5/08).

12. John Maynard Keynes, *General Theory of Employment, Interest and Money* (1936; repr. New York: Macmillan, 2007).

13. These figures come from the Congressional Budget Office, "Historical Budget Data," www.cbo.gov (accessed 4/18/08).

14. Office of Management and Budget, "Budget of the United States Government, fiscal year 2011," www.whitehouse.gov/omb/budget/Overview/ (accessed 2/16/10).

15. Board of Governors of the Federal Reserve System, *The Federal Reserve System: Purposes and Functions*, 9th ed., Washington, DC, June 2005, www.federalreserve.gov/pf/pdf/pf_1.pdf, p. 12 (accessed 9/24/12).

16. Milton Friedman, "The Quantity Theory of Money: A Restatement," in *The Optimum Quantity of Money and Other Essays* (Chicago: Aldine, 1969), p. 52.

17. In reality, under the Monetary Control Act (MCA) of 1980, the reserve requirement can range from 8 percent to 14 percent for all demand deposits greater than $25 million. In the original law, banks with demand deposits under $25 million had to have a reserve of only 3 percent. The amount that is subject to the lower reserve requirement is increased every year to reflect overall money supply and currently is about $71 million. See Board of Governors of the Federal Reserve System, "Reserve Requirement," www.federal reserve.gov/monetarypolicy/reservereq.htm#table1 (accessed 2/7/12).

18. In December 2002, the discount rate was effectively discontinued as an active policy tool and was pegged to 1 percent above the targeted FFR (which means that the "discount rate" is oddly named—it really should be called the "premium rate"). December 2002 *Federal Reserve Bulletin* (pp. 482–83). For an extended discussion of this move see Donald D. Hester, "U.S. Monetary Policy in the Greenspan Era: 1987–2003," unpublished paper, University of Wisconsin, Madison, November 14, 2003, http://ideas.repec.org/p/att/wimass/200323.html (accessed 8/10/08).

19. Board of Governors of the Federal Reserve System, Credit and Liquidity Programs and the Balance Sheet, www.federalreserve.gov/monetarypolicy/bst_recenttrends.htm (accessed 2/16/10).

20. See Federal Research Board, "Membership of the Board of Governors of the Federal Reserve System, 1914," www.federalreserve.gov/bios/boardmembership.htm, for a list of all Federal Reserve Board members (accessed 8/5/08).

21. Edward R. Tufte, *Political Control of the Economy* (Princeton, NJ: Princeton University Press, 1978); Douglas Hibbs, "The Partisan Model of Macroeconomic Cycles: More Theory and Evidence for the United States," *Economics and Politics* 6 (1994): 1–23.

22. Jim Granato, "The Effect of Policy-Maker Reputation and Credibility on Public Expectations," *Journal of Theoretical Politics* 8 (1996): 449–70; Irwin L. Morris, *Congress, the President, and the Federal Reserve: The Politics of American Monetary Policy-Making* (Ann Arbor: University of Michigan Press, 2000).

23. John B. Taylor, *Economics*, 4th ed. (New York: Houghton Mifflin, 2003), Chapter 10. Some economics textbooks also define regulation of externalities, such as pollution, as economic regulation.

24. Zachary A. Goldfarb, David Cho, and Binyamin Appelbaum, "Treasury to Rescue Fannie and Freddie," *Washington Post*, September 7, 2008, p. A1.

25. Peter Baker, "A Professor and a Banker Bury Old Dogma on Markets," *New York Times*, September 21, 2008, p. A1.

26. Renae Merle, "U.S. Stock Markets Soar on Financial Rescue Plan," *Washington Post*, September 19, 2008; Howard Schneider, Neil Irwin, and Binyamin Appelbaum, "Treasury to Temporarily Guarantee Money Market Funds," *Washington Post*, September 19, 2008.

27. Theda Skocpol, *Social Policy in the United States: Future Possibilities in Historical Perspective* (Princeton, NJ: Princeton University Press, 1995), p. 37.

28. Skocpol, *Social Policy in the United States*, pp. 145–60.

29. David M. Kennedy, *Freedom from Fear: The American People in Depression and War, 1929–1945* (New York: Oxford University Press, 2001); Byron W. Daynes, William Pederson, and Michael P. Riccards, eds., *The New Deal and Public Policy* (New York: St. Martin's Press, 1998).

30. Robert Dallek, *Flawed Giant: Lyndon Johnson and His Times, 1961–1973* (New York: Oxford University Press, 1998); Irving Berstein, *Guns or Butter: The Presidency of Lyndon Johnson* (New York: Oxford University Press, 1996).

31. Carmen DeNavas-Walt, Bernadette D. Proctor, and Jessica C. Smith, "Income, Poverty, and Health Insurance Coverage in the United States: 2009," September 2010, www.census.gov/prod/2010pubs/p60-238.pdf, p. 14 (accessed 10/18/10).

32. Larry Bartels, "Inequalities," *New York Times*, April 27, 2008, www.nytimes.com/2008/04/27/magazine/27wwln-idealab-t.html?_r=1&oref=slogin&pagewanted=print (accessed 5/10/08).

33. Congressional Budget Office, "Historical Effective Federal Tax Rates: 1979 to 2005," Summary Table 1, p. 6, December 2007 (accessed 8/8/08).

34. Eric J. Toder, Benjamin H. Harris, and Katherine Lim, "Distributional Effects of Tax Expenditure," Tax Policy Center, July 21, 2009, www.taxpolicycenter.org/UploadedPDF/411922_expenditures.pdf (accessed 6/17/10).

35. Dean Baker, *The Conservative Nanny State: How the Wealthy Use the Government to Stay Rich and Get Richer*, May 2006, www.conservative nannystate.org.

36. Chris Edwards and Jeff Patch, "Corporate Welfare," in *Cato Handbook for Policymakers*, 7th ed., Cato Institute, 2009, www.cato.org/pubs/handbook/hb111/hb111-26.pdf (accessed 9/24/12).

37. Paul N. Van de Water and Arloc Sherman, "Social Security Keeps 20 Million Americans Out of Poverty: A State-by-State Analysis," Center on Budget and Policy Priorities, August 11, 2010, www.cbpp.org/cms/?fa=view&id=3260 (accessed 9/16/10).

38. Social Security Administration, Office of Retirement and Disability Policy, and Office of Research, Evaluation, and Statistics, "Fast Facts & Figures about Social Security, 2009," SSA Publication No. 13–11785, July 2009, http://retirement.gov/policy/docs/chartbooks/fast_facts/2009/fast_facts09.pdf (accessed 2/19/10).

39. See the 2008 OASDI Trustees Report, www.ssa.gov/OACT/TR/TR08/II_project.html#wp105643 (accessed 8/10/08).

40. Social Security Administration, 2010 OASDI Trustees Report, Figure II D4, www.ssa.gov/OACT/TR/2010/trLOF.html (accessed 9/16/10).

41. See Congressional Budget Office, "Menu of Social Security Options," May 25, 2005, www.cbo.gov/publication/16532?, for a detailed account of the fiscal impact of the various proposals.

42. Carmen DeNavas-Walt, Bernadette D. Proctor, and Jessica C. Smith, "Income, Poverty, and Health Insurance Coverage in the United States: 2008," U.S. Census Bureau, September 2009, www.census.gov/prod/2009pubs/p60-236.pdf (accessed 6/18/10).

43. Department of Health and Human Services, Centers for Medicare and Medicaid Services, "Brief Summaries of Medicare and Medicaid," www.cms.hhs.gov/MedicaidGenInfo/03_TechnicalSummary.asp (accessed 8/11/08).

44. State spending figures are from National Governors' Association, *The Fiscal Survey of States, Spring 2012* Washington, DC, pp. vii–xi, www.nga.org/files/live/sites/NGA/files/pdf/FSS1206.PDF, and national spending figures are from Congressional Budget Office, "Medicaid Spending and Enrollment Detail for CBO's March 2012 Baseline, Washington, DC, www.cbo.gov/sites/default/files/cbofiles/attachments/43059_Medicaid.pdf (accessed 6/18/12).

45. A complete list of the Federal Medical Assistance Percentages may be found at Department of Health and Human Services, "Federal Financial Participation in State Assistance Expenditures, FY 2009," http://aspe.hhs.gov/health/fmap09.htm (accessed 8/11/08).

46. 2010 Medicare Trustees Report, Washington, DC, August, 2010, pp. 244–45, www.cms.gov/ReportsTrustFunds/tr2010.pdf (accessed 9/16/10).

47. Children's Health Insurance Program, Medicaid.gov, www.medicaid.gov/Medicaid-CHIP-Program-Information/By-Topics/Childrens-Health-Insurance-Program-CHIP/Childrens-Health-Insurance-Program-CHIP.html (accessed 3/13/12).

48. Congressional Budget Office, "Cost Estimates for H.R. 4872, Reconciliation Act of 2010 (Final Health Care Legislation)," March 20, 2010, www.cbo.gov/doc.cfm?index=11355 (accessed 9/24/12).

49. *Gonzales v. Oregon*, 546 U.S. 243 (2006).

50. U.S. Department of Agriculture, "Supplementary Assistance Nutrition Program: Program Data, Annual State Data FY2007-2011." www.fns.usda.gov/pd/snapmain.htm (accessed 3/1/2012).

51. U.S. Department of Labor, "Unemployment Insurance Data Summary," http://workforcesecurity.doleta.gov/unemploy/content/data.asp (accessed 3/15/12).

52. Internal Revenue Service, "EITC Awareness Day Fact Sheet," www.irs.gov/pub/irs-utl/eitc_day_fastfacts_011508.pdf (accessed 8/11/08).

53. Internal Revenue Service, "About EITC," www.eitc.irs.gov/central/abouteitc/ (accessed 3/15/12).

54. R. Kent Weaver, *Ending Welfare as We Know It* (Washington, DC: Brookings Institution Press, 2000).

55. See the analysis of welfare reform by the Center on Budget and Policy Priorities, www.cbpp.org/pubs/tanf.htm, or by the Urban Institute, www.urban.org/toolkit/issues/welfarereform.cfm (accessed 8/18/08).

56. U.S. Department of Education, Race to the Top fund, www2.ed.gov/programs/racetothetop/index.html (accessed 2/23/10).

57. Amanda Paulson, "The Next Race to the Top? Arne Duncan Outlines Vision for Teacher Reform," *Christian Science Monitor*, February 15, 2012, www.csmonitor.com/USA/Education/2012/0215/The-next-Race-to-the-Top-Arne-Duncan-outlines-vision-for-teacher-reform (accessed 3/14/12).

You Decide

a. John Tierney, "The Sagebrush Solution," *New York Times*, July 26, 2005, p. A19. Aditional information was drawn from www.highcountrynews.org.

b. A very detailed account of this saga may be found in Raymond B. Wrabley Jr., "Managing the Monument: Cows and Conservation in the Grand-Staircase-Escalante National Monument," *Journal of Land, Resources and Environmental Law* 29:2 (2009): 253–80.

CHAPTER 15

1. Helene Cooper and David Sanger, "Obama Says Afghan Policy Won't Change after Dismissal," *New York Times,* June 23, 2010, p. A1.

2. Mark Mazzeti and Eric Schmitt, "C.I.A Missile Strike May Have Killed Pakistan's Taliban Leader," *New York Times*, August 6, 2009, p. A7.

3. For an example of the isolationist approach, see Justin Raimondo, "Out of Iraq, into Darfur?" *American Conservative,* June 5, 2006. For a longer exposition of isolationism, see Patrick J. Buchanan, *A Republic, Not an Empire*, updated ed. (Washington, DC: Regnery Publishing, 2002).

4. Robert O. Keohane, *After Hegemony: Cooperation and Discord in the International System* (1984; repr. Princeton, NJ: Princeton University Press, 2005).

5. The distinction was first made in E. H. Carr, *The Twenty Years' Crisis, 1919–1939: An Introduction to the Study of International Relations* (London: Macmillan, 1939). Realism was elaborated as a general theory in Hans Morgenthau, *Politics among Nations: The Struggle for Power and Peace* (New York: Knopf, 1948). For a general overview, see Jonathan Haslam, *No Virtue like Necessity: Realist Thought in International Relations since Machiavelli* (New Haven, CT: Yale University Press, 2002).

6. A synoptic account of the United States as a world power, which takes the story up to the 2003 invasion of Iraq, is Niall Ferguson, *Colossus: The Price of America's Empire* (New York: Penguin Press, 2004).

7. Samuel Flagg Bemis, *John Quincy Adams and the Foundations of American Foreign Policy* (New York: Knopf, 1949); Ernest R. May, *The Making of the Monroe Doctrine* (Cambridge, MA: Harvard University Press, 1975). The latter stresses domestic political considerations and argues that the Monroe Doctrine was "actually the by-product of an election campaign."

8. Daniel M. Smith, *The Great Departure: The United States and World War I, 1914–1920* (New York: John Wiley, 1965).

9. Thomas J. Knock, *To End All Wars: Woodrow Wilson and the Quest for a New World Order* (New York: Oxford University Press, 1992).

10. Margaret MacMillan, *Paris 1919: Six Months That Changed the World* (New York: Random House, 2001).

11. John M. Cooper, *Breaking the Heart of the World: Woodrow Wilson and the Fight for the League of Nations* (New York: Cambridge University Press, 2001).

12. John Lewis Gaddis, *Strategies of Containment* (New York: Oxford University Press, 2005).

13. Tony Smith, "Making the World Safe for Democracy in the American Century," *Diplomatic History* 23:2 (1999): 173–88.

14. Winston Churchill, "Sinews of Peace (Iron Curtain)," Westminster College, Fulton, MO, March 5, 1946, available from the Churchill Centre at www.winstonchurchill.org/i4a/pages/index.cfm?pageid=429 (accessed 8/2/08). See also Klaus Larres, *Churchill's Cold War: The Politics of Personal Diplomacy* (New Haven, CT: Yale University Press, 2002).

15. George F. Kennan, "The Sources of Soviet Conduct," *Foreign Affairs* 25:4 (July 1947): 566–82.

16. Robert L. Beisner, *Dean Acheson: A Life in the Cold War* (New York: Oxford University Press, 2006); Dean Acheson, *Present at the Creation* (New York: Norton, 1969).

17. Michael J. Hogan, *The Marshall Plan: America, Britain, and the Reconstruction of Western Europe* (New York: Cambridge University Press, 1987). See also Martin Schain, ed., *The Marshall Plan: Fifty Years Later* (New York: Palgrave, 2001).

18. Marc Trachtenberg, *A Constructed Peace: The Making of the European Settlement, 1945–1963* (Princeton, NJ: Princeton University Press, 1999).

19. The balance of military power between NATO and the Warsaw Pact throughout the Cold War is traced in David Miller, *The Cold War: A Military History* (New York: St. Martin's Press, 1998).

20. Robert A. Packenham, *Liberal America and the Third World* (Princeton, NJ: Princeton University Press, 1973). For an overview, see David P. Forsythe, "Human Rights in U.S. Foreign Policy: Retrospect and Prospect," *Political Science Quarterly* 105:3 (Autumn, 1990): 435–54.

21. Lawrence Freedman, *Kennedy's Wars: Berlin, Cuba, Laos, and Vietnam* (Oxford: Oxford University Press, 2002).

22. William J. Duiker, *Sacred War: Nationalism and Revolution in a Divided Vietnam* (New York: McGraw-Hill, 1995).

23. Henry Kissinger, *Years of Upheaval* (Boston: Little, Brown, 1982); Jussi Hanhimäki, *The Flawed Architect: Henry Kissinger and American Foreign Policy* (New York: Oxford University Press, 2004).

24. Raymond Garthoff, *Détente and Confrontation: American-Soviet Relations from Nixon to Reagan* (Washington, DC: Brookings Institution Press, 1994).

25. Francis Fukuyama, *The End of History and the Last Man*, updated ed. (New York: Free Press, 2006).

26. For a summary of American human rights policy, see John W. Dietrich, "U.S. Human Rights Policy in the Post–Cold War Era," *Political Science Quarterly* 121: 2 (Summer, 2006): 269–94.

27. Samuel P. Huntington, *The Clash of Civilizations and the Remaking of World Order* (New York: Free Press, 2002).

28. Louis Fisher, *Presidential War Power* (Lawrence: University Press of Kansas, 2004).

29. David Hoffman and David B. Ottaway, "Panel Drops Covert-Acts Notification; In Compromise, Bush Pledges to Inform Hill in All but Rare Cases," *Washington Post*, October 27, 1989, p. A1.

30. See especially *Hamdan v. Rumsfeld,* 548 U.S. 557 (2006), and *Boumediene v. Bush,* 553 U.S. 723 (2008). For a discussion of these and related cases, see Dahlia Lithwick and Walter Dellinger, "A Supreme Court Conversation," *Slate*, June 22, 2007, www.slate.com/id/2168856/entry/2168959 (accessed 7/4/08); and James Risen, "The Executive Power Awaiting the Next President," *New York Times*, June 22, 2008.

31. Dahlia Lithwick, "The Enemy Within," *Slate*, June 12, 2008, www.slate.com/id/2193468 (accessed 8/12/08).

32. Somini Sengupta, "As Musharraf's Woes Grow, Enter an Old Rival, Again," *New York Times*, April 6, 2007, p. A3; Leslie Wayne, "Airbus Seeks a Welcome in Alabama," *New York Times*, June 19, 2007, p. C1.

33. Andrew Jacobs, "China Angered by U.S. Lobbying on Rights," *New York Times*, August 1, 2008.

34. Steven R. Weisman, "U.S. and China Agree to Ease Foreign Investment," *New York Times*, June 19, 2008.

35. American Israel Public Affairs Committee, "Legislation and Policy Update," www.aipac.org/Legislation_and_Policy/default.asp (accessed 8/3/08).

36. See Pew Research Center, "The U.S. Public's Pro-Israel History," July 19, 2006, http://pewresearch.org/pubs/39/the-u.s.-publics-pro-israel-history (accessed 8/2/08).

37. John Harwood, "War-Weary Public Wants Congress to Lead; Poll Shows Desire for Lawmakers to Set Policy Amid Growing Dismay over Iraq, President Bush," *Wall Street Journal*, December 14, 2006, p. A4; E. J. Dionne, "Slowly Sidling to Iraq's Exit; Many GOP Candidates Part Company with Bush," *Washington Post*, August 29, 2006, p. A15.

38. "Public Wary of Military Intervention in Libya," Pew Research Center, March 14, 2012, http://pewresearch.org/pubs/1927/strong-opposition-us-involvement-libya-military-overcommitted (accessed 9/25/12).

39. A directory of NGOs can be found at the Department of Public Information site, Nongovernmental Organization Section, www.un.org/dpi/ngosection/asp/form.asp (accessed 8/2/08).

40. See Amnesty International, "The Secretive and Illegal U.S. Programme of Rendition," April 5, 2006, www.amnesty.org/en/news-and-updates/feature-stories/secretive-and-illegal-us-programme-of-rendition-20060405 (accessed 8/12/08).

41. See the National Democratic Institute for International Affairs site at www.ndi.org and the International Republican Institute site at www.iri.org.

42. Elizabeth Bumiller, Eric Schmitt, and Thom Shanker, "U.S. Sends Top Iranian Leader a Warning on Strait Threat," *New York Times,* January 12, 2012, p. A1.

43. Johanna Neuman and Megan K. Stack, "Americans' Beirut Exodus Underway; Hundreds Are Evacuated by Ship and Helicopter," *Los Angeles Times*, July 20, 2006, p. A10. The Clinton administration resorted to cruise missile attacks five times: three against Iraq (1993, 1996, 1998), one in 1995 against Bosnian Serb forces in the former Yugoslavia, and one against targets in Afghanistan and Sudan in 1998. James Mann, "Foreign Policy of the Cruise Missile," *Los Angeles Times*, December 23, 1998, p. 5.

44. A comprehensive account of the Afghanistan invasion and its aftermath is in Barnett R. Rubin, "Saving Afghanistan," *Foreign Affairs* 86:1 (January/February, 2007): 57–78.

45. United States International Trade Commission, Harmonized Tariff Schedule of the United States (2010), Revision 2, www.usitc.gov/docs/tata/hts/bychapter/1002htsa.pdf (accessed 9/14/10).

46. Tyler Marshall, "Clinton to Nudge China on Rights Reform, Officials Say," *Los Angeles Times*, June 17, 1997, p. 7.

47. Colum Lynch, "U.N. Backs Broader Sanctions on Tehran; Security Council Votes to Freeze Some Assets, Ban Arms Exports," *Washington Post*, March 25, 2007, p. A1.

48. William B. Quandt, *Camp David: Peacemaking and Politics* (Washington, DC: Brookings Institution Press, 1986).

49. John Lewis Gaddis, *The Cold War: A New History* (New York: Penguin Press, 2005).

50. U.S. Department of State, *Treaties in Force*, January 1, 2007, www.state.gov/s/l/treaty/treaties/2007/index.htm (accessed 8/12/08).

51. Lisa L. Martin, "The President and International Commitments: Treaties as Signaling Devices," *Presidential Studies Quarterly* 35:3 (2005): 440–65.

52. P. J. Huffstutter, "A Town Gives until It Hurts," *Los Angeles Times*, November 7, 2003, p. A1.

53. Pew Research Center, "Fewer Americans See Solid Evidence of Climate Change," October 22, 2009, http://people-press.org/report/556/global-warming (accessed 2/17/10).

54. Steven Erlanger, "Syrian Conflict Poses the Risk of Wider Strife," *New York Times*, February 12, 2012, p. A1.

You Decide

a. See the International Criminal Court site at www.icc-cpi.int/home.html; for background on the ICC, see United Nations, UN News Centre, "The International Criminal Court," www.un.org/News/facts/iccfact.htm.

b. International Criminal Court, "The States Parties to the Rome Statute," June 1, 2008, http://hrw.org/campaigns/icc/ratifications.htm.

c. Thom Shanker and James Dao, "U.S. Might Refuse New Peace Duties without Immunity," *New York Times*, July 3, 2002.

d. David Clark, "U.S to Attend Hague Court Meeting as Observer," Reuters, November 16, 2009, www.reuters.com/article/idUSLG395050 (accessed 2/11/10).

e. Brett D. Schaefer, "Overturning Clinton's Midnight Action on the International Criminal Court," Heritage Foundation Executive Memorandum 708, January 9, 2001, www.heritage.org/Research/InternationalOrganizations/EM708.cfm.

f. Human Rights Watch, "Myths and Facts about the International Criminal Court," http://hrw.org/campaigns/icc/facts.htm.

g. Alan Cowell, "British Soldier Pleads Guilty to War Crime," *New York Times*, September 20, 2006.

h. Michael Lewis, "Military's Opposition to Harsh Interrogation Is Outlined," *New York Times*, July 28, 2005.

ANSWER KEY

CHAPTER 1

1. c
2. b
3. c
4. d
5. d
6. c
7. a
8. e

CHAPTER 2

1. b
2. e
3. c
4. c
5. b
6. d
7. b
8. d
9. b
10. d
11. b
12. a
13. a
14. c
15. b

CHAPTER 3

1. c
2. b
3. b
4. d
5. c
6. b
7. b
8. b
9. a
10. d
11. b
12. a
13. d

CHAPTER 4

1. d
2. b
3. b
4. a
5. d
6. c
7. a
8. a
9. b
10. c
11. c
12. b
13. c

CHAPTER 5

1. d
2. b
3. a
4. b
5. e
6. c
7. a
8. b
9. c
10. c
11. a
12. b
13. d
14. a
15. e
16. c
17. a

CHAPTER 6

1. a
2. e
3. b
4. b
5. e
6. a
7. a
8. e
9. c
10. c
11. a

CHAPTER 7

1. a
2. d
3. b
4. b
5. b
6. c
7. e
8. a
9. c
10. b
11. a
12. b
13. e

CHAPTER 8

1. e
2. a
3. c
4. b
5. e
6. c
7. a
8. b
9. d
10. b
11. a

CHAPTER 9

1. d
2. e
3. b
4. a
5. d
6. b
7. d
8. c
9. e
10. a
11. b
12. b

CHAPTER 10

1. a
2. c
3. d
4. a
5. c
6. e
7. b
8. b
9. a
10. c
11. d
12. b

CHAPTER 11	CHAPTER 12	CHAPTER 13	CHAPTER 14	CHAPTER 15
1. c	1. a	1. a	1. a	1. c
2. a	2. d	2. c	2. c	2. a
3. d	3. b	3. b	3. d	3. e
4. e	4. a	4. e	4. a	4. c
5. b	5. e	5. e	5. d	5. d
6. c	6. b	6. b	6. a	6. d
7. b	7. c	7. c	7. b	7. b
8. b	8. a	8. e	8. b	8. c
9. d	9. e	9. a	9. b	9. a
10. b	10. b	10. b	10. c	10. c
11. a	11. d	11. c	11. e	11. b
12. e	12. c	12. c	12. a	12. d
13. a	13. a	13. a	13. e	
14. b	14. b	14. d	14. b	
			15. a	
			16. b	

CREDITS

TABLES AND FIGURES

Figure 1.2: Robert J. Vanderbei, Map: 2008 Presidential Election, Purple America. Reprinted by permission of Robert J. Vanderbei, Princeton University. **Box 5.1:** From "Beyond Red vs. Blue: The 2005 Political Typology." Reprinted by permission of The Pew Research Center for the People & the Press. **Figure 5.1:** Pollster. com, Chart: National Job Approval: President Barack Obama, from http://pollster.com/Obama44JobApprovalr.php. Reprinted with permission. **Table 5.1:** From "American Attitudes Hold Steady in Face of Foreign Crises," August 17, 2006, p. 4. Reprinted by permission of The Pew Research Center for the People & the Press. **Table 5.3:** From "Abortion, the Court, and the Public," Oct. 3, 2005, p. 4. Reprinted by permission of The Pew Research Center for the People & the Press. **Tables 5.4:** From "Beyond Red vs. Blue: The 2005 Political Typology." Reprinted by permission of The Pew Research Center for the People & the Press. **Figure 13.5:** Stephen Jessee & Alexander Tahk, Figure "Current Beliefs" from Supreme Court Ideology Project, http://sct.tahk.us/current.html. Reprinted by permission of the authors.

PHOTOGRAPHS

Page 3 © White House Photo / Alamy; **5** Jose Luis Magana/AP; **7** (left) U.S. Army Photo by Staff Sgt. Russell Bassett; **7** (right) Houston Chronicle, Brett Coomer/AP Photo; **10** Charles Dharapak/AP ; **12** (top) Rick Wilking/AP; **15** © Leigh Vogel/Corbis; **16** (bottom) Erin Siegal/Reuters/Landov; **16** Flip Schulke/CORBIS; **23** © Peter Casolino / Alamy; **25** © North Wind Picture Archives / Alamy; **30** North Wind Picture Archives; **031** © Bettmann/CORBIS; **034** Leonard de Selva/CORBIS; **36** Corbis; **40** U.S. Army photo by Staff Sgt. Lynette Hoke, **1**st Brigade Combat Team, **34**th Infantry Division Public Affairs; **41** KEVIN DIETSCH/UPI /Landov; **45** National Archives/Time Life Pictures/Getty Images; **47** (left) © Everett Collection Inc / Alamy; **47** (right) ©Everett Collection Inc/ Alamy; **48** AP Photo/Gary Gardiner; **055** John Bazemore/AP; **57** Rex Features/AP; **62** © Spencer Grant / Alamy ; **64** © The Metropolitan Museum of Art. Image source: Art Resource, NY; **66** Bettmann/Corbis; **68** The Granger Collection, New York; **74** © Will & Deni McIntyre/CORBIS; **76** Karen Bleier/AFP/Getty Images;

78 Kevin Maloney/Getty Images; **79** Mario Tama/Getty Images; **81** Justin Sullivan/Getty Images; **84** David Zalubowski/AP; **89** Michael S. Williamson/The Washington Post/ Getty Images; **92** (left) AP Photo; **92** (right) William Thomas Cain/Getty Images; **93** Gettypx/Newscom; **95** AP Photo; **99** Al Crespo/Sipa Press/ Newscom; **100** William Campbell/Sygma/Corbis; **102** © Fred Mack / Alamy; **103** © Stacy Walsh Rosenstock / Alamy; **105** Stan Shebs/Wikimedia Commons; **108** Tom Green Defense Team/AP; **109** Alan Kim/The Roanoke Times/AP; **110** Mandel Ngan/AFP/ Getty Images; **115** Site Intelligence Handout/EPA/Newscom; **125** Alamy; **127** (left) Fox/Photofest; **127** Charles Dharapak/AP; **128** © Kenneth D Durden | Dreamstime.com ; **129** SHAWN THEW/ EPA/Newscom; **130** Charles Dharapak/AP; **132** Jeff Malet Photography/Newscom; **133** AP Photo/Paul Sakuma; **148** © Yunus Arakon/ istockphoto.com; **152** (left) Wide World Photos/AP; **152** (right) Karim Kadim/AP; **161** Ron Sachs - CNP/Newscom; **163** (left) © Chuck Burton/ /AP/Corbis; **163** (right) CHRIS LIVINGSTON/ EPA/Newscom; **163** (center) Chip Somodevilla/ Getty Images; **165** © North Wind Picture Archives / Alamy; **166** Corbis; **167** The Granger Collection, New York / The Granger Collection; **170** © Specimen / Alamy; **179** Kayte Deioma / Photo Edit; **180** M. Spencer Green, File/AP; **182** © ZUMA Wire Service / Alamy ; **184** Paul Sancya/AP; **185** CHRIS KLEPONIS/AFP/GETTY IMAGES/Newscom; **186** MARTIN FRIED/UPI/Newscom; **191** STAN HONDA/ AFP/Getty Images; **193** World Wide photos/AP; **195** Marcio Jose Sanchez/AP/Wide World Photos; **196** Mike Derer/AP; **198** © Ken Cedeno/Corbis; **202** Charlie Riedel/AP/Wide World Photos; **203** BRIAN SNYDER/REUTERS/Newscom; **204** © Chris Fitzgerald / Candidate Photos / Newscom; **205** Carolyn Kaster/AP; **206** Alamy; **211** Evan Vucci/AP; **213** © ZUMA Wire Service / Alamy ; **216** ROBYN BECK/AFP/Getty Images; **218** (top) Jamie Sabau/ Getty Images; **255** Alexis C. Glenn/UPI /Landov; **257** The Granger Collection, New York; **259** Jim Urquhart/AP; **263** Jon C. Hancock/AP; **267** (top) Lenny Ignelzi/AP; **267** (bottom) Kevin Wolf/ AP; **268** AP/Jeff Roberson; **272** AP Photo/J. Scott Applewhite; **273** Kevin Dietsch/UPI /Landov; **276** Julie Jacobson/AP; **282** Senate Television/AP; **287** Chip Somodevilla/Getty Images; **293** Erin A. Kirk-Cuomo/DOD Photo; **295** Brooklyn Museum/Corbis; **297** World History Archive/Newscom; **301** Jacquelyn Martin/AP; **303** © LAN HONGGUANG/Xinhua Press/Corbis; **306** © Ron Sachs/

INDEX

Human Rights Watch, 482
Hustler, 103

Idaho, 295
idealism, **469,** 470–71, *470,* 472, 487–88
identity politics, 130, 131–32, **134**
ideology, 16–17
    federalism and, 79, 81
    inconsistency of, 16–17, 128, 129
    polarization of, 139–40
    political conflict as a result of, 11, 139–40
    public opinion and, 17, 126, 128, 129, 139–40
    in Senate, **279**
"I Have a Dream" speech, *400,* 402
IHOP, 410
immigration, 16, 17, 65, 74, 129, 144, 161, 166, 260, 297, 355–56, *355,* 389–90, 395, 418, 419
    illegal, 419, *419,* 420
    reform debates on, 205, 419
impeachment, **41,** 287, 318, 337
imperial judiciary, 356
implied powers, 47, 58, 63, 65
income:
    inequality of, 451–52
    political influence of, **134**
    racial divide in, 397
    in South vs. North, 392
    state differences in, **82–83**
    of women vs. men, 410, **411**
income inequality, 425
income support, 459–61
income tax, 45, 439, 440
incumbency advantage, 268
incumbents, 193, 260–61
    election rates of, 215–16, **215**
    high reelection rates of, 202, **210**
    permanent campaign of, 202, *202*
    presidential nominations of, 198, 202
    retrospective evaluations of, 193, 213, 214
independent agencies, 335, 336, **336**
    number of employees in, 337, **338**
Independent Party, 184
independents, **139,** 140
    candidacy of, 193
independent voters, 174
Indiana, 198
Indian Removal Act, 394
individualism, economic, 14
industrialization, 67, 295
industry, 14
infant mortality, 399
inflation, 297, 432, 442, 454
    Misery Index of unemployment and, **435**
    prevention of, as economic policy goal, 434–35, 436
infrastructure:
    concurrent power over, **59**
    federal authority over, 38
    federal spending on, 9, 83
In re Oliver 333 U.S. 257, **96**
inside strategies, 239–42
intelligence gathering, 477
intelligent design, 14
intercontinental railroad, 395

interest groups, 10, 12, 14, *76,* 84, 202, 204, 229, *231,* **232**
    campaign ads run by, 206, 243, 245
    campaign contributions by, **210,** 231, 232, 243–46
    definition of, 231
    electioneering and, **244**
    financial expenditures of, 237–39, **238, 239, 240, 245,** 246, 249, 250
    foreign policy and influence of, 478–80
    as fundamental feature of democracy, 231
    funding of, 235
    growth in number of, 237, 250
    inside lobbying strategies of, 239–42, *241*
    membership size and role in, 233
    organizational models of, 231–33
    outside lobbying strategies of, *234,* 239, 242–46
    political influence and power of, 231, 235, 246, 247, 248–49, *248,* 446, 480
    political parties vs., 231
    public opinion and, 14, 132
    regulations imposed on, 207, 236, 244
    resources used by, 234–35
    social policy formation and role of, 428, 433–34
    staff and revolving door of, 235–37
    three types of, **232**
    see also lobbying, lobbyists
interest rates, 429, 432, 441, 442, 443–44
intergovernmental organizations (IGOs), 59–60, 481
intergovernmental relations, 67–68
Interior Department, U.S., **335, 338,** 446
    Endangered Species Act and, 363
intermediate scrutiny, 98
intermediate scrutiny test, 407, 408, **408**
Internal Revenue Code, 208
Internal Revenue Service (IRS), 9, 185, 244, 336–37
international aid, 16, 138
    see also foreign aid
International Criminal Court (ICC), 482, *482*
internationalism, 469, **469,** 470, 472
International Monetary Fund (IMF), 59, 402, 473, 481
international organizations, 481
International Republican Institute, 481
International Trade Commission, 485
Internet, **13,** 104, 111, 133, 136, 146–50, 151, 204, 217, 444
    fabricated photos on, 149
    fund-raising and, 217
    grassroots lobbying on, 243
    information gathering and availability as transformed by, 148–50, 154
    knowledge levels in users of, **147**
    Medicare Prescription Drug Benefit and, *329*
    photos on, 149
    questionable reliability of, 149
interrogation, 482
Interstate Commerce Act (1887), 444
Interstate Commerce Commission, 296, 332, 444
Iowa, 197, 205

Iran, *303*
    nuclear program of, 483, 485
Iranian Hostage Crisis, *316*
Iraq, 304, 305, 489
    democracy in, 469
    Persian Gulf War and, 297
    war in, 89, 316
Iraq War, 11, 149, 185, 217, 273, 317, 468, 469, 474, 476, 483, 489
    funding of, 317, 478, 480
    media coverage and, *152*
    public opinion on, 143, 144–45, *152,* 215, 480, 481, 488
    realist vs. idealist view on, 470–71, 487–88
    troop withdrawal issue in, 478, 480
    war powers and, *38,* 41, 302, 303
    weapons of mass destruction as motive for, 469
Ireland, **486**
isolationism, 469, **469,** 470, 471
Israel, 58, 480, 482, 485, 487
issue scale, 136
Italy, 58, **486**

Jack in the Box, 410
Jackson, Andrew, 165, *165,* 166, 258, 295
    bureaucracy and, 331–32, *332*
Jackson, Robert, 377
Japan, 58, 472, 482, **486**
Japanese Americans, 395
    internment of, 382, 395
Jay, John, 29
Jefferson, Thomas, 33, 63, 98, 104–5, 257
    compromises forged by, 295
    Marbury v. Madison and, 359
Jefferson, William, 266, *267*
Jews, 101, 167, 377
Jim Crow laws, *66,* 67, 393, 396
Joe Camel, 103, *103*
Johnson, Andrew, 287
Johnson, Lyndon, 72, 168, 202, 275, 276, 296, 333, 432, 449–50
    approval ratings of, **309**
    civil rights and, 296, 334, 412, 414, 416, 450
    War on Poverty program of, 296, 450, 461
Joint Committee on Taxation, 277
joint committees, 277
Jones, Antoine, 111
journalists, interest groups and, 246
JP Morgan Chase, 445
judicial activism, 380, 405–7
judicial branch, 26
    allocation of power to, 6, 8, **28, 35,** 40, 41, 42
    appointments to, 298–300, 367–72, **369, 370,** *371*
    checks and balances on, 40–42
    court fundamentals and, 361–64
    court structure and, 361, 364–67
    federal, development of an independent and powerful, 357–61, **360**
    foreign policy and role of, 478
    "imperial," 356
    influence on political process of, 12
    see also courts; Supreme Court, U.S.

judges appointed by, **369**
social policies of, 450
Reagan Revolution, 333, 334
realignments, in party systems, 168–69
realism, 469, **469,** 470–71, 472, 487–88
reasonable basis test, 405, 408, 410
reasonable vote, 213–14
recess appointments, 300
recession, *447,* 459, 474
    Keynesian economic theory for
      softening of, 437
Reconstruction, 66, 67, 167, 287, 358, 393
redistribution, fiscal policy's nature of, 14,
    134, 439–40, **441**
redistricting, 263–66
"red states," 14, 17
red tape, bureaucracy and, 329
reductions in force (RIF), 340–41
Reed, Stanley, 377–78
reelection:
    EOP role in, 312
    presidential approval and, 309, **309**
Reform Party, U.S., 184, *196*
regional primaries, 196–97
regions, political differences among, 30,
    131–32, **134**
regressive taxes, 439, 440
regulation, 326–28, *327,* 439
    of banking system, 440–42, 444
    business, 13, **13,** 14, **59,** 67, 75, 295–96,
      326
    campaign finance, 207–12, **208,** 209, 211,
      236, 244
    civil service, 339–41
    commerce, 9, **59,** 60, 63–64, 65, 67,
      77–78, **77,** 107, 327, 444
    currency, 9
    drug, 81, 327–28, 329, 330–31
    economic effects of, 444–45
    economic vs. social, 444–45
    environmental, 75, 444–45, 446, *446*
    everyday life affected by, 13, 327–28, *327*
    extent of, 297
    free market, 9, 436, 444
    ideological views on, 14, 16, 79
    Internet, 104
    of lobbying groups, 236, 244
    media, 14, 101–2, *103,* 150–52
    notice and comment procedure and, 326
    role in coercive federalism of, 73
    state power over, 75, 82
    trade, 9, **59**
    of water safety, 444
Rehnquist, William, 81
Reid, Harry, *276*
religion, **77**
    government and, 104–9
    political affiliation and, 174, **176**
    political conflict as a result of, 14
    political influence of, 14, 128, 129, 130
    see also freedom of religion
religious discrimination, **413**
religious displays, 14, 104, *105,* 106
Religious Freedom Restoration Act (1993),
    77, 107
remedial legislation, 76

reporters, *see* journalists; media
republican democracy, 6, 28, 31
Republican Governors' Association, 170
republicanism, 28
Republican Lawyers' Organization, 170
Republican National Committee (RNC),
    170–71
Republican Party, U.S., 12, 24, 132, **143,**
    161–62, 163–64, 192, 295–96,
    342, 371
    affiliations by race and gender with, 16,
      16, **176**
    as brand name, 170, 204
    bureaucratic control and, 348
    campaign fundraising and support
      provided by, 179, **180**
    Civil War amendments passed by, 393
    congressional conference of, 171–72
    culture wars reflected in election results
      of, 14
    economic policy and, 435, 446
    formation of, 295
    founding and history of, 164–68, **164**
    gay marriage and, 144
    global warming and, 144
    House controlled by, 74, 305, 312, 334
    identification with, 12, 14, 16, *16,* 17, 129,
      130, 132, 140, **140**
    ideology and, 14, 16, 17, 81, 172–73,
      172, 180
    Latinos in, 395, 415
    limited federal government and, 72
    limited government and, 426
    New Deal opposed by, 333
    party coalitions in, 174–75, **176**
    party identification in electorate of,
      173–74, **175**
    party in government of, 171–73
    party organizations of, 169–71
    position on regulation of, 14, 169
    position on spending of, 14
    position on taxes of, 14, 428, 437, 439
    poverty rates under leadership of, 452
    presidential platforms of, 179–80
    Senate controlled by, 297, 305, 312, 334,
      372
    smaller federal government favored by,
      167, 168, 169
    social policy approaches favored by, 452,
      455, 460
    see also elections, U.S.
research and development, 328
reservations, Native American, 394
reserved powers, 34
reserve requirement, 442
resources, national distribution of, 82–83
    see also spending
Respect for Fallen American Heroes Act, 89
RESPECT project, 461
restaurants, desegregation of, 401–2, 405
restrictive covenants, 404
retirement age, 453, 455
retrospective evaluations, 193, 213, 214
reverse discrimination, 374
revisionary power, 358
    see also judicial review

Revolutionary War, 359
    government during, 25–26
    influence on Constitutional Convention
      of, 25, 27, 28, 31
revolving door, 235, 237
Rhode Island, 32, 37
Richmond, Va., 416
right to bear arms, 96, **96,** 109–10
right to die, 117–18, 129, 459
right to petition, 96, **96, 108**
ripeness, 374–75
R. J. Reynolds, 103
Roberts, John G., 81 370, *375, 376, 380,* **381**
Robinson, Jackie, 394
Robinson v. California, **96**
robo-polls, 137
Roe v. Wade, 117
roll call votes, 274
Rolling Stone, 467
Romney, Mitt, 17, 135, 174, 191, 192, 197, **200,**
    207, 415, 425, 440
Roosevelt, Eleanor, *449*
Roosevelt, Franklin D., **68,** 167, *167,* 296, *297,*
    333, 355, 432, 449
    court-packing plan of, 368
    Supreme Court switch and, 382
Roosevelt, Theodore, 23, 295–96, 455
Ross, Gary, *414,* 415
Rove, Karl, 342
Ruby Tuesday, 410
rules, influence on political process of,
    9, 12, 24
rules and regulations, bureaucracy and, 349
runoff elections, 195
Rush Limbaugh Show, The, **147**
Russia, 481, 482
    nuclear weapons of, 473
Rutledge, Justice, 358
Rwanda, 297
Ryan, Paul, *425*

same-sex marriage, 14, 16, *23,* **44,** 45, 62, *62,*
    79, 125, 126, 144, 194, 355, 396, 399,
    410–11, 414, *414,* 419
samples:
    random, 135, **135,** 136
    survey, 135, **135**
sampling error, **135**
Sandanistas, 41
Sanders, Bernard, *284*
Santorum, Rick, 192, 197
Sarbanes-Oxley Act (2002), 334
satellite television, 151
Scalia, Antonin, 81, 356, *376,* 377, *380,* **381**
Schattschneider, E. E., 10
Schenk, Charles, 98–99
Schiavo, Michael, 117
Schiavo, Terri, 117
Schilb v. Kuebel, **96**
school desegregation, 382, 399, 401,
    403–5, 414
    Brown I and, 382, 394, 401, 404
    Brown II and, 394, 404
    busing and, 405, *410*
school prayer, 14, 45, 105, 381, *382*
school vouchers, 14, 17

South America, 471
South Carolina, 64, 112, *246*
Southern Ohio Correctional Facility, *48*
South Vietnam, 296, 473
sovereign power, 57
Soviet Union, 59, 472–73, 487
    fall of, 474
    Reagan policy toward, 297
    U.S. policy of containment and,
        472–74
    U.S. treaties with, 473, 487
space program, spending for, 337
Spain, **486**
Spanish-American War, 302
Speaker of the House, 272, 311
speech:
    commercial, 103, *103*, **108**
    hate, 100–101, *100*
    less protected, 102–4
    political, 98–99, 102, *103*, **108**
    protected, 97–101
    symbolic, 99–100, *99*, 100, **108**
    see also freedom of speech
speed limits, 57
spending:
    concurrent powers of, **59**
    congressional authority over, 40, **59**, 72,
        107, 429–31
    deficits and, **437, 438**
    federal, 13, 70, **71,** 72, 82, 138, 142, 161,
        162, **238, 239,** 337, **339,** 437, **438,**
        439, **440, 441,** 449, 453, 455,
        456–57, **457,** 459–61
    on health care, 455, 456–57, **457**
    ideological views on, 14, 16
    Keynesian economic theory and,
        437, 439
    on lobbying efforts, 237–39, **238, 239,**
        240, 250
    mandatory vs. discretionary,
        439, **440**
    1980s budget deficit and, 439
    public opinion on, 127, 138, 337
    on social policies, 449, 451–52, 456–57,
        459–61
    state and local, 71, **71,** 72, 83
split tickets, casting of, 215
spoils system, 166, 331–32, *332,* 333
sports, 112
spying:
    domestic, 93, 102, 111, 112–13, 119; *see*
        also surveillance
    foreign, 113
Stamp Act (1765), 25
Standard Oil, 444
standard operating procedures, 329
standing, 362–63
standing committees, 277
Stanton, Elizabeth Cady, 400
state capacity, 329
State Department, U.S., 331, **335,** 347,
    347, 429
    foreign policy and role of, 476
    number of employees in, **338**
state laws, judicial review of, 359, 360–61
State of the Union address, 304, 310, 311

states:
    economic differences among, 82, **82–83**
    income assistance and welfare
        administered by, 459
    Medicaid and discretionary
        power of, 456
    political differences among,
        14, **14,** 17, 109
    social policy formation and role of,
        433, 459
states' rights, 64–65, 68, 70–71, 74–83, 94, 95,
    96, 98, 109, 117–18, 359, 360
statutory interpretation, 361
stem cell research, 14, 17, 74, 459
Stevens, John Paul, 380, **381**
Stewart, Potter, 103–4
stimulus package, *see* economic stimulus
    package
stock markets, 449
    in financial crisis of 2008, 445–47
Stone, Harlan Fiske, 377
Stonewall Rebellion, 396
straight tickets, casting of, 215
Strategic Arms Limitation Treaty
    (SALT I), 473
street-level bureaucrats, 328
strict construction, 379, 382
strict scrutiny, 98, 407–8, **408,** 417
strip searches, 111
Student Nonviolent Coordinating Committee
    (SNCC), 402
substantive due process doctrine, 118, 410
substantive representation, 259
suicides, assisted, 57, 81
Sullivan, Kathleen, 45
supermajorities, 36
"Super PACs," 245
Supplemental Nutrition Assistance
    Program, 459
Supplemental Security Income (SSI), 459
supply-side economics, 439
Supreme Court, U.S., *40,* 48, 61, 148, 265,
    357–61, *357, 364,* 365–67, 372–83,
    429, 459
    ACA and, 56
    access to, 372–75, **373**
    allocation of power to, 8, **28,** 40, 42, 61, 62
    amicus curiae and, 376
    appellate jurisdiction of, 358, **360,** 365
    appointments to, *40,* 42, 75
    briefs for, 376
    campaign finance reforms and,
        99–100, 211
    case criteria of, 374–75
    chief justices of, 358
    civil liberties and, 95–119
    civil rights issues and, 392–93,
        394, 396, 401, 402, 403–11, 413,
        416, 418
    color-blind jurisprudence of, 405–7, 416
    constitutional amendments to overturn
        decisions of, 43, 45, 99
    constitutional interpretation by, 47–48,
        61, 63–65, 66–67, 75–79, **77,** *78,*
        79, 81, 93, 95–119, 294, 302–3, 361,
        366–67, 379, 380, 382, 419

    decision making of, 378–82
    docket of, 372
    executive privilege ruling of, 308
    FDR's court-packing plan for, 368
    federalism and, 61, 63–64, **65,** 66–67,
        66, 72, 75–79, *76,* **77,** 79, 81, 83, 94,
        95–96, 107, 109, 112, 359
    foreign policy and, 478
    G. W. Bush's appointments to, 300
    hearing cases before, 376–78, *376*
    interpretation of laws by, 8, 40, 42,
        63–64, 67, 75, 76, 79, 81, 103–4, 359
    judicial activism of, 380, 405–7
    judicial restraint of, 380
    judicial review by, 40, 42, 358–61,
        359, 383
    justices' conference in, 377
    legislative vetos and, 287
    opinion writing in, *375,* 377–78
    oral argument in, 376–77, *376*
    original jurisdiction of, 359, **360,** 372
    pocket vetos and, 285
    policy implications of composition of, 42,
        75–76, 79
    as policy-making institution, 355, 356
    as political institution, 355, 356, 378–83
    precedent overruled by, 362, **363**
    public knowledge of, *127*
    public opinion and, *375,* 378, 380, 381–82
    rules of access for, 372–73
    separation of powers and, 380–81
    speech protected by, 90
    strategic approach to, 380
    strict construction and, 379, 382
    2012 elections and, 355
    War Powers Resolution and, 303
    workload of, 372, **373**
    writ of certification and, 373
    writ of certiorari and, 373
    writ of mandamus issued by, 359
    see also judicial branch; *specific cases*
surge, in troops, *see* troop surge
surveillance, 102, 111, 112–13
    see also spying
surveys, 128, 133
    interpretation of, 138
    mass, 135–36, **135**
    problems with, 138, 480
    techniques of, 136–37
    wording of, 129, **137,** 141
    see also polls
suspension of rules, 286
Sweden, 58, **486**
Swezy, Dan, *414*
swing states, 198, **199**
Switzerland, **486**
Syria, 470, 471, 488

talk radio, 146
Tammany Hall, 166, *166*
Taney, Roger, 64–65
Tanzania, 474
tariffs, 31, 37, 64, 478, 485
    definition of, 485
TARP, *see* Troubled Asset Relief Program
Tax Day, 403

PRESIDENTS *& Vice Presidents*
OF THE UNITED STATES

	PRESIDENT	*Vice* PRESIDENT
1	George Washington (*Federalist 1789*)	John Adams (*Federalist 1789*)
2	John Adams (*Federalist 1797*)	Thomas Jefferson (*Dem.-Rep. 1797*)
3	Thomas Jefferson (*Dem.-Rep. 1801*)	Aaron Burr (*Dem.-Rep. 1801*) George Clinton (*Dem.-Rep. 1805*)
4	James Madison (*Dem.-Rep. 1809*)	George Clinton (*Dem.-Rep. 1809*) Elbridge Gerry (*Dem.-Rep. 1813*)
5	James Monroe (*Dem.-Rep. 1817*)	Daniel D. Tompkins (*Dem.-Rep. 1817*)
6	John Quincy Adams (*Dem.-Rep. 1825*)	John C. Calhoun (*Dem.-Rep. 1825*)
7	Andrew Jackson (*Democratic 1829*)	John C. Calhoun (*Democratic 1829*) Martin Van Buren (*Democratic 1833*)
8	Martin Van Buren (*Democratic 1837*)	Richard M. Johnson (*Democratic 1837*)
9	William H. Harrison (*Whig 1841*)	John Tyler (*Whig 1841*)
10	John Tyler (*Whig and Democratic 1841*)	
11	James K. Polk (*Democratic 1845*)	George M. Dallas (*Democratic 1845*)

	PRESIDENT	*Vice* PRESIDENT
12	Zachary Taylor (*Whig 1849*)	Millard Fillmore (*Whig 1849*)
13	Millard Fillmore (*Whig 1850*)	
14	Franklin Pierce (*Democratic 1853*)	William R. D. King (*Democratic 1853*)
15	James Buchanan (*Democratic 1857*)	John C. Breckinridge (*Democratic 1857*)
16	Abraham Lincoln (*Republican 1861*)	Hannibal Hamlin (*Republican 1861*) Andrew Johnson (*Unionist 1865*)
17	Andrew Johnson (*Unionist 1865*)	
18	Ulysses S. Grant (*Republican 1869*)	Schuyler Colfax (*Republican 1869*) Henry Wilson (*Republican 1873*)
19	Rutherford B. Hayes (*Republican 1877*)	William A. Wheeler (*Republican 1877*)
20	James A. Garfield (*Republican 1881*)	Chester A. Arthur (*Republican 1881*)
21	Chester A. Arthur (*Republican 1881*)	
22	Grover Cleveland (*Democratic 1885*)	Thomas A. Hendricks (*Democratic 1885*)
23	Benjamin Harrison (*Republican 1889*)	Levi P. Morton (*Republican 1889*)
24	Grover Cleveland (*Democratic 1893*)	Adlai E. Stevenson (*Democratic 1893*)

	PRESIDENT	*Vice* PRESIDENT		PRESIDENT	*Vice* PRESIDENT
25	William McKinley *(Republican 1897)*	Garret A. Hobart *(Republican 1897)* Theodore Roosevelt *(Republican 1901)*	36	Lyndon B. Johnson *(Democratic 1965)*	Hubert H. Humphrey *(Democratic 1963)*
26	Theodore Roosevelt *(Republican 1901)*	Charles W. Fairbanks *(Republican 1905)*	37	Richard M. Nixon *(Republican 1969)*	Spiro T. Agnew *(Republican 1969)* Gerald R. Ford *(Republican 1973)*
27	William H. Taft *(Republican 1909)*	James S. Sherman *(Republican 1909)*	38	Gerald R. Ford *(Republican 1974)*	Nelson Rockefeller *(Republican 1974)*
28	Woodrow Wilson *(Democratic 1913)*	Thomas R. Marshall *(Democratic 1913)*	39	James E. Carter *(Democratic 1977)*	Walter Mondale *(Democratic 1977)*
29	Warren G. Harding *(Republican 1921)*	Calvin Coolidge *(Republican 1921)*	40	Ronald Reagan *(Republican 1981)*	George H. W. Bush *(Republican 1981)*
30	Calvin Coolidge *(Republican 1923)*	Charles G. Dawes *(Republican 1925)*	41	George H. W. Bush *(Republican 1989)*	J. Danforth Quayle *(Republican 1989)*
31	Herbert Hoover *(Republican 1929)*	Charles Curtis *(Republican 1929)*	42	William J. Clinton *(Democratic 1993)*	Albert Gore Jr. *(Democratic 1993)*
32	Franklin D. Roosevelt *(Democratic 1933)*	John Nance Garner *(Democratic 1933)* Henry A. Wallace *(Democratic 1941)* Harry S. Truman *(Democratic 1945)*	43	George W. Bush *(Republican 2001)*	Richard Cheney *(Republican 2001)*
33	Harry S. Truman *(Democratic 1945)*	Alben W. Barkley *(Democratic 1949)*	44	Barack Obama *(Democratic 2009)*	Joseph R. Biden Jr. *(Democratic 2009)*
34	Dwight D. Eisenhower *(Republican 1953)*	Richard M. Nixon *(Republican 1953)*			
35	John F. Kennedy *(Democratic 1961)*	Lyndon B. Johnson *(Democratic 1961)*			

Governing California in the Twenty-First Century

THE POLITICAL DYNAMICS OF THE GOLDEN STATE

FOURTH EDITION

J. Theodore Anagnoson
CALIFORNIA STATE UNIVERSITY, LOS ANGELES

Gerald Bonetto
CALIFORNIA STATE UNIVERSITY, LOS ANGELES

J. Vincent Buck
CALIFORNIA STATE UNIVERSITY, FULLERTON

Richard E. DeLeon
SAN FRANCISCO STATE UNIVERSITY

Jolly Emrey
UNIVERSITY OF WISCONSIN–WHITEWATER

James J. Kelleher
CALIFORNIA STATE UNIVERSITY, DOMINGUEZ HILLS

Nadine Koch
CALIFORNIA STATE UNIVERSITY, LOS ANGELES

W. W. NORTON AND COMPANY
NEW YORK ★ LONDON

W. W. Norton & Company has been independent since its founding in 1923, when William Warder Norton and Mary D. Herter Norton first published lectures delivered at the People's Institute, the adult education division of New York City's Cooper Union. The firm soon expanded its program beyond the Institute, publishing books by celebrated academics from America and abroad. By midcentury, the two major pillars of Norton's publishing program—trade books and college texts—were firmly established. In the 1950s, the Norton family transferred control of the company to its employees, and today—with a staff of four hundred and a comparable number of trade, college, and professional titles published each year—W. W. Norton & Company stands as the largest publishing house owned wholly by its employees.

The text of this book is composed in Berlin
with the display set in Interstate.
Book design: Sandra Watanabe
Composition: Jouve International—Brattleboro, VT
Manufacturing: Courier—Westford, MA
Associate Editor: Jake Schindel
Copyeditor: Candace Levy
Project editor: Christine D'Antonio
Associate Director of Production, College: Ben Reynolds

Library of Congress Cataloging-in-Publication Data has been applied for.
  ISBN 978-0-393-91915-8 (pbk.)

W. W. Norton & Company, Inc., 500 Fifth Avenue, New York, N.Y. 10110
www.wwnorton.com

W. W. Norton & Company Ltd., Castle House, 75/76 Wells Street, London W1T 3QT

2 3 4 5 6 7 8 9 0

Contents

5 ★ The California Legislature 97

6 ★ The Governor and the Executive Branch *119*

Preface

We began this project over a decade ago with a working title asking whether California's political system and its politics were simply "broken." That is, politicians were caught within a system that was so contradictory in its rules, norms, and mores that budgets simply couldn't be passed on time or balanced, programs and departments couldn't be managed under the existing set of rules, and citizen expectations were so out of line with the ability of the political system to satisfy them that the level of negativism and cynicism was about as bad as could be found anywhere in the nation.

We think after a decade of false and halting starts that the picture needs some modification. California has begun to repair its infrastructure. The state has new incentives for politicians to be less ideologically extreme on the right or the left, in particular the "top two" primary system and the commission that is now drawing new districts for the Assembly, the state Senate, and congressional districts every 10 years after the Census. Decision rules in Sacramento still leave much to be desired, but at least a budget can be passed with majority rule instead of having to have two-thirds, a rule that necessitated some votes from the minority party and, unfortunately, some pork projects or other incentives to gain those votes. And the nation's strictest term-limit rules have been modified to allow members of the Assembly or state Senate to serve 12 years in a single house before being "termed out" and forced to seek another office outside the state legislature. Hopefully this will increase the level of expertise available among legislators.

At the same time, if the distance to be traveled to reach a political system that would actually "function" and make decisions is one mile, we have gone perhaps 1,000 feet. There still is no way to adjust the tax system without a two-thirds vote, and California's tax system badly needs modernization from its last overhaul more than 50 years ago. While the economy has moved toward a services base, California's tax system remains based on the manufacturing that was more common a half century ago. The income tax relies much too heavily on the capital gains tax, and that in turn creates revenue peaks and valleys that tempt Sacramento politicians to build the periodic surges of revenue into the base and in turn to run deficits when times are tough.

Proposition 13, passed in 1978, caused over the next decade a massive centralization of authority in Sacramento at the expense of cities, counties, and school districts. As a result, local governments have little authority over their own revenue. State government proved to be unable to provide local governments the revenue and authority they needed to deal with the recent recession, financial collapse, and defaulted mortgages that plague certain parts of the state, resulting in a number of local government bankruptcies, and in governments that are not bankrupt, the inability to help people in a genuine time of need. In some dire cases, state government cutbacks combined with the revenue-depleting impacts of home mortgage foreclosures, high unemployment, business failures, and grossly overburdened public sector pension and benefit obligations created local "perfect storms" of economic and political conditions that bankrupted Stockton and other cities and still threaten others. The state has been unable to help.

In these circumstances, the fourth edition of *Governing California in the Twenty-First Century* offers a ray of hope but the reality of a long distance to go. We hope you enjoy our analysis of California's politics, not quite "broken"—but not as yet "fixed" either—at this point.

We divided the writing of this book as follows:

1. California Government in Crisis—Anagnoson (tanagno@calstatela.edu)
2. The Constitution and the Progressive Legacy—Bonetto (Gerry@piasc.org)
3. Interest Groups and the Media in California—Bonetto
4. Parties and Elections in California—Koch (nkoch@calstatela.edu)
5. The California Legislature—Buck (vbuck@fullerton.edu)
6. The Governor and the Executive Branch—Buck
7. The California Judiciary—Emrey (emreyj@uww.edu)
8. The State Budget and Budgetary Limitations—Anagnoson
9. Local Government—DeLeon (rdeleon@sfsu.edu)
10. Public Policy in California—Anagnoson

There are websites for the second, third, and fourth editions of this book. For the fourth edition, go to http://www.silcom.com/~anag999/g4.html. For the second or third edition sites, substitute "g2" or "g3" (without the quotes) for "g4." The sites contain:

- A link to the publisher's own site for this book.

- A list of *errata*. If you find any error in the book, please email the lead author, J. Theodore Anagnoson, at anag999@silcom.com or tanagno@calstatela.edu.

- The answers to the short answer questions at the end of each chapter

- PowerPoint slides used by Anagnoson in Spring 2009 to teach an upper division course in California politics. These are up to date only to the end of Spring 2009.

We have constructed, in addition, a test bank for instructors. To gain access to the test bank, visit wwnorton.com/instructors.

We would like to acknowledge the helpful recommendations from a series of reviewers, whose comments have assisted us in updating events and materials. We would also like to thank the many students who have communicated their comments. I would also like to acknowledge the assistance of Alexandra Jimenez in gathering data used in Chapter 1. Any errors that remain are strictly our own, much as we would like to attribute them to others.

We would be glad to hear from you about the book. Use the e-mail addresses above to communicate with us.

J. Theodore Anagnoson
Professor of Political Science
California State University, Los Angeles

1 California Government in Crisis

WHAT CALIFORNIA GOVERNMENT DOES AND WHY IT MATTERS

Which of the following actions does not involve the use of an object or action regulated by the federal, state, or local government?

★ Driving on the freeway

★ Driving on a tollway

★ Driving across a bridge

★ Walking to the grocery store

★ Buying fruit at the grocery store

★ Going to school at any level, public or private

★ Working for the California Highway Patrol

★ Working for a private security guard service

★ Working for a grocery store

★ Eating dinner in a restaurant

[Answers at the end of the chapter.]

The California Dream?

For almost 200 years, the dream of California has attracted immigrants from the United States and abroad. Governor Arnold Schwarzenegger, in one of his state of the state speeches (2004), said that California represents "an empire of hope and aspiration," a place where "Californians do great things." To some, the California dream is sun and surf; to others, the warm winter season; to still others, a house on the coast in the redwoods and acres of untrammeled wilderness, or three or four cars per family. Many of these dreams can be summed up in the phrase *freedom from restraints* or *freedom from traditions*. These are typical themes in statewide elections and gubernatorial state of the state speeches—bringing back our image of an older, less crowded California.

The reality is that some of the dream is attainable for many—we live in a place with winter weather that is the envy of most of the rest of the nation—but much of it is not. One of the themes of this book is the conflict between the dream and the reality, between the ideals that we set for ourselves and the reality of our everyday lives. One conflict particularly vivid to politicians is the conflict between the expectations we have for them and the reality of the constraints and incentives we saddle them with, so that they cannot possibly meet our expectations.

The Crisis of California Politics

The question before us is whether California government is capable of making the decisions needed for California to thrive and preserve its standard of living through the twenty-first century. The general sentiment among informed observers is that California is hamstrung by voter-approved rules and regulations, all admirable individually but a nightmare collectively. However, during the Schwarzenegger administration from 2003 to 2011, some progress was made:

- Proposition 11, approved in November 2008, took the power to apportion the districts of the Assembly and State Senate away from those bodies and gave it to a citizens' commission. Later, the voters added congressional districts to the duties of the new citizens' commission. In 2012, the first year the new districts were used, they seemed to be fair (that is, not gerrymandered). Future years will establish whether unbiased districts will produce more moderate legislators willing to compromise for the good of the state as a whole, which was the goal of changing the reapportionment method. So far, we have had significantly more competition.

- In 2010, the voters decided to change the state's party primary elections from a party primary to a new top-two system, used for the first time in June 2012. Under the new system, there is no party primary. Instead the election system is like a swimming or track meet, in which there are preliminary heats and finals. Following the preliminary election, the top two candidates advance to the finals in November, even if they are from the same party or they are not in a major party.

- In 2010, the voters also approved changing the majority needed to approve the state budget in the legislature from a two-thirds vote of the total number of legislators in each chamber, the Assembly and the State Senate, to a simple majority (50 percent plus one). The budgets approved in June 2011 and June 2012 were the first to be approved using the new system. However, the state constitution still requires a two-thirds majority of both houses of the legislature, plus the governor's signature, to raise or lower taxes.

Schwarzenegger also made progress through the approval of reforms to the workers' compensation system in 2004 and several initiatives to rebuild California's infrastructure (levees in the Central Valley, highways) in 2006.

Yet under Governor Jerry Brown, elected in November 2010, the frustrating budget stalemate has continued in spite of the majority rule for passing the budget. As of June 2012, the budget gap was $16 billion, more than the total revenues received for the general fund in 40 of the 50 states. However, the Legislative Analyst's Office reported in January 2012 that although the deficit still persists, the long-term trend is moving in the right direction, toward smaller deficits. While the majority budget rule might not be the only factor, clearly it has helped in cutting the long-term deficits projected in Figure 1.1.

The downward trend is the result of difficult and tough decisions. Every college student in California knows some of them, having seen cut after cut after cut to the budgets of the community colleges, the California State University system, and the University of California system. These cuts have been partially replaced by tuition and fee increases. Other reductions have included Medi-Cal (California's medical program for the poor) rate and service reductions, many cost-containment measures in the state developmentally disabled programs, and the elimination of the state's local government redevelopment agencies and their state funding (see Chapter 9). Prisoners are being sent from the state prisons to local jails, and many state responsibilities are being devolved to the local level of government. Figure 1.1 reflects the results of those decisions and the continuing, if slow, improvement to the state's economy.

California state government thus faces a series of paradoxes. On the one hand, we see progress in cutting the deficit and in making the hard decisions necessary

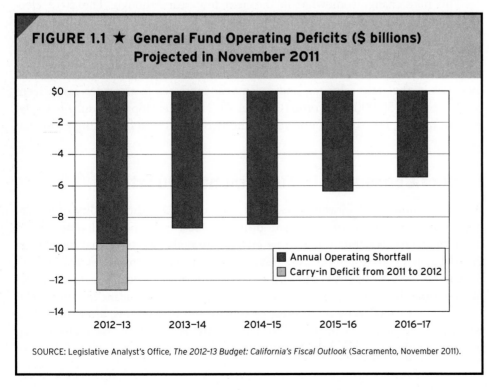

FIGURE 1.1 ★ General Fund Operating Deficits ($ billions) Projected in November 2011

SOURCE: Legislative Analyst's Office, *The 2012-13 Budget: California's Fiscal Outlook* (Sacramento, November 2011).

to weather the national economic storm. But on the other hand, the difficulty of those decisions and the fact that taxes can still be only raised by a two-thirds majority has meant that there has been a budget crisis for months every single year. And every decision in the state government is a budget decision—a decision made solely, or almost solely, on the basis of whether there is enough money and a budget source for the particular activity.

Let us take a closer look at some reasons we seem to have a continual crisis in California state government.

The Two-Thirds Requirement for Raising Taxes

As noted earlier, until November 2010, when the voters passed Proposition 25, California's constitution required a two-thirds vote of the total membership—not just those present and voting—in each house of the legislature to pass the budget. Proposition 25 lowered the vote required to pass the budget to 50 percent plus one. It will take several years to see if this change makes a substantial difference. So far, the first two budgets passed under the new rules—which penalize legislators' salaries if the budget is not passed on time—have been passed around June 15, the constitutional deadline, but have not been any more balanced than previous budgets. Obtaining a balanced budget clearly requires improving the quality of the state's economy and tax system as well as changing procedural deadlines.

Herein lies the problem. A two-thirds vote of the absolute number of legislators in both houses of the state legislature is still necessary to raise or lower any tax level. With a Republican Party that refuses to countenance any tax increases of any kind (plus the taxpayer groups that promise to sue the instant any tax increase is passed), the burden of balancing the state budget has fallen on low- and moderate-income state residents, who benefit disproportionately from state programs (which are now being cut). For higher-income state residents, state services are at least partially irrelevant, as the major "service" is a low tax rate, and this has not been raised in at least three years.

This may change somewhat in the next few years, though. The 2012 elections saw the Democrats win a supermajority of seats in the legislature, meaning they would have enough votes without any Republican support to raise taxes (see Chapter 4). Whether this supermajority will hold remains to be seen. Meanwhile, Proposition 30 on the November 2012 ballot passed, implementing four-year increases in the state sales tax and seven-year increases in tax rates for citizens making over $250,000 in income (Chapter 4). These developments may have significant impact, but they do not negate the two-thirds rule for raising taxes that currently exists.

Lack of Consensus in Fundamental Questions

Another reason for California's perpetual state of crisis is the inability of legislators to unify in matters of policy and principle. How can a political system overcome the inertia generated by narrow interests to make decisions that benefit the broader general interest of the public as a whole? In a large complex state like California, this issue will persist, but in the past, California politicians have been able to overcome the lack of consensus to make progress on significant questions. Has California changed? Why do interest groups cause impasse now, after the 2000s, when they did not back in the 1970s and 1980s? After all, we have always had interest groups, and we had the two-thirds decision rule for adopting the budget or raising taxes in the legislature from 1935 until 2010. Dan Walters suggests that the blame heaped on the legislature is inappropriate.

> In fact, California's governance maladies stem from the complex, often contradictory nature of the state itself. With its immense geographic, economic, and cultural diversity, California has myriad policy issues, but those same factors also have become an impediment to governance. The state lost its vital consensus on public policy issues, and without that civic compass, its politicians tend to ignore major issues and pursue trivial ones. . . . The real issue is whether the public's anger at Gray Davis will morph into a new sense of civic purpose or whether California is destined to be . . . ungovernable.[1]

So far, the experience since the recall of Governor Gray Davis in 2003 indicates very slow progress, with no "new sense of civic purpose." The same old problems seem to vex California's political class, over and over.

The Ease of Passing Initiatives

One factor is certainly the ease with which special interests propose and collect signatures, campaign for, and sometimes pass initiatives to help their own cause. The initiative was added to the California constitution by the Progressive movement just after the beginning of the twentieth century as a way to promote the involvement of the public in public policy and affairs. Two recent examples include Proposition 15 on the June 2010 ballot, ostensibly allowing taxpayers to have more control over their government but in fact designed to keep local public utilities from competing with PG&E, and Proposition 33 on the November 2012 ballot, ostensibly allowing insurance companies to give longevity discounts to drivers who had continuous insurance coverage from another insurance company but in fact designed to give one insurance company the ability to raise rates on drivers who had lapses in insurance coverage. In general, the initiative has ceased to be a measure promoting direct democracy for at least the last two decades. It is instead just one more method by which special interests convince voters who are paying little attention to government and politics that they should enact some rule, law, or constitutional amendment that will benefit the particular interest and hurt the public as a whole.

Term Limits

The term limit movement found fertile ground in California in the 1980s and 1990s. Proposition 140 in 1990 imposed the severest term limits in the nation on the legislature and the elected officials of the executive branch, and the voters in many cities in California enacted term limits as well. Part of the statewide anger was directed against Willie Brown, then Speaker of the California Assembly, whose flamboyant lifestyle and prolific fund-raising raised the ire of voters.

The theory of the term limits movement is that if term limits are imposed, members of the Assembly and state Senate will pay more attention to their jobs and raise less money for future campaigns, and the system will be opened up to more minority and female candidates. Since term limits have been imposed, the proportion of Latino legislators in particular has indeed risen, but paradoxically, members have much less expertise on the matters they vote on and many— perhaps most—members of the legislature spend a good deal of their time worrying about their next position and raising funds for those campaigns.

The result is that most observers think that term limits have worsened the legislature, not bettered it. By the time legislators acquire the expertise to make good decisions, they are term-limited out. One of the reasons our limits are the strictest in the nation is that there is a lifetime ban on running for the same position again. While voters strongly support term limits, they have recently taken steps to address some of the institutional problems they present. In June 2012, the voters approved Proposition 28, which allows legislators to serve as many as 12 years in the legislature, providing the 12 years is served in one house. (The previous total service time had actually been higher—14 years—but with caps of 6 years in the Assembly and 8 in the Senate.) Currently the term limits are 12 years (six terms) for the Assembly, 12 years (three terms) for the state Senate, and 8 years (two terms) for all statewide officials (governor, lieutenant governor, attorney general, controller, secretary of state, treasurer, superintendent of public instruction, insurance commissioner, and the four members of the Board of Equalization).

The Safe-Seat Reapportionment

Every 10 years, after the census, state legislatures realign their seats in accordance with the census numbers. In California, until recently, this process was usually partisan. In some reapportionments, the legislature came together across party lines to form a coalition in which most incumbent seats became safe seats—that is, seats for which the incumbent generally wins by more than a 10 to 15 percent margin (a 55 to 45 percent win is a 10 percent margin). Short of a surge in voter anger, most incumbents are safe, meaning that their votes in the Assembly or state Senate are not restricted by considerations of what their opponent will say about the vote in the next election campaign.

In November 2008, however, voters passed Proposition 11, which substituted a citizens' commission for the legislature itself in drawing up the Assembly and state Senate districts. It was expected to reduce the proportion of extremely safe seats in the 2012 and subsequent elections.

Here are the results from the 2010 and 2012 legislative elections, combining congressional, state Senate, and Assembly seats:

	WON BY	<10%	10–19.9%	20–29.9%	30–44.9%	45–99%	100%
2010	Total of 153 districts	10	21	38	49	28	7
	percent	7%	14%	25%	32%	18%	5%
2012		29	38	38	22	25	2
		19%	25%	25%	14%	16%	1%

SOURCE: Compiled by the author from the Secretary of State's website. Data from 2012 include one additional district, from a special state Senate election.

In 2010, 7 percent of the districts were competitive, won by less than 10 percent of the vote. That percentage was 19 percent for 2012, meaning roughly 80 percent of all districts were still safe. The category of districts that were won by 10–19.9 percent of the vote moved from 14 percent to 25 percent, and the districts won by 30 percent of the vote or more dropped from 55 percent in 2010 to 31 percent in 2012. The combination of the top two primary and the newly reapportioned seats has indeed produced more competitive races for the Assembly, state Senate, and House of Representatives in California.

Reform Ideas

In addition to the steps already taken (as discussed earlier), numerous additional reforms have been suggested over the years to address the institutional hindrances to effective California governance. Some of the standard ones are listed here. See how many you agree with as you begin this book.

On the liberal side:

- Instituting public financing of election campaigns.

- Loosening further the term limits for members of the Assembly and Senate.

- Lowering the required super-majority to raise taxes from two-thirds to some lower, more achievable percentage, such as 55 or 60 percent.

- Restricting the initiative process to allow more citizen participation and decreasing the necessity to hire professional firms to collect signatures and run initiative campaigns. This would require lengthening the time allowed to collect signatures.

- Making it more difficult to amend the state constitution, which now requires 807,615 valid signatures for an initiative and a 50 percent vote of those who turn out at the next election.

From California Forward, a politically moderate reform organization:

- Instituting performance-based budgeting, with clear goals and performance measures for all programs.

- Engaging in multi-year budget planning.

- Mandating that all new programs, including those in initiatives, should have budget sources identified.

- Using spikes in revenue for the state's "rainy-day fund" and for paying down debt.

- Realigning the tax structure to match the state's shift from a manufacturing economy to a service-based one (see Chapter 8).

- Decentralizing and devolving more power to local governments.

- Investing more in K–12 education.

- Encouraging state and local leaders to reform public pensions.

On the conservative side:

- Changing the legislature from full time to part time.

- Imposing caps on public sector pensions.

- Making all new programs pay-as-you-go.

- Lowering California's tax rates, making the system less progressive in the process.

- Improving California's business climate with lower taxes and fewer regulations.

- Making it easier to terminate incompetent public sector workers, including teachers.

Most of these ideas involve so much controversy that they have little chance of being enacted, at least in the short run. In general, enacting major reforms such as those just listed is much easier through the ballot box (that is, via an initiative) than it is through the legislature, where constitutional changes require a two-thirds vote of the Assembly and the Senate before being placed on the ballot for ratification.

Why Study California Politics?

We know the obvious answer to the question, Why study California politics?—the course meets some requirement for graduation or your major. The State of California decided that every college student should know something about the California Constitution and California government and politics. But more important—why?

- You are *the citizens and voters of the present and future*. The policies and political trends occurring today do and will continue to impact your lives, from university tuition fees to the strength of the job market.

- California politics is plagued by *low levels of participation and turnout*, so much so that the electorate is distinctly older and more conservative than would be the case if every eligible adult voted. Your vote and participation can make a difference.

- California politics also suffers from *too much interest-group participation and not enough citizen participation*. The general interests of large groups of citizens need to be represented at the Table.

That's the narrow answer. A broader answer as to why we study California politics is that California's government and politics are distinctive and worthy of study. How are we different?

- We have much *more cultural diversity* than other states, including a much higher proportion of Latino and Asian residents. By some measures, we are the multicultural trendsetter among states.

- We are *one of the 10 largest economies in the world*. We are much larger than other states and larger than most entire countries. The 38 million citizens of the state of California produce as much in goods and services as France or Great Britain. However, we need to be cautious about statements about the economy—not only are there different ways to measure the size of the economy but governors and state government have much less control over that economy than do nations. Nations can run deficits and print money; governors and states can't, at least not in the long run. Nations can influence the money supply through their reserve banks; governors and states cannot.

- We *are the most populous state, and we have grown more quickly than other states*. In 1960 New York had 41 members in the U.S. House of Representatives; California had 38. The 2010 Census resulted in California having 53 seats, followed by Texas with 36 and Florida and New York both with 27.

- We are *more majoritarian than other states*, meaning that we rely more on the measures for direct democracy—the initiative, the referendum, and the recall—that were added to the state constitution by the Progressive movement in 1912. Every state uses majority rule for most decisions, but when we use the term *majoritarian*, we mean that the public makes policy decisions, rather than our elected representatives.

Consider the following continuum:

Majoritarian   Republican

A *majoritarian* government is one that is highly influenced by the public at large, through public-opinion polls that politicians take and through such measures as the initiative, referendum, and recall that enable the public to decide government policies directly.

A *republican* government is one in which we elect representatives to make our decisions for us, very much based on the Madisonian model for the federal government.

California government has moved much more toward the majoritarian model than other states. Not only are initiatives to amend the constitution routine but interest groups often begin collecting signatures for an initiative just to pressure the legislature into voting on their legislation. Californians like being majoritarian: surveys show that most don't want to restrict use of the initiative, in spite of its extensive use by interest groups.[2]

A report from the nonpartisan Initiative and Referendum Institute at the University of Southern California shows that Oregon has had more initiatives in the period from 1904 to 2009 than any other state, with 351. California is close behind at 329, followed by Colorado (209), North Dakota (178), and Arizona (171). Twenty-seven states do not have the initiative at all, and the top five states account for more than half of all initiatives considered from 1904 to 2009.[3]

What Determines the Content and Character of California's Politics?

Three factors shape the content and character of California's politics:

- The underlying demographic and sociopolitical trends that affect California and the other states;

- The rules of the game, as set out in the federal and state constitutions and in state laws; and

- The decisions of voters and politicians.

In Chapters 1 and 2 we will discuss the underlying demographic and sociopolitical trends and the rules of the game. What voters and politicians do in different areas is the subject of the rest of the book.

Underlying Socioeconomic Trends

Socioeconomic trends have driven many of the problems that have faced California voters and politicians. Some of these are discussed in the following sections.

POPULATION GROWTH Except for the four years from 1993 to 1996, California's population has grown by about 450,000 people per year for more than two decades. The 2010 Census results show California's 2010 population as 37,691,912. Current growth is 350,000 people per year. This strong and consistent growth means that the political controversies that have plagued the state in the past cannot be expected to abate in the future. Some of those controversies include:

- *Housing and Transportation*—Even with the decline brought on by the recession of 2008–09, housing prices in many middle-class areas have skyrocketed since the early 1990s. Many lower- and middle-class people must live in the Central Valley and commute to work in the San Francisco Bay Area or live in Riverside and San Bernardino counties and commute to the Los Angeles area. In both of these places, commutes of one to two hours—and even more—each way are not uncommon. Our transportation systems have not kept pace and were built for a much smaller population.

- *Schools*—Population growth means more schoolchildren, and there is a high demand for teachers across the state, along with a lack of fully qualified or credentialed teachers in many urban areas. Projections of the educational requirements of the future job market show that approximately 35 percent of jobs will require a college degree. Budget cuts to the University of California, California State University, and community college systems are already resulting in fewer students receiving their degrees and will make it impossible to meet this employment goal. The proportion of students who receive a college degree should be rising to meet future job requirements, but instead the proportion is falling.

- *Immigration*—California has had high levels of immigration since the 1950s, so high in some areas that candidates for the presidency of Mexico have campaigned here. Between 1970 and 2010 the number of immigrants in the California population increased from 1.8 to about 10.2 million; 27 percent of the state's current population was born somewhere else, a much higher proportion than in any other state. Most immigrants in California are from Latin America or Asia, with 4.3 million from Mexico, some 43 percent of the total immigrant population in California. Immigrants live in all parts of California, with those from Latin America more likely to live in Southern California and those from Asia in Northern California. Immigrants are younger than nonimmigrant Californians and more likely to be poor, and although some have relatively high levels of education, most immigrants are less educated than the native population.[4] Table 1.1 shows the 11 largest countries of origin for immigrants in California in 2006.

As of 2009, there were approximately 2.6 million illegal immigrants in California's population of 38 million, estimated the Urban Institute, using the census figures on the foreign-born population and subtracting the numbers we know are naturalized or here on legal visas and work permits.[5] Illegal immigrants are a continuing political issue. In 1994, Proposition 187 would have refused public services to anyone who could not show documentation, but it was found to be unconstitutional. A driver-license bill allowing undocumented immigrants to receive licenses was so controversial in the 2003 that it contributed to the recall of Governor Gray Davis

TABLE 1.1 ★ Leading Countries of Origin of Immigrants in California, 2009

COUNTRY	NUMBER OF IMMIGRANTS IN CALIFORNIA	PERCENT NATURALIZED
Mexico	4,308,000	28
Philippines	783,000	68
China (including Taiwan)	681,000	68
Vietnam	457,000	82
El Salvador	413,000	37
India	319,000	46
Korea	307,000	55
Guatemala	261,000	28
Iran	214,000	76
Canada	132,000	49
United Kingdom	125,000	40

SOURCE: Public Policy Institute of California, "Just the Facts: Immigrants in California" (April 2011), www.ppic.org (accessed 7/17/12). PPIC cites the U.S. Census and the 2009 American Community Survey.

TABLE 1.2 ★ Undocumented Immigrants by State, 2009

STATE	NUMBER OF UNDOCUMENTED IMMIGRANTS	SHARE OF STATE'S TOTAL POPULATION (%)
California	2,600,000	7.0
Texas	1,680,000	6.8
Florida	720,000	3.9
Illinois	554,000	4.3
New York	550,000	2.8
Georgia	480,000	4.9
Arizona	460,000	7.0
New Jersey	360,000	4.1
North Carolina	370,000	3.9
Other states	2,976,000	1.9
All states	10,750,000	3.5

SOURCE: Public Policy Institute of California, "Just the Facts: Illegal Immigrants" (December 2010), www.ppic.org (accessed 7/17/12). Estimates shown are from the U.S. Department of Homeland Security.

and was repealed before it took effect. Times have changed sufficiently that Governor Brown signed a bill in October 2012 that would allow illegal immigrants to drive legally in California if they qualified for the new federal work permit program announced by the Obama administration earlier that year. However, during the presidential elections of both 2008 and 2012, several of the more conservative candidates took strong stands against immigration. Table 1.2 shows the number of undocumented immigrants by state, along with the share of that state's total population that they make up. Arizona and California have the highest proportion of undocumented immigrants at 7.0 percent.

Reflecting the controversies over immigration, both legal and undocumented, in recent years, California has seen a number of demonstrations on the immigration issue. They have taken both sides: against more immigration, in favor of closing the borders, in favor of a "path to citizenship," both for and against the Arizona immigration law of 2010, and so forth. At least one of the demonstrations was the largest ever seen in Southern California to that date—over 1 million people. Little policy action has taken place at the state level, however.

RACE AND ETHNICITY In many respects, California's population is notably diverse compared with the U.S. population (see Table 1.3). Latino or Hispanic is not a racial category in the official census, but a separate question asks about Hispanic or Latino origin. About 17 percent of the United States is Latino, but about 38 percent of California is. Almost 60 percent of California's Latino population is of Mexican heritage.

AGE California's population is relatively young, mostly because of immigration. Immigrants tend to be younger and to have larger families than those who have been residents for longer periods.

EDUCATION Californians are highly educated. A greater proportion of Californians have gone to college or completed a bachelor's or higher degree than in the United States in general.

MOBILITY AND FOREIGN-BORN About 60 percent of all Americans live in the state in which they were born, but only 50 percent of all Californians were born in California. One-quarter, in fact, were foreign born, a much higher percentage than in the United States as a whole (12 percent). Most foreign-born residents are not U.S. citizens; only 40 percent of the foreign-born in both the United States and California are citizens. As one might expect with such a large foreign-born population, only

---

TABLE 1.3 ★ Ethnic Composition of California and the United States, 2011

	CALIFORNIA	UNITED STATES
White persons	74%	78%
Black/African American persons	7%	13%
Asian persons	14%	5%
American Indian/Alaskan Native persons	2%	1%
Native Hawaiian/other Pacific Islander persons	1%	0%
Two or more races	4%	2%
Persons of Hispanic or Latino origin	38%	17%
White persons not Hispanic	40%	63%

SOURCE: U.S. Census Bureau, "California Quick Facts from the U.S. Census Bureau," http://quickfacts.census.gov/qfd/states/06000.html (accessed 11/12/12).

61 percent of those over age five speak English at home in California. In the United States as a whole, 82 percent of those over age five speak English at home. That is a substantial difference by the standards of social science. There have been many political issues over this, ranging from debates over whether local store signs should be in foreign languages to the "English as the official state language" movement.

INCOME The U.S. Census Bureau has estimated California's median household income at $60,883 for 2006–10, about $9,000 higher than the national figure of $51,914. The state poverty rate is almost the same as the national figure, 13.7 percent for 2008 (California) compared with 13.8 percent (United States).

Conclusion

In this book we are going to consider the real world of California politics and the possibilities, both fascinating and frustrating, of the present, as well as changes that might make the future more positive for both politicians and the public. We will investigate what makes California different from other states and examine its unique political problems, including

- the inability to balance the budget, year after year.
- the malapportioned districts for the California legislature that, in combination with the primary system, produce legislators who are more liberal than the public on the Democratic side and more conservative than the public on the Republican side. We shall see whether the new top-two primary system and the non-gerrymandered legislative districts make any difference in this area.
- the public's attachment to the strictest term limits in the nation.
- the public's attachment to extreme majoritarianism, which produces the longest ballots in the nation as well as some of the lowest turnout rates.

Our coverage includes subjects that the newspapers and bloggers discuss in great detail as well as some subjects, such as the California tax system and the impact of Proposition 13, that are taken for granted but that have kept the state from updating its structure and services. Welcome to the journey.

A Guide to This Book

Chapter 2, "The Constitution and the Progressive Legacy," deals with California's state constitutions and the Progressives, the two crucial factors that defined the shape and direction of today's California government.

Chapters 3 and 4 deal with the bodies outside government that influence what government can accomplish. Chapter 3, "Interest Groups and the Media in California," deals with the groups that are as prevalent and influential in California as they are in our nation's capital. Chapter 4, "Parties and Elections in California," deals with parties and voters, and how both influence government through elections and campaigns.

Chapters 5, 6, and 7 deal with the institutions of government. Chapter 5, "The California Legislature," deals with the legislature, the body we love to hate. We try in this book to understand the legislature and why it functions as it does rather than simply condemn it. Chapter 6, "The Governor and the Executive Branch," asks whether California has become ungovernable. Chapter 7, "The California Judiciary," deals with judges and the criminal justice system.

Chapters 8, 9, and 10 deal with some policy problems and governmental structures that are particularly relevant today. Chapter 8, "The State Budget and Budgetary Limitations," addresses taxes, spending, and the California budget, asking whether the budget can be controlled in today's political and policy environment with the tools we have available to us. Chapter 9, "Local Government," deals with local government and its dependency on the state, a dependency that localities are taking action to remove in part through the initiative process. Chapter 10, "Public Policy in California," deals with several contemporary public policy problems, illustrating how the institutions and voters have acted in these areas.

FOR FURTHER READING

"California in Crisis." *California Journal*, August 2003, pp. 18–27.

Davis, Mike. *City of Quartz: Excavating the Future in Los Angeles*. New York: Vintage, 1990.

Goldmacher, Shane. "New Rules, New Tactics, in U.S. Races: Lessons Learned in the Free-Spending State Campaigns Now Apply to Candidates Seeking Office at the Federal Level." *Los Angeles Times*, February 24, 2010, p. AA3.

Gramlich, John. "California's Worst Enemy: Its Own Political System." *Stateline*, May 17, 2011. http://stateline.org. Accessed 7/17/12.

Hofstadter, Richard. *The Age of Reform*. New York: Washington Square Press, 1988.

Horwitz, Sasha. *Termed Out: Reforming California's Term Limits*. Los Angeles: Center for Governmental Studies, October 2007. www.cgs.org. Accessed 7/17/12.

Legislation by Initiative vs. through Elected Representatives. San Francisco: Field Institute, November, 1999. www.field .com/fieldpollonline/subscribers/COI-99-Nov-Legislation .pdf. Accessed 7/17/12.

Lewis, Michael. "California *and* Bust." *Vanity Fair*, November 2011.

Matthews, Joe, and Mark Paul. *California Crack Up, How Reform Broke the Golden State and How We Can Fix It*. Berkeley: University of California Press, 2010.

McGhee, Eric, and Daniel Krimm. *California's Political Geography*. San Francisco: Public Policy Institute of California, February 2012.

Olin, Spencer C. *California's Prodigal Sons: Hiram Johnson and the Progressives, 1911–1917*. Berkeley: University of California Press, 1968.

Public Policy Institute of California. "Just the Facts: Illegal Immigrants." San Francisco: Public Policy Institute of California, December 2010. www.ppic.org. Accessed 7/17/12.

———. "Just the Facts: Immigrants in California." San Francisco: Public Policy Institute of California, April 2011. www.ppic .org. Accessed 7/17/12.

———. "Research Brief: How Have Term Limits Affected the California Legislature?" No. 94. San Francisco: Public Policy Institute of California, November 2004. www.ppic.org. Accessed 7/17/12.

Reyes, Belinda I., ed. *A Portrait of Race and Ethnicity in California, An Assessment of Social and Economic Well-Being*. San Francisco: Public Policy Institute of California, 2001.

Skelton, George. "California's Capitol—The Long View. A Columnist Looks Back on 50 Years Covering the Ups and Downs of Sacramento." *Los Angeles Times*, December 1, 2011.

Slater, Dashka, and Gary Rivlin. "Economy, California on the Brink." *Newsweek*, September 5, 2011, pp. 26–27.

Walters, Dan. "California Makes It Easier to Cut Taxes Than to Raise Them." *Sacramento Bee*, May 16, 2010.

Wilson, James Q. "A Guide to Schwarzenegger Country." *Commentary*, December 2003, 45–49.

ON THE WEB

California Choices: www.californiachoices.org (accessed 7/17/12).

California Forward: "The California Forward 2010 Reform Principles." www.cafwd-action.org (accessed 7/17/12).

Center for Governmental Studies: www.cgs.org (accessed 7/17/12). A think tank that specifically focuses on promoting citizen participation in government.

The Field (California) Poll: Field Institute. www.field.com (accessed 7/17/12).

Los Angeles Times: www.latimes.com (accessed 7/17/12).

Public Policy Institute of California: www.ppic.org (accessed 7/17/12). A think tank devoted to nonpartisan research on how to improve California policy.

Sacramento Bee: www.sacbee.com (accessed 7/17/12).

San Francisco Chronicle: www.sfgate.com (accessed 7/17/12).

SUMMARY

I. Many observers question whether California is governable, at least as far as budgets and taxes are concerned.
   A. The Democratic majority won't consider cutting programs substantially but does not constitute the two-thirds necessary to raise taxes.
   B. The Republican minority will not consider any tax increases and has more than one-third of the votes in both chambers, thus preventing any agreement that might be a compromise for both sides.

II. The crisis has many roots.
   A. The requirement that two-thirds of the total membership of each house of the legislature is needed to raise taxes.
   B. Interest-group impasse reflected in the legislature on many issues.
   C. The ease with which the voters can pass initiatives designed to help an interest group with its cause, set aside funds from the general fund for a single cause, etc.
   D. Severe term limits—the strictest in the nation—leading to a loss of knowledge and interest in staying in the legislature and learning the issues involved there.
   E. Gerrymandered districts that are safe for most legislatures. The districts for the 2012 election are the first in many decades that have not been gerrymandered by the legislature; the new citizens' commission proposed them in 2011.

III. Reform ideas are abundant. Several from both sides of the political spectrum are listed in the text.

IV. California's politics are important for several reasons.
   A. California is the biggest state, has an economy in the top 10 among nations of the world, and has a population more multicultural and diverse than the rest of the nation.
   B. California is strongly majoritarian, and its citizens like it that way.
   C. California has experienced some of the strongest population growth of any state, resulting in a number of political conflicts over the years.
   D. California has more immigrants—and more undocumented immigrants—than any other state, although Arizona has the same proportion of undocumented immigrants.
   E. California is younger than many states, has a greater percentage of its population that is college-educated, and is richer than most states.

PRACTICE QUIZ

1. The budget must be passed by a majority of those present and voting in both chambers of the legislature.
   a) true.
   b) false.

2. Most states require a two-thirds majority to pass their budgets each year.
   a) true.
   b) false.

3. What proportion of California legislative seats in 2012—those in the Assembly, state Senate, and Congress—were safe (that is, the won by a margin of 10 percent or more)?
   a) about 50 percent.
   b) about 65 percent.
   c) about 80 percent.
   d) 90+ percent.

4. California's population, the foreign-born population, and the approximate number of undocumented immigrants, according to the text are:
   a) 50 million, 5 million, 2 million.
   b) 34 million, 8.8 million, 2.4 million.
   c) 25 million, 20 million, 18 million.
   d) 38 million, 10.2 million, 2.6 million.

5. Latino or Hispanic has been a racial category in the U.S. Census that is taken every 10 years.
   a) true.
   b) false.

6. The proportion of immigrants in California who speak English at home as compared to the United States as a whole is
   a) greater.
   b) lesser.
   c) the same.

7. According to this book, the inability of the California legislature to make decisions that benefit the state as a whole is due to
   a) the number of interest groups.
   b) the two-thirds requirement to raise taxes.
   c) California's size.
   d) all of the above.

8. California's term limits are
   a) 8 years for the governor, 4 years for the Assembly, and 6 years for the state Senate.
   b) 6 years for the governor, 6 years for the Assembly, and 8 years for the state Senate.
   c) 8 years for the governor, 12 years for the Assembly, and 12 years for the state Senate.
   d) 8 years for the governor, 8 years for the Assembly, and 12 years for the state Senate.

9. Some undocumented immigrants can obtain a driver license in California.
   a) true.
   b) false.

CRITICAL-THINKING QUESTIONS

1. How distinctive is California compared with other states? Are we really that different?

2. California's population differs from that of other states on several levels: what are the two or three most significant, and why are they significant?

KEY TERMS

At this point you should have a general understanding of the following concepts and terms:

California dream (p. 2)
cultural diversity (p. 8)
foreign-born (p. 10)
Latino/Hispanic (p. 12)

majoritarian (p. 9)
racial and ethnic diversity (p. 12)
reapportionment (p. 6)
recall (p. 8)

safe seat (p. 6)
term limits (p. 5)
undocumented immigration (p. 10)

ANSWERS TO QUESTIONS IN "WHAT CALIFORNIA GOVERNMENT DOES AND WHY IT MATTERS"

Every action named involves government at some level and in some way:

- Driving on the freeway: Freeways are built by state government with federal and state funds; traffic is monitored by the California Highway Patrol.

- Driving on a tollway: California has several privately owned tollways; these are freeways built with private funds typically raised by selling bonds, itself a market regulated by government. State government approves the rights of way for these tollways and otherwise regulates their operations.

- Driving across a bridge: Standards for bridges come from both the federal government and the California Department of Transportation; most bridges were constructed with public funds.

- Walking to the grocery store: Sidewalks were constructed with public funds and to local government construction standards.

- Buying fruit at the grocery store: Scales are certified by county government; both imported and domestic fruit must meet U.S. Department of Agriculture and State Department of Agriculture standards.

- Going to school at any level, public or private: States have standards for what must be taught at each grade level, as well as tests to determine whether schools are meeting the standard.

- Working for the California Highway Patrol: The CHP is a state government agency.

- Working for a private security guard service: Security guards must meet local police department standards.

- Working for a grocery store: Wages, hours, and working conditions are governed by the state Department of Employment Security or by union contract.

- Eating dinner in a restaurant: County Departments of Health oversee restaurant food quality and cleanliness.

2 | The Constitution and the Progressive Legacy

WHAT CALIFORNIA GOVERNMENT DOES AND WHY IT MATTERS

The current problems in California are hard to miss. Look anywhere and you'll find a crisis. For many, the root cause is an age-old, deeply flawed constitution and particularly the ballot box initiative. The initiative was the result of the attempt to gain control of the state's political process over special interests. Ironically, nearly 100 years later, the initiative has become a means through which individuals, interest groups, and elected officials pursue outcomes they cannot achieve in the legislature.

Any individual or group can propose a statute or an amendment to the California constitution. Of course, having sufficient funds to wage an effective campaign and having an issue appealing enough to the voters to have one's measure approved are other matters. Only about a third of initiatives are approved by the voters, and the amount of money spent correlates only very loosely with the probability of approval.

In 2006, for example, California voters cast their ballots on Proposition 87, a high-profile initiative that was also the most costly in history, with over $156 million being spent. Supporters contributed $61.9 million (with $49.6 million alone coming from film producer Steve Bing), and opponents contributed $94.4 million (with Chevron Corporation, Aera Energy, and Occidental Oil and Gas contributing $38 million, $32.8 million, and $9.6 million, respectively).[1]

The initiative brought out celebrities on both sides, including prominent individuals, companies, and organizations. These included former President Bill Clinton, Brad Pitt, and the Coalition for Clean Air in support of the measure, and Governor Arnold Schwarzenegger, Chevron Corporation, and California Chamber of Commerce in opposition.

The measure established a $4 billion program, the primary goal of which was to reduce petroleum consumption by 25 percent, with research and production incentives for alternative energy, alternative-energy vehicles, and energy-efficient technologies, as well as funding for education and training. The program would be funded by a tax of 1.5 to 6.0 percent (depending on oil price per barrel) on California oil producers.

The stakes were high because California was the fourth largest oil-producing state in the nation: roughly 37 percent of California's oil was pumped in the state, and another 21 percent came from Alaska. The rest was imported.

The campaign was bitter and acrimonious. Accusations of dirty tactics thrived, and lawsuits were filed by both sides. Supporters alleged that the opposition's print and television advertisements created the false impression that it was financed by a broad coalition, including educators and public-safety officials, when in fact it was subsidized by the oil industry. On the other side, opponents to the measure accused their adversaries of illegally registering several "no" sites that, when accessed, redirected viewers to the "Yes-on-87" website. In the end, little came of either lawsuit; however, each helped sharpen and intensify feelings on both sides.

In the end, Proposition 87 failed to pass, getting 45.3 percent of the vote, as voters feared that passage of the initiative would cause higher gas prices, resulting in a greater demand for foreign oil. It is a prime example, however, of an issue that, rather than being debated by experts and elected officials in the legislature, was seized by wealthy individuals and interest groups in the name of direct democracy. Such examples abound in California politics.

In Chapter 1, we discussed some of the demographic differences between California and other states. We also mentioned that California's government is institutionally designed to foster (or at least not be able to solve) critical state issues. Here are some of the unique features in the political process:

- The **sheer size of the state** increases the cost of political campaigns and media cost.

- The **competing network of interest groups** causes groups to jockey for position and influence.

- The **increasing use of the initiative** significantly impacts state and local governance and policy.

- The **divided executive branch**, composed of nine separately elected officials, each with his or her own area of authority and responsibility, leads to overlapping responsibilities and fragmentation in the execution of state policy.

- The **widespread, almost universal use of nonpartisan elections at the local level of government** eliminates a valuable clue for voters to identify the policy positions of the candidates on the ballot.

Aside from the size of the state and the interest-group network, these other characteristics are a result of the Progressive movement, which flourished from 1900 to 1917. The leaders of this movement focused on one goal: making government more responsive to the political, social, and economic concerns of the people. Their reforms continue to shape California government and politics in ways that sharply differentiate it from other states. To some, these features hamper the political process and should be changed. To others, they are the essence of California, and if they were changed, California would be just another state.

The Rules of the Game: California's Constitution

The California constitution is long and very detailed, with numerous amendments added over the years, dealing with both the fundamental principles and power of government as well as commonplace issues such as the right to fish on government property, English as the state's official language, and grants for stem cell research. Today California has the second highest number of constitutional amendments, behind Alabama, and has the second longest state constitution, behind Louisiana. The California constitution is over 100 pages long.

The constitution defines the rules under which political actors and the citizens interact with each other to fulfill their goals as individuals, members of a group, or a population as a whole. Its long and storied history can be divided into four stages:

- **The 1849 constitution.** Written by residents of the territory in anticipation of statehood, this constitution contains many of the basic ideas underlying California government today.

- **The 1879 constitution.** Written by a constitutional convention in 1878, this is the basic document, with amendments, that is in force today.

- **From 1900 to 1917.** During this period, the Progressives amended the constitution and passed laws to return government to the people, temper the power of special interests, and make government responsive to the people's desires and needs. The most prominent reforms of this period were the initiative, referendum, and recall.

- **From 1918 to the present.** Amendment after amendment lengthened the state's constitution, resulting in a document that at one point was almost 100,000 words long. Several commissions proposed substantive changes, but the only changes adopted came from two constitutional revision commissions, one in the 1960s and the other in the 1990s, that shortened and clarified language in the constitution but made no substantial changes to its provisions.

The 1849 Constitution

By 1849, 80,000 unruly gold miners had moved to California, giving the area enough people to apply for territorial status, and the settlers of the territory drafted a constitution. Admitting California as a free state, however, would have upset the balance between free and slave states that had existed in the Union since 1820; therefore, admission as a territory was delayed. In 1849, the newly elected president of the United States Zachary Taylor proposed that California draft a constitution and apply for admission as a state directly to Congress, instead of applying as a territory first and moving to state status later. California citizens elected delegates to a constitutional convention; the delegates in turn met and drew up the proposed constitution in 43 days.

The constitutional convention, 48 elected men who met in Monterey in September of 1849, used a book of constitutions that contained the constitutions of the federal government and some 30 states. Several of the provisions were taken directly from the constitutions of New York and Iowa. The basic provisions of the 1849 constitution are still in force:

- The framework of the government rested on a separation of powers—executive, legislative, and judicial—and checks and balances, like the federal government.

- Executive power was divided, as it is today, with the separate election and jurisdiction of the governor, lieutenant governor, comptroller, treasurer, attorney general, surveyor general, and superintendent of public instruction. This division weakens the governor, who cannot appoint—or remove—senior members of his or her own administration. Moreover, each of these statewide officials is a potential competitor for the governor's office, and each can put out statements that contradict what the governor is saying.

- An extensive bill of rights begins the constitution.

- The legislature was elected and consisted of two houses, one called the Senate, the other the Assembly.

Features that were different from what we have today include

- The right to vote at that time was limited to white males 21 years of age or older who had lived in California for at least six months.

- The legislature by a two-thirds vote could grant Native Americans the right to vote "in such special cases as such proportion of the legislative body may deem just and proper."

- The judiciary was elected, as judges are today, but they were organized into four levels as was Mexico's judiciary at the time.

- All laws and other provisions were to be published in both English and Spanish, since California was a bilingual state.

The first California constitution read very much like any other state constitution—it had about 9,000 words, compared with the present U.S. Constitution's 4,500 words, plus another 3,100 words of amendments. Over time, as we shall see, the constitution evolved into a much longer document.

In 1850, the federal government passed a series of bills that made up the Compromise of 1850. These bills admitted California to the union as a free state, established territorial governments in Utah and New Mexico, allowed residents of those states to decide whether to be free or slave states, settled a dispute over the border between Texas and New Mexico, compensated Texas with $10 million to repay debts to Mexico, abolished the slave trade in the District of Columbia, and put the Fugitive Slave Act into effect.

The 1879 Constitution

Voters approved the convening of a constitutional convention in 1877, but the actual convention was held in 1879. A new political party, the Workingmen's Party, which supported many Populist ideas (see p. 24), and which held 51 of the 152 seats at the convention, played a significant role in the discussion.[2] The new party supported restrictions on corporations and railroads and was also strongly opposed to the presence of Chinese workers in California. One of its rallying cries was "The Chinese must go!"[3] The party also opposed centralized governmental power and a powerful legislature, proposing unsuccessfully to the convention that California collapse the two houses of the legislature into one, a unicameral legislature, and abolish the lieutenant governor's office.

All kinds of provisions were adopted. For example, stockholders were to be responsible for the debts of a corporation. The railroads could not give free passes to those holding political office; they could not raise rates on one line to compensate for reductions made to compete on alternative lines; and they would be regulated by a Railroad Commission. Other provisions restricted Chinese workers, prohibiting them from being employed on public works projects or by corporations chartered in California.

These additions added words—almost doubling the constitution's size—and policies that read very much like a series of laws rather than a fundamental framework within which laws would operate. By 1948, the California constitution, with amendments, reached 95,000 words.

The new constitution was approved by a 54 to 46 percent vote in May 1879, with 90 percent of those eligible to vote participating. In the end, however, most of the reform measures were not put into practice right away, as corporations and other special interests sued to block their implementation, continuing the domination of the state by corporate and railroad power. These setbacks were temporary, however. In a matter of three decades the broad reforms of the Progressive movement gained passage, weakening the grip of these special interests in the legislature and reshaping the landscape of California politics.

You can get a sense of California's constitution and how different it is from the federal constitution by examining California's bill of rights, called "Declaration of Rights." The federal bill of rights consists of the first 10 amendments to the U.S. Constitution, and while other amendments may be passed, the first 10 will remain the Bill of Rights as they were written. California's bill of rights, meanwhile, can be expanded or rewritten as times change. Because of this factor, California's bill of rights reflects the political changes and conflicts that have occurred over time, which means that some of the rights can be much more specific than the corresponding federal right. You can see the result of that specificity in the provisions for freedom of speech as they apply to a newspaper. The federal constitution has the familiar First Amendment:

> Amendment 1: Congress shall make no law respecting an establishment of religion, or prohibiting the free exercise thereof, or abridging the freedom of speech, or of the press; or the right of the people peaceably to assembly, and to petition the Government for a redress of grievances.

California's corresponding section has both more detail and more specificity, since it has been amended over time.

> SEC. 2. (a) Every person may freely speak, write and publish his or her sentiments on all subjects, being responsible for the abuse of this right. A law may not restrain or abridge liberty of speech or press.

(b) A publisher, editor, reporter, or other person connected with or employed upon a newspaper, magazine, or other periodical publication, or by a press association or wire service, or any person who has been so connected or employed, shall not be adjudged in contempt by a judicial, legislative, or administrative body, or any other body having the power to issue subpoenas, for refusing to disclose the source of any information procured while so connected or employed for publication in a newspaper, magazine, or other periodical publication, or for refusing to disclose any unpublished information obtained or prepared in gathering, receiving, or processing of information for communication to the public. Nor shall a radio or television news reporter or other person connected with or employed by a radio or television station, or any person who has been so connected or employed, be so adjudged in contempt for refusing to disclose the source of any information procured while so connected or employed for news or news commentary purposes on radio or television, or for refusing to disclose any unpublished information obtained or prepared in gathering, receiving, or processing of information for communication to the public.

Note the use of modern language, such as *wire service* and *television*.

California's Declaration of Rights can also be amended through the initiative process, which allows individuals or groups to put proposed changes before the voting public at any election.

From 1900 to 1917: The Progressive Movement

Pressure for political reform continued. Beginning with the turn of the twentieth century, the Progressives pursued three goals: to attack corporate political influence, eliminate the political corruption that went with such influence, and democratize the political process.[4]

They understood that these goals had to be accomplished before they could address equally pressing but more mundane concerns of the time. They accomplished all of this—and much more. Beginning with the 1911 legislative session, these reformers passed dozens of constitutional amendments and statutes that changed the face of California government and politics.[5] The most prominent of the political reforms were the following:

- **Nonpartisanship.** This is the norm in local elections, by which no party label is affixed to the candidates' names on the ballot. Of the more than 19,000 elected public officials in California, less than 300 are elected in partisan races.

- **Primary elections.** Before the institution of primary elections, political parties chose their candidates in party conventions (with their stereotypes of the smoky back rooms) or caucuses—meetings of party members at the local level. In a primary election, each prospective party nominee has to obtain more votes than any other prospective nominee to run as the party's candidate in the general election in November.

- **The office block ballot.** This is the ballot that we vote on today, with a "block" for each office and the candidates listed for that office. Before this reform, in some elections, voters cast ballots for their preferred party, not for individual candidates.

- **Direct democracy.** These grassroots processes—the initiative, referendum, and recall—give citizens the ability to rein in the abuse of power by elected officials or to ignite those same public officials if they are paralyzed by inaction and partisan bickering.

During this period, the California constitution grew substantially as the legislature enacted dozens of constitutional amendments and statutes. In the first three months of 1911 alone, the legislature passed more than 800 statutes and 23 constitutional amendments.

From 1960 to the Present: Late Revisions

In 1963, the legislature created a constitution revision commission as a result of an initiative passed in 1962. The commission, composed of 50 citizens, three state senators, and three Assembly members, submitted two major reports with recommended revisions to the state constitution. The legislature incorporated these into 14 constitutional amendments that were submitted to the voters for their approval between 1966 and 1976, and the voters approved 10 of these. These simplified, shortened, and reorganized the constitution but made few substantive changes in it.

In 1993, the legislature again established a constitution revision commission, which proposed a number of substantial changes to the constitution, provisions reformers had discussed in some cases for generations. For a variety of reasons, many having to do with the two-thirds vote in the Assembly and Senate to place them on the ballot, they were never submitted to the voters.

How well do the constitution of 1879 and the Progressive-era amendments fit a California that is 10 to 20 times larger than in the early twentieth century? Not terribly well, it must be admitted. The legislature is the same size, 40 state Senators and 80 Assembly members, but the districts have grown from just over 60,000 for the state Senate to almost 1,000,000 people, with much less personal service

---

BOX 2.1 | **Amending the California Constitution**

The constitution can be amended in one of three ways. In each case, the proposed amendment must be ratified by majority vote in the next statewide election.

1. **A constitutional convention can propose an amendment.** The convention can be called either by the legislature with a two-thirds vote or by a majority vote of the electorate through an initiative. Voters must ratify the amendment by majority vote in the next statewide election.

2. **Citizens can propose an amendment directly through the initiative.** The process requires the proponents to submit a petition with the signatures of 8 percent of the voters in the last gubernatorial election. The proposed amendment then is placed on the ballot for approval in the next statewide election.

3. **The legislature may propose an amendment to the constitution.** The process requires a two-thirds vote of both houses of the legislature. The proposed amendment is then placed on the ballot for approval in the next statewide election.

than what occurred in an earlier era. The initiative could be mounted by small amateur groups in the early twentieth century, but now it is strictly a tool for use by well-funded interest groups. Serious efforts to modernize state government, unfortunately, have been few and far between, and when they have occurred, as with the constitutional revision commission of the 1990s, the results were subject to partisan voting and insufficient majorities to send them to the people for a final decision.

The Progressive Movement and Its Impact on California Politics

The Progressive movement had its roots in the economic and political changes that swept the United States after the Civil War. It was foreshadowed by the Populist movement, which dominated American politics from 1870 to 1896.

Some of the political concerns and much of the moral indignation expressed by the Populists about the changes taking place in America are reflected in the Progressive movement. One major difference between the two movements is geographic. The Populist movement began in the rural areas of the country; the Progressive movement was urban, born in the major cities.[6] While the Progressive movement was identified mostly with the Republican Party, there were notable Progressive leaders in the Democratic Party as well, such as Woodrow Wilson.

The Progressives perceived many of the same problems as the Populists. From the Civil War on, the United States had rapidly industrialized, and wealth became concentrated in the hands of a new breed of corporate entrepreneurs. *Monopoly* was the word of the day. These corporate giants dictated economic policy, which in turn had significant social and political consequences. In California, one giant corporation, the Southern Pacific Railroad, stood above all others. It represented a concentration of wealth and power that gave it undue influence not only economically but also politically. To a degree perhaps unparalleled in the nation, the Southern Pacific Railroad and a web of associated interests ruled the state. The Southern Pacific Railroad had the money and resources to influence political decisions. Bribing public officials was not unusual, nor was handpicking candidates for the two major political parties.[7]

The Progressives countered the powerful corporations, specifically the Southern Pacific Railroad, by prosecuting the corrupt politicians who served them. Eventually, this tactic unraveled the railroad's domination of state and local politics and led to a series of regulatory reforms that loosened the choke hold that they—and specifically the Southern Pacific Railroad—had on state and local politics.

Local Politics

Progressive reforms began at the local level, in the cities of San Francisco and Los Angeles. The battle against the Southern Pacific Railroad and corporate influence in general started in San Francisco in 1906, with the reform movement fighting to rid city government of graft and bribery. President Theodore Roosevelt stepped in to help. Working hand in hand with James D. Phelan, the former mayor of San Francisco, Roosevelt sent in federal agents led by William J. Bums to investigate bribery and corruption charges.[8] Public officials were put on trial for the bribery, bringing to the public's attention the extent of graft and political corruption in municipal government.

Seventeen supervisors and a number of corporate leaders were indicted.[9] The mayor was forced to resign, and his henchman, Abraham Reuf, who implicated officials of the Southern Pacific Railroad and several utility companies, was convicted and sentenced to 14 years in jail. While Reuf was the exception, and the graft trials largely failed to convict those indicted, they were nonetheless an important step in breaking the power of the Southern Pacific Railroad and its political allies.

In 1906, the Southern Pacific Railroad also dominated Los Angeles.[10] During this time, a group dedicated to good government, the Non-Partisan Committee of One Hundred, was formed. They selected a reform candidate for mayor who was opposed by the two major parties, labor, and the *Los Angeles Times*. While the reform candidate lost his bid for the mayoralty, 17 of 23 reform candidates for other city positions were elected.[11] The nonpartisan reformers were on the way to ridding the city of the Southern Pacific machine.

State Politics

The 1907 legislative session was one of the most corrupt on record, with no action taken without the blessing of the political operatives of the Southern Pacific Railroad. At the end of the session, the editor of the Fresno *Republican*, Chester Rowell, wrote: "If we are fit to govern ourselves, this is the last time we will submit to be governed by the hired bosses of the Southern Pacific Railroad Company."[12]

At the same time, Rowell and Edward Dickson of the Los Angeles *Express* began to organize a statewide movement to attack the Southern Pacific's power. At Dickson's invitation, a group of lawyers, newspaper publishers, and other political reformers met in Los Angeles. They founded the Lincoln Republicans, later to become the League of Lincoln-Roosevelt Republican Clubs, dedicated to ending the control of California politics by the Southern Pacific Railroad and linking themselves to the national Progressive movement.

The Lincoln-Roosevelt League participated in the statewide legislative elections of 1908 and managed to elect a small group of reformers to the legislature. Two years later it fielded a full-party slate, from governor down to local candidates.

STATEHOUSE VICTORY In 1910, Hiram Johnson became the candidate for governor of the Lincoln-Roosevelt League. He campaigned up and down the state, focusing on one main issue: the Southern Pacific Railroad. He claimed the Southern Pacific Railroad, acting in concert with criminal elements, had corrupted the political process in California. He defined the battle as one between decent, law-abiding citizens and a few corrupt, powerful individuals who were determined to run the state in their own best interests.

Johnson won the election and met with leading national Progressives—Theodore Roosevelt, Robert La Follette, and Lincoln Steffens—to discuss a reform program for California. The new administration in Sacramento set out to eliminate every special interest from the government and to make government solely responsive to the people and Johnson. Through a series of legislative acts and constitutional amendments, they went a long way in that direction. In 1911, the voters passed the initiative, the referendum, and the recall. These three reforms, widely known as *direct democracy*, placed enormous power and control over government in the hands of the voters. Now citizens could write their laws or amend the constitution through the initiative, approve or disapprove constitutional amendments through the referendum, and remove corrupt politicians from office through the recall.

In addition to these reforms, a new law set up a railroad commission with power to fix rates beginning in 1911. Other reforms included the *direct primary*, which gave the power to ordinary citizens to select the candidates of the political parties for national and state offices. Women obtained the right to vote in California in 1911. Legislation was also enacted that limited women to an eight-hour workday, set up a workmen's compensation system, put into practice a weekly pay law, and required employers to inform strikebreakers that they were being hired to replace employees on strike (and thus might face verbal abuse and physical violence).

The Progressives in California more than kept their campaign promises to limit the influence of the corporations and the political parties in politics. In the first two years in office, the Johnson administration succeeded in breaking the power of the Southern Pacific Railroad.[13]

LAST HURRAH The national Progressive Party lost its bid to capture the White House in 1912, with a ticket of Theodore Roosevelt for president and Hiram Johnson for vice president. The failure to win an important national office weakened the party by lessening the enthusiasm of its supporters. It also meant that the party had no patronage with which to reward its followers between elections. Electoral failure was just one of several major problems that plagued the Progressives. Several other factors also contributed to the decline of the party: the public grew tired of reform, there was a major falling out among the leadership in California, the Progressives generally opposed World War I, and the party failed to support reforms that labor so badly wanted.

While the Progressives were hoping that Roosevelt would run again in 1916, he was working to prevent another third-party fiasco. When the Progressives learned that the Republican Party would not nominate Roosevelt, they offered him the nomination, but he turned them down. At a dinner in San Francisco in July 1916, the California Progressive Party disbanded. Hiram Johnson urged his followers to go back to either the Republican or the Democratic Party. Later that year Johnson, now a Republican, was elected to the U.S. Senate, where he served for 28 years.

If there was one major flaw in Progressive thinking, it was the belief in the active, informed citizen willing to participate in politics. Progressives believed that given the opportunity, citizens would be happy to support the democratic process and spend whatever time and effort was needed to participate in elections. Since the late 1940s, a host of studies has shown that large numbers of people don't vote or pay attention to politics. But the Progressives cannot be faulted for today's diminished interest in politics and government. In the end, they gave the people of California tremendous political power, if or when they choose to use it.

This political power was appropriate for 1910, when California had 2.4 million people. Since then, California has grown so much and so quickly that its constitution has been unable to catch up, and the reforms that allowed "the people" to propose initiatives and recall public officials in particular cannot be exercised on a *statewide*[14] level in a state of now 38 million people without money, organization, and professional help. We haven't had an initiative that did *not* use paid, professional signature gatherers since 1990, and that one needed a paid coordinator for the campaign. A totally volunteer initiative organization hasn't been successful since 1984.

Direct Democracy

The Progressives established civil service reforms, nonpartisan commissions to control key state regulatory functions, nonpartisan elections to cripple local machines, office block voting (a ballot listing all candidates for a given office under the name of that office), and primary elections. If these innovations failed to check the power of special interests, they gave voters the power of direct action through the initiative, referendum, and recall. These three mechanisms work in the same way. Citizens circulate petitions to gather a required number of signatures to bring the measure to statewide vote. The number of signatures, as we shall see, varies depending on the mechanism.

Initiative

THE PROCESS Of the three direct voices in government, the initiative is the most well known and most frequently used. The process, also known as direct legislation, requires the proponent to obtain a title (e.g., "Public Schools: English as Required Language of Instruction") and summary of the proposed initiative from the state attorney general. Upon obtaining the title and summary, the proponents have 150 days to circulate a petition to gather the required number of signatures to qualify for the ballot—5 percent of voters in the last gubernatorial election for statutes, and 8 percent for constitutional amendments. The secretary of state submits the measure at the next general election held at least 131 days after it qualifies or at any special election held before the next general election. The governor may call a special election for the measure.

Before 1960, initiatives appeared only on the general election ballot, thus limiting their use to the two-year election cycle. Since 1960, they have appeared on the primary, general, and special-election ballots, which allows for more frequent opportunities to qualify and vote on them. The freedom to qualify them in all elections keeps the public aware of them and excited about using them.

FREQUENCY OF USE Initiatives have become a staple of California's political fabric. From 1912 to 2012, over 1,600 initiatives were titled and summarized for circulation. Of this number, 360 qualified for the ballot, 3 were removed by court order, and 121 were approved by the voters—for an overall passage rate of 34 percent. Of the 121 initiatives approved, 40 were constitutional amendments and 10 were constitutional/stationary changes.[15]

Figure 2.1 presents the use of initiative by decade. Note these two points: the increasing frequency of initiatives since 1970, and the varying, but generally low, level of success for the measures that made it to the ballot.

For discussion purposes, we can compress the 100-year history of initiatives into four time periods: 1912–39, 1940–69, 1970–1999, and 2000–12.

1912–39 From the beginning, various individuals and special interests understood that the initiative could be used to forward their special causes. Social and cultural issues, such as outlawing gambling on horse races, professional fighting, prostitution, and land ownership by Asians, drew the highest voter turnout during this period. Labor issues (closed versus open shops) and tax propositions were also volatile issues.

No one issue, however, dominated the initiative process during this period more than the so-called liquor question.[16] These initiatives were among the most controversial, and they drew high voter turnouts. Twelve measures related

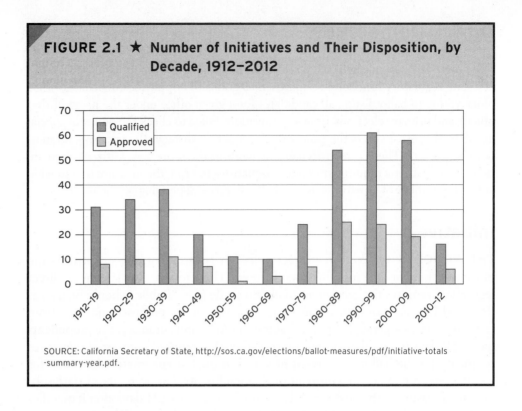

FIGURE 2.1 ★ Number of Initiatives and Their Disposition, by Decade, 1912–2012

SOURCE: California Secretary of State, http://sos.ca.gov/elections/ballot-measures/pdf/initiative-totals-summary-year.pdf.

to liquor control appeared on the ballot between 1914 and 1936, for and against full prohibition and antisoloon measures, and state regulation versus local control. Voting was consistent throughout this period, with the anti-Prohibition forces generally prevailing on every measure. The issue, however, wouldn't go away; in 1948, after many failures to qualify an initiative, the antiliquor forces qualified another local option measure, which was rejected by 70 percent of the voters. After this vote, the issue lost its appeal, never to appear on the ballot again.

1940–69 In this time period, use of the initiative declined markedly. Compared to the previous 27 years, a higher percentage of proposed measures failed to gather enough signatures to qualify for the ballot. The subject matter of the initiatives also varied from those of 1912–39. Newer issues came to the forefront: race and civil rights, property taxes, and labor and welfare issues.

Proposition 14 (1964) was the most prominent of a number of initiatives that dealt with fair housing. The initiative was drafted to nullify the Rumford Fair Housing Act, which prohibited discrimination in the rental, lease, or purchase of housing on the basis of race and national origin. The Rumford Act, supporters of Proposition 14 claimed, interfered with their private property rights. Real estate and homeowners' associations led the forces in support of the proposition and a coalition of Democratic Party leadership, organized labor, churches, and a variety of other groups led the forces against it. The broader issue of race, specifically African Americans, lingered in the background of the campaign; by all accounts, race was the deciding factor in how people voted. Proposition 14 passed by a 2–1 margin in November 1964. Its victory was a major factor in the Watts riots in the summer of 1965.[17] Over the next two years, Proposition 14 was overturned, first by the California Supreme Court and then by the U.S. Supreme Court, because it violated the Fourteenth Amendment.

1970–99 In this period initiatives abounded, with over 1,000 being titled, 141 qualifying, and 56 being approved. The subjects addressed social, cultural, and economic issues, including the death penalty, gun control, busing, property tax, nuclear power, water resources, air quality, coastal preservation, English as the official language, affirmative action, illegal immigrants, and gay marriage.

The most controversial initiative of this period was Proposition 13, titled the "People's Initiative to Limit Property Taxation" (1978). Sponsored by longtime antitax activists Howard Jarvis and Paul Gann, Proposition 13 was a reaction to the spiraling appreciation of property throughout the 1970s. In just one year, some properties were reassessed at a value 50 to 100 percent higher, and their owners' tax bills jumped correspondingly.

Proposition 13 was a grassroots effort. Nearly every state employee and labor union, and most Democratic leaders, opposed it. The pro side raised $2.2 million, and the con side raised $2 million. On June 6, 1978, nearly two-thirds of California's voters passed Proposition 13, reducing property tax rates by about 57 percent.

Now, 30 years later, Proposition 13 is still hotly debated. Critics argue that it creates tax inequities because it treats residential and commercial property the same and assesses similar properties differently based solely on when a homeowner bought a house. Supporters argue that pegging property taxes to the yearly assessed value of the property exposes homeowners to accelerated yearly property taxes, which leaves them vulnerable to losing their homes.

2000–12 During this period, California voters decided on 75 initiatives in 16 separate elections, 3 of which were special elections, including the special election to recall Governor Gray Davis. Twenty-five passed, including measures on farm animal confinement practices, redistricting the state legislative boundaries, victims' rights, and parole procedures.

The most controversial and long-lasting ballot issue deals with same-sex marriage. The issue goes back some 35 years. In 1977, the state legislature passed a law that said that marriage is a "personal relation arising out of a civil contract between a man and a woman." This was reaffirmed in 2000 when the voters passed Proposition 22, a statutory—not constitutional—amendment that revised the California Family Code to formally define marriage to be between a man and a woman.

In 2004, San Francisco Mayor Gavin Newsom began performing same-sex marriages, which were judicially annulled. However, in May 2008, the California Supreme Court ruled Proposition 22 invalid. At about the same time, fearing such a decision, the proponents of Proposition 8 ("Eliminates Right of Same-Sex Couples to Marry") had already begun to qualify the initiative for the ballot, anticipating this time that a constitutional amendment, not a statute, would put the issue to rest.

The campaign over Proposition 8 was fiercely contested. In the end, the initiative passed by a margin of 52.3 to 47.7 percent. Both sides attracted significant amounts of money: those supporting Proposition 8 contributed $40.3 million, and those opposing Proposition 8 contributed $64.4 million, making it the second most expensive initiative campaign—to Proposition 87 in 2006—in state history and the highest same-sex marriage initiative campaign expenditure ever nationally.

After the election six lawsuits were filed by gay couples and government bodies, with the California Supreme Court challenging the constitutionality of Proposition 8. Three of the six were accepted together to be heard by the court, but the court denied the request to stay the enforcement of Proposition 8. On May 26,

2009 (*Strauss v. Horton*), the court ruled that Proposition 8 was valid but allowed existing same-sex marriages to stand.

On August 4, 2010, a federal court declared the ban unconstitutional in *Perry v. Schwarzenegger* (now *Perry v. Brown*), and this decision was upheld by the Ninth Circuit in February 2012. The supporters of Proposition 8 had the choice of appealing the decision to the full 11-judge Ninth Circuit Court or appealing directly to the U.S. Supreme Court. They chose the former route, and this is where the issue stands today.

How can we account for the increase in initiatives over the past four decades? The simplest explanation is that it is a consequence of several factors—the complexity of modern society, the increased willingness to regulate and specify legally things that had been left to individual citizens in the first half of the twentieth century, and the move from a part-time to full-time legislature in 1968. As a result of the latter change, politics became a career, more legislation was passed, the budget grew, and decision making and power shifted to Sacramento.

These shifts, coupled with the other reforms started by the Progressives to rid the capital of political corruption and an unresponsive legislature—direct primaries, term limits, regulation of campaign contributions, and the various devices used to weaken political parties—undermined the influence voters have on elected officials. Accordingly, voters, frustrated by the action or inaction of the legislature, have turned to the initiative to get what they want.

During this time period, special interests also frequently turned to initiatives to promote policies they couldn't get through the legislature. More and more, all a group needs is the money to fund an initiative campaign. As a result, an industry of professional campaign managers and signature gatherers is flourishing. In fact, these so-called policy managers now identify hot issues and then go out and search for clients who will pay for the privilege of sponsoring the initiative.

Referendum

THE PROCESS A referendum allows voters to approve or reject statutes or amendments passed by the state legislature. The process is as follows: the measure may be proposed by presenting to the secretary of state a petition with signatures equal to 5 percent of the voters in the last gubernatorial election. The filing of the signatures must take place within a 90-day period after the enactment of the statute. If it qualifies to be on the ballot, the measure prevents the law from taking effect until the electorate decides whether it should become a law.

FREQUENCY OF USE The referendum is used infrequently. In fact, it has almost faded from use. Between 1912 and 2012, 48 referenda have appeared on the ballot. Using the same periods that we used for the initiative, there were 33 referenda from 1912 to 1939, 2 from 1940 to 1969, and 13 from 1970 to 2012.

Voters rejected a law 27 times; they approved a law 21 times. Moreover, only 14 referenda have appeared on the ballot since 1942: 1 in 1942, 1 in 1952, 4 in 1982, 3 in 2000, 1 in 2004, 4 in 2008, 2 in 2010 and 1 in 2012. Three of the 4 referenda of 1982 had to do with the redistricting of congressional, state Senate and state Assembly district boundaries. The Democratic state legislature had drawn district boundaries for all three bodies that the Republican believed were unfair. The voters concurred and rejected all three Democratic laws, forcing new boundaries to be drawn, which, from the Republican point of view, were more reflective of political reality.[18]

Recall

THE PROCESS The recall allows voters to determine whether to recall an elected official before his or her term expires. Proponents first submit a petition alleging the reason for recall. They have 150 days to present to the secretary of state a petition with the required number of signatures to qualify for the ballot. At the same time, if required, a successor is elected if the sitting official is recalled.

For statewide offices, the number of signatures must be equal to 12 percent of the last vote for the office, with signatures from at least five counties equal to 1 percent of the last vote for the office in the county. For the Senate, Assembly, members of the Board of Equalization, and judges, the number of signatures must be equal to 20 percent of the last vote for the office. Upon receiving the petitions, an election must be held between 60 and 80 days from the date of certification of sufficient signatures.

FREQUENCY OF USE Recalls of statewide offices or the state legislature are rare. There have been eight recalls out of 118 filings against state office holders. Seven of the eight were state legislators; Governor Davis was the other. Four of the state legislators were tossed out of office. The recall was put into use almost immediately after its passage against three state legislators—twice in 1913, against Senator Marshall Black for involvement in a banking scandal, which succeeded, and against Senator James Owen for corruption, which failed. The next year Senator Edwin Grant, who represented the red-light district in San Francisco, was recalled for opposing prostitution, which succeeded.

Four other state legislators faced a recall vote in 1994 and 1995. The National Rifle Association failed in its attempt to recall Senator David Roberti for his position on gun control legislation. Two Republican members of the Assembly, Doris Allen and Paul Horcher, were voted out of office for supporting Willie Brown for speaker in a battle between the parties for control of the Assembly. And an attempt to recall Democratic Assemblyman Mike Machado for backing Republicans failed.[19]

The most notorious recall, however, was that of Governor Gray Davis. He is the only California governor to have been recalled, although there had been over two dozen previous attempts to gather enough signatures to recall a governor, including three against Ronald Reagan in the 1960s and one against Pete Wilson in the 1990s. During the 2002 campaign for governor, Davis had claimed that the budget deficit was $18 billion, but a week after his election he revealed it was actually $35 billion. Proponents of the recall immediately accused Davis of misleading voters about the severity of the state's budget crisis during his reelection campaign.

Each of the direct democracy processes—initiative, referendum, and recall—is available as well in local politics, where they first appeared and where they still thrive today.

Debating the Merit of Direct Democracy

The debate about the merits of direct democracy—initiative, referendum, and recall—has been ongoing since its adoption in the early twentieth century. As we have seen, one device, the initiative, has been employed more than the other two and is generally the focus of the debate on the value of direct democracy.

Many scholars believe the initiative blurs the complexity of many issues and reduces them to clichés or sound bites upon which the voter is asked to make a yes/no choice. Furthermore, they are concerned about the influence of money in the initiative process. Some writers, like journalists David Broder and Peter Schrag, believe that special interests with deep pockets dominate the initiative process, undermining the efficacy of representative government, with its built-in checks and balances. Other writers, such as academics Elisabeth R. Gerber and Shaun Bowler, take a broader view, arguing that money plays a vital role in defeating initiatives but not in the passage of initiatives. They argue that successful initiatives are the product of grassroots movements that have more to do with visceral social and economic issues than with well-financed campaigns. Supporters of the initiative also claim that the initiative is a more effective means of serving the majority in California than the legislative process in any event. Therein lies the catch-22 that largely defines California politics: the legislature is argued to be hamstrung by the zealous use of direct democracy, while direct democracy is argued to be necessary to overcome an unproductive legislature.

A recent Field Poll[20] reveals that Californians still support the institution of direct democracy but not as strongly as in the past. In 1979, just after the passage of Proposition 13, 83 percent of voters viewed statewide ballot proposition elections as a good thing. While the favorable rating has dropped considerably since then, a majority of Californians (53 percent) still favor statewide ballot proposition elections.

Californians also think that the voting public trust fellow citizens, by use of initiatives, more than they do their elected representatives "to do what is right on important government issues" (63 percent), and especially when it comes to deciding on large-scale government programs and projects.

It's not surprising, then, that a majority of voters oppose two proposed changes to the initiative process. By a 59 to 33 percent margin, voters oppose giving the legislature the right to amend or repeal an initiative four years after its passage, and they also oppose the idea that the legislature should be able to amend an initiative after it qualifies for placement on the ballot.

In final analysis, according to the Field Poll, voters don't fully trust their elective representatives. They believe elected officials, by a 56 to 29 percent margin, "are more easily influenced by interest groups." Until that trust is gained or regained, Californians will continue to hold strong in their support of direct democracy.

California's Constitution: Where Are We Now?

California's constitution has been through three stages—establishment in the mid-1800s, rewriting in 1879, and extensive amendment during the Progressive era. Since then, a fourth, ongoing stage has been defined by political scientists and others—most notably the 1996 California Constitutional Revision Commission—making numerous suggestions to update the constitutional framework. The 1996 commission made many suggestions to strengthen the governor and make state government less susceptible to interest-group influence. These suggestions included:

- Having the governor and lieutenant governor run as a team.
- Having the other elected members of the executive branch be appointed by the governor.

- Merging the several tax administration agencies.

- Lengthening term limits for legislators.

- Requiring a simple majority instead of a two-thirds majority for the enactment of the budget each year.

Most of these proposals have never come before the voters. In 2010, however, with the state's decade-long budget crisis looming in the background, California voters passed Proposition 25, which changed the legislative requirement to pass the budget from two-thirds to a simple majority. Proposition 25 also requires state legislators to forfeit their pay in years in which they fail to pass a budget in a timely fashion. So Democrats—currently the majority party—can pass a budget without any Republican votes; however, they still can't raise taxes without a two-thirds vote. This makes the Democrats fully responsible for the budget, which, under current economic conditions, can be balanced only by cutting spending.

In the meantime, voters continue their love–hate relationship with the political parties. In 2008, the passage of Proposition 11 removed the legislature from the process of drawing its own district boundaries; a citizen commission will draw the boundaries beginning with the 2012 elections, based on the 2010 Census. And in 2010, the voters approved a top-two primary initiative, with candidates from all the parties listed on one ballot and the top two candidates, regardless of party, moving to a runoff in the November election.

FOR FURTHER READING

Allswang, John M., *The Initiative and Referendum in California, 1898–1998.* Stanford, CA: Stanford University Press, 2000.

Broder, David. *Democracy Derailed: Initiative Campaigns and the Power of Money.* New York: Harcourt, 2000.

California Secretary of State. "Initiative Totals by Summary Year 1912–March 2012." http://www.sos.ca.gov/elections/ballot-measures/pdf/initiative-totals-summary-year.pdf. Accessed 8/3/12.

Donovan, Todd, S. Bowler, D. McCuan and K. Fernandez. "Contending Players and Strategies: Opposition Advantages in Initiative Elections." In *Citizens as Legislators: Direct Democracy in the United States.* Ed. S. Bowler, T. Donovan, and C. Tolbert, pp. 133–52. Columbus: Ohio State University Press, 1998.

Gerber, Elisabeth. *The Populist Paradox: Interest Group Influence on the Promise of Direct Legislation.* Princeton, NJ: Princeton University Press, 1999.

Hofstadter, Richard. *The Age of Reform.* New York: Washington Square Press, 1988.

Johnson, Hiram. "First Inaugural Address." January 3, 1913. http://governors.library.ca.gov/addresses/23-hjohnson01.htm. Accessed 8/3/12.

Mowry, George. *The California Progressives.* Chicago: Quadrangle Paperbacks, 1963.

Olin, Spencer C., Jr. *California's Prodigal Sons: Hiram Johnson and the Progressives, 1911–1917.* Berkeley: University of California Press, 1968.

"Policy Forum: Do Ballot Initiatives Undermine Democracy?" *Cato Policy Report* (July–August 2000): 6–9. www.cato.org/pubs/policy_report/v22n4/initiatives.pdf. Accessed 6/20/12.

Schrag, Peter. *Paradise Lost: California's Experience, America's Future.* Berkeley: University of California Press, 1998.

Starr, Kevin. *Inventing the Dream: California through the Progressive Era.* New York: Oxford University Press, 1985.

Swisher, Carl Brent. Motivation and Political Technique in the California Constitutional Convention 1878–79. New York: Da Capo Press, 1969.

ON THE WEB

Ballot measure updates: www.sos.ca.gov/elections_j-htm (accessed 6/20/12).

California State Constitution: www.leginfo.ca.gov/const.html (accessed 6/20/12). This site makes the California State Constitution searchable by keyword.

Initiative & Referendum Institute: www.iandrinstitute.org (accessed 6/20/12).

LearnCalifornia.org: www.learncalifornia.org/doc.asp?id=1606 (accessed 6/20/12). LearnCalifornia.org offers a guide to the history of progressivism in California.

Southern Pacific Historical & Technical Society: www.sphts.org (accessed 6/20/12).

SUMMARY

I. The California constitution originated with the version of 1849.
  A. The basic structure of government is still the same.
  B. The most significant changes were the inclusion of the provisions for direct democracy, the initiative, referendum, and recall, in 1911.

II. The history of the constitution has four stages.
  A. 1849: basic structure of government established. Includes separation of powers, bicameralism, federalism, and popular election of most state offices.
  B. 1879: a constitutional convention added nine new articles and 8,000 words to respond to the reform needs of the time.
  C. 1910–17: the Progressive era added the initiative, referendum, and recall and hundreds of reform laws.
  D. 1960–present time: California voters have authorized a few significant reforms.

III. Proposing an amendment to the California constitution is easy.
  A. Amendments can be proposed in three ways:
    1. Through a constitutional convention. The legislature can convene the convention by a two-thirds vote or it can be convened by a majority vote of the electorate from an initiative. A Bay Area business group tried to collect sufficient signatures for a new constitutional convention in 2009–10 but gave up because professional signature-gathering firms refused to work with the group, feeling that the effort would imperil their future existence.
    2. Amendments may be proposed by collecting signatures through the initiative process.
      a) Signatures totaling 8 percent of the vote in the last gubernatorial election are required, collected over a five-month period.
      b) Most amendments are proposed this way. The cost is approximately $1 million to $2 million, mostly for signature gathering.
      c) The legislature may propose an amendment by a two-thirds vote.
  B. In each case, the electorate must then ratify the amendment before it goes into the constitution. A majority vote is required.

IV. The Progressive reformers had several key goals.
  A. Ending the dominance of big business over the state, especially the Southern Pacific Railroad.
  B. Reforming the corrupt political process.
  C. Removing from office corrupt political officials at the state and local levels of government.
  D. Returning political power to the people.

V. Progressive laws and constitutional amendments wrought many significant changes.
  A. Ended child labor.
  B. Established a state park system.
  C. Enacted protections for working people.
  D. Established nonpartisan elections.
  E. Instituted primary elections.
  F. Created office block voting.
  G. Set in motion the process of direct democracy—the initiative, referendum, and recall.
  H. Resulted in the vast bulk of the Progressive reforms that are still in operation today.

VI. Direct democracy is a vital aspect of California politics.
  A. The initiative is the most popular of the three direct democracy mechanisms.
    1. Proponents need to gather signatures equal to 5 percent of voters in the last gubernatorial election for statutes and 8 percent of the voters for constitutional amendments.
    2. Since 1912, roughly 33 percent of initiatives that are voted on pass.
    3. The initiative has increasingly become a mechanism by which special interests or wealthy individuals can pass legislation by circumventing the legislature.
  B. The referendum allows voters to approve or reject statutes or constitutional amendments passed by the legislature.
    1. Proponents need to gather signatures equal to 5 percent of voters in the last gubernatorial election.
    2. The referendum is infrequently used and has appeared on the ballot less than 50 times since 1912.
    3. In 2008, four referenda appeared on the ballot, all dealing with Indian gaming. All four passed.
  C. Recall allows voters to remove a public official from elected office before his or her term is up.
    1. The number of signatures that needs to be gathered depends on the office: 12 percent of the last vote for statewide office from at least five counties equal to 1 percent of the last vote in the

county; 20 percent of the last vote in for office for Senate, Assembly, and Board of Equalization.
2. Since 1912, there have been only eight recalls of statewide officials and legislative members.

3. Governor Gray Davis is the only statewide official to have been recalled.

PRACTICE QUIZ

1. The popular democracy process by which citizens can place a constitutional amendment or statute on the ballot is called a(n)
   a) referendum.
   b) initiative.
   c) recall.
   d) nonpartisan election.

2. The individual who served as governor during much of the Progressive period was
   a) Chester Rowell.
   b) Edward Dickson.
   c) Hiram Johnson.
   d) Samuel P. Huntington.

3. The process by which a certain percentage of those who vote in the last gubernatorial election can sign petitions to vote on a law enacted by the legislature is a(n)
   a) referendum.
   b) initiative.
   c) recall.
   d) nonpartisan election.

4. The process by which an elected official is removed from office before his or her term expires is called a(n)
   a) referendum.
   b) initiative.
   c) recall.
   d) nonpartisan election.

5. Progressive reformers pointed to this company whenever they spoke about machine politics and corporate privilege in Sacramento:
   a) Standard Oil Company.
   b) Bank of America.
   c) Southern Pacific Railroad.
   d) Northern Securities Company.

6. The only sitting California governor to be recalled from office was
   a) Ronald Reagan.
   b) Jerry Brown.
   c) Gray Davis.
   d) Pete Wilson.

7. Which of the following direct democracy devices allows voters to approve or reject statutes or amendments passed by the legislature?
   a) referendum
   b) direct primary
   c) initiative
   d) recall

8. In which historical block was the greatest number of initiatives titled?
   a) 1912–39
   b) 1940–69
   c) 1970–99
   d) 2000–12

9. Which of the following is not a Progressive Era reform?
   a) nonpartisan elections
   b) primary elections
   c) the office block vote
   d) party caucuses

10. Which of the following is not a legal way to amend the California constitution?
    a) The legislature can convene a constitutional convention by a two-thirds vote.
    b) The governor can sign into law a proposed amendment passed by the legislature.
    c) The legislature may propose a constitutional amendment by a two-thirds vote.
    d) The electorate can propose a constitutional amendment through the initiative process.

CRITICAL-THINKING QUESTIONS

1. The California constitution has gone through a series of revisions. Identify the periods of those revisions and discuss the contribution that each made to the state's political structure.

2. Suppose you worked for a coalition of interest groups supporting legislation to increase the state sales tax to fund a state-run health care system. The coalition is frustrated by the lack of action in the legislature. They come to you

for advice about the initiative process and the possibility of success. What would you tell them from what you've read in this chapter?

3. Some people argue that direct democracy provides citizens with another way to correct the behavior and decision making of public officials. Others argue that it is merely the instrument of those special interest groups that have enough money to manipulate the political process. Present an argument for each position. Where do you stand in this debate?

4. California is the model Progressive state. The key components, however, greatly weakened the role of political parties in the state. Identify and discuss how some of the reforms of this period have weakened the state's party system. Is this a good or a bad thing? Do you think there are any correlations between weak parties and the increasing use of the initiative process?

KEY TERMS

California Constitutional Revision
    Commission (p. 32)
direct democracy (p. 23)

initiative (p. 17)
Progressive movement (p. 18)
recall (p. 25)

referendum (p. 30)

3 Interest Groups and the Media in California

WHAT INTEREST GROUPS DO AND WHY THEY MATTER IN CALIFORNIA POLITICS

Consider the diversity of organizations that try to influence governmental policy or legislation:

★ A **student organization** opposes legislation to raise tuition at state universities

★ A **business trade association** supports legislation that would reform the state's workers' compensation insurance system

★ A **telecommunications company** opposes legislation mandating the use of hands-free telephones in cars and trucks

★ A **citizens' group** supports legislation that would impose stricter penalties on people convicted of drunk driving

★ An **association of county governments** opposes legislation that prohibits the placing of certain juvenile offenders into group homes that are located in residential neighborhoods

★ A **public employees' union** supports legislation that prohibits state agencies from contracting with businesses unless the businesses pay their employees the equivalent of a living wage

Each of these organizations is an interest group. Interest groups have always been part of California's (and America's) political landscape. They are a product of freedom of association that is a First Amendment right under our democratic system of government.

Interest groups are associations of individuals who seek to influence policy decisions primarily in the legislature, with the executive branch, at administrative agencies, and through direct legislation (the initiative). They are a way, in addition to voting, for individuals to voice their opinion on issues that concern them.

Interest groups are also called pressure groups, political advocacy groups, special-interest groups, and lobbying groups. Because they focus primarily on influencing policy decisions in the legislature, interest groups are often referred to as the third house, a term that describes their standing and influence in the legislative process.[1]

In California, interest groups are especially influential because of the state's unique political landscape. As we shall see, open primaries, top-two primary elections, term limits, and non-partisan elections at the local level have freed candidates from party dependence and turned candidates to interest groups for financial backing and mobilizing voters. At the same time, interest groups have realized that they could successfully use the initiative process to achieve political goals, and there has been no shortage of initiatives—and money spent—to do so, even if the propositions are in conflict with broad-based citizen interests.

Interest-Group Dynamics in Politics

All Californians are represented by interest groups, whether wittingly or not, such as county and city governments, trade associations, labor unions, professional and religious organizations, educational institutions, and environmental groups. When a government recognizes the right of association, citizens will exercise that right, and groups of all types will form. There is much debate about the influence of interest groups in the political arena, especially about whether the theories of pluralism or elitism best explain their status and power in the political process.

In pluralist theory, the political system is considered a marketplace in which a multitude of interests compete, with no one interest or combination of interests powerful enough to dominate, and in which government sits outside as an umpire or referee. Pluralist theory argues that power is dispersed. To achieve success, interests often have to join together to bargain and negotiate with opposition interests, and through bargaining and negotiating, policy decisions are made. Pluralist theory acknowledges that some groups are stronger and even more successful than others; however, it also contends that these groups do not necessarily succeed all or a majority of the time. They point out that weaker but well-organized groups do succeed in achieving their goals or checking stronger groups.

Elitist theory acknowledges that there are many interest groups active in the political process, but most of them have minimal power. Power rests in the hands of a few groups, such as large national and multinational corporations, universities, foundations, and public policy institutes, where leaders (elites) set the agenda and determine the policy outcomes of government. Accordingly, when it comes to important policy matters—the economy and noteworthy social policies—elites representing a narrow range of groups determine the basic direction of public policy. Still, elite theory recognizes that less powerful groups, most commonly in coalition with other less powerful groups, are occasionally able to check the proposals of elites. This is especially true when elites can't agree among themselves on policy choices.

Which theory best describes interest groups in California? Neither elitism nor pluralism fully explains California politics. In practice, California politics is a blend of pluralism and elitism. In each legislative session, there is widespread interest group activity, with literally thousands of interests competing for influence on more than 2,000 bills. Most of these groups, from child care facilities and auto repair shops to environmental organizations, trade unions, and businesses, focus on measures that directly affect their interest. Often these issues are of limited concern to the public at large. In these circumstances, the groups involved in the issue, whether for or against, work to create policy through competition and compromise. Here the pluralism theory fits well. Yet on some broad-based issues, a small number of (elite) groups, such as public employee unions and multinational corporations, influence decision making to favor their own special interests. They exert power downward, on the legislature, other groups, and the public. They are able to do this because of their economic clout and ability to contribute great sums of money to candidates, independent committees, ballot initiatives, and public relations campaigns. In the end, California politics is a mixture of pluralism and elitism, depending on the issue in question and the stakes presented.

Lobbying the Legislature

The people who do the work for interest groups are called lobbyists, and the work they do is called lobbying. Lobbyists have played a visible and sometimes controversial role in California politics. The most notorious figure was Arthur Samish, whose influence in the state legislature during the 1930s and 1940s drew national attention. Samish represented the most powerful industries in the state: oil, liquor stores, transportation, breweries, and racing. Samish was not shy about his influence. He once told a grand jury looking into his lobbying activities, "To hell with the governor of California. I'm the governor of the legislature."[2]

Samish's downfall came as a result of two articles in *Collier's* magazine in 1949 about "the man who secretly controls the state."[3] In the article, when asked who had more influence, himself or Samish, Governor Earl Warren responded, "On matters that affect his clients, Artie unquestionably has more power than the governor."[4]

Soon after the articles appeared Governor Warren asked for legislation to regulate lobbyists and require the disclosure of lobbyists' financial activities. The legislature obliged first with the Collier Act and later with the Erwin Act. The legislature also voted to ban Arthur Samish from the capitol building. Somewhat thereafter, Samish was convicted of income tax evasion and sentenced to three years in federal prison, thus ending his career as a Sacramento power broker.

Diversity of Interest Groups

The term *interest groups* is all inclusive, covering a wide range of businesses and organizations. The California secretary of state classifies interest groups into 19 categories and shows the amount spent by each category for lobbying for a two-year legislative session. Table 3.1 shows the figures for the 2009–10 session.

Many organizations openly state in their literature and on their websites that lobbying or advocacy is a major part of their activity and a principal reason why many individuals and businesses join the group. For example, the California Applicants' Attorneys Association claims to be "the most powerful and most knowledgeable legal voice for the injured workers of California"; the California Labor Federation, AFL-CIO, professes to promote "the interests of working people and

TABLE 3.1 ★ Lobbying Categories and Spending, 2009–10

CATEGORY	AMOUNT (MILLIONS)
1. Government	$89.3
2. Miscellaneous*	79.4
3. Health	61.5
4. Manufacturing, industrial	50.0
5. Education	37.6
6. Finance, insurance	33.3
7. Labor unions	32.8
8. Utilities	32.0
9. Professional, trade	31.4
10. Oil and gas	22.3
11. Transportation	13.6
12. Real estate	11.6
13. Entertainment, recreation	10.8
14. Agriculture	8.7
15. Merchandise, retail	8.5
16. Legal	6.5
17. Public employees	5.9
18. Lodging, restaurants	2.1
19. Political organizations	0.4

*Includes hundreds of interest groups, such as professional and trade associations, environmental organizations, and religious groups.

SOURCE: Data from California Secretary of State, http://cal-access.ss.ca.gov/Lobbying/Employers/list.aspx?view=category.

their families for the betterment of California communities"; and the California Alliance of Child and Family Services lobbies "on behalf of its member agencies and the children and families they serve."

Individual businesses and academic institutions, however, rarely identify lobbying as one of their activities. This is understandable and perfectly legitimate. Lobbying is not a primary reason for the existence of these organizations; profits are. They participate in politics to protect or expand their markets. They are careful not to call attention to their involvement in politics out of fear that they may alienate customers or tarnish their image. Accordingly, information about their lobbying activity must be obtained from newspaper accounts and public disclosure documents.

Many businesses do join professional or trade associations to give them a voice on issues that affect their industry. "We're the champion of California businesses, large and small," the California Chamber of Commerce proudly asserts on its website. "For more than 120 years, CalChamber has worked to make California a better place to do business by giving private-sector employers a voice in state politics." The more than 13,000 member businesses give the chamber tremendous clout and stature. In turn, individual members enjoy several advantages—sharing of cost, strength in numbers, and, perhaps most important, anonymity.

Government also lobbies government. Taxpayer protection groups have come to call these interests—education, health, special districts, local government, state agencies—"the spending lobby" because they are motivated by the desire to maintain or increase their revenue. In 2008, for instance, government was the highest spender among the 19 categories of lobbyist employers registered with the secretary of state.

According to governmental lobbyists, the passage in 1978 of Proposition 13, which limited the property tax revenues to local government, spurred the growth in governmental lobbying and the competition for funds. John P. Quimby Sr., a former Assemblyman who lobbies for San Bernardino County, told the *Riverside Press Enterprise* in 1997: "I wish government wasn't for sale like this, but the fact is you have to hustle to get your share. Local governments without lobbyists see the ones with representation doing better so they say, 'We need to get our butts on board and get one or they're going to steal everything from us.'"[5] Or, to put it another way, government agencies spend taxpayers' money to lobby government for more money to spend on taxpayers.

The Increase in Interest Groups

In California over the last two decades, the number of interest groups and lobbying expenditures has grown steadily. In 1990, lobbyists represented approximately 1,300 interest groups; in 2000, the number had nearly doubled to 2,552; and in 2010, it had increased to 3,094.[6] During the same period, lobbying expenditures also grew substantially, with just a slight dip in 2009–10, as seen in Table 3.2. However, during the first three-quarters of the 2011–12 legislative session, groups spent nearly $216 million on lobbying activity, a 5 percent increase over the first three-quarters of the 2009–10 session, which suggests that lobby spending for 2011–12 will again set a record amount.[7]

TABLE 3.2 ★ Growth in Lobbying Expenditures

LEGISLATIVE SESSION	LOBBYING EXPENDITURES	PERCENT INCREASE
1989–90	$193,575,480	
1991–92	233,872,097	20.8
1993–94	250,119,667	7.0
1995–96	266,939,559	6.7
1997–98	292,615,513	9.6
1999–2000	344,318,650	17.7
2001–02	386,829,719	12.4
2003–04	413,376,146	6.9
2005–06	500,326,710	21.0
2007–08	558,419,109	11.0
2009–10	538,638,251	–3.5

SOURCE: Data from California Secretary of State, http://cal-access.ss.ca.gov/Lobbying/Employers.

California continually ranks first nationally in number of interest groups and amount spent on lobbying activity. California accounts for one-third of all lobbyist activity in the country. Texas and New York rank second and third behind California, and together they spend around 60 percent of what is spent in California on lobbying activities.[8] What Carey McWilliams said about California politics during the 1930s and 1940s still holds true today: "Interests, not people, are represented in Sacramento. Sacramento is the marketplace of California where grape growers and sardine fishermen, morticians and osteopaths bid for allotments of state power."[9]

Several factors encouraged the proliferation of interest groups:

Weak Political Parties

California has weak parties for a variety of reasons, but largely because of the Progressive reforms of the 1910s. The reforms were directed at the spoils system in government, the control parties had over which candidates would represent the party in general elections, and the influence of interest groups in the legislature. To balance these influences, they gave voters the direct democracy practices of initiative, referendum, and recall. These measures and subsequent reforms—many of which were considered citizen initiatives, such as the direct primary, term limits, redistricting by an independent commission, and top-two open primary—greatly free officials from party structure and discipline and tie them to interest groups that can ensure their reelection. In this way, Progressive attempts to curb interest group influence actually strengthened it.

Growth of Government

California government has grown substantially over the past half century. Californians, like other Americans, initially were suspicious of government. They perceived government as a force whose powers had to be kept in check to protect individual rights. As time passed, however, citizens began to perceive government differently, as a force that could be used to solve myriad social and economic problems. The legislature has eagerly taken up the challenge.

Term Limits

In 1990, California voters approved term limits for all state and legislative offices. Term limits, it was argued, would break the cozy relationship between elected officials and lobbyists. Yet this is not what has happened. As legislators with years of institutional memory left office, the legislature became more chaotic and less efficient. "Experts say it is this institutional memory that has swung the legislature toward the 'third house' of special interests. In short, the lobbyists have it. Legislators don't." Legislators rely on lobbyists to write intricate legislation and counsel them on the flood of complex issues that come across their desks.[10]

Public Interest Groups

The growth of public interest groups, what some call the New Politics movement, began in the 1970s and continues through today. Examples of such groups are AARP, Sierra Club, and the Foundation for Taxpayers and Consumer Rights. As the textbook *We the People* explains, these "groups sought to distinguish themselves from other groups—business groups, in particular—by styling themselves as 'public interest groups,' terminology that suggests they served the general good rather than their own selfish interests." Although these so-called public interest groups claim to represent *only* the public interest, they should be judged critically, for they are sometimes facades behind which narrow private interests hide.

Interest-Group Politics

Today, in California, politics *is* interest groups. Not all interest groups, however, are equal. Some have considerably more clout than others. The success of an interest group depends on several factors: a clear message, group cohesiveness, the alignment of the group's interests with those of other groups and elected officials, an understanding of the political process, technical expertise, and money. As we shall see, money is especially important.

Table 3.3 shows the top employers of lobbyists. This list has remained relatively stable over the past several years, with four or five groups moving in and out of the ranks from one year to the next, depending on their agenda in the legislative session. By most standards, the lobbyists for these groups are some of the most successful in Sacramento.

It is not surprising that with the growth of the "lobbying industrial complex" in California, allegations of influence peddling follow and sometimes turn out to

TABLE 3.3 ★ Top 10 Lobbyist Employers, January 1, 2009–December 31, 2010

ORGANIZATION	CUMULATIVE EXPENDITURES
Western States Petroleum Association	$9,345,305
California Teachers Association	9,164,421
California State Council of Service Employees	8,665,881
California Chamber of Commerce	6,715,018
California Labor Federation, AFL-CIO	5,967,560
California Hospital Association	4,483,216
California School Employees Association	4,475,376
Kaiser Foundation Health Plan	4,255,622
California Manufacturers & Technology Association	3,950,754
Chevron Corporation	3,846,857

SOURCE: Data from California Secretary of State, http://cal-access.ss.ca.gov/Lobbying/Employers.

be true. For example, Clay Jackson, one of the most influential lobbyists in Sacramento, was accused of offering large campaign contributions to Senator Alan Robbins in return for the lawmaker's support on legislation benefiting Jackson's clients. The FBI uncovered Robbins's part in the plan, and he agreed to wear a wire to expose Jackson in exchange for a reduced sentence. In the end, Jackson, Robbins, and former State Senator Paul Carpenter (who funneled campaign money through a public relations firm for Robbins's personal use) were convicted of engaging in a money-laundering scheme.

The incident raised questions about the connections among interest groups, money, and power in Sacramento. It revealed how a legal fund-raising system can be used to benefit legislators, especially in an environment in which there is a fine line between campaign contributions and influence over the way in which legislators vote on issues—even when these processes are conducted legally.

Lobbyists

Lobbyists are at the forefront of interest-group activity. They coordinate the efforts to secure passage, amendment, or defeat of bills in the legislature and the approval or veto of bills by the governor. Having a good lobbyist is paramount to the success of any group.

There are citizen lobbyists and professional lobbyists. A citizen lobbyist is not paid to advocate for a particular issue or set of issues. Citizen lobbyists interact with their representatives to express their personal views on an issue and to attempt to influence legislation on that issue. Professional lobbyists are paid for their services and must register with the secretary of state. They also must submit quarterly disclosure reports detailing for whom they are working, the amount of money earned, and payment such as gifts and honoraria made to public officials they lobby.

There are two categories of professional lobbyists: contract and in-house. Contract lobbyists make up 50 percent of all lobbyists in Sacramento; in-house lobbyists account for the other half.[11] Contract lobbyists offer their services to the general public; they are advocates for hire and often represent multiple clients on a variety of issues at the same time. In-house lobbyists are employees of a trade, professional, or labor association and represent that group's interest only. Many of these interest groups also use contract lobbyists because the group is involved in too many issues for its in-house staff to handle, or it may want to use a lobbyist who specializes in a specific subject area such as health insurance or who has a close relation with a particular legislator or members of a specific committee whose support is vital for the group's success.

Lobbying

Few issues are just lobbied—that is, discussed with a public official or staff during the legislative process. Most issues are managed using a combination of techniques: public relations (marketing), grassroots mobilization, and coalition building.

The first job of the lobbyist is to know the group's objective. Is the goal new legislation? Is it to amend existing law? Or is it to stop another business or interest group from passing new legislation or amending an existing law that may affect the group's interest? The goal may not even be legislation. The group may want to amend current regulatory policy or shape the content of new regulations that will affect its members.

The lobbyist must also identify other groups that may have an interest in the issue, and assess whether these groups, legislators, the executive branch, regulators, or the general public will support or oppose the group's activity. Moreover, lobbyists who can rely on the group's members, especially if they reside in the legislator's district, can more easily influence policy making. The most successful efforts are built around networks of activists who have made it a point to know their elected officials. These relationships can be built in many ways: working on election campaigns, commending a representative in writing for an action he or she has taken, contributing to political campaigns, and connecting in other ways so as to have a positive relationship with these officials.

With this preparation in hand, the lobbyist has a greater chance of success. Of course, several other factors are also important: knowledge of the legislation process, strong communication skills, established relationships, credibility, adaptability to change, and the ability to negotiate.

Campaign Contributions to Candidates

Besides expenditures on lobbying to influence legislative action, interest groups also make campaign contributions, which enable them to become familiar with and gain access to legislators. They do so through political action committees (PACs).

There is a connection between lobbying success and campaign contributions. Those who invest heavily in lobbying generally invest heavily in PAC contributions, and vice versa.[12] Table 3.4 shows the top 10 contributors for the 2009–10 legislative year. The table shows only the amount directly contributed to candidates for the

TABLE 3.4 ★ Top 10 Contributors to Legislative Candidates, 2009–10	
California Association of Realtors	$781,354
AT&T	775,900
California Teachers Association	702,541
California Dental Association	671,049
California State Council of Laborers	604,035
Pechanga Band of Luiseño Mission Indians	562,699
California Medical Association	509,385
PG&E	488,816
California Professional Firefighters	477,018
California State Pipe Trades Council	474,737

SOURCE: National Institute on Money in State Politics, www.followthemoney.org/database/state_overview.phtml?s=CA&y=2010.

state legislature—the total of which was $105,822,734. This figure does not include what these organizations may have contributed to the Democratic or Republican Party committees ($67,574,985), candidates for statewide office, ($307,677,930), or ballot initiatives ($235,674,934), which, when totaled, comes to an additional $610,927,849.[13] Campaign contributions enable a lobbyist to gain access to legislators. The lobbyist can then make his or her argument—at which time he or she can provide the legislator with important, often technical information.

In 2010, the U.S. Supreme Court in *Citizens United v. Federal Election Commission* held that political action committees could raise unlimited funds from individuals, corporations, and unions to support or oppose candidates for office. Though a landmark case nationally, *Citizens United* had little impact on political spending in California because California had allowed such practice before the Supreme Court's ruling.

California's disclosure laws require independent committees to file the same financial reports as candidate committees and ballot measure committees. In a study of independent committees in California from 2005 to 2010, Linda Casey of the National Institute on Money in State Politics showed that independent spending amounted to 9 percent ($228.8 million) of the total amount spent directly for candidates and initiatives ($2.5 billion).

Jesse Unruh, former speaker of the Assembly, once said, "Money is the mother's milk of politics." This adage still holds true today. Most interest groups have PACs and carefully target their campaign contributions. They support individuals in positions of power (e.g., incumbent state officers, party leaders in the legislature, committee chairs, and rising stars). Contributions have little to do with the legislator's

TABLE 3.5 ★ Top 10 Independent Spenders on Initiatives, 2005–10

California Teachers Association	$101,738,213
Pharmaceutical Research & Manufacturers of America	70,819,206
PG&E	61,856,250
Pechanga Band of Lucerño Mission Indians	47,618,135
Morongo Band of Mission Indians	46,525,977
Chevron Corporation	43,607,500
California State Council of Service Employees	42,121,506
Philip Morris	38,079,500
Agua Caliente Band of Cahuilla Indians	34,840,025
AERA Energy	33,235,243

SOURCE: National Institute on Money in State Politics, www.followthemoney.org/database/state_overview.phtml?s=CA&y=2010.

or a party's political ideology. The only question is, Can this legislator help me achieve my goals?

An example of the dynamics of campaign contributions and lobbying can be seen in the California Correctional Peace Officers Association (CCPOA), one of the most powerful interest groups in Sacramento. It has achieved this status through a combination of aggressive lobbying, large campaign contributions, and skillful public relations.

The union is one of the biggest contributors to candidates running for statewide and legislative office. Over the past decade, the union has spent nearly $40 million in lobbying and campaign activities,[14] contributing aggressively to the campaigns of its supporters and just as aggressively to defeat those who oppose its agenda. The union is one of the few public employee groups to give generously to both Republicans and Democrats. For example, when Pete Wilson ran for governor in 1990, prison guards gave $1 million to his campaign. Wilson reciprocated with substantial pay increases and stronger sentencing policies. The union, however, really stepped forward with Gray Davis. Besides early endorsement in the primary, which guaranteed his selection as the Democrat candidate for governor, they contributed more than $3 million between 1998 and 2002 to his campaign war chest. During the same period, the union contributed millions of dollars to members of the legislature, with especially large sums going to the leadership of both parties. Governor Davis responded in kind. Correctional officers' wages were tied to those of highway patrol officers. Retirement benefits, sick leave and overtime provisions, and uniform allowances were greatly increased.

CCPOA also spent heavily—$1.8 million—in support of Jerry Brown's 2010 gubernatorial victory. In March 2012, the legislature and Governor Brown agreed on a new contract, which the union overwhelmingly approved. The contract increases pension contributions of officers, reduces pay in one year by requiring one day of unpaid leave each month, and eliminates a state-funded, $42 million-a-year 401(k)-type plan that correctional officers received in addition to their pensions. However, as the *San Francisco Chronicle* pointed out, the contract eliminates limitations on accrual of vacation time, currently estimated at more than 33 million hours and estimated to cost the state another $1 billion.[15]

Governor Brown argued that collective bargaining is about "give and take" and claimed the deal with the correctional officers was comparable to what other public employee unions received under Governor Schwarzenneger. Moreover, according to some, the union contract is a bargaining chip to gain union support for the governor's prison reform agenda, including closing youth prisons and transferring up to 30,000 low-level offenders from state prisons to local jails, which is intended to save the state millions of dollars. Still, the returns from CCPOA's campaign spending and lobbying suggest that the strategy has paid off handsomely. Today, "California's prison guards are the nation's highest paid, a big reason that spending on the state's prison system has rocketed from less than 4.3 percent of the budget in 1986 to more than 11 percent today."[16]

Regulating Interest Groups

With the passage of the Political Reform Act (PRA) of 1974, California lobbyist and interest groups are required to report campaign and lobbying expenditures. At the same time, the PRA shifted the filing of lobbying statements from the state legislature to the independent Fair Political Practice Commission.

Since its passage, the PRA has undergone numerous amendments, the most significant being in 2000 with the passage of Proposition 34. The following rules now govern interest groups and lobbyists:

- A lobbyist or lobbying firm cannot present a gift to a state-elected official or legislative official in aggregate of more than $10 a month. Anyone who is not a registered lobbyist can give up to $250 in gifts in any calendar year.

- A lobbyist cannot contribute to state candidates or officeholders if he or she are registered to lobby that candidate or officeholder's agency. However, the various interest groups that employ lobbyists have no such restrictions.

- Interest groups, individuals, and businesses have specific limits on election contributions to candidates or officeholders. The limits for legislative candidates are $3,200; for all state offices except the governor, $5,300; and for governor, $21,300.

Some public interest groups, such as Common Cause, Clean Money Campaign, and the League of Women Voters, have called for further restrictions on lobbying expenditures and campaign contributions by both individual and interest groups. Such measures, they argue, would constrain the power of special interests and allow public policy decision to reflect the overall interest of society.

Recommendations to restrict the power of interest groups fall into three categories: clean-money elections, contribution restrictions, and conflict-of-interest laws. The first category, clean-money elections, would provide public funding to candidates who demonstrate a base of public support by getting a qualifying number of voter signatures and a certain number of small contributions and who agree to forgo any other private donations. Such measures would cover all state legislative and statewide offices and have recently been adopted by Maine and Arizona. In California, it would be difficult to get the political parties and most legislators, who are tied to the current funding system, to support the idea. It would also be difficult to convince the public that they should subsidize campaigns for elective office. Over the years, only 35 to 40 percent of California voters have supported public financing of election campaigns.

The second category, contribution limits, has been a focal point of campaign reform for some time. Most of the effort has come from citizen groups disgruntled with the current system. Together they have established stricter reporting requirements and limits on campaign contributions and loans to state candidates and political parties. The changes have been accomplished almost wholly through initiatives sponsored by these groups over the past decade—Propositions 63 and 78 in 1993, Proposition 208 in 1996, and Proposition 34 in 2000. These efforts will continue in the future as various groups attempt to rein in the free flow of money into political campaigns.

One of the biggest issues involving campaign finance has been the rise of super PACs. Technically known as independent expenditure-only committees, super PAC committees may raise unlimited sums of money from corporations, unions, associations, and individuals and then spend unlimited sums to overtly advocate for or against political candidates. Super PACs must, however, report their donors to the Federal Election Commission on a monthly or quarterly basis—the super PAC's choice—as a traditional PAC would. Unlike traditional PACs, super PACs are prohibited from donating money directly to political candidates, though this has not prevented them from exhibiting enormous influence in elections.

The last category, conflict-of-interest laws, covers a multitude of situations. Sometimes simultaneous activity falls into this category. For example, the California Senate offers lobbyists who contribute to its charity the opportunity to travel with the lawmakers to various foreign countries.[17]

The Senate's California International Relations Foundation, a charity, helps fund the entertainment of foreign delegations that visit the state capital and a high school students' exchange between California and Japan. The idea is new in lobbyist-legislator relations.

Each donor contributes $2,000 to $3,000, which gives the donor a seat on the foundation's board of directors and the invitation to travel with legislators on trade and cultural trips to foreign countries. Since 2004, there have been 18 trips to places such as Tokyo, Jerusalem, and Rio de Janeiro.

The foundation operates out in the open, and it does not underwrite the expenses of either the traveling legislators or the supporters. Critics, however, contend that it provides a unique opportunity for supporters. They gain the goodwill of and access to legislators. This is especially convenient when the supporter's interest group has a bill pending in the legislature.

Outside the Legislature

Up until now, we have focused on the influence of interest groups on the state legislature. Interest groups, however, flex their muscles in other ways in the electoral process: through get-out-the-vote and initiative (direct legislation) campaigns.

GET OUT THE VOTE Many interest groups engage in get-out-the-vote (GOTV) operations among their members to help a candidate (and political party) or an issue win at the ballot box. This is especially true in what is perceived to be a hotly contested election. In such instances, GOTV can be the most important activity undertaken because there are many examples of an election being won or lost by a handful of votes.

GOTV operations are often considered "outsider strategies"—that is, they take place outside the traditional arena of interest-group activity, the legislature, and they are supported by groups that feel they have a vital stake in the outcome of the election, as Hispanics did in 1994 with Proposition 187, making illegal aliens ineligible for public services, and as the Protect Marriage Coalition did in 2008 with Proposition 8, eliminating same-sex couples' right to marry.

Some interest groups, like organized labor, religious denominations, and minorities, have a long history in mobilizing their members to vote—and to vote for or against a candidate or critical issue. Other interest groups, like gays, environmentalists, and gender-based groups, have more recently begun to participate in GOTV activities. They mobilize their supporters at the grassroots level, employing a variety of techniques, including direct mail, door-to-door canvassing, telemarketing, poll watching, pickup, phoning, and assistance. Months of work go into planning the campaign. While the goal is simple—delivering members' votes—the outcome is unpredictable until the final tally of ballots.

INITIATIVES Chapter 2 explored the history of the initiative and the impact of some of those that passed. What was initially considered a tool for citizens to check the actions of elected officials and indirectly the influence of interest groups in the legislature is still considered so today. The majority of voters support the initiative because they believe that the public, and not elected representatives, are better suited to decide "important government issues," although many also believe that a few narrow economic interests also shape public policy through the initiative process.[18]

Yet, as Elisabeth Gerber shows, this may not be as big of an issue as voters think. Although there are now more initiatives and considerably more money spent on them, groups with different goals use the initiative process differently. On the one hand, narrow (economic) interest groups, whose members join because of their occupation or professional status, rely primarily on the mobilization of money for initiative campaigns. They use these monetary resources and, to a lesser extent, personnel in two ways: "to protect the status quo or to pressure the legislature." When they sponsor initiatives, the measures generally fail. On the other hand, citizen groups, whose members join as free individuals committed to some personal belief or social issue, rely primarily on the mobilization of personnel who "volunteer their personal time and energy . . . to pass new laws by initiative."[19] In the end, the measures citizen groups back succeed at a higher rate than those sponsored by narrow economic interests.

For most Californians, the media—news stories, paid political commercials, public debate, direct mail—are the most influential sources of information on the activity of interest groups, the amount of money spent on lobbying and political campaigns, and the increasing frequency and amount of money spent on initiatives. The media keep citizens actively involved in politics.

The Media

The term *media* refers to the dispensers of information, including broadcast media (radio and television), print media (newspapers and magazines), and electronic media (the Internet). When we speak of these sources individually we refer to it as a *medium* (the Latin singular of *media*). Sometimes we speak about mass media but most often the limiting adjective (*mass*) is assumed.

Television

Today, television is the medium of choice for political information for the vast majority of Americans, and Californians are no exception. This medium can spread messages quickly, covering a wide variety of topics, including car chases, earthquakes, and the latest political scandal. Television is particularly important for conducting political campaigns in a large state with a diverse population, such as California. Yet for all its speed and ability to reach large numbers of viewers, television is a medium that provides little information on government.

Two facts account for this lack of information: (1) California is so big and diverse that it is difficult to cover statewide political and governmental news, and (2) Californians in general are not that interested in state government and policy. These dynamics, along with a fragmented political structure, produce a stark reality—the largest state in the nation, with some of the largest media resources and markets in the nation, provides relatively little political and governmental news, particularly on television news programs.[20] There are few media correspondents in Sacramento. More important, because there is no newspaper distributed statewide, there is no incentive to cover news on a statewide basis.

The nightly news stations compete with one another for viewers. But in reality, the news formats provide little in the way of important political information. The half-hour news format is crammed with commercials, weather reports, entertainment news, sports coverage, and a host of other topics that do little to inform the viewer about the political problems that affect the state and nation. Those topics that are reported with any depth are calculated to achieve ratings and are structured to last over several newscasts.

Each local station has its own version of some type of "action" news team or consumer protection group bringing audiences the latest artificially hyped crisis. From the nature of the issues covered, it is clear that local television, for the most part, has made a concerted effort to treat political news as a secondary issue. Issues related to political parties, government, or interest groups in California don't have the power to reach and energize large populations on a day-to-day basis.

Local television stations focus our attention on issues like crime in a way that government representatives cannot. Sensational undercover stories are frequently broadcast, such as the financial deceptions practiced by automobile dealers, the unsanitary conditions in local restaurants, and the health risks of cosmetic surgeries. These exposés help identify dishonest practices in our communities, but they are also examples of how the ability to identify important political issues has passed from the political parties to the media. The media place an issue on the agenda, often based more on its sensational appeal than its practical importance, and the next day government representatives are telling the public what must be done to fix the problem. They are reacting to the media's promotion of the issue.

In California, where voters have the ability to put statute and constitutional initiatives on the ballot, local television plays a major role by getting information to the voters about these issues through extensive advertising campaigns. These messages are drafted and paid for by the interest groups that support the initiatives, and the political parties may or may not play a role in the process. The broadcast media have the power to reach a vast audience, something the parties cannot do on their own.

Newspapers

The number of newspapers across the United States has fallen during the last 25 years, and newspaper circulations have declined in every recent year as well. Newspapers still remain active in identifying political corruption, reporting the workings of state and local government, covering political campaigns, and helping keep the public focused on important political issues. But newspapers in the final analysis are businesses and must be able to generate revenues and profits. To adequately cover state government, reporters and news staff have to be located in Sacramento. At the same time, on-the-spot coverage of county and local government requires a second set of reporters and news staff. The expense is prohibitive, and, over time, newspaper coverage at the state and local levels has noticeably declined. The public is not as fully informed about the activities of its various levels of government as it needs to be. The *Los Angeles Times* and the *Sacramento Bee* cover developments in Sacramento more extensively than other newspapers, but both have become victim to cost pressures and the need to reduce news reporting staffs in the 1990s and 2000s.

The drive for profits has reduced the news reporting capabilities of broadcast and print media, which cover only the big stories at the state government level. Ultimately, this means the public receives little information about the political activities of state and local government. This leads to a public that constantly finds itself surprised by political crises that seem to develop suddenly, such as rising state deficits, electricity shortages, declining state bond ratings, school facilities that are falling apart, and an overwhelmed freeway system. But for all their failings, broadcast and print media still play an important role in the election process and in formulating the political agenda. The media continue to identify the major political issues, report on the political progress of candidates at all levels, question the candidates and officeholders, and edit the replies the public gets to hear and read. These powers continue to undermine the role of political parties in California.

With Arnold Schwarzenegger's election as governor in October 2003, the public had a renewed interest in state politics. People were curious. A few stations that had closed their Sacramento news bureaus announced their reopening. This wasn't surprising. Nationally known figures have generally drawn more media attention than regional or local personalities. There was more coverage of Governors Edmund G. Brown, Ronald Reagan, and Jerry Brown, each of whom was a presidential contender, than of Governors Deukmejian, Wilson, and Davis, who were not.[21]

As time passed, however, the increase in coverage wasn't due to Schwarzenegger's celebrity but the state's economic woes: record budget deficits, sinking bond ratings, high unemployment, and staggering foreclosure filings. These concerns still persist today under Governor Jerry Brown. Local government, interest groups (especially public employee unions whose members are impacted by the budget deficits), and the general public have turned to Sacramento for solutions. Economic issues are the big concern, not the political personalities who have been thrust in the position of resolving these problems.

The Internet

Today the Internet offers instant access to political information and the opportunity to communicate one's views quickly to political leaders, news outlets, interest groups, and other individuals through blogs, Twitter, Tumblr, Facebook, and other social media channels. Many experts see the Internet as a catalyst for enhancing the democratic process. It offers candidates the opportunity to communicate rapidly with supporters and to recruit campaign workers. During the presidential election season, it has proven to be an excellent tool for raising campaign funds. The Internet offers political parties the opportunity to disseminate their issue positions to millions of potential voters in a quick and inexpensive fashion. Whether it will restore some of the power political parties have lost remains to be seen. The Internet is open to all users, and in that environment, political parties will still have lots of competition to control the political agenda.

With the growth of the Internet, access to California political and news sources has expanded exponentially. The major newspapers provide daily e-mails that focus on topics of the reader's interest, and research organizations, libraries, and blogs provide political information, background, and research beyond what any individual can absorb. A list of some of the major sources covering California politics is provided in Table 3.6.

Media and Political Campaigns

Running for office is a very expensive endeavor and it requires highly focused political messages. Because of these requirements, electronic media are the media of choice to reach large numbers of citizens. The media are also very useful in mobiliz-

TABLE 3.6 ★ Internet Sources Covering California Politics

MAJOR NEWSPAPERS

Los Angeles Times (www.latimes.com)
Sacramento Bee (www.sacbee.com)
San Francisco Chronicle (www.sfgate.com)
Capitol Weekly (capitolweekly.net)

ORGANIZATIONS

Rough & Tumble (www.rtumble.com)
California Progress Report (www.californiaprogressreport.com)
Flashreport (www.flashreport.org)
Fox & Hounds (www.foxandhoundsdaily.com)
Calitics (www.calitics.com)
Around the Capitol (www.aroundthecapitol.com)

PUBLIC POLICY SITES

Public Policy Institute of California (www.ppic.org)
California Health Care Foundation (www.chcf.org)
California Policy Inbox (http://inbox.berkeley.edu)

UNIVERSITIES

University of California at Berkeley (http://igs.berkeley.edu/)
California State University Bakersfield (www.csub.edu/library/)

MAJOR COLUMNISTS

Dan Walters, Daniel Weintraub, and Peter Schrag of the *Sacramento Bee* (www.sacbee.com)
George Skelton of the *Los Angeles Times* (www.latimes.com)

ing supporters on Election Day. Mobilizing a candidate's base of support is essential to winning elections. Without the media, no effective message is conveyed to the electorate, and consequently no money can be raised to fuel the modern type of media campaign that candidates must use to get elected. The media have the dual role of getting out the message to one's supporters and energizing them so they will contribute the money needed to win public office. Candidates cannot depend on local campaign appearances to reach enough people. They must depend on the power of electronic media to reach the mass audience needed to win elections.

In some cases, the media themselves and their coverage can become a central issue in the campaign, with a candidate running against the media and positioning himself or herself as outside the political establishment. During the recall election of 2003, the *Los Angeles Times* ran a story just before the election about inappropriate sexual behavior on the part of Schwarzenegger during his acting days. The reaction of many citizens was that the newspaper was taking incumbent Governor Gray Davis's side, not that it was uncovering important information that citizens might want to consider in their voting decisions.[22]

Interest-Group Politics in California: Where Are We Now?

Interest groups play an important and often dominant role in California politics. The continued growth in the number of groups and their lobbying expenditures attest to this fact. Moreover, if the past decade is any indication, the number of interest groups doing business in Sacramento will continue to grow, and lobbying expenditures will continue to increase. The size and structural deficit of the state budget, weak political parties, mandated term limits, increase in public interest groups, and continued dependence of local governments on Sacramento for financial assistance are all factors that will continue to promote interest group politics.

Much of the time, these groups are self-regulating, checking one another and forging broad-based coalitions of interests to achieve important policy decisions. Of course, interest groups will always be able to achieve advantages for narrow issues affecting their members, and the most powerful will generally be the most successful, as long as they can get a group of legislators to fall in behind them. That's why interest-group disclosure rules, campaign expenditure limits, and other reporting requirements are necessary. They enable us to keep these groups in check. That's the theory, at least.

Today, however, there is a disjunction between theory and practice. Interest groups have undue influence on politics in the state. Without some limit on the amount of money an interest group can spend on lobbying and campaign contributions, the only check on their power may be divided government, whereby one party controls the executive and one controls both or one house of the legislature, so that no one interest or coalition of interests can ride roughshod over government.

That's the state of affairs in California today. Although California's politics are not broken, unless these concerns are addressed, California will continue to hobble along, and interest groups will continue to flourish and prosper at the expense of the general public.

FOR FURTHER READING

Baldassare, Mark. "The California Initiative Process—How Democratic Is It?" Public Policy Institute of California, February 2002.

Gerber, Elisabeth R. "Interest Group Influence in the California Initiative Process." Public Policy Institute of California, 1998. www.ppic.org/main/publication.asp?i=49. Accessed 8/4/12.

McWilliams, Carey. *California: The Great Exception.* Berkeley: University of California Press, 1999.

Michael, Jay, Dan Walters, and Dan Weintraub. *The Third House: Lobbyists, Power, and Money in Sacramento.* Berkeley, CA: Berkeley Public Policy Press, 2000.

Rasky, Susan F. "Covering California: The Press Wrestles with Diversity, Complexity, and Change." In *Governing California: Politics, Government, and Public Policy in the Golden State.* Ed. Gerald C. Lubenow and Bruce E. Cain. Berkeley: Institute of Government Studies Press, University of California, 1997, pp. 157–88.

Samish, Arthur H., and Bob Thomas. *The Secret Boss of California.* New York: Crown Publishers, 1971.

ON THE WEB

Around the Capitol: www.aroundthecapitol.com (accessed 8/4/12). A portal to California legislative information.

California Alert: http://blogs.sacbee.com/capitolalertlatest/ California and national political news and commentary.

Capitol & California: www.sacbee.com/capitolandcalifornia (accessed 6/22/12).

Capital Weekly: www.capitolweekly.net (accessed 6/22/12).

Lobbying activity: http://cal-access.ss.ca.gov/lobbying (accessed 6/22/12); the secretary of state's office reports on lobbying in California politics.

SUMMARY

I. Interest groups are at the center of California's campaign and lobbying activities.
   A. Some believe they play a necessary role in our democratic society.
   B. Others see them as detrimental to our political system.

II. Interest groups exhibit the following characteristics:
   A. They are associations of individuals who join together for the purpose of influencing governmental or legislative policy.
   B. They can be individual businesses, trade and professional associations, or labor unions.
   C. They have proliferated over the past three decades for four reasons: growth in government, weak political parties, public interest groups, and term limits.

III. Lobbyists do the work of interest groups.
   A. The activity referred to as lobbying.
   B. There are three different categories of lobbyists.
     1. citizen lobbyists
     2. contract lobbyists
     3. in-house lobbyists
       a) Citizen lobbyists are individuals who have an interest in an issue and want to make their view known to their public official.
       b) Contract lobbyists and in-house lobbyists are professionals who must register with the secretary of state and submit a variety of disclosure statements yearly regarding their activities.

IV. The number of interest groups (and registered lobbyists) has grown substantially in each legislative session since 1990.
   A. In the 2007–08 legislature, interest groups employed over 3,200 lobbyists.
   B. In the same legislature, they spent over $500 million on lobbying activities.
   C. The public ranks lobbying at the bottom of professions for honesty and integrity.

V. Lobbyists perform a variety of activities to accomplish their goals.
   A. Preparation for the legislative or regulatory campaign:
     1. set campaign goals
     2. learn as much about the interest group as possible
     3. establish a grassroots network
     4. identify other organizations that could support or oppose the goals

   B. The campaign (lobbying basics):
     1. draft language, amendments, etc.
     2. prepare a fact sheet, position papers, etc.
     3. contact committee members before the committee hearing
     4. initiate a grassroots campaign to contact key legislators
   C. Legislative activity:
     1. testify in person
     2. bring expert witness from legislator's district

VI. There is a strong correlation between lobbying expenditure and campaign contributions.
   A. Interest groups that invest heavily in lobbying also invest heavily in political campaigns.
   B. The California Correctional Peace Officers Association is a prime example.

VII. Interest groups contribute to candidates' and officeholders' campaigns to leverage their influence.
   A. The Political Reform Act of 1974 was passed to regulate lobbying practices and requires the disclosure of lobbying financial activity.
   B. Proposition 34, the most recent initiative amendment to the act, includes new restrictions:
     1. Lobbyists cannot contribute to the campaigns of anyone they are lobbying for.
     2. Lobbyists are limited in the amount of money they can contribute during any election cycle.

VIII. The media are important vehicles in mobilizing and informing voters and candidates' supporters.
   A. Television and newspapers have traditionally had the greatest influence, with the Internet (through political websites and blogs) gaining in influence.
   B. Little of this mobilization, however, comes from news programs, which generally provide scant political information.
     1. It comes indirectly through the ability of television news programs to cover scandals and dishonest practices of politicians and focus viewers' attention on the latest special investigation.
     2. This demonstrates how the power to set the political agenda has passed from the political parties to the media.

PRACTICE QUIZ

1. The term *third house* refers to which of the following entities?
   a) judicial branch
   b) executive branch
   c) interest groups
   d) media

2. Over the past two decades, interest-group expenditures in California have
   a) declined.
   b) increased.
   c) remained relatively the same.
   d) fluctuated from year to year.

3. An individual who offers his or her lobbying services to multiple clients at the same time is called a(n)
   a) contract lobbyist.
   b) "hired gun."
   c) citizen lobbyist.
   d) in-house lobbyist.

4. The principal function of an interest group is to
   a) provide its members with educational and social opportunities.
   b) contribute money to candidates for public office who favor its programs.
   c) attain favorable decisions from government on issues that it supports.
   d) seek to inform the public on the role of interest in the economy.

5. Political action committees (PACs)
   a) have declined in popularity in recent years.
   b) must disclose campaign contributions and expenditures in connection with state and local elections.
   c) may make unlimited contributions to political candidates.
   d) provide candidates with public funding for their campaign.

6. According to the text, all of the following factors are involved in the media's decision not to cover more political and governmental news except
   a) Californians are not that interested in political and governmental news.

   b) the ratings for political and governmental news are lower than other kinds of news, such as the weather, consumer news, and sports coverage.
   c) so many news programs cover California political and governmental news that there is little for each station to report.
   d) political and governmental news, except during election campaigns, does not lend itself to sensational coverage.

7. What former speaker of the California Assembly said, "Money is the mother's milk of politics?"
   a) Jesse Unruh
   b) Willie Brown
   c) Antonio Villaraigosa
   d) Fabian Nuñez

8. Over the past two decades, the number of newspapers across the United States has _____, and newspaper circulations have _____ in every recent year as well.
   a) risen, increased
   b) remained the same, increased
   c) risen, declined
   d) fallen, declined

9. Which of the following is *not* a reason for the increase in interest groups in California?
   a) divided government
   b) weakness of political parties
   c) term limits
   d) growth of public interest groups

10. Many experts see the Internet as a catalyst for _____ the democratic process.
    a) threatening
    b) enhancing
    c) having little effect on
    d) undermining

CRITICAL-THINKING QUESTIONS

1. Over the past several decades, interest groups have grown and expanded their influence over public policy decisions in the legislature and at administrative agencies. Identify the reasons for this phenomenon.

2. Interest groups use a variety of techniques to accomplish their goal. Suppose you worked for an interest group that opposed stricter requirements for the recycling of plastic bottles. Outline a campaign to achieve your goal. Justify why you would take the action you propose.

3. Some people argue that interest groups provide citizens with another way in which to become involved in the political process. Others argue that interest groups undermine the political process. Discuss the arguments for both positions. Give your opinion on the controversy.
4. Interest groups play a significant role in the funding of political campaigns. Should more restriction be put on their activity? You decide that interest groups should be limited or altogether prohibited from contributing to political campaigns. How would this policy affect political campaigns? What would be the outcome of this reform?
5. What are the factors that have led to relatively low levels of coverage of politics and government in California?

KEY TERMS

California Political Reform Act (p. 47)
citizen lobbyist (p. 44)
contract lobbyist (p. 44)
in-house lobbyist (p. 44)

interest group (p. 37)
lobbying (p. 39)
media (p. 50)
political action committee (PAC) (p. 45)

public interest group (p. 42)
third house (p. 38)
trade association (p. 40)

4 Parties and Elections in California

WHAT CALIFORNIA GOVERNMENT DOES AND WHY IT MATTERS

As described in previous chapters, the Progressive movement brought to California three important tools of direct democracy: the initiative, the referendum, and the recall. All three of these have had a fundamental impact on electoral politics in our state. More recently, there has been a spate of initiatives and referenda that have dramatically changed how and when we conduct elections. In the abstract, many of these changes and reforms appear to strengthen the democratic process in California. However, some would argue that legislating by the ballot box (using initiatives or referenda to change policy) has produced some unanticipated consequences.

As this chapter will describe, California's primary election system has been changed numerous times as a result of various propositions. First, Proposition 198 in 1996 changed our long-held primary system to a new "open" primary. This new primary system was in place for the following two primary elections. Then, the new system was overturned by the U.S. Supreme Court and we reverted to a variation of the old primary election method. In 2010, voters, unhappy with the status quo, passed Proposition 14, which once again changed our primary system, this time in a very dramatic way (described in detail in this chapter). It is believed that this new primary system might very well be challenged in the courts, as was the previous one. June 2012 was the first time voters used this new primary system.

Initiatives brought additional changes to the 2012 primary election. It was the first election that manifested the results of the implementation of Propositions 11 and 20. Proposition 11, passed in 2008, mandated the creation of an independent, bipartisan Citizens Redistricting Commission that would be responsible for redrawing the boundaries of the state Senate and state Assembly districts after each U.S. Census. Proposition 20 added to the responsibility of the commission by granting it the authority to redraw U.S. House of Representative district boundaries in the state. Predictably, groups unhappy with the law—which was adopted through direct democracy—wanted voters to overturn it. So a new referendum appeared on the November 2012 ballot statewide that aimed to undo parts of Proposition 11. This ballot measure required that voters approve the revised state Senate boundaries set by the commission. If voters fail to approve the new districts, for which we've already held elections, court-appointed officials would set interim boundaries for use in the next statewide election until permanent boundaries can be set. Voters approved the measure by a wide margin.

One has to wonder how voters feel about all of these changes brought about through the ballot box. Our primary system has been changed four times over the past nine primaries; the ballot voters now receive looks very different as a result of Proposition 14, and votes now are tallied in a very unusual way; the ballot independent voters receive could potentially change with every primary election, depending on decisions made by the qualified political parties about ballot access, and newly redrawn state and federal legislative districts have included new neighborhoods and excluded others that had been historically part of the district.

Many observers believe voters are confused with all of these changes, and the result has been a decline in voter turnout rates. Case in point: the June 2012 primary, with its proposition-mandated changes, had one of the lowest voter turnout rates in state history, with only about 31 percent of registered voters casting ballots. Typically, primaries in which none of the candidates is a viable presidential nominee do not garner a lot of voter interest, and that was the case for the June 2012 primary. However, this turnout rate of less than one-third of registered voters broke the record low of 42 percent in 1996 by a wide margin. One has to wonder if all of these changes, brought to us by the initiative and referenda, are partly responsible for this dismal rate of voter participation. We have voters passing initiatives and referenda that change, in fundamental ways, our elections. Those who disagree with the outcome produced by direct democracy bring legal challenges or again use the initiative or referendum to change or undo what the voters had passed. The march of new initiatives and referenda, and lawsuits challenging them, just seems to continue. You have to ask, Is this any way to run a democracy?

Political Parties

A political party is an organization of people with roughly similar political or ideological positions who work to win elections to take control of the government and change public policy. Political parties perform many valuable functions in a democratic society. One of their most important roles is to mobilize voters at election time, helping to get out the vote. They also function as opposition points to the policies pursued by government at all levels, thereby promoting discussion of important political issues. Parties help recruit candidates for office and play a major role in the selection process. They are directly involved in political campaigns, providing workers, raising money, and identifying important political issues. Parties help bring about consensus on important political issues and serve as two-way communication channels between government and the people. Consequently, most political scientists consider them vital to the health of a democratic state.

California has a *winner-take-all* system of voting in which the candidate receiving the highest vote wins the election. Political scientists have long known that such a system promotes two dominant political parties. As a result, two major political parties dominate the political process in California: the Republicans and the

Democrats. *Third parties*, which are defined as any party other than the Republicans and Democrats, play only a limited role in California politics, although several third parties are considered qualified and are entitled to appear on the California ballot. They are the American Independent Party, the Americans Elect Party, the Peace and Freedom Party, the Green Party, and the Libertarian Party.

Party Organizations

All political parties in California have *state central committees*, which are made up of partisan officeholders and other party officials. The average political party member or supporter is not represented by this organization. The state central committee helps build support for the party's campaign efforts. Members of *county central committees* are elected by the voters in each assembly district. They generally help in campaigns. Because of the Progressive reforms, state and county committees are weak and play a diminished role in the party's affairs.

The Progressive Impact on Political Parties

The Progressive movement viewed political parties as corrupt organizations operating in concert with big corporations with the intent of controlling and manipulating the political system for their own benefit. Spencer Olin describes the attitude that Progressives had toward political parties:

> Accompanying their democratic faith in the wisdom of the individual voter was a distrust of formal party organizations, which were viewed as the media of special-interest power. . . . Furthermore, it was argued by progressives that science and efficient management would solve the problems of government; parties were irrelevant and unnecessary.[1]

The Progressives attacked the power of the political parties with reforms such as party primaries. Primaries were designed to take the power to select candidates for office away from the parties and put it into the hands of voters. The primary system also opened up the opportunity to run for office to anyone capable of meeting the basic qualifications, such as age and residency requirements. Instead of the party leadership and their corporate allies having the power to select candidates and subsequently manipulate them while they held office, the people now participated in a whole new class of elections, forcing candidates to direct their political messages and loyalty to the average voter.

Nonpartisan elections further weakened parties by preventing party designations from appearing on the ballot. Voters were no longer able to use their party loyalties to make voting decisions on Election Day at the county and city level. The Progressives wanted the electorate to do its homework and find out about the candidates. Instead of a party label on the ballot, voters were to be given only the current occupational status of the candidate. This meant that voters had to inform themselves by reading up on the candidates or even attending a candidate's forum.

The Progressives also installed a new ballot, the *office block ballot*. This type of ballot made it difficult to vote the straight party ticket, which was easy in many other states. Ballots that favored voting for one party, or voting the *straight ticket*, listed all the candidates running for each office by party. The use of the office block ballot in California discourages such behavior by listing each office separately and requiring the voter to make his or her choice.

The weakening of political parties in the form of nonpartisan elections at the county and city levels are believed to have an impact on voters. Contrary to the beliefs of the Progressives, voters are not known to devote a lot of time conducting research on each candidate in an attempt to determine how to cast their vote. However, we do know that voters who identify with a political party view the party affiliation of candidates as important and this information helps them in their vote decision. Typically, county and city races are not exciting, high-profile contests, and not allowing candidates to have their party label on the ballot means voters don't have that additional information to assist them in their vote choice. Researchers have found that a voter's attachment to a political party also may motivate them to vote. As Schaffner, Streb, and Wright describe it, "party identification is a, or even the, central component of voter decision making. As an effective attachment, it motivates individuals to participate as a display of party support."[2] Therefore, nonpartisan elections may have lower turnout rates than partisan ones.

Third Parties in California

Voters in California have long had the opportunity to vote for third-party candidates. In the 2012 presidential race, voters could vote for the Republican or Democratic candidates or for the candidates of four other parties: the American Independent Party, Green Party, Libertarian Party, and the Peace and Freedom Party.

Traditionally, third-party candidates do not win in a *winner-take-all* system like that in the United States. Both major parties make much of the fact that third parties do not win and warn voters against throwing their votes away. However, a significant percentage of voters reject their advice and continue to vote for third-party candidates anyway.

The American political system, which is a *federal system*, delegates power to three levels of government: national, state, and local. One of the powers that states retain is to determine how political parties may organize and gain access to the ballot. Because the legislature in California is dominated by the Republicans and Democrats, they have not made it easy for third parties to qualify to get on the ballot. As a consequence, California politics is almost totally dominated by the Republicans and Democrats.

There are two ways that political parties can qualify to get on the ballot in California. The first method is by *registration*; the second is by *petition*. Both methods are based on a percentage of those persons who voted in the last preceding gubernatorial election. In the election held in November 2010, some 10,300,392 persons turned out to vote. To qualify a new party by the registration method, the law requires that 103,004 persons or 1 percent of those who voted in the 2010 gubernatorial election officially register with the new party. The law also requires that the registrations be completed and mailed in by the 154th day preceding the upcoming primary. The second option, the petition method, is even more difficult and tedious. It requires a new political party to collect signatures equal to 10 percent of those who voted in the last gubernatorial election on petitions asking that the party be included in the upcoming primary. Currently, that number stands at over 1 million signatures. Obviously, qualifying as a new political party is not an easy task and requires time, manpower, expertise, and resources.

So what is the role of third parties in politics, particularly in California? One theory is that third parties act as spoilers. They may draw enough votes from one or the other of the two major parties to alter the election outcome. Third parties also help focus public attention on important political issues. Once an issue attracts

BOX 4.1 | **Qualified Political Parties in California**

AMERICAN INDEPENDENT PARTY	www.aipca.org
AMERICANS ELECT PARTY	www.americanselect.org
DEMOCRATIC PARTY	www.cadem.org
GREEN PARTY	www.cagreens.org
LIBERTARIAN PARTY	www.ca.lp.org
PEACE AND FREEDOM PARTY	www.peaceandfreedom.org
REPUBLICAN PARTY	www.cagop.org

enough public attention, it will be taken over by one or both of the two major political parties. Altering election outcomes and raising political issues relegates third parties to a lesser role in politics. Whether that will change over time remains to be seen. Box 4.1 provides the URLs of those parties currently qualified in California.

Party Affiliation of California Voters

A plurality of California voters identify with the Democratic Party. As of October 2012, about 44 percent of voters are registered with the Democratic Party compared to 29 percent affiliated with the Republican Party. A substantial 21 percent of voters have no party preference, and 6 percent identify with one of the minor parties. Party affiliation is fairly easy to determine in the state, because when you register to vote, you are asked to declare your political party. Of the seven political parties that have qualified for the ballot in California, two are major parties and five are minor or third parties. The Democratic and Republican parties receive the lion's share of votes and members.

As Figure 4.1 illustrates, since 1996, registration in the two major political parties has declined. Identification with the Democratic Party declined by only 3 percent compared to an 8 percent decline in those registering with the Republican Party. The most dramatic change has been among those who have no political party preference (also referred to as independent voters). This group has nearly doubled its size over the past 16 years; now more than one in five voters claim no party preference when they register to vote.

Now let us look at political-party affiliation and some demographic factors. Figure 4.2 presents the results of a California statewide survey conducted in July 2012 that asked respondents about their party affiliation, age, gender, race, educational level, and place of birth. The results suggest that nearly 45 percent of all young, middle-aged, and older Californians prefer the Democratic Party. Younger

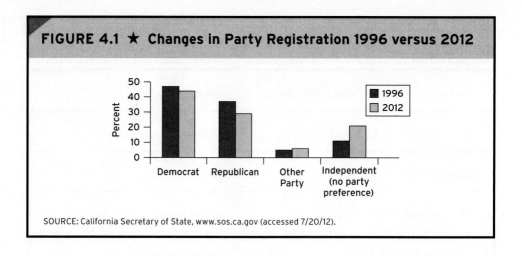

FIGURE 4.1 ★ Changes in Party Registration 1996 versus 2012

SOURCE: California Secretary of State, www.sos.ca.gov (accessed 7/20/12).

people are less inclined than are middle-aged and older people to affiliate with the Republican Party (19 percent compared to 36 percent and 34 percent), and younger people appear to be more likely than the other age groups not to affiliate with one of the major political parties, with 30 percent registering as independents. Conversely, a recent California Field Poll (2011) found that the Republican Party is becoming the party of senior citizens. Currently, those 50 years of age or older make up 54 percent of the party, and this number is growing annually as the population ages. Many are questioning what the Republican Party of the future will look like in California with the passing of these older Republicans. Will the party be able to survive this demographic trend?

We also observe gender differences in party affiliation, with a majority of women affiliating with the Democratic Party (compared to 37 percent of men) and more men than women registering as independents (27 percent and 16 percent, respectively). Educational level seems to have an impact on party preference. Regardless of educational level, the Democratic Party has more support than the Republican Party. However, a majority of those with a high school degree or less prefer the Democratic Party, and only 26 percent in this category identify with the Republican Party. Latinos, by over a 40 percent margin, prefer the Democratic Party over the Republican Party (57 percent Democratic versus 15 percent Republican), while whites are evenly split between the Democratic Party and the Republican Party (40 percent Democratic versus 39 percent Republican). In comparing the U.S.-born to immigrants, more U.S.-born Californians prefer the Republican Party (32 percent to 25 percent) and nearly equal numbers of U.S.-born and immigrants support the Democratic Party. It is interesting that more of the foreign-born identify themselves as independents, 27 percent, compared to 20 percent of U.S.-born.

Some of these demographic trends suggest that politics in our state will change in the future. Older white males' proportionate decline in the population will continue to have an impact on the Republican Party, a party that will continue to lose a large segment of its support. It is important to note another impact of changing demographics: the Latino population is increasing, and this portends well for the future of the Democratic Party. Recently released Census data showed that from 2000 to 2010 the Latino population grew by nearly 28 percent to 14 million, whereas the white population declined more than 5 percent to just under 15 million. Currently, Latinos favor the Democratic Party over the Republican Party by sizable percentages, and there is no reason to expect this to change in the future. Many are predicting an even stronger Democratic Party presence in the state.

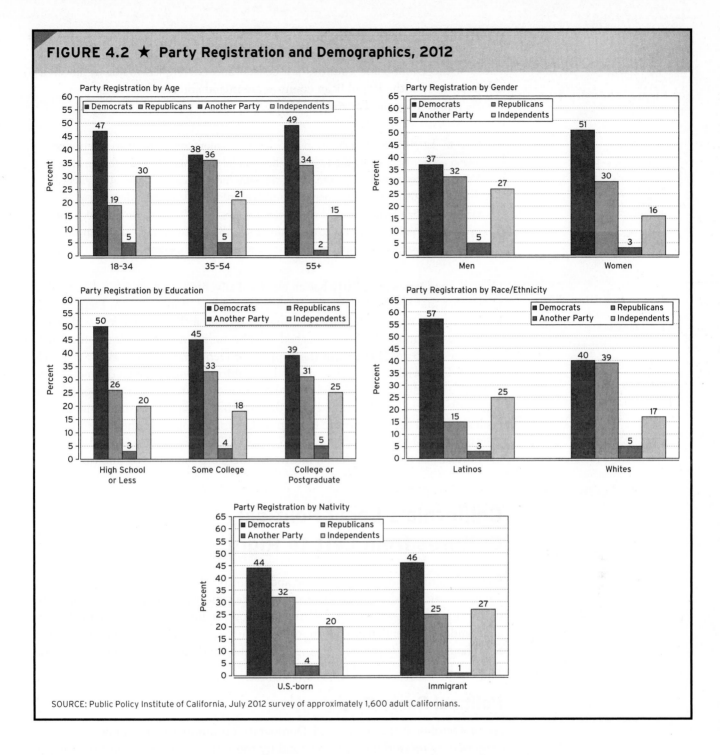

FIGURE 4.2 ★ Party Registration and Demographics, 2012

Party Registration by Age

Party Registration by Gender

Party Registration by Education

Party Registration by Race/Ethnicity

Party Registration by Nativity

SOURCE: Public Policy Institute of California, July 2012 survey of approximately 1,600 adult Californians.

THE RED AND THE BLUE IN CALIFORNIA Thinking back to the presidential election of 2012, you may recall that most television programs focusing on the election outcome had maps of the United States color-coded to represent the states that voted Republican (red) and those states that voted Democratic (blue). The map was very interesting—the West Coast and most of the Northeast as well as major urban areas of the United States were blue (Democratic) and the South, agricultural regions, and the Great Plains states were red (Republican). The map nicely illustrated the national split between urban areas, predominantly Democratic, and rural, agricultural, and suburban areas, mostly Republican.

As the map in Figure 4.3 shows, the same geographic split appears within the state of California—a split between the coastal counties and the inland counties. Most of the Democratic counties are coastal and encompass major urban areas, whereas most of the Republican counties are inland and rural.

As reported by the *Los Angeles Times*:

> Over the last decade, Republican influence has grown more concentrated in conservative inland California—largely the Central Valley and Inland Empire but also the Antelope Valley, the Sierra and rural north. . . . At the same time Democrats have strengthened their domination of counties along California's coastline, building overwhelming advantages in the San Francisco and Los Angeles areas as Latino voters have expanded the party's base. And from San Diego's beachfront suburbs to the Central Coast, Democrats have eroded Republican support among moderates, especially women.[3]

Overall, the Democratic Party has an electoral advantage in California, largely due to the fact that nearly 70 percent of the state's population resides in Democratic-leaning coastal regions. Republicans have an uphill battle winning statewide elections and are more likely to succeed if they nominate ideologically moderate candidates who are able to win the support of Democratic voters. What this suggests for California's political future is that California will remain a distinctly blue state. The fact that the urban and coastal population centers are largely Democratic and moderate to liberal, coupled with the fact that a majority of independent voters lean toward the Democratic Party, puts California solidly in the "blue" column. This is not to suggest that all populated coastal regions are the same politically and ideologically. As the next section illustrates, there are some interesting variations.

California's Local Political Cultures from Left to Right

Political culture is difficult to define and quantify. However, we can offer at least a few statistics to show how three of the state's most populous counties differ in terms of political partisanship, political ideology, political activism, political tolerance, and voting tendencies on important issues. Table 4.1 compares and contrasts San Francisco City/County, Los Angeles County, and San Diego County on those selected indicators of local political culture.

Political Party Registration

As of October 2012, registered Democrats outnumbered Republicans in San Francisco by more than six to one and by more than two to one in Los Angeles County. In San Diego County, however, Republicans and Democrats were nearly equal at 34 and 35 percent, respectively.

Political Ideology

Based on community surveys conducted in late 2000, about one in five San Franciscans identify themselves politically as "very liberal" and only 4 percent as "very conservative." In both Los Angeles County and San Diego County, conservatives outnumber liberals by about two to one.[4]

FIGURE 4.3 ★ Percent Difference between Democratic and Republican Registration by County (2012 Presidential Election)

SOURCE: California Secretary of State, October 22, 2012, www.sos.ca.gov.

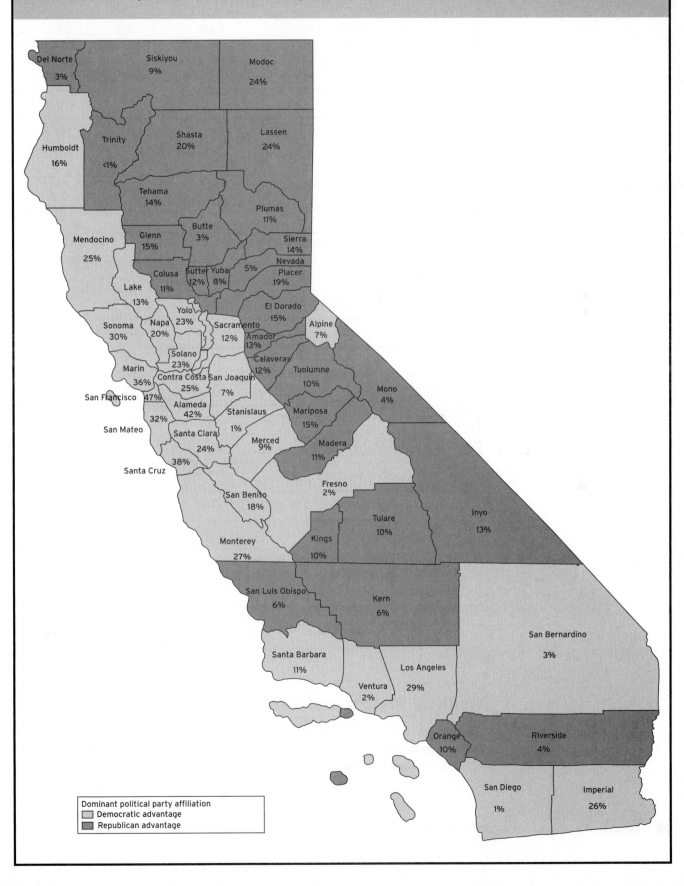

Dominant political party affiliation
- Democratic advantage
- Republican advantage

TABLE 4.1 ★ Regional Political Cultures: Three California Counties Compared from Left to Right

INDICATOR	SAN FRANCISCO	LOS ANGELES	SAN DIEGO
1. Percent Democrats (2012)	56	51	35
2. Percent Republicans (2012)	9	22	34
3. Percent very liberal (2000)	21	8	6
4. Percent very conservative (2000)	4	15	14
5. Percent high protest activity (2000)	47	30	30
6. Percent voter turnout (Nov. 4, 2008)	79	77	84
7. Percent voter turnout (Nov. 2, 2010)	62	53	64
8. Percent voter turnout (Nov. 6, 2012)	57	52	56
9. Percent yes on Proposition 13 (1978)	47	67	60
10. Percent yes on Proposition 187 (1994)	29	56	68
11. Percent yes on Proposition 209 (1996)	29	45	63
12. Percent yes on Proposition 215 (1996)	78	56	52
13. Percent yes on Proposition 22 (2000)	32	59	63
14. Percent yes on Proposition 8 (2008)	25	50	54
15. Percent yes on Proposition 30 (2012)	77	60	46
16. Percent yes on Proposition 34 (2012)	70	54	45
17. Percent vote Brown for governor (2010)	79	63	44
18. Percent vote Whitman for governor (2010)	18	32	50
19. Percent vote Obama for president (2012)	83	69	51

SOURCES: Indicators 1-2, 6-18: California Secretary of State, various official statements of vote. Indicators 3-5: Analysis of sample survey data obtained from the Social Capital Benchmark Survey 2000.

Political Protest and Voter Turnout

Those same surveys show that San Franciscans are much more inclined to engage in political protest than are their counterparts in the southland. Specifically, 47 percent of San Francisco citizens scored "high" on a nationally normed political protest activity index, as compared with only 30 percent in both Los Angeles and San

Diego Counties. In terms of more conventional forms of political participation, however, San Diego County's citizens are on top, with higher voter turnout rates than San Franciscans and Angelenos in both the November 4, 2008, general election and the November 2, 2010, general election. The November 6, 2012, general election saw both San Diego and San Francisco with near equal turnout rates, with Los Angeles lagging behind.

Support for Proposition 13

Proposition 13, the 1978 initiative that rolled back property tax rates and limited the government's ability to raise local property taxes in the future, regarded by some observers "as one of the most significant political events in California's history,"[5] won by a landslide vote nearly everywhere throughout the state, including a 67 percent yes vote in Los Angeles County and a 60 percent vote in San Diego County. In San Francisco, however, it mustered only 47 percent, not even a majority.

Political Tolerance and Support for Racial and Cultural Diversity

Table 4.1 reports county voting results on seven different statewide ballot propositions over the period 1994–2012. All seven can be viewed as indicators of political tolerance and support for racial and cultural diversity.

- Proposition 187 was a 1994 initiative constitutional amendment that made undocumented immigrants ineligible for various public social services. The state's voters approved it by a wide margin, with 56 percent voting yes in Los Angeles County and 68 percent in San Diego County. Only 29 percent voted for it in San Francisco.

- Proposition 209 was a 1996 initiative constitutional amendment that prohibited state and local government agencies from giving preferential treatment to any individual or group on the basis of race, sex, color, ethnicity, or national origin. Widely viewed by friends and foes alike as an attack on affirmative action, this measure also passed in the statewide vote, with 63 percent support in San Diego County. It received only 45 percent in Los Angeles County, however, and a mere 29 percent in San Francisco.

- Proposition 215 was a 1996 initiative statute that permitted the medicinal use of marijuana. This measure passed in the statewide vote, but only barely in San Diego County with 52 percent, more comfortably in Los Angeles County with 56 percent, and by a landslide 78 percent vote in San Francisco.

- Proposition 22 was a 2000 initiative statute declaring that only marriage between a man and a woman is valid or recognized in California. This measure was approved by a landslide statewide vote, with 59 percent support in Los Angeles County and 63 percent in San Diego County. In San Francisco, however, a resounding 68 percent voted no.

- Proposition 8 was a 2008 initiative constitutional amendment that eliminated the right of same-sex couples to marry. Backers of the proposition placed it on the ballot as a direct challenge to the California Supreme Court's ruling in May 2008 affirming the constitutionality of same-sex marriage. The measure was approved 52 to 48 percent in the statewide vote. Only 25 percent of San Francisco County's voters voted yes, however, compared with 50 percent in Los Angeles County and 54 percent in San Diego County.

- Proposition 30 was a 2012 initiative constitutional amendment that would temporarily raise taxes to fund education. Personal income taxes would increase on those earnings over $250,000 for seven years and the sales tax would increase by .25 cent for four years. This increased state revenue would be used to fund education at the K-12, community college, and university levels. Teacher unions and Governor Brown campaigned aggressively for the passage of this initiative. Failure of the proposition would result in extensive budget cuts to the already struggling public school and university systems. Proposition 30 was approved statewide by a 54-to-46 percent vote. Over three-quarters of San Francisco voters approved of the measure, as did 60 percent of Los Angeles county voters. In San Diego, however, only 46 percent voted yes.

- Proposition 34 was an initiative statute asking voters to approve the repeal of the death penalty and replace it with life imprisonment without the possibility of parole. This measure would apply retroactively to those inmates currently on death row. The measure failed to pass with a statewide vote of only 47 percent. Contrary to the statewide vote, 70 percent of voters in San Francisco and 54 percent of voters in Los Angeles voted in favor of this measure. In San Diego county, only 45 percent voted yes.

The Presidential Election of 2008

In the November 4, 2008, presidential election, California voters supported Barack Obama in a landslide over John McCain by 61 to 37 percent. Majorities in all three counties voted for Obama, with San Francisco County leading the pack with 84 percent for Obama, followed by Los Angeles County at 61 percent and San Diego County at 54 percent.

The Gubernatorial and U.S. Senate Elections of 2010

In the 2010 race for governor, the winner, Democrat Jerry Brown, easily beat Republican Meg Whitman, 79 percent to 18 percent in San Francisco and 63 percent 32 percent in Los Angeles County. In San Diego County, however, Whitman beat Brown 50 percent to 44 percent. In the race for U.S. Senate that year, the winner incumbent Democrat Barbara Boxer handily defeated Republican Carly Fiorina, 80 percent to 16 percent in San Francisco and 62 percent to 33 percent in Los Angeles County. But in San Diego County, Fiorina came out on top, 51 percent to 44 percent.

The Presidential Election of 2012

In the November 6, 2012, presidential election, voters preferred President Barack Obama over former Massachusetts Governor Mitt Romney by 59 to 38 percent. San Francisco county overwhelmingly voted for President Obama with a resounding 83 percent, voters in Los Angeles county supported him at 69 percent, and San Diego county at 51 percent.

To Sum Up

The statistics in Table 4.1 show that political life varies dramatically in California from region to region. If you happen to reside in San Francisco, you live in one of the nation's most liberal, tolerant, and activist political cultures.[6] The political environment in San Diego County, on the other hand, is more conservative, less tolerant, and more passive. Los Angeles County falls somewhere between these two extremes. These three counties reflect the range of political cultural differences that exist across the state. You can easily see why local representatives in the state legislature fight so much and so fiercely and have a very hard time agreeing on anything.

Elections in California

The Battle over the Primary

The past decade has seen much controversy, upheaval, and court challenges regarding the type of primary system used in California. In primary elections, voters cast votes to select who will run as their party's nominees in the general election. In the United States, there are three general types of primary-election systems, and states have the authority to determine which system they will operate under.

- *Closed primary system*—Only voters who declare a party affiliation when they register to vote are permitted to vote in their party's primary election. Each party has its own ballot, listing the names of the candidates from their party competing to be the party's candidate in the general election. Registered Democrats receive the Democratic ballot, registered Republicans receive the Republican ballot, and voters registered with minor parties receive their party's ballot. Voters who decline to state a party affiliation when they register are not eligible to receive a party ballot because it is only party members who have the privilege of electing the party's nominees.

- *Open primary system*—Registered voters, regardless of their party affiliation, can vote in the party primary of their choice on primary election day. As an example, a registered Democrat can decide he or she would like to vote in the Republican Party primary and request that ballot. The choice of party ballot on primary election day does not affect the voter's permanent party affiliation. Approximately 20 states operate under this system.

- *Blanket primary system*—One ballot lists all candidates from all of the parties. All registered voters, including those not affiliated with any party, are permitted to vote, and all voters receive the same ballot. For instance, a voter who is not affiliated with a party may vote for a Democrat to run as the nominee for governor and a Republican to run as the nominee for the U.S. Senate. Under this system, voters who are not affiliated with a party help choose that party's nominees. Alaska, Louisiana, and Washington State all use this primary system.

California operated under the closed primary system until the passage of Proposition 198 in 1996 (incorrectly named the "Open Primary" proposition). Proposition 198 instituted a blanket primary system in which all voters received a single ballot containing the names of all candidates from all parties. California held two blanket primaries—in June 1998 and March 2000—before the U.S. Supreme Court (in the case of *California Democratic Party v. Jones*) invalidated Proposition 198. The Court ruled that, based on the First Amendment's guarantee of freedom of association, California's political parties did have a right to exclude nonparty members from voting in party primaries. In an effort to include the growing number of nonaffiliated voters, California adopted a *modified closed primary system*. Beginning with the March 2002 primary election, political parties still had their own party ballots but now had the option of adopting a party rule that would allow unaffiliated voters to vote in their party primary. If an unaffiliated voter is not allowed to request a party's ballot, he or she is given a ballot containing only the names of candidates for nonpartisan races and ballot measures.

Proponents of the blanket primary were not satisfied with the modified closed primary system, arguing that the blanket primary system is the most inclusive one and would result in more-moderate candidates running in primary elections, thus producing more competitive races. The logic is that if independent, ideologically moderate voters participate in the primary election, they will bring a counterbalance to the more extreme and ideological views of traditional primary party voters, the party loyalists. Primary candidates would, therefore, need to moderate their positions to attract the votes of moderate, independent voters. So, in June 2010, voters once more passed a proposition that changes California's primary-election system.

Proposition 14 mandates a form of a blanket primary system known as the "top-two vote getters" system. This primary system would be used for state legislative and congressional seats as well as for statewide offices, such as governor and attorney general. All registered voters, even those stating no party preference, receive a ballot listing all candidates from all qualified political parties. The top two vote getters for each office are then in a runoff in November's general election. An interesting feature of this new primary election system is the possibility that the top two vote getters could be of the same political party, resulting in two Democrats or two Republicans competing against each other in the general election. California's new primary system does not apply to candidates running for the U.S. president, county central committee, or local offices. The June 5, 2012, primary election was the first statewide election held under this new system, and the results were quite interesting. Of the 53 primary elections for U.S. House seats, 8 of these races resulted in candidates from the same party being the top-two vote getters: November 2012 had 6 contests with Democrats pitted against each other and 2 contests featuring Republican candidates competing against each other. Of the 20 primary contests for the California state Senate, 5 resulted in November match-ups between two of the same party members (Democrats), and for the state Assembly, we had 15 contests with Democrats going head to head and 6 contests with two Republicans battling for the Assembly seat.

This new primary system also allows candidates to designate whether they have a political party preference and how it should be stated on the ballot. According to California law, "a candidate for nomination to a voter-nominated office shall have his or her party preference, or lack of party preference, stated on the ballot, but the party preference designation is selected solely by the candidate." What this means is that candidates can state the party they identify with or they can state they don't have a party preference. In this age of voter frustration, directed at party politics and legislative gridlock, having the ballot state "Party Preference: None" appears to be a strategy adopted by some candidates. This is what happened in a race for a hotly contested congressional seat in Ventura County. The redrawing of the state's congressional district boundaries created a new swing district in this area. A *swing district* is one in which there are near equal numbers of Republican and Democratic voters and a significant number of independent voters. This new district consisted of 41 percent Democrats, 35 percent Republicans, and 19 percent with no party preference (independent voters). In this type of a district it is usually the independent voters who often decide the winner. There is no electoral edge given to either party candidate—the district is competitive. There were four Democrats, one Republican, and one independent (no party preference) running in this primary. The "independent" candidate was actually a Republican who switched her party registration to no party preference just before filing her papers to run, hoping to win the support of enough independent and moderate voters to be one of the top two winners. A number of candidates have used this strategy, hoping voters wouldn't remember or even know that they had been party loyalists before the campaign. Unfortunately for this candidate, the only Republican on the ballot and the better-known Democrat captured the top two positions and competed against each other in the November general election.

Will this new primary system have the intended impact of encouraging more moderate candidates running in primaries and being elected to office? Louisiana and Washington operate under similar primary systems, and analyses of their election outcomes found that these states have not experienced the election of more moderate candidates. However, some argue that blanket primaries can boost voter turnout by 3 to 6 percent by attracting voters with no party preference. It is too soon to tell the impact of this new primary system on California electoral politics.

Presidential Primaries: Maximizing California's Clout?

Until 2000, California held its presidential primaries in June of election years, one of the last states to cast its votes for the parties' nominees. It was often the case that states holding earlier primaries and caucuses determined who the presidential nominees were before Californians had a chance to go to the polls. To have more influence in the nomination process, California changed its presidential primary election date to early March. Many believed it was only fitting that the most populous state should have an early primary date. Sadly, this earlier primary date did not result in California voters' having more clout in the presidential nomination process, as other states moved their primaries to even earlier dates. So California changed its primary date back to June, effective 2006. However, for the 2008 presidential primaries, California changed the date once again, from June 3 to February 5, the earliest permissible date under national party rules.

Many political analysts and journalists heralded the early-February presidential primary date. But did this move really have the intended impact, as hopefully reflected in a 2007 *Los Angeles Times* article titled, "Earlier Primary Gives California a Major Voice"? Many who had argued for the early-February 2008 presidential primary believed that candidates would have to campaign early and hard in the Golden State and would have to win support from a very racially and ethnically diverse population, especially the growing number of Latino voters. To win voters' support, issues important to Californians would need to be addressed, and all this would result in California's greater prominence in presidential campaign politics. Or so the theory went.

One of the unanticipated consequences of California's adoption of an early primary date was that a number of states with long-standing early primaries set their election dates even earlier, not wanting to be overshadowed by the most populous state in the nation. And 23 other states also moved their primaries to February 5, resulting in something akin to a national primary. California's dream of being in the electoral limelight quickly faded.

Another consequence of the early-February primary was that the June 2008 primary election for statewide offices cost the state and counties $100 million and resulted in a historically low voting turnout rate of less than 25 percent of the registered voters. Including the November 2008 general election, California voters were asked to vote in three elections in less than 10 months. Now California's presidential primary is once again back to the June date. Some believe this frequent changing of primary election dates contributes to California's less than spectacular voting turnout rates because voters might be confused as to when elections will be held.

Initiative Campaigns: Direct Democracy or Tool of Special Interests?

One legacy of California's early-twentieth-century reform movement is the initiative process. Californians can completely bypass the state legislature, their elected representatives, and place proposed policies on the ballot for direct vote by the people. As the name suggests, the electorate *initiates* initiatives. Most people think of the initiative process as direct democracy in action—concerned citizens circulate petitions to qualify their issue for the ballot and then hold an election allowing the public to state its preference for or against the proposed policy. In reality, only a small number of ballot initiatives emerge as a result of grassroots efforts. Initiatives are largely a political tool used by special-interest groups to achieve their policy goals. Depending on the issue, interest groups sometimes find it politically expedient to bypass the legislature altogether, believing they have a better chance of achieving their policy goals if they take the issue directly to the voters.

For example, many members of the California legislature would find it politically unwise to introduce legislation that would legalize marijuana or abolish the death penalty or raise taxes. Positions on these issues are sure to outrage some voters, making reelection more difficult. That is why these types of issues find their way onto our ballots as initiatives or referendums. Likewise, legislation that would curb the power of special interests, interests that make sizable campaign contributions to legislators, also are unlikely to be dealt with by our elected representatives. Recently, some local ballot measures have passed that reduce retirement benefits of public employees. If an elected official introduced this type of proposal, he or she would be targeted by unions representing public employees for reelection defeat. So, for many of these types of issues, interest groups realize the most productive route is to go directly to the voters via the initiative process. In addition, citizen groups have found the initiative process to be the only avenue for policy change in the areas of legislative term limits, nonpartisan redistricting, and the blanket primary system. These changes would never have been proposed or approved by legislators because these reforms would curb their own and their political party's powers.

Since 1912, the first year initiatives were permitted, over 350 statewide initiatives have appeared on the California ballot. These ballot initiatives have dealt with a wide range of issues, such as legalization of marijuana, campaign finance reform, same-sex marriage, taxation policy, legalization of gambling casinos, the establishment of a state lottery, environmental regulations, affirmative action policy, the criminal justice system, and labor issues. Of these hundreds of initiatives, only about one-third have been approved by the voters. In the past three decades, there has been a dramatic surge in the number of initiatives that have been proposed and that have qualified for the ballot. Many surmise that the reason for this increase is that special interests have become more sophisticated in their use of the initiative process to achieve their policy goals.

To qualify for the ballot, the state requires over 500,000 signatures of registered voters for initiatives creating new laws (statutes) and over 800,000 signatures for propositions that aim to amend the state constitution. Signatures are gathered on petitions, which are then submitted to the secretary of state's office for verification. Collecting hundreds of thousands of signatures of registered voters is a daunting task. Rarely is this a grassroots movement in which ordinary citizens fan out across the state, knock on doors, and stand in front of supermarkets, asking strangers to support their initiative by signing a petition. More common is the hiring of professional signature gatherers. There are political consulting firms who specialize in this very activity. They hire individuals to go to college campuses, supermarkets, malls, and other places where voters congregate, and they are paid an average of $1.50 per signature for every signature they acquire. This means that it costs over $750,000 just to collect the signatures to qualify a proposition for the ballot.

For the more controversial initiatives, in order to wage a successful campaign either in support of or in opposition to an initiative, one needs to have ample political resources. Money is probably the most important of these resources. Not only must a statewide initiative campaign hire political consultants, but it must also plan and implement a sustainable media campaign. Such campaigns are very costly because of California's size and expensive media markets. Therefore, it is not surprising to find the more high-profile and controversial initiative campaigns costing tens of millions of dollars. In 2008 slightly over $60 million was spent on the highly controversial initiative Proposition 8, a constitutional amendment that would eliminate same-sex marriage in California. Proposition 8 was put on the ballot in response to the State Supreme Court's May 2008 ruling (4–3) declaring that the state constitution protects a fundamental "right to marry" that extends equally to same-sex couples. Both sides of the issue collected near equal sums of contributions totaling $74 million, with the majority of the contributions in support of Proposition 8 coming from members of the Mormon Church throughout the United States.[7] As expensive as Proposition 8 was, it did not break the record for the most expensive initiative campaign. In 2006 both sides spent more than $150 million on Proposition 87, the alternative energy initiative, which was soundly defeated by a 55 percent vote. This was, by far, the most expensive proposition campaign not only in California history but in U.S. history.

It should be noted, however, that spending more money than the opposing side does not always guarantee victory. Case in point: Proposition 19, the legalization of marijuana initiative on the November 2010 ballot. Proponents had raised and spent nearly $4 million on the yes campaign, whereas the opposition spent only a paltry $300,000 in defeating this measure.

Political savvy is another important resource. The chances of winning an initiative campaign increase if one understands how the game is played. For example, the naming of the proposition can increase its chance of passage. In the November 1996 election, Proposition 209, officially titled "Prohibition against Discrimination or Preferential Treatment by State and Other Public Entities," appeared on the ballot. Its supporters referred to the proposition as the "California Civil Rights Initiative." Considering these titles alone, it would be difficult to imagine this proposition failing; in these progressive times, it is fair to say that most voters are opposed to discrimination and are supportive of civil rights. However, in reality, Proposition 209 was not what most would consider to be a civil rights statute. The proposition proposed to eliminate affirmative action programs in California for women and minorities in public employment, education (college admissions, tutoring, and outreach programs), and contracting. Proposition 209 passed and is now state law.

Critics of the initiative process believe that too many complicated issues are presented to the voters as ballot propositions. In some recent elections, voters have had to vote for candidates for federal, state, county, and city elective offices as well as cast their votes for over a dozen important state propositions and numerous county and city measures.

Some argue that many of the issues that appear as ballot initiatives are best suited for debate and deliberation by our elected representatives and should not be decided by misleading television ads aimed at the public. Sometimes the propositions are very confusing in name and in substance, and some question whether we are asking too much of the electorate to wade through all this information. Another problem with the initiative process is that the constitutionality of many propositions approved by the voters is later challenged. It takes years for the courts to render a decision, and it is not uncommon for the courts to declare the law based on the passage of the proposition to be unconstitutional, null, and void. Not only does this complicate the process; it also frustrates the public who voted for a new policy only to see the courts invalidate the public's will.

The legislature understands some of the problems associated with the initiative process and has created state commissions to investigate and reform the process. Some suggested reforms have been to prohibit the use of paid signature gatherers whom only the well-funded interest groups are able to afford; to increase the number of signatures required in an effort to reduce the number of initiatives; to restrict the types of issues that can appear as ballot initiatives; and to review the constitutionality of initiatives prior to placing them on the ballot. Although there have been a couple of commissions to examine these ideas, none of these reforms has been adopted.

The 2003 Gubernatorial Recall Election: A Perfect Political Storm

On October 7, 2003, Governor Gray Davis made history. Only 11 months after he successfully won his reelection bid, he was recalled from office. He was the first and only governor in the state of California and the second governor in the nation's history to be recalled. The recall movement and election of Arnold Schwarzenegger was in every sense dramatic, historic, and stunning.

Davis was reelected in November 2002, thanks to a very weak challenger, even though just before the election a majority of voters disapproved of his overall performance as governor.[8] Voters held Governor Davis responsible for the 2000–01 energy crisis during which Californians had to reduce their energy consumption while experiencing or being threatened by blackouts and, to add insult to injury, had to pay more for their electricity. News reports focused on this issue for many months and this issue had a negative impact on Davis's popularity. Compounding the problem was a dramatic decrease in state revenues. The governor had to announce that the state was short $23.6 billion and the 2003–04 budget shortfall would rise to nearly $35 billion. The state legislature could not produce a budget on time and voters were very uneasy about the economic future of the state. Davis entered his second term as a wounded, unpopular governor, viewed as distant, too beholden to special interests, and ineffectual.

Darrell Issa, a multimillionaire Republican member of Congress from the San Diego area, was a dominant force in the movement to recall Davis. He injected nearly $2 million into the recall effort and had hopes of running for governor if the recall succeeded. Nearly 1.5 million voter signatures were collected on recall petitions, meeting the state requirement for an October 2003 recall election. Unfortunately for Representative Issa's hopes of capturing the governorship, appearing on the scene was a well-known, highly likable, charismatic, moderate Republican antipolitician, antiestablishment actor/businessman: Arnold Schwarzenegger. In the summer of 2003, Schwarzenegger announced his candidacy and immediately became the front-runner among Republican candidates, making national and international headlines with his decision to run.[9] Politically, it was the making of a perfect storm: a weak and unpopular governor, an unhappy electorate, and an internationally known celebrity. Schwarzenegger was elected governor and was reelected again in November 2006. An unpopular war, a series of corruption and sex scandals implicating prominent Republican officeholders, and an unpopular president all contributed to the defeat of Republican candidates in the 2006 national elections. In contrast, Schwarzenegger won his reelection bid by a whopping 17 percent margin. His adoption of moderate positions—pro-choice on abortion, moderate on the environment, and cooperating with the Democratically controlled state legislature—placed him in sync with voters, resulting in his reelection victory.

The 2008 Election: Demographic and Ideological Shifts

The 2008 election was somewhat unusual, even by California standards. A very popular, young, charismatic candidate, Barack Obama, topped the ticket as the Democratic candidate for the presidency, winning 61 percent of the popular vote, the biggest margin in the state of California since 1964.

The *Los Angeles Times*, in an article aptly titled "State's Shifting Political Landscape," described the election results:

> Those unpredictable decisions by voters, however, were accompaniments to the election's main theme: the demographic and ideological shifts that have delivered the state into Democratic hands and demonstrated anew the tough road ahead for the Republican minority.[10]

The Democratic Party was hopeful that it could continue to win the support and allegiance of the overwhelming number of voters who cast their votes for Obama, especially 83 percent of first-time voters. Seventy-six percent of those 18–29 years of age voted for Obama compared to only 48 percent of those 65 and older. However, some analysts were not confident that future elections would see high percentages of young voters turning out to vote or see substantial increases in support for the Democratic Party.

By November 2, 2010, the evidence was in. The lead headline from Scott Fahey's *Elections 2010* blog from Southern California Public Radio read, "Low youth voter turnout hurts Democrats." As he described it, "In California, one of every five voters in 2008 was between the ages of 18 and 29, compared with about 1 in 10 on Tuesday." California reflected the overall national trend with fewer young, liberal, and black voters casting votes in the November 2010 general election.

The 2010 General Election

While the nation witnessed a historic "shellacking" of the Democratic Party, as President Obama called it, with an unprecedented loss of Democratically held seats in Congress, Californians voted to the beat of a different drummer. All of the Democratic candidates running for statewide elective office won and nearly all won by respectable margins. The *Los Angeles Times*, in an analysis of the vote based on exit poll data, concluded that the strength of the Latino vote was a key factor in the success of Democratic candidates. Latino voters made up 22 percent of the California voter pool, a record tally that mortally wounded many Republicans.

THE GOVERNOR'S RACE The costliest statewide race in the nation's history pitted novice politician and billionaire Meg Whitman against political insider Jerry Brown. Whitman spent a record-breaking $160 million on her general election campaign (see Table 4.2, p. 85), with over $140 million from her own personal wealth. Of this total, she poured nearly $110 million into TV and radio advertising, and Californians quickly became aware of her candidacy and voters easily recognized her name. In contrast, Jerry Brown, who had served two terms as governor (1975–83), had been mayor of Oakland (1999–2007), and more recently served as state attorney general, spent only $25 million on his campaign. In the end, Brown won by a very comfortable margin, 54 percent to 41 percent. Furthermore, Brown's cost per vote was only $1.24, whereas Whitman spent a whopping $51.82 per vote! What accounted for Brown's victory and Whitman's defeat?

- *Voters wanted an experienced leader*—Whitman, a politically inexperienced mega-wealthy businesswoman, believed her money and outsider status would win her the governorship. Exit polls, however, revealed that 54 percent of voters wanted "an insider who knows how to get things done" compared to only 36 percent who wanted "an outsider who wants to shake things up."[11] Voters were very concerned about the economy, and Brown campaigned as the candidate with the experience to deal with the state's fiscal crisis and legislative gridlock.

- *Immigration issue*—Just weeks before the election, Whitman, who ran on an anti-illegal immigration platform, was forced to admit that she had employed a housekeeper for nine years who did not have legal residency status. Whitman had fired her housekeeper and stated during her campaign that she would support deportation of her former employee. Any progress the Whitman campaign had made on reaching out to Latino voters dissipated with the news of this scandal. Exit polls found that Latinos, more than any other voting group, said it was the governor's race that impelled them to vote, with 60 percent voting for Brown and only 34 percent voting for Whitman. Likewise, independent voters, who tend to be anti-illegal immigration, were concerned that Whitman knew of her housekeeper's illegal status (evidence was presented to support this allegation) and yet took no action until it became a campaign issue. In order to win the election, Whitman needed the support of independent voters. Polling data suggest that this scandal, so close to election day, was the turning point in the governor's race.

- *Demographic divide*—Brown won the election with the support of women and Latino voters. Although male voters were evenly split between Brown and Whitman, a majority of female voters favored Brown (54 percent) over Whitman (42 percent). Anglo voters favored Whitman over Brown (53 to 45 percent) but Latino voters, who are largely credited with the electoral success of Democratic candidates in this election, overwhelmingly favored Brown. Analysts believe that Brown's experience and moderate positions on the issues attracted the support of women and Latino voters.

- *Political landscape*—It is not surprising that inland voters preferred Whitman and coastal and urban voters largely preferred Brown. Because most of California's population resides in the coastal regions and urban centers, Democratic candidates have a distinct edge over Republican candidates in statewide contests.

THE U.S. SENATE RACE Barbara Boxer, a liberal Democrat, running for her fourth term in the U.S. Senate, had a tough reelection challenge, the toughest of her political career. Boxer, a career politician, ran against outsider and novice campaigner Carly Fiorina, a Republican and former CEO of Hewlett-Packard (HP). Typically, incumbents such as Boxer, running for reelection in a state where her political party dominates, would have had a relatively easy time keeping their seat. The situation was different this time around. California's economy was in shambles; Boxer's popularity had been declining; and Fiorina was a formidable opponent. In the end, Boxer prevailed, winning reelection with 52 percent of the vote compared to Fiorina's 43 percent. Many pundits believe that Fiorina's failure to moderate her position on social issues (she was ardently anti-abortion and anti-illegal immigration) along with Boxer's stinging ads highlighting the layoff of 30,000 HP workers under Fiorina's stewardship were responsible for Fiorina's loss.

PROPOSITION 20: REDISTRICTING CONGRESSIONAL DISTRICTS VS. PROPOSITION 27: ELIMINATING THE STATE REDISTRICTING COMMISSION Propositions 20 and 27 were actually competing initiatives. Proposition 20 is an extension of Proposition 11, which passed in November 2008. Proposition 11 created the 14-member Citizens Redistricting Commission that would be in charge of drawing the boundaries of state Assembly and state Senate districts after each U.S. Census. November 2010's Proposition 20 asked voters to remove the authority for congressional redistricting from the legislature and give this power to the newly created Citizens Redistricting Commission. The commission would then be responsible for drawing congressional district lines as well as the already approved power of drawing state Assembly and state Senate district boundaries. The competing initiative, Proposition 27, on the other hand, would have eliminated the Citizens Redistricting Commission and returned to the legislature the power to draw state district boundaries (essentially repealing Proposition 11). California voters soundly endorsed the Citizens Redistricting Commission (defeating Proposition 27 with a 59 percent no vote) and gave the Commission the power to determine congressional districts as well (Proposition 25 passed with a 61 percent yes vote).

The Citizens Redistricting Commission completed its work in August 2011, and the impact of its work has been profound on a number of levels. As soon as the new district maps were finalized, lawsuits were filed against the commission's drawing of state Assembly and Senate district boundaries. A referendum was qualified for the November 2012 ballot that asked voters to prevent the revised state Senate boundaries from taking effect. Some of the most dramatic changes resulted from the redrawing of congressional district lines. Before the redrawing of district lines by this independent, bipartisan commission, very few house incumbents were ever defeated. They resided in safe districts with little or no reelection competition from challengers. The newly drawn political map has changed that. Some long-serving members of Congress have had their districts redrawn to where they are not guaranteed reelection. Some of the new districts are now electorally competitive, whereas others have been redrawn to where the voter demographics now favor the opposing political party. Take, for example, Representative David Drier, a Republican who chairs one of the most powerful committees in the House of Representatives. His congressional district was redrawn, and he would have faced a difficult reelection bid in this new district, which has more Democrats than Republicans. Rather than wage an expensive and likely losing reelection bid, he announced his retirement after serving 30 years in the House. One of the most watched congressional races in 2012 was between two well-known Democratic House members who found themselves in the same newly drawn congressional district in the San Fernando Valley. Representatives Howard Berman and Brad Sherman were forced to compete against each other in the primary election, which was nicknamed the "clash of the titans" or the "Erman Wars." They were the top two vote-getters and ran against each other again in November's general election, with Sherman winning over 60 percent of the vote. Overall, the new congressional district boundaries created by the commission resulted in 36 safe or leaning Democratic districts, 13 safe or leaning Republican districts, and 4 toss-up districts. In the November 2012 congressional elections, Democrats gained 4 more seats than they had before the redistricting, for a total of 38 seats compared to 15 Republican seats.

PROPOSITION 25: SIMPLE MAJORITY VOTE TO PASS BUDGET Proposition 25 changed the legislative vote requirement from two-thirds to pass the budget to a simple majority. In addition, all members of the legislature must permanently forfeit reimbursement for salary and expenses for every day the budget is late. California had not passed a state budget by the mandatory June 15 deadline in 23 years. Budget negotiations in 2010 extended 100 days past the deadline, just close enough to Election Day for it to be fresh in voters' minds. Californians passed Proposition 25, with a 55 percent affirmative vote. Supporters of this initiative were labor unions (especially teachers who received layoff notices when the budget was not passed on time), the League of Women Voters, groups representing retirees, and others who were able to devote resources to the "Yes on Prop. 25" campaign.

Since the passage of this proposition, the state budget has been passed on time and lawmakers were not forced to forfeit their pay or reimbursement for expenses. However, it is interesting to note that although lawmakers are technically in compliance with the law by meeting the June 15 deadline, they have fallen short of the intent of Proposition 25. As described by the *Sacramento Bee*, "While lawmakers sent Brown the main budget bill, Assembly Bill 1464, they did not send him the bulk of more than two dozen 'trailer' bills that actually explain how to cut programs and raise revenue"[12] to carry out the expenditures. Senate President Pro Tem

Darrell Steinberg (D-Sacramento) said that is because legislative Democrats and Brown still must resolve "small but important differences."

The 2012 Primary Election

The June 2012 primary was an interesting one. Usually, the major contest in the primary during a presidential election year is between the candidates competing for their party's nomination for the presidential race. But, as typically happens when states hold their primary late in the political season, Mitt Romney already had won enough delegates to secure his party's nomination, and President Obama had no Democratic challenger and was, by default, his party's nominee. Perhaps this explains why only 31 percent of California voters participated in this election with Los Angeles County having one of the lowest turnout rates, at less than 22 percent. There were two initiatives on the ballot, Propositions 28 and 29 and, as mandated by the passage of Proposition 14, this was the first statewide blanket primary using the new top-two vote-getter system. It was also the first election since the adoption of the newly drawn congressional and state legislative districts. The ballot looked different; all voters regardless of party affiliation were given the same ballot; the results were calculated differently; and some candidates found themselves running in new or very different districts. A very interesting election, indeed.

PROPOSITION 28: LIMITS ON LEGISLATORS' TERMS IN OFFICE; CONSTITUTIONAL AMENDMENT In 1990, voters passed Proposition 140, which implemented term limits for those elected to the California legislature. Legislators were limited to three 2-year terms in the Assembly and two 4-year terms in the Senate. This placed a 14-year limit of service in the California legislature. Proposition 28 is a constitutional amendment changing the term limit laws. This measure does two things: it reduces the total number of years an individual can serve in the legislature from 14 to 12 years, and it increases the number of years that can be served in either chamber. Six 2-year terms in the Assembly or three 4-year terms in the Senate are allowable. Individuals can still serve in both chambers but are not permitted to exceed the 12-year limit on service. Voters passed Proposition 28 by a rather wide margin of 61 to 39 percent. A major argument in support of this proposition was that allowing legislators to serve longer in the Assembly or Senate will reduce the habit of "flipping offices," by which individuals jump from one chamber to the other. Now, individuals can run for reelection for the same office and serve the maximum 12 years. Proponents also argued that serving 12 years in one chamber will allow members to pay more attention to the needs of their constituents and this focused attention might reduce the power of special-interest groups.

PROPOSITION 29: TAX ON CIGARETTES FOR CANCER RESEARCH Proposition 29 would raise the tax on a pack of cigarettes by $1. The revenue generated by the cigarette tax would be used for research on cancer and tobacco-related diseases. Antismoking advocates were frustrated that the legislature, in the past 30 years, had failed to pass more than 30 attempts to raise taxes on cigarettes. So, they decided to bypass an uncooperative legislature and go directly to the voters. Nearly $59 million was spent on ads supporting or opposing this proposition. The "no" campaign was very well funded thanks to the tobacco companies who contributed $44 million in hopes of defeating the measure. Groups supporting the measure, such as the American Cancer Society and the American Heart and Lung Associations, were able to raise only $12 million. The mayor of New York City, Michael Bloomberg, contributed $0.5 million to the yes campaign, and Lance Armstrong, well-known bicycling champion and cancer survivor, was its high-profile spokesperson. It was estimated that the cigarette tax would raise about $735 million annually. The *Los Angeles Times* did not endorse Proposition 29, and in its editorial stated a reason that seemed to resonate with voters: "It just doesn't make sense for the state to get into the medical research business to the tune of half a billion dollars a year when it has so many other important unmet needs."[13] Opponents argued that some of the revenue should be used to help California address its fiscal crisis. The budget crisis has resulted in the shortening of the school year, the closing of state parks, layoffs of teachers, and other difficult budgetary cuts in order to address the state's $16 billion deficit. Polls taken in March, before the onslaught of TV ads, showed 67 percent in support of the proposition. By election day, support had declined, and Proposition 29 failed to pass, with 50.8 percent voting no.[14]

The 2012 General Election: More Demographic and Ideological Shifts

THE PRESIDENTIAL RACE The outcome of the November 2012 presidential election looked similar to the 2008 presidential election, with young and minority voters favoring President Obama and older and white voters supporting Romney. Statewide, President Obama won 59 percent of the vote, slightly less than the 61 percent he won in 2008. He received 71 percent of the votes cast by 18–29-year-old Californians, which is close to the 76 percent he received in 2008. Of those 65 years of age and older, 48 percent voted for Obama, the same percentage as did in 2008. Other notable demographic results were based on race, marital status, and place of residence. Whereas only 45 percent of whites supported Obama, 79 percent of Asian Americans and 72 percent of Latinos voted for him. Marital status also made a difference in vote choice, with Obama receiving 67 percent of the votes of unmarried Californians and 51 percent of married voters. Voters living in urban areas voted to reelect the president by 65 percent compared to rural voters at 50 percent.

The 2012 election was interesting in terms of voter turnout rates. Although 5 percent fewer people voted in 2012 than in 2008, more young voters turned out to vote in 2012. The youth vote accounted for 20 percent of all votes cast in 2008 and 28 percent of all votes in 2012. That is a 40 percent increase in turnout among 18–29-year-old voters. Nationwide, there was a very slight increase in the youth vote, which grew from 17 percent in 2008 to 19 percent in 2012. What accounted for this dramatic increase in the turnout of young California voters?

According to Peter Levine, California's new online voter registration system (a description of which comes later in this chapter), made available shortly before the 2012 election, registered nearly 700,000 new voters, many of whom were young people.[15] Also, Proposition 30 (the initiative to fund higher education) was a salient issue for young voters. If the measure did not pass, college students were facing another round of tuition increases, crowded classes, and cuts in enrollment to the CSU and UC systems. This combination of an accessible online voter registration system and an important initiative impacting higher education motivated young voters.

CONGRESSIONAL RACES As mandated by the U.S. Constitution, all House members serve two-year terms in office. California has 53 House members, and in the November 2012 election, 11 new members were elected, the most new members in 20 years. Democrats won 38 of the 53 seats, and the number of seats held by Latinos also increased. These changes were a result of the recent remapping of House districts and changing demographics. A number of incumbent House members retired when their districts were redrawn after the 2010 Census, and they found themselves in competitive districts where their reelection was not assured. Prior to the 2012 election, only 1 House seat had changed between the parties during the last five Congressional elections. In 2012, Democratic candidates won 4 more House seats than they had in 2012. A second factor related to the strong showing by Democratic candidates is the growing number and clout of Latino voters, especially in southern California. As reported in the *Los Angeles Times*, "Voters in Riverside and San Bernardino counties elected three Democrats to Congress— two Latinos and a gay Asian American—after having sent only two Democrats to Washington in the last four decades."[16]

The Democratic Party had hopes of winning back control of the U.S. House of Representatives and needed to win 25 additional House seats around the country to reach this goal. California and its newly remapped competitive districts were seen as an opportunity for the Democratic Party to win some new seats. To that end, a whopping $53 million was spent on California House races by the political parties, interest groups, and individuals.[17]

CALIFORNIA LEGISLATIVE RACES The headline in the *Los Angeles Times* on November 8, 2012, read "Blue reign in Sacramento: Democrats' historic gains position them for unchecked power." Prior to the November 6 election Democrats had controlled both the state Assembly and the state Senate. They were expected to win enough seats to maintain their majority. Amazingly, the election not only allowed the Democratic Party to maintain their majority status but their electoral successes gave them *supermajority* status. Having a supermajority means that there are enough Democratic votes in each chamber to raise taxes without needing any votes from Republicans. Proposition 13, passed in 1978, mandates that legislation raising revenue must be passed by a two-thirds vote. As a result of this election, Democrats now control 70 percent of the seats in the state Senate and nearly 68 percent of the Assembly seats: a supermajority in both chambers. The last time a party had supermajority power was in 1933 when the Republicans were in charge. The Democrats last had this power in 1883.

PROPOSITIONS There were 11 measures on the November 2012 ballot. Voters were asked to weigh in on a number of issues ranging from increased taxes to fund educational programs to the repeal of the death penalty. A recordbreaking amount of money was spent on these campaigns. George Skelton, a *Los Angeles Times* columnist, wrote "It's almost unfathomable that $372 million was spent to promote or attack the 11 measures. To put it in perspective, that amount of money could pay for the annual tuitions of 31,000 undergrads at the University of California. The top 20 donors provided 69 percent of all initiative funding."[18] What follows is a description of some of the more high profile measures.

- *Proposition 30: Taxes to Fund Education versus Proposition 38: Tax to Fund Education and Early Childhood Programs*—These two competing propositions dealt with ways to raise revenue to fund education. Proposition 30, backed by the Governor, would temporarily raise the state sales tax for 4 years and increase taxes on the wealthy for 7 years. Proposition 38 would raise taxes on earnings for all Californians for 12 years. Since these were competing measures, if both passed, the one receiving the most votes would prevail. Proposition 30 passed with 55 percent of the vote. Proposition 38 received only 28 percent of the vote even though its sponsor spent $44 million of her own money on the measure. In addition, an outside political group from Arizona spent over $11 million to defeat both Propositions 30 and 38.

- *Proposition 32: Political Contributions by Payroll Deduction: Contributions to Candidates*—This measure would prohibit unions from using payroll deductions for political purposes. As expected, unions were opposed to this measure and poured over $50 million into campaigns to defeat this measure. They were ultimately victorious, as the initiative failed.

- *Proposition 34: Death Penalty*—This initiative statute would repeal the death penalty and replace it with life in prison without possibility of parole. Those currently on death row would have their sentences commuted to life imprisonment. Proponents of this measure spent over $8 million on this measure. Opponents spent a small fraction of that amount. The measure was defeated with a 52 percent "no" vote.

- *Proposition 36: Three Strikes Law: Repeat Felony Offenders*—This measure would revise the existing Three Strikes law to impose life sentences only when the offender is convicted of a new violent felony. Those previously convicted under this law for nonviolent felonies may have their sentences reviewed. The measure easily passed with 69 percent of the vote.

- *Proposition 37: Genetically Engineered Foods Labeling*—This proposition would require the labeling of food which is made from plants or animals containing genetically altered material. Agroscience opponents such as DuPont, Dow Agro, and Monsanto spent over $15 million to defeat this measure. The proposition failed, receiving only 48 percent of the vote.

Campaigning in California

California politics presents many challenges to those seeking elective office or the passage of a ballot measure. First, the immense size of the state means that state-wide propositions, candidates running for statewide office, and those running for federal offices, such as the U.S. Congress and the presidency, must plan campaigns that reach voters throughout the entire state. In fact, California has 13 distinct media markets, making it very expensive to communicate to its 38 million residents about politics. Second, California's population is very diverse, with many ethnicities, races, cultures, professions, occupations, and interests represented. Successful campaigns must find ways to effectively communicate their platform and messages to all of the 18 million registered voters in the state. And third, California has passed a number of political campaign reform acts in an attempt to regulate campaign spending and to provide public information on contributions and expenditures. These laws have proved beneficial to some and not as helpful to others.

Whatever the challenges of campaigning in California, one thing is certain: California's campaign politics are watched by the nation. California is a campaign trendsetter.

Money and Politics: California Style

As the record-breaking spending in the campaigns of 2010 showed, campaigning in California requires money, and lots of it. In fact, California is one of the most expensive states in which to conduct a political campaign. Table 4.2 compares the fund-raising of the 10 gubernatorial candidates who raised the most money in 2009–10. As you can see, amounts over $25 million landed a candidate on this list, and Whitman's $176 million is quite the anomaly. It is interesting to note that candidates running for governor in other large states, such as Texas and Florida, spent less than one-quarter of what Whitman spent on her campaign.

TABLE 4.2 ★ Fund-Raising by Top 10 Gubernatorial Candidates, 2009–10

CANDIDATE	STATE	PARTY	STATUS	TOTAL RAISED
Meg Whitman	California	Republican	Lost	176,684,951
Richard Scott	Florida	Republican	Won	67,421,942
Jerry Brown	California	Democrat	Won	40,556,608
Rick Perry	Texas	Republican	Won	39,328,540
Jon S. Corzine	New Jersey	Democrat	Lost	30,583,881
Tom Corbett	Pennsylvania	Republican	Won	28,561,987
Steve Poizner	California	Republican	Lost primary	26,660,173
Bill White	Texas	Democrat	Lost	26,291,532
Andrew Cuomo	New York	Democrat	Won	26,047,733
Dan Onorato	Pennsylvania	Democrat	Lost	25,116,397
			Total	487,253,745

SOURCE: *Follow the Money,* www.followthemoney.org/press/ReportView.phtml?r=487&ext=1#tableid3 (accessed 7/25/12).

Running for governor is not the only campaign that is costly. Running for the California legislature is also very expensive. Citing a Pew Center on the States study, Osorio notes that California is the costliest state in which to win a state Senate seat ($938,522). The least expensive state is North Dakota at $5,713. In Arizona it costs $36,696; in Wisconsin, $140,287; and in North Carolina, $234,031.[19] The prohibitive cost of campaigning in California restricts who can realistically run for office, another contributing factor to the state's governance challenges. Incumbents far outspend challengers, and incumbents' spending has increased over time while spending by challengers has not. On average, challengers spend only a fraction of what incumbents spend. This discrepancy helps to explain the high re-election rates of those elected to the California legislature. Some competitive races for the California legislature cost in excess of $1 million.

The following are some reasons that California campaigns are so expensive:

MEDIA-DOMINATED CAMPAIGNS Because of the size of the state and its 13 different media markets, candidates must spend enormous amounts of money producing political ads and buying the broadcast time to air them. During the 2003 gubernatorial recall election, it cost approximately $2 million a week to run political ads statewide.[20] In the 2006 governor's race, Schwarzenegger's campaign alone spent $9 million on TV ads in the short time span between July 1 and September 30. As is shown in Table 4.3, an astounding $138 million was spent in the November 2010 governor's race just on TV, cable, and radio airtime and production. This cost is in addition to the $57 million spent on the media during the primary campaign. As one media consultant described it, "There's a lot to be said for traditional politicking, kissing babies and shaking hands, but you have to get on TV to reach voters."[21]

POLITICAL CONSULTANTS Professional campaign managers and various consultants—media consultants, pollsters, fund-raisers, direct-mail experts, and voter mobilization professionals—cost money. Because of California's love of direct democracy, especially the initiative process, many well-known political consultants have established offices in California. There is money to be made in California politics, and candidates and supporters of ballot initiatives know that to win elections you must hire the costly services of top-notch political consultants.

WEAK POLITICAL PARTIES California has a comparatively weak political party system. The reform movement of Governor Hiram Johnson implemented many rules that reduced the organizational strength and clout of political parties within the state. Because of the weak party system in California, the party organizations are minimally involved in organizing and conducting the campaigns of candidates running for office. In addition, California has a relatively large number of registered voters who decline to affiliate with any political party and consider themselves politically independent. These unaffiliated, independent voters compose about 20 percent of all registered voters. The combination of weak party structure and less party attachment means that candidates themselves have to work harder—raise and spend more money—to reach these voters.

Campaign Finance Reform in California

To create more transparency in the electoral process and make public the flow of money in political campaigns, several campaign finance laws have been enacted in California over the past 100 years. Brief descriptions of the most recent laws follow.

TABLE 4.3 ★ Spending in California's Gubernatorial Election: How the Money Was Spent (spending through 10/16/10)

EXPENDITURE	WHITMAN ($)	BROWN ($)
Television and radio advertising	106,930,505.28	21,259,408.00
Campaign consultants	11,693,547.95	167,200.00
Campaign literature and mailings	10,582,303.93	2,532,801.36
Campaign workers' salaries	5,918,110.80	157,870.01
Radio airtime and production costs	5,472,228.17	0
TV or cable airtime and production costs	4,139,919.07	182,103.12
Information technology costs (Internet, e-mail)	3,177,977.76	23,345.51
Office expenses	2,321,340.46	132,023.40
Meetings and appearances	1,772,342.56	
Polling and survey research	1,410,893.36	93,728.30
Staff/spouse travel, lodging, and meals	1,260,616.12	2,618.30
Fundraising events	1,241,158.66	70,626.38
Candidate travel, lodging, and meals	950,890.17	12,071.76
Professional services (legal, accounting)	880,044.13	39,310.00
Postage, delivery, and messenger services	668,059.56	2,117.00
Campaign paraphernalia/miscellaneous	633,946.72	65,129.65
Phone banks	549,904.75	0
Contribution	252,500.00	0
Print ads	153,440.00	0
Voter registration	66,710.00	0
Civic donations	16,383.00	0
Returned contributions	0	99,364.14
Candidate filing/ballot fees	0	3,579.74
TOTAL	**160,092,822.45**	**24,843,296.67**

SOURCE: Campaign Watch, http://californiawatch.org/dailyreport/how-whitman-spent-160-million-6292.

1974: POLITICAL REFORM ACT In 1974 a group of reform-minded Californians crafted a statewide proposition that would require the most detailed campaign finance reporting in the nation. Proposition 9 appeared on the ballot during the Watergate scandal, and voters were ready for these reforms. Proposition 9 passed with an overwhelming majority of votes. This act created the Political Reform Division within the office of the secretary of state to administer and oversee key provisions of the law. A new independent state agency, the Fair Political Practices Commission, also was created for the purposes of interpreting and enforcing the act.

1988: PROPOSITION 73 In 1988 California voters overwhelmingly passed Proposition 73, which limited contributions to legislative and statewide candidates to $1,000 per donor, including individuals, labor unions, and corporations. A federal judge struck it down in 1990.

1996: PROPOSITION 208 Voters approved Proposition 208 by a 61 percent vote in 1996. Contributions to candidates from individuals, political parties, committees, corporations, unions, and political action committees (PACs) were limited. Spending limits also were imposed on candidates, although these were voluntary. Candidates who abide by the spending limits are allowed to collect larger contributions, whereas candidates who decide not to comply with the spending limits have lower contribution limits. Proposition 208 was being challenged in the courts when Proposition 34 was proposed and passed.

2000: PROPOSITION 34 Proposition 34 was placed on the ballot by the legislature. Spending limits were substantially increased, as were contribution limits. For example, under Proposition 208, individuals were permitted to contribute $1,000 to gubernatorial candidates—$500 if the candidate decided not to abide by the voluntary spending limits. Proposition 34 increased individual contributions to $21,200. Many reform-minded organizations that had supported Proposition 208, such as the League of Women Voters and Common Cause, were opposed to Proposition 34. They saw Proposition 34 as an attempt by the legislature to replace the more stringent Proposition 208 that was under review in the courts. Nevertheless, in November 2000, Proposition 34 passed with close to 60 percent of the popular vote and has replaced the provisions of Proposition 208.

Although it could be argued that Proposition 34 has resulted in less control of campaign financing, California does receive high marks when it comes to laws requiring public disclosure of campaign contributions and expenditures. The Campaign Disclosure Project conducted by UCLA in 2008 studied the campaign disclosure laws in all 50 states and ranked the states according to their campaign finance disclosure laws. California received a grade of A for its disclosure laws and ranked second in the nation; Washington State ranked first.

Campaign Contributions to Federal Candidates

As Table 4.4 illustrates, Californians are generous in their contributions to federal candidates and parties. In the 2012 election year, California ranked number one in the nation for its total amount of contributions. As the most populous state, California contributed nearly $300 million to federal candidates, with almost half of the contributions going to Democrats. Californians contributing to federal candidates and parties must abide by all federal campaign contribution laws, which limit the amount of money individuals and PACs may contribute to federal campaigns and parties.

TABLE 4.4 ★ Contributions by States to Federal Candidates in the 2012 Elections: The Top 10

RANK	STATE	TOTAL CONTRIBUTIONS ($)	TO DEMOCRATS (%)	TO REPUBLICANS (%)
1	California	297,098,839	49	37
2	Texas	242,325,942	18	51
3	District of Columbia	235,191,281	47	36
4	New York	222,137,461	48	34
5	Florida	150,831,110	29	57
6	Virginia	123,206,735	36	60
7	Illinois	104,654,233	42	45
8	Massachusetts	86,006,854	49	40
9	Pennsylvania	69,605,260	39	52
10	Nevada	62,123,429	11	22

Based on data released by the FEC on Oct 1, 2012 Totals include PAC and individual contributions to federal candidates and parties.

SOURCE: The Center for Responsive Politics, www.opensecrets.org.

Voting in California

Of California's nearly 39 million residents, approximately 17 million (72 percent) are registered to vote. To register to vote in the state of California you must meet the following criteria:

- You will be 18 years of age on or before Election Day.
- You are a citizen of the United States.
- You are a resident of California.
- You are not in prison or on parole for a felony conviction.
- You have not been judged by a court to be mentally incompetent to register and vote.

How You Can Register to Vote

Registering to vote is a simple process. Here are the options:

- Obtain a Voter Registration form from any U.S. post office or library. Forms are usually set out on counters. Fill out the preaddressed, stamped form and mail it in.

- Visit a California Department of Motor Vehicles office. The National Voter Registration Act of 1993 (also known as "Motor Voter") permits persons conducting business at a DMV office to register to vote or to update their voter registration information. In fact, since 1995 over 12.5 million people have registered or reregistered in conformance with this law.

- Register online. Go to the secretary of state's website, and use the new online voter registration system (registertovote.ca.gov). The process is very simple and completed entirely online if you have a California driver license or identification card. Since voter registration applications must be signed by the individual, the online system retrieves your signature from your driver license or ID card and electronically transfers it to your online registration application. This new system has proven to be so popular that of the record 1.4 million newly registered voters, over half of them registered online. California is one of only 15 states that offer electronic voter registration.

You will need to reregister to vote when

- you move;

- you change your name;

- you change your political party affiliation.

You must register at least 15 days before an election.

Who Votes in California?

Different groups vote at different rates. Figure 4.5 clearly illustrates this. Eight-five percent of white adults are registered to vote. The figure of African Americans is similar: a high registration rate of 82 percent. The number of Asian Americans voters has increased over the years with this group now having a 65 percent registration rate. Although Latino voter registration is increasing each year, only 38 percent of Latino adults are registered to vote. Over the decades the composition of the voting population has changed to where we have more minority voters. But overall the same pattern has held: whites vote at a higher rate than do Asian Americans and Latinos. Three factors help explain this discrepancy:

- *Eligibility*—A significant proportion of the Latino and Asian populations are not eligible to vote because they are not citizens.

- *Youth*—The Latino and Asian populations are both younger, and younger people are much less likely to vote than are older people.

- *Education*—The probability of voting increases significantly with a receipt of a college or advanced degree.

Research shows that if you control for these three factors, Latinos vote at rates comparable to whites.[22] The 2012 presidential election saw a decline in voter turnout. In 2008, 59 percent of eligible Californians turned out to vote. In 2012, nearly 2 million fewer adults voted, for a turnout rate of only 56 percent. As Figure 4.5 illustrates, the 2008 presidential election had the highest turnout rate since 1972. In analyzing voting statistics over the decades, political scientists have found that an exciting political

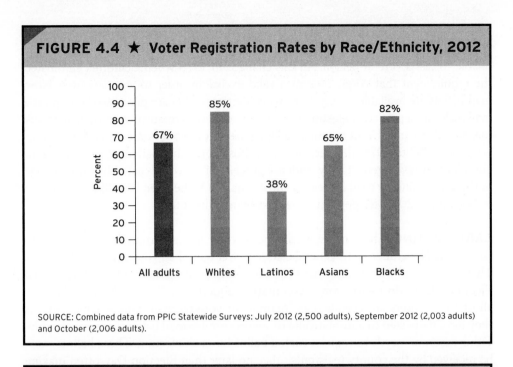

FIGURE 4.4 ★ Voter Registration Rates by Race/Ethnicity, 2012

SOURCE: Combined data from PPIC Statewide Surveys: July 2012 (2,500 adults), September 2012 (2,003 adults) and October (2,006 adults).

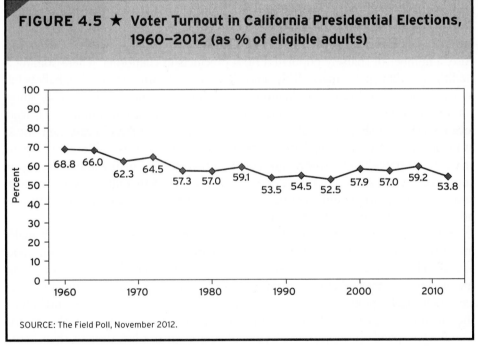

FIGURE 4.5 ★ Voter Turnout in California Presidential Elections, 1960–2012 (as % of eligible adults)

SOURCE: The Field Poll, November 2012.

race with charismatic candidates has the potential of encouraging more citizens to vote. Apparently, the 2008 presidential election was an example of this. Although more young adults and Latinos voted in 2012 than in 2008, the overall turnout rate declined, leading one to conclude that white voters did not come out to vote at the same rate as they had in 2008.

THE EVER-EXPANDING GROUP OF VOTERS: VOTING BY MAIL California now has very liberal vote-by-mail laws. Before 1978, a voter had to have a valid excuse for not voting at his or her designated polling place. You were eligible to receive a mail ballot if you signed a sworn statement that you were going to be away from your home precinct on Election Day or that you were infirm or bedridden and physically unable to cast a vote in person. All this changed in 1978 when California eliminated the requirement that voters present a valid excuse in order to vote absentee. Now, mail ballots are available to any voter who wants one. You are permitted to request a mail ballot for a particular election or you may request permanent vote-by-mail status, meaning that a mail ballot automatically will be sent to your home for each election.

From 1962 to 1978, the percentage of those voting by mail in primary and general elections averaged slightly under 4 percent of all votes cast. After the change in the law, voting by mail increased substantially. Of the over 10 million votes cast in November 2012, 51 percent were cast by mail ballots.

EARLY VOTING There is a special type of voter in California: the early voter. In fact, in the November 2012 general election, over half of all voters were early voters. There are several ways Californians can vote early (casting their votes before official Election Day). Most early voters voluntarily request vote-by-mail ballots. Virtually all of these voters are classified as "permanent vote-by-mail" voters, which means they have requested to automatically receive a vote-by-mail ballot for every election. Otherwise, one needs to request such a ballot for each election. These ballots must be received by the county registrar's office no later than Election Day, often making it necessary to mail in the completed ballot at least a few days before this deadline. And a number of voters fill out and mail their ballots weeks before Election Day because state law permits voting as early as twenty-nine days before an election. Also, a number of sparsely populated rural precincts in California, where staffing a traditional polling place makes little sense, have moved entirely to mail-in ballots for all voters. And in an attempt to lighten the volume of voters on Election Day, some counties have permitted "early voting," in which voters can go to various publicized locations (such as shopping malls, registrars' offices, civic centers) to cast their votes, again as early as twenty-nine days before an election. How does California compare to the other states? Well, twenty-nine states allow voting by mail without having an approved excuse, and California is one of only four states that allow for permanent voting by mail. Early voting, requiring no special excuse, is permitted by thirty-one other states and prohibited in fifteen states.

Many view these developments as positive changes, believing that by making voting more convenient, it will increase participation in this important civic activity. However, as with many reforms, there are unintended consequences. One major consequence is that early voting has had a direct impact on campaign strategy. Traditionally, political campaigns plan their strategy so that the weekend before the election is viewed as their last opportunity to communicate with the voters. Candidates spend an enormous amount of money in the last days of their campaigns trying to convince voters to vote for them or their initiative, or at least not to vote for their opponent or opposing side. During this time, they usually bombard viewers with TV ads and messages. Yet, in California, nearly half the voters have most likely already voted by mail or at an early-voting location. So candidates must now spend money earlier in the campaign cycle to reach these early voters before they cast their votes. As an example, State Senator Tom McClintock lost a race for state controller by less than one-half of a percentage point because he did not have enough money to buy TV ads until the final days of the campaign. Many absentee voters had already mailed in their ballots and did not see his campaign ads until after they had cast their vote. Earlier campaigning means more expensive campaigning in a state that is already prohibitively expensive.

HOW YOU CAN VOTE BY MAIL To apply for a mail ballot you may use the application form contained in the sample ballot mailed to your home before the election or you may apply in writing to your county elections official. Ballots can be returned by mail or in person to a polling place or elections office within your county on Election Day.

Modernizing Voting Machines

In the March 2002 election, voters approved Proposition 41, the Voting Modernization Bond Act. This act allocates $200 million to upgrade and modernize voting systems throughout the state. In the October 2003 recall election, three types of voting systems were used in California. Of California's 58 counties, 34 used some type of optical-scan ballot, 20 counties used some form of punch-card ballot, and only 4 counties used touch-screen ballots. After the controversial 2000 presidential election and the problem of punch-card voting in the state of Florida, the state legislature was concerned that if California did not replace its outmoded voting systems, the same calamity might strike here. Presumably, the remaining punch-card ballots and other outdated equipment will be replaced with more accurate voting machines.

What Reforms Are Needed?

It is fascinating to observe electoral politics in California. We live in a state where ballot initiatives are frequently used to make law, bypassing our duly elected representatives and the deliberative process of the legislature. In recent elections voters have been asked to weigh in on important policy matters such as same-sex marriage, abortion and parental notification, renewable energy, legalization of marijuana, the state budget process, tax issues, and the process by which state and congressional districts boundaries are determined. Many people question whether the initiative process is the best way to make public policy.

Although the legacy of the Progressives included the recall, referendum, and initiative, during the past few decades these tools of direct democracy have been taken over by special-interest groups. Some believe that reforms are needed to make it more difficult to recall an elected official or to bypass the legislative branch through the initiative process. Suggested reforms have included the prohibition of paid signature gatherers, judicial review of the proposed initiative before placement on the ballot and increasing the number of required signatures to qualify a recall or initiative for the ballot; for a recall to qualify for the ballot, California law requires the number of signatures to equal 12 percent of the votes cast in the last gubernatorial election, while other states require 25 to 40 percent.

Candidates and initiative campaigns spend enormous amounts of money in hopes of electoral victory. Proposition 34, the campaign finance initiative passed in 2000, substantially increased spending and contribution limits. California's limits on contributions to gubernatorial candidates are far more liberal than federal limits on contributions to presidential candidates. In fact, Californians can contribute more than 10 times the amount to gubernatorial candidates than they are permitted to contribute to presidential candidates ($25,900 versus $2,500). Many fear that these high limits will lead to spiraling campaign costs in a state where it is already expensive to campaign.

FOR FURTHER READING

Cain, B. "The California Recall." Interview, Brookings Institution, October 8, 2003.

Cain, Bruce E., and Elisabeth R. Gerber. *Voting at the Political Fault Line: California's Experiment with the Blanket Primary*. Berkeley: University of California Press, 2002.

California Fair Political Practices Commission. "Proposition 34." www.fppc.ca.gov. Accessed 7/25/12.

California Secretary of State's History of Political Reform Division, www.ss.ca.gov/elections. Accessed 7/25/12.

Douzet, Frédérick, Thad Kousser, and Kenneth P. Miller, eds. *The New Political Geography of California*. Berkeley, CA: Berkeley Public Policy Press, 2008.

Lubenow, Gerald C., ed. *California Votes: The 2002 Governor's Race and the Recall That Made History*. Berkeley, CA: Berkeley Public Policy Press, 2003.

Rarick, E. *California Votes: The 2010 Governor's Race*. Berkeley, CA: Institute of Governmental Studies, 2012.

Rasky, Susan. Introduction to "An Antipolitician, Antiestablishment Groundswell Elected the Candidate of Change." In *California Votes: The 2002 Governor's Race and the Recall That Made History*, ed. G. Lubenow.

UCLA School of Law, Center for Governmental Studies, and the California Voter Foundation. "Grading State Disclosure 2008: A Comprehensive, Comparative Study of Candidate Campaign Finance Disclosure Laws and Practices in the 50 States." 2008.

ON THE WEB

California Elections and Voter Information: www.sos.ca.gov/elections (accessed 7/25/12). The California Secretary of State offers a comprehensive guide to California elections, including information on how to register to vote.

California General Election Results: http://vote.sos.ca.gov (accessed 7/25/12). Detailed breakdowns of California election results.

The California Voter Foundation: http://calvoter.org (accessed 7/25/12).

Fair Political Practices Commission: www.fppc.ca.gov (accessed 7/25/12).

Join California: www.joincalifornia.com (accessed 7/25/12).

SUMMARY

I. Introduction
   A. There are several ways of voting in California.
      1. Voting by mail.
      2. Mail-in-ballot-only precincts.
      3. Early voting opportunities.
   B. Early voting has had an impact on candidates and campaign strategies.
      1. Traditional late spending on the weekend before Election Day is not as effective.
      2. Candidates must spend money earlier to communicate messages to early voters.

II. Political parties.
   A. Functions of parties.
   B. Two dominant parties: Democratic and Republican.
   C. Progressives' impact on parties was sizable.
      1. They disliked corrupt parties.
      2. They weakened the power of parties.
   D. Third parties struggle to compete.
      1. There are four certified minor parties.
      2. Third parties can impact the political agenda.

III. Party affiliation of California voters varies by region and demographics.
   A. The Democratic Party represents a plurality of voters.
   B. There has been an increase in the number of independents ("decline to state").
   C. Demographics and party affiliation.

1. Whites tend to vote Republican; Latinos tend to vote Democratic.
   2. Younger voters comprise the highest percentage of Independents, compared to other age groups.
   3. Women tend to prefer the Democratic Party, as do non–U.S.-born citizens.
   D. Blue and red in California.
      1. Coastal and urban areas tend to be Democratic.
      2. Inland and rural areas tend to be Republican.

IV. Elections in California.
   A. There have been many changes in the primary system used.
      1. Closed primary until Proposition 198 in 1996.
      2. Blanket primary 1998–2000. *California Democratic Party v. Jones*: in 2002, California Supreme Court ruled blanket primary unconstitutional.
      3. Modified closed primary system, 2002–10: "decline to state" voters permitted to vote in party primaries if party grants permission.
      4. Proposition 14, passed in 2010, replaced modified closed primary system with another version of blanket primary.
   B. Presidential primaries.
      1. Changes in date of primaries.
      2. 2008 presidential primary: more clout for state unrealized.
   C. Initiative campaigns.
      1. Tool of special interests or grass-roots movements.
      2. 1912–2010: over 350 ballot initiatives.

3. How to qualify an initiative for ballot.
    a) Over 500,000 signatures of registered voters needed for initiative, and over 800,000 for constitutional amendment.
    b) Costs and other political resources needed to be successful.
D. 2003 gubernatorial recall election.
    1. Major players.
    2. Issues.
        a) Challenge by wealthy congressman Issa.
        b) Budget deficit.
        c) Enron and energy crisis; rolling blackouts.
E. 2006 election: Schwarzenegger's reelection. Unpopular governor beats weak challenger.
F. 2008 election: ideological and demographic shift to Democrat. Long-term or situational?
G. 2010 election: most expensive governor's race in history. Brown, former governor, beats wealthy billionaire. Initiatives pass that will have an important impact on state budget process and political representation and party politics.
H. 2012 election: results similar to 2008 but more of a Democratic shift. Democratic Party gains supermajority status in state legislature. Young voters' turnout increased but overall turnout declined. New online voter registration system. An important measure, Proposition 30, passed, increasing the state sales tax and taxes on the wealthy to fund education.

V. Campaigning in California is expensive.
    A. Money and politics.
        1. Record-breaking spending.
            a) Wealthy candidates.
            b) Personal fortunes.
        2. Media-dominated campaigns.

3. Political consultants.
4. Weak political parties.
B. Campaign finance reform.
    1. 1974: Proposition 9, Political Reform Act.
        a) Created Political Reform Division.
        b) Established Fair Political Practices Commission.
    2. 1998: Proposition 73 limiting contributions passed; 1990 declared unconstitutional.
    3. 1996: Proposition 208 limiting contributions passed: Proposition 34 in 2000 invalidated Proposition 208.
    4. 2000: Proposition 34 passed increased spending and contribution limits.
    5. 2008: study of fifty states; California gets grade of A for campaign-finance disclosure laws.

VI. How to Register to vote in California.
    A. 39 million population, 17 million registered voters.
    B. How to register to vote: National Voter Registration Act (Motor Voter).
    C. Who votes?
        1. Whites overrepresented in voting population; Latinos and Asians underrepresented; African Americans vote in equal proportion to their percentage of population. Reasons: youth, eligibility, education.
        2. Voter turnout rates 1960–2012. November 2008 highest turnout since 1972.
        3. Absentee voter: over 50 percent of all registered voters.
        4. Modernizing voting machines: Proposition 41(2002) allocated $200 million to upgrade voting systems.

VII. Reforms may be necessary.
    A. Is initiative process best way to make policy?
    B. Need for campaign-finance reform to limit contributions and candidate spending.

PRACTICE QUIZ

1. In the 2012 general election, 18–29-year-olds voted at a higher rate than they did in 2008.
    a) true
    b) false
2. In running for the state legislature, winners and losers spend nearly the same amount of money on their political campaigns.
    a) true
    b) false
3. Political campaigns are so expensive in California because
    a) campaigns need to hire political consultants.
    b) campaigns need to spend a substantial amount of money on media advertising.
    c) political parties are not very involved in the planning and running of campaigns.
    d) all of the above

4. Special-interest groups often use the initiative process to achieve their policy objectives.
    a) true
    b) false
5. Which of the following is *not* true about Proposition 34, which deals with campaign finance:
    a) The League of Women Voters and Common Cause supported Proposition 34.
    b) Proposition 34 increased individual contributions to candidates to $21,200.
    c) Proposition 34 has resulted in less control on campaign financing.
    d) Proposition 34 replaced the stricter campaign finance law enacted through Proposition 208.
6. Of California's 38 million people, approximately how many are registered to vote?
    a) 30 million
    b) 25 million

c) 5 million
d) 18 million

7. Democrats are the plurality party in California.
   a) true
   b) false
8. The number of voters who decline to state a party affiliation at the time they register is declining.
   a) true
   b) false
9. Most of the Democratic counties encompass major urban areas, whereas most of the Republican counties are more rural in nature.
   a) true
   b) false

10. California presently operates under which of the following primary election systems:
    a) open primary
    b) blanket primary
    c) modified closed primary
    d) fully closed primary

CRITICAL-THINKING QUESTIONS

1. How might the cost of campaigning be reduced in California? Because incumbents spend much more money than challengers, what reforms might level the playing field of campaign politics?
2. What do you think have been the successes and failures of campaign finance laws in California? Do you think that additional reforms are needed? Why or why not?
3. How do you think the increase in unaffiliated voters and the increase in mail voters will affect campaigns and elections in the future?
4. Why do you think so many states follow California's lead in the areas of ballot propositions and recall efforts? Do you think this is a good or bad development? Explain why.

KEY TERMS

At this point you should have a general understanding of the following concepts and terms:

vote-by-mail ballot (p. 91)
ballot initiative (p. 74)
blanket primary (p. 71)
campaign finance reform (p. 86)
closed primary (p. 71)
decline to state (p. 71)
media-dominated campaign (p. 86)

media market (p. 75)
modified closed primary (p. 72)
Motor Voter (p. 90)
office block ballot (p. 61)
open primary (p. 71)
political consultant (p. 86)
political culture (p. 66)

political party affiliation (p. 60)
State Central Committees (p. 61)
Voting Modernization Bond Act (p. 93)
weak political parties (p. 86)
winner-take-all (p. 60)

5 The California Legislature

WHAT CALIFORNIA GOVERNMENT DOES AND WHY IT MATTERS

Consider the following activities of the legislature in 2011–12:

★ Passed legislation banning the sale of beer to which caffeine had been added. There had been incidents of severe intoxication from drinking this beverage.

★ Passed 1,884 bills. The governor vetoed 248 of them. No veto was overridden.

★ The Senate refused to confirm the reappointment of a member of the California State University Board of Trustees because he had supported a 12 percent increase in student fees while also supporting salaries in excess of $300,000 for campus presidents.

★ Passed legislation giving children age 12 and older the authority to get medical care for prevention of sexually transmitted diseases without parental consent.

★ Passed legislation making it illegal to sell live animals on any public right of way.

★ Passed a budget for the first time since the two-thirds vote requirement for budgets had been eliminated. Governor Brown vetoed the first attempt, saying it was not an honest budget.

Californians give little if any thought to their legislature. We have a general sense that it is made up of a group of elected individuals who write laws. Beyond that, our knowledge fades, although we believe strongly that the legislature does not work well. In fact, when the Field Poll has asked whether Californians approve of the job that the state legislature is doing overall in 20 different surveys since 2002, 40 percent or more of Californians have responded positively only once. In May 2010, only 16 percent approved, while 72 percent did not approve. At the same time, almost twice that number approved of the job that the U.S. Congress was doing.

Our lack of knowledge is related to the minimal coverage that legislatures receive in the media. The media find it difficult to cover institutions with multiple members who are doing many different things and have no single voice. They find it much easier to focus on a chief executive who has a press office to provide news-ready stories. In addition, media coverage of state politics is minimal. Although most people get their news from television, before the election of Governor Schwarzenegger no Los Angeles television station had a Sacramento bureau. But even the interest in a movie-star governor did not carry over to the legislature, and since his departure media interest in Sacramento in general has sharply declined.

Our dissatisfaction with the legislative process is related to the dysfunctional condition of our state. While the legislature is not the principal cause of this state of affairs, it is the most public arena in which the consequences are observed. Term limits and voting rules make it difficult for the legislature to function well, leading to gridlock and highly partisan disputes. Americans dislike politics in general and tend to believe that we should all be able to work together to achieve our common goals. Bipartisanship has a lot of appeal, but at the same time citizens want their individual interests forcefully represented against competing interests. We have conflicting expectations of legislatures, and the legislatures' attempts to balance these expectations often contribute to our dissatisfaction. The nineteenth-century German statesman Otto von Bismarck may well have been correct in suggesting that the making of laws, like the making of sausages, should not be observed.

In reality, legislatures, although poorly understood, play a critical role in our government. The framers of the national constitution, fearing a powerful executive, viewed Congress as the first branch of government and gave it the most significant and most explicit powers, including control of money and the writing of all laws. The fact that the president gets the most attention in the media today and that some congressional powers have gravitated to the president does not negate the fact that Congress is a very powerful body.

Most state legislatures have been modeled on the U.S. Congress in structure, process, and functions, and this is true in California, although there are some significant differences, explained later. Ours is a bicameral legislature (a two-house legislature) consisting of the 40-member Senate (sometimes called the upper house) and 80-member Assembly. Like Congress, members of both bodies represent geographically based districts and are elected by winner-take-all elections. As in Congress, bills become law by being approved by both houses and signed by the chief executive. The bulk of the work of each house is done in committees. Each house is organized by party and party leaders determine committee membership. Compared to Congress in Washington, in the state legislature seniority is much less important in determining committee memberships and chairs.

The recent history of the California legislature has been remarkable in its extremes. In the 1960s the legislature was changed from an often corrupt, amateur body to a well-paid, well-staffed professional legislature that was the envy of other states. It was regarded by many as the best state legislature in the country. This was accomplished under the leadership of the Assembly Speaker Jesse Unruh. Yet in 1990 the voters of California passed Proposition 140, imposing term limits on the legislature. Although this did not change the basic structure of the legislature, it did change the effectiveness and power of the legislature by reducing the time that legislators are permitted to serve and by reducing the size of the staff that makes legislative work possible.

Functions

Legislatures have two principal functions: representation and policy making. The tensions between these make it difficult for a legislature to perform as citizens might wish.

Representation

The legislature is the principal representative institution in our society, although the executive branch and interest groups also lay claim to this function. It is the duty of legislators (also called members, representatives, or assemblypersons or senators) to represent the voters and other residents (collectively known as constituents) within their districts, as well as the dominant interests within these districts. This is easier said than done. In the first place, the term *representation* has many meanings. Here we will simplify it to mean that our representative is our counterpart in Sacramento and that he or she will do what we would do were we there, especially when it comes to influencing legislation or voting. Of course, there are many of us, and we all do not see things the same way. Some of us are wealthy and educated; others, destitute. Some see government as the means to solve society's problems; others see government as the main problem.

Furthermore, representatives face many different and difficult issues—same-sex marriages, lower taxes versus improved services, new highways versus preservation of neighborhoods, more spending on prisons versus lower college tuition. We do not communicate with our representatives very well, and our wishes may have to be intuited rather than known. Under the best of circumstances, knowing what you should do for 450,000 or 900,000 constituents is difficult. Beyond that is the question of whether you should give your constituents what they want—maybe lower taxes and less regulation—or what they need—perhaps higher taxes and improved infrastructure. Political scientists talk about two polar forms of representation: the delegate who tries to find out what constituents want and does only that and the trustee who believes he or she is elected to use his or her own best judgment to do what is right. Delegates would most often try to provide what constituents want, whereas trustees would be more inclined to provide for their districts' needs as they perceive them. Both orientations involve difficulties because it is often impossible to know what constituents want, and determining district needs is often influenced by ideology or other subjective factors.

Some legislators identify closely with a particular group and view themselves as representatives of that group: women, ethnic minorities, sexual preference groups. There are others who want to get the representatives' ears: party leaders, the governor, campaign contributors, organized special interests. And those groups are better organized and have better access than average constituents. Large campaign contributors do not give their donations without expecting something in return, so the legislator is unable to ignore them. Ultimately it is the constituents who have the vote, but even this principle has been weakened in recent years because of big money, partisan gerrymandered districts, and term limits. Rarely do voters have a realistic chance to keep the good representatives and "throw the rascals out."

In addition to representing our policy views, representatives try to look out for us when we have specific problems with government—not getting an entitlement check, being treated unfairly by an inspector, worrying that a new highway will be built through our property, being opposed to liquor being sold near our

It is easy to stay on top of what is happening in the legislature by using the Internet. Both houses have Web pages. The Senate page is www.sen.ca.gov; the Assembly page is www.assembly.ca.gov. From these sites you can find out about the legislative process and about the status of individual bills. You can also find out how to stay in touch with your legislators. If you type in your address, the site will tell you who your legislators are and how you can contact them. Another useful site is that of the Legislative Counsel: www.leginfo.ca.gov.

State legislators are surprisingly accessible, especially in the district. If you have an issue for which you want to contact your legislator, be informed, call for an appointment, and be brief and forthright. Do not threaten. Information is helpful, and a good anecdote is always useful! Thoughtful letters are also helpful. E-mail is used too much, and staff can recognize form mail as soon as it is opened.

Of course, working through a lobby is also effective, and you may belong to an organization that lobbies; environmental groups, unions, and student organizations are just a few of many that write, track, and try to influence legislation in their area of concern.

kids' school. This ombudsman function is called "constituency service" or "case-work," and it involves intervening with the bureaucracy to solve specific problems. Representatives also try to get favorable treatment for economic interests in their districts—a restaurant owner wants a liquor license that he or she believes is being unfairly denied, or a construction company wants to build more buildings at the local state university. Representatives will also take stands on issues that are largely symbolic but still important to their constituents, such as flag burning or prayer in schools.

Another important part of representation is being available to constituents. Representatives spend much of their time in their districts, attending many functions; speaking to many groups to educate them about the activities of government; and listening to many constituents in their offices. Constituents and representatives of organized groups also visit with them in Sacramento.

Policy Making

The representatives described earlier come together to make policy, most obviously through the complex process of making laws, which involves writing bills, holding committee hearings, conducting legislative debates, and adding amendments.

Policy making also involves seeing that legislation is carried out by the bureaucracy as the legislature intended and looking out for potential problems in the implementation of policy. This function, called oversight, is carried out through a variety of means, including legislative hearings, staff follow-up on constituents' concerns, budgetary hearings, and confirmation hearings. Congressional hearings on the role of federal regulation in the Gulf of Mexico oil spill is an excellent example of this.

The job of the legislator involves both representing the district and making policy. It also involves fund-raising. Legislators live in two worlds, Sacramento and their districts, and they have offices in both places. Mail and phone messages are answered from both places. In the districts they listen to the concerns of their constituents on the one hand, and on the other they tell these constituents about government activities, policy, and politics. In Sacramento they also interact with those constituents who travel to the capital as well as representatives of interest groups. In addition, they work on policy, mostly in committee. Fund-raising takes place largely in the state capital, often involving important interest groups. Most often legislators are in Sacramento Monday through midday Thursday and return to the district for the remainder of the week; however, this varies with the time of the year. Special events often bring them back to their districts. It is necessary to keep a high profile in the district to discourage potential election opponents. The worst charge that can be brought against legislators is that they are ignoring their districts.

Members and Districts

Unlike Congress, in which each state has two seats in the Senate regardless of population, both houses of the California legislature are apportioned by population. The state is divided into 80 Assembly districts and 40 state Senate districts. In each of these districts a single representative is elected. This means that representatives will be paying attention to local interests because local voters determine who gets to go and stay in Sacramento. As a former speaker of the U.S. House of Representatives once said, "All politics is local." Local interests often take precedence over statewide interests. Our legislative system is designed to favor local interests (and interests with money).

Legislative elections are winner-take-all elections, which means that minor or third parties are generally excluded from the legislature, even though they may have substantial support statewide. If they cannot muster the most votes in any one district, they will not have a representative in Sacramento.

Most members, if they have any previous elective experience, have served on school boards, city councils, or county boards of supervisors. Many are self-selected. Others are tapped by party leaders or interests who see them as viable.

Campaigns can easily cost half a million dollars and campaign expenditures are likely to be much higher in the future given the Supreme Court ruling in *Citizens United* (see Chapter 3), which rejected corporate spending limits, and given that the California Citizens Redistricting Commission has created more competitive legislative districts. Fund-raising is one of the big obstacles to winning an election. The nature of California and the size of the districts make winning elections by old-fashioned precinct work unlikely. Use of electronic media is also impractical in the larger media markets because of cost. Most candidates have campaign consultants and engage in polling and targeted distribution of literature.

Because of the relatively small size of the legislature, the districts are among the largest in the country. Senate districts have over 900,000 constituents, Assembly districts over 450,000. Historically, district lines were drawn by the legislature, often leading to charges of gerrymandering, a term dating to the early 1800s, when Massachusetts Governor Elbridge Gerry oversaw a redistricting that benefited his party and resulted in district lines that resembled, in a famous cartoon of the day, a salamander. *To gerrymander* means to draw district lines in a manner that favors one party over another, generally by packing most of the opponent's voters into a few districts and spreading the remainder thinly over the remaining districts. The courts have generally accepted this practice, saying only that districts must be equal in population and must not be drawn to diminish the voting strength of any minority.

Redistricting is done following each census and until 2012 had to pass both houses and be signed by the governor, like any other piece of legislation. The Democrats controlled both houses and the governor's office after the 2000 census but chose to preserve the status quo, which maintained a majority with which they were comfortable. Because the incumbent Republicans were not in danger of losing their seats, they did not challenge the scheme in court. The result was that the vast majority of seats in the legislature were safe seats for one party or the other, and an incumbent was unlikely to be defeated in the general election.

Most action, therefore, took place in the primaries, but since the advent of term limits, incumbents rarely faced a serious challenge. Knowing that an incumbent assemblyperson would be out of office in no more than six years, the astute challenger waited for that vacancy to occur rather than engaging in an expensive, divisive challenge. If one believes that the real power of voters is to throw the rascals out, then term limits had an unintended consequence of insuring that that was unlikely to happen. The legislature was more immune from direct electoral challenge than ever before.

However, as of 2012, two steps have been taken that entirely change the situation described in the previous paragraphs, which created safe districts with highly partisan incumbents. Whether they will change the ultimate outcome remains to be seen. As a result of their continued frustration with the legislature—and not recognizing their own contributions to the problem by establishing term limits—the voters approved two measures, Proposition 11 in November 2008 and Proposition 14 in June 2010, that should impact who gets elected to the legislature. Proposition 11 takes the task of drawing legislative districts away from the legislature and places it with a 15-person commission (see Chapter 1). This committee created new districts that have a closer partisan balance and have at times pitted incumbents of the same party against one another. The expectation is that this will result in fewer seats that are safe for one party and that would previously have been filled by highly ideological partisans, but the true effect of Proposition 11 will not be known until the voting patterns of the newly elected legislature become clearer over the course of several years.

Proposition 14 carried this theme forward by eliminating partisan primaries and, perhaps, general elections. It provided for an open primary in which all candidates run and all voters take part. Voters vote in the primary or preliminary election for the candidate of their choice for each office from a single list of all candidates from every party, and the top two candidates go on to the November election, which is like a runoff. The expectation here is that, even if both of these candidates are in the same party, the more moderate candidate will win by appealing to voters in the minority party (see Chapter 4). If there are only two candidates in the first election they will have to run against each other for a second time. While this may seem absurd, the electorate in November is almost always larger (and therefore less Republican) than in June, which could affect the outcome. In 2012, the 65th Assembly District in Orange County was an excellent example of an incumbent—Republican in this case—challenged by a single opponent, a Democrat. They ran against each other in June and the Republican incumbent won with over 58 percent of the vote. In the run-off in November the Democratic challenger won with about 52 percent of the vote, and this was a key seat in the Democrats gaining a two-thirds majority in the Assembly. Many factors were at work in the district, not the least of which was that about 50,000 people voted in June while over 120,000 voted in November.

The hope was that the combination of Propositions 11 and 14 would result in legislators being elected who are more moderate and more willing to engage in bipartisan compromise, but it is too early for us to feel confident that this will occur. However, these measures did result in at least one huge change in 2012: the Democrats gained a two-thirds majority in both houses, meaning they can act on tax measures without any Republican votes. Still, many of these new legislators are from marginal seats (such as the 65th in Orange County and 32nd in Bakersfield) and may be reluctant to take bold action which might endanger their chances for reelection in two years when—because it is not a presidential election and therefore turnout will be lower—most likely fewer Democrats will vote. And the theory is that new legislators will in general be more moderate. A new chapter in California politics has been started, and no one knows what will be written in it.

Organization

Leadership

The leader of the Assembly is the speaker, and he or she has a remarkable array of powers, although these are now diminished because no member of the Assembly occupies his or her position for a long period of time. In an attempt to increase the power of the speaker by increasing his or her time in the position, in 2003 and again in 2009 the Democrats elected a first-term legislator to the speakership. The Assembly speaker's powers are considerably more extensive than the Speaker of the U.S. House of Representatives. Most notable of these powers—which begin with control over parking spaces and offices—is the almost complete control over establishing committees, assigning members to serve on committees, and removing them if the speaker chooses. Because the bulk of legislative work is done in committee, members are dependent on the speaker if they are to have any meaningful role in the legislature. The speaker is also the presiding officer when the full Assembly meets and in this role controls debate. If the speaker does not personally preside he or she designates the person who does. The speaker also appoints the majority floor leader, who assists in running legislative sessions.

It is difficult to overestimate the power of the speaker. This power is used to move bills and can be used to help supporters and hurt opponents. It is also used to raise money, which in turn is used to solidify support. Members find it advantageous to cooperate with the speaker. The speaker is elected by the entire membership of the Assembly, but in most cases the outcome is determined in advance by the majority party caucus, which consists of all of the members of the majority party meeting together. Only when the majority is split does the full Assembly vote become significant.

The minority caucus elects the Assembly minority leader, who is the public voice of the minority party and who works with the speaker to determine minority party assignments on committees. The speaker, however, has the final say.

The other important element of the leadership is the Assembly Rules Committee, which is made up of nine members, four elected by each caucus plus a chair appointed by the speaker. Its responsibilities include hiring staff and assigning bills to committees and reviewing legislative rules. Rarely does this committee operate independently of the speaker's wishes.

The organization of the Senate is similar, but the leader, the president pro tempore, does not have the absolute power that the Assembly speaker does. Many of the speaker's powers in the Assembly rest with the Rules Committee in the Senate. Yet in recent years the president pro tempore—most notably John Burton—has become the most influential legislator, largely because of the impact of term limits, which have created an Assembly that is far less experienced than the Senate. Assembly members have a maximum of 6 years' experience, and their leaders may have only 1 or 2 years' experience. Senators have often been in the Assembly first and then have an additional 8 years to serve. By the time a senator becomes a Senate leader, he or she may have had 10 or 12 years' experience in Sacramento. John Burton, who may be the last of his breed, had far more experience than that, including experience in the U.S. Congress.

Committees

The bulk of legislative work is done in committees. Committees allow for greater specialization, greater expertise of those involved, and greater attention to detail. In 2009–10 there were 30 standing or permanent committees in the Assembly and 22 in the Senate (see Table 5.1). Each member sits on several standing committees. In addition to standing committees, there are many select committees that exist to study specific issues, and joint committees to look at issues that concern both houses. Members may serve on a dozen or more of these less important committees.

Committees are at the heart of groups of players often referred to as issue networks. These networks consist of committee members and staff, senior members of the respective executive branch agency, and interest groups concerned with issues in a committee's jurisdiction. The bulk of policy details are worked out in these networks. Lobbyists and bureaucrats tend to be specialists. They generally spend their careers in a single subject area and are experts in this area. It would be unusual for someone who has spent a career in transportation to move to education. Previously, legislators would spend their careers in specific issue areas as well. Term limits have changed that, or rather have shortened the length of careers. While policy is still worked out in these networks, power has shifted to those with greater permanency, experience, and expertise—namely, lobbyists and bureaucrats. The less experienced and less knowledgeable legislator is now more dependent than before on these individuals for policy details. Experienced staff can help, but often staff members are no more experienced than legislators.

Staff

Before Proposition 140, the staff of the California legislature was the best in the nation. The proposition required a staff cut of 40 percent and resulted in layoffs and the departure of many of the best staffers, especially the experts on which the committees relied. Staff is still a significant factor in the legislature, and over the years, it has inched back toward its previous size.

Without staff, the legislature cannot effectively do its job. Staff is crucial in both the policy-making and representative functions of the legislature. All legislators have staff in both their Sacramento and district offices to help with constituency contacts, including casework, scheduling appearances, and answering mail and phone calls from constituents. In addition, committees have staff, called consultants,

TABLE 5.1 ★ Standing Committees of the California Legislature, 2009–10

STATE SENATE

Agriculture	Judiciary
Appropriations	Labor and Industrial Relations
Banking, Finance, and Insurance	Legislative Ethics
Budget and Fiscal Review	Natural Resources and Water
Business, Professions and Economic Development	Public Employment and Retirement
Education	Public Safety
Elections, Reapportionment, and Constitutional Amendments	Rules
Energy, Utilities, and Communications	Transportation and Housing
Environmental Quality	Veterans Affairs
Governance and Finance	
Governmental Organization	
Health	
Human Services	
Insurance	

ASSEMBLY

Committee on Accountability and Administrative Review	Committee on Insurance
Committee on Aging and Long-Term Care	Committee on Jobs, Economic Development, and the Economy
Committee on Agriculture	Committee on Judiciary
Committee on Appropriations	Committee on Labor and Employment
Committee on Arts, Entertainment, Sports, Tourism, and Internet Media	Committee on Local Government
Committee on Banking and Finance	Committee on Natural Resources
Committee on Budget	Committee on Public Employees, Retirement and Social Security
Committee on Business and Professions	Committee on Public Safety
Committee on Education	Committee on Revenue and Taxation
Committee on Elections and Redistricting	Committee on Rules
Committee on Environmental Safety and Toxic Materials	Committee on Transportation
Committee on Governmental Organization	Committee on Utilities and Commerce
Committee on Health	Committee on Veterans Affairs
Committee on Higher Education	Committee on Water, Parks, and Wildlife
Committee on Housing and Community Development	
Committee on Human Services	

to help with the policy work of that committee, and consultants are critical components of the issue networks. Each legislator is allotted an office budget for staffing. Additional staff depends on having a committee leadership role or on the generosity of the party leadership. In addition, the house leaders and caucuses have staff that may number more than 150 for the majority. This staff helps with bill analysis for individual members and public relations for individual members as well as the party.

There are over 2,000 legislative aides. It is not unusual for majority legislators to have 13 or 14 staff members. Minority members may have only 4 or 5. While most aides are modestly paid, some—especially highly valued committee consultants—make over $150,000. The total personnel budget for legislative workers in 2009 was

$129.3 million. The median salary for a staff member in the Assembly was about $51,000 and in the Senate, $61,000. These aides are supplemented with members of the prestigious Assembly and Senate Fellows program and many college interns.

There are three important and well-regarded groups of staff who are nonpartisan and work for the entire legislature. The first is the Legislative Analyst's Office, which analyzes budget proposals and the fiscal impact of ballot propositions. The second is the Legislative Counsel, which helps write bills, analyze ballot propositions, and provide legal advice. The third is the State Auditor's Office, which handles management and fiscal audits of the executive branch.

The Legislative Process

There are three types of items that may pass the legislature: bills, which if successful become laws; constitutional amendments, which require a two-thirds vote of both houses and a referendum by the voters; and resolutions, which are largely symbolic expressions of opinion. For the remainder of this section we are concerned primarily with bills.

Bills are introduced only by legislators, even if the content was originally proposed by someone as politically important as the governor. Indeed, bills are often not written by the person who introduces them. Many bills may be written by, or in conjunction with, lobbyists, and the nonpartisan Legislative Counsel's office may help in drafting language. Senators are limited to introducing 65 bills in a two-year session, whereas Assembly members may introduce only 30. Bills may be introduced for a variety of reasons, such as impressing constituents or paying off a political favor, and most go nowhere. In the 2009–10 legislative session, 1,495 bills were introduced in the Senate and 2,799 in the Assembly. Of these, 1,922 reached the governor's desk and 1,385 became laws. In the 2011–12 legislative session, 1,884 bills passed the legislature and reached the governor's desk. He signed 1,636 of them, vetoing 248, some of which were strongly supported by his allies. This is far fewer than was common 20 years ago. In 1989 and 1990, 3,174 new laws were enacted. Bills must pass both houses with identical language before they are forwarded to the governor for his or her signature.

Once bills are introduced, the rules committee of the appropriate house assigns the bill to a standing committee or perhaps two committees, depending on their content. The bill is also numbered and printed. Committees cannot act on a bill until it has been in print for 30 days to allow comment from interested parties. Committees hold hearings, scrutinize the language carefully to make sure that it says what members intend, add amendments, and pass or reject bills. An absolute majority of the committee must vote favorably to report a bill out. If a bill is reported out of committee, it goes to the floor for discussion by the entire house. Amendments may be added at this time. Amendments require only a majority vote. Bill passage requires an absolute majority (41 in the Assembly, 21 in the Senate). Once a bill has passed one house, it goes to the other house for similar consideration. If a bill is successful in both houses and the wording is the same, it goes to the governor for his or her signature. If the governor vetoes a bill, then it requires a two-thirds vote in each house to override the veto.

Most likely, a bill passing both houses will have different wording. In this case one house may acquiesce to the wording of the other house or a conference committee will be established to work out the differences. A conference committee

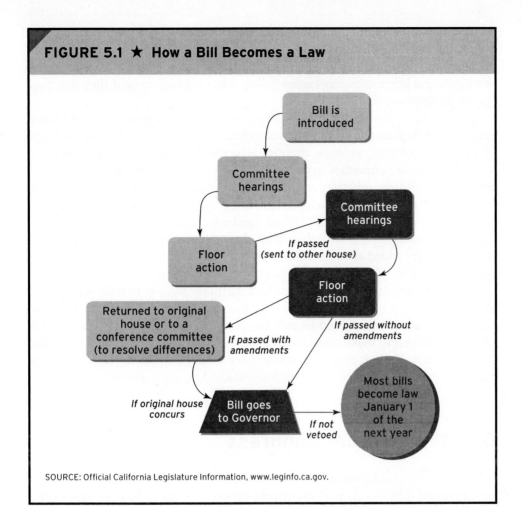

FIGURE 5.1 ★ How a Bill Becomes a Law

Bill is introduced

Committee hearings

Floor action

If passed (sent to other house)

Committee hearings

Floor action

If passed without amendments

Returned to original house or to a conference committee (to resolve differences)

If passed with amendments

If original house concurs

Bill goes to Governor

If not vetoed

Most bills become law January 1 of the next year

SOURCE: Official California Legislature Information, www.leginfo.ca.gov.

is a joint committee consisting of three members from each body. The Assembly members are appointed by the speaker, and Senate members are appointed by the Senate Rules Committee. They suggest compromise language that must pass both houses. If this attempt fails, two additional attempts may be made before the bill is put to rest.

This is the textbook approach. However, much legislation is able to shortcut some of these steps, especially near the end of a legislative session, when bills tumble over one another and deals are made in back rooms in a rush to adjourn. Many bills reappear as amendments to other bills, with even less public attention than in the normal process. At this time, the party leaders become more important because they are able to grease the skids for compromises and logrolling. (Logrolling is vote trading, the process by which members exchange votes—the classic "You vote for my bill, and I will vote for yours.")

A common end-of-session legislative tactic is to hijack a bill and then "gut and amend" it. A bill that started out to deal with state courts could suddenly reappear—with no public notice or hearings—as a bill offering in-state tuition to undocumented immigrants. Or take 2001 bill AB 1389 (insiders always refer to bills by numbers, like AB 1389 or SB 1785). This bill started out dealing with squid fishing and came back as a bill dealing with transferring public lands for development of a cruise ship terminal in San Francisco.[1]

End-of-session periods in Sacramento reflect quintessential American politics: a system that favors insiders, corporations, and big money. And while this goes on all year long, these back-room strategies work best when time is compressed and the media and other outsiders cannot follow what is going on or, if they can, they cannot do anything about it.

At the end of the session there is much pressure to get things done. As noted earlier, 988 bills passed in 2011 and many others were in play. Insiders and lobbyists know what is going on, and their attention is focused on a single bill or a small number of bills that are important to their clients. Large corporations and other interest groups hire full-time lobbyists and lawyers, sometimes a full platoon of them, to follow the important bills, develop the strategy, and take the necessary actions to ensure the desired outcome. All of which can be written off as business expenses.

These insiders work out deals behind the proverbial closed doors and provisions to bills are added and removed at the last minute. Often the junior members voting on the floor have no idea of what they are voting on.

Before the legislature was term-limited, members were extremely well-versed about their policy interests and had long memories about what tricks lobbyists and other legislators had tried to pull in previous sessions, which meant that it was more difficult to make unnoticed changes in legislation which would benefit a special interest. There is no such institutional memory now among legislators. The experience and skills rest mostly with lobbyists and agency representatives.

Differences from Congress

While the California legislature is modeled closely on the national legislature, there are important differences, and collectively, these make the California legislature a weaker body.

Term Limits

Unlike members of Congress, who can serve as long as they are reelected, California legislators are limited to three two-year terms in the Assembly and two four-year terms in the Senate. Term limits were enacted by the passage of Proposition 140 in 1990. There were numerous reasons for the success of this proposition. In part it was a reaction to the highly effective Assembly Speaker Willie Brown, a flamboyant politician who was immensely unpopular with conservative voters. In part it was a reaction against divided government (a Republican governor and a Democratic legislature) and gridlock. Partly it was a reaction against the large fund-raising efforts of incumbents. Partly it was a reflection of a national trend against entrenched incumbents. Finally, it was a belief among some Republicans that term limits would be a way to get rid of the Democratic majority. The effort has reduced the ability of the legislature to act effectively while neither reducing the Democratic majority nor eliminating gridlock.

Item Veto

In Washington, the president has to sign or reject bills passed by Congress in their entirety. He cannot approve parts that he likes and reject parts that he dislikes.

In California, as in most states, the governor has a line-item veto on appropriations, including those in the budget. This power allows the governor to reduce or eliminate a specific spending item, although he cannot increase items. This means that the legislature cannot force the governor's hand by including an item that he opposes in a larger bill, most of which he supports.

Apportionment and District Size

Both houses of the California legislature are apportioned by population, unlike Congress, in which the Constitution allots two senators to each state, regardless of size. Wyoming, with about the same number of residents as Long Beach, has the same number of senators as California, which is about 70 times larger. Because California is so populous (about 37 million people) and because its legislature is relatively small, its legislative districts are among the largest in the nation. Senate districts have over 900,000 constituents, while Assembly districts contain over 450,000 residents. New Hampshire, with 400 members in its lower house, has one representative for about every 3,000 residents. While its representatives are very accessible and elections are not expensive, most cannot wield very much influence in their very large chamber. California senators, unlike any other legislative body, represent more constituents than members of Congress and more than the U.S. senators of seven states. This means that they are considerably less accessible than their counterparts in other states and that their elections are considerably more expensive.

The fact that both houses are apportioned by population has led some informed observers to suggest that a unicameral legislature of 120 members would make more sense. This would result in smaller districts and increased accessibility among legislators.

Media Visibility

In Washington the president dominates the news. The media interpret the national government's actions by focusing on the president. Members of Congress are generally used to give more depth to a presidential story. Most often, these are party leaders, committee chairs, or the occasional legislator who has managed to make a name for himself or herself on a given issue.

The same is true in Sacramento, but the difference is that the statewide media, especially television, rarely cover news in Sacramento. Only the four party leaders receive air time, and because they hold their positions for so few years, the public has difficulty knowing who they are. Consequently, most of what happens in Sacramento occurs out of the spotlight.

Court Appointments

Some of the greatest legislative battles in Congress have been the Senate's hearings to confirm judicial appointments, especially to the Supreme Court. In California many judges are elected. Those who are appointed by the governor are approved by the Commission on Judicial Appointments. The Senate does get to approve many other gubernatorial appointments to executive positions and regulatory boards and commissions, including the governing boards of both the California State University and the University of California. For both bodies, they have rejected recent nominees over policy differences.

Filibusters

In the U.S. Senate—a body that is not apportioned on the basis of one person, one vote—41 percent of the members, potentially representing slightly more than 30 million people (fewer than the 37 million represented by California's two senators), can block the passage of most legislation through use of the filibuster. California has no such provision. Indeed, in most cases the majority rules. The principal exception is raising taxes, which requires a two-thirds vote.

Initiatives

Unlike the U.S. Constitution, the California constitution provides several means of taking issues directly to the voters. Most significant is the initiative. This is important in the legislative context because those who are thwarted in their attempts to get legislation passed can always threaten to take it or an even more extreme measure to the voters. This tactic can persuade the legislators to vote for measures that they would otherwise oppose and significantly weakens the legislature.

Seniority

In the U.S. Congress, seniority is used as an informal rule in appointing members to committees and choosing each committee's majority and minority leaders; once members are appointed to their committee positions, they are almost never removed. In the California legislature, both the appointment and removal power resides with the Assembly speaker and Senate majority leader, with seniority playing a much smaller role. Both the speaker and the Senate majority leader in 2007 and 2008 removed members of both parties from committee leadership roles for disagreeing with the leadership over various issues.

Problems, Real and Perceived

When voters pay attention to the legislature, it is most often to complain or criticize its actions. At times these objections are on target, at times not. State government currently is dysfunctional, and the legislature is an easy target. It is easy to be repulsed by the contentious process of arriving at legislative agreements. Moreover, the misbehavior of any one of the 120 legislators is amplified out of proportion and reflects badly on the whole institution. (In 2009, Orange County assemblyman Mike Duvall resigned after having been videotaped bragging about being in bed—literally—with a lobbyist.) Individual members often attack the legislature to play up their own importance, or they run for the legislature by running against it.

Among the most common valid criticisms of the legislature are the following:

Money

In the California legislature, as is the case throughout American politics, money carries a great deal of clout. Elections are expensive, and the money for elections comes from many sources, including the candidate's personal wealth, small contributions from many individual contributors, and larger contributions from business, unions, and other special interests. Large contributions are generally given to ensure support for a particular interest. Although legislators claim that their vote cannot be bought and that contributors are buying only access, that claim would be difficult to support, as the previous chapter has shown. Moreover, simply having access that the ordinary voter does not have is a significant advantage. We have the best legislature that money can buy, and short of moving to public financing of campaigns—an idea rejected by the voters in June 2010—those with money will always have an advantage over those who do not.

Money is usually distributed to those who support the position of a given interest or to those who might be swayed by the offer of monetary support. It also goes to party leaders, who then distribute it to solidify their support both within their party and against the other party. Indeed, it was the amassing of a large war chest that contributed to the distrust and dislike of Speaker Willie Brown and led to the proposing and passing of Proposition 140, setting term limits. However, term-limited legislators, having little background in fund-raising, have become more dependent than their predecessors on large donations from special interests. Jesse Unruh once said, "If you can't take their money, eat their food, drink their booze . . . and then vote against them, you don't belong here."[2] On this basis, there are probably more legislators now than before that "don't belong here."

Term Limits/Lack of Experience

It was believed that term limits would remove a remote professional class of legislators and bring in a new breed of legislators with closer ties to their districts. The ballot argument said that term limits "would remove the grip that vested interests have over the legislature" and create a "government of citizens representing their fellow citizens."[3] The expectations for this proposition were overhyped, and the results were unfortunate.

Legislative politics works best as an ongoing game among a relatively stable group of experienced players. Many of the aphorisms about politics, such as "Politics makes strange bedfellows" and "Don't burn your bridges," are based on ongoing relationships played out over a period of years. Over time legislators learn not only the game and how to play it but also whom they can trust, whom they can work with, and whom they should avoid. This knowledge facilitates cooperation across party lines. Legislators come to learn that not all good is on their side of the aisle and not all evil on the other side. In a short six years, legislators cannot all learn that; the players change too rapidly. The people who can work out effective compromises seldom emerge, and even if they were to emerge, they would not know with whom to work.

Nor can effective leadership emerge in six years. In recent years, to give leaders more time in office, the Assembly Democrats have chosen freshmen legislators as committee chairs and as speaker. But a freshman legislator, no matter how talented, cannot effectively lead a large collegial body. Contrast this with Congress, in which members may serve a decade or more before assuming a leadership position, and where Speaker Boehner and former Speaker Nancy Pelosi each served more than 20 years before assuming that position. Had they been in Sacramento, they would have been out of the Assembly for 14 years by that time.

Nor in 6 short years is there time to develop expertise in process or subject matter, the ordinary skills of a legislator. In Congress, by the time they assume leadership positions, members know the subject matter, the history, and the players. By the time 10 years have passed in Sacramento, members have been gone for 4 years. This dilemma was summed up by a lobbyist:

> I feel sorry for the first-term members who faced the energy crisis. They don't know who's smart; they don't know who knows what they're doing; they don't know the policy; they don't know the politics. And they are faced with a crisis.[4]

In Sacramento, effective power has shifted to the Senate, whose members are more experienced. Senators can spend eight years in the Senate, and many have already spent six years in the Assembly. But real power has shifted from the legislature to the permanent establishment—the bureaucracy and interest groups. Members in these institutions may spend a career in Sacramento outlasting five sets of Assembly members.

Much as they were dissatisfied with the legislature, it is doubtful that the voters wanted to shift power to either of those two groups. In June 2012 voters made a change in term limits which on balance may shift some power back to the legislature. Proposition 28 reduced the time a legislator could serve in Sacramento from 14 years (6 in the Assembly and 8 in the Senate) to 12 years, but now those years could all be served in one house. This will give each house more stability and should result in the selection of leaders with greater experience. It will probably mean that senators will generally be less experienced, but whatever is lost in that body will be gained by the much greater experience that Assembly members will be able to gain before being forced to leave. The result could be a more knowledgeable and effective legislature which is at least marginally better able to deal with lobbyists and bureaucrats.

If there has been a positive aspect to term limits, it is in the increased diversity of the legislature. The percentage of Latino legislators rose from 6 percent in 1990 to 25 percent in 2009, before declining to the current 19 percent. The percentage of women increased from 17.5 percent in 1990 to 32 percent in 2008 before dropping to the current 28 percent. The current speaker of the Assembly, John Pérez, is an openly gay Latino. The previous speaker, Karen Bass, is an African American woman. Members of ethnic groups and women regularly occupy positions in the Democratic leadership of both houses.[5]

Partisanship

Many believe that partisanship has increased in the legislature in recent years. This trend is often attributed to recent districts having been safe, where representatives were elected who couldn't lose in a general election and who were responsive to only their party's majority, which determines the primary election outcome and which is more extreme than the average voter. Safe districts resulted in increased partisanship and less willingness to compromise.

As usual, the issue is more complex than this, although the new more competitive general elections might result in the election of more moderates. The problem is not that there are strong partisans in the legislature, however. This has always been so. But in recent years, the quality of public discourse has become less civil, and the participants have come to have less regard for their opponents and have become less willing to work with them. Part of this incivility is a reflection of national politics brought on by the fact that the two national parties' leadership has become homogeneous and much more polarized. Part may also be attributed to term limits. Recognizing that they will not have to deal with them for years into the future, legislators make less effort to develop civil working relationships with their opponents.

But legislators should be partisan. We elect representatives on a partisan basis. Parties should stand for something. If we vote for Republicans rather than Democrats, then the Republicans should deliver on their partisan promises. Even those who rail against partisanship still want their interests to be forcefully proposed and protected.

Some of the greatest legislatures in the world, such as the British Parliament, are fiercely partisan and yet manage to govern. The difference is that in those bodies, the majority is permitted to rule. In our system, which permits a minority veto, bipartisan cooperation is essential; and when it is not forthcoming, the system cannot function.

Gridlock, Minority Rule, and Lack of Accountability

Although Democrats regularly control both legislative houses by majorities of more than 60 percent, our system has many checks and balances that make it difficult for a majority to rule. Our founding fathers distrusted the masses as much as they distrusted a strong executive. They were more comfortable with a system that did not work well than with a system that might do something that they did not like. While California does not have the filibuster that thwarts majority rule in Congress, it does have two major checks on effective majority governance. One is that the legislature and the governor are elected separately and may represent different parties. The second is that a two-thirds majority is required to get taxes raised, necessitating, in the absence of an overwhelming one-party majority (highly unusual, but which was achieved in the 2012 elections), that the two parties work together to produce realistic spending measures.

Perhaps no other provision of California governance has contributed more to the dysfunctional state of the state than this provision. Californians may elect a majority in the legislature and even a governor of the same party, but unless that party controls two-thirds of each house, it cannot control fiscal policy. Voters blame the majority party for gridlock, when in fact the control rests with the minority party. This provision is even more restrictive than the filibuster, which often locks up the U.S. Senate. The filibuster can only work with 40 percent of the Senate actively backing it, while California fiscal policy is held hostage to a one-third minority sitting on its collective hands, insuring gridlock. As Peter Schrag relates it:

> More than any other structural flaw, it [the two-thirds rule] diffused accountability and brought on much of the budgetary gridlock that California became notorious for in the 1980s and early 1990s.[6]

This structural flaw has been there for several decades, but one of the biggest changes in recent years and the one that contributes the most to our current state of dysfunction is that the minority party—using this "structural flaw"—refuses to compromise on the most critical issue before the state, the need for adequate and stable sources of revenue. Indeed it is this lack of compromise that has made this the critical issue.

Jerry Brown is one of the most experienced individuals to serve as governor. He is also a skilled negotiator. If he had the political culture of the 1970s, when he first served, he would be a successful governor. But skilled as he is, he is unable to find negotiating partners in the minority party leadership. According to a long-time associate of the governor, Jodie Evans, "He is aghast. He reports on some of his conversations like he couldn't believe the narrowness or lack of comprehending by public officials. . . . Some of my old tools are not going to work."[7] Brown himself says that the Republicans have a "perverse fidelity to each point in the Republican gospel."[8] These points are reinforced in the party caucuses.

The Republicans, of course, see it differently. Senator Bob Dutton says that "He's all talk and no go. He throws a few scraps out there . . . let's demonize the Republicans, and that's supposed to fix a problem?"[9] *Los Angeles Times* columnist George Skelton says, "The entire legislative system has been corrupted by Democrats' fear of angering labor unions and Republicans' subservience to a few anti-tax opportunists and entertainers."[10] But while the governor has shown a willingness to oppose the unions on pensions and organizing child care workers, the Republicans seem unwilling to agree to increasing revenues.

Initiatives

Initiatives are often used to bypass the legislative process. That this can be done reduces the need to carefully construct legislation that can pass. If an interest group believes that it can get an initiative proposition on the ballot with a populist appeal, however poorly worded—and there are many examples of such propositions—then they have little incentive to submit legislation for careful consideration of committees in each house of the legislature or to engage in legislative bargaining. Moreover, initiatives have passed that have weakened the legislature or weakened the legislature's ability to make responsible policy. Proposition 140, which instituted term limits, greatly weakened the ability of the legislature to function effectively, by ensuring that there are rarely any experienced legislators in Sacramento. Propositions 13 and 98 each limited the ability to make responsible fiscal policy, the first by limiting the use of a stable tax tool, the second by locking up a huge chunk of the available funds for a single purpose—education.

We will probably see many more propositions because it may be easier to get agreement with a majority of the voters than with two-thirds of the legislature. We appear to be in a destructive cycle. The voters feel dissatisfied with the legislature and pass a proposition that makes the legislature work less effectively. That makes voters more dissatisfied, and they vote for another proposition. And so on. An effort to put an initiative on the ballot in 2012 making the California legislature part-time failed.

California Legislature: Where Are We Now?

The legislature serves two principal functions: policy making and representation. The different requirements of these two functions create tensions. Legislators are also pressured by the needs versus the wants of the district; state versus local interests; the demands of interest groups, campaign contributors, party leaders, and the governor. California is a large state with many competing wants and needs. Legislative districts are among the largest anywhere. These factors turn the making of policy into a complex and often unseemly process. It is a process moved by imperfect humans who will always be somewhat flawed. Even the highly regarded legislature before term limits passed some bad legislation and left problems unaddressed.

Yet it could work better than it does. The state is dysfunctional, and in many ways the legislative process is key to this dysfunction. It is valid to ask if the legislature is the creator or the victim of this impaired system. In large part, this problem has been created by outside forces. Term limits and the two-thirds vote requirement for passing tax legislation are the most notable outside factors. The declining level of civility in the legislature is a reflection of the impact of term limits and of the increasing political polarization in the nation. But it is also caused in part by the safe districts created in the last legislative redistricting, a process carried out for the most part in the legislature. Legislators representing safe districts do not have to pay attention to moderate elements in their party or voters from the opposition party. Perhaps Propositions 11 and 14 will moderate this. Perhaps not. And 2012 may prove a crucial year in testing these changes. Finally, individuals are responsible for their own behavior. Regardless of outside forces, individual legislators of goodwill could make a difference.

As long as we have the current structure and policy limits placed on the legislature, often by initiatives, it is difficult to see how the system can improve. Given the diverse nature of the state and an electorate that is itself divided and tends to elect a legislature that is also divided on many important issues—which in a democracy should be a plus—positive change cannot be anticipated. Moreover, the public has little understanding of legislative functions or the legislative process, making positive change through the initiative process even more unlikely. Indeed, as mentioned, more draconian measures, such as a part-time legislature, have been suggested. As the popular cartoonist Walt Kelly's Pogo said, "We have met the enemy and he is us."

FOR FURTHER READING

Cain, Bruce E., and Roger G. Noll, eds. *Constitutional Reform in California: Making State Government More Effective and Responsive.* Berkeley, CA: Institute of Governmental Studies Press, 1995.

California Journal and State Net. *Roster and Government Guide.* Sacramento: California Journal, 2004.

de Sá, Karen. "How Our Laws in California Are Really Made." *San Jose Mercury News,* July 10, 2010. www.mercurynews.com/politics-government/ci_15452125. Accessed 6/26/12.

Institute of Governmental Affairs. "IGS Goes to Sacramento to Assess Ten Years of Term Limits." *Public Affairs Reports* 42, no. 3 (fall 2001).

Mathews, Joe, and Mark Paul. *California Crackup: How Reform Broke the Golden State and How We Can Fix It.* Berkeley: University of California Press, 2010.

Muir, William K., Jr. *Legislature: California's School for Politics.* Chicago: University of Chicago Press, 1982.

Schrag, Peter. *California: America's High-Stakes Experiment.* Berkeley: University of California Press, 2006.

———. *Paradise Lost: California's Experience, America's Future.* New York: New Press, 1998.

Wilson, E. Dotson. *California's Legislature.* Sacramento: Office of the Chief Clerk, California State Assembly, 2000.

ON THE WEB

California State Assembly Democratic Caucus: www.asmdc.org

California State Assembly Republican Caucus: www.republican.assembly.ca.gov

California Choices.org: http://californiachoices.org (accessed 6/26/12).

California State Senate: www.sen.ca.gov (accessed 6/26/12).

California State Assembly: www.assembly.ca.gov (accessed 6/26/12).

Capitol and California: www.sacbee.com/capitolandcalifornia (accessed 6/27/12).

Legislative Counsel: www.leginfo.ca.gov (accessed 6/26/12). The Legislative Counsel of California's official site, maintained by law.

Rough & Tumble: www.rtumble.com (accessed 6/27/12). Daily summary of California news.

Senate Democrats: www.democrats.sen.ca.gov

Senate Republicans: www.republicans.sen.ca.gov

University of California, Berkeley, Institute of Governmental Studies Library: http://igs.berkeley.edu/library (accessed 6/27/12).

SUMMARY

I. Legislatures are not well understood, but are critical to a democratic form of government. Indeed, a working legislature is practically a definition of a democratic government.

II. The California legislature is, for the most part, modeled on the U.S. Congress.
   A. It is bicameral.
   B. Members are elected from single-member, geographically based districts.
   C. Unlike the U.S. Congress, both houses are based on population.

III. Legislators must both represent their constituents and make policy.
   A. These two items are not always compatible.
   B. In representing their districts, members must decide whether to follow the wants or the needs of their constituents and whether to follow directions from the district or use their own best judgment.
   C. Poor communication from constituents makes these actions difficult.
   D. Legislators have offices both in Sacramento and in their districts.

IV. The California legislature was once the most professional of all state legislatures.
   A. Proposition 140, the term-limit proposition, greatly weakened the legislature by limiting members to serving six years in the Assembly and eight in the Senate.
   B. As a result, legislators are always inexperienced, compared to the bureaucracy and lobbyists.

V. The California legislature is relatively small.
   A. Therefore, it has some of the largest legislative districts in the world (863,000 for the Senate and 431,000 for the Assembly).
   B. Districts are gerrymandered to provide safe seats for both Republicans and Democrats.

VI. The leader of the Assembly is the speaker; the leader of the Senate the president pro tempore.
   A. Each is elected by all of the members in that body, but the majority party caucus usually determines the outcome.
   B. The speaker controls most of the resources and is very powerful.
   C. The speaker and the president pro tempore are term-limited.
   D. The president pro tempore shares powers with the Senate Rules Committee.

VII. The bulk of legislative work is done in committees.
   A. Bills are read and amended here.
   B. Committees are made up of a group of individuals— lobbyists, staffers, members, and bureaucrats—who make and control policy in a given substantive area.

VIII. Professional staff members make the legislature possible.
   A. Some of them work in districts, some in members' offices, some for committees, and some for the leadership.
   B. The best-paid staff members are usually subject-matter experts working for committees.

IX. The legislative process has several steps.
   A. Bills are first introduced by members and sent to committees.
   B. Bills must pass the floors of both houses (with identical wording) before they are sent to the governor for his signature.
   C. If the governor vetoes a bill, it takes a two-thirds vote of each house to override it.
   D. Budget, appropriation, and tax bills also require a two-thirds vote, giving the minority party immense power in the legislature and making it difficult for the majority party to govern.

X. The state legislature is different from the U.S. Congress.
   A. Members are term limited.
   B. The governor has an item veto (he can cut or eliminate any item in a budget bill, while not rejecting the entire bill).
   C. Both houses are based on population.
   D. The legislature does not have a filibuster, unlike the U.S. Senate (which requires an absolute 60 percent vote to cut off debate and pass a bill).
   E. The two-thirds money-bill requirement has a similar impact in thwarting the majority.
   F. California also has the initiative process, which allows the legislative process to be bypassed, most often by interests with deep pockets.

XI. The effectiveness of the California legislature is limited
   A. by term limits and lack of experience.
   B. by the two-thirds-vote rule, which keeps the majority party from governing and makes accountability difficult.
   C. by increasing partisanship.
   D. by the power of big money.
   E. by district size, making communication difficult.

PRACTICE QUIZ

1. An item veto allows
   a) the governor to reject any single item in an appropriations or budget bill.
   b) the speaker or the president pro tempore to pull any single item from the agenda.
   c) a single member to block a single piece of legislation by signing a written objection.
   d) a petition by a group of 10 legislators to block any single piece of legislation.

2. Proposition 140
   a) limits the time that legislators can serve in Sacramento.
   b) limits the legislature from raising property taxes.
   c) sets aside 40 percent of the budget for education purposes.
   d) requires the speaker to assign staff to the minority party.

3. The legislature is composed of
   a) 80 members in the Senate and 40 in the Assembly.
   b) 120 members in a single body.
   c) 60 members in each body.
   d) 80 members in the Assembly and 40 in the Senate.

4. A two-thirds vote is needed to pass
   a) appropriation bills.
   b) budget bills.
   c) tax bills.
   d) all of the above.

5. Partisanship in the legislature
   a) has declined because of apportionment.
   b) has declined because of the blanket primary now in effect.
   c) has led to greater ease in getting budgets improved.
   d) has increased in recent years.

6. The power of the speaker of the California Assembly includes all of the following *except*
   a) the power to assign parking spaces.
   b) the power to assign office space.
   c) the power to assign members to committees but not to remove them during the current term.
   d) the power to assign a member to a committee against both the member's wishes and the wishes and needs of his or her constituency.

7. Proposition 140 resulted in all of the following *except*
   a) an increase in office budgets.
   b) the establishment of term limits.
   c) a reduction of committee staff and personal staff.
   d) laying off some of the most knowledgeable staff experts from committees.

8. The legislative process is biased in favor of
   a) issues favored by the public.
   b) the status quo.
   c) change that interest groups favor.
   d) legislation proposed by the governor, who can introduce a limited number of bills directly to both houses, bypassing some of the steps of the legislative process.

9. California has some of the largest legislative districts in the nation. This means that
   a) elections in California tend to be expensive.
   b) citizen access to legislators is unusually good because legislators need to face the voters so often.
   c) staff levels are unusually high to handle the volume of business from constituents.
   d) California has an unusually large number of legislators.

10. Term limits have resulted in the following:
    a) an increase in expertise among legislators, who have only a few years to make a name for themselves
    b) an increase in citizen legislators, people with little or no political experience who are able to run because seats are open
    c) an increase in staff members, who are needed to help legislators with little experience
    d) a decline in the knowledge needed to pass good-quality legislation

CRITICAL-THINKING QUESTIONS

1. Should a legislator vote for what his or her constituents want or what his or her constituents need?
2. Who should apportion the legislature?
3. What criteria should be used to apportion a legislature?
4. Should a legislator take orders from constituents or use his or her own best judgment, even if it is unpopular?
5. How much access should lobbyists have to legislators?
6. When should a legislature have rules that allow a minority to block legislation?

KEY TERMS

At this point you should have a general understanding of the following concepts and terms:

apportionment (p. 109)
Assembly Rules Committee (p. 103)
Assembly Speaker (p. 103)
bicameralism (p. 98)
committees (p. 104)
gerrymander (p. 101)

gridlock (p. 113)
"gut and amend" (p. 107)
lack of accountability (p. 113)
line-item veto (p. 108)
minority rule (p. 113)
representation (p. 99)

Senate president pro tempore (p. 104)
staff (p. 104)
term limits/Proposition 140 (p. 108)
two-thirds vote (p. 106)
veto (p. 106)

6 The Governor and the Executive Branch

WHAT CALIFORNIA GOVERNMENT DOES AND WHY IT MATTERS

Consider the following activities in the executive branch of our state government:

★ After complaints from the oil industry about delays in permitting, Governor Jerry Brown fired the head of the Division of Oil, Gas, and Geothermal Resources, who had expressed concerns about "fracking."

★ Governor Brown commuted the prison sentence of a grandmother who spent a decade in prison for a crime she probably did not commit involving the death of her grandson.

★ The governor vetoed a bill requiring kids to wear helmets while skiing, stating that "Not every human problem deserves a law."

★ Upon entering office, Governor Brown reduced the size of the governor's press staff from 17 to 3, yet is widely seen as more accessible than was Governor Schwarzenegger.

★ Attorney General Kamala Harris, through hard, independent bargaining, got a better deal for the state and homeowners from banks in a home foreclosure abuse settlement than did her fellow attorneys general.

★ In 2010, when the U.S. District Court ruled that Proposition 8, which outlawed same-sex marriage, was unconstitutional, the attorney general and governor at the time—Jerry Brown and Arnold Schwarzenegger, respectively—declined to appeal the ruling.

Governor Brown commemorated the first anniversary of his third term in office with no press release trumpeting the milestone to the press. Blogger William Bradley says that no one talks much about Brown.[1] Brown likes it that way and substantially reduced the governor's press staff when he entered office. He need not have bothered because the press corps, never large, has declined drastically in recent years as newspapers retrench. TV has never paid much attention to Sacramento, and fewer viewers pay attention to TV news. Rarely is there more than a single out-of-town TV reporter in Sacramento.

California government operates largely out of the public view and it does not operate well. The term-limited legislature and the two-thirds vote requirement for passing revenue measures make it difficult for even a skilled governor to put together working coalitions on important budgetary matters—and Jerry Brown is a skilled governor. When governing fails, political leaders often turn to the initiative process, asking the public to make the final decision. But the members of the public have been kept largely uninformed up to this point and often do not understand the issues that they are asked to vote on.

Uninformed voters, inexperienced legislators, constitutional provisions that do not facilitate majority decision making, and an invisible executive. It is not a surprise that our state government does not work well.

The Invisible Governor?

While he is the most visible political figure in the state, the governor is almost invisible in comparison to the president of the United States. There are a number of reasons for this invisibility. We depend on the media for most of what we know about our government, and for the most part the media in the state are not interested in state politics or governance. From the media's perspective, there is little that is newsworthy about Sacramento: it is a long way from the major population centers of the state, and what happens there just does not capture the audience the way a good car chase does. The media work best by focusing on a well-known or riveting personality. But the governor is often perceived as boring—think of governors Davis, Wilson, and Deukmejian, and if you cannot remember them, that may have something to do with the media coverage they received. With the exception of U.S. senators, long-serving, high-visibility politicians are rare in our term-limited government.

The president's job is analytically divided into two roles: head of government and head of state. So, too, the governor, but while the head-of-government role is similar in both cases, the head-of-state role is vastly different, and it is that role that gives the president most of his visibility.

The role of the head of government is to govern—that is, to develop policy, get it passed through the legislature, and implement it via the bureaucracy. It is often divisive. Think of the prime minister of Great Britain, who not only develops policy, gets it passed, and implements it but actually appears on the floor of Parliament to answer questions, often shouted, from his own and opposition parties. In contrast, the queen is the head of state in Great Britain. Her role is highly visible, ceremonial, important for bringing people together. She cuts ribbons, attends public events, greets foreign visitors, participates in parades. In fact, this is her major role. Most of the time when you see the president between campaigns, it is in his role as head of state: welcoming the troops home, attending funerals, dedicating buildings, posing for pictures with foreign dignitaries, dipping his hands in Gulf oil, or making major or minor public announcements. Being head of state is largely a symbolically positive, noncontroversial role offering lots of photo ops for the media. In this role the president represents the entire nation, acting for all of us.

The governor does not have this range of opportunities for public visibility, or, if he or she does, the events are at so low a level that no one cares. Few dignitaries of note visit Sacramento, and the press simply does not warm to filming the governor talking to teachers or highway patrolmen, although pictures of Governor Schwarzenegger congratulating Jet Propulsion Laboratory scientists on a successful Mars landing were in all the papers in 2004. It is hard to imagine similar coverage if Governor Brown did the same thing. It is not worth the cost for profit-oriented TV stations to keep reporters and camera crews in Sacramento for these largely uninspiring moments—unless the governor has his own star power, as Schwarzenegger did. Jerry Brown is much more at home with governing and the minutiae of policy and has little interest in photo ops and the other elements of being head of state.

Nothing else so clearly demonstrates the difference between the chief executive of the United States and the chief executive of one of the most important states in the union than this difference in visibility.

There are important similarities between the two positions as well, and most notable here is that these are offices of limited powers. It is hard for the public to understand that the most powerful political leader of the most powerful nation on earth has strictly limited powers; the same is true of the governor of the most populous state in the union. Just as the president does not run the nation, the governor does not run the state. Our founding fathers feared a strong executive, having experienced such rule under a king and under capricious colonial governors. Consequently, they created a system in which the powers of the executive were secondary to the legislature and where the powers of all institutions were strictly limited.

The governor does have important powers, in some cases more than the president, but as Richard Neustadt has documented for the president, the governor's power is mostly the power to persuade.[2] His power to command and direct in any way he chooses is seriously limited.

As with the president, people have many incomplete, incorrect, and conflicting views of the governor. Tom Cronin and Michael Genovese compiled a list of what they call the paradoxes of the presidency:

- We want the president to be an effective politician while being above politics.

- We want him to be a common person and an extraordinary person at the same time.

- We want him to be powerful but not too powerful.[3]

In part, we want the president to be all things at all times, and, of course, this is not possible.

The governor is not burdened with as much symbolic baggage as is the president, and yet many misperceptions carry over to this office as well. These misperceptions are amplified by the fact that people think that they understand the office. After all, it is an executive office, a position with which all of us who work in organizations have some familiarity. But it is much more than, and much different from, being president of a corporation. It is a *political* executive office, and that is an entirely different position in an entirely different organization, an organization that does not respond well, if at all, to direct orders.

Our greatest misperception is thinking that the governor is more powerful than he or she in fact is. Our state government is modeled on the weak executive federal government that our founding fathers created. The governor does not control the legislature, and it is difficult to make policy without the cooperation, or at least acquiescence, of legislators who may have little reason to support the governor. He or she can get this cooperation only through persuasion—perhaps hardball persuasion, but persuasion nonetheless. Within the executive branch, it is possible to be more direct. But the executive branch is large and in many cases very remote from the governor. How does the governor get a highway patrolman in San Diego or a park ranger in Marin County to do what he or she wants?

Moreover, much of the executive branch is insulated from direct gubernatorial influence. The executive branch comprises many independently elected executives, known as the plural executive, often from the opposing party of the governor. And some organizations, such as the University of California, are governed by boards that can be influenced only by appointments, budgetary threats, or strongly voiced public opinion.

Besides, we often elect governors who are not especially knowledgeable about government agencies, Sacramento politics, or the many interests in our very large and diverse state. Arnold Schwarzenegger held no political office before being elected governor, and the 2010 Republican nominee for governor, Meg Whitman, did not even vote for many years. More important than formal powers are political skills, political resources, a favorable environment, and luck. Ability to bargain, friends in important positions, a good economy, and an absence of natural disasters, collectively and individually, are sometimes more important than formal powers.

Schwarzenegger was nearly unique in California politics initially, even exceeding the popularity of Ronald Reagan. By sheer dint of personality and the threat to go to the public with initiatives, he managed a series of impressive victories—in the early days. But it did not last. He overreached himself, and he antagonized the members of his own party with his moderate positions on many issues. His attempt to pass four initiatives in a special—and costly—election in November 2005 was a disaster. Near the end of his time in office, his approval ratings had reached a low of 23 percent in a Public Policy Institute of California poll.[4]

Jerry Brown is the polar opposite of Arnold Schwarzenegger. He is one of the most knowledgeable governors California has had in recent years. He loves the details of policy making, knows the intricacies of governing, and does not need the limelight. He knows how to bargain and make deals, but he is faced with a bad economy, huge revenue shortfalls, and an opposition party that will not bargain on revenue issues. It is too early to assess his success or failure in office, but in his first two years he was unable to put together the necessary support to address the long-term revenue crisis facing the state.

Formal Powers of the Governor

The formal powers of the governor, while limited, are still formidable. The governor has powers—most important, the line-item veto—that are denied to the president. Yet impressive as this list of powers is, these powers are most important as vantage points on which the governor bases his informal powers or powers to persuade. A governor who expects to use only his formal powers to govern will not accomplish much. He must use those powers as a basis to persuade other political actors to support his goals. For instance, he can use his appointment power to try

The governor has important formal and informal powers, among which are

FORMAL POWERS

organizing and managing the executive branch, including appointing many top executives

independent executive actions

commander in chief of the National Guard

appointing people to head executive agencies, to independent boards and commissions, and to the judiciary

drawing up the budget

making legislative recommendations

vetoing legislation

line-item vetoes of budget and appropriation items

granting of clemency, including pardons and reprieves

INFORMAL POWERS

bargaining with legislators and other independent power sources

access to the public to make his case

developing a vision or agenda for the state

raising money for political campaigns

to persuade an important legislator to support his budget by promising to appoint one of the legislator's supporters to an important state commission.

The state constitution vests supreme executive power in the governor. What those words mean is not clear, but it probably is both more and less than meets the eye. Less, because the governor's office is an office of limited powers in which nothing is supreme. More, because executives often reach beyond what was constitutionally intended. When a governor overreaches, recourse through the legislature or the judiciary takes time, and the results are often unclear.

Organizing and Managing the Executive Branch

The governor is empowered to organize and manage the executive branch. *Organize* means he can make a number of administrative appointments. *Manage* means that many of these appointees must report to the governor, at least indirectly, and he can remove them from office. Again, this power can be overstated. First, the state government does not do as much as one might think. Much of the money that it collects is passed on to local government and school districts to spend. Second, the rest of the elected executive branch, most notably the attorney general, limits his actions, and some state employees report to these elected officials—5,000 to the attorney general alone. Third, some of the appointments that the governor makes are to boards that can, and do, act independently of the governor; these appointments may be for fixed terms. The best known of these independent boards is the Regents of the University of California. This 26-member board consists of 7 ex officio members, who sit on the board because they occupy another office, including the governor himself; one student; and 18 members appointed by the governor for 12-year terms—terms that are longer than his. Control over this board, if he wishes to exert it, is possible only through new appointments, through the loyalty of previously appointed members, and through persuasion. Fourth, the governor must make appointments to agencies about which he knows little, often appointing individuals about whom he knows little. Information coming out of these agencies is limited, so the governor is often in the dark about what is happening until something goes terribly wrong and appears in the press.

Independent Executive Actions

The governor's powers are constitutionally restricted by the legislature, but he is able to act independently of the legislature in some cases. These are actions permitted by the constitution or under laws passed by the legislature. They are most significant in times of an emergency.

Few laws passed by the legislature are self-implementing. Most require positive action on the part of the administration. This process of implementation involves clarification of the law and the assembling of finances and an administrative structure to allow action to take place. All of this requires prioritization and the finding of funds, decisions that will have to be made by the governor's appointees or by the governor himself. This is a process that allows for far more influence by the governor than might be apparent on the surface.

Commander in Chief

The governor is the commander in chief of the California National Guard. This role is of little significance until times of civil disorder or natural disaster; and then the significance is in the calling out of the guard rather than actually directing its actions.

Appointments

Making appointments is one of the governor's most significant powers. The governor appoints four distinct groups of individuals: his personal staff, heads of major administrative divisions, some judges, and members of a variety of boards and commissions. Some of these appointments require confirmation by other bodies, some do not; some appointees work at his pleasure, whereas others serve for fixed terms; some are answerable directly to the governor, and others are several steps removed or protected from his intervention. Over the course of his administration, a governor can make more than 2,500 appointments. At the start of his term there will be about 500 positions to be filled.

The governor appoints his personal staff, which consists of about 100 individuals who make the governor's life possible—the individuals who structure the life of the governor, package him, and present him to the public. Governors hire, fire, and move these individuals about at will. No confirmation is required.

Next closest to the governor are the members of his cabinet. The governor determines who will serve in the cabinet and what role, if any, the cabinet plays in policy development. The heads of the superagencies of state government are in the cabinet as well as the director of finance and others whom the governor finds useful and appropriate. These positions require confirmation by the Senate, but the governor can fire them as he wishes.

The governor also appoints the heads of major departments, most of whom are in the superagencies. These individuals have the responsibility of overseeing more than 200,000 state employees.

In addition, the governor appoints members to more than 325 boards and commissions, important and unimportant, visible and invisible. Once appointed, individuals do not have to answer to the governor, although political pressure, including budget pressure, can be brought to bear in many ways.

Stating that "The state's bureaucracy is a labyrinth of disjointed boards, commissions, agencies and departments,"[5] Governor Brown in 2012 proposed a restructuring and consolidation of agencies. The previous year he eliminated 25 boards and commissions. There is no political payoff in this. Few outside of the government will notice. But it is important and illustrative of Brown's attention to policy detail.

Legislative Powers

Much of the success of the governor depends on his ability to persuade the legislature to go along with his programs. This is a difficult task because the legislature owes him little. He does not help elect them. They represent smaller and different constituencies, with legislators often looking out for local rather than statewide issues. They are on different career paths with different time constraints. Because they are term limited, they are relatively inexperienced in bargaining and do not have a long-term commitment to the Sacramento governing process. Their next jobs may be in the private sector, perhaps as lobbyists.

The governor's ability to persuade legislators depends on his political skills as well as many factors beyond his control, including the partisan makeup of the legislature and the political and economic environment. Although much of this influence depends on the governor's informal powers and the use of his other formal powers, he does have several specific powers that are directed primarily toward influencing the legislature, including preparing the budget, vetoing bills or provisions of bills, and making legislative recommendations.

Budget

Perhaps the governor's most significant power is that of preparing the budget, along with the line-item veto of budget provisions. At the federal level, the president presents Congress with a budget proposal, but it is only that, a proposal; the House of Representatives has constitutional authority over fiscal matters. The California constitution gives the power of preparing the budget to the governor. This means that all budget requests from executive branch agencies must pass through the governor. The actual work on this process is done by the Department of Finance.

The budget is prepared and sent to the legislature by January 10, with revisions following later in the spring (the May revise) as the financial picture becomes clearer. The governor then has the job of getting the budget approved by the legislature. Until 2012, a super majority of two-thirds was required to approve a budget (now only a simple majority plus one is required). Although a super-majority vote is no longer needed to pass a budget, it is still required to raise new revenues. Because current budgets do not have adequate revenues, the support of the minority party remains critical. Obtaining this support may require some expensive trade-offs with recalcitrant legislators who withhold their support until they receive an offer they cannot refuse. There are in effect five major players in the budget game—the governor and the leaders of both parties in both houses of the legislature. The need for one or two marginal votes may introduce even more major players. Because of his role at both ends of the budgetary process, and because one person needs to broker the deal, the governor usually has the key role, but even he can be held hostage by recalcitrant legislators. In recent years, Republican legislators have become adamant about not supporting tax increases, which, more than anything else, has led to the current system being unworkable. Any system that permits a minority to block action on important legislation requires compromise and bipartisan cooperation. Neither Schwarzenegger, a Republican, nor Brown, a Democrat, have been able to persuade the two parties to work together to shape revenue legislation.

Veto and Line-Item Veto

The second most significant power of the governor is the veto. Just as in Congress, all bills passed by the legislature can be vetoed by the governor. The legislature passes about 1,000 bills each year and the governor may veto up to one-third of them. The veto can be overridden only by a two-thirds majority of each house of the legislature, but that rarely happens. Equally important, and unlike the national government, the governor has a line-item veto, which permits the governor to reduce or delete any appropriation in a spending bill. That means that legislators cannot force the governor to accept funding for programs that he does not like by burying them inside a large spending bill that he must sign. The governor cannot add items, but the ability to reduce or eliminate the favorite programs of legislators is a powerful tool. It is a key item in the governor's box of bargaining tools, one that no other player has.

Legislative Recommendations

At the beginning of a legislative session, as required by the constitution, the governor presents a State of the State speech to the legislature. This speech may be short or long, general or specific. It is normally not covered in detail by the media, unlike the president's State of the Union speech. This speech may contain the governor's legislative program, but whether or not it is spelled out there, most governors have a program that addresses the problems of the state as they see them and that they hope to get passed through the legislature.

The governor cannot introduce legislation but can readily get allies to introduce his specific proposals. As the most prominent political figure in the state, he is in a position to press for action on these proposals. His success once again depends on a variety of factors, including his political skills. Because of his star power, Governor Schwarzenegger had greater access to the public through the media and could bring more outside pressure to bear on the legislature than most governors. But he squandered those resources, in part by supporting ill-advised initiatives, and in the end his governorship is widely seen as being filled with wasted opportunities. Jerry Brown prefers to work on the inside, using his not insignificant personal political skills. But he, too, needs public support for tax increases, and his public appearances may have more impact simply because they are so rare.

Judicial Powers

The governor has the power to grant pardons and commute or shorten sentences. He can also reverse parole decisions or delay a death sentence. These are significant powers, but they are used relatively rarely and with extreme caution because such decisions can have serious political consequences. Among other judicial powers of the governor is that of nominating justices to the supreme court and appellate courts and appointing other judges if positions are opened by retirement or resignation.

Public Roles of the Governor

While the governor's role as head of state does not provide as much access to the public as the president has, he still is occasionally seen cutting a ribbon, bestowing an honor upon some citizen, attending a funeral, or observing a natural disaster. These and other ceremonial and symbolic appearances may have little policy content, but they keep the governor in the public eye and give the impression that he is on top of things and that the state is in good hands. While far less visible than the president, governors do not underestimate these appearances. They remind people that the governor is on the job, that he does care about their concerns, and that, in the case of a disaster, the governor and the resources of the state will be available.

Occasionally there are some issues of such overwhelming importance—the budget crises are prime examples—that the media are willing to give the governor significant air time. On other occasions he can stage policy-related events, such as showing up at a school to emphasize his education policies (or to mask his actual opposition to certain education policies).

The governor also moves into the public spotlight during elections, and not only when he is campaigning for reelection. California governors often think they have a chance to become president—and why not, since governors of far less populous or attention-getting states have been elected. When governors sense a chance for the presidency, they try to get in the national media as much as possible. Jerry Brown did this regularly during his first two terms in office, to the detriment of his governing.

Governors also campaign for political allies—perhaps a candidate for president or a loyal endangered assemblyperson. Finally, they may take an active role in an initiative or referendum campaign, either to bolster the chances of an initiative that they support or to gain more public attention. In spite of his mixed success in this arena, Governor Schwarzenegger continued to be involved right through the elections of 2010, endorsing the successful Proposition 14 in June and leading the successful effort in November to defeat Proposition 23, which would have suspended an air pollution control law (AB 32).

The governor's extensive fund-raising appearances also may gain significant public attention. This attention is useful because it shows the opposition that the governor has a formidable war chest and shows the party faithful that the governor is out there stumping on their behalf.

Jerry Brown as Governor

Jerry Brown is the son of Pat Brown, one of California's most popular governors, who in the 1960s helped develop the education system and infrastructure that made California the envy of the nation. In 1974, seven years after his father left office, Jerry Brown was elected governor for two consecutive terms. He earned a reputation as a fiscal conservative as well as a visionary and as a bold politician who could ignore the wishes of his allies. He was also a frequent candidate for the Democratic Party nomination for president.

As a visionary, he was often parodied as Governor Moonbeam for advocating such things as establishing a space academy and purchasing a communications satellite for the state. His advocacy of fiscal restraints (which reflected his personal lifestyle) did not go over well in a state that still remembered his father, who had presided over an era of seemingly unlimited promise.

After a long time in the political wilderness, Brown reestablished his career, starting at the local level as mayor of the troubled city of Oakland and continuing on to be attorney general from 2007 to 2011. He was elected governor to a third term in 2010, after a hard-fought campaign against billionaire eBay entrepreneur Meg Whitman. Whitman had little political experience but a lot of money, and her self-financed campaign was the most expensive in California history. Brown won with far less money by emphasizing his political experience and an ability to work with the opposition Republicans.

Jerry Brown's predecessor in office, Arnold Schwarzenegger, was elected in the October 2003 recall of Governor Gray Davis. Davis was recalled due in part to the state's inadequate response to a manipulated energy crisis, to legislative budgetary stalemates, to fund-raising scandals, and to his own remoteness. Hoping for change, the voters turned to the inexperienced but flamboyant movie actor who stood out in a weak field of possible replacements.

Schwarzenegger's first and biggest challenge was to deal with the budget crisis. He proposed two financial initiatives for the March 2004 ballot, both of which the legislature endorsed and the voters approved, and that first year he balanced the state budget through a combination of cuts, borrowing, moving funds from one fiscal year to another, and the other traditional means that many governors use to balance the budget without raising taxes.

But the following year, he attacked the political establishment and called for a special election, asking voters to approve several propositions that came from the conservative part of the political spectrum. The result of the special election was a stunning defeat for the governor and his supporters. Not only did all four propositions that the governor supported fail but the governor's approval ratings fell from over 50 percent in January 2005 to between 30 and 40 percent by August and September of that year.

Most of the Schwarzenegger years were characterized by extreme state budget deficits that the governor and legislature were unable to close on a long-term basis. Year after year, the deficits were $15 billion or more of the approximately $100 billion general fund. There were yearly standoffs lasting for months between two groups: the governor and the Democrats on one hand, both willing to close a good portion of the gap with budget cuts and (in one year) revenue increases of approximately equal size, and the Republicans on the other hand, unwilling to raise taxes and revenues under any circumstances and demanding that budget cuts close at least half the gap before negotiations could begin.

In the end, the Schwarzenegger governorship failed to resolve the crises in California politics. Certainly the state was no better off when he left office than when Gray Davis was removed.

In 2010, the state voters had the opportunity to select between an experienced Democratic politician in Brown and a successful Republican Internet entrepreneur in Meg Whitman. The voters chose political experience over business acumen.

Although Brown is perhaps the most experienced nonincumbent elected to governor, his time in office has not been easy. Although he has achieved real accomplishments, the dysfunctions of the state have impeded his ability to make the degree of progress toward solving the state's problems that both he and the voters had anticipated.

From his predecessor, Brown inherited a budget deficit of $25 billion as well as an established pattern of constructing budgets largely with smoke and mirrors. Perhaps Brown's greatest accomplishments to date have been to cut the structural deficit by more than half while offering budgets that are far more honest than those of recent years. But he has had to do this with no support from Republican legislators and has had to make deep cuts in popular government programs, including cuts to higher education.

As of late 2012, Brown has signed 1884 new bills into law, vetoed 248 bills cut 5,500 positions from government, gotten Amazon.com to agree to pay state sales tax, "realigned" many services back to the local level, eliminated local redevelopment agencies, and persuaded the electorate to increase taxes to close a huge budget gap. He has also taken symbolic actions, such as eliminating a few boards and cutting back on issuing cell phones and state cars to public employees.

He remains visionary and is a strong supporter of such future-oriented programs as a high-speed rail and making California a leader in green energy and technology. But as former Senate President Pro Tempore John Burton pointed out, "'You cannot be proactive from a Democratic standpoint unless you have money.'" Burton concluded, as many political observers have, that Brown "'did as good as he could do with the cards that were dealt him.'"[6]

The cards were different from those he had when he was first governor. First, the legislature is now term limited, and as such its members are far less skilled at legislating and making deals than earlier legislators. Even more important is that the Republican legislators have become united and adamant about not raising taxes or creating any new ones. Because the California constitution requires a two-thirds vote on tax measures, the minority party generally has a veto, and without its support, creating an adequate and stable source of revenue is not possible. And that support will not be given. The Republicans do pay a price for this stance, however; their votes are not relevant on legislation that requires only a majority vote.

It is more the system than the individual politicians who are to blame for this longstanding political stalemate. Our system does not let the majority rule, and the minority in recent years has demonstrated an unwillingness to compromise on tax and revenue increases. Until the system is changed, or until the Republicans are willing to compromise on taxes, or until the Democrats are willing to disassemble most of the state functions, our state will remain in gridlock.

The highly unusual—and likely temporary—supermajority that the Democrats gained in 2012 may make at least a difference. So long as this lasts, Republican votes are not needed for tax changes. Yet, as noted in Chapter 5, several of the new Democrats are from marginal districts and may be reluctant to cast votes for unpopular tax measures that will be used against them in the next election. Further, the new changes in how districts are formed were intended to produce more moderate legislators, meaning these new Democrats may not be as adamant about tax increases as Democrats in the legislature have generally been in recent years.

Structure of the Executive Branch

The executive branch of California has several significant divisions: the governor's personal staff, the appointed cabinet and other department heads, the other elected officials of the executive branch, appointed boards and commissions, and the more than 300,000 state employees, divided into more than 85 agencies and 30 educational institutions. Not all of these agencies and employees are under the control of the governor. Figure 6.1 provides a graphic representation of the executive branch.

Personal Staff

Closest to the governor is his or her personal staff. The members of this staff include schedulers, speechwriters, and press officers. In addition there are individuals who oversee the appointments process, the general development of policy, and liaison with the legislature. They structure the governor's day, develop statements for the press and the public, arrange relations with various groups, and set up appearances throughout the state. Members of this staff are expendable, and they tend to be young and transient. Their positions totally depend on staying in the governor's good graces.

The Cabinet and Agency Heads

The governor uses his cabinet as he determines. It has no official policy function as a body but can be used to help formulate policy. The cabinet is often more a symbolic body than an integral structure of governing. The executive branch is divided into seven superagencies, and the heads of these agencies, called secretaries, are generally in the cabinet. These are State and Consumer Services; Youth and Adult Corrections; Environmental Protection; Health and Human Services; Labor and Workforce Development; Business, Transportation, and Housing; and Resources. These superagencies contain most of the agencies of the state. It is the individual agencies, not the umbrella superagencies, that actually carry out functions, and they may act independently of the superagency secretaries. The governor appoints these agency heads, although he often does not have a free choice. He needs to appoint someone with expertise in the area, and sometimes the qualifications are spelled out in law. These agencies and superagencies are called *line agencies*, the term used to describe organizations with their own statutory authority to carry out functions and provide services.

In addition, the governor has several staff advisory agencies, including the Department of Finance, the Office of Planning and Research, and the Department of Personnel Administration. Perhaps the most important of these is the Department of Finance, which prepares the governor's budget.

The Plural Elected Executive

One of the most notable features of California government is the number of statewide elected administrative offices. It has seven of these positions, plus the Board

FIGURE 6.1 ★ Executive Branch of the California State Government

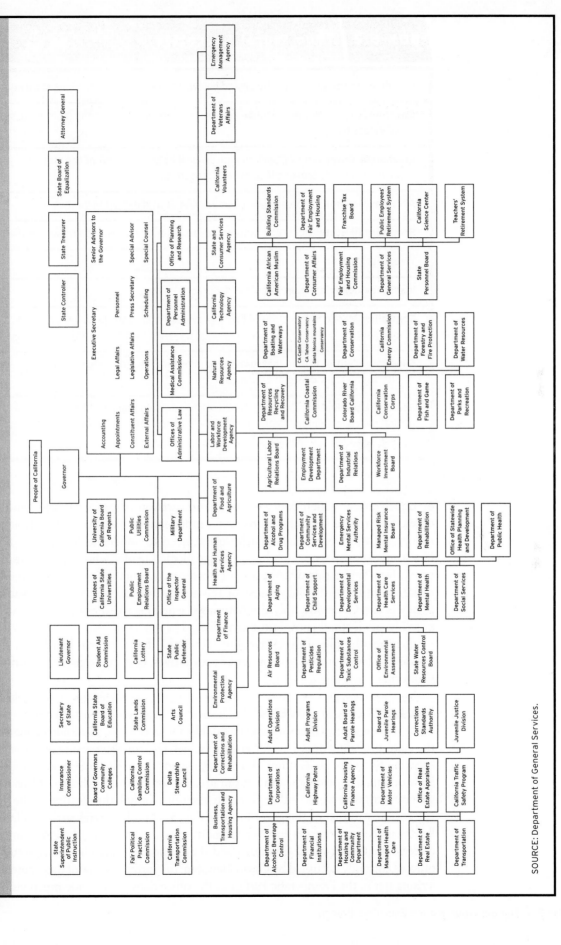

SOURCE: Department of General Services.

BOX 6.2 | The Plural Executive

In addition to the selected duties listed below, all sit ex officio on various state boards.

Governor: Organizes the executive branch, prepares the budget and legislation, signs or vetoes bills

Lieutenant Governor: Replaces the governor if he or she is out of the state or incapacitated or leaves office for any reason

Attorney General: Enforces laws, oversees and assists district attorneys

Secretary of State: Holds elections and oversees the records and archives of the state

Treasurer: Manages state money

Insurance Commissioner: Regulates insurance companies

Controller: Monitors collection of taxes, provides fiscal controls for receipts and payments

Superintendent of Public Instruction: Administers the state role in public education, sits on the state Board of Education

Board of Equalization: Oversees the assessment and administration of property taxes and the collection and distribution of sales taxes and the collection of excise taxes. The controller is a member of this body.

of Equalization, which oversees the administration of property, sales, and excise taxes. This means that there are seven independent bases of power that do not report to the governor and which do not need to adhere to his wishes. This differs from other states which have a single elected leader who appoints lesser state executives. While this distribution of power may limit the governor's freedom to make or implement policy, most of these positions do not deal with substantial policy issues. Generally, only the Attorney General is a real policy competitor (and possibly an electoral competitor as well).

It is not the plural executive, but rather the dysfunctional legislature and the restraints placed on the government by initiatives, that make governing difficult in California.

THE LIEUTENANT GOVERNOR The lieutenant governor exists to replace the governor if he or she becomes incapacitated. He also acts in the governor's absence from the state, providing occasions for great mischief. He can also preside over the Senate, breaking tie votes. He is often of a different party from the governor. Perhaps more than others, this position captures the imagination of those who would restructure government, who would either eliminate the office or link the election of the lieutenant governor to that of the governor, as is the case in other states such as Illinois. The lieutenant governor serves on several important boards, including the governing boards of both the University of California and the California State University system. The office is currently occupied by Gavin Newsom, the former mayor of San Francisco and a rising star in the Democratic Party, but the office does not provide much visibility.

THE ATTORNEY GENERAL The attorney general oversees the department of justice, which employs more than 5,000 persons and has responsibility to see that the laws are enforced. She has the freedom to set priorities for which areas get the most attention and resources. She has oversight responsibilities for local district attorneys and county sheriffs. She is legal counsel to the state and defends the state in lawsuits. She has no obligation to cooperate with the governor and is often viewed as a rival. In 2004 the governor ordered the attorney general to intercede with the state supreme court to stop gay marriages in San Francisco. The governor had no statutory basis for giving such an order, and although the attorney general ultimately did just that, he did it on his own authority. This office is very powerful, and incumbents often see themselves as leading candidates for governor—Jerry Brown used this office to launch his campaign for governor in 2010—although few have successfully made this transition. The attorney general is able to set her own

---

BOX 6.3   How Many State Employees Are There?

How many people are employed by the state of California? We actually don't know. The national ratings of how well the state is managed are C at best, in the lower half of the states nationally, symbolic of the fact that one reason we don't know how many employees there are is because the state is not well managed and its computer systems are out of date. The estimates range from 176,000 to almost 500,000.

First, when most people speak of "state employees," they mean those who report to the governor. But in fact because of the plural executive branch, UC/CSU, the legislative and judicial branches, and other independent boards, only half to two-thirds of state employees report to the governor.

The state also lacks a consistent definition of an employee. Some employees are full-time and have civil service protection. Others are full-time and temporary. Others are part-time with long-term contracts. Still others are part-time and temporary—although some of them work for years. (And some are nonstate employees who are employed under state contracts, just to complicate the situation.) Many, definitely not counted as state employees, actually work for local government but with state funding.

The bottom line is that without modern management practices and a consistent definition of who is who over time, we are left with estimates. The California Budget Project estimates the total personnel-years for state employment as 350,609 in 2008–09, but part-time employees here would be included only as a proportion of full-time, so the total number of people employed by the state is even higher. The budget crisis is no doubt lowering this figure.

Compared with other states, California has relatively few employees. The U.S. Census Bureau comparison tables show that in 2005, the latest figures available, California is fourth from the bottom, with 107 state employees per 10,000 population, compared with the national average of 142 and the highest state, Hawaii, with 426. The average for the top 10 states was 271. Most of the states that are most "efficient" are larger states, suggesting that economies of scale for larger states will yield fewer employees to do similar amounts of work. For total state and local employees, California is seventh from the bottom in 2005, with 490 total employees per 10,000 population, compared with the national average of 537 and the average for the top 10 states of 699.[a]

[a]California Budget Project, *Budget Backgrounder–Professors and Prison Guards: An Overview of California's State Workforce*, April 2010, www.cbp.org/pdfs/2010/1004_bbg_Professors_and_Prison_Guards.pdf (accessed June 2010).

agenda, and it may run counter to the governor's agenda. She can use her substantial powers to counter or even embarrass the governor.

The current attorney general is Kamala Harris, another rising Democratic star, but unlike the lieutenant governor she has been able to grab the headlines on several occasions with settlements against major corporations.

THE SECRETARY OF STATE The secretary of state's office oversees the records and archives of the state. It also has the responsibility for holding elections, including publishing election pamphlets, certifying initiative petitions, keeping records, and publishing the results of elections.

THE CONTROLLER The controller is the fiscal officer for the state and oversees the state's money and the collection of taxes. The controller sits on a large number of boards, including the very important Board of Equalization and Franchise Tax Board, discussed later.

THE TREASURER The treasurer manages the money after it comes in and before it is spent. It manages the investment of this money and the sale of bonds.

THE SUPERINTENDENT OF PUBLIC INSTRUCTION The superintendent is the chief administrator of the Department of Education. Unlike the other elected statewide officers, the superintendent is elected on a nonpartisan basis. Education administration is a confusing policy area; the superintendent shares power with an appointed Board of Education. This arrangement ensures controversy and was even more confusing until Governor Brown eliminated the position of the appointed secretary of education in 2011.

THE INSURANCE COMMISSIONER The insurance commissioner's office was made elective by Proposition 103 in 1988, the only position of the plural executive created by an initiative. The commissioner regulates the insurance industry, and Proposition 103 passed because the public felt that the appointed commissioner was not doing his job. It is not clear that making this an elective post has improved matters because most of the contributions to the campaigns for this position come from the insurance industry.

In addition to these positions, voters elect by district four members to the Board of Equalization, which oversees the assessment and administration of property taxes, although much of the work is done at the county level; collection and distribution of sales taxes; and the collection of excise taxes. Income taxes are handled by a different nonelected body, the Franchise Tax Board.

Agencies and the Bureaucracy

Most of the work of California state government is carried out by more than 200,000 state employees housed in over 85 agencies. Most of these agencies are located within the seven superagencies, and most are invisible to the general public, leading to the idea that state government runs by itself. A few agencies, such as the DMV and Caltrans, are well known if not well understood. Others, such as the Office of Small Business Development or the Department of Aging, rarely make it into the news or the public consciousness. Few Californians could name anyone in the executive branch up to and including department heads; few governors could do that either. Many of these individuals are permanent experts on policy subjects who quietly go about doing their jobs.

Most California employees have civil service protection. Many are also represented by unions. A few of these unions, notably the prison guards' union, are very powerful and politically well connected to the point at which the wishes and desires of the union are more likely to become state policy than the wishes and desires of the governor, the head of the Department of Corrections, or the administration of the department.

There are more than 325 state boards and commissions. Positions on these boards are filled by the governor subject to approval of another body, most often a legislative body. These boards and commissions include important ones, such as the Air Resources Board, the Public Utilities Commission, and the Gambling Control Commission. Again, probably the most visible are the Board of Regents of the University of California and the Trustees of the California State University, which together are responsible for more than 100,000 employees. On the other hand, boards such as the Board of Chiropractic Examiners and the Apprenticeship Council are probably known only to those with a direct interest in that area. Most members serve for fixed terms, some as long as 12 years, and, once appointed, do not have to respond to the governor's wishes.

California Executive Branch: Where Are We Now?

As of 2012, several tentative steps have been taken toward tackling the biggest long-term structural problems facing the state and providing the governor with a greater capacity to lead. First, Proposition 25 removed the two-thirds vote requirement to pass a budget. An important step, it loses much of its impact when revenues cannot be similarly raised. (And it may come back to haunt the Democrats some day, should the Republicans control all parts of the state government and can cut programs at will).

Second, although some doubt it will have any real impact, Proposition 11, approved in November 2008, has taken the power to draw the state legislative districts from the legislature and given it to a citizens' commission. This committee has created new districts that have a closer partisan balance and have at times pitted incumbents of the same party against one another. The hope is a legislature willing to cooperate and compromise both with itself and with the governor. (see Chapter 5).

Along similar lines, Proposition 14, approved in June 2010, substitutes a system of preliminary and final elections for the party primary (see Chapter 4). Voters will vote in the "primary" or preliminary election for the candidate of their choice for each office from a single list of all candidates from every party, and the top two candidates will go on to the November election, which will be like a runoff. Again, the ambition is to create a less partisan legislature. The unexpected consequence of these two propositions has been to create supermajorities for the Democrats in both houses of the legislature. How that will play out cannot be predicted at this time.

However, with the exception of Proposition 28 in June of 2012, which shortened the time that legislators could stay in Sacramento but permitted them to serve that entire time in one house, no firm steps have been taken toward addressing the lowered competence of the term-limited legislature. Indeed, there was a 2012 proposal to make the legislature operate only on a part-time basis, though it failed to get on the ballot. If such a motion ever passed, it would carry its own risks. A term-limited, largely inexperienced legislature has resulted in increased difficulty in reaching agreement and in much more power being wielded by experienced professional lobbyists. A part-time legislature will only exacerbate this situation without necessarily giving the executive branch more power to realize its agenda or enact crucial policies.

Finally, nothing has been done about fixing the distortions caused by both Proposition 13, the 1978 proposition that limited property tax increases, and the series of initiatives that have locked in certain parts of the budget and made creating a stable and adequate revenue stream close to impossible. California's revenues are far more volatile than those of other states, and Californians' willingness to govern by initiative remains undaunted.

The ineffectiveness of both Governors Schwarzenegger and Brown at working with the legislative minority to address the state's needs starkly demonstrates what is wrong with our political system: although this is a democracy, ordinary majorities are not able to govern. It remains to be seen if extra-ordinary majorities will do better.

FOR FURTHER READING

Cain, Bruce E., and Roger G. Noll, eds. *Constitutional Reform in California: Making State Government More Effective and Responsive*. Berkeley, CA: Institute of Governmental Studies Press, 1995.

California Performance Review. *Prescription for Change, Report of the California Performance Review*. Vols. I–IV. Sacramento: California Performance Review, 2004. http://cpr.ca.gov/#cpr. Accessed 6/30/12.

Gerston, Larry N., and Terry Christensen. *Recall! California's Political Earthquake*. Armonk, NY: M. E. Sharpe, 2004.

Lubenow, Gerald C., ed. *Governing California: Politics, Government, and Public Policy in the Golden State*. 2nd ed. Berkeley: Institute of Governmental Studies Press, University of California, 2006.

Mathews, Joe. *The People's Machine: Arnold Schwarzenegger and the Rise of Blockbuster Democracy*. New York: Public Affairs Press, 2006.

Schrag, Peter. *California: America's High-Stakes Experiment*. Berkeley: University of California Press, 2006.

————. *Paradise Lost: California's Experience, America's Future*. New York: New Press, 1998.

ON THE WEB

California Choices.org: http://californiachoices.org (accessed 6/30/12).

California Department of Finance: www.dof.ca.gov (accessed 6/30/12).

Center for Governmental Studies, Los Angeles: www.cgs.org (accessed 6/30/12).

Governor of California: www.gov.ca.gov (accessed 6/30/12). The official site of the Office of the Governor, where you can find background information and up-to-date news, and even e-mail the governor.

Public Policy Institute of California: www.ppic.org (accessed 6/30/12).

Rough & Tumble: www.rtumble.com (accessed 6/30/12). Daily summary of California news.

University of California, Berkeley, Institute of Governmental Studies Library: http://igs.berkeley.edu/library/.

SUMMARY

I. The office of the governor is modeled on that of the U.S. president. There are significant differences between the two offices, mostly having to do with visibility.

II. Each job has two analytical roles.
   A. Head of state, which is largely ceremonial, symbolizing the unity of the state or country. In this role, the governor or president makes public appearances

in activities that bring people together. The president, in this role, is on TV almost every evening. The governor has less opportunity to play this role, and even when he does, the state TV stations seem uninterested.

B. Head of government, which involves making policy and trying to get it passed by the legislature and implemented by the executive branch. That role is partisan and divisive. It is also an almost invisible role.

III. The formal powers of the office are greater for the governor than for the president.

A. The governor's formal powers include making appointments and organizing the executive branch; having independent executive actions permitted by law; being commander in chief; proposing the budget; making legislative recommendations; and exercising the veto, including the line-item veto.

B. The governor has most of the powers of the president in domestic policy but also has a line-item veto, which gives him or her more control over the political process of the budget.

C. But California has an initiative process that a popular governor can use to bludgeon a legislature into action.

D. California is different, too, in requiring a two-thirds vote of the legislature to pass a budget that may hamper the governor.

IV. The governor's public roles (head of state) include cutting ribbons, signing bills, observing natural disasters. Non-head-of-state public roles include campaigning and fund-raising, and advocating for initiatives.

V. Like the presidency, the office of governor is one of limited powers, which are restricted by the legislature, the judiciary, the plural elected executive, and the permanent executive branch.

VI. The structure of the state government includes the following:

A. the governor's personal staff

B. the governor's cabinet, which includes the heads of major departments

C. the 385 or more agencies that make up these departments

D. more than 300 boards and commissions, including the Public Utilities Commission and the Regents of the University of California

VII. In addition to the governor, the state is headed by a plural elected executive, which includes the lieutenant governor, the attorney general, the secretary of state, the controller, the treasurer, the superintendent of public education, the insurance commissioner, and the state board of equalization.

VIII. California employs the equivalent of more than 300,000 full-time employees to staff the government.

PRACTICE QUIZ

1. Which of the following is *not* part of the plural executive?
   a) the chancellor of the California State University
   b) the secretary of state
   c) the attorney general
   d) the controller
2. Which power does the governor have that the president does not have?
   a) legislative veto
   b) line-item veto
   c) power to declare war
   d) power to appoint judges
3. Which of the following activities of the governor would be considered part of his role as head of government?
   a) proposing a budget
   b) vetoing legislation
   c) proposing new air quality standards
   d) all of the above
4. Which of the following group of employees are under administrative control and report ultimately to the governor?
   a) legislative aides
   b) supreme court clerks
   c) highway patrol
   d) professors at California State University, Fullerton
5. How many state boards and commissions are there?
   a) fewer than 50
   b) between 50 and 150
   c) between 150 and 250
   d) between 250 and 350
6. The California governor is "invisible" under normal conditions for all of the following reasons *except*:
   a) California's governors appear in events where they are visible to the public, but for the most part, there is little interest in them.

b) for almost every recent governor, there has been little media interest in Sacramento.

c) the governor splits his or her power with other state executives, who are also trying to attract the media.

d) the governor's star power is only of interest to those who like superhero movies.

7. The governor manages the executive branch, but this power is limited by all of the following *except*:

a) the governor appoints so many people that many of them will be appointed to agencies the governor doesn't know much about.

b) some of California government is outside the power of the governor to supervise, like the University of California and the California State University.

c) the boards and commissions that the governor makes appointments to are mostly, except in extreme cases, outside of his power.

d) the attorney general must approve appointments to many boards and commissions, and that appointment power is difficult to obtain.

8. The line-item veto allows the governor to adjust any appropriations item up or down, including reducing it to zero.

a) true
b) false

9. All of the following are true of the governor's appointments to the cabinet *except*:

a) most cabinet appointments are routine, given to the governor's political supporters and campaign contributors.

b) the cabinet as a whole has no official policy function, unless the governor wants to give it a role.

c) some cabinet and subcabinet positions require an appointment of someone with qualifications that are spelled out in law.

d) the superagency heads are usually considered part of the governor's cabinet.

10. The job of the lieutenant governor, one columnist wrote not entirely in jest, consists of getting up in the morning, checking that the governor is still alive, and then making arrangements for lunch!

a) likely to be true.
b) likely to be false.

CRITICAL-THINKING QUESTIONS

1. Is the state government too large?

2. Does the plural elected executive contribute to effective or efficient government?

3. What is the value of having independent boards such as the Regents of the University of California that employ large numbers of people?

4. Which is more important for governing, the formal or informal powers of the governor? Think about this question in terms of "necessary" versus "sufficient" powers.

KEY TERMS

At this point you should have a general understanding of the following concepts and terms:

boards and commissions (p. 135)
cabinet (p. 124)
formal powers (p. 122)

head of government (p. 120)
head of state (p. 120)
informal powers (p. 122)

line-item veto (p. 126)
personal staff (p. 130)
superagencies (p. 130)

7 The California Judiciary

WHAT CALIFORNIA GOVERNMENT DOES AND WHY IT MATTERS

While the judiciary is ostensibly the least political of all of the branches of government, state courts are not insulated from a state's political culture or the actions of other state institutions. Moreover, state courts, although independent, do make judgments and rulings that become part of our larger, federal political system. This is because most law in the United States is enacted by states, and most legal challenges or cases appear in state courts first. Because of this, state courts are commonly called on to mediate important political issues that affect politics beyond their borders and become issues of national importance. This is especially true for California courts given the types of legal questions they are asked to address and the number of cases they handle each year. Two issues in particular reflect the dynamics of the relationship we find when we examine politics, courts, and federalism in California: medical marijuana (which we discuss later in this chapter) and same-sex marriage.

On May 15, 2008, the California Supreme Court ruled in the case *In re Marriage Cases* that the state of California does not have a compelling state interest to limit marriage to the traditional definition—one man and one woman—and that prohibiting same-sex couples from marrying is a violation of the equal protection clause. The repercussions from this ruling have been significant. Mobilization of interest in opposition to the ruling was swift, and as a result Proposition 8, which sought to eliminate same-sex marriage in California, appeared on the November 2008 ballot. This ballot measure was written specifically to overturn the California Supreme Court's ruling. The 2008 California "Official Voter Information Guide," which provides arguments for and against ballot propositions, quoted Proposition 8 advocates Ron Prentice of the California Family Council and Rosemarie Avila, governing board member of the Santa Ana Unified School District: "It overturns the outrageous decision of four activist Supreme Court judges who ignored the will of the people." Over 52 percent of the electorate agreed and Proposition 8 passed.

Politics are dynamic, however. The California courts, including the California Supreme Court, have ruled several times on the constitutionality of Proposition 8. In May 2009, the California Supreme Court addressed three consolidated cases involving the constitutionality of the state's ban on gay marriage (see *Strauss v. Horton, Tyler v. State of California*, and *City and County of San Francisco v. Horton*). In summary, the court ruled 6 to 1 that the amendment was not unconstitutional. But it also added that the amendment did not apply retroactively. This means that those 18,000 same-sex couples who married before the date that Proposition 8 went into effect are still legally married in the state of California.

But the saga didn't end there. In 2010, a federal district court judge found Proposition 8 to indeed be unconstitutional because it violated the Equal Protection and Due Process clauses of the U.S. Constitution by denying same-sex couples the right to marry (*Perry v. Brown*, formerly *Perry v. Schwarzenegger*). This decision was appealed and went to the Circuit Court of Appeals for the Ninth Circuit. A three-judge panel of the ninth circuit upheld the district court judge's ruling. Another appeal was filed with the ninth circuit for a rehearing of the case, which is referred to as an *en banc* (full court) hearing, but the court refused to review and reconsider its prior ruling, issuing an order to that effect on June 5, 2012. The U.S. Supreme Court is the only remaining legal venue for appeal for this particular case. Because the justices on the U.S. Supreme Court have what is called "discretion," they will have to vote to decide whether they wish to review *Perry v. Brown*; it will take at least four "yes" votes from the nine justices for them to review the case.

The consequences for action or inaction on the part of the highest court in the nation vary. For example, if the Supreme Court decides not to review the case, the ruling of the ninth circuit will remain in effect, which means that same-sex marriage is legal in California. If the Supreme Court chooses to review the case, they could rule in four possible ways. First, they could overturn the ninth circuit's ruling, which would have the effect of reinstating Proposition 8 and making same-sex marriage illegal again in California. Second, they could uphold the decision of the ninth circuit but limit the scope of that ruling to only California. Third, they could uphold the decision but apply it to only those states in the Ninth Circuit's jurisdiction. Fourth, and most dramatic, they could uphold the decision and apply the ruling broadly to all states, legalizing same-sex marriage nationally. Considering Proposition 8 itself was a product of California's unique reliance on direct democracy, we can see how the state's institutional design touches even the judiciary, with far-ranging consequences.

Judges and State Government

State courts are an integral and necessary component of state government. They exist and function to ensure that a state's citizenry is guaranteed due process of law and that the other branches and levels of government within the state uphold the state's statutes and code as well as the provisions in the state constitution. Therefore, judges play a much larger role than simply punishing criminals or imposing fines on a polluting company. Courts make decisions that are often political and sometimes very controversial. These decisions have the potential to affect more individuals than simply the parties to a case. Their rulings can have far-reaching consequences that not only ignite more political debate but also have an iterative effect. This is especially true in California, where the politics can be very contentious and the state witnesses a high rate of litigation. And while some cases that come before the California courts gain a significant amount of statewide and national media attention, other cases may remain under the radar yet still have an impact on our daily lives.

For example, on June 21, 2010, the California Supreme Court announced its ruling in *Kleffman v. Vonage Holdings Corp.* At issue in this case was the legality of commercial electronic advertising. Craig E. Kleffman sued Vonage on the basis that its use of multiple domain names to advertise its product and services through unsolicited e-mails (or spam) violated provisions in the California state code. The California high court ruled unanimously that "sending commercial e-mail advertisements from multiple domain names for the purpose of bypassing spam filters is not unlawful under [the state code]." This recent ruling, as well as the Proposition 8 cases discussed in the introduction, serves to illustrate the importance of the California judiciary. When individual citizens or groups of citizens believe that private entities or government have trampled on state law or on their civil liberties or civil rights, they turn to the courts. The judges serving on California's courts must decide if the state's laws or the rights of Californians have been violated.

There is also a recent trend to criminalize more behavior and increase the penalties for offenders. For example, California, like many other states, has modified its laws to allow juveniles to be tried as adults in some criminal cases. Although the intent of this law may have been to let juveniles know that California has little tolerance for certain types of crime, regardless of the defendant's age, the effect has been to shift cases from the courts of judges who deal exclusively with juveniles to the already overburdened courts handling crimes involving adults. In addition, victims' rights legislation, which has elevated some misdemeanors (nonserious crimes) to felonies (serious crimes), increases not only the severity of the penalties for the accused but also the workload for the courts. California's three-strikes law, which was enacted to punish repeat offenders, has had a similar impact. Keep in mind that these are just a few examples.

To be sure, most of the civil cases filed in California's civil courts will be resolved through negotiation between the parties and their attorneys. The courts are still involved, however, in processing the paperwork and dealing with the other administrative issues each civil case may involve.

It is also true that in reality, most of the criminal cases in the state's criminal courts will be resolved through plea bargaining, in spite of what we see in film or on television. Full court trials for the prosecution of high-profile crimes, like that of the music producer Phil Spector, who was charged with murdering Lana Clarkson in 2003 and was later convicted in 2009 after an earlier mistrial, are rare. A plea bargain is the norm. Even so, the courts are still involved in the process. Even if a criminal case never goes beyond the formal filing of charges against a defendant, judges are part of a plea bargain. As a referee, the judge's job is to determine if the plea bargain is appropriate and if the defendant entered into the plea bargain knowingly. The judge asks defendants if they understand the terms of the plea bargain and if they agreed to the terms voluntarily. If the judge decides that the terms of the plea bargain are inappropriate, it may be thrown out. The same applies to the defendant's ability to comprehend the terms of the plea and whether it was truly entered into voluntarily. If the judge concludes that any of these elements are problematic, then a new plea may have to be negotiated or the case may actually go to trial. Regardless, this single case involves many people in the criminal courts, from clerks to administrators and, of course, a judge.

To understand the role courts play in California government and politics, consider the following: from 2009 through 2010, approximately 10,075,000 cases were filed in California Superior Courts (trial courts of general jurisdiction).[1] Of these, over 85 percent were criminal in nature. And each one of these approximately 10,075,000 cases had to be handled individually by the appropriate state court in one way or another until it was resolved. To put this into context, let's consider the number of people living in this state. According to the U.S. Census Bureau, California's population was estimated at 37,691,912 as of September 2012. This number includes all persons who could be counted from newborns to the very old, people who are incarcerated and institutionalized, small children, and people with challenges that may inhibit them from participating in a range of activities.[2] Age, health, disabilities, and other factors exclude a number of Californians from committing crimes. Even if we grant that some individuals may be involved in more than 1 of 9.5 million lawsuits, almost 11 million cases filed in one state's courts in a single year is phenomenal. What is more, despite the incredible workload, California's criminal courts typically resolve cases involving felonies within 12 months. Civil cases are also resolved fairly quickly; on average, 65 percent of civil cases filed in a given year are resolved within a year.

It is easier for an individual to go to criminal court—just drive over the speed limit and get caught—than to civil court. Civil courts have rules about the types of cases they can hear. In civil disputes, parties must also have what is known as "standing to sue." To bring a case to court, an individual must suffer personal and real injury. Typically, one cannot sue on the behalf of another. As well as requiring standing, California courts, like the federal courts, will not handle collusive suits. Collusive suits are lawsuits in which both parties want a similar or the same outcome. Our legal system is an adversarial one, in which it is presumed that parties want opposite outcomes, and when one party wins, the other loses.

Both criminal and civil courts in California are limited as to the cases and controversies they handle because of jurisdiction. *Jurisdiction* refers to the kind of law the court handles. For example, there are criminal courts that deal with violations of state and local laws, and there are civil courts that hear cases involving disputes between individuals or classes of individuals. Civil courts may rule on cases involving breach of contract, tort liability, and wrongful-death suits, to name a few. *Jurisdiction* also refers to geographic boundaries. There are 58 superior court divisions in California, with at least one branch in each county. Cases are assigned to these courts depending on where the parties in civil suits reside or where alleged crimes have been committed in criminal cases.

Federalism and the California Courts: The Case of Medicinal Marijuana

In 1996 through the initiative, voters in California approved Proposition 215, the Compassionate Use Act (CUA). This act provides for the medical use of marijuana for seriously ill persons. It requires that a physician recommend that a patient's health would benefit from using marijuana to alleviate symptoms of serious illness. In addition, the act also shields patients and their caregivers from criminal prosecution for cultivating or possessing marijuana for use approved under the act.

Confusion ensued shortly after the act was implemented. First, there were many (successful) attempts at expanding the scope of the law. Second, the state law came directly in conflict with federal law that classifies marijuana as a controlled substance and makes its cultivation, possession, sale, and consumption illegal.

Seven years after the CUA was passed, Governor Gray Davis signed Senate Bill 420, the Medical Marijuana Program Act (MMPA) into law. The MMPA was designed to flesh out the parameters of the CUA. Among other things, the MMPA sought to create collective cooperatives in the state where marijuana could be cultivated and sold to qualified patients and caregivers. The cooperatives would be regulated by state and local agencies and the patients and caregivers would be issued identification cards that would help law enforcement more easily determine whether persons were covered by the CUA and, therefore, not subject to criminal prosecution under state law. The MMPA also allows for persons who fall under the classifications of cooperatives, caregivers, or patients, to raise a defense if they are charged with violating state laws involving the cultivation, possession, sale, or consumption of medical marijuana.

The MMPA had immediate implications regarding federalism. Although both the CUA and the MMPA are technically "good law" (meaning they are still current and enforceable), various attempts have been made by the national government to exercise preemption (this involves the national government claiming that it has authority over a particular policy area when it comes to legislation and thus preempts state and local regulations) over the issue of medical marijuana. For example, in 2005, the U.S. Supreme Court reviewed the case *Gonzales v. Raich*. At issue was whether Congress's power to regulate the manufacture and possession of marijuana under the Controlled Substances Act (21 U.S.C. §§ 801) allowed the national government to preempt California's laws on medicinal use of marijuana. The Supreme Court ruled in a 6 to 3 decision that the Commerce Power gives Congress the authority to regulate and to punish the manufacture and cultivation of marijuana despite California law that allows for compassionate use. It is worth noting that the dissenting Supreme Court justices argued that this was a violation of federalism and that the state law should prevail because no interstate commerce was taking place and this was purely local or *intrastate* commerce.

Since this ruling in 2005, many local governments have seized on the opportunity to create new zoning ordinances to limit the expansion of dispensaries. In fact, one tactic commonly used by local governments to close down marijuana dispensaries involves calling the U.S. attorney's office. The U.S. attorney has the authority to order these shops to discontinue their operations under the threat of having their property forfeited or seized, as well as other criminal sanctions under federal law.

Despite the U.S. Supreme Court's ruling in *Gonzales v. Raich*, California courts have continued to try medical marijuana cases according to state law. For example, a 2009 case, *People v. Colvin*, involved a co-owner (William Frank Colvin) of two nonprofit medical marijuana dispensaries, Holistic I (in Santa Monica) and Holistic 2 (in Hollywood). The dispensaries are registered with the city of Los Angeles and have been incorporated for several years. In addition, they are often reviewed by local law enforcement to ensure they meet the requirements and restrictions of the MMPA. Like other similar dispensaries, and according to the MMPA, Holistic 1 and 2 grow some of their marijuana on site but also belong to a cooperative that includes growers in Los Angeles and Humboldt. In March 2009, Colvin was less than a block from Holistic 2 en route to Holistic 1. He was stopped by police, taken into custody, and charged with violating state laws for possession of cocaine, sale or transportation of marijuana, and possession of marijuana. He did have an identification card for medicinal use and showed it to the arresting officer at the time. He also presented evidence to the trial court that he was registered to run the Holistic dispensaries. The trial court judge agreed that Colvin's dispensaries seemed to be in compliance with both the CUA and the MMPA, which are still California law despite the decision in *Raich* which gives the national government the power to preempt them with its own policy. Colvin's attorneys argued that he was only transporting the marijuana (one pound) from one dispensary to another. However, the trial court judge disagreed and ruled that the MMPA did not cover the transportation of marijuana. Colvin was found guilty of all three charges, placed on probation, and given community service. Colvin appealed this conviction, and the court of appeals determined that the transportation of marijuana from one dispensary to another fell within the scope of the MMPA. Because Colvin's possession of the pound of marijuana was for purposes of transporting it from one dispensary to another, it was also protected by the act. Therefore, the court of appeals reversed the trial court's decision with respect to two of Colvin's convictions (transportation and possession; the cocaine conviction was not appealed).

However, both parties to a case have the right to appeal, and the state appealed the decision of the court of appeals. The California Supreme Court had to determine whether it would take the case and rule on its merits or if it would choose not to hear the case and allow the court of appeals decision to stand (remain in effect). In May 2012, the California Supreme Court denied review, noting that medicinal marijuana remains an issue that has important implications for local, state, and federal law. It also cited that the *Colvin* case is only one of many that continue to be filed in the courts dealing with this policy issue. It is an interesting case study in the principle of federalism, particularly in those circumstances in which state and national law clearly conflict over a very controversial issue.[3]

How Are the California Courts Structured?

California courts have three levels: superior courts (trial courts), courts of appeals, and the California Supreme Court.

Superior courts adjudicate cases that involve violations of state and local criminal and civil law. These are the trial courts of California. When cases come before the superior courts, a jury or judge reviews the facts of the case and determines guilt or innocence in a criminal proceeding. If it is a civil case, the jury or judge determines which side presents the best case and awards damages accordingly. There are 400 courts located in the state, with approximately 1,500 judges presiding. The superior courts are also staffed with commissioners and referees. The superior courts are also the busiest courts of the state court system.

The California Courts of Appeals are intermediate appellate courts; those who lose their cases at the superior court can appeal first to the California Courts of Appeals. The purpose of this intermediate appellate court is to review the trial or the superior court records for error. California courts of appeals are divided into six districts across the state; 105 justices preside over these courts. These judges sit in 3-judge panels to review cases.

The California Supreme Court is the highest court in the state. Like the California Courts of Appeals, it is an appellate court that reviews appeals from losing parties in the lower courts. When a party to a case is unhappy with the ruling of

Member of the California State Supreme Court as of December 31, 2010. In January 2011, Tani Gorre Cantil-Sakauye (seated, center) succeeded Ronald George as Chief Justice of the Court. The Court's newest member, Justice Goodwin Liu (standing, far right), replaced retiring Justice Carlos Moreno in September 2011. (Courtesy of the Supreme Court of California. Photo by Wayne Woods.)

the California courts of appeals, the next step would be to appeal to the California Supreme Court. In California, the supreme court has what is known as discretion. Discretion allows the justices on the state supreme court to decide which cases they wish to review. Therefore, there is no guarantee that an appeal filed with the California Supreme Court will automatically get reviewed. This is the only court in California that has discretionary authority that provides the high court with a tool to moderate its workload. Justices on the supreme court cannot exercise discretion regarding death-penalty sentences or disciplinary cases involving judges or attorneys. All death-penalty sentences are automatically appealed and go directly to the California Supreme Court for review. Four out of the seven justices must agree in order for a party to win the case. The supreme court includes one chief justice and seven associate justices. (Table 7.1 provides a list of current California Supreme Court members.)

The court is diverse in regard to gender and race/ethnicity: four of the justices are women and three are nonwhite. On July 14, 2010, Chief Justice Ronald M. George publicly announced that he would not be seeking retention on the California Supreme Court in the November 2010 election. This announcement created a future vacancy, and Governor Schwarzenegger appointed Tani Gorre Cantil-Sakauye to replace Chief Justice George. Her appointment was confirmed by the Commission on Judicial Appointments on August 25, 2010, and Justice Cantil-Sakauye was retained by the voters on the November 2010 ballot. She became the 28th chief justice of California on January 3, 2011. Governor Brown appointed Goodwin Liu in 2011 to replace retired Justice Carlos Moreno.

However, the court is not as diverse ideologically. Five of the seven justices seated on the court were appointed by Republican governors. Why should this matter? Generally, Republicans are more conservative than Democrats on issues of ideological preference, such as civil rights or civil liberties. For example, a liberal judge is more likely to uphold laws that involve regulating business than a conservative judge. This expectation, that ideology or party identification translates into differences in judicial decision making, is even more important when we consider issues such as affirmative action, voting rights, freedom of expression, and capital punishment. Because the decisions of the California Supreme Court are binding on all persons residing in the state, the composition of the state's high court and the judges' political ideology can be very important.

Governors who have the opportunity to appoint judges to the courts take advantage of this possibility and put qualified jurists on the bench whose political beliefs most closely resemble their own. From time to time, a governor may be very open about who should be serving on the state supreme court. In the 1980s, former governor George Deukmejian spoke out to the press and public about his desire to put more conservatives on the state supreme court because the liberals serving on the bench at the time were making decisions he vehemently disagreed with. In addition, governors may have other political goals for the bench. They may, for example, seek to place more women and minorities on the state supreme court so that it is more representative of the state's diverse population.

From time to time, judges who have served on the California Supreme Court have had success at being promoted to the federal bench. The most recent promotion from the state high court to the federal courts of appeals met with significant political opposition. Janice Rogers Brown's appointment to the U.S. Court of Appeals for the District of Columbia Circuit was nonetheless confirmed in June 2005. Her confirmation was a result of a political compromise after a two-year bipartisan battle between Democrats and Republicans in the Senate over several of President Bush's judicial nominees. Janice Brown, a Republican and conservative, was appointed to the California Supreme Court in 1996 by Governor Pete Wilson. President George W. Bush attempted to nominate Judge Brown to the D.C. Circuit Court of Appeals in 2003, but he was unable to get her nomination confirmed by the U.S. Senate. The reason her nomination was initially unsuccessful was political. Justice Brown's detractors argued that her voting record as an appellate judge on California's Supreme Court reflected a much too conservative bias. In addition, organized interests such as the National Organization for Women (NOW) noted that Justice Janice Brown received an "unqualified" rating from the California State

Bar Association. She is the only member of the state supreme court to receive such a rating since the state bar has been evaluating judicial nominees.

Justice Brown's confirmation struggle also illustrates the debate regarding judicial independence versus judicial accountability that we will address later in this chapter. Federal court judges are appointed by the president and confirmed by the Senate for terms of life with good behavior. This selection method was designed to protect the federal judiciary from political influences, including public opinion. Because their appointments are for life terms, many interest groups and other interested members of the Senate pay close attention to judicial appointments and the nominee's positions on important issues and voting records. Appointments to the federal bench, unlike elections to state courts, are often the topic of heated partisan debate. Once a judge is appointed to a federal court, the only way to remove him or her is through impeachment. Thus it isn't possible to hold federal judges to the same level of accountability as most state judges. Therefore, partisans and interest groups act as gatekeepers, blocking nominations of those jurists whose political preferences differ from their own.

Judicial Selection

California's court system is the largest in the nation. Serving on the bench involves two things: (1) a person must be qualified, and (2) the qualified person must be selected to serve. The qualifications for judge are the same for the three court levels. Potential jurists in California must have at least 10 years of practice of law in the state of California or service as a judge of a court of record.

Judges serving on the California Supreme Court and California Courts of Appeals are initially nominated to serve on the appellate bench by the governor. The Commission on Judicial Appointments must approve the governor's nominations. The Commission on Judicial Appointments consists of the chief justice of the supreme court, the attorney general, and a presiding judge on the California Courts of Appeals. In addition, all nominees for California's appellate courts are reviewed by the State Bar of California's Commission on Judicial Nominees Evaluation. This body evaluates the nominees by conducting thorough background checks on their qualifications as judges and as citizens. The governor may use the commission's decision as a source of information when making his or her selections but is not bound by the commission's findings. After a judge's appointment is confirmed, the judge holds office until the next retention election. To remain on the appellate courts in California, judges must face a retention election. These elections are noncompetitive; the voters are simply asked whether the judge should remain on the appellate bench.

Likewise, judges serving on California's superior courts must face nonpartisan retention elections. However, in most cases, as with the appellate bench judges initially come to the superior court bench by gubernatorial nomination. Vacancies on the superior court occur because a judge retires, leaves due to poor health, or dies. Although judges are elected to the trial courts of California, the reality is that these elections typically draw very little attention. California voters are not highly aware of the judicial candidates for these positions, nor are they as concerned about judicial offices as they are about other political offices, such as state representatives or executive officials. From time to time, however, voter awareness about a judge's performance on a particular case or rulings in a specific issue area may lead voters to remove a judge from the bench.

Removing Judges from the Bench

As we have already discussed in this chapter, voters may remove judges from the bench during an election. There are other means for removing judges if there are concerns regarding judicial misconduct or judicial competency.

- *Impeachment*—California's judges may be impeached by the assembly and convicted by a two-thirds majority of the state Senate.

- *Recall election*—Like the governor, California judges are subject to recall election if the voters petition a recall.

- *Regulatory commission investigation*—The Commission on Judicial Performance may, after investigation of complaints regarding misconduct or incapacity, punish, censure, or remove a judge from office.

Who Has Access to the Court?

The California constitution and its statutes provide rights to the people of California regarding access to the courts. Former Chief Justice Ronald M. George had become engaged in overseeing the pursuit of reforms to statewide court access. According to "California Courts, Reference—How to Use: Guide to California Courts" Californians have:

- the right to sue for money owed and for other relief;

- the right to defend oneself against a lawsuit;

- the right to be presumed innocent if charged with a crime;

- the right to defend oneself against all criminal charges;

- the right to a public and speedy trial by jury if charged with a misdemeanor or a felony;

- the right to an attorney at public expense if one is charged with a felony or misdemeanor and cannot afford an attorney.

These rights apply to citizens of the state and noncitizens alike. These rights do not mitigate against concerns about quality of legal representation for indigent persons. The lack of resources in some local court jurisdictions, especially in smaller localities, and the impact of the current budget crisis on the state's judiciary as a whole, will affect the access to the courts.

Judicial Independence versus Judicial Accountability

Unlike the federal judiciary, which consists of appointed judges who serve life terms with good behavior, many states have some form of election system for selecting their judges. The reason federal judges are appointed is to allow for an independent judiciary. Theoretically, appointed judges are less likely to be influenced by politics in their decision making because they do not have to rely on the electorate to maintain their jobs on the bench. Most of the states, however, adopted some kind of election system for selecting their judges or retaining their judges, because states wanted judicial accountability. Elections allow for accountability by giving the voters the opportunity to select members of their courts and also to remove them through the election process if the jurists make decisions that are contrary to the public's preferences.

Although the voters rarely pay much attention to competitive judicial races or judicial retention elections, there have been instances when judges have lost their seats on the bench because of voters' perceptions about judicial rulings. In the November 1986 election, six of the seven justices serving on the California Supreme Court were seeking retention. Of these six, Governor George Deukmejian targeted three and spoke out publicly against their retention on the state supreme court. Deukmejian criticized these judges for their rulings in death-penalty cases. The governor was especially critical of Rose Bird, who was the chief justice of the California Supreme Court at that time. He warned Bird and two associate justices, Cruz Reynoso and Joseph Grodin, that if they didn't change their rulings in death-penalty appeals and uphold the death-penalty sentences, he would oppose their retention elections. Numerous interest groups and political action committees joined the governor's campaign against Rose Bird and her two colleagues. Political advertisements against the retention of Bird, Grodin, and Reynoso aired on radio and television. In response, Chief Justice Rose Bird produced a television ad explaining her decision-making record to the voters. Her explanations did not satisfy the electorate, however, and on November 4, 1996, Bird, Grodin, and Reynoso lost their seats on the California Supreme Court. Shortly thereafter, Governor Deukmejian appointed three justices to replace them, including Malcolm Lucas, who was nicknamed "Maximum Malcolm" because of his rulings sentencing convicted criminals to maximum penalties, including death.

Despite the low visibility of judicial elections, these elections have many political scientists and jurists concerned, particularly over the amount of money being spent by candidates in judicial elections.

A 1995 study of contested elections in Los Angeles County Superior Court reported that campaign spending by trial court judges had risen a great deal in the years between 1976 and 1994. In 1976, the median cost of a judicial campaign for a Los Angeles County Superior Court seat was approximately $3,000. By 1994, the median skyrocketed to $70,000. Incumbents running for reelection spent, on average, $20,000 more than the median challenger, or $95,000 in 1994. Compare that to the $1,000 median campaign expenditure of an incumbent in 1976.

The Civil Justice Association of California (CJAC), a group of citizens, taxpayers, and professionals, reviewed campaign contributions to the California judiciary from 1997 to 2000 and found the following:

- from 1997 to 2000, contributions to candidates in contested superior court elections totaled over $3 million for four counties;

- in a single race in Sacramento County, over $1 million was raised;

- attorneys are the largest contributors to most judicial races;

- two supreme court justices seeking retention in 1998—remember, these are uncontested elections—received contributions of $887,000 and $710,000.

The escalation of campaign spending in judicial elections is controversial, because it usually requires judicial candidates to seek funding support from outside sources. Like candidates seeking election to state legislative or executive offices, judges are now receiving and even soliciting financial support from organized interests. This phenomenon has even spilled over into retention elections for the state supreme court, even though they are noncompetitive. Judges must solicit campaign contributions to retain their seats on the bench. Contributors often include trial lawyers' associations and other special interests. This connection has raised concern because when interest groups contribute financially to a judge's campaign the potential for influence over judicial decision making arises. Although elections allow for accountability, the notion is that accountability is to the citizens or voters, not to the more narrow preferences of an organized interest group. This concern has mobilized a national movement for reform. One of the most active advocates is former Associate Justice of the U.S. Supreme Court Sandra Day O'Connor. Retired Justice O'Connor has been a vocal critic of state judicial elections because of the amounts that judicial candidates are soliciting and spending, and because of the public perception that money buys influence.

Most people consider the judiciary the least political of all of the branches of government, yet the increased spending in competitive and noncompetitive elections for judgeships compromises this assumption. Even judges are expressing concern. In 2001, an opinion survey, "Justice at Stake Campaign," revealed that 53 percent of California judges are dissatisfied with the current climate of judicial campaigning in the state. Over 80 percent of the judges surveyed believed that voters knew little about candidates for the bench and were electing judges based on criteria other than qualifications for office. The majority of judges polled agreed that reform of campaign financing of judicial elections is necessary and that public financing of these elections would be an appropriate alternative.

In response to stories in the media, including a series of articles published in the *Los Angeles Times,* and the concerns of the public, judges, public officials, and others, a task force was created to examine judicial campaigns in California. The Judicial Campaign Task Force for Impartial Courts was established in 2007. It consists of 14 members appointed by former California Supreme Court Chief Justice Ronald M. George, and it is investigating several issues, including the structure of California judicial elections as well as the filing, reporting, and accessibility of judicial campaign contributions and spending. The findings to date of this commission were reported in a 408-page volume in December 2009.[4] Many problems were noted with respect to judicial campaigns and elections, most notably the amount of money spent by candidates for judicial elections and, ironically, the poor quality or low level of information disseminated by judicial candidates to the public. The commission is not finished with its work, and additional reports are expected. It is also worthwhile to note that reforms and current state policies include the following:

- Judicial candidates are prohibited from making statements that commit or appear to commit them with respect to cases, controversies, or issues that could come before the courts.

- Judicial candidates may not knowingly misrepresent the identity, qualifications, present position, or other facts concerning themselves or an opponent.

- Judicial candidates are not prohibited from soliciting campaign contributions.

- Like all other state political candidates, judicial candidates are required to report all campaign contributions and expenditures.

- Any contributions to or expenditures of judicial candidates of $100 or more must be itemized. Judicial candidates for superior court may file a candidate statement to be included in the voter's pamphlet. These statements are very expensive, however, and the cost is prohibitive for most candidates.

There is one further caveat that should be mentioned. Whenever limits or rules are placed on campaign spending, the rights of freedom of expression and freedom of association guaranteed by both the California and U.S. constitutions may be abridged. Campaigning for political office is guaranteed by the right to speak freely, and in today's political contests, it is becoming increasingly expensive. Therefore, it is almost impossible to impose limits on campaign spending. So judges running for retention on the California Supreme Court or running to serve on the state's trial courts must exercise their own restraint—not an easy thing to do if your opponent or opposing forces are spending a lot of money to keep you off the bench.

The Politicization of the Judiciary

Every term, judges serving on the California bench across all court levels (trial, intermediate appellate, and supreme) are confronted with cases that require them to make political decisions or decisions that have political effects. One example of this is political redistricting. The redrawing of electoral districts is always a political process. Political parties seek either to maintain or to increase their odds of getting candidates reelected through the redrawing of district lines. It is very common for redistricting plans to end up contested in the courts by political parties, elected officials, candidates seeking political office, and/or organized special interests. Since the 1980s, the California courts have been involved in many cases and controversies regarding redistricting. Perhaps the most controversial was in 2005, when Governor Schwarzenegger and others proposed an initiative, Proposition 77, that would reform redistricting procedures in the state. Rather than having legislators redraw district lines after each census, the responsibility would be given to a panel of three retired judges (selected by legislative officials). This ballot measure was contested in the California Courts of Appeals before it even appeared on the ballot. Those opposed to the measure argued that judges should not be put in the role of redrawing or creating new political districts. Although there was some success with procedural challenges to the initiative at the courts of appeals, attempts to block the initiative from the ballot finally failed, and the voters had the opportunity to decide in November 2005 whether retired judges should be redrawing the state's electoral district lines. The voters vetoed the measure by a margin of approximately 19 percent.

As we can see, there are certainly political dimensions of the judiciary. While it is most common for us to consider the "political branches" such as the legislature and the executive first when we think about politics, it is important to remember that courts play a significant role in political processes and that this is especially true in California. The presence of the initiative, referendum, and recall facilitate this role further. The increased spending on judicial campaigns at the trial and appellate levels adds another dimension that may call some of these other political actions into question.

Judicial Review and the Statewide Initiative

Another issue of concern regarding the judiciary in California is the relationship between direct democracy and judicial review. It is vitally important to keep in mind that, regardless of the method of selection of judges, judicial decisions or rulings may have far-reaching consequences for all of us. California is one of 26 states in the United States that allows for citizens to propose and enact their own legislation through the initiative. Moreover, the California state constitution permits citizens to use the initiative to enact statutes and constitutional amendments.

The popular initiative was implemented in this state during the early twentieth century by Progressives such as the Lincoln-Roosevelt League, along with other like-minded groups seeking political reform in California government. As an alternative policy-making tool, the initiative allows citizens to circumvent the legislature and write and enact policies reflecting their own political preferences. Theoretically, the initiative performs as another check against unresponsive government. Therefore, when citizens believe the legislature is not responding to their demands—that is, when the legislature is not enacting the laws that they would like them to—the people may propose their own laws and, if they are successful at getting them on the ballot, persuade the voters to enact them.

The initiative, however, is also subject to judicial interpretation and judicial review, just like a piece of legislation coming out of the state legislature. Since the success of Proposition 13, the property tax reform initiative, in 1978, the use of the initiative in California has increased greatly. Organized interests and citizen-based movements have attempted to use the initiative to enact policies in California in nearly every conceivable issue area. Victim's rights and penalty enhancements for criminals, such as the three-strikes law, have been enacted through the initiative. The decriminalization of marijuana for medicinal purposes was adopted via the initiative. Term limits for many of California's elected officials were also ballot initiatives. Voters in California have also enacted policies for insurance reform, registration of sex offenders, harsher penalties for human trafficking in the sex trade industry, anti-affirmative action laws, and most recently, a temporary tax to fund education and modifications to the state's "three strikes and you're out" law over the past 30 years. While it is erroneous to argue that all initiatives in California reflect controversial issues such as those listed, it is clear that the initiative has been used increasingly in the past to enact a wide array of policies that reflect citizen dissatisfaction with elected state government.

When the initiative is used to enact controversial policies, it is usually debated in the press, and if that controversial initiative is successful at getting voter approval, there is a very strong likelihood it will be contested in the courts. In fact, the constitutional validity of each of the initiatives described in the preceding paragraph has been challenged in at least one court of law. The outcomes of these court cases have varied. But what is important is this: just like judges on federal courts, state court judges have the power of judicial review. When state judges have the power to overturn laws enacted by the people as well as laws composed by state legislators, the tension between lawmaking and law reviewing is heightened.

Is this tension all that important? Many scholars and many voters would argue that it is. In fact, the common opinion among the electorate in California is that the initiative as an alternative policy-making tool has become an exercise in futility, precisely because of legal intervention. The consensus among California voters is that once an initiative passes at the ballot box, it ends up in a court of law. In truth, courts are reactive bodies. Judges must wait until a case comes to their courtrooms to make a legal decision. So why do so many initiatives end up in the California courts? The answer is simply politics. California is a very diverse state, and our diversity can be measured in a number of ways. We are diverse in race and ethnicity, we are diverse in culture, we are diverse economically, we are even diverse in terrain and climate. Given so many dimensions of diversity, there is no dearth of conflict in our state regarding which political problems are important and which solutions to these problems should be adopted. Hence California courts also function as another arena for the continuation of political debate. The response to the State Supreme Court's 4–to–3 ruling in *In re Marriage Cases* and the subsequent proposal, adoption, and reversal of Proposition 8 illustrate this well.[5]

California Courts: Where Are We Now?

A number of issues currently confront California's courts. As discussed earlier, the caseload continues to increase for all court levels. And while the superior courts and appellate courts have been managing this load fairly efficiently, there are legitimate concerns about the system's ability to continue to do so, given the state's continued fiscal crisis.

Courts are also subject to similar constraints that affect state agencies. It is fairly easy to argue that the greatest of these constraints, setting jurisdiction (decision-making power and authority) aside, is the state's economy and budget. Most recently, the court system in California has found itself constrained by the extraordinary challenges of the state's budget. Chapter 8 discusses the budgetary process and more of the political implications in greater detail, but here we can examine the impact of this budgetary crisis on the courts.

On the face of it, a discussion about budgets and courts may not appear all that interesting. However, when Governor Brown signed the budget on June 27, 2012, it included $6 billion of automatic cuts—hundreds of millions to the court system— severely affecting both its day-to-day operations and its future construction plans. It is important to note that these cuts come on top of other actions that have been taken to reduce the size of court administration throughout the state. Because most courts are obviously located at the local level, counties and municipalities have taken the brunt of these budget cuts. Responses to the ramifications of these cuts have included threatened strikes by state court administrative personnel and the elimination of some innovative, albeit controversial, programs at the local level. One such program involves nonviolent misdemeanor crimes by juvenile offenders in the Los Angeles area. This program is part of a relatively recent, legal movement known as "problem-solving justice," or the good courts movement. It served as an alternative to more punitive, traditional forms of dealing with juvenile low-level crime. The nontraditional court served more than 100,000 children each year, but has been shut down by the county because of budget cuts.[6]

In addition, the new chief justice, Tani Gorre Cantil-Sakauye, has had to respond to some criticisms by organized interests and other parties about wasteful spending on projects and the growth of the state's Administrative Office of the Courts (AOC). A relatively new (2009) interest organization, The Alliance of California Judges, has been pressuring the chief justice and the judicial council to respond to past and present budget cuts more proactively. The alliance has been arguing that both should pay closer attention to wasteful spending, predicting (accurately) that like his predecessors, Governor Brown would include more cuts to the state courts' budgets in the new fiscal year. More specifically, this organization targeted the now defunct electronic Court Case Management System. According to the *Courthouse News Service*, "even as trial courts were closing, the [Judicial] Council voted repeatedly, with only one or two dissenting votes, to continue pouring hundreds of millions into that now failed IT project. That money came primarily from trial court funds." The *Courthouse News Service* article goes on to claim that "over half a billion" dollars was spent before the Court Management Case System was terminated.[7]

On top of this, C. J. Cantil-Sakauye released a report "prepared by a committee of state judges" in late May 2012 criticizing the AOC for understating the number of its employees and for paying "hundreds" of its personnel six-figure salaries. The report noted that this growth in both size and salaries paid was taking place during a hiring freeze. The investigation concluded, among other things, that the AOC had circumvented the hiring freeze and had violated some of its own personnel rules. It also recommended that there be significant cuts in the staff and that the organization be consolidated to allow for more oversight and, presumably, more efficiency.[8]

Finally, reforming judicial campaigns in the state is also a critical agenda item. Some attempts at reform, such as campaign finance reporting, have been implemented and have not been found unconstitutional. However, when voters amended the state constitution in 1986 to prohibit political parties from endorsing judges, who run in nonpartisan elections, the California Supreme Court found the initiative unconstitutional because it violated our rights to freedom of expression and freedom of association. Obviously, judges have a lot of say when it comes to these reforms, and it is up to the individual judge to decide how much is too much when it comes to campaign spending.

FOR FURTHER READING

American Judicature Society (AJS). "Judicial Selection in the States." www.judicialselection.us. Accessed 8/16/12.

Bonneau, Christopher W., and Melinda Gann Hall. *In Defense of Judicial Elections*. New York: Routledge Press. 2009. This book is a critique of previous empirical studies of judicial elections. Bonneau and Hall argue that elections as a selection method for judges is actually beneficial to democratic society.

California Courts, Guide to California Courts. www.courtinfo.ca.gov/courts. Accessed 9/27/12.

Civil Justice Association of California. "Campaign Contributions to the California Judiciary 1997–2000." Accessed 8/16/12.

The National Organization for Women. "NOW Opposes Extremist Judicial Nominees—Regardless of Gender." www.now.org/press/11-03/11-13.html.

Streb, Matthew J., ed. *Running for Judge: The Rising Political, Financial and Legal Stakes of Judicial Elections*. New York: New York University Press. 2007. This edited book is a collection of contemporary research conducted by professors who study state courts and judicial elections. Each chapter examines current issues and controversies that are confronted by state courts and state court judges.

ON THE WEB

The American Judicature Society (AJS): www.ajs.org. Accessed 8/16/12. The AJS is a nonpartisan organization made up of legal professionals and citizens. It seeks to provide a better understanding of the judiciary and the justice system.

The California Supreme Court Historical Society (CSCHS): http://cschs.org. Accessed 8/16/12. CSCHS catalogs and archives information about the California Supreme Court's history.

The National Center for State Courts (NCSC): http://ncsconline.org. Accessed 8/16/12. NCSC is an organization that provides services for court administrators, practitioners, and others interested in state courts. The website includes information, datasets, and articles about state courts and court-related topics.

SUMMARY

I. Introduction: judges and state government.
   A. Judges play an integral role in California politics.
   1. Court rulings can impact all Californians, such as the recent rulings on Proposition 8 (the ban on gay marriage).
   2. Controversial rulings can lead to political mobilization against the justices serving on California's courts. In some instances, justices have lost their retention election bids to keep their seats on the California Supreme Court.
   B. California courts have a very high caseload.
   1. Increase in criminalization and penalties increase the caseload.
   2. Despite the high workload, California courts remain fairly efficient and are able to dispose of a significant percentage of their criminal and civil caseload at all court levels.

II. Federalism and California Courts
   A. Legal challenges to Proposition 215, the Compassionate Use Act (CUA), illustrate the tension between state and federal government. California permits the use of medical marijuana under certain conditions, but the federal government does not. There are many continuous attempts by federal law enforcement to close marijuana dispensaries that would otherwise be operating legally under the CUA.
   B. Local governments are also adopting ordinances to regulate or even prohibit dispensaries from operating in their communities. At times, local governments will even use federal law enforcement to assist them with closing dispensaries.
   C. The California courts currently have a number of cases across all levels examining this policy.

III. Structure of the California courts.
   A. Superior courts are the trial courts of the California court system. They are courts of "first instance" and triers of fact. The California Courts of Appeals are intermediate appellate courts. They are divided into six districts across the state. All cases except for death-penalty cases are first appealed to the California Courts of Appeals. The supreme court is the highest court in the state. It is composed of seven justices and, like the courts of appeals, is an appellate court—that is, it reviews cases that were first heard in lower state courts such as the courts of appeals or a superior court.
   B. The California courts are diverse in terms of both gender and race. In July 2010, Chief Justice Ronald M. George announced that he would not seek to be retained on the California Supreme Court. This announcement created a vacancy, and Governor Schwarzenegger nominated Tani Gorre Cantil-Sakauye to fill this vacancy. She is the first female chief justice on the supreme court. Her appointment also creates a female majority, with four female justices and three males.
   C. Justices serving on the California Supreme Court have been promoted to the federal bench from time to time. Some of these appointments have been met with little opposition, and some have been unsuccessful, such as President George W. Bush's nomination of Janice Brown to the U.S. Courts of Appeals in 2003.

IV. Judicial selection.
   A. Methods of selection for the California courts include nonpartisan elections for superior court and merit selection for appellate courts.
   B. Methods of removal from the bench include recall elections and impeachment. In addition, because all judges in California face some sort of election (direct or retention), voters may choose to vote for another judicial candidate or they may choose to vote against retaining an appellate court judge.
   C. Access to California courts is widely available. However, there is concern about the cost of litigation and legal representation.

V. Judicial independence versus judicial accountability.
   A. There are two competing theories regarding judicial selection—appointment and election. Those who favor judicial independence argue that appointment is a better method for selecting judges because it insulates them from politics. Conversely, those who favor accountability argue that election as a method of selection is essential in a democracy and that judicial elections allow citizens to hold judges accountable for their decision making similar to the way other elected officials are held accountable for their actions in office.
   B. Recent controversies about judicial campaigning and campaign finance have led to some high-profile jurists (for example., retired U.S. Supreme Court Associate Justice Sandra Day O'Connor) and others to call for reforms. The most radical reforms proposed would eliminate judicial elections entirely. The increasing cost of judicial campaigns, which are low-saliency and low-turnout elections, have many members of the bar and legal community concerned.
   C. The politicization of the California courts is another issue of concern. Judges on California courts are increasingly asked to decide on cases involving very controversial issues such as the death penalty and gay marriage.

PRACTICE QUIZ

1. All death-penalty sentences are automatically appealed directly to the California Supreme Court for review.
   a) true
   b) false
2. The California Supreme Court is similar to the U.S. Supreme Court in that it has nine justices.
   a) true
   b) false
3. Most criminal cases in California are resolved through plea bargaining.
   a) true
   b) false
4. Voters in California are highly informed about the candidates running in judicial elections.
   a) true
   b) false
5. Initiatives passed in California are not subject to judicial interpretation and judicial review.
   a) true
   b) false
6. In recent years, campaign spending in judicial elections
   a) has increased.
   b) has decreased.
   c) has remained the same.
   d) cannot be determined.

7. Chief Justice Rose Bird and Associate Justices Cruz Reynoso and Joseph Grodin were voted out by voters who were angry about the judges' decisions concerning
   a) same-sex marriage.
   b) the death penalty.
   c) Proposition 13.
   d) term limits.
8. Judges selected by the governor to serve on the supreme court and the courts of appeals in California must be approved by
   a) the state legislature.
   b) the attorney general.
   c) the Commission on Judicial Appointments.
   d) none of the above.
9. Superior courts in California adjudicate the following types of actions:
   a) civil and criminal cases.
   b) only civil cases.
   c) only criminal cases.
   d) appeals only.
10. One method of removing judges in the state of California is
    a) removal by the governor.
    b) censure by the state legislature.
    c) agreement between the speaker of the Assembly and the attorney general.
    d) a recall election.

CRITICAL-THINKING QUESTIONS

1. Given the concern over the role of money in judicial elections, what kinds of reforms might be implemented that would still allow for accountability? Is it possible to keep money or special interests out of judicial elections?
2. What factors do you believe are responsible for the tremendous criminal caseload in the California superior courts?

3. Is judicial independence important for state court judges?
4. What kinds of checks are there on the California judiciary? How do the other branches and other political actors hold the state courts accountable?

KEY TERMS

At this point you should have a general understanding of the following concepts and terms:

appellate jurisdiction (p. 144)
civil courts (p. 141)
judicial accountability (p. 148)

judicial discretion (p. 145)
judicial independence (p. 148)

retention election (p. 147)
superior courts (p. 144)

8

The State Budget and Budgetary Limitations

WHAT CALIFORNIA GOVERNMENT DOES AND WHY IT MATTERS

Why Does Student Tuition Keep Rising?

The answer to rising student tuition is actually simple. Higher education is a major category, the third or fourth largest in most years, of the state budget, and charts that float around Sacramento make it look as if students, until very recently, paid relatively low tuitions/fees by national standards. The charts came from the California Postsecondary Education Commission, a research agency created by the legislature to be independent of the three systems of higher education, or from the Legislative Analyst's Office. Figure 8.1 presents an example from the 2006-07 school year. Everyone involved in higher education policy sees this chart: the governor's department of finance, the legislative committees and their staff, the bureaucracy, and one of this book's authors, who was on the California State University (CSU) statewide academic senate for several years. Once you have seen the chart, there is very little you can argue to legislators on the hunt for an extra several hundred million dollars to cut from the budget that can prevent them from saying, "Well, the students are paying relatively little by U.S. standards; just increase the university's fees to cover the difference."

And that was the process that occurred, year after year, for over a decade. By 2012, CSU's fees were no longer at the bottom of the list, but rather the middle. The University of California (UC) started higher on the list, but the same process has operated. All told, the legislature has cut hundreds of millions of dollars from the UC, CSU, and community college budgets. Table 8.2 on page 169 shows the expenditures for 2012–13 at $10.1 billion and 7 percent of total state expenditures. Over the four years from 2008 to 2012, higher education lost $2.8 billion in funding, about 22 percent of its total. Some of this has been replaced by student fee and tuition increases, but the budget cuts are

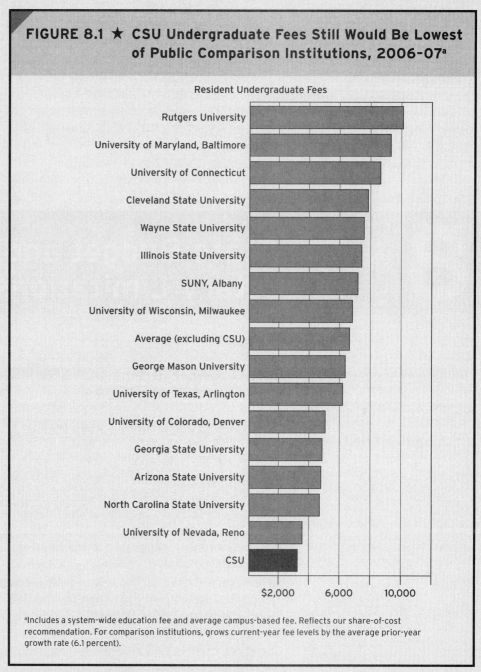

FIGURE 8.1 ★ CSU Undergraduate Fees Still Would Be Lowest of Public Comparison Institutions, 2006-07[a]

Resident Undergraduate Fees

Rutgers University
University of Maryland, Baltimore
University of Connecticut
Cleveland State University
Wayne State University
Illinois State University
SUNY, Albany
University of Wisconsin, Milwaukee
Average (excluding CSU)
George Mason University
University of Texas, Arlington
University of Colorado, Denver
Georgia State University
Arizona State University
North Carolina State University
University of Nevada, Reno
CSU

$2,000   6,000   10,000

[a]Includes a system-wide education fee and average campus-based fee. Reflects our share-of-cost recommendation. For comparison institutions, grows current-year fee levels by the average prior-year growth rate (6.1 percent).

the reasons classes are difficult to obtain and there seems to be less money available for other projects.

Students aren't the only citizens heavily impacted by California's budget woes. With a budget of over $130 billion, California represents one of the largest economies in the world. Its projected *deficit in* recent years has been larger than the entire budgets of all but the 5 to 10 largest states. Over 2.5 million workers in California—1 out of 6—work for the federal, state, or local governments, and some of the rest are indirectly funded by the public sector.[1]

For something this important to so many people, it is amazing that the process to approve the budget and some of the items in it is so controversial. The public itself is split—most Californians are opposed to spending cuts in public programs as well as increases in taxes or fees. They are also distrustful of state government and disapprove of the job their politicians are doing. One political party won't increase taxes under any circumstances; indeed, one group of legislators considers the entire budget so illegitimate that it won't vote for the budget under any realistic set of circumstances (in fact, at least one of them didn't vote for a budget for over a decade). The legislature came within one vote of increasing the sales tax in 2002, but that one vote couldn't be found. The amount—and intensity—of political controversy over this budget, a document that embodies the values and decisions of the citizens, its legislature, and its leaders, is truly remarkable.

Passing the budget is at the center, both in difficulty and in scope, of what state government does each year. Since the passage of Proposition 13, state government has received less revenue, which has become more volatile, rising and falling with the economy. The state constitution states that the legislature is to pass the budget by June 15. Since 1990, the legislature has met the deadline only six times. Two of those were budget surplus years, when it is easier to pass a budget. The other two were 2011 and 2012, when Proposition 25 required only a majority vote to pass the budget.

How Is the Budget Formed?

The process of forming a budget has four steps. Most governments today follow a similar process—proposal by the executive branch, enactment by the legislature, approval by the governor, and implementation by the executive branch. Box 8.1 shows the process. Note that the preparation, enactment, and implementation of a single fiscal year's budget takes almost three calendar years.

Executive Proposal

Each fall, state agencies send their budget proposals to the governor through the State Department of Finance. The governor formulates his budget proposal and sends it to the legislature in January. In late spring, he revises the proposal in what is called "the May revise."

Actually, before 1922, agencies proposed their budgets directly to the legislature; there was no unified state budget proposed by the governor or anyone else. "Budgeting was the domain of interest groups, department heads, and ranking committee members."[2] Progressive Governor Hiram Johnson in 1911 asked for justification for the amounts contained in the appropriations bills sent to him. Finding little or no justification, he created the Board of Control to advise him on the fiscal justification for each appropriation.

In 1922, California adopted its own version of new federal legislation (1921) *unifying* the budget process. The legislation called for a consolidated administration proposal in the form of a governor's budget that must be balanced, contain justifications for the amounts proposed, and be accompanied by bills in each house that legislative leaders are required to introduce, thus providing a starting point for the

BOX 8.1 / **California's Budget Process**

CALENDAR YEAR 1

JULY–SEPTEMBER

- Agencies prepare requests, proposals.
- Requests sent to Department of Finance.

OCTOBER–DECEMBER

- Department of Finance reviews requests, consults governor.

CALENDAR YEAR 2

JANUARY–MARCH

- California constitution requires governor to send a balanced budget to the legislature by January 10.
- Governor's budget proposal is introduced in both houses as identical budget bills.
- Legislative Analyst's Office prepares extensive analysis.
- Extensive budget hearings held in both houses.

APRIL–JUNE

- May—Governor sends revised and updated projections of revenues and expenditures to legislature (the May revise).
- June 15—California constitution requires legislature to pass (by a majority vote) a balanced budget by this date. As of November 2010, all members of the legislature permanently forfeit salary and expenses every day until the budget is passed.
- Governor signs budget, uses item veto, if desired, to lower any appropriation items. Legislature can override by a two-thirds vote.

JULY–SEPTEMBER

- July 1—California's fiscal year begins. This is the first quarter. (The federal fiscal year, in contrast, begins October 1.)

OCTOBER–DECEMBER

- Second quarter of California's fiscal year.

CALENDAR YEAR 3

JANUARY–MARCH

- Third quarter of California's fiscal year.

APRIL–JUNE

- Fourth quarter of California's fiscal year.

negotiations and decisions each year. The existence of a governor's budget was an improvement over the situation before 1900, when "government structures . . . hid more than they revealed to the public."[3]

Legislative Adoption

The legislature adopts a balanced budget based on the governor's proposal. As of 2011, both the Assembly and the state senate must adopt the budget by a majority of the entire membership of the body. The Assembly and senate budget committees and their subcommittees hold hearings on the budget bills, receiving testimony and input from individuals and groups, including the affected departments and agencies, the Department of Finance, the Legislative Analyst's Office, committee staff, and interest groups.

The Legislative Analyst's Office provides nonpartisan and independent review of the entire budget, including alternative ways to accomplish the same goals and objectives. The former legislative analyst Elizabeth Hill was called "the Budget Nun . . . because her fiscal reports are incorruptible. They're the bible. The one source of truth. . . . She's the most influential non-elected official in the Capitol."[4] The current legislative analyst, Mac Taylor, was appointed in 2008 and has 30 years of experience in the office.

Before 2011, when the Assembly and senate budget bills differed, a Budget Conference Committee was appointed to work out the differences. However, with the passage of Proposition 25 in 2010, only a majority vote is required to pass the budget, so the endless compromising with the Republican Party that used to occupy Sacramento through the summer in the 1990s and 2000s is over. In 2011 and 2012, the budget passed by June 15, the official deadline in Proposition 25 to prevent legislators from losing their salaries on every day that the budget is late. Raising a tax, however, still requires a two-thirds vote of both the Assembly and the state Senate. In 2012, the Democrats achieved majorities of over two-thirds in both the Assembly and Senate, allowing them for the time being to raise taxes without any Republican support.

The "Big 5" group, consisting of the governor, Assembly speaker, senate president pro tempore, and the Assembly and senate minority leaders, that used to be so important in soliciting a few Republican votes to pass the budget under the old two-thirds requirement, is now irrelevant, or at least it was in the first two years under the new system.

Gubernatorial Action

The governor may use the line-item veto to lower any line-item appropriation in the budget, including lowering it to zero. The legislature may override the governor's veto by a two-thirds majority in each of the two houses and replace the lowered number with its own amount, although doing so is rare.

Implementation

Agencies implement the budget as passed, with the fiscal year beginning July 1. The Department of Finance states explicitly that agencies and departments are expected to operate within their budgets and comply with any provisions enacted

BOX 8.2 The Constitutional Requirements for California's Budget

1. Within the first 10 days of the calendar year, the governor must submit to the legislature a unified budget that is balanced, contains an explanation for each proposed expenditure, and is accompanied by a budget bill itemizing the recommended expenditures.

2. The budget bills must be introduced immediately in each house by the respective appropriations chairs.

3. The legislature must pass the budget by June 15 of each year. As of 2004, the budget must be balanced.

4. Appropriations from the general fund must be passed in each house by a majority vote of the membership. Note that the requirement is "of the membership," not just those present and voting.

5. When the governor signs the budget bill(s), he or she is allowed to reduce or eliminate an appropriated dollar amount. This is the line-item veto, a powerful tool.

by the legislature. "The general expectation is that state agencies comply with the legislative intent."[5] There is some flexibility in implementation, but, compared to other states, the governor's flexibility is limited, as we shall see.

Other Groups Involved in the Budget Process

In addition to the governor and legislature, who are at the center of the process, the agencies mentioned earlier—the Department of Finance on the executive side and the Legislative Analyst's Office on the legislative side—are closely involved in the process, as are two other groups:

- The courts have sometimes ruled on the constitutionality of particular budget actions, particularly on proposed administrative actions taken in the absence of a budget when the legislature has been late. They have also had to decide the constitutionality of various budget provisions, like the Proposition 13 limits.

- Moody's, Fitch Ratings, and Standard & Poor's rate the ability of the states to repay their bond issues. The rating is one of several factors that influence the cost of selling a bond issue. The lower the credit rating, the higher the interest rate that must be paid to induce investors to purchase the bonds. In 2003, Moody's rating of California's bonds was the lowest rating given for any state. Nothing symbolizes the state's continuing inability to reconcile its desire for high services with its desire to pay low taxes than the fact that its bond rating continues to be in the bottom two or three among all states, one or two steps above "junk-bond status." The budget crises of 2009 and 2010, in which the state had to issue IOUs to its creditors in 2009, brought the rating back down to the lowest level of any state in 2010, although the bonds were still considered to be "investment-grade." In 2012, the state still had one of the lowest state credit ratings.

What Is in the Budget?

Every state budget contains the following information:

- economic assumptions—how the economy should respond during the forthcoming fiscal year, and what that response means for revenues and expenditures
- revenues expected in the various categories
- expenditures appropriated by department and program

Revenues

Looking at all sources of revenue, both general funds and special funds, we see the revenue sources are as follows, according to the governor's budget proposal in January and May 2012 (see Table 8.1 and Figure 8.2):

PERSONAL INCOME TAX California's personal income tax ranges from 0 to 9.3 percent of income, with a substantial credit per child or dependent. The income tax is considered highly progressive, with the top 5 percent of taxpayers

---

TABLE 8.1 ★ Revenue Sources, 2012–13 Budget, May 2012 Governor's Revise

REVENUE SOURCES	DOLLARS (IN BILLIONS)	PERCENT OF TOTAL REVENUE
Personal income tax	61.6	46
Sales tax	31.0	23
Corporation tax	8.5	6
Highway users' taxes	5.7	4
Motor vehicle fees	5.7	4
Insurance tax	2.5	2
All others	17.7	13
Total	132.7	

SOURCE: California Department of Finance, "2012-13 Enacted Budget," www.ebudget.ca.gov (accessed 9/9/12).

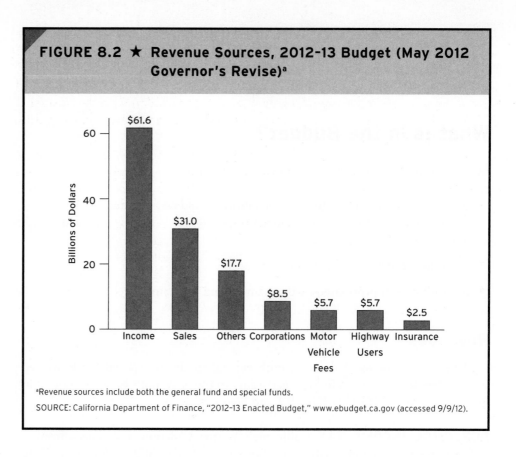

FIGURE 8.2 ★ Revenue Sources, 2012-13 Budget (May 2012 Governor's Revise)[a]

[a]Revenue sources include both the general fund and special funds.

SOURCE: California Department of Finance, "2012-13 Enacted Budget," www.ebudget.ca.gov (accessed 9/9/12).

paying about two-thirds of the income tax, while the bottom 40 percent pay less than 1 percent.[6] This is one of the most progressive personal income taxes in the nation. Regular income (salaries and wages) does not vary that much from year to year, but capital gains income (income from selling stock that has appreciated in value, for example) varies considerably from one year to the next, making revenues from the income tax fluctuate considerably.

Governor Jerry Brown's initiative proposal on the November 2012 ballot established three new brackets for taxpayers who make more than $250,000 per year: at 10.3, 11.3, and 12.3 percent of income. The new brackets are temporary, lasting for seven years, from 2012 to 2018. They make the California state income tax even more progressive than it is at present, reflecting the income level of the state (higher than the nation's; see Chapter 1).

SALES TAX The state sales tax is 7.5 percent. Counties or taxing districts are allowed to add between 0.13 and 0.5 percent per local district for local services. In some areas there is more than one district tax in effect. The average sales tax in California is 7.75 percent. The minimum in any area is 7.5 percent. The maximum is in two cities in Los Angeles County, Pico Rivera and South Gate, at about 10 percent. Economists consider the sales tax regressive—that is, as individual or household income increases, the proportion of income paid through the tax decreases, because lower-income households spend a higher proportion of their incomes on consumption goods that are taxed compared with higher income households. In California, the state refunds 1.25 percent of its share to the local city and county;

this feature has led many cities to search for businesses that are both clean industries and have a high sales volume, such as big-box shopping centers and automobile dealerships.

A state sales tax has existed in California since 1933, with the rate being raised on the average every five years. Governor Jerry Brown's proposal on the November 2012 ballot raised the state sales tax one-quarter of 1 percent temporarily, from 2013 to 2015.

The sales tax is based on an older conception of the economy in which most of the economy consists of goods that are bought and sold. The modern economy is over half services, but these are not taxed at all in California, as the sales tax was developed over 50 years ago and has not been updated. In many states, at least some services are taxed. Having a broader base on the sales tax would enable the rate to be lowered from its current high level, but finding a two-thirds majority in the legislature to pass a tax reform act is close to impossible.

PROPERTY TAX All owners of property pay California's property tax, limited under Proposition 13 to 1 percent of the assessed value in 1975 or the value of a more recent sale. Once acquired, annual tax increases are limited to 2 percent or the amount of inflation, whichever is less. Proposition 13 passed overwhelmingly in 1978 and contains provisions requiring special votes greater than 50 percent for legislators and voters to raise taxes. Proposition 13 rolled back property taxes in California by more than half, and the state has endeavored to make up the difference ever since. Local property tax revenue available for cities, counties, and school districts has been substantially reduced. As a result, all local government entities are more reliant on the state for revenue, and decision-making power has substantially shifted, in the eyes of virtually all observers, from the local level to the state level. School districts are an excellent example of the effects. Whereas California once had some of the best-quality and best-funded schools in the nation, its expenditures per pupil have fallen in comparison to the rest of the nation, its staff per student ratio is now 70 percent of the average for other states, its student achievement levels lag behind the rest of the nation, and a substantially greater proportion of high-income families send their children to private schools compared to the pre-1978 period. At the same time, teacher salaries are relatively high because of the cost of living, in particular housing prices, and the desire to attract good-quality recruits to the profession. The infrastructure discussion in Chapter 10 has more examples.

CORPORATION TAX The corporation tax taxes corporate profits and provides about 6 percent of state revenues, according to Table 8.1 and Figure 8.2. The corporation tax structure is cited favorably by *Governing* magazine in its appraisal of the state's tax system as "tough on the creation of tax-dodge subsidiaries, and the law covers a firm's property and assets, not just its sales."[7] Almost 500,000 corporations filed tax returns in 1999, but "the 1.9 percent with taxable incomes in excess of $1 million paid 80.1 percent of the tax. The ten largest corporations pay 20 percent of the tax in any given year."[8]

The overall tax structure, compared to other states, depends more on taxes that are volatile—that is, they go up and down with the economy (income tax, sales tax)—and less on taxes that don't vary with the economy (the property tax) because of the Proposition 13 limits. The average state obtains 29 percent of its total state and local tax funds from the property tax, but because of Proposition 13's limits, California obtains only 22 percent.

INDIAN GAMBLING Governor Schwarzenegger attempted to increase the amount of revenue received for the General Fund from Indian gambling operations in California. In 2005–06, the state received only $27 million for the General Fund of the $301 million the state got as a result of the tribal–state gambling compacts negotiated by the governor and ratified by the legislature. In 2008–09, the governor's budget projected $430 million in revenues, but much less was actually received. In the current budget, the subject isn't even mentioned.

How Well Does the Taxing System Function?

The taxing system seems to be functioning poorly. *Governing* magazine's February 2003 analysis, "The Way We Tax," gave California one star out of four in the category "Adequacy of Revenue," two out of four in "Fairness to Taxpayers," and two out of four in "Management of System."[9] Only Tennessee received a lower overall rating, and four other states were tied with California. Some of the problem areas:

- The "highly progressive—and volatile" income tax depends too much on capital gains being taxed at the same level as regular income. Thus, when the stock market soared in 2000, tax revenues soared also, but the state received only half this amount the very next year. In 2008, for example, the forecast for the income tax dropped 13 percent in just six months due to the downturn in the economy.

- Although the state income tax is highly progressive, the sales tax is highly regressive and the entire tax system is regressive as a whole, meaning that those at the bottom of the income distribution pay a higher proportion of their incomes as taxes to the state than those at the top. Figure 8.3 shows the percentage that each quintile, or fifth, paid to the state in all taxes in 2009: sales tax, business taxes, property tax, and personal and corporate income taxes.

- In 2009, Governor Schwarzenegger and the legislative leadership agreed to establish the Commission on the 21st Century Economy to suggest ways to modernize California's out-of-date revenue structure. A majority of the bipartisan commission recommended reducing the personal income tax substantially and eliminating the state sales tax and corporate tax, substituting in their place a "business net receipts tax," not to exceed 4 percent, that would be applied to the net receipts of all businesses. Small businesses with less than $500,000 in annual receipts would be exempt. Perceived as a conservative report, it was thoroughly rejected by liberals in the legislature. As a result, nothing came of the recommendations.

- "The state tax structure is highly elastic and, increasingly, . . . spending is inelastic," according to John Ellwood, a professor at the University of California, Berkeley. An elastic tax structure is one that would vary considerably as the economy expands and contracts, whereas an inelastic structure would not vary in those circumstances. So taxes received go up and down as the economy changes over time, but expenditures for the most part do not change, or change very slowly.

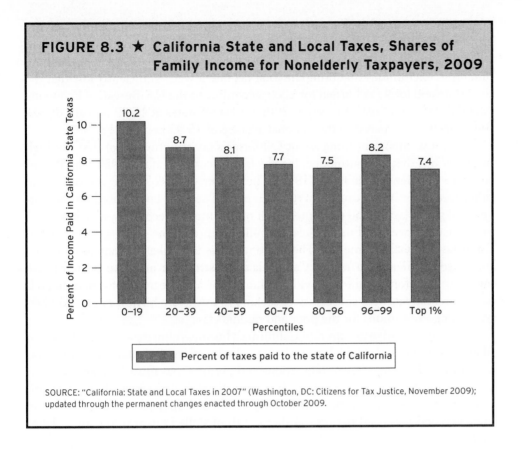

FIGURE 8.3 ★ California State and Local Taxes, Shares of Family Income for Nonelderly Taxpayers, 2009

Percent of Income Paid in California State Texas

Percentiles	Value
0–19	10.2
20–39	8.7
40–59	8.1
60–79	7.7
80–96	7.5
96–99	8.2
Top 1%	7.4

■ Percent of taxes paid to the state of California

SOURCE: "California: State and Local Taxes in 2007" (Washington, DC: Citizens for Tax Justice, November 2009); updated through the permanent changes enacted through October 2009.

- The sales tax focuses on goods that are sold, reflecting the manufacturing economy in place when the tax was developed. But the modern economy has shifted toward services, which are not taxed—for example, a doctor's office visit or the labor charge when your automobile is fixed. Broadening the base of the sales tax would enable the high rate (compared to other states) to be lowered.

- "Ballot measures have imposed rigid spending demands" (discussed in the section "Budgetary Limitations," later in the chapter).

- Tax subsidies have proliferated as the legislature has added them in recent years as inducements to obtain the two-thirds majority necessary to pass the budget.

- Tax administration is split among the Franchise Tax Board, the Board of Equalization, and the Employment Development Department, considered an inefficient arrangement.

Is California Overtaxed?

Conservatives certainly think California is overtaxed. The California Taxpayers Association makes the case that "the extraordinary level of taxation in California can provide more than enough in tax revenue to fund police and fire services, education for our children, and public works projects and health and welfare services for California's poor."[10] Taxes are so high, in their view, that the state is becoming economically uncompetitive with other states.

California is a relatively rich state. Its household and median family incomes are some $5,000 (or more) higher than the U.S. averages. The income and sales tax rates are among the higher tax rates of all American states. However, there are numerous exemptions that bring the total tax rate lower—sufficiently low that the total state and local tax burden for 2009, according to the U.S. Bureau of Economic Analysis and the Census Bureau, is 20th among all states at 15.99 percent of personal income, compared to the national average of 15.43 percent.[11]

The most important thing about California's tax structure is not that it is high or higher but that it is outmoded. It reflects the economy of the 1950s and Proposition 13 decisions made in the 1970s. The property tax collects less money than other wealthy states because of Proposition 13. The sales tax is based on the purchase of goods (with food exempted), not on the modern economy, which is based on services. Lower- and middle-class families with children are largely exempted from the personal income tax. The bottom line is that, like so many areas of the state's governmental structure, California's tax structure needs to be reformed. Without tax reform, California will continue to be a battleground for both liberals and conservatives, with conservatives seeking to lower the highest rates, and liberals seeking exemptions for the poor and middle class.

Most conservative groups rate California's business climate as one of the worst of any state due to the high levels of taxes; the taxation of capital gains at regular tax rates; and the number of regulations and permits that must be taken account of to establish, run, and expand a business. Nevertheless, many large corporations are located in California, particularly in Silicon Valley (the area between San Francisco and San Jose) because of the wealth of skilled talent in the area's labor market.

Moreover, business has many benefits in the tax system. Although the bank and corporation tax is almost 9 percent, there are so many exemptions that the tax rate on the $1 trillion California economy is about two-thirds of 1 percent. Proposition 13 gives businesses relatively low property tax rates, especially because the turnover rate for business and commercial property is much lower than the rate for private homes. All told, however, most do not find that the benefits for business outweigh the poor business climate. Whether California can simplify the vast array of permitting and regulatory agencies characteristic of large, diverse states is another question. So far, little progress has been made.

One question is whether California's level of taxes reduces the growth the state would otherwise experience. An analysis of the growth rates of nine states with a high rate of personal income taxation compared to the nine states that lack any personal income tax shows that there is no conclusive relationship. In fact, the states that grow the most seem to be those that have high rates of population growth, and several of the nonincome tax states have economic resources (oil in particular, which is why they don't have a state income tax) not available to other states.[12]

Expenditures

Again looking at all expenditures, the following are the major categories of the budget for 2012–13:

Table 8.2 indicates that the largest category is "health and human services," at $44.9 billion for 2012–13 and about 32 percent of the entire budget. This category includes Medi-Cal, California's Medicaid program, which provides health cover-

TABLE 8.2 ★ State Expenditures by Category, 2012–13 Budget[a]

EXPENDITURES	DOLLARS (IN BILLIONS)	PERCENT OF TOTAL EXPENDITURES
Health and human services	44.9	32
Education (K–12)	39.6	28
Business, transportation, housing	15.8	11
Higher education	10.1	7
Corrections and rehabilitation	9.0	7
Legislative, judicial, executive	6.1	5
Resources	6.0	5
Environmental protection	1.9	2
General government	2.6	2
Others	1.8	1
Total	122.6	

[a]Includes the General Fund, special funds, and bond funds.
SOURCE: California Department of Finance, "2012–13," www.ebudget.ca.gov (accessed 9/9/12).

age for the poor as well as for senior citizens in nursing homes; the public health system; Healthy Families, California's state children's health insurance program; welfare; Temporary Assistance for Needy Families; and the state contribution to food stamps and the Women, Infants, and Children (WIC) supplemental food program, among many others.

"Education (K–12)" is the second largest portion of the state budget at $39.6 billion and 28 percent of total expenditures. There is a long, gradual upward trend in the proportion of the budget devoted to education, although there is a slight decline in the last several fiscal years because of declining state revenues. With the passage of Proposition 13, a gradually increasing proportion of the state general fund has been spent on K–12 education. The money in this category supplements property tax revenues for education, collected by each county.

The third largest category is "business, transportation, and housing," at $15.8 billion or 11 percent of the state budget. This area includes Caltrans, which maintains the state's roads; the Department of Motor Vehicles (DMV); and the departments that regulate corporations, alcoholic beverages, real estate, managed health care, and high-speed rail, among others. (The high-speed rail area includes only $15 million for state positions to manage the high-speed rail authority; if the high-speed railroad is actually implemented, construction funds will come from the federal government and bond issues.) Most programs in the business, transportation, and housing area are largely funded by special funds and taxes, not through the general fund.

"Higher education" is the fourth largest category at $10.1 billion and 7 percent of total expenditures. Higher education includes funding for the community college system (112 campuses), the CSU system (23 campuses), and the UC system (10 campuses). Since 1980–81 there has been a trend downward in the proportion of the budget devoted to higher education. In recent years, state funding for higher education has been cut severely, as indicated in the opening vignette to this chapter. Tuition increases have partially replaced the lost state funding.

The "corrections and rehabilitation" category provides funding for the state prisons and youth authorities. This category increased steadily from 1980–81 through the mid-1990s as the public demanded three-strikes laws and similar measures, but has since leveled off.

The "others" category provides funding for everything else in the state budget, from the coastal commissions to the state bureaucracy.

Figure 8.4 depicts the 2012–13 budget.

Why Do Revenues Vary So Much?

California's budget goes up and down each year, soaring when the economy is healthy and plunging in even the mildest recessions. Here is why:

- The economy. Revenues from the sales tax and the personal income tax depend on how the state economy performs each year.

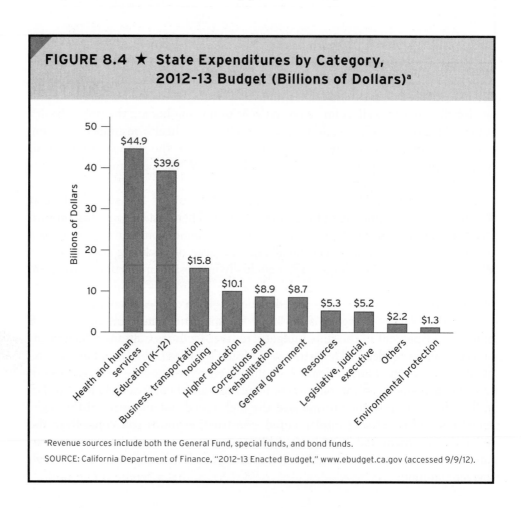

FIGURE 8.4 ★ State Expenditures by Category, 2012-13 Budget (Billions of Dollars)[a]

[a]Revenue sources include both the General Fund, special funds, and bond funds.

SOURCE: California Department of Finance, "2012-13 Enacted Budget," www.ebudget.ca.gov (accessed 9/9/12).

- Compared to other states, the budget relies more on the personal income tax, the capital gains portion of which soars when stock options are cashed out, than on the property tax, limited in 1978 by Proposition 13.

Budgetary Limitations

In addition to passing bond issues, through initiatives California voters have limited what the state government can do in some very significant areas. Here are the most significant:[13]

- **Proposition 13 (1978)** cut property taxes to 1 percent of the assessed valuation of the property in 1975 and allows reassessment only when the property is sold. If justified by inflation, the tax can rise a maximum of 2 percent in between assessments.

- **Proposition 62 (1986)** requires a vote of the electorate on all taxes that might be used to replace revenues lost under Proposition 13.

- **Proposition 98 (1988)** requires that at least 40 percent of the general fund be devoted to K–14 education, including community colleges; annual increases are to be at least equal to the increase in school enrollment and the cost of living.

- **Proposition 99 (1988)** mandated a 25¢ tax on cigarettes, with the proceeds to be spent on antismoking campaigns and medical research.

- **Proposition 111 (1990)** increased the gas tax and trucking fees, with the proceeds required to be spent on transportation projects.

- **Proposition 5 (1998)** mandated the state to negotiate a compact to allow tribal casinos in California.

- **Proposition 42 (2002)** requires that the sales tax on gasoline be devoted to transportation-related projects.

- **Proposition 49 (2002)**, supported by actor and (at that point) potential Republican candidate for governor Arnold Schwarzenegger, requires that several hundred million dollars be spent on after-school programs.

- **Proposition 71 (2004)** authorizes the sale of $3 billion in bonds to fund stem-cell research in the state.

- **Propositions 1A, 1B, 1C, 1D, 1E, 84 (2006)** authorizes over $40 billion in bonds to be spent on infrastructure improvements in the state. The interest on these bonds is paid from the budget each year.

- **Proposition 1A (2008)**, the "Safe, Reliable High-Speed Passenger Train Bond Act for the 21st Century," authorizes the sale of $9.9 billion in bonds to build a high-speed train connecting San Diego, Los Angeles, Bakersfield, San Francisco, and Sacramento. The interest from the bonds, when sold, will be $600 million per year out of the General Fund.

Of these, the two that have had the most effect are Propositions 13 and 98. Proposition 13 has made the state budget more reliant on taxes that vary with the economy and less reliant on sources of income that don't vary with the economy, particularly the property tax. Proposition 98 dictated that a certain proportion of the budget, almost half when higher education is included, must be devoted to one policy area.

Because the initiative requires only a majority vote, it is relatively easy to authorize expenditures through the initiative compared with going through the legislature. California has become a state in which it is easy to lower taxes/budget items and to authorize expenditures through the initiative but increasingly difficult to raise the funds to pay for all these items that the voters find so popular.

Recent California Budgets and the Budget Process

In each of the recent years, California lawmakers and the governor have closed the budget gap with the standard techniques used in other states—incremental tax increases; cuts in education, health, and social services, the largest portions of the budget; and borrowing through bond issues that are repaid over a 5- to 10-year period to cover a portion of the yearly deficit. California Forward, a new bipartisan group aimed at fixing some of California's perennial budget process problems, stated in 2008 that

> the current budget process is largely a relic of the mid-20th Century, with the focus on how much to increase spending (or how much to cut), rather than the value that public services bring to Californians over time. These annual budget decisions often either push California's fiscal systems toward long-term solvency or away from it. The ongoing and chronic imbalance between revenues and expenditures is one indicator of system failure. Changing how budget process decisions are made could enable public leaders to deal with the more intractable and complex problems involving the revenue system and the state-local relationship.

They identify, as we have, the key problems of budgeting:

> The costs of operating state programs are growing faster than the revenue base that supports them. The revenue system is highly sensitive to changes in the economy, producing significant volatility. The single-year budgeting horizon encourages short-term fixes, rather than long-term solutions. The budget does not take a strategic approach to ensure a return on public investments and there is a lack of public and legislative review of how money is spent.[14]

Many commentators noted the cumulative effect of the fees and caps that have been proposed more and more frequently in recent years.[15] Traditionally, California tried to supply sufficient services for all, on the principle that "if you're eligible, we'll serve you." The community colleges guarantee, for example, that any high school graduate can go to college. That principle has been shifting, though. The Schwarzenegger budget for 2004–05 in particular had caps on the number of individuals who can be served in various programs; immigrants in Medi-Cal and the program that supplies drugs for those with AIDS are both capped at the level of January 1, 2004. California's fees for students attending CSU and community colleges used to be among the lowest in the nation; they have increased substantially in recent years. Measures are often proposed as emergency measures, but few emergency measures have been repealed in the past. In short, there is a lowered expectation for services that has become particularly apparent in the Schwarzenegger and Jerry Brown eras but has been in the background for the last decade or more.

BOX 8.3 | **What Exactly Is Proposition 13?**

Proposition 13, passed overwhelmingly by the voters in June 1978, had the following provisions:

- All property taxes are rolled back to a maximum of 1 percent of the value of the property in 1975-76.

- The value of the property, and thus the tax paid, was allowed to increase by the rate of inflation, but the inflation rate was capped at 2 percent per year.

- When ownership changed, property would be revalued at the current market value.

- No new property taxes could be imposed, either by the state or by local governments.

- Any "special taxes" could be imposed only by a two-thirds margin of the voters in the particular area (the state legislature was already under a two-thirds approval rule for raising taxes, a rule in force since 1933).

- All property taxes collected were to be distributed "according to law," and because no law existed, the legislature had to create one, which it did in 1978 and 1979.

The most immediate change was to local governments. Before 1978, they had each established their own property tax rate, designed to produce sufficient revenues to accomplish the particular function of the agency. Now, instead, each agency's property tax rate was irrelevant; the state would decide "according to law" which agency got which amount of money. The total property tax collected fell by over half. The state, however, had a $5 billion surplus, which helped bridge the gap for several years.

The single biggest change is that the state assumed considerable authority over what used to be local government issues.[a] Local governments used to set the local tax rate to produce sufficient funds for the level of public services that each locality desired. Instead, those decisions are now made by the state, and "clearly, the property tax is now really a state tax."[b]

Another consequence flows from the provision that requires a two-thirds vote of the local area to impose or raise a tax. Many localities have had votes of 60 to 66 percent, just short of the required two-thirds, and have not been able to do such things as acquire land for parks. School bond issues, however, require only a 55 percent vote as a result of Proposition 39 in 2000, which authorized bonds for the repair and construction of school facilities if approved by 55 percent of the local voters, rather than two-thirds.

One of the most important consequences is called "the fiscalization of land use"—that is, the tendency of local governments not only to evaluate land use changes in terms of how much money will be brought to the local government but to make decisions on that basis. Because localities receive a share of the state sales tax, land use changes that produce a lot of sales tax revenues are preferred. Big-box shopping centers and auto malls have been favored by many cities in preference to housing developments. Along with favoring certain kinds of developments, development fees and other ways to obtain revenue that is not available through the property tax have increased substantially.

Finally, we have seen the development of many "arcane" financing techniques, those intricate enough to be understood only by a few. These are also designed to help obtain revenues to replace property taxes.

a. The best description of Proposition 13 and its implications is Jeffrey I. Chapman, "Proposition 13: Some Unintended Consequences," Public Policy Institute of California, September 1998, www.ppic.org (accessed 7/27/12).
b. Chapman, "Proposition 13," p. 22.

The California Budgetary Process: Where Are We Now?

As of 2012, the budgetary process needed substantial reform. Dan Walters, a respected California journalist, states that the inability of the legislature to deal with the budget crisis and fiscal matters in general seems to be a reflection of three structural factors:

1. The extremely short term limits on the legislature, meaning that few politicians present in the twenty-first century were also present in the early 1990s during the last budget crisis. The leadership is inexperienced compared to other states, and "current members [are relieved] of responsibility for past decisions."[16]
2. The bipartisan gerrymander of legislative districts after the 2000 Census, which produced an overwhelming number of safe districts and seems to have reduced the willingness of legislators to work for bipartisan solutions and compromise. In 2008, voters approved Proposition 11, which formed a citizens' commission to draw the state's Assembly and Senate districts after the 2010 Census. The 2012 election results showed that more of California's legislative districts were competitive than in earlier elections.
3. The two-thirds majority requirement for passing budgets and imposing tax increases. This, as we know, was modified by Proposition 25 in November 2010 to require only a majority to pass the budget each year. The two-thirds requirement still holds for tax increases and for the badly needed tax reform that would broaden the tax base and lower tax rates.

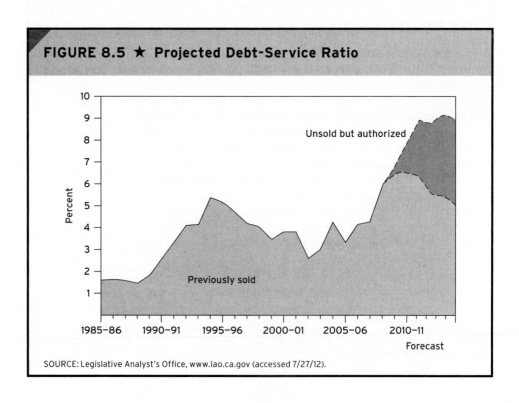

FIGURE 8.5 ★ Projected Debt-Service Ratio

SOURCE: Legislative Analyst's Office, www.lao.ca.gov (accessed 7/27/12).

In addition, there is a fourth factor—the citizens of California, who are willing to authorize all manner of financial allocations from the General Fund through the initiative process. These allocations vary from the self-serving to those with which no one would argue. But none has a dedicated new revenue source—each is an additional allocation from the General Fund, reducing the funds available for existing programs. Higher education, in particular, has been hurt by these actions. The willingness of the voters to authorize bond issues is leading to substantial additional debt payments from the General Fund, as pictured in Figure 8.5 from the Legislative Analyst's Office.

Data from the Census and Moody's show that California's net tax supported debt per capita and its debt as a proportion of 2010 personal income are number two in the nation, after New York.[17] The national median tax supported debt per capita is $1,066; California's is $2,542. The national median for net tax supported debt per capita as a proportion of 2010 personal income is 2.8 percent; California's is 6.8 percent. California's debt is high by any standard. While Californians may no longer feel that they can have every service imaginable without paying any higher taxes, they clearly haven't decided to pay for their past debts.

FOR FURTHER READING

Barrett, Katherine, Richard Greene, Michele Mariani, and Anya Sostek. "The Way We Tax." *Governing* (February 2003): 20.

Baldassare, Mark, and Christopher Hoene. *Local Budgets and Tax Policies in California and U.S. Cities: Surveys of City Officials*. San Francisco: Public Policy Institute of California, December 2004.

Baldassare, Mark, and Matthew Newman. *The State Budget and Local Health Services in California: Surveys of Local Health Officials*. San Francisco: Public Policy Institute of California, September 2005.

———. "Budget Backgrounder, A Mini-Primer on Bonds." Sacramento: California Budget Project, February 2006.

———. *A Budget for All Californians: Improving the Transparency and Accountability of the State Budget*. Sacramento: California Budget Project, May 2006.

———. "Governor Releases Proposed 2008–09 Budget." Sacramento: California Budget Project, January 2008.

California Budget Project. "Who Pays Taxes in California?" Sacramento: California Budget Project, April 2008. www.cbp.org. Accessed 7/30/12.

California Taxpayers Association. "Cal-Tax: Taxes Are Heavy Burden in California." www.caltax.org/California.htm. Accessed 7/30/12.

Howard, John. "The Schwarzenegger Budget." *California Journal* (February 2004): 44–47.

Legislative Analyst's Office. "California's Tax System: A Primer," April 2007. www.lao.ca.gov/2007/tax_primer/tax_primer_040907.aspx. Accessed 7/30/12.

Public Policy Institute of California. "Just the Facts: California's State Budget." San Francisco: Public Policy Institute of California, April 2010. www.ppic.org. Accessed 7/30/12.

———. "Just the Facts: Proposition 13, 30 Years Later." San Francisco: Public Policy Institute of California, June 2008. www.ppic.org. Accessed 7/30/12.

ON THE WEB

California Budget Project: www.cbp.org (accessed 7/30/12).

California Forward: www.cafwd.org (accessed 11/5/12). California Forward promotes better financial policy and quality public services.

Howard Jarvis Taxpayers Association: www.hjta.org (accessed 11/5/12).

Legislative Analyst's Office: www.lao.ca.gov (accessed 7/30/12).

State of California, Department of Finance–budget update site: www.ebudget.ca.gov (accessed 7/30/12).

State of California, Department of Finance: www.dof.ca.gov/Research/Research.php (accessed 7/30/12). California statistics and demographic information site

SUMMARY

I. What is the California budget?
   A. The governor's and legislature's views of the future.
      1. The future of the state's economy (economic assumptions).
      2. The future income of the state (revenues).
      3. Future spending of the state (expenditures).
   B. The budget is at the center of what the state does each year.

II. How is the budget formulated?
   A. Agencies send their requests to the governor each fall.
   B. The governor sends a balanced budget request to the legislature each January for the fiscal year starting the next July 1.
   C. The legislature adopts a balanced budget by June 15 each year, for the fiscal year to start July 1.
      1. The budget is almost always late. Only four budgets have been on time in the last two decades, and those were budget-surplus years.
      2. In recent years, the volatility of the state's revenues has caused the budget to be substantially readjusted during the fiscal year.
   D. The governor has a line-item veto, allowing him or her to reduce any line-item dollar amount downward, even to zero. However, the governor may not raise any line item.
   E. The legislature is assisted by its own neutral budget office—the Legislative Analyst's Office.
   F. If the Assembly and state senate versions of the budget differ, a "budget conference committee" will attempt to iron out the differences.
      1. If this fails, the Big 5 (the governor and the majority and minority leaders of both the Assembly and senate) will meet.
      2. Until 2011, this process was not successful, with budgets approved in late summer or early fall at best.
      3. In 2011 and 2012, because only a simple majority was needed to approve the budget, budgets were approved close to the deadline of June 15.
   G. Agencies then implement the approved budget, including studies to be carried out and presented to the legislature.

III. Revenues.
   A. Personal income tax—the largest source of income for the general fund and highly progressive.
   B. Sales tax—the next largest source of income, increased by 1 percent for 2009–10 and 2010–11. Local governments can add a small amount to the state sales tax. A portion of the tax is refunded to them. Many localities have added to their communities sales-tax-producing businesses such as big-box shopping centers and automobile dealerships specifically because of the revenues they would receive from the state.
   C. Corporate tax—the third largest source of revenues. A new method of calculating what is owed may reduce the state's revenues from this tax substantially starting in 2011–12.
   D. The California tax system is very volatile, compared to other states. It depends on the ups and downs of the economy and produces greater surges in revenue and precipitous falls when the economy booms or a recession takes place.

IV. Expenditures.
   A. Education (K–12)—the largest single expenditure. Proposition 98 requires K–12 expenditures to be over 40 percent of the state General Fund. K–12 education and higher education expenditures together equal or are greater than 50 percent of the state General Fund.
   B. Health and human services is the next highest category.
   C. Business, transportation, and housing is the third-highest category.

V. Limitations on the budget.
   A. The most substantial limitations have come from initiatives passed by the voters.
   B. Proposition 13, which limits the property tax to 1 percent of the value of one's house, and Proposition 98, which guarantees a certain amount to K–12 education, are the most important of these limitations.
   C. Cumulatively, the limitations have guaranteed well over half the General Fund and at least half of all expenditures, giving the governor and legislature less flexibility than they would have in other states. That was the intent of the initiatives—to limit what the governor and legislature can do. The level of distrust the voters have for the governor and legislature is very high in California.

VI. Recent state budgets have been characterized by huge and fluctuating gaps between revenues and expenditures.
   A. These have made it difficult to find the middle ground necessary to obtain a two-thirds vote in the legislature for a budget. Starting in 2011, only a majority will be required.
   B. Legislators and the governor have rolled over part of the debt in some recent years by borrowing against the future, through a bond issue. In general, this is a poor practice because the interest payments on the bonds become another amount that is "locked in" next year's budget and those of subsequent years as well.

VII. Why is budgeting such a problem in California?
    A. California's term limits are too short. Legislators do not get enough time to learn the intricacies of their jobs.
    B. Gerrymandered legislative districts have produced safe seats, so that legislators generally do not have to worry about losing in the next election. The process has produced even more partisan legislators than we would see otherwise. Proposition 8, approved in 2008, authorized the formation of a citizens' commission to redistrict the Assembly and state senate in 2011, after receiving the results of the 2010 Census. The first election held under the new seats was in 2012.
    C. The two-thirds majority for passing a budget and raising taxes has made the process difficult for both parties.
      1. Because one party generally supports high levels of services and taxes, and another takes the opposite approach, compromise has been difficult.
      2. Few states require a two-thirds majority to pass the budget. More do so to raise taxes.
    D. The initiative process makes it relatively easy for interest groups to sponsor initiatives to allocate proportions of the General Fund for themselves. The state's voters are too willing to approve such initiatives.

PRACTICE QUIZ

1. Both the governor and the legislature are obliged by the California state constitution to pass a balanced budget.
    a) true
    b) false
2. The state of California cannot pass its budget each year starting in 2011 unless the Assembly and state Senate pass the budget by
    a) 50 percent plus 1 vote.
    b) 55 percent.
    c) 66.7 percent.
    d) 75 percent.
3. The state of California cannot raise state taxes unless the Assembly and state Senate pass the relevant law by
    a) 50 percent plus 1 vote.
    b) 55 percent.
    c) 66.7 percent.
    d) 75 percent.
4. Proposition 13 requires
    a) property taxes to be lowered to the level when the property was last sold. Property tax values can rise 2 percent per year.
    b) property taxes to be set at 1975 levels; property is reassessed when it is sold. Property tax values can rise 2 percent per year.
    c) property taxes to be lowered to 1945 levels; property is reassessed when it is sold. The level of the tax can rise 3 percent per year.
    d) Property taxes to be raised to the appropriate level when the property on both sides of a house or business has been sold—all the property is then reassessed at current values. The level of the tax can rise 2 percent per year if the property is not sold.
5. Proposition 98 requires education spending to be at least
    a) 50 percent of the entire state budget.
    b) 50 percent of the general fund.
    c) 33.3 percent of the general fund.
    d) 40 percent of the general fund.
6. How do term limits affect the budget process?
    a) More minority and female legislators are elected, and they are more willing to compromise to enact the budget.
    b) Former senior legislators, while not able to hold their current seats, return to the legislature each year to offer their ideas about how to solve the budget crisis.
    c) Term limits have produced majority and minority leaders in both the Assembly and Senate who are willing to compromise and get the job done.
    d) Term limits have produced a less experienced leadership who have found it difficult to compromise and enact the budget.
7. The governor's line-item veto allows
    a) the governor to lower any appropriation item.
    b) the governor, in conjunction with an agency, to veto any bill in its entirety.
    c) the governor to "pencil out" any line or sentence in any bill.
    d) the governor to raise or lower any appropriation item, including lowering the item to zero.
8. The governor's line-item veto may be overridden by a 50 percent plus one vote in both houses of the legislature.
    a) true
    b) false
9. The credit rating assigned to the state of California by Moody's, Fitch Ratings, or Standard & Poor's is important because
    a) the credit rating influences the size of the deficit or surplus California may have in any given fiscal year.
    b) when the credit rating goes down, the interest rate that the state pays to float its bonds goes up.

c) when the credit rating goes up, the amount of interest the state pays goes down.
d) all of the above
e) none of the above
f) a and b above, but not c

10. Indian gambling revenues have become an extremely significant source of income for the state of California.
a) true
b) false

CRITICAL-THINKING QUESTIONS

1. How might California's tax system be made more predictable and less dependent on the economy than it is now? How might *Governing* magazine rate your proposed changes?
2. How should the budget process in California be reformed, assuming it should be reformed? What goals are important in reforming the process, and what changes in the process might achieve those goals?
3. Should the governor have more authority in the budget process? One of the key differences between California and Georgia was the difference in the power of the governor. Leaving aside the opinion you might have of the current incumbent, what reforms might help with the long-term budget process in California?
4. The other major player in the budget process is the legislature. How might the legislature's consideration of the budget be changed to make California's budget more predictable and timely?

KEY TERMS

At this point you should have a general understanding of the following concepts and terms:

big-box shopping centers/automobile dealerships (p. 165)
Budget Conference Committee (p. 161)
Department of Finance (p. 159)
governor's budget (p. 159)

Legislative Analyst's Office (p. 161)
line-item veto (p. 161)
May revise (p. 159)
Moody's, Fitch Ratings, Standard & Poor's ratings (p. 162)

personal income tax (p. 163)
progressive (p. 163)
regressive (p. 164)
sales tax (p. 164)
unified budget (p. 159)

9 Local Government

WHAT CALIFORNIA'S LOCAL GOVERNMENTS DO AND WHY THEY MATTER

Governing California would be hard to imagine without the more than 5,000 local governments that help run the state. Local officials and workers in cities, counties, school districts, special districts, and regional bodies all play an essential role. By late spring 2012, however, many local governments were in trouble, especially in the cities, and some of them were struggling to survive.

The complexity of the state's local government system makes it hard to generalize about what local governments do. But a short list would include the following:

★ General-purpose local governments, like cities and counties, do everything from putting out fires to cleaning the streets and seeing that the buses run on time. They protect the health, safety, welfare, and overall quality of life of all who live within their jurisdictions.

★ Limited-purpose governments, such as school districts and other special districts, deliver specific public services such as public education, pest abatement, and irrigation to meet particular needs within defined territorial boundaries.

★ Regional governments address problems such as air pollution and population growth that affect broad areas across many jurisdictions and that require comprehensive study and planning to solve.

★ Many local governments do the actual work involved in implementing state and federal laws, from control of water quality and production of affordable housing to homeland security.

★ Most local governments provide citizens with opportunities to learn about public problems, express their opinions, practice hands-on democracy, and collectively exercise some degree of popular control on issues they really care about close to home.

★ Some local governments experiment and innovate to pioneer new ways of serving citizens better or improving the democratic process. Often these local initiatives spread and can have major impacts in reforming how government works at the state and national levels.

Times have been hard for Californians the last few years. A prolonged and severe economic recession had taken its toll. But by spring 2012 things seemed to be getting better. For local government officials, however, hard times had become even harder as they coped with slashed budgets, reduced staffing, cutbacks in services, and projected revenue shortfalls as far as the eye could see. Many local officials, especially in the state's larger cities, also discovered, sometimes too late, that they faced unsustainable financial obligations to their current and retired employees. In some cases the projected costs of promised pensions and health benefits had already escalated out of control. One city, Vallejo, faced with such problems, had already declared bankruptcy in 2008. Another, Stockton, filed for bankruptcy in June 2012, followed by San Bernardino, in August 2012. Making things worse, an important source of revenues for many cities was suddenly extinguished in 2011. The state government, backed by the California Supreme Court, terminated the existence of nearly 400 community redevelopment agencies in one fell swoop and seized their money to help solve its own budget crisis. The state government was in trouble, too, and local governments would have to fend for themselves. If local government leaders could expect little support from the state, they could expect even less from the federal government, which continued to be paralyzed by legislative gridlock and polarized partisan politics.

On top of these multiple hardships, the youth-led Occupy Wall Street Movement that erupted in September 2011 in New York City had inspired scores of Occupy demonstrations and encampments in cities across the nation. This spontaneous grassroots movement gave voice to the anger and resentment of the 99 percent toward the rich and powerful 1 percent. It shifted the focus of national political discourse from important concerns about deficits and austerity to the even deeper issues of expanding income inequality, social injustice, and the plutocracy our democracy had seemingly become. But in many California cities, even the more liberal ones like San Francisco and Oakland, local governments bore the brunt of protest demands, the occasional outbreaks of violence, and the financial impact of all this disruption on local budgets and commerce. On December 12, 2011, for example, an estimated 3,000 marchers from Occupy Oakland, for the second time, shut down the Port of Oakland for a day. A few months later, on May 1, 2012, a band of self-described anarchists infiltrated an Occupy San Francisco protest in the city's Mission district and damaged over 30 businesses. (Occupy San Francisco leaders condemned the violence and raised funds to partially reimburse business owners for the costs of repairs.) Occupy demonstrations also flared up on some state college campuses. In November 2011, for example, student activists at UC Berkeley and UC Davis put up tents on their campuses and helped organize student protests of recent education budget cuts and skyrocketing tuitions. Later attempts by police to remove these encampments resulted in violent confrontations, including a notorious pepper-spraying incident at UC Davis.

Despite these challenges, if there is hope for economic recovery and democratic renewal in California, much of it lies with the state's local governments, especially in the cities, where most people live and work, where democracy still thrives, and where protests often give rise to needed political reforms. Local governments do a lot under extremely harsh conditions, and all of it matters.

The Legal Framework: Dillon's Rule, Home Rule, and Local Powers of Governance

The U.S. Constitution assigns power and authority to the national and state governments, but it says nothing about local governments. Counties, cities, special districts, and other forms of local government have no inherent rights or powers. What rights and powers they do have are conferred on them by the state constitution or state legislature.

The constitutional doctrine that gives states ultimate authority over local governments is known as Dillon's Rule. In 1868, Iowa judge John F. Dillon ruled that "municipal corporations" such as counties and cities are mere "creatures of the state" and may exercise only those powers delegated to them by the state.[1] Upheld by the U.S. Supreme Court in 1903 and again in 1923, Dillon's Rule is firmly established, at least in theory, as the basic legal framework for relations between state and local governments. In practice, however, only a few states, like Alabama, Idaho, and Nebraska, demand strict obedience to Dillon's Rule and require local governments to seek their permission in order to act. California, like most states, has passed government codes and home-rule laws that allow significant local discretion and autonomy. Within broad limits, county and city residents can select their own form of government, manage their own elections, raise their own revenues, and choose what kinds of functions to perform and at what levels of service.[2]

In California, under the provisions of Article XI, Section 5, of the state constitution and various court rulings,[3] most of the more populous cities and counties have adopted home-rule charters, which allow the maximum discretion and autonomy to local governments. The others are designated as general law cities and counties that fall more directly under state authority and control. To get an idea of just how far home-rule powers can be taken in asserting local autonomy, see Box 9.1 on home rule and local autonomy in San Francisco.

A more practical restraint on state meddling in local government is based on the maxim that all politics is local. State legislators, after all, are elected by local constituencies to protect their local interests, and they won't last long if they forget who brought them to the dance. These political realities have shielded local governments from the full blast of arbitrary state authority.[4] Finally, as part of the so-called devolution revolution that began in the 1970s, federal and state authorities have been only too eager to delegate responsibility to local governments to fend for themselves and solve their own problems, using their own money.

In sum, Dillon's Rule is very liberally construed in California. The state's constitutional and legal framework confers broad formal powers of local governance, especially in charter cities and counties. Home rule on paper, however, does not necessarily translate into home rule in reality. In recent years, as we shall see, the state's chronic budget crises and other financial disasters have been strangling the life out of some local governments and crippling the powers of others to govern. Formal authority minus needed resources equals impotent local government. That equation threatens to reduce the ideal of home rule and local autonomy to a myth.

BOX 9.1 | San Francisco: Pushing the Envelope of Home-Rule Powers

As a consolidated city and county, San Francisco has pushed the limits of home-rule powers about as far as they can go. Some examples:

CITY OF REFUGE LAWS

In the early 1980s, San Francisco declared itself a "sanctuary city." It has since passed a number of "city of refuge" laws to protect immigrants from illegal search and seizure by state and federal authorities.

LIMITS ON GROWTH AND NEW LABOR STANDARDS

Since the 1980s, San Francisco has imposed increasingly severe restrictions on high-rise construction, waterfront development, and land use generally. The city also began charging developer fees to raise new local revenues for affordable housing and public-transit improvements. In 2003, the city required all city employers to pay a high minimum wage and in 2006 to provide paid sick leave to all employees. In 2007, the city began offering affordable health care to all uninsured city residents.

GOVERNMENT REORGANIZATION AND ELECTORAL REFORMS

In 1995, San Francisco voters approved a charter amendment that consolidated the city's divided bureaucracy under mayoral authority. The following year, voters changed how they elected their Board of Supervisors, rejecting the at-large system in favor of district elections. In 2002, the city adopted ranked choice voting for district elections and citywide offices, the first major city in the nation to do so.

SOCIAL AND CULTURAL POLICY

In 1996, San Francisco passed its landmark Equal Benefits law, which requires all businesses and nonprofits that have contracts with the city to provide equal benefits to married employees and those with same-sex domestic partners. In February 2004, Mayor Gavin Newsom directed that official marriage licenses be granted to same-sex couples. A month later, more than 4,000 gay and lesbian couples had been married under the new local policy. The California Supreme Court ordered the city to halt the practice, pending judicial review. In May 2008, the court ruled that the state's ban on same-sex marriage was unconstitutional and that such marriages would be legal effective June 2008 for residents and nonresidents. On November 4, 2008, however, the state's voters approved an initiative constitutional amendment, Proposition 8, eliminating the right of same-sex couples to marry. The California Supreme Court ruled in 2009 that Proposition 8 was constitutional. On appeal, a federal district judge ruled in August 2010 that Proposition 8 violated the U.S. Constitution. Ban supporters, in turn, appealed to the U.S. Ninth Circuit Court of Appeals, which affirmed the District Court ruling in 2012. It is highly likely this case will reach the U.S. Supreme Court for final resolution.

As these examples illustrate, San Francisco often acts as if it were a state unto itself and not merely the creature of one. The decision to certify gay marriages, in particular, created a storm of legal challenge and political controversy across the nation. San Franciscans, however, seem to enjoy sparking conflict by pushing the envelope of their home-rule powers. Where they succeed, others may follow.

SOURCES: Richard Edward DeLeon, *Left Coast City: Progressive Politics in San Francisco, 1975–1991* (Lawrence: University Press of Kansas, 1992).
"San Francisco and Domestic Partners: New Fields of Battle in the Culture War," in *Culture Wars and Local Politics*, ed. Elaine B. Sharp (Lawrence: University Press of Kansas, 1999), pp. 117–36.
Rich DeLeon, "Only In San Francisco?: The City's Political Culture in Comparative Perspective," *SPUR Newsletter*, Report 411, November 12, 2002, www.spur.org/documents/pdf/021101_article_01.pdf (accessed 8/2/12).
"San Francisco: The Politics of Race, Land Use, and Ideology," in *Racial Politics in American Cities*, ed. Rufus P. Browning, Dale Rogers Marshall, and David H. Tabb, 3d ed. (New York: Longman, 2003), pp. 167–98.
Dean E. Murphy, "San Francisco Mayor Exults in Move on Gay Marriage," *New York Times*, February 19, 2004.

County Governments

At the first meeting of the California legislature in 1850, lawmakers divided the state into 27 counties for the purpose of administering state laws. Since then many new counties have been created, mostly by subdivision. The state's current 58 counties have been with us since 1907, when the last addition, Imperial County, was carved out of the old San Diego County (see Figure 9.1). Political movements have arisen from time to time that attempted to split an existing county to make a new one. An 1894 amendment to the state constitution, however, made it virtually impossible to do so by requiring a favorable majority vote in both the entire county affected and in the territory of the proposed new county.[5]

FIGURE 9.1 ★ The 58 California Counties

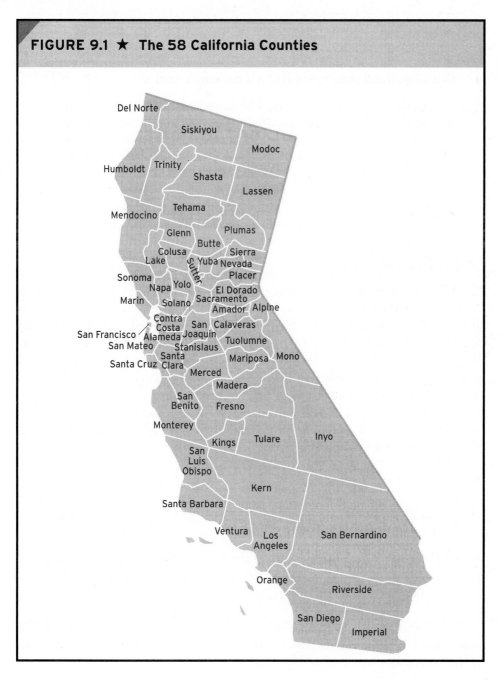

California's 58 counties vary greatly in their territory, population, and demographic characteristics.

- *Territory*—Just in terms of size, the differences are vast. For example, you could fit 427 areas the size of San Francisco County (47 square miles) within the borders of San Bernardino County (20,053 square miles). The differences in physical geography are equally extreme, ranging from deserts to rain forests, from flat farmlands to tall mountains. Some counties are densely urban and covered with cities, whereas others are so rural that coyotes outnumber people.

- *Population*—Alpine County's grand total of 1,061 residents could all live comfortably in one San Francisco precinct. Los Angeles County, at the other extreme, is bursting with nearly 10 million people, representing more than 28 percent of the state's entire population. The lowest-ranking 29 counties combined contain only 5 percent of the state's total population; the 5 most populous counties (Los Angeles, Orange, San Diego, San Bernardino, and Santa Clara) hold about 55 percent of the state's total.

- *Demography*—If you tour the state's 58 counties, you'll discover vastly different social and economic worlds. The populations of some counties are relatively poor, others relatively rich. Some are mostly white, others mainly nonwhite. Some are dominated by homeowners, others—for example, San Francisco—by renters.

Table 9.1 reports the lowest- and highest-ranking counties on these and other selected indicators to illustrate the extremes observed among California's counties.

Legal Framework

The state constitution provides a general legal framework for the governing of most counties, which are known as *general-law counties*. It prescribes the number and functions of elected county officials, how they are selected, and what they may or may not do in raising revenue, spending money, delivering services, and so on. Fourteen counties, however, have adopted a *home-rule charter*, which gives voters greater control over the selection of governing bodies and officers, more flexibility in raising taxes and revenues, and broader discretion in organizing to deliver services. All of the state's most populous counties and one small county, Tehama, with its 57,000 residents, are now *charter counties*. Voters can adopt a charter for their county government by a majority vote.

- Long content to live without a charter, the voters of Orange County finally adopted one in March 2002. They did so mainly to prevent the governor from appointing his own choice to fill a vacancy on the county board of supervisors, which he had the authority to do under the general-law provisions.

- San Francisco is an unusual case. It is governed under a single charter as a consolidated county and city, an arrangement that is unique in the state and rare in the country.

County charters vary widely in content and in the range of powers claimed for local control. When a charter does not mention a subject, that subject is governed by the general law.

TABLE 9.1 ★ Comparing the Counties of California

	LOWEST	HIGHEST
Total population (2011)	1,102 (Alpine)	9,889,056 (Los Angeles)
Land area (square miles)	47 (San Francisco)	20,053 (San Bernardino)
Population density (2011)	1.6 (Alpine)	17,179 (San Francisco)
White non-Hispanic (2011)	16.3% (Imperial)	87% (Sierra)
Hispanic (2011)	7.4% (Trinity)	80.6% (Imperial)
Asian/Pacific Islands (2011)	0.5% (Sierra)	34.4% (San Francisco)
Black (2008)	0.1% (Alpine)	15.2% (Solano)
Homeowners (2008)	39.5% (San Francisco)	73.1% (Placer)
Aged 25+ years with BA degree (2008)	10.1% (Kings)	56.9% (Marin)
Median family income (2008)	$37,936 (Imperial)	$91,982 (Marin)
Below poverty (2008)	6.1% (Marin)	22.9% (Imperial)
Unemployment (2012)	6.6% (Marin)	28.2% (Imperial)

SOURCES: 2008 data: U.S. Census Bureau, American Factfinder, 2008 American Community Survey 1-Year Estimates. http://factfinder.census.gov; 2011 data: U.S. Census Bureau, http://quickfacts.census.gov/qfd/states/06/06025 .html; 2012 data: California Economic Development Department, www.labormarketinfo.edd.ca.gov/Content .asp?pageid=170 (all accessed 8/2/12).

Government Organization

In all counties except San Francisco, an elected five-member board of supervisors exercises both legislative and executive authority. Given the extremes in the size of county populations, it shouldn't surprise you that small five-member boards yield huge disparities in political representation. For example, each board member in tiny Alpine County represents, on average, only 212 residents. In mammoth Los Angeles County, on the other hand, each board member represents nearly 2 million people, a number greater than the entire population of New Mexico.

County boards of supervisors, whose members are elected by districts for staggered four-year terms, not only pass laws, called *ordinances* at the local level, but also control and supervise the departments charged with administering them. This combination of legislative and executive authority gives county supervisors great power. From time to time, someone suggests a formal separation of powers and greater executive accountability. But nothing has changed in this regard and probably never will.

FIGURE 9.2 ★ Los Angeles County Organizational Chart

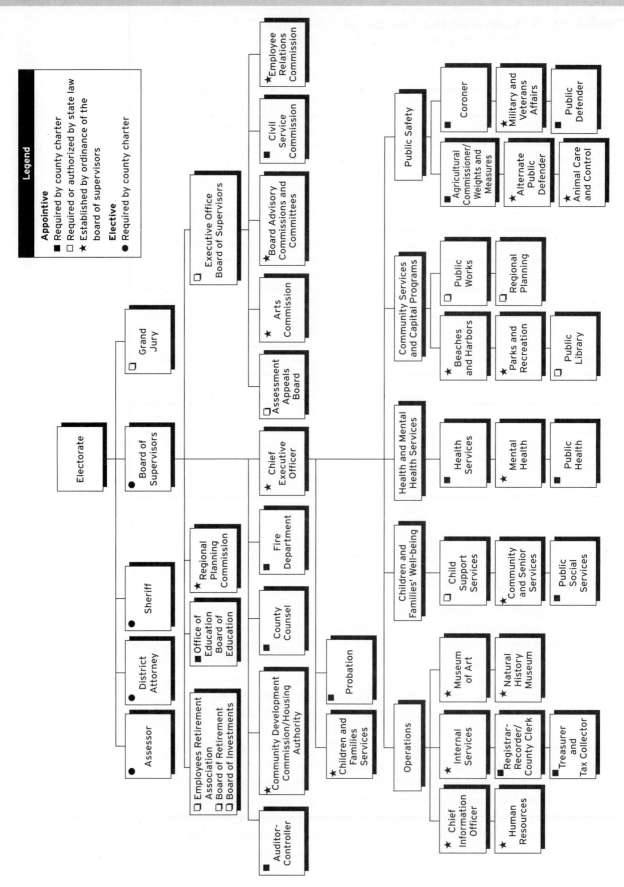

SOURCE: *County of Los Angeles Annual Report 2009–2010*, p. 5. Several departments report directly to the Board of Supervisors or are headed by elected officials, but work with the chief executive office through the clusters. These are assessor, auditor-controller, executive office of the Board of Supervisors, county counsel (Operations), community development commission (Community and Municipal Services); sheriff, district attorney, and fire (Public Safety).

As always, there is an exception: In the consolidated city and county government of San Francisco, an elected 11-member board of supervisors has legislative authority. An independently elected mayor has executive authority and some control, shared with many boards and commissions, over the bureaucracy.

In addition to the board of supervisors, other elected county officers required by general law include a sheriff, who enforces the law in areas outside the cities; a district attorney; and an assessor. A 1998 constitutional amendment consolidated municipal and superior trial courts into a single layer of superior court judges elected by county voters. Elections for all offices are nonpartisan. In terms of appointed positions, charter counties have considerable latitude in creating departments and agencies to serve their needs, either by charter provision or by ordinance. Other offices are required or authorized by state law. Some charter counties, like Los Angeles County, have appointed a chief administrative officer to manage their sprawling bureaucracies under board supervision.

Figure 9.2 shows Los Angeles County's organization chart. It illustrates the complexity of local government authority and responsibility that can be found in counties with large and diverse populations. By way of contrast, Figure 9.3 shows Placer County's organizational chart, which is much simpler and more typical of counties with small populations.

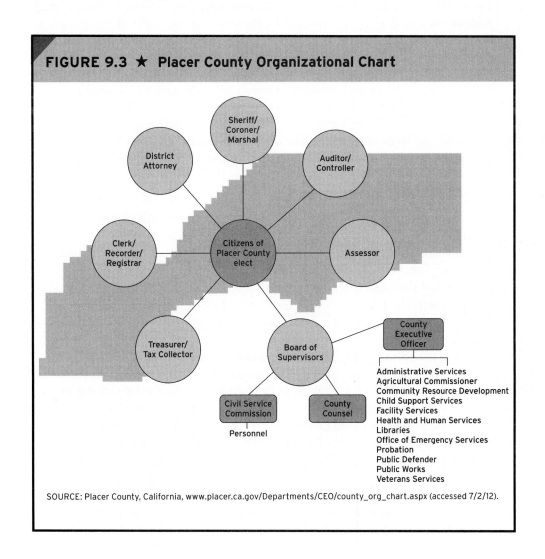

FIGURE 9.3 ★ Placer County Organizational Chart

SOURCE: Placer County, California, www.placer.ca.gov/Departments/CEO/county_org_chart.aspx (accessed 7/2/12).

County Government Functions and Responsibilities

County governments have major functions and responsibilities, most of them mandated by state or federal law, especially outside the jurisdictions of cities. County responsibilities include bridges and highways, public safety, public health, employment, parks and recreation, welfare and public assistance, public records, tax collection, general government, court administration, and land use. In the larger counties, the public workforce required to manage all this can be truly massive. Los Angeles County, for example, now has over 101,296 employees. The revenues needed to pay for their efforts can be equally huge. In 2011–12, for example, Los Angeles County raised and spent over $23.3 billion. Most of this money was received from intergovernmental transfers ($10.2 billion) and property taxes ($4.6 billion). Most of it was spent on public assistance ($5.9 billion), public safety ($6.2 billion), and health services ($6.7 billion).[6]

Decisions on land-use policy are perhaps the most important and controversial ones a county board of supervisors can make. If you're ever in the mood to watch a good political fight, attend a typical county board of supervisors meeting in places like Napa County or San Diego County. Areas like these still have plenty of open land outside the cities and fast-growing populations that fuel a demand for new housing construction, schools, and public infrastructure (sewers, highways, etc.). Landowners and developers typically badger the county board of supervisors to allow them to build, often with the result that conservationists, environmentalists, and other groups mobilize in opposition to push them back.

- In January 2010, Napa County supervisors were the target of several developer and environmentalist lawsuits related to land use. The economic downturn in the Napa Valley wine industry had created pressure to convert agricultural lands into homes. The developers sued the county to block overregulation of such lands and to protect private property rights. The environmentalists sued the county, charging that officials were failing to protect such lands from development.[7]

- More recently, on July 31, 2012, the Riverside County Board of Supervisors met to decide whether to "fast track" approval of Granite Construction's application to build a surface mine known as Liberty Quarry near the small town of Temecula. Fast-tracking would allow skipping the county planning commission's standard review and thus expedite the board's final decision on the project. The public debate at the crowded meeting was impassioned on both sides. Orange-shirted opponents faced off against green-shirted supporters. Representatives of the chamber of commerce, labor unions, and other groups backed the proposal, arguing that the quarry would stimulate the local economy and create badly need jobs. Temecula city officials, environmentalists, and leaders of the Pechanga Band of Luiseño Indians contended that the quarry would pollute the air, wreck the economy, and destroy a nearby sacred tribal site. One supervisor called Liberty Quarry "the most divisive project in county history." The board voted 3–2 to fast-track approval, prompting cheers from the green shirts and cries of outrage from the orange shirts. This story then ended abruptly and happily for all concerned. On November 15, 2012, just days before the board was scheduled to give its final approval, leaders of the Pechanga Band announced that they had reached an agreement with Granite Construction to purchase the Liberty Quarry site for $3 million and pay the firm an additional $17.35 million to cover its project costs. Granite was permitted to build its mine elsewhere miles from Temecula and the sacred tribal lands. The Pechanga Band promised to preserve the original site as it was. And Temecula officials would drop their lawsuit to stop the board from voting on a controversial decision it no longer had to make.[8]

As California's population continues to grow and to spread from the cities into the state's remaining farmlands and rural areas, you can expect to see more land-use battles erupting in the political arenas of county governments.

Local Agency Formation Commissions

All 58 California counties have a local agency formation commission (LAFCo), whose members are appointed by the county board of supervisors. These commissions play a critical role in resolving conflicts among the many local governments that often compete with one another for power and resources within their county jurisdictions. A county's LAFCo is responsible for

- reviewing and approving the incorporations of new cities, the formation of new special districts, and any proposed changes of jurisdictional boundaries, including annexations and detachments of territory, secessions, consolidations, mergers, and dissolutions.

- reviewing and approving contractual service agreements between local governments and between local governments and the private sector.

- defining the official spheres of influence for each city and special district.

- initiating proposals for consolidation, dissolution, mergers, and reorganizations if such changes seem necessary or desirable.

These powerful commissions are especially busy in counties that are rocked by large-scale land-use battles, such as San Diego County, Napa County, and Contra Costa County, or that teem with masses of people, multitudes of governments, and major secession movements, such as Los Angeles County.

City Governments

Legal Framework

Like counties, California's cities derive their powers as municipal corporations from the state constitution and state legislature. Within that legal framework, as of June 2010, the state's 481 incorporated cities fell into three categories: general-law cities (371), charter cities (109), and the unique case of San Francisco's consolidated city and county. The state Government Code, enacted by the legislature, specifies the general powers and structure of general-law cities. Broader home-rule powers are granted to charter cities, giving citizens more direct control over local affairs. Under these different arrangements, all cities have the power to legislate, as long as their local policies don't conflict with state or federal law. They have the power to raise revenues, levy taxes, charge license and service fees, and borrow. They may also hire personnel as needed; exercise police powers to enforce local, state, and federal laws; and condemn property for public use.

Incorporation: How Cities Are Born

The state grants powers to cities, and in that sense cities are indeed creatures of the state. But cities themselves are created only by the request, and with the consent, of the residents in a given area. In California, this process of *municipal incorporation* is typically initiated by a citizen petition or by a resolution of the county board of supervisors. Landowner petitions are also possible but rare. Some of the more important reasons that motivate residents to seek incorporation are

- to limit population growth, or perhaps to accelerate it.
- to provide more or better-quality services than those provided by the county.
- to prevent annexation by a nearby city.
- to create a unit of government more responsive to local needs and concerns.

A petition for municipal incorporation must be submitted to the county's LAFCo. The LAFCo panel reviews the proposed plans for the new city, its boundaries, service provisions, governing capacity, and financial viability. The LAFCo also studies the likely financial and other impacts of the proposed incorporation on neighboring local governments, including the county itself. If the petition for incorporation survives this initial review and a later public hearing and possible protests, it moves to an election. If a majority of voters living within the boundaries of the proposed new city approve, a new city is legally born.

New cities are created by incorporation quite frequently. Between 1962 and 2011, the number of cities in the state grew from 373 to 482.[9] Most recently, for example, on March 8, 2011, the residents of Jurupa Valley, an unincorporated community of about 95,000 in Riverside County, voted for cityhood effective July 1 that year. Residents in other unincorporated places, however, have rejected the opportunity to incorporate as a city and run their own show. The prospect of rapid growth and development, for example, scared many of the 57,000 residents of Castro Valley. In November 2002, they voted three to one against incorporation. They were happy to remain Northern California's largest unincorporated community and to continue being governed locally by the Alameda County Board of Supervisors.

City Government Functions and Responsibilities

City governments provide a wide range of services and facilities that directly affect the lives of their residents: fire and police protection; street construction and maintenance; sewage and waste disposal; health, social, and recreational programs; and planning and zoning to determine land use consistent with a community's needs and values. Most city governments provide water, and some run public transit systems. A few, like Los Angeles and Sacramento, own and manage municipal electricity or natural gas utilities.

Residents in most cities are content if the basic services, such as police, fire, and waste management, are provided reliably and efficiently, either directly by the municipality itself or, as in many smaller cities, by contracting services from other local governments and the private sector.[10] In some places, however, residents demand more from their city government than just the basics. In some cities, for example, business leaders and entrepreneurs often pressure city hall to promote rapid economic growth and development. In other cities, such as Berkeley and San Francisco, community activists often pressure city hall to limit growth and development and to pursue ambitious social agendas on the world stage.

City Government Revenues and Expenditures

As shown in Table 9.2, the typical city budget in California relies most heavily on current service charges and taxes for most of its revenues. Most of what it spends goes for public safety, community development and health, public utilities, and transportation. We will have more to say about city finances later in this chapter in the context of the state's continuing budget crisis.

Forms of City Government and the Legacy of Progressive Structural Reforms

The overall vision and structural reforms advanced by the Progressives nearly a century ago have had an enduring impact on the form of municipal government in California. Progressive reformers sought to replace government by corrupt bosses running partisan, ward-based, big-city political machines with government by reputable civic leaders and nonpartisan experts managing local affairs in the public interest. The structural reforms implementing that vision called for

- strong managers and weak mayors.

- nonpartisan elections.

TABLE 9.2 ★ Typical Sources and Uses of Municipal Funding (Excluding City and County of San Francisco)

REVENUES		EXPENSES	
Taxes	31.8%	Public safety	26.7%
Current service charges	37.9%	Community development and health	17.4%
Intergovernmental agencies	9.5%	Public utilities	19.8%
Revenues from use of money and property	2.7%	Transportation	18.0%
Special benefit assessments, licenses and permits, fines and forfeitures	3.5%	Culture and leisure	8.0%
		General government	9.5%
Other revenues and other financing sources	14.6%	Other	0.6%
	_____		_____
	100%		101%*

*Total expenses add up to over 100 percent due to rounding.
SOURCE: California Controller's Office, *Cities Annual Report FY 2009–2010*, www.sco.ca.gov/Files-ARD-Local/LocRep/0910cities.pdf, pp. v, xx (accessed 8/2/12).

- at-large council elections.

- nonconcurrent elections.

- the tools of direct democracy (the initiative, referendum, and recall).

Other Progressive reforms included civil service (merit-based) systems of municipal employment and, especially in the larger cities, professionally run city planning commissions and departments.[11] Reformers were particularly successful in the southwestern states, where populations were growing fast and new cities were popping up everywhere, isolated from the influence of eastern-style partisanship and urban machine politics.[12] Municipalities that have all or most of these institutional features are known as *reform governments*. Most medium-size American cities and nearly all of California's cities qualify for that label.

COUNCIL-MANAGER PLAN VERSUS MAYOR-COUNCIL SYSTEM Under the *council-manager* form of government, the voters elect a city council, which in turn appoints a professionally trained city manager to run the administration. The city manager directly controls the bureaucracy and supervises the performance of department heads. The council restricts itself to legislative policy making, while retaining the ultimate authority to fire or replace the appointed manager. Fully 96 percent of the 456 California cities surveyed in 2002 are governed by the council-manager plan,[13] including some big ones like San Diego and San Jose. Mayors are directly elected in about a third of these cities, but with few exceptions (e.g., San Jose) they perform mainly ceremonial duties and have no independent executive powers, such as the veto or budgetary control.

The rest of California's cities are governed by *mayor-council systems*. Most are very small cities that can't afford a professional city manager. In the larger cities that have mayor-council systems, like San Francisco and Los Angeles, the voters elect a mayor and a city council in separate elections. The mayor serves as the city's overall chief executive and exercises independent veto and budgetary powers. The council (or, in the case of San Francisco, the board of supervisors) is responsible for legislative policy making. Typically, as in Los Angeles and San Francisco, various appointive boards and commissions set overall policy and supervise administration of important city departments, such as police and fire, thus limiting the mayor's direct control of the bureaucracy.

In practice, formal and informal power arrangements vary markedly across both systems. In recent years, many council-manager cities have strengthened mayoral authority to become more responsive to their political environments.[14] Some mayor-council cities, on the other hand, have hired professional managers to achieve greater administrative control and efficiency. Personal ambition, political skill, and leadership style are key factors that determine just how powerful a given mayor or manager really is in running things and shaping public policy.[15]

NONPARTISAN ELECTIONS California law requires that all local elections be officially nonpartisan. In nonpartisan elections, no information about a candidate's political party membership is shown on the ballot. Unofficially, of course, many local contests are fiercely partisan, especially because the courts some years ago permitted political party organizations to endorse candidates in local races. For example, in San Francisco's 1999 mayoral runoff election between Willie Brown and Tom Ammiano, the local Republican Party reluctantly endorsed the state GOP's archenemy, Democrat and former Assembly Speaker Willie Brown.

Shocked and humiliated by this action, some outraged GOP leaders sought to expel the local chapter from the state party organization.[16]

AT-LARGE VERSUS DISTRICT COUNCIL ELECTIONS A recent survey found that nearly all California cities (93 percent) conduct at-large council elections, in which voters elect council members citywide rather than by districts or wards.[17] Under the *at-large system*, for example, if a number of candidates compete for one of the three vacant seats on the council, all of the city's voters have the opportunity to vote for any three of them, and the top three vote-getters are declared the winners. About 5 percent of cities use the *district election method*, which divides the city into districts and requires the voters in each district to elect one of the candidates running in that district to represent them on the council. The remaining cities—Oakland is an example—use some hybrid combination of at-large and district elections to elect their councils.

Some cities, most prominently San Francisco in 2000, have changed from at-large to district elections. San Francisco's switch to the district system was a response to voter demand for greater representation of neighborhoods and minority groups, reduced influence of big money on elections, and a wider field of candidates who otherwise could not afford to run citywide campaigns.[18] Of course, the district system by itself doesn't guarantee a more neighborhood-oriented council, less costly campaigns, or political life on a smaller scale. The 15 members of the Los Angeles City Council, for example, are elected by districts. But each council member represents nearly a quarter of a million residents on average and must run expensive campaigns over vast territories to get elected.

NONCONCURRENT ELECTIONS Progressive reformers sought to insulate local government from the corrupting influence of national partisan politics. One way they accomplished this goal was to require many cities to conduct nonconcurrent elections for council seats. That is, they scheduled local elections in nonpresidential election years or at odd times, deliberately out of sync with the national election calendar. A recent survey found that only about 19 percent of California cities hold council elections concurrently with the presidential general election or presidential primaries.[19] As discussed later, nonconcurrent elections have been blamed as the number one structural cause of the dismally low voter turnout rates in California cities.

DIRECT DEMOCRACY At the local level of government, just as at the state level, ordinary citizens have access to the tools of direct democracy (the initiative, referendum, and recall) bequeathed to them by Progressive Era reformers. Specifically, if citizens gather the required number of valid signatures on formal petitions, they can

- initiate direct legislation, including proposed ordinances and charter amendments, by placing such measures on the ballot for voter approval.

- suspend implementation of council legislation until the voters approve it at a referendum election.

- subject incumbent elected officials to a recall vote and possible dismissal before the next scheduled regular election.

Local referenda are quite rare. Local recall elections are even rarer, except in places like the contentious little town of Pacifica, where voters have successfully petitioned for five recall elections over the last 30 years. The use of local ballot initiatives,

BOX 9.2   The Brown Act

The Ralph M. Brown Act of 1953 required that "all meetings of the legislative body of a local agency shall be open and public, and all persons shall be permitted to attend any meeting of the legislative body of a local agency, except as otherwise provided in this chapter." The intent of the Brown Act, also known as the "open meetings law," was to support transparency and prevent secret meetings and backroom dealings of local government officials in the conduct of public business. (The Bagley-Keene Act of 1967 later extended the same open-meetings requirement to state government agencies.) The Brown Act did allow closed meetings for personnel decisions and the like to protect community and individual rights. Critics like Peter Scheer, however, argue that the original narrow exemptions were stretched too far in the 1990s to include meetings negotiating local collective-bargaining agreements, which the public may see only after they are signed—often too late to raise hard questions and objections about the financial implications. Despite its limitations, the Brown Act is consistent with the state's Progressive reform tradition. It gives citizens timely access to vital information about what local government officials say and do in their name.

SOURCES: League of California Cities, *Open & Public IV: A Guide to the Ralph M. Brown Act* (2007). Peter Scheer, "Public Employee Unions: Losing the Image Battle," *San Francisco Chronicle*, June 13, 2010, p. N5.

however, is much more frequent and widespread, although not nearly to the extent observed at the state level. Direct legislation by citizen initiative has become almost routine in some cities, such as San Francisco, especially around land-use issues. A recent study, however, found that only 43 of 387 cities surveyed (11 percent) had even one citizen initiative on their most recent ballot.[20] Also see Box 9.2 on the Brown Act, the "open meetings law," which gives citizens yet another tool of direct democracy for becoming more informed about the decision-making process and for holding their local government officials accountable.

LOCAL VOTER TURNOUT AND POLITICAL REPRESENTATION Voter participation is low and still falling at all levels of government in California. At the local level, a recent survey revealed that only 48 percent of a city's registered voters, on average, cast ballots in the most recent council elections. That same survey found that "California residents who are highly educated, wealthy, old, and white are much more likely to participate than residents who are poor, young, less educated, and nonwhite."[21] The political exclusion of the state's large and growing noncitizen immigrant population only adds to the problem of achieving democracy for all (see Box 9.3). Clearly, at least at the local level, California's active electorate is not very large and is demographically not representative of the state's population.

Certain institutional reforms could boost voter turnout and eventually produce more representative and responsive local government. One electoral reform in particular would likely have a major impact: the rescheduling of local nonconcurrent elections to coincide with high-turnout presidential elections. Doing so in a given city "could well mean a doubling of voter turnout."[22] A number of California cities have recently moved to concurrent elections, partly as a cost-saving measure.

California's large noncitizen population poses a particular challenge to local leaders who seek to increase political participation, fair representation, and government responsiveness in their communities. Using 2000 U.S. Census data (the latest available at this time), Joaquin Avila found that the state had at least 85 cities in which noncitizens made up more than 25 percent of the adult population. Noncitizens were the majority in 12 of these cities. In Los Angeles, noncitizens made up an astounding 32 percent of the adult residents. Noncitizens are constitutionally banned from voting in elections, denied formal political representation, and excluded from the policy-making process. Even in San Francisco, the self-proclaimed "sanctuary city," the voters rejected a local ballot initiative in 2003 that would have allowed noncitizen parents of public school children to vote in school board elections. Some critics argue that the exclusion of noncitizens from the political process violates the democratic principle of rule by the consent of the governed. Joaquin Avila contends that the "ultimate product of such exclusion is a political apartheid." What do you think?

SOURCES: Joaquin Avila, "Political Apartheid in California: Consequences of Excluding a Growing Noncitizen Population," Latino Policy & Issues Brief No. 9, UCLA Chicano Studies Research Center (December 2003). Ron Hayduk, *Democracy for All: Restoring Immigrant Voting Rights in the United States* (New York: Routledge, 2006).

Without such electoral reform or some kind of new political mobilization of the inactive electorate, the unrepresentative active electorate will continue to choose who governs at the local level.

Special Districts

Special districts are limited-purpose local governments. They fill the need or desire for services that general-purpose governments such as counties and cities cannot or will not provide. If residents or landowners desire new or better services, they can take steps to establish a special district to pay for them. As a popular guide to special districts notes: "Special districts *localize* the costs and benefits of public services. Special districts allow local citizens to obtain the services they want at a price they are willing to pay."[23] Examples of special districts include fire protection districts, cemetery districts, water districts, recreation and park districts, storm water drainage and conservation districts, irrigation districts, and mosquito abatement districts.

School and Community College Districts

California's school and community college districts are a unique type of special district. As of 2010–11, there were 1,037 K–12 school districts in the state, a number whittled down, mostly by consolidation, from the 1,630 districts that operated in 1962.[24] School districts derive their authority from the state Education Code and are governed by locally elected school boards. Each board sets general policies and appoints a superintendent as chief executive officer, who serves at the pleasure of the board. The superintendent has overall responsibility for managing the system and its various schools and programs. In 2012, the state's community college system of two-year public institutions had 112 colleges organized into 72 districts. Serving more than 2.6 million students, nearly 25 percent of the nation's community college student population, it is the largest system of higher education in the world. In 1988, the legislature enacted Assembly Bill 1725, giving community colleges status as institutions of higher education. AB 1725 also strengthened the advisory role of local academic senates and of the Student Senate for California Community Colleges in working with state government officials in making higher-education policy. Each community college district is governed by a locally elected board of trustees that sets general policies and appoints a chancellor as chief executive officer. As discussed elsewhere in this book, the state of the state's K–14 public education system and especially the financial crises that surround it continue to be a major focus of policy debate and political battle.

Nonschool Special Districts

Excluding the school districts, the state had 4,792 special districts in 2009–10, according to the most recent California State Controller's report on special districts.[25] These special districts can be classified in three different ways: single-purpose versus multiple-purpose special districts, enterprise versus nonenterprise special districts, and independent versus dependent special districts.

- About 85 percent of the state's special districts perform a single function, such as fire protection or mosquito abatement. The others are multifunctional, such as the state's nearly 900 County Service Areas (CSAs), which provide two or more services, such as enhanced recreation services and extended police protection.

- About one in four special districts are enterprise districts, which are run like businesses and charge user fees for services. Nearly all water, waste, and hospital districts are enterprise districts of this sort. The state's many nonenterprise districts provide public services such as fire protection and pest control that benefit the entire community, not just individual residents. Typically, property taxes rather than user fees pay the costs.

- About two-thirds of the state's special districts are independent districts. An independent district is governed by its own separate board of directors elected by the district's voters. Dependent districts are governed by existing legislative bodies. All CSAs, for example, are governed by a county board of supervisors.

These three ways of classifying special districts are not mutually exclusive, and examples of all possible combinations exist.

Legal Framework

Like all local governments in the state, special districts must conform to the state constitution and the legislature's Government Code. Statutory authority for special districts derives either from a principal act or a special act of the state legislature. A *principal act* is a general law that applies to all special districts of a given type. For example, the Fire Protection District Law of 1987 in the state Health and Safety Code governs all 386 fire districts. About 60 of these principal law statutes are on the books and can be used to create a special district anywhere in the state. Another 120 or so *special acts* have been passed by the legislature to adapt a special district's structure, financing, and authority to unique local circumstances. The Alameda County Flood Control and Water District, for example, was formed under such a special act.

How Special Districts Are Created

To form a special district, the voters in the proposed district must apply to their county's LAFCo. After the LAFCo reviews and approves the proposal, it moves to an election in which only the voters residing inside the proposed district boundaries may vote. A simple majority is required for approval in most cases. A two-thirds majority is required if new special taxes are involved. The total number of special districts has increased only slightly in recent years, from 4,750 in 2005–06 to 4,792 in 2009–10, according to the latest available reports. However, the modest net change in total numbers can conceal a considerable churning of old districts dying and new ones being born. During the 2009–10 fiscal year, for example, 50 new districts were created and 27 were dissolved.[26]

The Advantages and Disadvantages of Special Districts

The advantages claimed for special districts include

- the flexibility that such districts allow in tailoring the level and quality of service to citizen demands.

- the linking of costs to benefits, so that those who don't benefit from a district's services don't have to pay for them.

- the greater responsiveness of special districts to their constituents, who often reside in smaller geographic areas of larger city and county jurisdictions.

The disadvantages of special districts include

- the overlapping of jurisdictions and the resulting duplication of services already provided by cities and counties or by other special districts.

- the reduced incentives for needed regional planning, especially in providing water, sewer, and fire protection services, which are typically offered by a host of special districts governed by independent boards without any central coordination.

- the decreased accountability that results from the sheer multiplicity of limited special districts, which overwhelms the average citizen's ability to find out who is in charge of delivering specific services.

These critics would abolish most special districts and centralize their functions in established general-purpose city and county governments. One contends that special districts "make a mockery of the natural connections that people have with a specific place. Special districts lie beyond the commonsense experience of most citizens; their very purpose is to divorce a narrow element of policy from the consideration of those charged with the maintenance of the common interest."[27]

Regional Governments

A number of regional governments have formed in California to cope with problems such as air pollution, waste management, growth control, affordable housing production, and transportation gridlock—problems that affect large geographical areas and millions of people living in many different city and county jurisdictions. Some of these regional bodies have strong regulatory powers. Others are mainly advisory in function.

Regulatory Regional Governments

Examples of state regional governments that have strong regulatory powers include the California Coastal Commission, the South Coast Air Quality Management District, and the San Francisco Bay Conservation and Development Commission.

CALIFORNIA COASTAL COMMISSION (CCC) Appointed by the governor and the state legislature, the 12-member CCC has state-empowered regulatory authority to control all development within the 1,000-yard-wide shoreline zone along the entire California coast. Exercising its powers to grant or withhold permits for development, the CCC has succeeded over the years in opening public access to beaches, protecting scenic views, and restoring wetlands.

SOUTH COAST AIR QUALITY MANAGEMENT DISTRICT (SCAQMD) The 12-member SCAQMD board has state-granted regulatory authority to control emissions from stationary sources of air pollution (e.g., power plants, refineries, gas stations) in the state's south coast air basin. This region encompasses all of Los Angeles and Orange Counties and parts of Riverside and San Bernardino Counties, an area of 12,000 square miles and home to more than 12 million people, nearly half the state's total population. This area also has the worst smog problem in the nation. Over the years, the board, which is appointed by city governments in the basin area, has conducted many studies, monitored air pollution levels, developed regional pollution abatement plans, and vigorously enforced federal and state air pollution laws. In large part thanks to its efforts, the maximum level of ozone in the basin has been cut to less than half of what it was in the 1950s, despite the tripling of population and quadrupling of vehicles in the region over that same period.

SAN FRANCISCO BAY CONSERVATION AND DEVELOPMENT COMMISSION (BCDC) The 27-member BCDC was created by the state legislature in 1965 in response to growing public concern about the future of San Francisco Bay, which was rapidly being dredged and polluted at an alarming rate by landfill projects. The commission includes members appointed by the governor, legislature, and various state and federal agencies, as well as four city representatives appointed by the Association of Bay Area Governments and nine county supervisors—one from each of the nine bay area counties. The commission is charged with regulating all filling and dredging in the bay; protecting the Suisun Marsh, the largest wetlands in California; regulating proposed new development within the first 100 feet inland from the bay to ensure maximum public access; enforcing the federal Coastal Zone Management Act; and other regulatory functions. By exercising its permit powers, BCDC not only stopped development that eventually could have reduced the bay to a pond but also actually added hundreds of acres of new open water.

Advisory Regional Governments

In addition to regional regulatory bodies, the state also has a number of regional planning, research, and advisory institutions. The most important are various regional councils of government (COGs). COGs are assemblies of delegates representing a region's counties and cities who join voluntarily and meet regularly to discuss common problems and regional issues. The state's two most prominent COGs are the Southern California Association of Governments (SCAG), the nation's largest COG, and the Association of Bay Area Governments (ABAG).

SCAG's regional jurisdiction encompasses 15 million people living in an area of more than 38,000 square miles, while ABAG's boundaries include 6 million people living in an area of 7,000 square miles. Both SCAG and ABAG have general assemblies that represent the broad membership of counties and cities located in each region. In both COGs, the serious work is done by smaller executive committees, a 75-member regional council in the case of SCAG and a 38-member executive board in the case of ABAG. Like most COGs, both SCAG and ABAG have professional staffs that conduct extensive research and planning studies of regional problems. Both regularly host regional conferences and forums on a range of substantive issues. And both have been designated by the federal government as metropolitan planning organizations for their regions, with the mandate to draw up plans for regional transportation, air quality, growth management, hazardous waste management, and production of affordable housing.

Both SCAG and ABAG have raised public awareness of regional problems and issues. They have also encouraged more regional planning and collaborative decision making. Neither COG, however, has the effective power or authority to enforce its policy recommendations on other local governments in their regions. Many Bay Area local officials, for example, pay lip service to ABAG's recommended fair-share quotas for production of affordable housing but then routinely ignore them when making decisions.

Occasionally, a serious organized effort is made to create a truly comprehensive regional government with broad regulatory authority and strong enforcement powers. In the early 1990s, for example, an attempt was made to establish a powerful Bay Area regional government under the banner of BayVision 2020.[28] That proposal failed, like all the others, because most of the region's local governments were unwilling to surrender local autonomy and delegate some of their powers to a new, higher authority.

On a more hopeful note, Governor Schwarzenegger signed Senate Bill 375 into law in September 2008, moving the state at least a few steps in the direction of creating stronger regional governments, particularly in the areas of transportation, housing, and environmental protection. This landmark legislation requires the state's Air Resources Board to collaborate with metropolitan planning organizations and local government officials in developing "sustainable community strategies" and setting regional targets for the reduction of greenhouse gas emissions.

Progress in implementing SB 375 over the next few years will depend on economic conditions and mostly voluntary cooperation from city and county officials. But SB 375 also comes armed with an array of penalties and incentives that might actually work in time to nudge local officials into some form of regional governance that can make a difference.[29]

Indeed, by early summer 2012, the Air Resources Board had set precise regional targets for reducing greenhouse gas emissions by 2020 and 2035. Even more encouraging, the board had already approved the sustainable community strategies proposed by the Sacramento and Southern California metropolitan planning organizations (MPOs), and the state's other MPOs were lining up to get the board's green light.

California's Community Redevelopment Agencies, R.I.P.

In late December 2011, nearly 400 redevelopment agencies operated throughout the state in sponsoring cities and counties. By May 2012, only a few months later, they were all gone. What happened to them is the subject of a mini-case study starting on page 202. Here we'll offer only a short obituary explaining how they were born, what they did, and why their death was greeted with both cheers and jeers, along with some tears.

California's redevelopment agencies were born on paper in 1945 when the state legislature passed the Community Redevelopment Act, which authorized the formation of such agencies "to prepare and carry out plans for the improvement, rehabilitation, and redevelopment of blighted areas."[30] These new agencies were to be placed under the control of sponsoring local governments, mainly cities and counties, and were authorized to acquire property by the power of eminent domain, dispose of it by lease or sale without public bidding, clear the land, construct infrastructure needed for building on project sites, and make other improvements. To ensure that these powerful agencies served a public interest priority, they were required to spend at least 20 percent of their funds on affordable housing. As to their funding, redevelopment agencies did not have the power to tax, but they could issue revenue bonds. The first redevelopment agencies received most of their funding from federal grants. Later they would be allowed to earn revenues through property tax-increment financing. If a project site generated higher property tax revenues than it otherwise might have produced without redevelopment, the increment in revenues over the baseline would be returned to the agency to pay for the project site investments. In time, many of these agencies became flush with cash. Following passage of Proposition 13 in 1978, fiscally starved cities and counties began using their redevelopment agencies to raise additional property tax revenues, which were otherwise forbidden under the limits imposed by that landmark constitutional amendment.

In the typical case, redevelopment agencies would buy and assemble parcels of land, enhance the infrastructure, and then transfer the land to private parties "on favorable terms for residential and/or commercial development."[31] Over the years, the state's redevelopment agencies produced a lot of affordable housing, rescued a lot of land from blight and decay, and often became engines of local economic development. Their collective track record was blemished, however, by instances of abuse of agency power and misuse of funds for projects that served only private interests and profits. These projects destroyed more affordable housing than they created and bulldozed entire communities out of their neighborhoods. In some cases, as happened recently in Oakland, financially desperate city officials dipped into their redevelopment funds to pay basic salaries for police officers and to cover other expenses unrelated to the purpose of fighting blight and urban decay.[32] Moreover, some studies showed that redevelopment projects really didn't stimulate new economic development but merely relocated it from one poor area to another within a region with no net gain in jobs or tax revenues. Madeline Janis, a former commissioner on the Los Angeles Community Redevelopment Agency, offers the example of "a garment factory that was given CRA/LA-owned land and a $2-million subsidy in 2009 to move from South Gate to South Los Angeles, creating very few new jobs—and taking jobs away from another needy community."[33]

By 2010, redevelopment agencies had become chronically controversial, loved by some and hated by others. The precise mix of love and hate was determined by an agency's location and its history there. When the state government dipped down that year to take its own big bite out of redevelopment funds, redevelopment officials and their allies chose to fight rather than compromise. It was a political battle they couldn't win.

Two Case Studies in Local Government Revolt

The following two mini-case studies dramatically illustrate how California's local governments have coped with recent crises that have threatened to tear cities apart and undermine home rule. The first looks at what happened when the citizens of San Fernando Valley attempted to secede from the city of Los Angeles in 2002. The second examines the revolt of local officials against the state government in 2010 when Sacramento legislators tried, once again, to balance the state budget by grabbing property tax money from the cities, counties, and redevelopment agencies. The revolt turned out well for the cities and counties, but not so well, to say the least, for the redevelopment agencies.

Breaking Up Is Hard to Do: The San Fernando Valley Secession Movement

Nearly all of California's local governments have developed stress fractures of one kind or another from trying to cope with growing populations, increased demands for service, shrinking financial resources, and a state government that seems determined to make things worse rather than better. On top of all that, the state's largest city, Los Angeles, has been beset by internal conflicts that threaten to tear it apart. On November 5, 2002, that city's voters rejected a citizen referendum that would have allowed the San Fernando Valley and its 1.35 million residents to secede from Los Angeles and become a separate city. If the measure had passed, the new city would immediately have ranked as America's sixth-largest city, while what remained of Los Angeles south of the Santa Monica mountains would have fallen from second- to third-largest in terms of population.

This secessionist revolt did not come out of the blue. It was only the latest in a long string of failed secession attempts that began 30 years earlier with the predominantly white valley's opposition to Los Angeles's school integration and busing policies. Since then, however, the valley's population has grown in size and diversity. Its political and business leaders have become more organized and sophisticated. And its list of grievances against Los Angeles city hall, codified in a latter-day "Declaration of Independence," have expanded to include complaints and demands that can no longer be easily dismissed by Los Angeles power elites as narrow, selfish, or racist.

Encouraged by a 1997 state law that prevented city councils from simply vetoing secession attempts, Valley Voters Organized toward Empowerment (Valley VOTE) and other secession groups gathered over 100,000 signatures to place the referendum on the ballot. They secured LAFCo approval based on studies showing that both cities, old and new, would be economically viable following the split. They argued their case that valley residents paid more in taxes than they received in services from the distant, unresponsive politicians and bureaucrats who ruled Los Angeles city hall. And key leaders, including many developers and business owners, most of them white, appealed to Los Angeles voters to "Free the Valley!" by giving valley residents control of their own city government—presumably more friendly to small businesses, more inclined to cut taxes and improve services, and more responsive to the valley's needs and aspirations.

Los Angeles mayor James Hahn and other city officials were slow to take this latest secession attempt seriously and respond to it. Alarmed, downtown business leaders, city hall lobbyists, and public service employee union chiefs organized "LA United Together" to fight the valley secession referendum and another one by Hollywood on the same ballot. They raised over $7 million for the antisecession campaign, outspending the valley and Hollywood cityhood advocates by more than two to one. They unleashed a blitz of TV ads declaring that secession would not solve any problems and would only make things worse. In the middle of a statewide economic downturn and budget crunch, Mayor Hahn warned, valley secession would cause a citywide financial disaster of "biblical proportions." Among other complications of the proposed "divorce," valley kids would still belong to the Los Angeles Unified School District, Los Angeles city departments and agencies would have to provide a wide range of contractual services to valley residents until the new city established its own bureaucracy, and the new city would also be required to pay Los Angeles an "alimony" totaling $2 billion over 20 years under LAFCo-arranged compensation for lost revenue. Leading up to the referendum vote, these arguments gave pause to many valley residents, especially Latinos who depended on jobs and services dispensed by Los Angeles city hall.

Under the 1997 state law, formal secession required majority approval both from the entire Los Angeles city voter population and from the breakaway subpopulation of Valley voters themselves. The referendum passed narrowly in San Fernando Valley, achieving at least a moral victory. The measure failed by a wide margin in the citywide vote, however, thus squelching this latest secession attempt. Nonetheless, the stresses and strains that had given rise to the movement in 2002 were still active in 2012 and could erupt once again in the years ahead.[34]

The Great Redevelopment Agency Massacre of 2011

The second case study illustrates just how complicated and combative the process of governing California can be when budgets are involved and when local governments fight the state government over money. This case features just about every major governing institution and political actor covered in the textbook, including the governor, the state legislature, the court system, many local governments of different types, and the workings of direct democracy, public opinion, interest groups, elections, and the state constitution itself. All were brought together in a collision in 2011 caused by only the latest in a seemingly never-ending cascade of budget crises. The study also shows how a local government revolt against the state can succeed—and then go awry. At the end of the story, the budget crisis will have been only partly solved, nearly 400 local government agencies will have been erased, and the future of state and local government relations will have been plunged even deeper into turbulence and uncertainty. It is a revealing case, sad in its way, and full of irony.

BRIEF HISTORICAL BACKGROUND In February 2004, the state's budget deficit had grown massive and out of control. Herb Wesson Jr., speaker of the state Assembly at the time, wrote that the staggering $35 billion deficit was "a hole so deep and so vast that even if we fired every single person on the state payroll, we would still be billions short."[35] The story of how that hole was dug starts in 1978, when the state's voters passed Proposition 13. Most of the state's fiscal misery, short term and long term, branches out from there (see Chapter 8). Surveying the damage that Proposition 13 had caused over the last 25 years, Peter Schrag recited the familiar list: reduced public services at all levels of government, the declining quality of public education, the neglected and rotting infrastructure, and so on. But as bad as that was, Schrag wrote, the biggest impact "was the seismic shift in California's governmental structure, accountability and power: from local to state government; from representative democracy to direct democracy through the initiative process; from a communitarian ethic in how we paid for public services to a fee ethic."[36]

The next major chapter in this story was written in 1988, when the state's voters passed Proposition 98, which required the state's annual budget to allocate approximately 40 percent of the general fund to the schools. When the state later faced serious revenue shortfalls, the legislators found a way to balance the state budget while also complying with Proposition 98. They deposited a major portion of the collected local property tax revenues into educational revenue augmentation funds (ERAFs) and directed that those funds be spent on schools to meet the obligations imposed by Proposition 98. But what about the financial needs of other local governments, whose property tax revenues (thanks to Proposition 13) were now placed under state government control and being handed out to the schools? In what can only be described as a shell game, the state tried to solve that problem by giving some money back to local governments from other funds. That solution might have worked, except that most of those other funds had strings attached, including paying for state-mandated programs that had little or nothing to do with local priorities. To make matters worse, the state and federal politicians continued to crank out new mandated programs for local governments to administer without providing any additional funding—so-called unfunded mandates.

According to one study, California's cities and counties had become "net donors to the state general fund" and were "at the mercy of the state as long as the Legislature is in session." Put bluntly, from the local government point of view, the state budget process had been lowered to the level of a "fiscal street mugging."[37] To some critics these trends spelled doom for effective home rule.[38] To adapt and survive, many local governments were forced to slash public services, lay off employees, defer infrastructure maintenance, and charge new user fees wherever they could. Many also pursued the "fiscalization of land use."[39] That is, they changed

BOX 9.4

Like all cities with storm drains that flow to rivers and oceans, the small City of Bellflower (population 73,000) must comply with the federal Clean Water Act. That law prohibits municipal storm water discharges without a National Pollutant Discharge Elimination System (NPDES) permit. In California, the NPDES permit program is administered by the State Water Resources Control Board and nine regional water quality control boards. To obtain the needed permit, a city must at minimum develop and implement storm water pollution prevention plans that include management and monitoring programs, controls on industrial runoff, and public education. In recent years, the state regional boards have imposed even more stringent and costly requirements on municipal storm drain operators. The Los Angeles regional board, for example, required Bellflower and other cities seeking NPDES permits to eliminate all litter from their storm drains. "If a single Styrofoam cup should reach the ocean," wrote Charles Summerell, "these agencies would be in violation of federal law." While imposing this new mandate with the best of intentions, the federal and state governments refused to fund it. Local governments had to pay for it out of their own hides. For many cities, reported Summerell, the effects of this unfunded mandate have been "financially devastating." In October 2002, for example, the City of Bellflower was forced to cut $358,000 from its limited budget to comply with the new regulations. To prevent that plastic foam cup from reaching the ocean, Bellflower residents paid the price in terms of one fewer gang specialist deputy probation officer ($24,013); one fewer recreation staff position ($54,500); reduced law enforcement overtime ($15,000); reduced sidewalk, curb, and gutter improvements ($40,791); postponed purchase of an emergency generator ($55,000); and slashed funding for other important local services.

SOURCE: Charles Summerell, *The Fiscal Condition of California Cities: 2003 Report* (Sacramento: The Institute for Local Self Government, 2003), p. 34.

their economic development and land use policies to discourage new residential housing (whose property taxes now go to the state, not to the local governments) in favor of attracting new businesses, such as shopping malls and automobile dealerships, that would capture sales tax revenues for starved local treasuries.

By early 2004, local government officials had grown tired of the governor and state legislators using local government property tax revenues to balance out-of-control state budgets. Leaders of the League of California Cities, the California State Association of Counties, and other local government organizations formed a political coalition that forced Governor Arnold Schwarzenegger and the state legislature to place a proposed constitutional amendment, Proposition 1A, on the November 2004 ballot. In return for local government acceptance of two more years of reduced funding to help balance the state budget, Proposition 1A would prohibit the state from reducing local sales tax rates or altering the method of allocation, from shifting property taxes from local governments to schools or community colleges, from decreasing local-earmarked vehicle license fee revenues without providing replacement funding, and from enforcing unfunded state government mandates. Redevelopment agencies, it is important to note, were not explicitly covered by these protections. Proposition 1A would further require a declared fiscal emergency, a two-thirds vote of both houses of the legislature, and the governor's approval to shift local government property tax revenues to the schools. In such an emergency, those diverted revenues would have to be repaid, with interest, within three years.[40] In the November election, Proposition 1A passed overwhelmingly with 84 percent of the vote. Many of California's local government officials celebrated Proposition 1A as the new Magna Carta of state–local fiscal relations. It was a landmark constitutional amendment that would "restore predictability and stability to local government budgets."[41]

YET MORE BUDGET CRISES, PROPOSITION 22, AND THE DEATH OF REDEVELOPMENT AGENCIES We now fast forward to December 2008. Governor Schwarzenegger, confronted with yet another budget crisis, declared a fiscal emergency. The state legislature quickly invoked Proposition 1A to borrow $2 billion in property taxes from local governments to help close a $20 billion gap in the state's 2009–10 budget. Under the terms of Proposition 1A, that money presumably would be repaid with interest (set at 2 percent) within three years. The governor and legislature also tapped another $2 billion from the state's many local redevelopment agencies, which were not covered under Proposition 1A and thus not entitled to any reimbursement, much less with interest.

Advocates of redevelopment agencies fought these mandated givebacks, mainly through the courts. They called such givebacks a form of theft and pointed out that these agencies were funnels for a lot of federal economic stimulus money. The capacity to leverage tens of billions of dollars in new jobs and investments, they argued, would be lost if redevelopment projects were defunded.[42] The most furious reaction to the state legislature's perceived money grab, however, came once again from the cities and counties. Leaders of county and city governments, redevelopment agencies, labor and business groups, and urban professional associations formed the Californians to Protect Local Taxpayers and Vital Services Coalition to mobilize for political war with state government officials. Coalition leaders expressed their total lack of trust in the good intentions of state government officials: "The borrowing [under Proposition 1A] was meant to provide an outlet in short-term budget emergencies," the Coalition's website declared, "but it's instead being used to paper over structural budget problems. For example, the State has no clear way to pay back the $2 billion plus interest in local property taxes that the state is borrowing as part of this year's 2009–2010 State budget, yet lawmakers borrowed these funds anyway."[43] The League of California Cities derided the state's all-too-familiar budget fix as an illegal and reckless Ponzi scheme.[44] The coalition gathered 1.1 million qualifying signatures to place a new initiative constitutional amendment, Proposition 22, on the November 2010 election ballot. The official voter guide summarized the proposition's intent: "Prohibits the State, even during a period of severe fiscal hardship, from delaying the distribution of tax revenues for transportation, redevelopment, or local government projects and services."[45] If approved by the voters, the proposed constitutional amendment would close the loopholes in Proposition 1A that had allowed the state to continue borrowing money from local treasuries with no intention of paying it back. Proposition 22 would block such borrowing even under conditions of "severe fiscal hardship." Further, unlike Proposition 1A, Proposition 22 explicitly protected the state's redevelopment agencies. Their funds would also be placed in the lockbox of property tax revenues to be reserved for local government use only, safe from the sticky fingers of desperate state legislators.

Representatives of the state's teachers, nurses, and firefighters wrote the argument against Proposition 22 in the official voter guide. They warned that the proposed amendment would significantly reduce funding for public schools, affordable health care, and public safety. The prohibition on state borrowing of local funds particularly worried them because in a "real fiscal crisis" such inflexibility would leave "schools, children's health care, seniors, the blind and disabled with even less hope." Their most vehement objection to Proposition 22, however, was that it "locks protections for redevelopment agencies into the State Constitution forever. These agencies have the power to take your property away with eminent domain. They skim off billions in local property taxes, with much of that money ending up in the hands of local developers." "Your tax dollars," they concluded, "should go first to schools, public safety, and health care. They should go LAST to the developers and the redevelopment agencies that support this proposal."[46]

On November 2, 2010, Proposition 22 passed easily with 61 percent of the vote. Feckless state legislators could never again balance their state budgets on the backs of the cities, counties, and redevelopment agencies. Or so it might have seemed to the victors. Perhaps forgotten, however, was a very important point made at the beginning of this chapter. Dillon's Rule established that local governments are creatures of the state. And the state's power to create local political entities is also the power to destroy them.

When Jerry Brown became governor (for the second time) in January 2011, he faced yet another huge budget deficit of $25 billion. As part of his response, he announced a plan to terminate the state's nearly 400 redevelopment agencies and redirect their property tax revenues to pay for schools, health services, and other programs placed in jeopardy by the budget crisis. Those property tax revenues totaled $5.7 billion (about 12 percent of all property tax revenues collected by the state). Governor Brown's goal the first year, however, was to transfer only $1.7 billion to the state, leaving the remaining funds to the agencies to complete redevelopment projects underway and to close up shop.

To execute Governor Brown's plan, two bills were introduced in the state Assembly. The first, AB 26, would dissolve all the redevelopment agencies. The second, AB 27, was a compromise measure pushed mainly by legislators who worried that killing the redevelopment agencies would eliminate a major source of funding for new affordable housing. This bill would allow cities and counties to reconstitute their redevelopment agencies on a smaller scale but only on the condition that they make substantial payments twice a year to a state fund set up to benefit schools and other programs. Redevelopment officials might have worked with legislators at this stage to make a better deal, but they were in no mood to compromise. As AB 26 and AB 27 made their way through the legislative process, local redevelopment officials across the state, seeing the writing on the wall, rushed to lock in funds before the curtain came down and their money taken. In San Diego, for example, these preemptive lock-in moves were made not only to guarantee funding for current projects but also for those set to start in the distant future, as far away as 2048.[47]

After AB 26 and AB 27 became law in June 2011, the California Redevelopment Association, League of California Cities, and other petitioners promptly sued the state and took their case to the California Supreme Court. Based in large part on their claim that these two laws violated the provisions of Proposition 22, they challenged the constitutionality of both laws and requested a stay of action. The state supreme court justices granted the stay, heard oral arguments in November, and announced their ruling on December 29, 2011.[48] First, the court ruled that AB 26 was constitutional. As creatures of the state, redevelopment agencies could be dissolved by the state. Nothing in Proposition 22 or the rest of the state constitution explicitly protected these agencies from such dissolution. The state's redevelopment agencies as they stood then were toast. Second, the court ruled that AB 27 was unconstitutional because it required newly reconstituted redevelopment agencies to make payments to the state as a condition for survival. Such mandatory "pay to play" payments violated Proposition 22, which prohibited the state from making such "raids" on redevelopment funds. The court's decision was the worst possible outcome for redevelopment agency supporters. The state could kill redevelopment agencies with AB 26, but it could not resurrect them with AB 27 because of Proposition 22. Redevelopment agency officials, the most aggressive advocates of Proposition 22, were thus hoisted by their own petard.[49]

By May 2012, redevelopment agencies no longer existed in California. The 1,500 or so employees who had worked for them were laid off or reassigned to other positions. Some agency funds were distributed to cities and counties to complete existing projects, and the rest were transferred to the state. City and county officials immediately began pleading with state legislators to pass a new and improved version of the old redevelopment program that might survive legal scrutiny. As summer approached, however, there was no response, at least no response that might win Governor Brown's approval. Meanwhile, some cities and counties began launching new redevelopment projects under their own more limited authority and using their own resources.[50] And the budget crisis? As of late May 2012, the governor and the state legislators still had to find another $16 billion to close the gap. The money squeezed from the now-extinct redevelopment agencies turns out to have been only a drop in the bucket.

Local Government: Where Are We Now?

California's local governments, especially the cities, face three major problems, all related. First is the continuing economic distress caused by the collapse of the housing market bubble and the meltdown of national financial institutions. Second is the long-term destructive impact of unsustainable local government pension and benefit programs. And third, by far the most important problem but also the least solvable, is the lack of support from the state and federal governments as cities and other local governments try to fend for themselves while bearing the brunt of economic hard times and national political upheaval. Despite these formidable challenges, however, some local government leaders are seizing the opportunity found in crisis to adapt and innovate and inspire new movements of political and social reform.

The Great Recession and Its Impact on Local Governments

The Great Recession, which officially began in December 2007, hit California especially hard. This fact should not be surprising because California was a "pivotal site" and one of the "wellsprings" of the Great Recession itself.[51] Across the state, 95 percent of voters reported in January 2010 that California's economy was in "bad times" (up from 52 percent in 2007), 79 percent that unemployment was a "very serious" problem (up from 39 percent in 2007), and 59 percent that their personal financial well-being was "worse off" than the year before (up from

33 percent in 2007).[52] The Associated Press reported that between October 2007 and April 2010 the state's unemployment rate increased from 5.4 to 12.3 percent, residential and commercial property foreclosure rates from 1.5 to 3.2 percent, and bankruptcy fillings from 0.5 to 1.7 percent.[53] All the state's 58 counties suffered economic hardship during this period, but some much more than others. The Associated Press Economic Stress Index, which combines statistics on unemployment, foreclosures, and bankruptcies, rose from 7.2 points to 16.6 points for the state as a whole between October 2007 and April 2010. This index of hard times increased by "only" about 6 points in the relatively well-off counties of Santa Barbara and San Francisco. The index jumped more than 14 points (from 12.0 to 24.2) in Merced County, however, and even higher in less populated counties like San Benito (15 points) and Colusa (16 points). And in Imperial County, a shift from 21.8 to 32.0 points on the index reflected very bad times there becoming even worse.

At the national level, the widespread fear and anger triggered by deepening recession helped fuel the political mobilization that gave Barack Obama his stunning victory in the November 2008 presidential election. At the level of California's 27 most populous counties, the link between the severity of economic stress and the demand for political reform was particularly clear. As Figure 9.4 shows, the counties hit hardest by the recession tended to be those whose voters shifted most toward supporting the Democratic Party's candidate in the 2008 election. This spike in voter support for Democrats proved to be quite durable. The Democratic candidate gained an average of 7 percentage points in these counties from 2004 to 2008. And despite a recovering state economy and lower unemployment, voter support for President Obama fell back by only an average of 2 points from 2008 to 2012, when he was reelected. Politically, therefore, these county electorates had become 5 points more "blue," on net, since just before the Great Recession.

At the level of cities, the recession caused many business failures, massive job losses, widespread home foreclosures, a rising demand for local government services, and a plunge in the tax revenues needed to pay for them. The recession's negative impacts were so severe in some cities that local governments were pushed to the brink of bankruptcy. The city of Vallejo, for example, buckled under the burden of unrestrained spending, reduced tax revenues, and out-of-control pension and benefit costs. In 2008, this city of 117,000 finally surrendered to the inevitable and declared bankruptcy. Three years later, after a federal judge released the city from bankruptcy, Vallejo's fiscal condition had improved but was still bleak. City leaders grappled with austerity budgets, reduced staff, unhappy citizens, and lingering anger from the public employee labor union leaders who had sued to stop the bankruptcy in the first place. The bankruptcy had cost Vallejo $8 million in legal fees alone, money that could have been spent on urgently needed services. City leaders now had to search for new revenue sources while coping with the stigma of management failure that has repelled investors and would-be new residents alike.[54]

Stockton, a city of 290,000, suffered an even worse fate than Vallejo's. By late May 2012, the city was in dire financial straits because of its depressed local economy, 20 percent unemployment rate, projected large budget deficits with no reserves, and unsustainable pension and benefit liabilities. Most daunting were the mounting debt-service costs to be paid on gross overinvestment in poorly conceived and wildly optimistic redevelopment projects like a new baseball park, marina, sports arena, and city hall.[55] On top of those financial miseries, the state government's recent dismantling of Stockton's redevelopment agency had reduced the city's property tax revenues from that source by 60 percent. Finding no other

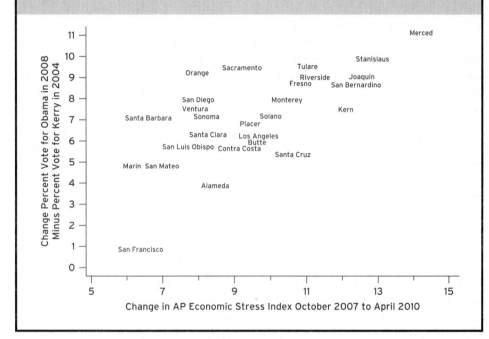

FIGURE 9.4 ★ Economic Stress Triggers Voter Support for Political Change in California Counties

This scatter plot shows the shift in voter support for the Democratic Party's presidential candidate from 2004 to 2008 (*left scale*) versus the shift in the AP Economic Stress Index from October 2007 to April 2010 (*bottom scale*). (Technical note: The data point labels are slightly jittered for readability. The correlation is *R* = .66, and the linear regression model fit is *y* = 0.80 + 0.66*x*, indicating that a 1 percent increase in the AP Economic Stress Index was associated with a 0.66 percent increase in voter support for the Democratic Party's candidate.)

way to escape financial disaster, city officials prepared to declare bankruptcy. They negotiated with the city's creditors in a process mandated by a new state law (AB 506) that forces municipalities to take more time and explore more alternatives before seeking bankruptcy protection. After those negotiations failed to produce a better solution, the city council voted on June 26, 2012, to declare bankruptcy. That decision, according to *The Economist*, made Stockton "the biggest municipal insolvency in American history."[56] Only a month later, San Bernardino, a city of 210,000 coping with its own financial emergency, also filed for bankruptcy protection.[57] By late fall 2012, no additional cities had filed for bankruptcy. A widely quoted analysis by Moody's Investor Service, however, showed that Modesto, Riverside, and other cities in the severely stressed Inland Empire were following exactly the same path Stockton took into bankruptcy. Moody's outlook for the future of this region was grim: "In the current environment, as more municipalities approach the economic or political limit to raising taxes or adjusting spending, we expect an increase in defaults and bankruptcies over the next few years." It is possible that further economic recovery combined with the recent passage of Proposition 30 in the 2012 election will sufficiently improve the "current environment" to allow cities like Modesto and Riverside to escape Stockton's fate. But much will depend on how quickly and how well city leaders can bring their employee compensation packages and pension obligations under stricter control.[58]

"Where Politicians Fear to Tread": GASB and Pension Reform

Financial horror stories like those of Vallejo and Stockton worry local government leaders around the state, particularly in areas where economic recovery from the prolonged recession has been slow.[59] Even in the more economically robust cities like Los Angeles and San Francisco, however, the projected long-term costs of local government pension and health benefit programs could lead to financial ruin and bring them down unless painful but necessary reforms are made.

Until fairly recently, most local politicians were blissfully unaware of (or in denial about) the long-term implications of their pension plans and health benefits for current and retired employees. In 2006, however, the national Governmental Accounting Standards Board (GASB) issued new accounting and reporting rules that required all U.S. local governments (starting first with the big cities) to estimate and report the full long-term costs of health benefits and other nonpension-related contracts over 30 years. Local officials, once they were informed about those projected costs, were expected to begin immediately storing away funds each year to pay for them. The old "pay–go" system—that is, thinking and budgeting only one year ahead—was out the window.[60] In his article, "Where Politicians Fear to Tread," John Diaz of the *San Francisco Chronicle* called attention to the new GASB rules and wrote: "If you want to see a California politician run for cover, ask him or her about the acronym 'GASB.'"[61] Most elected politicians operate with very short time horizons. What they were forced to see when GASB took their blinders off was shocking.

Former mayor Richard Riordan, for example, warned in 2010 that his city of Los Angeles would face the prospect of bankruptcy in four years if the city didn't stand tough against the public employee unions and convert their pension funds from defined benefits to 401(k)s.[62] Local politicians on the left, who typically rely heavily on public employee labor unions for votes, may have a tougher time confronting and coping with such harsh fiscal realities. In liberal San Francisco, for example, a civil grand jury report in 2010 warned about the coming "Pension Tsunami." The study projected that the city's pension and health care costs would increase from $413 million in 2010 to nearly $1 billion in five years, devouring fully a third of the city's current general fund.[63] Simply telling the truth about such matters can be politically risky, especially in what one reporter accurately described as a "political culture that routinely rewards public employee unions with little thought about the future."[64] After the city's progressive public defender, Jeff Adachi, appealed to fellow progressives to support pension reform, he was branded as a traitor by the city's public employee labor union leaders and shunned by the *San Francisco Bay Guardian* and other media voices on the left.[65] The city's voters, however, demanded action. In the November 2011 election they overwhelmingly supported a modest pension reform package placed on the ballot by interim mayor Edwin Lee. At the same time, the voters also chose Lee, a political moderate, to become the city's new permanent mayor. During his campaign, Lee had announced that negotiations with the public employee unions on pension reform "must save at least $300 million to $400 million per year to save the city from near-certain bankruptcy."[66] Hard times, both economically and politically, lay ahead for San Francisco. And if wealthy San Francisco is in trouble, so are, to an even greater extent, many other California local governments confronting the same kinds of problems with weaker economies, fewer resources, and little or no political support.

On the Brighter Side

Despite hard times, California's local government officials and community activists have taken positive steps to solve their own problems, while also trying to clean up the various messes made by the state and federal governments. For example, by mid-June 2010, the mayors of 136 California cities had signed the U.S. Conference of Mayors Climate Protection Agreement. This initiative was launched by Seattle Mayor Greg Nickels on February 16, 2005, the day that the Kyoto Protocol became law for the 141 countries that had, by that date, ratified it. President George W. Bush had rejected the protocol and dismissed the science of global warming that had prompted it. But these California mayors, along with 906 others from across the country, pledged to meet or beat the Kyoto Protocol targets in their own cities and to urge their state governments and the federal government to do the same.[67]

San Francisco, in particular, has arguably become the nation's vanguard city of progressive reform and social change. In 2002, for example, San Francisco became the first major U.S. city to adopt ranked choice voting for local elections. In 2003, the voters required all city employers to pay their employees a high minimum wage, and in 2006 also to provide them with paid sick leave. In 2004, then-mayor Gavin Newsom boldly authorized same-sex marriages in San Francisco, an action that met with strong opposition at the time and that continues to have legal and political repercussions at the state and national levels. In 2007, Supervisor Tom Ammiano and Newsom initiated a pioneering universal health care program serving the city's estimated 73,000 uninsured residents. "Cities shouldn't have to do this," Newsom said, "but I'm very proud that our city is doing it."[68]

But Local Governments Cannot Do It Alone:
The State, the Feds, and the Occupy Movement

Gavin Newsom's comment that "cities shouldn't have to do this" prompts one last point on the topic of where we are now in California local government. The point is simply that California's local governments can't function very well or for very much longer without major support from the state and federal governments. Yet the state government remains in perpetual crisis mode, coping with one massive budget deficit after another and repeatedly calling on local governments to bail it out of financial disaster rather than the other way around. And the federal government has neglected urban problems for decades, slashed most of its urban assistance programs, and provided little in the way of direct stimulus funding to state and local governments to help them help their local economies pull out of recession. The continuing political paralysis, polarization, and gridlock at both the state and federal levels of government is eroding the foundations of American federalism by allowing, through neglect, one city after another, like Vallejo and Stockton, to sink beneath the waves.

The Occupy Movement and all of its diverse branches in American cities may prove to be the political catalyst needed to restore a sense of democratic renewal,

Occupy San Francisco encampment near Justin Herman Plaza, November 2011. (Photo by Richard DeLeon.)

national community, and shared responsibility for collectively mobilizing to do something about the root causes of income inequality and social injustice in this country. In California, however, the relative success of the various urban-based Occupy movements has varied greatly with the local political culture, economic circumstances, and leadership skills found in each city.

In San Francisco, for example, most of the city's elected officials supported the first Occupy San Francisco demonstrations and encampments near the federal reserve building and Justin Herman Plaza. Interim Mayor Edwin Lee and his police chief waited a long time and negotiated patiently with the occupiers before dismantling the encampments in December 2011 with relatively few arrests. The Occupy San Francisco movement since then has diversified and specialized in targeting specific neighborhoods (e.g., Occupy Bernal), financial institutions (e.g., Occupy Wells Fargo), and types of actions, such as preventing bank foreclosures on homes. There have been sporadic flare-ups of violence in some city neighborhoods, particularly the Mission, but the self-described anarchists who instigated them have been condemned by the local Occupy leaders.

In Oakland, on the other hand, just across the bay, the Occupy Oakland movement took root in a more economically distressed city and with many more working-class and unemployed participants than in San Francisco. Occupy Oakland also operated on a much larger scale, with more outbreaks of violence and greater economic disruption, including a general strike involving thousands of protesters who closed down the city's port for a day, and with a more repressive response from city officials, especially the police. Reflecting the distrust many protesters felt toward the city's police, they renamed Frank H. Ogawa Plaza, the site of their main encampment in front of city hall, the Oscar Grant Plaza after a young man killed on the BART system by a police officer in 2009. The dismantling of that encampment and others was accompanied by violent resistance and many arrests. Mayor Jean Quan, a progressive elected in 2011, has had difficulty controlling events and mediating between angry protesters, angry business owners, the police, and others. In late May 2012, a signature-gathering campaign to recall Mayor Quan was under way, even as Occupy Oakland leaders continued to refuse to make a pledge of nonviolence or to screen their participants for weapons.[69]

As this brief comparison of two Occupy protests in California cities suggests, the Occupy Movement itself is too volatile and uncoordinated and leaderless to have much of a direct impact in transforming America's political system and governing institutions. Indeed, by late 2012, nearly all of the Occupy encampments in California cities had disappeared. Many of the original protestors had moved on to agitate for social change in more conventional ways, including active engagement in the November election campaigns. The visible face of the movement had largely faded from view. In retrospect, the Occupy Movement may come to be seen mainly as a short-lived but vital catalyst of urban-based democratic renewal and progressive reform. It forced the issues of income inequality and social justice into the spotlight of the 2012 presidential election, and it moved government leaders at all levels, including the local, to pay more attention to the forgotten 99 percent.

FOR FURTHER READING

Baldassare, Mark. *A California State of Mind: The Conflicted Voter in a Changing World.* Berkeley: University of California Press, 2002.

Bridges, Amy. *Morning Glories: Municipal Reform in the Southwest.* Princeton, NJ: Princeton University Press, 1997.

DeLeon, Richard Edward. *Left Coast City: Progressive Politics in San Francisco, 1975–1991.* Lawrence: University Press of Kansas, 1992.

Hajnal, Zoltan L., Paul G. Lewis, and Hugh Louch. *Municipal Elections in California: Turnout, Timing, and Competition.* San Francisco: Public Policy Institute of California, 2002.

Rodriguez, Daniel B. "State Supremacy, Local Sovereignty: Reconstructing State/Local Relations under the California Constitution." In *Constitutional Reform in California: Making State Government More Effective and Responsive.* Ed. Bruce E. Cain and Roger G. Noll. Berkeley: Institute of Governmental Studies Press, University of California, 1995, pp. 401–29.

Sonenshein, Raphael J. *Politics in Black and White: Race and Power in Los Angeles.* Princeton, NJ: Princeton University Press, 1993.

ON THE WEB

California Department of Finance/Research: www.dof.ca.gov/Research/Research.php (accessed 7/6/12). The Department of Finance produces detailed and up-to-date statistical reports and studies on local government finances, the state budget process and its impacts on localities, and a wide range of demographic and economic information on cities and counties.

California Employment Development Department: www.edd.ca.gov (accessed 7/7/12). Valuable source of up-to-date statewide and county-level information on employment and labor market conditions.

California Secretary of State: www.sos.ca.gov/elections (accessed 7/7/12). Excellent source of information on county-level election results for statewide candidate races and ballot propositions.

California Special Districts Association: www.csda.net (accessed 7/7/12).

California State Association of Counties: www.csac.counties.org (accessed 7/7/12). Useful source of wide-ranging news and information on California's counties, with a main focus on policy and administration.

Institute for Local Government: www.ca-ilg.org (accessed 8/4/12). The research arm and affiliate of the League of California Cities and the California State Association of Counties. Very good source of in-depth studies of key policy issues facing the state's local governments.

League of California Cities: www.cacities.org/index.jsp (accessed 7/7/12). An excellent source of news, information, and data on all aspects of governing California's cities.

U.S. Conference of Mayors: www.usmayors.org (accessed 7/7/12).

SUMMARY

I. Overview of California local governments.
 A. California has more than 5,000 local governments of various types, including general-purpose governments like counties and cities, specific-purpose governments like school districts and special districts, and regional governments.
 B. Local governments provide essential services, ranging from law enforcement and fire protection to waste management and street maintenance to air- and water-quality control.

II. Legal framework for local government: the state has ultimate authority over local governments.
 A. Under Dillon's Rule, local governments are "creatures of the state" and have no inherent rights or powers except those given to them by the state constitution or legislature.
 B. California, like most states, gives counties and cities significant powers to govern themselves, make policies, enforce laws, raise revenues, borrow, and generally control local affairs as long as their decisions don't conflict with state or federal laws.
 C. The more populous cities and counties have adopted home-rule charters, which allow maximum local autonomy in self-governance.
 D. The other cities and counties operate as general-law counties and cities, which have to abide more strictly to the state legislature's local government code.

III. County governments.
 A. California's 58 counties are extremely diverse in terms of territorial extent, population size, demographic characteristics, and political culture.
 B. Except for the unique case of San Francisco's consolidated county/city government, all counties are governed by five-member boards of supervisors that exercise both legislative and executive powers.
 C. Counties perform important functions, many of them required by state government laws and mandates.
 D. Counties also provide essential services, especially in unincorporated areas outside the cities and other jurisdictions, and they are major arenas for making large-scale land-use and development policies.
 E. Each county also has a local agency formation commission (LAFCo), which plays a critical role in creating, merging, or dissolving new local governments, like cities and special districts, and resolving disputes among competing jurisdictions.

IV. City governments.
 A. The state has 481 cities, most of them general-law cities, the rest charter cities that have significant home-rule powers and local autonomy.

 B. Cities are legally created through a process of municipal incorporation that requires LAFCo review and approval, and a final majority vote of the community seeking formal city status.
 C. Nearly all cities have a form of government modeled on the vision of Progressive Era reformers. Called reform cities, most have strong city managers, weak mayors, nonpartisan elections, at-large council elections, nonconcurrent elections, and direct democracy (the initiative, referendum, and recall). Important exceptions to such reform cities are cities like Los Angeles and San Francisco, which have strong mayors and, in the case of San Francisco, district elections.

V. Citizen participation in local government.
 A. The Brown Act of 1953, known as the "open meetings law," requires that all meetings of local legislative bodies be open and public unless specifically exempted, and that all citizens be permitted to attend such meetings.
 B. Voter turnout in city elections has been steadily declining in recent years.
  1. Those who do vote in city elections tend to be whiter, older, richer, and more educated than those who don't.
  2. In particular, the state's growing population of noncitizens have little political voice or formal representation in local government.
  3. Certain electoral reforms, such as a shift from nonconcurrent to concurrent elections, could markedly increase voter turnout levels.

VI. Special districts.
 A. Special districts are limited-purpose local governments.
 B. Excluding the state's 1,042 K–12 school districts and 72 community-college districts, California has nearly 5,000 special districts.
 C. Special districts provide a range of services—for example, irrigation, pest abatement, parks and recreation, water, fire protection—which are not provided at all (or in sufficient amounts) by general-purpose governments like counties and cities.
 D. Special districts are created by a LAFCo-approved citizen petition and a majority vote.
 E. Most special districts are independent agencies that provide one type of service received and paid for by residents in smaller territories of larger jurisdictions, like counties.
 F. Some special districts are enterprise districts that charge individual user fees for service.
 G. Most special districts are funded by taxes or special assessments from service recipients.
 H. The advantages of special districts include greater flexibility and responsiveness in tailoring service and the levels of cost and benefit to citizen demands.

I. The disadvantages of special districts include duplication of services, lack of coordination, and unclear structures of authority and accountability.

VII. Regional governments.
A. The state's regional governments address problems like air pollution and population growth that affect large areas and multiple local government jurisdictions.
B. Some regional governments, like the San Francisco Bay Conservation and Development Commission and the California Coastal Commission, have strong regulatory authority and enforcement powers.
C. Other regional governments, like the Southern California Association of Governments, the Association of Bay Area Governments, and other councils of government (COGs), mainly perform research, planning, and advisory functions and have little or no power or authority to impose their decisions on local jurisdictions.

VIII. Community redevelopment agencies.
A. Nearly 400 redevelopment agencies were active throughout the state in 2011.
B. They no longer exist. How and why they disappeared are discussed in the text.

IX. Five major problems facing local governments.
A. The challenge posed by internal conflicts and secessionist movements exists in some local jurisdictions, as illustrated by the last San Fernando Valley secession attempt in Los Angeles.
B. A second problem is figuring out how to cope with the continuing impact of the Great Recession on local economies, housing markets, employment, and local government revenues and services.
C. Lawmakers routinely try to fix the state government's chronic budget crisis by raiding local government treasuries, thus depriving cities and counties of needed resources and undermining effective home rule.
D. If the long-term costs of local government pension and health benefit plans are not controlled soon, the result could be financial ruin and even bankruptcy.
E. Local governments cannot function effectively without state and federal government support, which is unlikely to come in today's political climate. The Occupy Movement might change things—or not.

PRACTICE QUIZ

1. Cities and counties that have home-rule charters have the authority to make their own laws even if they violate state and federal laws.
   a) true
   b) false
2. The U.S. Constitution gives local governments inherent rights and powers which cannot be taken away by state governments.
   a) true
   b) false
3. County boards of supervisors have both legislative and executive authority.
   a) true
   b) false
4. Most cities are governed by manager-council systems.
   a) true
   b) false
5. At the local government level, citizens cannot petition for a referendum or recall election.
   a) true
   b) false
6. Which of the following is *not* a characteristic of reform government at the local level?
   a) at-large council elections
   b) nonpartisanship
   c) city manager plan
   d) concurrent elections
7. Which of the following counties operates under a single charter as a consolidated city and county?
   a) Los Angeles
   b) Sacramento
   c) San Francisco
   d) Orange
8. Which of the following is *not* a tool of direct democracy?
   a) referendum
   b) incorporation
   c) initiative
   d) recall
9. Which of the following elected officials will be found only in county governments?
   a) sheriff
   b) mayor
   c) council member
   d) manager
10. The fiscalization of land use is one way some local governments have found to
    a) encourage the construction of new affordable housing.
    b) prevent the building of new shopping malls.
    c) promote new businesses that will return a local share of state-collected sales taxes.
    d) raise property taxes to pay for new schools and sewage systems.

CRITICAL-THINKING QUESTIONS

1. Do you think the Progressive Era reform vision for local governments is still a good one today and that the state's local governments should continue to be run by professional managers and insulated as much as possible from state and national party politics? Why or why not?

2. Should local governments, such as cities, be given more home-rule powers and greater local autonomy free of state interference? Test case: Would it be okay with you if all California cities asserted their home-rule powers and local autonomy to the extent that San Francisco has? Why or why not?

3. Do you agree with some critics that most special districts should be abolished and their functions centralized under the control of county and city governments? Why or why not?

4. Do you agree with some observers that California needs more and stronger regional governments? Why or why not? If you agree, what are some of the problems facing those who seek to form such governments, and what steps would you take to create them? How would you balance your recommendations with the principles of home rule and local autonomy?

5. Do you think communities such as those in San Fernando Valley should be allowed to secede from established jurisdictions and form their own cities? If so, do you think it should be easier or harder for them to do so than it is now?

6. Do you support or oppose the rebellion of local governments against the state as a response to the state's attempt to use local government property tax revenues to solve its budget deficit problem? Why or why not?

KEY TERMS

At this point you should have a general understanding of the following concepts and terms:

advisory regional governments (p. 199)
at-large elections (p. 193)
charter cities and counties (p. 181)
cities (p. 189)
council-manager plan (p. 192)
councils of government (COGs) (p. 199)
counties (p. 183)
Dillon's Rule (p. 181)
direct democracy (p. 193)
district elections (p. 193)
educational revenue augmentation funds (ERAFs) (p. 203)

enterprise districts (p. 196)
fiscalization of land use (p. 203)
general-law cities (p. 189)
general-law counties (p. 184)
Governmental Accounting Standards Board (GASB) (p. 210)
home rule (p. 181)
independent districts (p. 196)
local agency formation commission (LAFCo) (p. 189)
mayor-council plan (p. 192)
municipal incorporation (p. 190)
nonconcurrent elections (p. 193)

nonpartisanship (p. 192)
Occupy Movement (p. 211)
ordinances (p. 185)
redevelopment agencies (p. 200)
reform governments (p. 192)
regional governments (p. 198)
regulatory regional governments (p. 198)
school districts (p. 195)
secession (p. 201)
special districts (p. 195)
tax-increment financing (p. 200)
unfunded mandates (p. 203)
user fees (p. 196)

10 Public Policy in California

WHAT GOVERNMENT DOES AND WHY IT MATTERS

Duroville

Riverside County, east of Los Angeles, has some 300+ trailer parks, many inhabited by migrant agricultural workers who pick the vegetables and fruit that grow so abundantly in the county's irrigated valleys. In 1999, the county cracked down on several trailer parks that cater to migrant workers, finding that they had substandard and dangerous conditions. Harvey Duro Sr., a member of the Torres Martinez Desert Cahuilla Indian Reservation, spread the word of a new trailer park on reservation land where the displaced workers could move. Many farm workers moved in; they pay about $500 a month per trailer to live there.[1]

The conditions aren't good. The trailer park, officially called Desert Mobile Home Park but unofficially known as Duroville, is next to a dump that burns from time to time. There have been heaps of tires and construction debris piled in the area, the streets are dusty (and muddy when it rains), and the area's sewage goes into a pond next door. In 2002, the teachers in the local schools noticed many students from the park with asthma and rashes; the likely culprit was determined to be the dump. The Bureau of Indian Affairs, which had jurisdiction because the trailer park was on the reservation, moved to close the park because of the unsanitary conditions. In 2009 the local U.S. attorney said in court that the park had "leaking sewage, 800 feral dogs, piles of debris and fire hazards," along with 5,000 tenants. The cost of bringing it into compliance would be more than $4 million, which the owner could not afford.

After several years of litigation, a federal judge in 2009 decreed that there was no other place for the residents to go, and the park could stay open. It holds anywhere from 2,000 to 6,000 people, depending on the time of year and economic conditions. Many of them are undocumented. Many earn less than $10,000 per year. And many of them are Purépechas, an indigenous people from Michoacán, Mexico. Many, in fact, are from a single town in Michoacán.

By 2010, most of those selling drugs in the park were gone, the feral dog problem was substantially reduced, and the rotting garbage had been cleared. But there was still no place for the residents to move, and the quality of the trailers was no better.

Riverside County has a public housing project under construction intended for Duroville residents, but public housing projects require residents to be in the United States legally, and many residents of Duroville are not. In addition, the project requires more money to be finished; $12 million in redevelopment agency money has been targeted as the source, but as we saw in Chapter 9, the governor and the state department of finance convinced the legislature to end redevelopment agencies in California in 2012, and there is no money to finish the project. The $12 million, according to the *Desert Sun* newspaper, was intended to purchase new double-wide trailer homes for 181 families from Duroville.[2]

Duroville still exists, and whether it will close remains undecided. It has up to 6,000 residents, its own Wikipedia entry, and new resident councils and representatives to help ensure that residents adhere to the rules. Articles about the community occasionally appear in the *New York Times* and *Los Angeles Times* as well as in the local newspapers. The residents have been encouraged to leave, but they are not compelled to do so. The issue of housing, and many other policy areas in California politics, reveals the challenges posed throughout this book, challenges related to California's enormous diversity and unique institutions.

You may have concluded by now that California is a land of contrasts. The same state that has Beverly Hills and the communities of Silicon Valley also has its Durovilles. Public policy in California includes areas that are like Duroville—that is, areas that are not doing so well—and other areas that are in better shape. It is difficult to generalize as to what the average state of affairs is.

We know from earlier chapters in this book that California has been close to being ungovernable during the last two decades. We have a public that demands a high level of services but refuses consistently to pay for them. Many members of the public still feel that the free tuition and low fees in higher education during the Pat Brown era are still possible in an era when the state's people and politics have changed profoundly. The public is often willing to approve initiatives to undertake new projects that lack funding and is even more willing to curtail the use of taxes except for special functions, many of which happen to benefit the interests sponsoring the relevant initiative. The latter fact doesn't seem to bother the voters.

We have institutions that function, but in some cases barely so. The legislature still makes decisions but is paralyzed on restructuring the state's tax structure, which is now over 50 years old. Some new institutional changes—most the top-two primary system and the new nonpartisan legislative redistricting system notably—will benefit the functioning of the legislature, but we will have to see over the next few years how they perform. The 50 percent majority necessary to pass a budget has already ended the needless budget haggling that used to paralyze Sacramento all summer and for part of the fall, but the cost is cuts that have devastated the state's public schools.

We also know that major steps have been taken to improve the quality of the political process in California. The top-two primary, the 50 percent rule for passing the state's budget in the legislature, and the commission to handle redistricting every 10 years in a neutral and nonpartisan fashion may be just the beginning of a wave of reform that could take most of the next decade to straighten out the state.

Meanwhile, our question in this chapter is the current state of public policy in California. *Public policy* means what government actually does or "produces" in various policy areas, such as health, welfare, education, higher education, water, and the like. These areas are different in each state. For the California of the 1950s and 1960s, education and water policy were proud, if politically difficult, achievements, and the state was one of the nation's leaders in solving its problems and supporting its schools and colleges. For the California of the 2000s, these are areas of profound disappointment.

For example, even with Proposition 98 of 1988 "guaranteeing" the public schools some 40 percent of the general fund, California's finances have been so tight that K-12 spending is among the lowest of the 50 states. Spending per student in 2010-11 was 46th out of the states, at $8,908 per student, compared with a national average of $11,761. The number of K-12 students per teacher was 50th, and California has the largest class sizes in the entire country at 20.5 students per teacher, compared with the national average of only 13.8. The number of students per guidance counselor was 810; the national average is 433.[3]

Likewise, the University of California, the California State University, and the state's extensive community college system have all seen cutbacks in pay and course offerings as well as substantially higher tuition and fee payments. How much higher these can go is a major and unanswered question, but there are few alternatives in the current economic climate.

One could write several books about California public policy, so in this chapter we have picked four areas that are interesting. They are typical in the sense that they show some of the best and worst areas in which the state is involved. The first of these is health insurance. The second is immigration, a problem that affects several areas of public policy. The third is the state's infrastructure, widely assumed to be experiencing similar spending issues as K-12 education. And the fourth is gambling, sanctioned by the state on Indian reservations.

Health Insurance in California

One of the problems that the legislature and governor have had to face the last several decades is that many people in California, over 20 percent of the population, do not have health insurance. The reasons vary, but two stand out. One is that many people in California, more than the national average, work in small firms, and small firms tend not to offer health insurance nearly as often as large firms. The second is that California's population has a large proportion of immigrants, and immigrants tend to have a much lower probability of having health insurance than are native-born Americans. Figure 10.1 shows the last 10 years of health insurance in California, with figures from 2000 and 2010. The graph includes only people under 65 because those 65 years and over have a 0.99-plus probability of having Medicare.

California has the highest proportion of noncitizens in the nation, at 15 percent, and almost half of them don't have health insurance (47 percent), but four other states have a higher proportion of their noncitizens uninsured, led by Texas at almost 62 percent. The categories are discussed in the following sections.

Employer-Sponsored Insurance

About 53 percent of Californians under age 65 have employer-sponsored insurance (ESI)—that is, they get their insurance through their employer, who will typically subsidize some of the cost. ESI has been declining nationally, and the recession of 2008–09 accelerated the process, which means that there could be

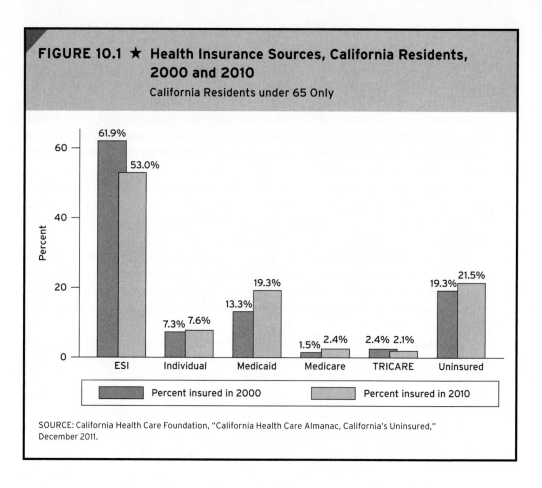

FIGURE 10.1 ★ Health Insurance Sources, California Residents, 2000 and 2010

California Residents under 65 Only

ESI: 61.9% (2000), 53.0% (2010)
Individual: 7.3% (2000), 7.6% (2010)
Medicaid: 13.3% (2000), 19.3% (2010)
Medicare: 1.5% (2000), 2.4% (2010)
TRICARE: 2.4% (2000), 2.1% (2010)
Uninsured: 19.3% (2000), 21.5% (2010)

Percent insured in 2000 | Percent insured in 2010

SOURCE: California Health Care Foundation, "California Health Care Almanac, California's Uninsured," December 2011.

some improvement over the next few years. Only seven states have a higher proportion of their population uninsured than California: Texas (which leads the nation at more than 27 percent), New Mexico, Florida, Nevada, Mississippi, Arizona, and Arkansas. In 2009, individuals paid $428 per month for health insurance, with employers paying all but $47 of that cost. Families paid $1,127, with employers paying all but $283 of the cost.

Individual Health Insurance Marketplace

In the individual health insurance marketplace, people purchase a health insurance policy directly from the insurance company. Two and a half million Californians, 8 percent of the population, participate in this market, which in California has been characterized by extremely large price increases from year to year (one large insurer asked for a 39 percent price increase from 2010 to 2011) and by insurers that have dropped policyholders who have become sick and filed large claims, on the grounds that their applications were not truthful. So many of these situations were highlighted in the newspapers that the new federal health insurance law, the Patient Protection and Affordable Care Act of 2010, specifically outlawed dropping policyholders when they get sick—called a *rescission*—effective September 23, 2010.

Medi-Cal

Medi-Cal is California's version of the federal Medicaid plan for the poor. The federal government sponsors two large federal health insurance programs, Medicare and Medicaid. Medicare, aimed primarily at senior citizens, is paid for with federal funds and beneficiary premiums, deductibles, and co-pays. Medicaid, in contrast, is aimed at low-income people, and the financing is split between the federal government and the states, with the federal government providing an average of 57 percent of the funding and some national standards, and the states providing the other 43 percent of the funding plus basic program administration and decision making. The proportion of the funding that each state provides is determined by a formula based on state per capita income, and because California is a relatively rich state, it receives 50 percent federal funding, the minimum. (Mississippi received the maximum federal funding rate at 74.2 percent in 2012.)

California's policy makers face a higher proportion of uninsured residents compared with other states, and the legislature and governor have attempted, successfully, to fill in the gap by expanding Medi-Cal. Medi-Cal now covers almost 30 percent of the population, compared with the national average of 22 percent.[4]

However, the downside to this expansion is that California's average cost per Medi-Cal recipient is the lowest of any state, mostly because provider payments—the payment to each hospital and doctor for providing a Medi-Cal-covered service—is the lowest in the country. Consequently, access to doctors, particularly specialists, is limited for Medi-Cal beneficiaries in many parts of the state because many medical practices either will not take Medi-Cal beneficiaries at all or limit the numbers they are able to see for financial reasons.[5]

Medicare

Figure 10.1 shows that about 2 percent of Californians are on Medicare. Remember that the chart shows only those under 65 years of age; for those 65 and over, Medicare is universal, and over 4 million Californians 65 and over are on it. For those under 65, anyone with ALS (Lou Gehrig's disease) or end-stage renal disease is immediately eligible for Medicare, and those who are on Social Security disability are eligible for Medicare after a two-year wait. Those under 65 who are on Medicare thus have a disability of some kind, although not all those with disabilities are eligible for Medicare.

TRICARE

In Figure 10.1, the TRICARE bar includes TRICARE and other military-related programs. These are the health care programs for military retirees and their dependents, including some members of the military reserves, with some civilian health benefits for military personnel as well. The category also includes those who receive their health care from the U.S. Department of Veterans Affairs (VA).

Uninsured

The last bars in Figure 10.1 are for those who lack health insurance—almost 22 percent of the under-65 population of California. This proportion is significantly higher than that of the United States as a whole, where 17 to 18 percent of the population is uninsured. The following are some facts about the uninsured:

- Some 23 percent of workers lack insurance in California, compared with 19 percent in the nation.

- Most heads of household without insurance have a job. The proportion who work full time for the whole year in California, some 62 percent, is about the same as the national figure of 61 percent.

- Only 14 percent of heads of household without insurance did not work, compared with the national figure of 17 percent.

- It is estimated that most *children* without insurance are eligible for Medi-Cal or Healthy Families, California's State Children's Health Insurance Program (SCHIP, which is a federal program aimed at those whose incomes are just above the Medicaid/Medi-Cal eligibility levels). Between 58 percent and 69 percent of children without insurance are eligible for either program; between 4 percent and 11 percent of adults are eligible.

- The 25- to 34-year-olds are the largest age group represented among the uninsured (26 percent), but every age group under 65 is represented. So-called preretirees, 55- to 64-year-olds, are 9 percent of the total.

- Of those without health insurance, 41 percent have incomes under $25,000 per year. Most of them will be covered by Medicaid/Medi-Cal under the new federal health insurance law when it comes into full effect by 2014.

- Ethnically, most people without health insurance in California are Latino (about 58 percent). Whites represent the next most frequent group, at 24 percent. Asians compose 11 percent of the total, and African Americans 5 percent.

- Of those without health insurance, 63 percent are American citizens; 37 percent are not.

The new federal health insurance law contains a requirement that all Americans have health insurance as of 2014. Those who are poor will be covered by an expanded Medicaid (Medi-Cal in California), mostly at federal expense. Those who lack the funds to purchase health insurance will receive a federal subsidy. Employers are encouraged to continue their coverage of those who have ESI as of this point. Whether the new law will eliminate those without health insurance in California is an open question. It seems likely that a good number of those who lack health insurance now will have it in 2015. We shall have to wait and see.

Immigrants in California

When a large proportion of a state's population is born in other countries and a substantial proportion of that population is not in the United States legally, there are many public-policy implications. In Chapter 1 we noted that

- 27 percent, or 10.2 million people, of the state's population in 2010 was born outside the United States. Of those, almost half are from Mexico.

- of the 38 million people in California, 2.6 million, almost one-quarter of the foreign-born population, are undocumented.

What issues arise from immigration?

Work Issues

Because one-quarter of all Californians are immigrants and because the immigrant population is concentrated among those of working age—25- to 64-years-old—

many jobs at all levels are held by immigrants, and policy issues arise as to how employers check that the applicant has the proper legal documentation to work and so forth. Immigrants are such an important part of the California labor force that the legalization of some undocumented workers, the so-called path to citizenship, has been noticeably more popular in California than in other states. One of the largest demonstrations in the nation took place recently in Los Angeles, where over a million people demonstrated for immigrants' rights. But legalization is *not* a cure-all. A Public Policy Institute of California study of the effects of legalizing some unauthorized immigrants concluded, based on a survey of immigrants who became legal permanent residents in 2003, that "legalization is not likely to increase the occupational mobility or wages of most unauthorized immigrants, at least in the short run."[6]

Campaign Issues

Immigration itself is an issue in many state campaigns. Governor Pete Wilson ran for reelection in 1994 in part on a stance opposing illegal immigration, as did 2010 Republican gubernatorial candidate Meg Whitman. Recent governors have actually sent bills to the federal government for extra payments that they allege arise from the level of immigration, which is a federal government responsibility.

School Issues

Immigrants tend to have more children than those who have lived in this country for several generations, and consequently areas that have more immigrants need more schools. Schools entail both construction costs and ongoing expenses for teachers and supplies. In six of California's largest cities, immigrants make up a majority: Glendale, Santa Ana, Daly City, El Monte, Union City, and Alhambra. Santa Clara (36 percent), San Francisco (36 percent), and Los Angeles (35 percent) are the counties with the highest percentages.

Costs of State Welfare and Health Programs

Because immigrants tend to be poorer than those born in the United States, the state's costs for welfare, Medi-Cal, and public health programs are substantially higher than they would be otherwise. The immigrant population's poverty rate is 18 percent, compared with 12 percent for those born in the United States.[7] These costs are the basis for the state's asking the federal government for assistance because of the disproportionate impact of immigration, a federal government responsibility.

We should note that *undocumented* immigrants are not eligible for welfare or Medi-Cal, although their U.S.-born children are eligible and may receive services. Hospitals must take care of those who arrive sick at the emergency room. Schools, by law, educate children without regard to citizenship status. And, of course, if you commit a crime and are caught, undocumented immigrants as well as others are sent to jail or the state's prisons. Overall, there is no reliable study of the fiscal effect of illegal immigration.[8]

Driver Licenses

Should noncitizens, particularly those who are not legally in this country, receive driver licenses? A decision by the legislature and the Davis administration to grant driver licenses to undocumented immigrants in 2003 was a major issue in the vote to recall Governor Davis in October of that year. The law required applicants to have other forms of identification, such as a federal individual taxpayer identification number, and the DMV was given discretion to specify the type of identification required. After the recall in 2003, Governor Schwarzenegger asked the legislature to repeal the law, and it did.

Voting

A policy issue that could arise in the future is the question of whether noncitizens should be allowed to vote in any elections at the state or local level. The options include allowing noncitizens to vote in all state and local elections, city elections only, neighborhood councils within cities only, or something similarly restricted. While *federal law* and the U.S. Constitution do not allow noncitizens to vote in federal elections for president, U.S. senator, or congressional representative, the *state* could change its constitution and laws to allow noncitizens to vote in state and local elections, using the differences between the total population and the voting population as justification. Maryland allows noncitizens to vote in state and local elections, and the question was debated in 2004 in New York, another large state with a substantial immigrant population. UCLA's Chicano Studies Research Center issued a policy paper in 2003 stating that immigrants were more than 25 percent of the population in over 85 California cities and calling for efforts to increase their political participation.[9]

It is not immigration per se that has led to these public-policy problems. What makes immigration such a difficult issue is the concentration of immigrants, both legal and illegal, in certain border states, producing costs that are higher than those of the average state. These costs are a result of federal immigration policies, over which the states have little control. Although the federal government formulates and implements immigration policy, it does not reimburse states for costs that are above the average level of other states as a result of those policies.

California's Infrastructure

Infrastructure is the part of government that citizens come into contact with the most—highways, schools, universities, commuter buses, and rail. California's infrastructure deteriorated significantly into the mid-2000s, but the five bond issues approved by the voters in November 2006, totaling over $40 billion, for infrastructure improvements to transportation systems, housing, public education, higher education, and disaster/flood control should make a significant difference in these systems over time as the bonds are issued and construction takes place. One factor that makes the maintenance of the state's infrastructure difficult is what Bruce Cain of University of California, Berkeley's Institute of Governmental Studies calls California's "infrastructure ambivalence." On the one hand, Californians want modern facilities and infrastructure, but "we don't want what often comes with those things. There are, for instance, unavoidable environmental costs. Water projects can endanger fisheries in the Delta. New roads and housing can separate and destroy ecosystems."[10] Consider the following examples.

Highways

California's public road system is worth approximately $300 billion. The American Association of State Highway and Transportation Officials, using Federal Highway Administration data, issued a report in 2009 indicating California's pavement conditions, including interstates, freeways, and major urban routes, as 35 percent poor, 31 percent mediocre, 16 percent fair, and 18 percent good. The "good" percentage is tied for the lowest in the nation with Rhode Island. The national average of the "poor" percentage is 13 percent; California's 35 percent is exceeded only by New Jersey's at 46 percent. A 2008 survey of the nation's bridges found 25 percent of them structurally deficient or functionally obsolete, with some 6,977, or 29 percent, of California's bridges falling into the deficient/obsolete category. Some progress is being made using funding from the 2006 infrastructure bond issues.

Fire Prevention

In early March 2004, voters in San Diego County considered seven attempts to raise more money for fire prevention and to "beef up fire departments that were overwhelmed in the deadly wildfires of last fall."[11] The city of San Diego is a good example. The proposal was to increase the hotel room tax, what is often called the tourist tax, from 10.5 percent to 13 percent of the price of a hotel room, a rate similar to what is charged in other large tourist-oriented cities in California. It attracted a 61 percent positive vote, a landslide in most elections, but the state constitution and laws, as amended by Proposition 13 and its follow-up legislation and constitutional amendments, require any new tax or increase in any existing local tax to be approved by two-thirds of the voters (see Chapter 8). The increase would have provided an extra $8 million for the fire department, $3 million for the police, and $7 million for tourism promotion projects.

Meanwhile, in the unincorporated areas of the county, many now served by volunteer fire departments that were overwhelmed by the fires of fall 2003, three tax increases failed. In one of them, the ballot statement opposing the $50 a year per parcel increase read: "Taxes won't stop. Next year, another tax. Taxing will continue until they break you financially." After the fires in fall 2003, the consensus was that the poor communications, volunteer fire departments, lack of coordination among agencies, and poor training had been major contributors to the quick spread of the fires and to the hundreds of homes lost. In spite of that, supporters could not muster a two-thirds vote.

In 2010, San Diego County remained the only county in the state *without* a unified countywide fire department, and in 2008 the county needed more than 20 additional fire stations and 800 additional firefighters to meet national fire-service accreditation standards. A *Los Angeles Times* series in mid-2008 pointed out that not only were fire departments across the state short of firefighters and equipment but a major factor in the increased losses from forest fires was the tendency of new developments to be located adjacent to wildlands. The state Department of Forestry and Fire Protection now estimates that "about 40% of the more than 12 million homes in the state are on land with a high or extreme threat of wildfire."[12] In wealthier areas, the recent tendency is to pay a private firefighting service a premium of "at least $10,000 per year . . . [to protect] homes with a value of at least $1 million."[13]

Levees

In 1986, a levee broke along the Yuba River and inundated the small town of Linda in the Central Valley, causing several hundred million dollars' worth of damage. In 2004, 18 years later, the state supreme court ratified a court of appeal decision that found the state of California liable because it had not repaired the stretch of levee that broke. While the state resisted liability for the break and its consequences, the courts have found that the state will have to pay for the consequences of its neglect.[14]

The *Sacramento Bee* published a series of articles that detailed the several governmental agencies that were responsible for flood control and maintenance of the levees along the Sacramento River. Although the agencies have not been able to find the funds to repair over 150 sites where the levees could fail during a major flood, builders and developers have continued to construct large developments in the Central Valley near Sacramento in areas where levees hold back rivers that are capable of flood damage to thousands of homes and businesses.[15]

In mid-2004, just after the publication of the *Sacramento Bee* series, a dirt levee broke suddenly in the Delta region, instantly changing 12,000 acres of farmland into a 12,000-acre lake. Officials found that a second levee was in danger of breaking, and a third needed to be shored up to prevent a road from being flooded, cutting the only connection to two islands housing 178 residents.[16] Total damage: $35 million to buildings and crops, plus another $36.5 million to fix the levees.

The Future of California's Infrastructure

The neglect of the state's infrastructure in these instances is obvious. The reasons why infrastructure repair and upkeep are not a higher priority are less obvious. One is that infrastructure is a long-term problem, and our political system, based on two- and four-year terms of office, thinks short term. This factor is magnified by the term limits imposed on the legislature, traditionally a body in which legislators spent several decades of their careers and could think in longer terms than the governor and the executive-branch officials, who are elected for only one or two four-year terms. Now with term limits, the members of the legislature are subject to the same short-term time constraints.

A second factor is the impact over time of the public employee unions that represent potential votes for politicians and whose emphasis, as one would imagine, is on maintaining or increasing personnel in the public sector, not on fixing infrastructure.

All of this changed with the destruction wreaked by Hurricane Katrina on the Gulf Coast and the subsequent failure of government in many places to fulfill its emergency responsibilities. The public-works package of bond issues approved by the voters in November 2006 included Proposition 1E, the Disaster Preparedness and Flood Prevention Act of 2006, which authorized $4.1 billion in bonds to rebuild flood-control structures, including the delta levees. The money authorized is providing a solid start toward rebuilding the eroding facilities.

Every governor in recent years has appealed to the federal government for extra help. Except for the Clinton administration's response to the Northridge earthquake in 1994, the federal government has not responded with anything out of the ordinary. California remains a relatively wealthy state that pays more to the federal government in taxes than it receives in federal benefits.

Many current construction projects in California were funded by the 2006 initiatives and the Obama administration's stimulus act of 2009. These have made some progress in upgrading the state's infrastructure, although much more remains to be done.

Indian Gaming in California

In 1931 the first casino opened in Nevada. Only Nevada had gambling casinos until 1976, when New Jersey voters legalized gambling in Atlantic City. Nine more states legalized gambling between 1989 and 1998, and there are now over 400 *non-tribal* casinos in 11 states. In the early 1980s, Indian tribes in Florida and California began to operate bingo games with larger prizes than state regulators allowed. The cases in both states went to court; the result was a Supreme Court decision in 1987 and in 1988 the passage by Congress of the Indian Gambling Regulatory Act. The act requires tribes to have a compact with the state specifying the type of gambling permitted on their lands. Today, at least 233 of the 562 federally recognized Indian tribes run about 500 gambling casinos and other facilities, "generating about $26.5 billion per year in revenue, or one-seventh of all gambling proceeds."[17]

In California, former Governor Pete Wilson negotiated in 2009 the first compact in 1998. It placed such severe restrictions on slot machines that the tribes qualified an initiative, Proposition 5, for the November 1998 ballot, taking the issue to the voters. The campaign was the most expensive in California at that time, with $90 million spent by both sides, and Proposition 5 was approved by a substantial majority. It required the governor to approve any tribal casino proposal. It placed no limits on the number of casinos statewide or the number of gambling machines or tables each casino could operate. It lowered the gambling age to 18 and allowed the tribes to continue using the video slot machines that the state and federal governments had deemed illegal. Tribal casinos would be self-regulated, governed by a tribal-appointed gaming board. There would be no direct state or local involvement in casino operations. The California Supreme Court struck down Proposition 5 in 1999. The court said the proposition violated an existing initiative law that banned casino gambling in California.

The tribes, however, found Wilson's successor, Gray Davis, more willing to negotiate compacts. He negotiated with 60 tribes, "allowing them to expand current gambling operations, allowing Nevada-style gambling . . . , legalizing video slot machines, [and] allowing casino employees to unionize." The compacts depended on the approval of Proposition 1A on the March 2000 ballot; it passed with a 65 percent majority. At this point, it is estimated that the tribes are generating revenues of approximately $7 billion per year, and they have become major contributors to California election campaigns. "Gaming has become so lucrative that hundreds of Native Americans are petitioning the Bureau of Indian Affairs for recognition of new California tribes to buy land and build casinos."[18] In 2012, the state's 109 tribes operated 67 casinos. Many more casinos are planned.

The major policy issue is the percentage of gaming revenues that should be returned to the state of California. At present, the tribes pay approximately $200 million per year, about 2.5 percent of their revenues, to the state to help other tribes that do not have gaming operations. They also make voluntary contributions to the local governments in the area of their casinos to offset increased expenses that may result from the casino. Connecticut receives 25 percent of the revenues from the Foxwoods Casino in that state; other states receive less. A recent court decision involving the Rincon tribe of San Diego County held that California could not extract taxes from Indian casinos in return for permission to expand.

Another casino-related issue is the lack of knowledge of the odds of winning at the various kinds of gambling available in California. In other states, non-Indian gambling operations must reveal their odds, but among the states with Indian gaming, only Connecticut requires the tribes to reveal the odds of winning.[19]

Tribal casinos are not required to address environmental problems, such as "damage to local roads, animal and plant life, and over demands . . . casinos placed on water supplies and public services." On his last day in office, after being recalled, Governor Davis wrote a letter releasing the tribes from any obligation to negotiate over these issues.[20]

Another contentious issue is the exclusion of hundreds of persons who thought they were members of Indian tribes and thus entitled to receive the substantial annual payments generated from casino profits that go to lawful members. Several tribes in recent years voted former members out of membership on the grounds that they were not lineal descendants of the original members of the tribe. The governor has been urged to investigate the disenrollments, which in some cases are contravened by DNA evidence, and the disenrolled members have threatened to sue in state, federal, or Bureau of Indian Affairs courts, although none of these courts normally takes on membership issues.

One interesting feature of Indian casinos in California is that because of federal law and a U.S. Supreme Court decision, the tribes have "sovereign" immunity from lawsuits filed by those who work in the casino or by patrons of the casino. Injured employees and customers have sued the casinos, but the suits have been routinely dismissed because of the sovereign immunity law. Congress has been unable or unwilling to update the law, meaning that the tribes are not required to obey laws relating to environmental quality, workers' compensation, and so forth. They are required to obey alcohol control laws, however.

Contrasting the casinos in California and Nevada, we note the following:

- Indian casinos in California do not pay property tax, sales tax, personal property tax, corporate tax, or state income tax. Persons living on Indian reservations pay federal income tax only. In contrast, Nevada casinos pay the same taxes as other businesses, and anyone who benefits from a Nevada casino has to pay the same tax as other citizens.

- Nevada casinos are regulated and policed by the state. Indian casinos in California have almost no regulation by the state and are policed by their own force, which follows its own tribal rules and is not subject to review by courts outside the reservation.

- Nevada casinos have known rates of return, regulated by the state, for slot machines and other games. Indian casinos in California operate under their own rules. The odds for slot machines in particular are not known and can be changed by the management at will.

In general, both patrons and employees have many more "rights" in Nevada because of the state's willingness to regulate the "gaming" industry and the inapplicability of the federal laws governing Indian reservations to gambling in Nevada.

The major issue facing the state and federal government in 2012 is that some of the tribes want to expand their casinos closer to urban areas. The Obama administration has loosened the rules on adding land to existing reservations. The U.S. Supreme Court in 2009 issued a ruling that the Interior Department, which houses the Bureau of Indian Affairs, could not create reservations for tribes that were not recognized in 1914, but legislation could overturn that ruling. Senator Dianne Feinstein has expressed concern over the expansion of the existing number of casinos, saying that "Enough is enough. Sixty casinos, it seems to me, is enough, more than enough."[21]

Indian gaming, then, raises a host of issues about whether private entities that profit from public infrastructure and legal rights granted by state government have any obligation to support the state in return. These are difficult issues, particularly given the history of the treatment of Native Americans in California, and they promise to be in the news for years to come.

Conclusion

We can learn something from these areas of public policy. First, there are major areas of public policy that operate reasonably well given the constraints on budgets that operate in California. Both the health care area and higher education fit this category. In health care, the state, confronted with a huge number of people without health insurance, expanded its Medicaid program, Medi-Cal, to accommodate some of these people. Because the federal government subsidizes half of all Medi-Cal costs, this is a very rational solution.

In infrastructure, the state is beginning to make progress, thanks to the bond issues approved in 2006 under Governor Schwarzenegger. We shall see if this continues in the future.

K–12 education, however, is another story. The side effect of Proposition 13 is that every policy area is more dependent on state-level policies and budgets than it was before 1978, and with that dependence the funds spent on K–12 education, in spite of the Proposition 98 guarantee, have fallen relative to what other states spend. Combined with the higher salaries paid in the public sector generally in California to compensate for the high cost of housing, the effect has been to make California's K–12 class sizes significantly higher than the norms nationally. The long-term effects of not having a well-educated workforce can be negative, as the students who are educated today are the people who will contribute to the Social Security and pension payments of the older generations.

Duroville is an example of an area where the state is hamstrung by inadequate revenues and an inability to control what happens on federal lands, in this case Indian reservations. Indian reservations are also relevant to the Indian casinos, where an interest did not like what the state had as its public policy, so it funded an initiative to change things, which passed. The initiative was written to benefit the interest, as we saw with the lack of information about betting odds and other areas that are public and regulated in Nevada, but secret and not regulated in California.

"We have met the enemy and he is us," said Pogo in a comic strip set in the Okefenokee swamp. Pogo made that statement on the first Earth Day, when he was confronted with an ocean of trash. But the same is true of contemporary California. Every few years, the voters seem to rise up against state government and approve initiatives that express their anger but tie up the government in knots that no one can undo. Consider the following:

- Proposition 13, limiting property taxes to 1 percent of the value of the property (1978)
- The failure to reconfirm three supreme court justices (1986)
- Proposition 98, requiring minimal K–12 education funding (1988)
- Proposition 140, legislative term limits (1990)
- Proposition 187, restricting services to undocumented immigrants (1994)
- Recall of Gray Davis as governor (2003)

Indeed, the goal of many initiatives is to keep the legislature from doing anything at all. As long as California is a state where it is easy to fund initiatives and difficult to enact policy through the legislature, the initiative will remain the public policy tool of choice for special interests.

We began this book with the idea that California was essentially ungovernable, that the voters had tied up state government in such a way that reasonable officials could not enact middle-of-the-road policies that would benefit the public as a whole. We have made some progress with the enactment of the top-two primary, the 50 percent legislative requirement to enact the budget, and the commission to reapportion the state's legislative districts after the census every 10 years. But we still have a way to go.

What else can be done? It is still too difficult to raise taxes, at a two-thirds majority of the legislature. The two-thirds should be lowered to somewhere in the 50 to 60 percent range, by which you would still need a supermajority to take such a serious action, but a minority of just a third could no longer hamstring the legislature. The governor still does not control the other members of the executive branch. We should be electing a governor and lieutenant governor on the same ticket and then having the governor appoint the other officials to head up the various elements of the executive. And the legislative term limits, even at 12 years in one house, are too short for legislators to invest sufficiently in learning—indeed, mastering—legislation. The legislature, compared with other states, is very small because the districts are the biggest in the nation; at a minimum, we should have a unicameral legislature with 120 seats, each a third smaller than a present Assembly seat.

The initiative process should be reformed, in the words of *The Economist*, so that "the initiative process and the legislature work together, rather than against each other."[22] The initiative should be taken at least partially out of the hands of the professional fund-raising and political consultant firms that dominate it. They do so because five months is too short a time for amateurs to collect signatures. You need paid professionals to do the job in that time. The number of signatures required is too few. And the legislature cannot amend the proposed initiative typically even decades after it is enacted. In other states legislatures can place competing and presumably better-written initiatives on the ballot themselves; this might well be an experiment worth taking given the number of poorly written initiatives that have been approved in the last two decades.

We end with our theme from Chapter 1. We have begun the long road to reform, and there is hope for a state more governable in the future. But more steps have to be taken, and we need both visionary leadership and voters who pay attention and are interested in change. We hope the readers of this book will be those voters.

FOR FURTHER READING

"Arnold's Big Chance: A Survey of California." *The Economist*, May 1, 2004, pp. 1–16.

Barrera, E. A. "A Firestorm of Controversy—Still No County Fire Department Five Years after Cedar Blaze." *East County Magazine*, August 2008, www.eastcountymagazine.org (accessed 8/17/12).

Hill, Laura E., Magnus Lofstrom, and Joseph M. Hayes. "Immigrant Legalization: Assessing the Labor Market Effects." San Francisco: Public Policy Institute of California, 2010, www.ppic.org/content/pubs/report/R_410LHR.pdf. Accessed 8/17/12.

Hans Johnson and Laura Hill. "At Issue, Illegal Immigration." San Francisco: Public Policy Institute of California, July 2011. www.ppic.org/content/pubs/atissue/AI_711HJAI.pdf. Accessed 8/17/12.

Kaiser Commission on Medicaid and the Uninsured. "Citizenship Documentation Changes." Co-published with the Georgetown University Health Policy Institute, May 2009, www.kff.org/medicaid/7896.cfm. Accessed 8/17/12.

———. "Five Basic Facts on Immigrants and Their Health Care." March 2008, www.kff.org/medicaid/upload/7761.pdf. Accessed 8/17/12.

Light, Steven Andrew, and Kathryn R. L. Rand. *Indian Gaming and Tribal Sovereignty: The Casino Compromise*. Lawrence: University Press of Kansas, 2005.

Pear, Robert. "Lacking Papers, Citizens Are Cut from Medicaid." *New York Times*, March 12, 2007.

Schrag, Peter. *California: America's High-Stakes Experiment*. Berkeley: University of California Press, 2006.

Simmons, Charlene Wear. *Gambling in the Golden State, 1998 Forward*. Sacramento: California Research Bureau, California State Library, May 2006.

"Special Report: Democracy in California, The People's Will," *The Economist*, April 23, 2011.

State of California, Legislative Analyst's Office. *A Primer: The State's Infrastructure and the Use of Bonds*. Sacramento: Legislative Analyst's Office, January 2006.

ON THE WEB

American Association of State Highway and Transportation Officials: www.transportation.org. Accessed 8/17/12.

California Progress Report: www.californiaprogressreport.com. Accessed 11/6/12. A daily briefing on politics and policy.

Center on Policy Initiatives, San Diego: www.onlinecpi.org/index.php. Accessed 8/17/12.

Public Policy Institute of California: www.ppic.org. Accessed 8/17/12.

UCLA Chicano Studies Research Center: www.chicano.ucla.edu/center.htm. Accessed 8/17/12.

SUMMARY

I. Duroville is a trailer park located on an Indian reservation in Riverside County. Many of its residents are agricultural workers, and the park has had particularly squalid conditions in its 12 years of existence.
    A. The federal government has filed suit to close it, but the lack of an alternative location that the several thousand residents could afford has stymied federal and state efforts to do so.
    B. The state and county have constructed a new trailer park using redevelopment funds, but the $12 million that the county would need to finish the park has been eliminated in the state budget crisis, and many of the present Duroville residents would not be able to move because they are undocumented.

II. California has a higher-than-average proportion of people without health insurance.

A. Employer-sponsored insurance is lower in California in part because California has more small firms and in part because the state has so many noncitizens.
B. Proportionally, more people buy their own health insurance in California than in other states. The health insurance market has been characterized by a large percentage of price increases from year to year and by "rescissions," the cancellation of policies because of inaccurate applications (the insurance company view) or because high claims have been filed (the state view).
C. Medi-Cal covers 30 percent of Californians, a larger proportion than in other states, but the average cost per beneficiary is among the lowest among the states because provider payments are so low.
D. In California, Medicare covers some 600,000 persons under 65 with disabilities. A similar number is covered

by TRICARE or the Department of Veterans Affairs (VA).

E. Almost 22 percent of the state's population lack health insurance, significantly more than in other states. Most people without health insurance work full time all year, are Latino, and are American citizens. Most children without health insurance are eligible for Medi-Cal or Healthy Families.

F. The new federal health insurance law is likely to ensure that many more people in California have health insurance by 2015.

III. California has the highest number and proportion of immigrants of any state. Twenty-seven percent, or 9.9 million people, of California's 37 million were born outside the United States. Almost half of those are from Mexico.

A. A quarter of those born abroad—2.6 million—are estimated to be undocumented.

B. Many issues arise from the high proportion of immigrants in California, including who pays the extra costs for them (the federal government or the state government), whether they should be allowed to have driver's licenses, who pays to build schools for them, whether they should be allowed to vote in local elections in towns or cities where noncitizens make up a majority, and so forth.

IV. California's infrastructure has noticeably deteriorated in the last 50 years.

A. The issue affects vital state services, such as fire prevention. San Diego County is particularly affected because its citizens are reluctant to pay for adequate fire protection.

B. The state's highways are in poor condition but are being gradually upgraded through bond issues passed in 2006 at Governor Schwarzenegger's urging and through federal Recovery Act funds.

C. The levees in the Delta and the Central Valley of California are being attended to by state funds provided in bond issues passed in 2006.

V. Indian casinos are widespread in California and have provided a few of the state's Indians with relatively high incomes.

A. There are presently 67 Indian casinos, with over 60,000 slot machines.

1. Some 2 to 3 percent of the proceeds from the casinos are paid to the state, mostly to a fund that compensates tribes that do not have casinos. The state General Fund receives about $25 million per year, in spite of then-Governor Schwarzenegger's efforts to increase the amount. The $25 million is less than one-tenth of 1 percent of the General Fund total.

2. The odds of winning in Indian casinos in California are not known, in contrast to Nevada's casinos, which are strongly regulated. California Indian casinos are weakly regulated.

B. *Sovereign immunity* means that those who work at or who patronize Indian casinos do not have the right to sue them for injuries or other problems.

C. The tribes determine who is and is not a member, and some tribes have excluded previous members after the casino has opened, thus increasing the money received by the other members.

VI. The book concludes with a look at the fundamental problems confronting California government, symbolized by Pogo's statement that "we have met the enemy and he is us." The voters have been willing to approve any number of initiatives that have tied the state government in knots, expressing their anger every few years with property tax limitations, the strictest term limits in the nation, recalling the governor, and approving patently unconstitutional restrictions on the services received by immigrants. However, three steps represent some hope in making California governable again: the top-two primary, the commission that has redistricted the state after the 2010 census, and the 50 percent approval rule for the budget in the legislature. More steps remain.

PRACTICE QUIZ

1. Medicaid is
   a) a national program, administered by the federal government, with little state input.
   b) a state program, administered with little federal government guidance or funds.
   c) a federal/state program, with over half the money coming from the federal government.
   d) a federal/state program, with over half the money coming from the states.

2. Duroville is a particularly difficult public policy problem because
   a) the trailer park is located on an Indian reservation, taking it out of state jurisdiction.
   b) many of the residents are undocumented, meaning they will have a difficult time qualifying for public housing.
   c) the many other trailer parks in Riverside County indicate that the problems symbolized by Duroville may be widespread.
   d) all of the above

3. In California, ESI
   a) has historically been higher proportionately than in other states because of the size and structure of California's employers and the number of noncitizens in the state.
   b) has historically been about the same as in other states.
   c) has historically been lower than in other states because of the size and structure of California's employers and the number of noncitizens in the state.
   d) has historically been higher than in other states because of the generosity of the state's medical programs.
4. The individual health insurance market in California is a model that other states might emulate.
   a) true
   b) false
5. More immigrants in California are from Mexico than any other country of origin.
   a) true
   b) false
6. Just as immigrants are spread throughout California, they are also spread throughout the United States on a roughly equivalent basis.
   a) true
   b) false
7. California's infrastructure has been neglected for all of the following reasons *except*
   a) most recent budgets have had to cut expenses, and infrastructure is among the easier items to cut.
   b) the state legislature does not put a high priority on infrastructure issues because infrastructure does not vote.
   c) most politicians in California have long time horizons.
   d) public employee unions have emphasized their members, who are voters, rather than infrastructure issues.
8. Indian gaming in California operates under the same general set of rules as the casinos in Nevada do.
   a) true
   b) false
9. Indian gaming issues in California have involved the following *except*
   a) tribal-sponsored initiatives
   b) federal court decisions over the legality of Indian casinos in California
   c) compacts negotiated by the governor and ratified by the state senate
   d) substantial gaming revenues received by local governments in California
10. According to the book, California voters are unwilling to support sufficient fire protective services in some counties because
   a) more than 33 percent of voters are opposed to paying increased taxes for this purpose.
   b) private fire protective services have largely replaced those in the public sector in these counties.
   c) only about 10 percent of existing housing in California is located in areas classified as "high" or "extreme" fire danger.
   d) it is rare for California counties to have unified countywide fire departments.

CRITICAL-THINKING QUESTIONS

1. Discuss the condition of California's highways, both in your experience and as presented in the book. What does the condition of our highway system have in common with the other infrastructure problems mentioned, such as fire prevention, city swimming pools, school buildings, and levees?
2. The involvement of many different groups makes Indian gaming a significant public-policy problem. Indicate the different groups that are involved; their goals, which may be different or conflicting; and something about their success thus far.
3. Discuss the ways in which undocumented immigration is a problem for localities (counties, cities, towns, unincorporated areas) in California. What in general can be done to solve these problems?
4. What are the two most important reforms of California government to consider in the future?

KEY TERMS

At this point you should have a general understanding of the following concepts and terms:

employer-sponsored insurance (ESI)
(p. 219)
Indian Gambling Regulatory Act
(p. 227)
individual insurance market (p. 220)
infrastructure (p. 224)
legal permanent resident (p. 223)

Medicaid (p. 220)
Medi-Cal (p. 220)
Medicare (p. 221)
nonpartisan legislative redistricting
(p. 218)
nontribal casinos (p. 227)
Proposition 5 (p. 227)

public policy (p. 218)
redistricting (p. 218)
rescissions (p. 220)
sovereign immunity (p. 228)
tribal casinos (p. 227)
undocumented immigrant (p. 222)
unicameral legislature (p. 230)

Answer Key

Chapter 1

1. c
2. b
3. c
4. d
5. b
6. b
7. d
8. c
9. a

Chapter 2

1. b
2. c
3. a
4. c
5. c
6. c
7. a
8. c
9. d
10. b

Chapter 3

1. c
2. b
3. a
4. c
5. b
6. c
7. a
8. d
9. a
10. b

Chapter 4

1. a
2. b

3. d
4. a
5. a
6. d
7. a
8. b
9. a
10. b

Chapter 5

1. a
2. a
3. d
4. c
5. d
6. c
7. a
8. c
9. a
10. d

Chapter 6

1. a
2. b
3. d
4. c
5. d
6. d
7. d
8. b
9. a
10. b

Chapter 7

1. a
2. b
3. a
4. b
5. b
6. a

7. b
8. c
9. a
10. d

Chapter 8

1. a
2. a
3. c
4. b
5. d
6. d
7. a
8. a
9. d
10. b

Chapter 9

1. b
2. b
3. a
4. a
5. b
6. d
7. c
8. b
9. a
10. c

Chapter 10

1. c
2. d
3. c
4. b
5. a
6. b
7. c
8. b
9. d
10. a

Notes

Chapter 1

1. Dan Walters, "Ex-Governors Miss Chance to Discuss Complexities," *Santa Barbara News-Press*, February 21, 2004, p. A11.
2. James Q. Wilson, "A Guide to Schwarzenegger Country," *Commentary* (December 2003), pp. 45–49. Field Institute, *Legislation by Initiative vs. through Elected Representatives* (San Francisco: Field Institute, November 1999), www.field.com/fieldpollonline/subscribers/COI-99-Nov-Legislation.pdf (accessed 7/17/12).
3. Initiative and Referendum Institute, "Initiative Use" (Los Angeles: University of Southern California Gould School of Law, September 2010), www.iandrinstitute.org (accessed 7/17/12).
4. "Just the Facts: Immigrants in California," PPIC (Public Policy Institute of California), July 2002.
5. Jeffrey S. Passel, Randy Capps, and Michael Fix, *Undocumented Immigrants: Facts and Figures* (Washington, DC: Urban Institute Immigration Studies Program, January 12, 2004), www.urban.org/UploadedPDF/1000587_undoc_immigrants_facts.pdf (accessed 7/17/12).

Chapter 2

1. Follow the Money, "National Institute on Money in State Politics," www.followthemoney.org (accessed 6/20/12).
2. Amanda Meeker, "An Overview of the Constitutional Provisions Dealing with Local Government, Report of the California Constitutional Review Commission," (1996), pp. 87–92, www.californiacityfinance.com/CCRChistory.pdf (accessed 12/3/12).
3. Carl Brent Swisher, *Motivation and Political Technique in the California Constitutional Convention 1878–79* (New York: Da Capo Press, 1969).
4. Spencer C. Olin Jr., *California's Prodigal Sons: Hiram Johnson and the Progressives, 1911–1917* (Berkeley: University of California Press, 1968), p. 70.
5. John M. Allswang, *The Initiative and Referendum in California, 1898–1998* (Stanford CA: Stanford University Press, 2000), p. 15.
6. Richard Hofstadter, *The Age of Reform* (New York: Washington Square Press, 1988), p. 23.
7. George Mowry, *The California Progressives* (Chicago: Quadrangle Paperbacks, 1963), pp. 9, 12–13.
8. Kevin Starr, *Inventing the Dream: California through the Progressive Era* (New York: Oxford University Press, 1985), pp. 242–43.
9. Dean R. Cresap, *Party Politics in the Golden State* (Los Angeles: The Haynes Foundation, 1954), p. 12.
10. Mowry, *The California Progressives*, p. 12.
11. Mowry, *The California Progressives*, p. 15.
12. Quoted in Mowry, *The California Progressives*, p. 65.
13. Starr, *Inventing the Dream*, p. 254.
14. Many recalls take place at the local level, where volunteer groups organize recalls of city council or school board members because they simply feel strongly about a particular issue. Statewide recalls, however, are rare.
15. Debra Bowen, California Secretary of State News Release, "99 Years of California Initiatives, One Day Left to Qualify for June 8 Ballot," www.sos.ca.gov/admin/press-releases/2010/db10-015.pdf (accessed 6/20/12).
16. Allswang, *The Initiative and Referendum in California*, p. 33.
17. Allswang, *The Initiative and Referendum in California*, p. 75.

18. California Secretary of State Debra Bowen, "Referendum," www.sos.ca.gov/elections/ballot-measures/referenda.htm (accessed 6/20/12).

19. Jim Puzzanghera, "History of Recall Adds Fuel to Both Sides," *The San Jose Mercury News*, June 18, 2003, http://digital.library.ucla.edu/websites/2003_999_022/latest.news/94/index.htm (accessed 8/3/12)

20. Field Research Corporation, "Statewide Ballot Proposition Elections," October 2011, http://field.com/fieldpollonline/subscribers/COI-11-Oct-California-Ballot-Propositions.pdf (accessed 6/20/12).

Chapter 3

1. Jay Michael, Dan Walters, and Dan Weintraub, *The Third House: Lobbyists, Power, and Money in Sacramento* (Berkeley, CA: Berkeley Public Policy Press, 2002), p. 13.

2. Cary McWilliams, *California: The Great Exception* (Berkeley: University of California Press, 1999), p. 198.

3. Arthur H. Samish and Bob Thomas, *The Secret Boss of California* (New York: Crown Publishers, 1971), p. 13.

4. Debra Bowen, California Secretary of State, "History of the Political Reform Division," 2004, www.ss.ca.gov/prd/about_the_division/history.htm (accessed 6/22/12).

5. Sam Dotson, "Some Call Spending Money to Get Money Respectable but Necessary for Inland Cities and Schools," *Riverside Press Enterprise*, July 6, 1997, p. A2.

6. Debra Bowen, California Secretary of State, "Lobbying Activity: Employers of Lobbyists," http://cal-access.ss.ca.gov/Lobbying/Employers (accessed 6/22/12).

7. Chase Davis, "State Lobby Spending on Pace to Set Records," *California Watch*, November 3, 2011, http://californiawatch.org/dailyreport/state-lobby-spending-pace-set-records-13402 (accessed 6/22/12).

8. "California Lobbyist Control Gets a C," *Silicon Valley/San Jose Business Journal*, May 19, 2003.

9. McWilliams, *California*, p. 213.

10. Mark Sappenfield, "Why Clout of Lobbyists Is Growing," *Christian Science Monitor*, July 23, 2003, news.corporate.findlaw.com/csmonitor/s/20030723/23jul2003084412.html; www.csmonitor.com/2003/0722/p01s02-uspo.html (accessed 6/22/12).

11. Debra Bowen, California Secretary of State, "Lobbying Activity: Lobbying Firms," 2007–08, http://cal-access.ss.ca.gov/Lobbying/Employers (accessed 6/22/12).

12. Stephen Ansolabehere, James Snyder Jr., and Mickey Tripathi, "Are PAC Contributions and Lobbying Linked? New Evidence from the 1995 Lobby Disclosure Act," http://www.tandfonline.com/doi/abs/10.1080/1369525022000015586#preview (accessed 8/4/12).

13. National Institute on Money in State Politics, "State Overview: California 2009–10," www.followthemoney.org.

14. California Fair Political Practices Commission, "Big Money Talks," March 2010, p. 41, www.fppc.ca.gov/reports/Report31110.pdf (accessed 6/22/12).

15. Maria Lagos, "Result of Furloughs—$1 Billion Liability," *San Francisco Chronicle*, April 23, 2011, www.sfgate.com/cgi-bin/article.cgi?f=/c/a/2011/03/07/MNSQ1I2ASB.DTL&ao=all (accessed 6/22/12).

16. Steven Malanga, "The Beholden State," *City Journal* 20 (Spring 2010), www.city-journal.org/2010/20_2_california-unions.html (accessed 6/22/12).

17. Patrick McGreevy and Nancy Vogel, "Senate Travel Perks for Sales," *Los Angeles Times*, March 16, 2008.

18. Field Research Corporation, "Statewide Ballot Proposition Elections," October 2011, http://field.com/fieldpollonline/subscribers/COI-11-Oct-California-Ballot-Propositions.pdf (accessed 6/22/12).

19. Elisabeth R. Gerber, "Interest Group Influence in the California Initiative Process," Public Policy Institute of California, 1998, www.ppic.org/main/publication.asp?i=49 (accessed 8/4/12).

20. Susan F. Rasky, "Covering California: The Press Wrestles with Diversity, Complexity, and Change," in *Governing California: Politics, Government, and Public Policy in the Golden State*, ed. Gerald C. Lubenow and Bruce E. Cain (Berkeley: Institute of Governmental Studies Press, University of California, 1997), pp. 157–88.

21. Rasky, "Covering California," p. 182.

22. Jim Rutenberg, "Working to Spin Distrust of Media into Votes," *New York Times*, October 12, 2003.

Chapter 4

1. Spencer C. Olin, *California's Prodigal Sons: Hiram Johnson and the Progressives, 1911–1917* (Berkeley: University of California Press, 1968).

2. Schaffner, Brian F., Streb, Matthew, and Wright, Gerald, "Teams without Uniforms: The Nonpartisan Ballot in State and Local Elections," *Political Research Quarterly* 54, no. 1 (2001), pp. 7–30.

3. Michael Finnegan, "The Race for the White House," *Los Angeles Times*, September 8, 2004, p. A1.

4. Roper Center for Public Opinion Research, *Social Capital Community Benchmark Survey: Methodology and Documentation*, February 17, 2001, www.ropercenter.uconn.edu/scc_bench.html (accessed 8/13/12).

5. Mark Baldassare, *A California State of Mind: The Conflicted Voter in a Changing World* (Berkeley: University of California Press, 2002), p. 47.

6. Richard Edward DeLeon, *Left Coast City: Progressive Politics in San Francisco, 1975–1991* (Lawrence: University Press of Kansas, 1992).

7. "The Mormon Money behind Proposition 8," October 23, 2008, www.theatlantic.com/daily-dish/archive/2008/10/the-mormon-money-behind-proposition-8/209748/ (accessed 8/13/12).

8. S. Rasky, "Introduction to 'An Antipolitician, Antiestablishment Groundswell Elected the Candidate of Change,'" in *California Votes: The 2002 Governor's Race and the*

Recall That Made History, ed. G. Lubenow (Berkeley: Berkeley Public Policy Press, 2003).

9. Rasky, "Introduction."

10. Decker, C., "State's Shifting Political Landscape," *Los Angeles Times*, November 6, 2008, p. A1.

11. Decker, C., "Money Simply Is Not Enough," *Los Angeles Times*, November 7, 2010, p. A41.

12. Kevin Yamamura, and Torey Van Dot "California Lawmakers Secure Pay with Unfinished Budget," , *Sacramento Bee*, June 16, 2012, p. 1A, www.sacbee.com/2012/06/16/4566229/california-lawmakers-secure-continued.html (accessed 7/20/12).

13. "No on Prop. 29," *Los Angeles Times*, April 27, 2012, articles.latimes.com/2012/apr/27/opinion/la-ed-prop29-20120427 (accessed 12/3/12).

14. Adam Nagourney, "Vote on $1 Cigarette Tax Starts $47 Million California Brawl," *New York Times*, June 4, 2012.

15. "Young Voters Help Secure Obama Victory, Passage of Progressive Ballot Measures," Huffington Post, November 7, 2012.

16. Phil Willon, "GOP Loses Grip on Inland Empire," *Los Angeles Times*, November 11, 2012, p. A37.

17. Jean Merl, "California No Longer on Sidelines in Congressional Races," *Los Angeles Times*, November 5, 2012, p. AA3.

18. George Skelton, "Time for Initiative Reforms," *Los Angeles Times*, November 15, 2012, p. A2.

19. D. P. Osorio, "The Cost of Winning a Senate Race," DPOsorio.com, May 9, 2012, http://dposorio.com/blog/822/the-cost-of-winning-a-senate-race (accessed 7/20/12).

20. Rasky, "Introduction."

21. William Booth, "In Calif. Governor's Race, It's Ads Infinitum," *Washington Post*, May 29, 1998, p. A1.

22. Carol A. Cassel, "Hispanic Turnout: Estimates from Validated Voting Data," *Political Research Quarterly* 55, no. 2 (June 2002), pp. 391–408. Michael A. Jones-Correa and David L. Leal, "Political Participation: Does Religion Matter?" *Political Research Quarterly* 54, no. 4 (2001), pp. 751–70.

Chapter 5

1. Emily Bazar, "A Mad Dash into Confusion: As Lawmakers Race to Wrap Up for the Year the Public Often Gets Left in the Dark," *Sacramento Bee*, September 16, 2001.

2. Lou Cannon, *Governor Reagan: His Rise to Power* (New York: Public Affairs, 2003), p. 166.

3. Peter Schrag, *Paradise Lost: California's Experience, America's Future* (New York: New Press, 1998), p. 244.

4. Institute of Governmental Studies, "IGS Goes to Sacramento to Assess Ten Years of Term Limits," *Public Affairs Report* 42, no. 3 (fall 2001).

5. National Conference of State Legislators, www.ncsl.org/default.aspx?tabid=18248 (accessed 6/28/12).

6. Schrag, *Paradise Lost*, p. 143.

7. Adam Nagourney, "Political Shift in California Trips Brown," *New York Times*, September 20, 2011, www.nytimes.com/2011/09/21/us/politics/brown-says-california-gop-is-harder-to-work-with-decades-later.html?pagewanted=all (accessed 6/24/12).

8. Anthony York, "Brown and Obama Find Bipartisanship a Difficult Goal to Reach," *Los Angeles Times*, February 24, 2012, http://articles.latimes.com/2012/feb/24/local/la-me-jerry-brown-20120224 (accessed 6/24/12).

9. Nagourney, "Political Shift in California Trips Brown."

10. George Skelton, "California's Capitol—the Long View: A Columnist Looks Back on 50 Years Covering the Ups and Downs of Sacramento," *Los Angeles Times*, December 1, 2011, p. A2.

Chapter 6

1. William Bradley, "Jerry Brown 2.0 at 1," Huffington Post, January 7, 2012, www.huffingtonpost.com/william-bradley/jerry-brown-2012_b_1190844.html (accessed 6/29/12).

2. Richard E. Neustadt, *Presidential Power and the Modern Presidents: The Politics of Leadership from Roosevelt to Reagan* (New York: Macmillan, 1990).

3. Thomas E. Cronin and Michael A. Genovese, *The Paradoxes of the American Presidency* (New York: Oxford University Press, 1998).

4. Public Policy Institute of California, "Job Approval Ratings for Governor Schwarzenegger" www.ppic.org/content/pubs/other/APR_Schwarzenegger0510.pdf (accessed 8/30/12).

5. "Press Release: Governor Brown Delivers Plan to Streamline and Simplify State Government to Little Hoover Commission," March, 30, 2012, http://gov.ca.gov/news.php?id=17476 (accessed 8/30/12).

6. Nicolas Riccardi, "Brown's 2011: Tall Hopes but Taller Hurdles," *Los Angeles Times*, December 27, 2011, p. A1.

Chapter 7

1. 2011 Court Statistics Report, http://www.courts.ca.gov/documents/2011CourtStatisticsReport.pdf.

2. U.S. Census Bureau, American Fact Finder, http://factfinder2.census.gov/faces/nav/jsf/pages/index.xhtml

3. *People v. Colvin*, 203 Cal.App.4th 1029 (2012).

4. Judicial Council of California, http://www.courts.ca.gov/policyadmin-jc.htm?genpubtab.

5. 2008 Court Statistics Report.

6. "California Courts Wrestle with Budget Cuts Old and New." Retrieved from http://latimesblogs.latimes.com/california-politics/2012/06/california-court.html

7. "IT Project Sinks in Sea of Criticism." Retrieved from http://www.courthousenews.com/2012/03/27/45079.htm

8. See "Judges Criticize Court Bureaucracy in Blistering Report." Retrieved from http://www.law.com/jsp/ca/PubArticleCA.jsp?id=1202556419264&Judges_Criticize_Court_Bureaucracy_in_Blistering_Report.

Chapter 8

1. Marla Dickerson, "State Fiscal Woes Threaten Cities' Budgets and a Leading Job Engine," *Los Angeles Times*, January 17, 2003, pp. C1, C4.
2. California Department of Finance, "History of Budgeting," February 24, 1998, www.dof.ca.gov (accessed 7/27/12).
3. California Department of Finance, "History of Budgeting."
4. George Skelton, "The 'Budget Nun' Earns Her Pay and Bipartisan Respect," *Los Angeles Times*, May 26, 2003, p. B5.
5. California Department of Finance, "California's Budget Process," October 10, 2000, www.dof.ca.gov/fisa/bag/process.htm (accessed 7/27/12).
6. Public Policy Institute of California, "California's Tax Burden," 2003, www.ppic.org (accessed 7/30/12).
7. Katherine Barrett, Richard Greene, Michele Mariani, and Anya Sostek, "The Way We Tax," *Governing* (February 2003), p. 20.
8. *Silicon Valley/San Jose Business Journal*, "Analysis details who pays taxes in California," www.bizjournals.com/sanjose/stories/2002/04/08/daily60.html (accessed 9/11/12).
9. Barrett et al., "The Way We Tax," p. 20.
10. California Taxpayers Association, "Cal-Tax: Taxes Are Heavy Burden in California," www.caltax.org/California.htm (accessed 7/30/12).
11. California Budget Project, "Who Pays Taxes in California?" (Sacramento: California Budget Project, updated April 2012).
12. Institute for Taxation and Economic Policy, "'High Rate' Income Tax States Are Outperforming No-Tax States," February 2012, www.itepnet.org (accessed 7/27/12).
13. James D. Savage, "California's Structural Deficit Crisis," *Public Budgeting and Finance* 12, no. 2 (summer 1992), pp. 82–97.
14. California Forward, "Curing Deficits and Creating Value: Principles for Improving State Fiscal Decisions," s3.amazonaws.com/zanran_storage/www.caforward.org/ContentPages/1903423.pdf (accessed 12/3/12).
15. Peter Nicholas and Virginia Ellis, "Budget Signals Narrowed Ambitions," *Los Angeles Times*, February 18, 2004, p. A1.
16. Dan Walters, "California's Crisis of Governance Undermines Democratic Theory," *Sacramento Bee*, July 4, 2004, p. A16.
17. Texas Bond Review Board, "Debt Affordability Study," February 2012, Appendix F, www.brb.state.tx.us/pub/bfo/DAS2012.pdf (accessed 7/27/12).

Chapter 9

1. Bernard H. Ross and Myron A. Levine, *Urban Politics: Power in Metropolitan America*, 6th ed. (Itasca, IL: F. E. Peacock, 2001), p. 90.
2. Dale Krane, Platon N. Rigos, and Melvin B. Hill Jr., *Home Rule in America: A Fifty-State Handbook* (Washington, DC: CQ Press, 2001).
3. Daniel B. Rodriguez, "State Supremacy, Local Sovereignty: Reconstructing State/Local Relations under the California Constitution," in *Constitutional Reform in California: Making State Government More Effective and Responsive*, ed. Bruce E. Cain and Roger G. Noll (Berkeley: Institute of Governmental Studies Press, University of California, 1995), pp. 401–29. Krane, Rigos, and Hill, *Home Rule in America*. Melvin B. Hill, *State Laws Governing Local Government Structure and Administration* (Washington, DC: U.S. Advisory Commission on Intergovernmental Relations [ACIR], 1993).
4. Ross and Levine, *Urban Politics*, p. 91.
5. John Taylor, "What Happened to Branciforte County?" (Sacramento: California State Association of Counties, 2000), www.counties.org/defaultasp?id=52 (8/4/12).
6. *County of Los Angeles Annual Report 2011–2012*, http://lacounty.gov/wps/portal/lac/employees/ (accessed 8/2/12). See also for budget figures http://ceo.lacounty.gov/pdf/11-12/2011-12%20Adopted%20Budget%20Charts.pdf (accessed 8/2/12).
7. Jillian Jones, "County's Legal Troubles Tied to the Value of the Land," *Napa Valley Register*, January 30, 2010, http://napavalleyregister.com/news/local/article_31d6dfe0-0d71-11df-a0e3-001cc4c03286.html (accessed 8/4/12).
8. Aaron Claverie and David Downey, "Pechanga to Buy Quarry Site," *The Californian*, November 15, 2012, www.nctimes.com/news/local/swcounty/region-pechanga-to-buy-quarry-site/article_a17a4dde-0a5a-597d-a8f9-057ba5c3eddf.html (accessed 11/16/12).
9. U.S. Census Bureau, *2007 Census of Governments* (Washington, DC: Government Printing Office, 2007). California Association of Local Agency Formation Commissions, "California Cities by Incorporation Date," www.calafco.org/resources.htm#incorp (accessed 8/4/12).
10. Zoltan L. Hajnal, Paul G. Lewis, and Hugh Louch, *Municipal Elections in California: Turnout, Timing, and Competition* (San Francisco: Public Policy Institute of California, 2002), pp. 23–24.
11. Ross and Levine, *Urban Politics*, pp. 165–78.
12. Amy Bridges, *Morning Glories: Municipal Reform in the Southwest* (Princeton, NJ: Princeton University Press, 1997).
13. International City/County Management Association (ICMA), "Officials in U.S. Muncipalities 2,500 and Over in Population," in *The Municipal Year Book 2003* (Washington, DC: ICMA, 2003), pp. 195–200.
14. H. George Frederickson and Gary Alan Johnson, "The Adapted American City: A Study of Institutional Dynamics," *Urban Affairs Review* 36, no. 6 (2001): 872–884. Susan A. McManus and Charles S. Bullock III, "The Form, Structure, and Composition of America's Municipalities in the New

Millennium," in *The Municipal Yearbook 2003*, ed. ICMA, pp. 3–18.

15. Bruce E. Cain, Megan Mullin, and Gillian Peele, "City Caesars? An Examination of Mayoral Power in California," presented at the 2001 annual meeting of the American Political Science Association, August 29–September 2, San Francisco.

16. Richard Edward DeLeon, *Left Coast City: Progressive Politics in San Francisco, 1975–1991* (Lawrence: University Press of Kansas, 1992).

17. Hajnal et al., *Municipal Elections in California*, p. 25.

18. DeLeon, *Left Coast City*. A recent study of over 7,000 U.S. cities found that district systems were better than at-large systems in achieving diversity on city councils only where underrepresented groups are highly concentrated geographically and constitute a sizable share of the population. See Jessica Trounstine and Melody Ellis Valdini, "The Context Matters: The Effects of Single-Member Versus At-Large Districts on City Council Diversity," *American Journal of Political Science* 52, no. 3 (July 2008): 554–69.

19. Hajnal et al., *Municipal Elections in California*, p. 19.

20. Hajnal et al., *Municipal Elections in California*, p. 26.

21. Hajnal et al., *Municipal Elections in California*, p. 3.

22. Hajnal et al., *Municipal Elections in California*, p. 64.

23. Senate Local Government Committee, *What's So Special about Special Districts? A Citizen's Guide to Special Districts in California*. 3rd ed. (Sacramento: California State Senate, 2002), p. 3.

24. California Department of Education, http://www.cde.ca.gov/ds/sd/cb/ceffingertipfacts.asp (accessed 8/2/12).

25. California State Controller's Office, *Special Districts Annual Report 2009–2010*, http://www.sco.ca.gov/Files-ARD-Local/LocRep/districts_reports_0910_specialdistricts.pdf, p. vi (accessed 8/2/12).

26. California State Controller's Office, *Special Districts Annual Report 2009–2010*.

27. Brian P. Janiskee, "The Problem of Local Government in California," *Nexus, a Journal of Opinion* (Spring 2001), pp. 219–33.

28. Gabriel Metcalf, "An Interview with Joe Bodovitz," *SPUR* report no. 378 (September 1999).

29. The text of the SB 375 law is available at www.leginfo.ca.gov/pub/07-08/bill/sen/sb_0351-0400/sb_375_bill_20080930_chaptered.pdf (accessed 8/2/12). The Institute for Local Government provides a useful resource center with detailed background on SB 375. See http://www.ca-ilg.org/sb-375-resource-center (accessed 8/2/12). To track progress in implementing SB 375, see http://www.arb.ca.gov/cc/sb375/sb375.htm (accessed 8/2/12).

30. California Supreme Court, quoting from the Community Redevelopment Act, in *Cal. Redevelopment Assn. v. Matosantos*, S194861, December 29, 2011, http://www.courtinfo.ca.gov/opinions/archive/S194861.PDF, p. 9 (accessed 5/23/12).

31. *Cal. Redevelopment Assn. v. Matosantos*, S194861 (December 29, 2011), www.courtinfo.ca.gov/opinions/archive/S194861.PDF, p. 9 (accessed 5/13/12).

32. Marisa Lagos, "Calif. Wins OK to Abolish Redevelopment Agencies," *San Francisco Chronicle*, December 30, 2011, p. A-1.

33. Madeline Janis, "Rethinking Redevelopment in California," *Los Angeles Times*, February 8, 2012, http://articles.latimes.com/print/2012/feb/08/opinion/la-oe-janis-redevelopment-20120208 (accessed 5/13/12).

34. For more information on the secession movement and its outcome, see Tom Hogen-Esch, "Urban Secession and the Politics of Growth: The Case of Los Angeles," *Urban Affairs Review* 36, no. 6 (2001): 783–809. Martin Kasindorf, "L.A. Secession Drives Faltering as City Hall Warns about Risks," *USA Today*, October 30, 2002, p. 3A. William Booth, "L.A. Secession Campaign Tests Hahn's Mettle," *Washington Post*, September 22, 2002, p. A4. David Devoss, "Secession Is Dead, but Self-Rule Dream Lives," *Los Angeles Times*, November 9, 2002, p. 3.

35. Herb J. Wesson Jr., "Cutting to the Bone," *Western City* (February 2003).

36. Peter Schrag, "25 Years Later," *San Diego Union-Tribune*, June 22, 2003, p. G1.

37. Michael Coleman and Bob Leland, "State Intrusion Creates Fickle Fiscal Future for Cities," *Western City* (April 2003).

38. Michael Coleman and Michael G. Golantuono, "Local Fiscal Authority and Stability: Control and Risk in California City Revenues," *Western City* (August 2003).

39. Dean J. Misczynski, "The Fiscalization of Land Use," in *California Policy Choices*, ed. John J. Kirlin and Donald R. Winkler, vol. 3 (Los Angeles: University of Southern California, 1986). Paul Lewis and Elisa Barbour, *California Cities and the Local Sales Tax* (San Francisco: Public Policy Institute of California, 1999), www.ppic.org/content/pubs/report/R_799PLR.pdf (accessed 8/4/12).

40. For a detailed analysis of Proposition 1A, see League of Women Voters of California Education Fund, "Proposition 1A," November 2004, http://ca.lwv.org/lwvc/edfund/elections/2004nov/pc/prop1A.html (accessed 7/6/12).

41. Michael Coleman, "A Primer on California City Finance," *Western City*, March 2005.

42. Keeley Webster, "Controversial CRA Givebacks Hinder Development," *California Lawyer Magazine* (April 2010). For a contrary perspective, see Steven Greenhut, "Court Wise to Take Redevelopment Cash," CalWatchdog.com, May 23, 2010.

43. Californians to Protect Local Taxpayers and Vital Services Coalition, "Questions & Answers," www.savelocalservices.com/node/27 (accessed 6/14/10).

44. League of California Cities, "League of California Cities Condemns Proposed State Budget As Reckless Ponzi Scheme," press release, July 21, 2009.

45. Attorney General, "Proposition 22: Official Title and Summary," http://voterguide.sos.ca.gov/past/2010/general/propositions/22/title-summary.htm (accessed 5/22/12).

46. Attorney General, "Proposition 22: Arguments and Rebuttals," http://voterguide.sos.ca.gov/past/2010/general/propositions/22/arguments-rebuttals.htm (accessed 5/22/12).

47. Liam Dillon, "San Diego to Brown: How You Like Them $4 Billion?" *Voice of San Diego*, February 17, 2011, www.voiceofsandiego.org/government/thehall/article_95760260-3b01-11e0-bbac-001cc4c03286.html (accessed 5/19/12).

48. *Cal. Redevelopment Assn. v. Matosantos*, S194861 (December 29, 2011), www.courtinfo.ca.gov/opinions/archive/S194861.PDF (accessed 5/23/12).

49. See Marisa Lagos, "Calif. Wins OK to Abolish Redevelopment Agencies," *San Francisco Chronicle*, December 30, 2011, p. A-1.

50. For a thoughtful essay on the uncertain future of redevelopment in Los Angeles and other cities, see Madeline Janis, "Rethinking Redevelopment in California," *Los Angeles Times*, February 8, 2012, http://articles.latimes.com/print/2012/feb/08/opinion/la-oe-janis-redevelopment-20120208 (accessed 5/13/12).

51. Ashok Bardhan and Richard A. Walker, "California, Pivot of the Great Recession," Working Paper Series (Berkeley: Institute for Research on Labor and Employment, University of California, March 2010).

52. Field Research Corporation, *The Field Poll, Release #2320*, January 19, 2010.

53. Associated Press, *AP Economic Stress Index: Measuring Financial Strain across the U.S.*, http://hosted.ap.org/specials/interactives/_national/stress_index/ (accessed 6/14/10).

54. Maria LaGanga, "Lessons of Hard Times in Vallejo," *Los Angeles Times*, May 26, 2010. Carolyn Jones, "Vallejo's Bankruptcy Ends after 3 Tough Years," *San Francisco Chronicle*, November 2, 2011, p. C-5.

55. Alison Vekshin, "The Building Boom That's Sinking Stockton," *BusinessWeek.com*, April 12, 2012, www.businessweek.com/articles/2012-04-12/the-building-boom-thats-sinking-stockton.html (accessed 5/24/12).

56. "Stockton's Bankruptcy: California's Greece," *The Economist*, June 30, 2012, www.economist.com/node/21557768 (accessed 8/3/12).

57. "San Bernardino Officially Files for Bankruptcy Protection," *Los Angeles Times*, August 1, 2012, http://latimesblogs.latimes.com/lanow/2012/08/san-bernardino-officially-files-for-bankruptcy-protection.html (accessed 8/2/12).

58. Moody's Investor Service, "Why Some Cities Are Choosing Bankruptcy," August 17, 2012, www.cacities.org/UploadedFiles/LeagueInternet/d4/d49b287c-0939-48ae-b8bc-834aaf6a0eeb.pdf (accessed 11/16/12). Also see Dan Walters, "Bankruptcy Filings by California Cities May Spread," *Modesto Bee*, October 22, 2012, www.modbee.com/2012/10/22/2423407/dan-walters-bankruptcy-filings.html (accessed 11/16/12).

59. Jim Christie, "Bankruptcy Talk Spreads Among Calif. Muni Officials," Reuters, May 27, 2010.

60. Robert Locke, "How GASB 45 Will Affect Your City or Agency: What You Need to Know," *Western City Magazine*, November 2006.

61. John Diaz, "Where Politicians Fear to Tread," *San Francisco Chronicle*, December 9, 2007, p. C-4.

62. Maria L. LaGanga, "Lessons of Hard Times in Vallejo," *Los Angeles Times*, May 26, 2010. Jim Christie, "Bankruptcy Talk Spreads among Calif. Muni Officials," Reuters, May 27, 2010. Richard Riordan and Alexander Rubalcava, "Los Angeles on the Brink of Bankruptcy," *Wall Street Journal*, May 5, 2010.

63. Civil Grand Jury (2009–10), "Pension Tsunami: The Billion Dollar Bubble." City and County of San Francisco, June 2010, p. 4.

64. Joshua Sabatini, "San Francisco's Public Pension System Is Drowning in Red Ink," *San Francisco Examiner*. August 14, 2011, www.sfexaminer.com/local/2011/08/san-franciscos-public-pension-system-drowning-red-ink (accessed 5/12/12).

65. Jeff Adachi, "Why Progressives Should Support Pension Reform," *Fog City Journal*, March 14, 2011, www.fogcityjournal.com/wordpress/2700/why-progressives-should-support-pension-reform (accessed 4/11/12).

66. Quoted in Corey Marshall, "Will the City's Pension Proposal Really Solve the Pension Crisis?" SPUR Blog, June 14, 2011, http://spur.org/blog/2011-06-14/will-citys-pension-proposal-really-solve-pension-crisis (accessed 7/15/11).

67. U. S. Conference of Mayors, "U. S. Conference of Mayors Climate Protection Agreement," www.usmayors.org/climateprotection/agreement.htm (accessed 6/14/10).

68. Wyatt Buchanan, "734 Businesses Sign Up for S.F. Health Program," *San Francisco Chronicle*, May 2, 2008.

69. Matthai Kuruvila, "Unruly Meeting on Occupy, Violence," *San Francisco Chronicle*, May 26, 2012, p. C-1. Wikipedia offers useful histories and valuable guides to the Occupy movement in general and the Oakland and San Francisco Occupy movements in particular, http://en.wikipedia.org/wiki/Occupy_movement, http://en.wikipedia.org/wiki/Occupy_Oakland, and http://en.wikipedia.org/wiki/Occupy_San_Francisco (all accessed 5/26/12).

Chapter 10

1. Dan Barry, "Beside a Smoldering Dump, a Refuge of Sorts," *New York Times*, October 21, 2007, www.nytimes.com/2007/10/21/us/21land.html?_r=1 (accessed 7/10/12).

2. Marcel Honoré, "Duroville Relocation Effort Suffers Blow," *Desert Sun*, May 1, 2012.

3. California Budget Project, "School Finance Facts, a Decade of Disinvestment: California Education Spending Nears the Bottom," Sacramento: California Budget

Project, October 2011, www.cbp.org/pdfs/2011/111012 _Decade_of_Disinvestment_SFF.pdf (accessed 8/10/12).

4. See Medicaid.gov for information on state enrollments in Medicaid, www.medicaid.gov/Medicaid-CHIP-Program -Information/By-State/By-State.html (accessed 9/11/12).

5. For more information about Medi-Cal, see the many publications of the California HealthCare Foundation at their website, www.chcf.org (accessed 8/17/12), or the Kaiser Family Foundation, www.kff.org (accessed 8/17/12).

6. Laura E. Hill et al., "Immigrant Legalization: Assessing the Labor Market Effects," summary (San Francisco: Public Policy Institute of California, April 2010).

7. Public Policy Institute of California, "Just the Facts, Immigrants in California," July 2002, www.ppic.org (accessed 8/17/12).

8. Hans Johnson and Laura Hill, "At Issue: Illegal Immigration," Public Policy Institute of California, July 2011, www .ppic.org/main/publication.asp?i=676. (accessed 7/2012).

9. Joaquin Avila, "Political Apartheid in California: Consequences of Excluding a Growing Noncitizen Population," Latino Policy and Issues Brief No. 9 (Los Angeles: UCLA Chicano Studies Research Center, December 2003).

10. Bruce E. Cain, "Searching for the Next Pat Brown: California Infrastructure in the Balance," in *California's Future in the Balance*, California Policy Issues Annual, special ed. (Los Angeles: Edmund G. "Pat" Brown Institute of Public Affairs, November 2001).

11. "Penny-Wise, Fire-Foolish" [editorial], *Los Angeles Times*, March 8, 2004, p. B10.

12. Bettina Boxall, "A Santa Barbara Area Canyon's Residents Are among Many Californians Living in Harm's Way in Fire Prone Areas," *Los Angeles Times*, July 31, 2008, p. A1.

13. Kimi Yoshino, "Buying a Quick Response," *Los Angeles Times*, October 26, 2007, pp. A1, A21.

14. Stuart Leavenworth, "Logjam May Break on Mending Levees," *Sacramento Bee*, April 2, 2004.

15. Stuart Leavenworth, "Defenses Decayed: Neglected Levees Pushed Past Limits," *Sacramento Bee*, March 28, 2004.

16. Sara Lin and William Wan, "Crews Shore Up Levees as Concerns Rise over Upkeep," *Los Angeles Times*, June 10, 2004, pp. B1, B8.

17. Craig Lambert, "Trafficking in Chance," *Harvard Magazine* (July–August 2002), p. 40, http://500nations.com (accessed 8/17/12).

18. "Proposition 97," Institute of Governmental Studies, University of California, Berkeley, igs.berkeley.edu/library/ elections/proposition-97 (accessed 12/17/12).

19. Paul Pringle, "Players at Indian Slots Have No Clue on Payout," *Los Angeles Times*, February 10, 2003, p. B1.

20. Pringle, "Players."

21. Dan Morain, "Obama's Policies Help Indians, but Payback Is Iffy," *Sacramento Bee*, July 15, 2012.

22. "Special Report: Democracy in California, The People's Will," *The Economist*, April 23, 2011, p. 15.